NEGIMA!
OMNIBUS 7

Ken Akamatsu

TRANSLATED BY
Toshifumi Yoshida & Ikoi Hiroe

ADAPTED BY
Ikoi Hiroe

LETTERING AND RETOUCH BY
Steve Palmer

KC
KODANSHA
COMICS

D0925127

Negima! Omnibus volume 7 is a work of fiction. Names, characters, places, and incidents are the products of the author's imagination or are used fictitiously. Any resemblance to actual events, locales, or persons, living or dead, is entirely coincidental.

A Kodansha Comics Trade Paperback Original.

Negima! Omnibus volume 7 copyright © 2007-2008 Ken Akamatsu
English translation copyright © 2013 Ken Akamatsu

All rights reserved.

Published in the United States by Kodansha Comics, an imprint of Kodansha USA Publishing, LLC, New York.

Publication rights for this English edition arranged through Kodansha Ltd., Tokyo.

First published in Japan in 2007-2008 by Kodansha Ltd., Tokyo, as *Maho sensei Negima!* volumes 19, 20 and 21.

ISBN 978-1-61262-999-5

Printed in the United States of America.

www.kodanshacomics.com

9 8 7 6 5 4 3 2 1

Translator: Toshifumi Yoshida & Ikoi Hiroe
Adaptor: Ikoi Hiroe
Lettering: Steve Palmer

Honorifics Explained

Throughout the Kodansha Comics books, you will find Japanese honorifics left intact in the translations. For those not familiar with how the Japanese use honorifics and, more important, how they differ from American honorifics, we present this brief overview.

Politeness has always been a critical facet of Japanese culture. Ever since the feudal era, when Japan was a highly stratified society, use of honorifics—which can be defined as polite speech that indicates relationship or status—has played an essential role in the Japanese language. When addressing someone in Japanese, an honorific usually takes the form of a suffix attached to one's name (example: "Asuna-san"), is used as a title at the end of one's name, or appears in place of the name itself (example: "Negi-sensei," or simply "Sensei!").

Honorifics can be expressions of respect or endearment. In the context of manga and anime, honorifics give insight into the nature of the relationship between characters. Many English translations leave out these important honorifics and therefore distort the feel of the original Japanese. Because Japanese honorifics contain nuances that English honorifics lack, it is our policy at Kodansha Comics not to translate them. Here, instead, is a guide to some of the honorifics you may encounter in Kodansha Comics books.

-san: This is the most common honorific and is equivalent to Mr., Miss, Ms., or Mrs. It is the all-purpose honorific and can be used in any situation where politeness is required.

-sama: This is one level higher than "-san" and is used to confer great respect.

-dono: This comes from the word "tono," which means "lord." It is an even higher level than "-sama" and confers utmost respect.

-kun: This suffix is used at the end of boys' names to express familiarity or endearment. It is also sometimes used by men among friends, or when addressing someone younger or of a lower station.

-chan: This is used to express endearment, mostly toward girls. It is also used for little boys, pets, and even among lovers. It gives a sense of childish cuteness.

Bozu: This is an informal way to refer to a boy, similar to the English terms "kid" and "squirt."

Sempai/
Senpai: This title suggests that the addressee is one's senior in a group or organization. It is most often used in a school setting, where underclassmen refer to their upperclassmen as "sempai." It can also be used in the workplace, such as when a newer employee addresses an employee who has seniority in the company.

Kohai: This is the opposite of "sempai" and is used toward underclassmen in school or newcomers in the workplace. It connotes that the addressee is of a lower station.

Sensei: Literally meaning "one who has come before," this title is used for teachers, doctors, or masters of any profession or art.

-[blank]: This is usually forgotten in these lists, but it is perhaps the most significant difference between Japanese and English. The lack of honorific means that the speaker has permission to address the person in a very intimate way. Usually, only family, spouses, or very close friends have this kind of permission. Known as yobisute, it can be gratifying when someone who has earned the intimacy starts to call one by one's name without an honorific. But when that intimacy hasn't been earned, it can be very insulting.

CONTENTS

Negima! Volume 19 1

Negima! Volume 20 165

Negima! Volume 21 327

Bonus Section 490

Translation Notes.........526

A Word from the Author

Following in the footsteps of the animation and video games, *Negima!* is finally becoming a live-action drama series!

Now as to what kind of show it's going to be…!?

For more information, please look online, including on my own home page.

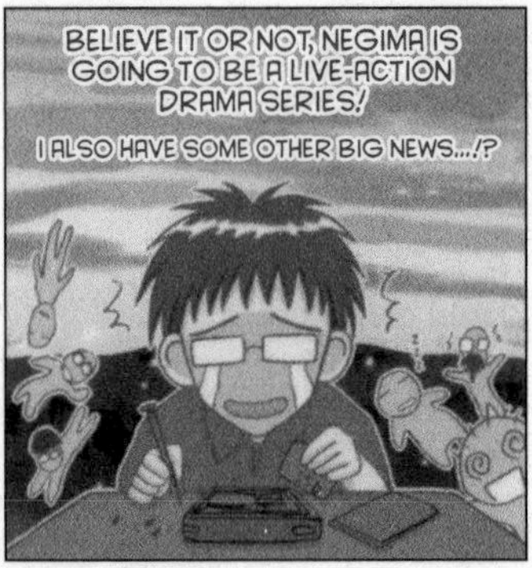
BELIEVE IT OR NOT, NEGIMA IS GOING TO BE A LIVE-ACTION DRAMA SERIES!
I ALSO HAVE SOME OTHER BIG NEWS...!?

On the manga front, as of volume 19, we enter into the summer vacation chapters, and a whole new story arc is about to begin. Please look forward to what I have in store for the Negi party and the other classmates in the chapters to come!

Ken Akamatsu
www.ailove.net

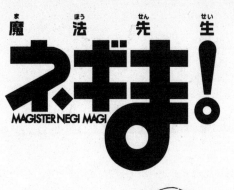

魔法先生ネギま!

MAGISTER NEGI MAGI

19

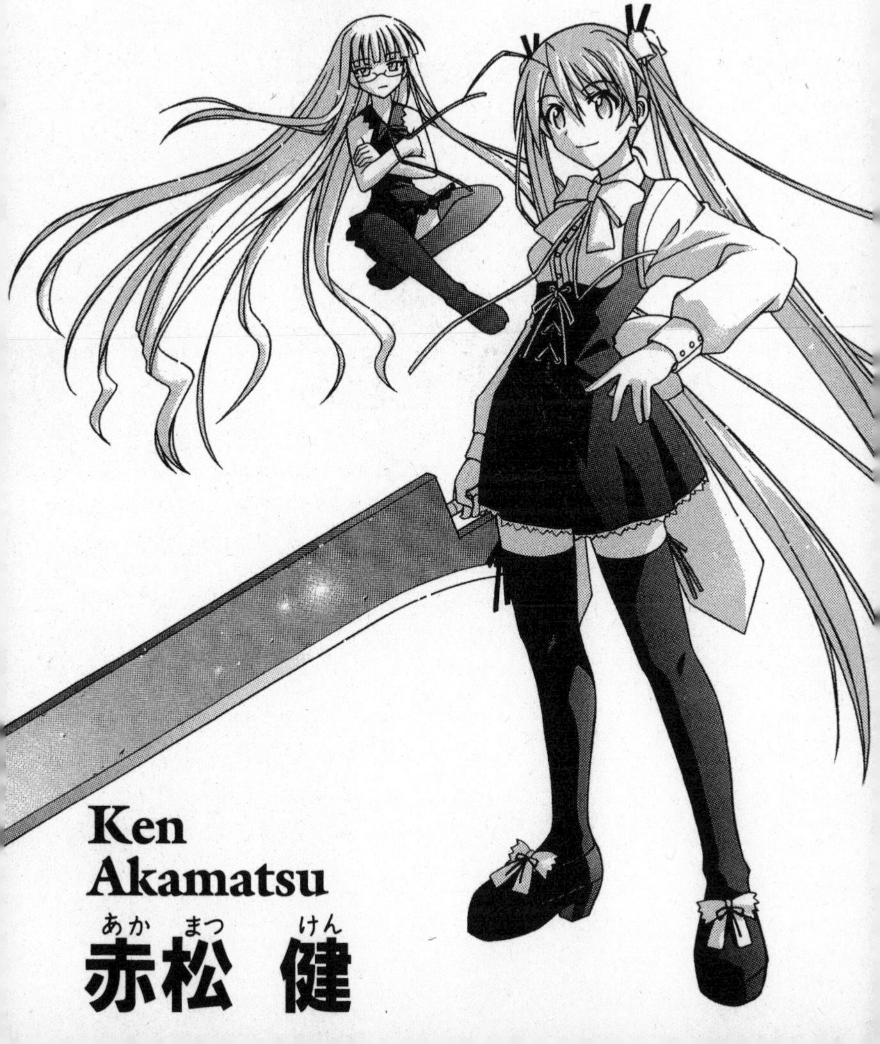

Ken Akamatsu

赤松 健

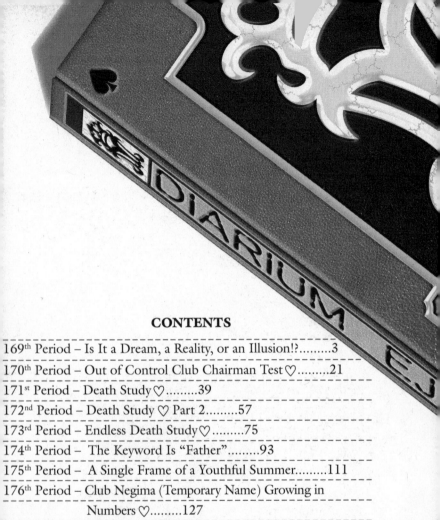

CONTENTS

169th Period – Is It a Dream, a Reality, or an Illusion!?.........3

170th Period – Out of Control Club Chairman Test ♡.........21

171st Period – Death Study ♡.........39

172nd Period – Death Study ♡ Part 2.........57

173rd Period – Endless Death Study ♡.........75

174th Period – The Keyword Is "Father".........93

175th Period – A Single Frame of a Youthful Summer.........111

176th Period – Club Negima (Temporary Name) Growing in
Numbers ♡.........127

177th Period – Dead or Alive.......145

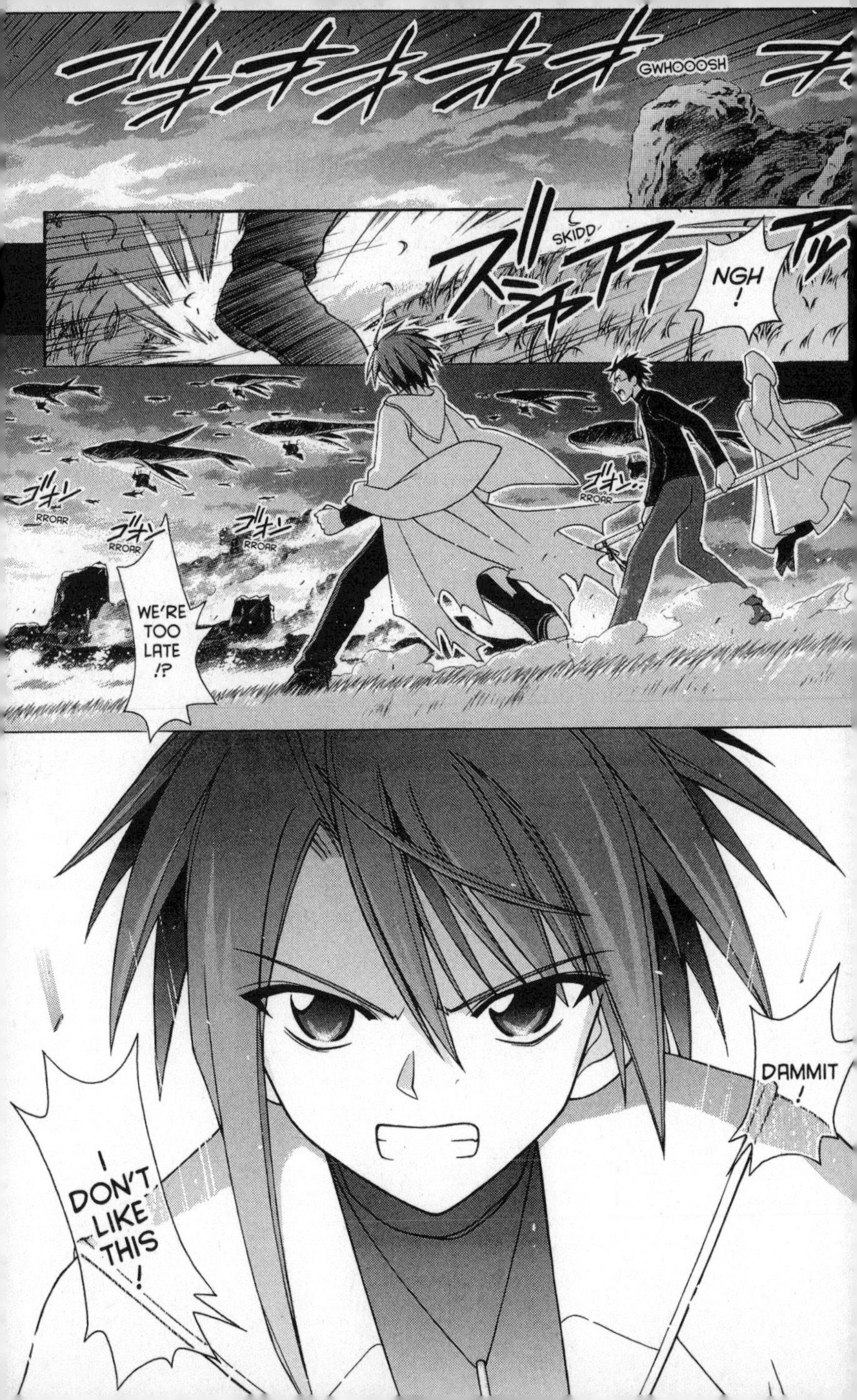
GWHOOOSH
SKIDD
NGH!
RROAR
RROAR
RROAR
RROAR
WE'RE TOO LATE!?
DAMMIT!
I DON'T LIKE THIS!

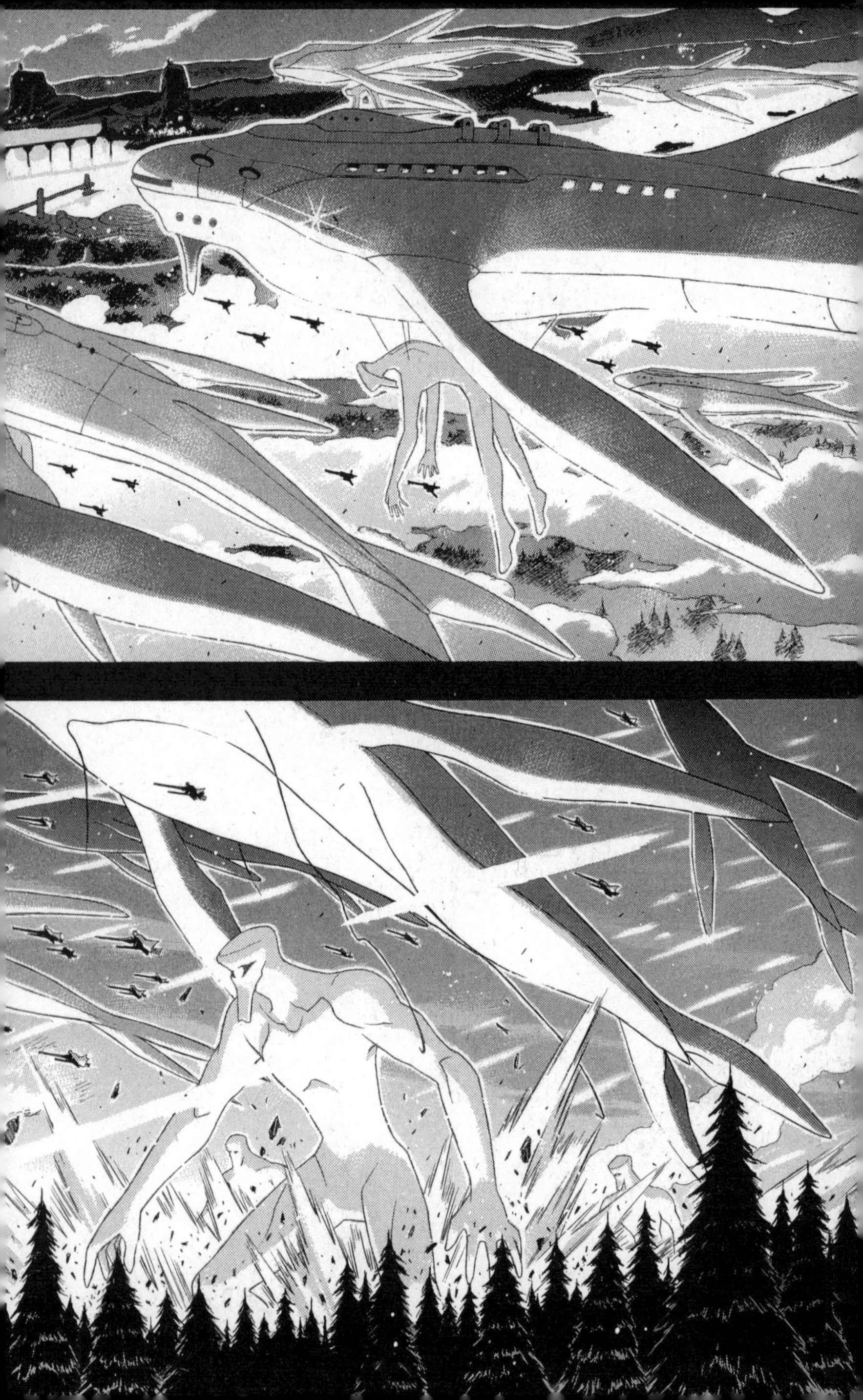

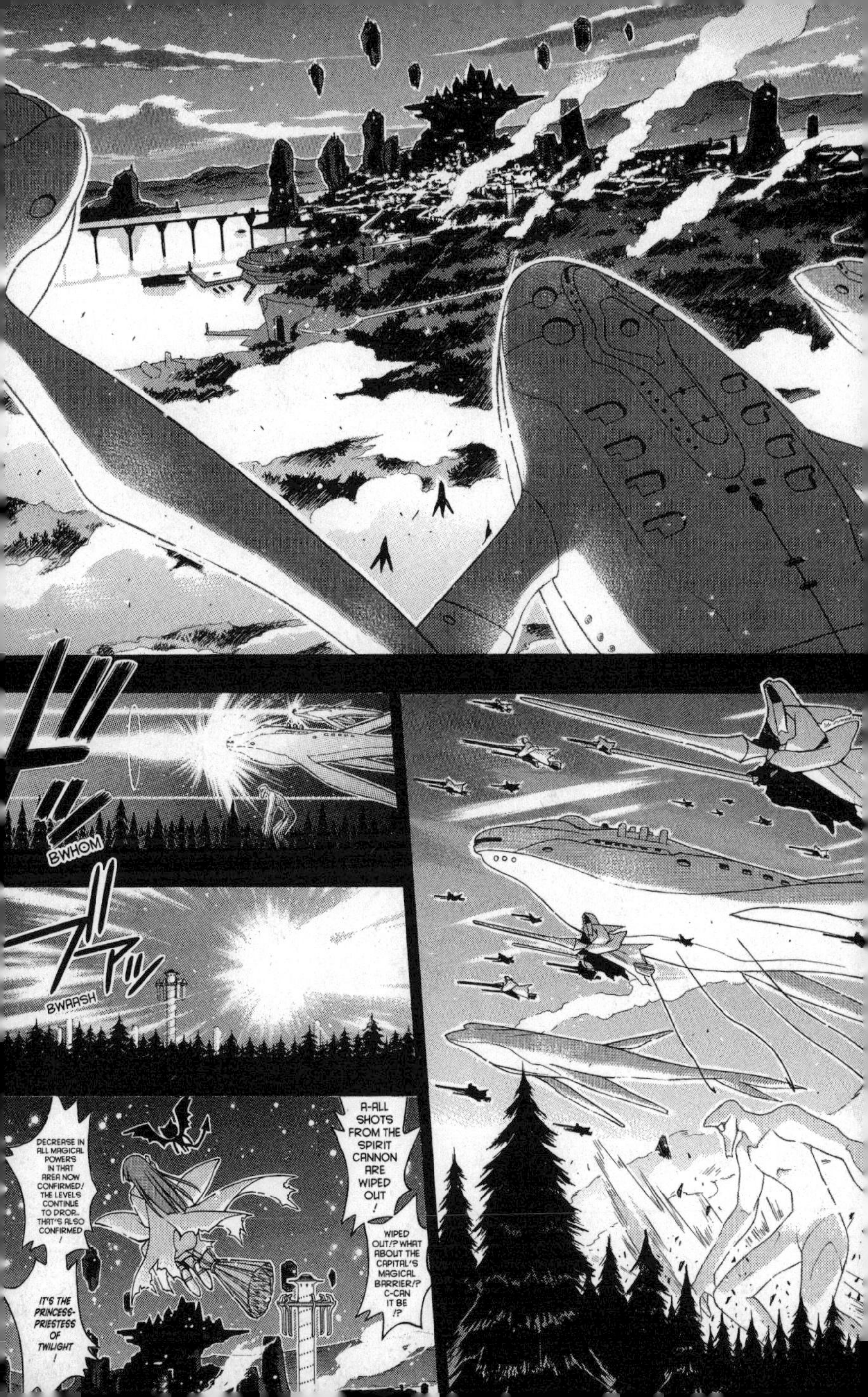
BWHOM
BWAASH
A-ALL SHOTS FROM THE SPIRIT CANNON ARE WIPED OUT!
WIPED OUT!? WHAT ABOUT THE CAPITAL'S MAGICAL BARRIER!? C-CAN IT BE!?
DECREASE IN ALL MAGICAL POWERS IN THAT AREA NOW CONFIRMED! THE LEVELS CONTINUE TO DROP... THAT'S ALSO CONFIRMED!
IT'S THE PRINCESS-PRIESTESS OF TWILIGHT!

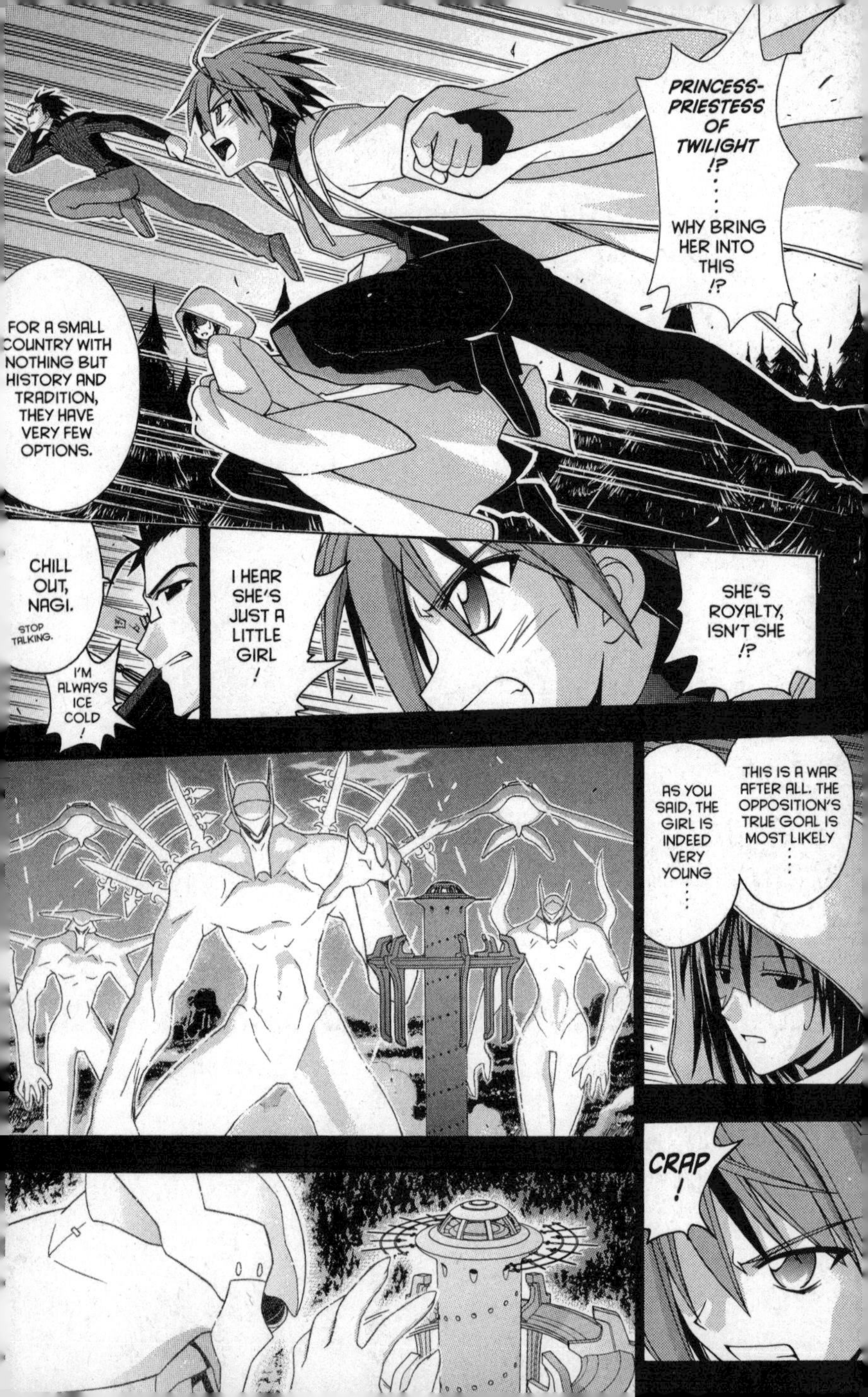
PRINCESS-PRIESTESS OF TWILIGHT!? ... WHY BRING HER INTO THIS!?
FOR A SMALL COUNTRY WITH NOTHING BUT HISTORY AND TRADITION, THEY HAVE VERY FEW OPTIONS.
SHE'S ROYALTY, ISN'T SHE!?
I HEAR SHE'S JUST A LITTLE GIRL!
CHILL OUT, NAGI.
STOP TALKING.
I'M ALWAYS ICE COLD!
THIS IS A WAR AFTER ALL. THE OPPOSITION'S TRUE GOAL IS MOST LIKELY...
AS YOU SAID, THE GIRL IS INDEED VERY YOUNG...
CRAP!

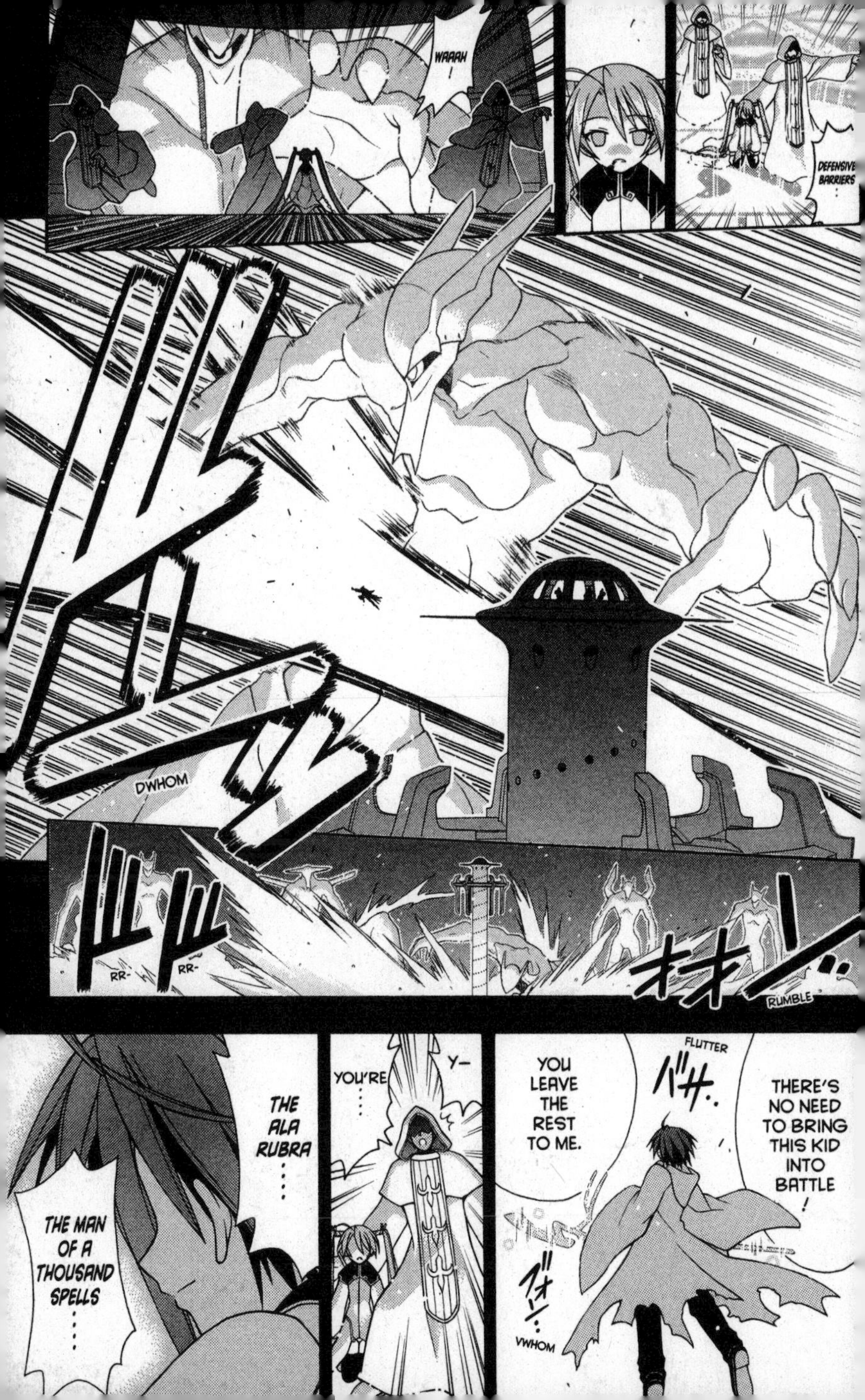

DEFENSIVE BARRIERS
WAAAH!
DWHOM
RUMBLE
RR-
RR-
THERE'S NO NEED TO BRING THIS KID INTO BATTLE!
FLUTTER
YOU LEAVE THE REST TO ME.
VWHOM
Y—
YOU'RE...
THE ALA RUBRA...
THE MAN OF A THOUSAND SPELLS...

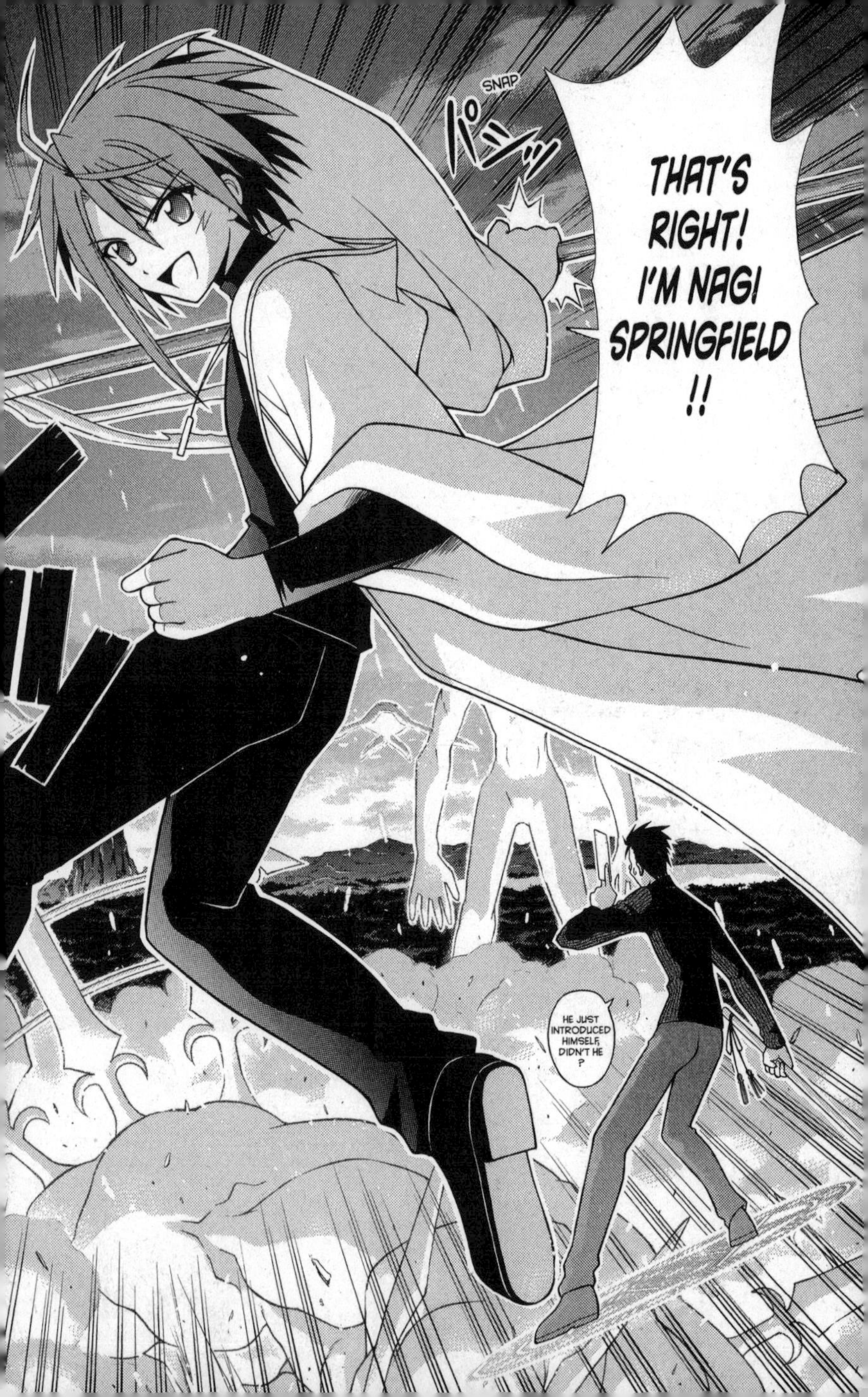
SNAP
パシッ
THAT'S RIGHT! I'M NAGI SPRINGFIELD !!
HE JUST INTRODUCED HIMSELF, DIDN'T HE ?

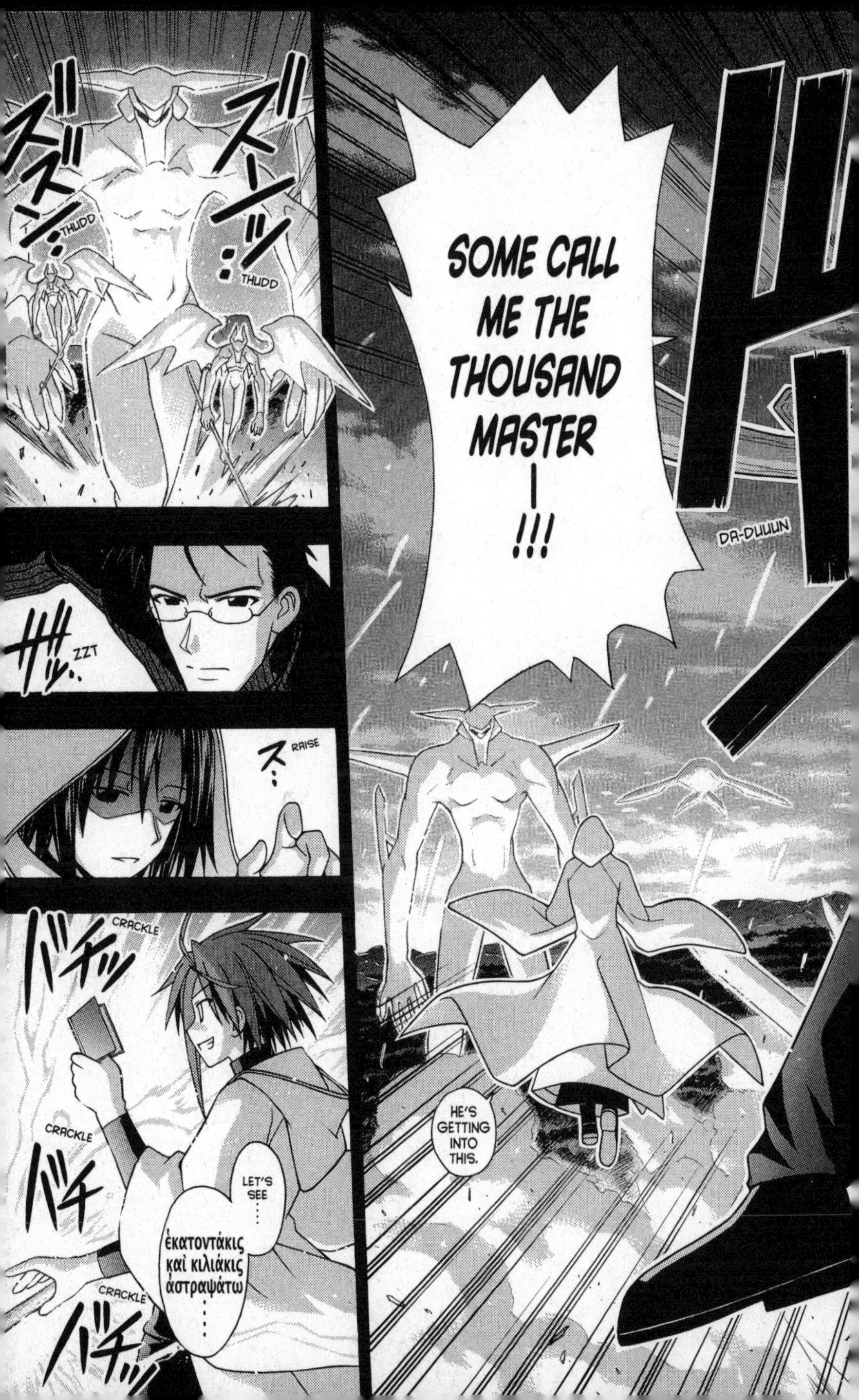
SOME CALL ME THE THOUSAND MASTER—!!!
DA-DUUUN
HE'S GETTING INTO THIS.
THUDD
THUDD
ZZT
RAISE
CRACKLE
LET'S SEE...
ἑκατοντάκις καὶ χιλιάκις ἀστραψάτω...
CRACKLE
CRACKLE

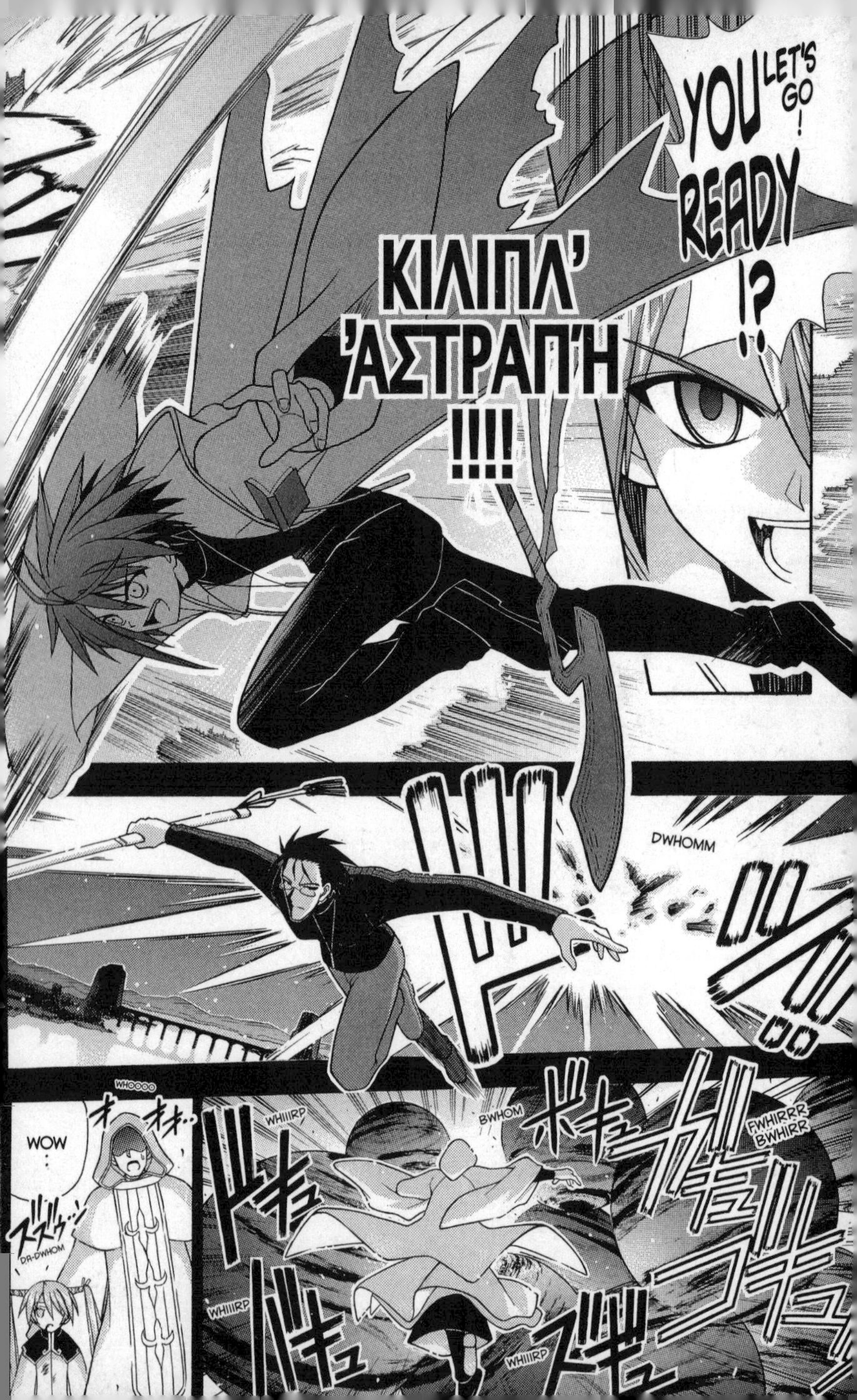
YOU READY!?
LET'S GO!
ΚΙΛΙΠΛ' 'ΑΣΤΡΑΠ'Η!!!!
DWHOMM
FWHIRRR BWHIRR
BWHOM
WHIIIRP
WHIIIRP
WHIIIRP
WHOOOO
WOW...
DA-DWHOM

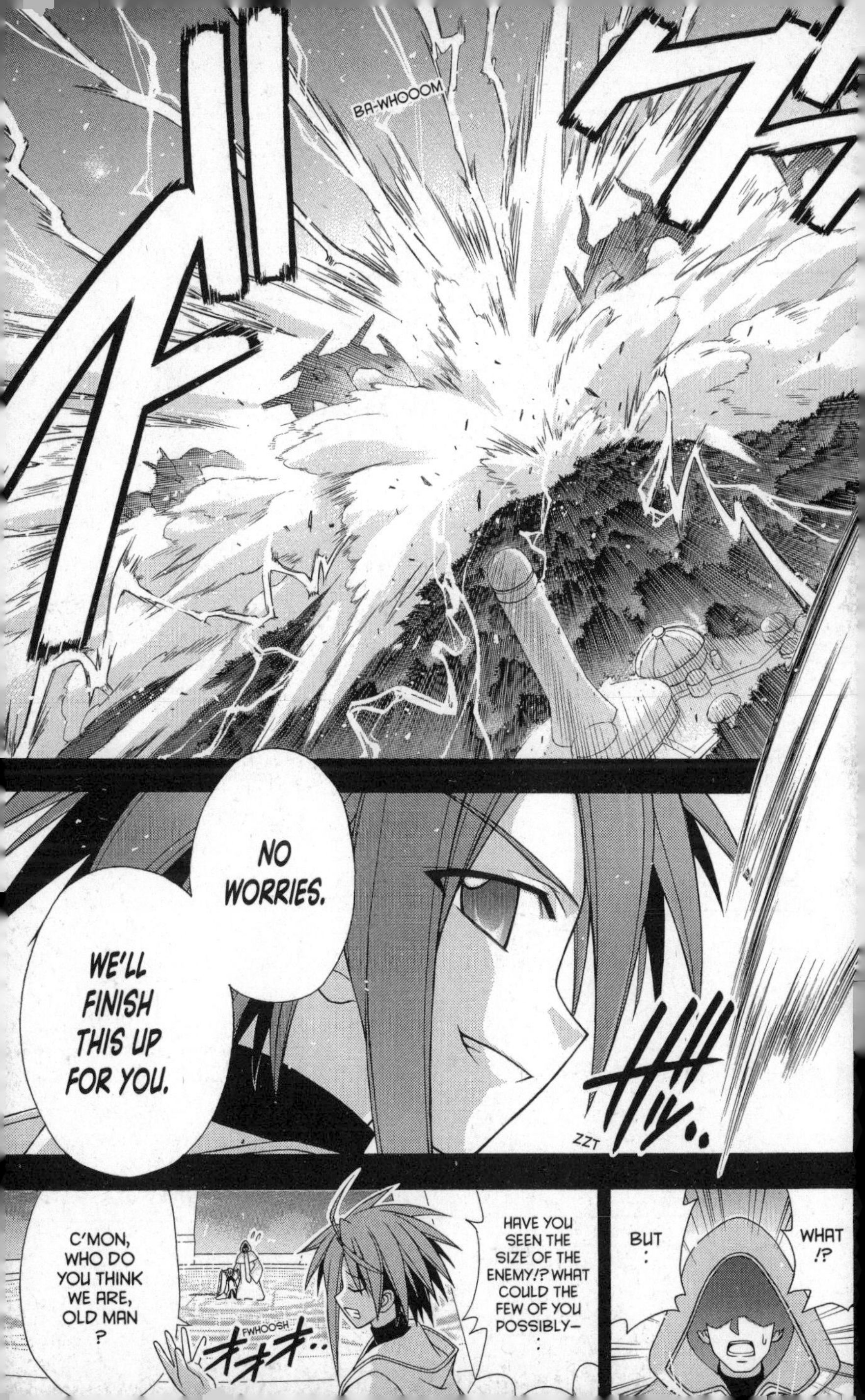
BA-WHOOOM
NO WORRIES.
WE'LL FINISH THIS UP FOR YOU.
ZZT
WHAT!?
BUT...
HAVE YOU SEEN THE SIZE OF THE ENEMY!? WHAT COULD THE FEW OF YOU POSSIBLY—...
C'MON, WHO DO YOU THINK WE ARE, OLD MAN?
FWHOOSH

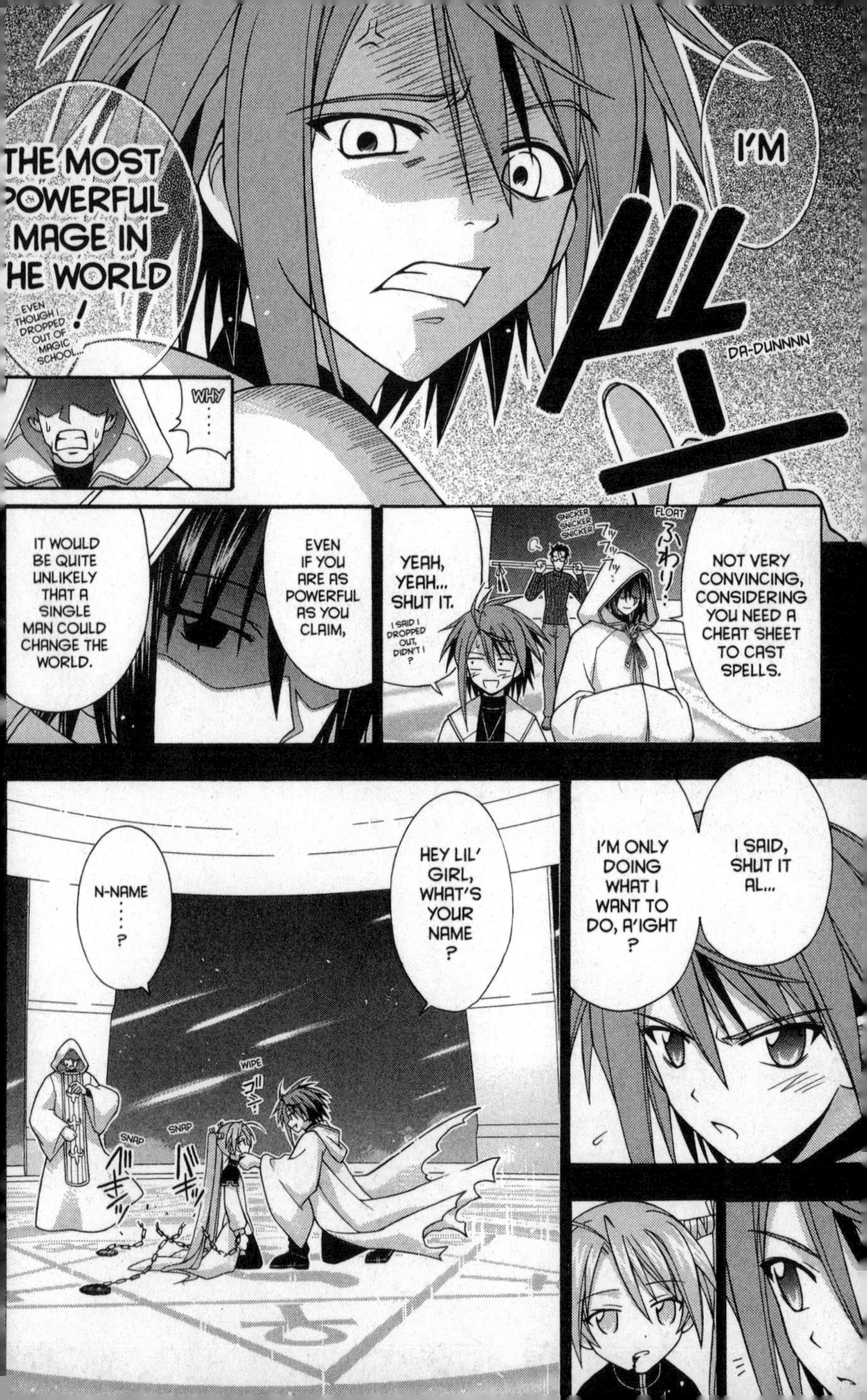
I'M
THE MOST POWERFUL MAGE IN THE WORLD!
EVEN THOUGH I DROPPED OUT OF MAGIC SCHOOL...
DA-DUNNNN
WHY....
FLOAT
ふわり…
NOT VERY CONVINCING, CONSIDERING YOU NEED A CHEAT SHEET TO CAST SPELLS.
SNICKER SNICKER SNICKER
YEAH, YEAH... SHUT IT.
I SAID I DROPPED OUT, DIDN'T I?
EVEN IF YOU ARE AS POWERFUL AS YOU CLAIM,
IT WOULD BE QUITE UNLIKELY THAT A SINGLE MAN COULD CHANGE THE WORLD.
I SAID, SHUT IT AL...
I'M ONLY DOING WHAT I WANT TO DO, A'IGHT?
HEY LIL' GIRL, WHAT'S YOUR NAME?
N-NAME....?
WIPE
SNAP
SNAP

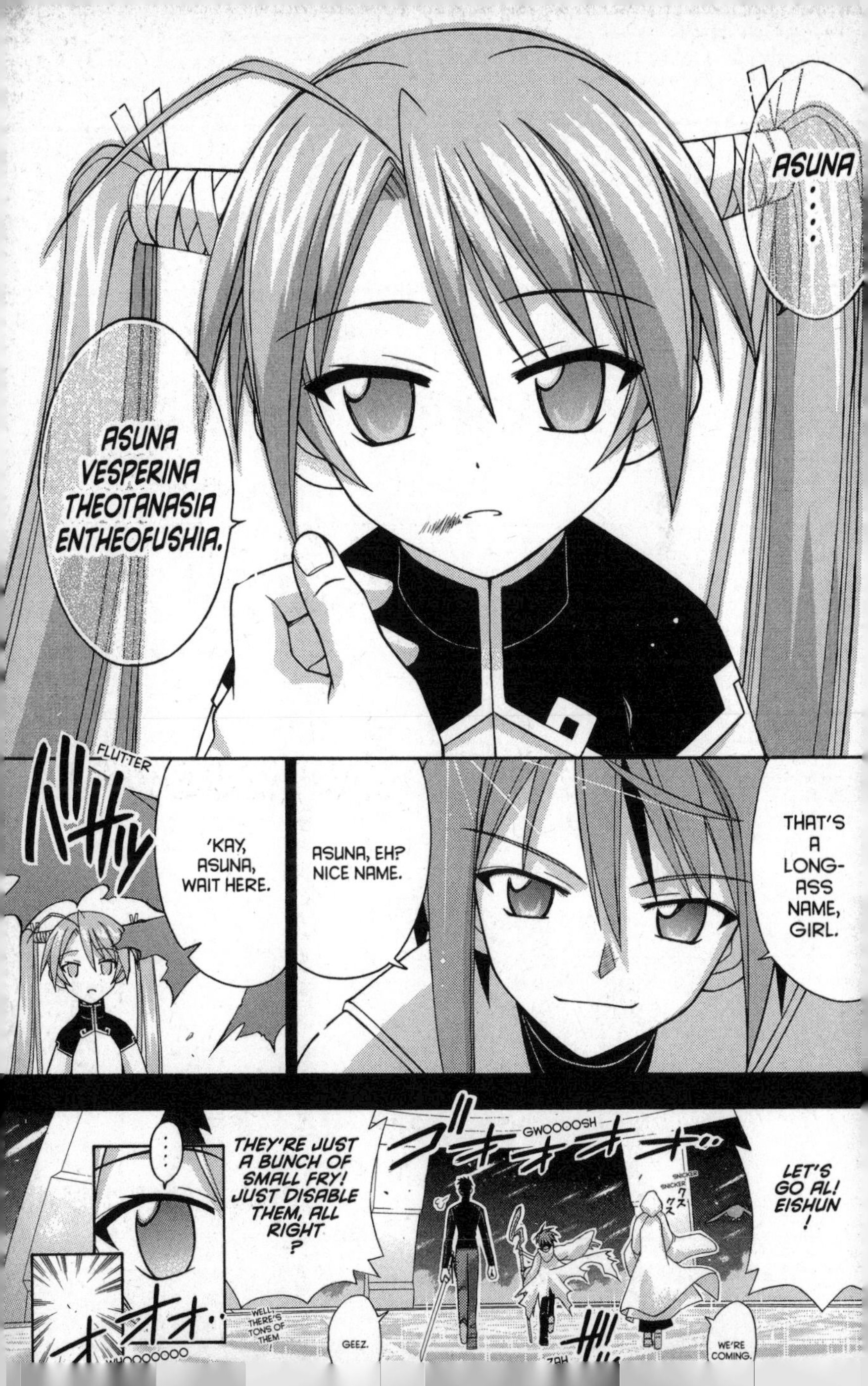
ASUNA
....
ASUNA VESPERINA THEOTANASIA ENTHEOFUSHIA.
THAT'S A LONG-ASS NAME, GIRL.
ASUNA, EH? NICE NAME.
FLUTTER
'KAY, ASUNA, WAIT HERE.
LET'S GO AL! EISHUN!
GWOOOOSH
SNICKER SNICKER
THEY'RE JUST A BUNCH OF SMALL FRY! JUST DISABLE THEM, ALL RIGHT?
WE'RE COMING.
GEEZ.
WELL, THERE'S TONS OF THEM
....
WHOOOOOOO

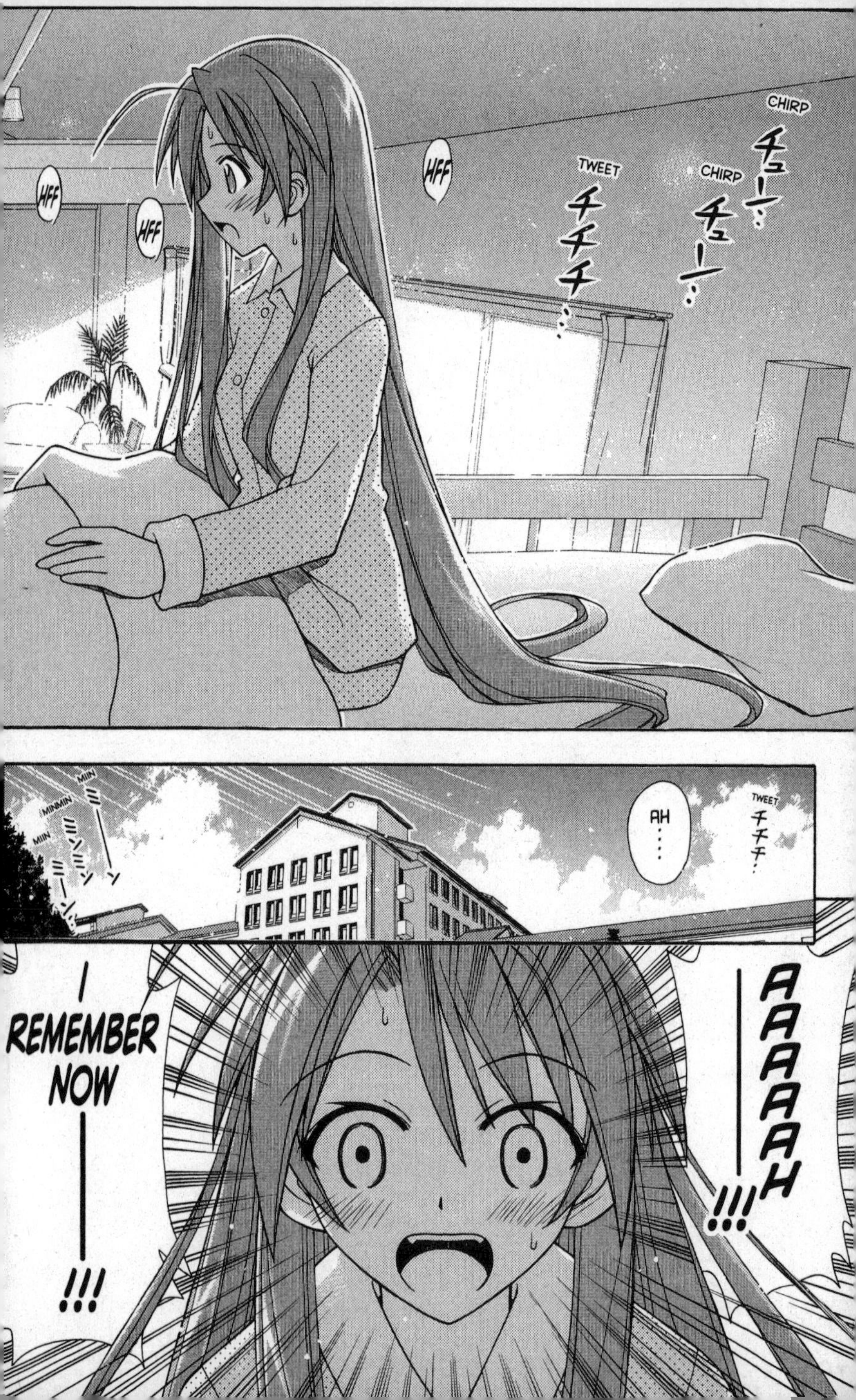

CHIRP
チュー…
CHIRP
チュー…
TWEET
チチチ…
HFF
HFF
HFF
TWEET
チチチ…
AH…
MIN
ミーン
MINMIN
ミンミン
MIN
ミーン
AAAAAAH!!!
I REMEMBER NOW!!!

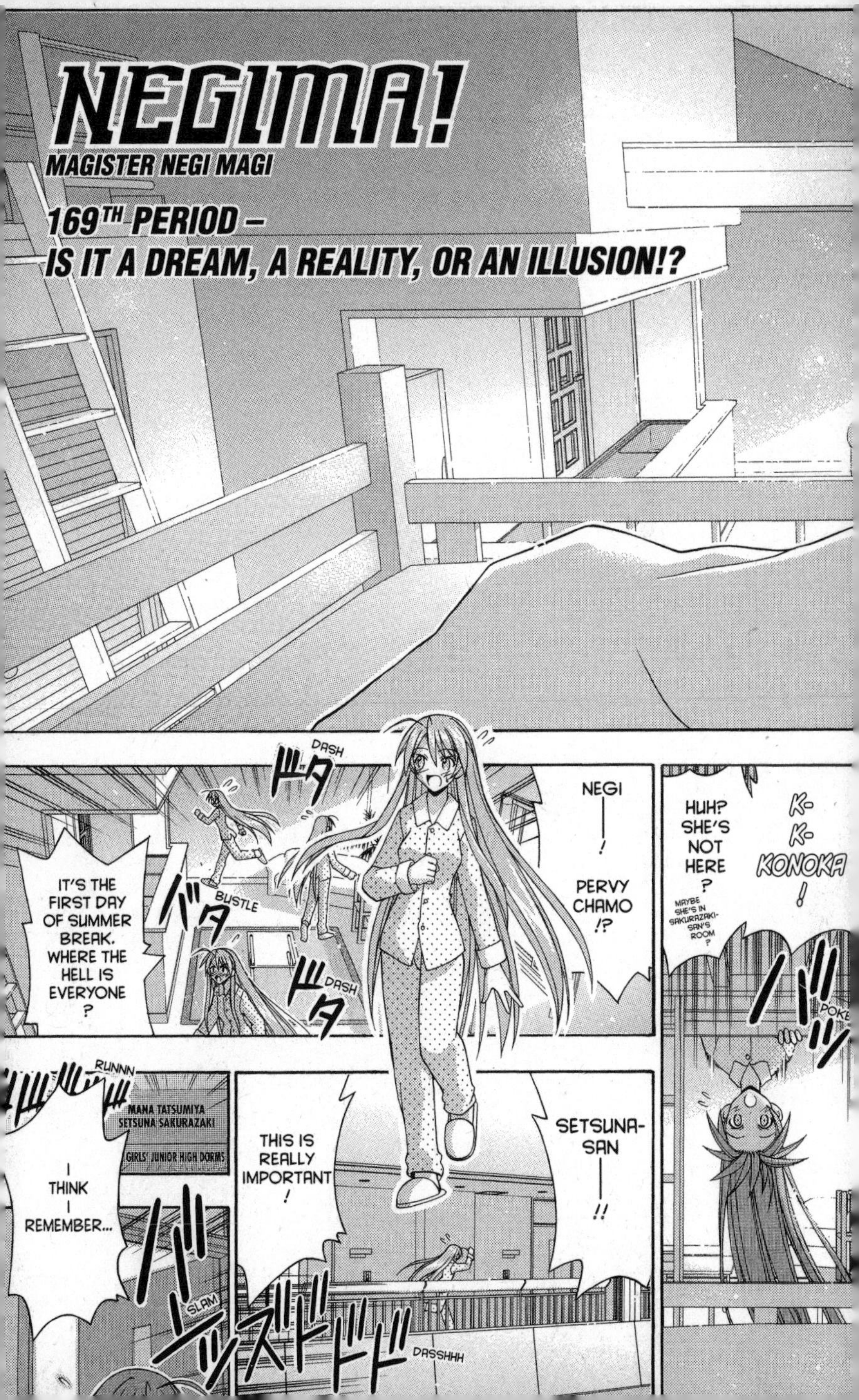
NEGIMA!
MAGISTER NEGI MAGI
169TH PERIOD –
IS IT A DREAM, A REALITY, OR AN ILLUSION!?
HUH? SHE'S NOT HERE?
MAYBE SHE'S IN SAKURAZAKI-SAN'S ROOM?
K-K-KONOKA!
POKE
NEGI—!
PERVY CHAMO!?
DASH
BUSTLE
DASH
IT'S THE FIRST DAY OF SUMMER BREAK. WHERE THE HELL IS EVERYONE?
SETSUNA-SAN—!!
THIS IS REALLY IMPORTANT!
SLAM
DASSHHH
RUNNN
MANA TATSUMIYA
SETSUNA SAKURAZAKI
GIRLS' JUNIOR HIGH DORMS
I THINK I REMEMBER...

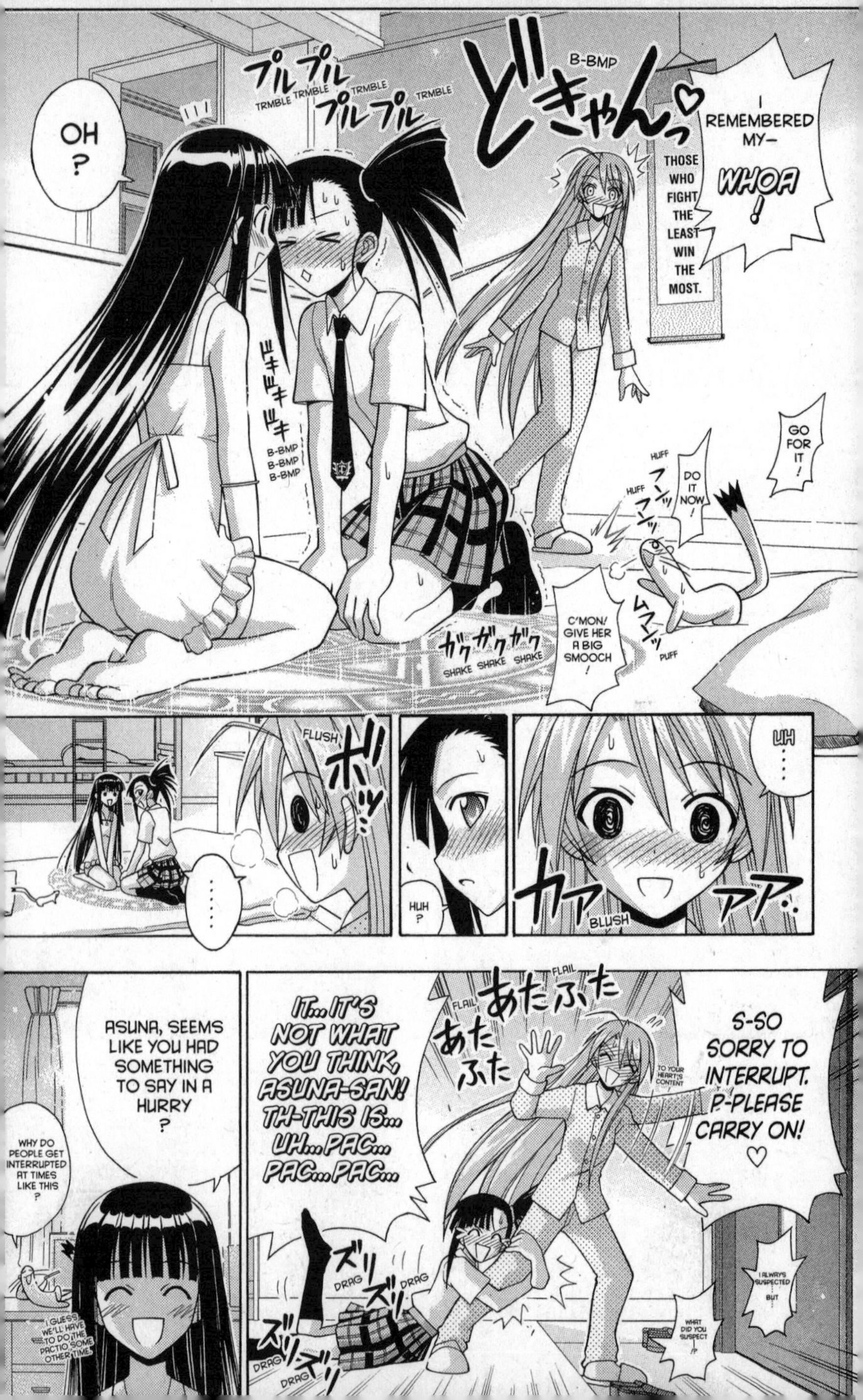
I REMEMBERED MY—
WHOA!
THOSE WHO FIGHT THE LEAST WIN THE MOST.
どきゃんっ♡
B-BMP
プルプル
TRMBLE TRMBLE
プルプル
TRMBLE TRMBLE
OH?
GO FOR IT!
DO IT NOW!
フンッ HUFF
フンッ HUFF
ドキドキドキ
B-BMP B-BMP B-BMP
C'MON! GIVE HER A BIG SMOOCH!
ムフンッ
PUFF
ガクガクガク
SHAKE SHAKE SHAKE
UH......
カァァ..
BLUSH
HUH?
ボッ
FLUSH
......
S-SO SORRY TO INTERRUPT. P-PLEASE CARRY ON! ♡
TO YOUR HEART'S CONTENT
あたふた
FLAIL
あたふた
FLAIL
IT... IT'S NOT WHAT YOU THINK, ASUNA-SAN! TH-THIS IS... UH... PAC... PAC... PAC...
I ALWAYS SUSPECTED... BUT...
WHAT DID YOU SUSPECT!?
ズリズリ
DRAG DRAG
ズリズリ
DRAG DRAG
ASUNA, SEEMS LIKE YOU HAD SOMETHING TO SAY IN A HURRY?
WHY DO PEOPLE GET INTERRUPTED AT TIMES LIKE THIS?
I GUESS WE'LL HAVE TO DO THE PACTIO SOME OTHER TIME.

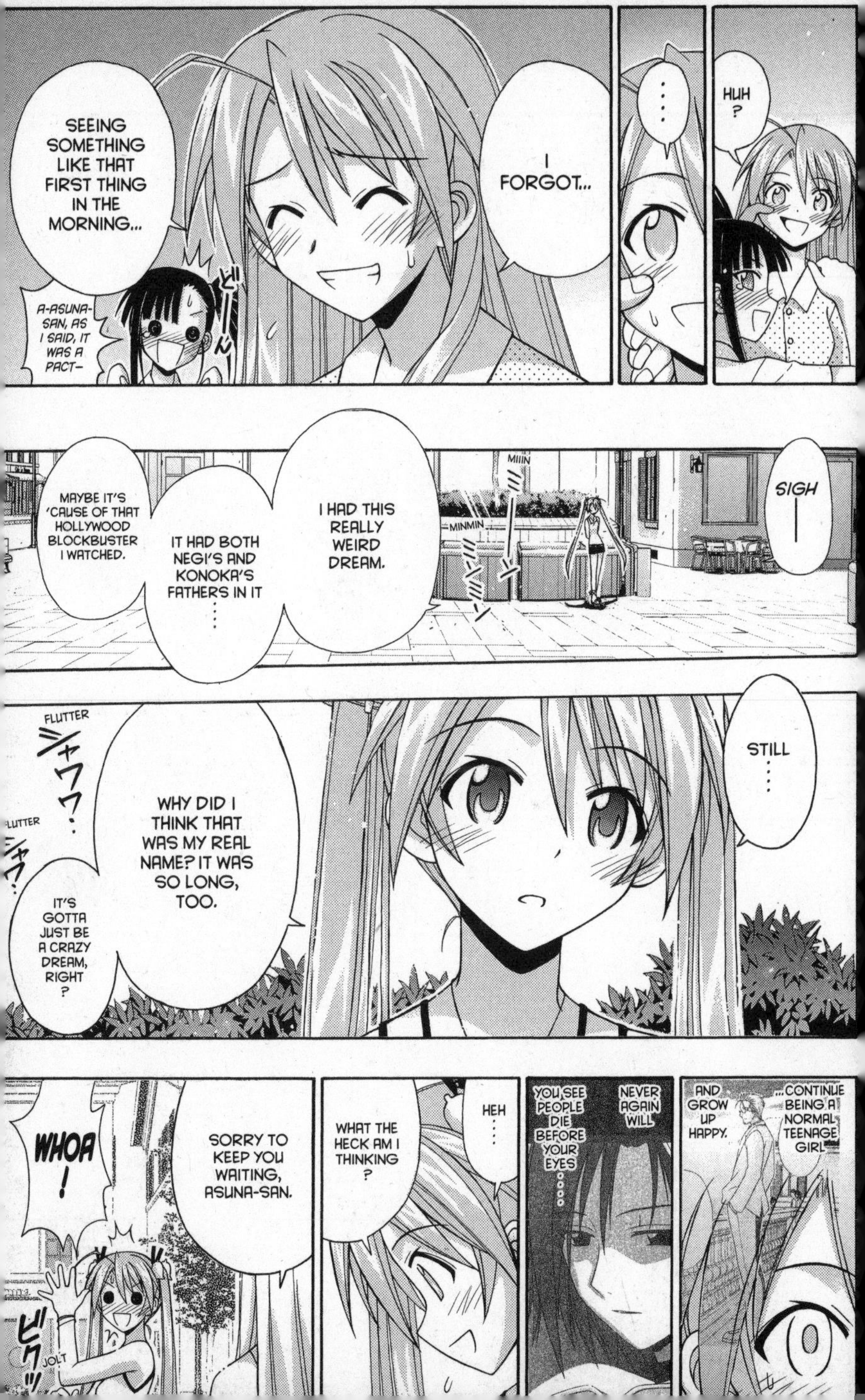
HUH ?
...
I FORGOT...
SEEING SOMETHING LIKE THAT FIRST THING IN THE MORNING...
A-ASUNA-SAN, AS I SAID, IT WAS A PACT—
SIGH
MIIN
MINMIN
I HAD THIS REALLY WEIRD DREAM.
IT HAD BOTH NEGI'S AND KONOKA'S FATHERS IN IT ...
MAYBE IT'S 'CAUSE OF THAT HOLLYWOOD BLOCKBUSTER I WATCHED.
STILL ...
WHY DID I THINK THAT WAS MY REAL NAME? IT WAS SO LONG, TOO.
FLUTTER
FLUTTER
IT'S GOTTA JUST BE A CRAZY DREAM, RIGHT ?
...CONTINUE BEING A NORMAL TEENAGE GIRL
AND GROW UP HAPPY.
NEVER AGAIN WILL
YOU SEE PEOPLE DIE BEFORE YOUR EYES .....
HEH ...
WHAT THE HECK AM I THINKING ?
SORRY TO KEEP YOU WAITING, ASUNA-SAN.
WHOA !
JOLT

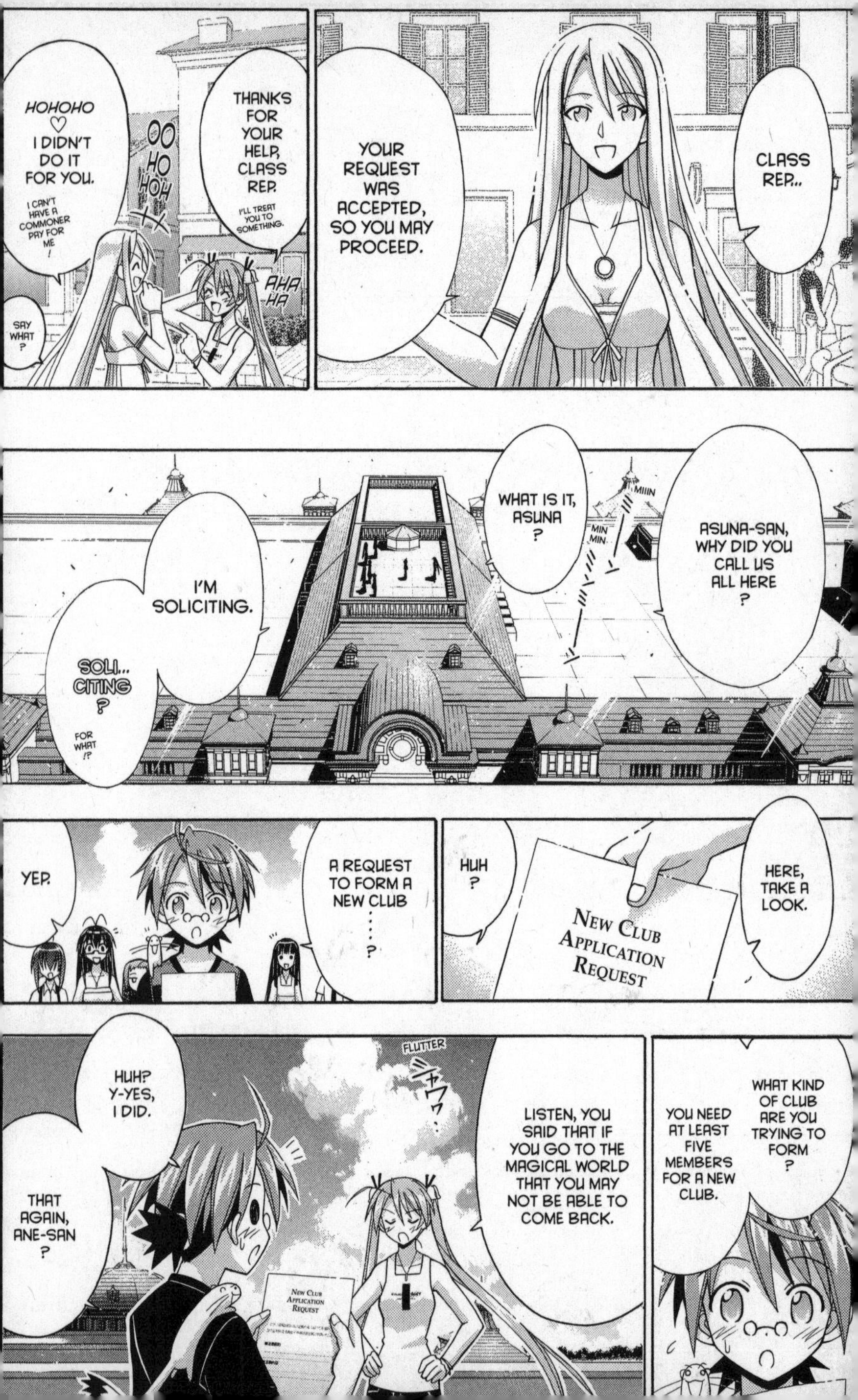
CLASS REP...
YOUR REQUEST WAS ACCEPTED, SO YOU MAY PROCEED.
THANKS FOR YOUR HELP, CLASS REP.
I'LL TREAT YOU TO SOMETHING.
AHA HA
OO HO HOH
HOHOHO ♡ I DIDN'T DO IT FOR YOU.
I CAN'T HAVE A COMMONER PAY FOR ME!
SAY WHAT?
ASUNA-SAN, WHY DID YOU CALL US ALL HERE?
MIIIN
MIN MIN
WHAT IS IT, ASUNA?
I'M SOLICITING.
SOLI... CITING?
FOR WHAT!?
HERE, TAKE A LOOK.
NEW CLUB APPLICATION REQUEST
HUH?
A REQUEST TO FORM A NEW CLUB...?
YEP.
WHAT KIND OF CLUB ARE YOU TRYING TO FORM?
YOU NEED AT LEAST FIVE MEMBERS FOR A NEW CLUB.
LISTEN, YOU SAID THAT IF YOU GO TO THE MAGICAL WORLD THAT YOU MAY NOT BE ABLE TO COME BACK.
FLUTTER
HUH? Y-YES, I DID.
THAT AGAIN, ANE-SAN?
NEW CLUB APPLICATION REQUEST

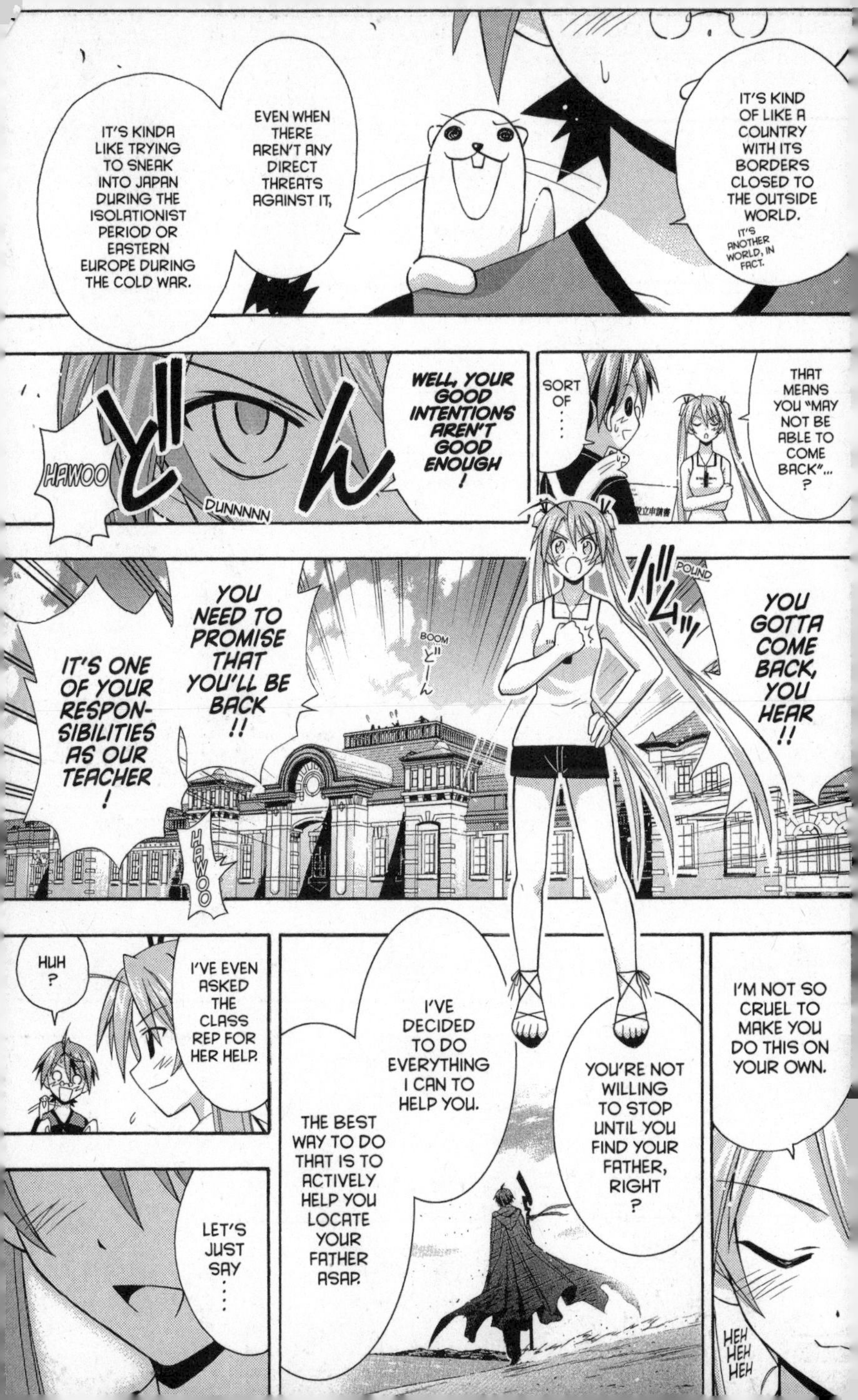
IT'S KIND OF LIKE A COUNTRY WITH ITS BORDERS CLOSED TO THE OUTSIDE WORLD.
IT'S ANOTHER WORLD, IN FACT.
EVEN WHEN THERE AREN'T ANY DIRECT THREATS AGAINST IT,
IT'S KINDA LIKE TRYING TO SNEAK INTO JAPAN DURING THE ISOLATIONIST PERIOD OR EASTERN EUROPE DURING THE COLD WAR.
THAT MEANS YOU "MAY NOT BE ABLE TO COME BACK"...?
SORT OF....
WELL, YOUR GOOD INTENTIONS AREN'T GOOD ENOUGH!
HAWOO
DUNNNNN
YOU GOTTA COME BACK, YOU HEAR!!
POUND
BOOM
YOU NEED TO PROMISE THAT YOU'LL BE BACK!!
IT'S ONE OF YOUR RESPONSIBILITIES AS OUR TEACHER!
HAWOO
I'M NOT SO CRUEL TO MAKE YOU DO THIS ON YOUR OWN.
HEH HEH HEH
YOU'RE NOT WILLING TO STOP UNTIL YOU FIND YOUR FATHER, RIGHT?
I'VE DECIDED TO DO EVERYTHING I CAN TO HELP YOU.
THE BEST WAY TO DO THAT IS TO ACTIVELY HELP YOU LOCATE YOUR FATHER ASAP.
I'VE EVEN ASKED THE CLASS REP FOR HER HELP.
HUH?
LET'S JUST SAY....

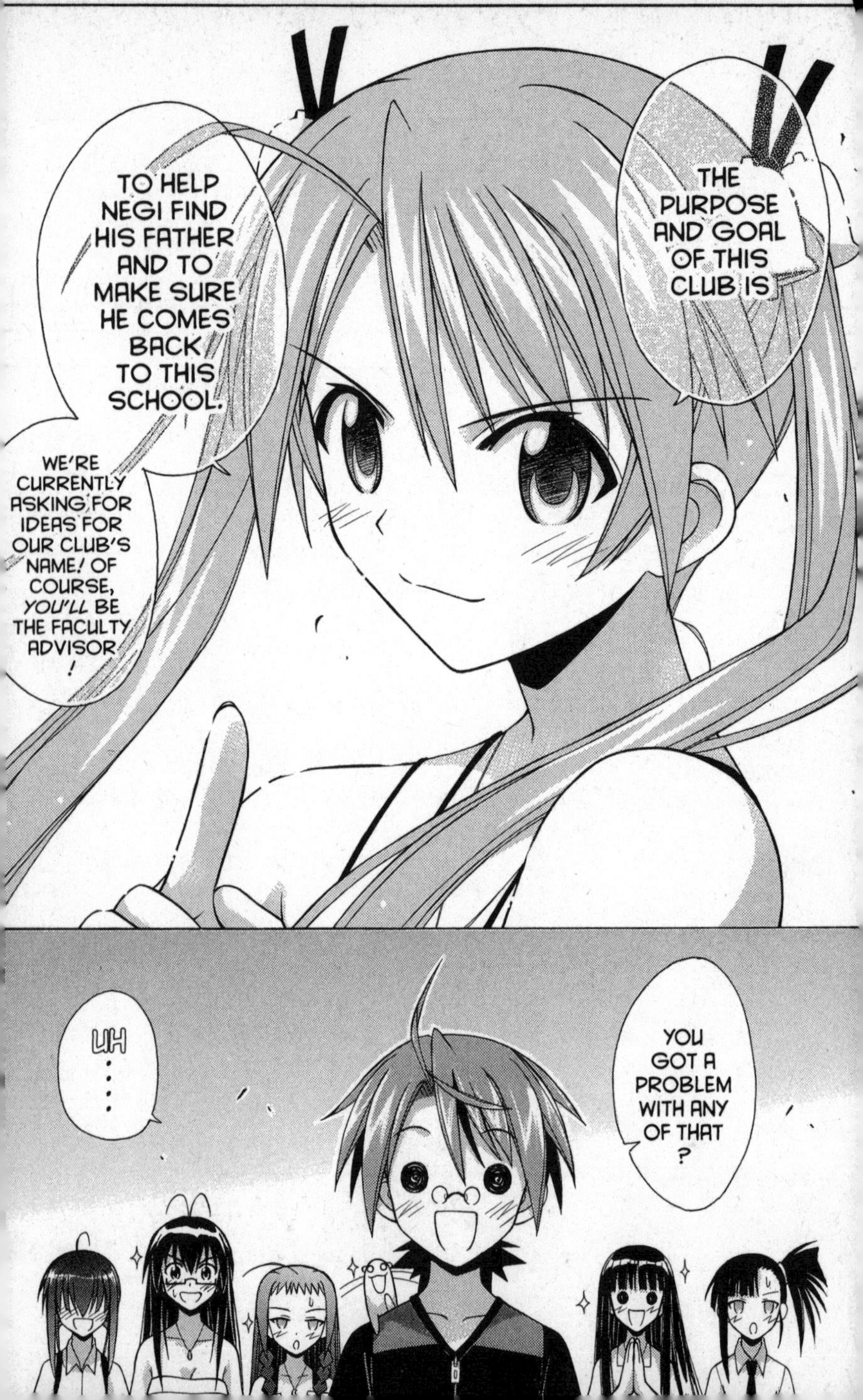
THE PURPOSE AND GOAL OF THIS CLUB IS
TO HELP NEGI FIND HIS FATHER AND TO MAKE SURE HE COMES BACK TO THIS SCHOOL.
WE'RE CURRENTLY ASKING FOR IDEAS FOR OUR CLUB'S NAME! OF COURSE, *YOU'LL* BE THE FACULTY ADVISOR!
YOU GOT A PROBLEM WITH ANY OF THAT?
UH....

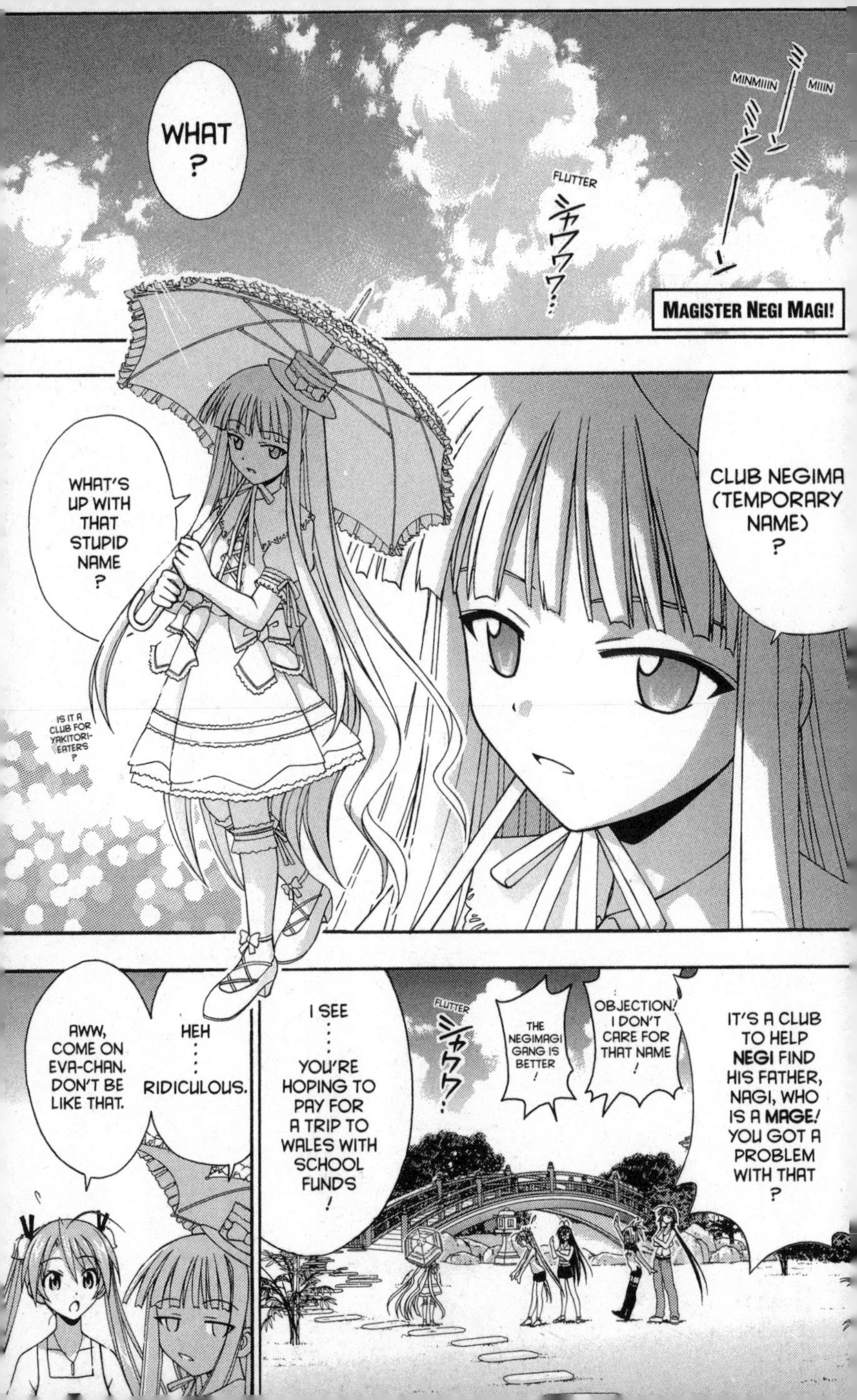

MAGISTER NEGI MAGI!
MINMIIIN MIIIN
FLUTTER
WHAT?
CLUB NEGIMA (TEMPORARY NAME)?
WHAT'S UP WITH THAT STUPID NAME?
IS IT A CLUB FOR YAKITORI-EATERS?
IT'S A CLUB TO HELP NEGI FIND HIS FATHER, NAGI, WHO IS A MAGE! YOU GOT A PROBLEM WITH THAT?
OBJECTION! I DON'T CARE FOR THAT NAME!
THE NEGIMAGI GANG IS BETTER!
FLUTTER
I SEE... YOU'RE HOPING TO PAY FOR A TRIP TO WALES WITH SCHOOL FUNDS!
HEH... RIDICULOUS.
AWW, COME ON EVA-CHAN. DON'T BE LIKE THAT.

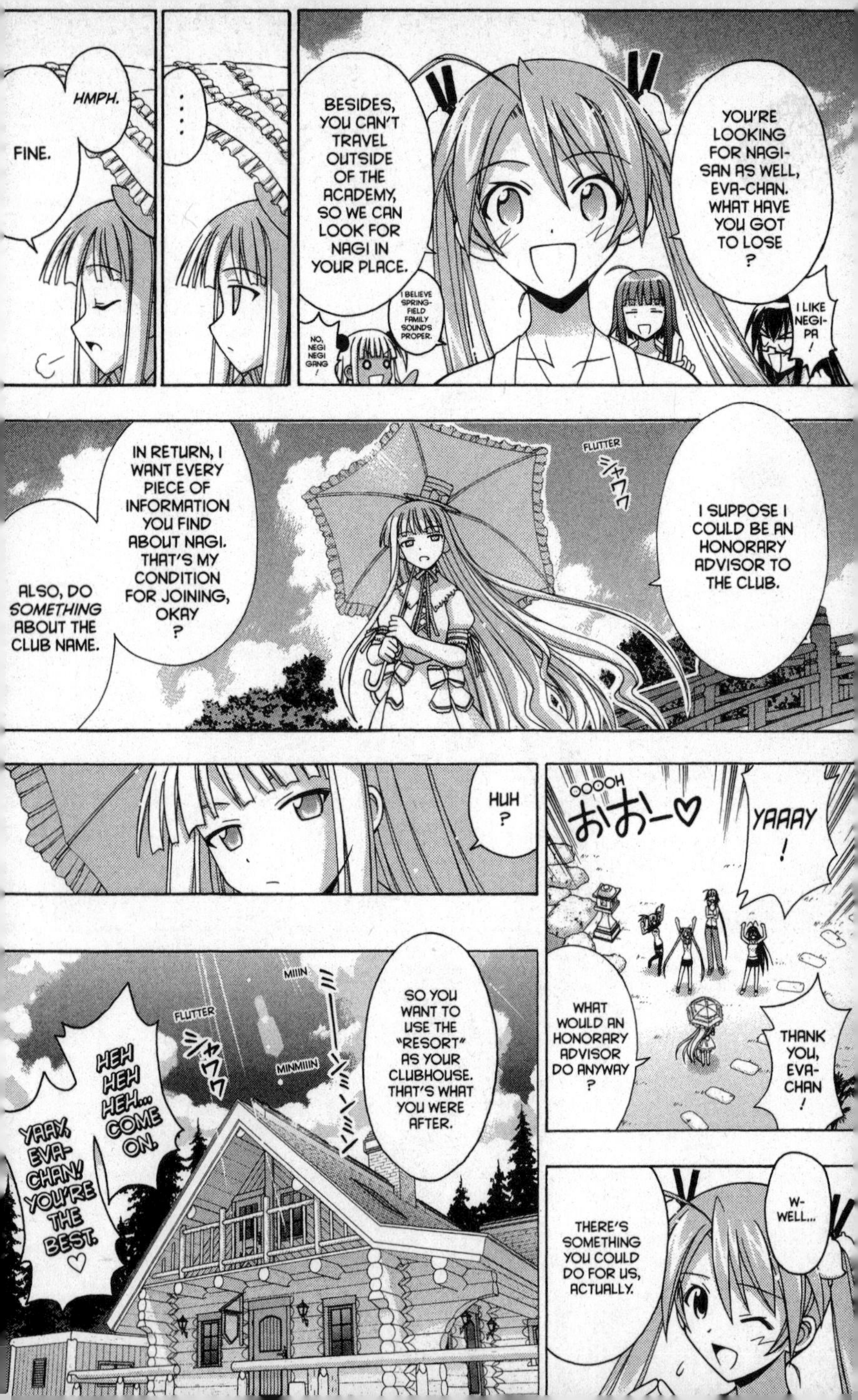

YOU'RE LOOKING FOR NAGI-SAN AS WELL, EVA-CHAN. WHAT HAVE YOU GOT TO LOSE?
I LIKE NEGI-PA!
BESIDES, YOU CAN'T TRAVEL OUTSIDE OF THE ACADEMY, SO WE CAN LOOK FOR NAGI IN YOUR PLACE.
I BELIEVE SPRING-FIELD FAMILY SOUNDS PROPER.
NO, NEGI NEGI GANG!
....
HMPH.
FINE.
I SUPPOSE I COULD BE AN HONORARY ADVISOR TO THE CLUB.
FLUTTER
シャワワ
IN RETURN, I WANT EVERY PIECE OF INFORMATION YOU FIND ABOUT NAGI. THAT'S MY CONDITION FOR JOINING, OKAY?
ALSO, DO *SOMETHING* ABOUT THE CLUB NAME.
YAAAY!
OOOOH
おおー♡
THANK YOU, EVA-CHAN!
WHAT WOULD AN HONORARY ADVISOR DO ANYWAY?
W-WELL...
THERE'S SOMETHING YOU COULD DO FOR US, ACTUALLY.
HUH?
MIIIN
MINMIIIN
ミーンミンミン
SO YOU WANT TO USE THE "RESORT" AS YOUR CLUBHOUSE. THAT'S WHAT YOU WERE AFTER.
FLUTTER
シャワワ
HEH HEH HEH... COME ON.
YAAAY, EVA-CHAN! YOU'RE THE BEST. ♡

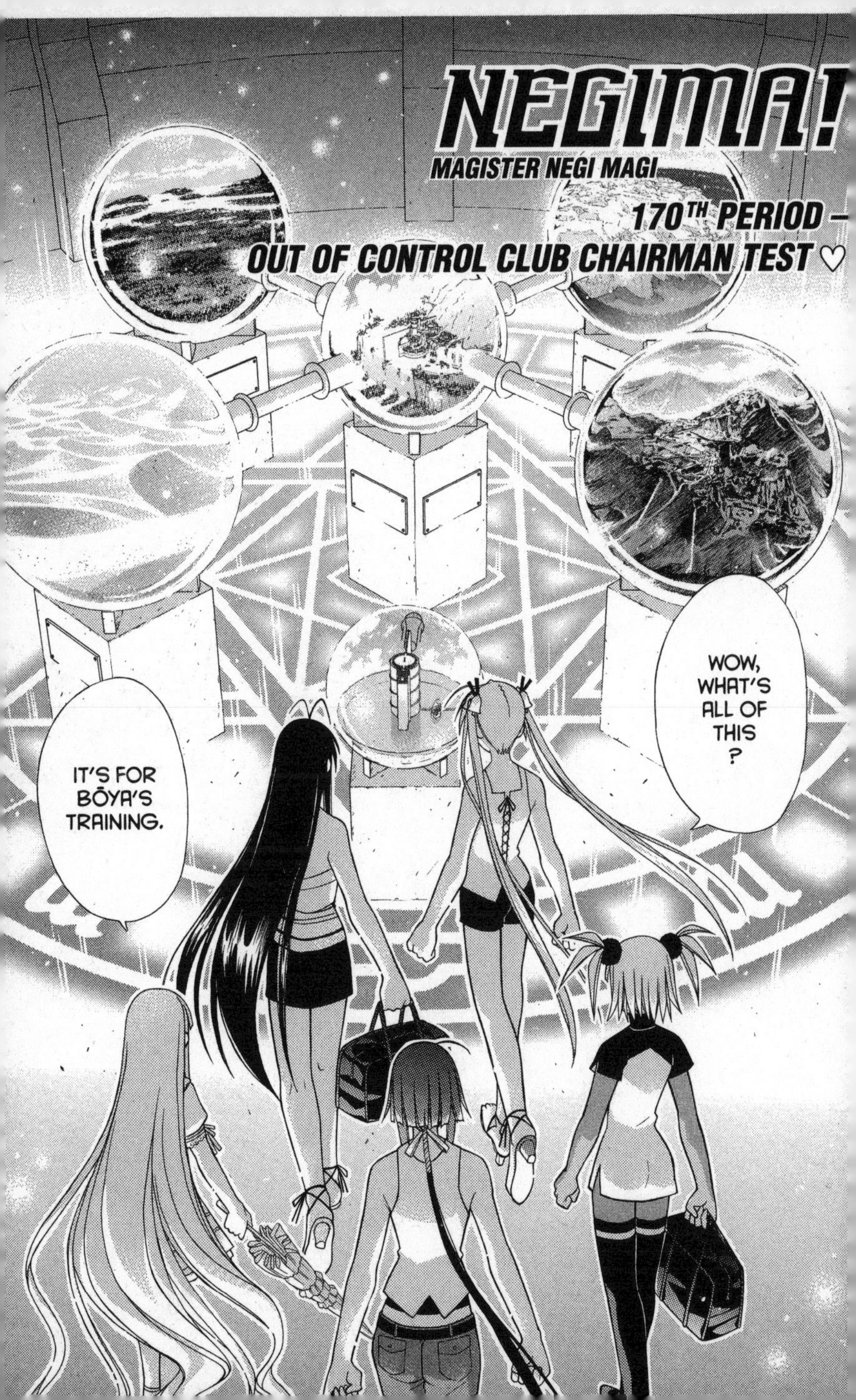
NEGIMA!
MAGISTER NEGI MAGI
170TH PERIOD – OUT OF CONTROL CLUB CHAIRMAN TEST ♡
WOW, WHAT'S ALL OF THIS?
IT'S FOR BŌYA'S TRAINING.

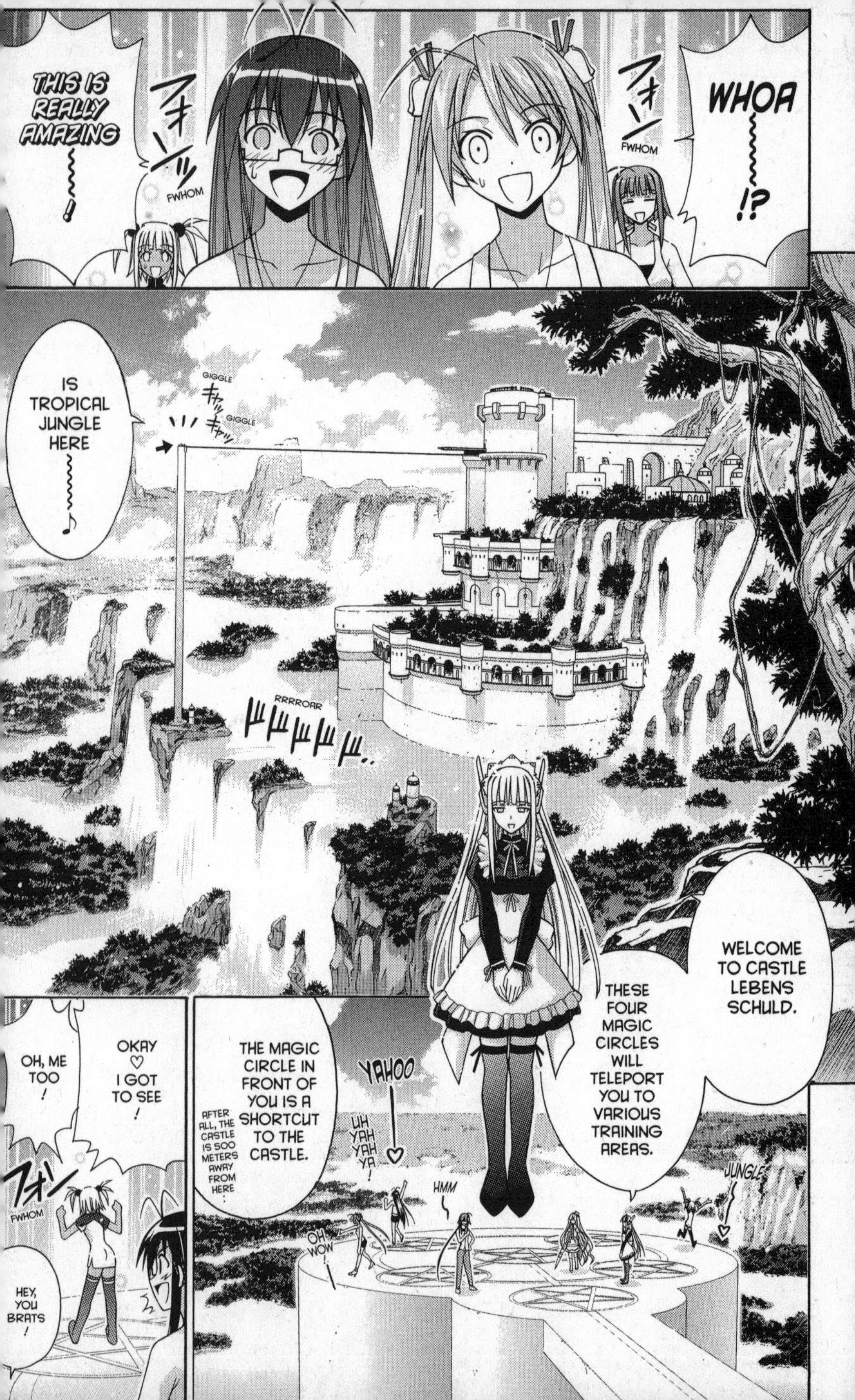
WHOA~~~!?
FWHOM
THIS IS REALLY AMAZING~~~!
FWHOM
IS TROPICAL JUNGLE HERE~~~♪
GIGGLE GIGGLE
RRRROAR
WELCOME TO CASTLE LEBENS SCHULD.
THESE FOUR MAGIC CIRCLES WILL TELEPORT YOU TO VARIOUS TRAINING AREAS.
THE MAGIC CIRCLE IN FRONT OF YOU IS A SHORTCUT TO THE CASTLE.
AFTER ALL, THE CASTLE IS 500 METERS AWAY FROM HERE.
YAHOO ♡
UH YAH YAH YA!
JUNGLE! ♡
HMM
OH WOW!
OKAY ♡ I GOT TO SEE!
OH, ME TOO!
FWHOM
HEY, YOU BRATS!

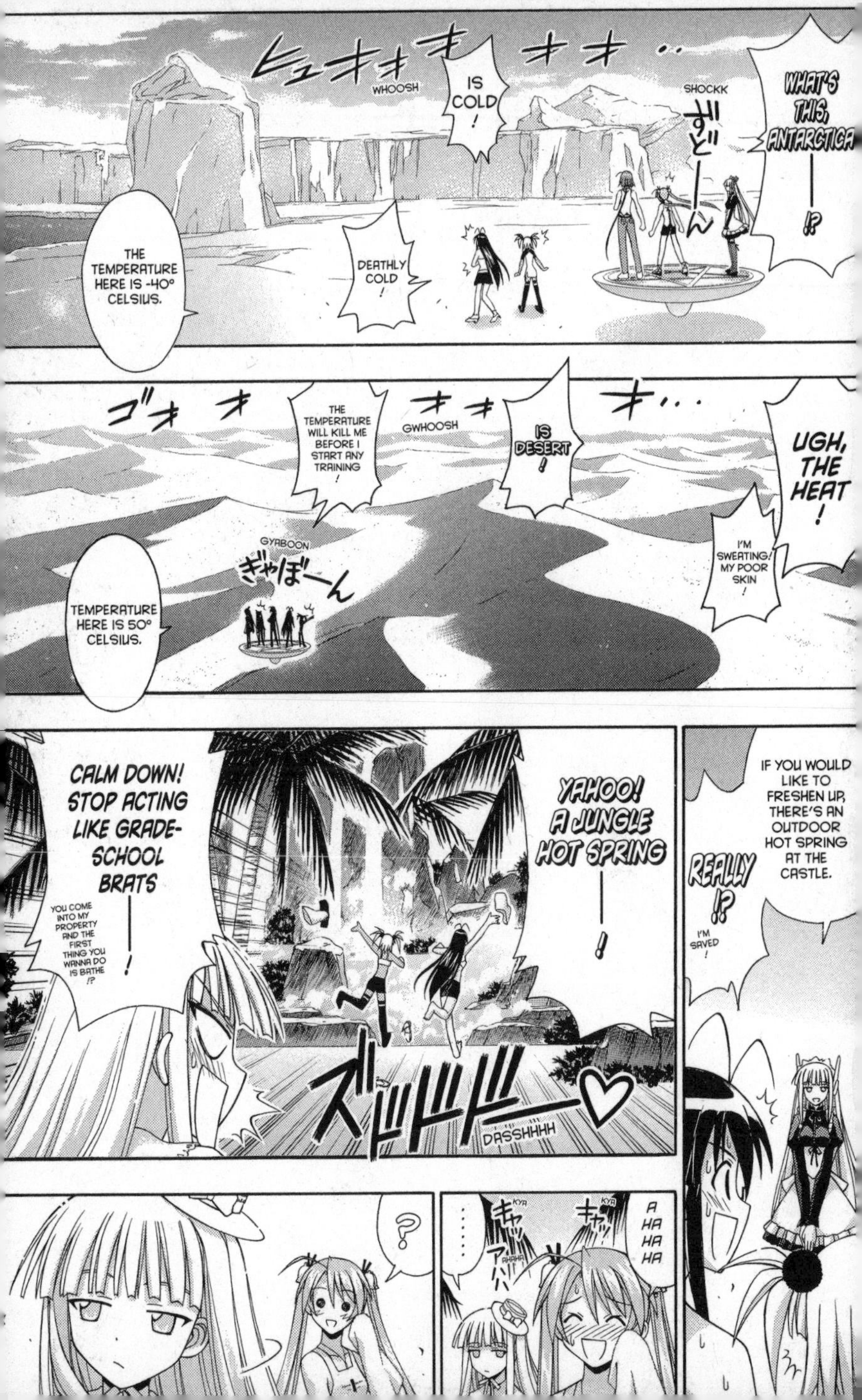
WHAT'S THIS, ANTARCTICA —!?
SHOCKK
ずどーん
IS COLD!
ヒュオオオオオ..
WHOOSH
DEATHLY COLD!
THE TEMPERATURE HERE IS -40° CELSIUS.
UGH, THE HEAT!
I'M SWEATING! MY POOR SKIN!
IS DESERT!
ゴオオオオオ...
GWHOOSH
THE TEMPERATURE WILL KILL ME BEFORE I START ANY TRAINING!
GYABOON
ぎゃぼーん
TEMPERATURE HERE IS 50° CELSIUS.
IF YOU WOULD LIKE TO FRESHEN UP, THERE'S AN OUTDOOR HOT SPRING AT THE CASTLE.
REALLY!?
I'M SAVED!
YAHOO! A JUNGLE HOT SPRING —!
CALM DOWN! STOP ACTING LIKE GRADE-SCHOOL BRATS —!
YOU COME INTO MY PROPERTY AND THE FIRST THING YOU WANNA DO IS BATHE!?
ズドドドー
DASSHHHH
A HA HA HA
キャッ
KYA
キャッ
KYA
アハハ
AHAHA
......
?

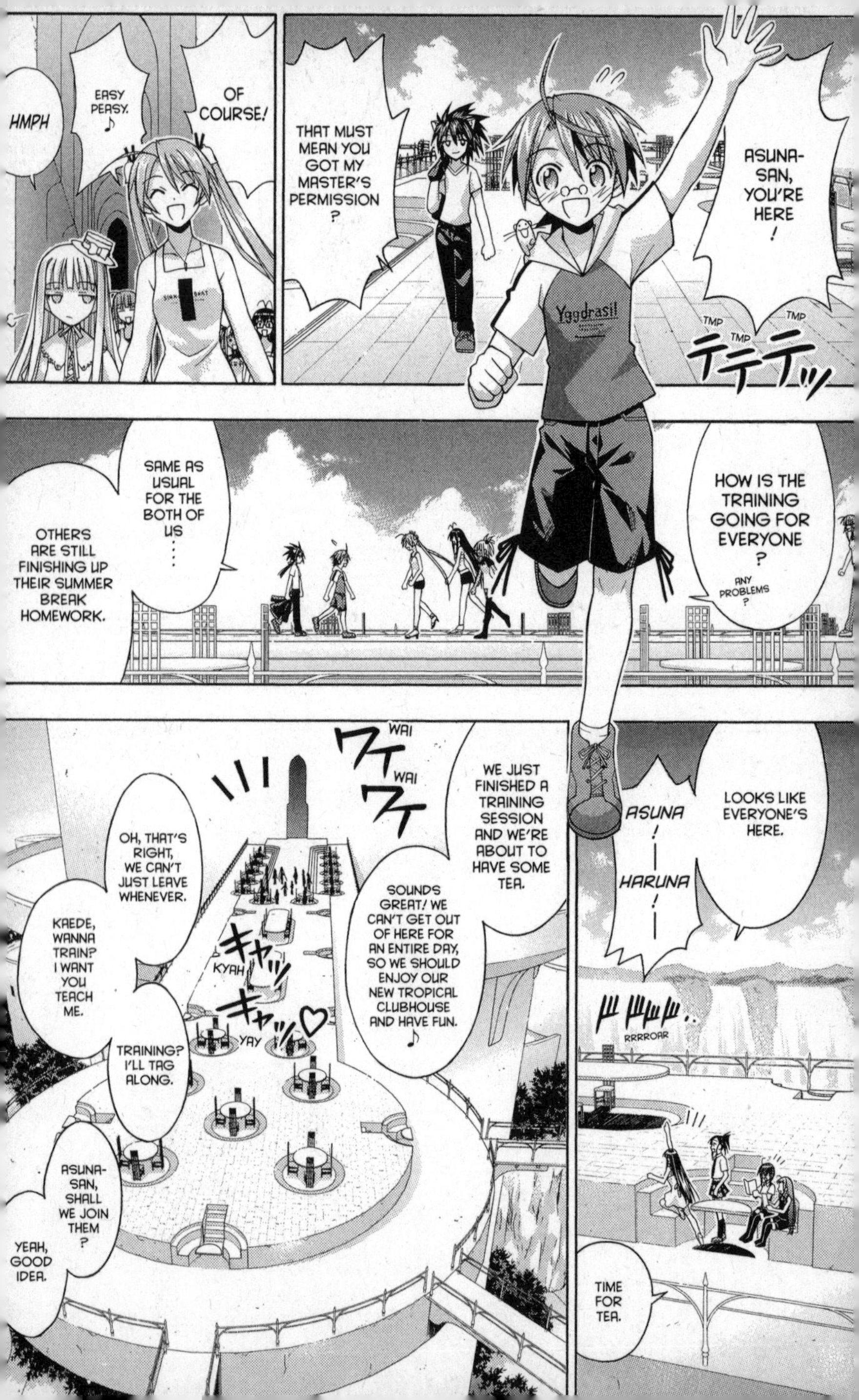
ASUNA-SAN, YOU'RE HERE!
TMP
TMP
TMP
テテテッ
THAT MUST MEAN YOU GOT MY MASTER'S PERMISSION?
OF COURSE!
EASY PEASY. ♪
HMPH
HOW IS THE TRAINING GOING FOR EVERYONE?
ANY PROBLEMS?
SAME AS USUAL FOR THE BOTH OF US...
OTHERS ARE STILL FINISHING UP THEIR SUMMER BREAK HOMEWORK.
LOOKS LIKE EVERYONE'S HERE.
ASUNA!
HARUNA!
RRRROAR
TIME FOR TEA.
ワイワイ
WAI WAI
WE JUST FINISHED A TRAINING SESSION AND WE'RE ABOUT TO HAVE SOME TEA.
SOUNDS GREAT! WE CAN'T GET OUT OF HERE FOR AN ENTIRE DAY, SO WE SHOULD ENJOY OUR NEW TROPICAL CLUBHOUSE AND HAVE FUN. ♪
OH, THAT'S RIGHT, WE CAN'T JUST LEAVE WHENEVER.
KAEDE, WANNA TRAIN? I WANT YOU TEACH ME.
キャッ
KYAH
キャッ♡
YAY
TRAINING? I'LL TAG ALONG.
ASUNA-SAN, SHALL WE JOIN THEM?
YEAH, GOOD IDEA.

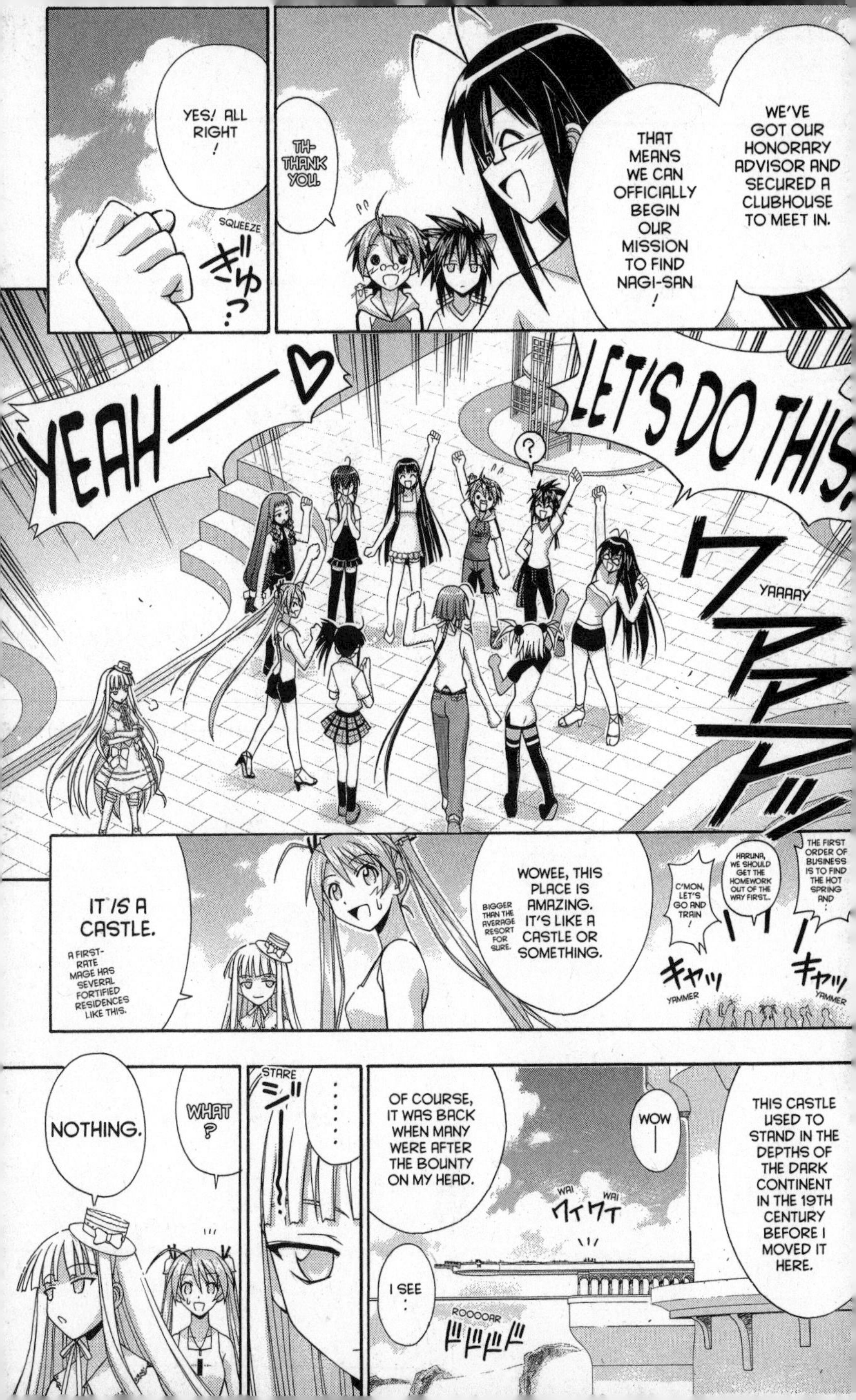
WE'VE GOT OUR HONORARY ADVISOR AND SECURED A CLUBHOUSE TO MEET IN.
THAT MEANS WE CAN OFFICIALLY BEGIN OUR MISSION TO FIND NAGI-SAN!
TH-THANK YOU.
YES! ALL RIGHT!
ぎゅっ…
SQUEEZE
LET'S DO THIS!
?
YEAH—♥
ワァアァッ
YAAAAY
THE FIRST ORDER OF BUSINESS IS TO FIND THE HOT SPRING AND
HARUNA, WE SHOULD GET THE HOMEWORK OUT OF THE WAY FIRST...
C'MON, LET'S GO AND TRAIN!
キャッ
YAMMER
キャッ
YAMMER
WOWEE, THIS PLACE IS AMAZING. IT'S LIKE A CASTLE OR SOMETHING.
BIGGER THAN THE AVERAGE RESORT FOR SURE.
IT IS A CASTLE.
A FIRST-RATE MAGE HAS SEVERAL FORTIFIED RESIDENCES LIKE THIS.
THIS CASTLE USED TO STAND IN THE DEPTHS OF THE DARK CONTINENT IN THE 19TH CENTURY BEFORE I MOVED IT HERE.
WOW—
ワイワイ
WAI WAI
OF COURSE, IT WAS BACK WHEN MANY WERE AFTER THE BOUNTY ON MY HEAD.
I SEE...
ドドドド
ROOOOAR
......
ジ
STARE
!
WHAT?
NOTHING.

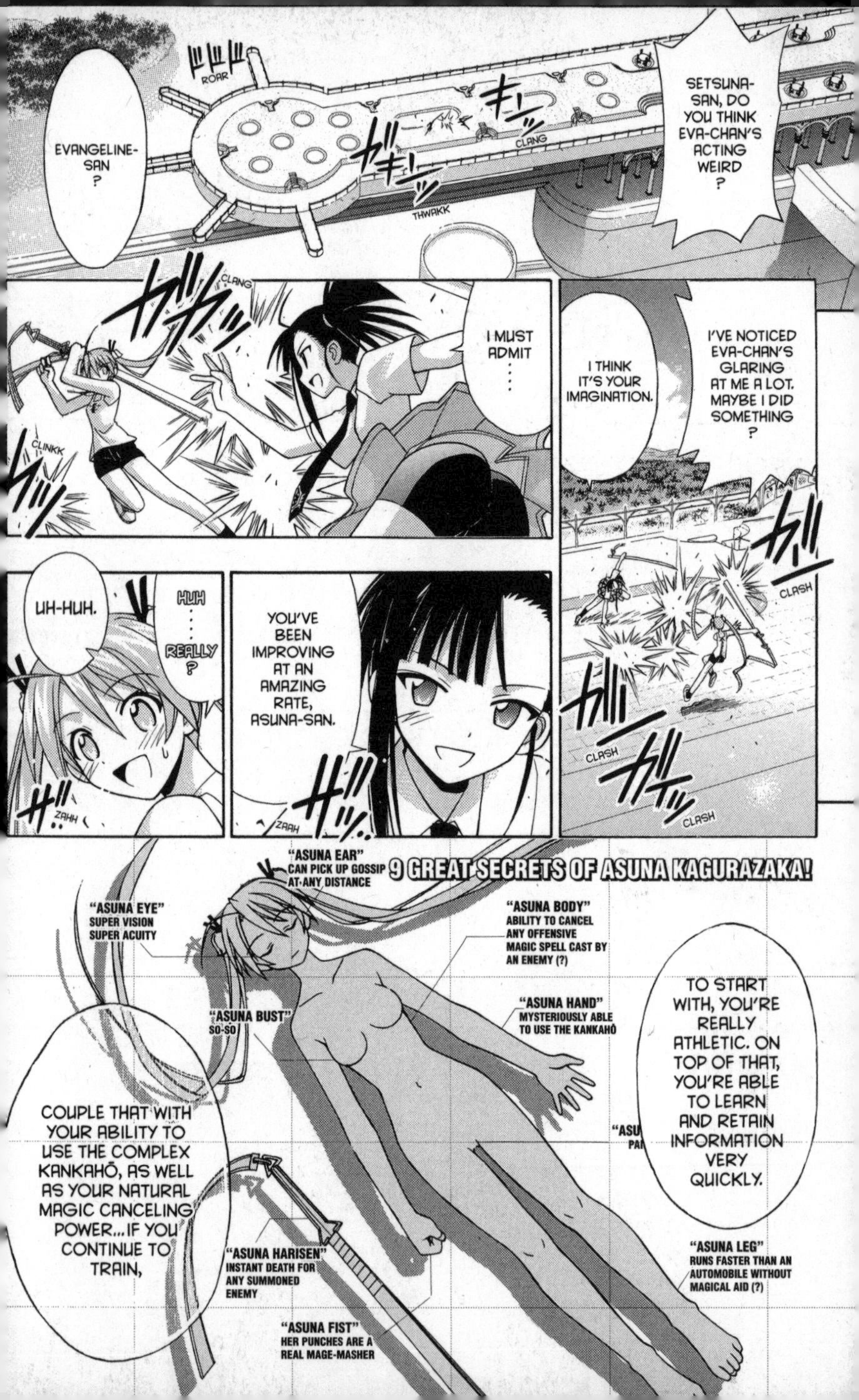
SETSUNA-SAN, DO YOU THINK EVA-CHAN'S ACTING WEIRD?
CLANG
THWAKK
ROAR
EVANGELINE-SAN?
I'VE NOTICED EVA-CHAN'S GLARING AT ME A LOT. MAYBE I DID SOMETHING?
I THINK IT'S YOUR IMAGINATION.
CLASH
CLASH
CLASH
I MUST ADMIT....
CLANG
CLINKK
YOU'VE BEEN IMPROVING AT AN AMAZING RATE, ASUNA-SAN.
ZAAH
HUH... REALLY?
UH-HUH.
ZAHH
TO START WITH, YOU'RE REALLY ATHLETIC. ON TOP OF THAT, YOU'RE ABLE TO LEARN AND RETAIN INFORMATION VERY QUICKLY.
9 GREAT SECRETS OF ASUNA KAGURAZAKA!
"ASUNA EAR" CAN PICK UP GOSSIP AT ANY DISTANCE
"ASUNA BODY" ABILITY TO CANCEL ANY OFFENSIVE MAGIC SPELL CAST BY AN ENEMY (?)
"ASUNA HAND" MYSTERIOUSLY ABLE TO USE THE KANKAHŌ
"ASUNA LEG" RUNS FASTER THAN AN AUTOMOBILE WITHOUT MAGICAL AID (?)
"ASUNA EYE" SUPER VISION SUPER ACUITY
"ASUNA BUST" SO-SO
"ASUNA HARISEN" INSTANT DEATH FOR ANY SUMMONED ENEMY
"ASUNA FIST" HER PUNCHES ARE A REAL MAGE-MASHER
COUPLE THAT WITH YOUR ABILITY TO USE THE COMPLEX KANKAHŌ, AS WELL AS YOUR NATURAL MAGIC CANCELING POWER...IF YOU CONTINUE TO TRAIN,

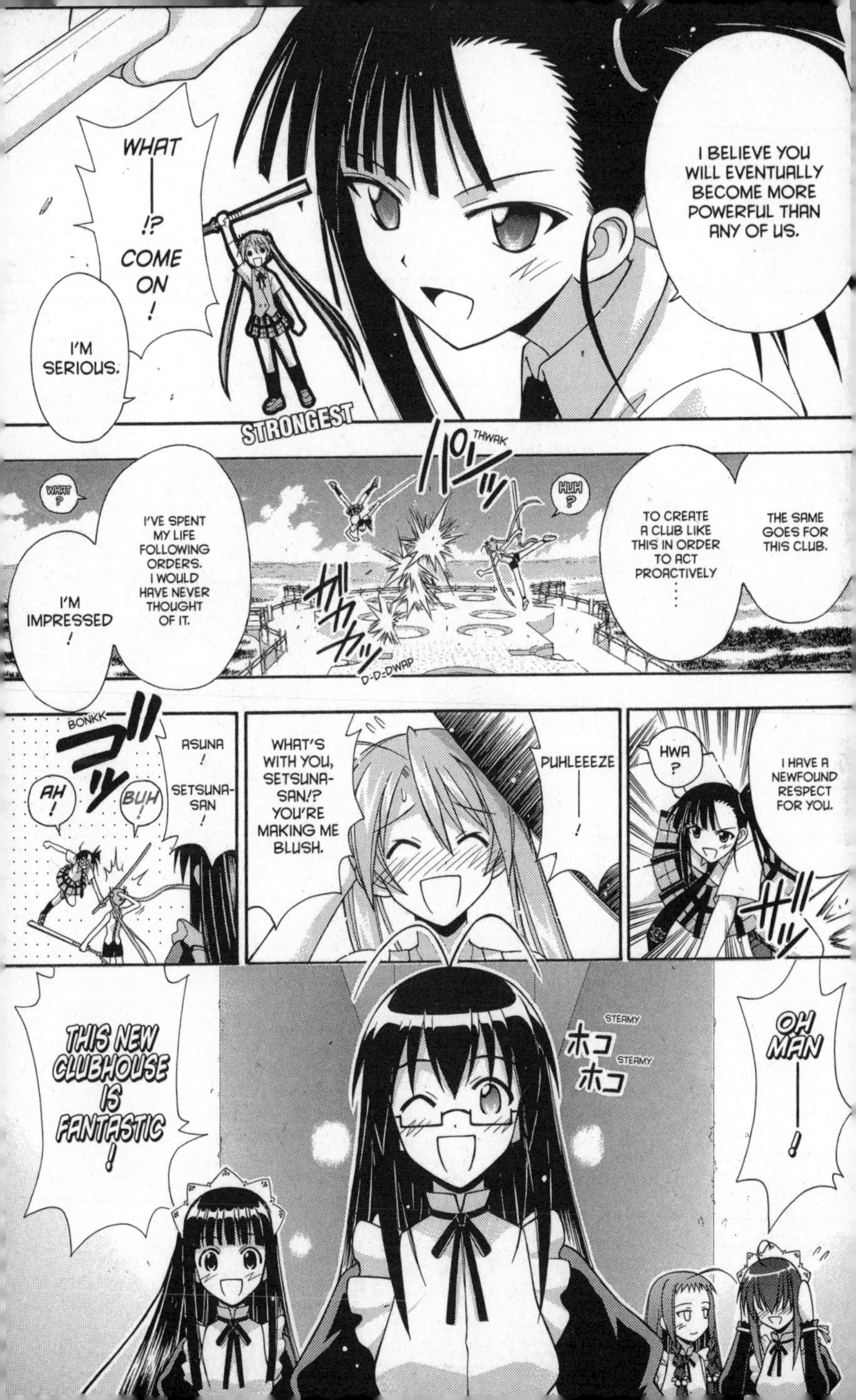
I BELIEVE YOU WILL EVENTUALLY BECOME MORE POWERFUL THAN ANY OF US.
WHAT—!? COME ON!
I'M SERIOUS.
STRONGEST
THE SAME GOES FOR THIS CLUB.
TO CREATE A CLUB LIKE THIS IN ORDER TO ACT PROACTIVELY......
HUH?
THWAK
WHAT?
I'VE SPENT MY LIFE FOLLOWING ORDERS. I WOULD HAVE NEVER THOUGHT OF IT.
I'M IMPRESSED!
D-D-DWAP
I HAVE A NEWFOUND RESPECT FOR YOU.
HWA?
PUHLEEEZE—!
WHAT'S WITH YOU, SETSUNA-SAN!? YOU'RE MAKING ME BLUSH.
ASUNA! SETSUNA-SAN!
BONKK
BUH!
AH!
OH MAN——!
STEAMY
STEAMY
THIS NEW CLUBHOUSE IS FANTASTIC!

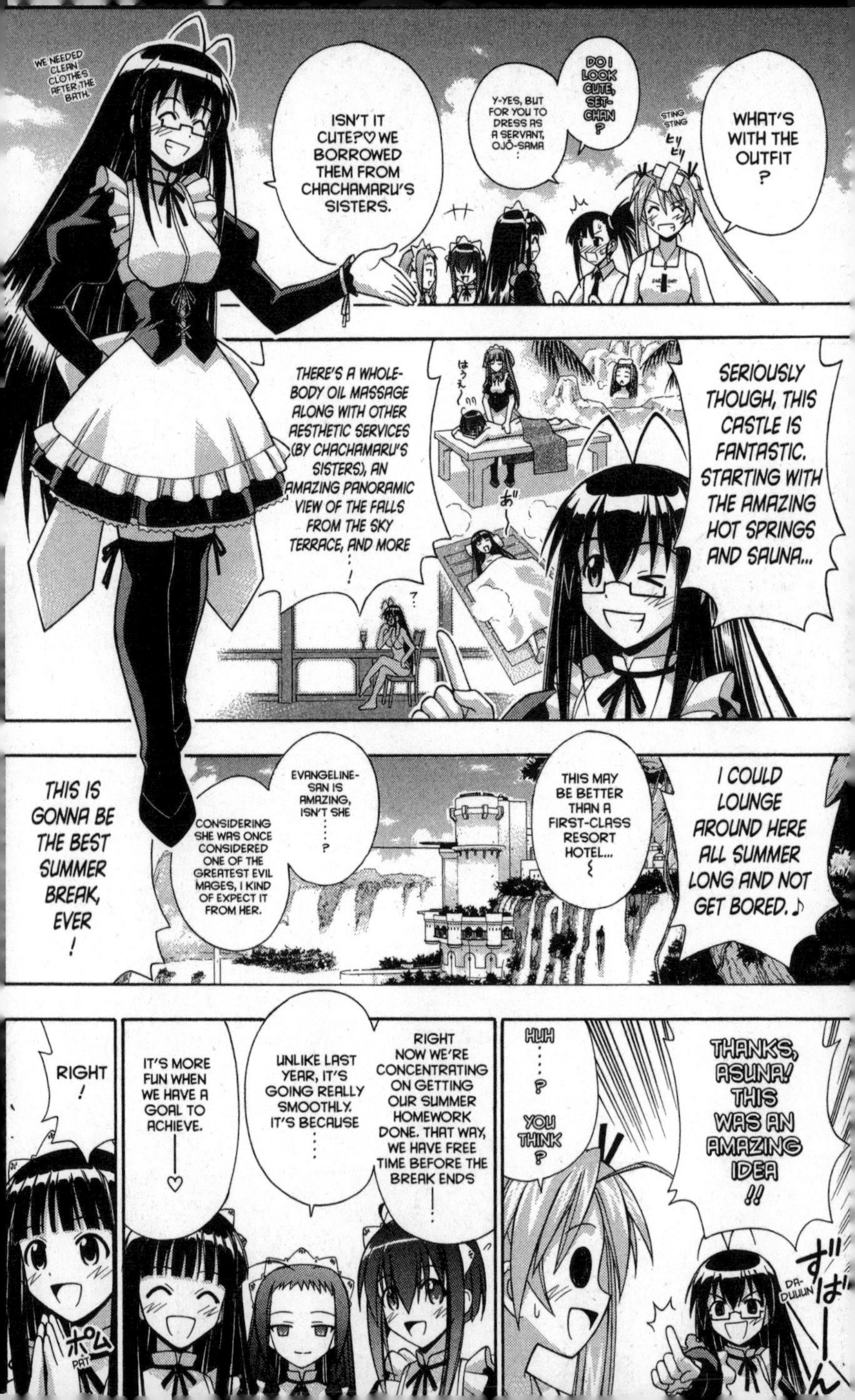
WHAT'S WITH THE OUTFIT?
STING STING
ピリピリ
DO I LOOK CUTE, SET-CHAN?
Y-YES, BUT FOR YOU TO DRESS AS A SERVANT, OJŌ-SAMA...
ISN'T IT CUTE?♡ WE BORROWED THEM FROM CHACHAMARU'S SISTERS.
WE NEEDED CLEAN CLOTHES AFTER THE BATH.
SERIOUSLY THOUGH, THIS CASTLE IS FANTASTIC. STARTING WITH THE AMAZING HOT SPRINGS AND SAUNA...
はうぇ～
あ～
THERE'S A WHOLE-BODY OIL MASSAGE ALONG WITH OTHER AESTHETIC SERVICES (BY CHACHAMARU'S SISTERS), AN AMAZING PANORAMIC VIEW OF THE FALLS FROM THE SKY TERRACE, AND MORE...!
I COULD LOUNGE AROUND HERE ALL SUMMER LONG AND NOT GET BORED.♪
THIS MAY BE BETTER THAN A FIRST-CLASS RESORT HOTEL...~
EVANGELINE-SAN IS AMAZING, ISN'T SHE...?
CONSIDERING SHE WAS ONCE CONSIDERED ONE OF THE GREATEST EVIL MAGES, I KIND OF EXPECT IT FROM HER.
THIS IS GONNA BE THE BEST SUMMER BREAK, EVER!
THANKS, ASUNA! THIS WAS AN AMAZING IDEA!!
ずばーん
DA-DUUUN
HUH...? YOU THINK?
RIGHT NOW WE'RE CONCENTRATING ON GETTING OUR SUMMER HOMEWORK DONE. THAT WAY, WE HAVE FREE TIME BEFORE THE BREAK ENDS!
UNLIKE LAST YEAR, IT'S GOING REALLY SMOOTHLY. IT'S BECAUSE...
IT'S MORE FUN WHEN WE HAVE A GOAL TO ACHIEVE.♡
RIGHT!
ポム
PAT

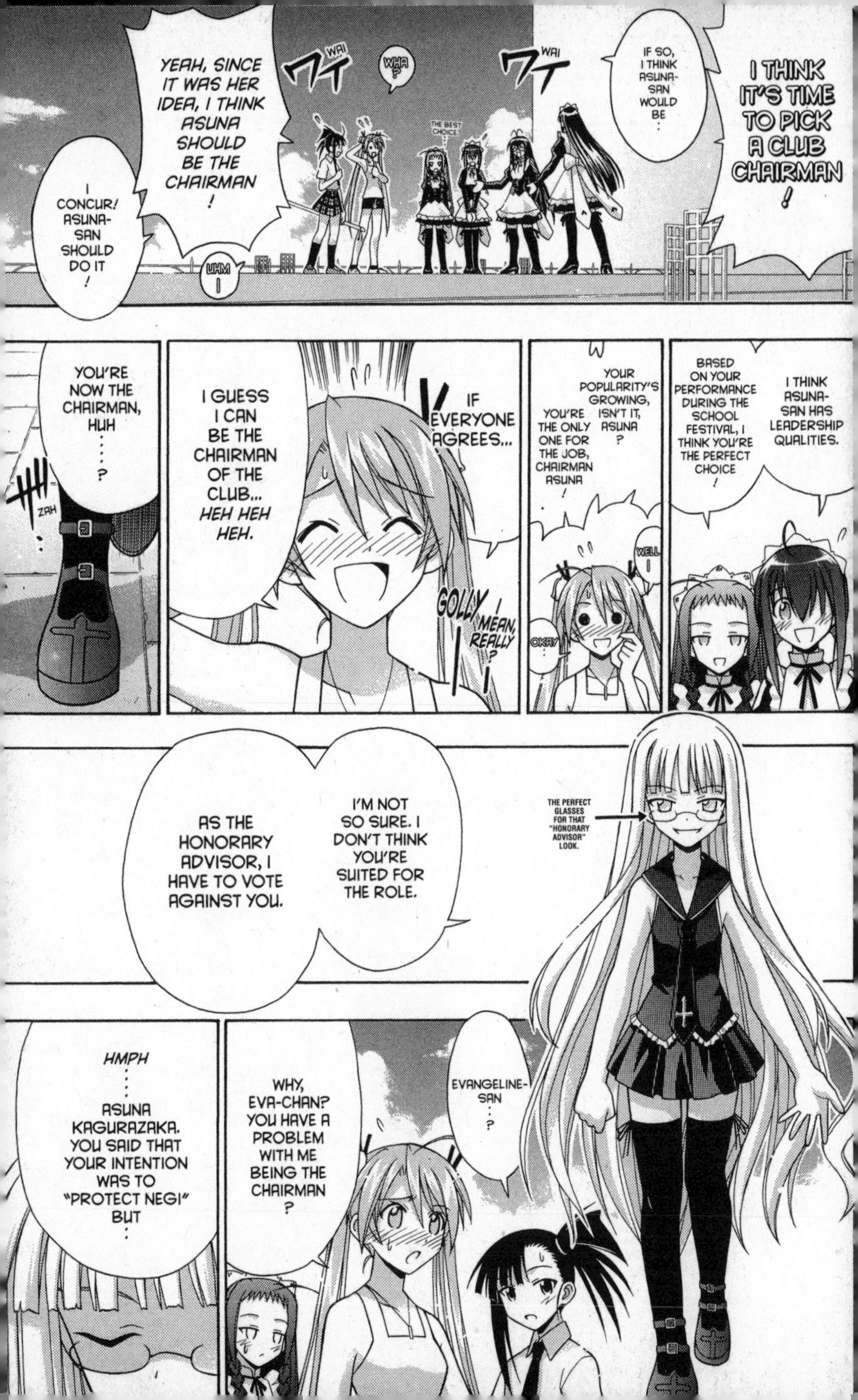
I THINK IT'S TIME TO PICK A CLUB CHAIRMAN!
IF SO, I THINK ASUNA-SAN WOULD BE...
WAI
THE BEST CHOICE...
WHA?
WAI
YEAH, SINCE IT WAS HER IDEA, I THINK ASUNA SHOULD BE THE CHAIRMAN!
UHM
I CONCUR! ASUNA-SAN SHOULD DO IT!
I THINK ASUNA-SAN HAS LEADERSHIP QUALITIES.
BASED ON YOUR PERFORMANCE DURING THE SCHOOL FESTIVAL, I THINK YOU'RE THE PERFECT CHOICE!
YOUR POPULARITY'S GROWING, ISN'T IT, ASUNA?
YOU'RE THE ONLY ONE FOR THE JOB, CHAIRMAN ASUNA!
WELL
OKAY...
IF EVERYONE AGREES...
GOLLY
I MEAN, REALLY?
I GUESS I CAN BE THE CHAIRMAN OF THE CLUB... HEH HEH HEH.
YOU'RE NOW THE CHAIRMAN, HUH...?
ZAH
THE PERFECT GLASSES FOR THAT "HONORARY ADVISOR" LOOK.
I'M NOT SO SURE. I DON'T THINK YOU'RE SUITED FOR THE ROLE.
AS THE HONORARY ADVISOR, I HAVE TO VOTE AGAINST YOU.
EVANGELINE-SAN...?
WHY, EVA-CHAN? YOU HAVE A PROBLEM WITH ME BEING THE CHAIRMAN?
HMPH... ASUNA KAGURAZAKA. YOU SAID THAT YOUR INTENTION WAS TO "PROTECT NEGI" BUT...

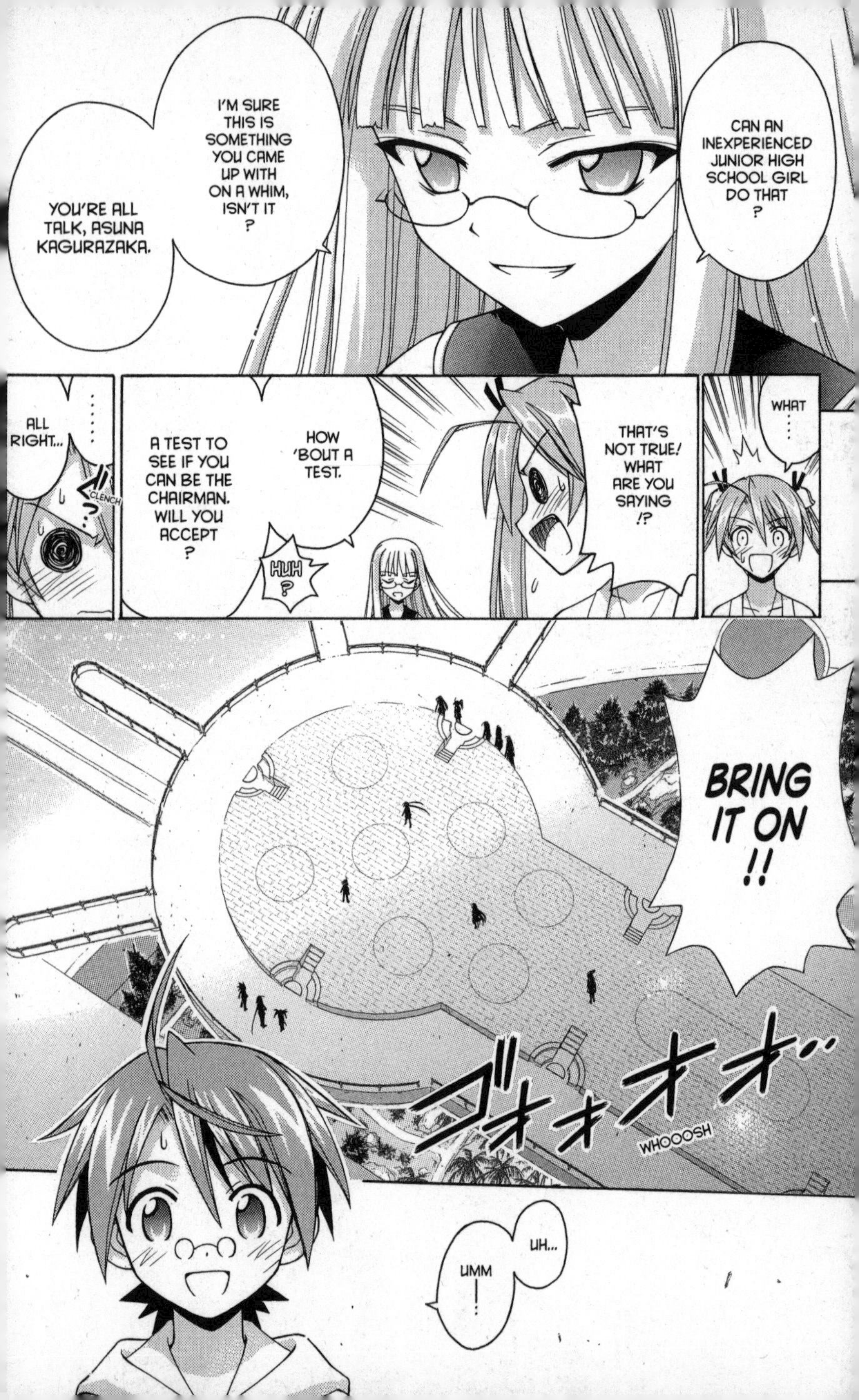
CAN AN INEXPERIENCED JUNIOR HIGH SCHOOL GIRL DO THAT?
I'M SURE THIS IS SOMETHING YOU CAME UP WITH ON A WHIM, ISN'T IT?
YOU'RE ALL TALK, ASUNA KAGURAZAKA.
WHAT...
THAT'S NOT TRUE! WHAT ARE YOU SAYING!?
HOW 'BOUT A TEST.
HUH?
A TEST TO SEE IF YOU CAN BE THE CHAIRMAN. WILL YOU ACCEPT?
......
ALL RIGHT...
CLENCH
BRING IT ON!!
ゴォォオオ
WHOOOSH
UH... UMM!

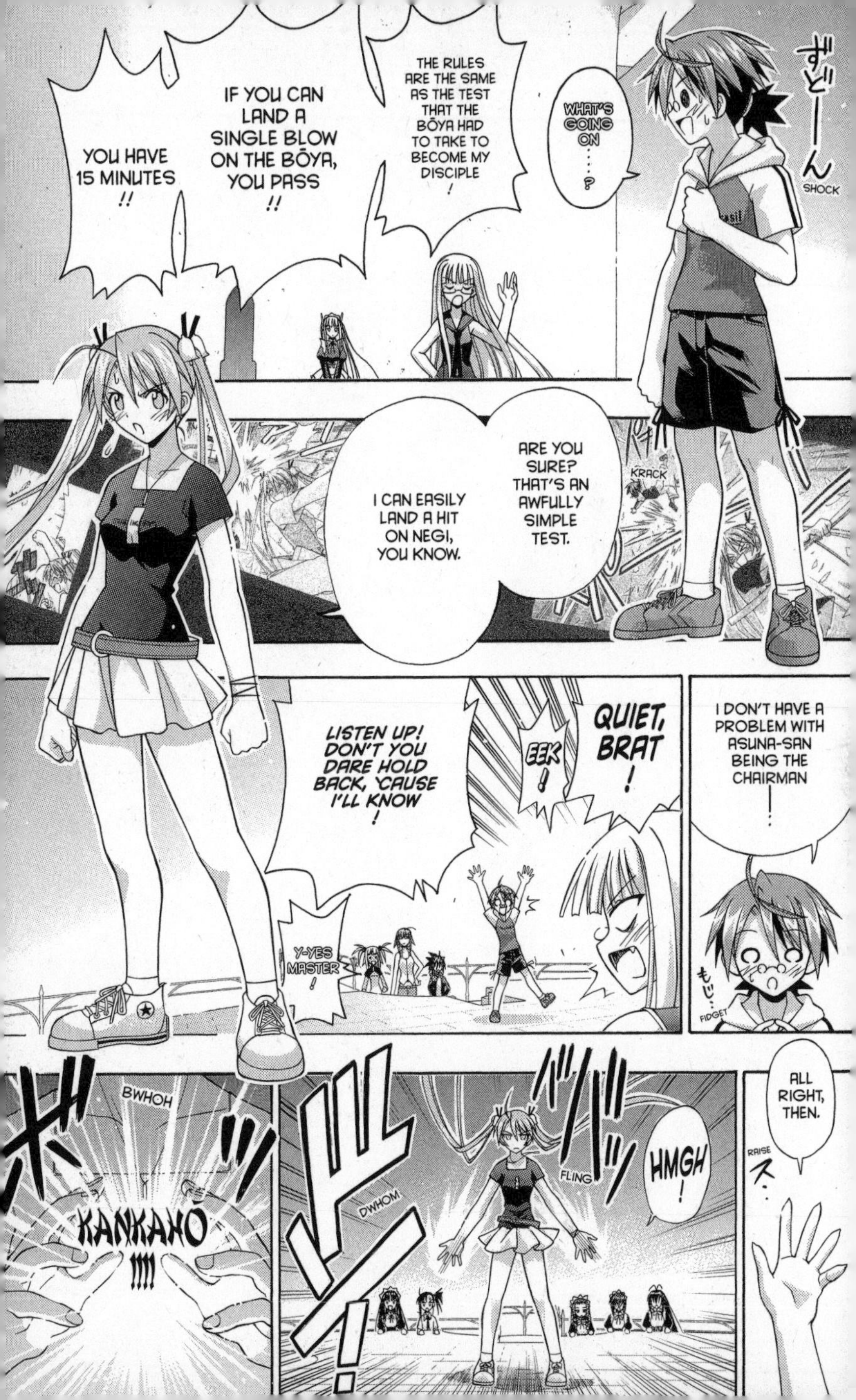

ずどーん
SHOCK
WHAT'S GOING ON...?
THE RULES ARE THE SAME AS THE TEST THAT THE BŌYA HAD TO TAKE TO BECOME MY DISCIPLE!
IF YOU CAN LAND A SINGLE BLOW ON THE BŌYA, YOU PASS!!
YOU HAVE 15 MINUTES!!
KRACK
ARE YOU SURE? THAT'S AN AWFULLY SIMPLE TEST.
I CAN EASILY LAND A HIT ON NEGI, YOU KNOW.
I DON'T HAVE A PROBLEM WITH ASUNA-SAN BEING THE CHAIRMAN...
もじ…
FIDGET
QUIET, BRAT!
EEK!
LISTEN UP! DON'T YOU DARE HOLD BACK, 'CAUSE I'LL KNOW!
Y-YES MASTER!
ALL RIGHT, THEN.
RAISE
ス…
HMGH!
FLING
DWHOM
BWHOH
KANKAHŌ!!!!

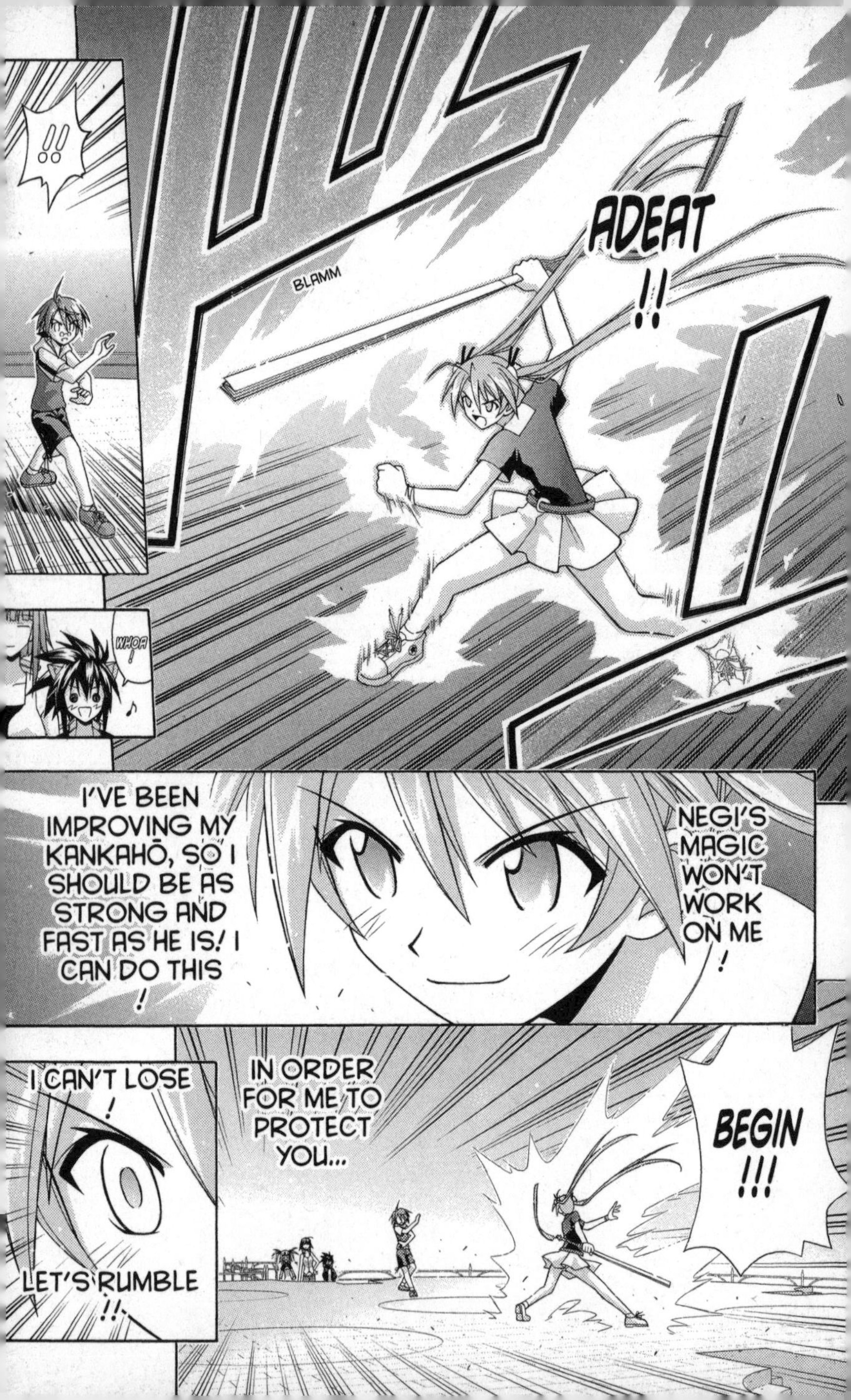
ADEAT!!
BLAMM
!!
WHOA!
NEGI'S MAGIC WON'T WORK ON ME!
I'VE BEEN IMPROVING MY KANKAHŌ, SO I SHOULD BE AS STRONG AND FAST AS HE IS! I CAN DO THIS!
BEGIN!!!
IN ORDER FOR ME TO PROTECT YOU...
I CAN'T LOSE!
LET'S RUMBLE!!

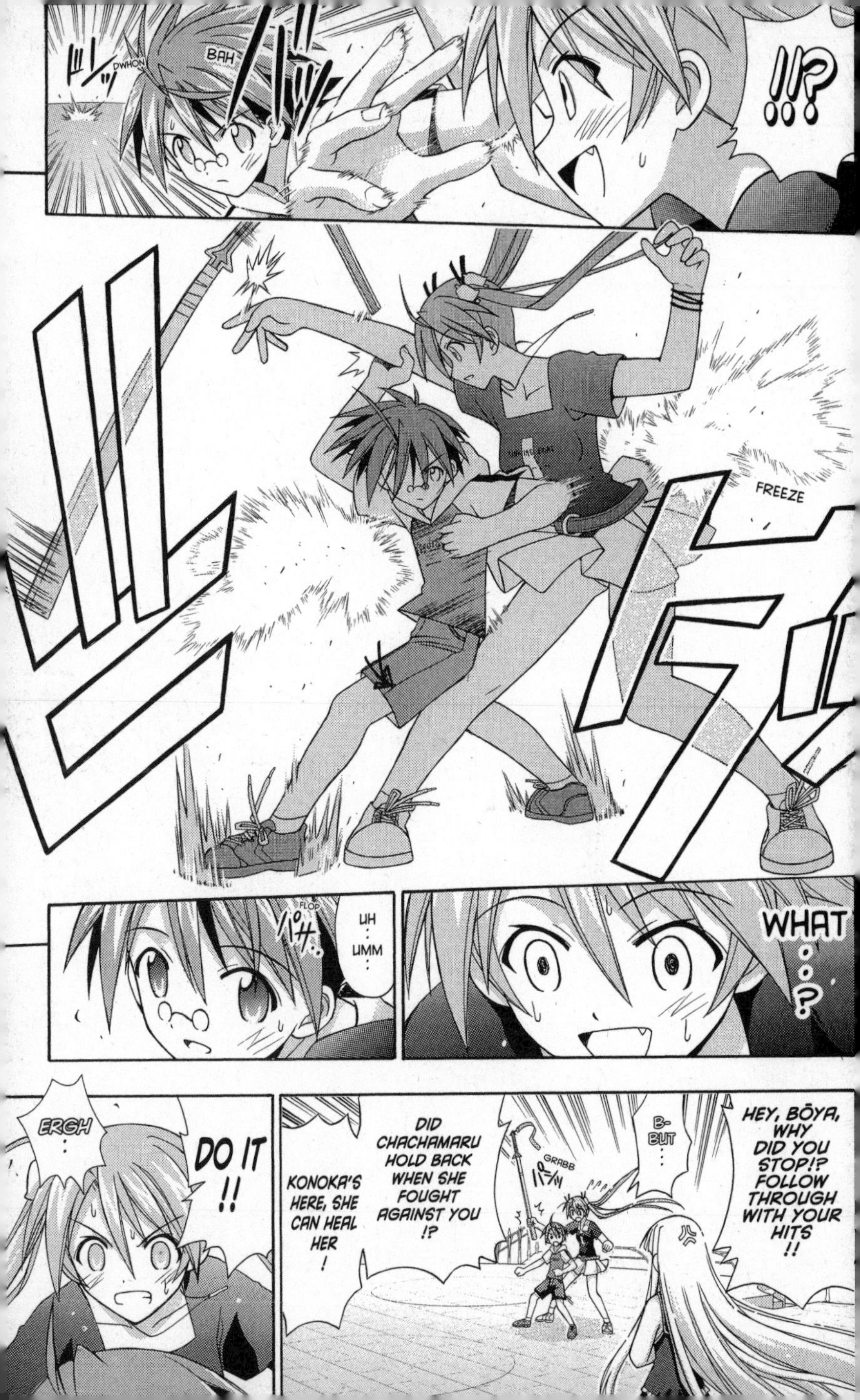

!!?
DWHON
BAH
FREEZE
WHAT...?
FLOP
UH... UMM...
HEY, BŌYA, WHY DID YOU STOP!? FOLLOW THROUGH WITH YOUR HITS!!
B-BUT...
GRABB
DID CHACHAMARU HOLD BACK WHEN SHE FOUGHT AGAINST YOU!?
KONOKA'S HERE, SHE CAN HEAL HER!
DO IT!!
ERGH...

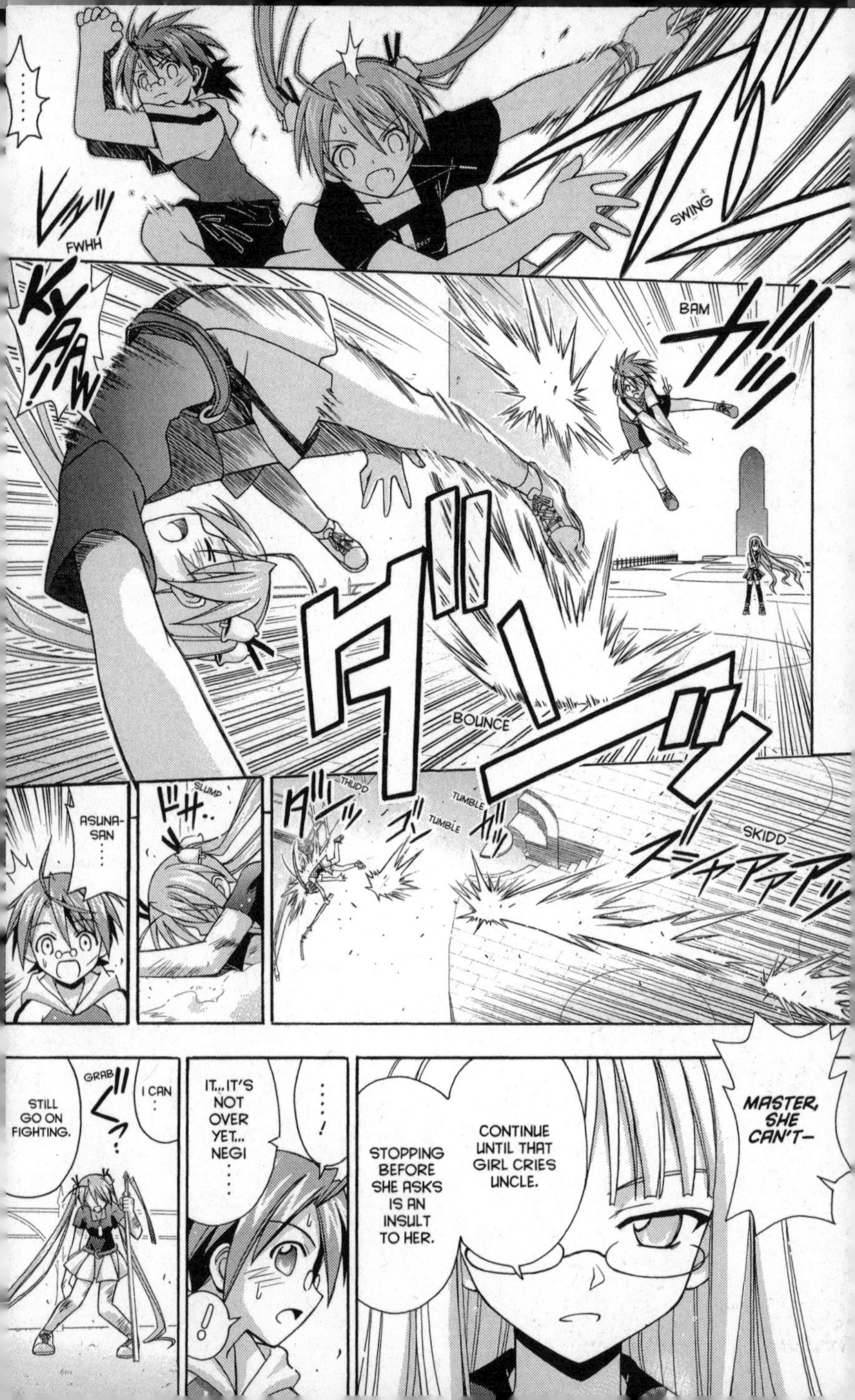
SWING
FWHH
......!
BAM
KYAAW!!
BOUNCE
THUDD
TUMBLE
TUMBLE
SKIDD
SLUMP
ASUNA-SAN......
MASTER, SHE CAN'T—
CONTINUE UNTIL THAT GIRL CRIES UNCLE.
STOPPING BEFORE SHE ASKS IS AN INSULT TO HER.
....!
IT...IT'S NOT OVER YET... NEGI......
I CAN...
GRAB
STILL GO ON FIGHTING.

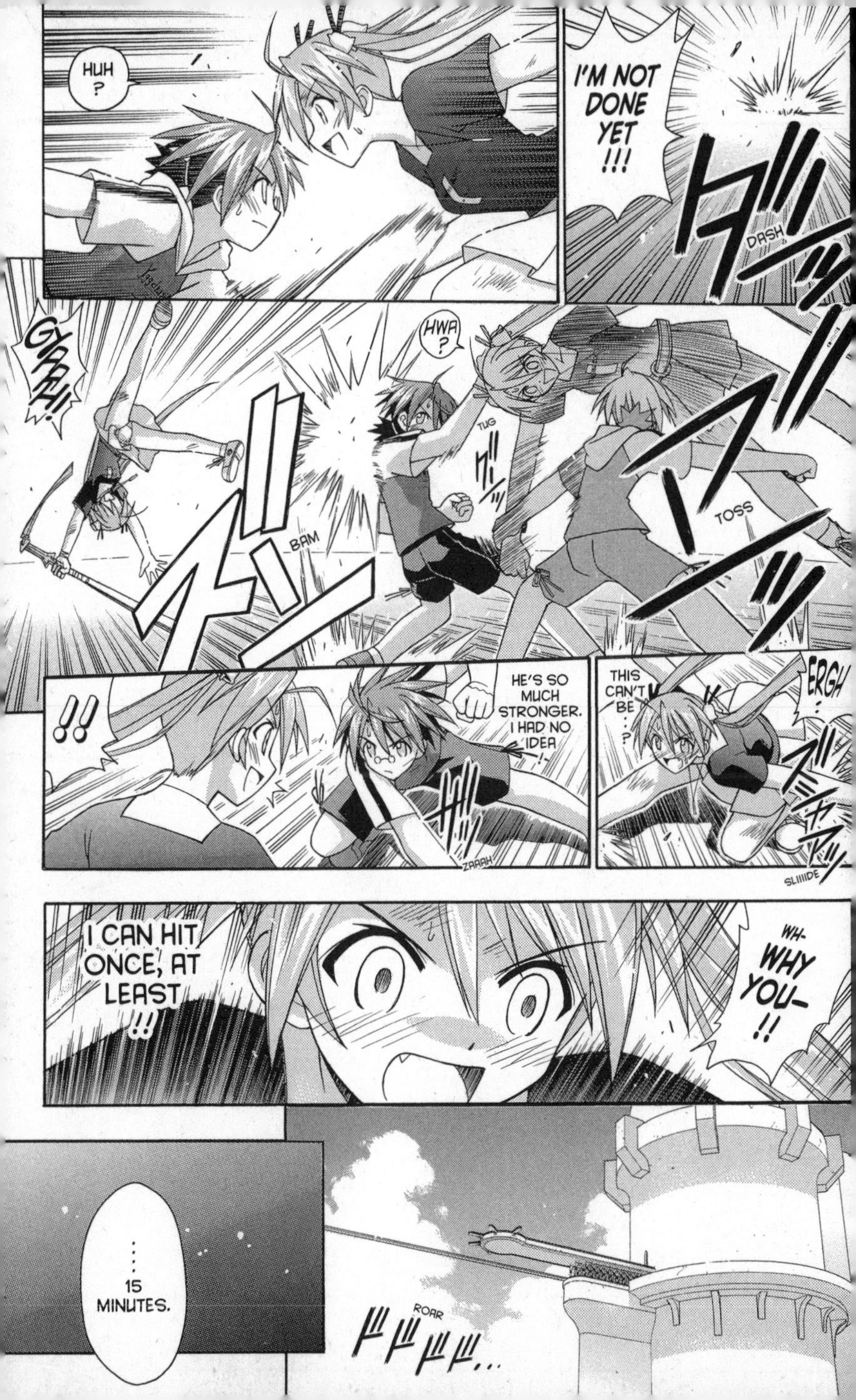
I'M NOT DONE YET!!!
DASH
HUH?
HWA?
TOSS
TUG
BAM
GYAAAH!!
ERGH...!
THIS CAN'T BE...?
SLIIIDE
HE'S SO MUCH STRONGER. I HAD NO IDEA...!
!!
ZAAAH
WH-WHY YOU-!!
I CAN HIT ONCE, AT LEAST!!
...15 MINUTES.
ROAR

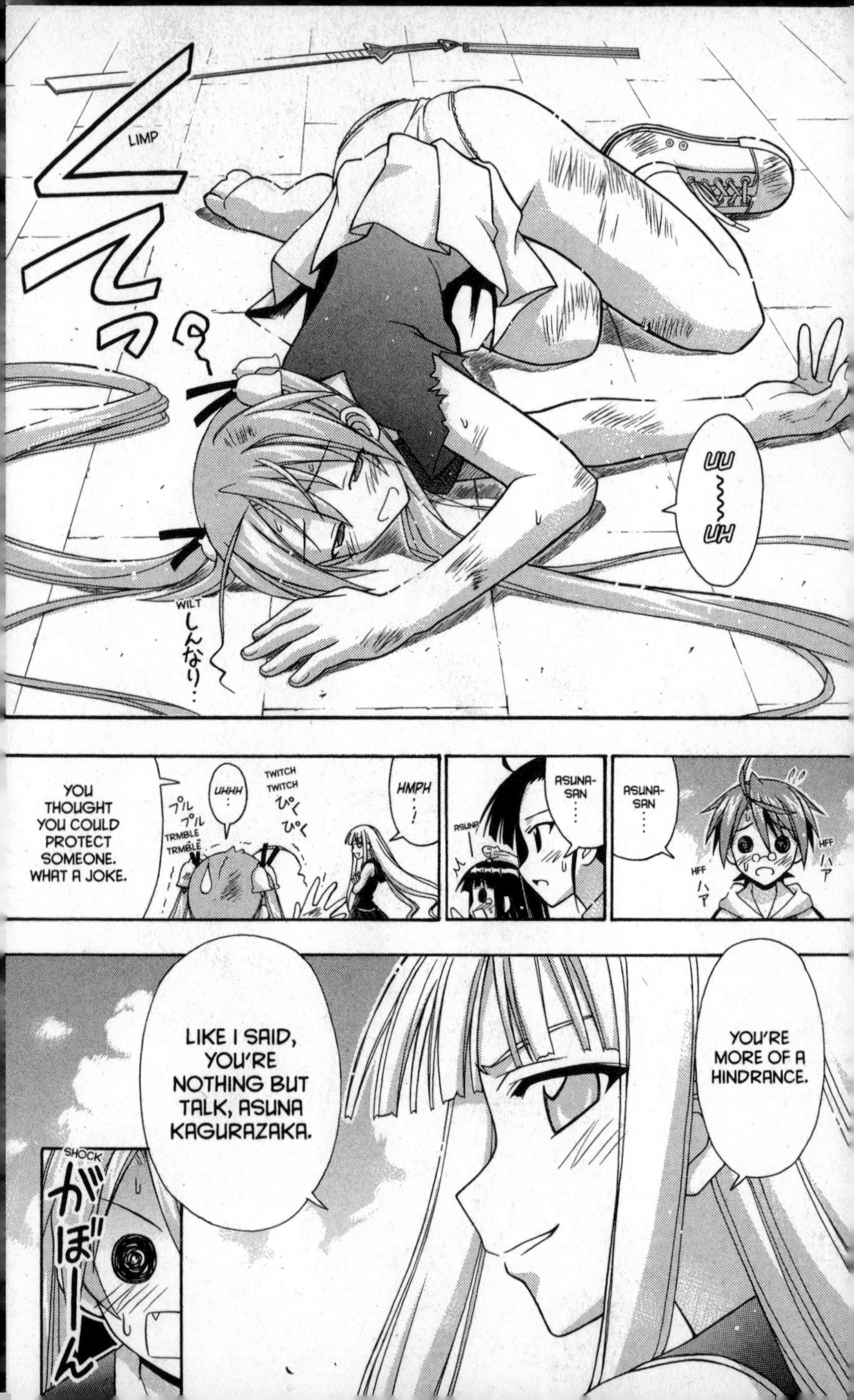
LIMP
UU~~~H
WILT
しんなり…
ASUNA-SAN……
HFF
ハァ
HFF
ハァ
ASUNA-SAN……
ASUNA!
HMPH…!
TWITCH TWITCH
ぴくぴく
UHHH…
TRMBLE TRMBLE
プルプル
YOU THOUGHT YOU COULD PROTECT SOMEONE. WHAT A JOKE.
YOU'RE MORE OF A HINDRANCE.
LIKE I SAID, YOU'RE NOTHING BUT TALK, ASUNA KAGURAZAKA.
SHOCK
がぼーん

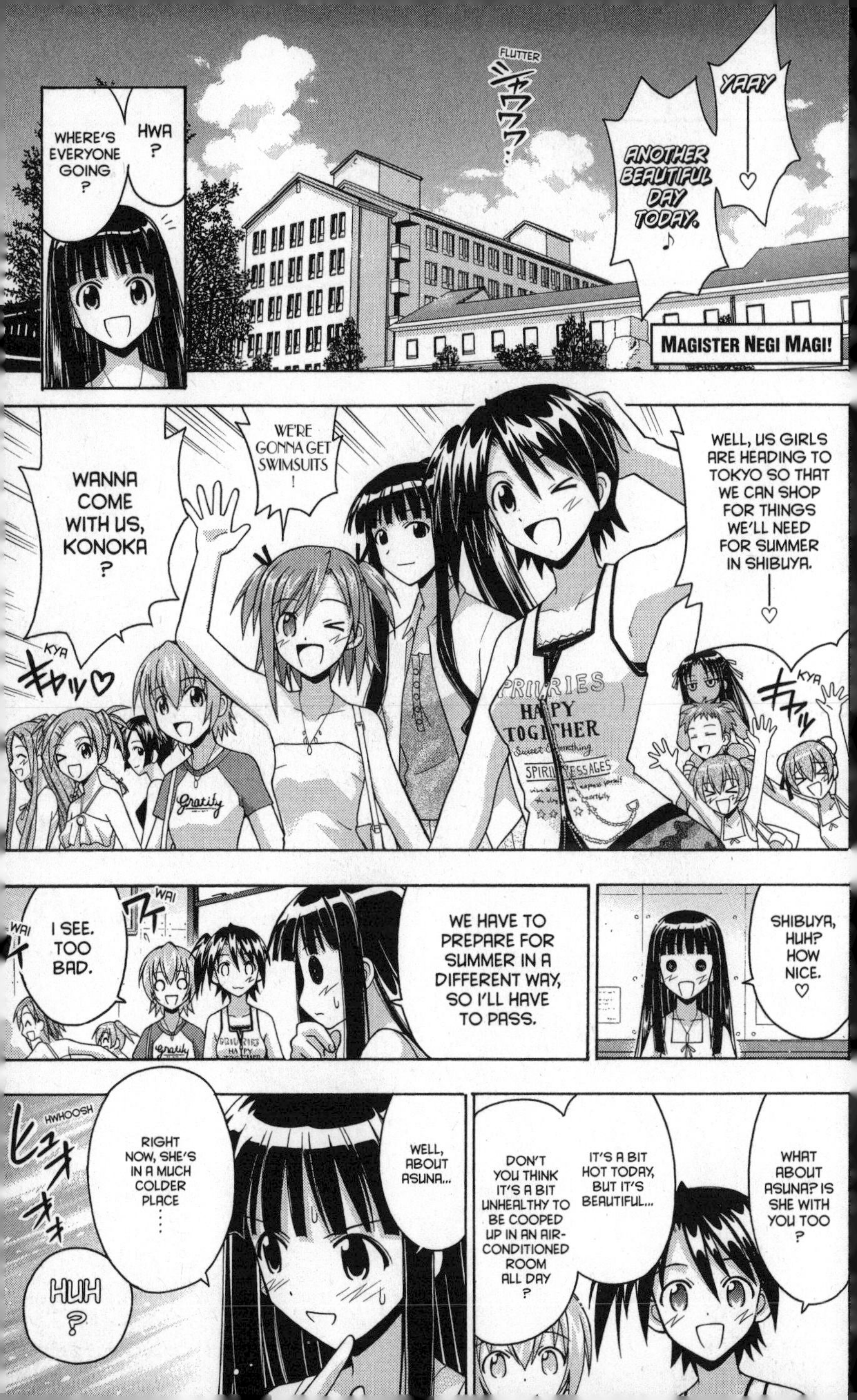
YAAY ♡
ANOTHER BEAUTIFUL DAY TODAY. ♪
FLUTTER
MAGISTER NEGI MAGI!
HWA?
WHERE'S EVERYONE GOING?
WELL, US GIRLS ARE HEADING TO TOKYO SO THAT WE CAN SHOP FOR THINGS WE'LL NEED FOR SUMMER IN SHIBUYA. ♡
KYA
WE'RE GONNA GET SWIMSUITS!
WANNA COME WITH US, KONOKA?
KYA
SHIBUYA, HUH? HOW NICE. ♡
WE HAVE TO PREPARE FOR SUMMER IN A DIFFERENT WAY, SO I'LL HAVE TO PASS.
WAI
I SEE. TOO BAD.
WAI
WHAT ABOUT ASUNA? IS SHE WITH YOU TOO?
IT'S A BIT HOT TODAY, BUT IT'S BEAUTIFUL...
DON'T YOU THINK IT'S A BIT UNHEALTHY TO BE COOPED UP IN AN AIR-CONDITIONED ROOM ALL DAY?
WELL, ABOUT ASUNA...
RIGHT NOW, SHE'S IN A MUCH COLDER PLACE....
HWHOOSH
HUH?

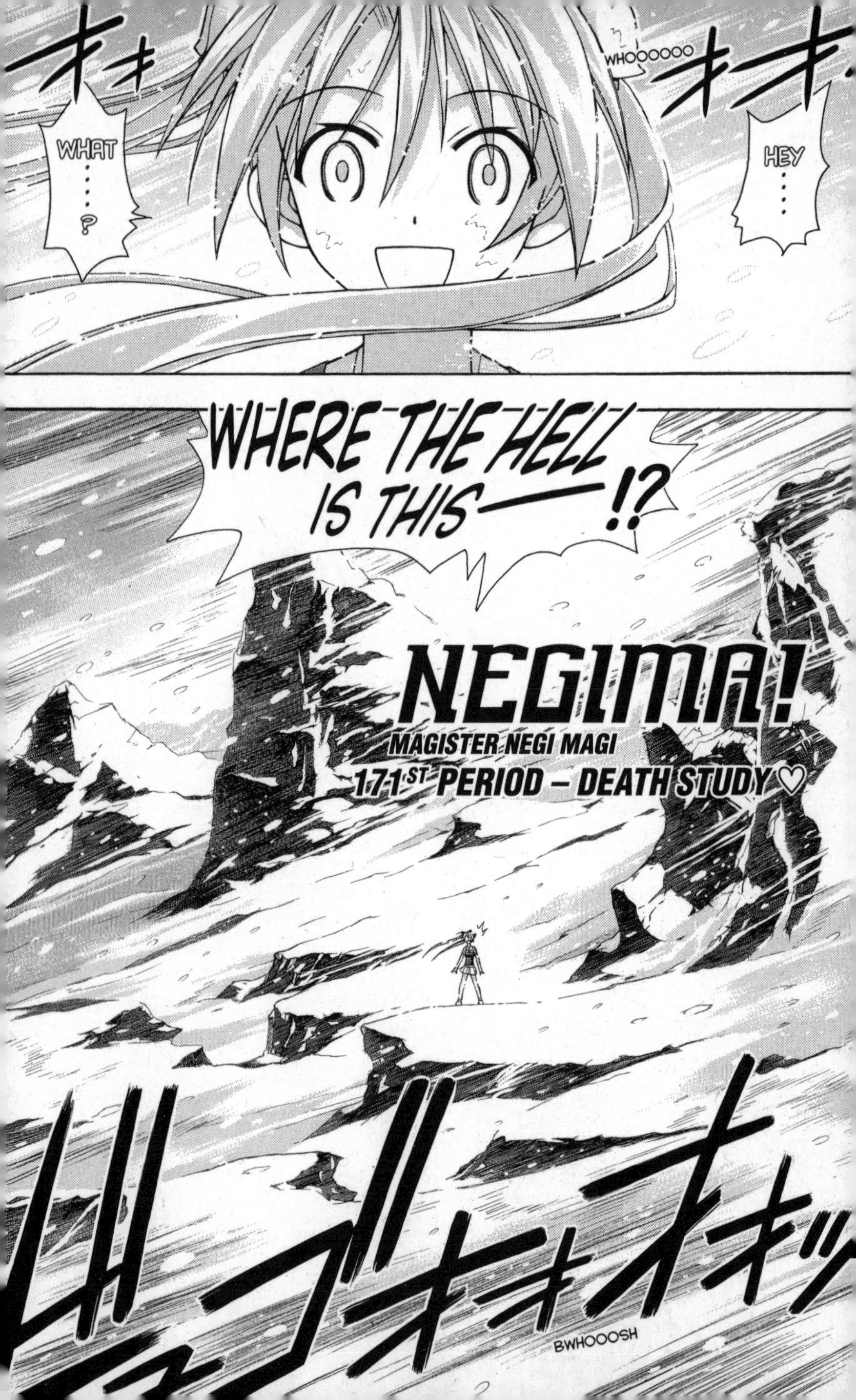
WHOOOOOO
HEY ....
WHAT .... ?
WHERE THE HELL IS THIS——!?
NEGIMA!
MAGISTER NEGI MAGI
171ST PERIOD – DEATH STUDY ♡
BWHOOOSH

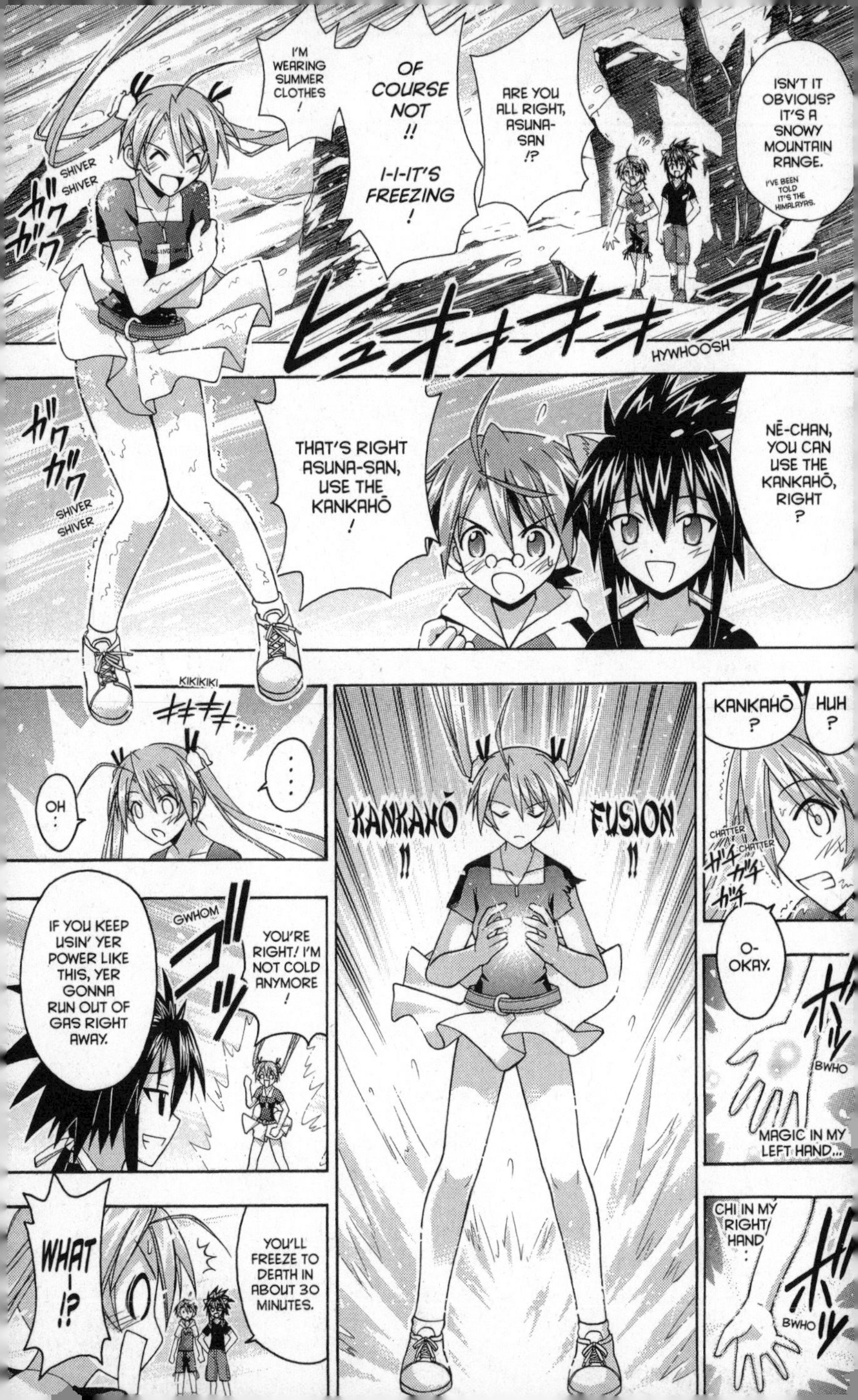
ISN'T IT OBVIOUS? IT'S A SNOWY MOUNTAIN RANGE.
I'VE BEEN TOLD IT'S THE HIMALAYAS.
ARE YOU ALL RIGHT, ASUNA-SAN!?
OF COURSE NOT!!
I-I-IT'S FREEZING!
I'M WEARING SUMMER CLOTHES!
SHIVER SHIVER
HYWHOOSH
NĒ-CHAN, YOU CAN USE THE KANKAHŌ, RIGHT?
THAT'S RIGHT ASUNA-SAN, USE THE KANKAHŌ!
SHIVER SHIVER
HUH?
KANKAHŌ?
CHATTER CHATTER
O-OKAY.
BWHO
MAGIC IN MY LEFT HAND...
CHI IN MY RIGHT HAND...
BWHO
KANKAHŌ FUSION!!
KIKIKIKI
....
OH...
YOU'RE RIGHT! I'M NOT COLD ANYMORE!
GWHOM
IF YOU KEEP USIN' YER POWER LIKE THIS, YER GONNA RUN OUT OF GAS RIGHT AWAY.
YOU'LL FREEZE TO DEATH IN ABOUT 30 MINUTES.
WHAT!?

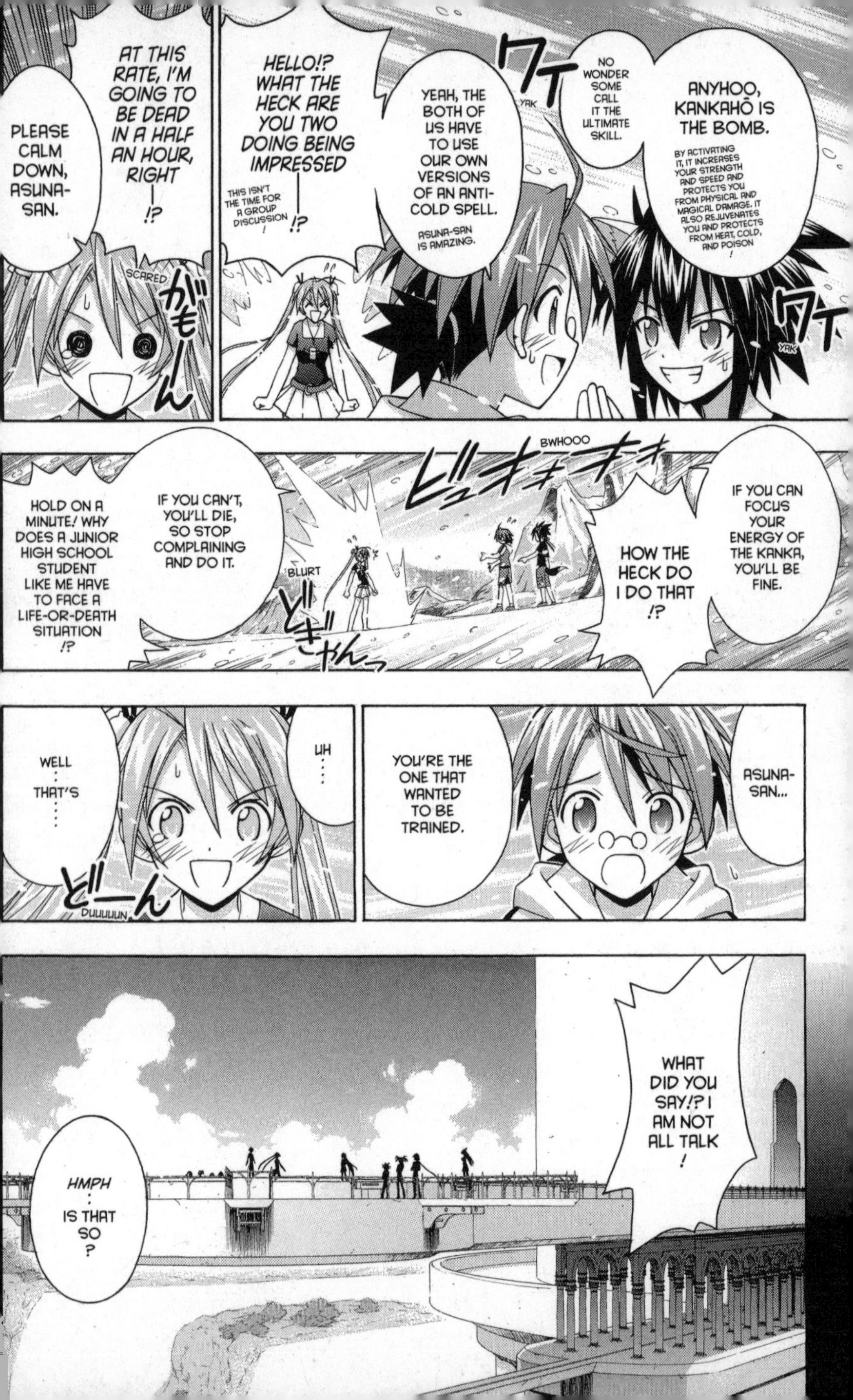
ANYHOO, KANKAHŌ IS THE BOMB.
BY ACTIVATING IT, IT INCREASES YOUR STRENGTH AND SPEED AND PROTECTS YOU FROM PHYSICAL AND MAGICAL DAMAGE. IT ALSO REJUVENATES YOU AND PROTECTS FROM HEAT, COLD, AND POISON!
ワイ
YAK
NO WONDER SOME CALL IT THE ULTIMATE SKILL.
ワイ
YAK
YEAH, THE BOTH OF US HAVE TO USE OUR OWN VERSIONS OF AN ANTI-COLD SPELL.
ASUNA-SAN IS AMAZING.
HELLO!? WHAT THE HECK ARE YOU TWO DOING BEING IMPRESSED—!?
THIS ISN'T THE TIME FOR A GROUP DISCUSSION!
AT THIS RATE, I'M GOING TO BE DEAD IN A HALF AN HOUR, RIGHT—!?
PLEASE CALM DOWN, ASUNA-SAN.
がもーん
SCARED
IF YOU CAN FOCUS YOUR ENERGY OF THE KANKA, YOU'LL BE FINE.
ビュオォォォ
BWHOOO
HOW THE HECK DO I DO THAT!?
どぎゃんっ
BLURT
IF YOU CAN'T, YOU'LL DIE, SO STOP COMPLAINING AND DO IT.
HOLD ON A MINUTE! WHY DOES A JUNIOR HIGH SCHOOL STUDENT LIKE ME HAVE TO FACE A LIFE-OR-DEATH SITUATION!?
ASUNA-SAN...
YOU'RE THE ONE THAT WANTED TO BE TRAINED.
UH...
WELL... THAT'S...
どーん
DUUUUUN
WHAT DID YOU SAY!? I AM NOT ALL TALK!
HMPH... IS THAT SO?

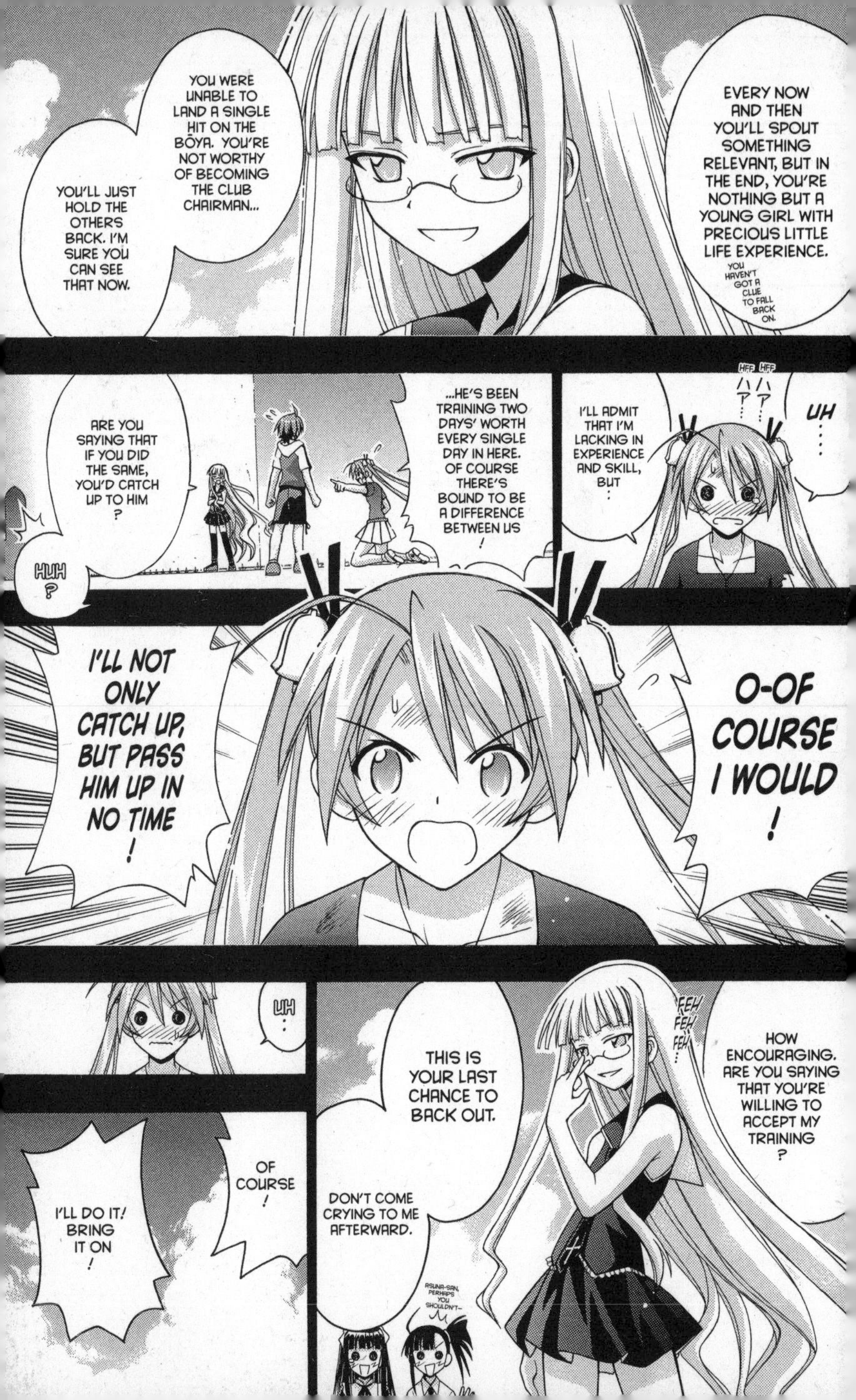

EVERY NOW AND THEN YOU'LL SPOUT SOMETHING RELEVANT, BUT IN THE END, YOU'RE NOTHING BUT A YOUNG GIRL WITH PRECIOUS LITTLE LIFE EXPERIENCE.
YOU HAVEN'T GOT A CLUE TO FALL BACK ON.
YOU WERE UNABLE TO LAND A SINGLE HIT ON THE BŌYA. YOU'RE NOT WORTHY OF BECOMING THE CLUB CHAIRMAN...
YOU'LL JUST HOLD THE OTHERS BACK. I'M SURE YOU CAN SEE THAT NOW.
HFF HFF
UH...
I'LL ADMIT THAT I'M LACKING IN EXPERIENCE AND SKILL, BUT...
...HE'S BEEN TRAINING TWO DAYS' WORTH EVERY SINGLE DAY IN HERE. OF COURSE THERE'S BOUND TO BE A DIFFERENCE BETWEEN US!
ARE YOU SAYING THAT IF YOU DID THE SAME, YOU'D CATCH UP TO HIM?
HUH?
O-OF COURSE I WOULD!
I'LL NOT ONLY CATCH UP, BUT PASS HIM UP IN NO TIME!
FEH FEH FEH...
HOW ENCOURAGING. ARE YOU SAYING THAT YOU'RE WILLING TO ACCEPT MY TRAINING?
THIS IS YOUR LAST CHANCE TO BACK OUT.
DON'T COME CRYING TO ME AFTERWARD.
ASUNA-SAN, PERHAPS YOU SHOULDN'T—
UH...
OF COURSE!
I'LL DO IT! BRING IT ON!

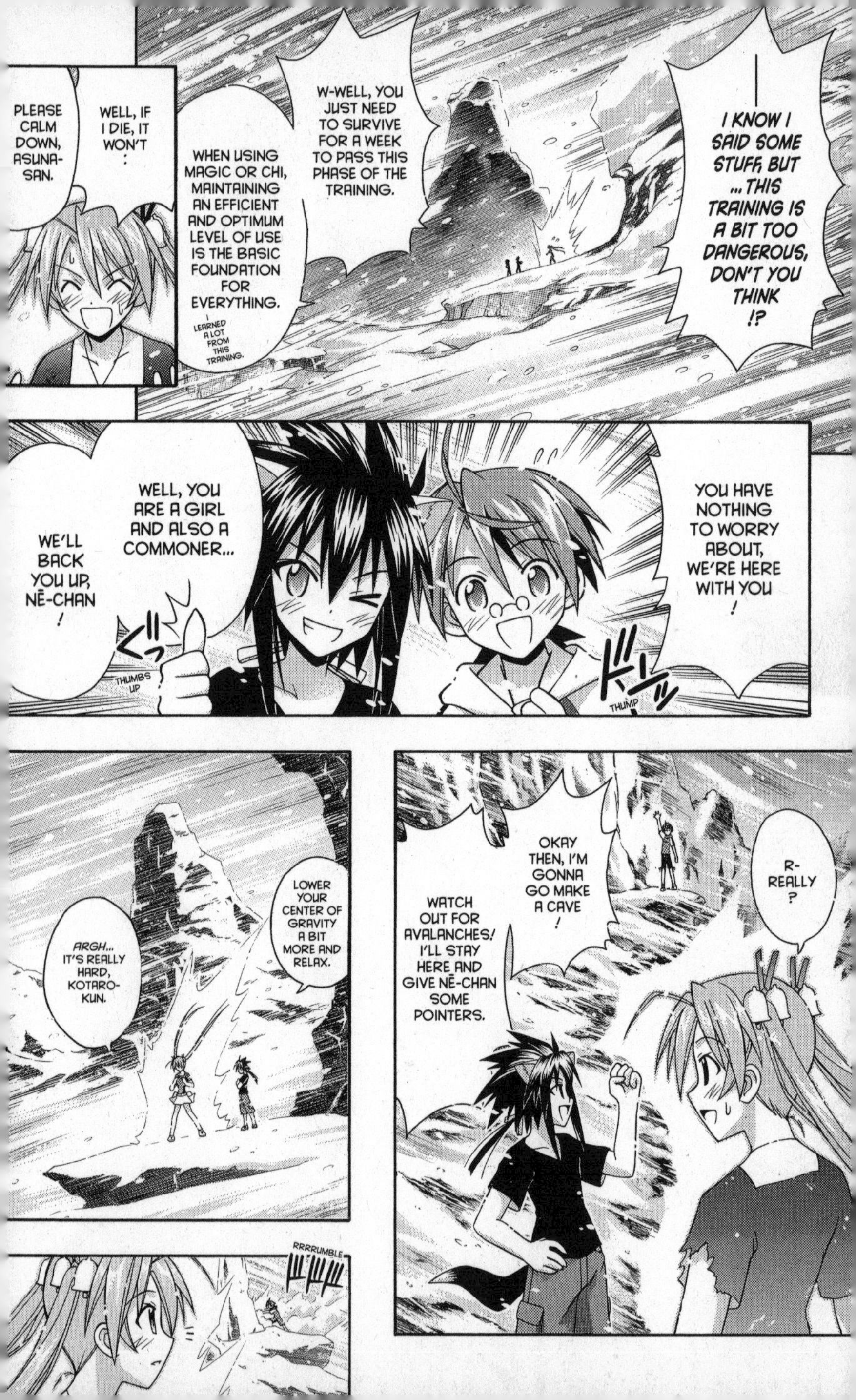

I KNOW I SAID SOME STUFF, BUT ...THIS TRAINING IS A BIT TOO DANGEROUS, DON'T YOU THINK!?
W-WELL, YOU JUST NEED TO SURVIVE FOR A WEEK TO PASS THIS PHASE OF THE TRAINING.
WHEN USING MAGIC OR CHI, MAINTAINING AN EFFICIENT AND OPTIMUM LEVEL OF USE IS THE BASIC FOUNDATION FOR EVERYTHING.
I LEARNED A LOT FROM THIS TRAINING.
WELL, IF I DIE, IT WON'T :
PLEASE CALM DOWN, ASUNA-SAN.
YOU HAVE NOTHING TO WORRY ABOUT, WE'RE HERE WITH YOU!
THUMP
WELL, YOU ARE A GIRL AND ALSO A COMMONER...
WE'LL BACK YOU UP, NĒ-CHAN!
THUMBS UP
R-REALLY?
OKAY THEN, I'M GONNA GO MAKE A CAVE!
WATCH OUT FOR AVALANCHES! I'LL STAY HERE AND GIVE NĒ-CHAN SOME POINTERS.
LOWER YOUR CENTER OF GRAVITY A BIT MORE AND RELAX.
ARGH... IT'S REALLY HARD, KOTARO-KUN.
RRRRUMBLE

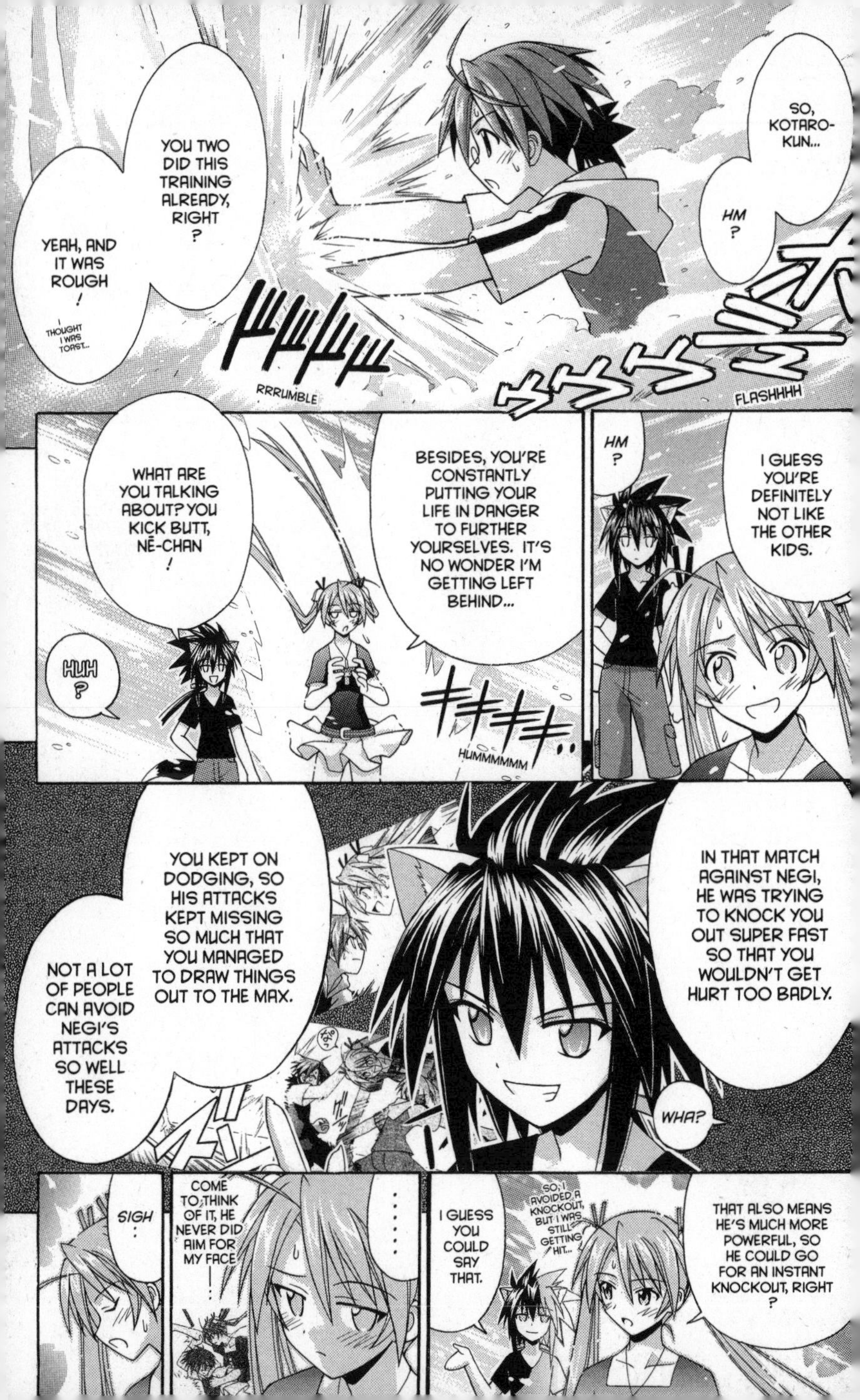
SO, KOTARO-KUN...
HM?
FLASHHHH
YOU TWO DID THIS TRAINING ALREADY, RIGHT?
YEAH, AND IT WAS ROUGH!
I THOUGHT I WAS TOAST...
RRRUMBLE
I GUESS YOU'RE DEFINITELY NOT LIKE THE OTHER KIDS.
HM?
BESIDES, YOU'RE CONSTANTLY PUTTING YOUR LIFE IN DANGER TO FURTHER YOURSELVES. IT'S NO WONDER I'M GETTING LEFT BEHIND...
HUMMMMMM
WHAT ARE YOU TALKING ABOUT? YOU KICK BUTT, NĒ-CHAN!
HUH?
IN THAT MATCH AGAINST NEGI, HE WAS TRYING TO KNOCK YOU OUT SUPER FAST SO THAT YOU WOULDN'T GET HURT TOO BADLY.
WHA?
YOU KEPT ON DODGING, SO HIS ATTACKS KEPT MISSING SO MUCH THAT YOU MANAGED TO DRAW THINGS OUT TO THE MAX.
NOT A LOT OF PEOPLE CAN AVOID NEGI'S ATTACKS SO WELL THESE DAYS.
THAT ALSO MEANS HE'S MUCH MORE POWERFUL, SO HE COULD GO FOR AN INSTANT KNOCKOUT, RIGHT?
SO, I AVOIDED A KNOCKOUT, BUT I WAS STILL GETTING HIT...
I GUESS YOU COULD SAY THAT.
......
COME TO THINK OF IT, HE NEVER DID AIM FOR MY FACE...!
SIGH...

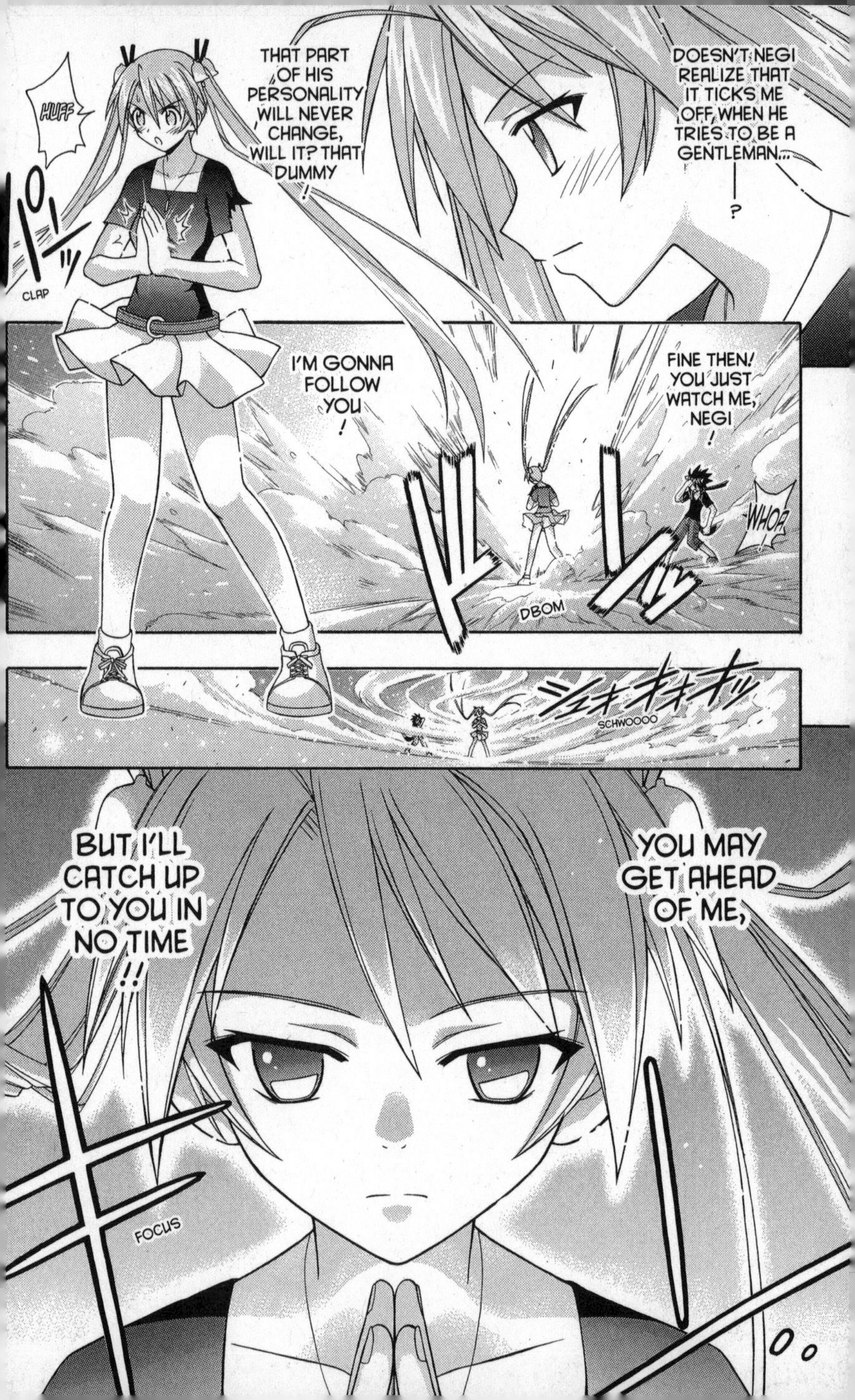
DOESN'T NEGI REALIZE THAT IT TICKS ME OFF WHEN HE TRIES TO BE A GENTLEMAN...?
THAT PART OF HIS PERSONALITY WILL NEVER CHANGE, WILL IT? THAT DUMMY!
HUFF
CLAP
FINE THEN! YOU JUST WATCH ME, NEGI!
WHOA
DBOM
I'M GONNA FOLLOW YOU!
SCHWOOOO
YOU MAY GET AHEAD OF ME,
BUT I'LL CATCH UP TO YOU IN NO TIME!!
FOCUS

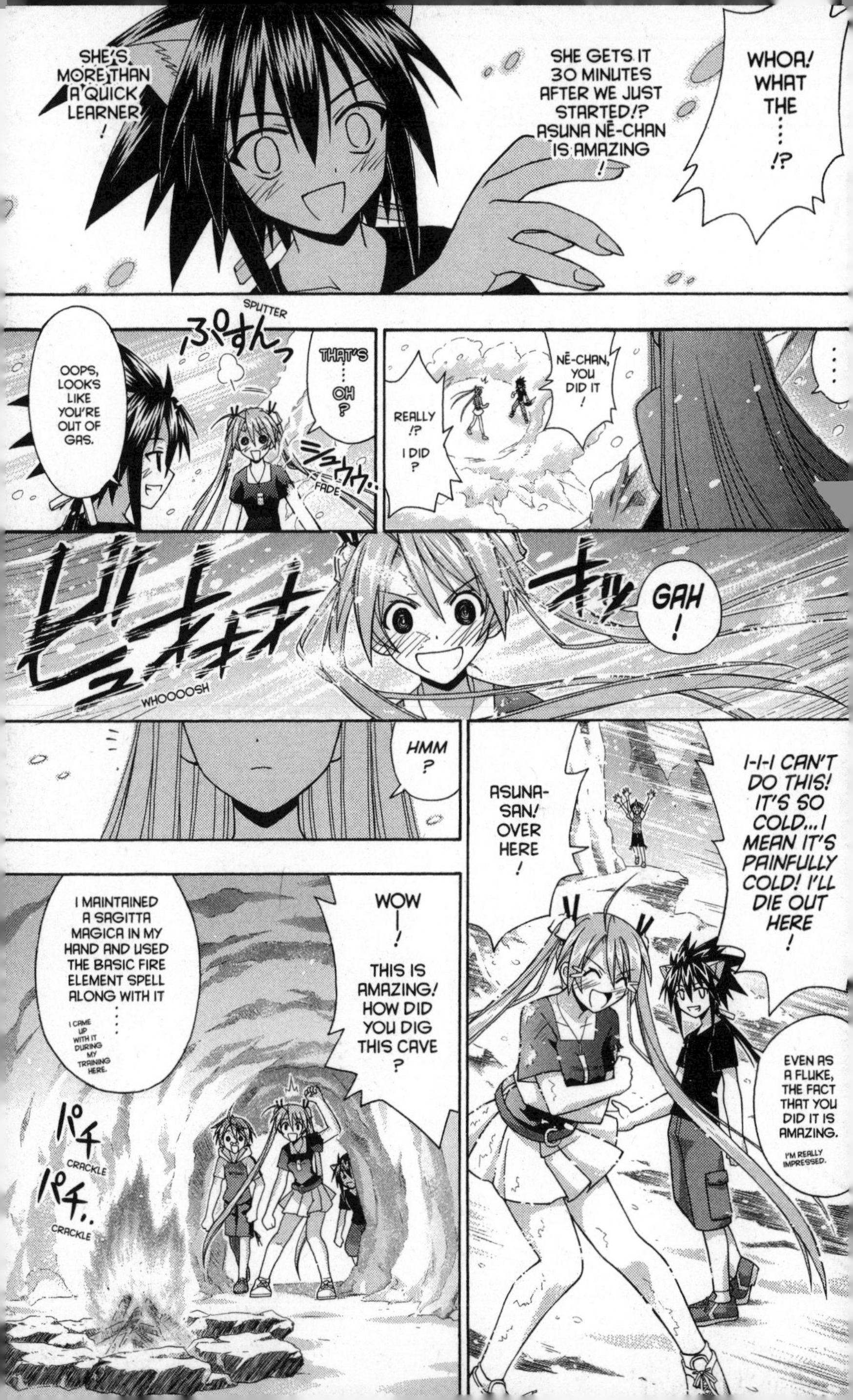
WHOA! WHAT THE......!?
SHE GETS IT 30 MINUTES AFTER WE JUST STARTED!? ASUNA NĒ-CHAN IS AMAZING!
SHE'S MORE THAN A QUICK LEARNER!
....
NĒ-CHAN, YOU DID IT!
REALLY!? I DID?
SPUTTER
THAT'S... OH?
FADE
OOPS, LOOKS LIKE YOU'RE OUT OF GAS.
GAH!
WHOOOOSH
I-I-I CAN'T DO THIS! IT'S SO COLD...I MEAN IT'S PAINFULLY COLD! I'LL DIE OUT HERE!
ASUNA-SAN! OVER HERE!
EVEN AS A FLUKE, THE FACT THAT YOU DID IT IS AMAZING.
I'M REALLY IMPRESSED.
HMM?
WOW!
THIS IS AMAZING! HOW DID YOU DIG THIS CAVE?
I MAINTAINED A SAGITTA MAGICA IN MY HAND AND USED THE BASIC FIRE ELEMENT SPELL ALONG WITH IT...
I CAME UP WITH IT DURING MY TRAINING HERE.
CRACKLE
CRACKLE

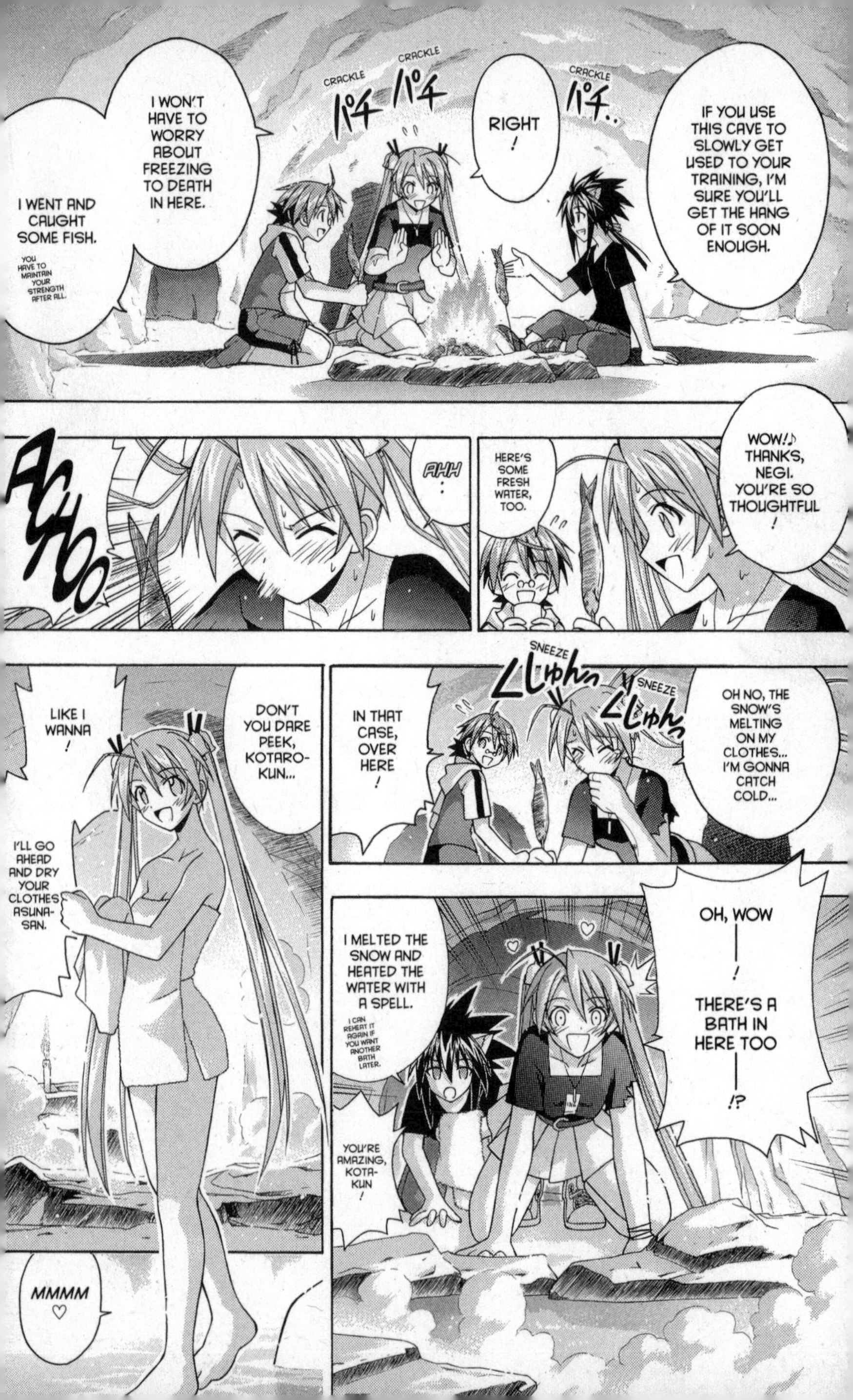

IF YOU USE THIS CAVE TO SLOWLY GET USED TO YOUR TRAINING, I'M SURE YOU'LL GET THE HANG OF IT SOON ENOUGH.
CRACKLE パチ..
RIGHT!
CRACKLE パチ
CRACKLE パチ
I WON'T HAVE TO WORRY ABOUT FREEZING TO DEATH IN HERE.
I WENT AND CAUGHT SOME FISH.
YOU HAVE TO MAINTAIN YOUR STRENGTH AFTER ALL.
WOW!♪ THANKS, NEGI. YOU'RE SO THOUGHTFUL!
HERE'S SOME FRESH WATER, TOO.
AHH...
ACHOO
OH NO, THE SNOW'S MELTING ON MY CLOTHES... I'M GONNA CATCH COLD...
SNEEZE くしゅん
SNEEZE くしゅん
IN THAT CASE, OVER HERE!
OH, WOW—! THERE'S A BATH IN HERE TOO—!?
I MELTED THE SNOW AND HEATED THE WATER WITH A SPELL.
I CAN REHEAT IT AGAIN IF YOU WANT ANOTHER BATH LATER.
YOU'RE AMAZING, KOTA-KUN!
DON'T YOU DARE PEEK, KOTARO-KUN...
LIKE I WANNA!
I'LL GO AHEAD AND DRY YOUR CLOTHES ASUNA-SAN.
MMMM ♡

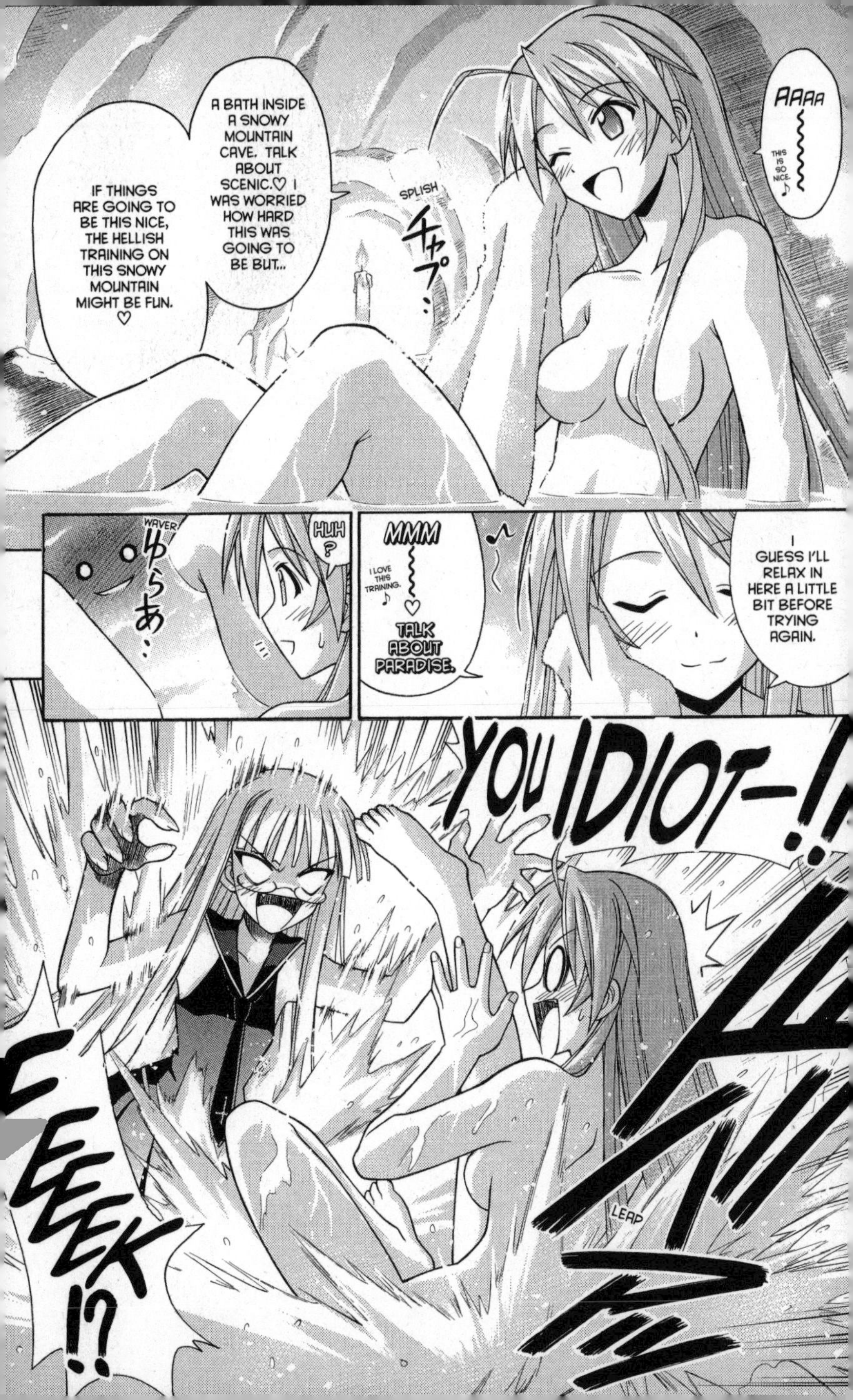
AAAA~ THIS IS SO NICE. ♪
SPLISH
チャプ…
A BATH INSIDE A SNOWY MOUNTAIN CAVE. TALK ABOUT SCENIC.♡ I WAS WORRIED HOW HARD THIS WAS GOING TO BE BUT...
IF THINGS ARE GOING TO BE THIS NICE, THE HELLISH TRAINING ON THIS SNOWY MOUNTAIN MIGHT BE FUN. ♡
I GUESS I'LL RELAX IN HERE A LITTLE BIT BEFORE TRYING AGAIN.
MMM~ I LOVE THIS TRAINING. ♪ ♡ TALK ABOUT PARADISE.
HUH?
WAVER
ゆらあ…
YOU IDIOT—!!
LEAP
EEEEK!!?

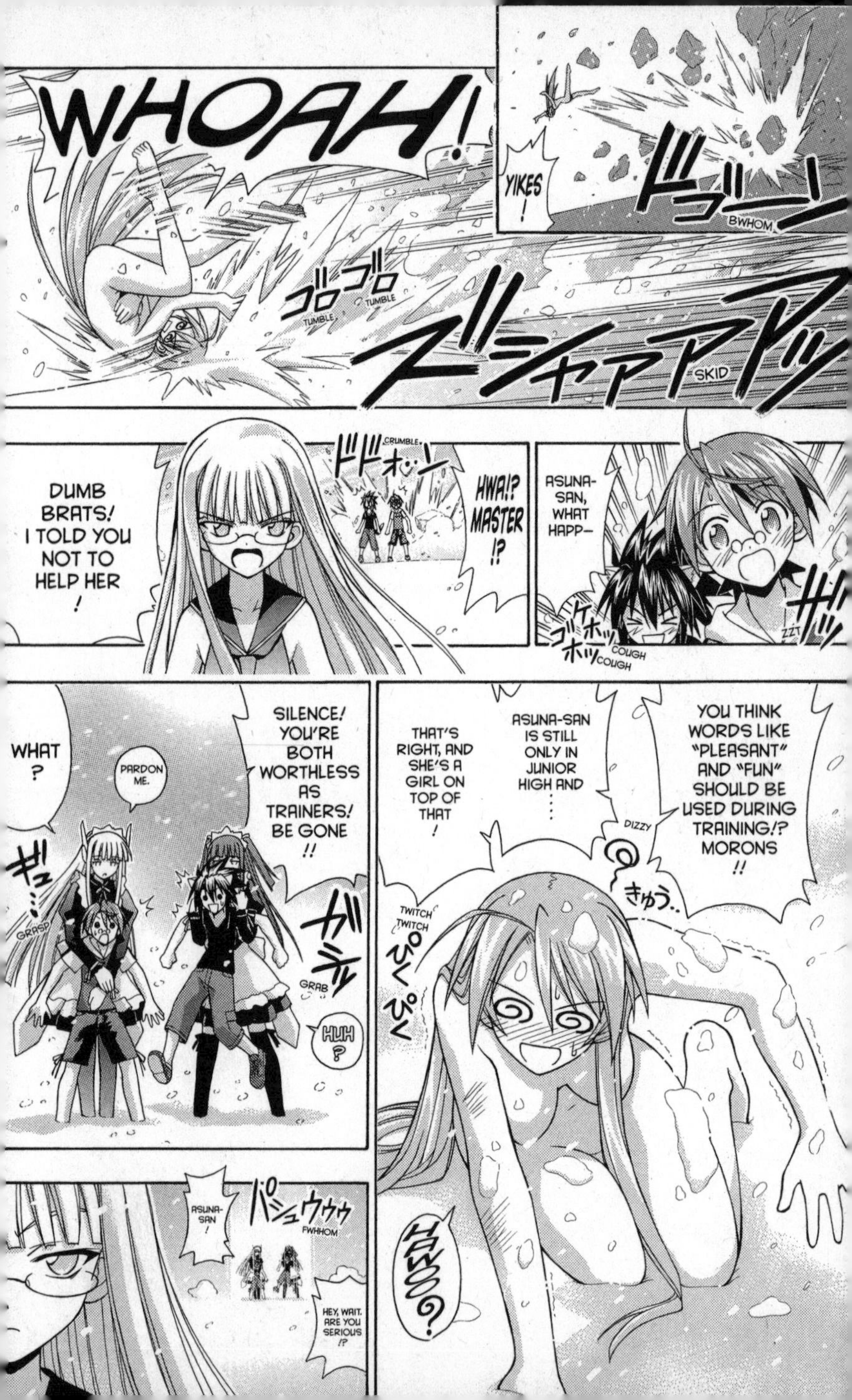
YIKES!
ドゴーン
BWHOM
WHOAH!
ゴロゴロ
TUMBLE TUMBLE
ズシャアアッ
SKID
ASUNA-SAN, WHAT HAPP—
ザッ
ZZT
ケホッ ゴホッ
COUGH COUGH
HWA!? MASTER!?
ドドオン
CRUMBLE
DUMB BRATS! I TOLD YOU NOT TO HELP HER!
YOU THINK WORDS LIKE "PLEASANT" AND "FUN" SHOULD BE USED DURING TRAINING!? MORONS!!
ASUNA-SAN IS STILL ONLY IN JUNIOR HIGH AND......
THAT'S RIGHT, AND SHE'S A GIRL ON TOP OF THAT!
DIZZY
きゅう..
TWITCH TWITCH
ぴくぴく
HAWOOO?
SILENCE! YOU'RE BOTH WORTHLESS AS TRAINERS! BE GONE!!
WHAT?
PARDON ME.
ギュ...
GRASP
ガシッ
GRAB
HUH?
ASUNA-SAN!
パシュウウウ
FWHHOM
HEY, WAIT. ARE YOU SERIOUS!?

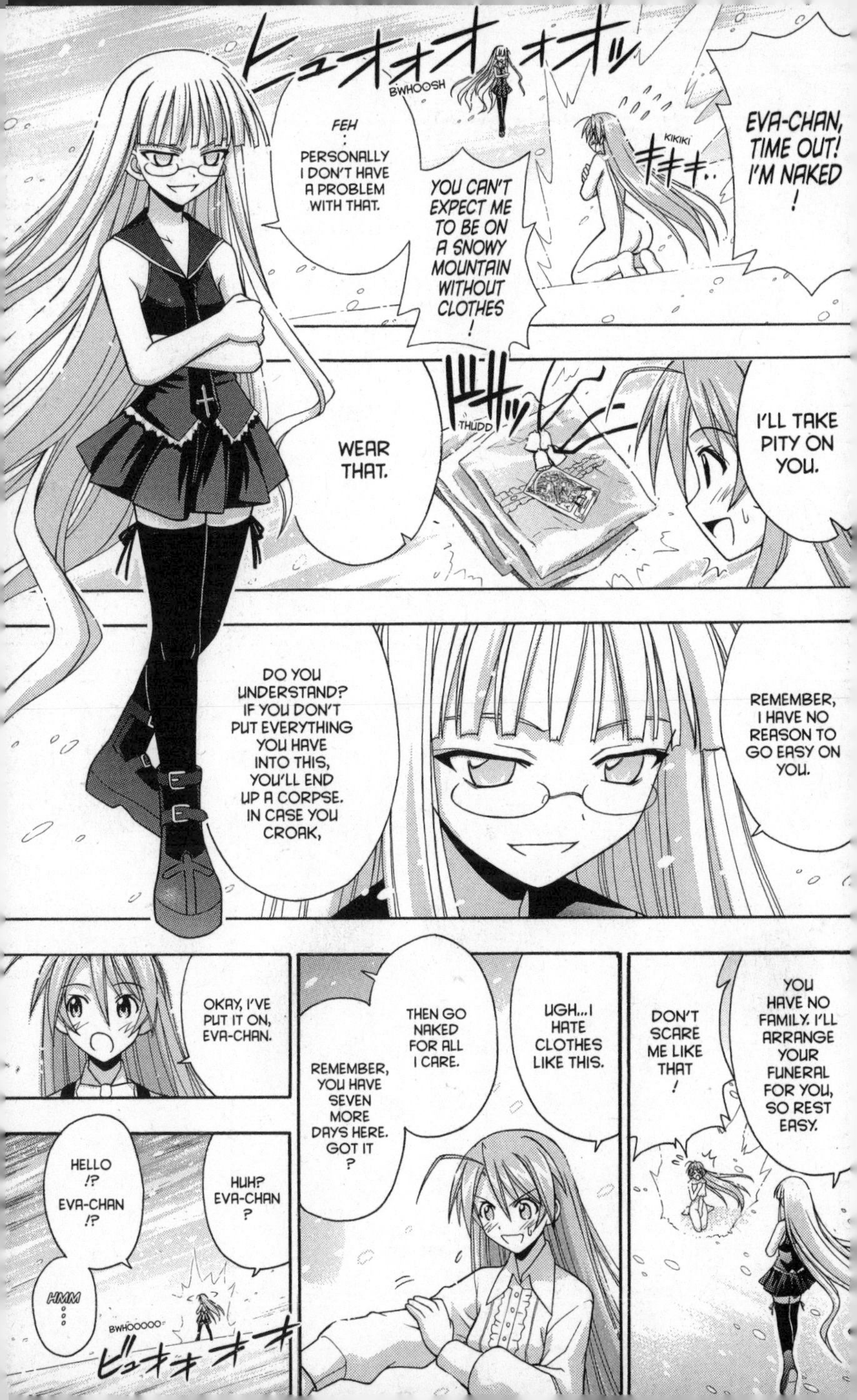
EVA-CHAN, TIME OUT! I'M NAKED!
KIKIKI
YOU CAN'T EXPECT ME TO BE ON A SNOWY MOUNTAIN WITHOUT CLOTHES!
BWHOOSH
FEH: PERSONALLY I DON'T HAVE A PROBLEM WITH THAT.
I'LL TAKE PITY ON YOU.
THUDD
WEAR THAT.
REMEMBER, I HAVE NO REASON TO GO EASY ON YOU.
DO YOU UNDERSTAND? IF YOU DON'T PUT EVERYTHING YOU HAVE INTO THIS, YOU'LL END UP A CORPSE. IN CASE YOU CROAK,
YOU HAVE NO FAMILY. I'LL ARRANGE YOUR FUNERAL FOR YOU, SO REST EASY.
DON'T SCARE ME LIKE THAT!
UGH...I HATE CLOTHES LIKE THIS.
THEN GO NAKED FOR ALL I CARE.
REMEMBER, YOU HAVE SEVEN MORE DAYS HERE. GOT IT?
OKAY, I'VE PUT IT ON, EVA-CHAN.
HUH? EVA-CHAN?
HELLO!? EVA-CHAN!?
HMM...
BWHOOOOO

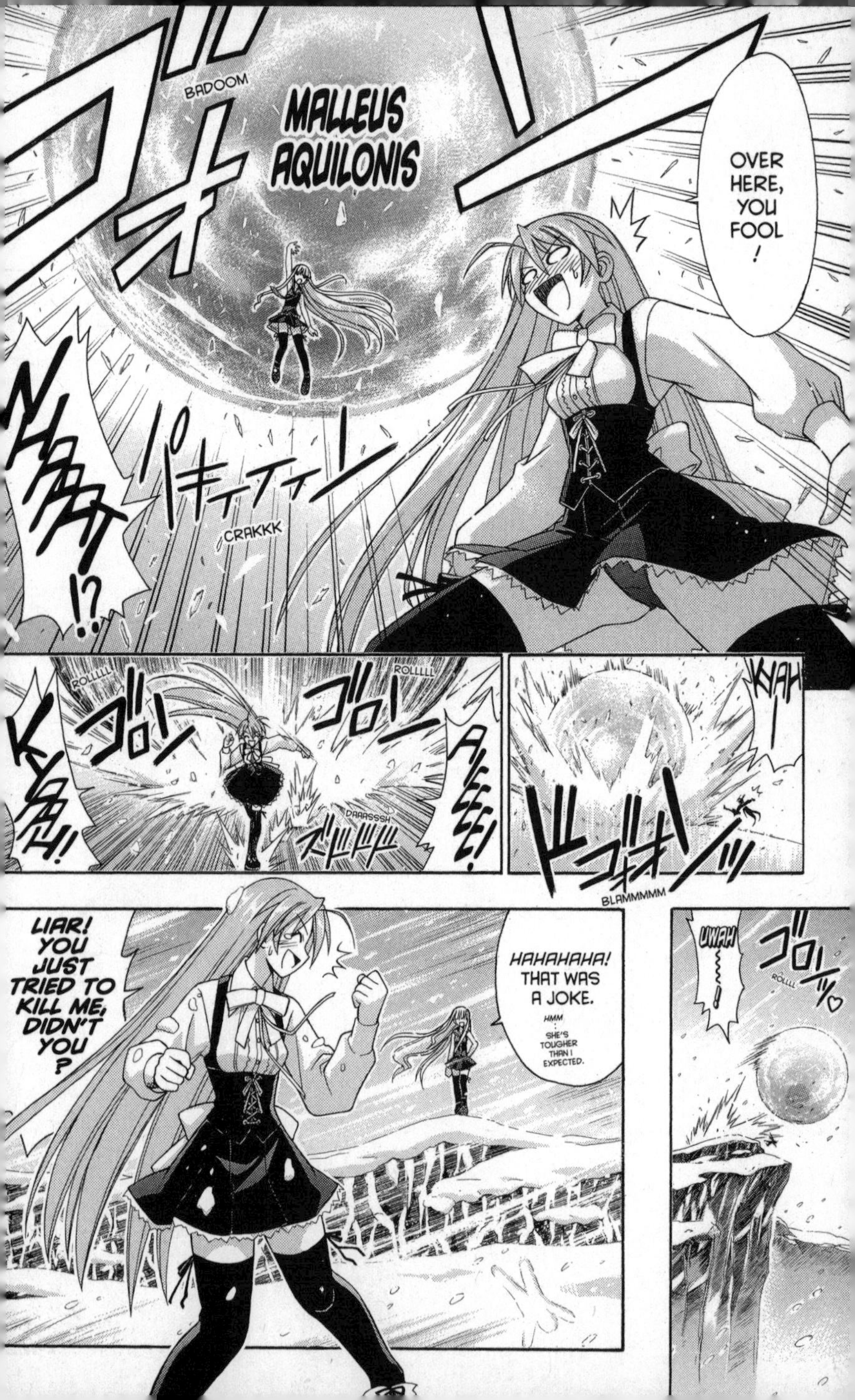
OVER HERE, YOU FOOL!
BADOOM
MALLEUS AQUILONIS
CRAKKK
KYAH!
BLAMMMMM
ROLLLLL
ROLLLLL
AIEEE!
DAAASSSH
KYAAAH!
UWAH~!
ROLLL
HAHAHAHA! THAT WAS A JOKE.
HMM... SHE'S TOUGHER THAN I EXPECTED.
LIAR! YOU JUST TRIED TO KILL ME, DIDN'T YOU?

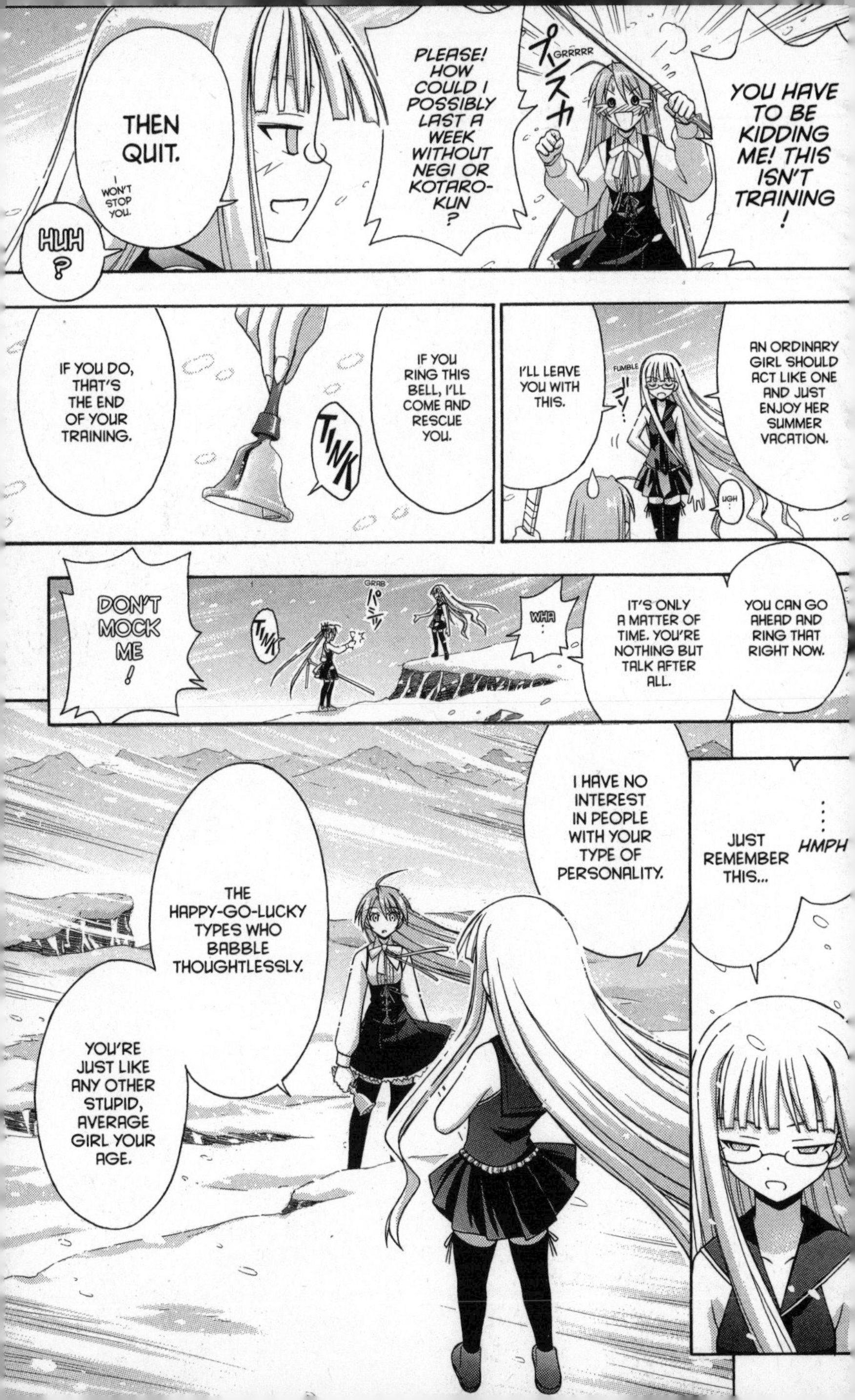
YOU HAVE TO BE KIDDING ME! THIS ISN'T TRAINING!
GRRRRR
PLEASE! HOW COULD I POSSIBLY LAST A WEEK WITHOUT NEGI OR KOTARO-KUN?
THEN QUIT.
I WON'T STOP YOU.
HUH?
AN ORDINARY GIRL SHOULD ACT LIKE ONE AND JUST ENJOY HER SUMMER VACATION.
UGH
FUMBLE
I'LL LEAVE YOU WITH THIS.
IF YOU RING THIS BELL, I'LL COME AND RESCUE YOU.
TINK
IF YOU DO, THAT'S THE END OF YOUR TRAINING.
YOU CAN GO AHEAD AND RING THAT RIGHT NOW.
IT'S ONLY A MATTER OF TIME. YOU'RE NOTHING BUT TALK AFTER ALL.
WHA...
GRAB
TINK
DON'T MOCK ME!
...HMPH
JUST REMEMBER THIS...
I HAVE NO INTEREST IN PEOPLE WITH YOUR TYPE OF PERSONALITY.
THE HAPPY-GO-LUCKY TYPES WHO BABBLE THOUGHTLESSLY.
YOU'RE JUST LIKE ANY OTHER STUPID, AVERAGE GIRL YOUR AGE.

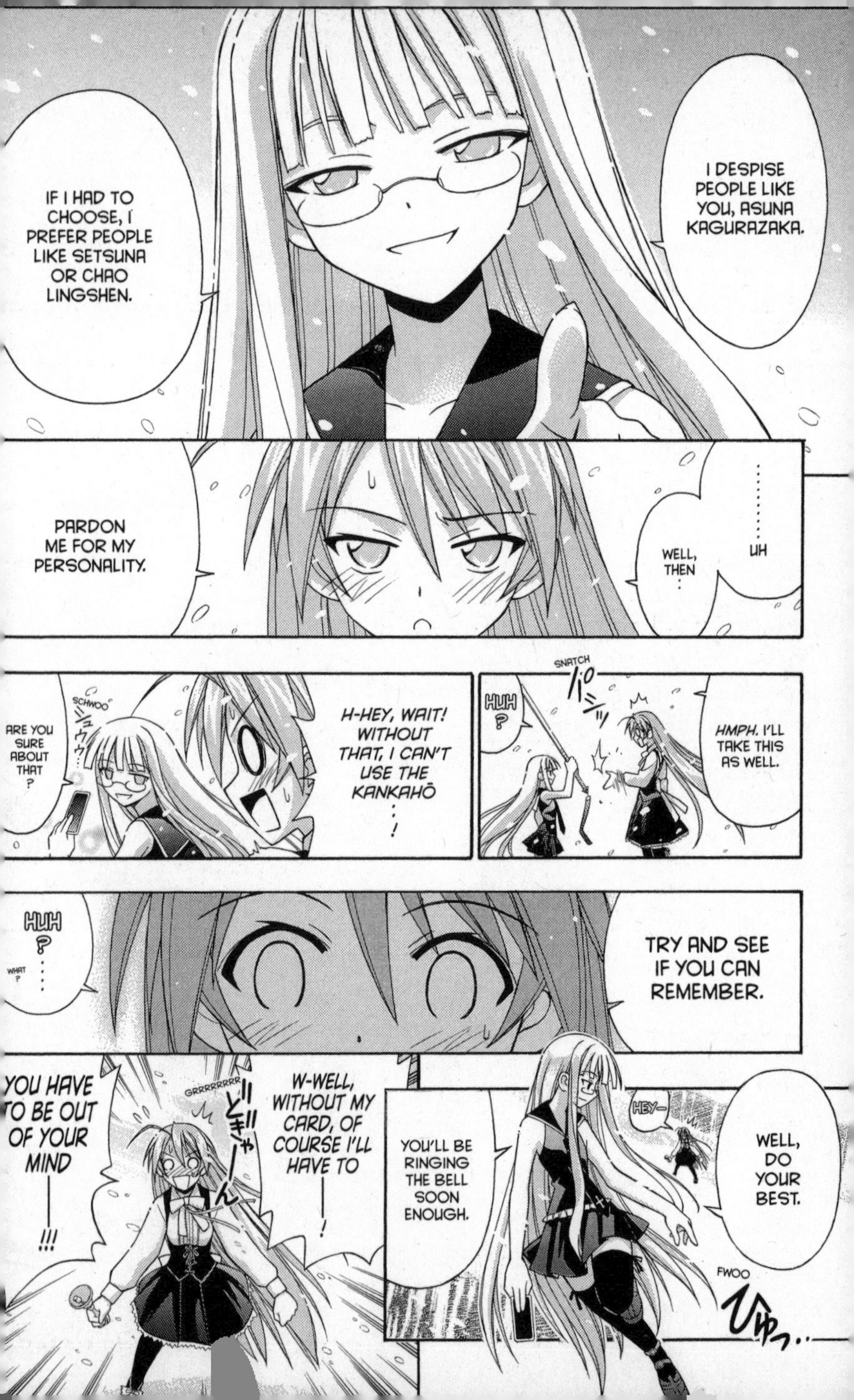
I DESPISE PEOPLE LIKE YOU, ASUNA KAGURAZAKA.
IF I HAD TO CHOOSE, I PREFER PEOPLE LIKE SETSUNA OR CHAO LINGSHEN.
……UH
WELL, THEN…
PARDON ME FOR MY PERSONALITY.
SNATCH
HMPH. I'LL TAKE THIS AS WELL.
HUH?
H-HEY, WAIT! WITHOUT THAT, I CAN'T USE THE KANKAHŌ…!
SCHWOO
ARE YOU SURE ABOUT THAT?
TRY AND SEE IF YOU CAN REMEMBER.
HUH?
WHAT?…
WELL, DO YOUR BEST.
HEY—
FWOO
YOU'LL BE RINGING THE BELL SOON ENOUGH.
W-WELL, WITHOUT MY CARD, OF COURSE I'LL HAVE TO—!
GRRRRRRR
YOU HAVE TO BE OUT OF YOUR MIND—!!!

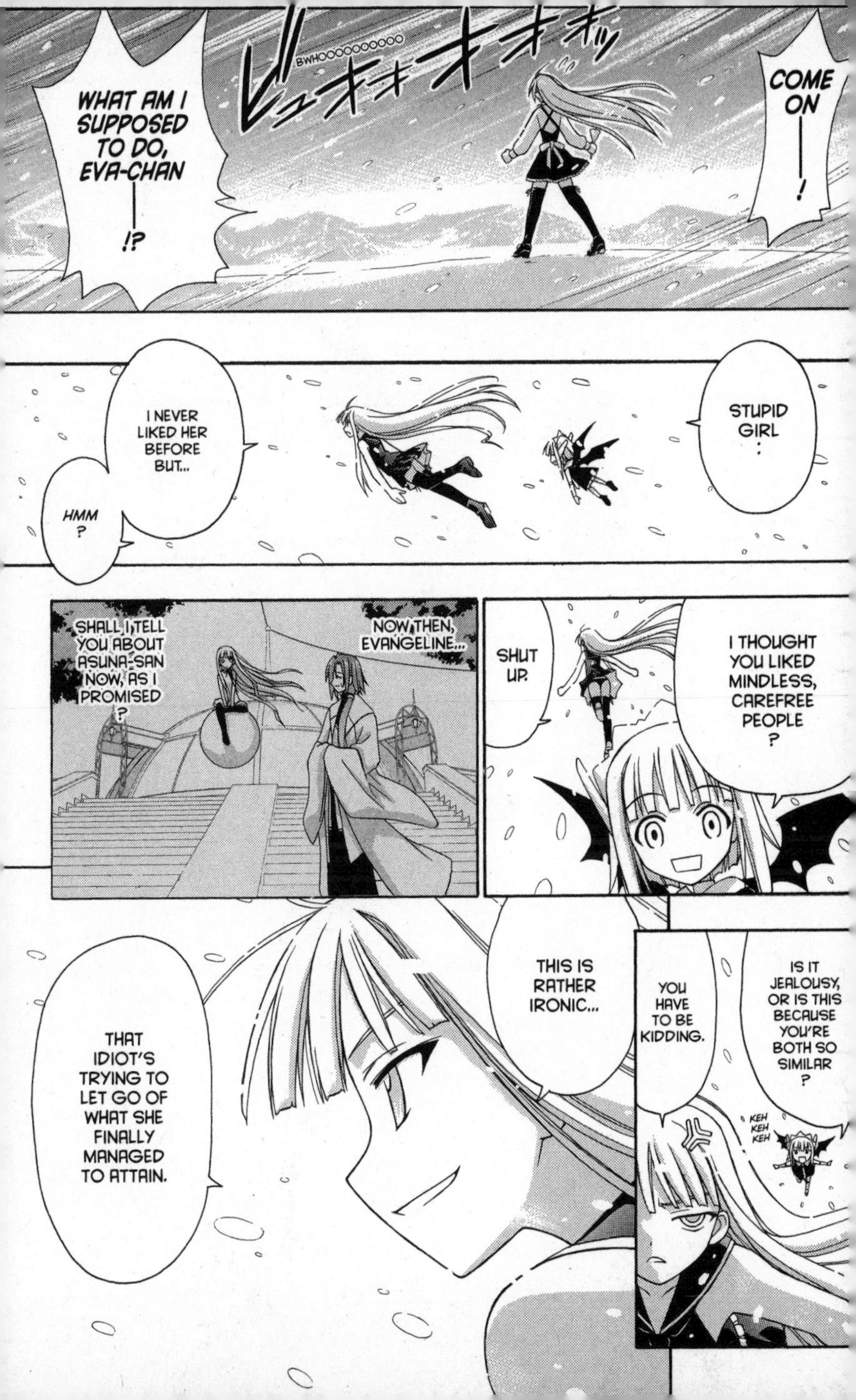
COME ON—!
BWHOOOOOOOOOO
WHAT AM I SUPPOSED TO DO, EVA-CHAN—!?
STUPID GIRL:
I NEVER LIKED HER BEFORE BUT...
HMM?
I THOUGHT YOU LIKED MINDLESS, CAREFREE PEOPLE?
SHUT UP.
NOW, THEN, EVANGELINE...
SHALL I TELL YOU ABOUT ASUNA-SAN NOW, AS I PROMISED?
IS IT JEALOUSY, OR IS THIS BECAUSE YOU'RE BOTH SO SIMILAR?
KEH KEH KEH
YOU HAVE TO BE KIDDING.
THIS IS RATHER IRONIC...
THAT IDIOT'S TRYING TO LET GO OF WHAT SHE FINALLY MANAGED TO ATTAIN.

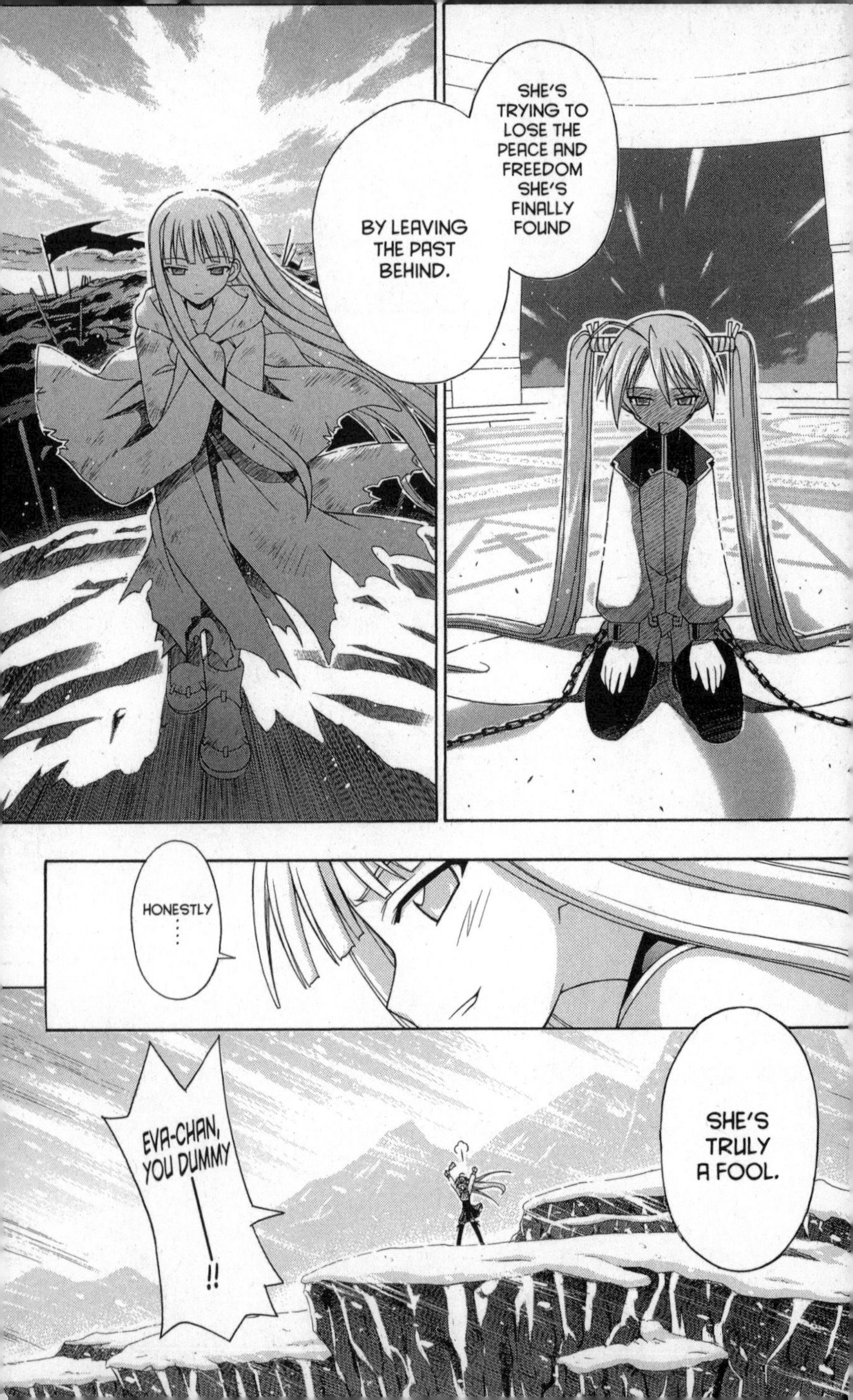
SHE'S TRYING TO LOSE THE PEACE AND FREEDOM SHE'S FINALLY FOUND
BY LEAVING THE PAST BEHIND.
HONESTLY ....
SHE'S TRULY A FOOL.
EVA-CHAN, YOU DUMMY —!!

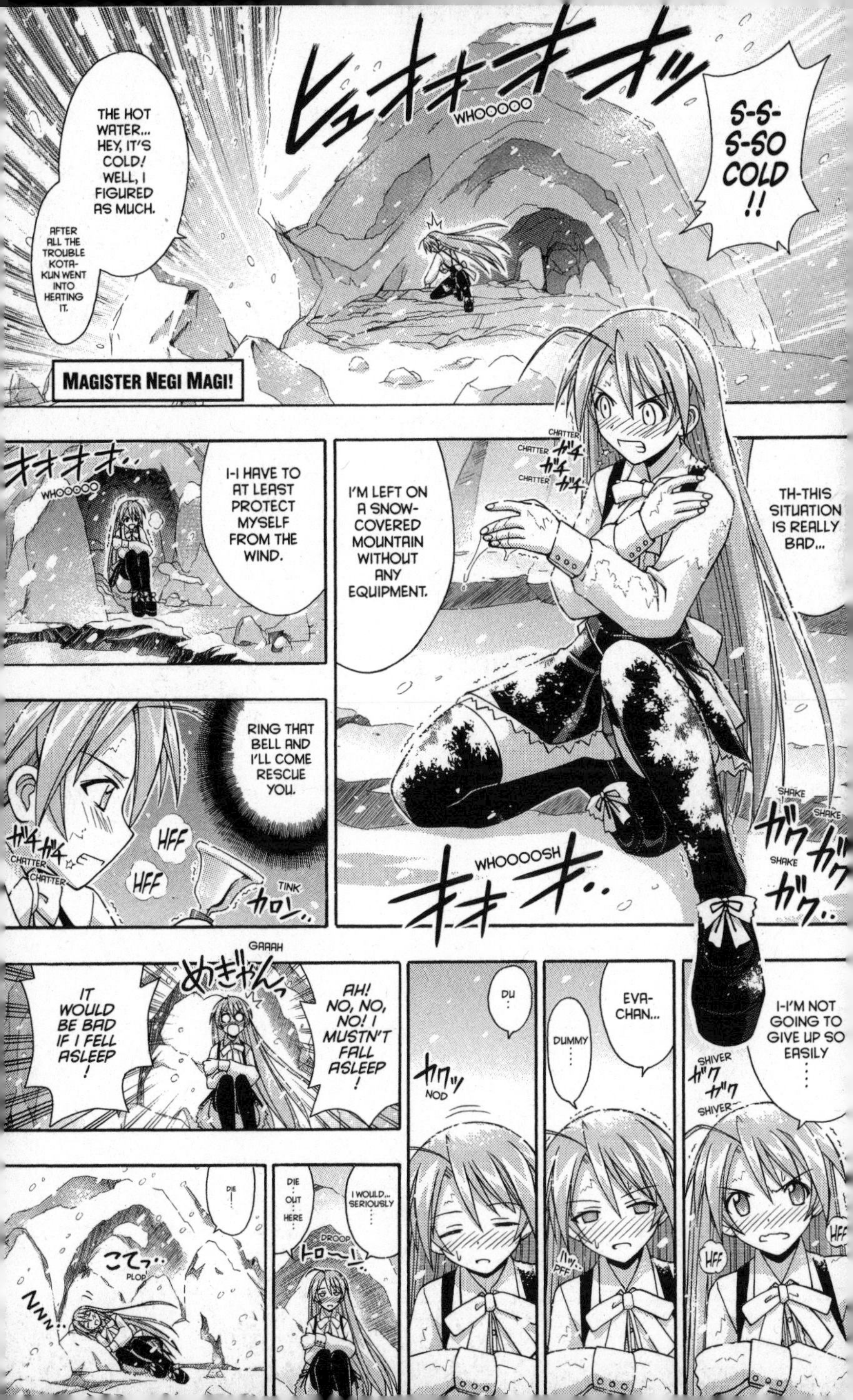

WHOOOOO
S-S-S-SO COLD!!
THE HOT WATER... HEY, IT'S COLD! WELL, I FIGURED AS MUCH.
AFTER ALL THE TROUBLE KOTA-KUN WENT INTO HEATING IT.
MAGISTER NEGI MAGI!
TH-THIS SITUATION IS REALLY BAD...
CHATTER CHATTER CHATTER
I'M LEFT ON A SNOW-COVERED MOUNTAIN WITHOUT ANY EQUIPMENT.
SHAKE SHAKE SHAKE
WHOOOOSH
I-I HAVE TO AT LEAST PROTECT MYSELF FROM THE WIND.
WHOOOOO
RING THAT BELL AND I'LL COME RESCUE YOU.
HFF
HFF
TINK
CHATTER CHATTER
I-I'M NOT GOING TO GIVE UP SO EASILY....
SHIVER SHIVER
HFF
HFF
EVA-CHAN...
DUMMY...
PFF
DU...
NOD
AH! NO, NO, NO! I MUSTN'T FALL ASLEEP!
GAAAH
IT WOULD BE BAD IF I FELL ASLEEP!
I WOULD... SERIOUSLY...
DIE OUT HERE...
DROOP
DIE...
PLOP
NNN...

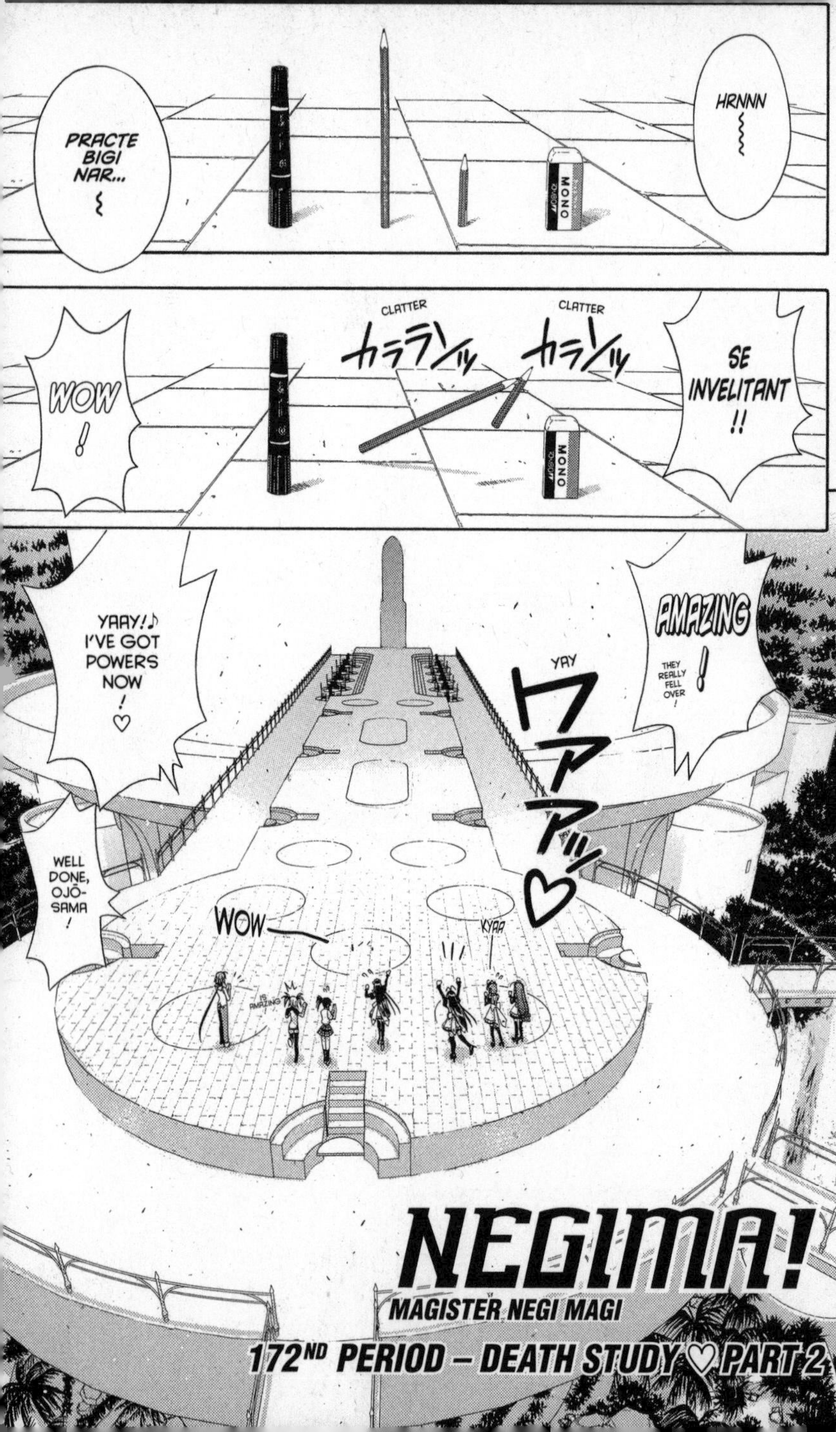
HRNNN
PRACTE BIGI NAR...
SE INVELITANT!!
CLATTER
カランッ
CLATTER
カラランッ
WOW!
AMAZING!
THEY REALLY FELL OVER!
YAY
ワァアッ♡
YAAY!♪ I'VE GOT POWERS NOW!♡
WELL DONE, OJŌ-SAMA!
KYAA
IS AMAZING
WOW—
NEGIMA!
MAGISTER NEGI MAGI
172ND PERIOD – DEATH STUDY ♡ PART 2

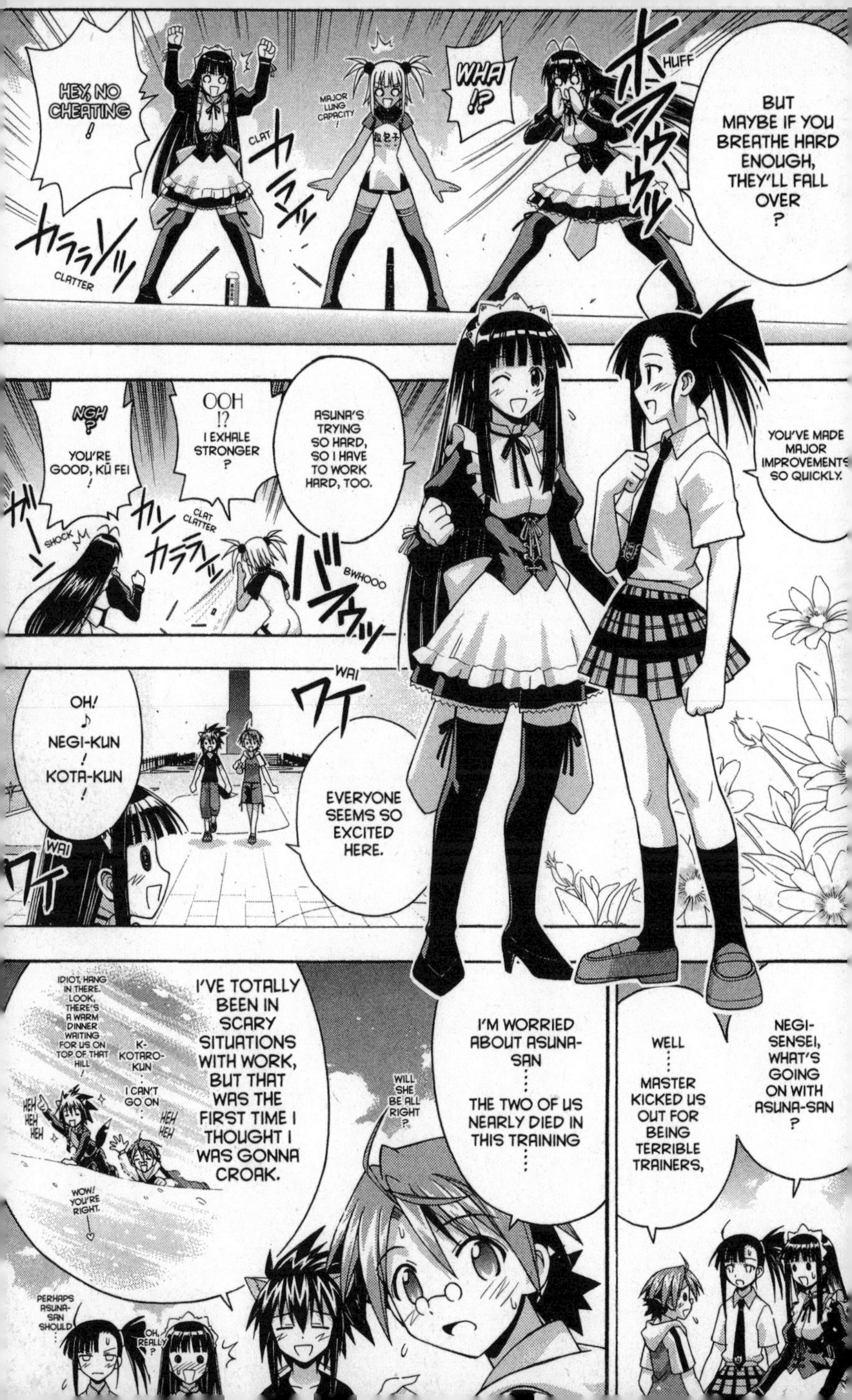

BUT MAYBE IF YOU BREATHE HARD ENOUGH, THEY'LL FALL OVER?
HUFF
WHA!?
MAJOR LUNG CAPACITY!
CLAT
HEY, NO CHEATING!
CLATTER
YOU'VE MADE MAJOR IMPROVEMENTS SO QUICKLY.
ASUNA'S TRYING SO HARD, SO I HAVE TO WORK HARD, TOO.
WAI
EVERYONE SEEMS SO EXCITED HERE.
BWHOOO
OOH!? I EXHALE STRONGER?
CLAT CLATTER
NGH? YOU'RE GOOD, KŪ FEI!
SHOCK
OH! ♪ NEGI-KUN! KOTA-KUN!
WAI
NEGI-SENSEI, WHAT'S GOING ON WITH ASUNA-SAN?
WELL... MASTER KICKED US OUT FOR BEING TERRIBLE TRAINERS,
I'M WORRIED ABOUT ASUNA-SAN... THE TWO OF US NEARLY DIED IN THIS TRAINING...
WILL SHE BE ALL RIGHT?
I'VE TOTALLY BEEN IN SCARY SITUATIONS WITH WORK, BUT THAT WAS THE FIRST TIME I THOUGHT I WAS GONNA CROAK.
K-KOTARO-KUN I CAN'T GO ON...
HEH HEH
IDIOT, HANG IN THERE. LOOK, THERE'S A WARM DINNER WAITING FOR US ON TOP OF THIS HILL!
HEH HEH HEH
WOW! YOU'RE RIGHT. ♡
OH, REALLY?
PERHAPS ASUNA-SAN SHOULD...

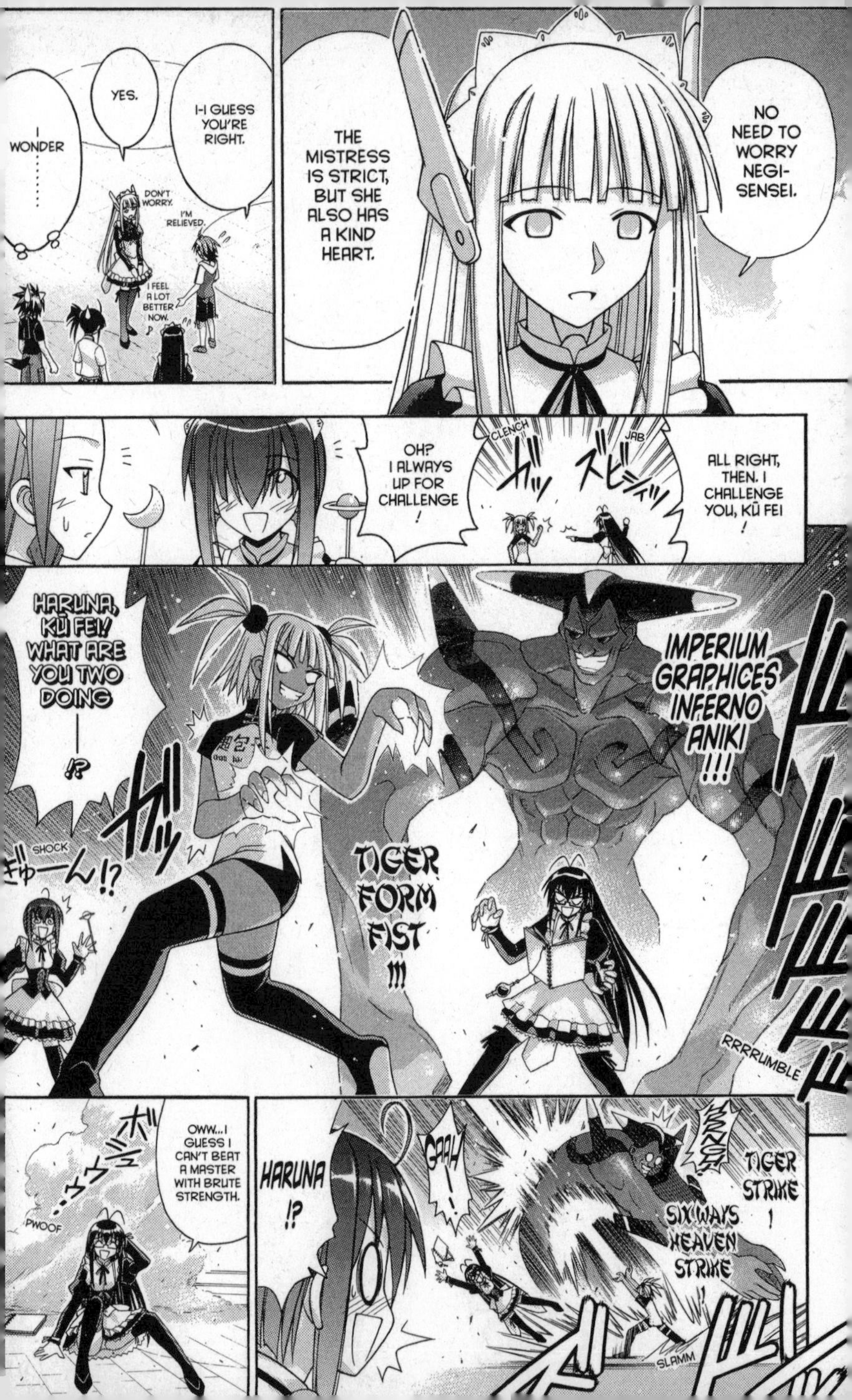

NO NEED TO WORRY NEGI-SENSEI.
THE MISTRESS IS STRICT, BUT SHE ALSO HAS A KIND HEART.
I-I GUESS YOU'RE RIGHT.
YES.
I WONDER......
DON'T WORRY.
I'M RELIEVED.
I FEEL A LOT BETTER NOW.
ALL RIGHT, THEN. I CHALLENGE YOU, KŪ FEI!
JAB
CLENCH
OH? I ALWAYS UP FOR CHALLENGE!
IMPERIUM GRAPHICES INFERNO ANIKI!!!
RRRUMBLE
TIGER FORM FIST!!!
HARUNA, KŪ FEI! WHAT ARE YOU TWO DOING——!?
SHOCK
TIGER STRIKE!
SIX WAYS HEAVEN STRIKE!
GAAH!
SLAMM
HARUNA!?
OWW...I GUESS I CAN'T BEAT A MASTER WITH BRUTE STRENGTH.
PWOOF

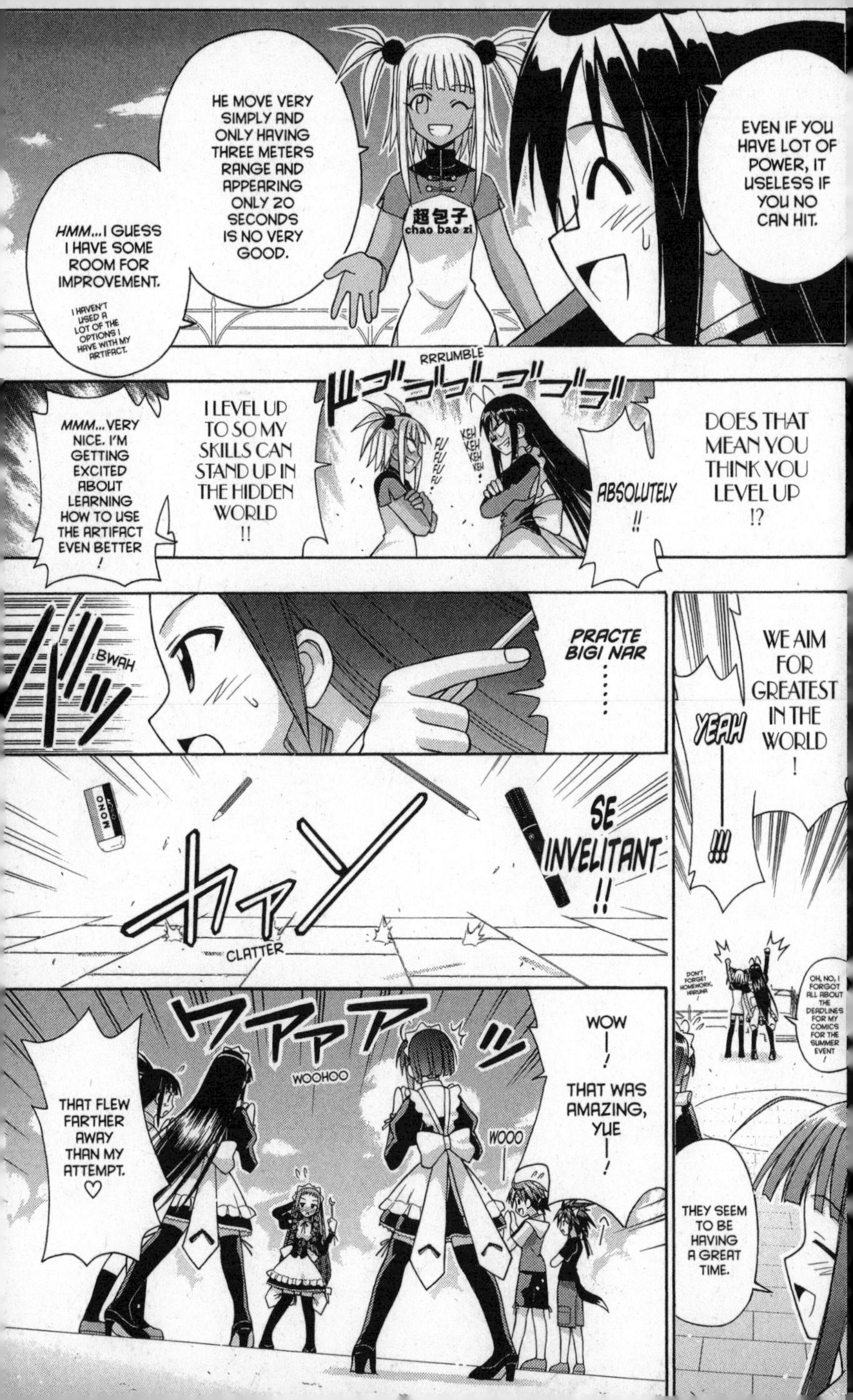
EVEN IF YOU HAVE LOT OF POWER, IT USELESS IF YOU NO CAN HIT.
HE MOVE VERY SIMPLY AND ONLY HAVING THREE METERS RANGE AND APPEARING ONLY 20 SECONDS IS NO VERY GOOD.
超包子
chao bao zi
HMM...I GUESS I HAVE SOME ROOM FOR IMPROVEMENT.
I HAVEN'T USED A LOT OF THE OPTIONS I HAVE WITH MY ARTIFACT.
DOES THAT MEAN YOU THINK YOU LEVEL UP !?
ABSOLUTELY !!
RRRUMBLE
KEH KEH KEH KEH
FU FU FU FU
I LEVEL UP TO SO MY SKILLS CAN STAND UP IN THE HIDDEN WORLD !!
MMM...VERY NICE. I'M GETTING EXCITED ABOUT LEARNING HOW TO USE THE ARTIFACT EVEN BETTER !
WE AIM FOR GREATEST IN THE WORLD !
YEAH —!!!
OH, NO, I FORGOT ALL ABOUT THE DEADLINES FOR MY COMICS FOR THE SUMMER EVENT !
DON'T FORGET HOMEWORK, HARUNA !
THEY SEEM TO BE HAVING A GREAT TIME.
PRACTE BIGI NAR ......
BWAH
SE INVELITANT !!
MONO
CLATTER
WOW —! THAT WAS AMAZING, YUE —!
WOOHOO
WOOO
THAT FLEW FARTHER AWAY THAN MY ATTEMPT. ♡

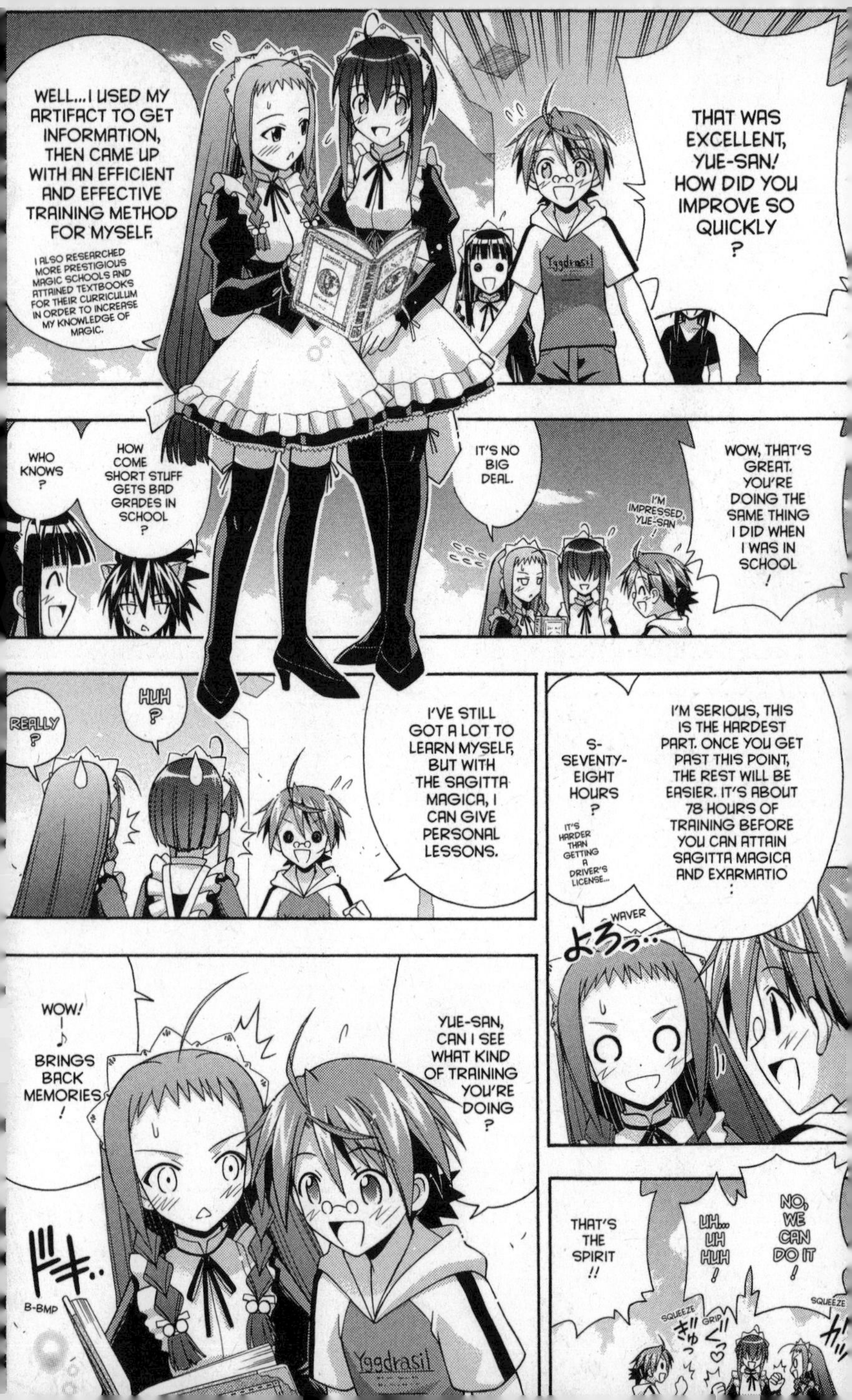
THAT WAS EXCELLENT, YUE-SAN! HOW DID YOU IMPROVE SO QUICKLY?
WELL...I USED MY ARTIFACT TO GET INFORMATION, THEN CAME UP WITH AN EFFICIENT AND EFFECTIVE TRAINING METHOD FOR MYSELF.
I ALSO RESEARCHED MORE PRESTIGIOUS MAGIC SCHOOLS AND ATTAINED TEXTBOOKS FOR THEIR CURRICULUM IN ORDER TO INCREASE MY KNOWLEDGE OF MAGIC.
WOW, THAT'S GREAT. YOU'RE DOING THE SAME THING I DID WHEN I WAS IN SCHOOL!
I'M IMPRESSED, YUE-SAN!
IT'S NO BIG DEAL.
HOW COME SHORT STUFF GETS BAD GRADES IN SCHOOL?
WHO KNOWS?
I'M SERIOUS, THIS IS THE HARDEST PART. ONCE YOU GET PAST THIS POINT, THE REST WILL BE EASIER. IT'S ABOUT 78 HOURS OF TRAINING BEFORE YOU CAN ATTAIN SAGITTA MAGICA AND EXARMATIO:
S-SEVENTY-EIGHT HOURS?
IT'S HARDER THAN GETTING A DRIVER'S LICENSE...
WAVER
よろっ
I'VE STILL GOT A LOT TO LEARN MYSELF, BUT WITH THE SAGITTA MAGICA, I CAN GIVE PERSONAL LESSONS.
HUH?
REALLY?
YUE-SAN, CAN I SEE WHAT KIND OF TRAINING YOU'RE DOING?
WOW! ♪ BRINGS BACK MEMORIES!
ドキ..
B-BMP
NO, WE CAN DO IT!
UH... UH HUH!
THAT'S THE SPIRIT!!
SQUEEZE
GRIP
ぎゅっ
ぐっ
SQUEEZE

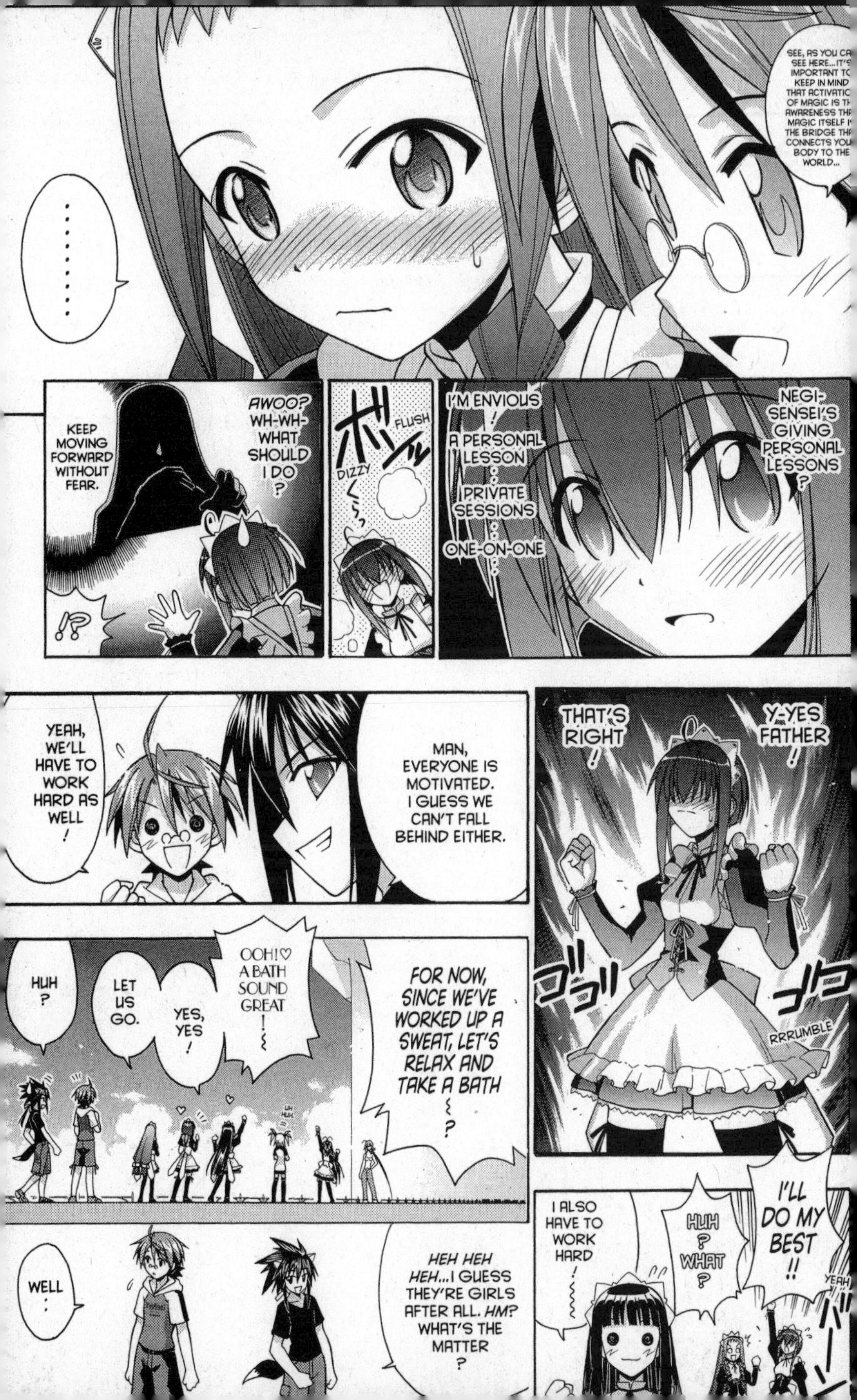

SEE, AS YOU CA SEE HERE...IT'S IMPORTANT TO KEEP IN MIND THAT ACTIVATIC OF MAGIC IS TH AWARENESS TH MAGIC ITSELF I THE BRIDGE TH CONNECTS YOU BODY TO THE WORLD...
....
NEGI-SENSEI'S GIVING PERSONAL LESSONS?
I'M ENVIOUS!
A PERSONAL LESSON...
PRIVATE SESSIONS...
ONE-ON-ONE...
FLUSH
DIZZY
AWOO? WH-WH-WHAT SHOULD I DO?
KEEP MOVING FORWARD WITHOUT FEAR.
!?
Y-YES FATHER!
THAT'S RIGHT!
RRRUMBLE
MAN, EVERYONE IS MOTIVATED. I GUESS WE CAN'T FALL BEHIND EITHER.
YEAH, WE'LL HAVE TO WORK HARD AS WELL!
FOR NOW, SINCE WE'VE WORKED UP A SWEAT, LET'S RELAX AND TAKE A BATH~?
OOH!♡ A BATH SOUND GREAT!~
YES, YES!
LET US GO.
HUH?
UH HUH.
I'LL DO MY BEST!!
YEAH
HUH? WHAT?
I ALSO HAVE TO WORK HARD!~
HEH HEH HEH...I GUESS THEY'RE GIRLS AFTER ALL. HM? WHAT'S THE MATTER?
WELL...

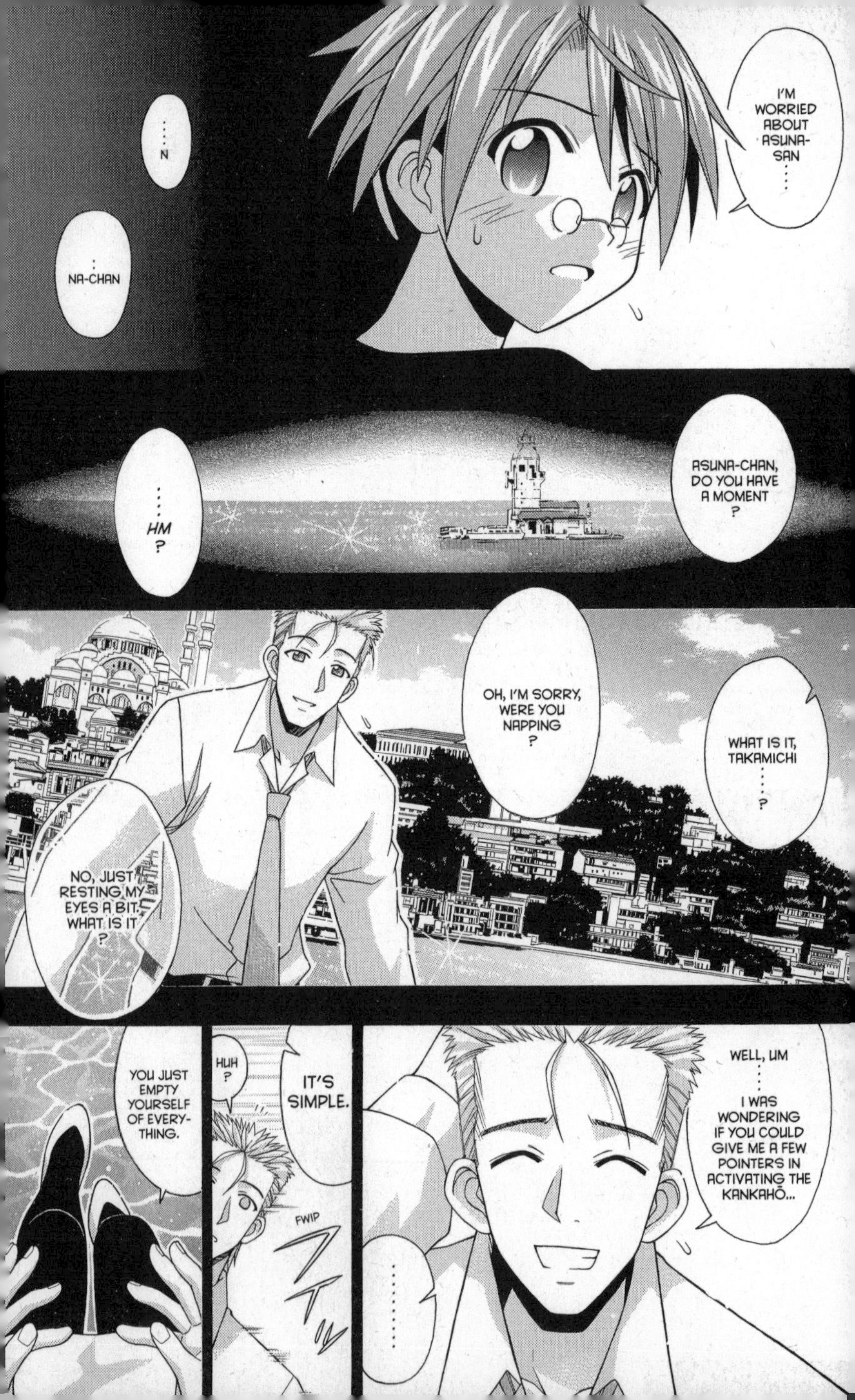
I'M WORRIED ABOUT ASUNA-SAN ......
...N
...NA-CHAN
ASUNA-CHAN, DO YOU HAVE A MOMENT ?
......HM ?
WHAT IS IT, TAKAMICHI ......?
OH, I'M SORRY, WERE YOU NAPPING ?
NO, JUST RESTING MY EYES A BIT. WHAT IS IT ?
WELL, UM ......
I WAS WONDERING IF YOU COULD GIVE ME A FEW POINTERS IN ACTIVATING THE KANKAHŌ...
......
IT'S SIMPLE.
HUH ?
FWIP
YOU JUST EMPTY YOURSELF OF EVERY-THING.

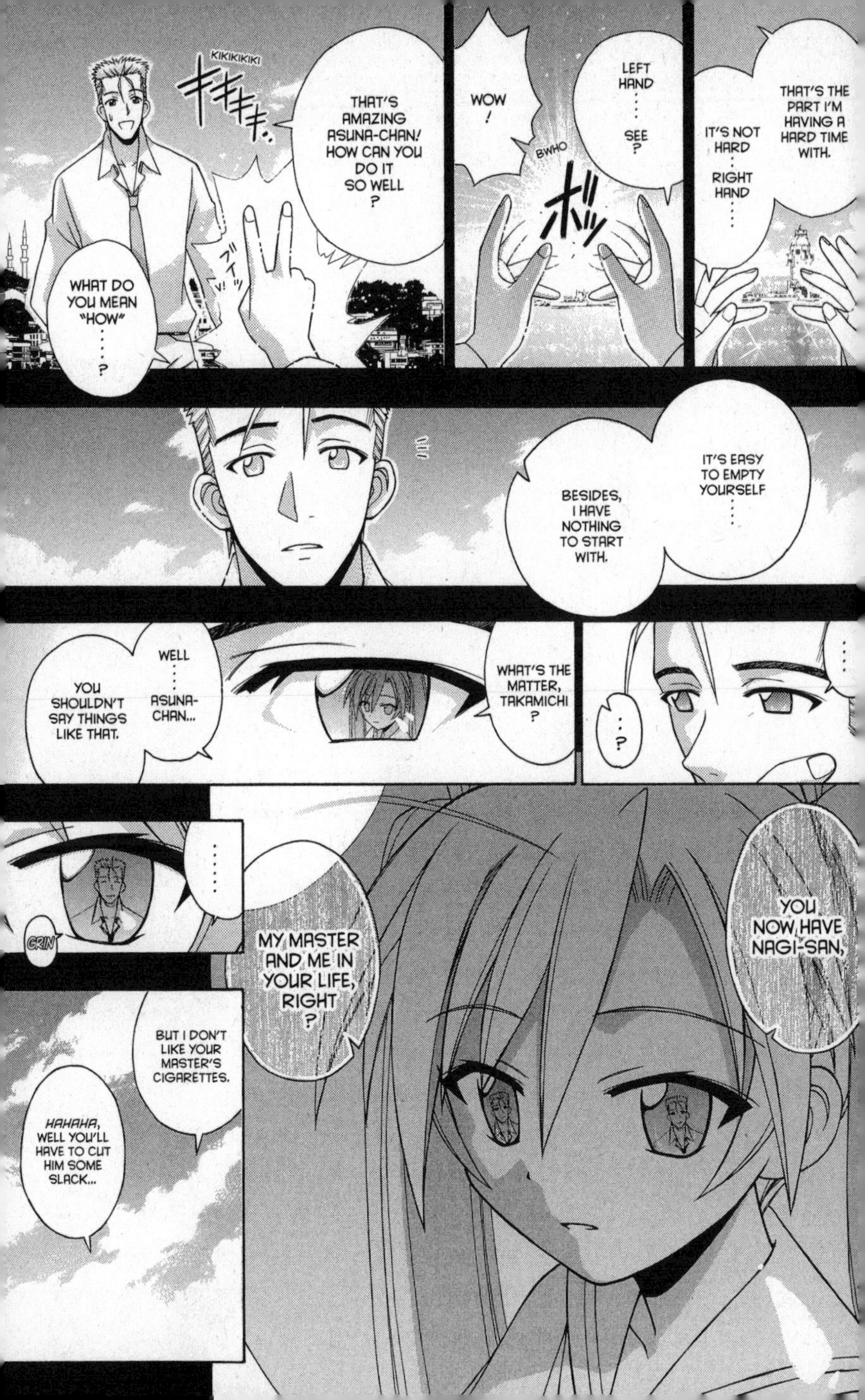
THAT'S THE PART I'M HAVING A HARD TIME WITH.
IT'S NOT HARD ... RIGHT HAND ...
LEFT HAND ... SEE?
WOW!
BWHO
KIKIKIKIKI
THAT'S AMAZING ASUNA-CHAN! HOW CAN YOU DO IT SO WELL?
V!
WHAT DO YOU MEAN "HOW" ...?
IT'S EASY TO EMPTY YOURSELF ...
BESIDES, I HAVE NOTHING TO START WITH.
...
...?
WHAT'S THE MATTER, TAKAMICHI?
WELL ... ASUNA-CHAN...
YOU SHOULDN'T SAY THINGS LIKE THAT.
YOU NOW HAVE NAGI-SAN,
MY MASTER AND ME IN YOUR LIFE, RIGHT?
......
GRIN
BUT I DON'T LIKE YOUR MASTER'S CIGARETTES.
HAHAHA, WELL YOU'LL HAVE TO CUT HIM SOME SLACK...

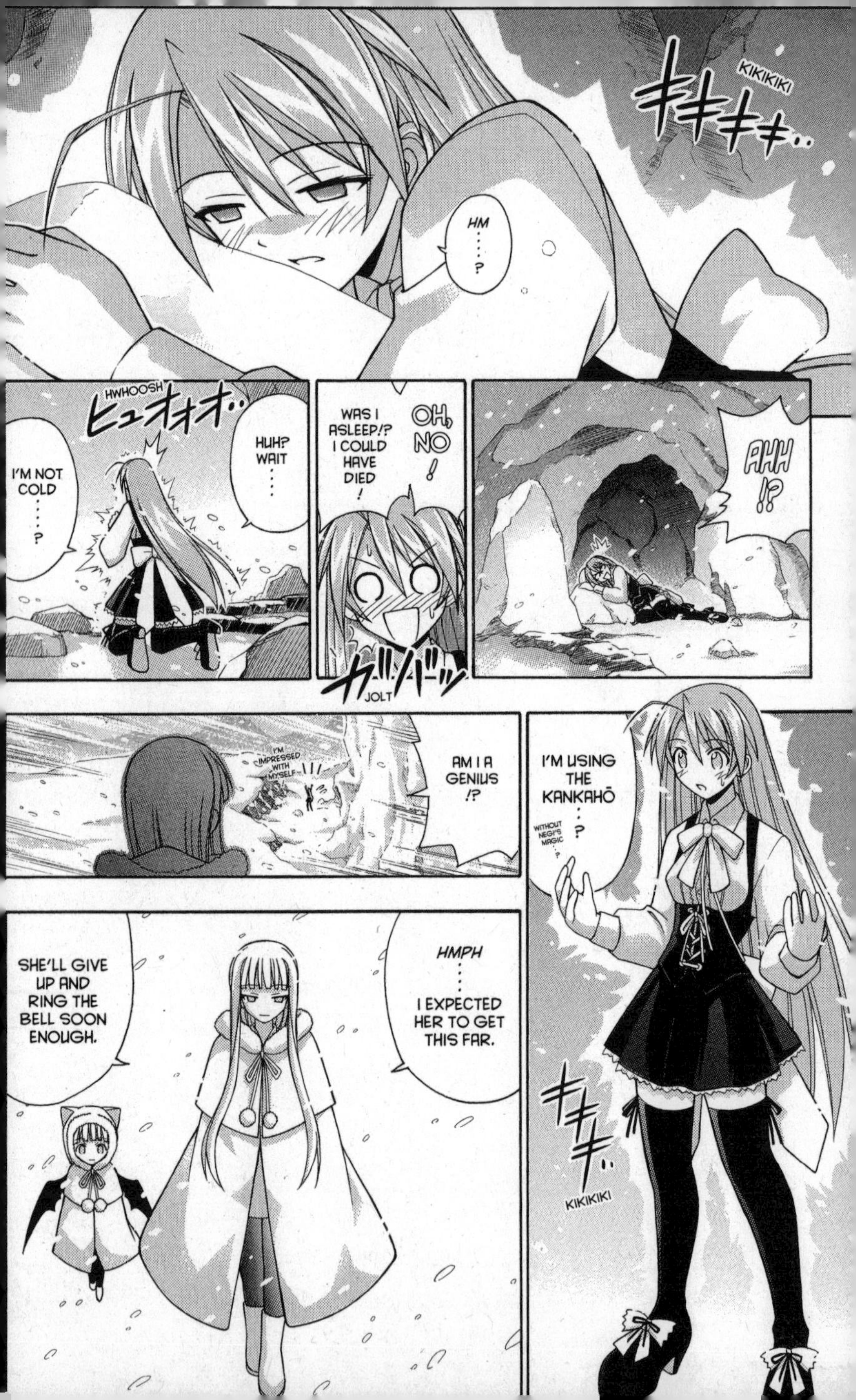
KIKIKIKI
HM....?
AHH!?
OH, NO!
WAS I ASLEEP!? I COULD HAVE DIED!
JOLT
HUH? WAIT....
I'M NOT COLD....?
HWHOOSH
I'M USING THE KANKAHŌ...?
WITHOUT NEGI'S MAGIC...?
KIKIKIKI
AM I A GENIUS!?
I'M IMPRESSED WITH MYSELF
HMPH... I EXPECTED HER TO GET THIS FAR.
SHE'LL GIVE UP AND RING THE BELL SOON ENOUGH.

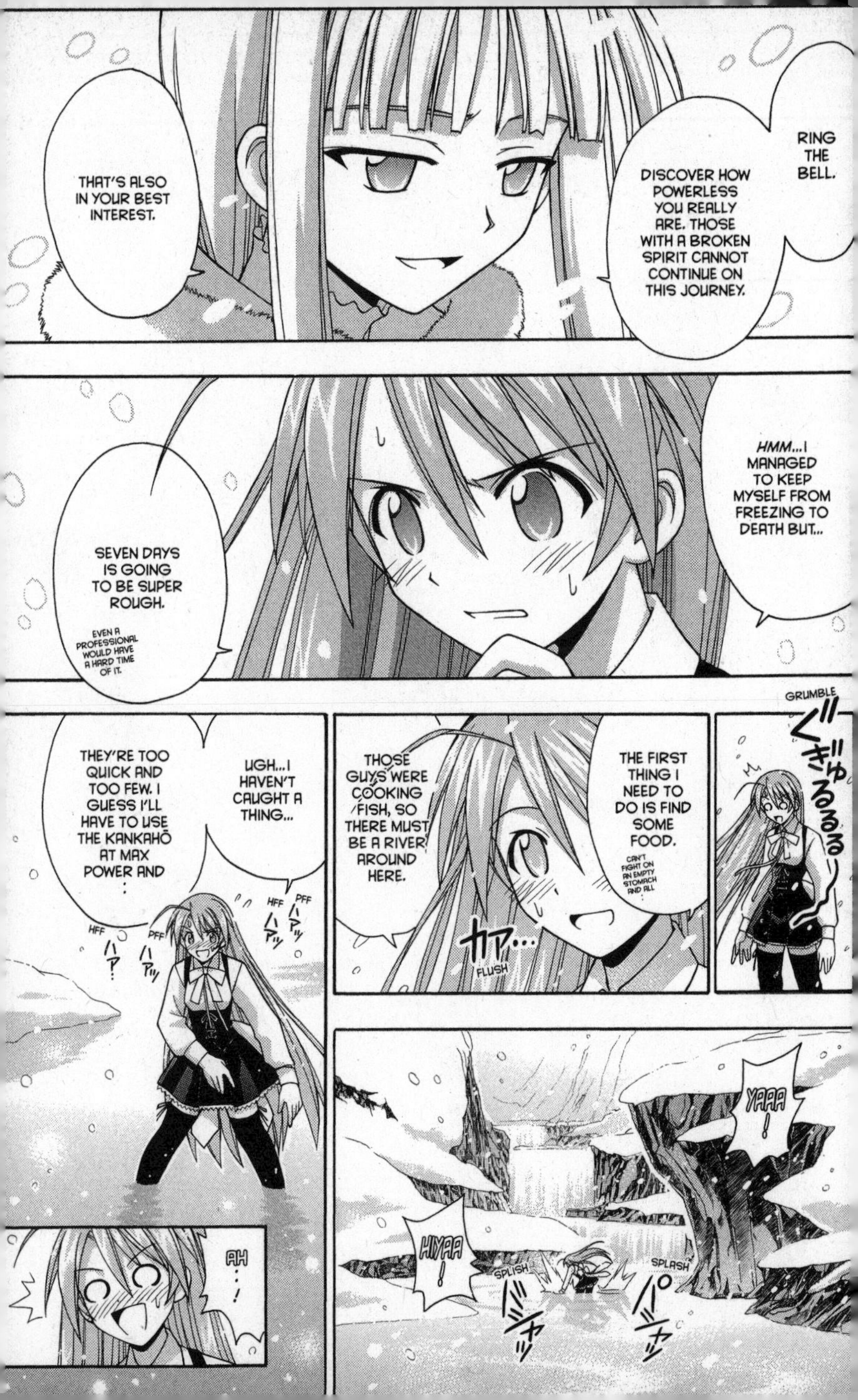

RING THE BELL.
DISCOVER HOW POWERLESS YOU REALLY ARE. THOSE WITH A BROKEN SPIRIT CANNOT CONTINUE ON THIS JOURNEY.
THAT'S ALSO IN YOUR BEST INTEREST.
HMM...I MANAGED TO KEEP MYSELF FROM FREEZING TO DEATH BUT...
SEVEN DAYS IS GOING TO BE SUPER ROUGH.
EVEN A PROFESSIONAL WOULD HAVE A HARD TIME OF IT.
GRUMBLE
ぐぎゅるるる
THE FIRST THING I NEED TO DO IS FIND SOME FOOD.
CAN'T FIGHT ON AN EMPTY STOMACH AND ALL
THOSE GUYS WERE COOKING FISH, SO THERE MUST BE A RIVER AROUND HERE.
カア…
FLUSH
YAAA!
HIYAA!
SPLISH
バシャッ
SPLASH
パシャッ
UGH...I HAVEN'T CAUGHT A THING...
THEY'RE TOO QUICK AND TOO FEW. I GUESS I'LL HAVE TO USE THE KANKAHŌ AT MAX POWER AND...
HFF
ハアッ
PFF
ハアッ
HFF
ハア
PFF
ハアッ
AH...!

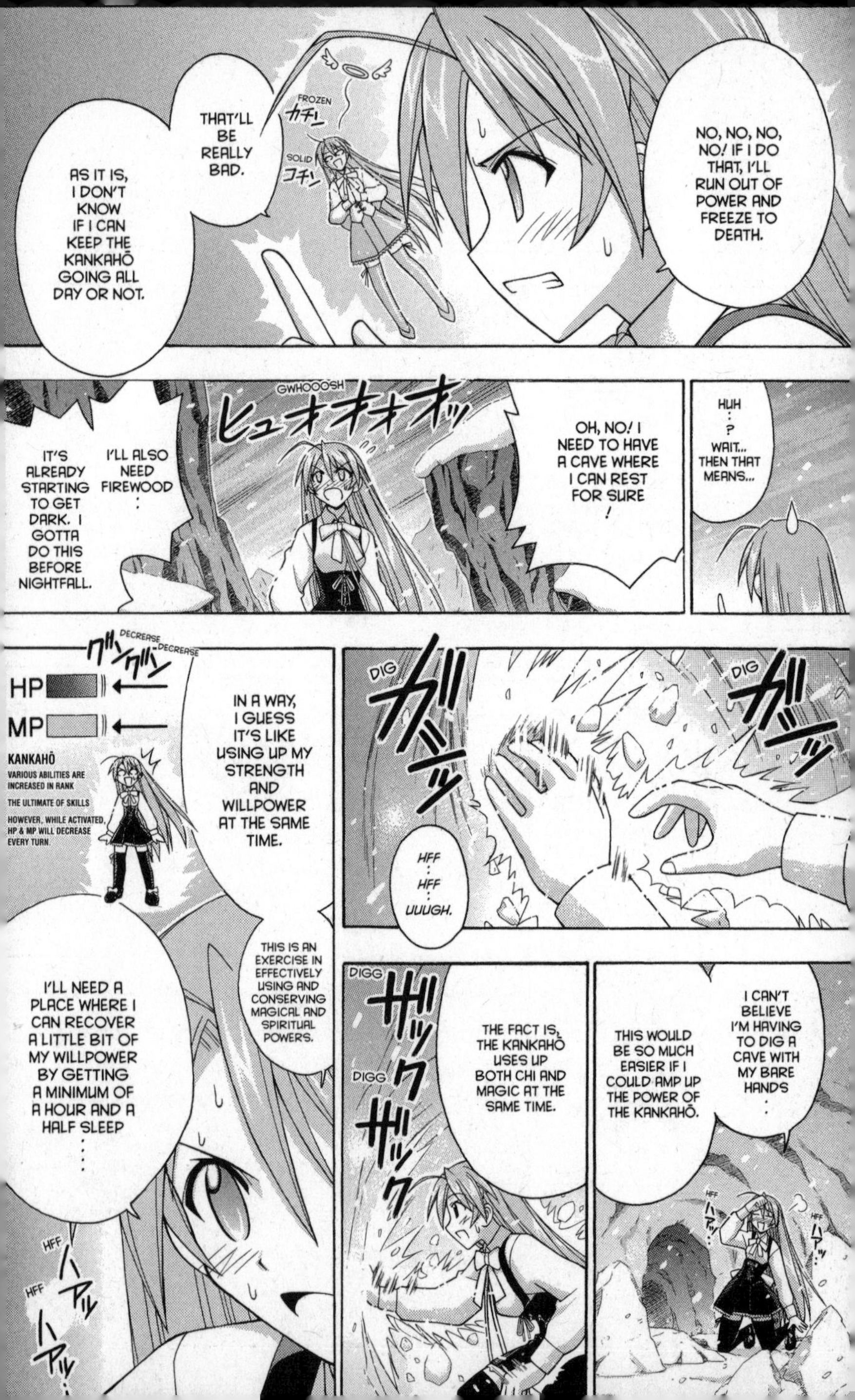
NO, NO, NO, NO! IF I DO THAT, I'LL RUN OUT OF POWER AND FREEZE TO DEATH.
THAT'LL BE REALLY BAD.
FROZEN カチン
SOLID コチン
AS IT IS, I DON'T KNOW IF I CAN KEEP THE KANKAHŌ GOING ALL DAY OR NOT.
HUH...? WAIT... THEN THAT MEANS...
OH, NO! I NEED TO HAVE A CAVE WHERE I CAN REST FOR SURE!
GWHOOOSH ヒュオオオオオッ
I'LL ALSO NEED FIREWOOD...
IT'S ALREADY STARTING TO GET DARK. I GOTTA DO THIS BEFORE NIGHTFALL.
DIG ガッ
DIG ガッ
HFF... HFF... UUUGH.
I CAN'T BELIEVE I'M HAVING TO DIG A CAVE WITH MY BARE HANDS...
THIS WOULD BE SO MUCH EASIER IF I COULD AMP UP THE POWER OF THE KANKAHŌ.
THE FACT IS, THE KANKAHŌ USES UP BOTH CHI AND MAGIC AT THE SAME TIME.
DIGG ザック
DIGG ザック
HFF ハァッ
HFF ハァッ
DECREASE DECREASE グングン
HP
MP
KANKAHŌ
VARIOUS ABILITIES ARE INCREASED IN RANK
THE ULTIMATE OF SKILLS
HOWEVER, WHILE ACTIVATED, HP & MP WILL DECREASE EVERY TURN.
IN A WAY, I GUESS IT'S LIKE USING UP MY STRENGTH AND WILLPOWER AT THE SAME TIME.
THIS IS AN EXERCISE IN EFFECTIVELY USING AND CONSERVING MAGICAL AND SPIRITUAL POWERS.
I'LL NEED A PLACE WHERE I CAN RECOVER A LITTLE BIT OF MY WILLPOWER BY GETTING A MINIMUM OF A HOUR AND A HALF SLEEP...
HFF ハァッ
HFF ハァッ

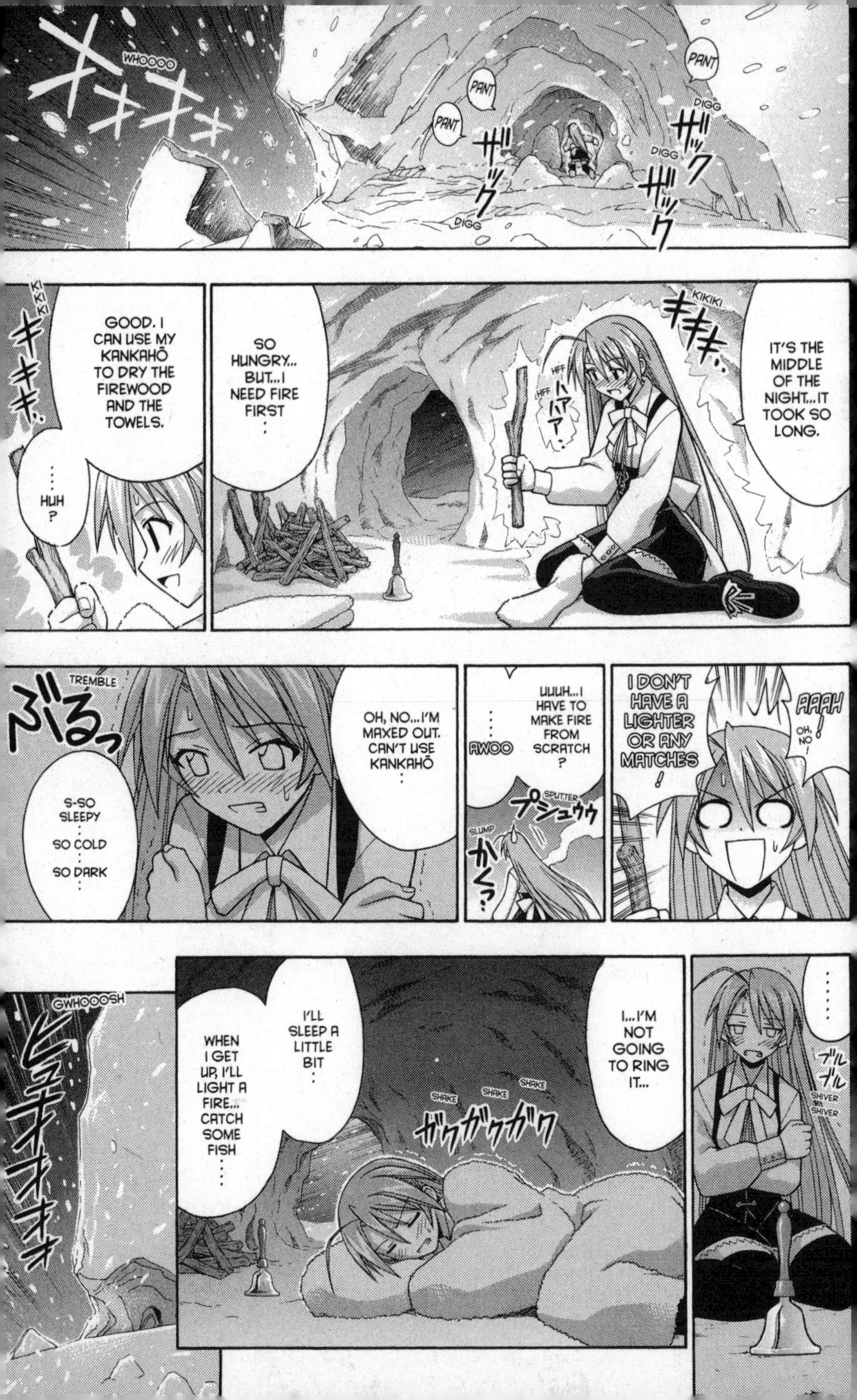
WHOOOO
PANT
PANT
PANT
DIGG
DIGG
DIGG
KIKIKI
IT'S THE MIDDLE OF THE NIGHT...IT TOOK SO LONG.
HFF HFF
SO HUNGRY... BUT...I NEED FIRE FIRST...
KIKIKI
GOOD. I CAN USE MY KANKAHŌ TO DRY THE FIREWOOD AND THE TOWELS.
...HUH?
AAAH
OH, NO!
I DON'T HAVE A LIGHTER OR ANY MATCHES!
UUUH...I HAVE TO MAKE FIRE FROM SCRATCH?
...AWOO
SPUTTER
SLUMP
TREMBLE
OH, NO...I'M MAXED OUT. CAN'T USE KANKAHŌ...
S-SO SLEEPY... SO COLD... SO DARK...
......
SHIVER SHIVER
I...I'M NOT GOING TO RING IT...
SHAKE SHAKE SHAKE
I'LL SLEEP A LITTLE BIT...
WHEN I GET UP, I'LL LIGHT A FIRE... CATCH SOME FISH...
GWHOOOSH

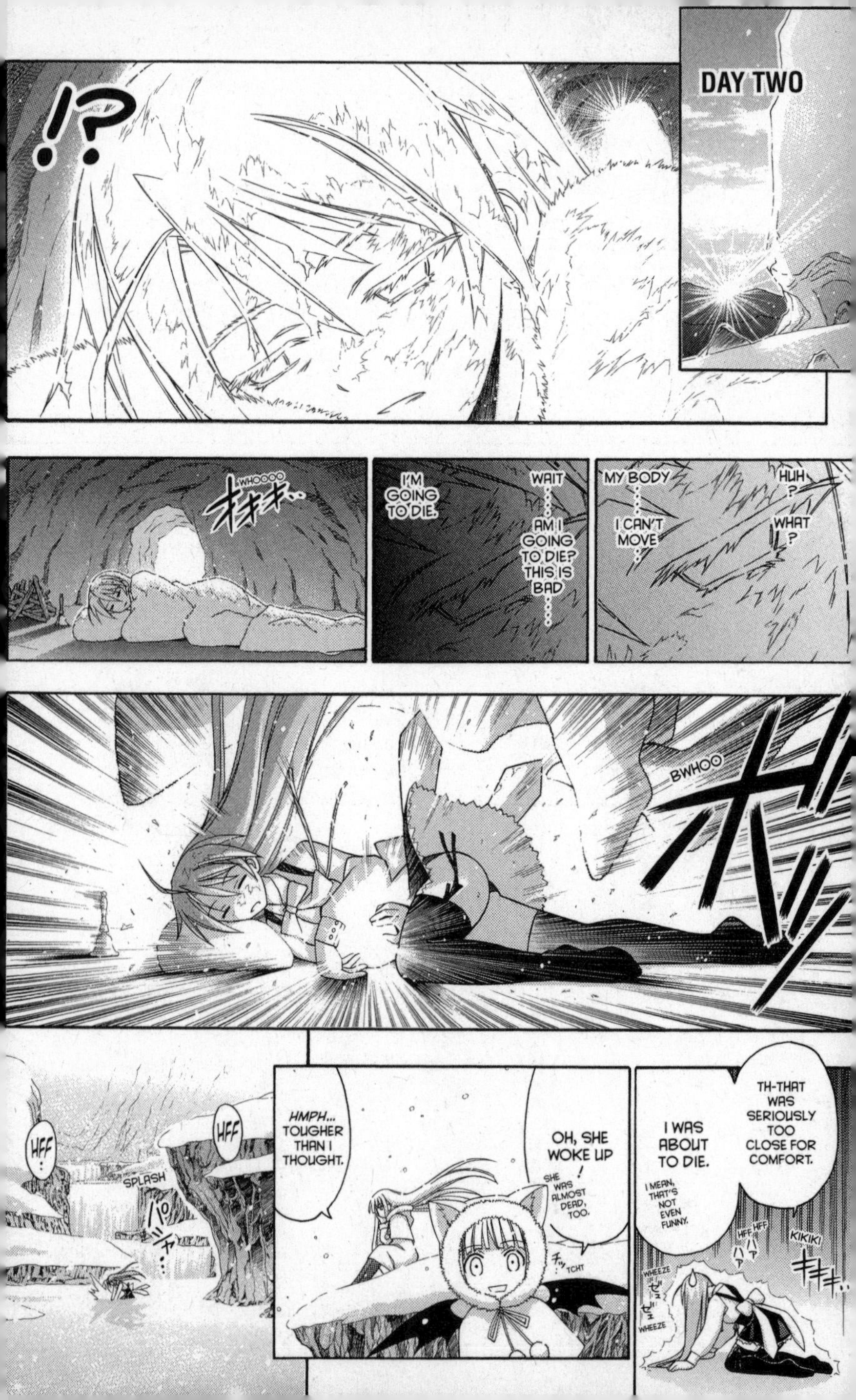

DAY TWO
!?
HUH? WHAT?
MY BODY... I CAN'T MOVE...
WAIT... AM I GOING TO DIE? THIS IS BAD.....
I'M GOING TO DIE.
WHOOOO
オキキ..
BWHOO
ボッ
TH-THAT WAS SERIOUSLY TOO CLOSE FOR COMFORT.
I WAS ABOUT TO DIE.
I MEAN, THAT'S NOT EVEN FUNNY.
KIKIKI
キキキ
HFF
ハァ ハァ
WHEEZE
ゼェ ゼェ
WHEEZE
OH, SHE WOKE UP!
SHE WAS ALMOST DEAD, TOO.
HMPH... TOUGHER THAN I THOUGHT.
チッ
TCHT
HFF
HFF
SPLASH
パシャ...

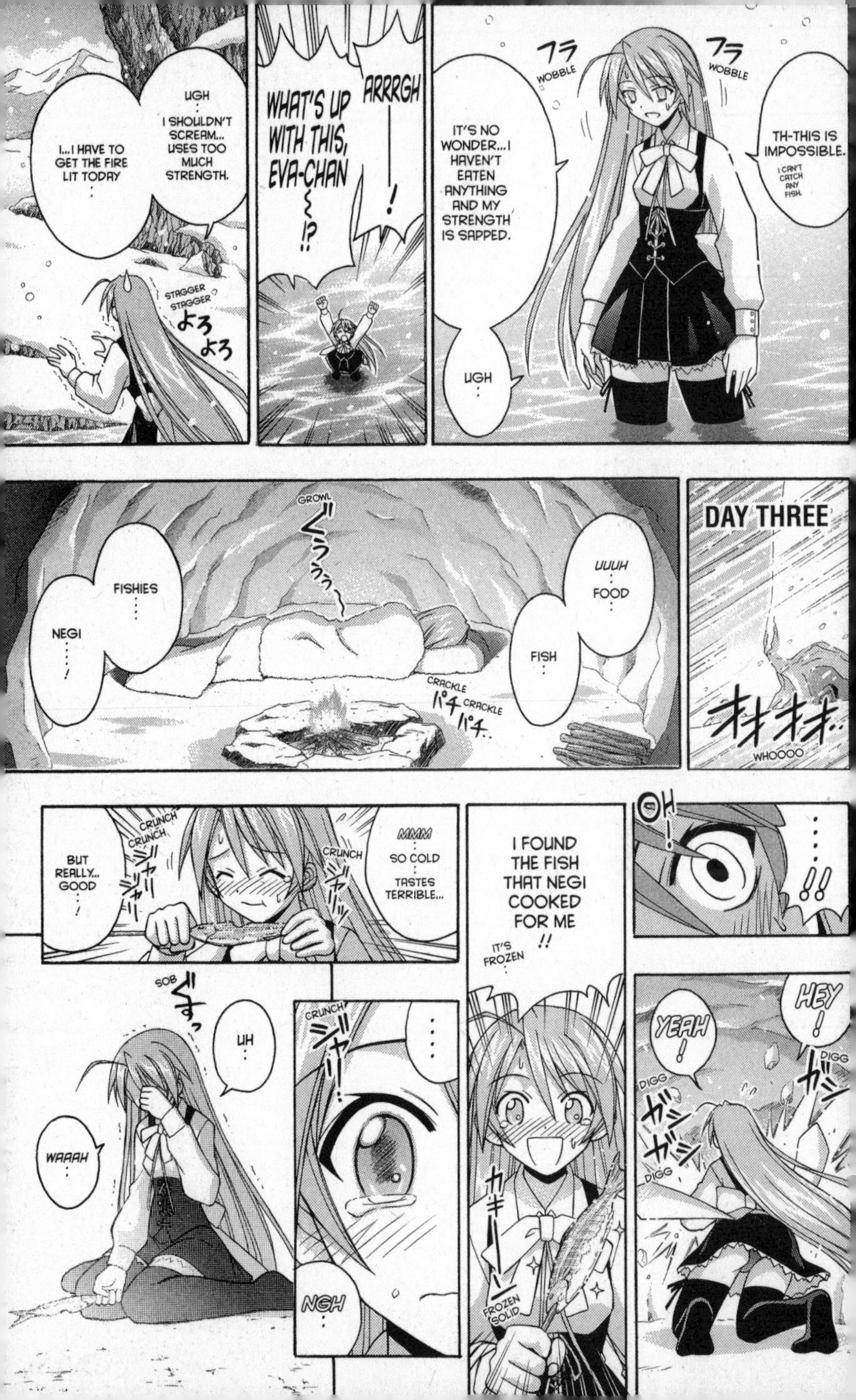
フラ
WOBBLE
フラ
WOBBLE
TH-THIS IS IMPOSSIBLE.
I CAN'T CATCH ANY FISH.
IT'S NO WONDER...I HAVEN'T EATEN ANYTHING AND MY STRENGTH IS SAPPED.
UGH...
ARRRGH—!
WHAT'S UP WITH THIS, EVA-CHAN~!?
UGH... I SHOULDN'T SCREAM... USES TOO MUCH STRENGTH.
I...I HAVE TO GET THE FIRE LIT TODAY...
STAGGER STAGGER
よろよろ
DAY THREE
オオオオ…
WHOOOO
UUUH... FOOD...
FISH...
GROWL
ぐうううう~
FISHIES...
NEGI...!
CRACKLE
パチ
CRACKLE
パチ…
OH—!
...!!
HEY!
YEAH!
DIGG
ガシ
DIGG
ガシ
DIGG
ガシ
I FOUND THE FISH THAT NEGI COOKED FOR ME!!
IT'S FROZEN...
カキーン
FROZEN SOLID
MMM... SO COLD... TASTES TERRIBLE...
CRUNCH
ジャリッ
BUT REALLY... GOOD...!
CRUNCH CRUNCH
ジャリジャリ
....
CRUNCH
ジャリッ!
NGH
UH...
SOB
ぐすっ
WAAAH...

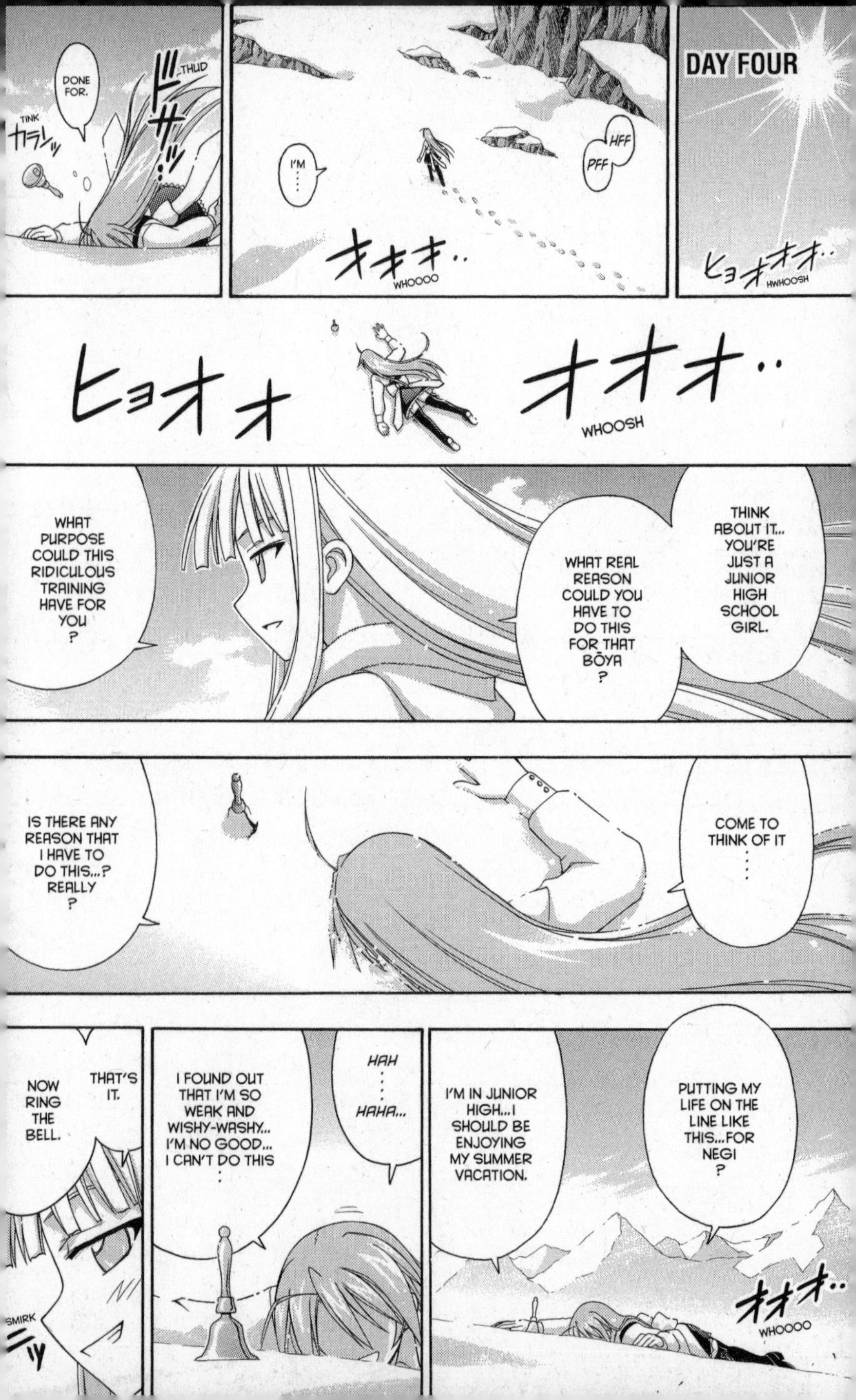
DAY FOUR
ヒョオオオ..
HWHOOSH
HFF
PFF
I'M . . .
オォォ..
WHOOOO
DONE FOR.
ドサッ
THUD
カランッ
TINK
ヒョオオ オオオ..
WHOOSH
THINK ABOUT IT... YOU'RE JUST A JUNIOR HIGH SCHOOL GIRL.
WHAT REAL REASON COULD YOU HAVE TO DO THIS FOR THAT BŌYA ?
WHAT PURPOSE COULD THIS RIDICULOUS TRAINING HAVE FOR YOU ?
COME TO THINK OF IT . . .
IS THERE ANY REASON THAT I HAVE TO DO THIS...? REALLY ?
PUTTING MY LIFE ON THE LINE LIKE THIS...FOR NEGI ?
I'M IN JUNIOR HIGH...I SHOULD BE ENJOYING MY SUMMER VACATION.
オオオ..
WHOOOO
HAH . . . HAHA...
I FOUND OUT THAT I'M SO WEAK AND WISHY-WASHY... I'M NO GOOD... I CAN'T DO THIS . .
THAT'S IT.
NOW RING THE BELL.
ニッ
SMIRK

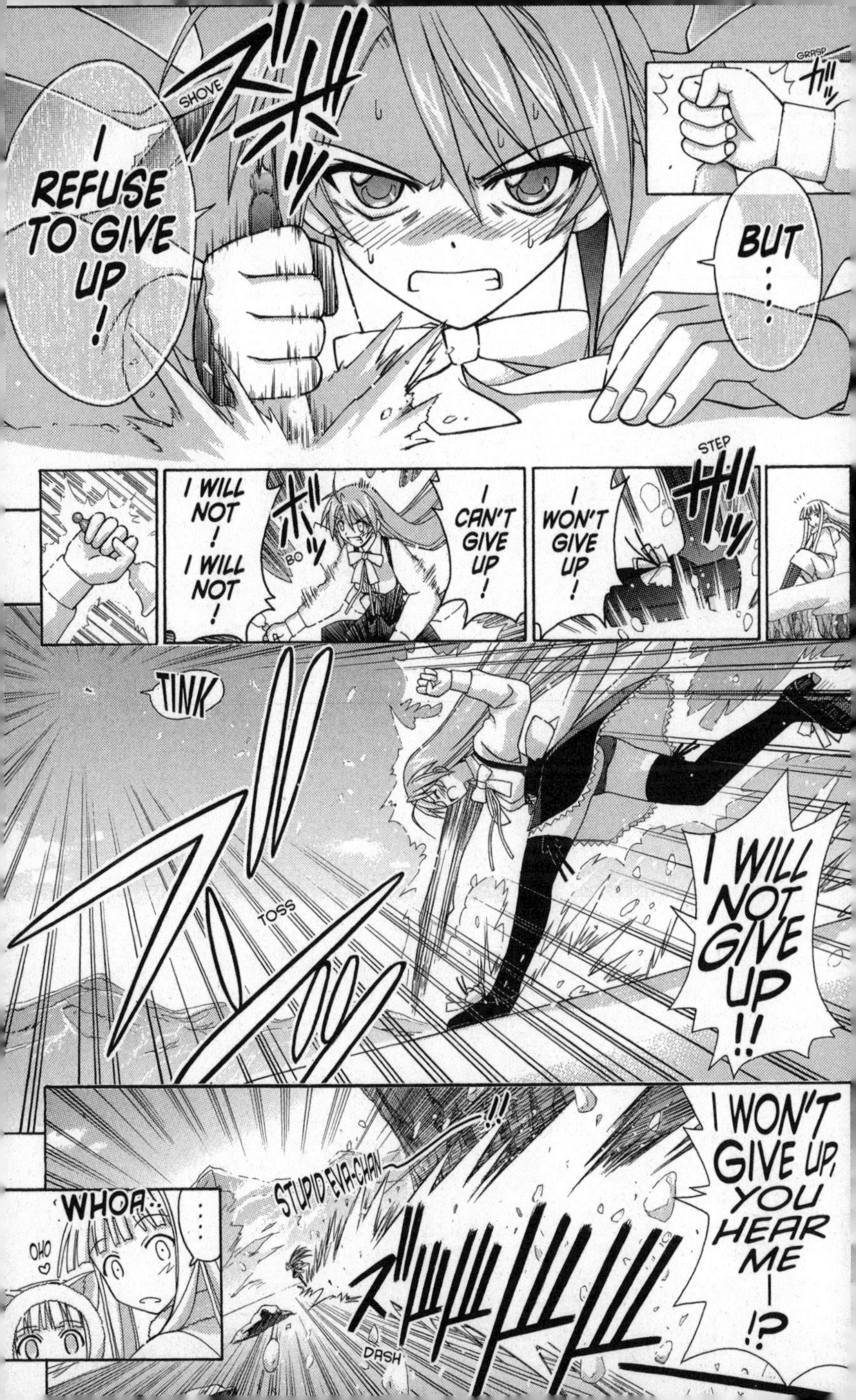
GRASP
BUT...
SHOVE
I REFUSE TO GIVE UP!
STEP
I WON'T GIVE UP!
I CAN'T GIVE UP!
BO
I WILL NOT! I WILL NOT!
I WILL NOT GIVE UP!!
TOSS
TINK
I WON'T GIVE UP, YOU HEAR ME—!?
!!
STUPID EVA-CHAN
DASH
...
WHOA...
OHO ♡

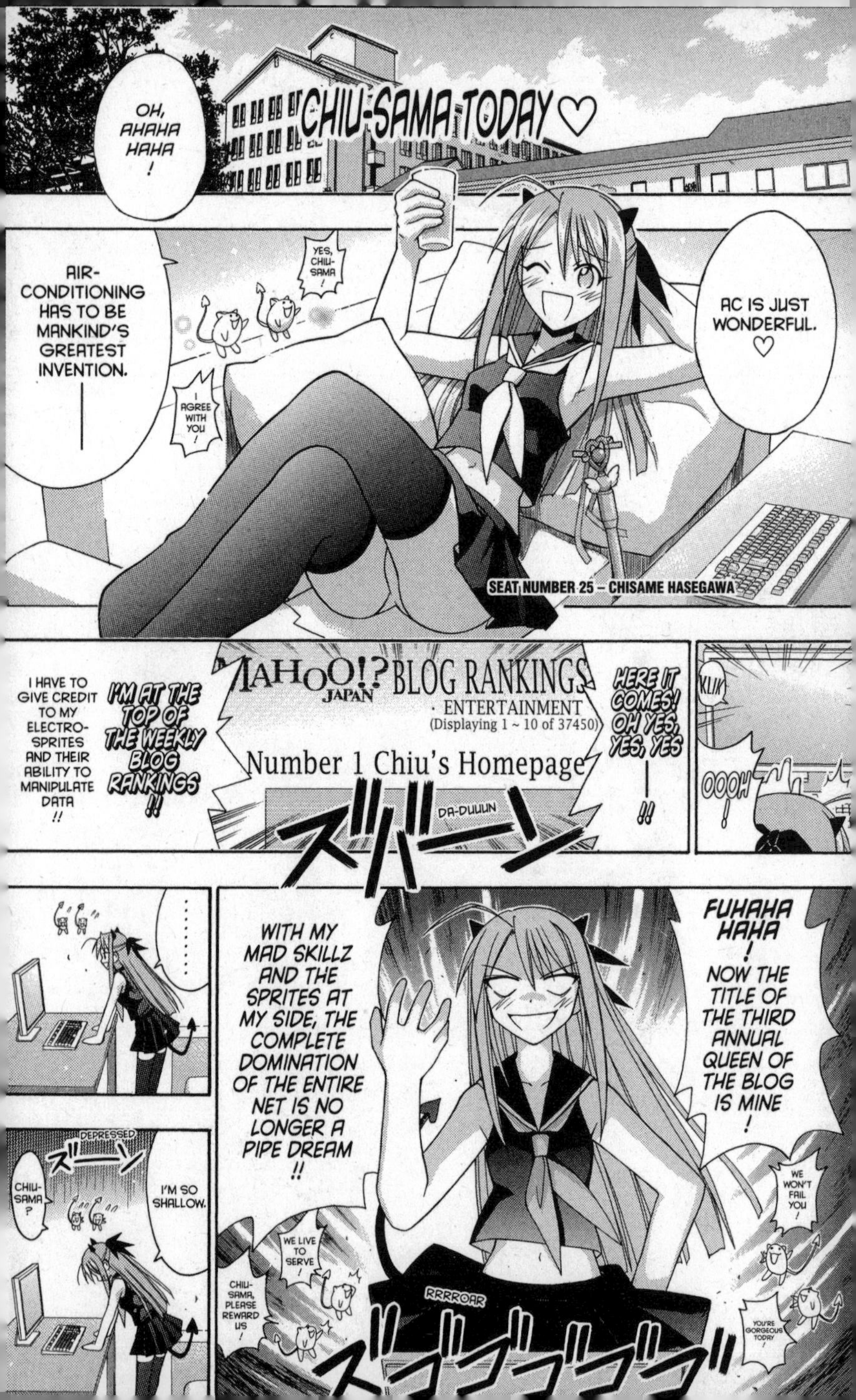
CHIU-SAMA TODAY♡
OH, AHAHA HAHA!
AC IS JUST WONDERFUL. ♡
YES, CHIU-SAMA!
I AGREE WITH YOU!
AIR-CONDITIONING HAS TO BE MANKIND'S GREATEST INVENTION.—
SEAT NUMBER 25 – CHISAME HASEGAWA
KLIK
OOOH!
HERE IT COMES! OH YES, YES, YES—!!
MAHOO!? JAPAN BLOG RANKINGS
· ENTERTAINMENT
(Displaying 1 ~ 10 of 37450)
Number 1 Chiu's Homepage
DA-DUUUN
I'M AT THE TOP OF THE WEEKLY BLOG RANKINGS!!
I HAVE TO GIVE CREDIT TO MY ELECTRO-SPRITES AND THEIR ABILITY TO MANIPULATE DATA!!
FUHAHA HAHA! NOW THE TITLE OF THE THIRD ANNUAL QUEEN OF THE BLOG IS MINE!
WITH MY MAD SKILLZ AND THE SPRITES AT MY SIDE, THE COMPLETE DOMINATION OF THE ENTIRE NET IS NO LONGER A PIPE DREAM!!
WE WON'T FAIL YOU!
WE LIVE TO SERVE!
CHIU-SAMA, PLEASE REWARD US!
YOU'RE GORGEOUS TODAY
RRRROAR
......
DEPRESSED
I'M SO SHALLOW.
CHIU-SAMA?

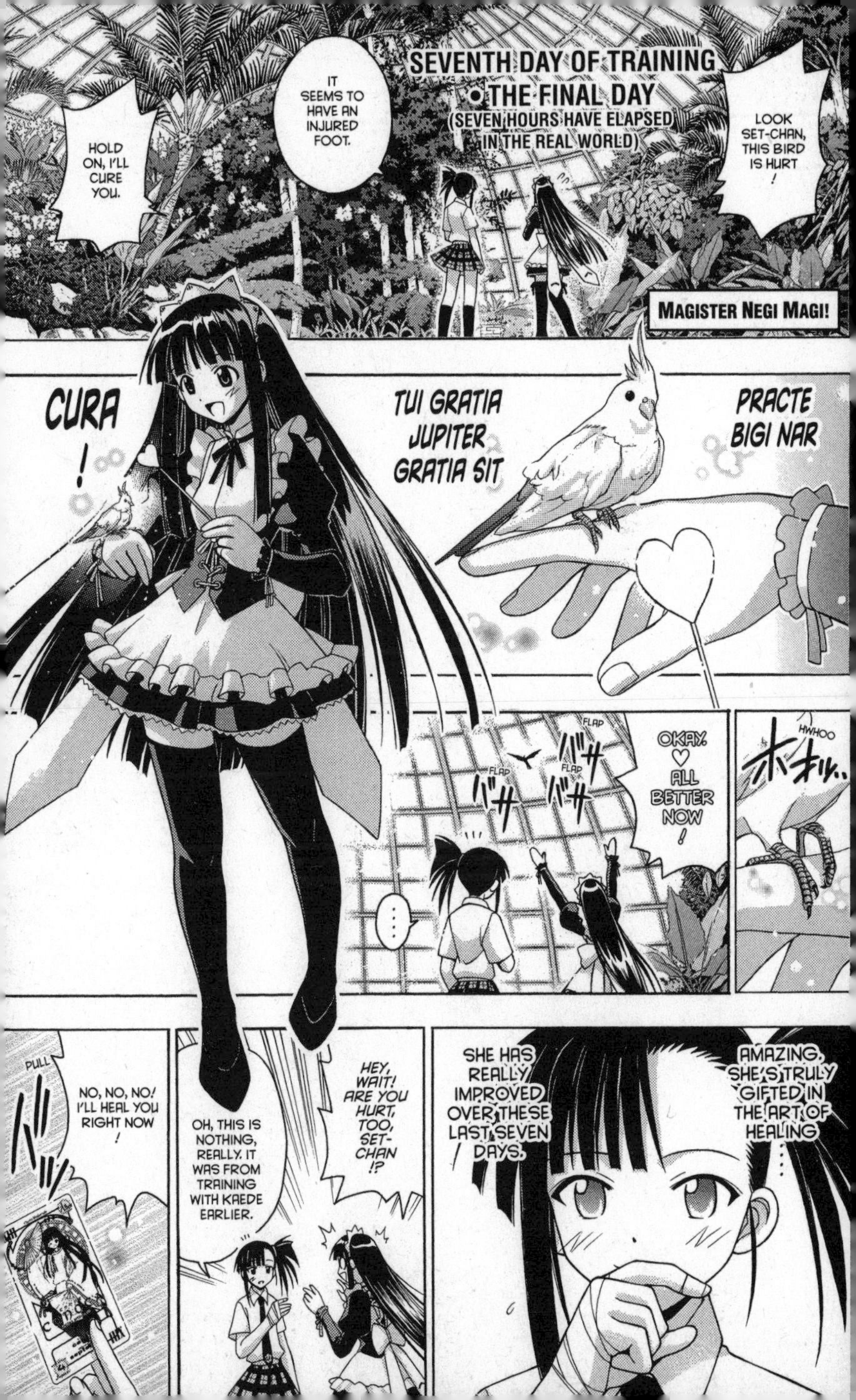

LOOK SET-CHAN, THIS BIRD IS HURT!
SEVENTH DAY OF TRAINING
• THE FINAL DAY
(SEVEN HOURS HAVE ELAPSED IN THE REAL WORLD)
IT SEEMS TO HAVE AN INJURED FOOT.
HOLD ON, I'LL CURE YOU.
MAGISTER NEGI MAGI!
PRACTE BIGI NAR
TUI GRATIA JUPITER GRATIA SIT
CURA!
HWHOO
OKAY. ♡ ALL BETTER NOW!
FLAP
FLAP
FLAP
...
AMAZING. SHE'S TRULY GIFTED IN THE ART OF HEALING
...
SHE HAS REALLY IMPROVED OVER THESE LAST SEVEN DAYS.
HEY, WAIT! ARE YOU HURT, TOO, SET-CHAN!?
OH, THIS IS NOTHING, REALLY. IT WAS FROM TRAINING WITH KAEDE EARLIER.
PULL
NO, NO, NO! I'LL HEAL YOU RIGHT NOW!

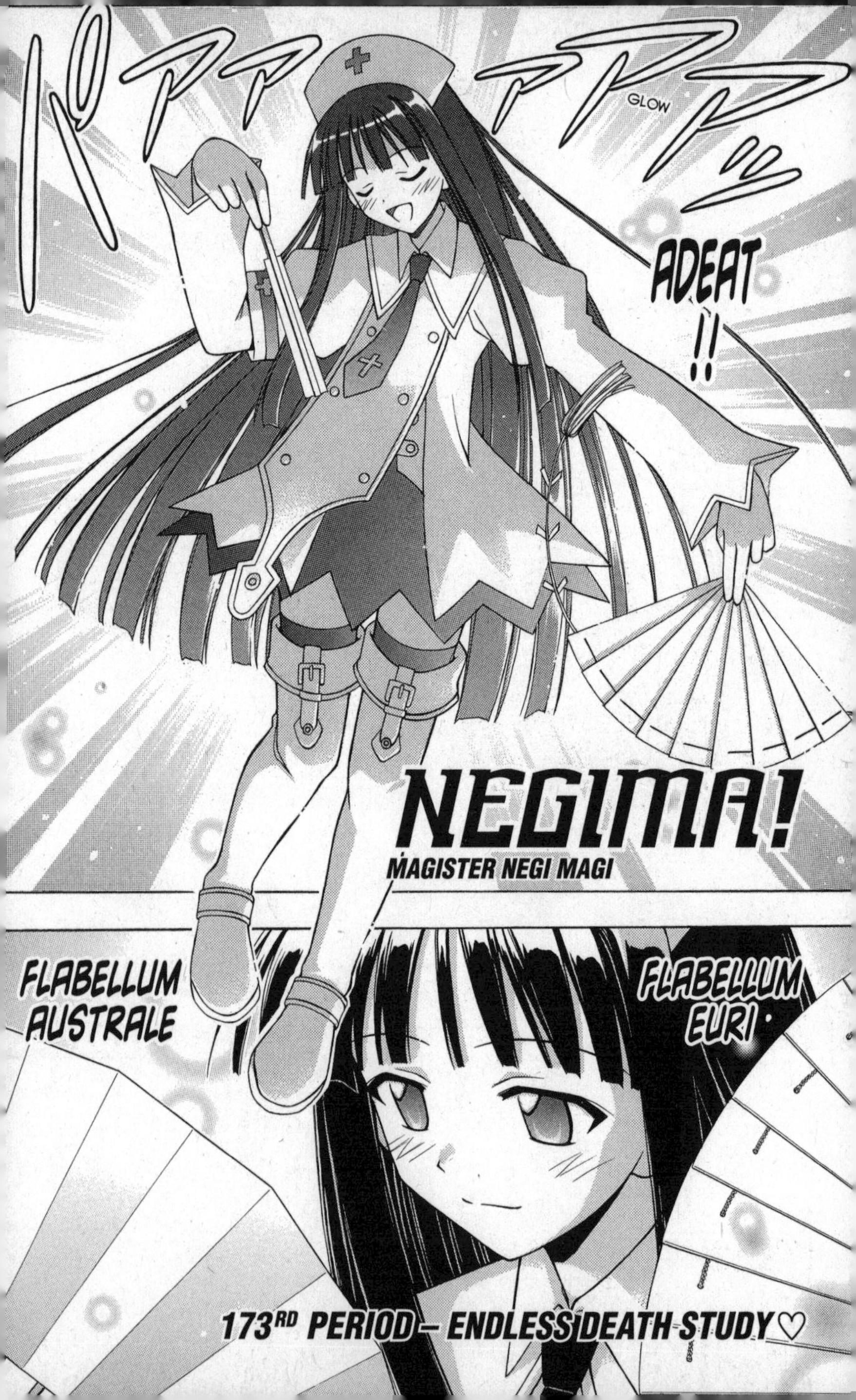

パァァァァァァッ
GLOW
ADEAT !!
NEGIMA!
MAGISTER NEGI MAGI
FLABELLUM EURI
FLABELLUM AUSTRALE
173RD PERIOD – ENDLESS DEATH STUDY♡

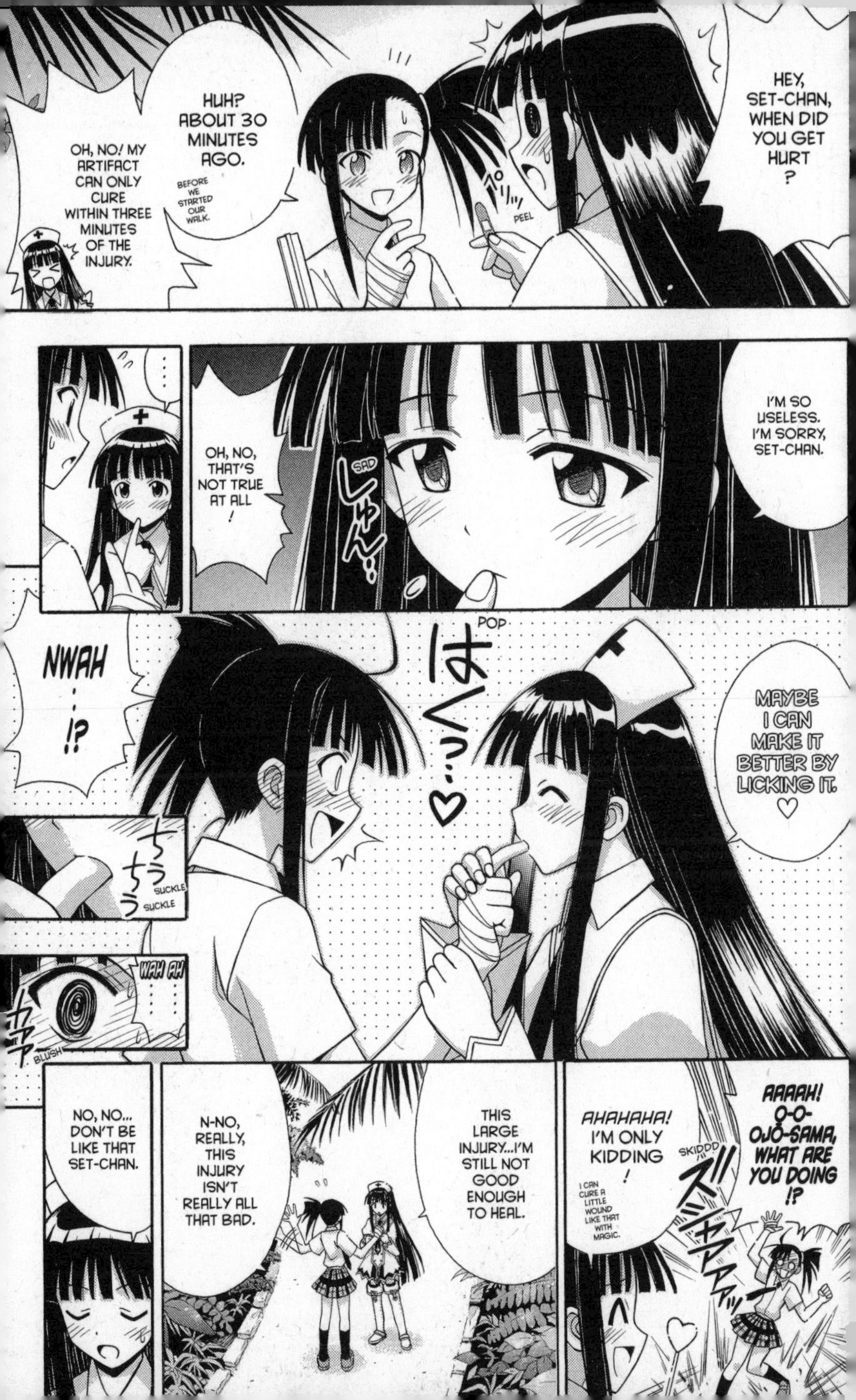

HEY, SET-CHAN, WHEN DID YOU GET HURT?
ペリッ
PEEL
HUH? ABOUT 30 MINUTES AGO.
BEFORE WE STARTED OUR WALK.
OH, NO! MY ARTIFACT CAN ONLY CURE WITHIN THREE MINUTES OF THE INJURY.
I'M SO USELESS. I'M SORRY, SET-CHAN.
しゅん…
SAD
OH, NO, THAT'S NOT TRUE AT ALL!
...
MAYBE I CAN MAKE IT BETTER BY LICKING IT. ♡
はくっ…♡
POP
NWAH...!?
ちう ちう
SUCKLE SUCKLE
WAH AH...
カァ
BLUSH
AAAAH! O-O-OJŌ-SAMA, WHAT ARE YOU DOING!?
ズザァァッ
SKIDDD
AHAHAHA! I'M ONLY KIDDING!
I CAN CURE A LITTLE WOUND LIKE THAT WITH MAGIC.
THIS LARGE INJURY...I'M STILL NOT GOOD ENOUGH TO HEAL.
N-NO, REALLY, THIS INJURY ISN'T REALLY ALL THAT BAD.
NO, NO... DON'T BE LIKE THAT SET-CHAN.

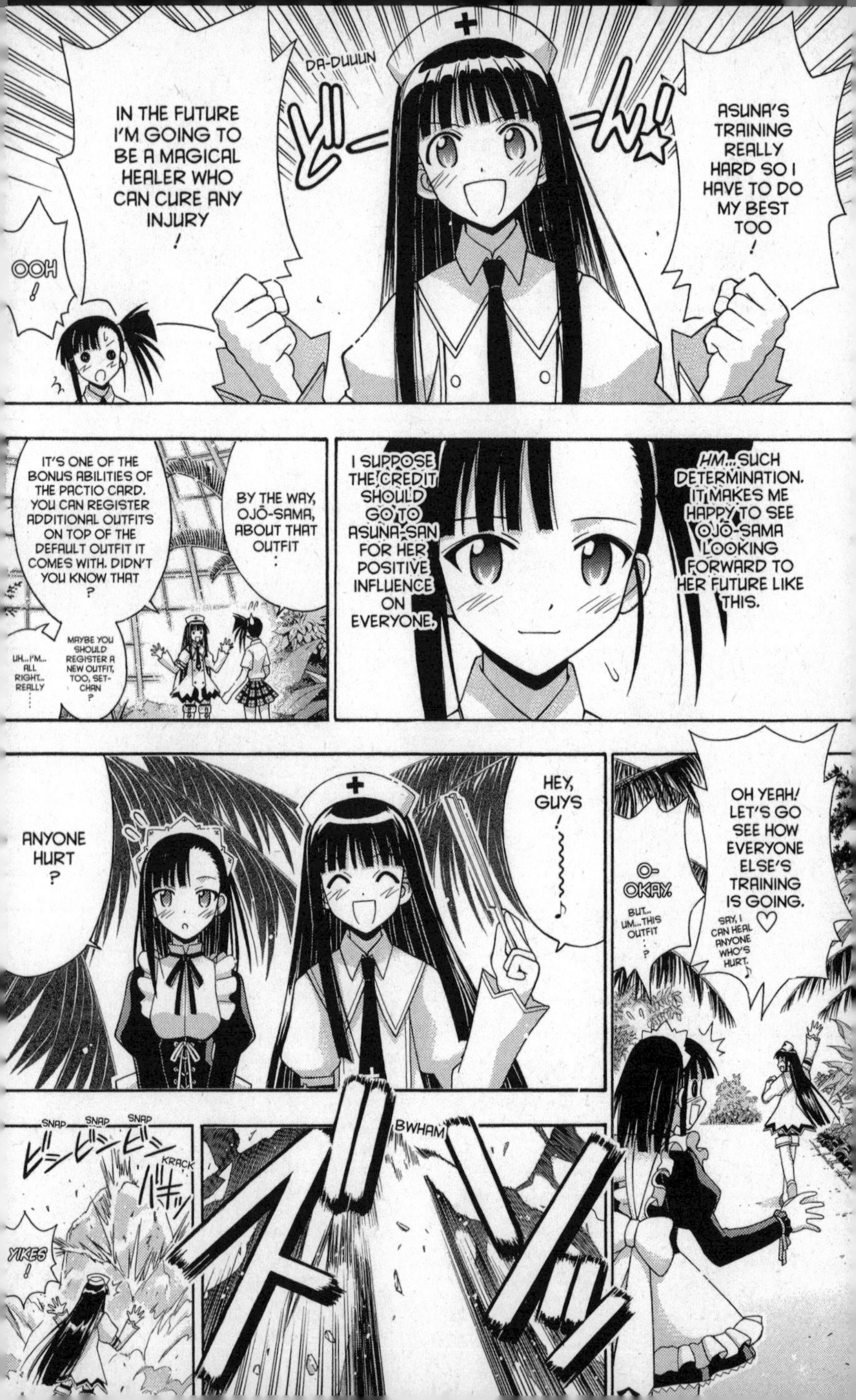
DA-DUUUN
ASUNA'S TRAINING REALLY HARD SO I HAVE TO DO MY BEST TOO!
IN THE FUTURE I'M GOING TO BE A MAGICAL HEALER WHO CAN CURE ANY INJURY!
OOH!
HM... SUCH DETERMINATION. IT MAKES ME HAPPY TO SEE OJŌ-SAMA LOOKING FORWARD TO HER FUTURE LIKE THIS.
I SUPPOSE THE CREDIT SHOULD GO TO ASUNA-SAN FOR HER POSITIVE INFLUENCE ON EVERYONE.
BY THE WAY, OJŌ-SAMA, ABOUT THAT OUTFIT...
IT'S ONE OF THE BONUS ABILITIES OF THE PACTIO CARD. YOU CAN REGISTER ADDITIONAL OUTFITS ON TOP OF THE DEFAULT OUTFIT IT COMES WITH. DIDN'T YOU KNOW THAT?
MAYBE YOU SHOULD REGISTER A NEW OUTFIT, TOO, SET-CHAN?
UH...I'M... ALL RIGHT... REALLY...
OH YEAH! LET'S GO SEE HOW EVERYONE ELSE'S TRAINING IS GOING.
SAY, I CAN HEAL ANYONE WHO'S HURT. ♪
O-OKAY. BUT... UM... THIS OUTFIT...?
HEY, GUYS! ♪
ANYONE HURT?
BWHAM
KRACK
SNAP SNAP SNAP
YIKES!

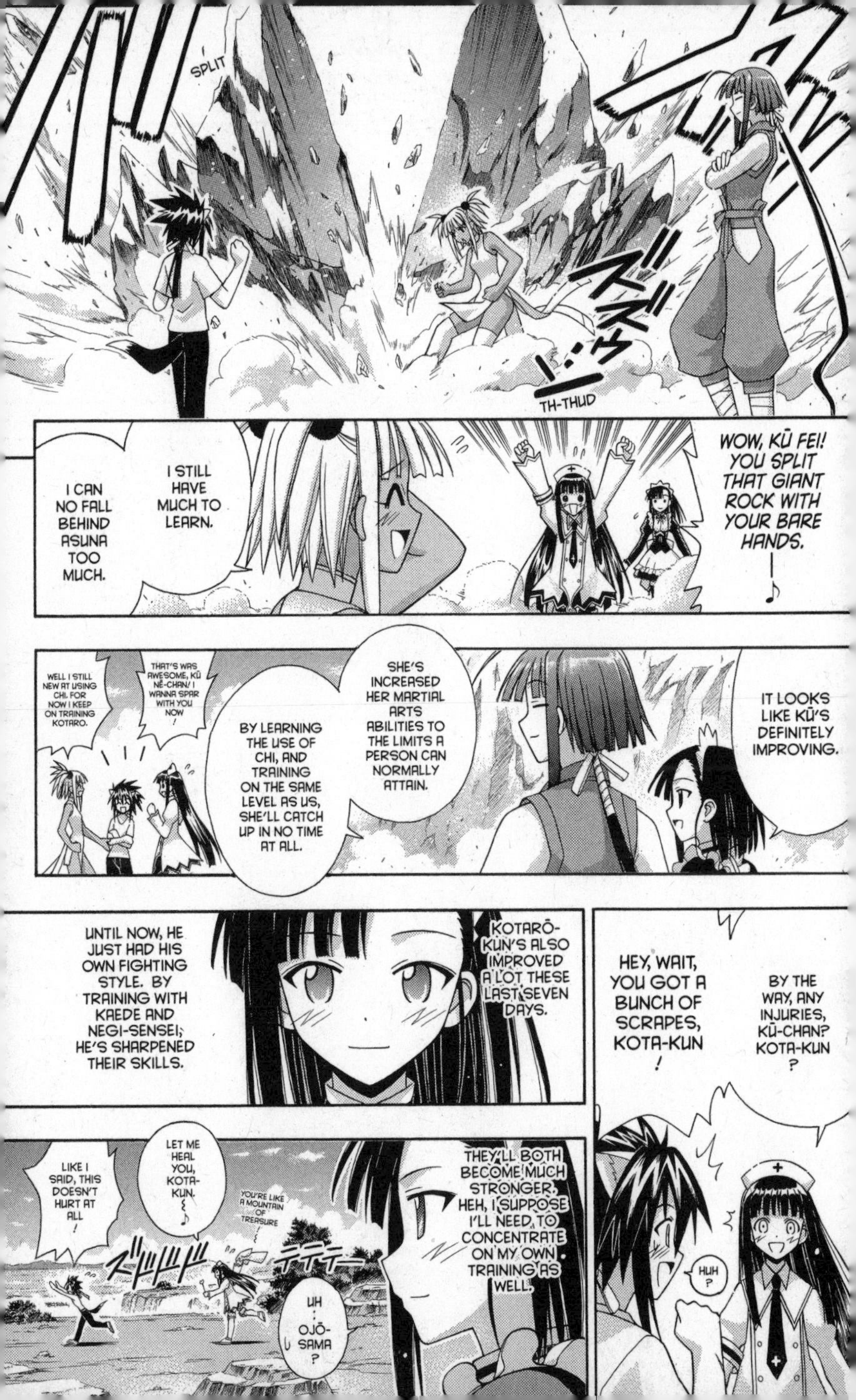
SPLIT
TH-THUD
WOW, KŪ FEI! YOU SPLIT THAT GIANT ROCK WITH YOUR BARE HANDS. ♪
I STILL HAVE MUCH TO LEARN.
I CAN NO FALL BEHIND ASUNA TOO MUCH.
IT LOOKS LIKE KŪ'S DEFINITELY IMPROVING.
SHE'S INCREASED HER MARTIAL ARTS ABILITIES TO THE LIMITS A PERSON CAN NORMALLY ATTAIN.
BY LEARNING THE USE OF CHI, AND TRAINING ON THE SAME LEVEL AS US, SHE'LL CATCH UP IN NO TIME AT ALL.
THAT'S WAS AWESOME, KŪ NĒ-CHAN! I WANNA SPAR WITH YOU NOW!
WELL I STILL NEW AT USING CHI. FOR NOW I KEEP ON TRAINING KOTARO.
BY THE WAY, ANY INJURIES, KŪ-CHAN? KOTA-KUN?
HEY, WAIT, YOU GOT A BUNCH OF SCRAPES, KOTA-KUN!
HUH?
KOTARŌ-KUN'S ALSO IMPROVED A LOT THESE LAST SEVEN DAYS.
UNTIL NOW, HE JUST HAD HIS OWN FIGHTING STYLE. BY TRAINING WITH KAEDE AND NEGI-SENSEI, HE'S SHARPENED THEIR SKILLS.
THEY'LL BOTH BECOME MUCH STRONGER. HEH, I SUPPOSE I'LL NEED TO CONCENTRATE ON MY OWN TRAINING AS WELL.
UH... OJŌ-SAMA?
LET ME HEAL YOU, KOTA-KUN. ♪
YOU'RE LIKE A MOUNTAIN OF TREASURE
LIKE I SAID, THIS DOESN'T HURT AT ALL!

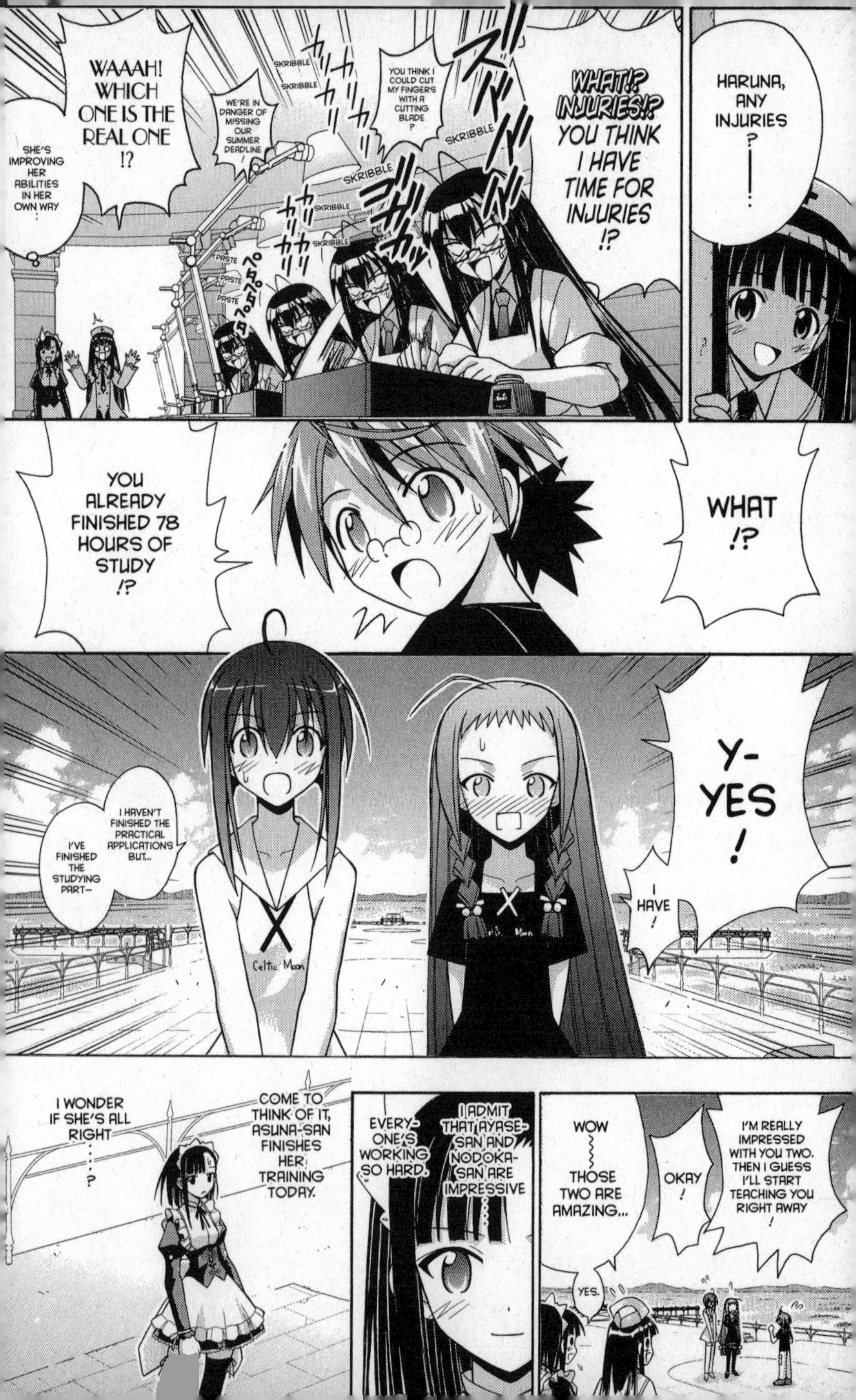
HARUNA, ANY INJURIES?
WHAT!? INJURIES!? YOU THINK I HAVE TIME FOR INJURIES!?
SKRIBBLE
YOU THINK I COULD CUT MY FINGERS WITH A CUTTING BLADE?
SKRIBBLE
SKRIBBLE
SKRIBBLE
SKRIBBLE
SKRIBBLE
WE'RE IN DANGER OF MISSING OUR SUMMER DEADLINE!
PASTE
PASTE
PASTE
WAAAH! WHICH ONE IS THE REAL ONE!?
SHE'S IMPROVING HER ABILITIES IN HER OWN WAY...
WHAT!?
YOU ALREADY FINISHED 78 HOURS OF STUDY!?
Y-YES!
I HAVE!
I HAVEN'T FINISHED THE PRACTICAL APPLICATIONS BUT...
I'VE FINISHED THE STUDYING PART–
Celtic Moon
I'M REALLY IMPRESSED WITH YOU TWO. THEN I GUESS I'LL START TEACHING YOU RIGHT AWAY!
OKAY!
WOW~ THOSE TWO ARE AMAZING...
YES.
I ADMIT THAT AYASE-SAN AND NODOKA-SAN ARE IMPRESSIVE...
EVERYONE'S WORKING SO HARD.
COME TO THINK OF IT, ASUNA-SAN FINISHES HER TRAINING TODAY.
I WONDER IF SHE'S ALL RIGHT...?

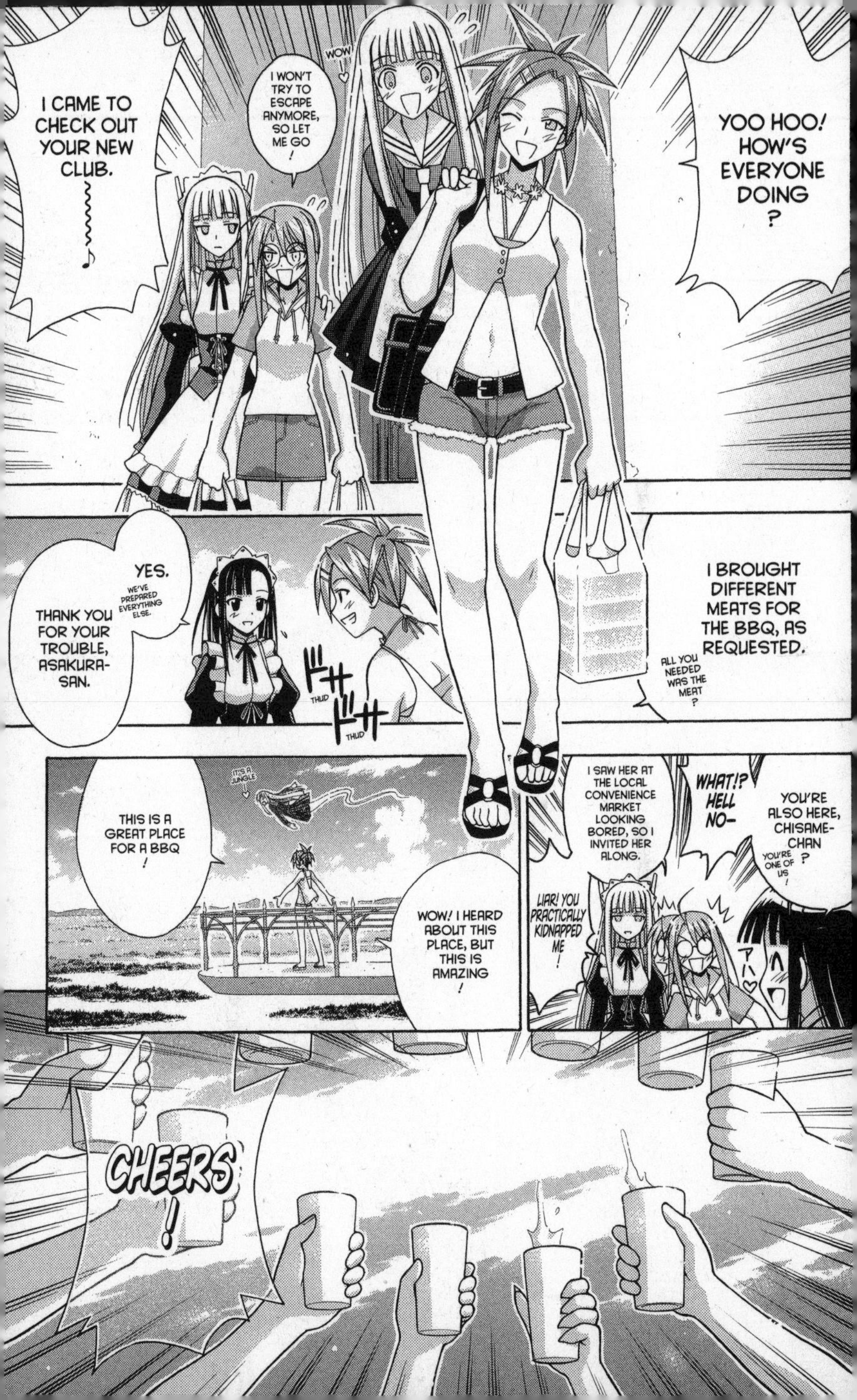
YOO HOO! HOW'S EVERYONE DOING?
WOW ♡
I WON'T TRY TO ESCAPE ANYMORE, SO LET ME GO!
I CAME TO CHECK OUT YOUR NEW CLUB. ♪
I BROUGHT DIFFERENT MEATS FOR THE BBQ, AS REQUESTED.
ALL YOU NEEDED WAS THE MEAT?
ドサ THUD
ドサ THUD
YES.
WE'VE PREPARED EVERYTHING ELSE.
THANK YOU FOR YOUR TROUBLE, ASAKURA-SAN.
YOU'RE ALSO HERE, CHISAME-CHAN?
YOU'RE ONE OF US!
WHAT!? HELL NO-
I SAW HER AT THE LOCAL CONVENIENCE MARKET LOOKING BORED, SO I INVITED HER ALONG.
LIAR! YOU PRACTICALLY KIDNAPPED ME!
アハ♡
WOW! I HEARD ABOUT THIS PLACE, BUT THIS IS AMAZING!
IT'S A JUNGLE ♡
THIS IS A GREAT PLACE FOR A BBQ!
CHEERS!

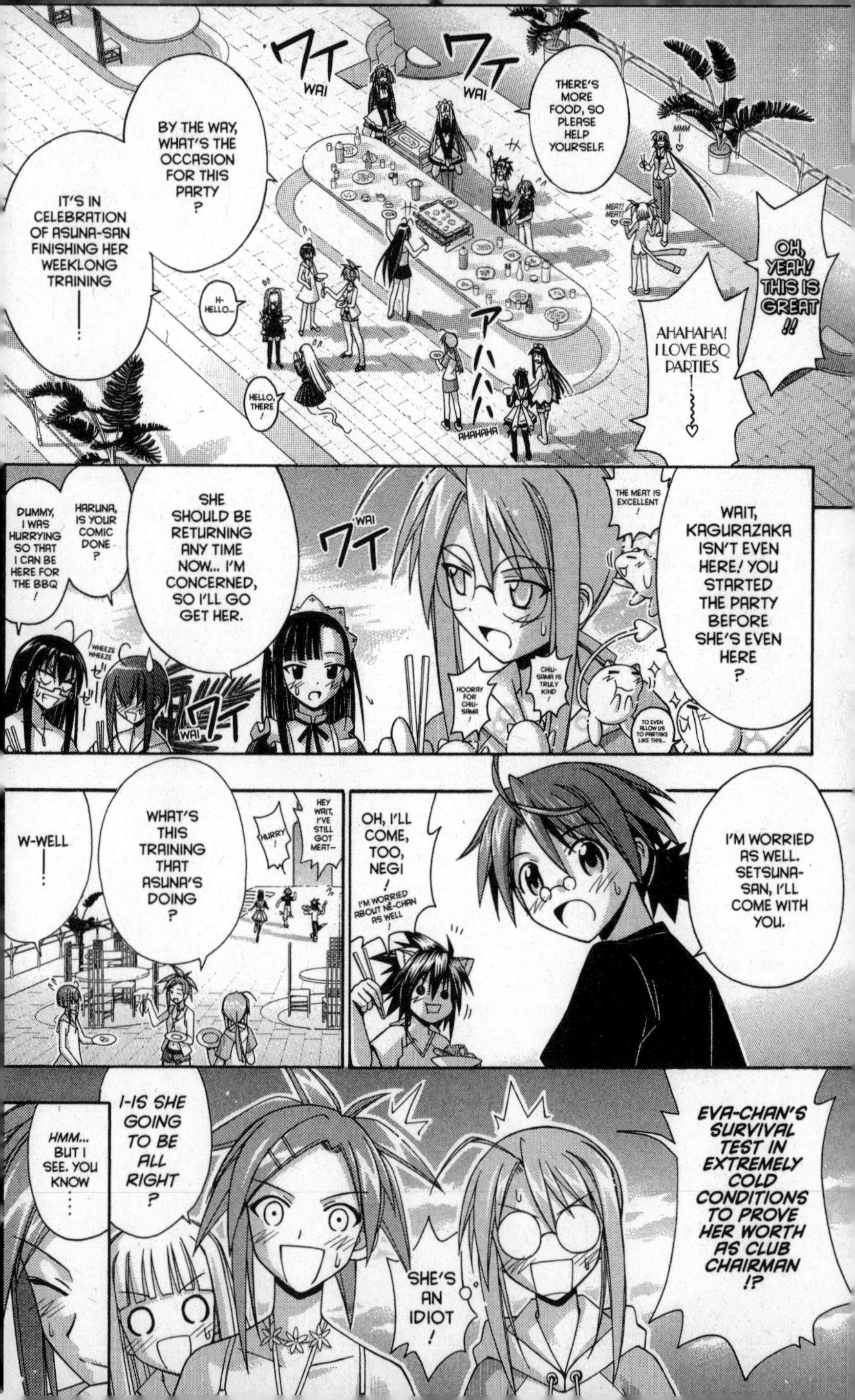
MMM ♡
OH, YEAH! THIS IS GREAT!!
AHAHAHA! I LOVE BBQ PARTIES ♡
THERE'S MORE FOOD, SO PLEASE HELP YOURSELF.
MEAT! MEAT! ♡
WAI
WAI
BY THE WAY, WHAT'S THE OCCASION FOR THIS PARTY?
IT'S IN CELEBRATION OF ASUNA-SAN FINISHING HER WEEKLONG TRAINING!
H-HELLO...
AHAHAHA
HELLO, THERE!
WAIT, KAGURAZAKA ISN'T EVEN HERE! YOU STARTED THE PARTY BEFORE SHE'S EVEN HERE?
THE MEAT IS EXCELLENT!
CHIU-SAMA IS TRULY KIND!
TO EVEN ALLOW US TO PARTAKE LIKE THIS...
HOORAY FOR CHIU-SAMA!
WAI
SHE SHOULD BE RETURNING ANY TIME NOW... I'M CONCERNED, SO I'LL GO GET HER.
WAI
HARUNA, IS YOUR COMIC DONE?
DUMMY, I WAS HURRYING SO THAT I CAN BE HERE FOR THE BBQ!
WHEEZE WHEEZE
I'M WORRIED AS WELL. SETSUNA-SAN, I'LL COME WITH YOU.
OH, I'LL COME, TOO, NEGI!
I'M WORRIED ABOUT NÉ-CHAN AS WELL!
HEY WAIT, I'VE STILL GOT MEAT—
HURRY!
WHAT'S THIS TRAINING THAT ASUNA'S DOING?
W-WELL!
EVA-CHAN'S SURVIVAL TEST IN EXTREMELY COLD CONDITIONS TO PROVE HER WORTH AS CLUB CHAIRMAN!?
SHE'S AN IDIOT!
I-IS SHE GOING TO BE ALL RIGHT?
HMM... BUT I SEE. YOU KNOW....

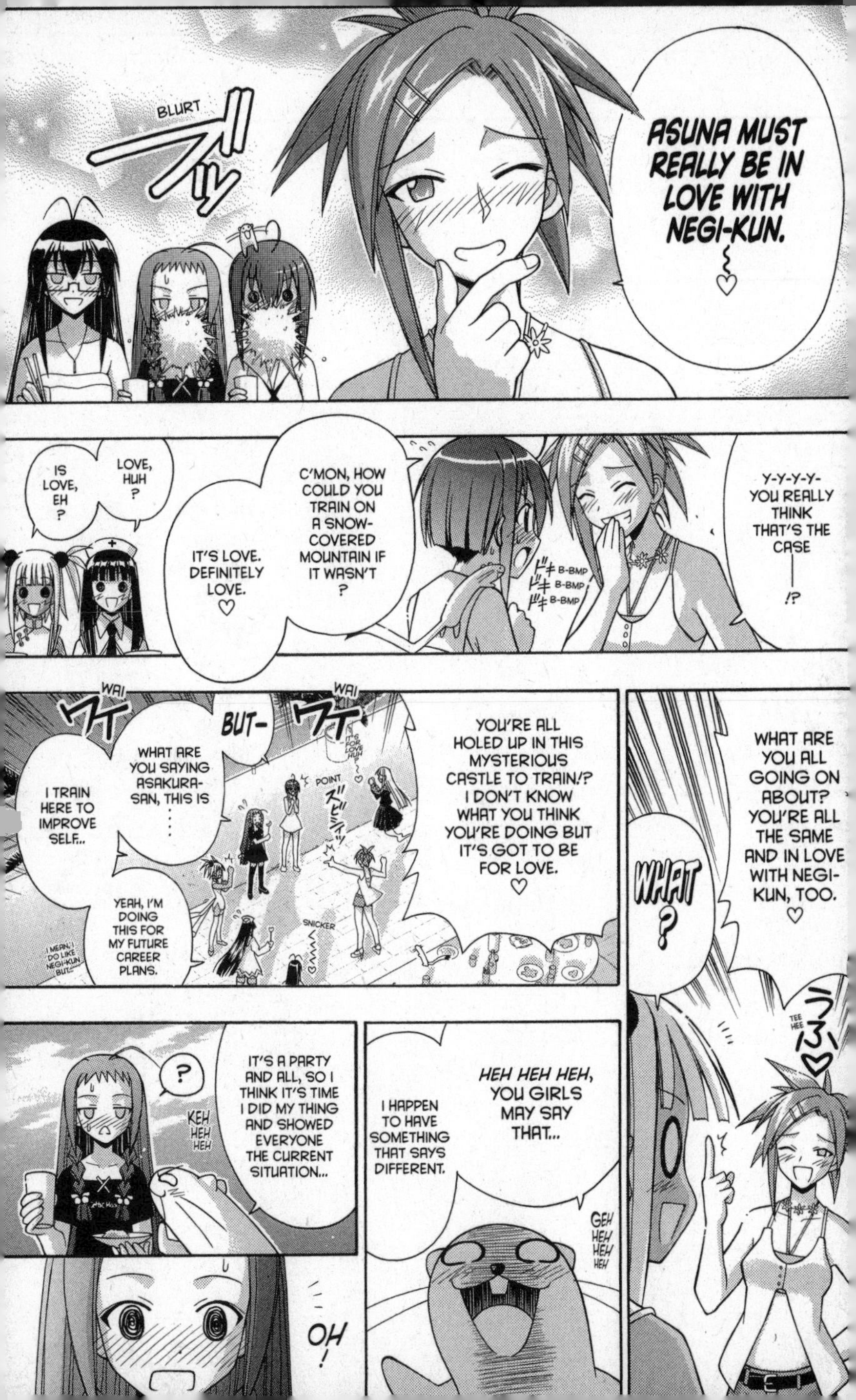

ASUNA MUST REALLY BE IN LOVE WITH NEGI-KUN. ♡
BLURT
Y-Y-Y-Y-YOU REALLY THINK THAT'S THE CASE—!?
B-BMP B-BMP B-BMP
C'MON, HOW COULD YOU TRAIN ON A SNOW-COVERED MOUNTAIN IF IT WASN'T?
IT'S LOVE. DEFINITELY LOVE. ♡
LOVE, HUH?
IS LOVE, EH?
WHAT ARE YOU ALL GOING ON ABOUT? YOU'RE ALL THE SAME AND IN LOVE WITH NEGI-KUN, TOO. ♡
WHAT?
YOU'RE ALL HOLED UP IN THIS MYSTERIOUS CASTLE TO TRAIN!? I DON'T KNOW WHAT YOU THINK YOU'RE DOING BUT IT'S GOT TO BE FOR LOVE. ♡
WAI
IT'S FOR LOVE HUH ♡
WAI
BUT-
POINT
WHAT ARE YOU SAYING ASAKURA-SAN, THIS IS......
I TRAIN HERE TO IMPROVE SELF...
YEAH, I'M DOING THIS FOR MY FUTURE CAREER PLANS.
I MEAN, I DO LIKE NEGI-KUN BUT...
SNICKER
TEE HEE
HEH HEH HEH, YOU GIRLS MAY SAY THAT...
I HAPPEN TO HAVE SOMETHING THAT SAYS DIFFERENT.
GEH HEH HEH HEH
IT'S A PARTY AND ALL, SO I THINK IT'S TIME I DID MY THING AND SHOWED EVERYONE THE CURRENT SITUATION...
?
KEH HEH HEH
OH!

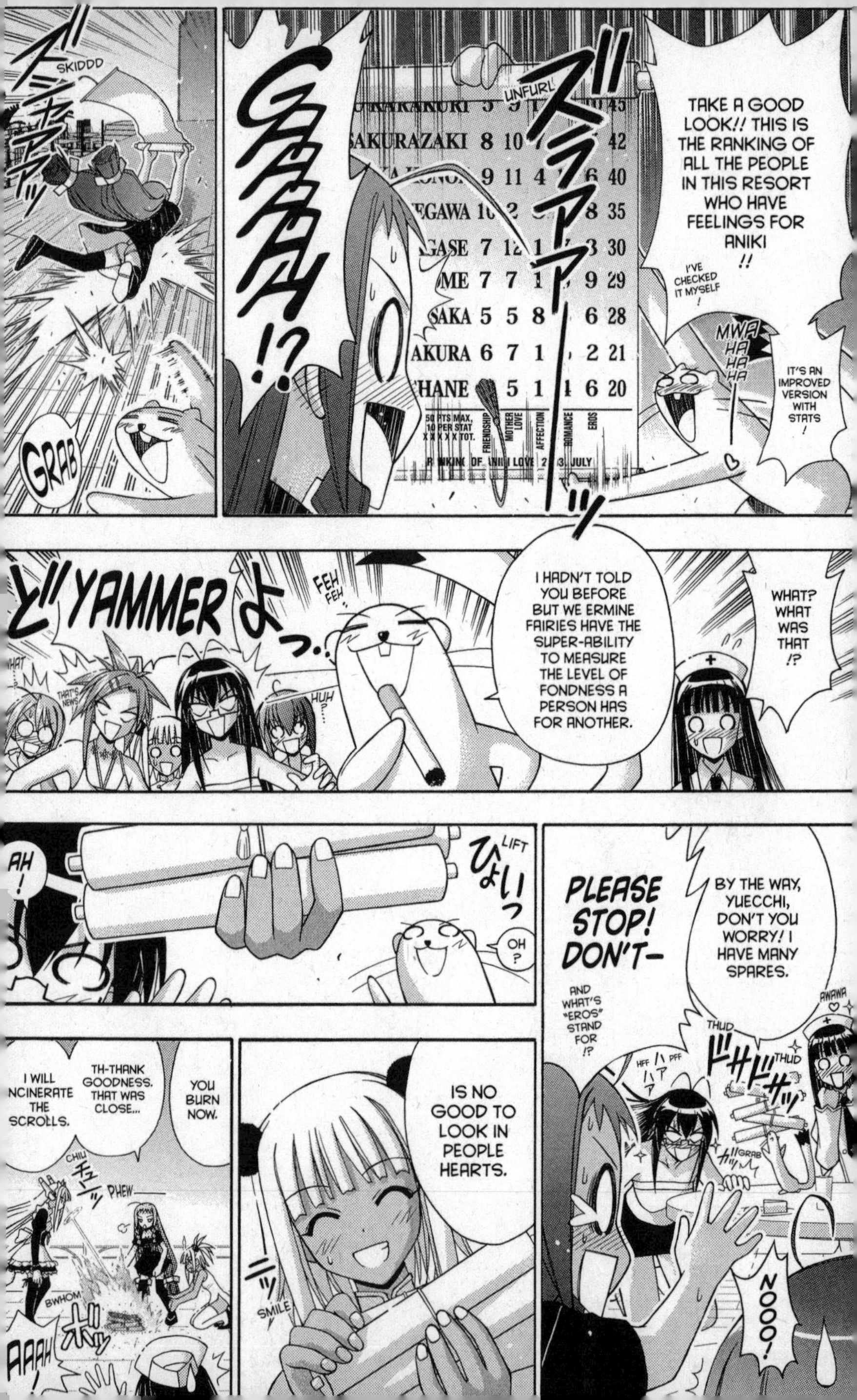

TAKE A GOOD LOOK!! THIS IS THE RANKING OF ALL THE PEOPLE IN THIS RESORT WHO HAVE FEELINGS FOR ANIKI!!
I'VE CHECKED IT MYSELF!
MWA HA HA HA
IT'S AN IMPROVED VERSION WITH STATS!
UNFURL
SAKURAZAKI 8 10 42
EGAWA 35
GASE 7 12 1 3 30
ME 7 7 1 9 29
SAKA 5 5 8 6 28
AKURA 6 7 1 2 21
HANE 5 1 4 6 20
50 PTS MAX, 10 PER STAT
FRIENDSHIP
MOTHER LOVE
AFFECTION
ROMANCE
EROS
GAAAH!?
SKIDDD
GRAB
WHAT? WHAT WAS THAT!?
I HADN'T TOLD YOU BEFORE BUT WE ERMINE FAIRIES HAVE THE SUPER-ABILITY TO MEASURE THE LEVEL OF FONDNESS A PERSON HAS FOR ANOTHER.
FEH FEH
YAMMER
HUH?
THAT'S NEWS
WHAT
BY THE WAY, YUECCHI, DON'T YOU WORRY! I HAVE MANY SPARES.
PLEASE STOP! DON'T-
AND WHAT'S "EROS" STAND FOR!?
AWAWA
THUD
THUD
HFF PFF
GRAB
NOOO!
LIFT
OH?
AH!
IS NO GOOD TO LOOK IN PEOPLE HEARTS.
SMILE
YOU BURN NOW.
TH-THANK GOODNESS. THAT WAS CLOSE...
I WILL NCINERATE THE SCROLLS.
CHIU
PHEW
BWHOM
AAAH!

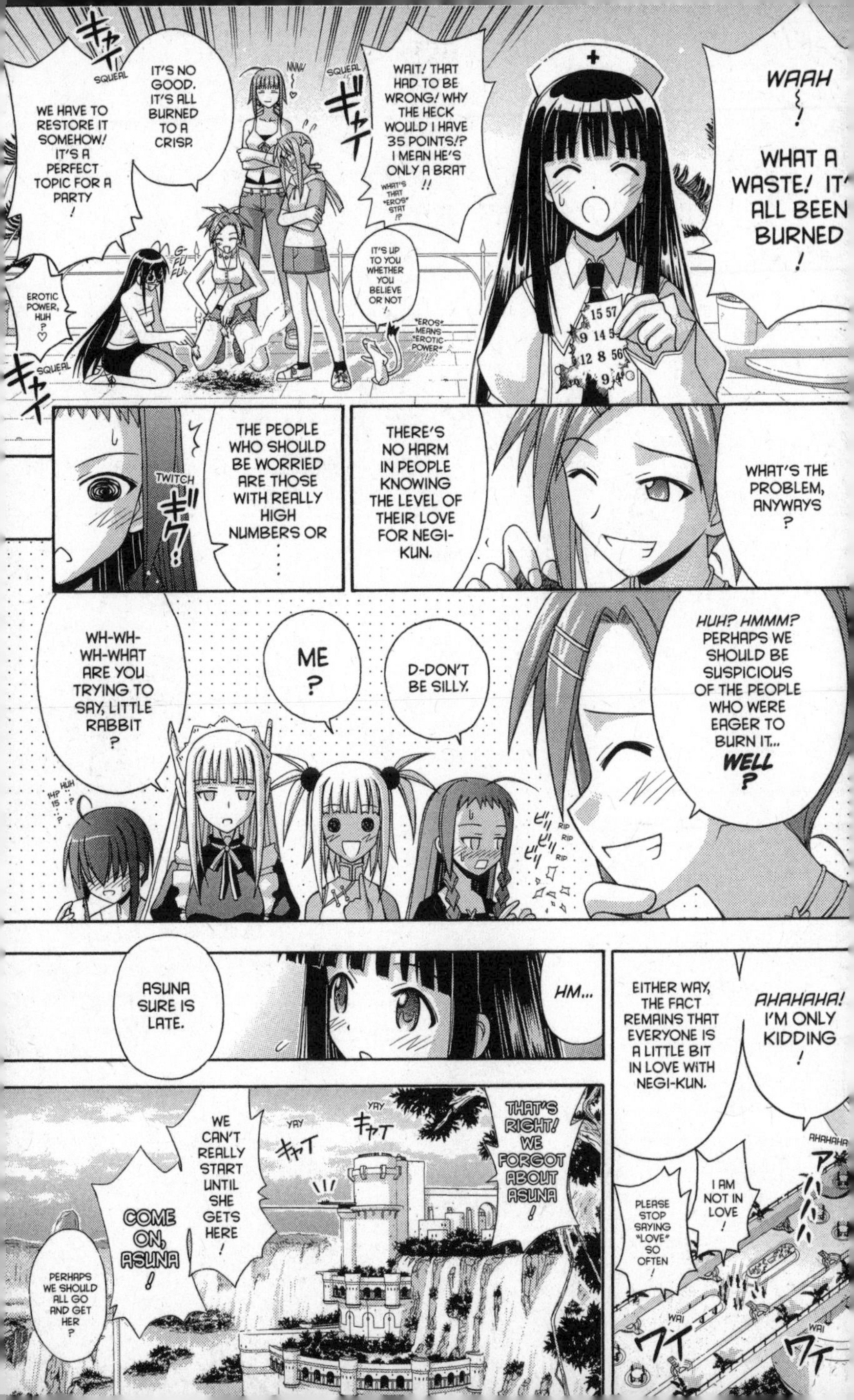
WAAH ~!
WHAT A WASTE! IT' ALL BEEN BURNED!
WAIT! THAT HAD TO BE WRONG! WHY THE HECK WOULD I HAVE 35 POINTS!? I MEAN HE'S ONLY A BRAT!!
SQUEAL
WHAT'S THAT "EROS" STAT!?
IT'S UP TO YOU WHETHER YOU BELIEVE OR NOT!
EROS MEANS *EROTIC POWER*
NNH ♡
IT'S NO GOOD. IT'S ALL BURNED TO A CRISP.
SQUEAL
WE HAVE TO RESTORE IT SOMEHOW! IT'S A PERFECT TOPIC FOR A PARTY!
G-FU FU
EROTIC POWER, HUH ♡
SQUEAL
WHAT'S THE PROBLEM, ANYWAYS?
THERE'S NO HARM IN PEOPLE KNOWING THE LEVEL OF THEIR LOVE FOR NEGI-KUN.
THE PEOPLE WHO SHOULD BE WORRIED ARE THOSE WITH REALLY HIGH NUMBERS OR ......
TWITCH
HUH? HMMM? PERHAPS WE SHOULD BE SUSPICIOUS OF THE PEOPLE WHO WERE EAGER TO BURN IT... WELL?
RIP RIP RIP
D-DON'T BE SILLY.
ME?
WH-WH-WH-WHAT ARE YOU TRYING TO SAY, LITTLE RABBIT?
AHAHAHA! I'M ONLY KIDDING!
EITHER WAY, THE FACT REMAINS THAT EVERYONE IS A LITTLE BIT IN LOVE WITH NEGI-KUN.
AHAHAHA
I AM NOT IN LOVE!
PLEASE STOP SAYING "LOVE" SO OFTEN!
WAI
WAI
HM...
ASUNA SURE IS LATE.
THAT'S RIGHT! WE FORGOT ABOUT ASUNA!
YAY
YAY
WE CAN'T REALLY START UNTIL SHE GETS HERE!
COME ON, ASUNA!
PERHAPS WE SHOULD ALL GO AND GET HER?

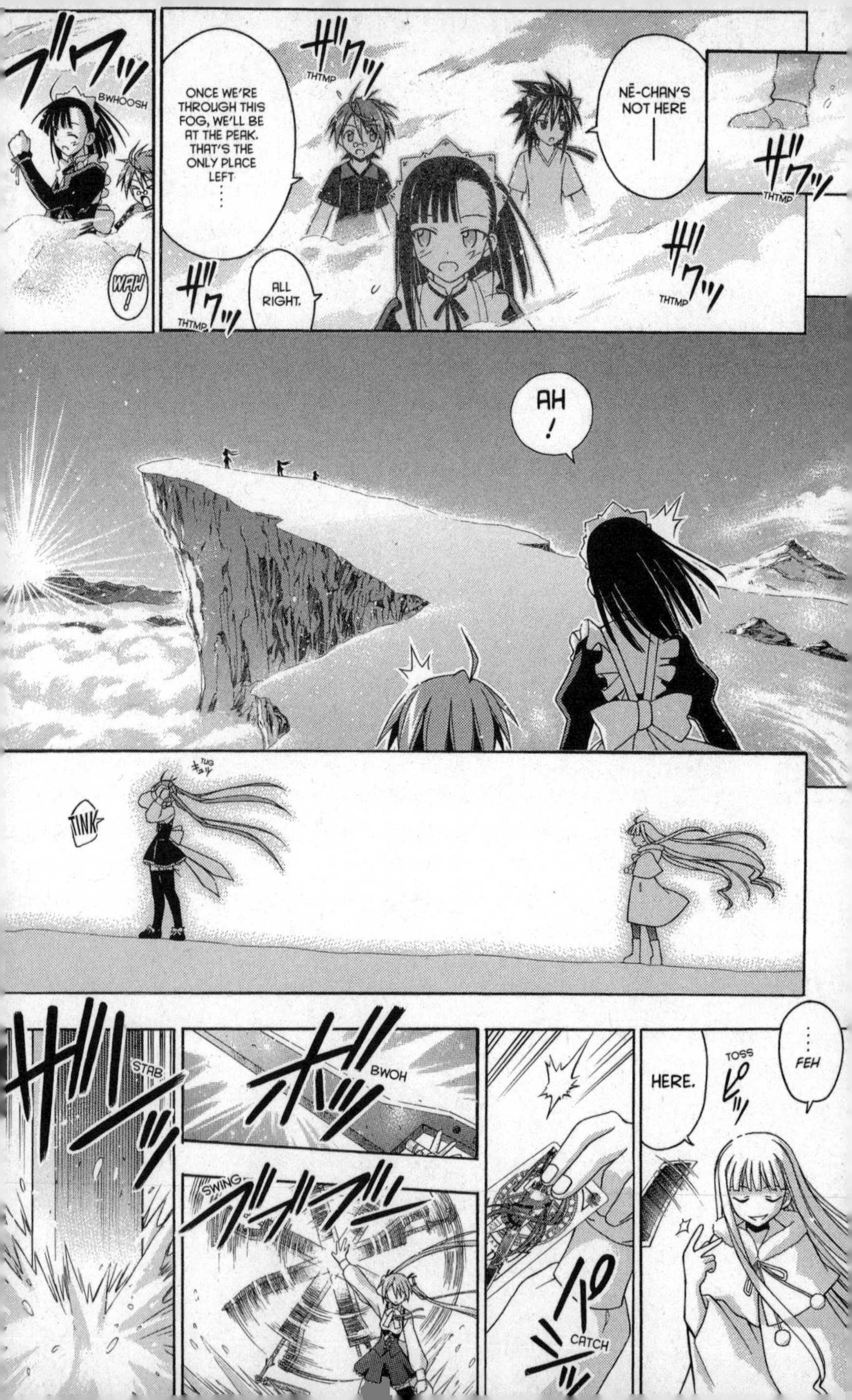
THTMP
NĒ-CHAN'S NOT HERE —
THTMP
THTMP
ONCE WE'RE THROUGH THIS FOG, WE'LL BE AT THE PEAK. THAT'S THE ONLY PLACE LEFT . . . .
ALL RIGHT.
THTMP
BWHOOSH
WAH!
AH!
TUG
TINK
. . . FEH
TOSS
HERE.
CATCH
BWOH
SWING
STAB

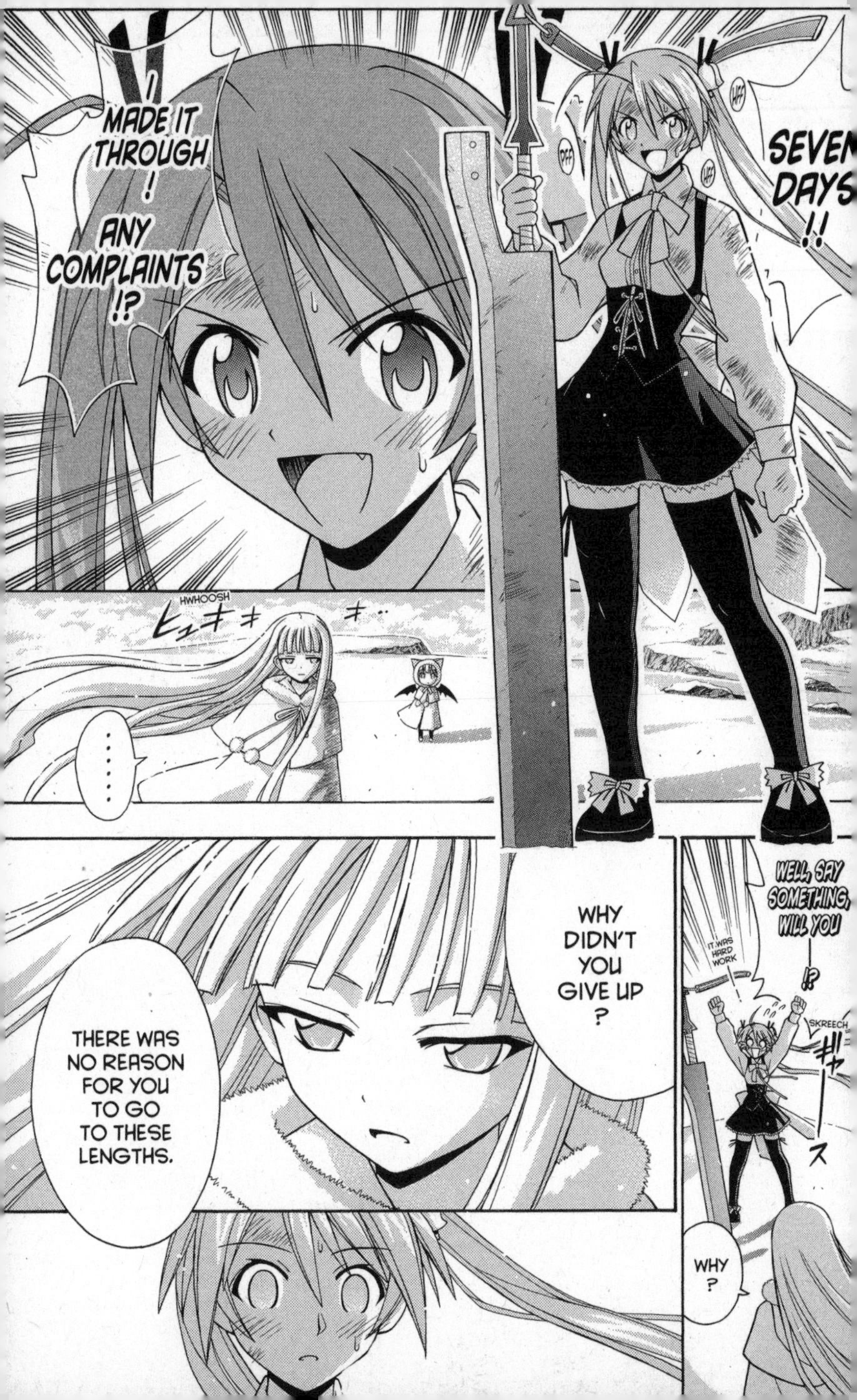
HFF
PFF
HFF
SEVEN DAYS!!
I MADE IT THROUGH!
ANY COMPLAINTS!?
HWHOOSH
......
WELL, SAY SOMETHING, WILL YOU—!?
IT WAS HARD WORK
SKREECH
WHY?
WHY DIDN'T YOU GIVE UP?
THERE WAS NO REASON FOR YOU TO GO TO THESE LENGTHS.

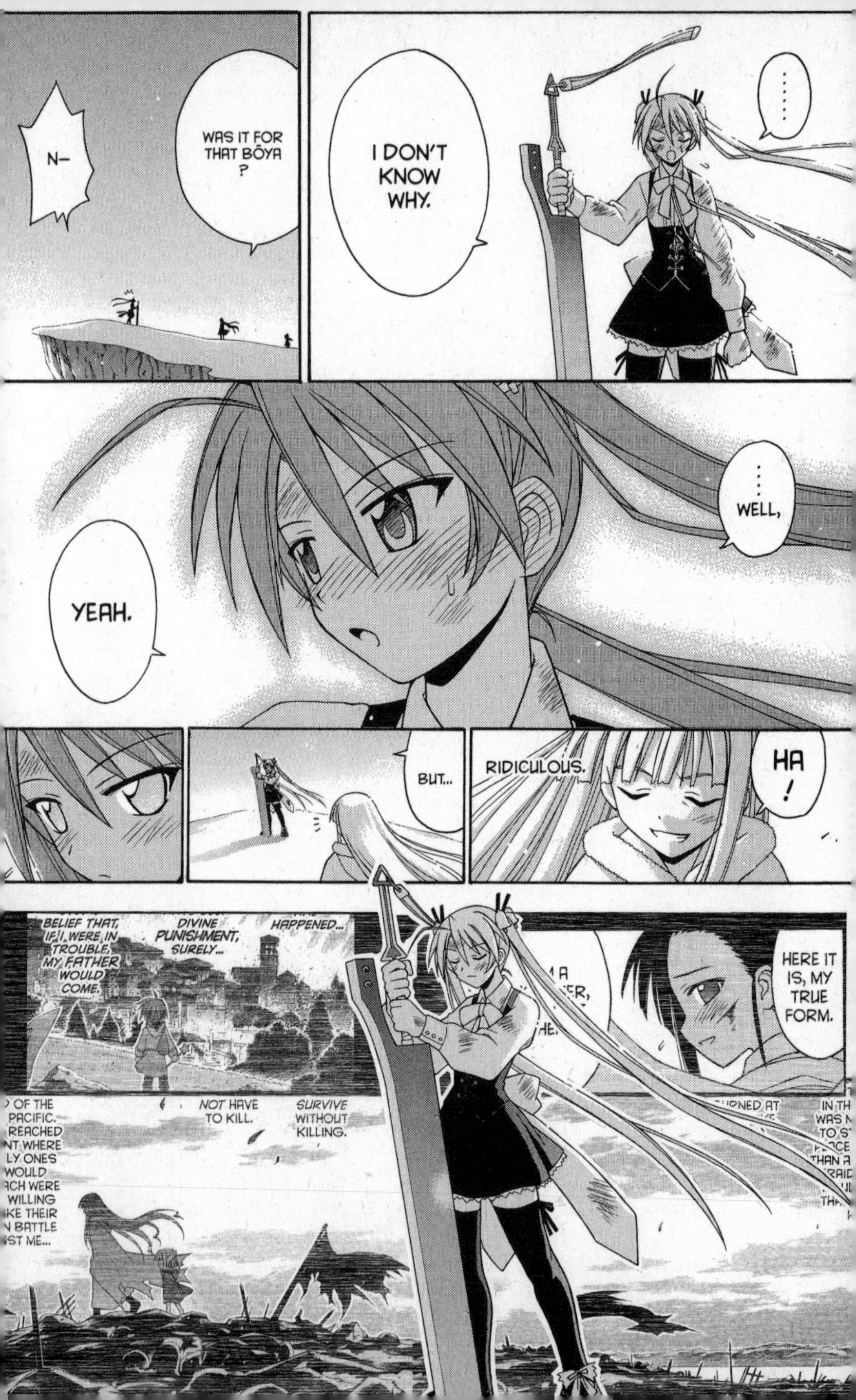
……
I DON'T KNOW WHY.
WAS IT FOR THAT BŌYA ?
N–
…WELL,
YEAH.
HA!
RIDICULOUS.
BUT…
HERE IT IS, MY TRUE FORM.
HAPPENED…
DIVINE PUNISHMENT, SURELY…
BELIEF THAT, IF I WERE IN TROUBLE, MY FATHER WOULD COME.
SURVIVE WITHOUT KILLING.
NOT HAVE TO KILL.

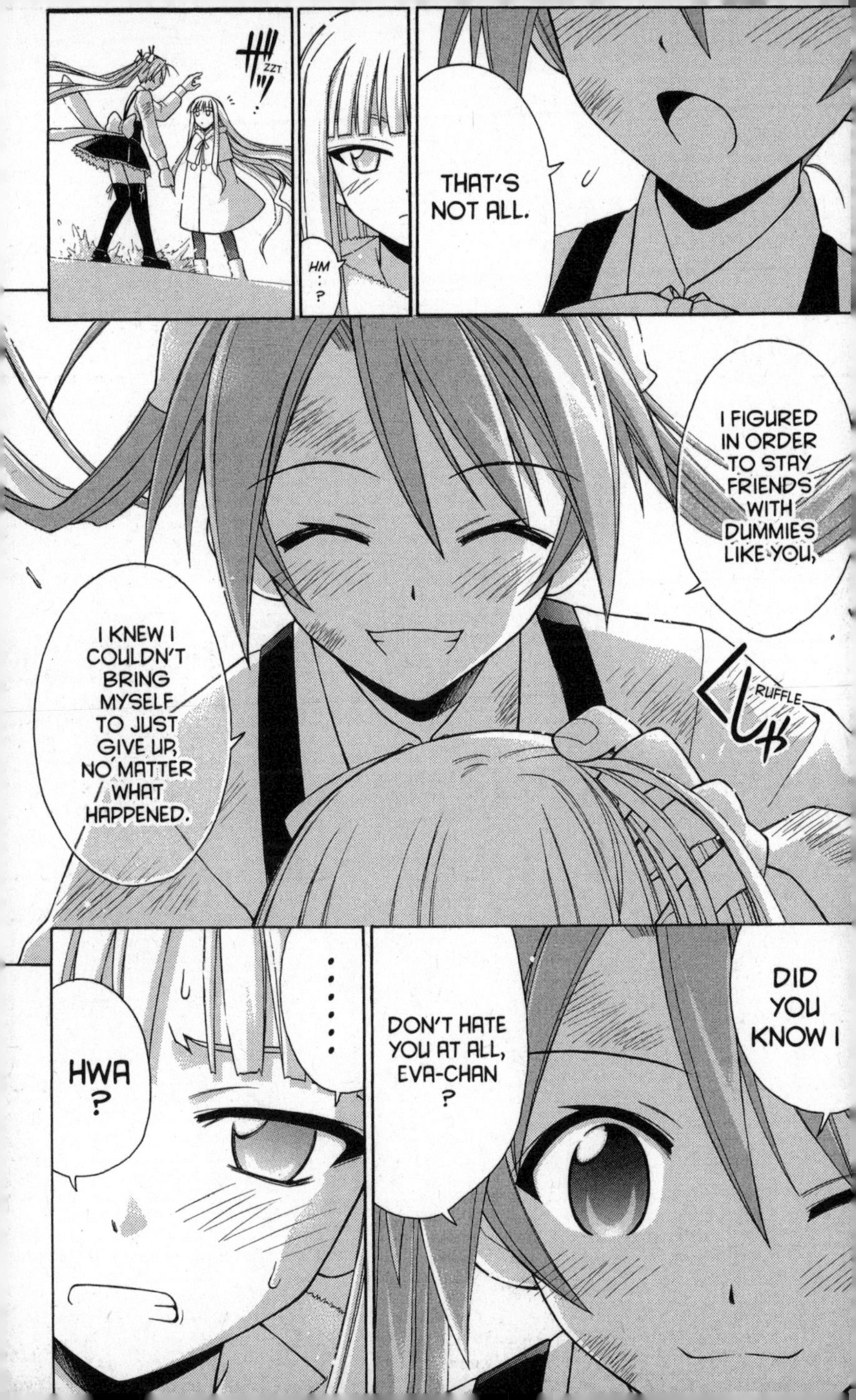
THAT'S NOT ALL.
HM..?
ZZT
I FIGURED IN ORDER TO STAY FRIENDS WITH DUMMIES LIKE YOU,
RUFFLE
I KNEW I COULDN'T BRING MYSELF TO JUST GIVE UP, NO MATTER WHAT HAPPENED.
DID YOU KNOW I
DON'T HATE YOU AT ALL, EVA-CHAN?
......
HWA?

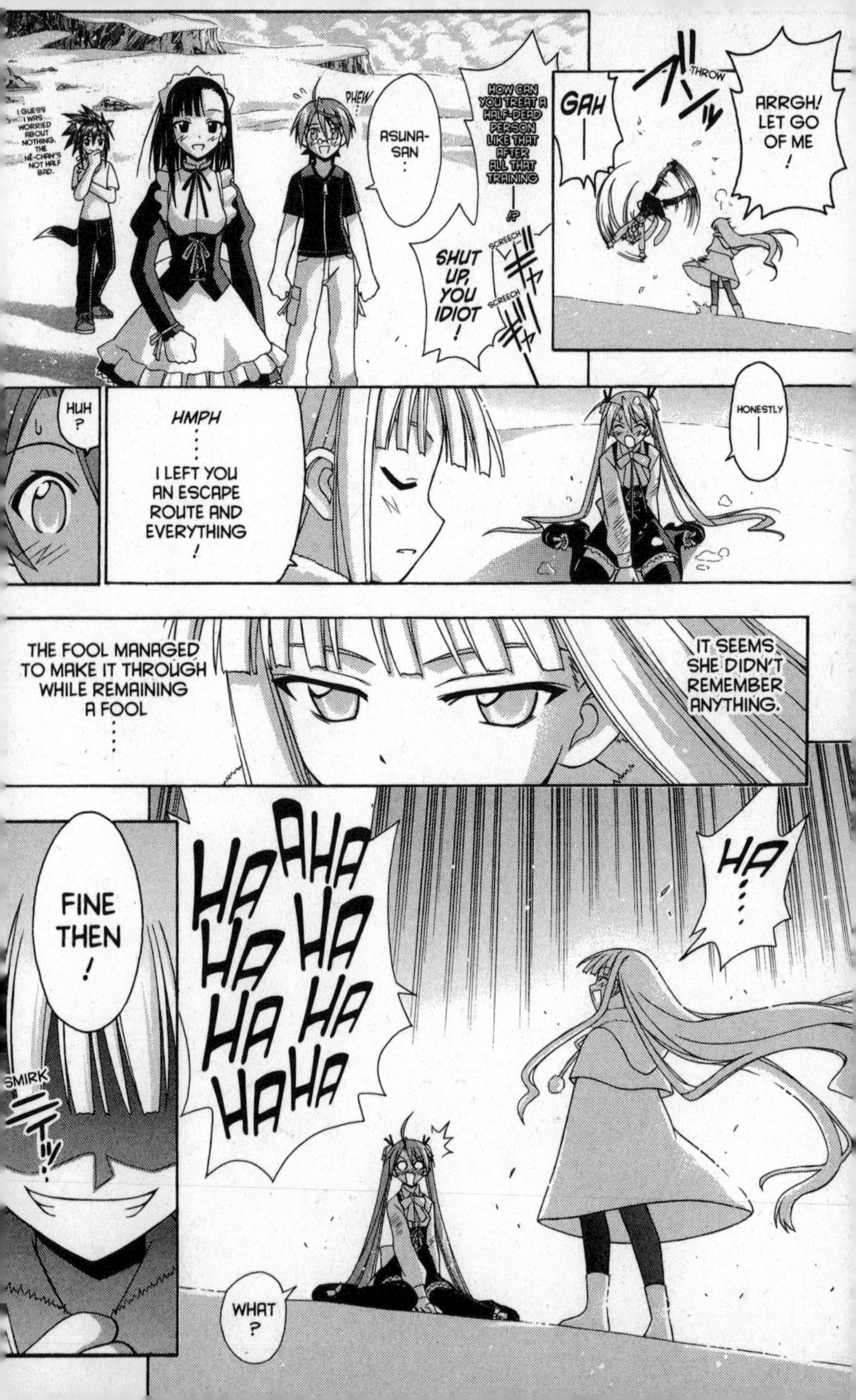
ARRGH! LET GO OF ME!
THROW
GAH—
HOW CAN YOU TREAT A HALF-DEAD PERSON LIKE THAT AFTER ALL THAT TRAINING—!?
SCREECH
SCREECH
SHUT UP, YOU IDIOT!
ASUNA-SAN...
PHEW
I GUESS I WAS WORRIED ABOUT NOTHING. THE NÉ-CHAN'S NOT HALF BAD.
HONESTLY—
HMPH... I LEFT YOU AN ESCAPE ROUTE AND EVERYTHING!
HUH?
IT SEEMS SHE DIDN'T REMEMBER ANYTHING.
THE FOOL MANAGED TO MAKE IT THROUGH WHILE REMAINING A FOOL...
HA...
HAHAHA HA HA HA HA HA HA HAHA
WHAT?
FINE THEN!
SMIRK

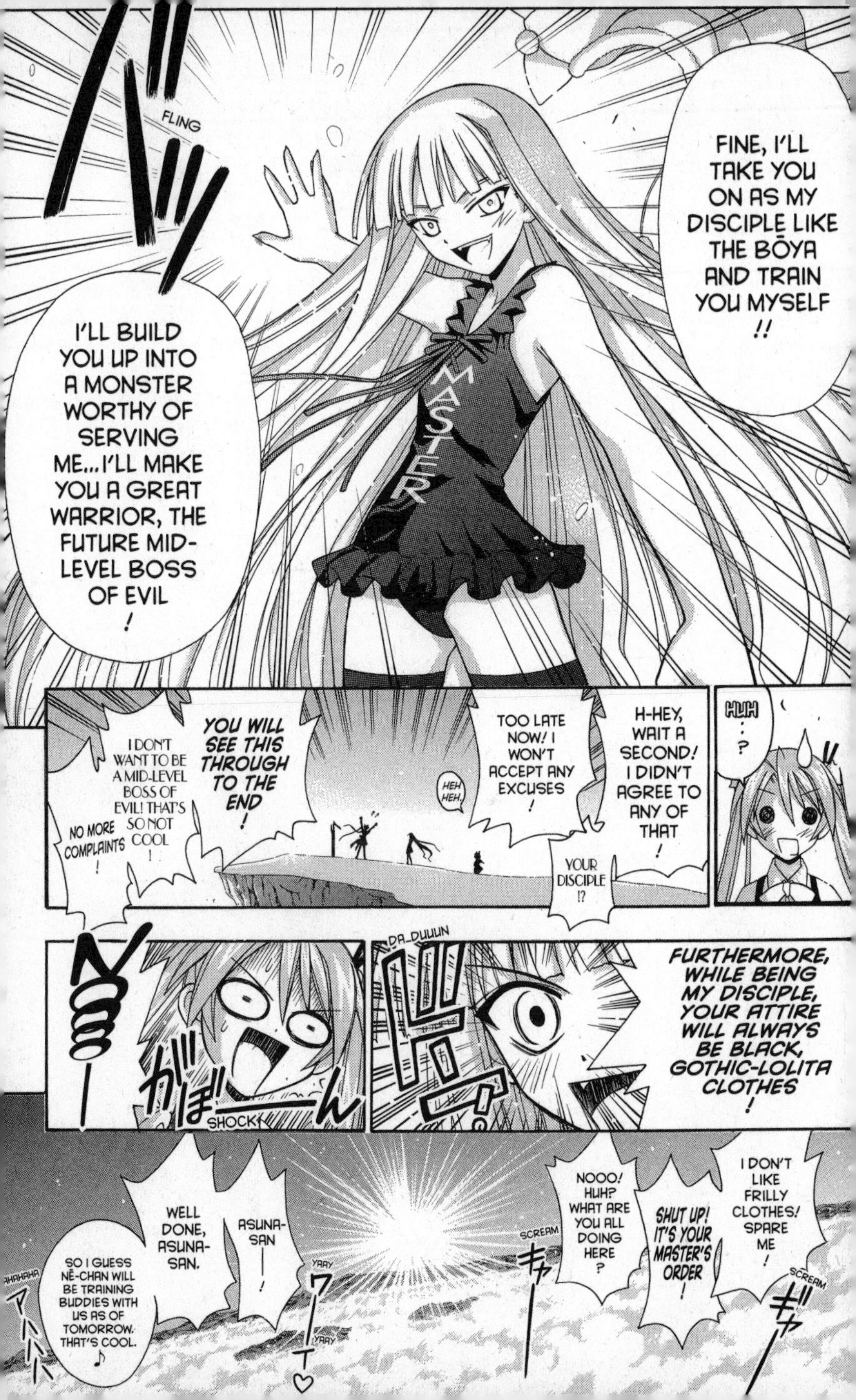
FINE, I'LL TAKE YOU ON AS MY DISCIPLE LIKE THE BŌYA AND TRAIN YOU MYSELF!!
FLING
I'LL BUILD YOU UP INTO A MONSTER WORTHY OF SERVING ME...I'LL MAKE YOU A GREAT WARRIOR, THE FUTURE MID-LEVEL BOSS OF EVIL!
HUH...?
H-HEY, WAIT A SECOND! I DIDN'T AGREE TO ANY OF THAT!
YOUR DISCIPLE!?
TOO LATE NOW! I WON'T ACCEPT ANY EXCUSES!
HEH HEH.
YOU WILL SEE THIS THROUGH TO THE END!
I DON'T WANT TO BE A MID-LEVEL BOSS OF EVIL! THAT'S SO NOT COOL!
NO MORE COMPLAINTS!
FURTHERMORE, WHILE BEING MY DISCIPLE, YOUR ATTIRE WILL ALWAYS BE BLACK, GOTHIC-LOLITA CLOTHES!
DA-DUUUN
SHOCK
I DON'T LIKE FRILLY CLOTHES! SPARE ME!
SCREAM
SHUT UP! IT'S YOUR MASTER'S ORDER!
NOOO! HUH? WHAT ARE YOU ALL DOING HERE?
SCREAM
ASUNA-SAN!
WELL DONE, ASUNA-SAN.
YAAY
YAAY
SO I GUESS NĒ-CHAN WILL BE TRAINING BUDDIES WITH US AS OF TOMORROW. THAT'S COOL. ♪
AHAHAHA

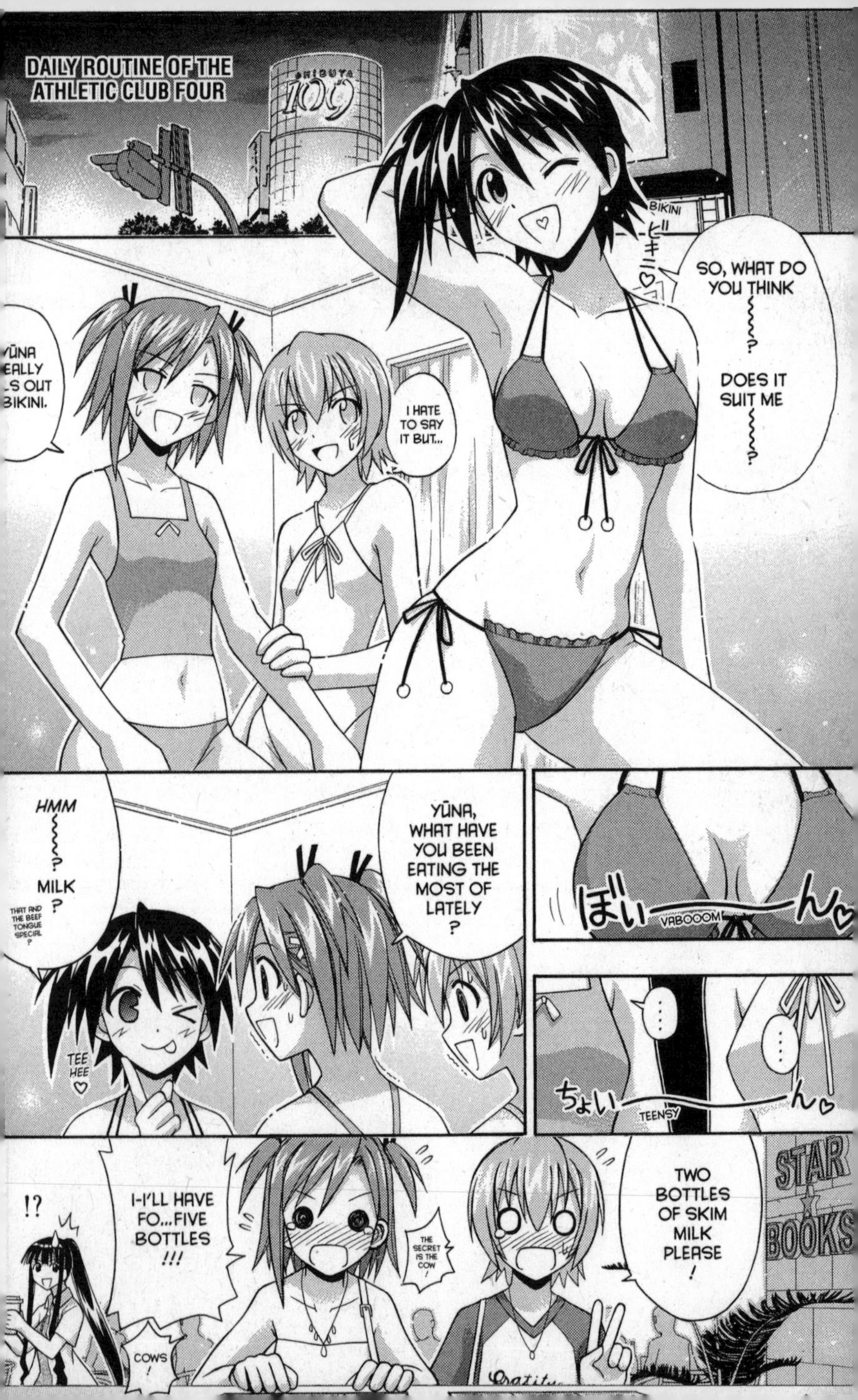
DAILY ROUTINE OF THE ATHLETIC CLUB FOUR
SHIBUYA 109
BIKINI ビキニ
SO, WHAT DO YOU THINK ~~~? DOES IT SUIT ME ~~~?
I HATE TO SAY IT BUT...
YŪNA EALLY LS OUT BIKINI.
ぼいーん VABOOOM
.....
.....
ちょいーん TEENSY
YŪNA, WHAT HAVE YOU BEEN EATING THE MOST OF LATELY?
HMM ~~~? MILK?
THAT AND THE BEEF TONGUE SPECIAL?
TEE HEE
STAR BOOKS
TWO BOTTLES OF SKIM MILK PLEASE!
THE SECRET IS THE COW!
I-I'LL HAVE FO...FIVE BOTTLES!!!
COWS!
!?

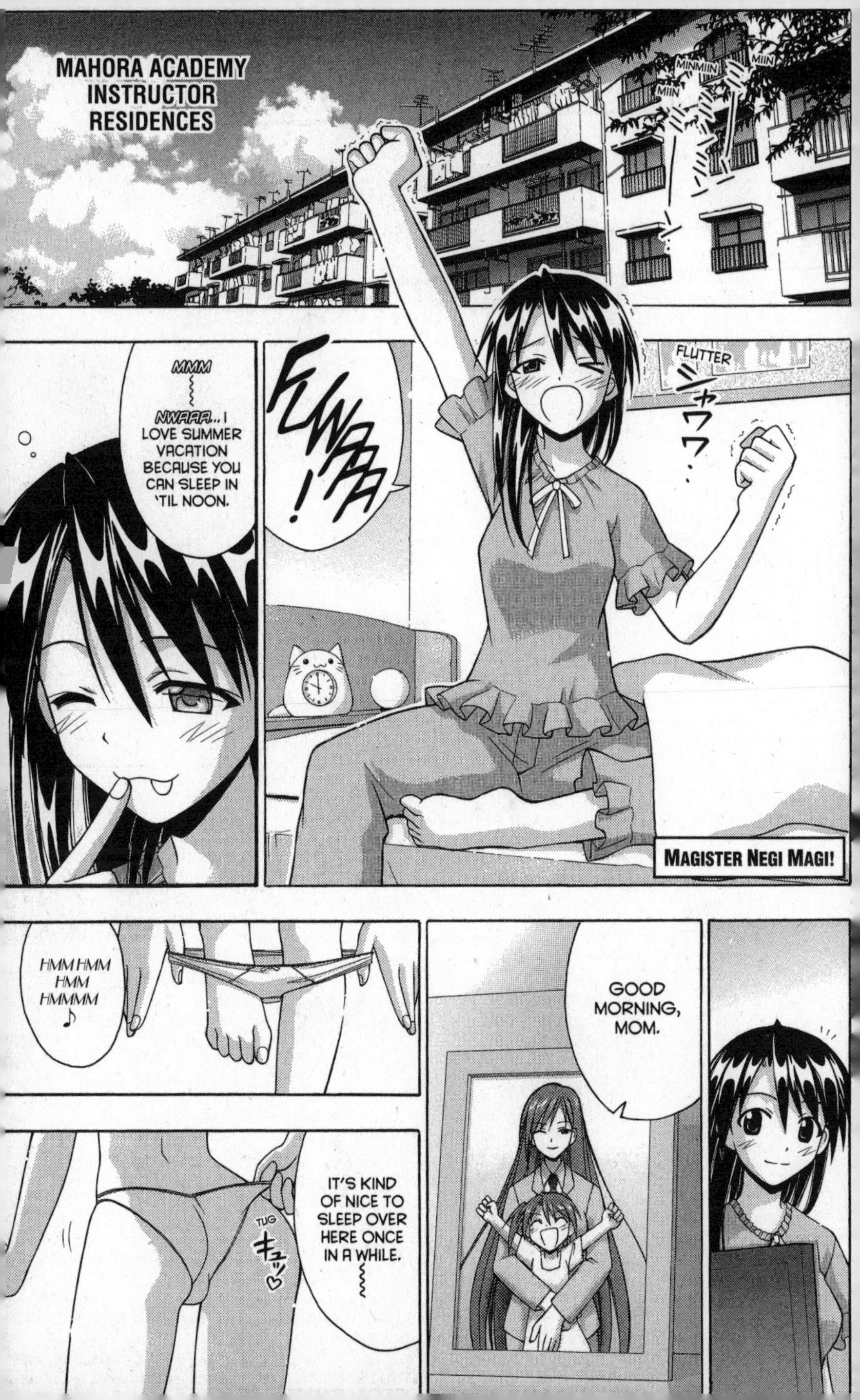
MAHORA ACADEMY INSTRUCTOR RESIDENCES
MINMIIN MIIN MIIN
FUWAAA!
FLUTTER
MMM... NWAAAA... I LOVE SUMMER VACATION BECAUSE YOU CAN SLEEP IN 'TIL NOON.
MAGISTER NEGI MAGI!
GOOD MORNING, MOM.
HMM HMM HMM HMMMM ♪
IT'S KIND OF NICE TO SLEEP OVER HERE ONCE IN A WHILE.
TUG

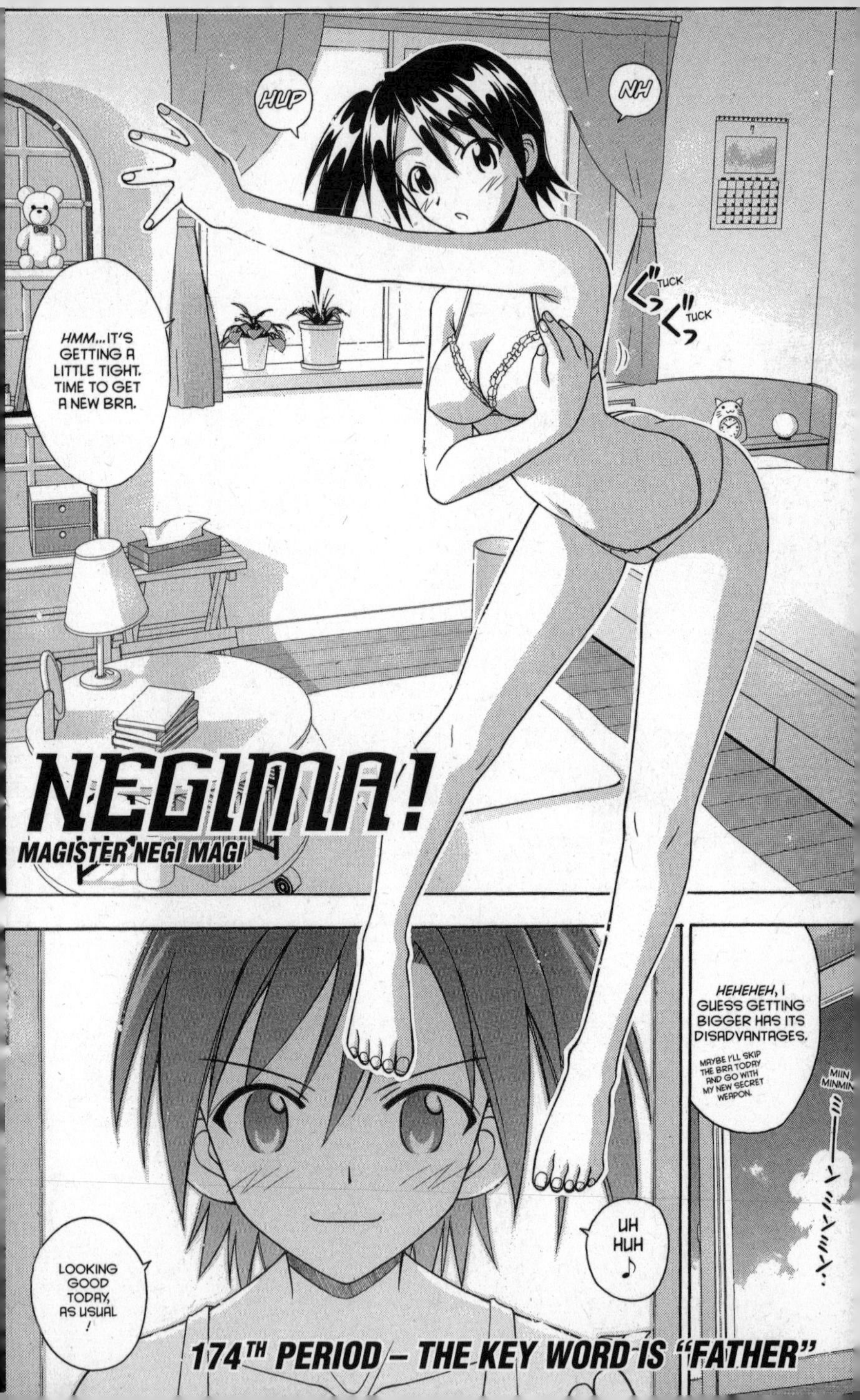
NH
TUCK
TUCK
HUP
HMM...IT'S GETTING A LITTLE TIGHT. TIME TO GET A NEW BRA.
NEGIMA!
MAGISTER NEGI MAGI
MIIN MINMIN
HEHEHEH, I GUESS GETTING BIGGER HAS ITS DISADVANTAGES.
MAYBE I'LL SKIP THE BRA TODAY AND GO WITH MY NEW SECRET WEAPON.
UH HUH ♪
LOOKING GOOD TODAY, AS USUAL!
174TH PERIOD – THE KEY WORD IS "FATHER"

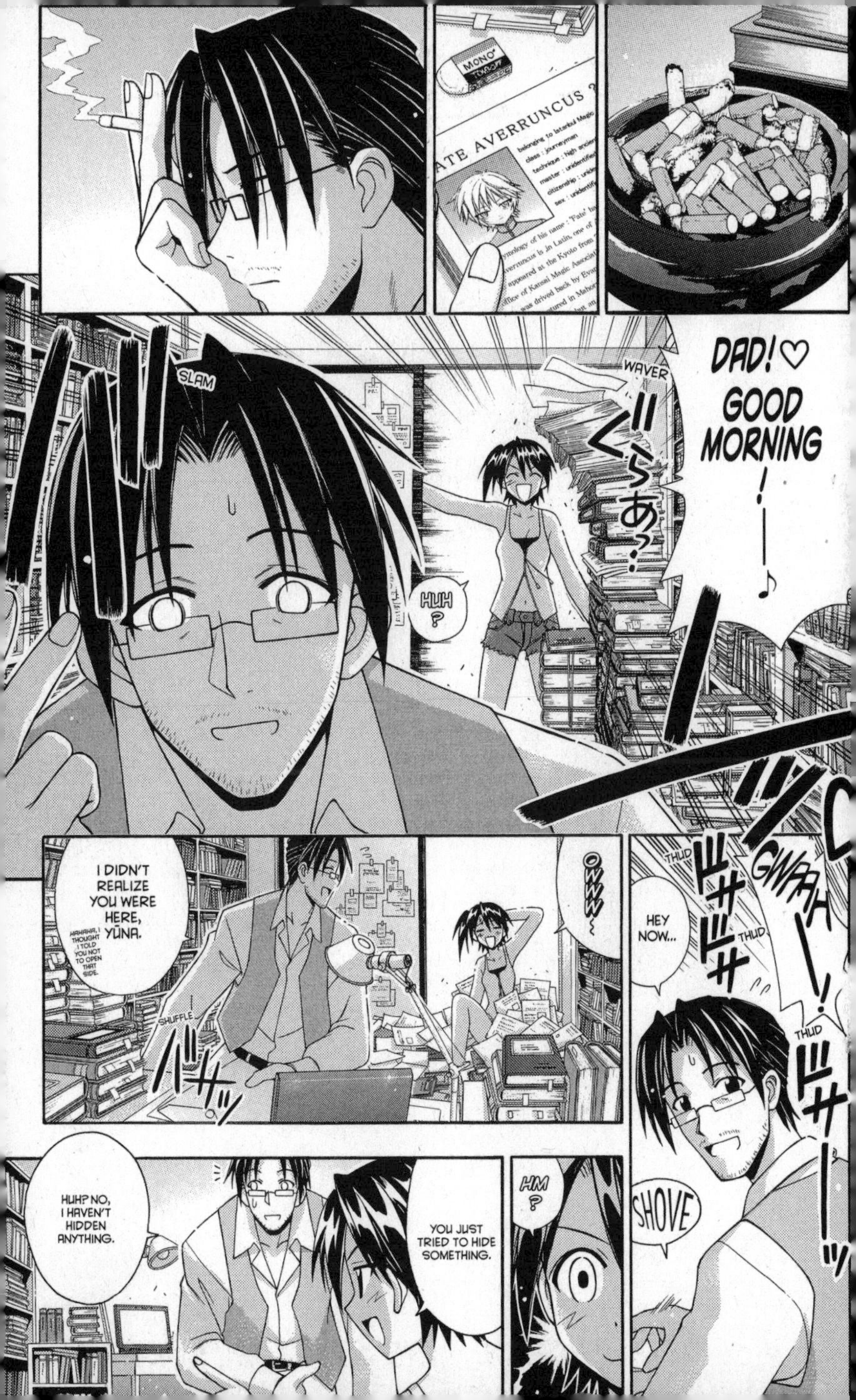
MONO
ATE AVERRUNCUS
belonging to Istanbul Magic
class : journeyman
DAD! ♡ GOOD MORNING! ♪
WAVER
HUH?
SLAM
GWAAAH!
THUD
HEY NOW...
THUD
THUD
SHOVE
OWWW~
I DIDN'T REALIZE YOU WERE HERE, YŪNA.
HAHAHA, I THOUGHT I TOLD YOU NOT TO OPEN THAT SIDE.
SHUFFLE
HM?
YOU JUST TRIED TO HIDE SOMETHING.
HUH? NO, I HAVEN'T HIDDEN ANYTHING.

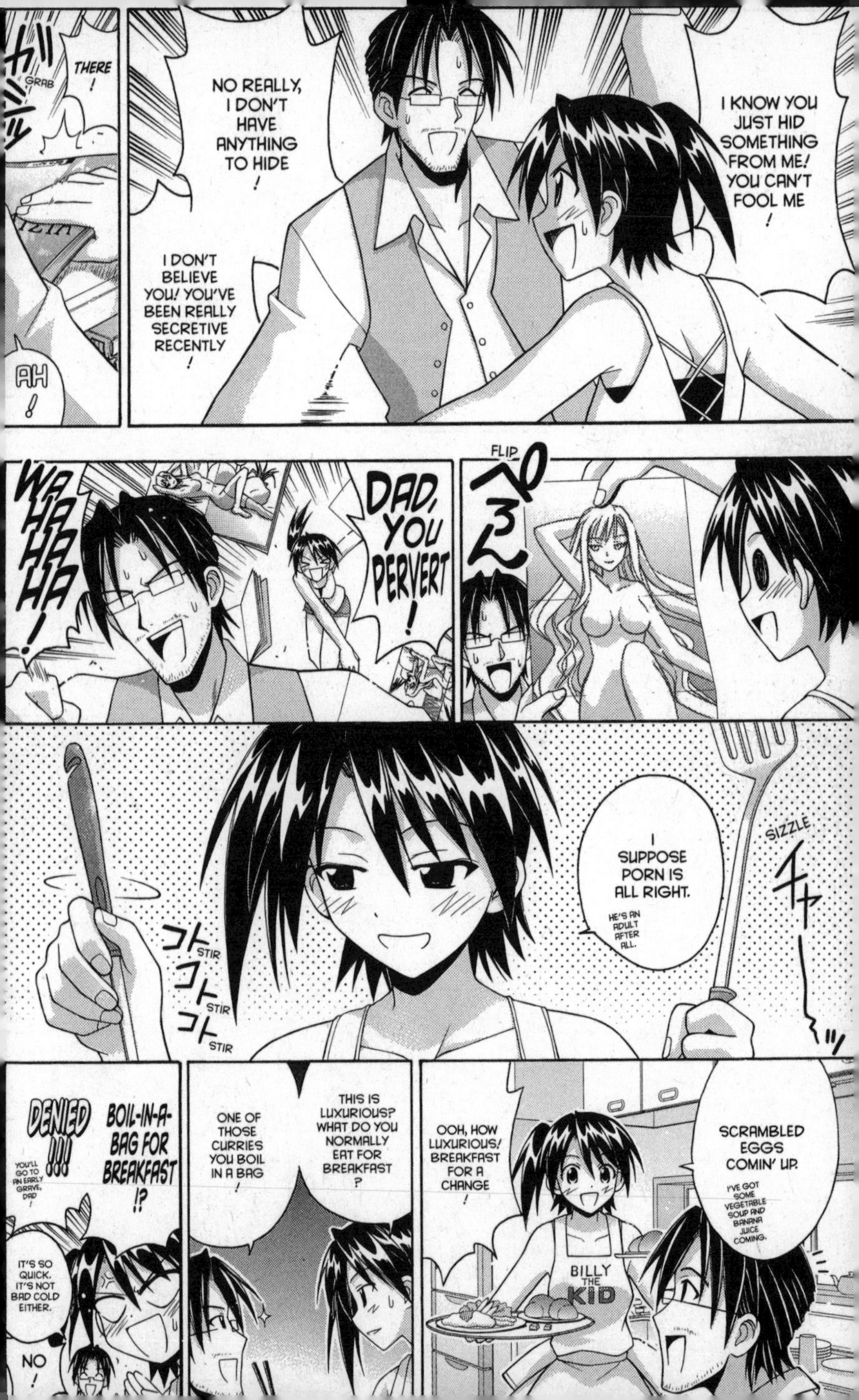
I KNOW YOU JUST HID SOMETHING FROM ME! YOU CAN'T FOOL ME!
NO REALLY, I DON'T HAVE ANYTHING TO HIDE!
I DON'T BELIEVE YOU! YOU'VE BEEN REALLY SECRETIVE RECENTLY!
THERE!
GRAB
AH!
FLIP
DAD, YOU PERVERT!
WAHAHAHA!
I SUPPOSE PORN IS ALL RIGHT.
HE'S AN ADULT AFTER ALL.
SIZZLE
STIR
STIR
STIR
SCRAMBLED EGGS COMIN' UP.
I'VE GOT SOME VEGETABLE SOUP AND BANANA JUICE COMING.
OOH, HOW LUXURIOUS! BREAKFAST FOR A CHANGE!
BILLY THE KID
THIS IS LUXURIOUS? WHAT DO YOU NORMALLY EAT FOR BREAKFAST?
ONE OF THOSE CURRIES YOU BOIL IN A BAG!
BOIL-IN-A-BAG FOR BREAKFAST!?
DENIED!!!
YOU'LL GO TO AN EARLY GRAVE, DAD!
IT'S SO QUICK. IT'S NOT BAD COLD EITHER.
NO!

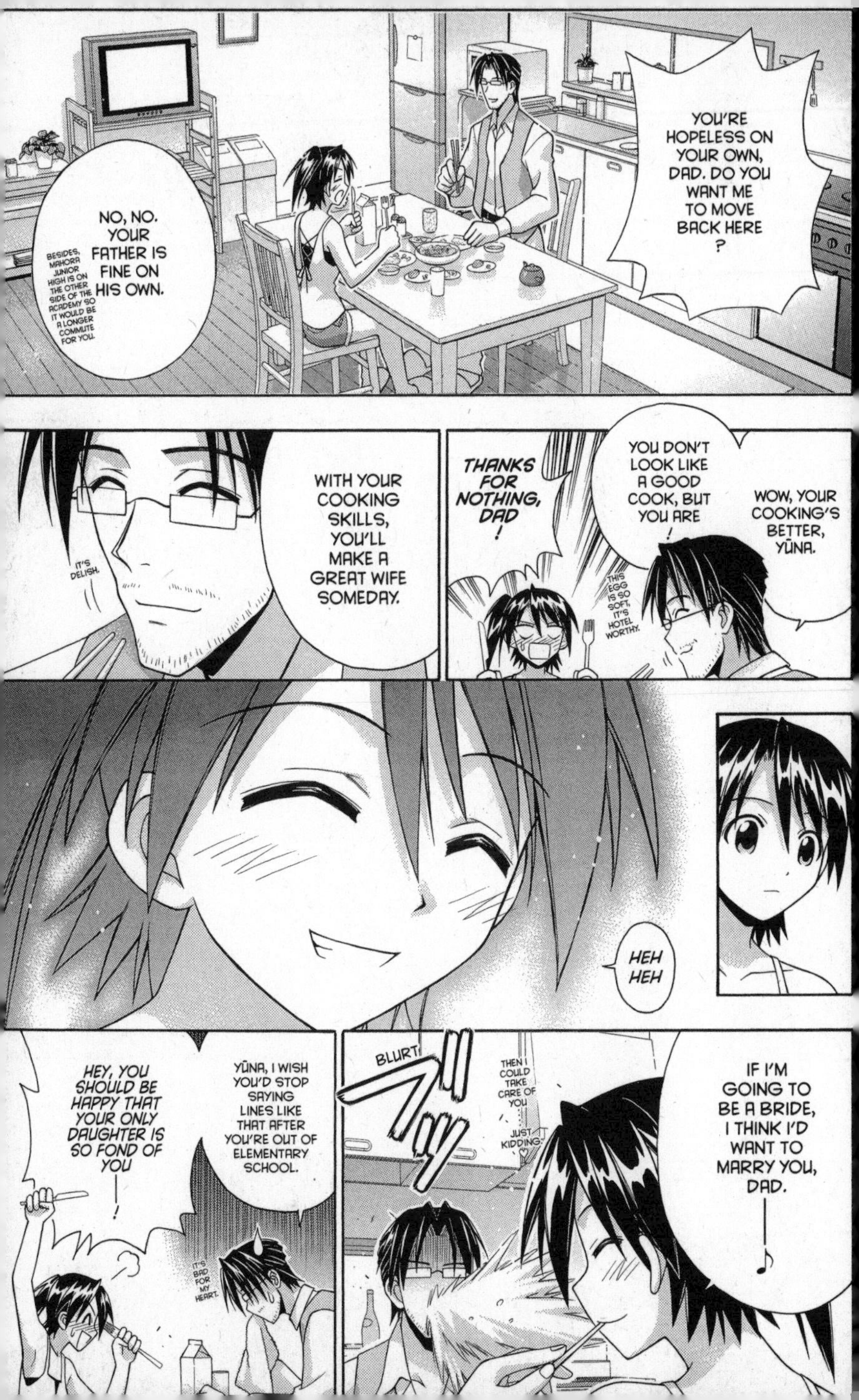
YOU'RE HOPELESS ON YOUR OWN, DAD. DO YOU WANT ME TO MOVE BACK HERE?
NO, NO. YOUR FATHER IS FINE ON HIS OWN.
BESIDES, MAHORA JUNIOR HIGH IS ON THE OTHER SIDE OF THE ACADEMY SO IT WOULD BE A LONGER COMMUTE FOR YOU.
WOW, YOUR COOKING'S BETTER, YŪNA.
YOU DON'T LOOK LIKE A GOOD COOK, BUT YOU ARE!
THIS EGG IS SO SOFT, IT'S HOTEL WORTHY.
THANKS FOR NOTHING, DAD!
WITH YOUR COOKING SKILLS, YOU'LL MAKE A GREAT WIFE SOMEDAY.
IT'S DELISH.
HEH HEH
IF I'M GOING TO BE A BRIDE, I THINK I'D WANT TO MARRY YOU, DAD! ♪
THEN I COULD TAKE CARE OF YOU.
JUST KIDDING. ♡
BLURT
YŪNA, I WISH YOU'D STOP SAYING LINES LIKE THAT AFTER YOU'RE OUT OF ELEMENTARY SCHOOL.
HEY, YOU SHOULD BE HAPPY THAT YOUR ONLY DAUGHTER IS SO FOND OF YOU!
IT'S BAD FOR MY HEART.

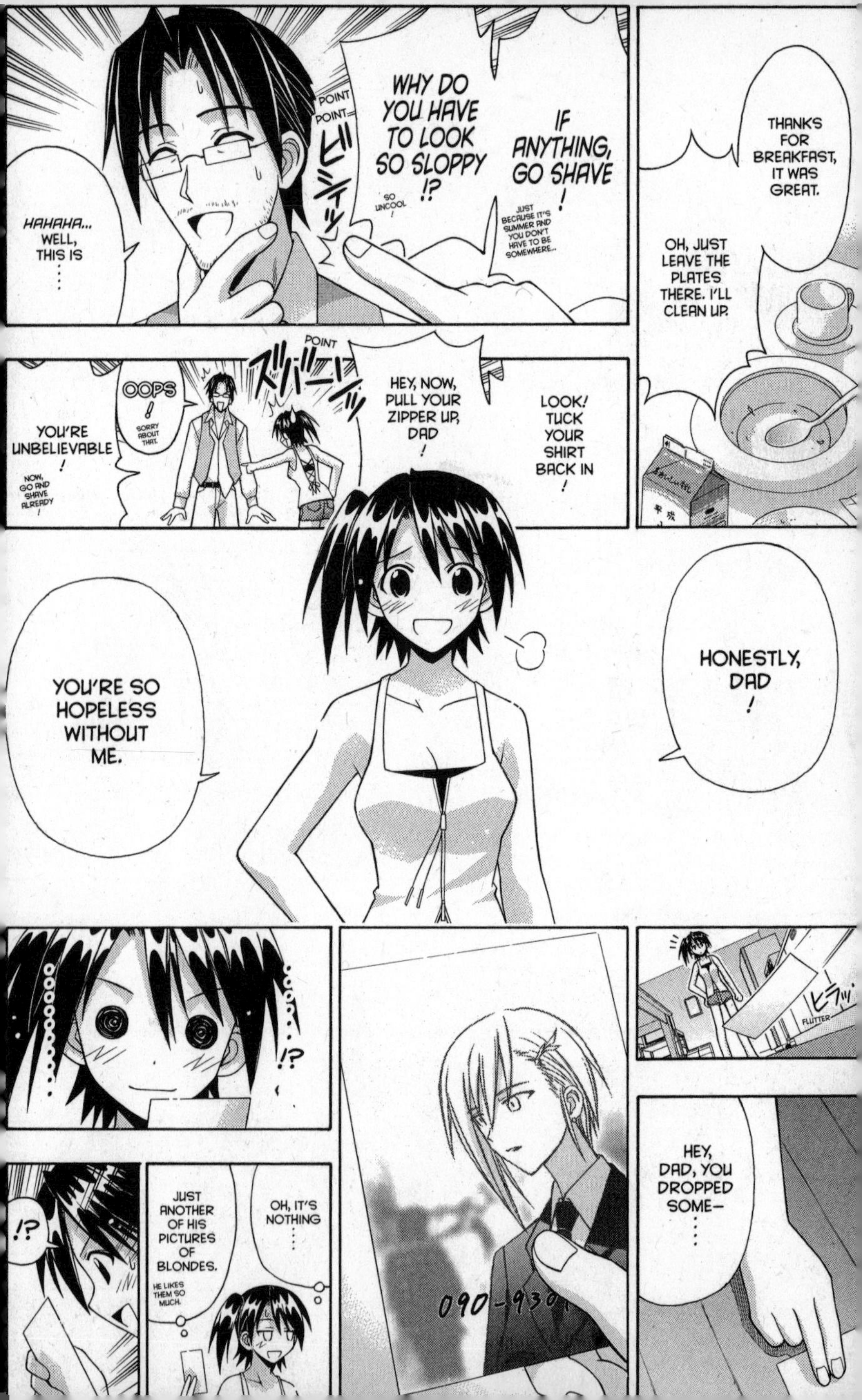
THANKS FOR BREAKFAST, IT WAS GREAT.
OH, JUST LEAVE THE PLATES THERE. I'LL CLEAN UP.
IF ANYTHING, GO SHAVE!
JUST BECAUSE IT'S SUMMER AND YOU DON'T HAVE TO BE SOMEWHERE...
WHY DO YOU HAVE TO LOOK SO SLOPPY!?
SO UNCOOL!
POINT POINT
HAHAHA... WELL, THIS IS...
LOOK! TUCK YOUR SHIRT BACK IN!
HEY, NOW, PULL YOUR ZIPPER UP, DAD!
POINT
OOPS! SORRY ABOUT THAT.
YOU'RE UNBELIEVABLE! NOW, GO AND SHAVE ALREADY!
HONESTLY, DAD!
YOU'RE SO HOPELESS WITHOUT ME.
FLUTTER
HEY, DAD, YOU DROPPED SOME—...
090-9301
...!?
OH, IT'S NOTHING...
JUST ANOTHER OF HIS PICTURES OF BLONDES.
HE LIKES THEM SO MUCH.
!?

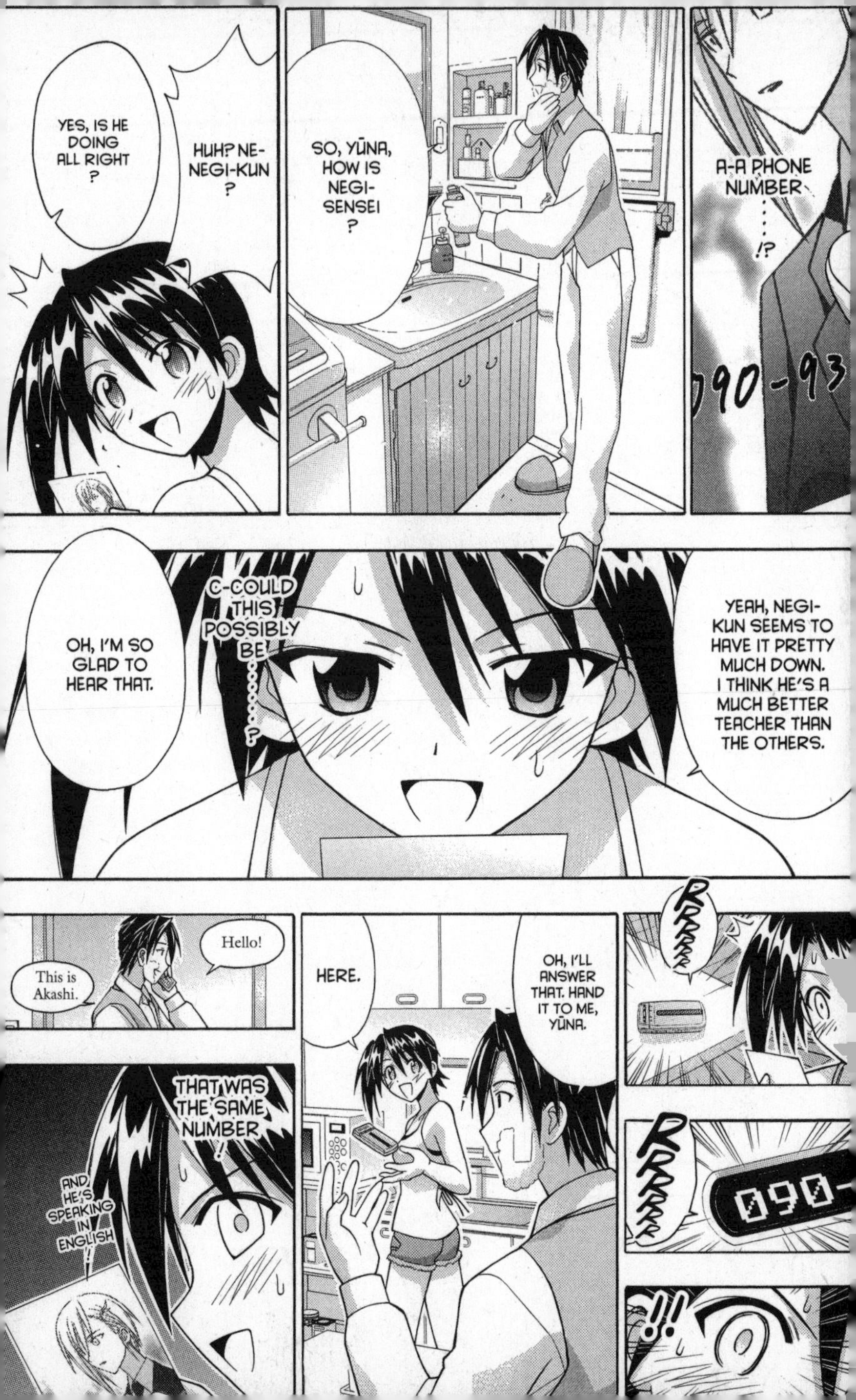
A-A PHONE NUMBER......!?
090-93
SO, YŪNA, HOW IS NEGI-SENSEI?
HUH? NE-NEGI-KUN?
YES, IS HE DOING ALL RIGHT?
YEAH, NEGI-KUN SEEMS TO HAVE IT PRETTY MUCH DOWN. I THINK HE'S A MUCH BETTER TEACHER THAN THE OTHERS.
C-COULD THIS POSSIBLY BE......?
OH, I'M SO GLAD TO HEAR THAT.
RRRRRRR
RRRRRRR
090-
!!
OH, I'LL ANSWER THAT. HAND IT TO ME, YŪNA.
HERE.
Hello!
This is Akashi.
THAT WAS THE SAME NUMBER!
AND HE'S SPEAKING IN ENGLISH!

Thank you!
SORRY, YŪNA, SOMETHING CAME UP. I HAVE TO GO.
I MIGHT BE HOME LATE, SO GO AHEAD AND HAVE DINNER WITHOUT ME, OKAY?
DOOOM
TH-THERE'S NO DOUBT ABOUT IT!!
HUH...?
WHAT!?
YOUR FATHER'S HAVING AN AFFAIR—!?
HUH? BUT, YŪNA, ISN'T YOUR DAD...
YEAH... HE'S SINGLE, RIGHT?
IF I SAY HE'S HAVING AN AFFAIR, HE IS! OKAY? HE'S CHEATING ON VARIOUS LEVELS!!
TAILING HIM IS A BIT EXTREME, ISN'T IT?
うん
SHH!
SHE'S HERE!

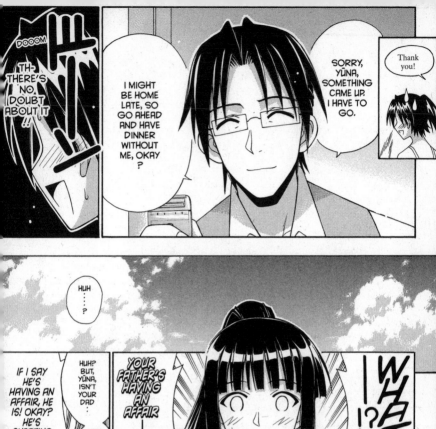

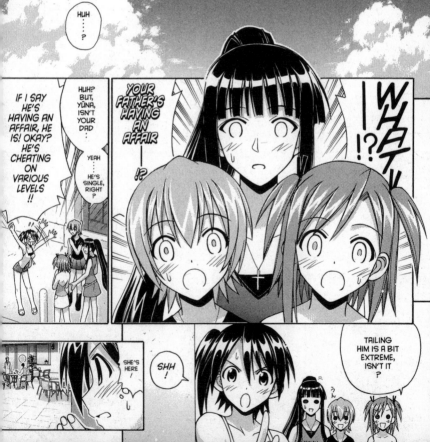

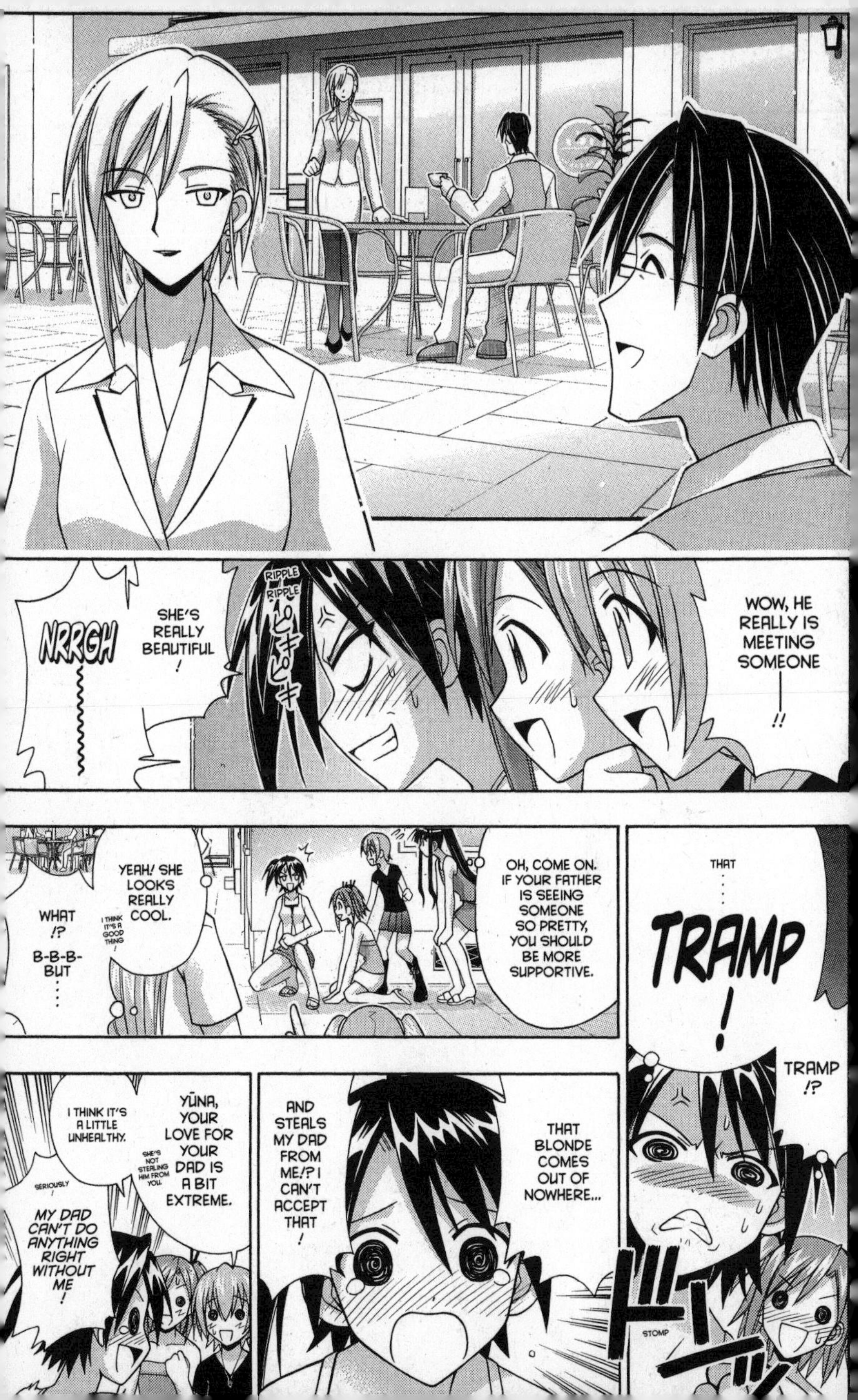
WOW, HE REALLY IS MEETING SOMEONE—!!
RIPPLE RIPPLE
SHE'S REALLY BEAUTIFUL!
NRRGH
THAT... TRAMP!
TRAMP!?
STOMP
OH, COME ON. IF YOUR FATHER IS SEEING SOMEONE SO PRETTY, YOU SHOULD BE MORE SUPPORTIVE.
YEAH! SHE LOOKS REALLY COOL.
I THINK IT'S A GOOD THING!
WHAT!? B-B-B-BUT....
THAT BLONDE COMES OUT OF NOWHERE...
AND STEALS MY DAD FROM ME!? I CAN'T ACCEPT THAT!
YŪNA, YOUR LOVE FOR YOUR DAD IS A BIT EXTREME.
SHE'S NOT STEALING HIM FROM YOU.
I THINK IT'S A LITTLE UNHEALTHY.
SERIOUSLY!
MY DAD CAN'T DO ANYTHING RIGHT WITHOUT ME!

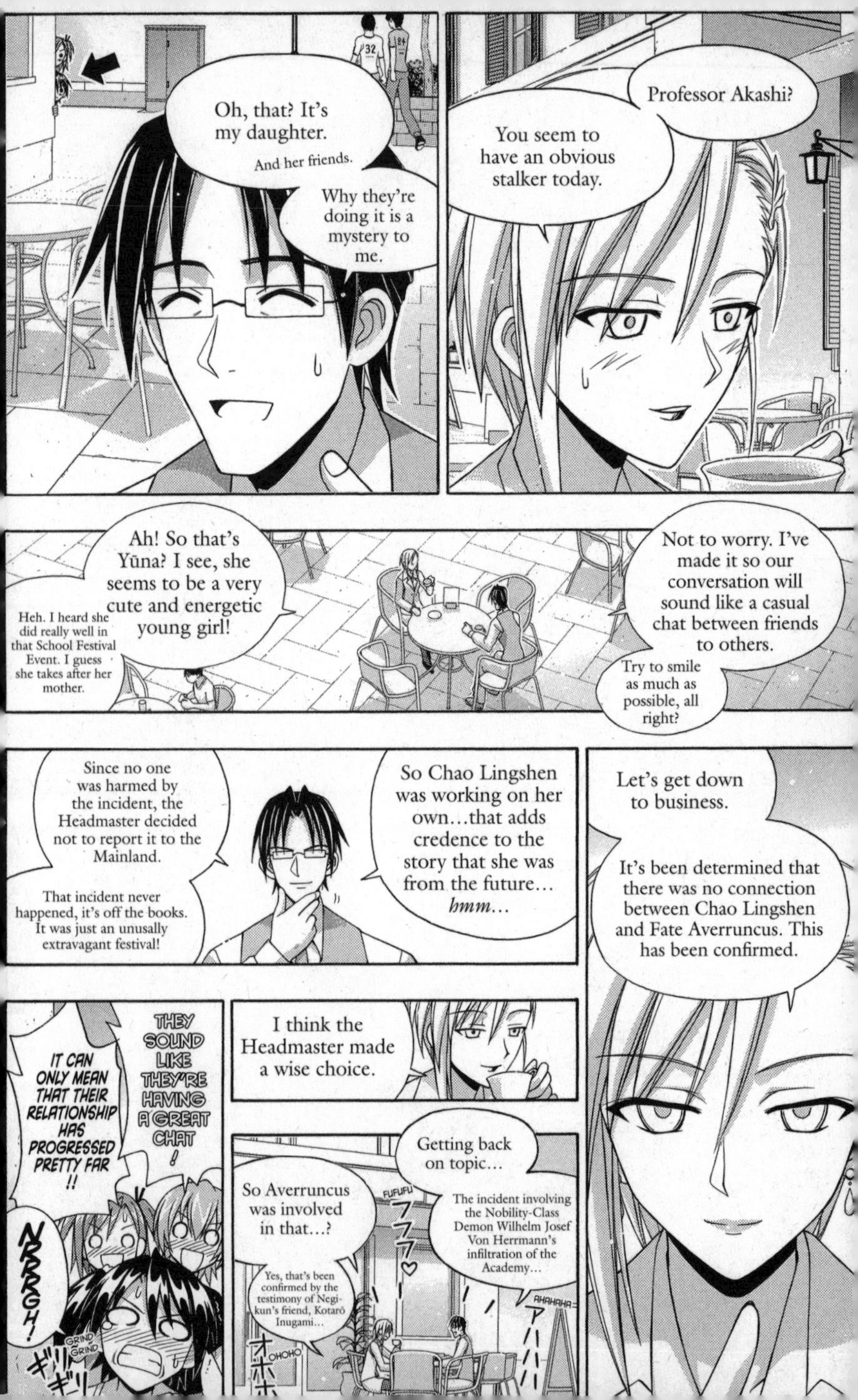
Professor Akashi?
You seem to have an obvious stalker today.
Oh, that? It's my daughter.
And her friends.
Why they're doing it is a mystery to me.
Not to worry. I've made it so our conversation will sound like a casual chat between friends to others.
Try to smile as much as possible, all right?
Ah! So that's Yūna? I see, she seems to be a very cute and energetic young girl!
Heh. I heard she did really well in that School Festival Event. I guess she takes after her mother.
Let's get down to business.
It's been determined that there was no connection between Chao Lingshen and Fate Averruncus. This has been confirmed.
So Chao Lingshen was working on her own…that adds credence to the story that she was from the future… *hmm*…
Since no one was harmed by the incident, the Headmaster decided not to report it to the Mainland.
That incident never happened, it's off the books. It was just an unusally extravagant festival!
I think the Headmaster made a wise choice.
Getting back on topic…
The incident involving the Nobility-Class Demon Wilhelm Josef Von Herrmann's infiltration of the Academy…
AHAHAHA
So Averruncus was involved in that…?
FUFUFU
Yes, that's been confirmed by the testimony of Negi-kun's friend, Kotarō Inugami…
OHOHO
THEY SOUND LIKE THEY'RE HAVING A GREAT CHAT!
IT CAN ONLY MEAN THAT THEIR RELATIONSHIP HAS PROGRESSED PRETTY FAR!!
NRRRGH!
GRIND GRIND

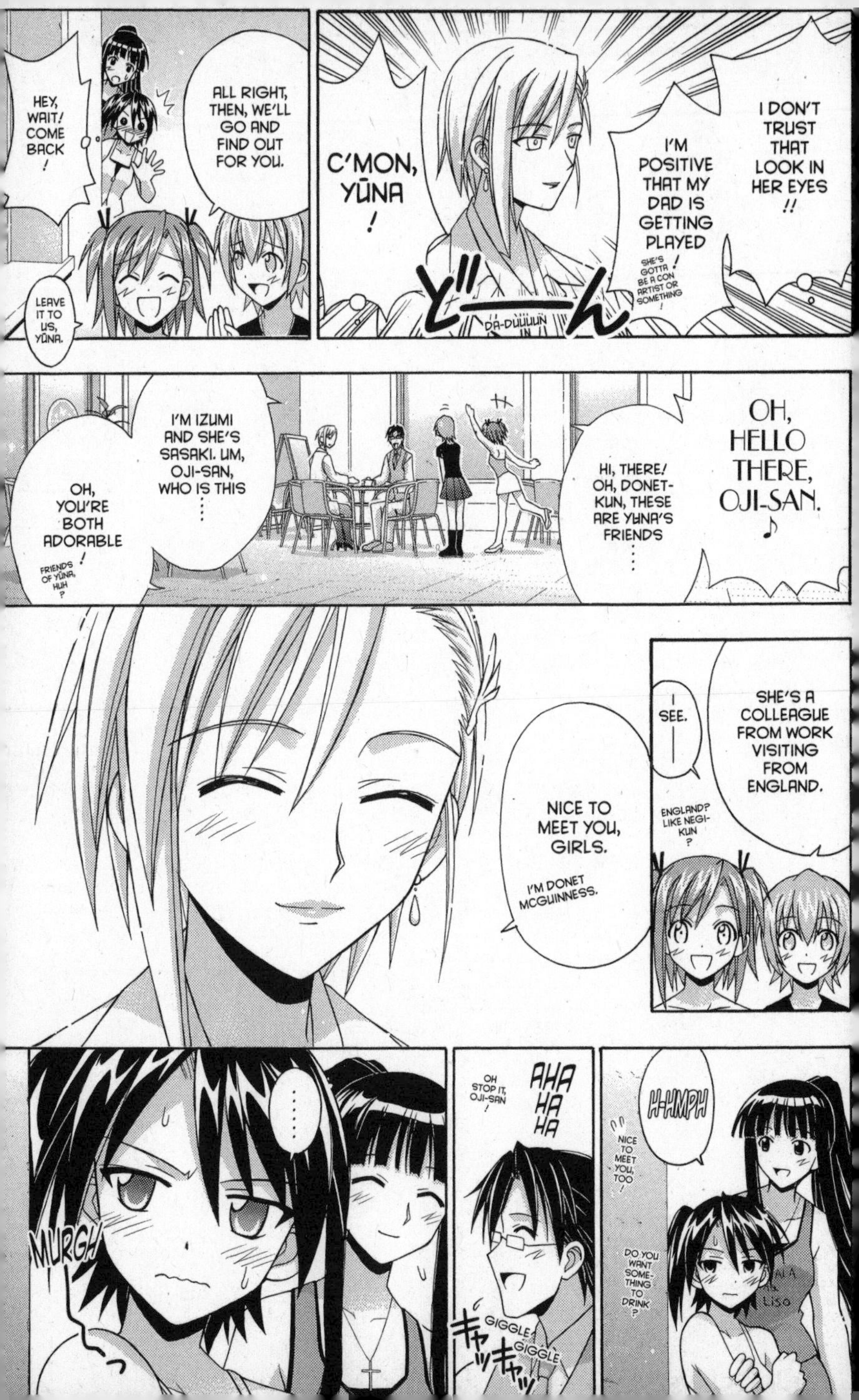
I DON'T TRUST THAT LOOK IN HER EYES!!
I'M POSITIVE THAT MY DAD IS GETTING PLAYED!
SHE'S GOTTA BE A CON ARTIST OR SOMETHING!
C'MON, YŪNA!
どーん
DA-DUUUUN
ALL RIGHT, THEN, WE'LL GO AND FIND OUT FOR YOU.
HEY, WAIT! COME BACK!
LEAVE IT TO US, YŪNA.
OH, HELLO THERE, OJI-SAN. ♪
HI, THERE! OH, DONET-KUN, THESE ARE YUNA'S FRIENDS...
I'M IZUMI AND SHE'S SASAKI. UM, OJI-SAN, WHO IS THIS...
OH, YOU'RE BOTH ADORABLE!
FRIENDS OF YŪNA, HUH?
SHE'S A COLLEAGUE FROM WORK VISITING FROM ENGLAND.
I SEE.
ENGLAND? LIKE NEGI-KUN?
NICE TO MEET YOU, GIRLS.
I'M DONET MCGUINNESS.
H-HMPH
NICE TO MEET YOU, TOO!
DO YOU WANT SOMETHING TO DRINK?
AHA HA HA
OH STOP IT, OJI-SAN!
ギャッキャッ
GIGGLE GIGGLE
......
MURGH

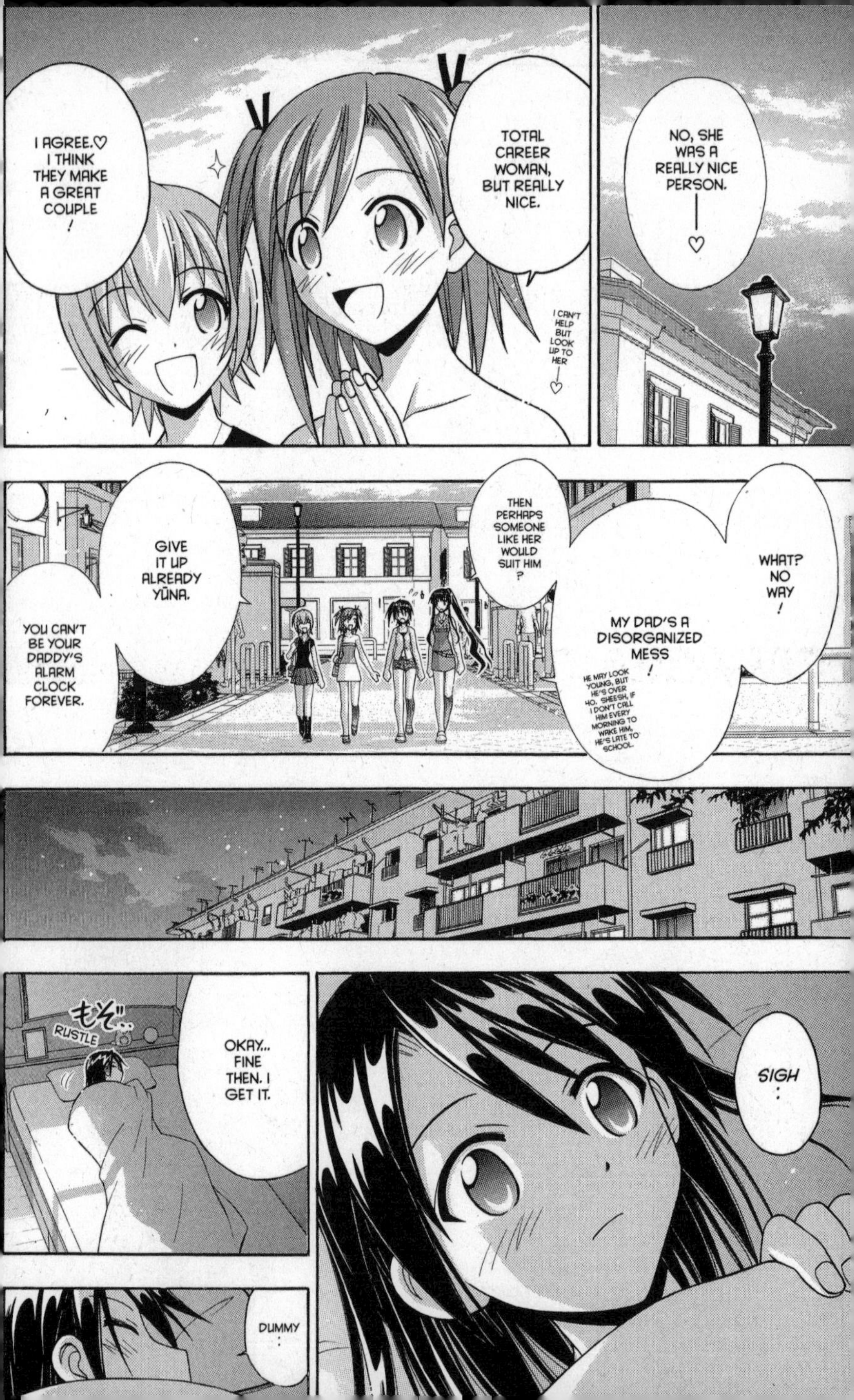
NO, SHE WAS A REALLY NICE PERSON. —♡
TOTAL CAREER WOMAN, BUT REALLY NICE.
I CAN'T HELP BUT LOOK UP TO HER —♡
I AGREE.♡ I THINK THEY MAKE A GREAT COUPLE!
THEN PERHAPS SOMEONE LIKE HER WOULD SUIT HIM?
WHAT? NO WAY!
MY DAD'S A DISORGANIZED MESS!
HE MAY LOOK YOUNG, BUT HE'S OVER 40. SHEESH, IF I DON'T CALL HIM EVERY MORNING TO WAKE HIM, HE'S LATE TO SCHOOL.
GIVE IT UP ALREADY YŪNA.
YOU CAN'T BE YOUR DADDY'S ALARM CLOCK FOREVER.
SIGH...
もぞ...
RUSTLE
OKAY... FINE THEN. I GET IT.
DUMMY...

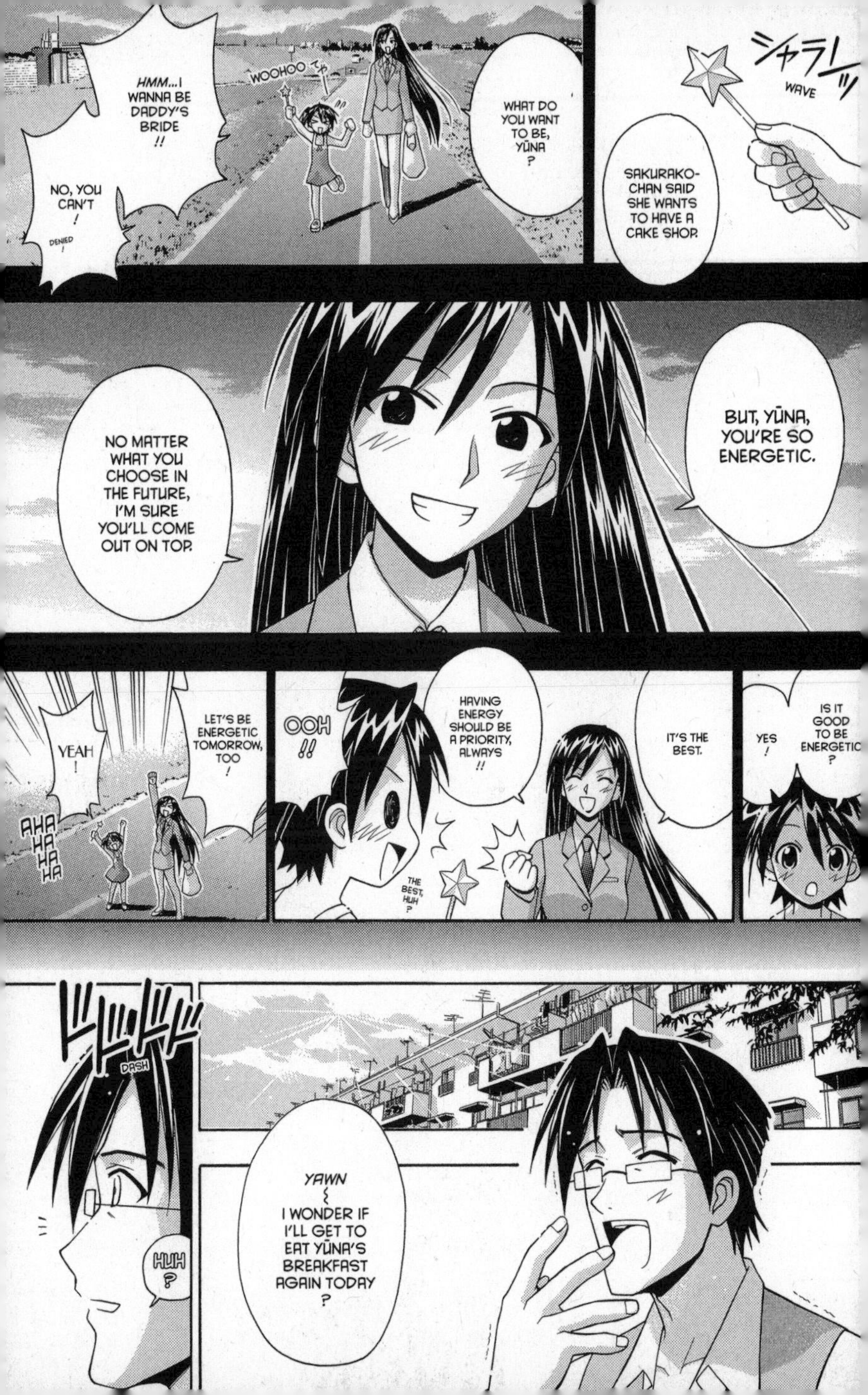
WAVE
SAKURAKO-CHAN SAID SHE WANTS TO HAVE A CAKE SHOP.
WHAT DO YOU WANT TO BE, YŪNA?
WOOHOO
HMM...I WANNA BE DADDY'S BRIDE!!
NO, YOU CAN'T!
DENIED!
BUT, YŪNA, YOU'RE SO ENERGETIC.
NO MATTER WHAT YOU CHOOSE IN THE FUTURE, I'M SURE YOU'LL COME OUT ON TOP.
IS IT GOOD TO BE ENERGETIC?
YES!
IT'S THE BEST.
THE BEST, HUH?
HAVING ENERGY SHOULD BE A PRIORITY, ALWAYS!!
OOH!!
LET'S BE ENERGETIC TOMORROW, TOO!
YEAH!
AHAHAHAHA
YAWN~ I WONDER IF I'LL GET TO EAT YŪNA'S BREAKFAST AGAIN TODAY?
DASH
HUH?

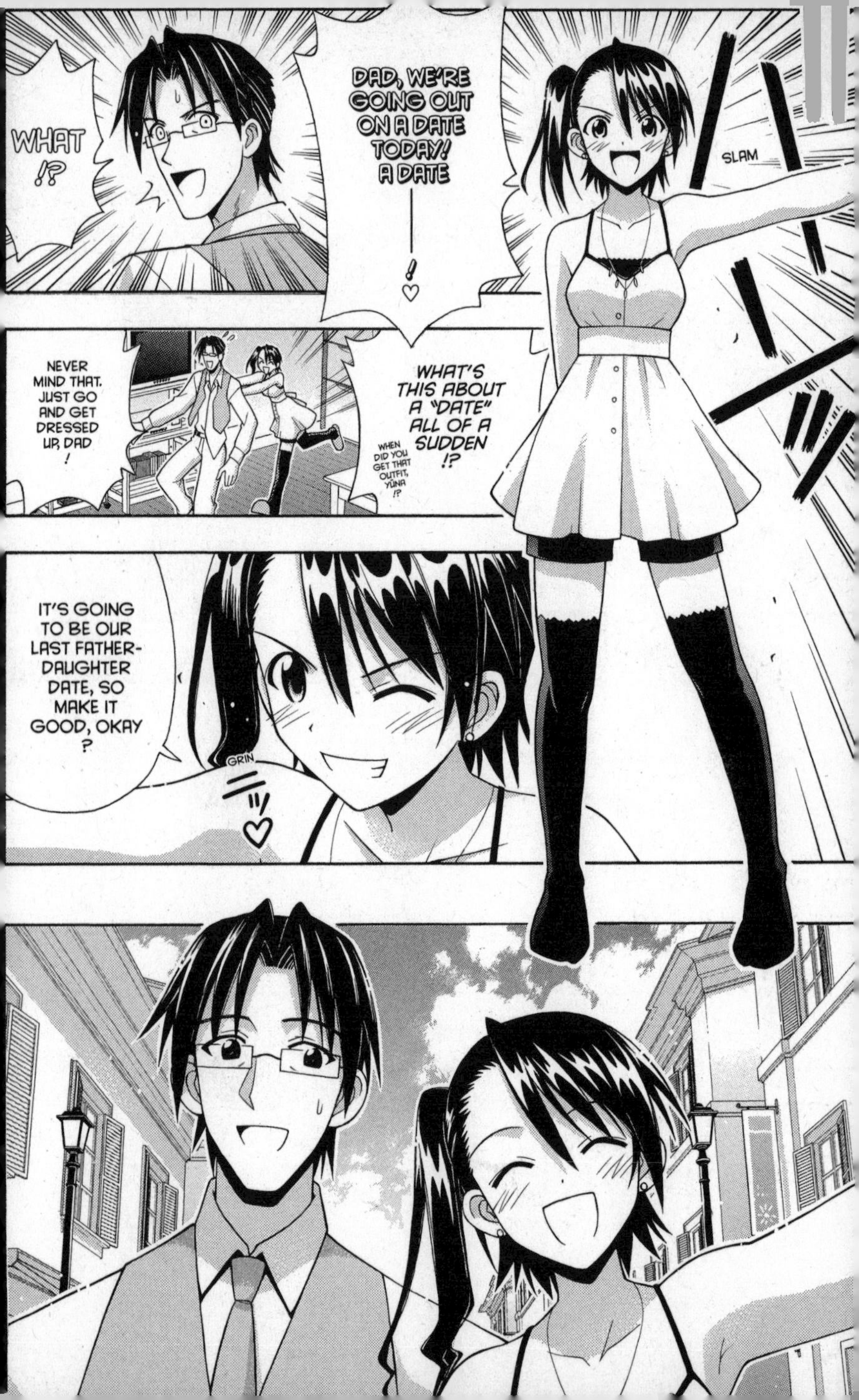
SLAM
DAD, WE'RE GOING OUT ON A DATE TODAY! A DATE !♥
WHAT !?
WHAT'S THIS ABOUT A "DATE" ALL OF A SUDDEN !?
WHEN DID YOU GET THAT OUTFIT, YŪNA !?
NEVER MIND THAT. JUST GO AND GET DRESSED UP, DAD !
IT'S GOING TO BE OUR LAST FATHER-DAUGHTER DATE, SO MAKE IT GOOD, OKAY ?
GRIN ♥

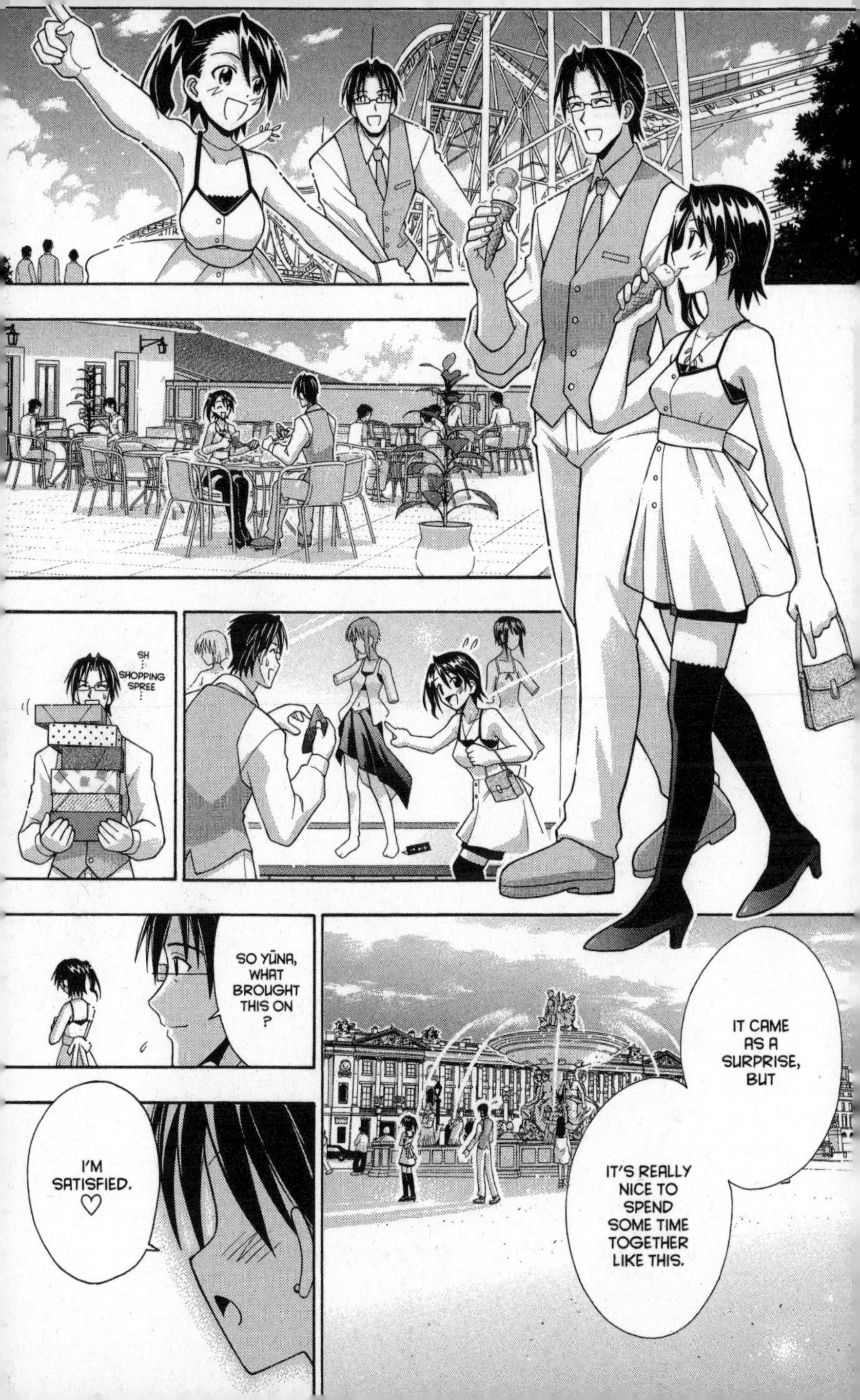
SH... SHOPPING SPREE...
IT CAME AS A SURPRISE, BUT
IT'S REALLY NICE TO SPEND SOME TIME TOGETHER LIKE THIS.
SO YŪNA, WHAT BROUGHT THIS ON?
I'M SATISFIED. ♡

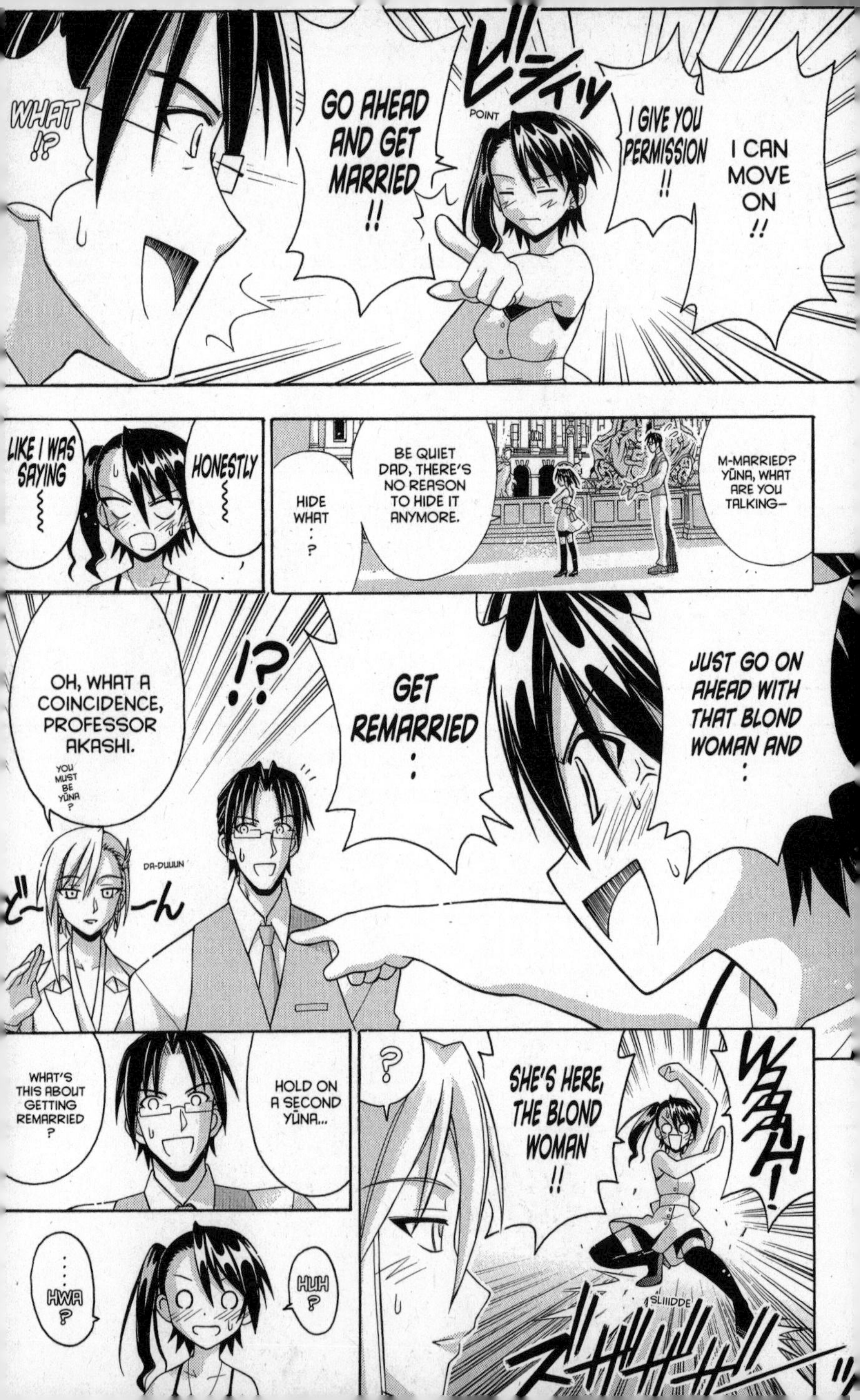
I CAN MOVE ON !!
I GIVE YOU PERMISSION !!
POINT
GO AHEAD AND GET MARRIED !!
WHAT !?
M-MARRIED? YŪNA, WHAT ARE YOU TALKING—
BE QUIET DAD, THERE'S NO REASON TO HIDE IT ANYMORE.
HIDE WHAT . . . ?
HONESTLY ~~~
LIKE I WAS SAYING ~~~
JUST GO ON AHEAD WITH THAT BLOND WOMAN AND :
GET REMARRIED :
!?
OH, WHAT A COINCIDENCE, PROFESSOR AKASHI.
YOU MUST BE YŪNA ?
DA-DUUUN
SHE'S HERE, THE BLOND WOMAN !!
?
SLIIIDDE
HOLD ON A SECOND YŪNA...
WHAT'S THIS ABOUT GETTING REMARRIED ?
HUH ?
. . . . HWA ?

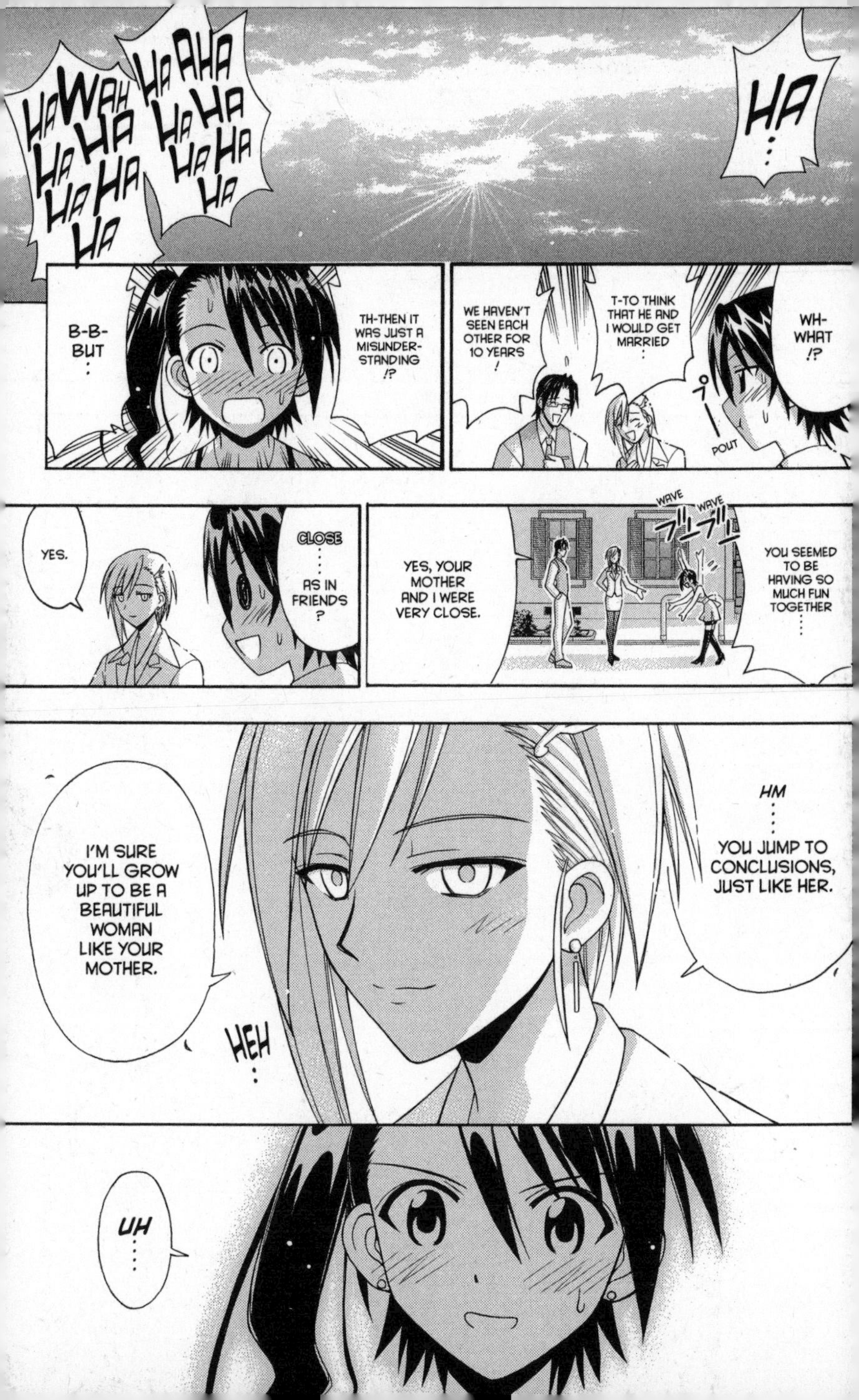
HA...
HA AHA HA HA HA HA HA
HAWAH HA HA HA HA HA HA HA
WH-WHAT!?
T-TO THINK THAT HE AND I WOULD GET MARRIED...
WE HAVEN'T SEEN EACH OTHER FOR 10 YEARS!
POUT
TH-THEN IT WAS JUST A MISUNDER-STANDING!?
B-B-BUT...
YOU SEEMED TO BE HAVING SO MUCH FUN TOGETHER...
WAVE WAVE
YES, YOUR MOTHER AND I WERE VERY CLOSE.
CLOSE... AS IN FRIENDS?
YES.
HM... YOU JUMP TO CONCLUSIONS, JUST LIKE HER.
I'M SURE YOU'LL GROW UP TO BE A BEAUTIFUL WOMAN LIKE YOUR MOTHER.
HEH...
UH...

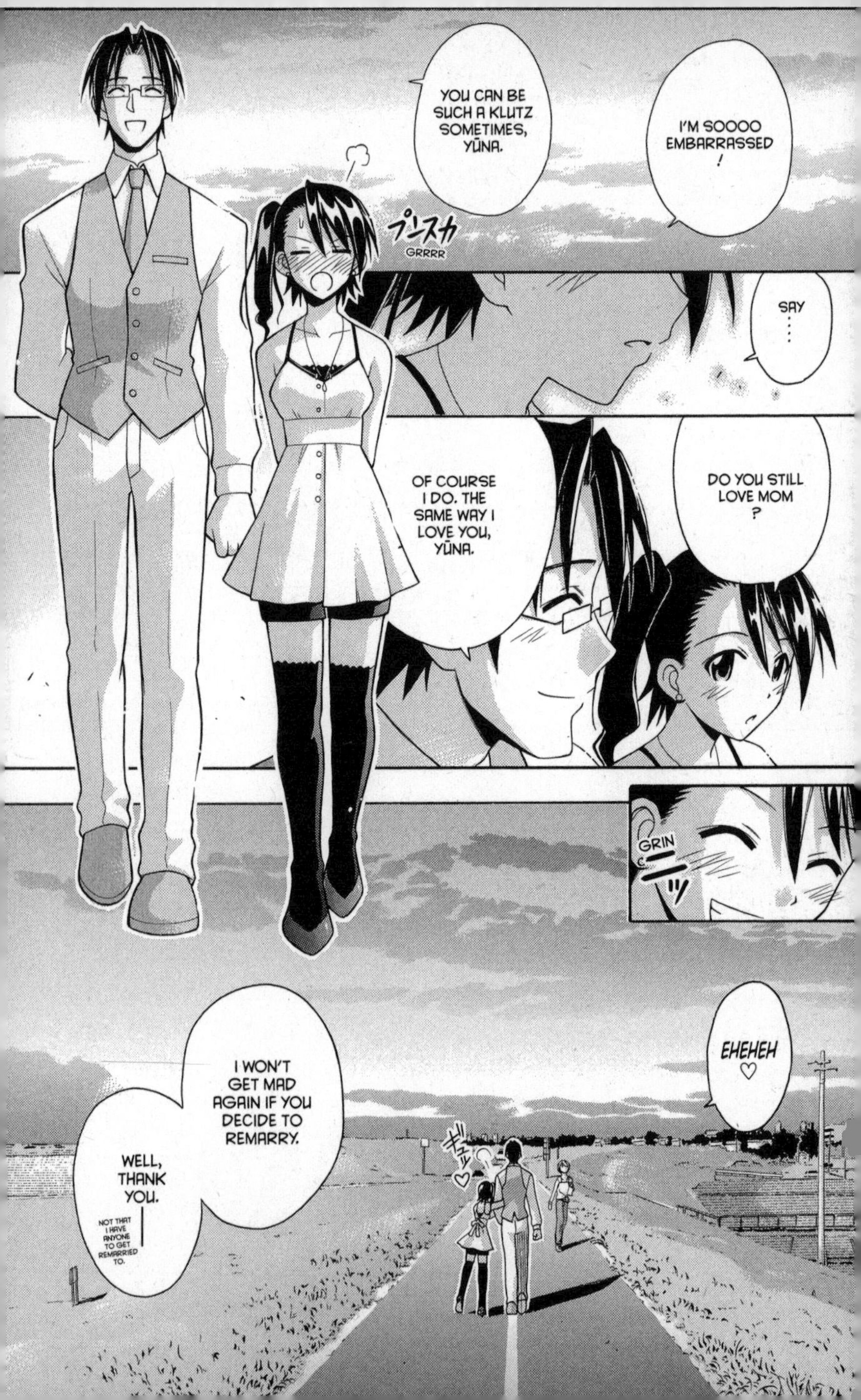
I'M SOOOO EMBARRASSED !
YOU CAN BE SUCH A KLUTZ SOMETIMES, YŪNA.
プンスカ
GRRRR
SAY ....
DO YOU STILL LOVE MOM ?
OF COURSE I DO. THE SAME WAY I LOVE YOU, YŪNA.
GRIN
EHEHEH ♡
I WON'T GET MAD AGAIN IF YOU DECIDE TO REMARRY.
WELL, THANK YOU.
NOT THAT I HAVE ANYONE TO GET REMARRIED TO.

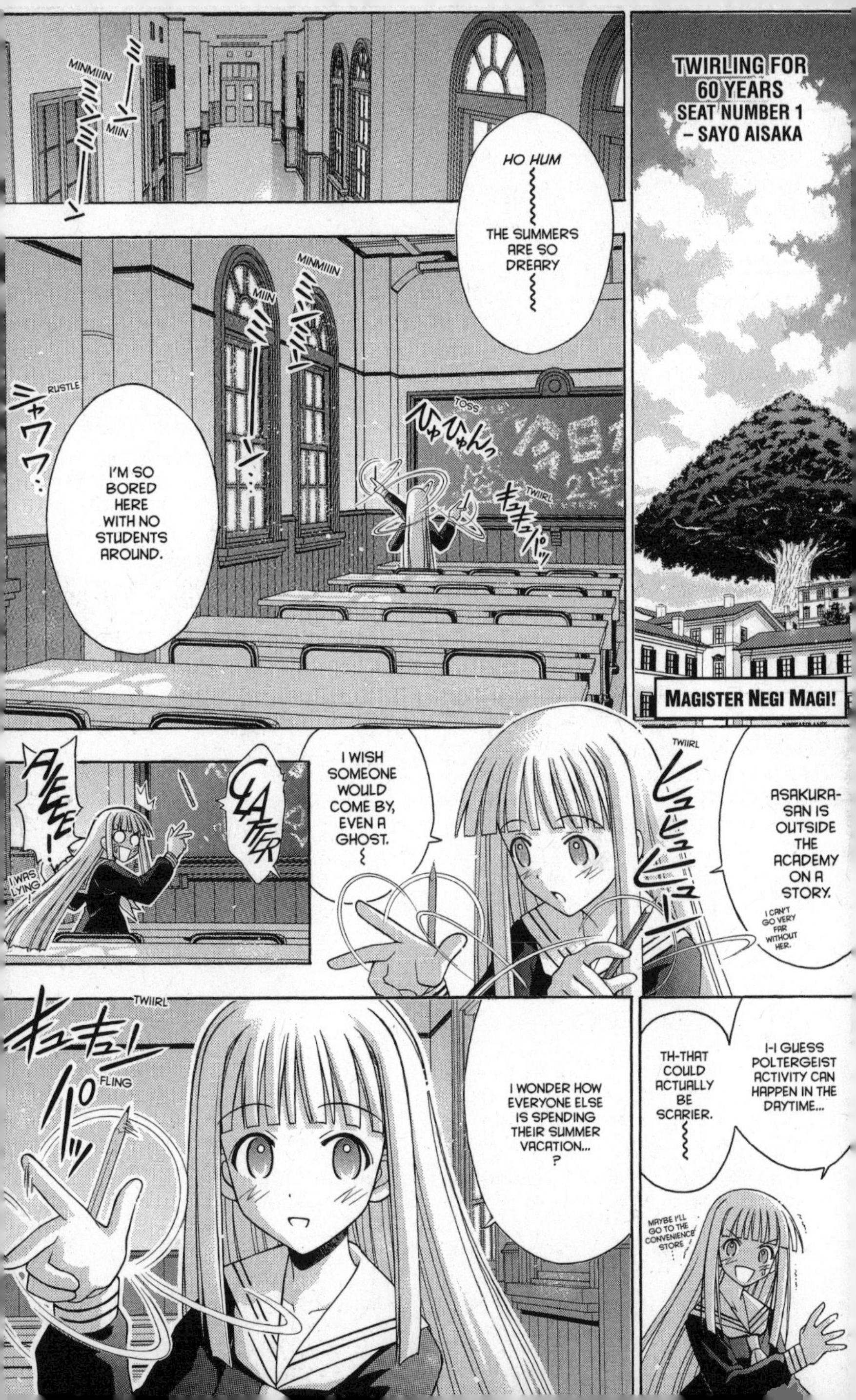
TWIRLING FOR 60 YEARS
SEAT NUMBER 1 – SAYO AISAKA
MAGISTER NEGI MAGI!
MINMIIIN
MIIN
HO HUM~ THE SUMMERS ARE SO DREARY~
MINMIIIN
MIIN
RUSTLE
I'M SO BORED HERE WITH NO STUDENTS AROUND.
TOSS
TWIRL
TWIIRL
ASAKURA-SAN IS OUTSIDE THE ACADEMY ON A STORY.
I CAN'T GO VERY FAR WITHOUT HER.
I WISH SOMEONE WOULD COME BY, EVEN A GHOST.
CLATTER
AIEEE!
I WAS LYING!
I-I GUESS POLTERGEIST ACTIVITY CAN HAPPEN IN THE DAYTIME...
TH-THAT COULD ACTUALLY BE SCARIER.
MAYBE I'LL GO TO THE CONVENIENCE STORE
I WONDER HOW EVERYONE ELSE IS SPENDING THEIR SUMMER VACATION...?
TWIIRL
FLING

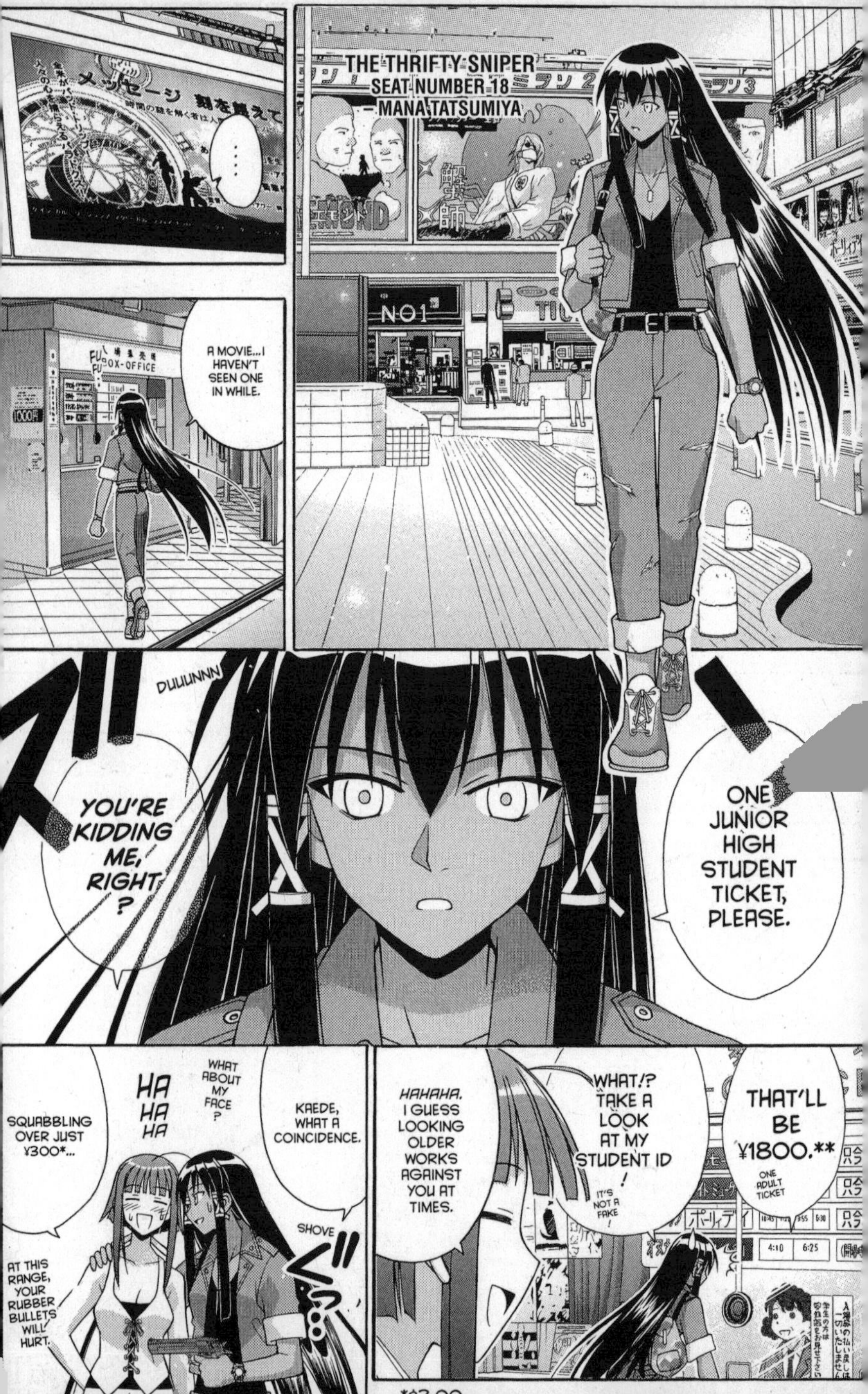
THE THRIFTY SNIPER
SEAT NUMBER 18
MANA TATSUMIYA
NO1
...
FU FU
BOX-OFFICE
A MOVIE...I HAVEN'T SEEN ONE IN WHILE.
ONE JUNIOR HIGH STUDENT TICKET, PLEASE.
DUUUNNN
YOU'RE KIDDING ME, RIGHT?
THAT'LL BE ¥1800.**
ONE ADULT TICKET
WHAT!? TAKE A LOOK AT MY STUDENT ID!
IT'S NOT A FAKE!
HAHAHA. I GUESS LOOKING OLDER WORKS AGAINST YOU AT TIMES.
KAEDE, WHAT A COINCIDENCE.
WHAT ABOUT MY FACE?
HA HA HA
SQUABBLING OVER JUST ¥300*...
SHOVE
AT THIS RANGE, YOUR RUBBER BULLETS WILL HURT.

*$3.00

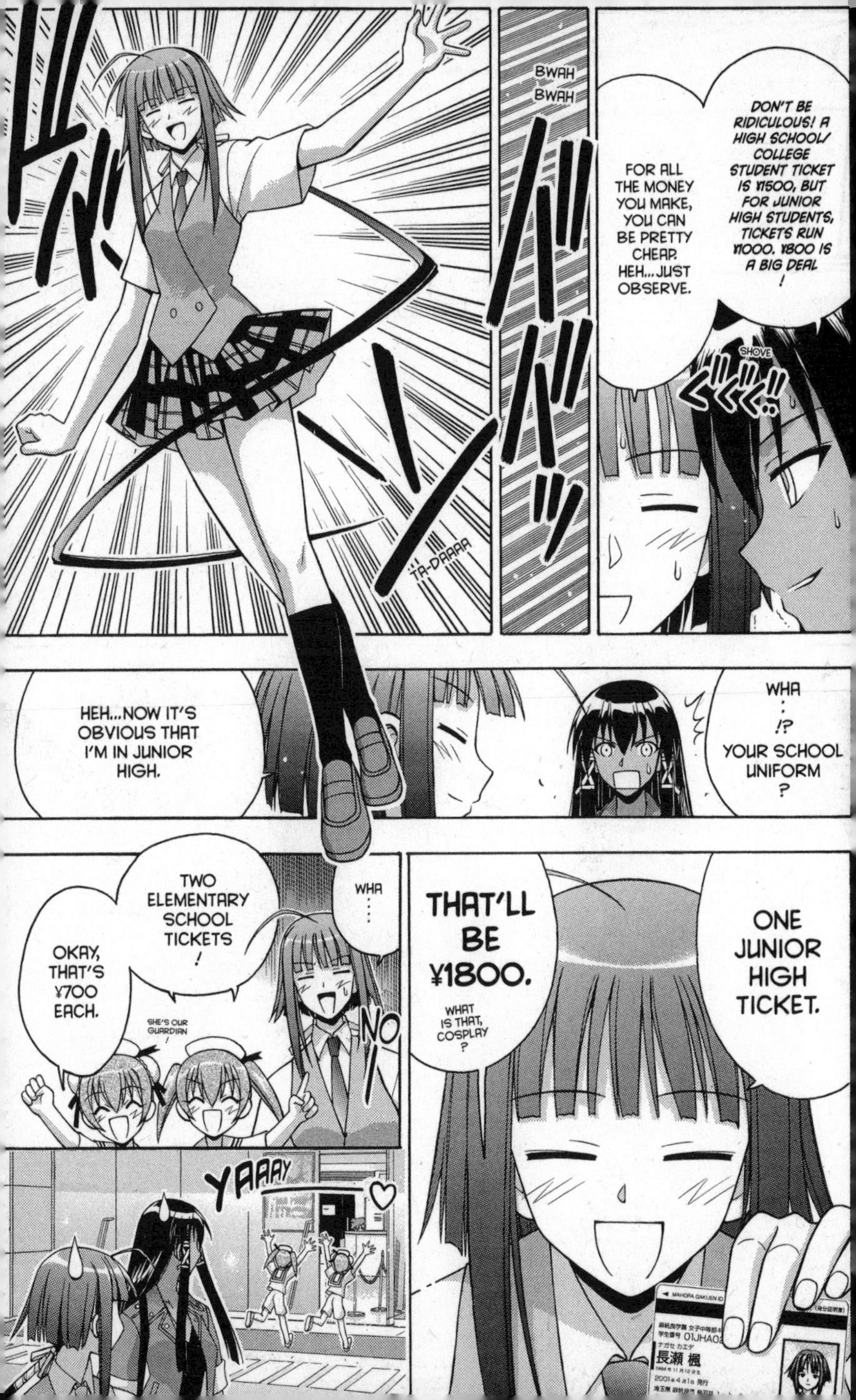

DON'T BE RIDICULOUS! A HIGH SCHOOL/ COLLEGE STUDENT TICKET IS ¥1500, BUT FOR JUNIOR HIGH STUDENTS, TICKETS RUN ¥1000. ¥800 IS A BIG DEAL!
FOR ALL THE MONEY YOU MAKE, YOU CAN BE PRETTY CHEAP. HEH...JUST OBSERVE.
SHOVE
BWAH BWAH
TA-DAAAA
WHA... !? YOUR SCHOOL UNIFORM?
HEH...NOW IT'S OBVIOUS THAT I'M IN JUNIOR HIGH.
ONE JUNIOR HIGH TICKET.
THAT'LL BE ¥1800.
WHAT IS THAT, COSPLAY?
TWO ELEMENTARY SCHOOL TICKETS!
WHA...
OKAY, THAT'S ¥700 EACH.
SHE'S OUR GUARDIAN!
NO!
YAAAY

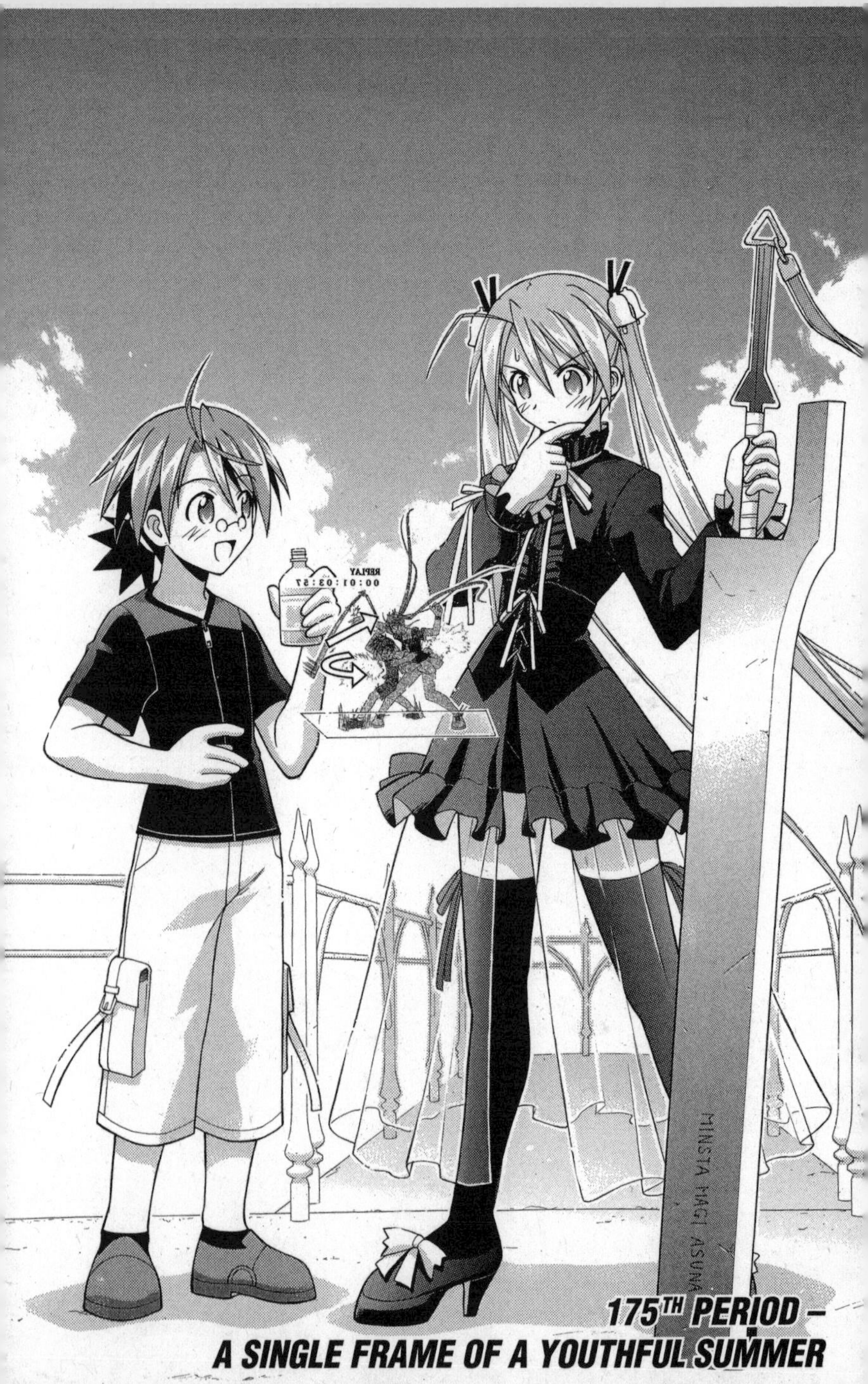
REPLAY
00:01:03:57
MINSTA MAGI ASUNA

175TH PERIOD – A SINGLE FRAME OF A YOUTHFUL SUMMER

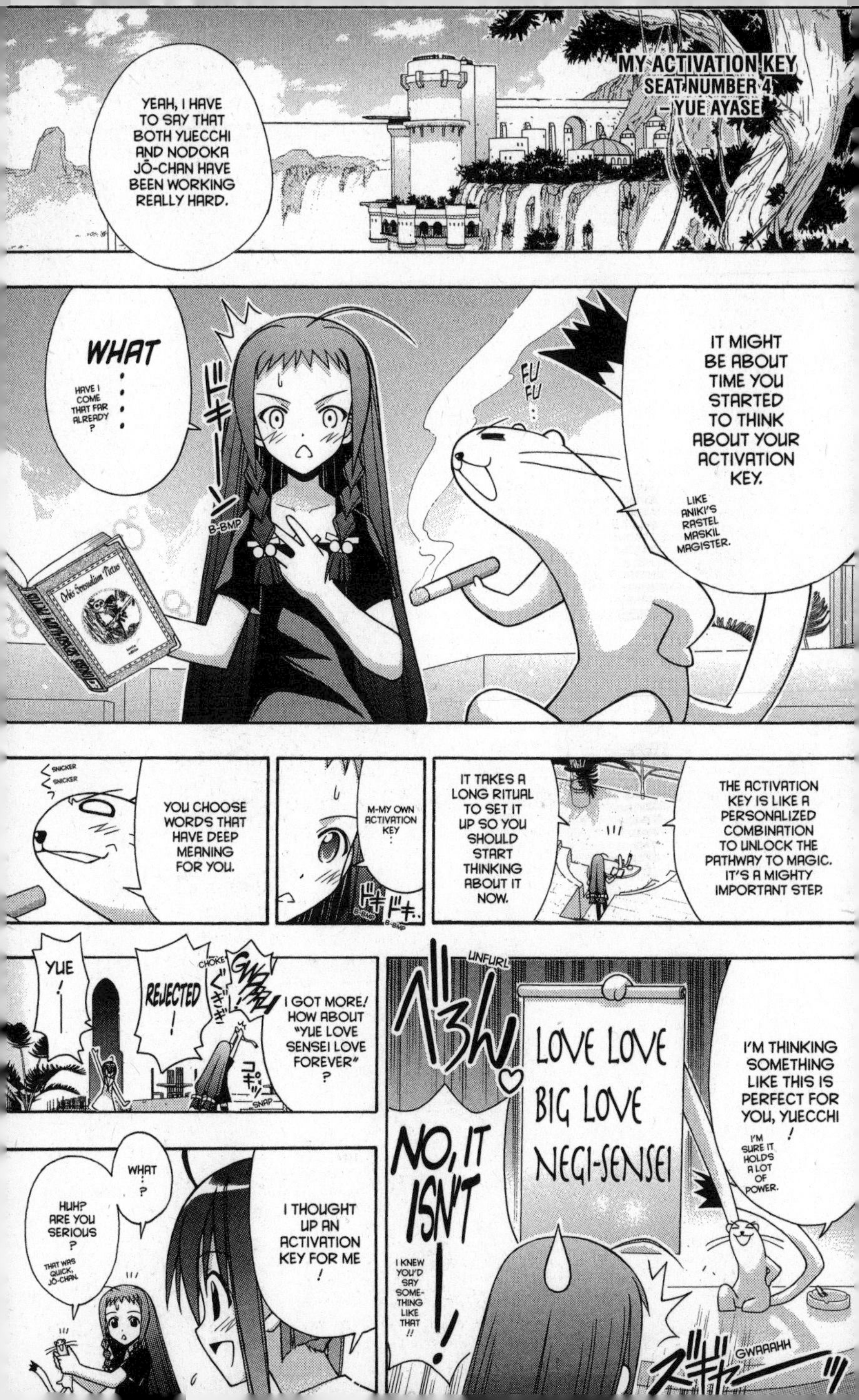
MY ACTIVATION KEY SEAT NUMBER 4 – YUE AYASE
YEAH, I HAVE TO SAY THAT BOTH YUECCHI AND NODOKA JŌ-CHAN HAVE BEEN WORKING REALLY HARD.
IT MIGHT BE ABOUT TIME YOU STARTED TO THINK ABOUT YOUR ACTIVATION KEY.
LIKE ANIKI'S RASTEL MASKIL MAGISTER.
FU FU...
B-BMP
WHAT...
HAVE I COME THAT FAR ALREADY?
THE ACTIVATION KEY IS LIKE A PERSONALIZED COMBINATION TO UNLOCK THE PATHWAY TO MAGIC. IT'S A MIGHTY IMPORTANT STEP.
IT TAKES A LONG RITUAL TO SET IT UP SO YOU SHOULD START THINKING ABOUT IT NOW.
M-MY OWN ACTIVATION KEY...
B-BMP B-BMP
SNICKER SNICKER
YOU CHOOSE WORDS THAT HAVE DEEP MEANING FOR YOU.
I'M THINKING SOMETHING LIKE THIS IS PERFECT FOR YOU, YUECCHI!
I'M SURE IT HOLDS A LOT OF POWER.
UNFURL
LOVE LOVE BIG LOVE NEGI-SENSEI
NO, IT ISN'T!
I KNEW YOU'D SAY SOMETHING LIKE THAT!!
GWAAAHH
I GOT MORE! HOW ABOUT "YUE LOVE SENSEI LOVE FOREVER"?
CHOKE
GWAAH!
SNAP
REJECTED!
YUE!
I THOUGHT UP AN ACTIVATION KEY FOR ME!
WHAT...?
HUH? ARE YOU SERIOUS?
THAT WAS QUICK, JŌ-CHAN.

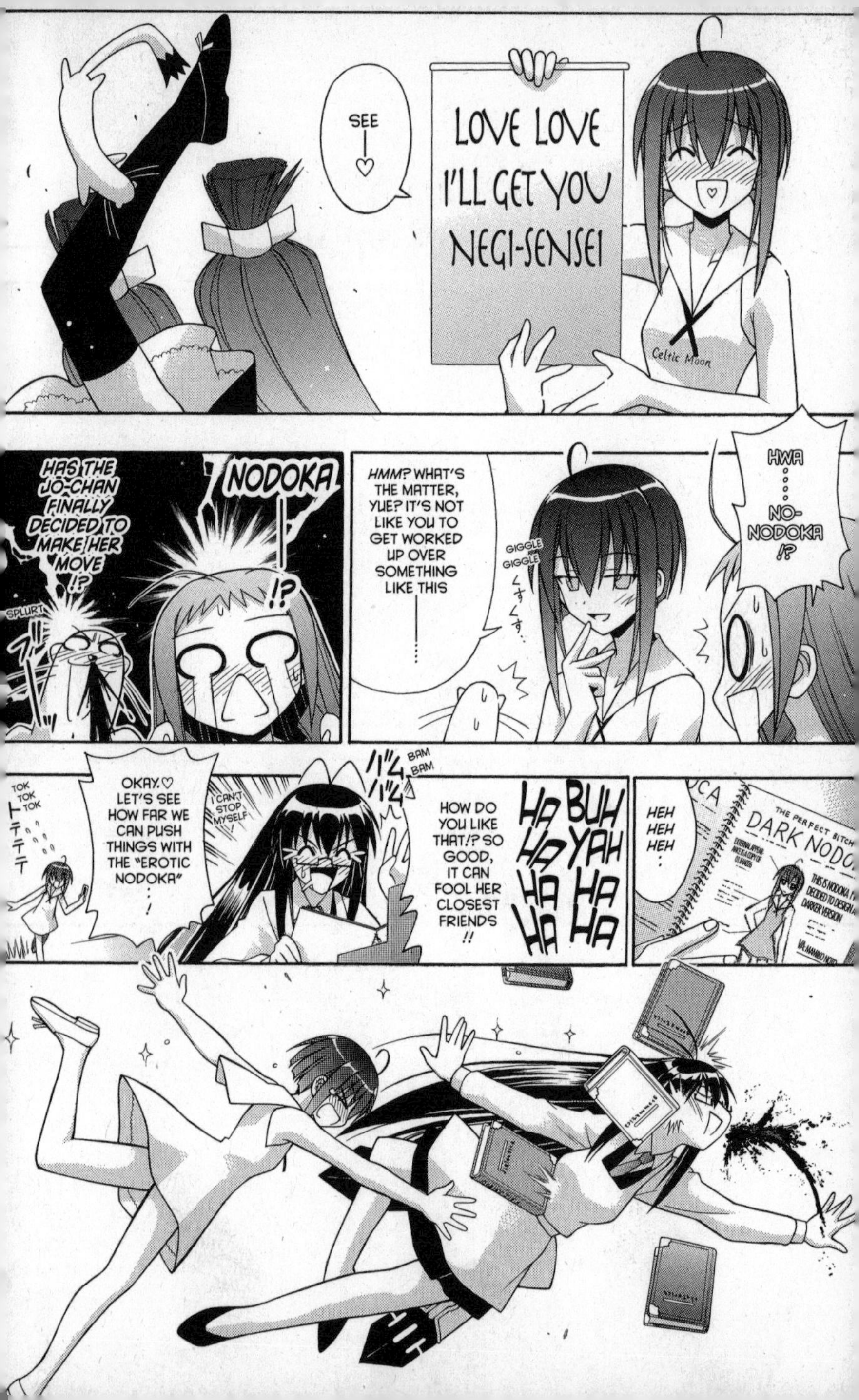
LOVE LOVE I'LL GET YOU NEGI-SENSEI
Celtic Moon
SEE ♡
HWA.... NO-NODOKA!?
HMM? WHAT'S THE MATTER, YUE? IT'S NOT LIKE YOU TO GET WORKED UP OVER SOMETHING LIKE THIS......
GIGGLE GIGGLE
くすくす…
NODOKA!?
HAS THE JŌ-CHAN FINALLY DECIDED TO MAKE HER MOVE!?
SPLURT
THE PERFECT BITCH
DARK NODO
HEH HEH HEH...
BUH YAH HA HA
HA HA HA HA
HOW DO YOU LIKE THAT!? SO GOOD, IT CAN FOOL HER CLOSEST FRIENDS!!
BAM BAM
I CAN'T STOP MYSELF!
OKAY.♡ LET'S SEE HOW FAR WE CAN PUSH THINGS WITH THE "EROTIC NODOKA"...!
TOK TOK TOK

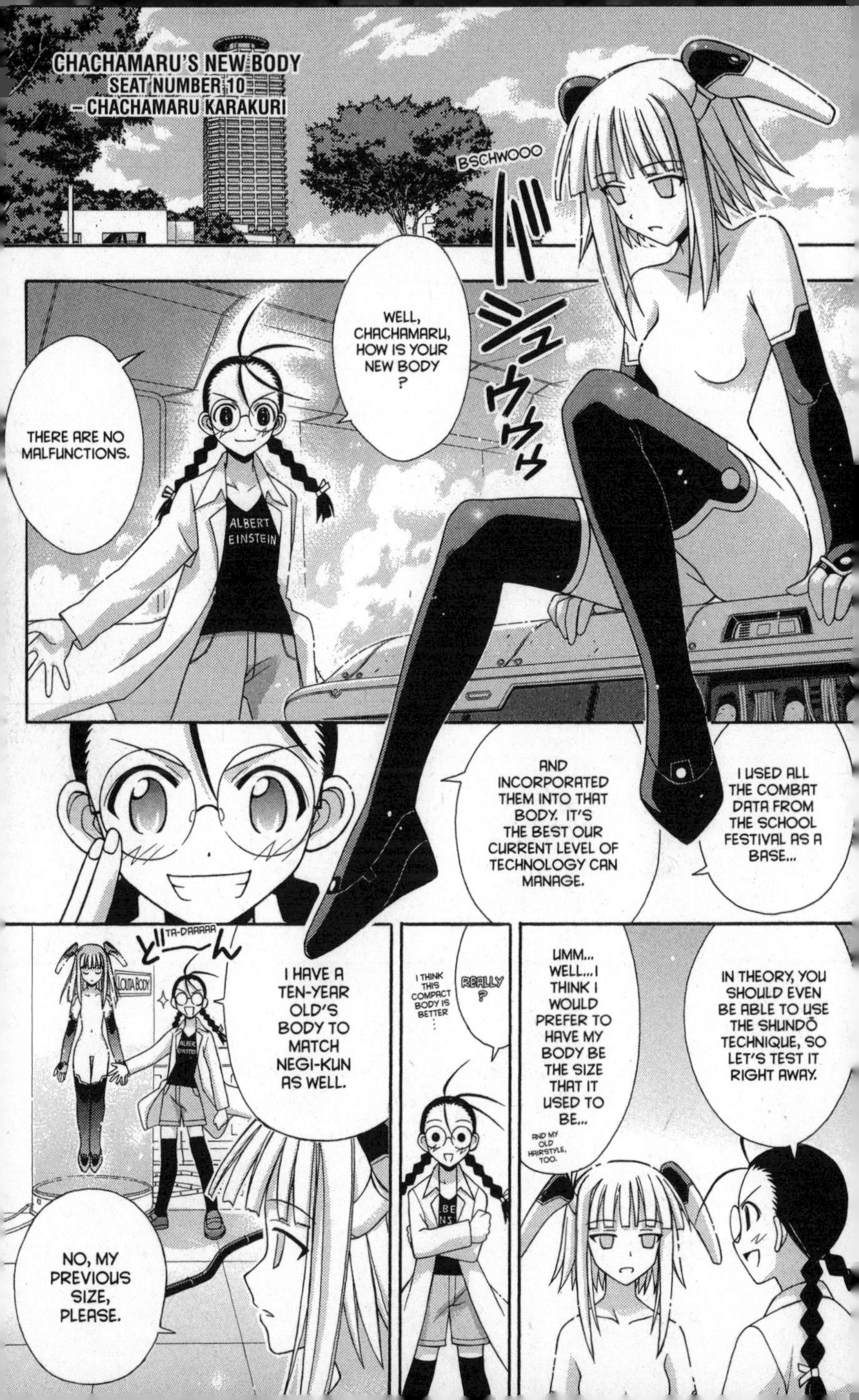
CHACHAMARU'S NEW BODY
SEAT NUMBER 10
– CHACHAMARU KARAKURI
ジュウゥゥ
BSCHWOOO
WELL, CHACHAMARU, HOW IS YOUR NEW BODY ?
THERE ARE NO MALFUNCTIONS.
ALBERT EINSTEIN
I USED ALL THE COMBAT DATA FROM THE SCHOOL FESTIVAL AS A BASE...
AND INCORPORATED THEM INTO THAT BODY. IT'S THE BEST OUR CURRENT LEVEL OF TECHNOLOGY CAN MANAGE.
IN THEORY, YOU SHOULD EVEN BE ABLE TO USE THE SHUNDŌ TECHNIQUE, SO LET'S TEST IT RIGHT AWAY.
UMM... WELL... I THINK I WOULD PREFER TO HAVE MY BODY BE THE SIZE THAT IT USED TO BE...
AND MY OLD HAIRSTYLE, TOO.
REALLY ?
I THINK THIS COMPACT BODY IS BETTER . . .
ど〜ん
TA-DAAAAA
LOLITA BODY
I HAVE A TEN-YEAR OLD'S BODY TO MATCH NEGI-KUN AS WELL.
NO, MY PREVIOUS SIZE, PLEASE.

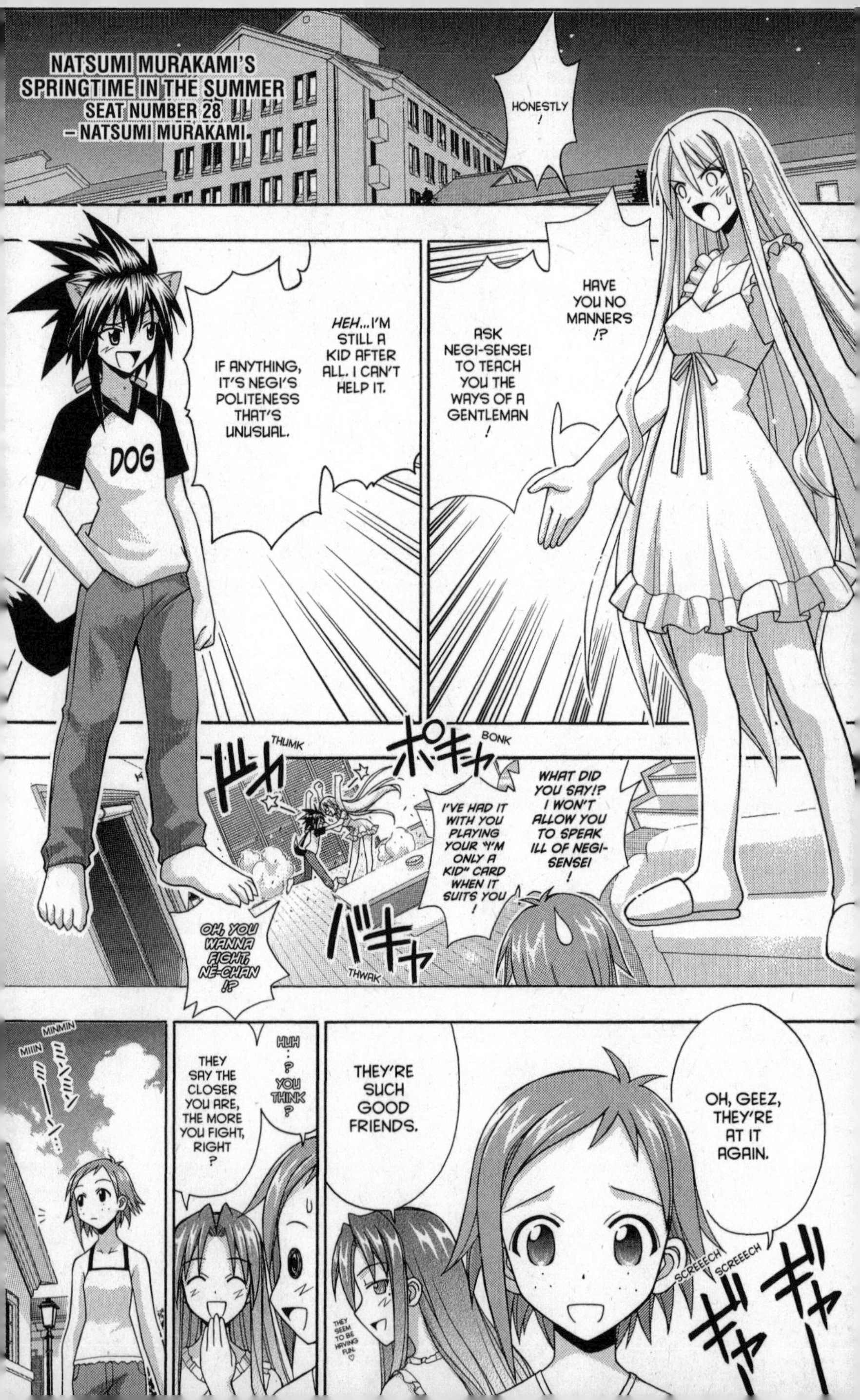

NATSUMI MURAKAMI'S SPRINGTIME IN THE SUMMER
SEAT NUMBER 28 – NATSUMI MURAKAMI
HONESTLY!
HAVE YOU NO MANNERS!?
ASK NEGI-SENSEI TO TEACH YOU THE WAYS OF A GENTLEMAN!
HEH...I'M STILL A KID AFTER ALL. I CAN'T HELP IT.
IF ANYTHING, IT'S NEGI'S POLITENESS THAT'S UNUSUAL.
WHAT DID YOU SAY!? I WON'T ALLOW YOU TO SPEAK ILL OF NEGI-SENSEI!
BONK
I'VE HAD IT WITH YOU PLAYING YOUR "I'M ONLY A KID" CARD WHEN IT SUITS YOU!
THUMK
OH, YOU WANNA FIGHT, NE-CHAN!?
THWAK
OH, GEEZ, THEY'RE AT IT AGAIN.
SCREEECH
SCREEECH
THEY'RE SUCH GOOD FRIENDS.
HUH? YOU THINK?
THEY SAY THE CLOSER YOU ARE, THE MORE YOU FIGHT, RIGHT?
THEY SEEM TO BE HAVING FUN.
MINMIN
MIIIN

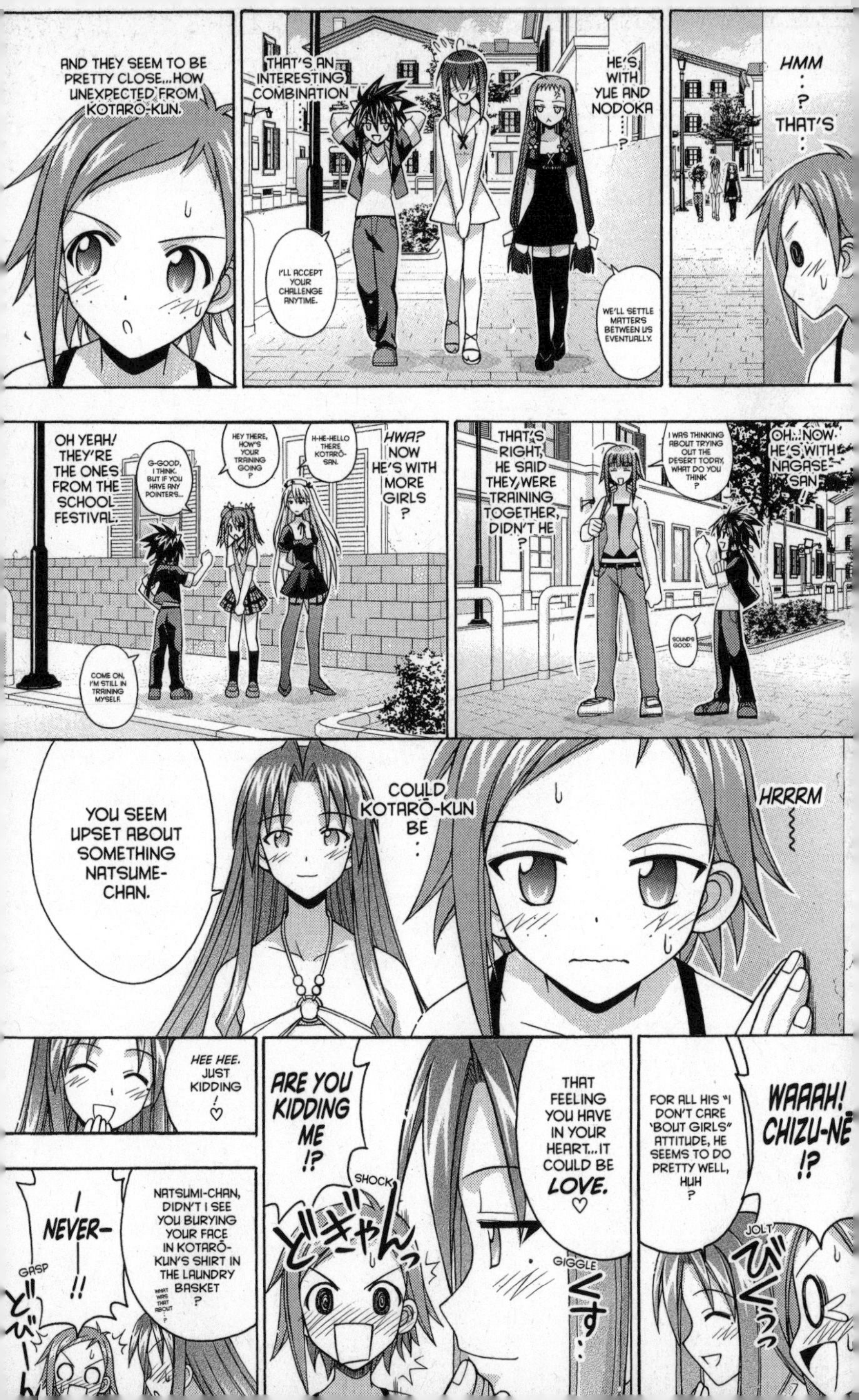
HMM..? THAT'S..
HE'S WITH YUE AND NODOKA...?
WE'LL SETTLE MATTERS BETWEEN US EVENTUALLY.
THAT'S AN INTERESTING COMBINATION
I'LL ACCEPT YOUR CHALLENGE ANYTIME.
AND THEY SEEM TO BE PRETTY CLOSE...HOW UNEXPECTED FROM KOTARŌ-KUN.
OH...NOW HE'S WITH NAGASE-SAN!?
I WAS THINKING ABOUT TRYING OUT THE DESERT TODAY, WHAT DO YOU THINK?
THAT'S RIGHT, HE SAID THEY WERE TRAINING TOGETHER, DIDN'T HE?
SOUNDS GOOD.
HWA? NOW HE'S WITH MORE GIRLS?
H-HE-HELLO THERE KOTARŌ-SAN.
HEY THERE, HOW'S YOUR TRAINING GOING?
G-GOOD, I THINK. BUT IF YOU HAVE ANY POINTERS...
OH YEAH! THEY'RE THE ONES FROM THE SCHOOL FESTIVAL.
COME ON, I'M STILL IN TRAINING MYSELF.
HRRRM
COULD KOTARŌ-KUN BE..
YOU SEEM UPSET ABOUT SOMETHING NATSUME-CHAN.
WAAAH! CHIZU-NĒ!?
FOR ALL HIS "I DON'T CARE 'BOUT GIRLS" ATTITUDE, HE SEEMS TO DO PRETTY WELL, HUH?
JOLT
THAT FEELING YOU HAVE IN YOUR HEART...IT COULD BE LOVE. ♡
GIGGLE
くす..
ARE YOU KIDDING ME!?
SHOCK
どぎゃんっ
HEE HEE. JUST KIDDING! ♡
NATSUMI-CHAN, DIDN'T I SEE YOU BURYING YOUR FACE IN KOTARŌ-KUN'S SHIRT IN THE LAUNDRY BASKET?
WHAT WAS THAT ABOUT..?
I NEVER--!!
GASP

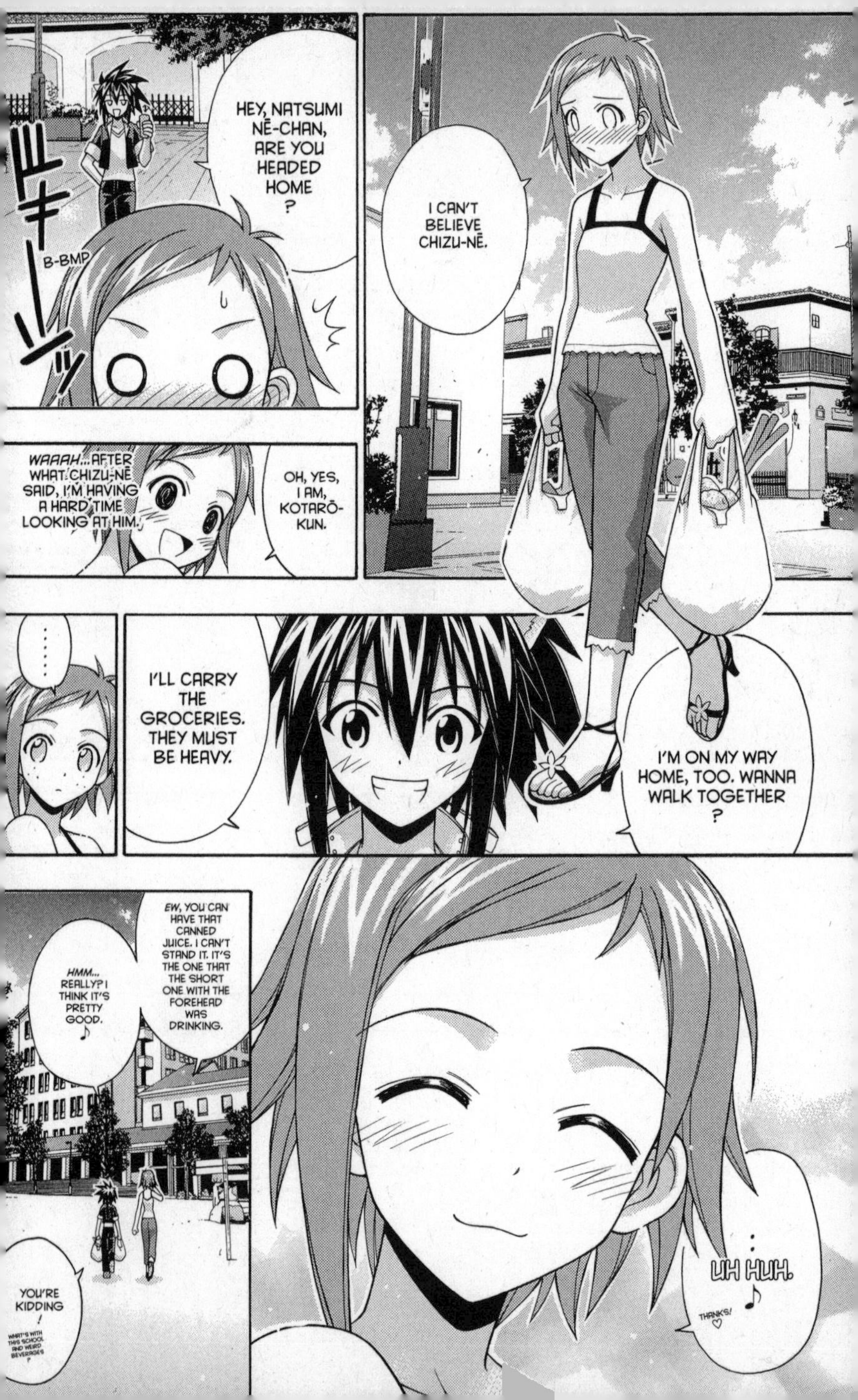
I CAN'T BELIEVE CHIZU-NĒ.
HEY, NATSUMI NĒ-CHAN, ARE YOU HEADED HOME?
B-BMP
OH, YES, I AM, KOTARŌ-KUN.
WAAAH... AFTER WHAT CHIZU-NĒ SAID, I'M HAVING A HARD TIME LOOKING AT HIM.
I'M ON MY WAY HOME, TOO. WANNA WALK TOGETHER?
I'LL CARRY THE GROCERIES. THEY MUST BE HEAVY.
......
UH HUH.
THANKS! ♡
EW, YOU CAN HAVE THAT CANNED JUICE. I CAN'T STAND IT. IT'S THE ONE THAT THE SHORT ONE WITH THE FOREHEAD WAS DRINKING.
HMM... REALLY? I THINK IT'S PRETTY GOOD. ♪
YOU'RE KIDDING!
WHAT'S WITH THIS SCHOOL AND WEIRD BEVERAGES?

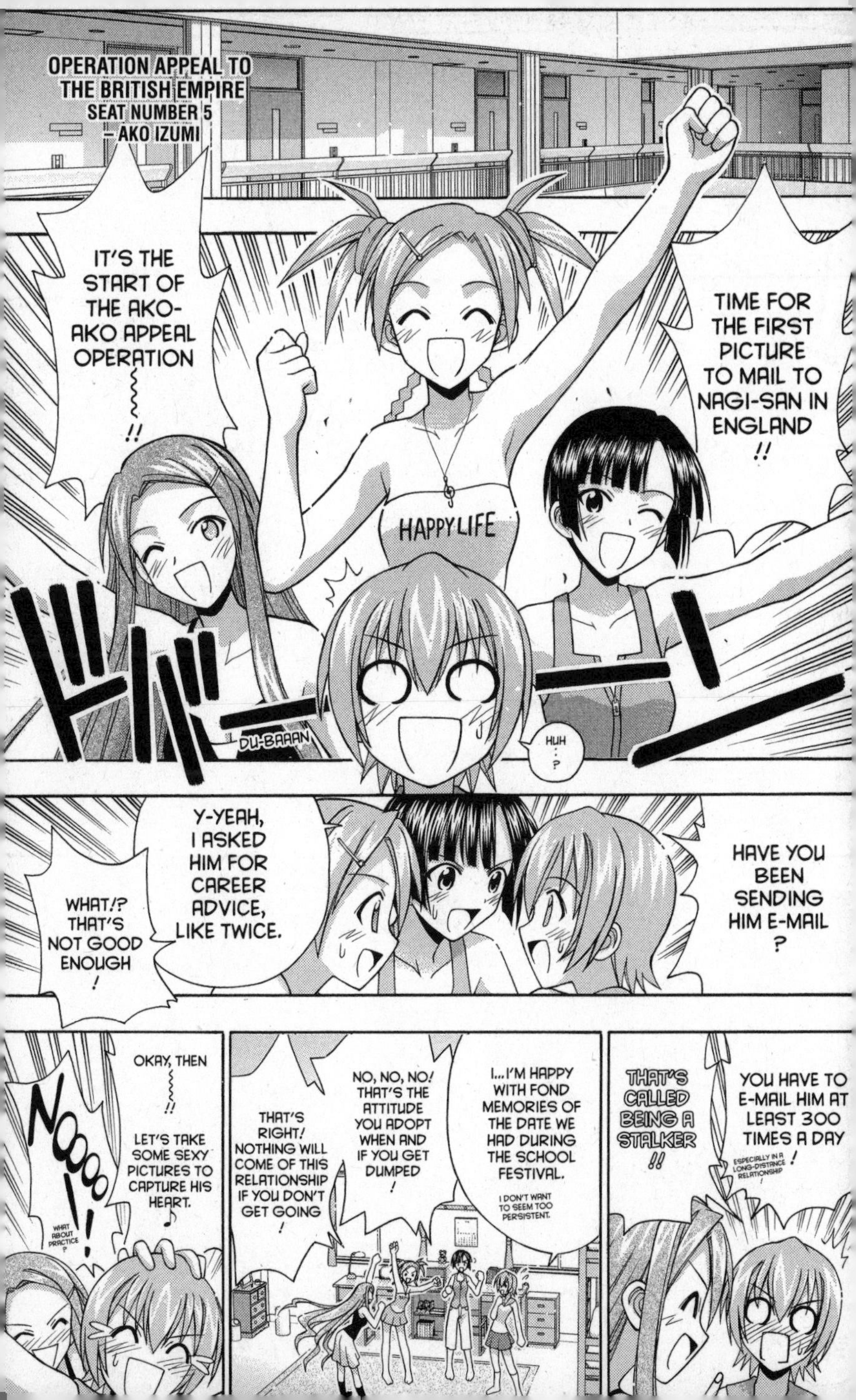
OPERATION APPEAL TO THE BRITISH EMPIRE SEAT NUMBER 5 – AKO IZUMI
TIME FOR THE FIRST PICTURE TO MAIL TO NAGI-SAN IN ENGLAND!!
IT'S THE START OF THE AKO-AKO APPEAL OPERATION~!!
HAPPY LIFE
DU-BAAAN
HUH...?
HAVE YOU BEEN SENDING HIM E-MAIL?
Y-YEAH, I ASKED HIM FOR CAREER ADVICE, LIKE TWICE.
WHAT!? THAT'S NOT GOOD ENOUGH!
YOU HAVE TO E-MAIL HIM AT LEAST 300 TIMES A DAY!
ESPECIALLY IN A LONG-DISTANCE RELATIONSHIP!
THAT'S CALLED BEING A STALKER!!
I...I'M HAPPY WITH FOND MEMORIES OF THE DATE WE HAD DURING THE SCHOOL FESTIVAL.
I DON'T WANT TO SEEM TOO PERSISTENT.
NO, NO, NO! THAT'S THE ATTITUDE YOU ADOPT WHEN AND IF YOU GET DUMPED!
THAT'S RIGHT! NOTHING WILL COME OF THIS RELATIONSHIP IF YOU DON'T GET GOING!
OKAY, THEN~!!
LET'S TAKE SOME SEXY PICTURES TO CAPTURE HIS HEART. ♪
NOOOO!!
WHAT ABOUT PRACTICE?

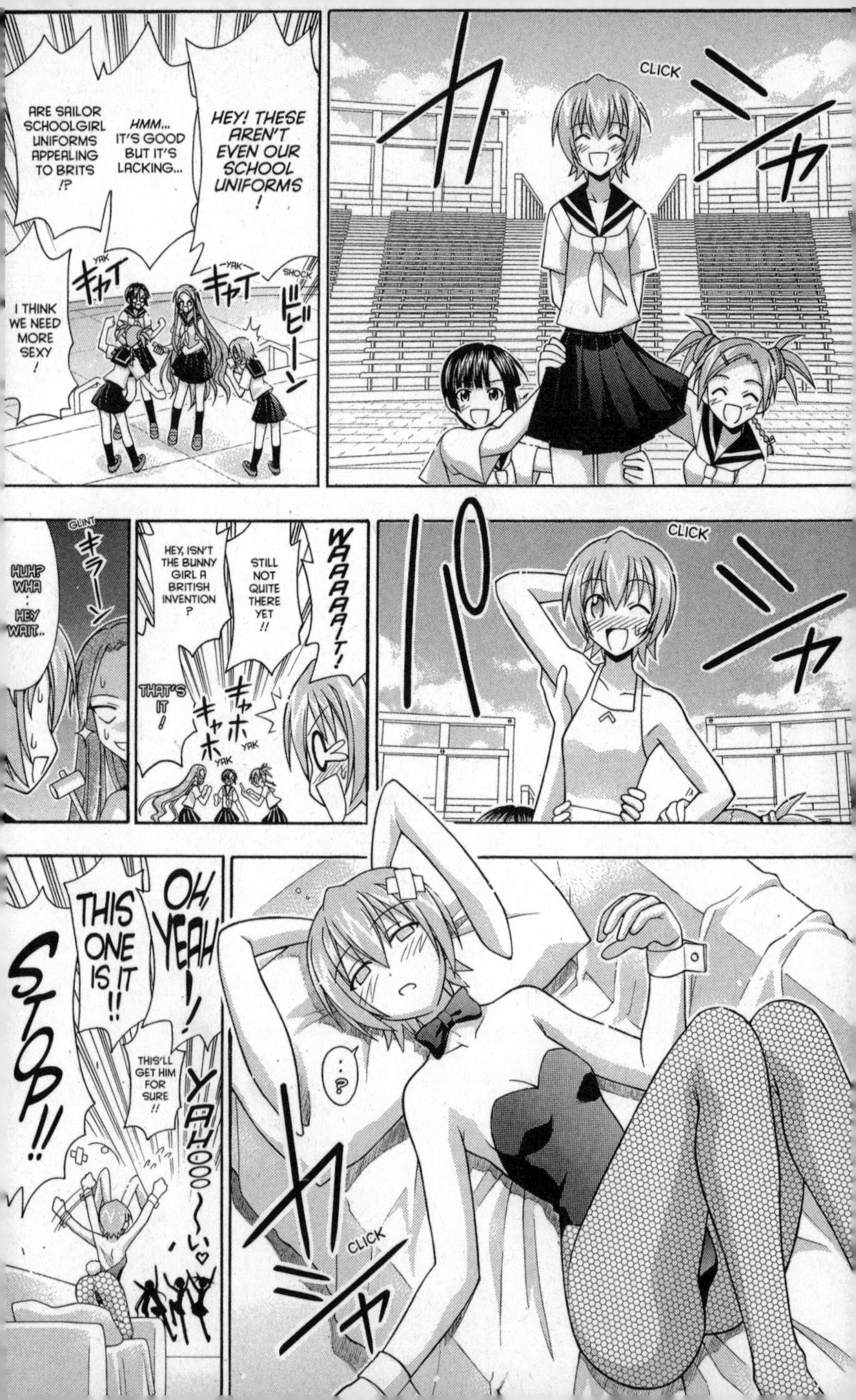
CLICK
HEY! THESE AREN'T EVEN OUR SCHOOL UNIFORMS!
HMM... IT'S GOOD BUT IT'S LACKING...
ARE SAILOR SCHOOLGIRL UNIFORMS APPEALING TO BRITS!?
SHOCK
YAK
YAK
I THINK WE NEED MORE SEXY!
CLICK
WAAAAAAIT!
STILL NOT QUITE THERE YET!!
HEY, ISN'T THE BUNNY GIRL A BRITISH INVENTION?
THAT'S IT!
YAK
YAK
GLINT
HUH? WHA... HEY WAIT..
...?
YAHOOO~!♡
CLICK
OH, YEAH!!
THIS ONE IS IT!!
STOP!!
THIS'LL GET HIM FOR SURE!!

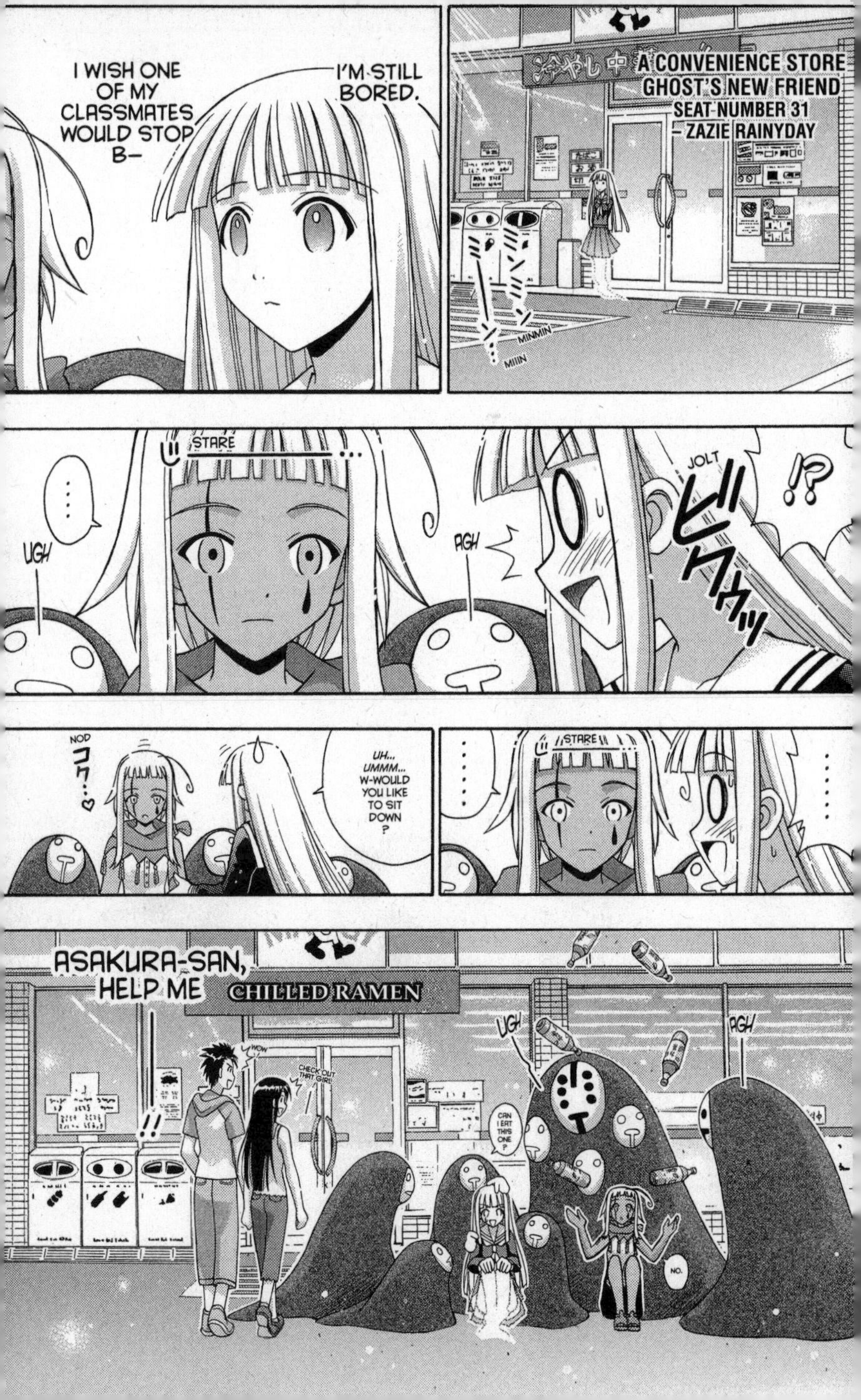
A CONVENIENCE STORE GHOST'S NEW FRIEND
SEAT NUMBER 31 – ZAZIE RAINYDAY
MINMIN
MIIN
I'M STILL BORED.
I WISH ONE OF MY CLASSMATES WOULD STOP B—
!?
JOLT
AGH
STARE
...
....
UGH
STARE
......
UH... UMMM... W-WOULD YOU LIKE TO SIT DOWN?
NOD
AGH
UGH
CAN I EAT THIS ONE?
NO.
CHECK OUT THAT GIRL!
WOW
!!
ASAKURA-SAN, HELP ME
CHILLED RAMEN

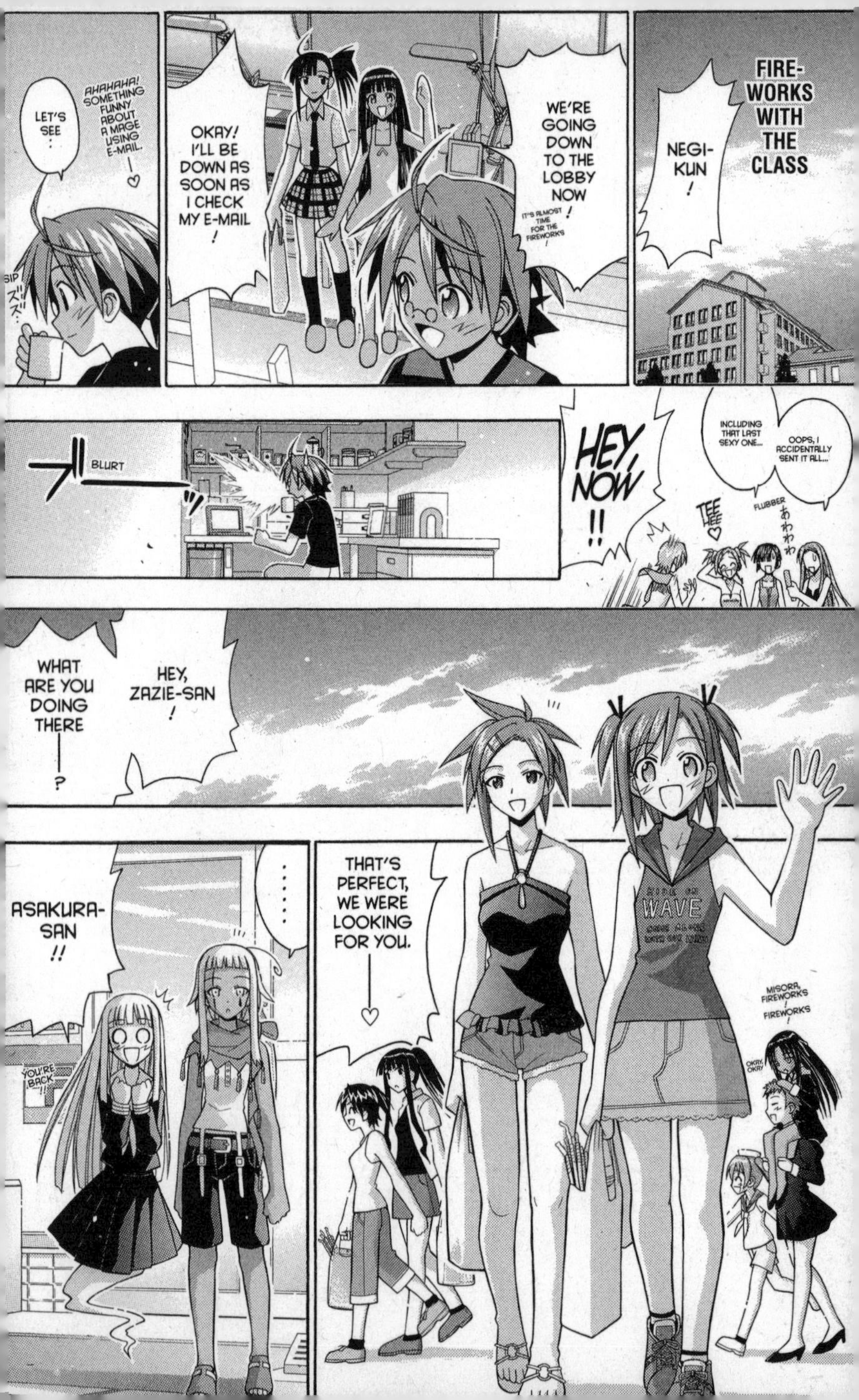
FIRE-WORKS WITH THE CLASS
NEGI-KUN!
WE'RE GOING DOWN TO THE LOBBY NOW!
IT'S ALMOST TIME FOR THE FIREWORKS!
OKAY! I'LL BE DOWN AS SOON AS I CHECK MY E-MAIL!
LET'S SEE...
AHAHAHA! SOMETHING FUNNY ABOUT A MAGE USING E-MAIL. —♡
SIP
OOPS, I ACCIDENTALLY SENT IT ALL...
INCLUDING THAT LAST SEXY ONE...
FLUBBER
TEE HEE ♡
HEY, NOW!!
BLURT
HEY, ZAZIE-SAN!
WHAT ARE YOU DOING THERE—?
MISORA, FIREWORKS! FIREWORKS!
OKAY, OKAY
THAT'S PERFECT, WE WERE LOOKING FOR YOU. —♡
......
ASAKURA-SAN!!
YOU'RE BACK—!!

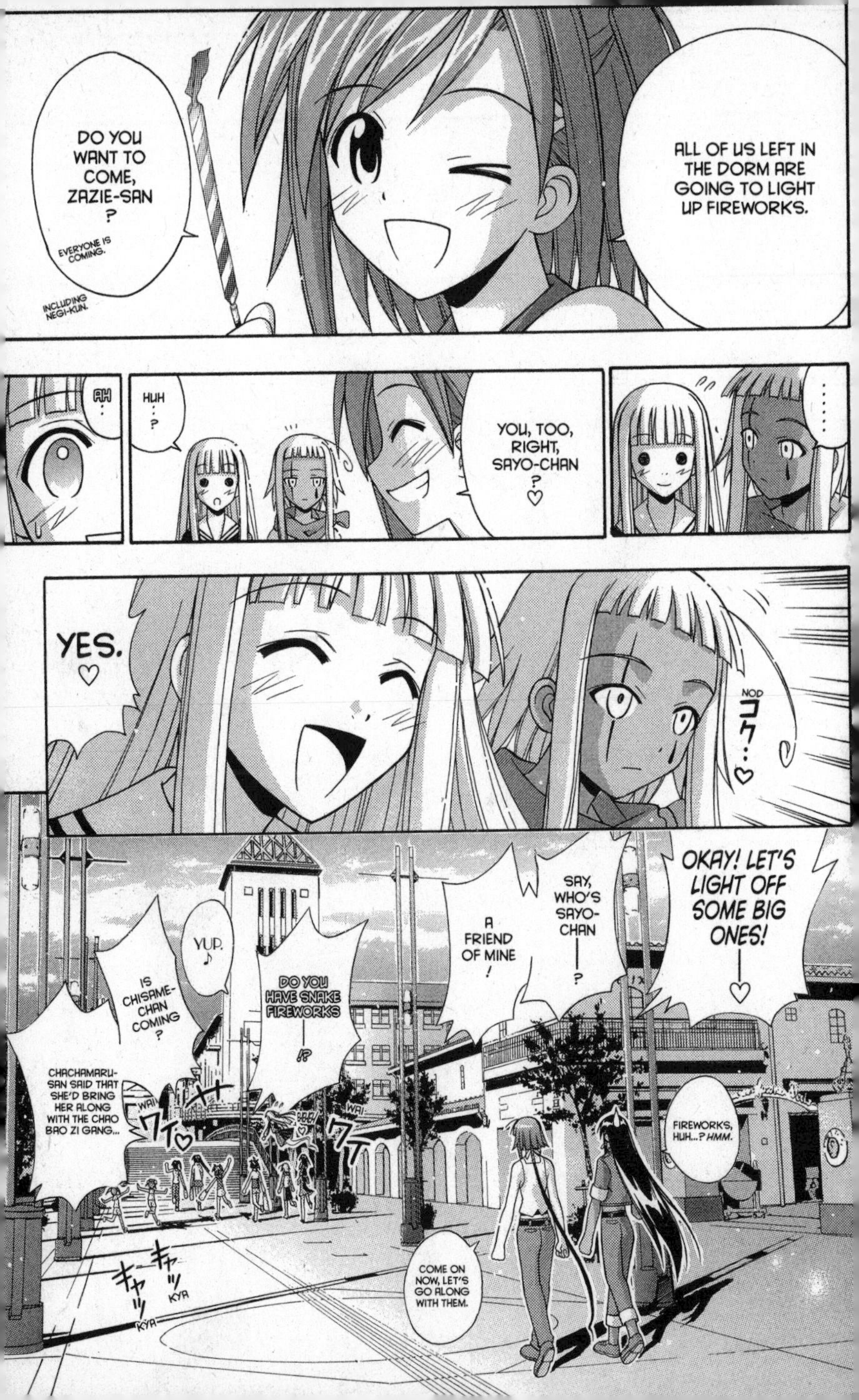
ALL OF US LEFT IN THE DORM ARE GOING TO LIGHT UP FIREWORKS.
DO YOU WANT TO COME, ZAZIE-SAN ?
EVERYONE IS COMING.
INCLUDING NEGI-KUN.
......
YOU, TOO, RIGHT, SAYO-CHAN ? ♡
HUH..?
AH...
NOD
YES. ♡
OKAY! LET'S LIGHT OFF SOME BIG ONES! ♡
SAY, WHO'S SAYO-CHAN ?
A FRIEND OF MINE!
YUP. ♪
DO YOU HAVE SNAKE FIREWORKS !?
IS CHISAME-CHAN COMING ?
FIREWORKS, HUH...? HMM.
CHACHAMARU-SAN SAID THAT SHE'D BRING HER ALONG WITH THE CHAO BAO ZI GANG...
WAI
WAI
COME ON NOW, LET'S GO ALONG WITH THEM.
KYA
KYA

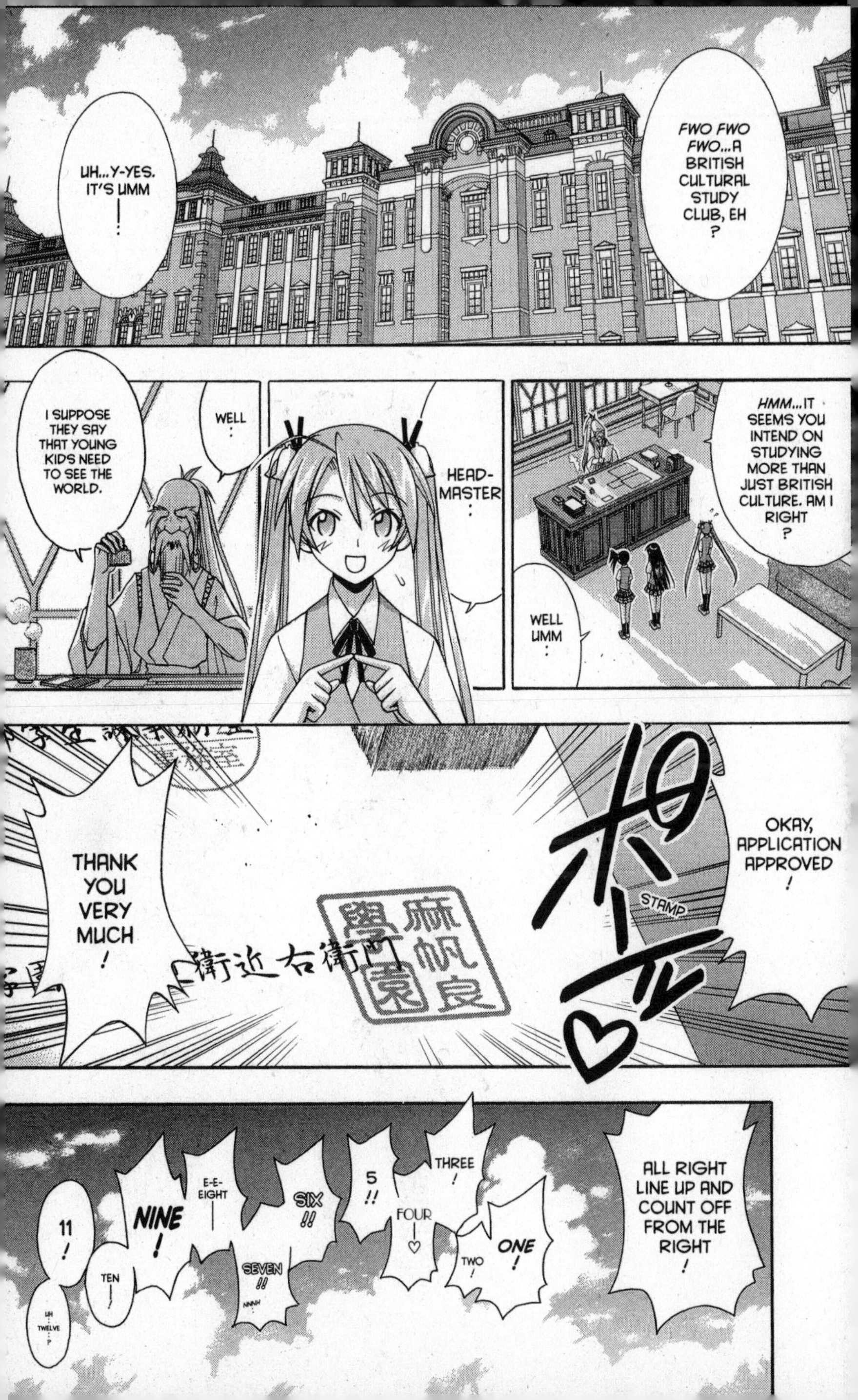
FWO FWO FWO...A BRITISH CULTURAL STUDY CLUB, EH ?
UH...Y-YES. IT'S UMM —!
HMM...IT SEEMS YOU INTEND ON STUDYING MORE THAN JUST BRITISH CULTURE. AM I RIGHT ?
WELL UMM :
HEAD-MASTER :
WELL :
I SUPPOSE THEY SAY THAT YOUNG KIDS NEED TO SEE THE WORLD.
OKAY, APPLICATION APPROVED !
STAMP
麻帆良學園
THANK YOU VERY MUCH !
ALL RIGHT LINE UP AND COUNT OFF FROM THE RIGHT !
ONE !
TWO !
THREE !
FOUR —♡
5 !!
SIX !!
SEVEN !!
NNNH
E-E-EIGHT —
NINE !
TEN —!
11 !
UH : TWELVE : P

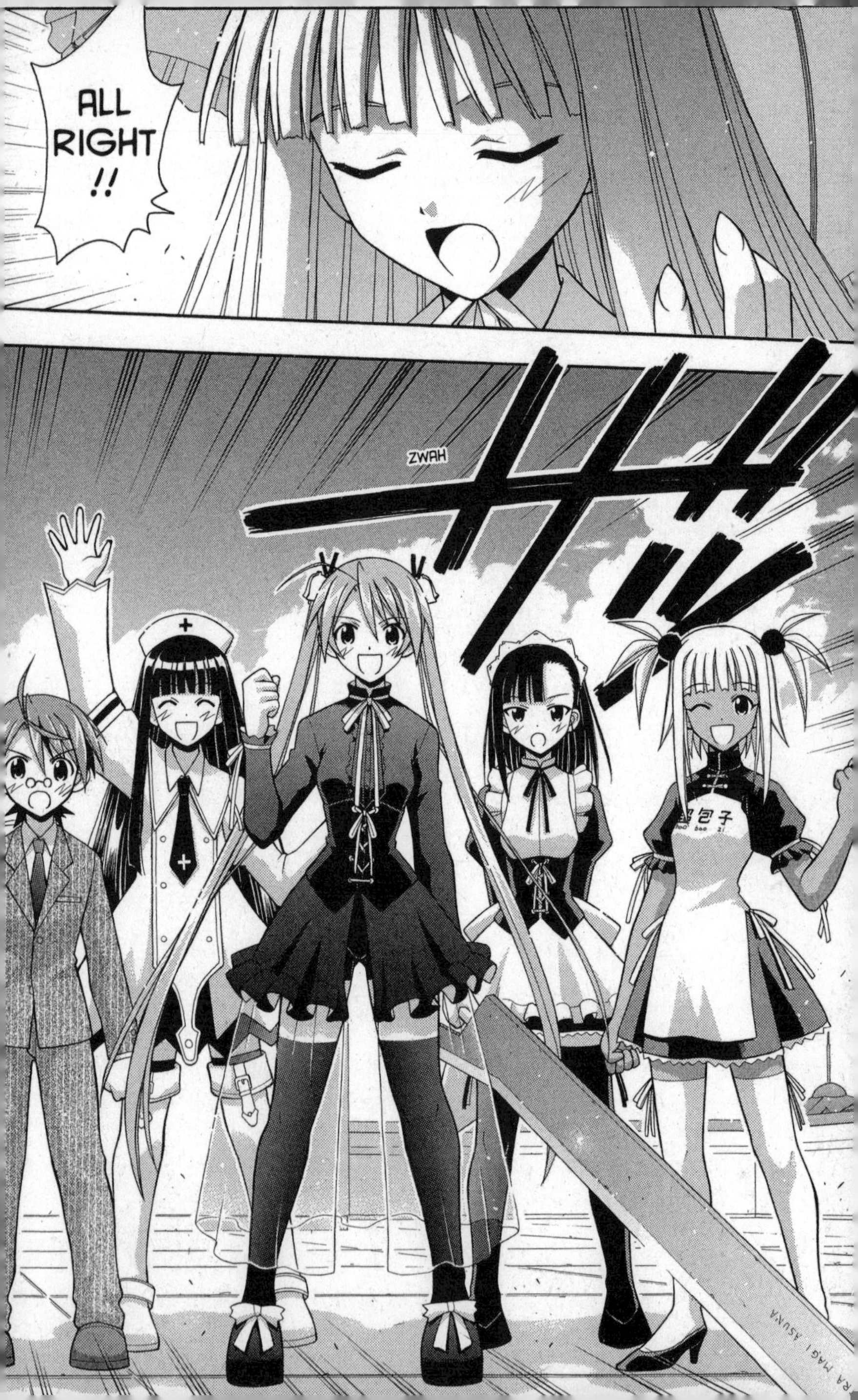
ALL RIGHT !!
ZWAH

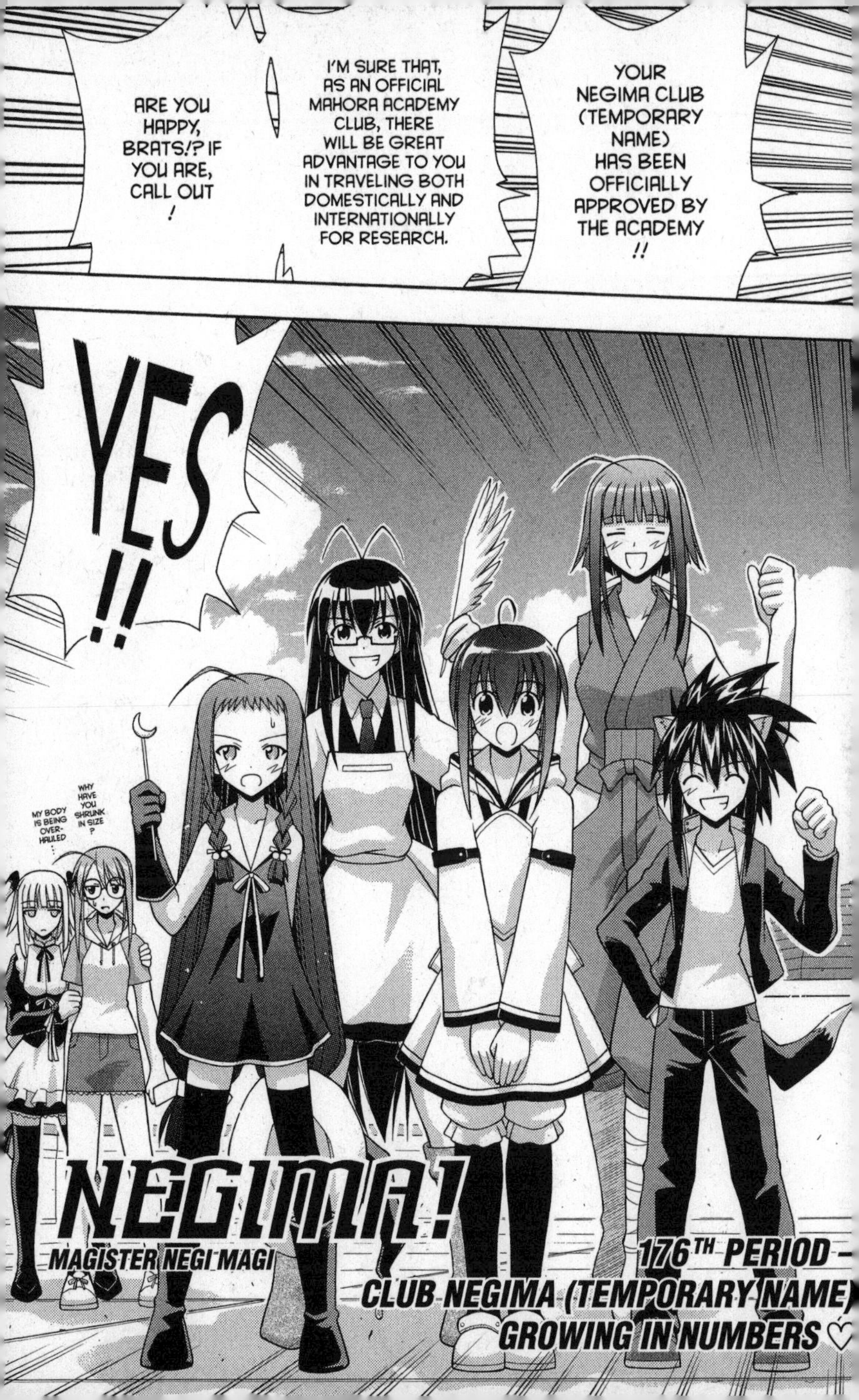
YOUR NEGIMA CLUB (TEMPORARY NAME) HAS BEEN OFFICIALLY APPROVED BY THE ACADEMY !!
I'M SURE THAT, AS AN OFFICIAL MAHORA ACADEMY CLUB, THERE WILL BE GREAT ADVANTAGE TO YOU IN TRAVELING BOTH DOMESTICALLY AND INTERNATIONALLY FOR RESEARCH.
ARE YOU HAPPY, BRATS!? IF YOU ARE, CALL OUT !
YES !!
WHY HAVE YOU SHRUNK IN SIZE ?
MY BODY IS BEING OVER-HAULED ...
NEGIMA!
MAGISTER NEGI MAGI
176TH PERIOD – CLUB NEGIMA (TEMPORARY NAME) GROWING IN NUMBERS ♡

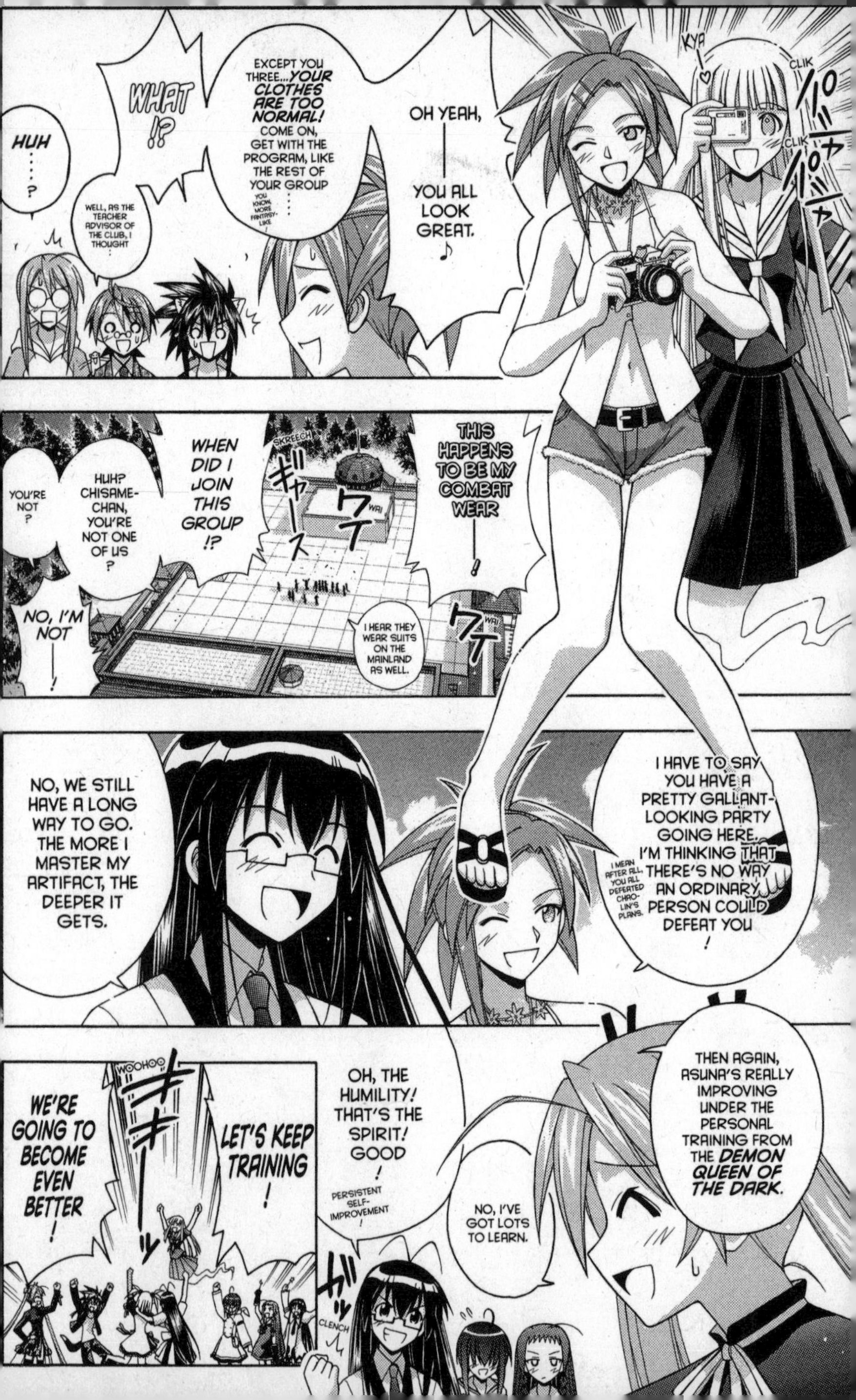
KYA ♡
CLIK
CLIK
OH YEAH, YOU ALL LOOK GREAT. ♪
EXCEPT YOU THREE... YOUR CLOTHES ARE TOO NORMAL! COME ON, GET WITH THE PROGRAM, LIKE THE REST OF YOUR GROUP...
YOU KNOW, MORE FANTASY-LIKE
WHAT!?
WELL, AS THE TEACHER ADVISOR OF THE CLUB, I THOUGHT...
HUH...?
THIS HAPPENS TO BE MY COMBAT WEAR!
WAI
WAI
I HEAR THEY WEAR SUITS ON THE MAINLAND AS WELL.
WHEN DID I JOIN THIS GROUP!?
SKREECH
HUH? CHISAME-CHAN, YOU'RE NOT ONE OF US?
YOU'RE NOT?
NO, I'M NOT!
I HAVE TO SAY YOU HAVE A PRETTY GALLANT-LOOKING PARTY GOING HERE. I'M THINKING THAT THERE'S NO WAY AN ORDINARY PERSON COULD DEFEAT YOU!
I MEAN AFTER ALL, YOU ALL DEFEATED CHAO-LIN'S PLANS.
NO, WE STILL HAVE A LONG WAY TO GO. THE MORE I MASTER MY ARTIFACT, THE DEEPER IT GETS.
THEN AGAIN, ASUNA'S REALLY IMPROVING UNDER THE PERSONAL TRAINING FROM THE DEMON QUEEN OF THE DARK.
NO, I'VE GOT LOTS TO LEARN.
OH, THE HUMILITY! THAT'S THE SPIRIT! GOOD!
PERSISTENT SELF-IMPROVEMENT!
CLENCH
LET'S KEEP TRAINING!
WOOHOO
WE'RE GOING TO BECOME EVEN BETTER!

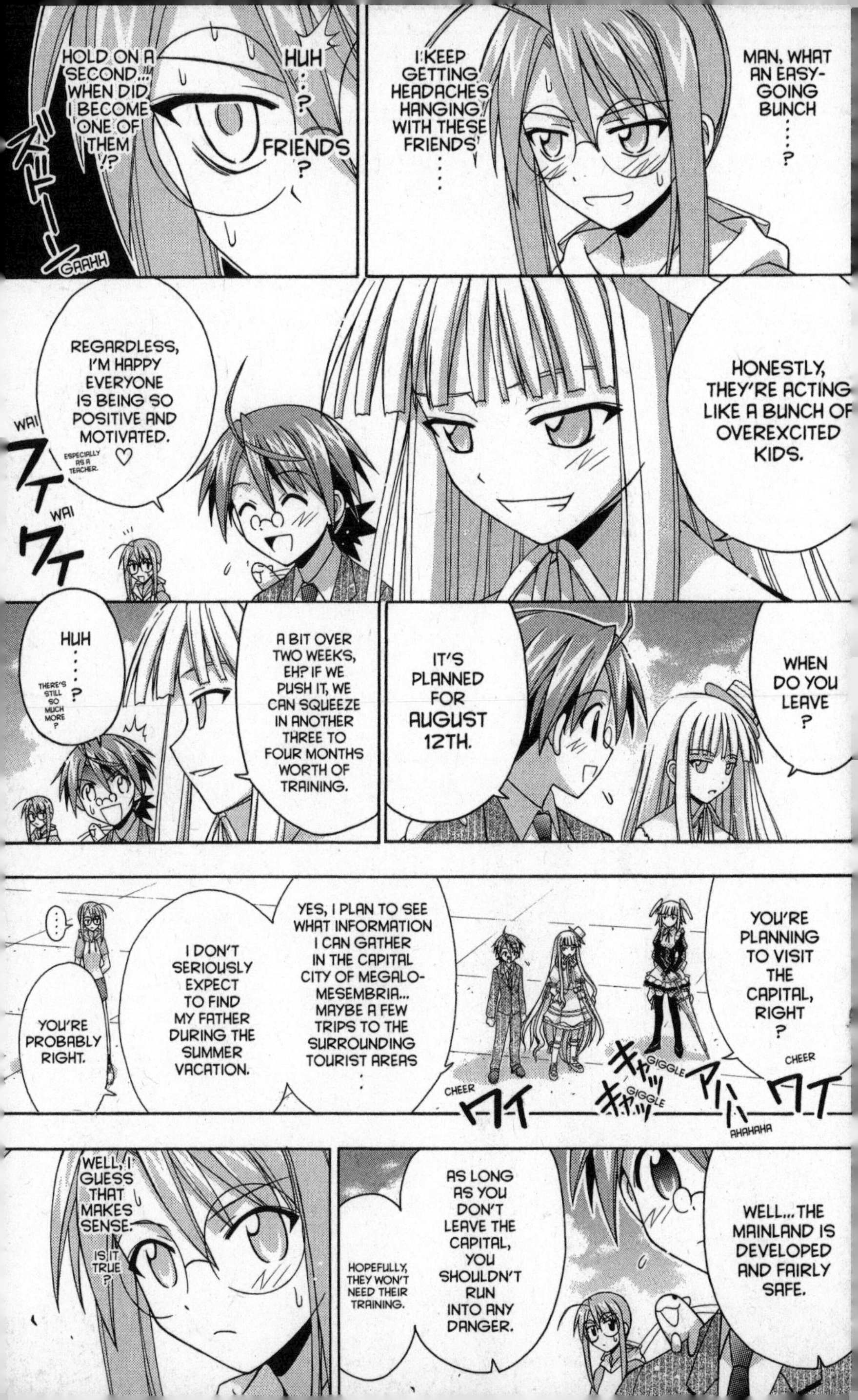
MAN, WHAT AN EASY-GOING BUNCH...?
I KEEP GETTING HEADACHES HANGING WITH THESE FRIENDS'...
HUH...? FRIENDS?
HOLD ON A SECOND... WHEN DID I BECOME ONE OF THEM!?
GAAHH
HONESTLY, THEY'RE ACTING LIKE A BUNCH OF OVEREXCITED KIDS.
REGARDLESS, I'M HAPPY EVERYONE IS BEING SO POSITIVE AND MOTIVATED. ♡
ESPECIALLY AS A TEACHER.
WAI
WAI
WHEN DO YOU LEAVE?
IT'S PLANNED FOR AUGUST 12TH.
A BIT OVER TWO WEEKS, EH? IF WE PUSH IT, WE CAN SQUEEZE IN ANOTHER THREE TO FOUR MONTHS WORTH OF TRAINING.
HUH...?
THERE'S STILL SO MUCH MORE?
YOU'RE PLANNING TO VISIT THE CAPITAL, RIGHT?
CHEER
AHAHAHA
GIGGLE
GIGGLE
CHEER
YES, I PLAN TO SEE WHAT INFORMATION I CAN GATHER IN THE CAPITAL CITY OF MEGALO-MESEMBRIA... MAYBE A FEW TRIPS TO THE SURROUNDING TOURIST AREAS...
I DON'T SERIOUSLY EXPECT TO FIND MY FATHER DURING THE SUMMER VACATION.
YOU'RE PROBABLY RIGHT.
...
WELL... THE MAINLAND IS DEVELOPED AND FAIRLY SAFE.
AS LONG AS YOU DON'T LEAVE THE CAPITAL, YOU SHOULDN'T RUN INTO ANY DANGER.
HOPEFULLY, THEY WON'T NEED THEIR TRAINING.
WELL, I GUESS THAT MAKES SENSE.
IS IT TRUE?

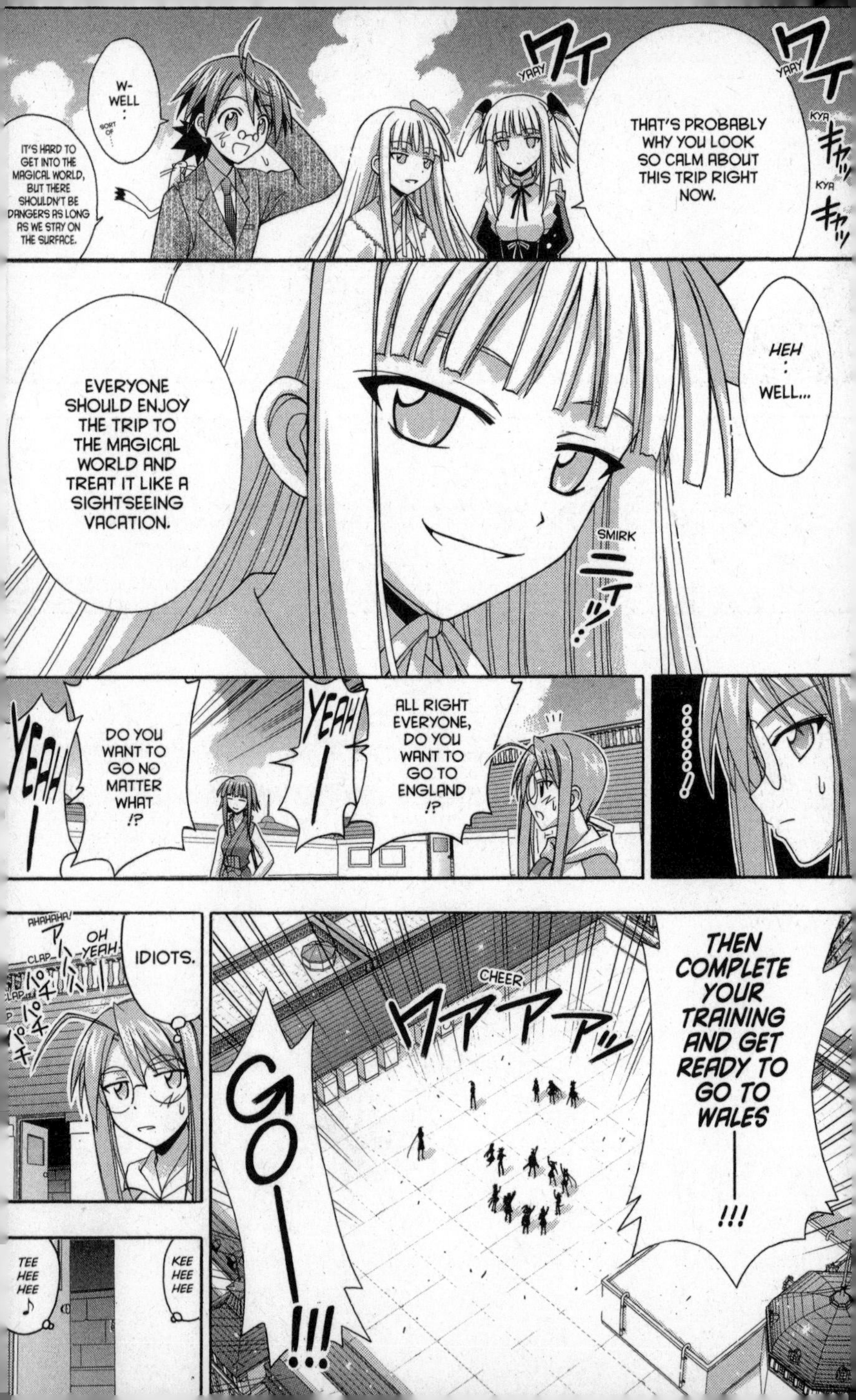
YAAY
YAAY
KYA
KYA
THAT'S PROBABLY WHY YOU LOOK SO CALM ABOUT THIS TRIP RIGHT NOW.
W-WELL...
SORT OF...
IT'S HARD TO GET INTO THE MAGICAL WORLD, BUT THERE SHOULDN'T BE DANGERS AS LONG AS WE STAY ON THE SURFACE.
HEH... WELL...
SMIRK
EVERYONE SHOULD ENJOY THE TRIP TO THE MAGICAL WORLD AND TREAT IT LIKE A SIGHTSEEING VACATION.
OOOOOO...!
ALL RIGHT EVERYONE, DO YOU WANT TO GO TO ENGLAND!?
YEAH!
DO YOU WANT TO GO NO MATTER WHAT!?
YEAH!
THEN COMPLETE YOUR TRAINING AND GET READY TO GO TO WALES—!!!
CHEER
GO—!!!
IDIOTS.
AHAHAHA!
OH YEAH!
CLAP
CLAP
KEE HEE HEE
TEE HEE HEE ♪

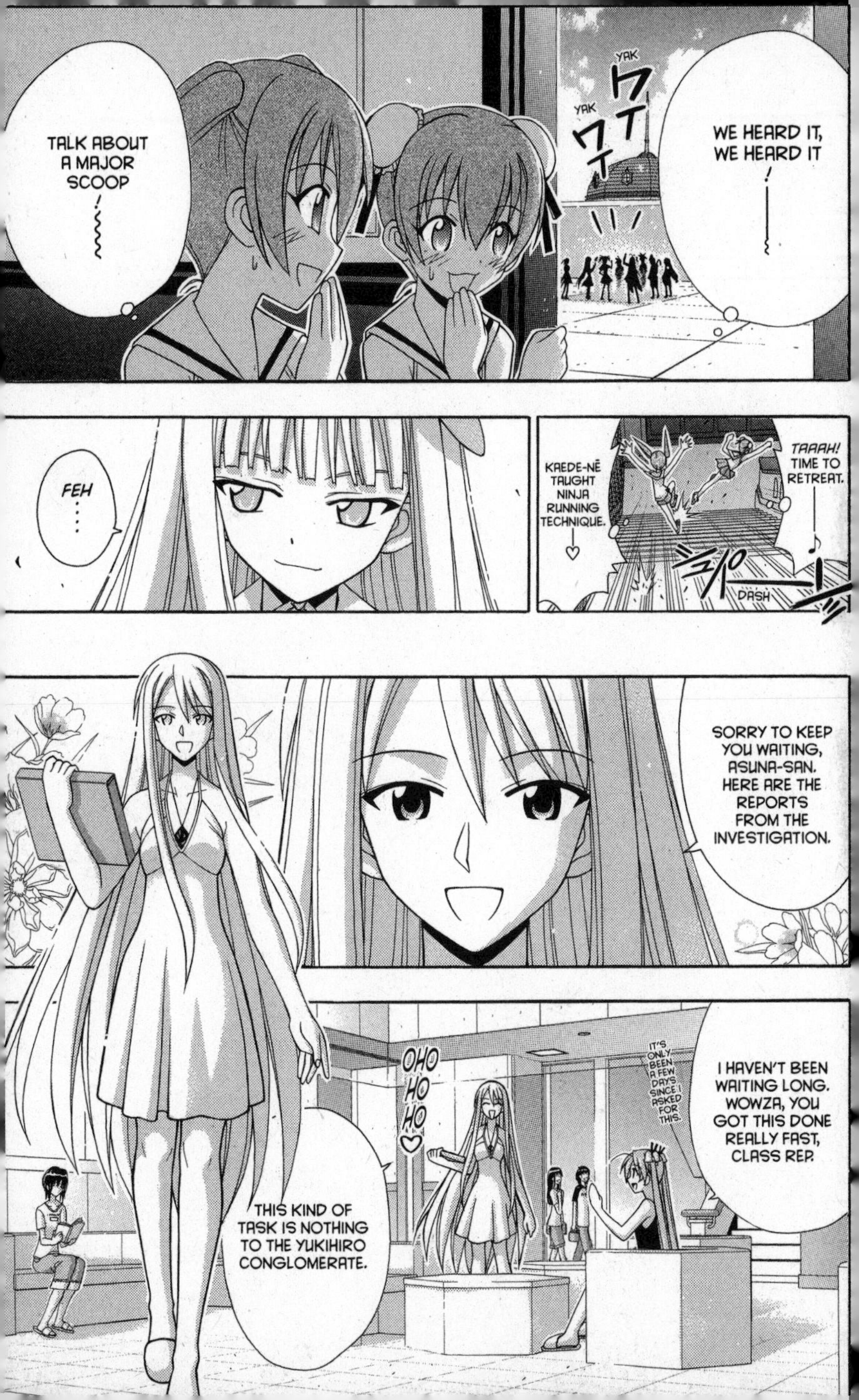
WE HEARD IT, WE HEARD IT!
YAK
YAK
TALK ABOUT A MAJOR SCOOP!
TAAAH! TIME TO RETREAT.
KAEDE-NĒ TAUGHT NINJA RUNNING TECHNIQUE.
DASH
FEH...
SORRY TO KEEP YOU WAITING, ASUNA-SAN. HERE ARE THE REPORTS FROM THE INVESTIGATION.
I HAVEN'T BEEN WAITING LONG. WOWZA, YOU GOT THIS DONE REALLY FAST, CLASS REP.
IT'S ONLY BEEN A FEW DAYS SINCE I ASKED FOR THIS.
OHO HO HO
THIS KIND OF TASK IS NOTHING TO THE YUKIHIRO CONGLOMERATE.

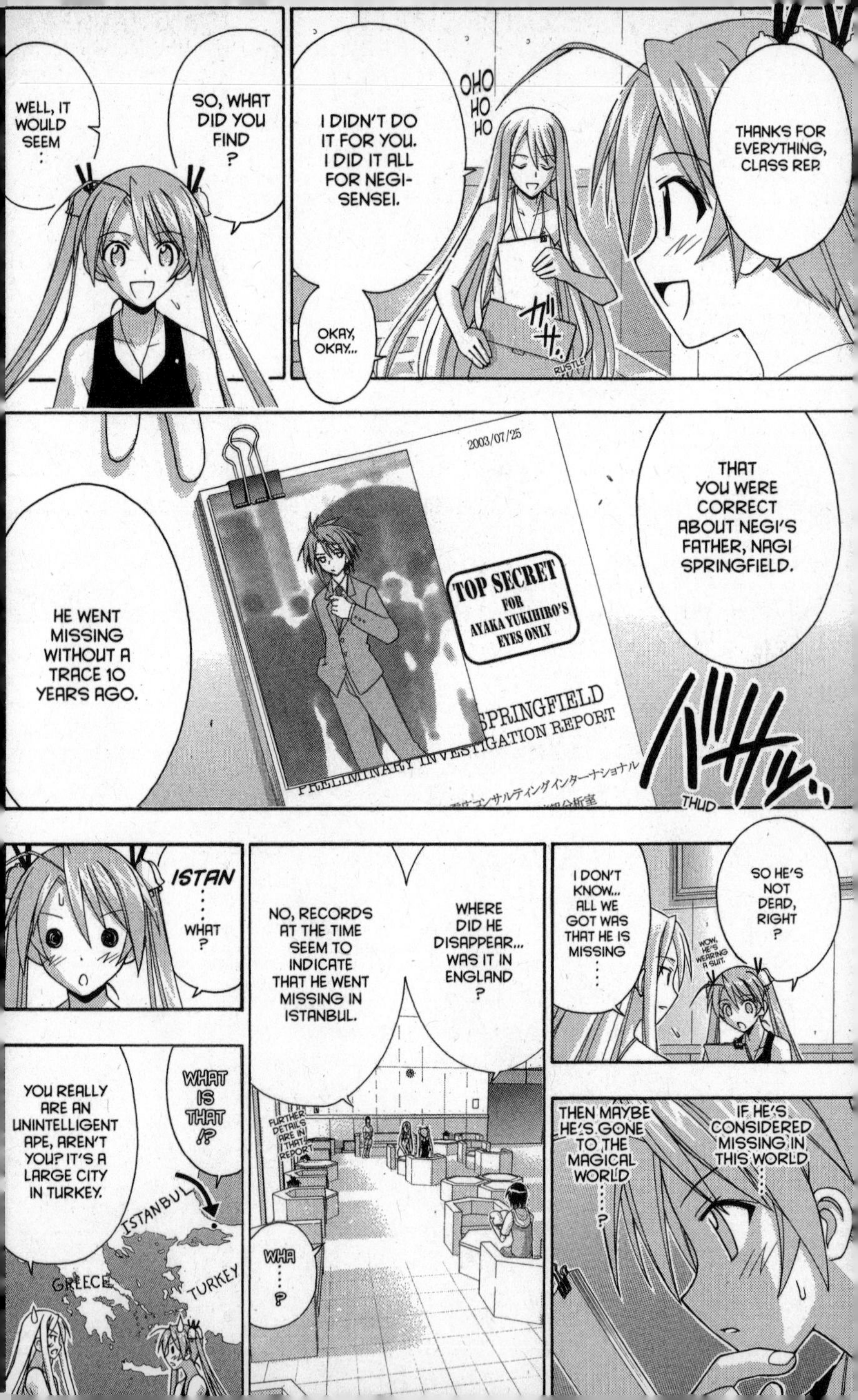
THANKS FOR EVERYTHING, CLASS REP.
OHO HO HO
I DIDN'T DO IT FOR YOU. I DID IT ALL FOR NEGI-SENSEI.
RUSTLE
OKAY, OKAY...
SO, WHAT DID YOU FIND?
WELL, IT WOULD SEEM :
THAT YOU WERE CORRECT ABOUT NEGI'S FATHER, NAGI SPRINGFIELD.
THUD
2003/07/25
TOP SECRET FOR AYAKA YUKIHIRO'S EYES ONLY
SPRINGFIELD
PRELIMINARY INVESTIGATION REPORT
HE WENT MISSING WITHOUT A TRACE 10 YEARS AGO.
SO HE'S NOT DEAD, RIGHT?
WOW, HE'S WEARING A SUIT.
I DON'T KNOW... ALL WE GOT WAS THAT HE IS MISSING ...
IF HE'S CONSIDERED MISSING IN THIS WORLD
THEN MAYBE HE'S GONE TO THE MAGICAL WORLD ...?
WHERE DID HE DISAPPEAR... WAS IT IN ENGLAND?
NO, RECORDS AT THE TIME SEEM TO INDICATE THAT HE WENT MISSING IN ISTANBUL.
FURTHER DETAILS ARE IN THAT REPORT.
WHA...?
ISTAN ... WHAT?
WHAT IS THAT!?
YOU REALLY ARE AN UNINTELLIGENT APE, AREN'T YOU? IT'S A LARGE CITY IN TURKEY.
ISTANBUL
GREECE
TURKEY

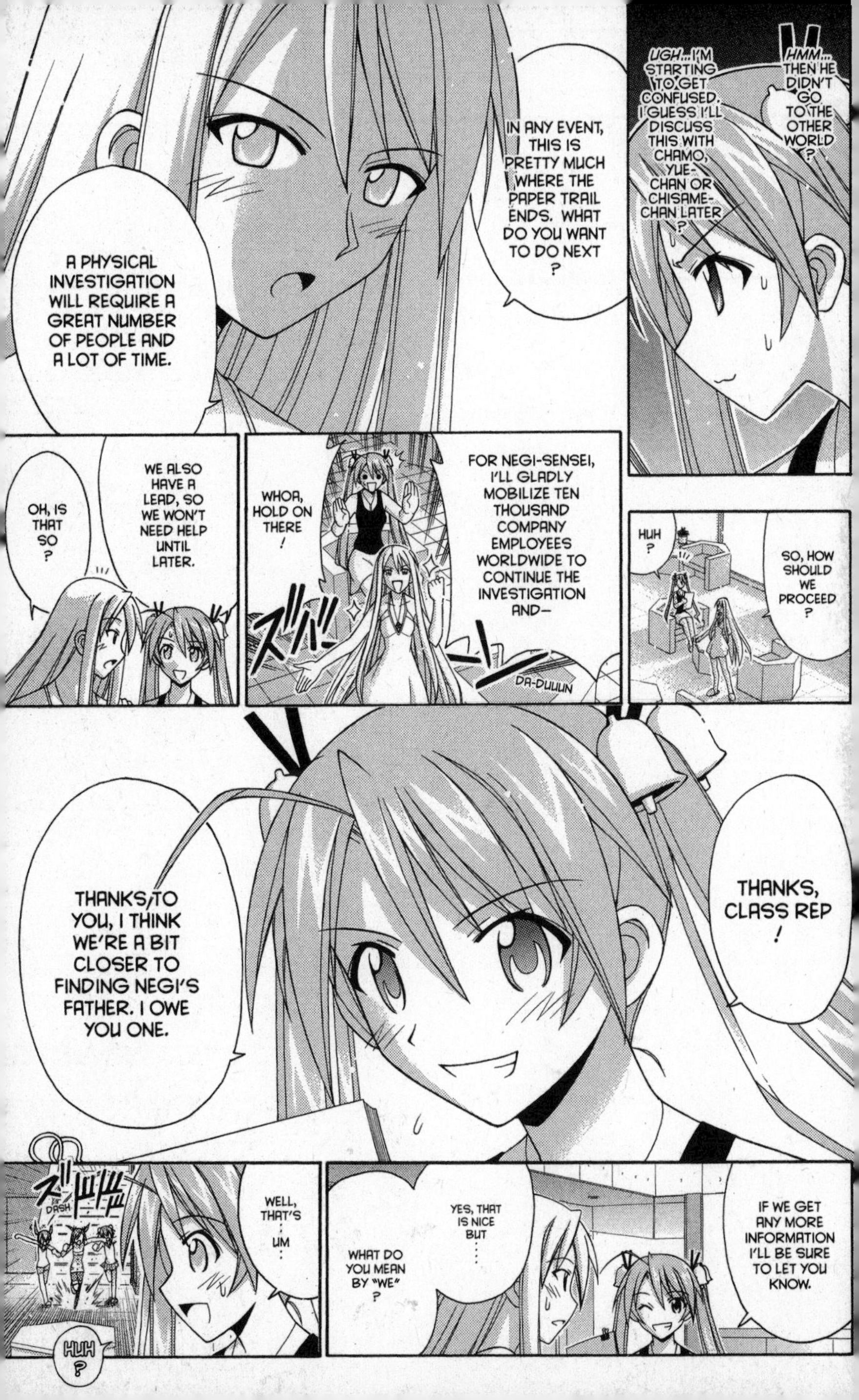
HMM... THEN HE DIDN'T GO TO THE OTHER WORLD?
UGH... I'M STARTING TO GET CONFUSED. I GUESS I'LL DISCUSS THIS WITH CHAMO, YUE-CHAN OR CHISAME-CHAN LATER?
IN ANY EVENT, THIS IS PRETTY MUCH WHERE THE PAPER TRAIL ENDS. WHAT DO YOU WANT TO DO NEXT?
A PHYSICAL INVESTIGATION WILL REQUIRE A GREAT NUMBER OF PEOPLE AND A LOT OF TIME.
SO, HOW SHOULD WE PROCEED?
HUH?
FOR NEGI-SENSEI, I'LL GLADLY MOBILIZE TEN THOUSAND COMPANY EMPLOYEES WORLDWIDE TO CONTINUE THE INVESTIGATION AND—
WHOA, HOLD ON THERE!
DA-DUUUN
WE ALSO HAVE A LEAD, SO WE WON'T NEED HELP UNTIL LATER.
OH, IS THAT SO?
THANKS, CLASS REP!
THANKS TO YOU, I THINK WE'RE A BIT CLOSER TO FINDING NEGI'S FATHER. I OWE YOU ONE.
IF WE GET ANY MORE INFORMATION I'LL BE SURE TO LET YOU KNOW.
YES, THAT IS NICE BUT...
WHAT DO YOU MEAN BY "WE"?
WELL, THAT'S... UM...
DASH
HUH?

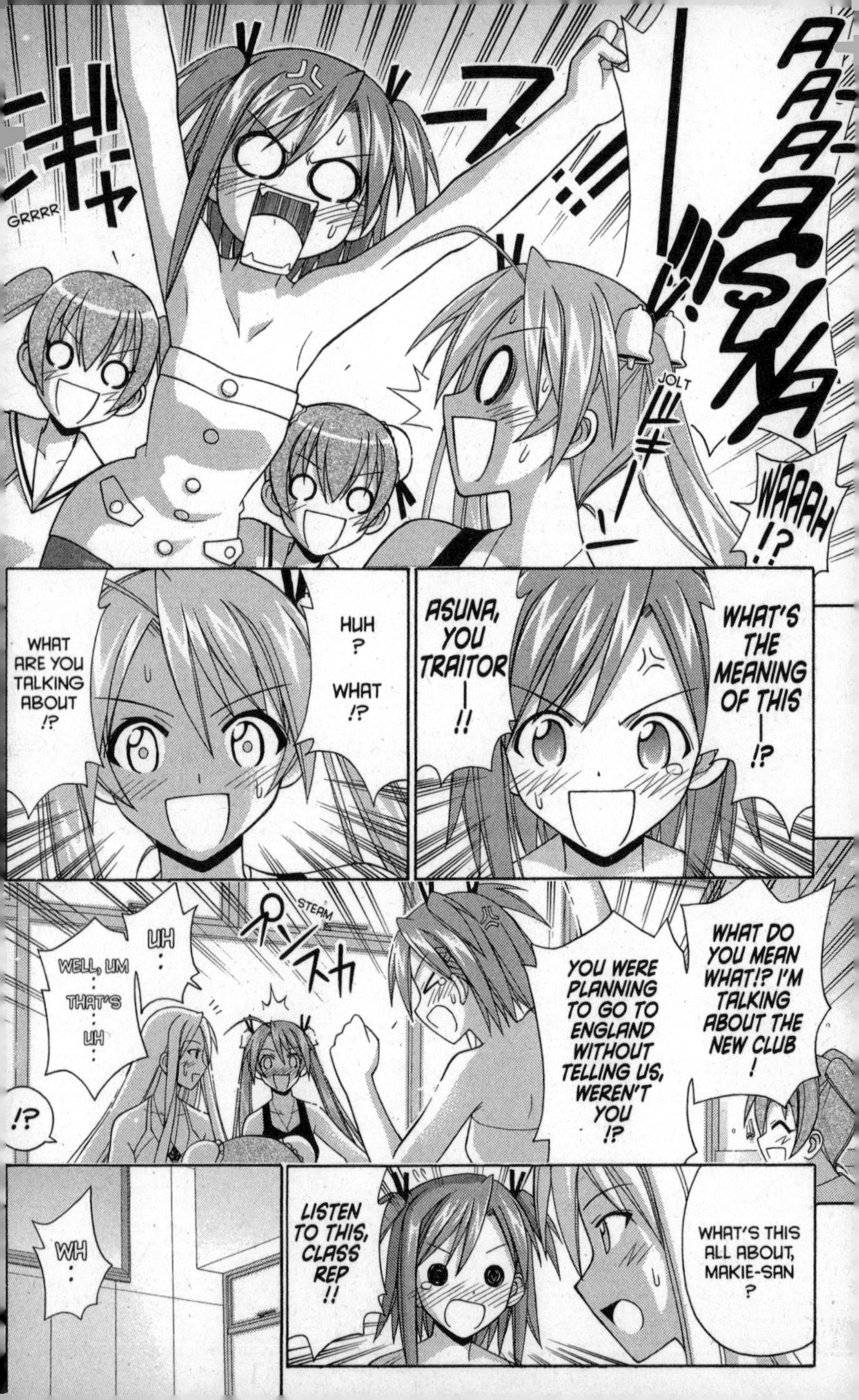
AAA-ASUNA!!
JOLT
WAAAH!?
GRRRR
WHAT'S THE MEANING OF THIS—!?
ASUNA, YOU TRAITOR—!!
HUH? WHAT!?
WHAT ARE YOU TALKING ABOUT!?
WHAT DO YOU MEAN WHAT!? I'M TALKING ABOUT THE NEW CLUB!
YOU WERE PLANNING TO GO TO ENGLAND WITHOUT TELLING US, WEREN'T YOU!?
STEAM
UH...
WELL, UM... THAT'S... UH...
!?
WHAT'S THIS ALL ABOUT, MAKIE-SAN?
LISTEN TO THIS, CLASS REP!!
WH...

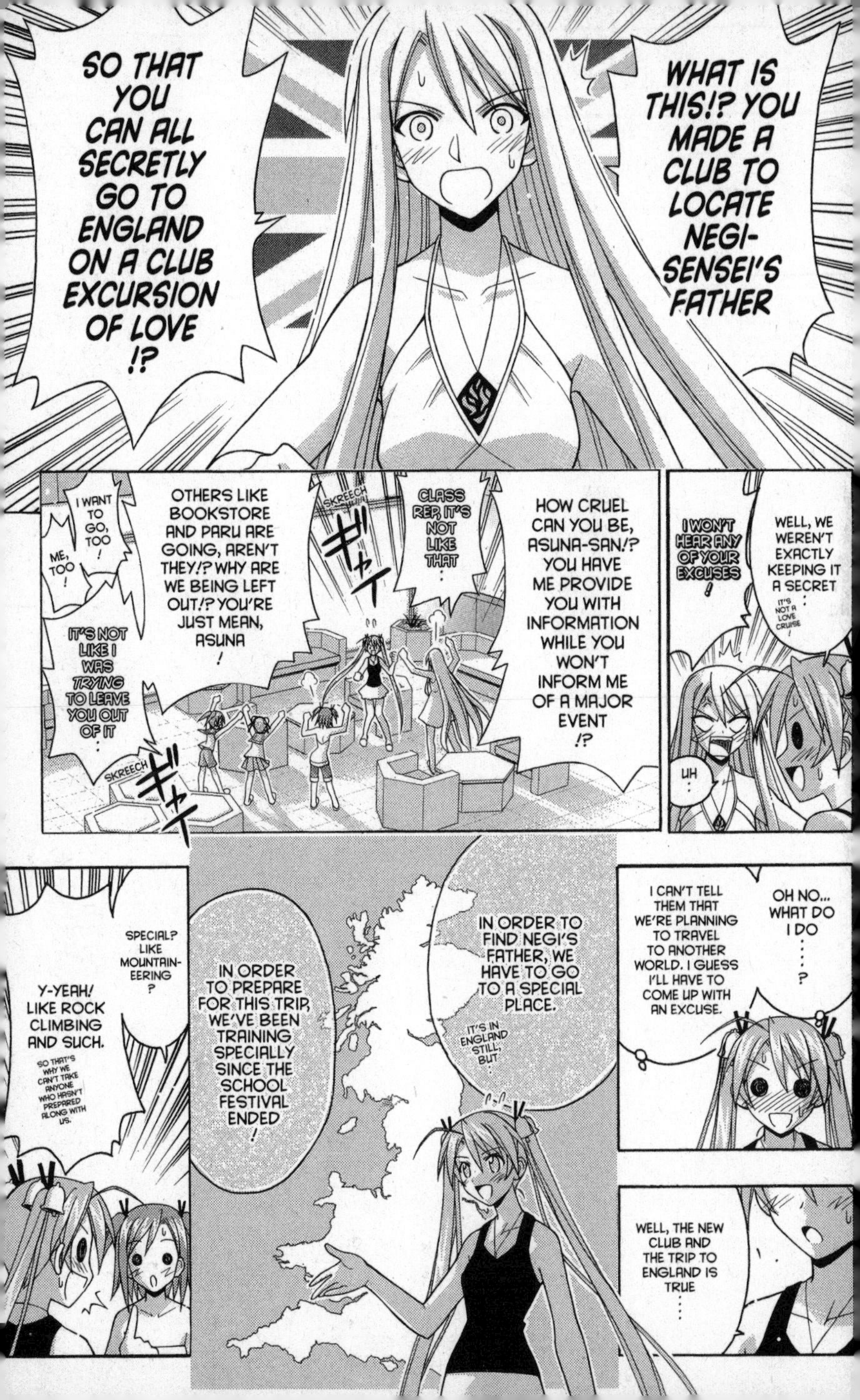
WHAT IS THIS!? YOU MADE A CLUB TO LOCATE NEGI-SENSEI'S FATHER
SO THAT YOU CAN ALL SECRETLY GO TO ENGLAND ON A CLUB EXCURSION OF LOVE !?
WELL, WE WEREN'T EXACTLY KEEPING IT A SECRET...
IT'S NOT A LOVE CRUISE!
I WON'T HEAR ANY OF YOUR EXCUSES!
UH...
HOW CRUEL CAN YOU BE, ASUNA-SAN!? YOU HAVE ME PROVIDE YOU WITH INFORMATION WHILE YOU WON'T INFORM ME OF A MAJOR EVENT !?
CLASS REP, IT'S NOT LIKE THAT...
SKREECH
OTHERS LIKE BOOKSTORE AND PARU ARE GOING, AREN'T THEY!? WHY ARE WE BEING LEFT OUT!? YOU'RE JUST MEAN, ASUNA!
I WANT TO GO, TOO!
ME, TOO!
IT'S NOT LIKE I WAS TRYING TO LEAVE YOU OUT OF IT...
SKREECH
OH NO... WHAT DO I DO.....?
I CAN'T TELL THEM THAT WE'RE PLANNING TO TRAVEL TO ANOTHER WORLD. I GUESS I'LL HAVE TO COME UP WITH AN EXCUSE.
WELL, THE NEW CLUB AND THE TRIP TO ENGLAND IS TRUE....
IN ORDER TO FIND NEGI'S FATHER, WE HAVE TO GO TO A SPECIAL PLACE.
IT'S IN ENGLAND STILL, BUT...
IN ORDER TO PREPARE FOR THIS TRIP, WE'VE BEEN TRAINING SPECIALLY SINCE THE SCHOOL FESTIVAL ENDED!
SPECIAL? LIKE MOUNTAIN-EERING?
Y-YEAH! LIKE ROCK CLIMBING AND SUCH.
SO THAT'S WHY WE CAN'T TAKE ANYONE WHO HASN'T PREPARED ALONG WITH US.

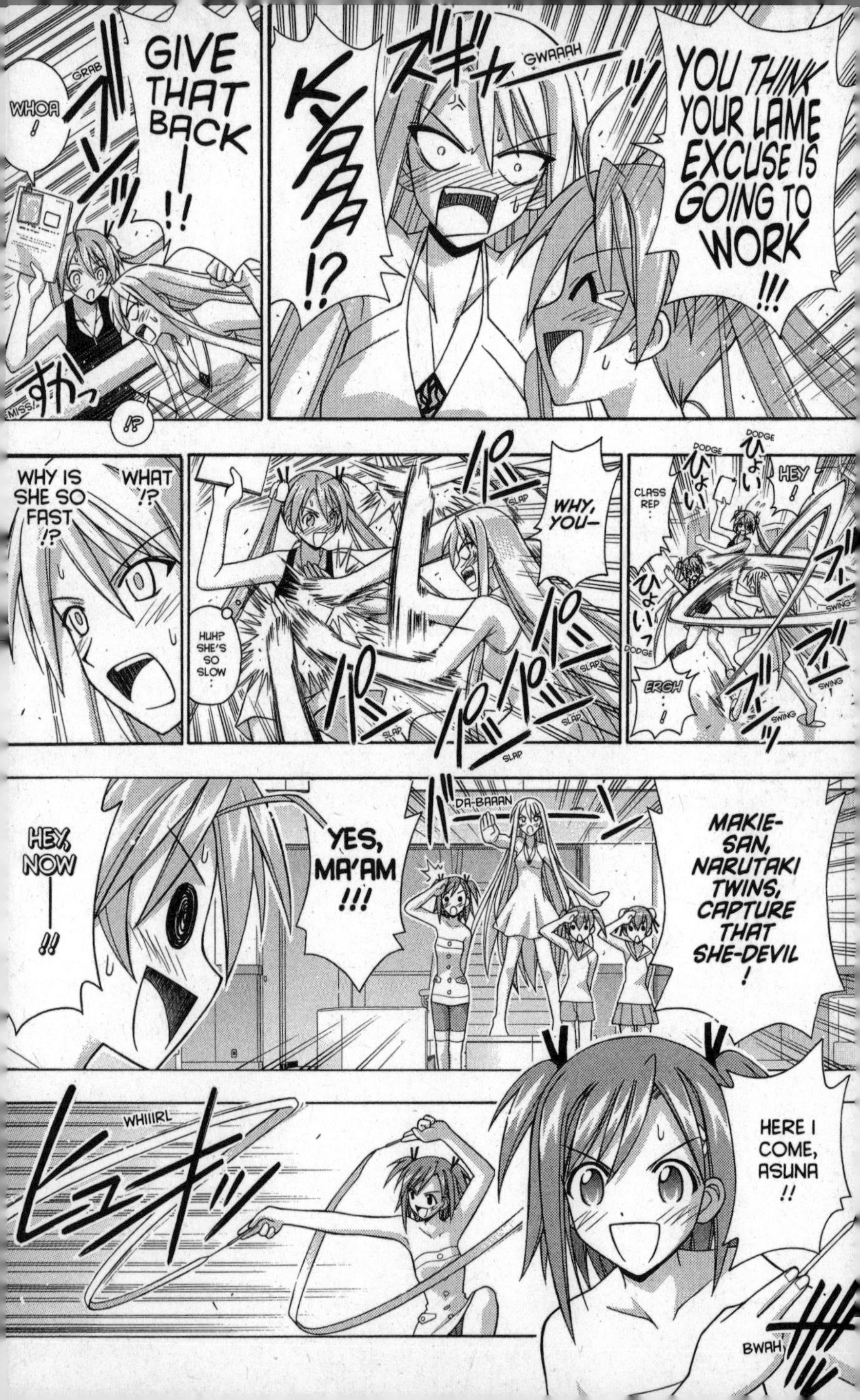
GWAAAH
YOU THINK YOUR LAME EXCUSE IS GOING TO WORK!!!
KYAAA!?
GIVE THAT BACK—!!
GRAB
WHOA!
MISS!
!?
DODGE
DODGE
HEY!
CLASS REP...
DODGE
SWING
SWING
SWING
ERGH...!
WHY, YOU—
SLAP
SLAP
SLAP
SLAP
SLAP
HUH? SHE'S SO SLOW...
WHAT!?
WHY IS SHE SO FAST!?
MAKIE-SAN, NARUTAKI TWINS, CAPTURE THAT SHE-DEVIL!
DA-BAAAN
YES, MA'AM!!!
HEY, NOW—!!
HERE I COME, ASUNA!!
BWAH
WHIIIRL

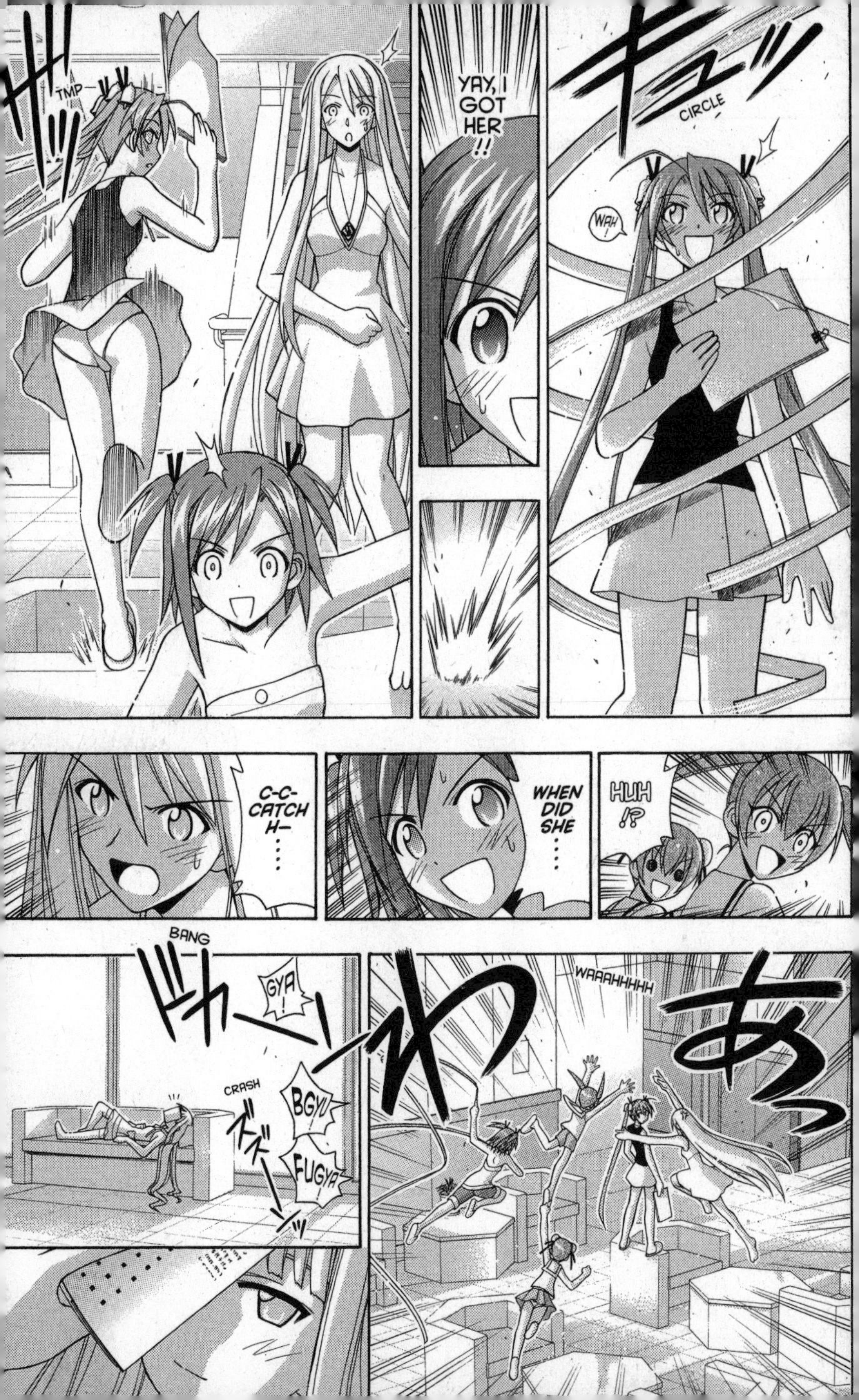
CIRCLE
WAH!
YAY, I GOT HER!!
TMP—
HUH!?
WHEN DID SHE.....
C-C-CATCH H—.....
WAAAHHHHH
BANG
GYA!
CRASH
BGYU!
FUGYA!

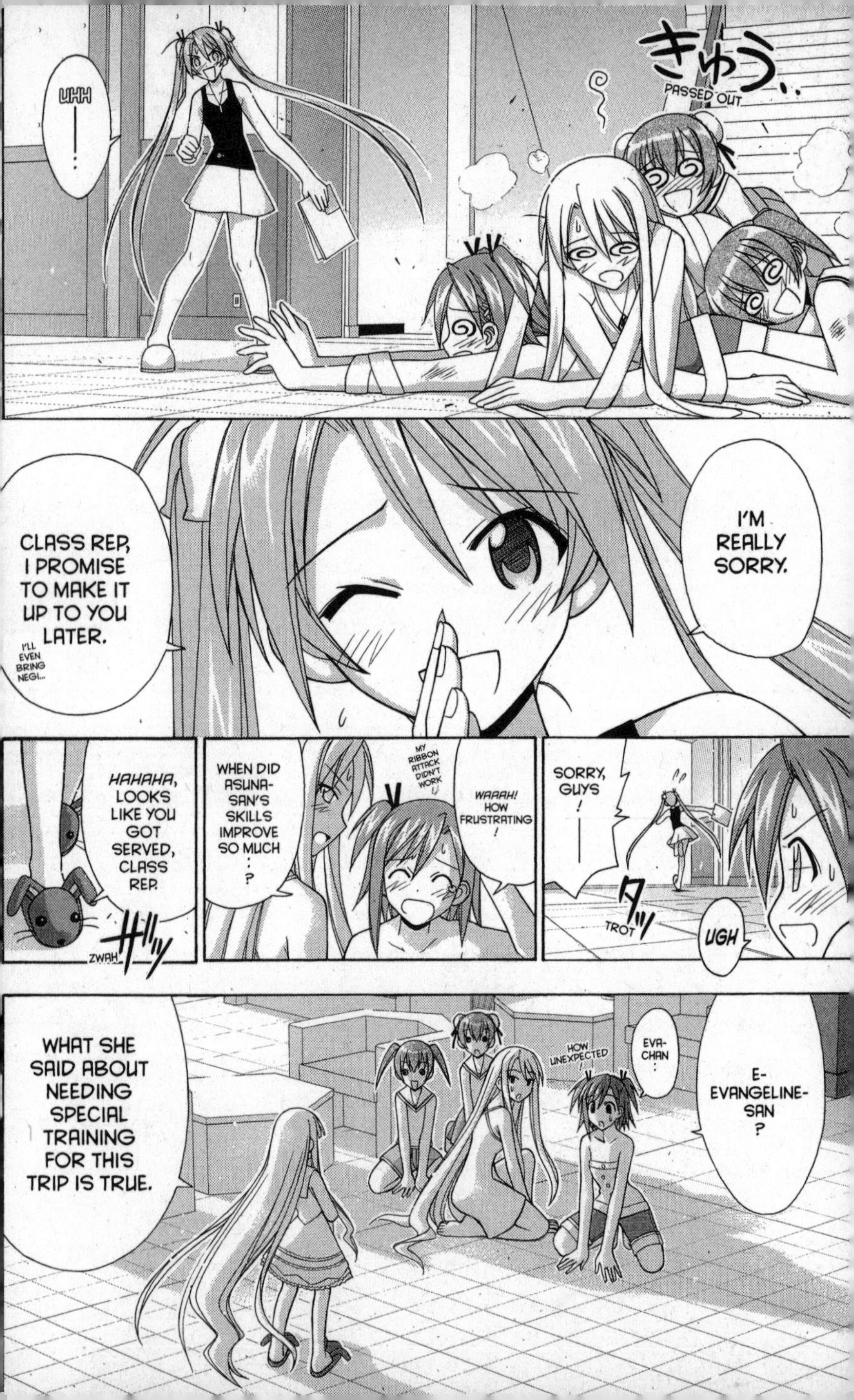
きゅう
PASSED OUT
UHH...!
I'M REALLY SORRY.
CLASS REP, I PROMISE TO MAKE IT UP TO YOU LATER.
I'LL EVEN BRING NEGI...
SORRY, GUYS!
タッ
TROT
UGH
WAAAH! HOW FRUSTRATING!
MY RIBBON ATTACK DIDN'T WORK!!
WHEN DID ASUNA-SAN'S SKILLS IMPROVE SO MUCH...?
HAHAHA, LOOKS LIKE YOU GOT SERVED, CLASS REP.
ザッ
ZWAH
E-EVANGELINE-SAN?
EVA-CHAN...
HOW UNEXPECTED
WHAT SHE SAID ABOUT NEEDING SPECIAL TRAINING FOR THIS TRIP IS TRUE.

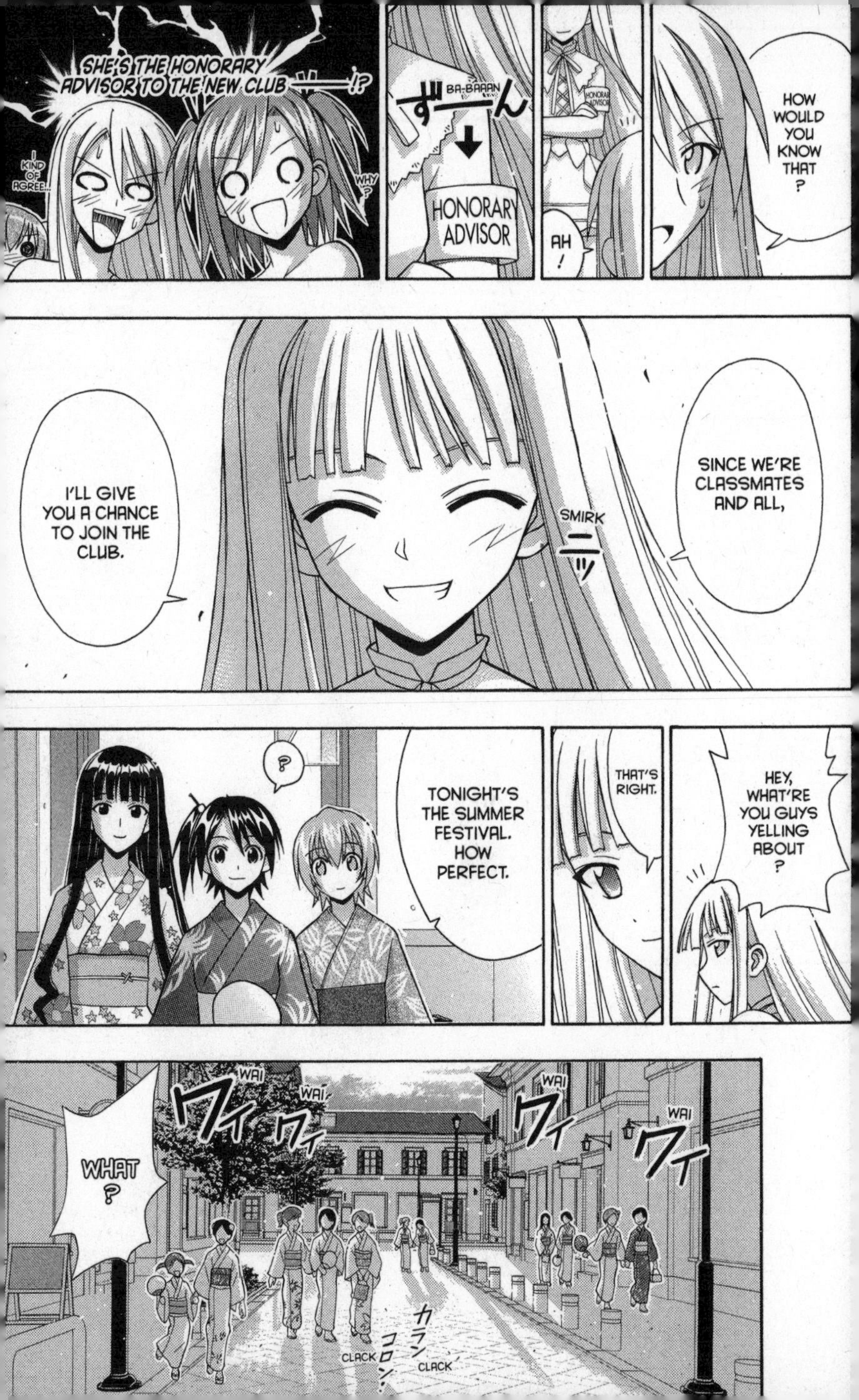
HOW WOULD YOU KNOW THAT?
AH!
BA-BAAAN
HONORARY ADVISOR
SHE'S THE HONORARY ADVISOR TO THE NEW CLUB—!?
WHY?
I KIND OF AGREE...
SINCE WE'RE CLASSMATES AND ALL,
SMIRK
I'LL GIVE YOU A CHANCE TO JOIN THE CLUB.
HEY, WHAT'RE YOU GUYS YELLING ABOUT?
THAT'S RIGHT.
TONIGHT'S THE SUMMER FESTIVAL. HOW PERFECT.
?
WAI
WAI
WAI
WAI
WHAT?
CLACK
CLACK

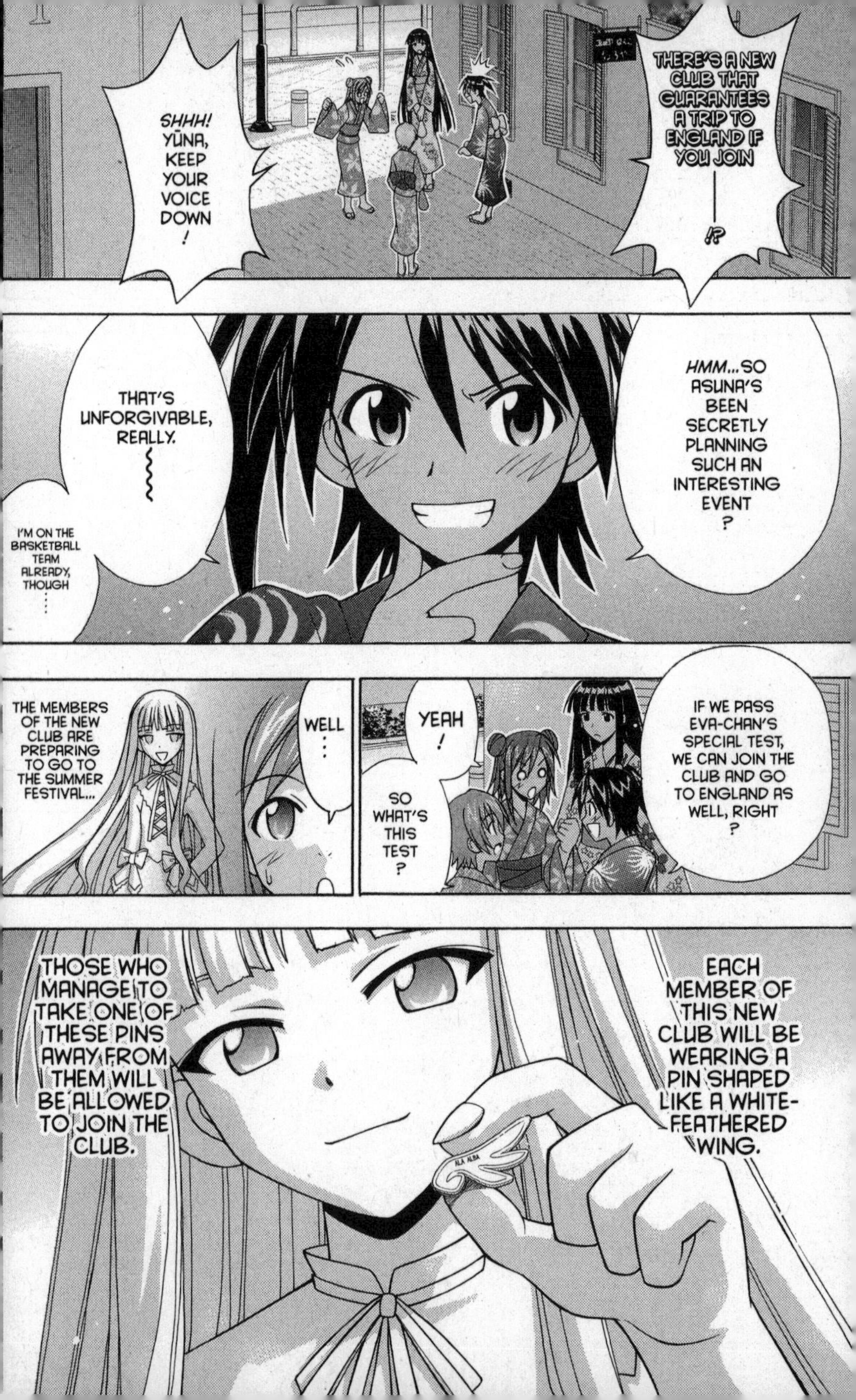
THERE'S A NEW CLUB THAT GUARANTEES A TRIP TO ENGLAND IF YOU JOIN —— !?
SHHH! YŪNA, KEEP YOUR VOICE DOWN!
HMM... SO ASUNA'S BEEN SECRETLY PLANNING SUCH AN INTERESTING EVENT?
THAT'S UNFORGIVABLE, REALLY.
I'M ON THE BASKETBALL TEAM ALREADY, THOUGH...
IF WE PASS EVA-CHAN'S SPECIAL TEST, WE CAN JOIN THE CLUB AND GO TO ENGLAND AS WELL, RIGHT?
YEAH!
SO WHAT'S THIS TEST?
WELL...
THE MEMBERS OF THE NEW CLUB ARE PREPARING TO GO TO THE SUMMER FESTIVAL...
EACH MEMBER OF THIS NEW CLUB WILL BE WEARING A PIN SHAPED LIKE A WHITE-FEATHERED WING.
ALA ALBA
THOSE WHO MANAGE TO TAKE ONE OF THESE PINS AWAY FROM THEM WILL BE ALLOWED TO JOIN THE CLUB.

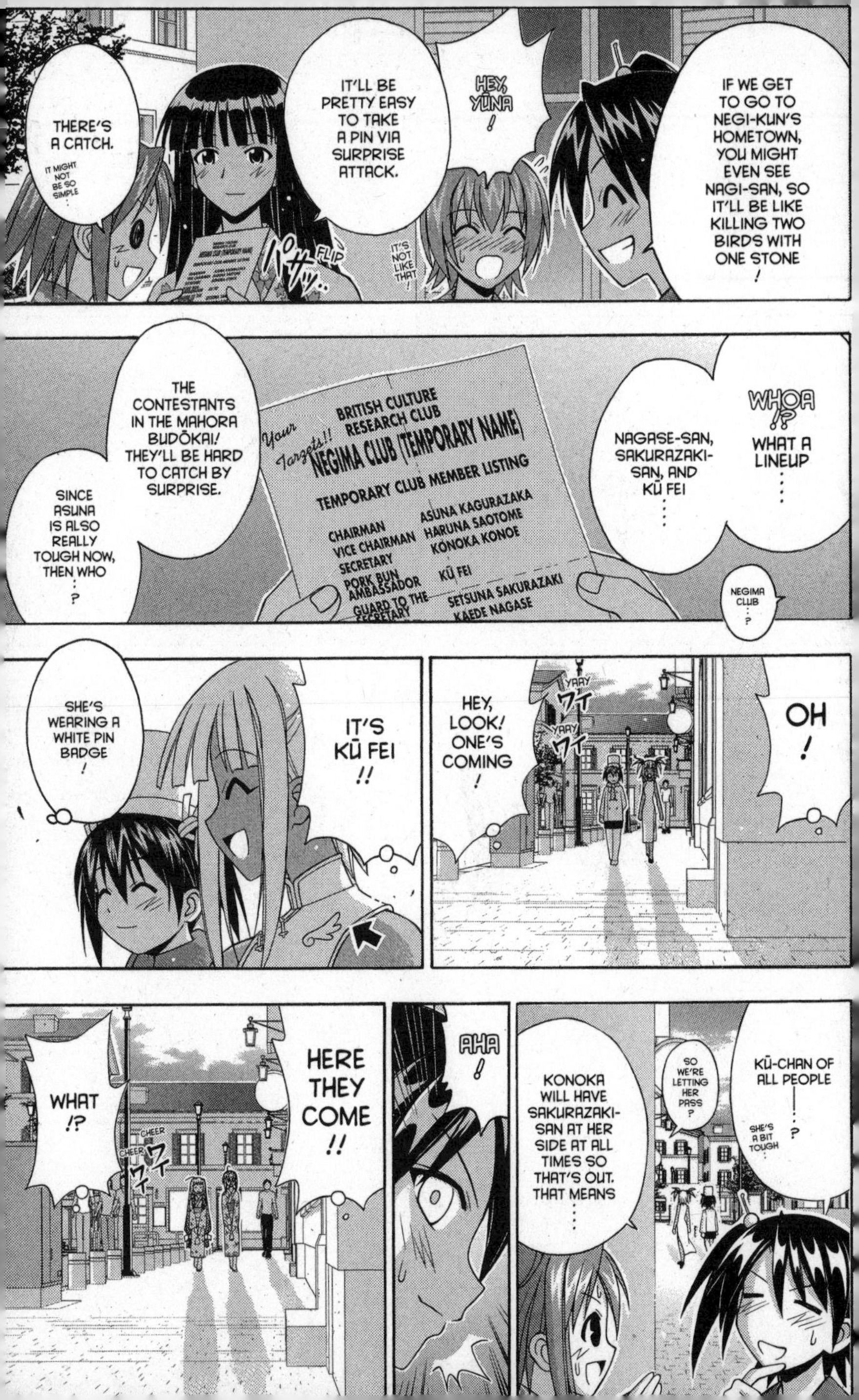
IF WE GET TO GO TO NEGI-KUN'S HOMETOWN, YOU MIGHT EVEN SEE NAGI-SAN, SO IT'LL BE LIKE KILLING TWO BIRDS WITH ONE STONE!
HEY, YŪNA!
IT'S NOT LIKE THAT
IT'LL BE PRETTY EASY TO TAKE A PIN VIA SURPRISE ATTACK.
FLIP
THERE'S A CATCH.
IT MIGHT NOT BE SO SIMPLE...
WHOA!? WHAT A LINEUP...
NAGASE-SAN, SAKURAZAKI-SAN, AND KŪ FEI...
NEGIMA CLUB...?
Your Targets!!
BRITISH CULTURE RESEARCH CLUB
NEGIMA CLUB (TEMPORARY NAME)
TEMPORARY CLUB MEMBER LISTING
CHAIRMAN ASUNA KAGURAZAKA
VICE CHAIRMAN HARUNA SAOTOME
SECRETARY KONOKA KONOE
PORK BUN AMBASSADOR KŪ FEI
GUARD TO THE SECRETARY SETSUNA SAKURAZAKI
KAEDE NAGASE
THE CONTESTANTS IN THE MAHORA BUDŌKAI! THEY'LL BE HARD TO CATCH BY SURPRISE.
SINCE ASUNA IS ALSO REALLY TOUGH NOW, THEN WHO...?
OH!
HEY, LOOK! ONE'S COMING!
YAAY
YAAY
IT'S KŪ FEI!!
SHE'S WEARING A WHITE PIN BADGE!
KŪ-CHAN OF ALL PEOPLE...?
SHE'S A BIT TOUGH
SO WE'RE LETTING HER PASS?
KONOKA WILL HAVE SAKURAZAKI-SAN AT HER SIDE AT ALL TIMES SO THAT'S OUT. THAT MEANS...
AHA!
HERE THEY COME!!
WHAT!?
CHEER
CHEER

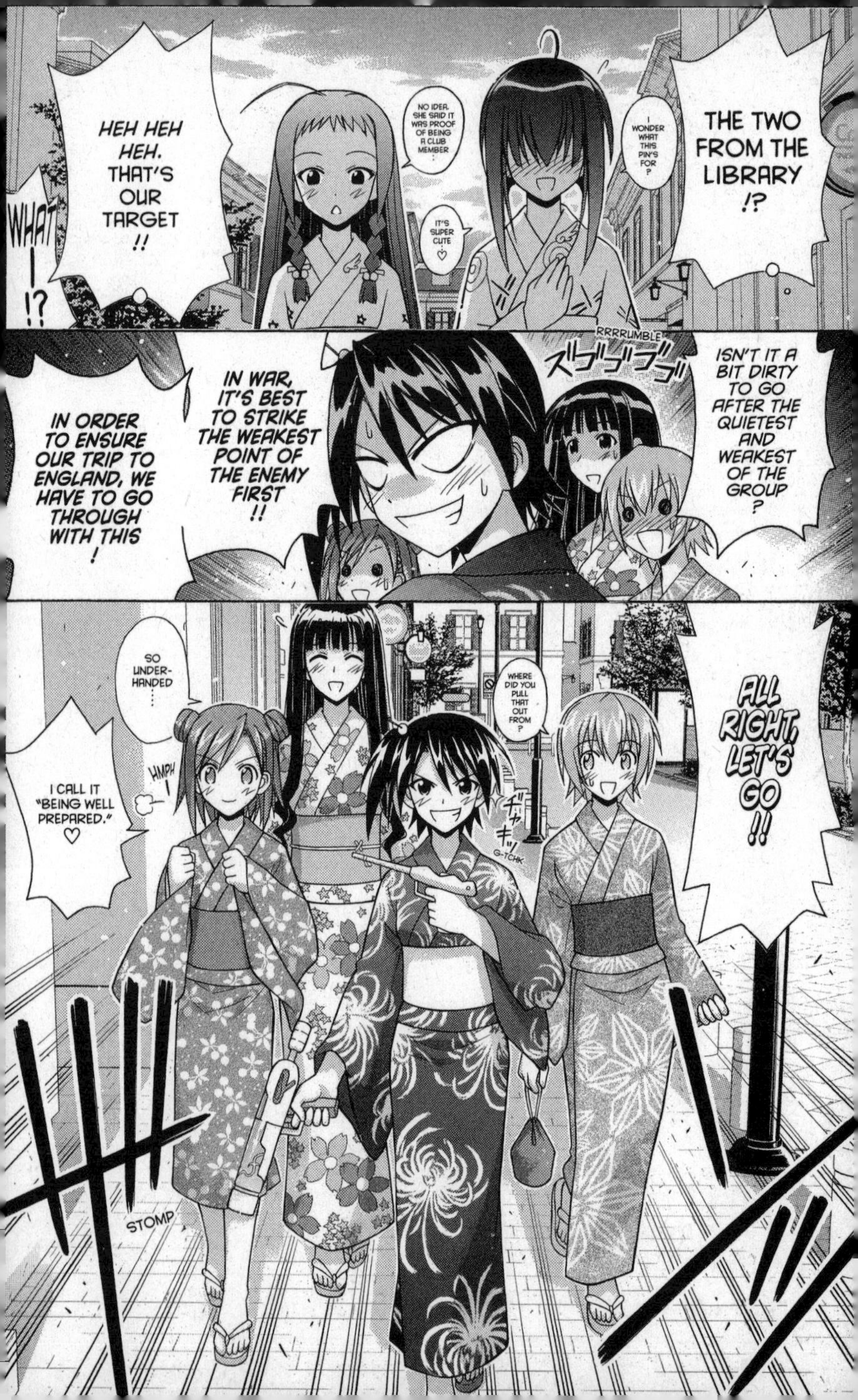
THE TWO FROM THE LIBRARY !?
I WONDER WHAT THIS PIN'S FOR ?
NO IDEA. SHE SAID IT WAS PROOF OF BEING A CLUB MEMBER ...
IT'S SUPER CUTE ♡
HEH HEH HEH. THAT'S OUR TARGET !!
WHAT !?
ISN'T IT A BIT DIRTY TO GO AFTER THE QUIETEST AND WEAKEST OF THE GROUP ?
RRRRUMBLE
IN WAR, IT'S BEST TO STRIKE THE WEAKEST POINT OF THE ENEMY FIRST !!
IN ORDER TO ENSURE OUR TRIP TO ENGLAND, WE HAVE TO GO THROUGH WITH THIS !
ALL RIGHT, LET'S GO !!
WHERE DID YOU PULL THAT OUT FROM ?
G-TCHK
SO UNDER-HANDED ......
HMPH !
I CALL IT "BEING WELL PREPARED." ♡
STOMP

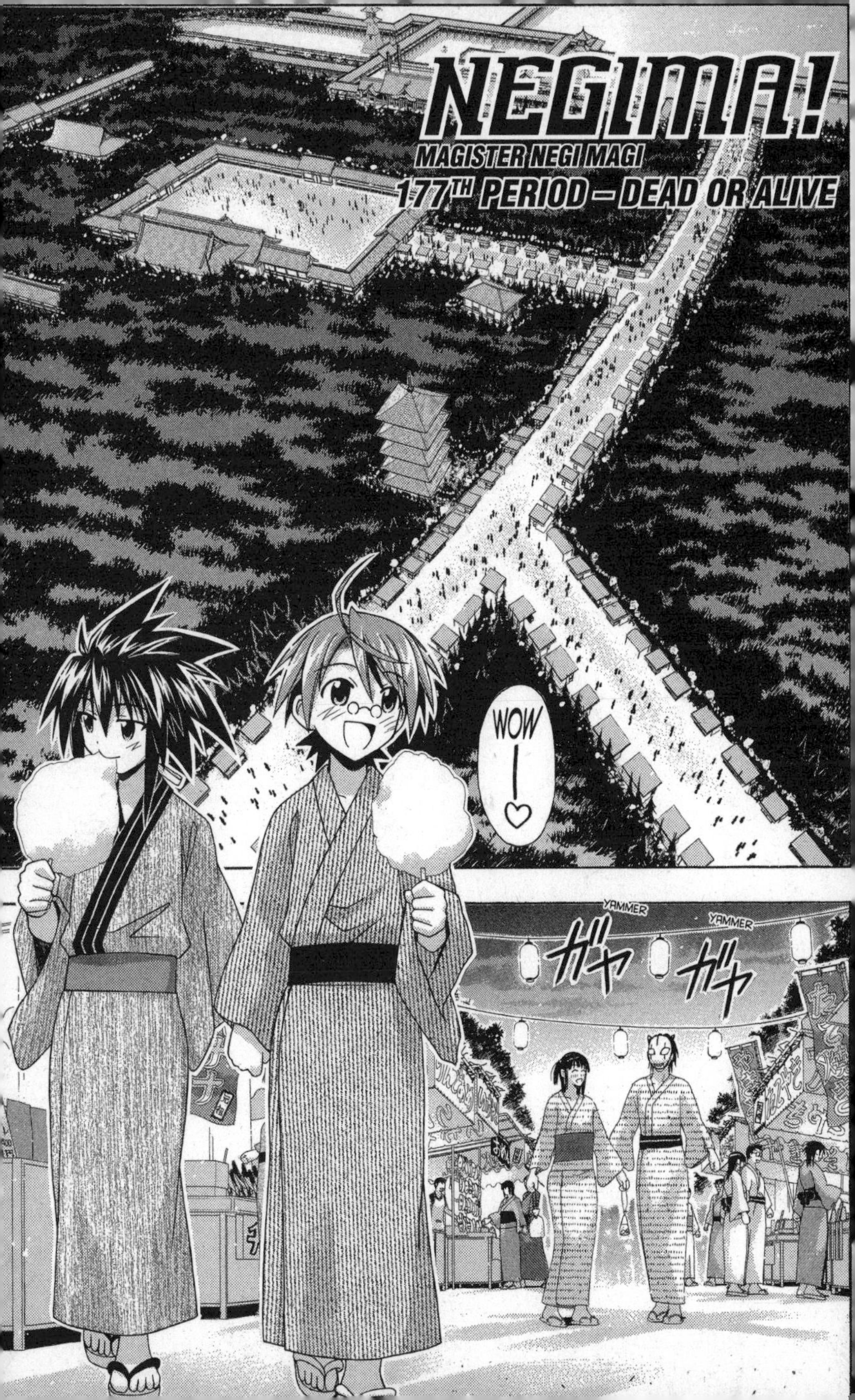
NEGIMA!
MAGISTER NEGI MAGI
177TH PERIOD – DEAD OR ALIVE
WOW! ♡
YAMMER YAMMER
ガヤ ガヤ

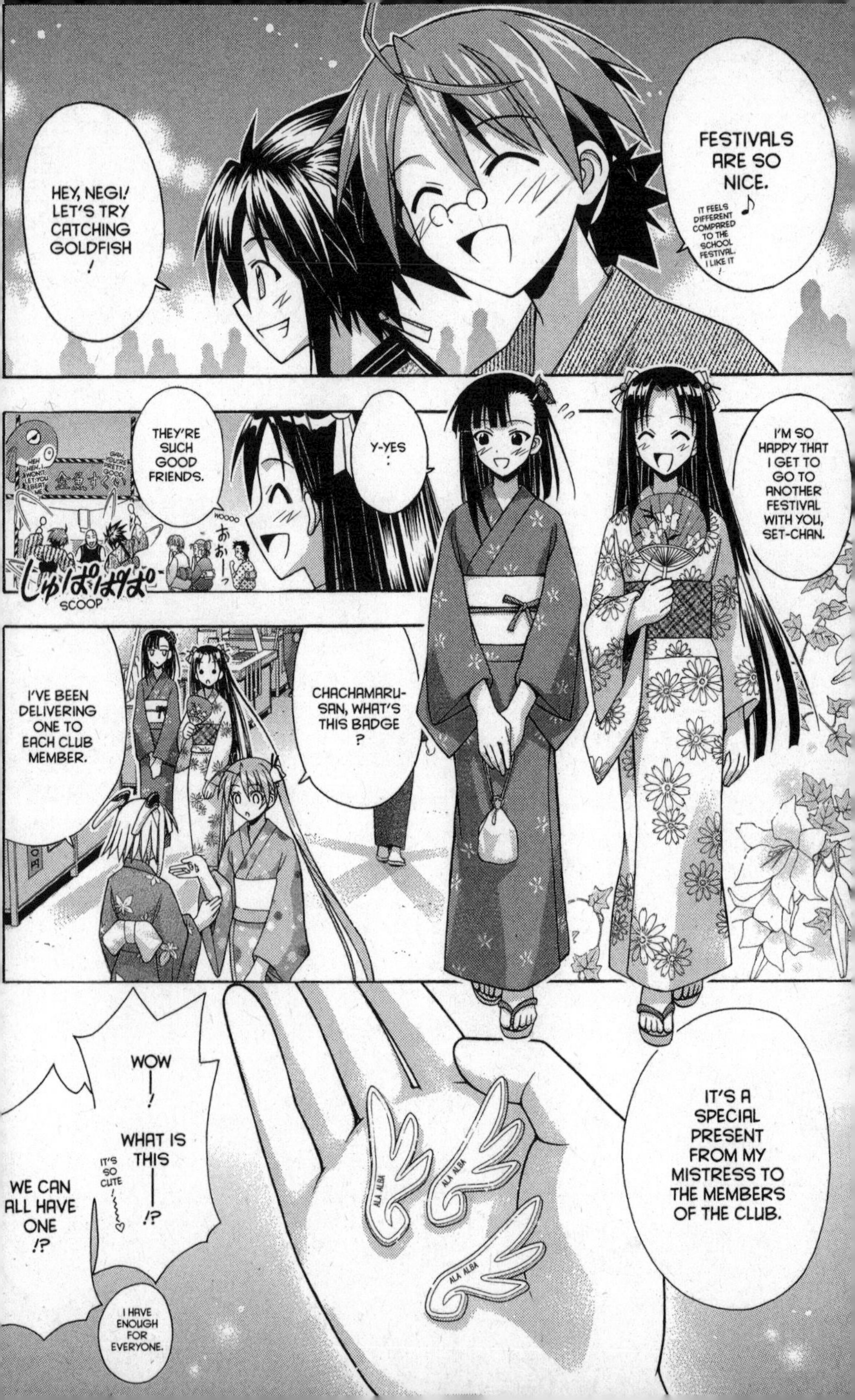
FESTIVALS ARE SO NICE. ♪
IT FEELS DIFFERENT COMPARED TO THE SCHOOL FESTIVAL. I LIKE IT!
HEY, NEGI! LET'S TRY CATCHING GOLDFISH!
I'M SO HAPPY THAT I GET TO GO TO ANOTHER FESTIVAL WITH YOU, SET-CHAN.
Y-YES:
THEY'RE SUCH GOOD FRIENDS.
WOOOO
おおーっ
GAH, YOU'RE PRETTY GOOD
金魚すくい
HEH HEH, I WON'T LET YOU BEAT ME
しゅぱぱぱ
SCOOP
CHACHAMARU-SAN, WHAT'S THIS BADGE?
I'VE BEEN DELIVERING ONE TO EACH CLUB MEMBER.
IT'S A SPECIAL PRESENT FROM MY MISTRESS TO THE MEMBERS OF THE CLUB.
ALA ALBA
ALA ALBA
ALA ALBA
WOW! WHAT IS THIS—!?
IT'S SO CUTE!~♡
WE CAN ALL HAVE ONE!?
I HAVE ENOUGH FOR EVERYONE.

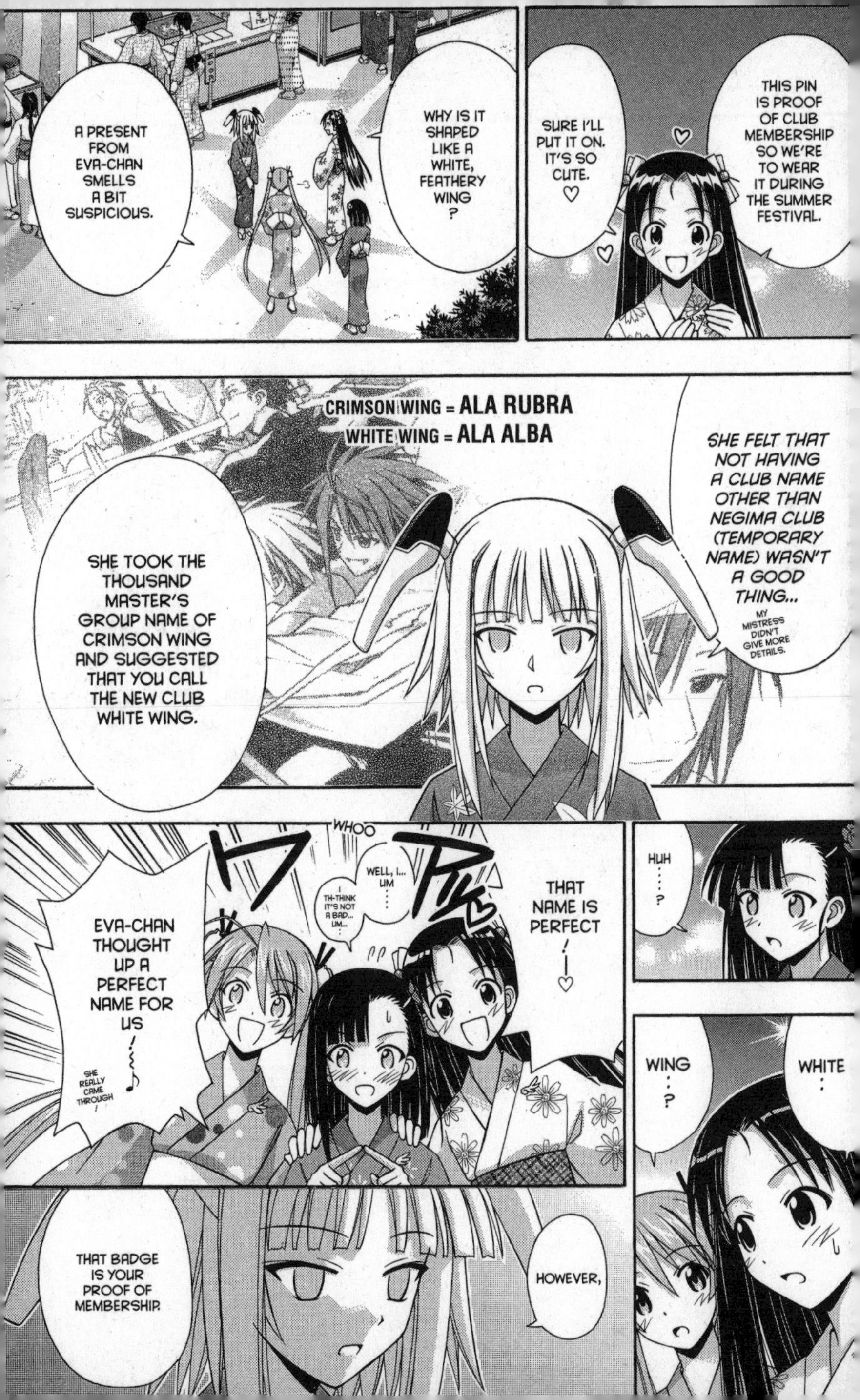
THIS PIN IS PROOF OF CLUB MEMBERSHIP SO WE'RE TO WEAR IT DURING THE SUMMER FESTIVAL.
SURE I'LL PUT IT ON. IT'S SO CUTE. ♡
WHY IS IT SHAPED LIKE A WHITE, FEATHERY WING?
A PRESENT FROM EVA-CHAN SMELLS A BIT SUSPICIOUS.
SHE FELT THAT NOT HAVING A CLUB NAME OTHER THAN NEGIMA CLUB (TEMPORARY NAME) WASN'T A GOOD THING...
MY MISTRESS DIDN'T GIVE MORE DETAILS.
CRIMSON WING = ALA RUBRA
WHITE WING = ALA ALBA
SHE TOOK THE THOUSAND MASTER'S GROUP NAME OF CRIMSON WING AND SUGGESTED THAT YOU CALL THE NEW CLUB WHITE WING.
HUH...?
WHITE...
WING...?
THAT NAME IS PERFECT! ♡
WHOO
WELL, I... UM...
I TH-THINK IT'S NOT A BAD... UM...
EVA-CHAN THOUGHT UP A PERFECT NAME FOR US!
SHE REALLY CAME THROUGH!
HOWEVER,
THAT BADGE IS YOUR PROOF OF MEMBERSHIP.

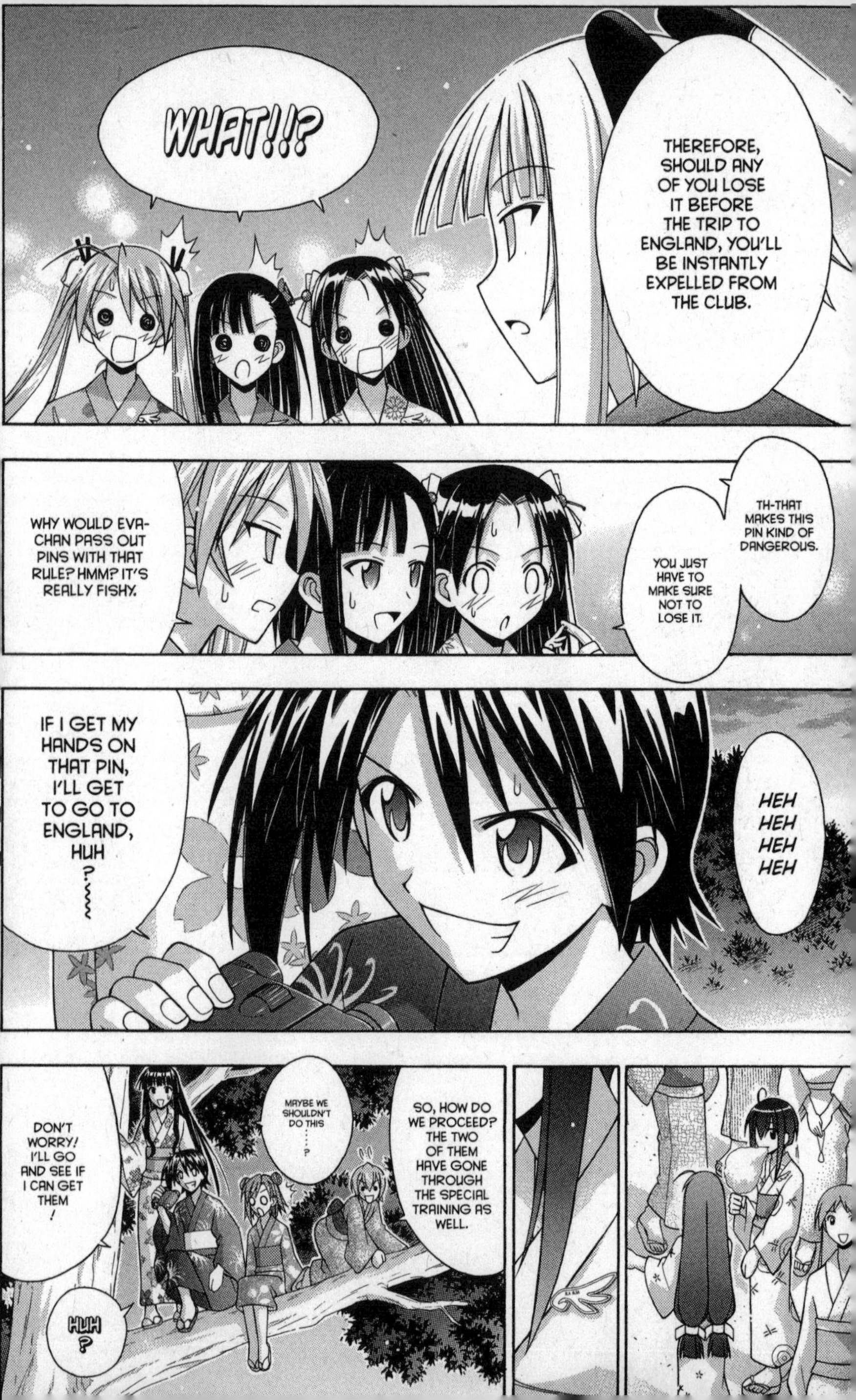
THEREFORE, SHOULD ANY OF YOU LOSE IT BEFORE THE TRIP TO ENGLAND, YOU'LL BE INSTANTLY EXPELLED FROM THE CLUB.
WHAT!!?
TH-THAT MAKES THIS PIN KIND OF DANGEROUS.
YOU JUST HAVE TO MAKE SURE NOT TO LOSE IT.
WHY WOULD EVA-CHAN PASS OUT PINS WITH THAT RULE? HMM? IT'S REALLY FISHY.
HEH HEH HEH HEH
IF I GET MY HANDS ON THAT PIN, I'LL GET TO GO TO ENGLAND, HUH?......
SO, HOW DO WE PROCEED? THE TWO OF THEM HAVE GONE THROUGH THE SPECIAL TRAINING AS WELL.
MAYBE WE SHOULDN'T DO THIS.....?
DON'T WORRY! I'LL GO AND SEE IF I CAN GET THEM!
HUH?

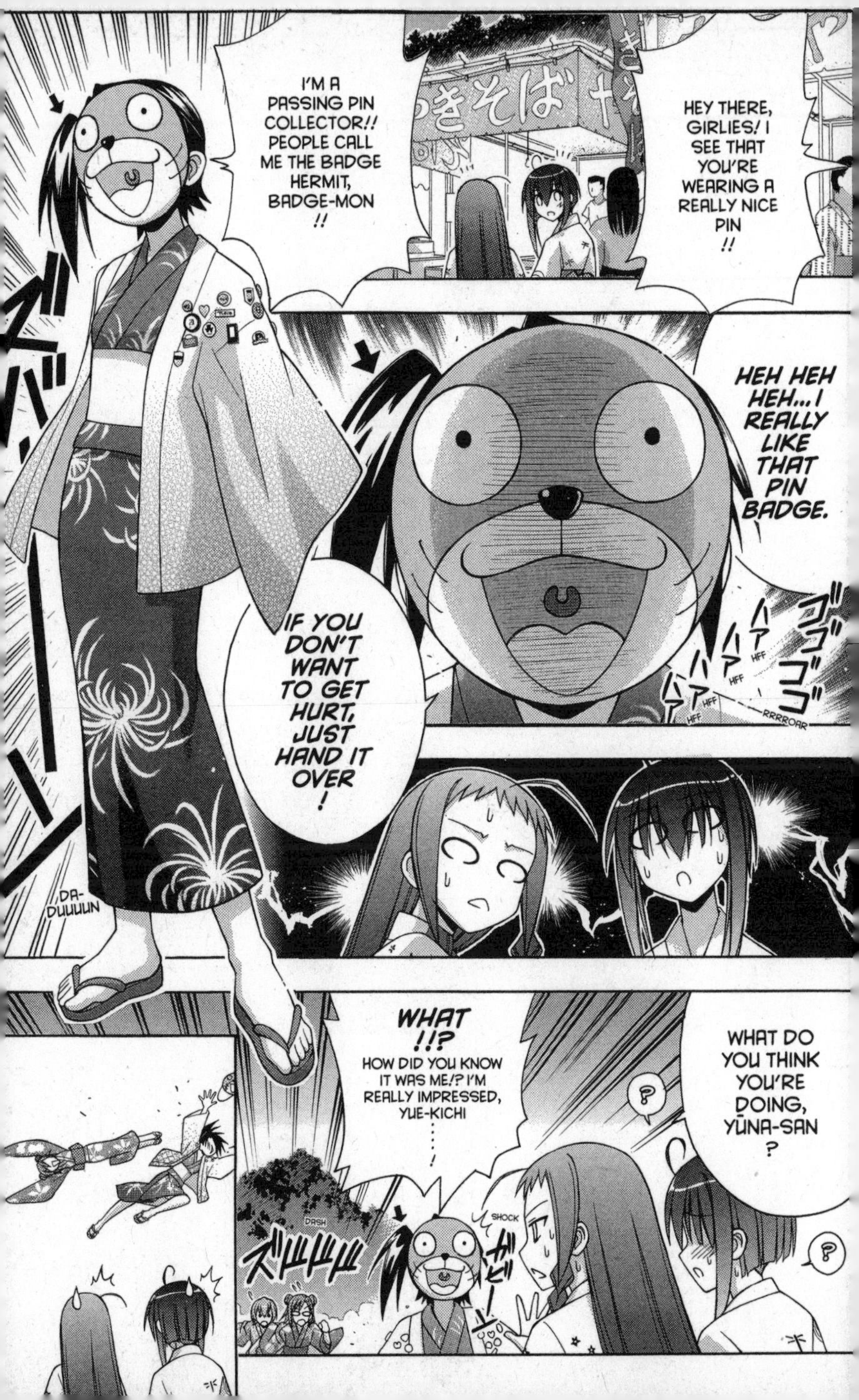
HEY THERE, GIRLIES! I SEE THAT YOU'RE WEARING A REALLY NICE PIN!!
HEH HEH HEH... I REALLY LIKE THAT PIN BADGE.
IF YOU DON'T WANT TO GET HURT, JUST HAND IT OVER!
HFF HFF HFF HFF
RRRROAR
I'M A PASSING PIN COLLECTOR!! PEOPLE CALL ME THE BADGE HERMIT, BADGE-MON!!
DA-DUUUUN
WHAT DO YOU THINK YOU'RE DOING, YŪNA-SAN?
?
?
WHAT!!?
HOW DID YOU KNOW IT WAS ME!? I'M REALLY IMPRESSED, YUE-KICHI
......!
SHOCK
DASH

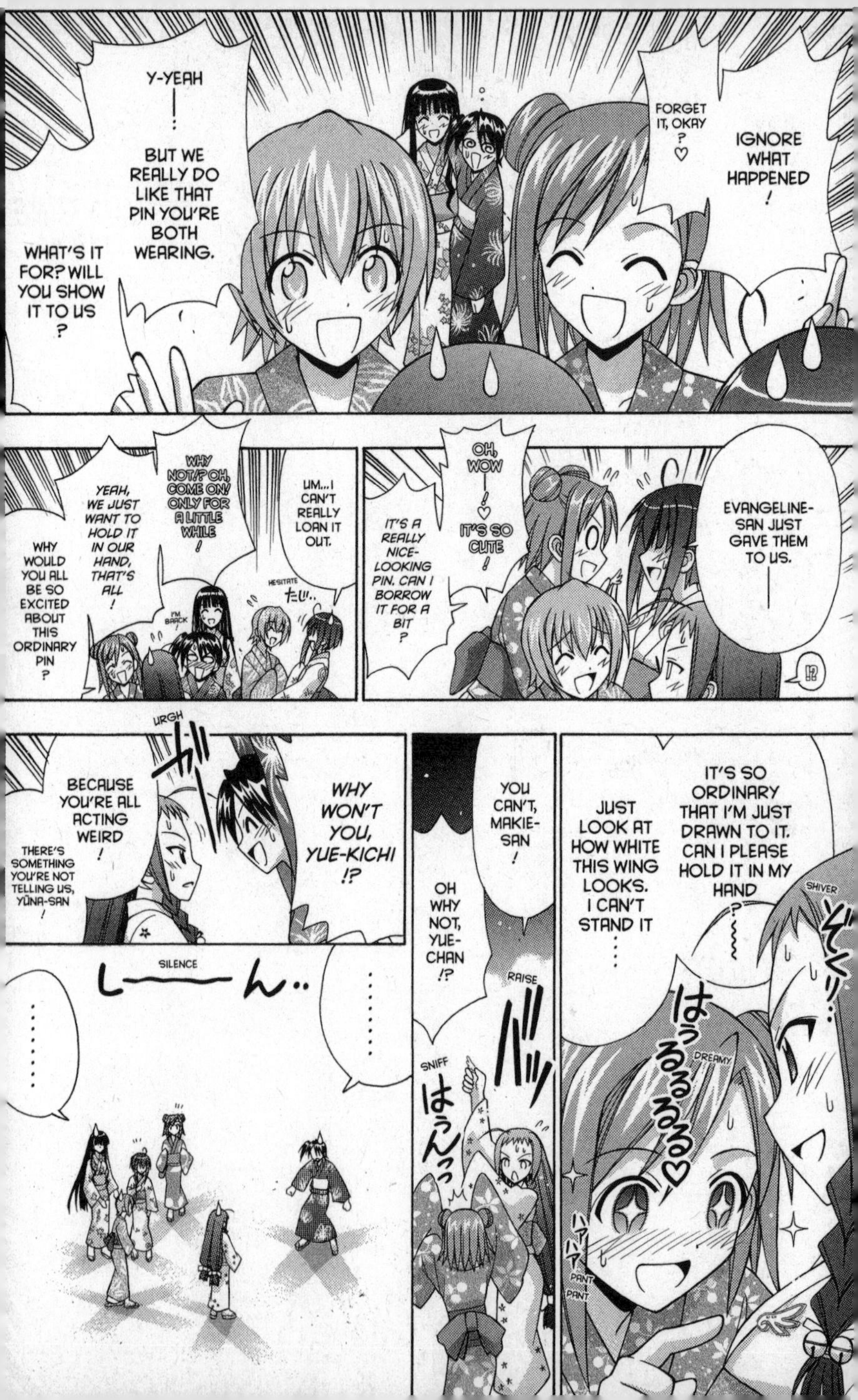
IGNORE WHAT HAPPENED!
FORGET IT, OKAY?♡
Y-YEAH—...
BUT WE REALLY DO LIKE THAT PIN YOU'RE BOTH WEARING.
WHAT'S IT FOR? WILL YOU SHOW IT TO US?
EVANGELINE-SAN JUST GAVE THEM TO US.—
!?
OH, WOW—!♡
IT'S SO CUTE!
IT'S A REALLY NICE-LOOKING PIN. CAN I BORROW IT FOR A BIT?
UM...I CAN'T REALLY LOAN IT OUT.
HESITATE
たじ..
WHY NOT!? OH, COME ON! ONLY FOR A LITTLE WHILE!
YEAH, WE JUST WANT TO HOLD IT IN OUR HAND, THAT'S ALL!
I'M BAACK!
WHY WOULD YOU ALL BE SO EXCITED ABOUT THIS ORDINARY PIN?
IT'S SO ORDINARY THAT I'M JUST DRAWN TO IT. CAN I PLEASE HOLD IT IN MY HAND?~~
JUST LOOK AT HOW WHITE THIS WING LOOKS. I CAN'T STAND IT....
SHIVER
DREAMY
PANT PANT
YOU CAN'T, MAKIE-SAN!
OH WHY NOT, YUE-CHAN!?
RAISE
SNIFF
WHY WON'T YOU, YUE-KICHI!?
URGH
BECAUSE YOU'RE ALL ACTING WEIRD!
THERE'S SOMETHING YOU'RE NOT TELLING US, YŪNA-SAN!
......
SILENCE
しーーーん..
......

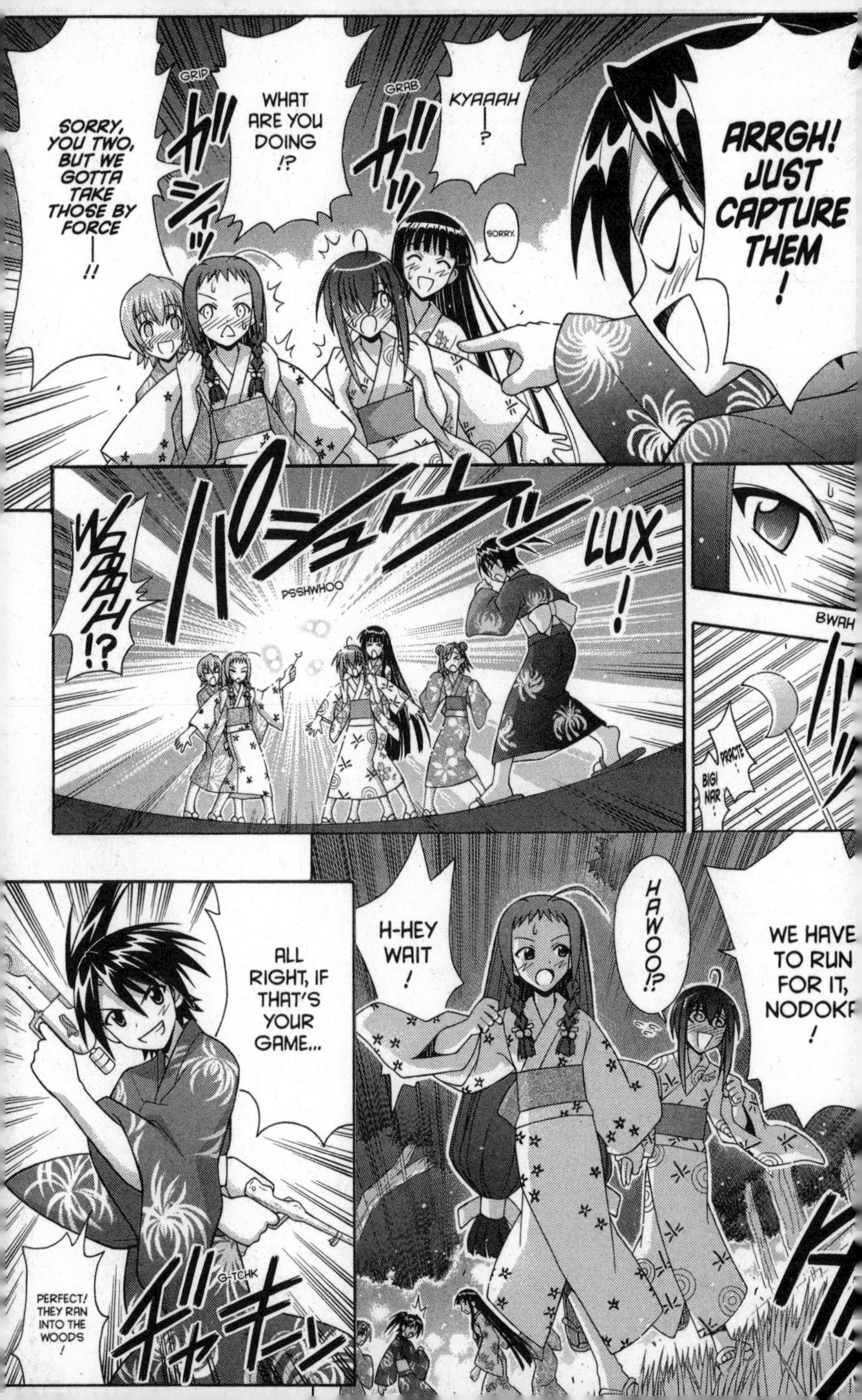
ARRGH! JUST CAPTURE THEM!
SORRY.
GRAB
KYAAAH—?
GRIP
WHAT ARE YOU DOING!?
SORRY, YOU TWO, BUT WE GOTTA TAKE THOSE BY FORCE—!!
BWAH
PRACTE BIGI NAR!
LUX!
PSSHWHOO
WAAH!?
WE HAVE TO RUN FOR IT, NODOKA!
HAWOO!?
H-HEY WAIT!
ALL RIGHT, IF THAT'S YOUR GAME...
G-TCHK
PERFECT! THEY RAN INTO THE WOODS!

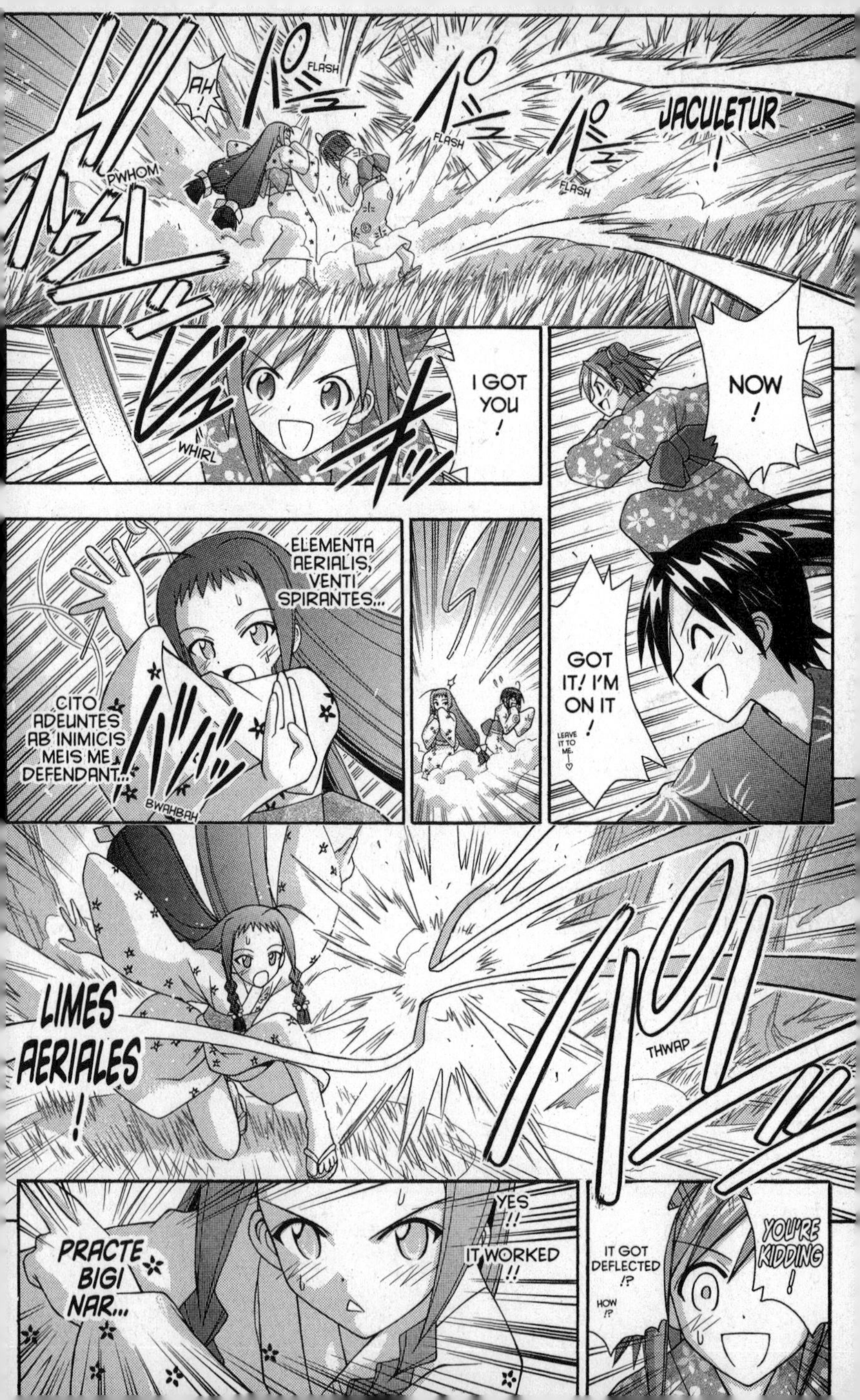
JACULETUR!
FLASH
FLASH
FLASH
AH!
PWHOM
NOW!
GOT IT! I'M ON IT!
LEAVE IT TO ME. ♡
I GOT YOU!
WHIRL
ELEMENTA AERIALIS, VENTI SPIRANTES...
CITO ADEUNTES AB INIMICIS MEIS ME DEFENDANT...
BWAHBAH
THWAP
LIMES AERIALES!
YOU'RE KIDDING!
IT GOT DEFLECTED!?
HOW!?
YES!!
IT WORKED!!
PRACTE BIGI NAR...

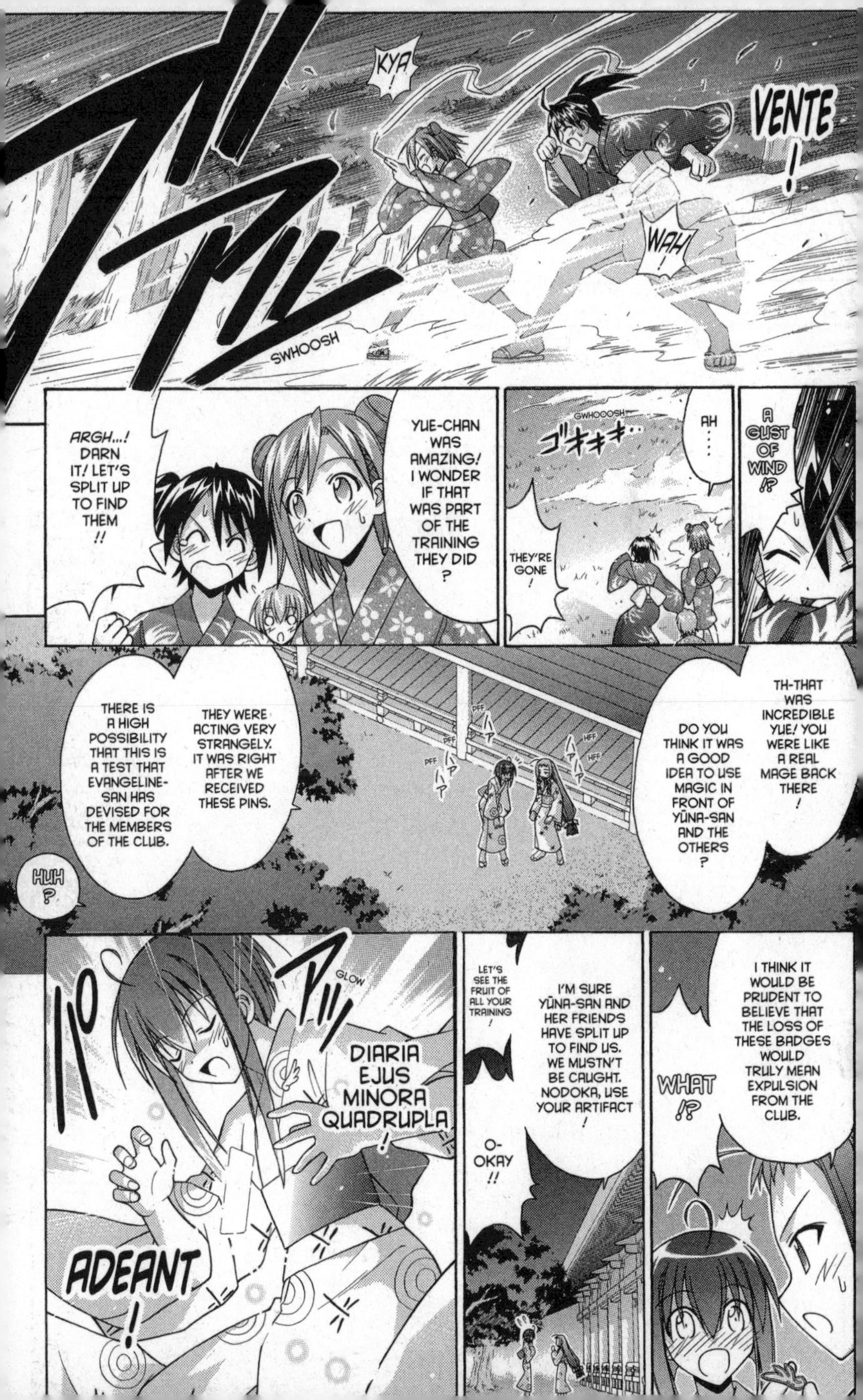
VENTE!
KYA!
WAH!
SWHOOSH
A GUST OF WIND!?
GWHOOOSH
AH...
THEY'RE GONE!
YUE-CHAN WAS AMAZING! I WONDER IF THAT WAS PART OF THE TRAINING THEY DID?
ARGH...! DARN IT! LET'S SPLIT UP TO FIND THEM!!
TH-THAT WAS INCREDIBLE YUE! YOU WERE LIKE A REAL MAGE BACK THERE!
DO YOU THINK IT WAS A GOOD IDEA TO USE MAGIC IN FRONT OF YŪNA-SAN AND THE OTHERS?
HFF HFF
PFF PFF PFF
THEY WERE ACTING VERY STRANGELY. IT WAS RIGHT AFTER WE RECEIVED THESE PINS.
THERE IS A HIGH POSSIBILITY THAT THIS IS A TEST THAT EVANGELINE-SAN HAS DEVISED FOR THE MEMBERS OF THE CLUB.
HUH?
I THINK IT WOULD BE PRUDENT TO BELIEVE THAT THE LOSS OF THESE BADGES WOULD TRULY MEAN EXPULSION FROM THE CLUB.
WHAT!?
I'M SURE YŪNA-SAN AND HER FRIENDS HAVE SPLIT UP TO FIND US. WE MUSTN'T BE CAUGHT. NODOKA, USE YOUR ARTIFACT!
LET'S SEE THE FRUIT OF ALL YOUR TRAINING!
O-OKAY!!
GLOW
DIARIA EJUS MINORA QUADRUPLA!
ADEANT!

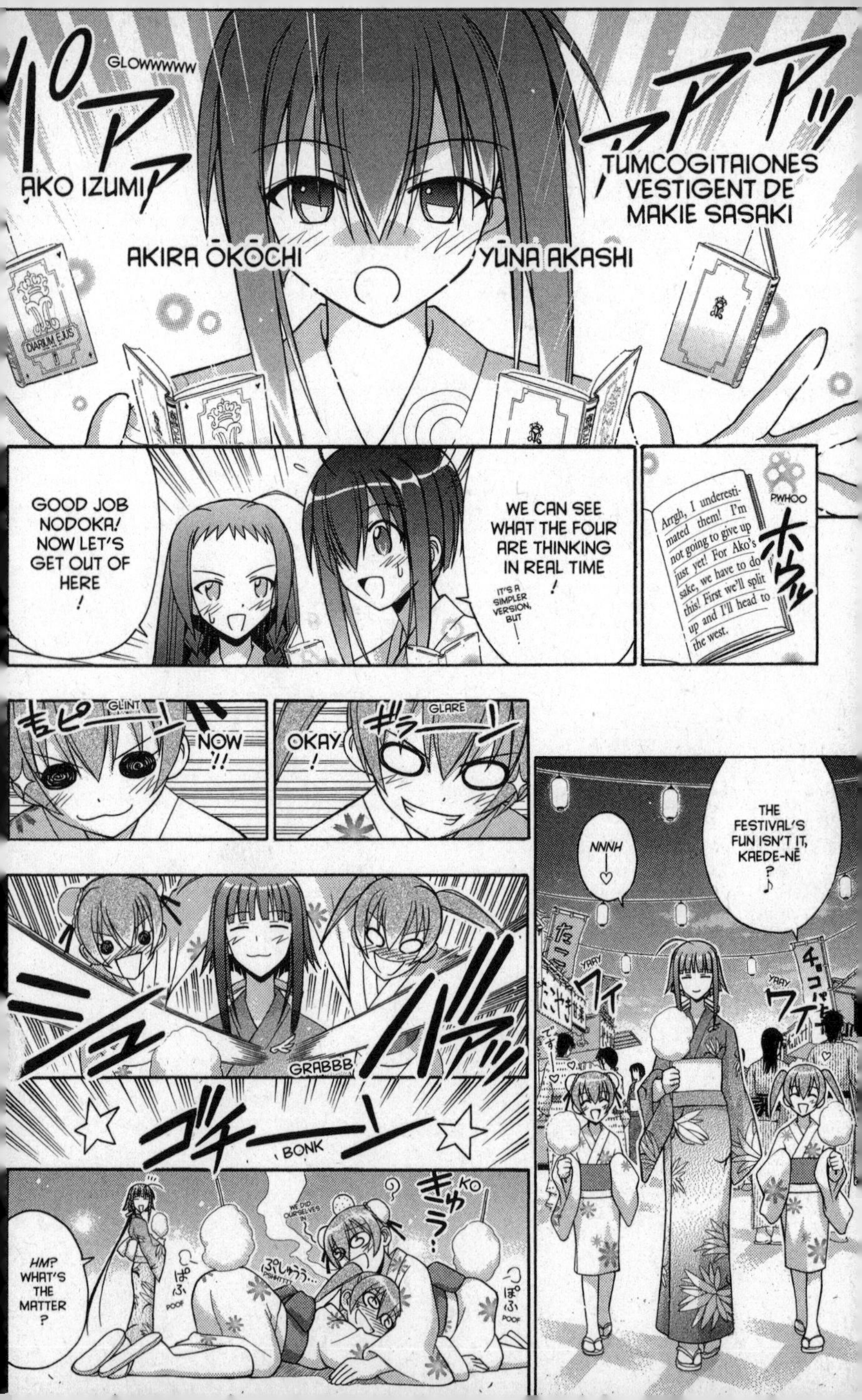
TUMCOGITAIONES VESTIGENT DE MAKIE SASAKI
YŪNA AKASHI
AKIRA ŌKŌCHI
AKO IZUMI
GLOWWWWW
DIARIUM EJUS
PWHOO
Arrgh, I underestimated them! I'm not going to give up just yet! For Ako's sake, we have to do this! First we'll split up and I'll head to the west.
WE CAN SEE WHAT THE FOUR ARE THINKING IN REAL TIME!
IT'S A SIMPLER VERSION, BUT
GOOD JOB NODOKA! NOW LET'S GET OUT OF HERE!
THE FESTIVAL'S FUN ISN'T IT, KAEDE-NĒ?♪
NNNH ♡
YAAY
YAAY
GLARE
OKAY!
GLINT
NOW!!
GRABBB
BONK
KO
WE DID OURSELVES IN...
POOF
POOF
HM? WHAT'S THE MATTER?

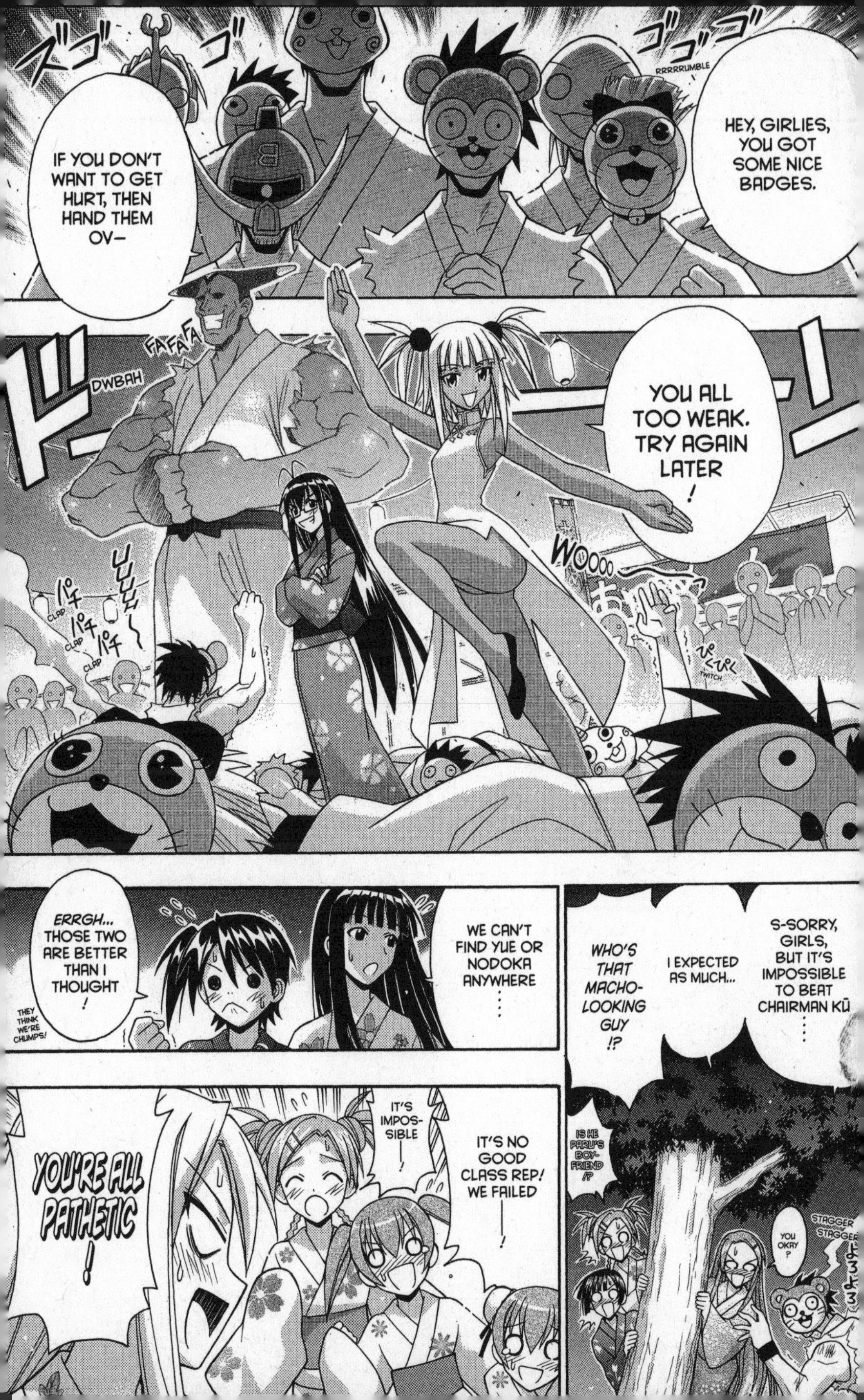
RRRRRUMBLE
HEY, GIRLIES, YOU GOT SOME NICE BADGES.
IF YOU DON'T WANT TO GET HURT, THEN HAND THEM OV–
FA FA FA
DWBAH
YOU ALL TOO WEAK. TRY AGAIN LATER!
WOOOO
CLAP CLAP CLAP
TWITCH
S-SORRY, GIRLS, BUT IT'S IMPOSSIBLE TO BEAT CHAIRMAN KŪ...
I EXPECTED AS MUCH...
WHO'S THAT MACHO-LOOKING GUY!?
WE CAN'T FIND YUE OR NODOKA ANYWHERE...
ERRGH... THOSE TWO ARE BETTER THAN I THOUGHT!
THEY THINK WE'RE CHUMPS!
STAGGER STAGGER
YOU OKAY?
IS HE PARU'S BOY-FRIEND!?
IT'S NO GOOD CLASS REP! WE FAILED—!
IT'S IMPOSSIBLE—!
YOU'RE ALL PATHETIC!

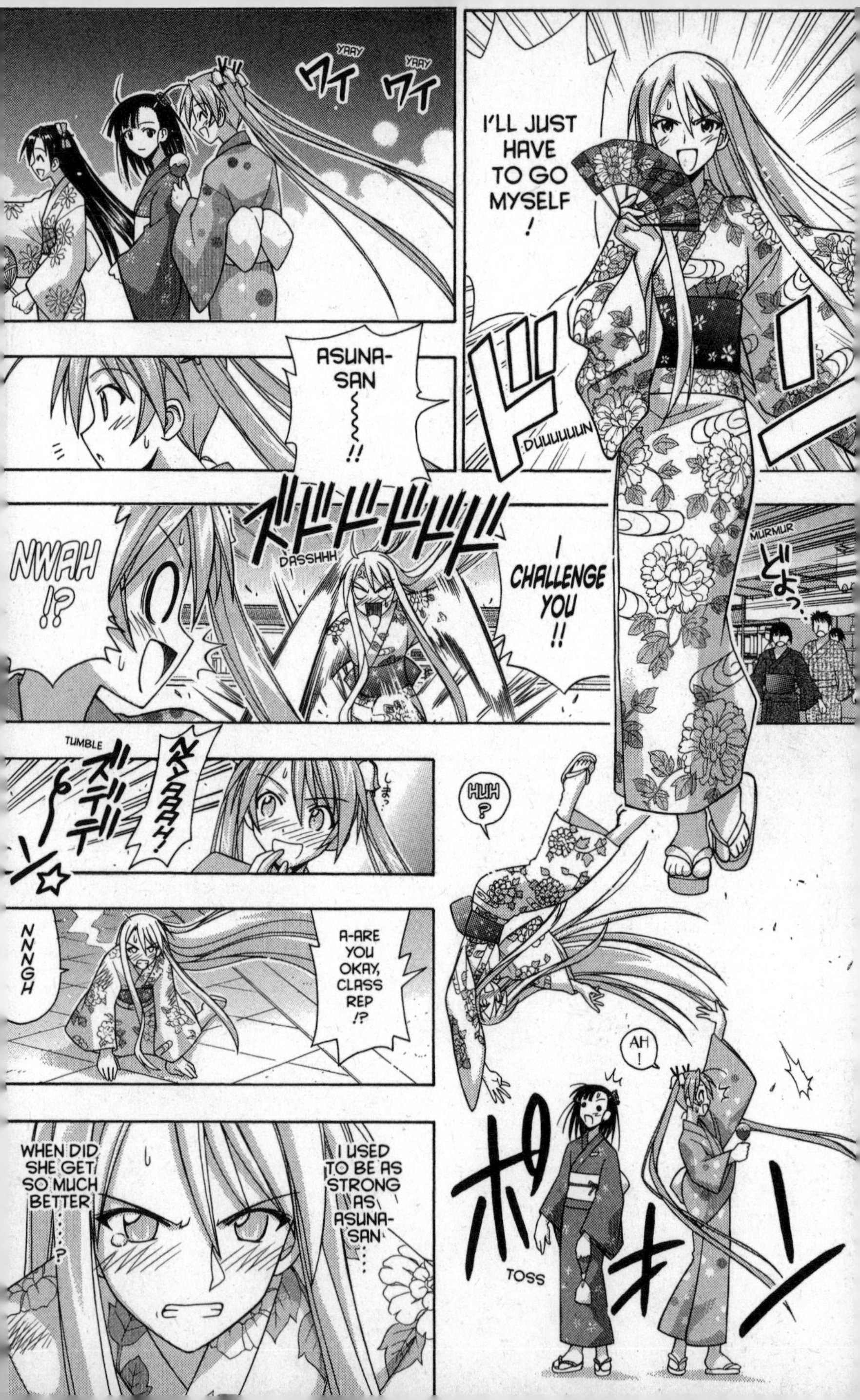

I'LL JUST HAVE TO GO MYSELF!
DUUUUUUN
YAAY
YAAY
ASUNA-SAN ~~!!
MURMUR
I CHALLENGE YOU!!
DASSHHH
NWAH!?
HUH?
AH!
TOSS
TUMBLE
A-ARE YOU OKAY, CLASS REP!?
NNNGH
I USED TO BE AS STRONG AS ASUNA-SAN...
WHEN DID SHE GET SO MUCH BETTER...?

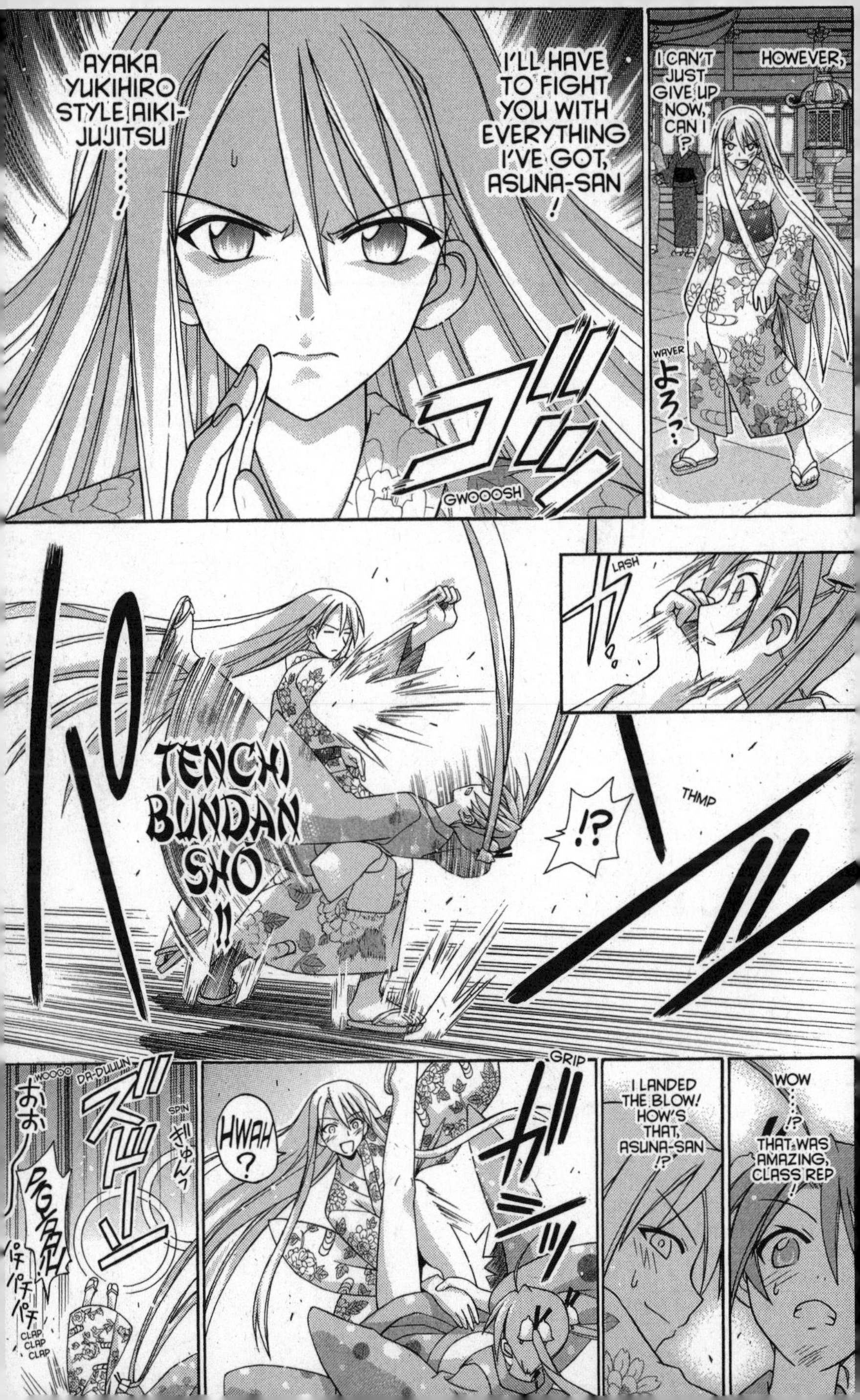

HOWEVER,
I CAN'T JUST GIVE UP NOW, CAN I!?
WAVER
よろっ…
I'LL HAVE TO FIGHT YOU WITH EVERYTHING I'VE GOT, ASUNA-SAN!
AYAKA YUKIHIRO STYLE AIKI-JUJITSU……!
GWOOOSH
LASH
THMP
!?
TENCHI BUNDAN SHO!!
WOW……!? THAT WAS AMAZING, CLASS REP!
I LANDED THE BLOW! HOW'S THAT, ASUNA-SAN!?
GRIP
HWAH?
SPIN
ぎゅんっ
DA-DUUN
WOOOO
おお～
CLAP CLAP CLAP
パチパチパチ

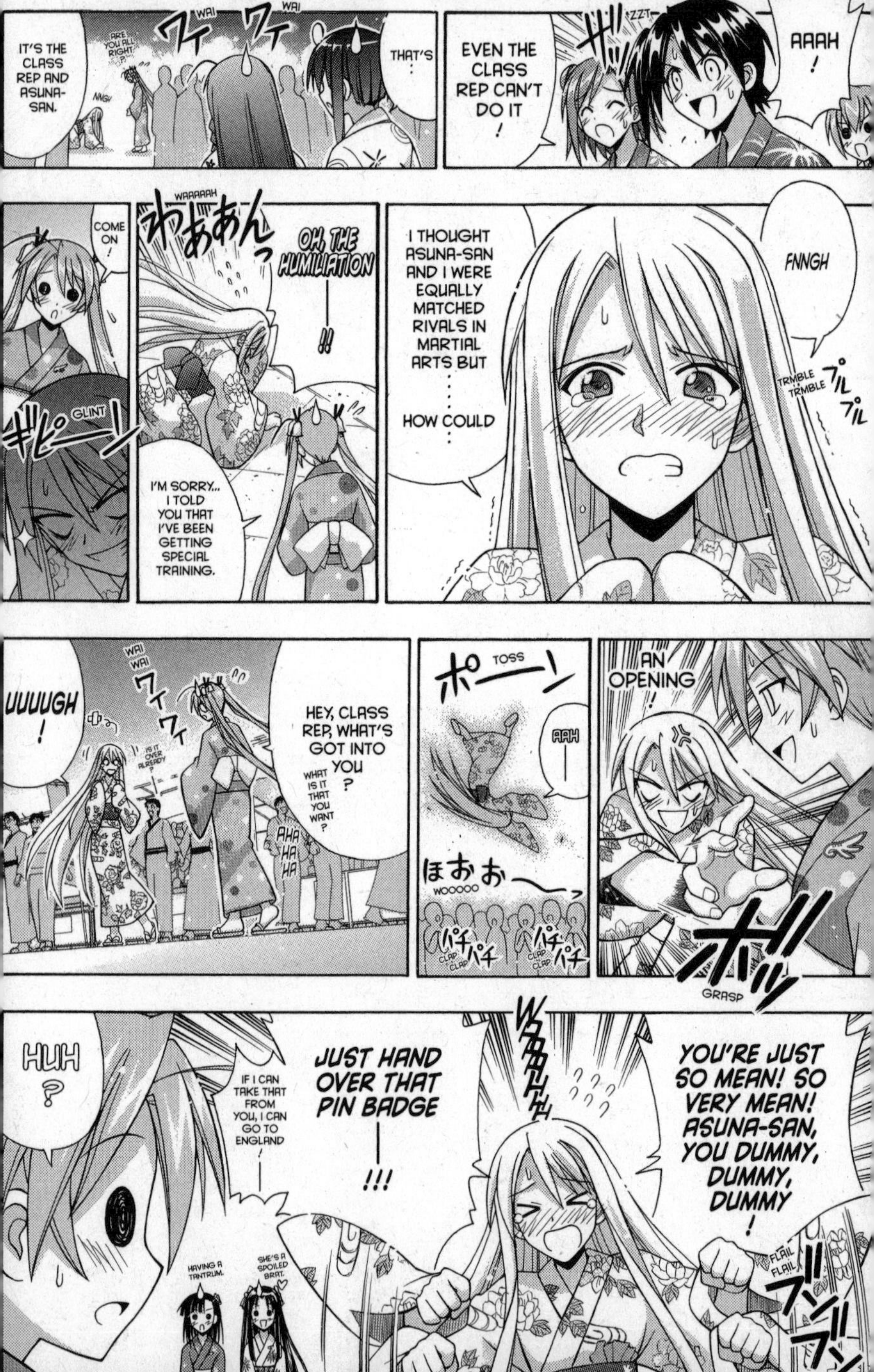
AAAH!
ZZ-T
EVEN THE CLASS REP CAN'T DO IT!
THAT'S...
WAI
WAI
ARE YOU ALL RIGHT?
NNGH
IT'S THE CLASS REP AND ASUNA-SAN.
FNNGH
TRMBLE TRMBLE
I THOUGHT ASUNA-SAN AND I WERE EQUALLY MATCHED RIVALS IN MARTIAL ARTS BUT...... HOW COULD
WAAAAAH
OH, THE HUMILIATION—!!
I'M SORRY... I TOLD YOU THAT I'VE BEEN GETTING SPECIAL TRAINING.
COME ON!
GLINT
AN OPENING!
GRASP
TOSS
AAH—
WOOOOO
CLAP CLAP
CLAP CLAP
HEY, CLASS REP, WHAT'S GOT INTO YOU?
WHAT IS IT THAT YOU WANT?
AHA HA HA
WAI WAI
IS IT OVER ALREADY
UUUUGH!
YOU'RE JUST SO MEAN! SO VERY MEAN! ASUNA-SAN, YOU DUMMY, DUMMY, DUMMY!
FLAIL FLAIL
JUST HAND OVER THAT PIN BADGE—!!!
IF I CAN TAKE THAT FROM YOU, I CAN GO TO ENGLAND—
SHE'S A SPOILED BRAT.
HAVING A TANTRUM.
HUH?

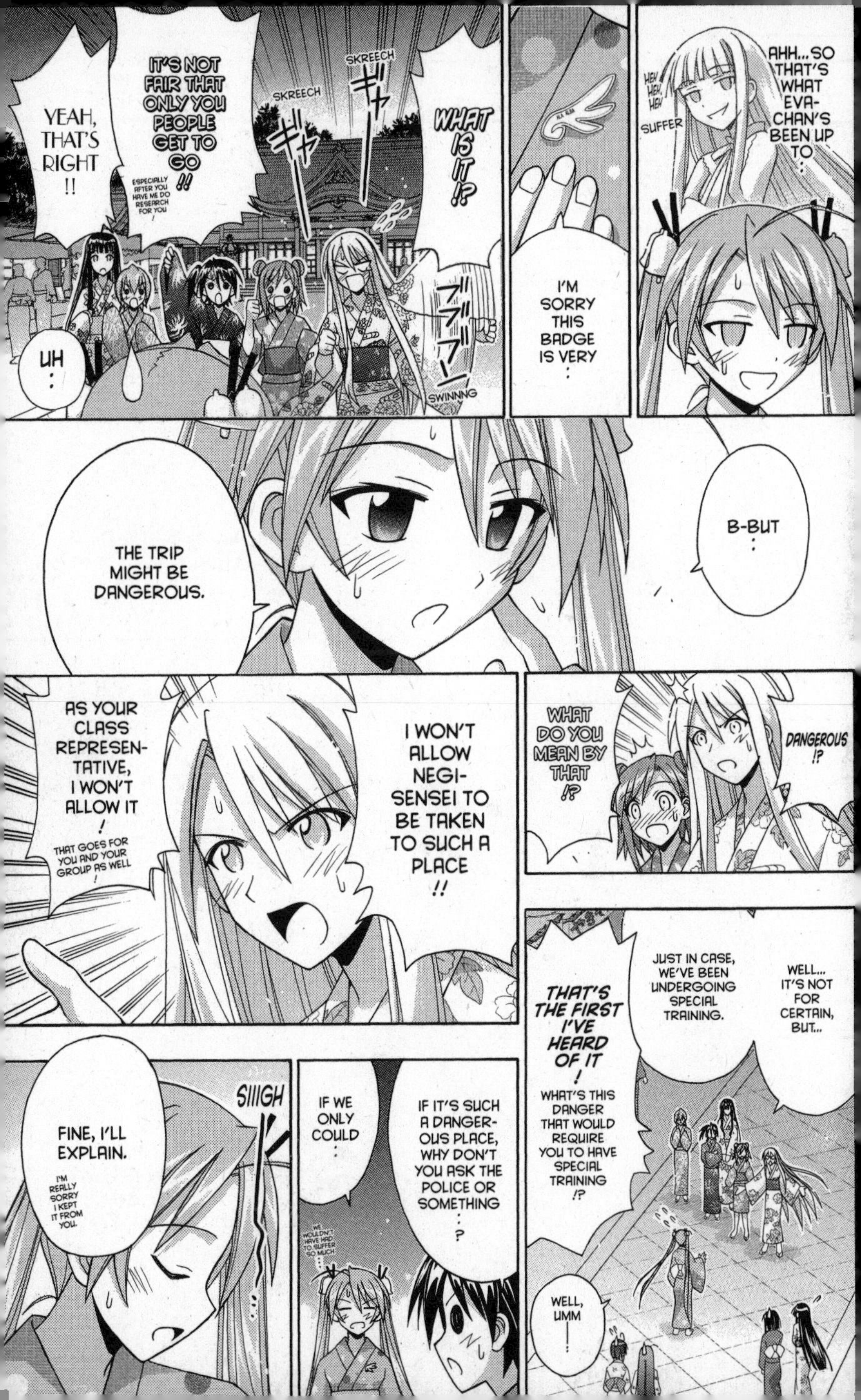

AHH... SO THAT'S WHAT EVA-CHAN'S BEEN UP TO...
HEH HEH HEH
SUFFER
I'M SORRY THIS BADGE IS VERY...
WHAT IS IT!?
SKREECH
SKREECH
IT'S NOT FAIR THAT ONLY YOU PEOPLE GET TO GO!!
ESPECIALLY AFTER YOU HAVE ME DO RESEARCH FOR YOU!
YEAH, THAT'S RIGHT!!
SWINNNG
UH...
B-BUT...
THE TRIP MIGHT BE DANGEROUS.
DANGEROUS!?
WHAT DO YOU MEAN BY THAT!?
I WON'T ALLOW NEGI-SENSEI TO BE TAKEN TO SUCH A PLACE!!
AS YOUR CLASS REPRESENTATIVE, I WON'T ALLOW IT!
THAT GOES FOR YOU AND YOUR GROUP AS WELL!
WELL... IT'S NOT FOR CERTAIN, BUT...
JUST IN CASE, WE'VE BEEN UNDERGOING SPECIAL TRAINING.
THAT'S THE FIRST I'VE HEARD OF IT!
WHAT'S THIS DANGER THAT WOULD REQUIRE YOU TO HAVE SPECIAL TRAINING!?
WELL, UMM!
IF IT'S SUCH A DANGEROUS PLACE, WHY DON'T YOU ASK THE POLICE OR SOMETHING..?
IF WE ONLY COULD...
WE WOULDN'T HAVE HAD TO SUFFER SO MUCH
SIIIGH
FINE, I'LL EXPLAIN.
I'M REALLY SORRY I KEPT IT FROM YOU.

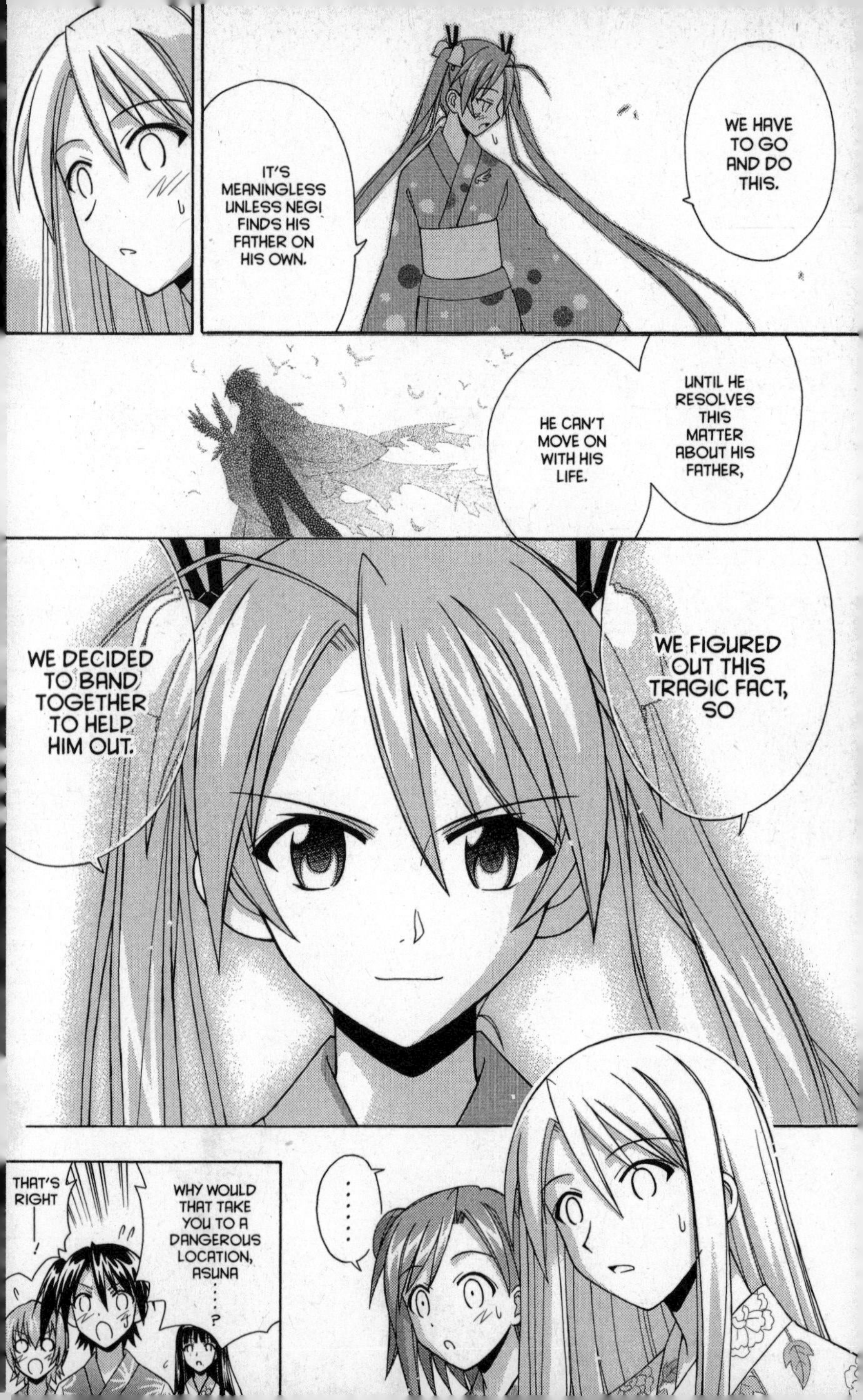

WE HAVE TO GO AND DO THIS.
IT'S MEANINGLESS UNLESS NEGI FINDS HIS FATHER ON HIS OWN.
UNTIL HE RESOLVES THIS MATTER ABOUT HIS FATHER,
HE CAN'T MOVE ON WITH HIS LIFE.
WE FIGURED OUT THIS TRAGIC FACT, SO
WE DECIDED TO BAND TOGETHER TO HELP HIM OUT.
......
WHY WOULD THAT TAKE YOU TO A DANGEROUS LOCATION, ASUNA .....?
THAT'S RIGHT —!

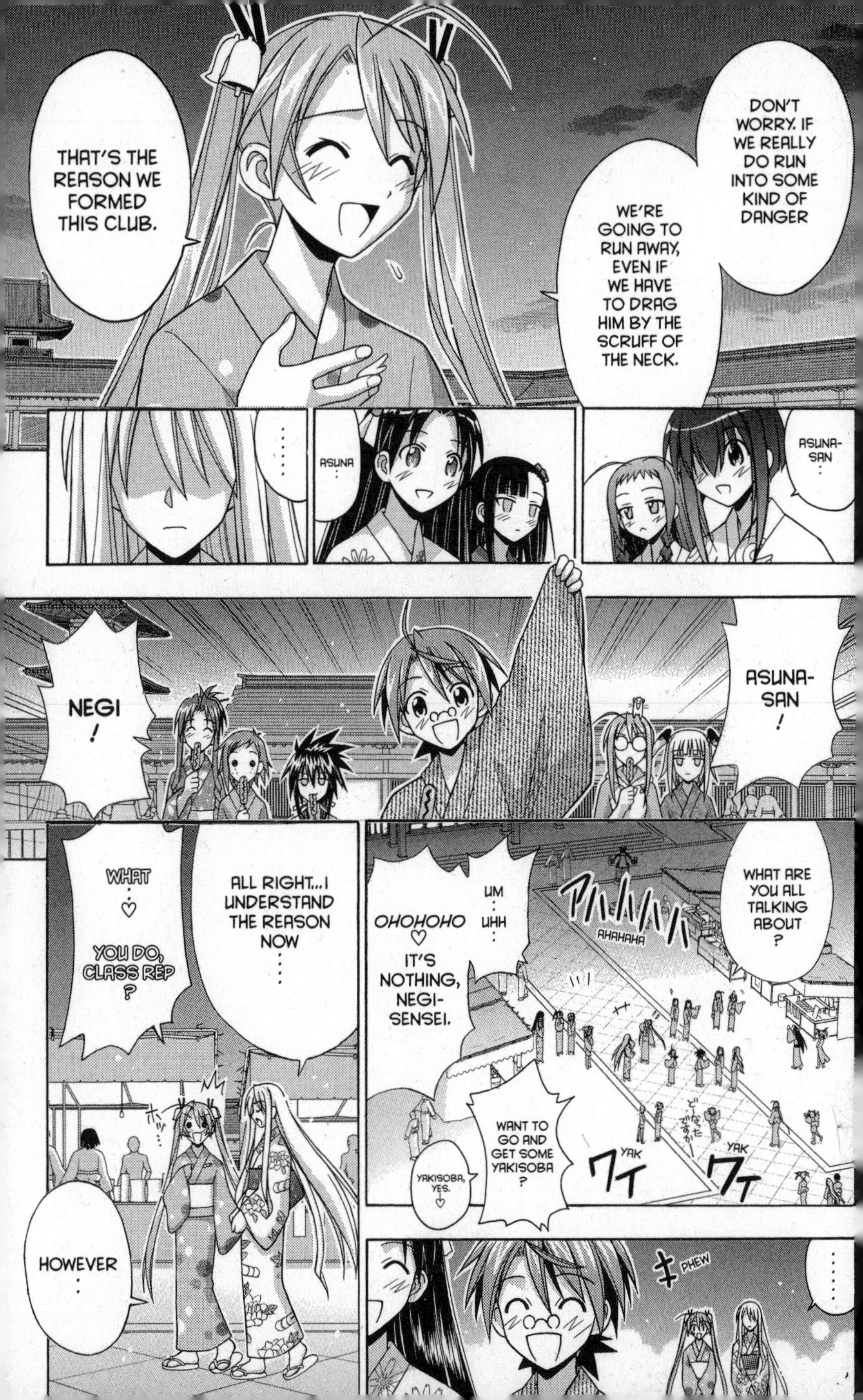
DON'T WORRY. IF WE REALLY DO RUN INTO SOME KIND OF DANGER
WE'RE GOING TO RUN AWAY, EVEN IF WE HAVE TO DRAG HIM BY THE SCRUFF OF THE NECK.
THAT'S THE REASON WE FORMED THIS CLUB.
ASUNA-SAN...
ASUNA...
......
ASUNA-SAN!
NEGI!
WHAT ARE YOU ALL TALKING ABOUT?
UM... UHH...
OHOHOHO ♡ IT'S NOTHING, NEGI-SENSEI.
AHAHAHA
WANT TO GO AND GET SOME YAKISOBA?
YAK
YAK
YAKISOBA, YES. ♡
PHEW
......
ALL RIGHT...I UNDERSTAND THE REASON NOW....
WHAT...♡
YOU DO, CLASS REP?
HOWEVER...

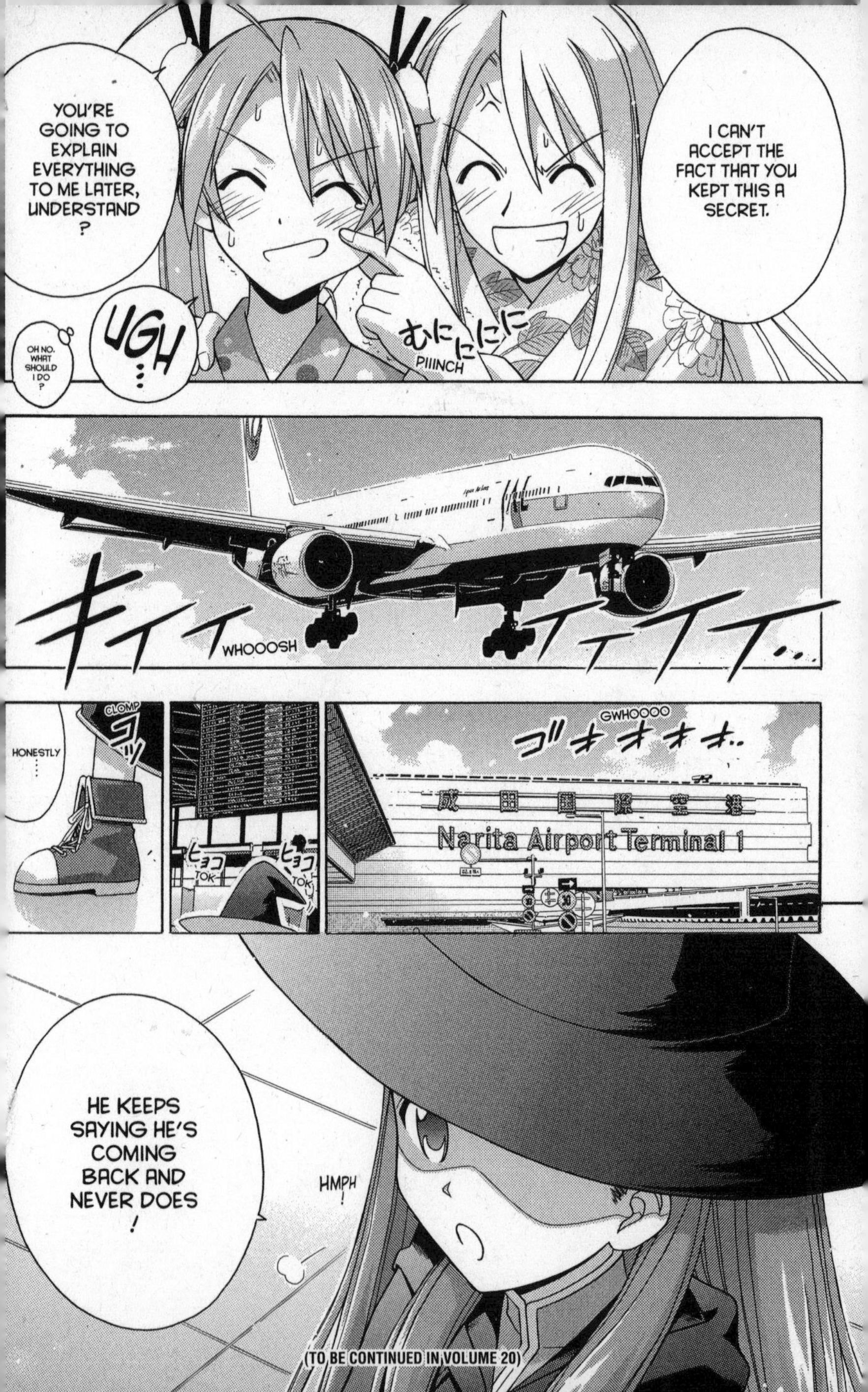
I CAN'T ACCEPT THE FACT THAT YOU KEPT THIS A SECRET.
YOU'RE GOING TO EXPLAIN EVERYTHING TO ME LATER, UNDERSTAND?
むにににに
PIIINCH
UGH...
OH NO. WHAT SHOULD I DO?
キイイ
WHOOOSH
イイイイ...
GWHOOOO
ゴォォォォ..
成田国際空港
Narita Airport Terminal 1
ヒョコ
TOK
ヒョコ
TOK
CLOMP
コッ
HONESTLY....
HE KEEPS SAYING HE'S COMING BACK AND NEVER DOES!
HMPH!
(TO BE CONTINUED IN VOLUME 20)

A Word from the Author

Negima! is finally heading into Volume 20. Starting with this volume, his childhood friend enters the picture... which shakes things up dramatically! We also get to see the results of the Negi Party's training!

And you can expect even more excitement in the *next* volume!

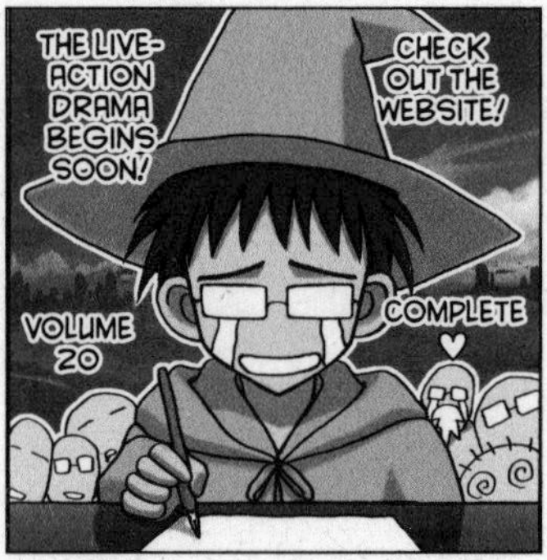
CHECK OUT THE WEBSITE!
THE LIVE-ACTION DRAMA BEGINS SOON!
COMPLETE
VOLUME 20

The *Negima!* live-action TV series is making its debut! All heck will break loose as thirty-one girls compete to capture Negi's (played by an adorable thirteen-year-old girl) affection. And keep an eye out for Takamichi and Shizuna-Sensei! For more information, visit my website!

Ken Akamatsu's website
http://www.ailove.net

20

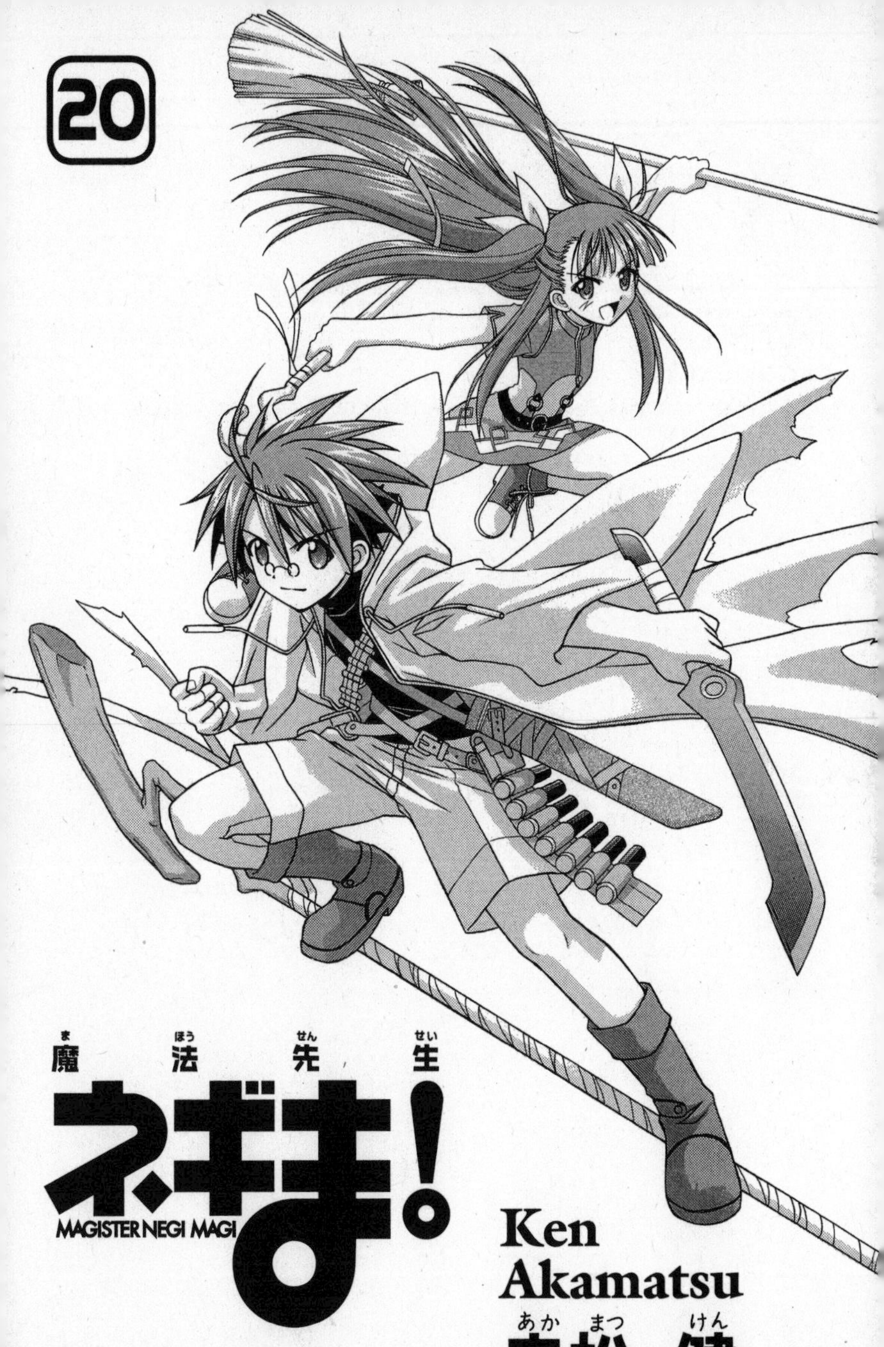

魔法先生ネギま!

MAGISTER NEGI MAGI

Ken Akamatsu

赤松 健

CONTENTS

178th Period – Summer! Beach! Confession!?.........167

179th Period – She's the One for Negi!?.........185

180th Period – Explosion! Negi Wars ♡ 203

181st Period – I Need to Tell You Something!.........219

182nd Period – Negi Party, All Ready!.........237

183rd Period – Full of Memories ♡ 255

184th Period – Negi Party Departs to London!!.........271

185th Period – Starting Point for the Future!!.........289

186th Period – Welcome to Another World!!.........307

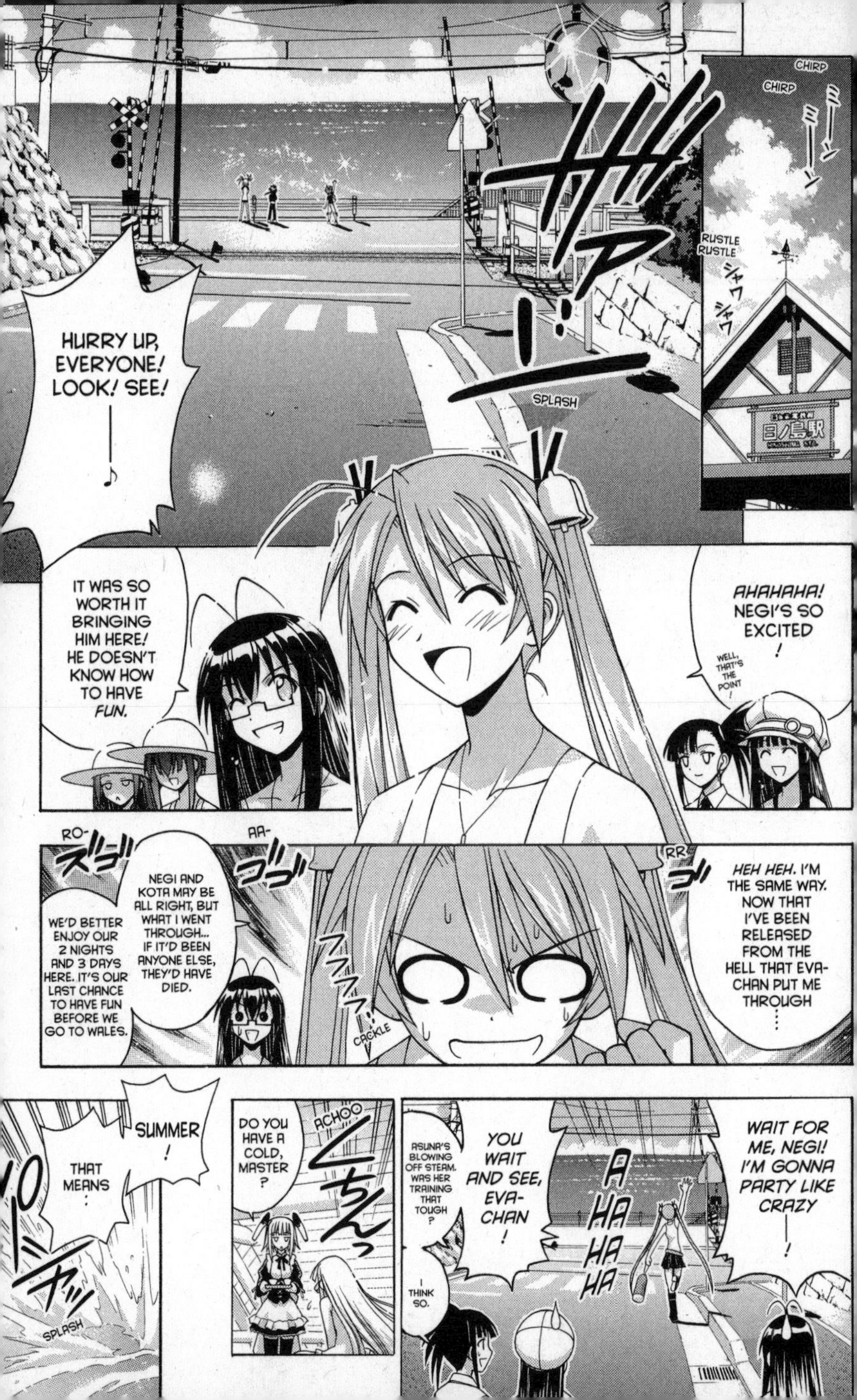
CHIRP
CHIRP
RUSTLE
RUSTLE
SPLASH
HURRY UP, EVERYONE! LOOK! SEE! ♪
AHAHAHA! NEGI'S SO EXCITED!
WELL, THAT'S THE POINT!
IT WAS SO WORTH IT BRINGING HIM HERE! HE DOESN'T KNOW HOW TO HAVE FUN.
RR-
HEH HEH. I'M THE SAME WAY. NOW THAT I'VE BEEN RELEASED FROM THE HELL THAT EVA-CHAN PUT ME THROUGH...
CACKLE
AA-
NEGI AND KOTA MAY BE ALL RIGHT, BUT WHAT I WENT THROUGH... IF IT'D BEEN ANYONE ELSE, THEY'D HAVE DIED.
RO-
WE'D BETTER ENJOY OUR 2 NIGHTS AND 3 DAYS HERE. IT'S OUR LAST CHANCE TO HAVE FUN BEFORE WE GO TO WALES.
WAIT FOR ME, NEGI! I'M GONNA PARTY LIKE CRAZY!
AHAHAHAHA
YOU WAIT AND SEE, EVA-CHAN!
ASUNA'S BLOWING OFF STEAM. WAS HER TRAINING THAT TOUGH?
I THINK SO.
ACHOO
DO YOU HAVE A COLD, MASTER?
SUMMER!
THAT MEANS...
SPLASH

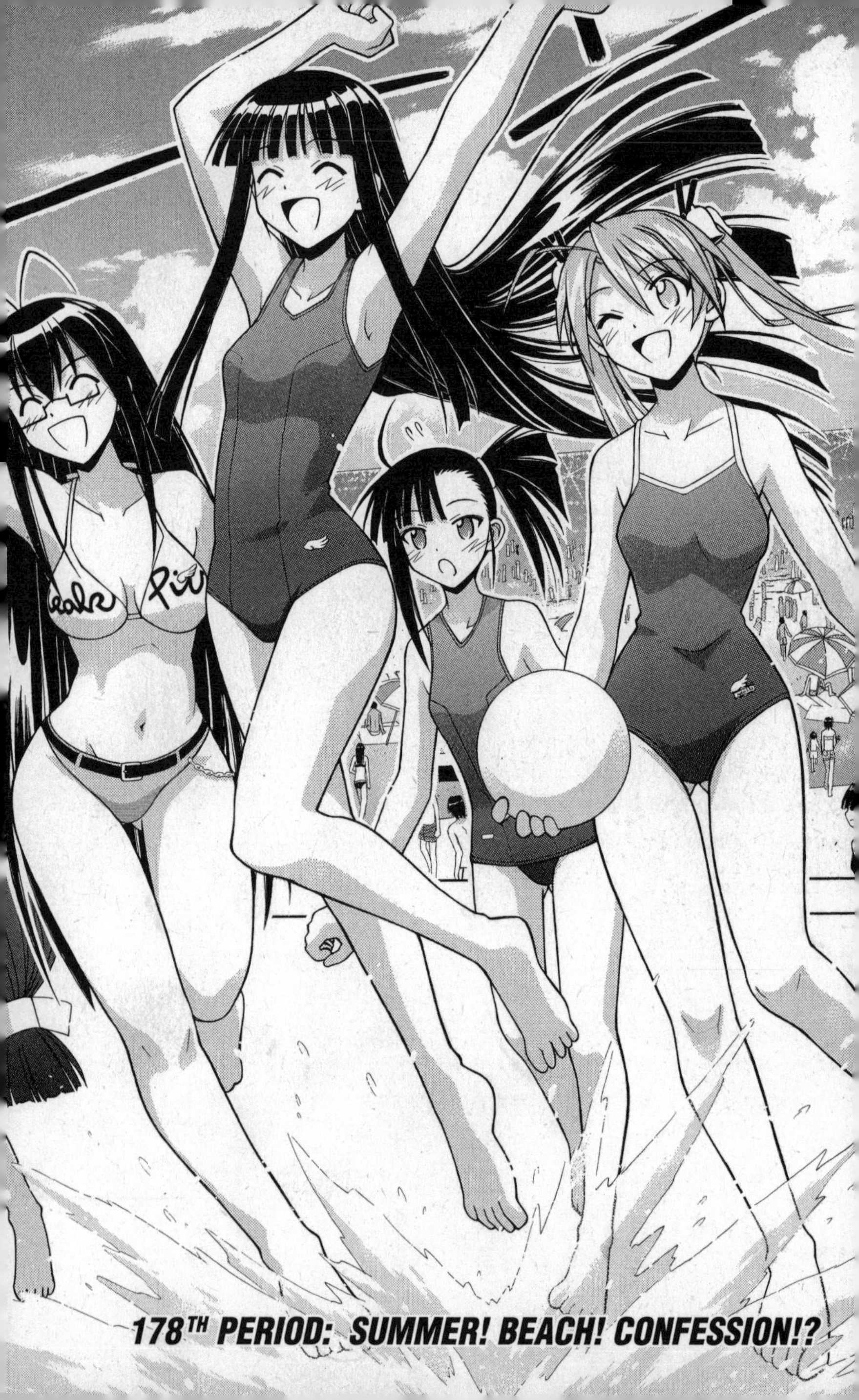
178TH PERIOD: SUMMER! BEACH! CONFESSION!?

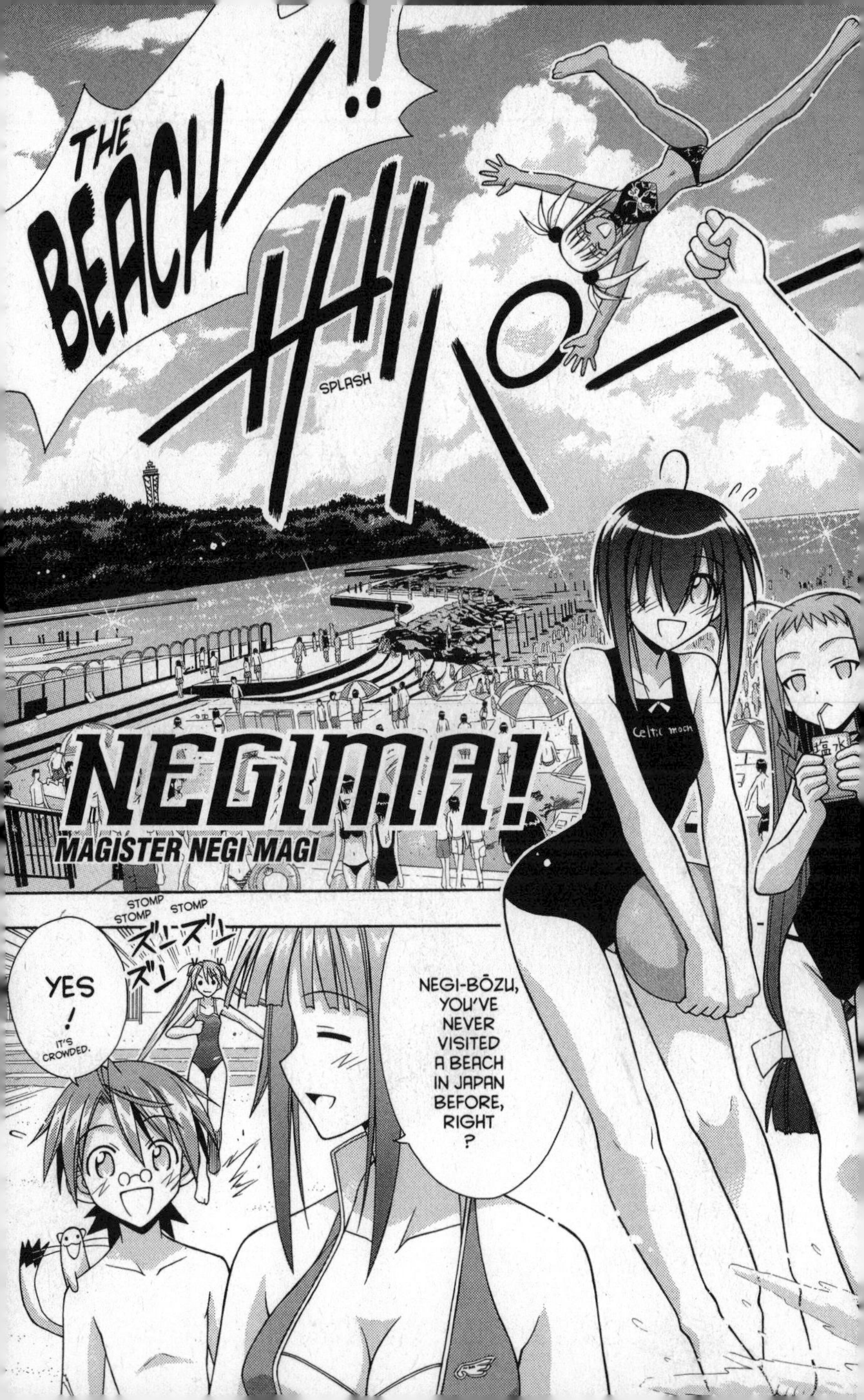
THE BEACH—!!
SPLASH
NEGIMA!
MAGISTER NEGI MAGI
NEGI-BŌZU, YOU'VE NEVER VISITED A BEACH IN JAPAN BEFORE, RIGHT?
STOMP STOMP STOMP
YES!
IT'S CROWDED.

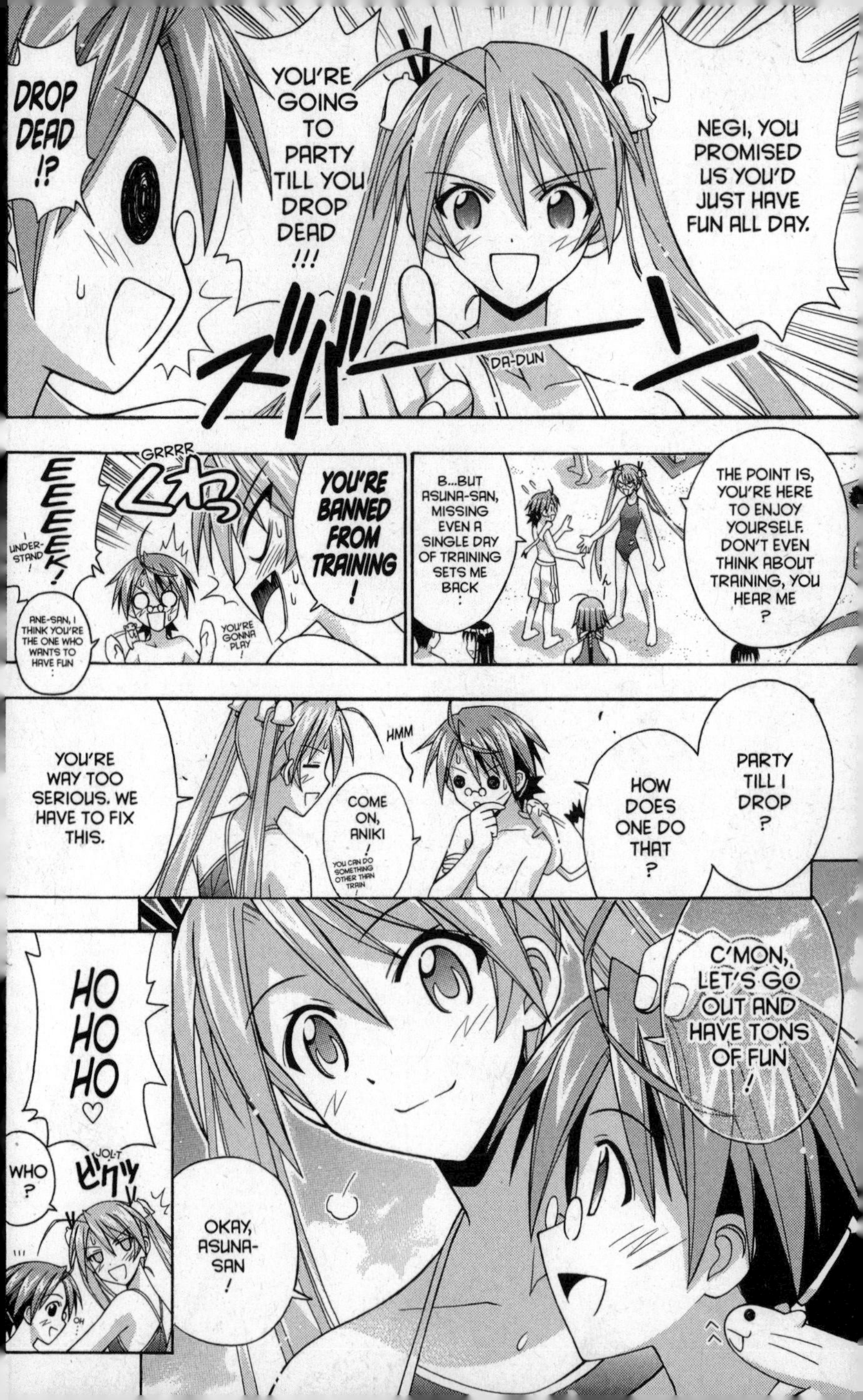
NEGI, YOU PROMISED US YOU'D JUST HAVE FUN ALL DAY.
YOU'RE GOING TO PARTY TILL YOU DROP DEAD!!!
DA-DUN
DROP DEAD!?
THE POINT IS, YOU'RE HERE TO ENJOY YOURSELF. DON'T EVEN THINK ABOUT TRAINING, YOU HEAR ME?
B...BUT ASUNA-SAN, MISSING EVEN A SINGLE DAY OF TRAINING SETS ME BACK
YOU'RE BANNED FROM TRAINING!
GRRRR
YOU'RE GONNA PLAY!
EEEEEK!
I UNDER-STAND!
ANE-SAN, I THINK YOU'RE THE ONE WHO WANTS TO HAVE FUN:
PARTY TILL I DROP?
HOW DOES ONE DO THAT?
HMM
COME ON, ANIKI!
YOU CAN DO SOMETHING OTHER THAN TRAIN!
YOU'RE WAY TOO SERIOUS. WE HAVE TO FIX THIS.
C'MON, LET'S GO OUT AND HAVE TONS OF FUN!
OKAY, ASUNA-SAN!
HO HO HO ♡
WHO?
JOLT
OH

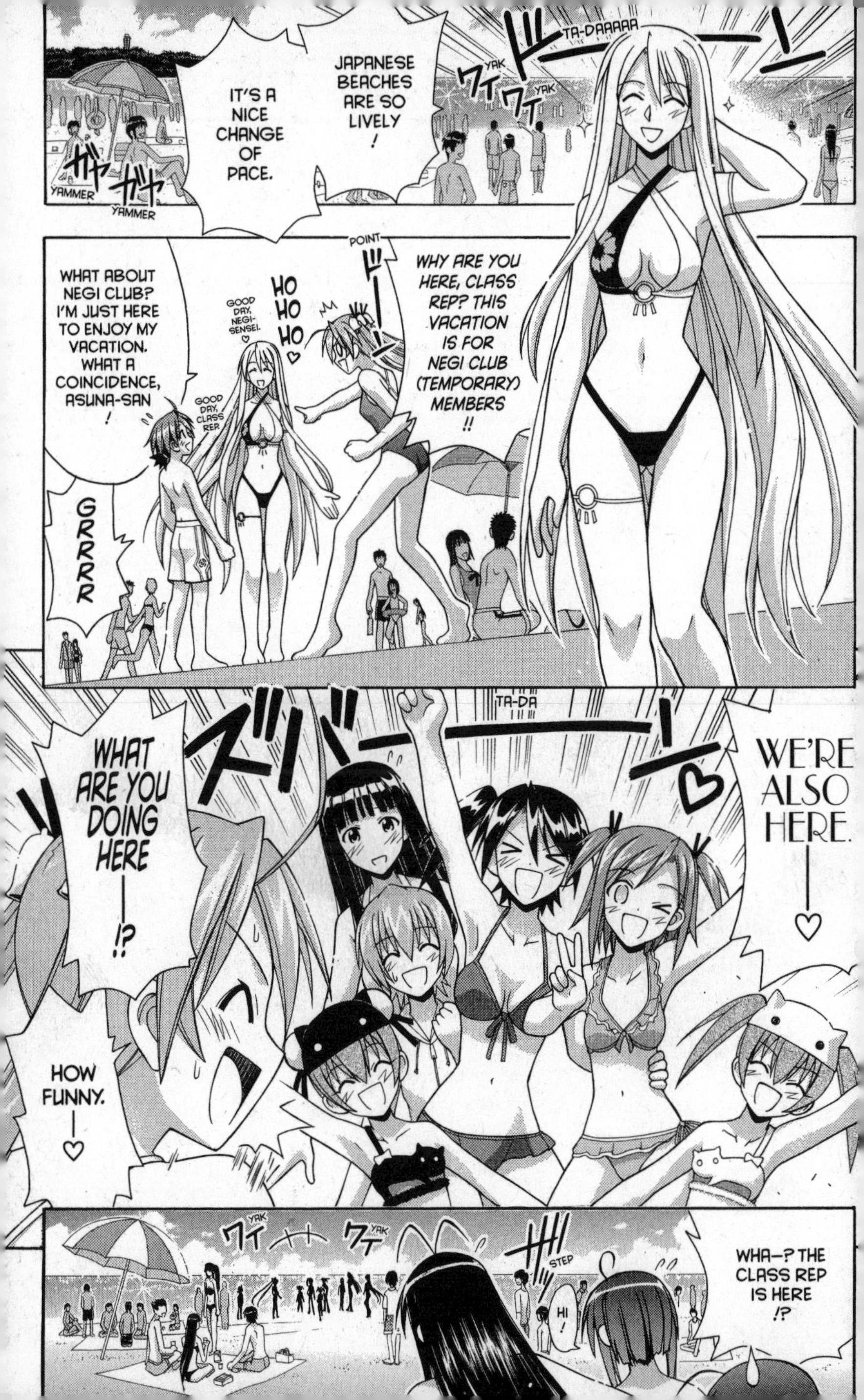
TA-DAAAAA
YAK
YAK
JAPANESE BEACHES ARE SO LIVELY!
IT'S A NICE CHANGE OF PACE.
YAMMER
YAMMER
WHY ARE YOU HERE, CLASS REP? THIS VACATION IS FOR NEGI CLUB (TEMPORARY) MEMBERS!!
POINT
HO HO HO
GOOD DAY, NEGI-SENSEI.
GOOD DAY, CLASS REP.
WHAT ABOUT NEGI CLUB? I'M JUST HERE TO ENJOY MY VACATION. WHAT A COINCIDENCE, ASUNA-SAN!
GRRRR
WE'RE ALSO HERE.
TA-DA
WHAT ARE YOU DOING HERE!?
HOW FUNNY.
WHA-? THE CLASS REP IS HERE!?
STEP
HI!
YAK
YAK

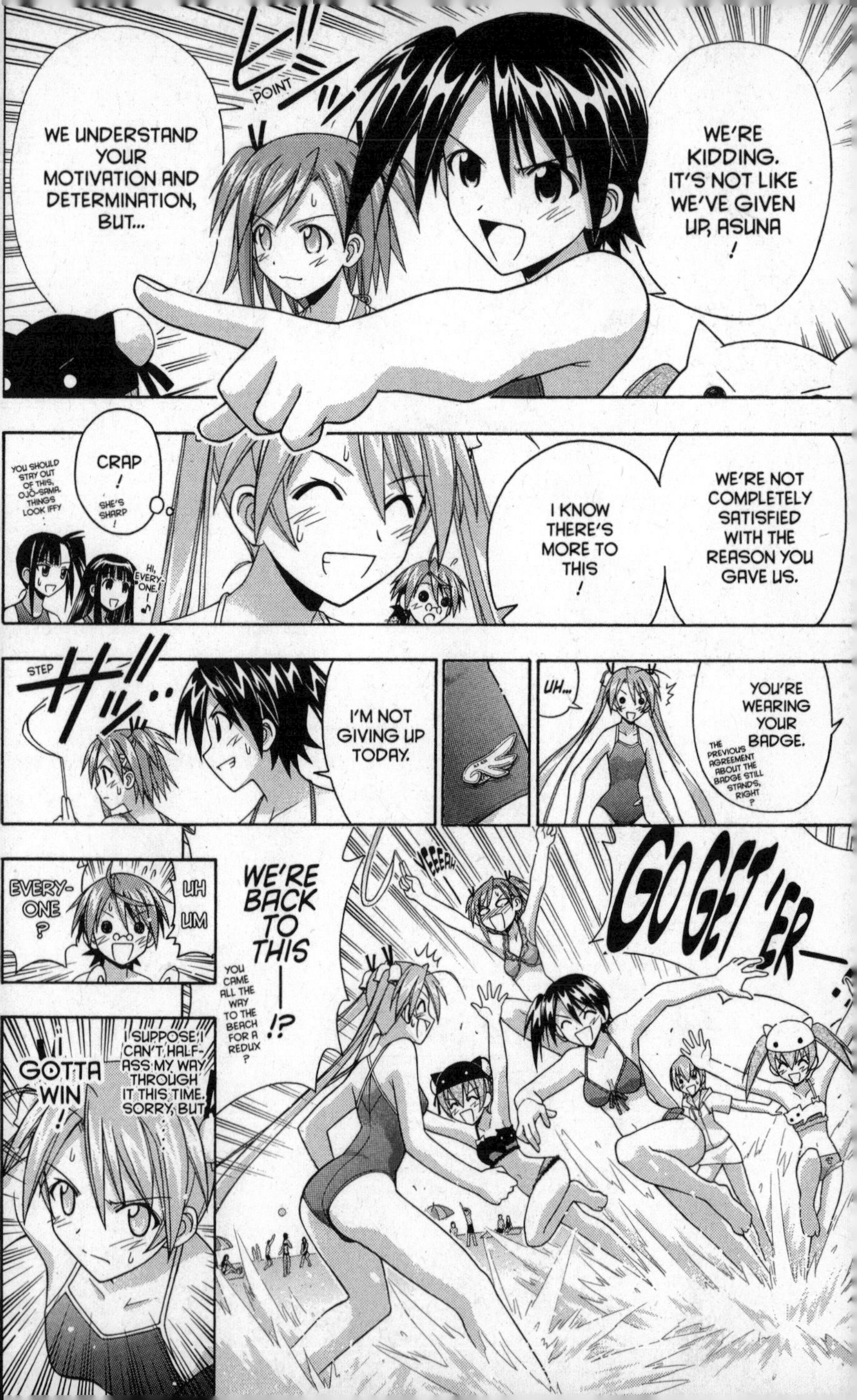
WE'RE KIDDING. IT'S NOT LIKE WE'VE GIVEN UP, ASUNA!
POINT
WE UNDERSTAND YOUR MOTIVATION AND DETERMINATION, BUT...
WE'RE NOT COMPLETELY SATISFIED WITH THE REASON YOU GAVE US.
I KNOW THERE'S MORE TO THIS!
CRAP!
SHE'S SHARP!
YOU SHOULD STAY OUT OF THIS, OJŌ-SAMA. THINGS LOOK IFFY.
HI, EVERYONE ♪
YOU'RE WEARING YOUR BADGE.
THE PREVIOUS AGREEMENT ABOUT THE BADGE STILL STANDS, RIGHT?
UH...
I'M NOT GIVING UP TODAY.
STEP
GO GET 'ER—!!
YEEEAH
WE'RE BACK TO THIS—!?
YOU CAME ALL THE WAY TO THE BEACH FOR A REDUX?
UH UM
EVERY-ONE?
I SUPPOSE I CAN'T HALF-ASS MY WAY THROUGH IT THIS TIME. SORRY, BUT...
I GOTTA WIN!

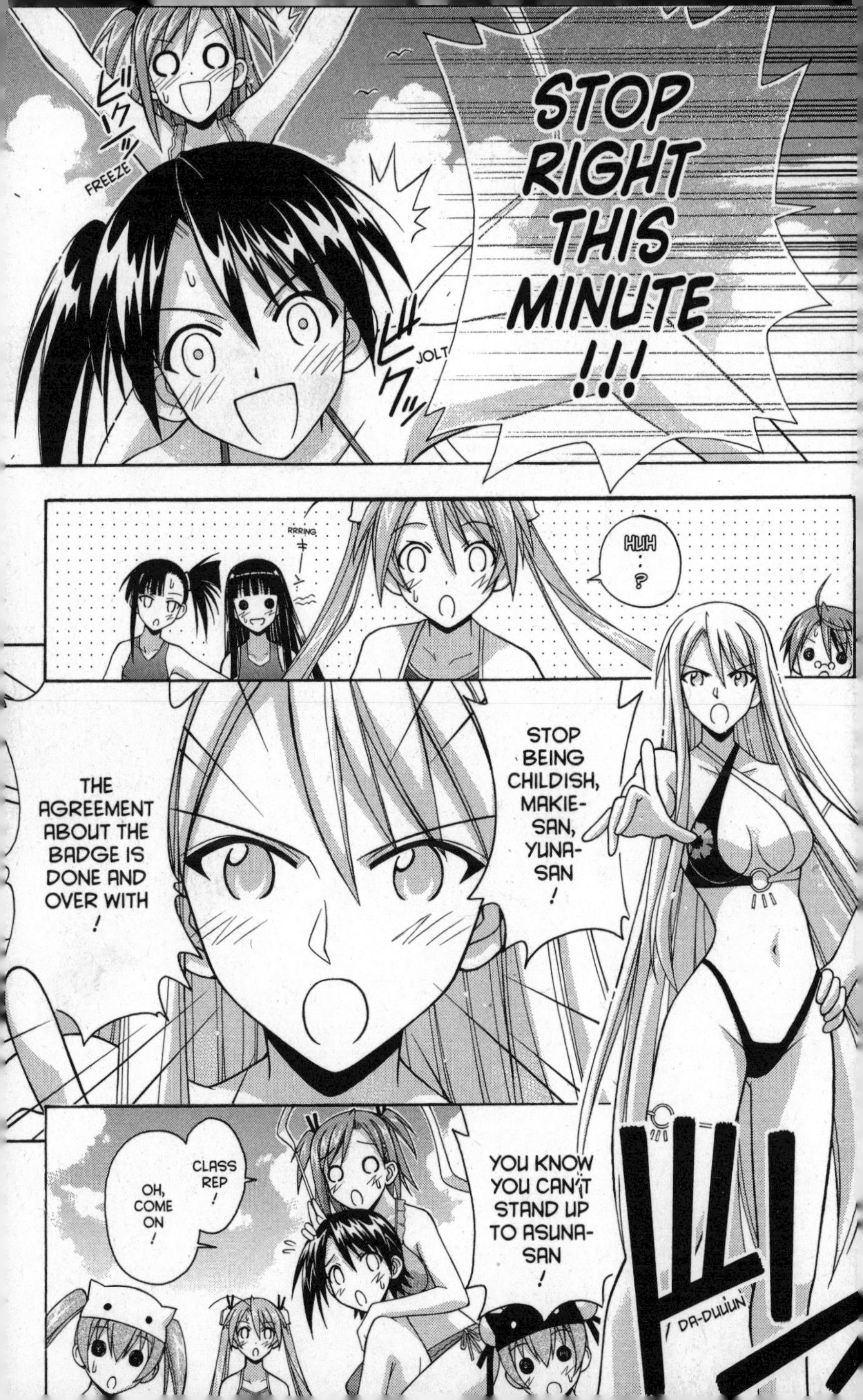
STOP RIGHT THIS MINUTE!!!
JOLT
FREEZE
HUH...?
RRRING
STOP BEING CHILDISH, MAKIE-SAN, YUNA-SAN!
THE AGREEMENT ABOUT THE BADGE IS DONE AND OVER WITH!
YOU KNOW YOU CAN'T STAND UP TO ASUNA-SAN!
DA-DUUUN
CLASS REP!
OH, COME ON!

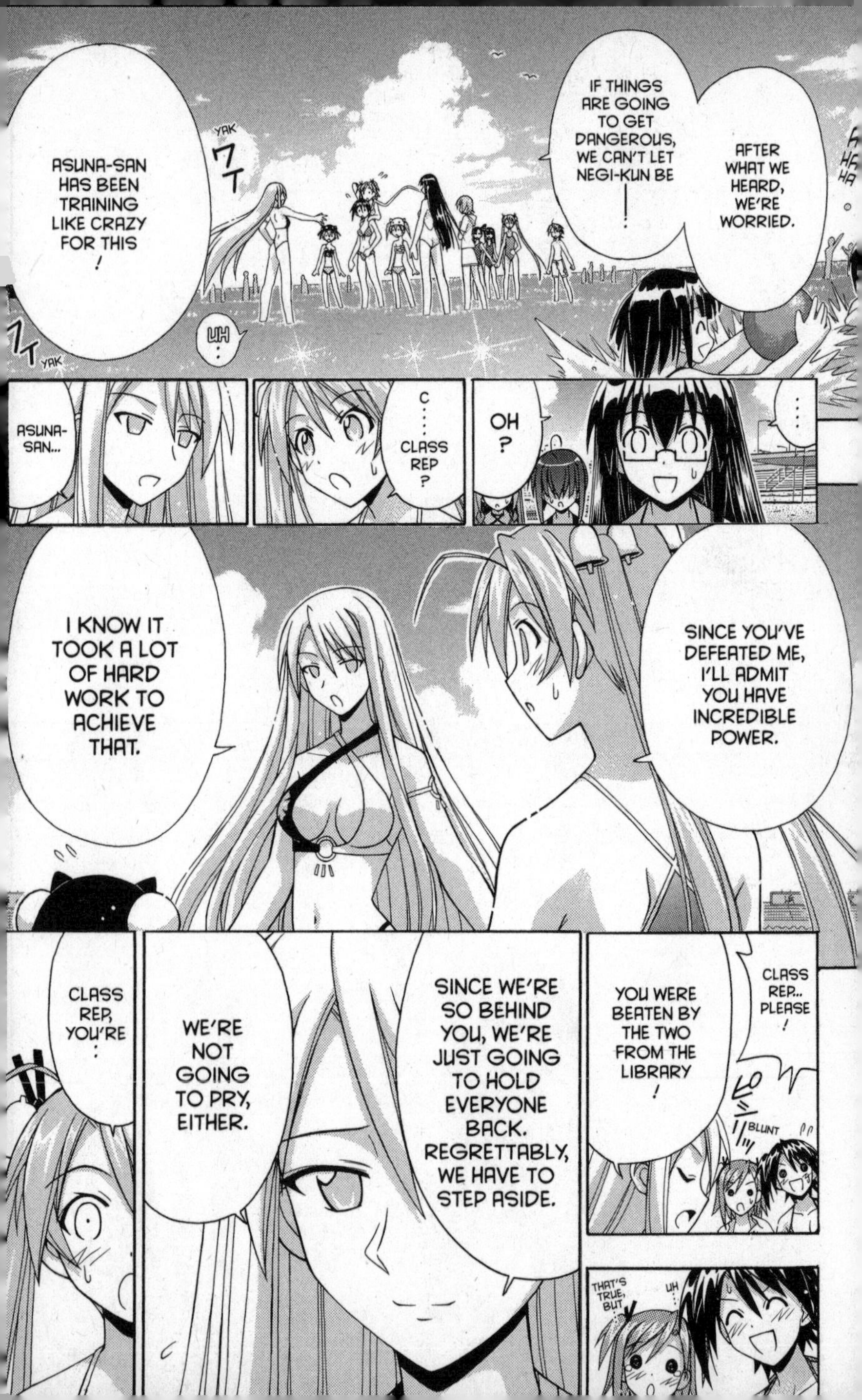
AFTER WHAT WE HEARD, WE'RE WORRIED.
IF THINGS ARE GOING TO GET DANGEROUS, WE CAN'T LET NEGI-KUN BE—!
HA HA HA
YAK
UH...
ASUNA-SAN HAS BEEN TRAINING LIKE CRAZY FOR THIS!
YAK
......
OH?
C...... CLASS REP?
ASUNA-SAN...
SINCE YOU'VE DEFEATED ME, I'LL ADMIT YOU HAVE INCREDIBLE POWER.
I KNOW IT TOOK A LOT OF HARD WORK TO ACHIEVE THAT.
CLASS REP... PLEASE!
YOU WERE BEATEN BY THE TWO FROM THE LIBRARY!
BLUNT
UH...
THAT'S TRUE, BUT...
SINCE WE'RE SO BEHIND YOU, WE'RE JUST GOING TO HOLD EVERYONE BACK. REGRETTABLY, WE HAVE TO STEP ASIDE.
WE'RE NOT GOING TO PRY, EITHER.
CLASS REP, YOU'RE...

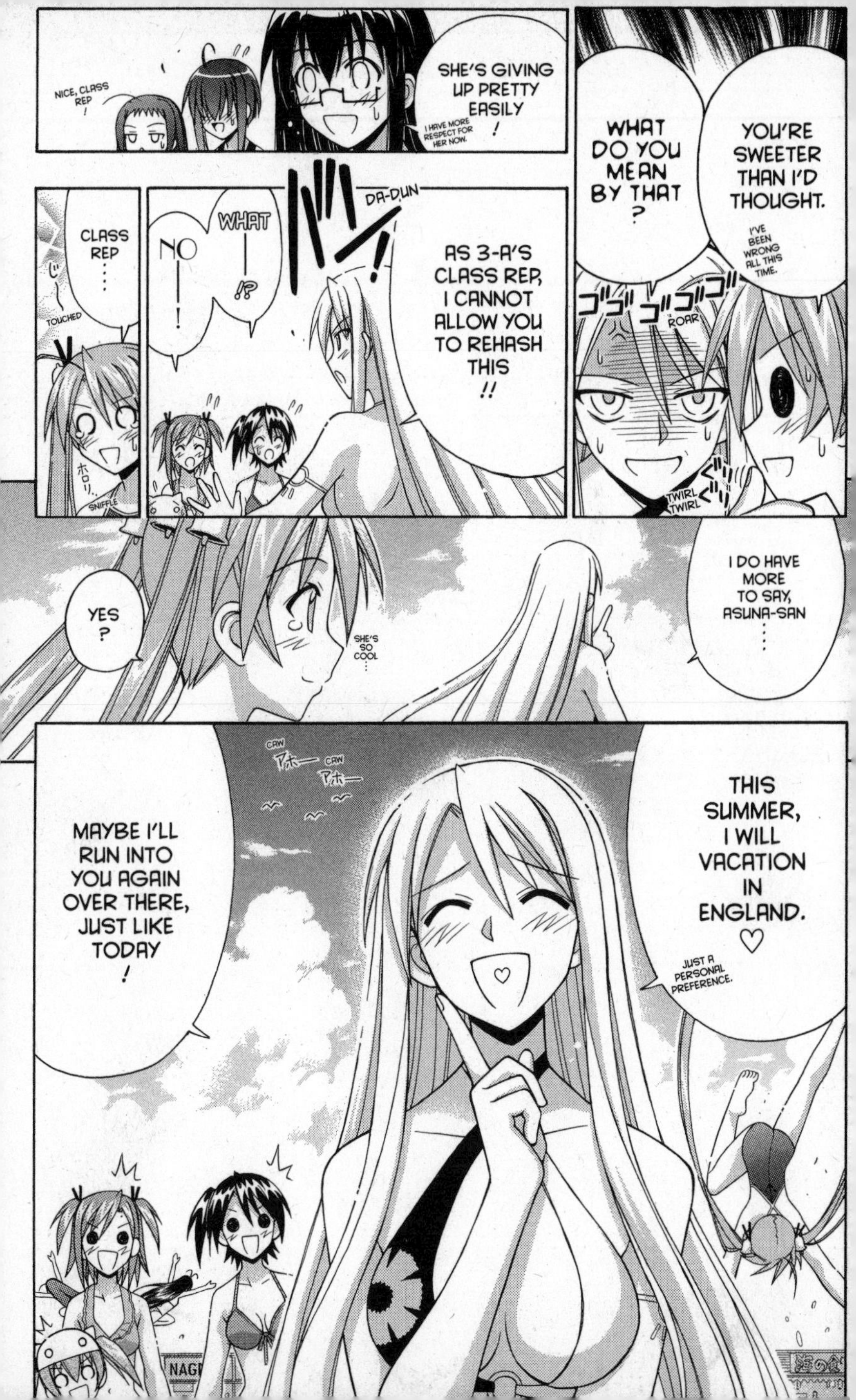
YOU'RE SWEETER THAN I'D THOUGHT.
I'VE BEEN WRONG ALL THIS TIME.
WHAT DO YOU MEAN BY THAT?
ROAR
TWIRL TWIRL
SHE'S GIVING UP PRETTY EASILY!
I HAVE MORE RESPECT FOR HER NOW.
NICE, CLASS REP!
DA-DUN
AS 3-A'S CLASS REP, I CANNOT ALLOW YOU TO REHASH THIS!!
WHAT—!?
NO—!
CLASS REP...
TOUCHED
SNIFFLE
I DO HAVE MORE TO SAY, ASUNA-SAN...
SHE'S SO COOL...
YES?
THIS SUMMER, I WILL VACATION IN ENGLAND. ♡
JUST A PERSONAL PREFERENCE.
CAW
CAW
MAYBE I'LL RUN INTO YOU AGAIN OVER THERE, JUST LIKE TODAY!
NAGI

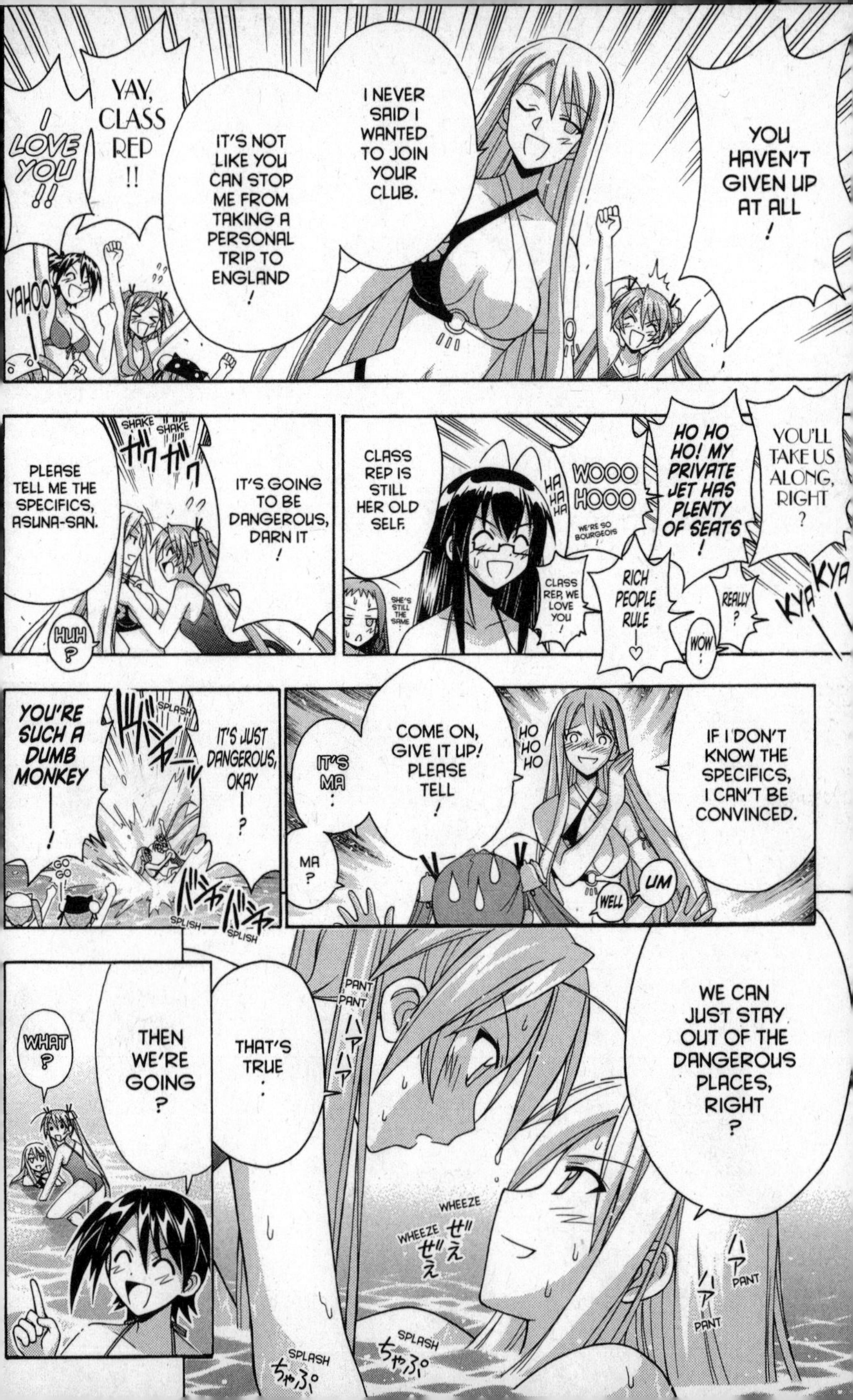

YOU HAVEN'T GIVEN UP AT ALL!
I NEVER SAID I WANTED TO JOIN YOUR CLUB.
IT'S NOT LIKE YOU CAN STOP ME FROM TAKING A PERSONAL TRIP TO ENGLAND!
YAY, CLASS REP!!
I LOVE YOU!!
YAHOO!
YOU'LL TAKE US ALONG, RIGHT?
HO HO HO! MY PRIVATE JET HAS PLENTY OF SEATS!
KYA KYA
WOOO HOOO
HA HA HA
WE'RE SO BOURGEOIS!
REALLY?
RICH PEOPLE RULE ♡
WOW!
CLASS REP, WE LOVE YOU!
CLASS REP IS STILL HER OLD SELF.
SHE'S STILL THE SAME
IT'S GOING TO BE DANGEROUS, DARN IT!
SHAKE SHAKE
PLEASE TELL ME THE SPECIFICS, ASUNA-SAN.
HUH?
IF I DON'T KNOW THE SPECIFICS, I CAN'T BE CONVINCED.
HO HO HO
COME ON, GIVE IT UP! PLEASE TELL!
UM
WELL
IT'S MA...
MA?
IT'S JUST DANGEROUS, OKAY!?
SPLASH
YOU'RE SUCH A DUMB MONKEY!!
GO GO!
SPLASH SPLASH
WE CAN JUST STAY OUT OF THE DANGEROUS PLACES, RIGHT?
PANT PANT
PANT PANT
THAT'S TRUE...
WHEEZE WHEEZE
SPLASH SPLASH
THEN WE'RE GOING?
WHAT?

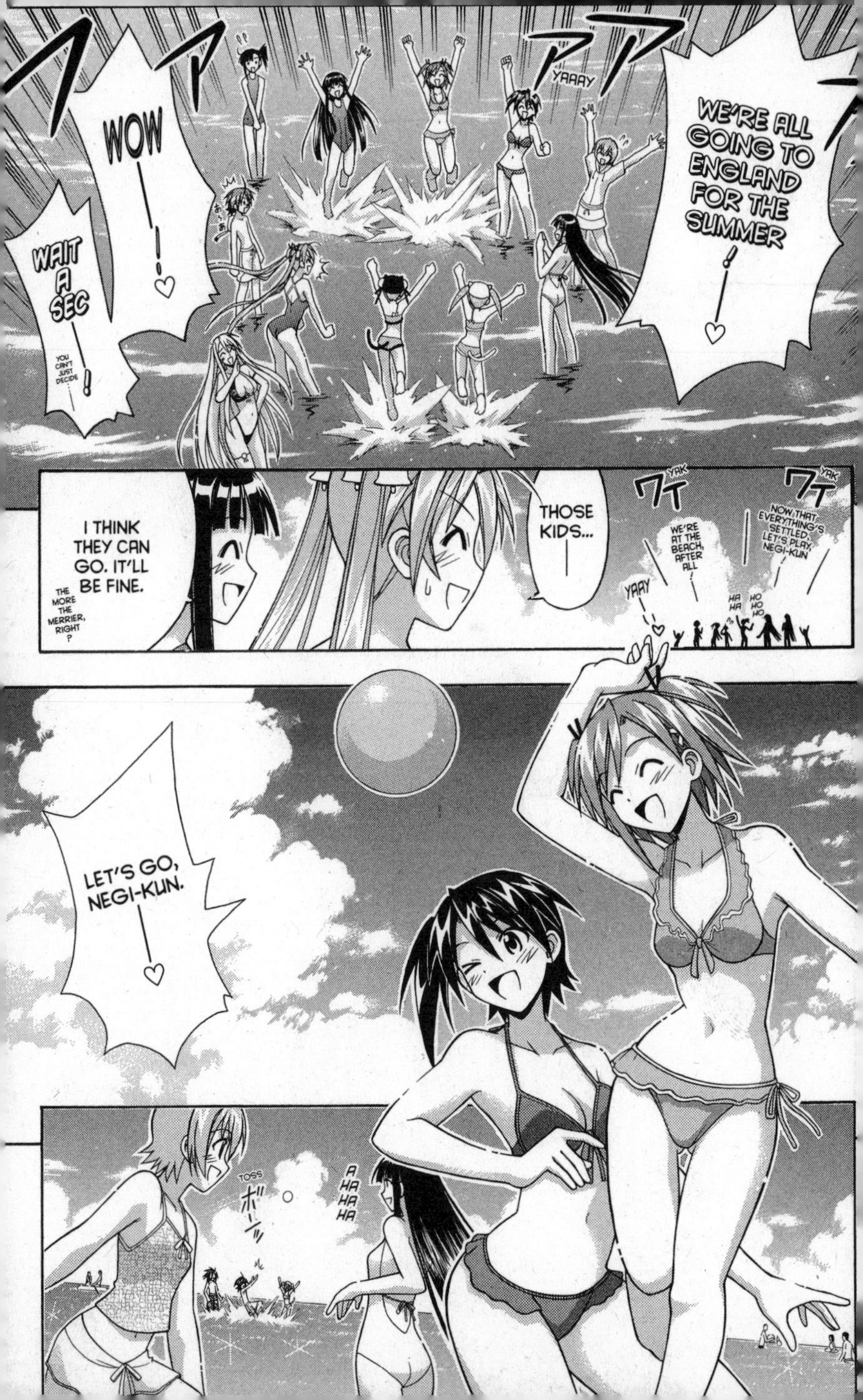
WE'RE ALL GOING TO ENGLAND FOR THE SUMMER!
YAAAY
WOW!
WAIT A SEC!
YOU CAN'T JUST DECIDE...
YAK
YAK
NOW THAT EVERYTHING'S SETTLED, LET'S PLAY, NEGI-KUN!
HO HO HO
HA HA
WE'RE AT THE BEACH, AFTER ALL!
YAAY
THOSE KIDS...
I THINK THEY CAN GO. IT'LL BE FINE.
THE MORE THE MERRIER, RIGHT?
LET'S GO, NEGI-KUN.
A HA HA HA
TOSS

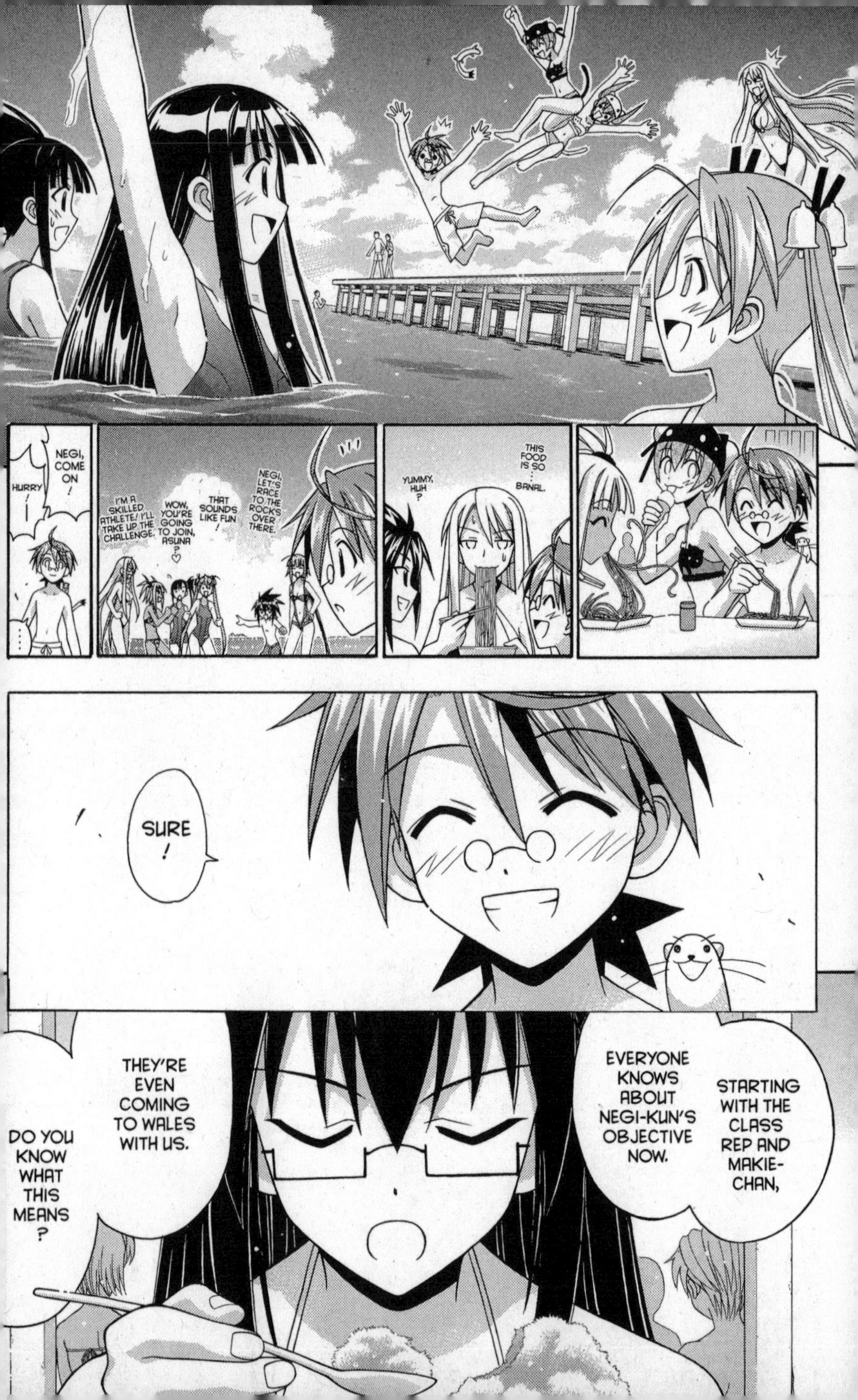

THIS FOOD IS SO... BANAL.
YUMMY, HUH?
NEGI, LET'S RACE TO THE ROCKS OVER THERE.
THAT SOUNDS LIKE FUN!
WOW, YOU'RE GOING TO JOIN, ASUNA?♡
I'M A SKILLED ATHLETE! I'LL TAKE UP THE CHALLENGE.
NEGI, COME ON!
HURRY!
...
SURE!
STARTING WITH THE CLASS REP AND MAKIE-CHAN,
EVERYONE KNOWS ABOUT NEGI-KUN'S OBJECTIVE NOW.
THEY'RE EVEN COMING TO WALES WITH US.
DO YOU KNOW WHAT THIS MEANS?

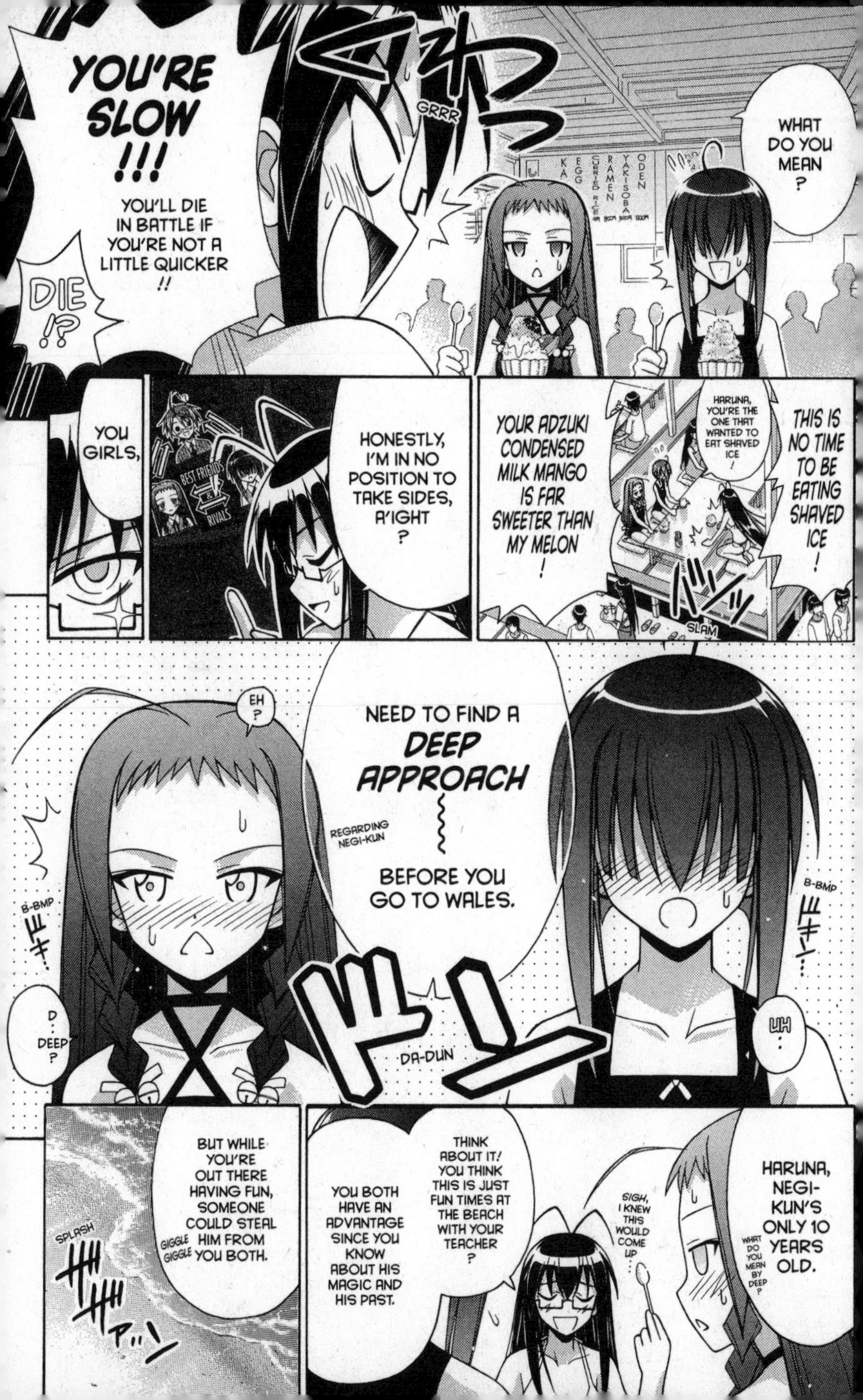
WHAT DO YOU MEAN?
GRRR
YOU'RE SLOW!!!
YOU'LL DIE IN BATTLE IF YOU'RE NOT A LITTLE QUICKER!!
DIE!?
ODEN
YAKISOBA
RAMEN
CURRIED RICE
EGG
THIS IS NO TIME TO BE EATING SHAVED ICE!
HARUNA, YOU'RE THE ONE THAT WANTED TO EAT SHAVED ICE!
YOUR ADZUKI CONDENSED MILK MANGO IS FAR SWEETER THAN MY MELON!
SLAM
HONESTLY, I'M IN NO POSITION TO TAKE SIDES, A'IGHT?
BEST FRIENDS & RIVALS
YOU GIRLS,
B-BMP
UH...
NEED TO FIND A DEEP APPROACH
REGARDING NEGI-KUN
BEFORE YOU GO TO WALES.
EH?
DA-DUN
B-BMP
D... DEEP?
HARUNA, NEGI-KUN'S ONLY 10 YEARS OLD.
WHAT DO YOU MEAN BY DEEP?
SIGH, I KNEW THIS WOULD COME UP...
THINK ABOUT IT! YOU THINK THIS IS JUST FUN TIMES AT THE BEACH WITH YOUR TEACHER?
YOU BOTH HAVE AN ADVANTAGE SINCE YOU KNOW ABOUT HIS MAGIC AND HIS PAST.
BUT WHILE YOU'RE OUT THERE HAVING FUN, SOMEONE COULD STEAL HIM FROM YOU BOTH.
GIGGLE GIGGLE
SPLASH

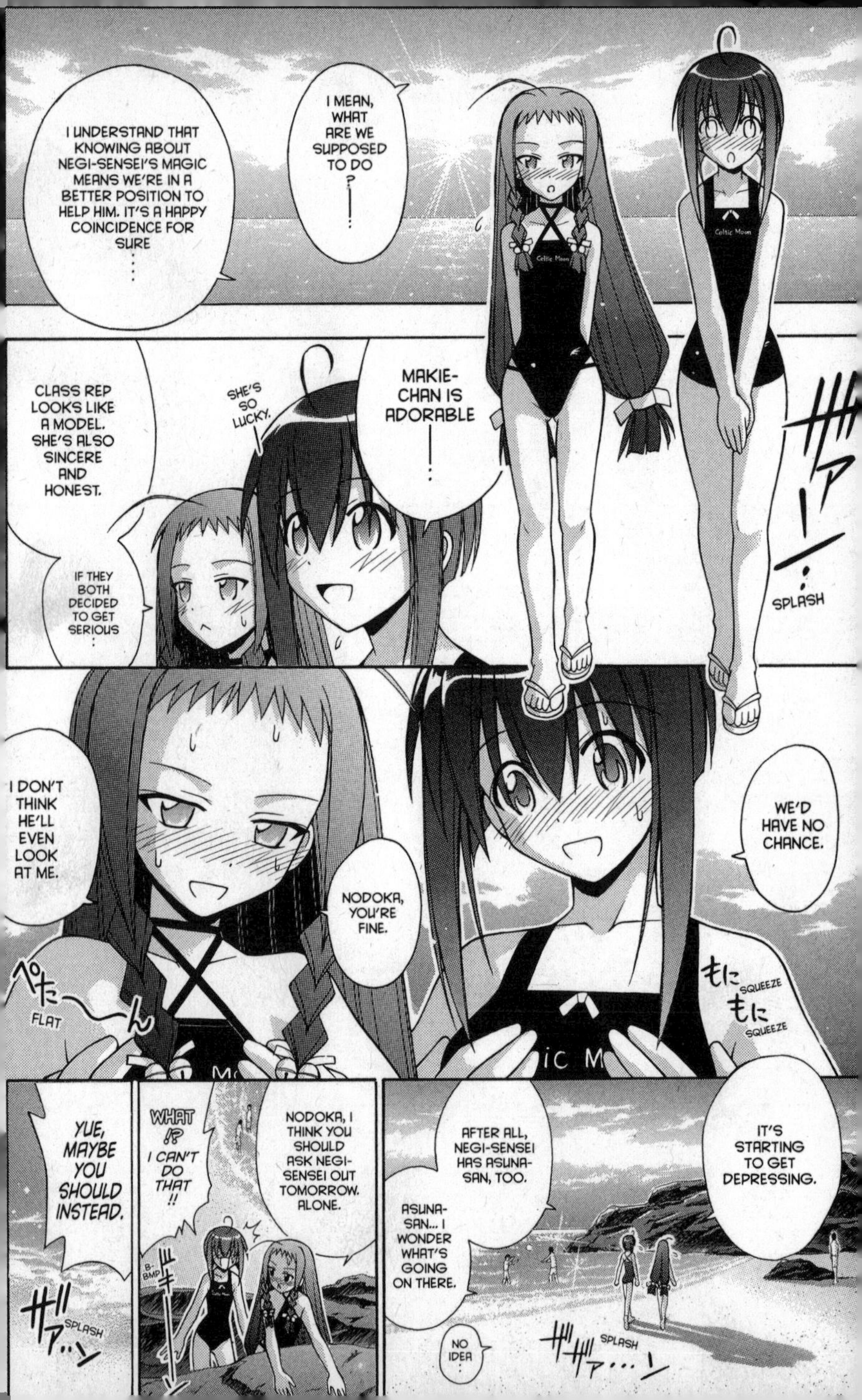

I MEAN, WHAT ARE WE SUPPOSED TO DO?......
I UNDERSTAND THAT KNOWING ABOUT NEGI-SENSEI'S MAGIC MEANS WE'RE IN A BETTER POSITION TO HELP HIM. IT'S A HAPPY COINCIDENCE FOR SURE...
Celtic Moon
Celtic Moon
SPLASH
MAKIE-CHAN IS ADORABLE......
SHE'S SO LUCKY.
CLASS REP LOOKS LIKE A MODEL. SHE'S ALSO SINCERE AND HONEST.
IF THEY BOTH DECIDED TO GET SERIOUS...
WE'D HAVE NO CHANCE.
もに SQUEEZE
もに SQUEEZE
NODOKA, YOU'RE FINE.
I DON'T THINK HE'LL EVEN LOOK AT ME.
ぺた〜ん FLAT
IT'S STARTING TO GET DEPRESSING.
AFTER ALL, NEGI-SENSEI HAS ASUNA-SAN, TOO.
ASUNA-SAN... I WONDER WHAT'S GOING ON THERE.
NO IDEA...
SPLASH
NODOKA, I THINK YOU SHOULD ASK NEGI-SENSEI OUT TOMORROW. ALONE.
WHAT!? I CAN'T DO THAT!!
B-BMP
SPLASH
YUE, MAYBE YOU SHOULD INSTEAD.

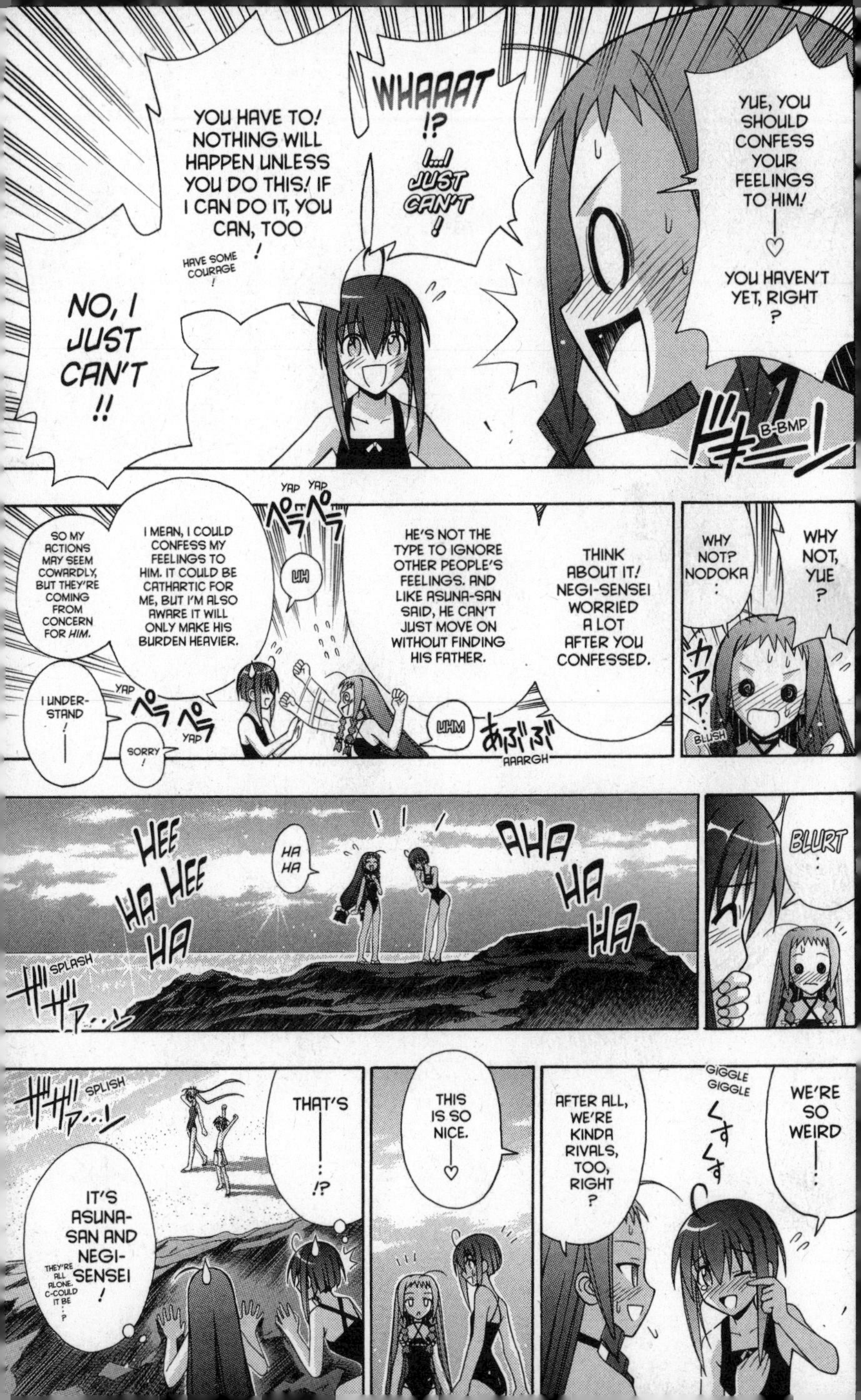
YUE, YOU SHOULD CONFESS YOUR FEELINGS TO HIM! ♡
YOU HAVEN'T YET, RIGHT?
B-BMP
WHAAAT!?
I...! JUST CAN'T!
YOU HAVE TO! NOTHING WILL HAPPEN UNLESS YOU DO THIS! IF I CAN DO IT, YOU CAN, TOO!
HAVE SOME COURAGE!
NO, I JUST CAN'T!!
WHY NOT, YUE?
WHY NOT? NODOKA...
BLUSH
THINK ABOUT IT! NEGI-SENSEI WORRIED A LOT AFTER YOU CONFESSED.
HE'S NOT THE TYPE TO IGNORE OTHER PEOPLE'S FEELINGS. AND LIKE ASUNA-SAN SAID, HE CAN'T JUST MOVE ON WITHOUT FINDING HIS FATHER.
UHM
AAARGH
YAP YAP
UH
I MEAN, I COULD CONFESS MY FEELINGS TO HIM. IT COULD BE CATHARTIC FOR ME, BUT I'M ALSO AWARE IT WILL ONLY MAKE HIS BURDEN HEAVIER.
SO MY ACTIONS MAY SEEM COWARDLY, BUT THEY'RE COMING FROM CONCERN FOR *HIM*.
YAP
YAP
SORRY!
I UNDERSTAND!
BLURT...
AHA HA HA
HA HA
HEE HA HEE HA
SPLASH
WE'RE SO WEIRD...!
GIGGLE GIGGLE
AFTER ALL, WE'RE KINDA RIVALS, TOO, RIGHT?
THIS IS SO NICE. ♡
THAT'S...!?
SPLISH
IT'S ASUNA-SAN AND NEGI-SENSEI!
THEY'RE ALL ALONE. C-COULD IT BE...?

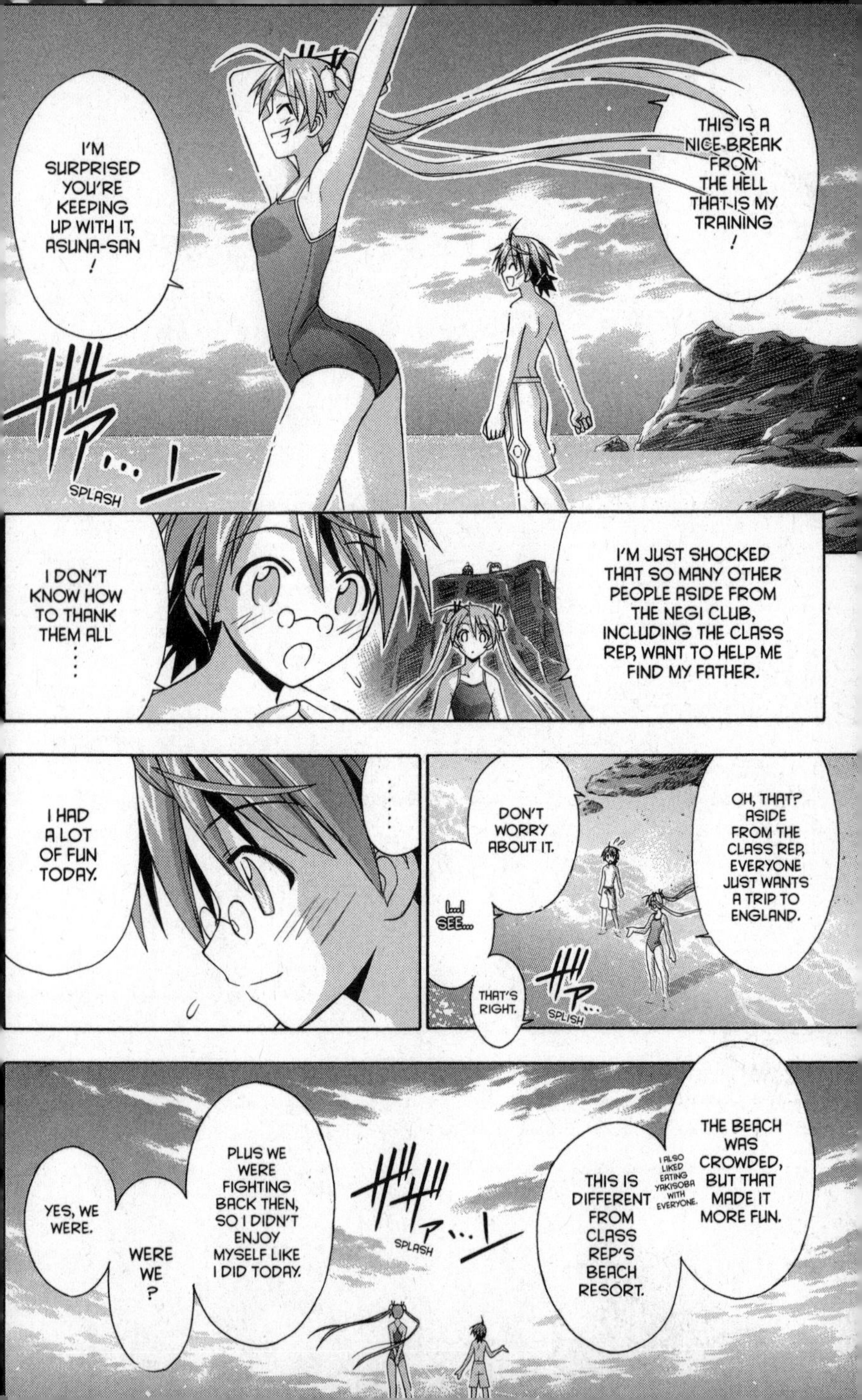
THIS IS A NICE BREAK FROM THE HELL THAT IS MY TRAINING!
I'M SURPRISED YOU'RE KEEPING UP WITH IT, ASUNA-SAN!
SPLASH
I'M JUST SHOCKED THAT SO MANY OTHER PEOPLE ASIDE FROM THE NEGI CLUB, INCLUDING THE CLASS REP, WANT TO HELP ME FIND MY FATHER.
I DON'T KNOW HOW TO THANK THEM ALL....
OH, THAT? ASIDE FROM THE CLASS REP, EVERYONE JUST WANTS A TRIP TO ENGLAND.
DON'T WORRY ABOUT IT.
I...I SEE...
THAT'S RIGHT.
SPLISH
......
I HAD A LOT OF FUN TODAY.
THE BEACH WAS CROWDED, BUT THAT MADE IT MORE FUN.
I ALSO LIKED EATING YAKISOBA WITH EVERYONE.
THIS IS DIFFERENT FROM CLASS REP'S BEACH RESORT.
SPLASH
PLUS WE WERE FIGHTING BACK THEN, SO I DIDN'T ENJOY MYSELF LIKE I DID TODAY.
WERE WE?
YES, WE WERE.

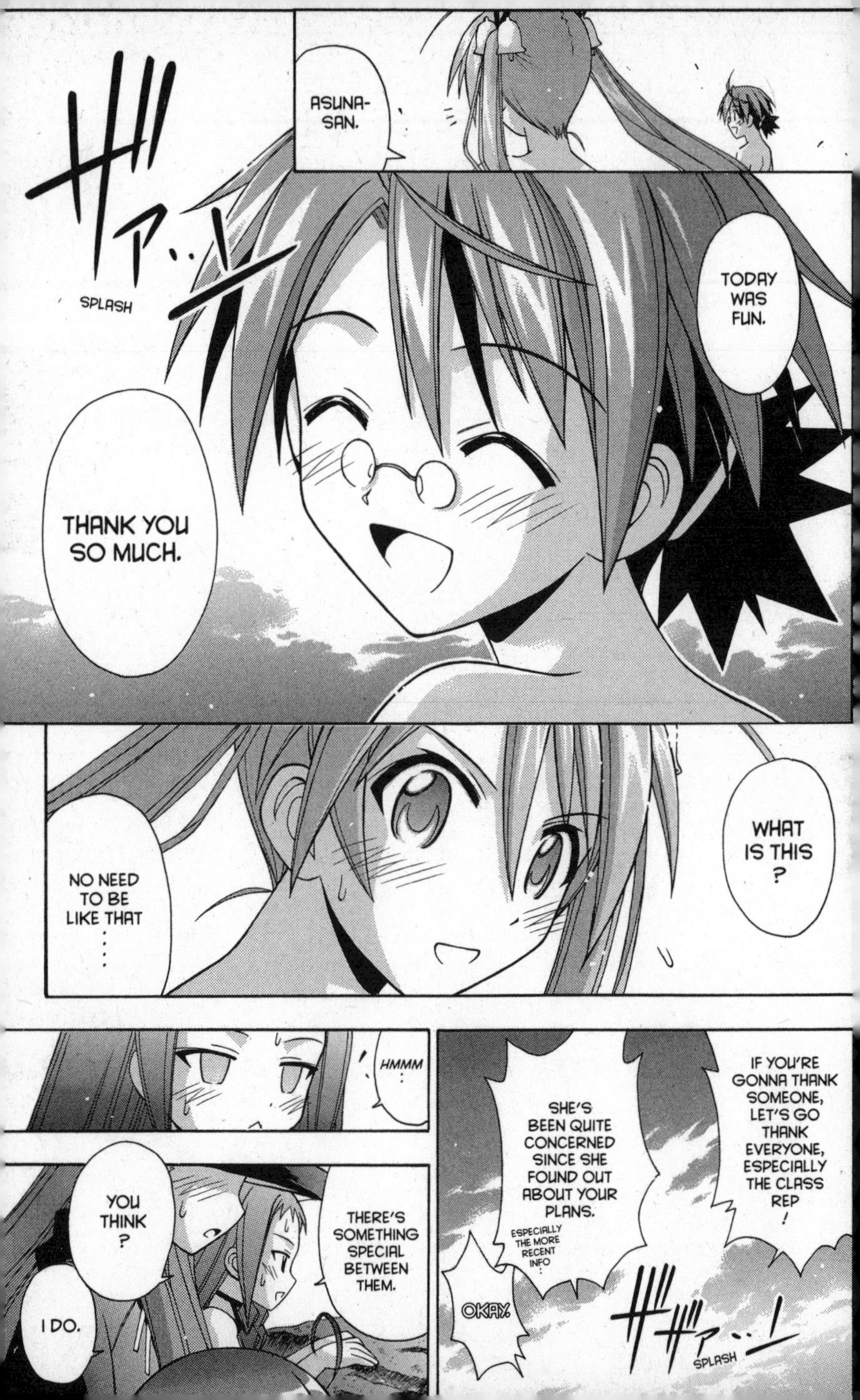
ASUNA-SAN.
TODAY WAS FUN.
THANK YOU SO MUCH.
SPLASH
WHAT IS THIS ?
NO NEED TO BE LIKE THAT ...
IF YOU'RE GONNA THANK SOMEONE, LET'S GO THANK EVERYONE, ESPECIALLY THE CLASS REP !
SHE'S BEEN QUITE CONCERNED SINCE SHE FOUND OUT ABOUT YOUR PLANS.
ESPECIALLY THE MORE RECENT INFO ...
OKAY.
SPLASH
HMMM ...
THERE'S SOMETHING SPECIAL BETWEEN THEM.
YOU THINK ?
I DO.

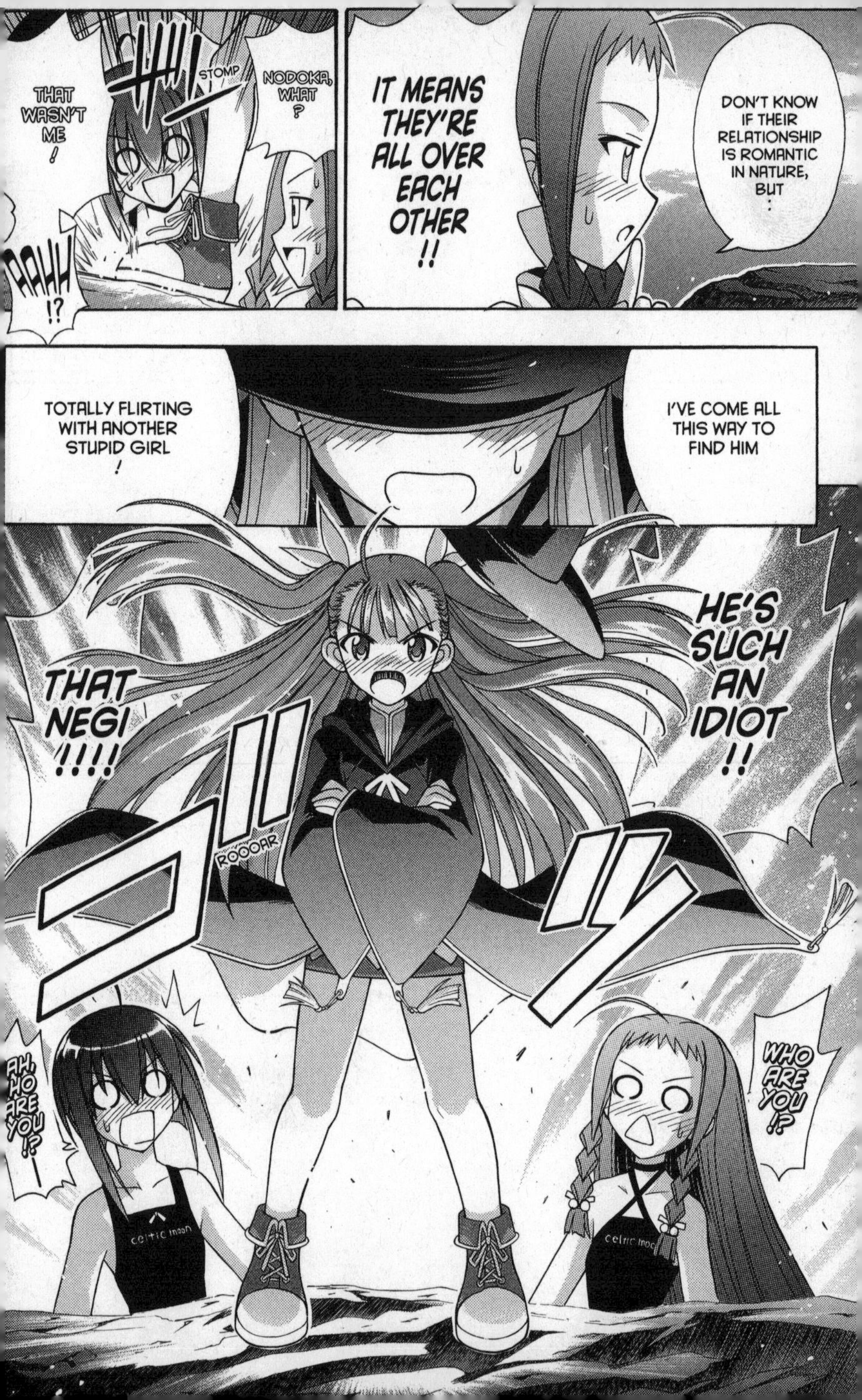
DON'T KNOW IF THEIR RELATIONSHIP IS ROMANTIC IN NATURE, BUT :
IT MEANS THEY'RE ALL OVER EACH OTHER !!
NODOKA, WHAT ?
STOMP
THAT WASN'T ME !
AAHH !?
I'VE COME ALL THIS WAY TO FIND HIM
TOTALLY FLIRTING WITH ANOTHER STUPID GIRL !
HE'S SUCH AN IDIOT !!
THAT NEGI !!!!
ROOOAR
WHO ARE YOU !?
AH, HO ARE YOU !?
celtic moon
celtic moon

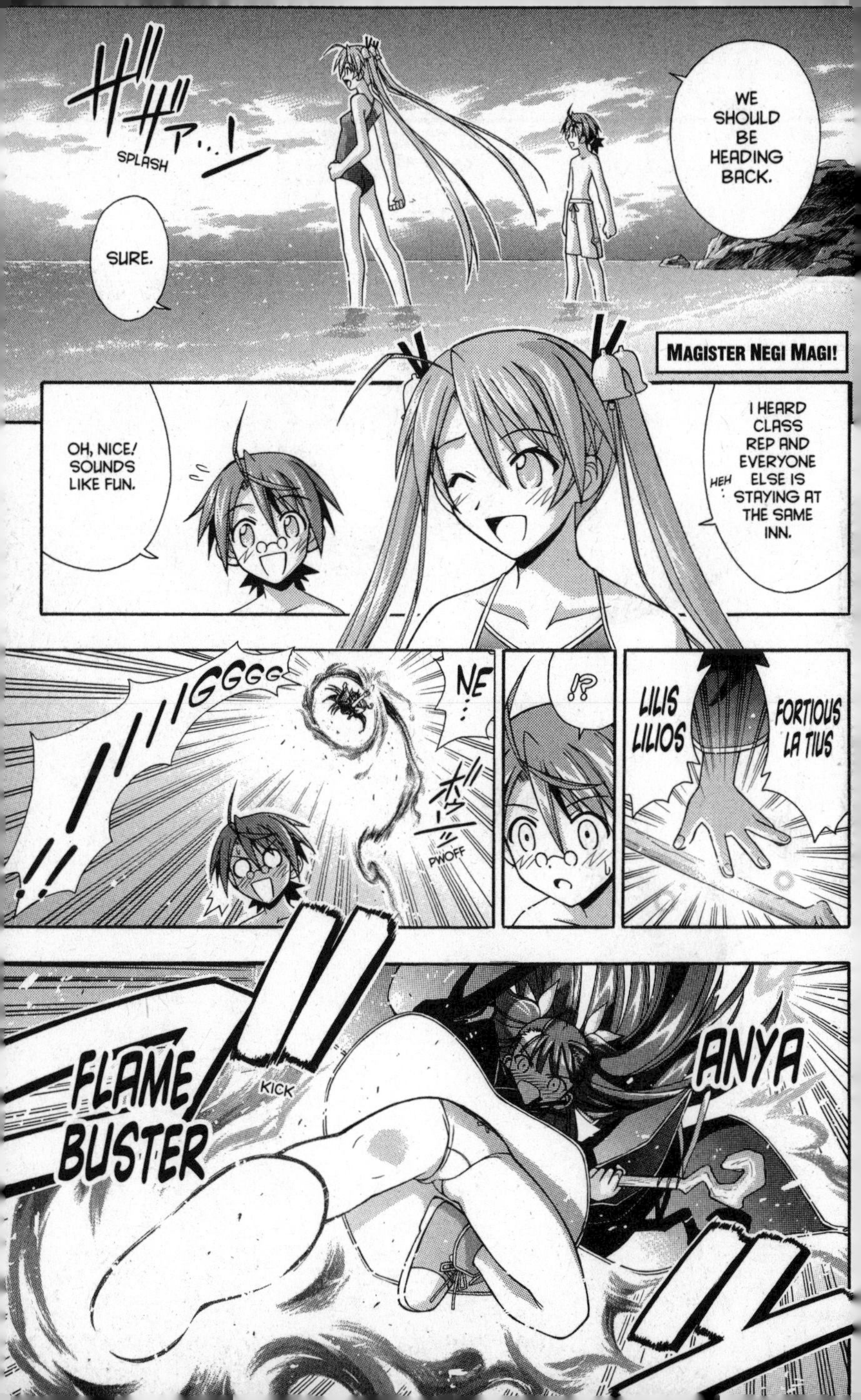
WE SHOULD BE HEADING BACK.
SPLASH
SURE.
MAGISTER NEGI MAGI!
I HEARD CLASS REP AND EVERYONE ELSE IS STAYING AT THE SAME INN.
HEH
OH, NICE! SOUNDS LIKE FUN.
FORTIOUS LA TIUS
LILIS LILIOS
!?
NE...
PWOFF
IGGGG
!!
ANYA
KICK
FLAME BUSTER

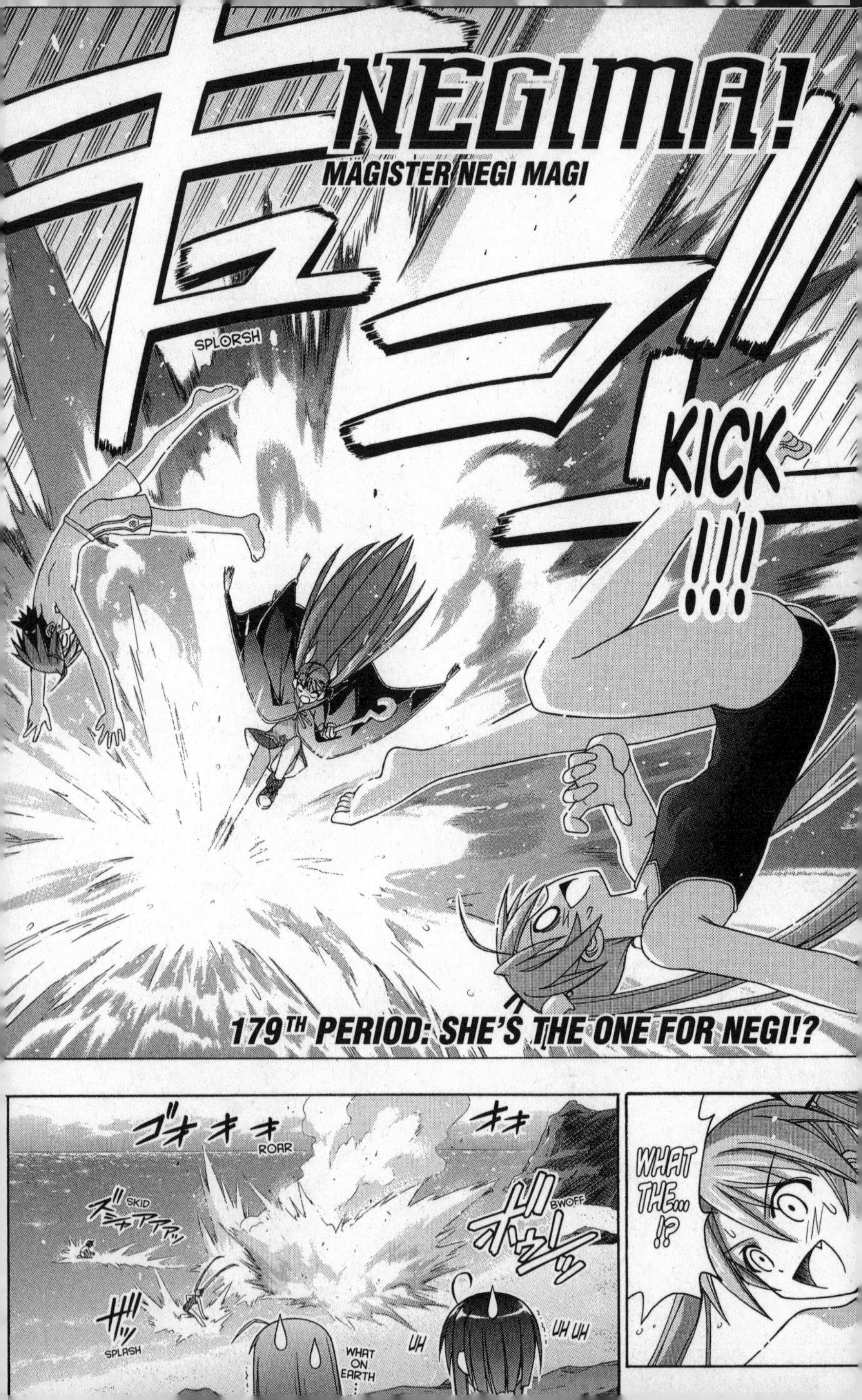
NEGIMA!
MAGISTER NEGI MAGI
KICK !!!
SPLORSH
179TH PERIOD: SHE'S THE ONE FOR NEGI!?
WHAT THE... !?
ROAR
BWOFF
SKID
UH UH
UH
WHAT ON EARTH
SPLASH

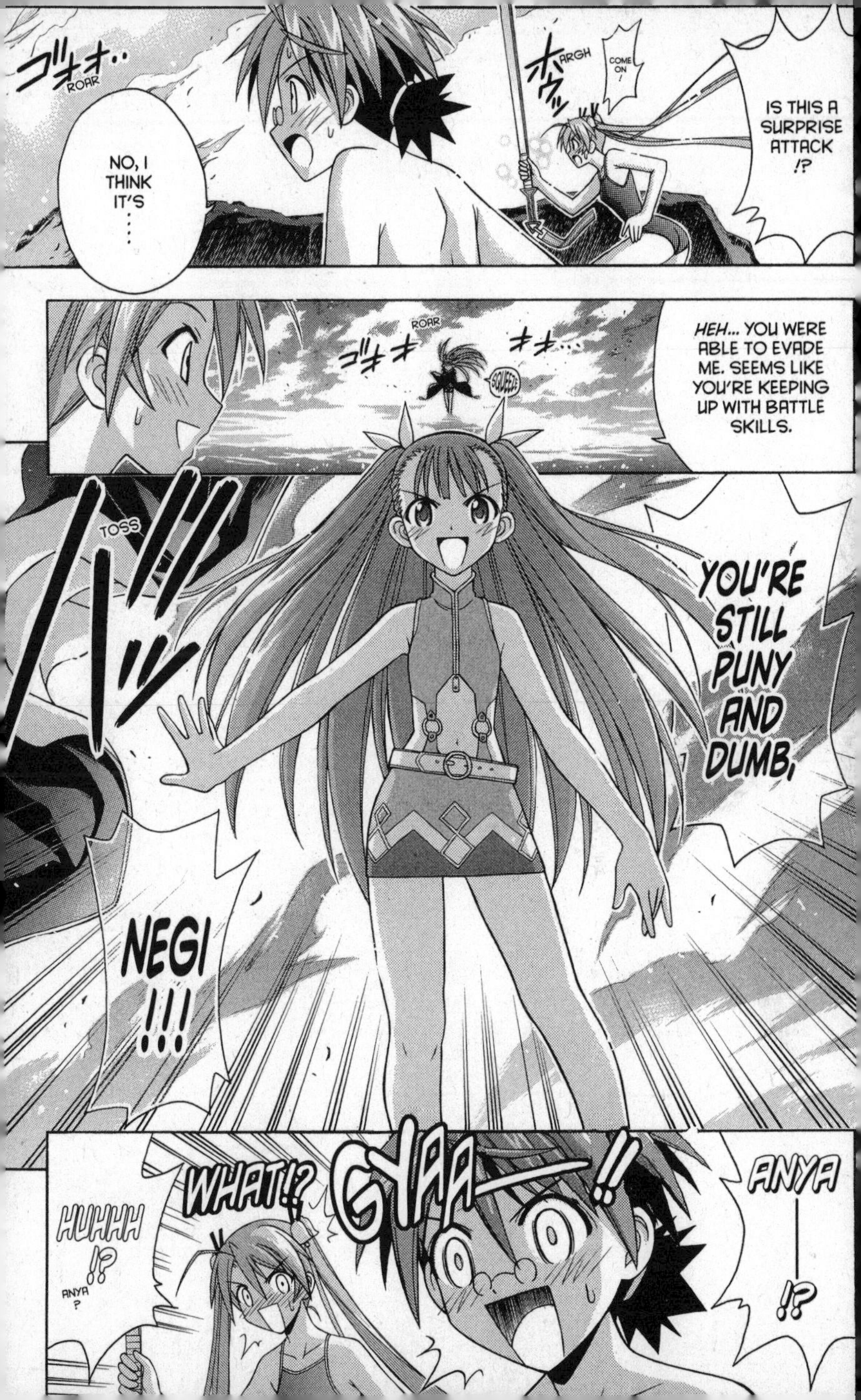
IS THIS A SURPRISE ATTACK !?
COME ON !
ARGH
ROAR
NO, I THINK IT'S ....
HEH... YOU WERE ABLE TO EVADE ME. SEEMS LIKE YOU'RE KEEPING UP WITH BATTLE SKILLS.
ROAR
SQUEEZE
YOU'RE STILL PUNY AND DUMB,
TOSS
NEGI !!!
ANYA——!?
GYAA——!!
WHAT!?
HUHHH !?
ANYA ?

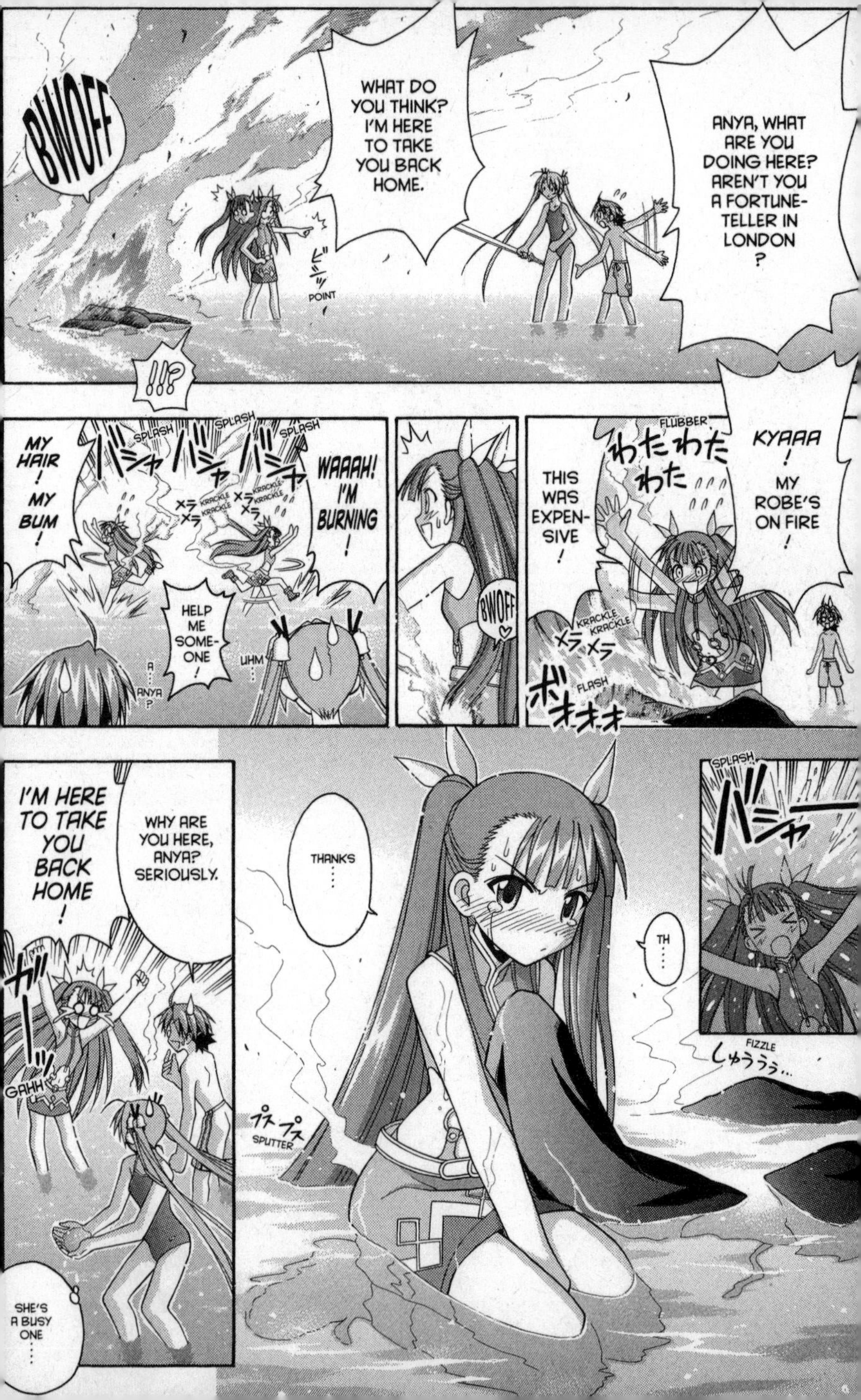
ANYA, WHAT ARE YOU DOING HERE? AREN'T YOU A FORTUNE-TELLER IN LONDON?
WHAT DO YOU THINK? I'M HERE TO TAKE YOU BACK HOME.
ビシッ
POINT
BWOFF
!!!?
KYAAA! MY ROBE'S ON FIRE!
わたわたわた
FLUBBER
THIS WAS EXPENSIVE!
メラ メラ
KRACKLE KRACKLE
ボオオオ
FLASH
BWOFF ♥
WAAAH! I'M BURNING!
バシャ バシャ バシャ
SPLASH SPLASH SPLASH
MY HAIR! MY BUM!
メラメラ メラメラ
KRACKLE KRACKLE KRACKLE KRACKLE
HELP ME SOMEONE!
UHM....
A... ANYA?
バシャー
SPLASH
しゅうううう...
FIZZLE
TH....
THANKS....
プスプス
SPUTTER
WHY ARE YOU HERE, ANYA? SERIOUSLY.
I'M HERE TO TAKE YOU BACK HOME!
ガー
GAHH
SHE'S A BUSY ONE....

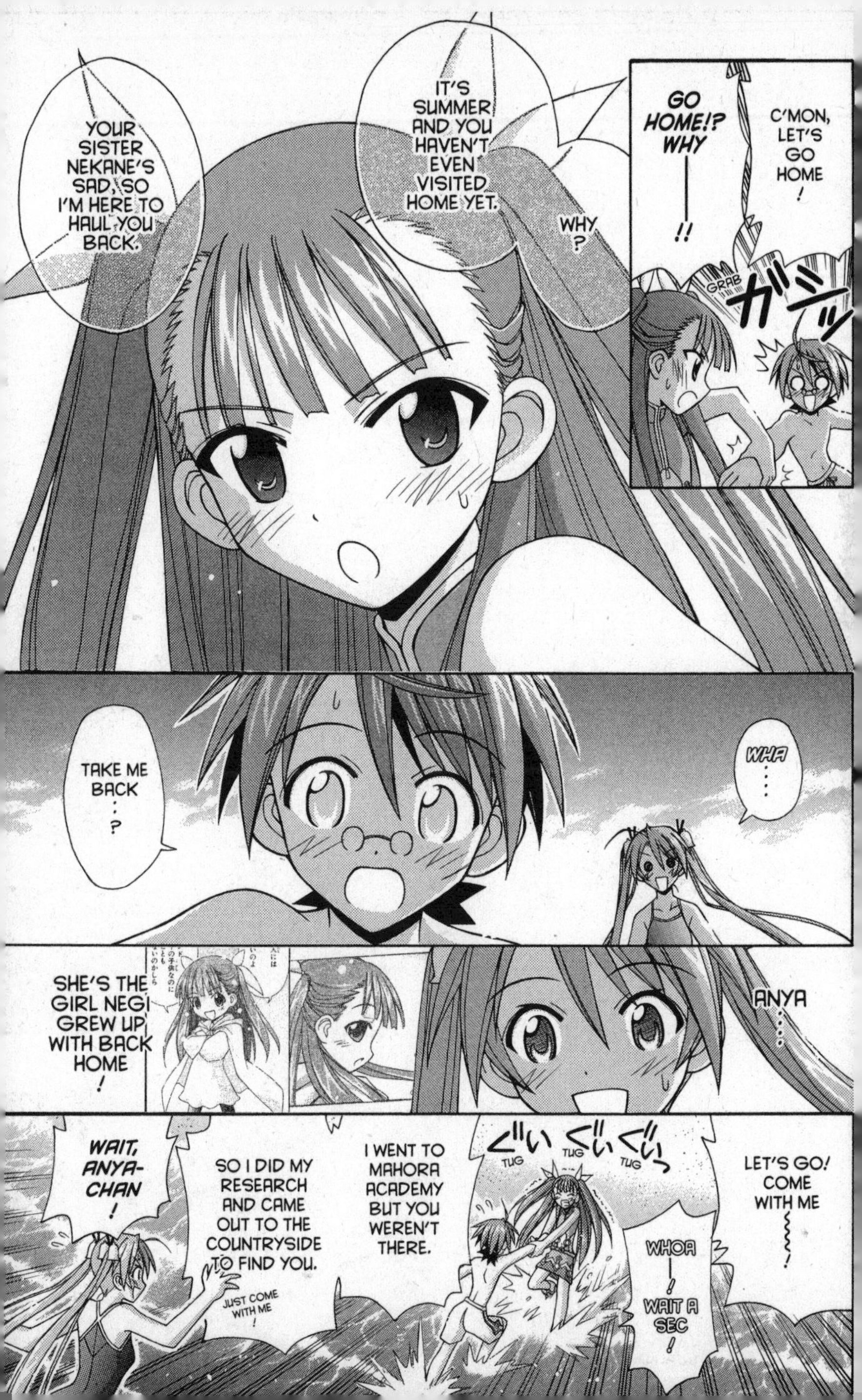
C'MON, LET'S GO HOME!
GO HOME!? WHY—!!
GRAB
ガシッ
WHY?
IT'S SUMMER AND YOU HAVEN'T EVEN VISITED HOME YET.
YOUR SISTER NEKANE'S SAD, SO I'M HERE TO HAUL YOU BACK.
WHA...
TAKE ME BACK...?
ANYA....
SHE'S THE GIRL NEGI GREW UP WITH BACK HOME!
LET'S GO! COME WITH ME~!
WHOA—! WAIT A SEC!
ぐいぐいぐいっ
TUG TUG TUG
I WENT TO MAHORA ACADEMY BUT YOU WEREN'T THERE.
SO I DID MY RESEARCH AND CAME OUT TO THE COUNTRYSIDE TO FIND YOU.
JUST COME WITH ME!
WAIT, ANYA-CHAN!

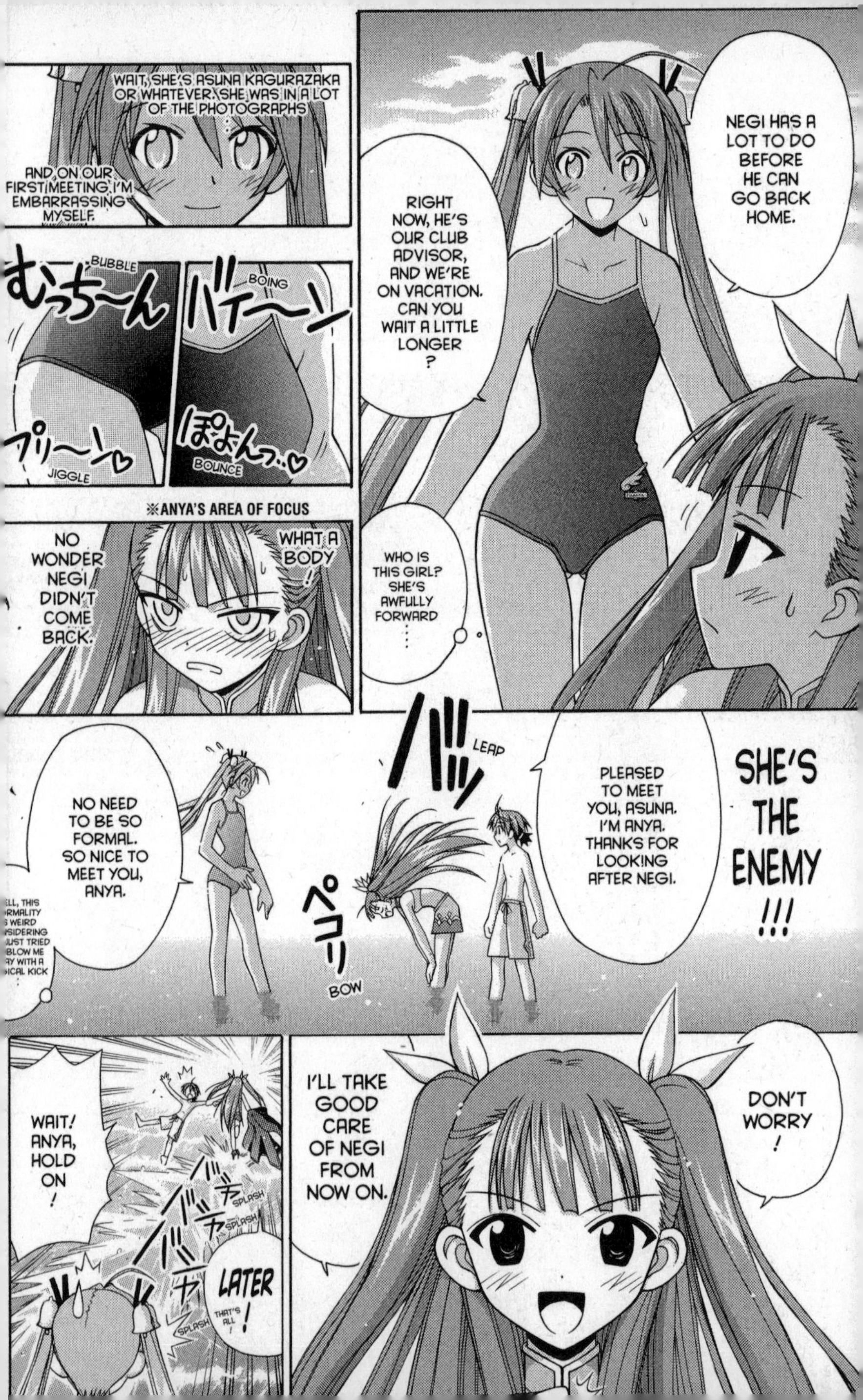
NEGI HAS A LOT TO DO BEFORE HE CAN GO BACK HOME.
RIGHT NOW, HE'S OUR CLUB ADVISOR, AND WE'RE ON VACATION. CAN YOU WAIT A LITTLE LONGER?
WHO IS THIS GIRL? SHE'S AWFULLY FORWARD...
WAIT, SHE'S ASUNA KAGURAZAKA OR WHATEVER. SHE WAS IN A LOT OF THE PHOTOGRAPHS...
AND ON OUR FIRST MEETING, I'M EMBARRASSING MYSELF.
バイーン
BOING
ぽよんっ♡
BOUNCE
むっちーん
BUBBLE
プリーン♡
JIGGLE
※ANYA'S AREA OF FOCUS
WHAT A BODY!
NO WONDER NEGI DIDN'T COME BACK.
SHE'S THE ENEMY!!!
PLEASED TO MEET YOU, ASUNA. I'M ANYA. THANKS FOR LOOKING AFTER NEGI.
バッ
LEAP
ペコリ
BOW
NO NEED TO BE SO FORMAL. SO NICE TO MEET YOU, ANYA.
DON'T WORRY!
I'LL TAKE GOOD CARE OF NEGI FROM NOW ON.
WAIT! ANYA, HOLD ON!
SPLASH
SPLASH
SPLASH
LATER!
THAT'S ALL!

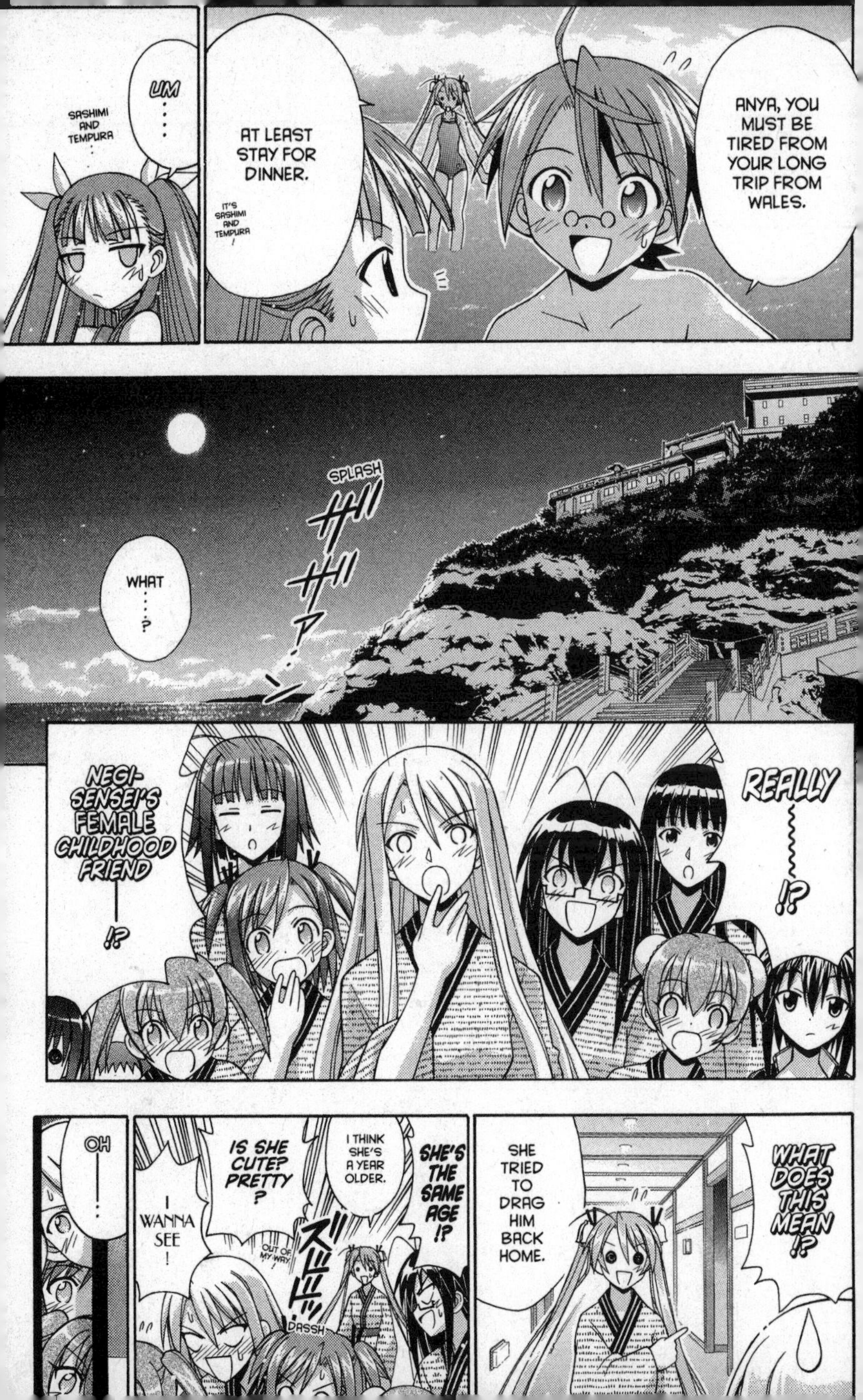
ANYA, YOU MUST BE TIRED FROM YOUR LONG TRIP FROM WALES.
AT LEAST STAY FOR DINNER.
IT'S SASHIMI AND TEMPURA!
UM....
SASHIMI AND TEMPURA...
SPLASH
WHAT...?
REALLY~!?
NEGI-SENSEI'S FEMALE CHILDHOOD FRIEND—!?
WHAT DOES THIS MEAN!?
SHE TRIED TO DRAG HIM BACK HOME.
SHE'S THE SAME AGE!?
I THINK SHE'S A YEAR OLDER.
IS SHE CUTE? PRETTY?
OUT OF MY WAY!
DASSH
I WANNA SEE!
OH—....

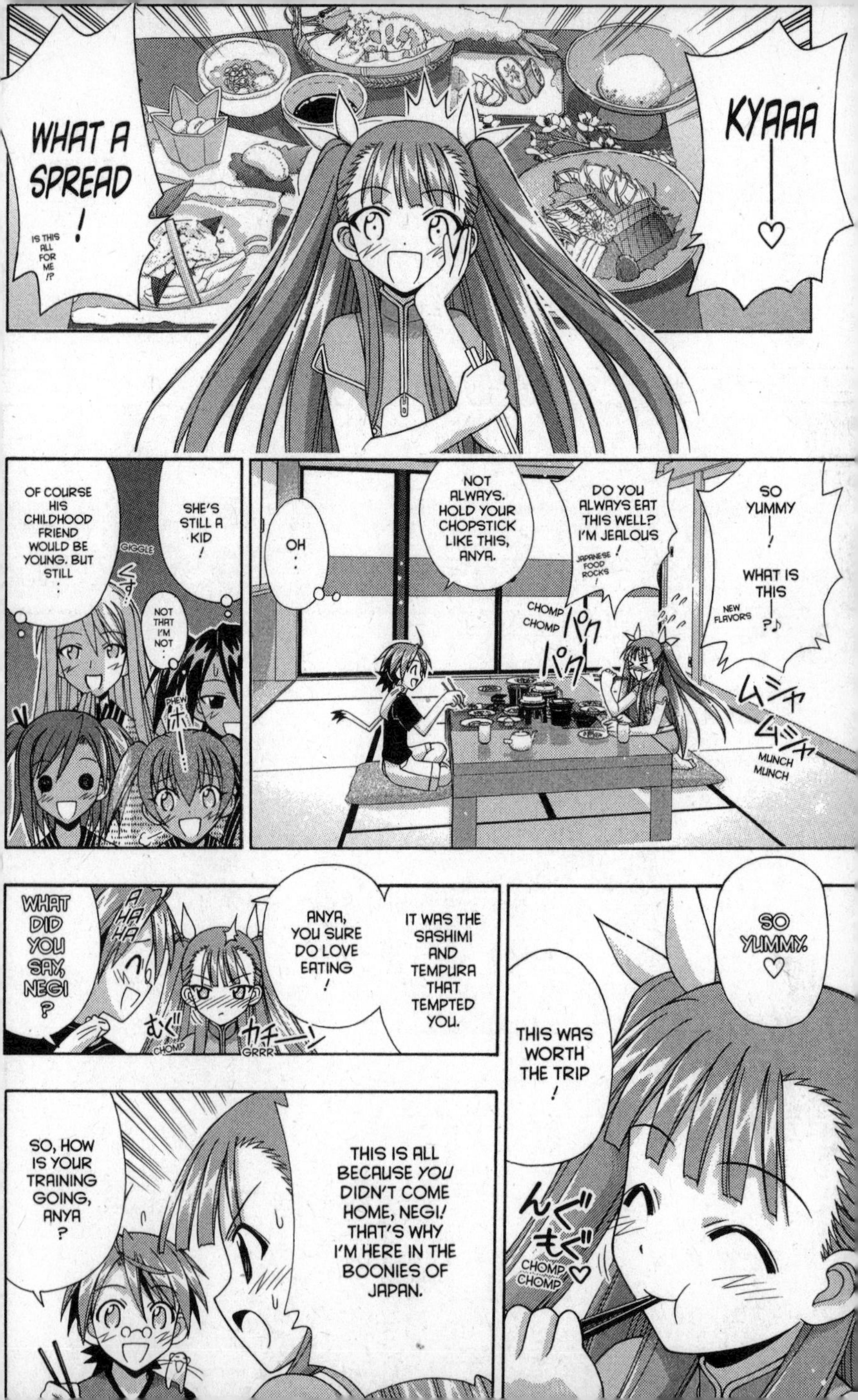
KYAAA ♡
WHAT A SPREAD!
IS THIS ALL FOR ME!?
SO YUMMY! WHAT IS THIS?♪
NEW FLAVORS
DO YOU ALWAYS EAT THIS WELL? I'M JEALOUS!
JAPANESE FOOD ROCKS!
NOT ALWAYS. HOLD YOUR CHOPSTICK LIKE THIS, ANYA.
OH...
パクパク
CHOMP CHOMP
ムシャムシャ
MUNCH MUNCH
SHE'S STILL A KID!
OF COURSE HIS CHILDHOOD FRIEND WOULD BE YOUNG. BUT STILL...
くすっ
GIGGLE
NOT THAT I'M NOT...
ホッ
PHEW
SO YUMMY. ♡
THIS WAS WORTH THE TRIP!
んぐもぐ♡
CHOMP CHOMP
ANYA, YOU SURE DO LOVE EATING! IT WAS THE SASHIMI AND TEMPURA THAT TEMPTED YOU.
AHAHA
WHAT DID YOU SAY, NEGI?
むぐ
CHOMP
カチーン!
GRRR
THIS IS ALL BECAUSE YOU DIDN'T COME HOME, NEGI! THAT'S WHY I'M HERE IN THE BOONIES OF JAPAN.
SO, HOW IS YOUR TRAINING GOING, ANYA?

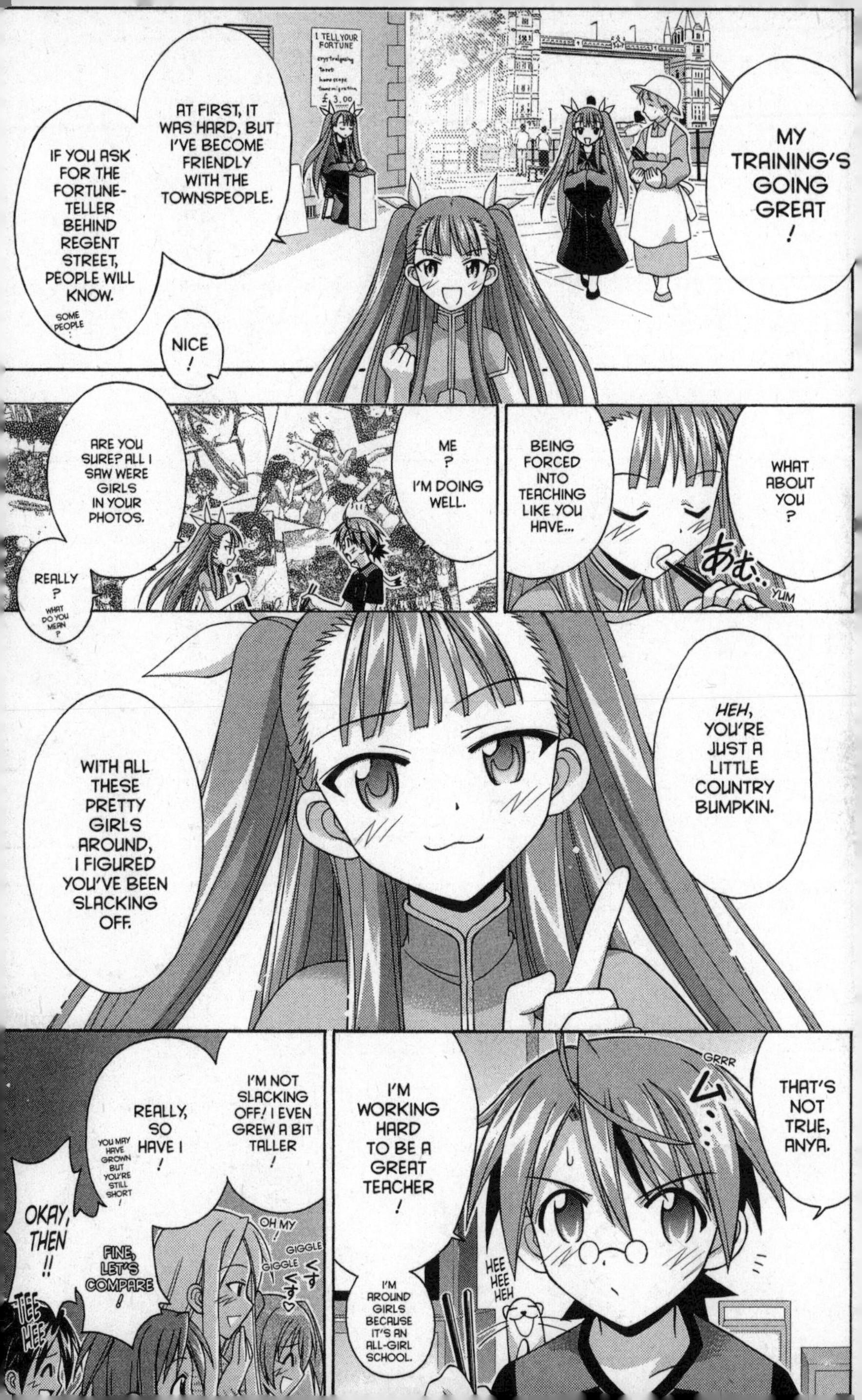
MY TRAINING'S GOING GREAT!
I TELL YOUR FORTUNE
£3.00
AT FIRST, IT WAS HARD, BUT I'VE BECOME FRIENDLY WITH THE TOWNSPEOPLE.
IF YOU ASK FOR THE FORTUNE-TELLER BEHIND REGENT STREET, PEOPLE WILL KNOW.
SOME PEOPLE...
NICE!
WHAT ABOUT YOU?
BEING FORCED INTO TEACHING LIKE YOU HAVE...
あむ…
YUM
ME? I'M DOING WELL.
ARE YOU SURE? ALL I SAW WERE GIRLS IN YOUR PHOTOS.
REALLY?
WHAT DO YOU MEAN?
HEH, YOU'RE JUST A LITTLE COUNTRY BUMPKIN.
WITH ALL THESE PRETTY GIRLS AROUND, I FIGURED YOU'VE BEEN SLACKING OFF.
THAT'S NOT TRUE, ANYA.
ム…
GRRR
I'M WORKING HARD TO BE A GREAT TEACHER!
HEE HEE HEH
I'M AROUND GIRLS BECAUSE IT'S AN ALL-GIRL SCHOOL.
I'M NOT SLACKING OFF! I EVEN GREW A BIT TALLER!
REALLY, SO HAVE I!
YOU MAY HAVE GROWN BUT YOU'RE STILL SHORT!
OH MY!
GIGGLE
くす
GIGGLE
くす♡
FINE, LET'S COMPARE!
OKAY, THEN!!
TEE HEE

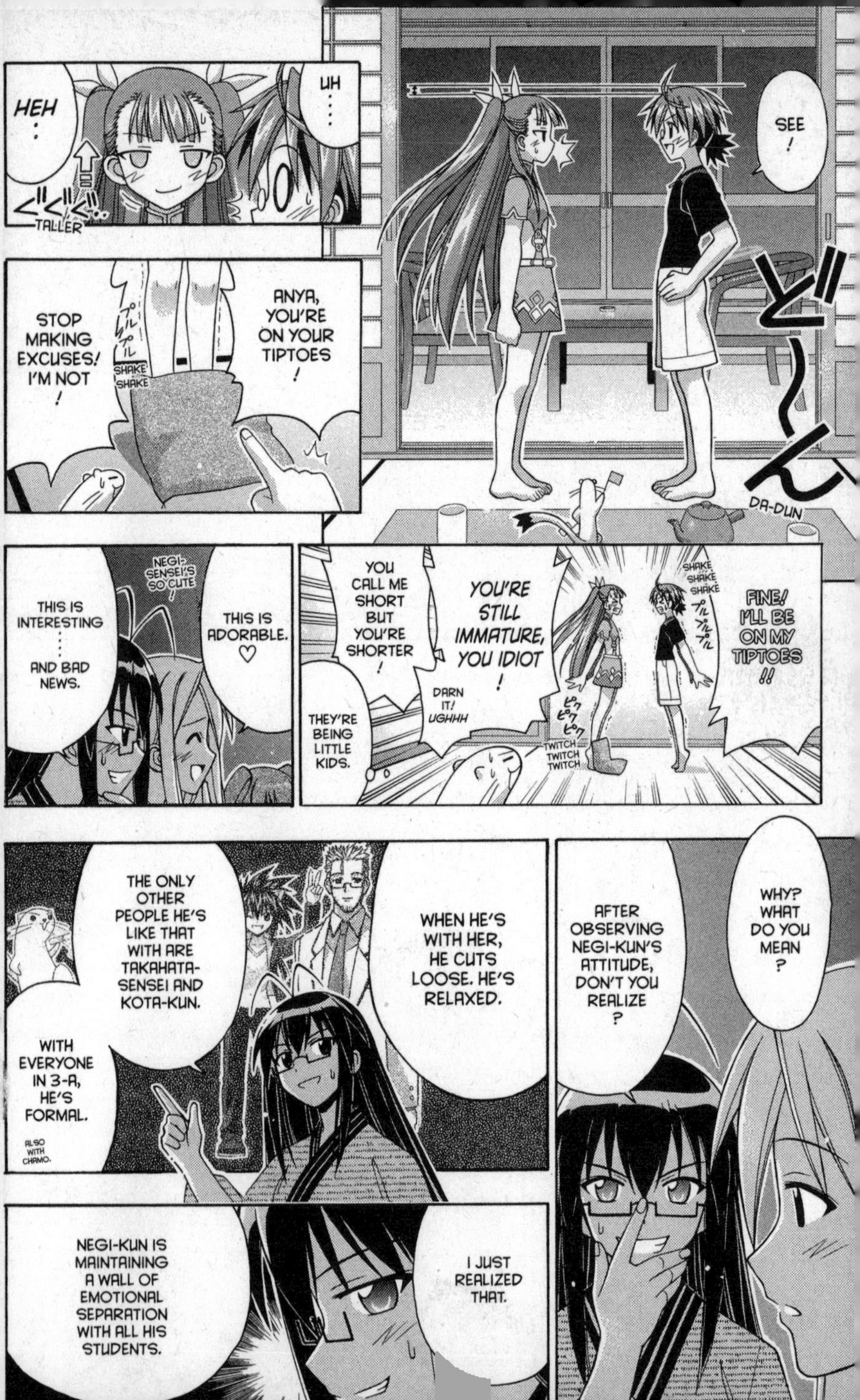
SEE!
どーん
DA-DUN
UH...
HEH...
ぐぐぐ...
TALLER
ANYA, YOU'RE ON YOUR TIPTOES!
STOP MAKING EXCUSES! I'M NOT!
プルプル
SHAKE SHAKE
FINE! I'LL BE ON MY TIPTOES!!
SHAKE SHAKE SHAKE
YOU'RE STILL IMMATURE, YOU IDIOT!
YOU CALL ME SHORT BUT YOU'RE SHORTER!
DARN IT! UGHHH
TWITCH TWITCH TWITCH
THEY'RE BEING LITTLE KIDS.
THIS IS ADORABLE. ♡
NEGI-SENSEI'S SO CUTE!
THIS IS INTERESTING... AND BAD NEWS.
WHY? WHAT DO YOU MEAN?
AFTER OBSERVING NEGI-KUN'S ATTITUDE, DON'T YOU REALIZE?
WHEN HE'S WITH HER, HE CUTS LOOSE. HE'S RELAXED.
THE ONLY OTHER PEOPLE HE'S LIKE THAT WITH ARE TAKAHATA-SENSEI AND KOTA-KUN.
WITH EVERYONE IN 3-A, HE'S FORMAL.
ALSO WITH CHAMO.
I JUST REALIZED THAT.
NEGI-KUN IS MAINTAINING A WALL OF EMOTIONAL SEPARATION WITH ALL HIS STUDENTS.

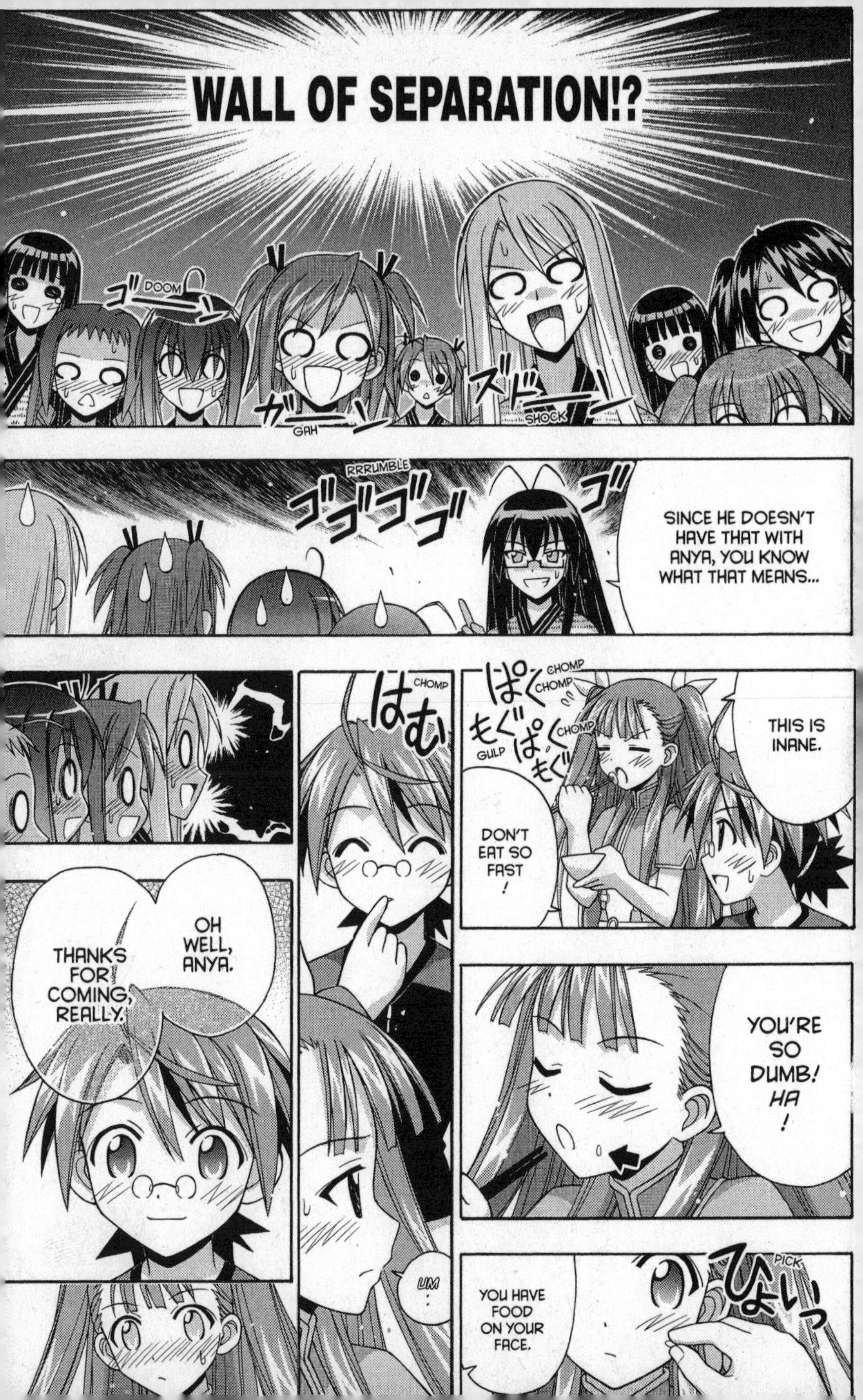
WALL OF SEPARATION!?
SHOCK
GAH
DOOM
SINCE HE DOESN'T HAVE THAT WITH ANYA, YOU KNOW WHAT THAT MEANS...
RRRUMBLE
CHOMP
CHOMP
CHOMP
GULP
THIS IS INANE.
DON'T EAT SO FAST!
CHOMP
YOU'RE SO DUMB! HA!
OH WELL, ANYA.
THANKS FOR COMING, REALLY.
UM...
PICK
YOU HAVE FOOD ON YOUR FACE.

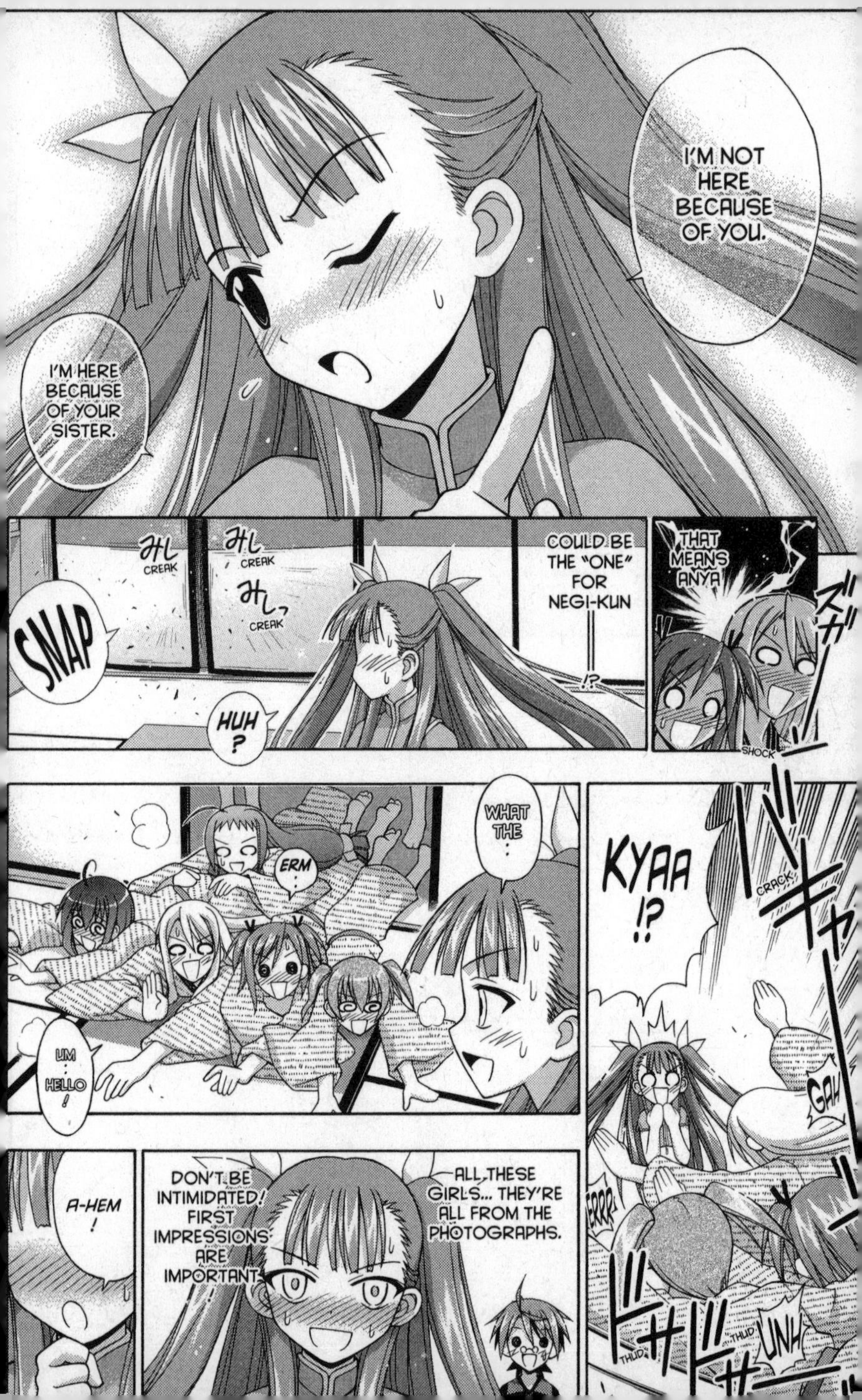
I'M NOT HERE BECAUSE OF YOU.
I'M HERE BECAUSE OF YOUR SISTER.
THAT MEANS ANYA
ズガ
SHOCK
COULD BE THE "ONE" FOR NEGI-KUN ‖ !?
みし CREAK
みし CREAK
みしっ CREAK
SNAP
HUH?
KYAA!?
CRACK
GAH
ERRR
THUD
THUD
UNH
WHAT THE...
ERM...
UM... HELLO!
ALL THESE GIRLS... THEY'RE ALL FROM THE PHOTOGRAPHS.
DON'T BE INTIMIDATED! FIRST IMPRESSIONS ARE IMPORTANT.
A-HEM!

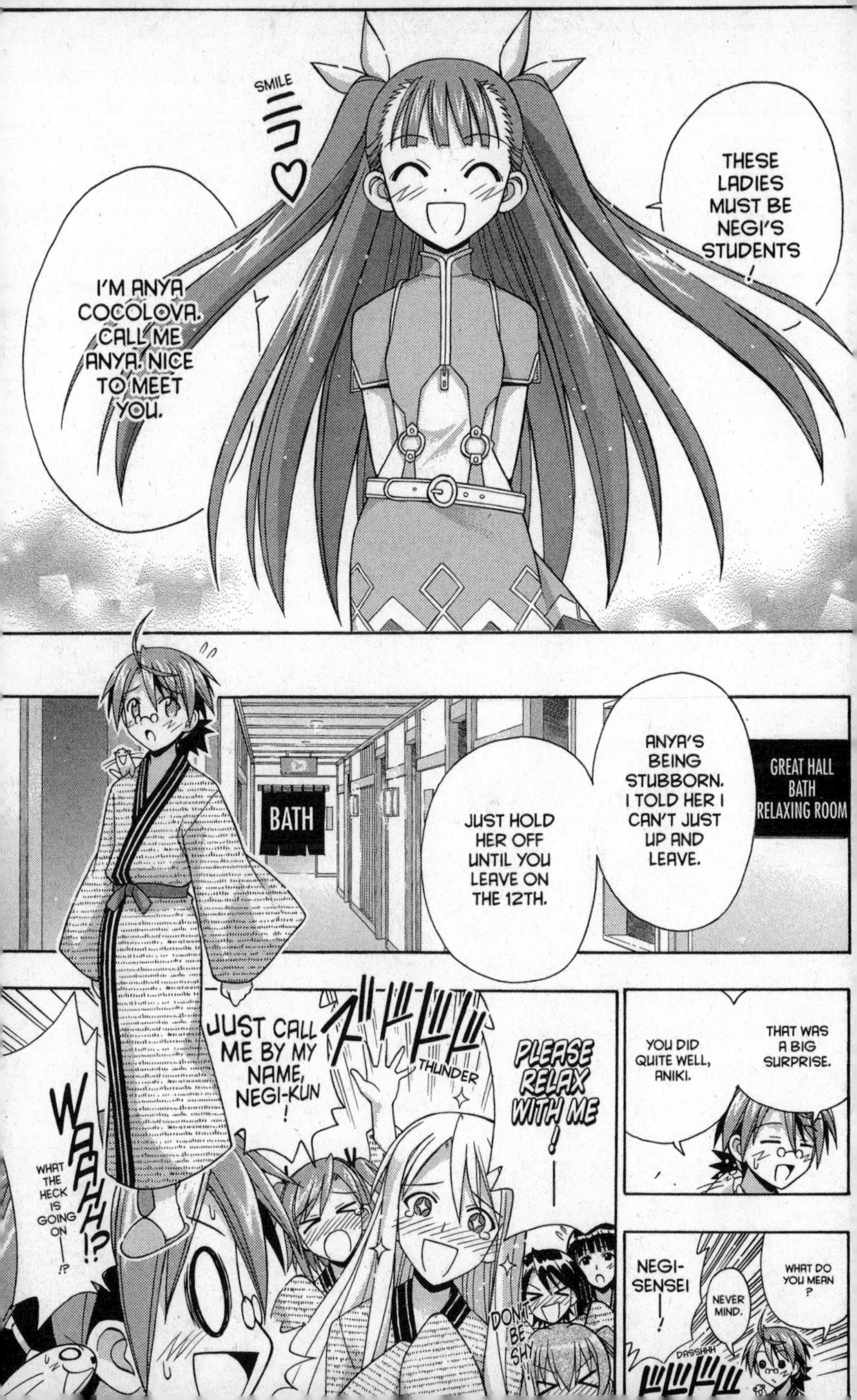
THESE LADIES MUST BE NEGI'S STUDENTS!
SMILE
I'M ANYA COCOLOVA. CALL ME ANYA. NICE TO MEET YOU.
GREAT HALL BATH RELAXING ROOM
ANYA'S BEING STUBBORN. I TOLD HER I CAN'T JUST UP AND LEAVE.
JUST HOLD HER OFF UNTIL YOU LEAVE ON THE 12TH.
BATH
THAT WAS A BIG SURPRISE.
YOU DID QUITE WELL, ANIKI.
WHAT DO YOU MEAN?
NEGI-SENSEI!
NEVER MIND.
DASSHHH
PLEASE RELAX WITH ME!
THUNDER
JUST CALL ME BY MY NAME, NEGI-KUN!
DON'T BE SHY!
WAAAH!?
WHAT THE HECK IS GOING ON!?

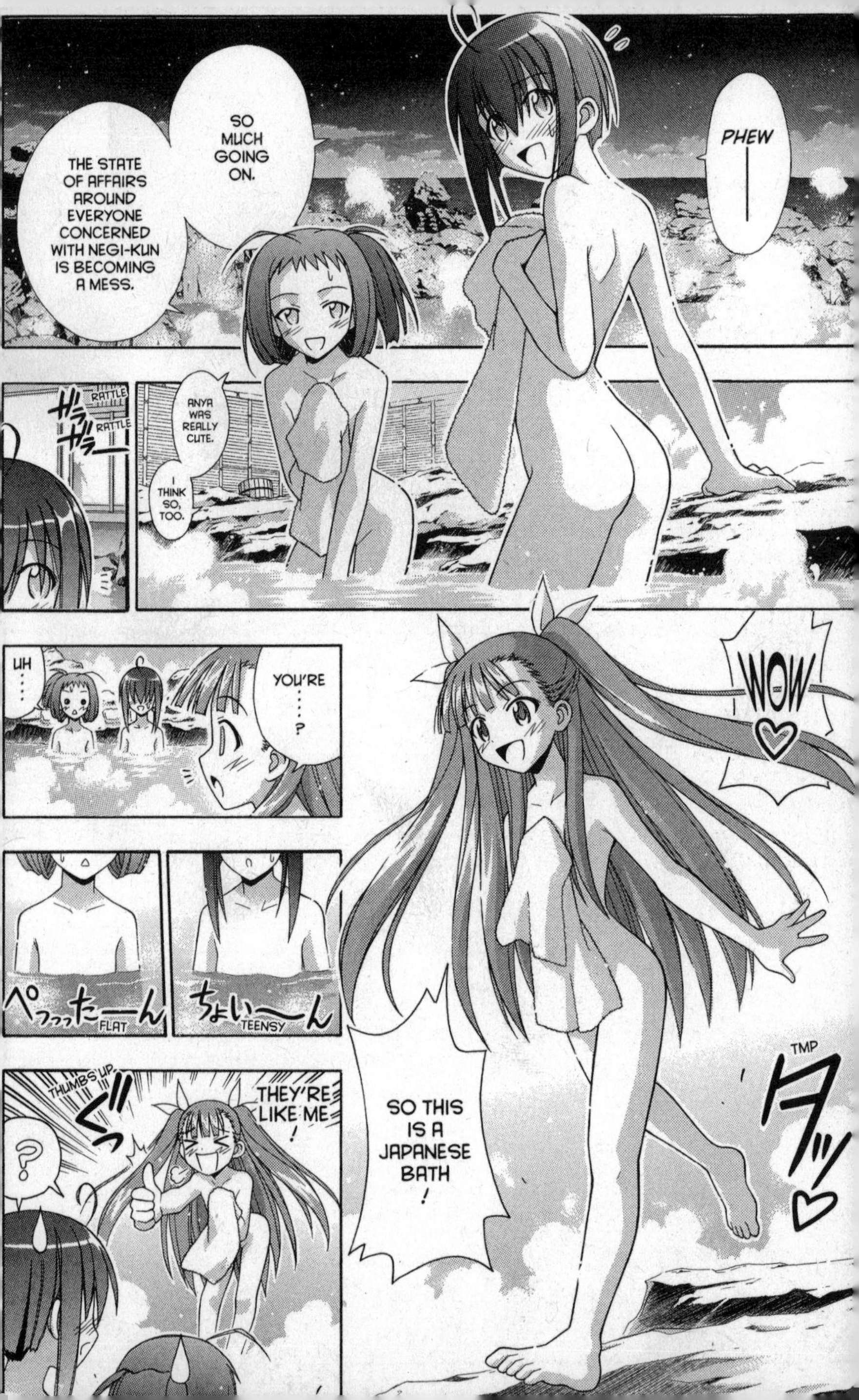
PHEW
SO MUCH GOING ON.
THE STATE OF AFFAIRS AROUND EVERYONE CONCERNED WITH NEGI-KUN IS BECOMING A MESS.
ANYA WAS REALLY CUTE.
I THINK SO, TOO.
RATTLE
RATTLE
WOW ♥
SO THIS IS A JAPANESE BATH!
TMP
YOU'RE ...?
UH ...
TEENSY
FLAT
THEY'RE LIKE ME!
THUMBS UP
?

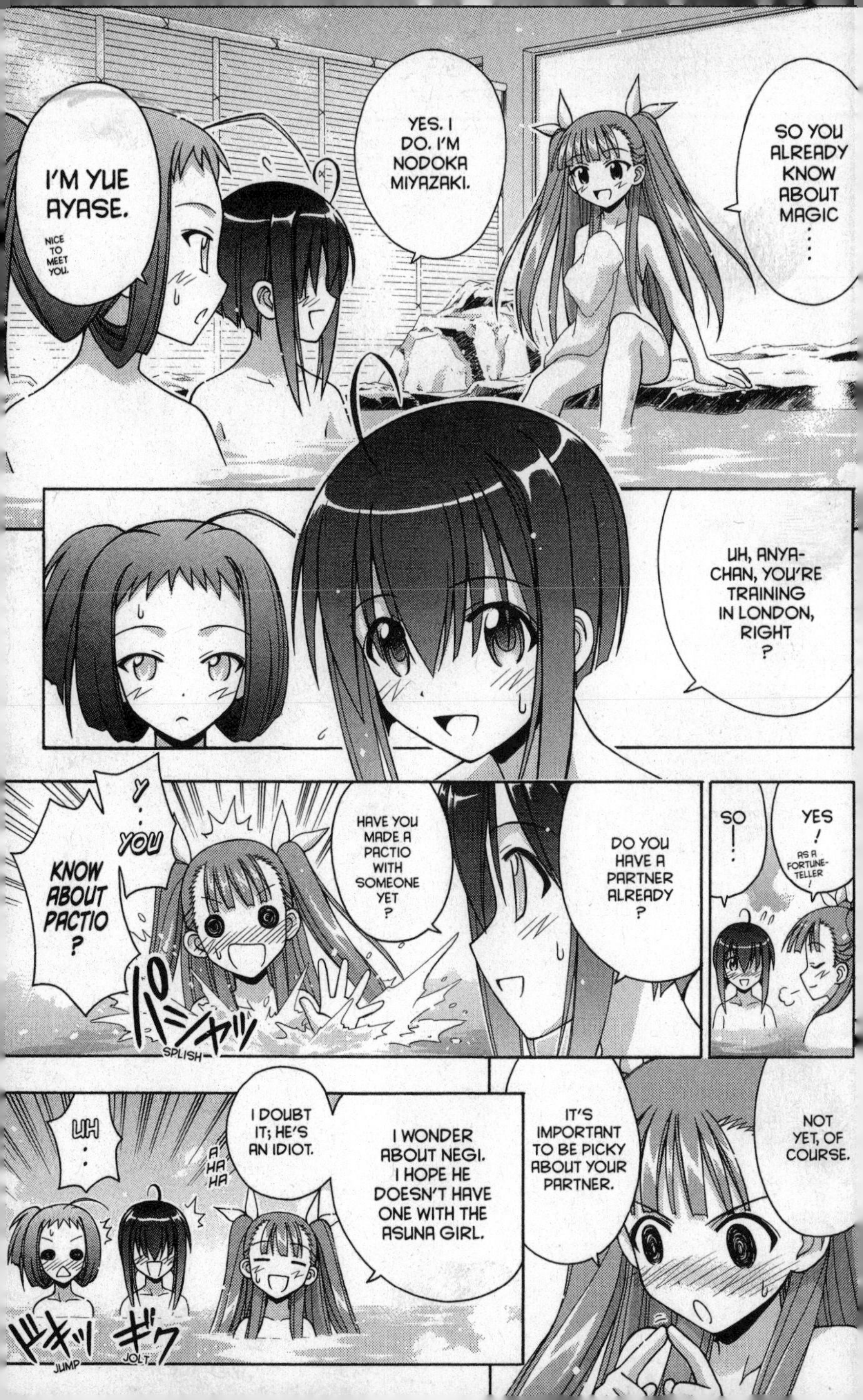

SO YOU ALREADY KNOW ABOUT MAGIC...
YES. I DO. I'M NODOKA MIYAZAKI.
I'M YUE AYASE.
NICE TO MEET YOU.
UH, ANYA-CHAN, YOU'RE TRAINING IN LONDON, RIGHT?
YES!
AS A FORTUNE-TELLER!
SO...!
DO YOU HAVE A PARTNER ALREADY?
HAVE YOU MADE A PACTIO WITH SOMEONE YET?
Y... YOU KNOW ABOUT PACTIO?
SPLISH
NOT YET, OF COURSE.
IT'S IMPORTANT TO BE PICKY ABOUT YOUR PARTNER.
I WONDER ABOUT NEGI. I HOPE HE DOESN'T HAVE ONE WITH THE ASUNA GIRL.
I DOUBT IT; HE'S AN IDIOT.
A HA HA
UH...
JOLT
JUMP

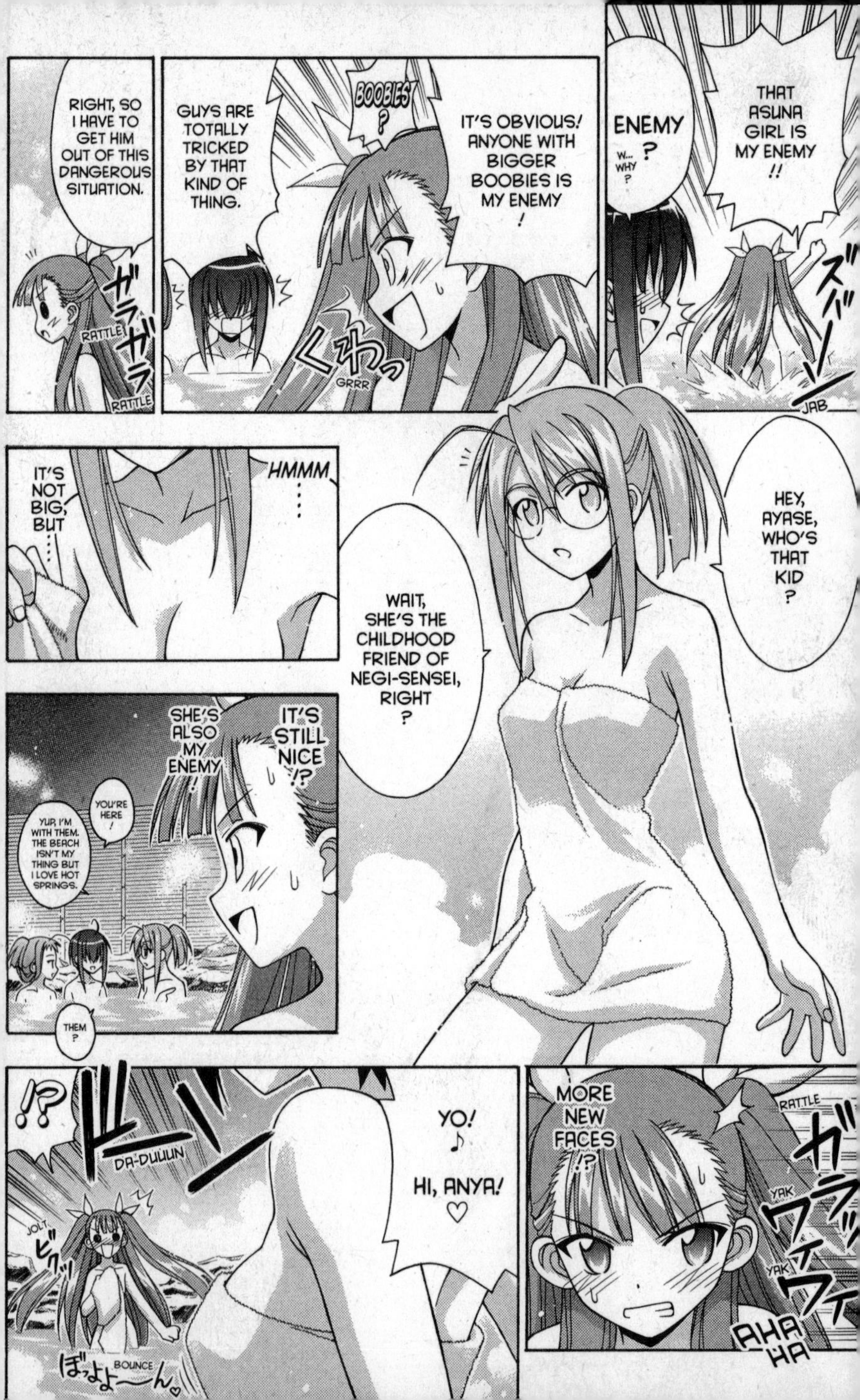
THAT ASUNA GIRL IS MY ENEMY!!
ENEMY?
W... WHY?
JAB
IT'S OBVIOUS! ANYONE WITH BIGGER BOOBIES IS MY ENEMY!
BOOBIES?
GUYS ARE TOTALLY TRICKED BY THAT KIND OF THING.
GRRR
RIGHT, SO I HAVE TO GET HIM OUT OF THIS DANGEROUS SITUATION.
RATTLE
RATTLE
HEY, AYASE, WHO'S THAT KID?
WAIT, SHE'S THE CHILDHOOD FRIEND OF NEGI-SENSEI, RIGHT?
HMMM...
IT'S NOT BIG, BUT...
IT'S STILL NICE!?
SHE'S ALSO MY ENEMY!
YOU'RE HERE!
YUP, I'M WITH THEM. THE BEACH ISN'T MY THING BUT I LOVE HOT SPRINGS.
THEM?
MORE NEW FACES!?
RATTLE
YAK
YAK
AHA HA
YO! ♪
HI, ANYA! ♡
DA-DUUUN
!?
JOLT
BOUNCE

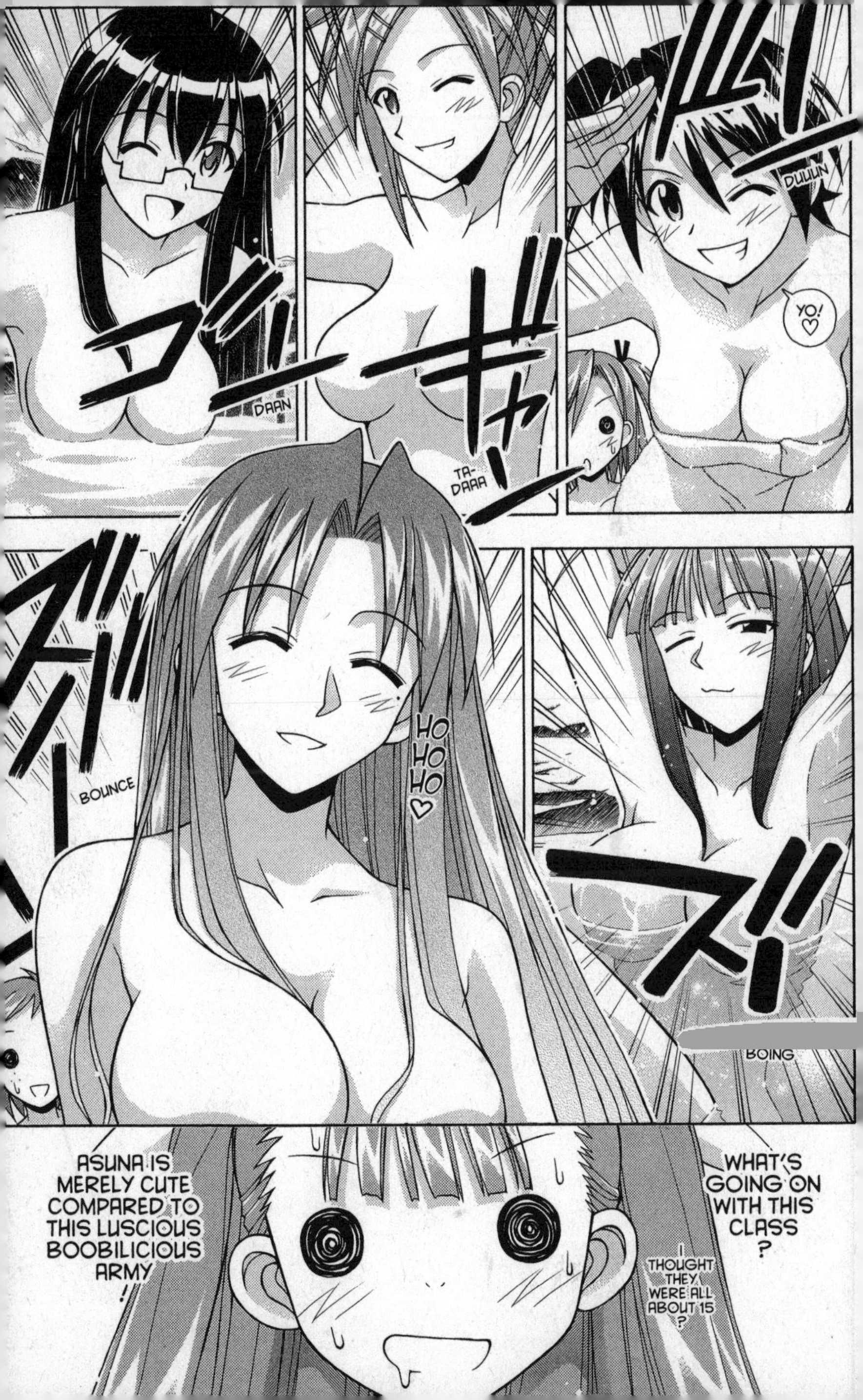
DUUUN
YO! ♡
TA-DAAA
DAAN
BOING
HO HO HO ♡
BOUNCE
WHAT'S GOING ON WITH THIS CLASS?
I THOUGHT THEY WERE ALL ABOUT 15?
ASUNA IS MERELY CUTE COMPARED TO THIS LUSCIOUS BOOBILICIOUS ARMY!

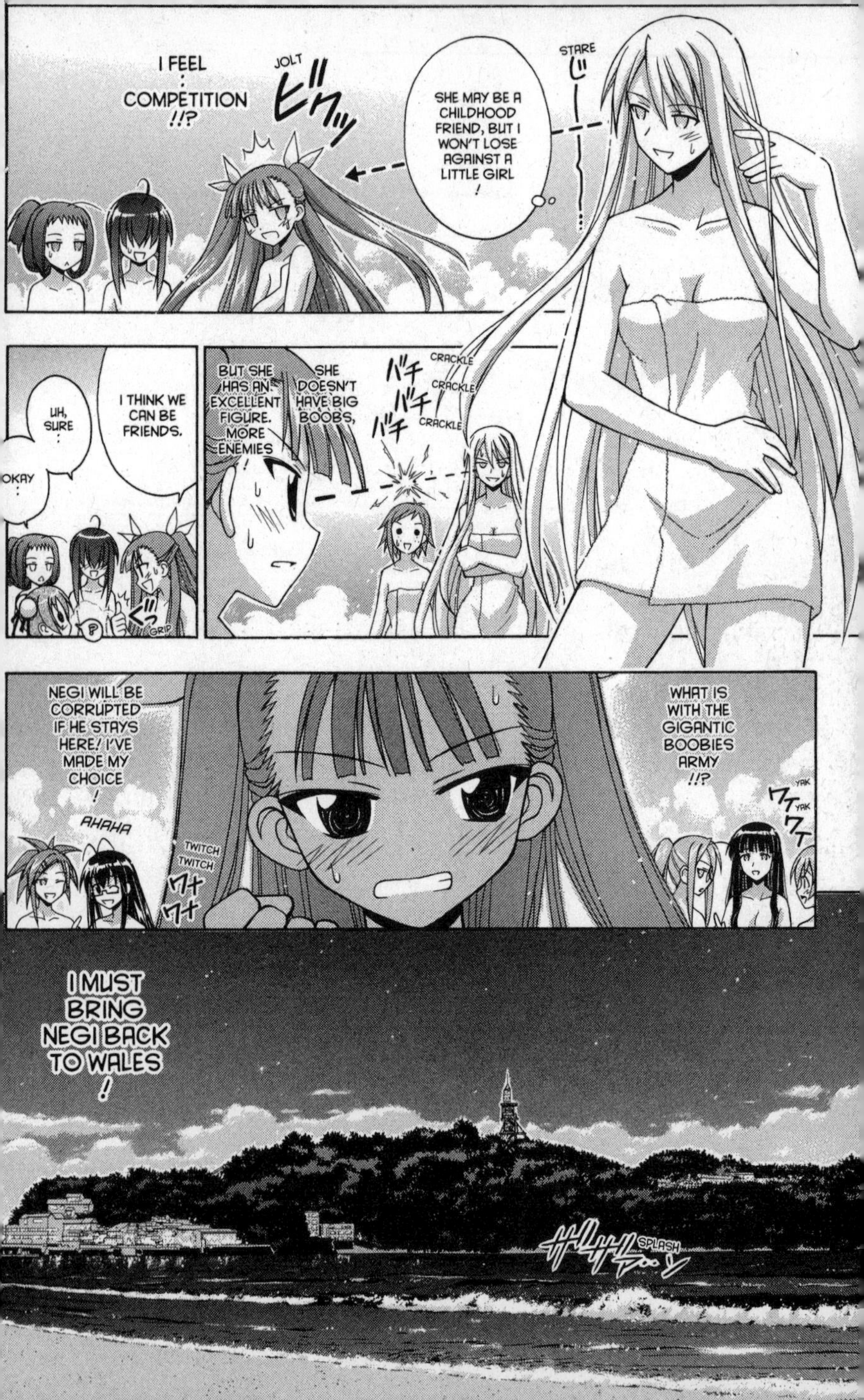
STARE
SHE MAY BE A CHILDHOOD FRIEND, BUT I WON'T LOSE AGAINST A LITTLE GIRL!
JOLT
I FEEL... COMPETITION!!?
CRACKLE CRACKLE CRACKLE
SHE DOESN'T HAVE BIG BOOBS,
BUT SHE HAS AN EXCELLENT FIGURE. MORE ENEMIES!
I THINK WE CAN BE FRIENDS.
UH, SURE...
OKAY...
GRIP
WHAT IS WITH THE GIGANTIC BOOBIES ARMY!!?
YAK YAK
NEGI WILL BE CORRUPTED IF HE STAYS HERE! I'VE MADE MY CHOICE!
TWITCH TWITCH
AHAHA
I MUST BRING NEGI BACK TO WALES!
SPLASH

ANYA
ANYA YURIENA COCOLOVA
Аня (Анна Юрьевна Коколова)
BIRTHDAY 11/25/92
BLOOD TYPE A
LIKES HIGH TEA AND TEA SNACKS
GRADUATED MERDIANA SCHOOL OF MAGIC 2002

NEGIMA!

MAGISTER NEGI MAGI

180TH PERIOD: EXPLOSION! NEGI WARS ♡

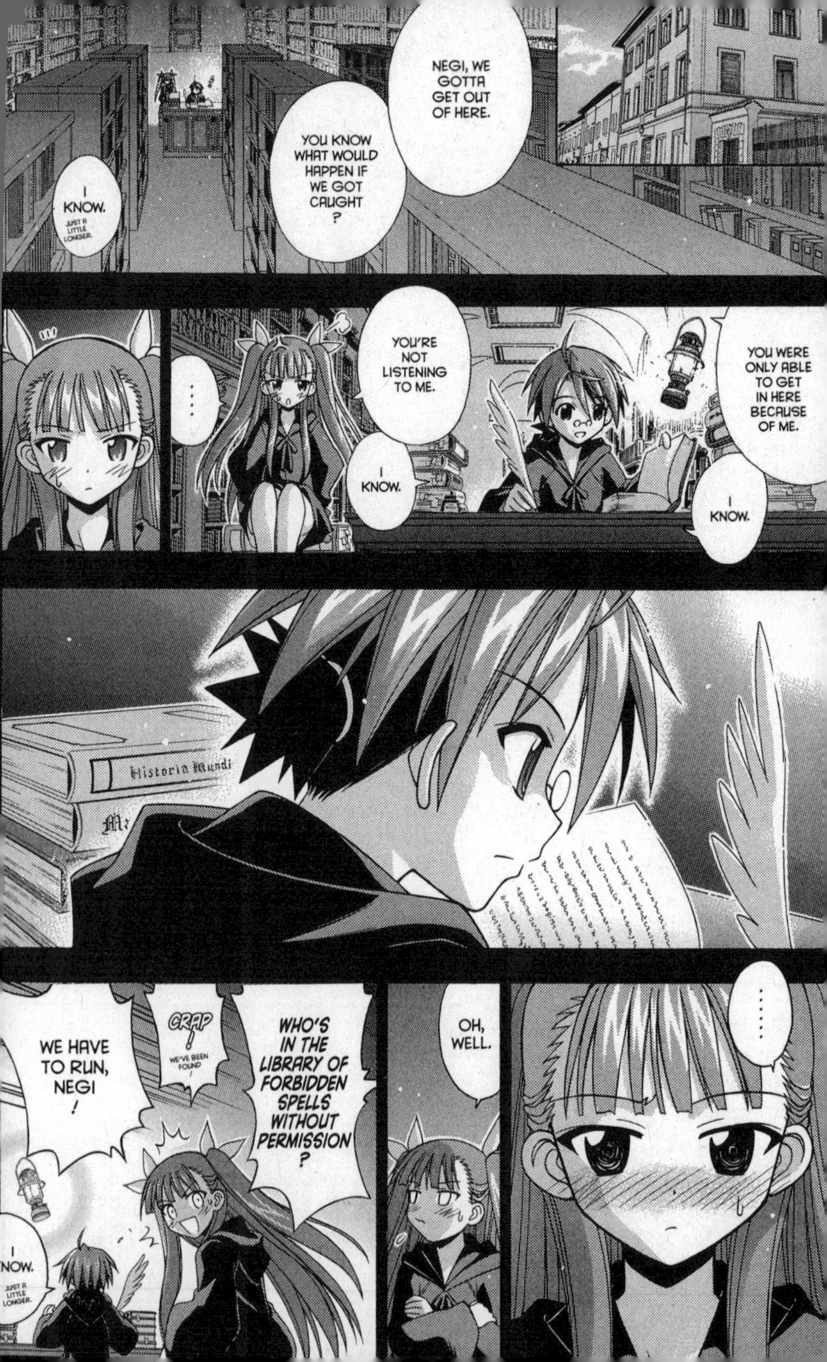

NEGI, WE GOTTA GET OUT OF HERE.
YOU KNOW WHAT WOULD HAPPEN IF WE GOT CAUGHT?
I KNOW.
JUST A LITTLE LONGER.
YOU WERE ONLY ABLE TO GET IN HERE BECAUSE OF ME.
I KNOW.
YOU'RE NOT LISTENING TO ME.
I KNOW.
....
Historia Mundi
......
OH, WELL.
WHO'S IN THE LIBRARY OF FORBIDDEN SPELLS WITHOUT PERMISSION?
CRAP!
WE'VE BEEN FOUND!
WE HAVE TO RUN, NEGI!
I KNOW.
JUST A LITTLE LONGER.

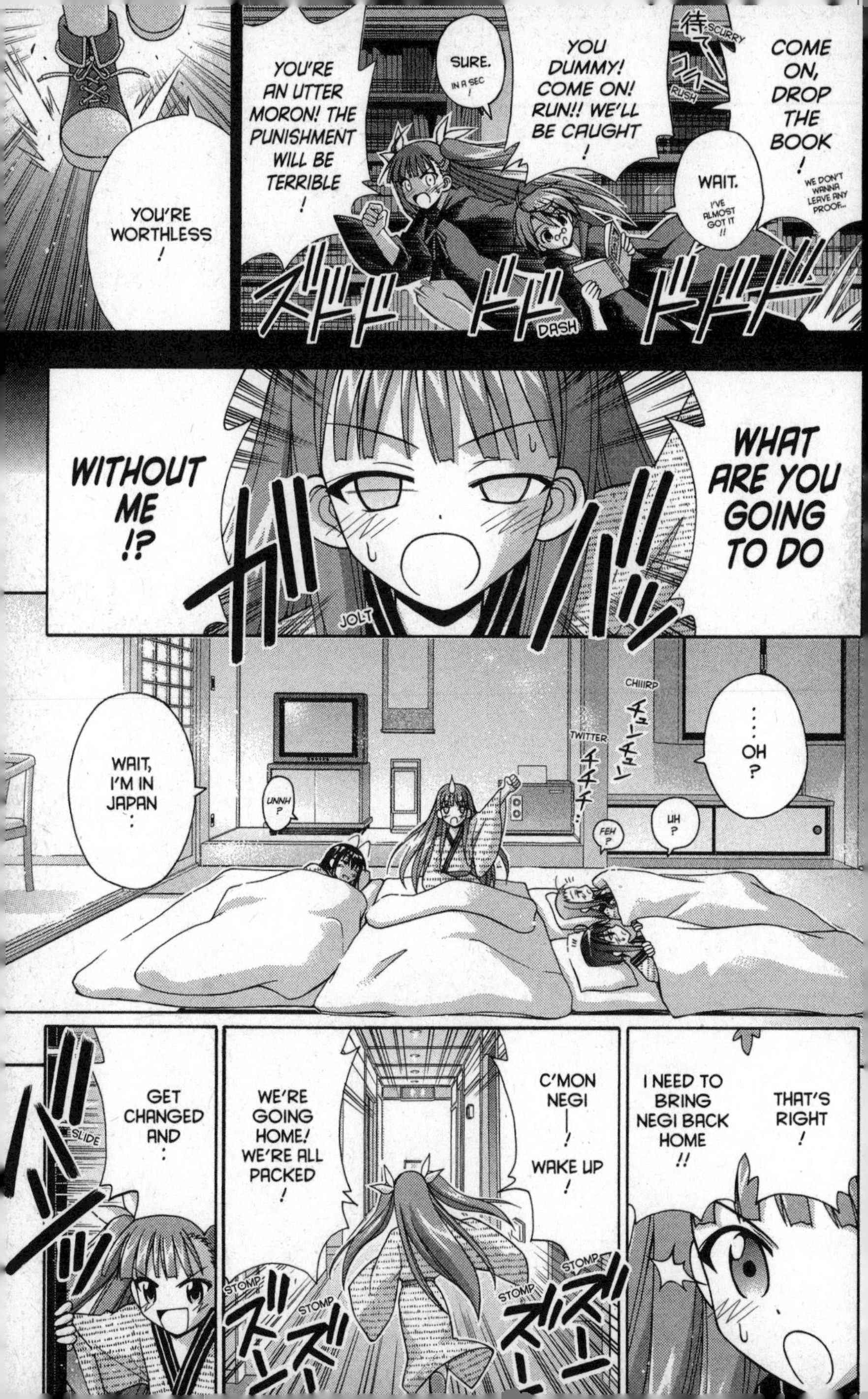
COME ON, DROP THE BOOK!
WE DON'T WANNA LEAVE ANY PROOF...
SCURRY
RUSH
WAIT. I'VE ALMOST GOT IT!!
YOU DUMMY! COME ON! RUN!! WE'LL BE CAUGHT!
SURE. IN A SEC!
YOU'RE AN UTTER MORON! THE PUNISHMENT WILL BE TERRIBLE!
DASH
YOU'RE WORTHLESS!
WHAT ARE YOU GOING TO DO
WITHOUT ME!?
JOLT
...OH?
CHIIIRP
TWITTER
UH?
FEH?
UNNH?
WAIT, I'M IN JAPAN...
THAT'S RIGHT!
I NEED TO BRING NEGI BACK HOME!!
C'MON NEGI—!
WAKE UP!
STOMP
STOMP
STOMP
STOMP
WE'RE GOING HOME! WE'RE ALL PACKED!
GET CHANGED AND...
SLIDE

WHAT
:

DA-DAAAN

WHAT ARE YOU DOING HERE!?

NEGI, THIS AGAIN!?

EH:!

OH:!

UHHH!?

ON:

WHAT

YA!!?

BLAMMMMM

BAGYA——

ANYA FLAME KNUCKLE!!!

WHAT ARE YOU DOING, NEGI!?

WOW

OH

WHAT!?

ANYA-CHAN, ASUNA LOOKS LIKE NEGI-KUN'S SISTER, SO:

WHAT ARE YOU DOING FIRST THING IN THE MORNING?

SCREECH

DA-DUUUN

WAIT, ANYA!!?

SHE'S EXPLOSIVE

I'M SORRY, ASUNA-SAN. IT'S A HABIT :

SPLURT SPLURT

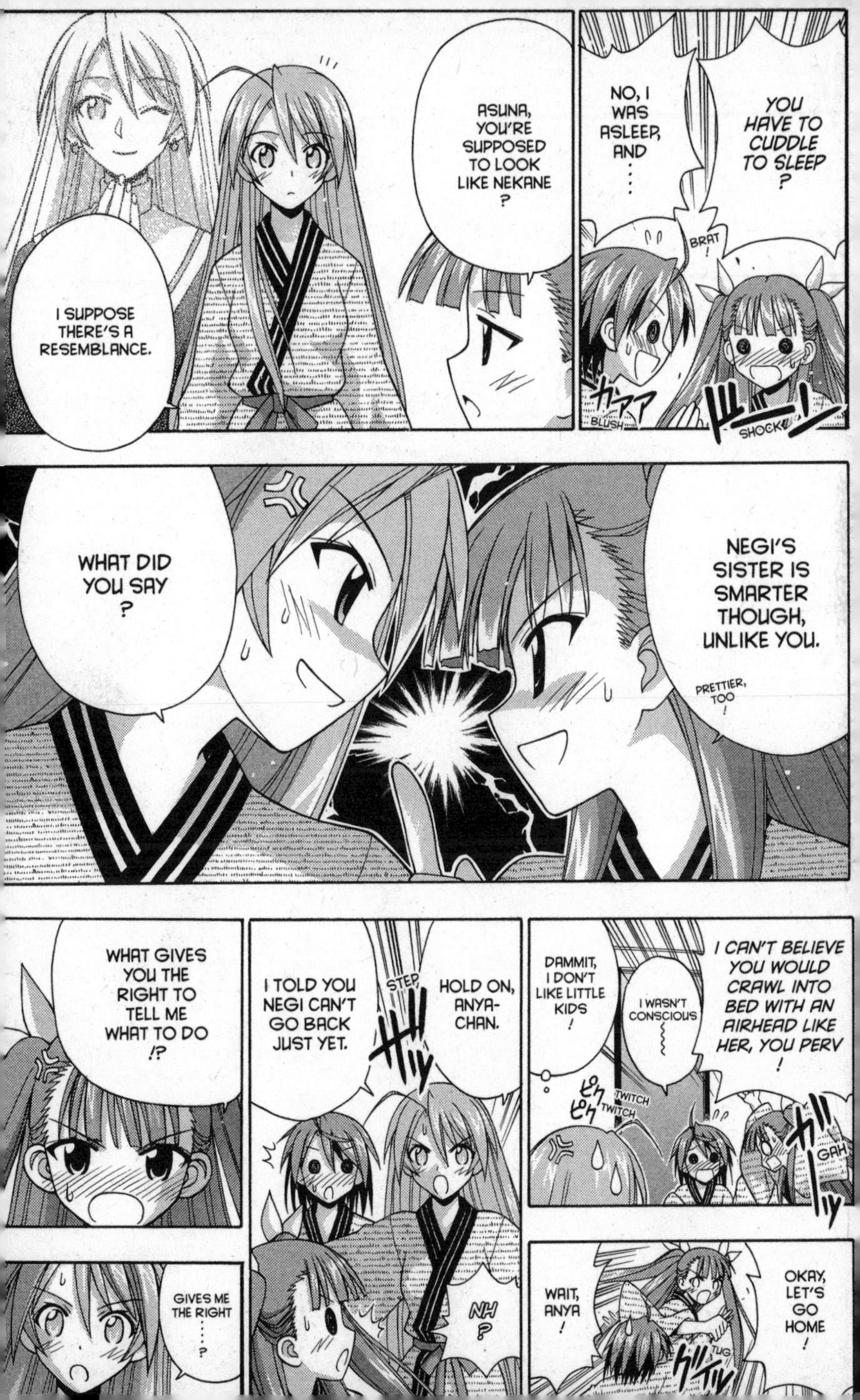
YOU HAVE TO CUDDLE TO SLEEP?
NO, I WAS ASLEEP, AND ....
BRAT!
BLUSH
SHOCK
ASUNA, YOU'RE SUPPOSED TO LOOK LIKE NEKANE?
I SUPPOSE THERE'S A RESEMBLANCE.
NEGI'S SISTER IS SMARTER THOUGH, UNLIKE YOU.
PRETTIER, TOO!
WHAT DID YOU SAY?
I CAN'T BELIEVE YOU WOULD CRAWL INTO BED WITH AN AIRHEAD LIKE HER, YOU PERV!
GAH
I WASN'T CONSCIOUS ~~~
DAMMIT, I DON'T LIKE LITTLE KIDS!
TWITCH TWITCH
OKAY, LET'S GO HOME!
TUG
WAIT, ANYA!
HOLD ON, ANYA-CHAN.
STEP
I TOLD YOU NEGI CAN'T GO BACK JUST YET.
NH?
WHAT GIVES YOU THE RIGHT TO TELL ME WHAT TO DO!?
GIVES ME THE RIGHT....?

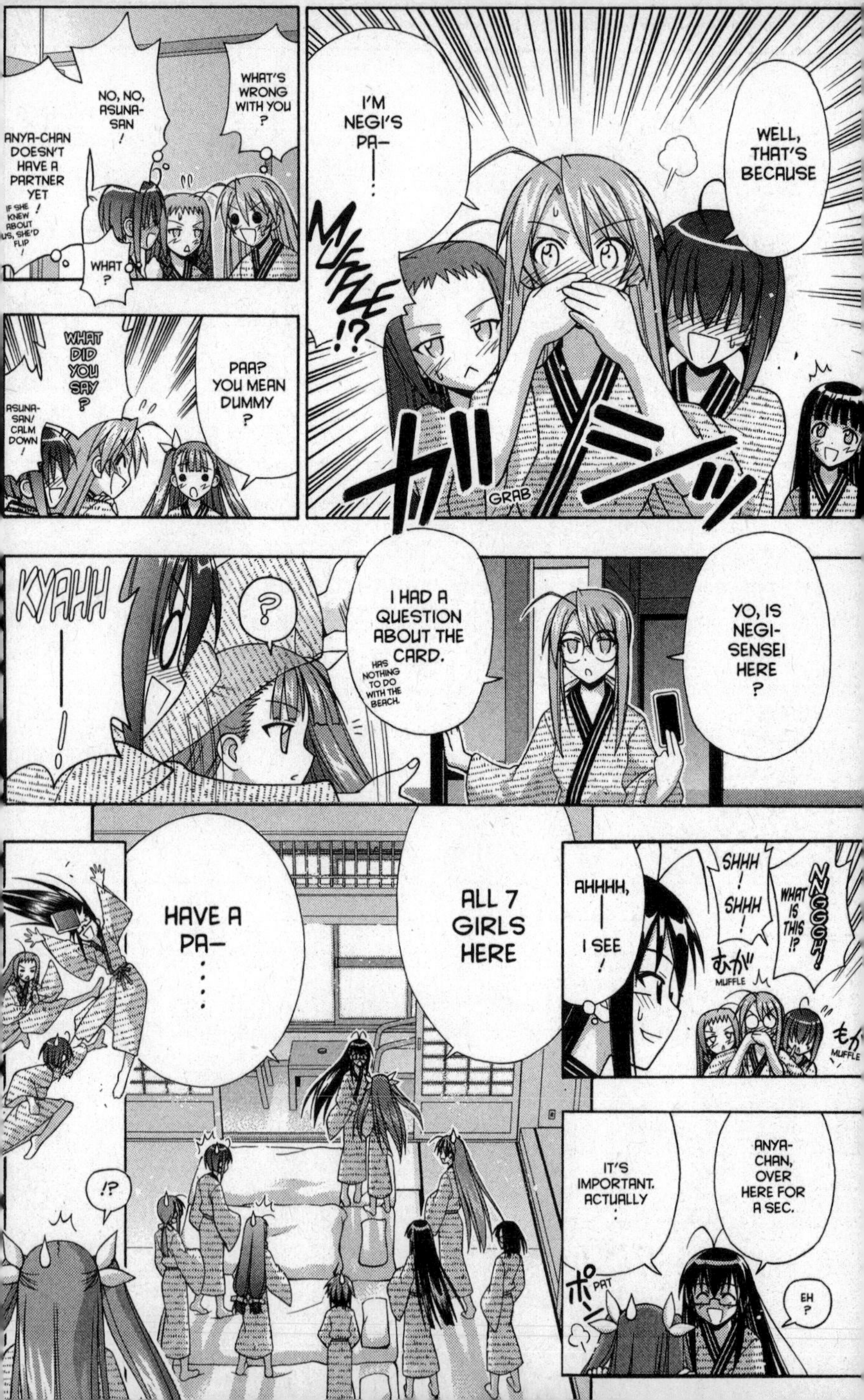

WELL, THAT'S BECAUSE
I'M NEGI'S PA—!
MUFFLE!?
GRAB
WHAT'S WRONG WITH YOU?
NO, NO, ASUNA-SAN!
ANYA-CHAN DOESN'T HAVE A PARTNER YET!
IF SHE KNEW ABOUT US, SHE'D FLIP!
WHAT?
PAA? YOU MEAN DUMMY?
WHAT DID YOU SAY?
ASUNA-SAN/ CALM DOWN!
YO, IS NEGI-SENSEI HERE?
I HAD A QUESTION ABOUT THE CARD.
HAS NOTHING TO DO WITH THE BEACH.
?
KYAHH—!
SHHH! SHHH!
NNGGGH!
WHAT IS THIS!?
AHHHH, —I SEE!
MUFFLE
MUFFLE
ANYA-CHAN, OVER HERE FOR A SEC.
IT'S IMPORTANT. ACTUALLY...
EH?
PAT
ALL 7 GIRLS HERE
HAVE A PA—....
!?

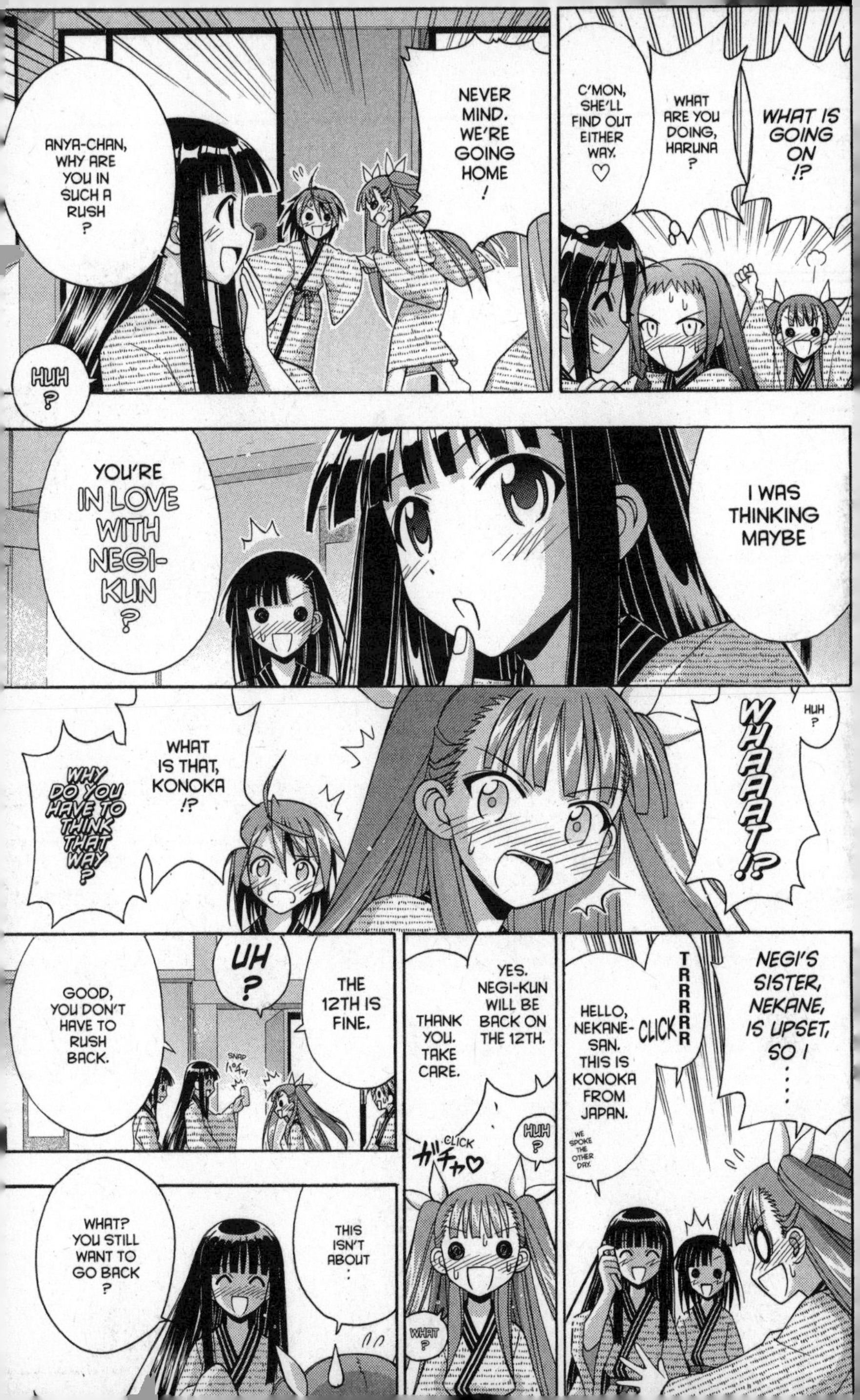
WHAT IS GOING ON !?
WHAT ARE YOU DOING, HARUNA ?
C'MON, SHE'LL FIND OUT EITHER WAY. ♡
NEVER MIND. WE'RE GOING HOME !
ANYA-CHAN, WHY ARE YOU IN SUCH A RUSH ?
HUH ?
I WAS THINKING MAYBE
YOU'RE IN LOVE WITH NEGI-KUN ?
HUH ?
WHAAAAT !?
WHAT IS THAT, KONOKA !?
WHY DO YOU HAVE TO THINK THAT WAY ?
NEGI'S SISTER, NEKANE, IS UPSET, SO I ...
TRRRRR
CLICK
HELLO, NEKANE-SAN. THIS IS KONOKA FROM JAPAN.
WE SPOKE THE OTHER DAY.
YES. NEGI-KUN WILL BE BACK ON THE 12TH.
THANK YOU. TAKE CARE.
HUH ?
CLICK ガチャ♡
WHAT ?
THE 12TH IS FINE.
UH ?
SNAP パチッ
GOOD, YOU DON'T HAVE TO RUSH BACK.
THIS ISN'T ABOUT ...
WHAT? YOU STILL WANT TO GO BACK ?

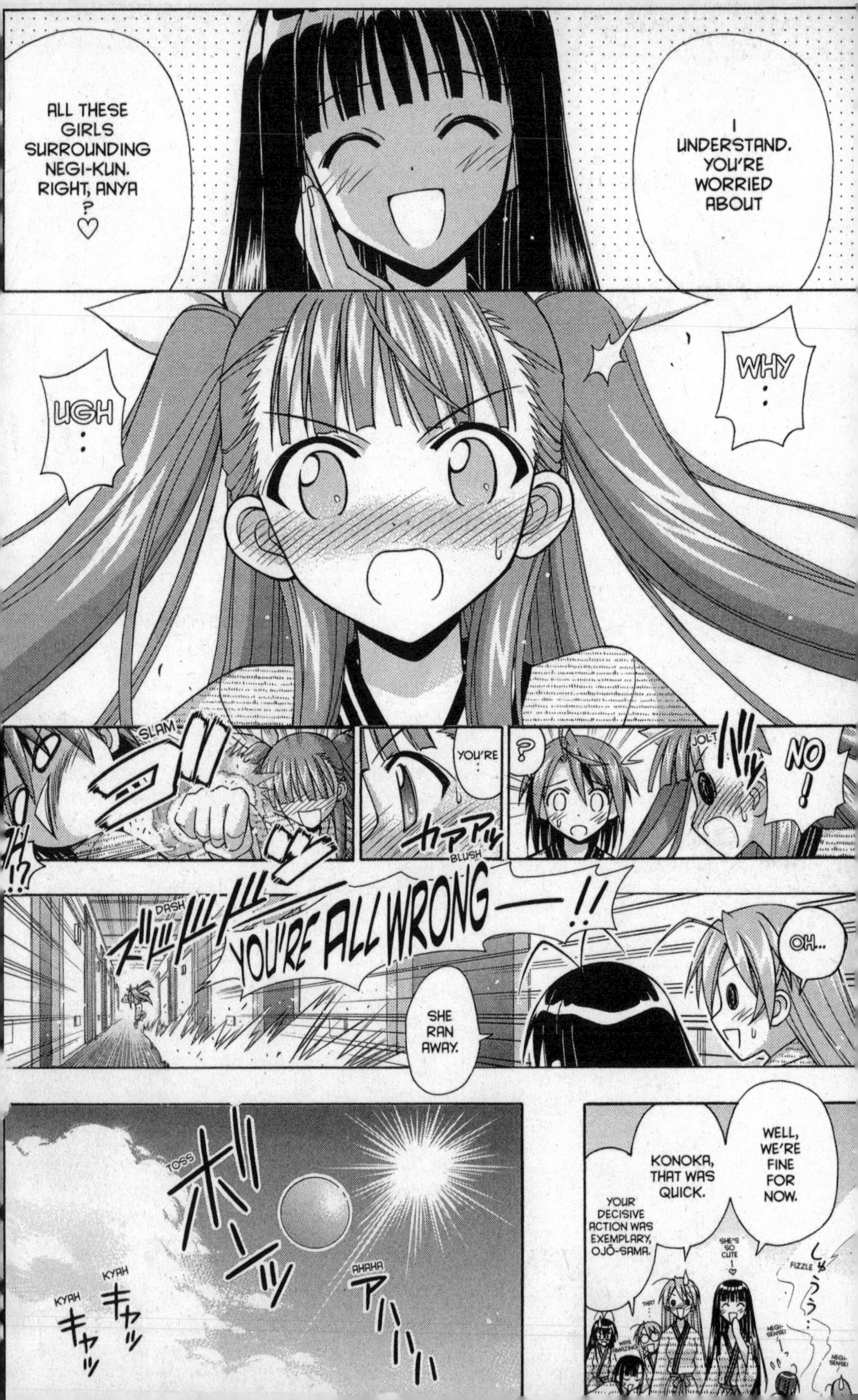
I UNDERSTAND. YOU'RE WORRIED ABOUT
ALL THESE GIRLS SURROUNDING NEGI-KUN. RIGHT, ANYA? ♡
WHY...
UGH...
NO!
JOLT
?
YOU'RE...
BLUSH
SLAM
!?
OH...
YOU'RE ALL WRONG——!!
SHE RAN AWAY.
DASH
WELL, WE'RE FINE FOR NOW.
KONOKA, THAT WAS QUICK.
YOUR DECISIVE ACTION WAS EXEMPLARY, OJŌ-SAMA.
SHE'S SO CUTE ♡
FIZZLE
NEGI-SENSEI!
NEGI-SENSEI!
THAT...
WAS AMAZING
TOSS
AHAHA
KYAH
KYAH

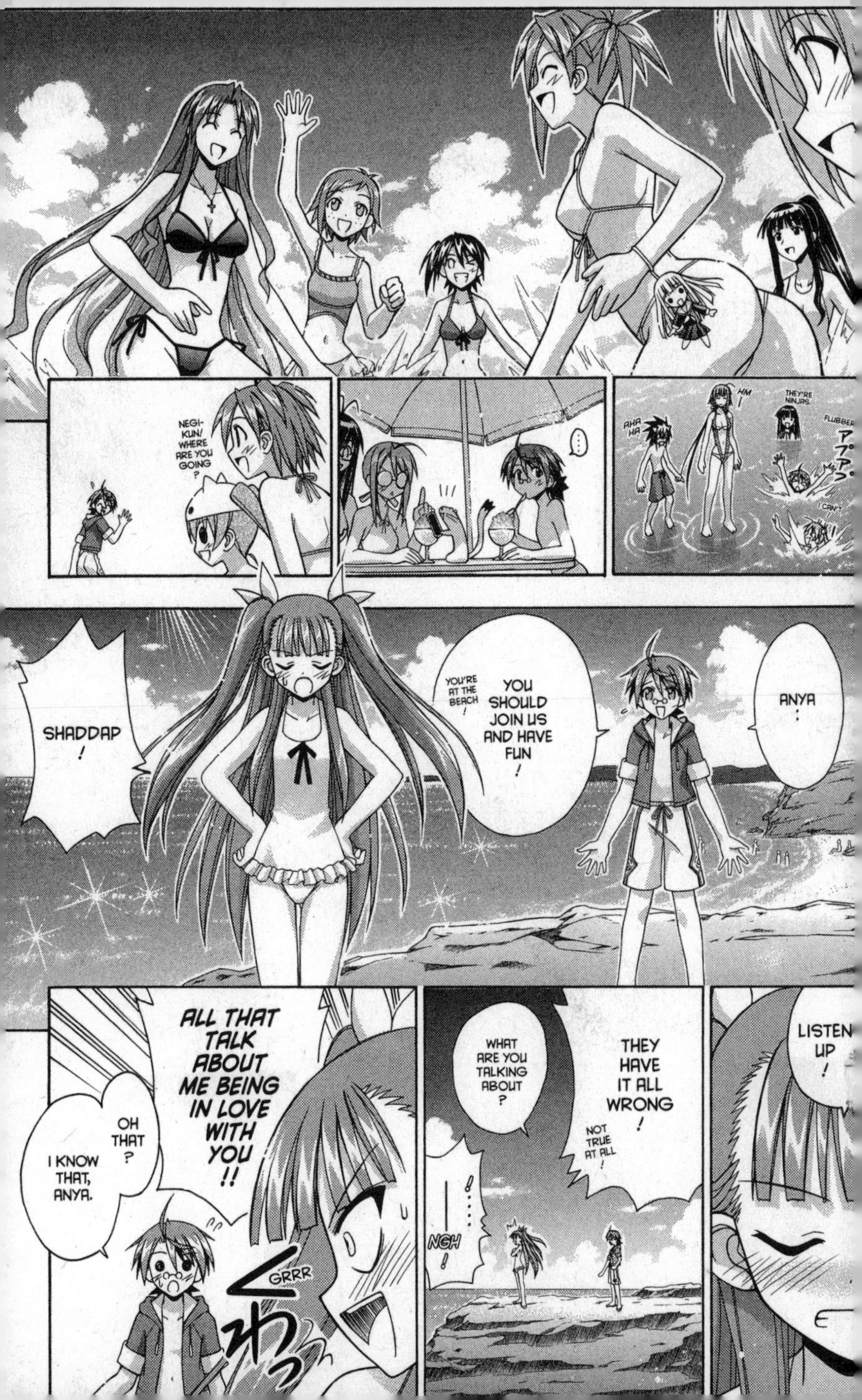
FLUBBER
アプアプ
I CAN'T!
THEY'RE NINJAS.
HM!
AHA HA
...
NEGI-KUN! WHERE ARE YOU GOING?
ANYA...
YOU'RE AT THE BEACH!
YOU SHOULD JOIN US AND HAVE FUN!
SHADDAP!
LISTEN UP!
THEY HAVE IT ALL WRONG!
NOT TRUE AT ALL!
WHAT ARE YOU TALKING ABOUT?
!.....
NGH!
ALL THAT TALK ABOUT ME BEING IN LOVE WITH YOU!!
OH THAT?
I KNOW THAT, ANYA.
GRRR

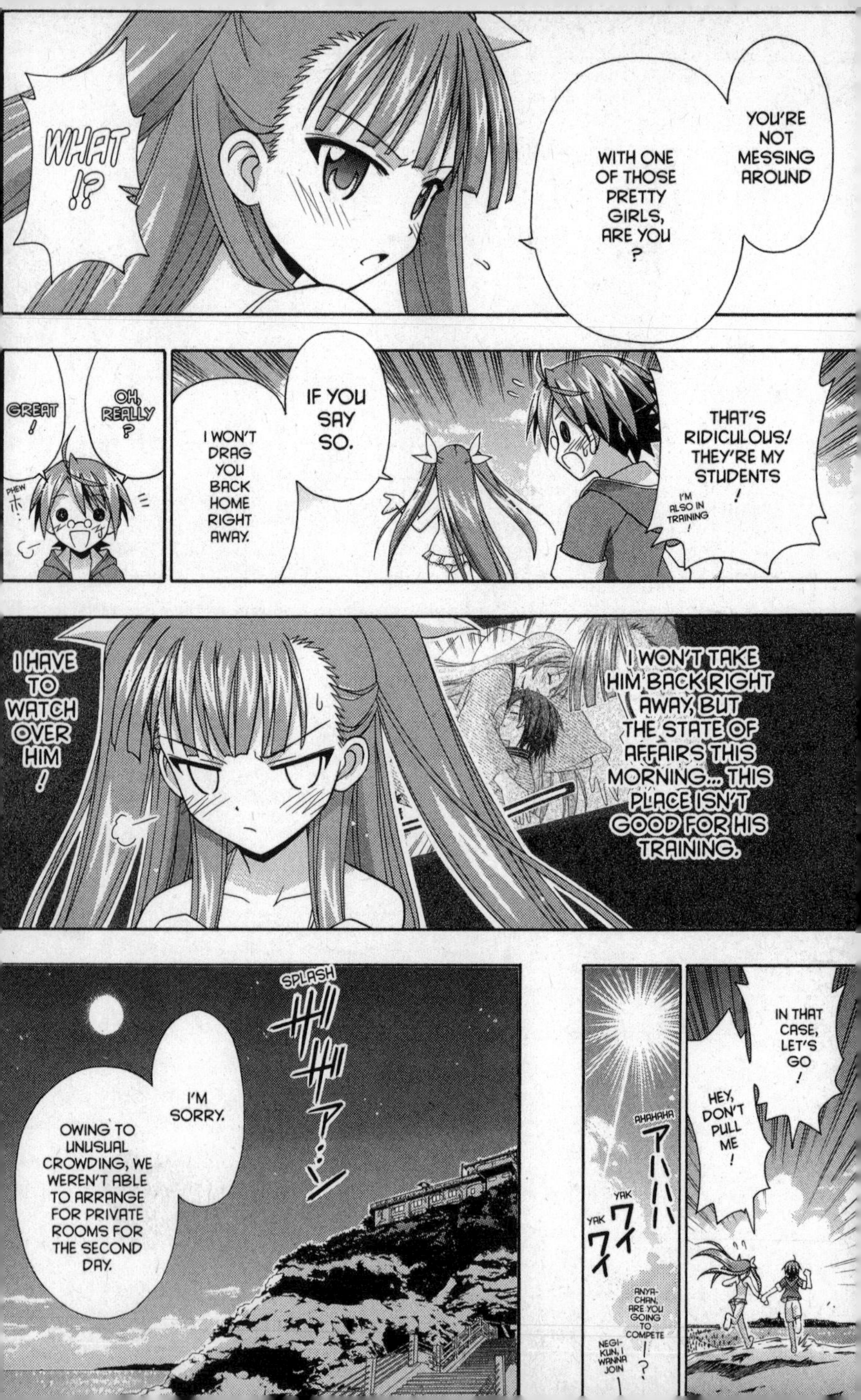
YOU'RE NOT MESSING AROUND WITH ONE OF THOSE PRETTY GIRLS, ARE YOU?
WHAT!?
THAT'S RIDICULOUS! THEY'RE MY STUDENTS!
I'M ALSO IN TRAINING!
IF YOU SAY SO.
I WON'T DRAG YOU BACK HOME RIGHT AWAY.
OH, REALLY?
GREAT!
PHEW ホッ
I WON'T TAKE HIM BACK RIGHT AWAY, BUT THE STATE OF AFFAIRS THIS MORNING... THIS PLACE ISN'T GOOD FOR HIS TRAINING.
I HAVE TO WATCH OVER HIM!
IN THAT CASE, LET'S GO!
HEY, DON'T PULL ME!
AHAHAHA アハハ
YAK YAK ワイワイ
ANYA-CHAN, ARE YOU GOING TO COMPETE!?
NEGI-KUN, I WANNA JOIN!
SPLASH ザザァ～ン
I'M SORRY.
OWING TO UNUSUAL CROWDING, WE WEREN'T ABLE TO ARRANGE FOR PRIVATE ROOMS FOR THE SECOND DAY.

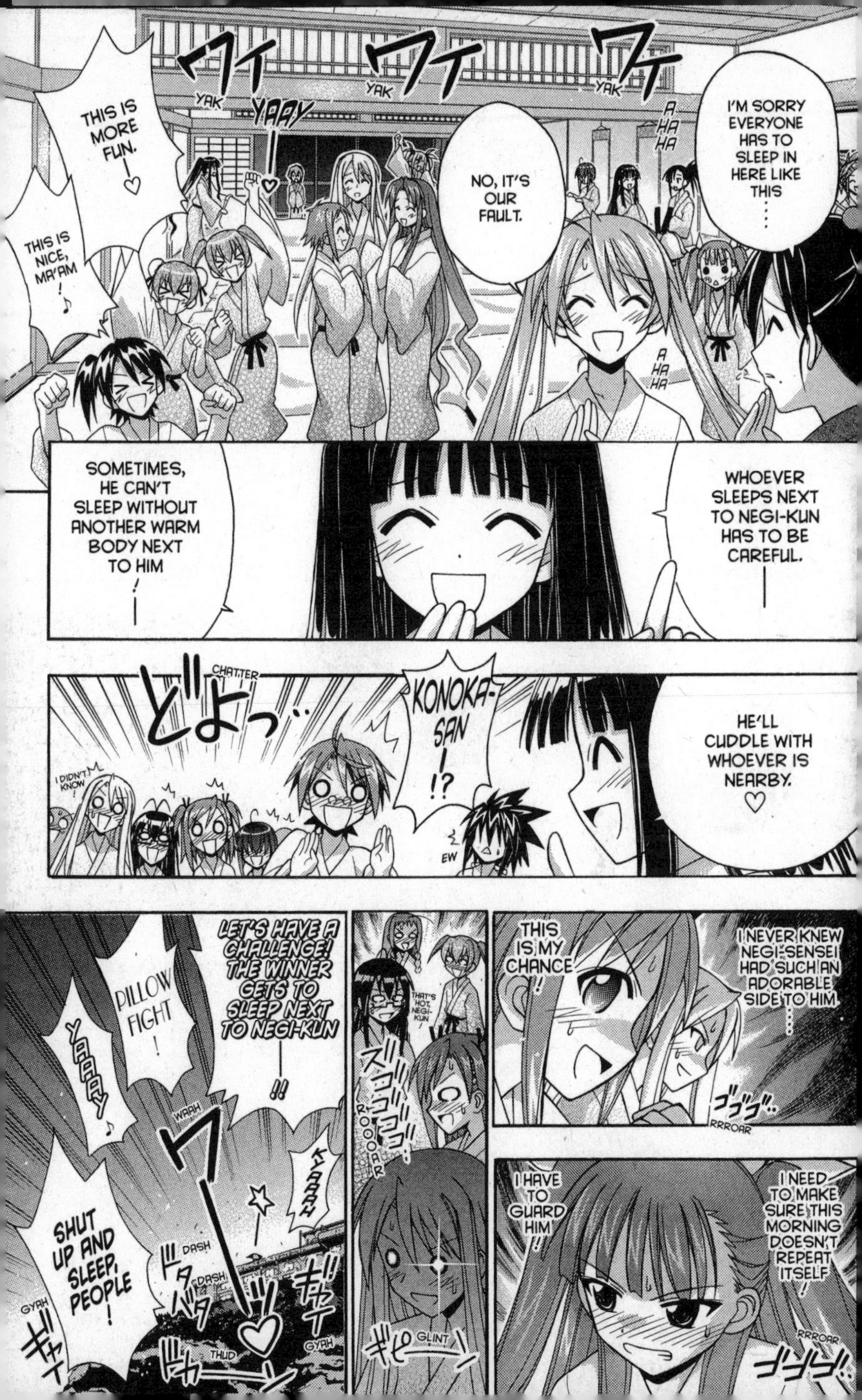
YAK
YAK
YAK
I'M SORRY EVERYONE HAS TO SLEEP IN HERE LIKE THIS......
A HA HA
NO, IT'S OUR FAULT.
A HA HA
YAAAY
THIS IS MORE FUN. ♡
THIS IS NICE, MA'AM! ♪
WHOEVER SLEEPS NEXT TO NEGI-KUN HAS TO BE CAREFUL.
SOMETIMES, HE CAN'T SLEEP WITHOUT ANOTHER WARM BODY NEXT TO HIM!
HE'LL CUDDLE WITH WHOEVER IS NEARBY. ♡
EW
KONOKA-SAN!!?
CHATTER
I DIDN'T KNOW!
I NEVER KNEW NEGI-SENSEI HAD SUCH AN ADORABLE SIDE TO HIM......
THIS IS MY CHANCE!
RRROAR
I NEED TO MAKE SURE THIS MORNING DOESN'T REPEAT ITSELF!
I HAVE TO GUARD HIM!
RRROAR
THAT'S HOT, NEGI-KUN!
RROOOAR
GLINT
LET'S HAVE A CHALLENGE! THE WINNER GETS TO SLEEP NEXT TO NEGI-KUN!!
PILLOW FIGHT!
YAAAAY ♪
WAAH
KYAAAH
SHUT UP AND SLEEP, PEOPLE!
DASH
DASH
GYAH
THUD
GYAH

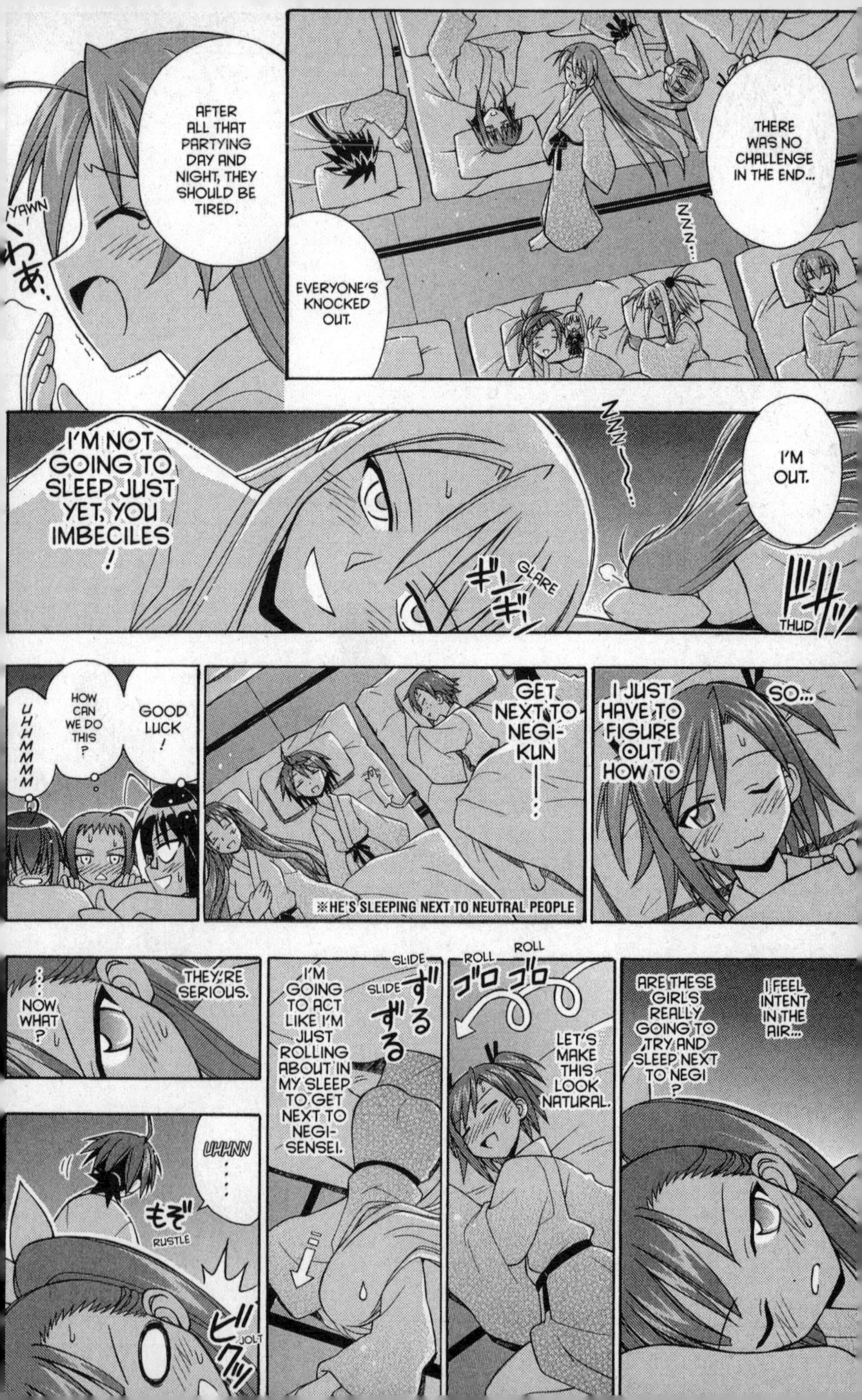
THERE WAS NO CHALLENGE IN THE END...
ZZZ...
EVERYONE'S KNOCKED OUT.
AFTER ALL THAT PARTYING DAY AND NIGHT, THEY SHOULD BE TIRED.
わあ…
YAWN
I'M OUT.
ドサッ
THUD
ZZZ~~...
ギン ギン
GLARE
I'M NOT GOING TO SLEEP JUST YET, YOU IMBECILES!
SO...
I JUST HAVE TO FIGURE OUT HOW TO
GET NEXT TO NEGI-KUN...!
※HE'S SLEEPING NEXT TO NEUTRAL PEOPLE
GOOD LUCK!
HOW CAN WE DO THIS?
UHHMMMM
I FEEL INTENT IN THE AIR...
ARE THESE GIRLS REALLY GOING TO TRY AND SLEEP NEXT TO NEGI?
ゴロ ゴロ
ROLL ROLL
LET'S MAKE THIS LOOK NATURAL.
ずる ずる
SLIDE SLIDE
I'M GOING TO ACT LIKE I'M JUST ROLLING ABOUT IN MY SLEEP TO GET NEXT TO NEGI-SENSEI.
THEY'RE SERIOUS.
...NOW WHAT?
UHHNN...
もぞ
RUSTLE
ビクッ
JOLT

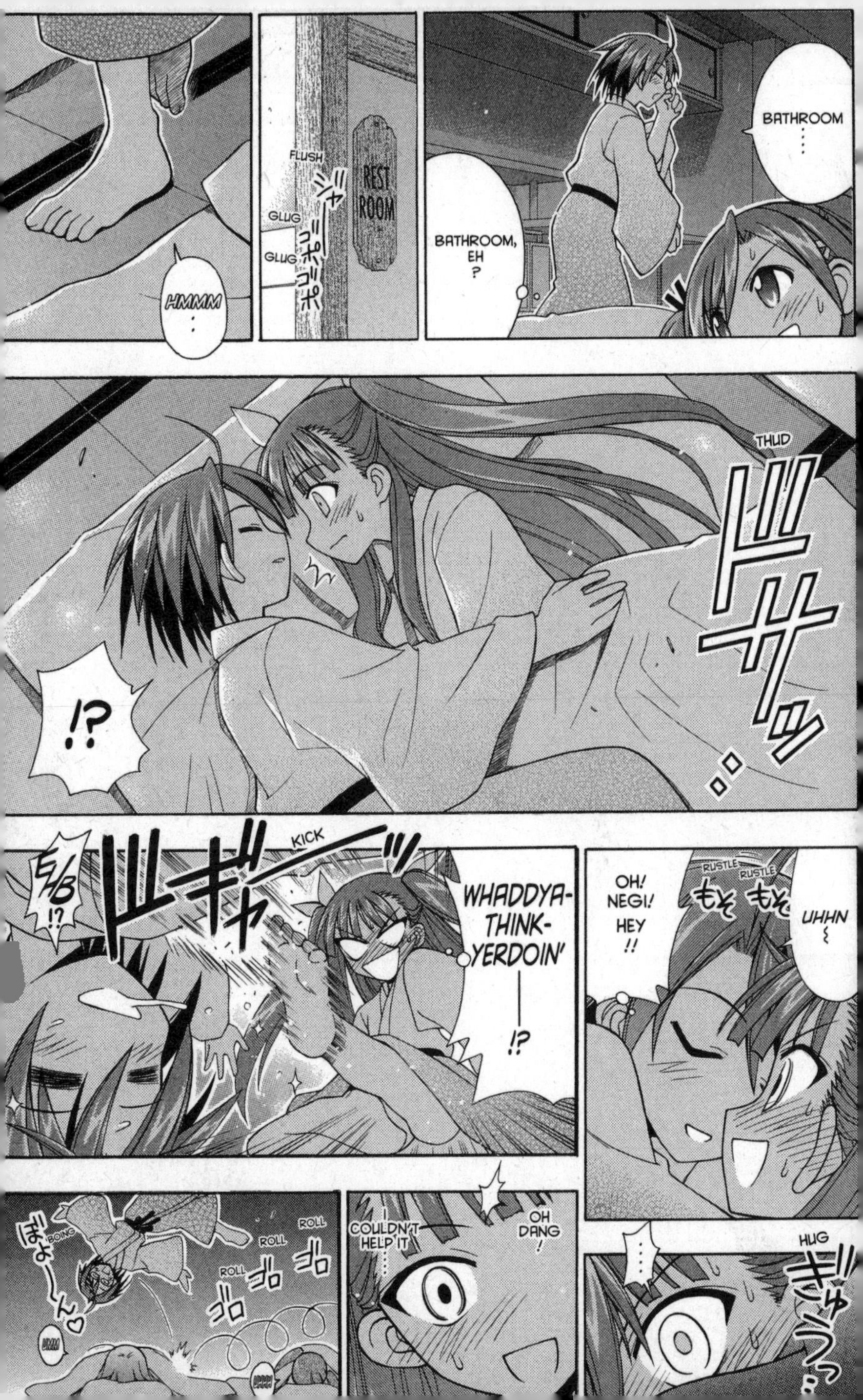

BATHROOM ....
BATHROOM, EH ?
FLUSH
GLUG GLUG
ジャーゴポゴポ
REST ROOM
HMMM ..
THUD
ドサッ
!?
RUSTLE RUSTLE
もそもそ
UHHN ~
OH! NEGI! HEY !!
WHADDYA-THINK-YERDOIN' ——!?
KICK
HUG
ぎゅうっ
....
OH DANG !
I COULDN'T HELP IT ....
ROLL
ゴロ
ROLL
ゴロ
ROLL
ゴロ
BOING
ぼよ〜ん♡
UMM

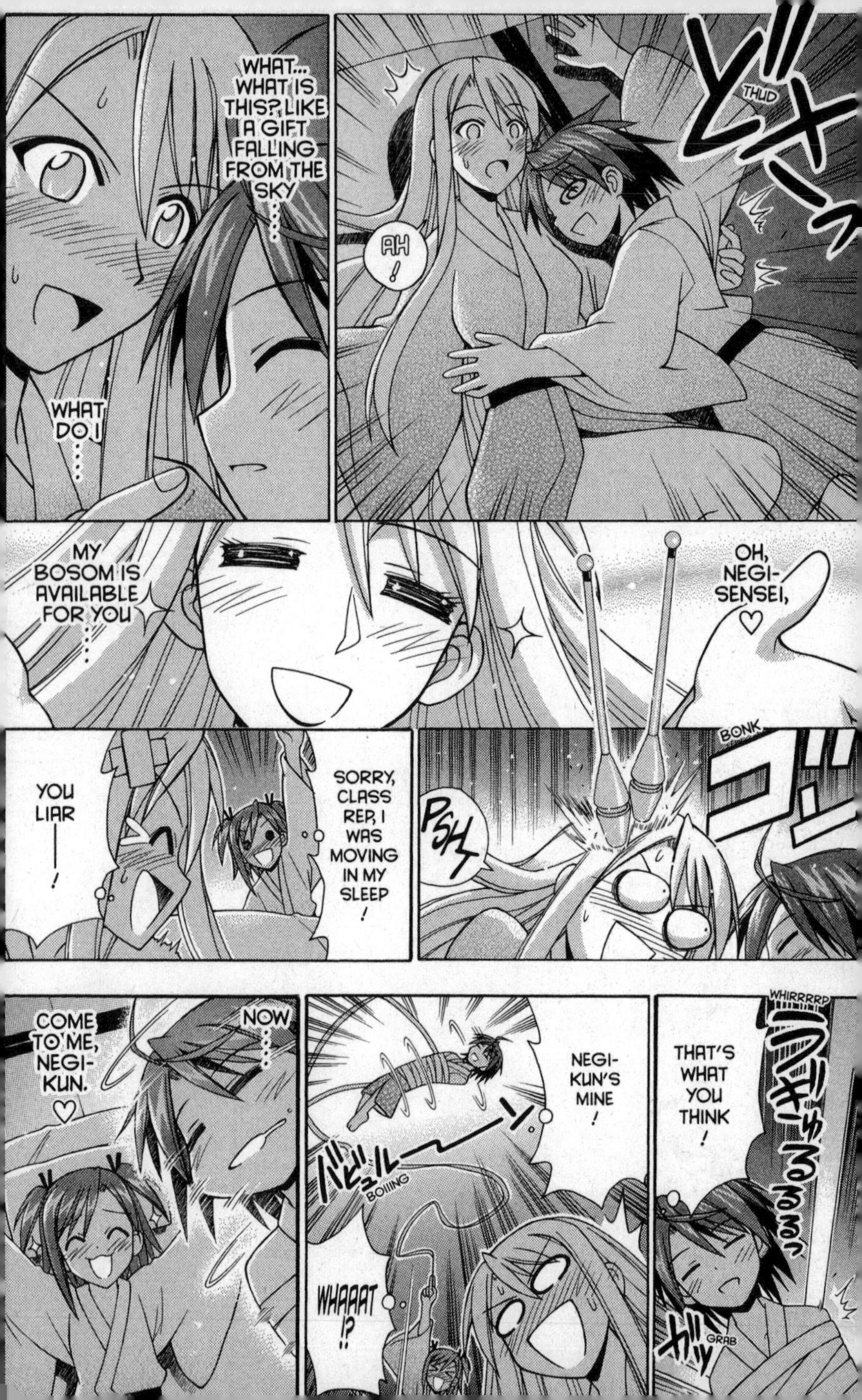
THUD
AH!
WHAT... WHAT IS THIS? LIKE A GIFT FALLING FROM THE SKY...
WHAT DO I...
OH, NEGI-SENSEI, ♡
MY BOSOM IS AVAILABLE FOR YOU...
BONK
PSHT
SORRY, CLASS REP, I WAS MOVING IN MY SLEEP!
YOU LIAR—!
WHIRRRRP
THAT'S WHAT YOU THINK!
GRAB
NEGI-KUN'S MINE!
BOIIING
WHAAAT!?
NOW...
COME TO ME, NEGI-KUN. ♡

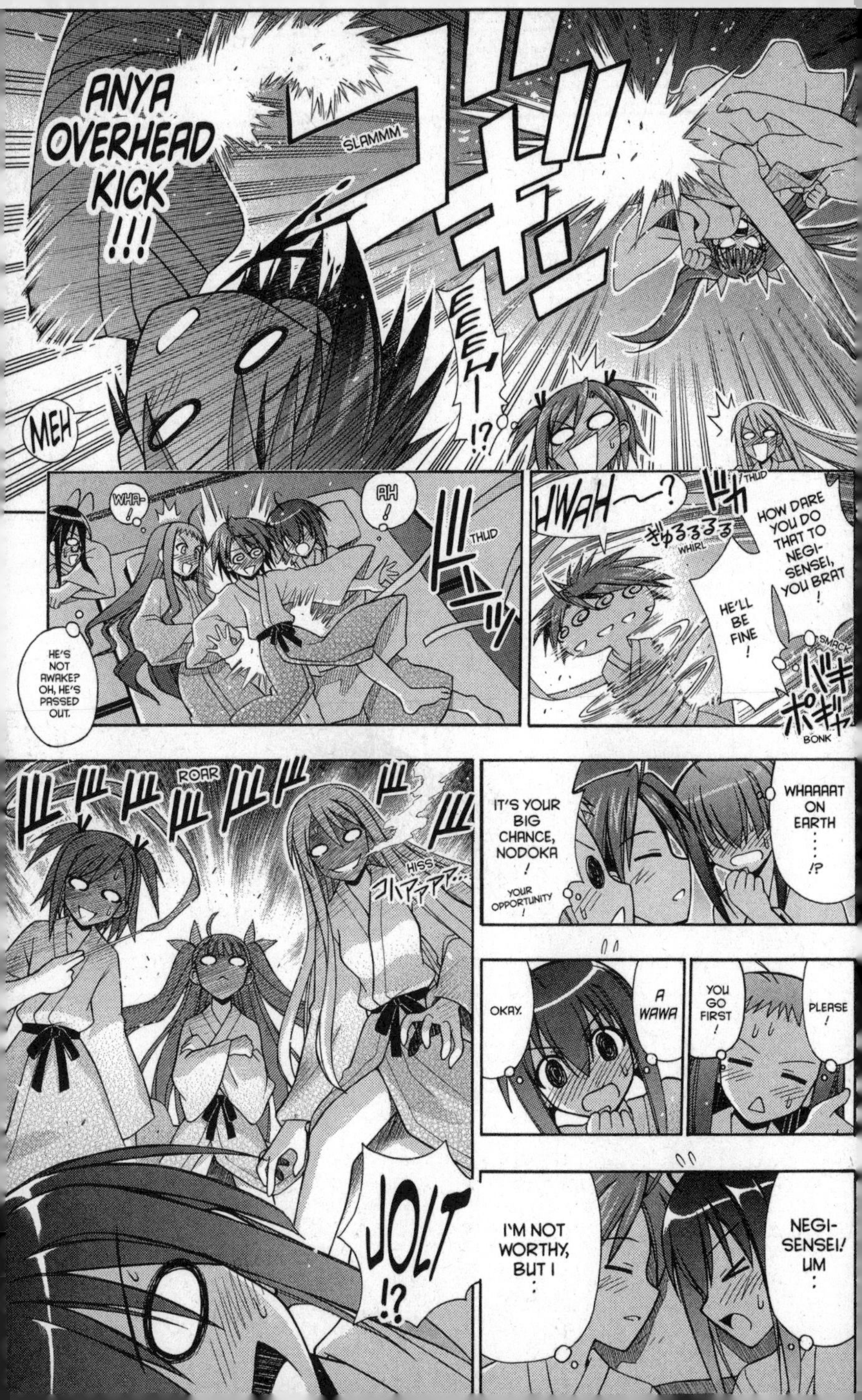
SLAMMM
ANYA OVERHEAD KICK!!!
EEEEH—!?
MEH
HOW DARE YOU DO THAT TO NEGI-SENSEI, YOU BRAT!
THUD
HWAH~~?
ぎゅるるるる
WHIRL
HE'LL BE FINE!
SMACK
BONK
THUD
AH!
WHA-!
HE'S NOT AWAKE? OH, HE'S PASSED OUT.
WHAAAAT ON EARTH.....!?
IT'S YOUR BIG CHANCE, NODOKA!
YOUR OPPORTUNITY!
PLEASE!
YOU GO FIRST!
A WAWA
OKAY.
NEGI-SENSEI! UM...
I'M NOT WORTHY, BUT I...
ROAR
HISS
JOLT!?

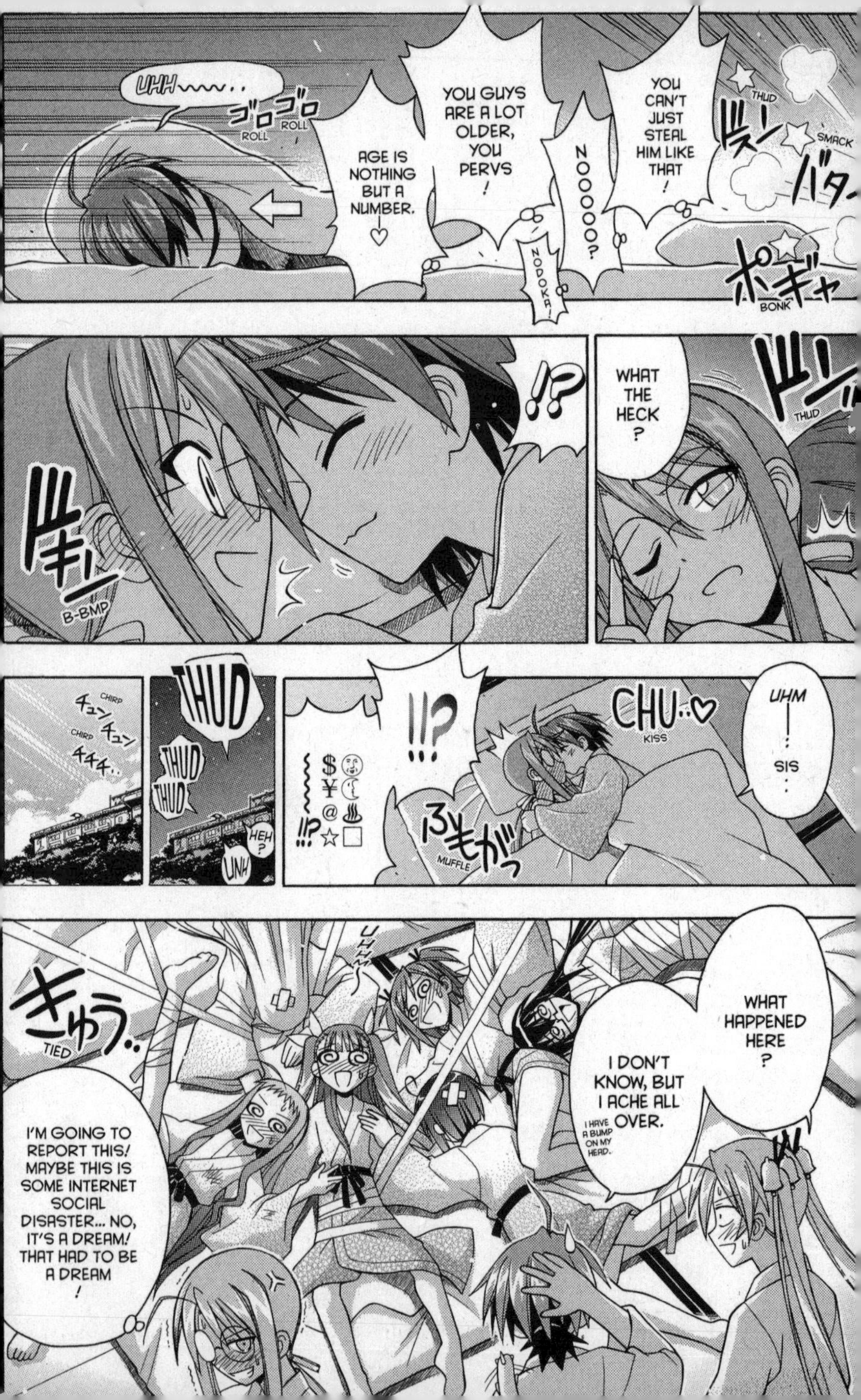
THUD
SMACK
BONK
YOU CAN'T JUST STEAL HIM LIKE THAT!
NOOOOOO?
NODOKA!
YOU GUYS ARE A LOT OLDER, YOU PERVS!
AGE IS NOTHING BUT A NUMBER. ♡
UHH~~..
ROLL ROLL
THUD
WHAT THE HECK?
!!?
B-BMP
UHM... SIS...
CHU..♡
KISS
!!?
$ ¥ @ !!? ☆
MUFFLE
THUD
THUD THUD
HEH?
UNH
CHIRP CHIRP
WHAT HAPPENED HERE?
I DON'T KNOW, BUT I ACHE ALL OVER.
I HAVE A BUMP ON MY HEAD.
UHHM~
TIED
I'M GOING TO REPORT THIS! MAYBE THIS IS SOME INTERNET SOCIAL DISASTER... NO, IT'S A DREAM! THAT HAD TO BE A DREAM!

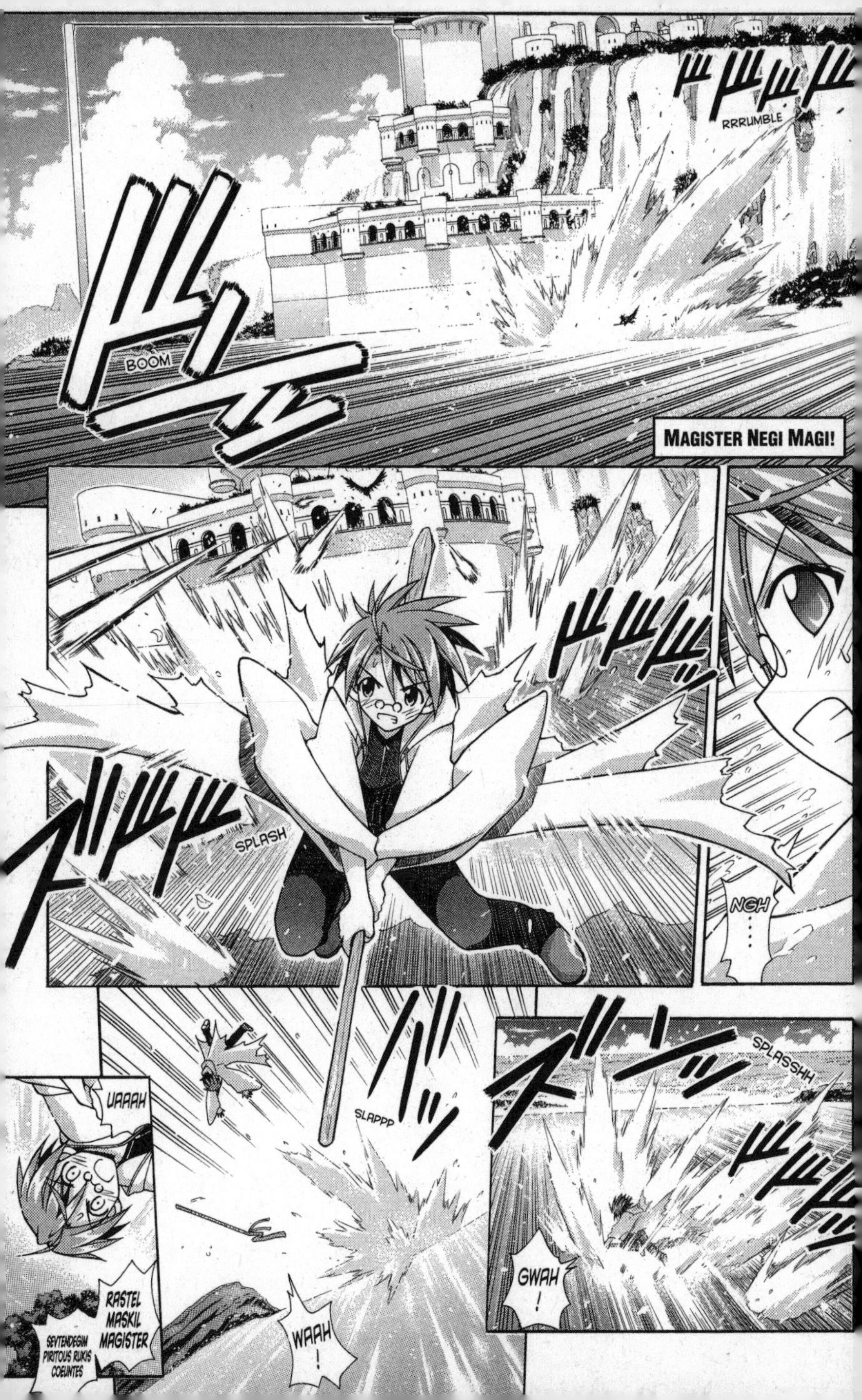
RRRUMBLE
BOOM
MAGISTER NEGI MAGI!
NGH ...
SPLASH
SPLASSHH
GWAH!
SLAPPP
UAAAH
RASTEL MASKIL MAGISTER
SEYTENDEGIM PIRITOUS RUKIS COEUNTES
WAAH!

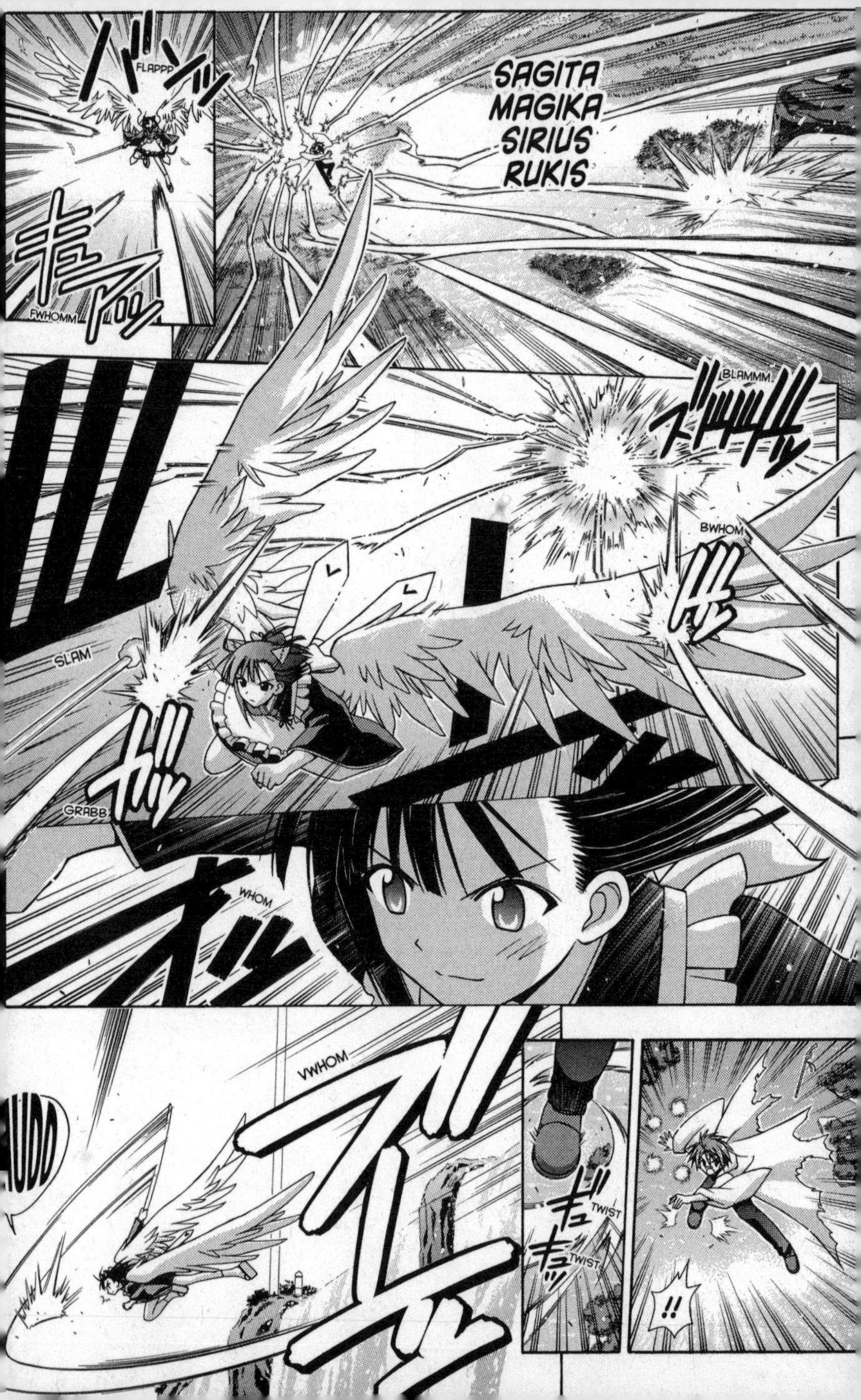
SAGITA MAGIKA SIRIUS RUKIS
FLAPPP
FWHOMM
BLAMMM
BWHOM
SLAM
GRABB
WHOM
!!
TWIST
TWIST
VWHOM

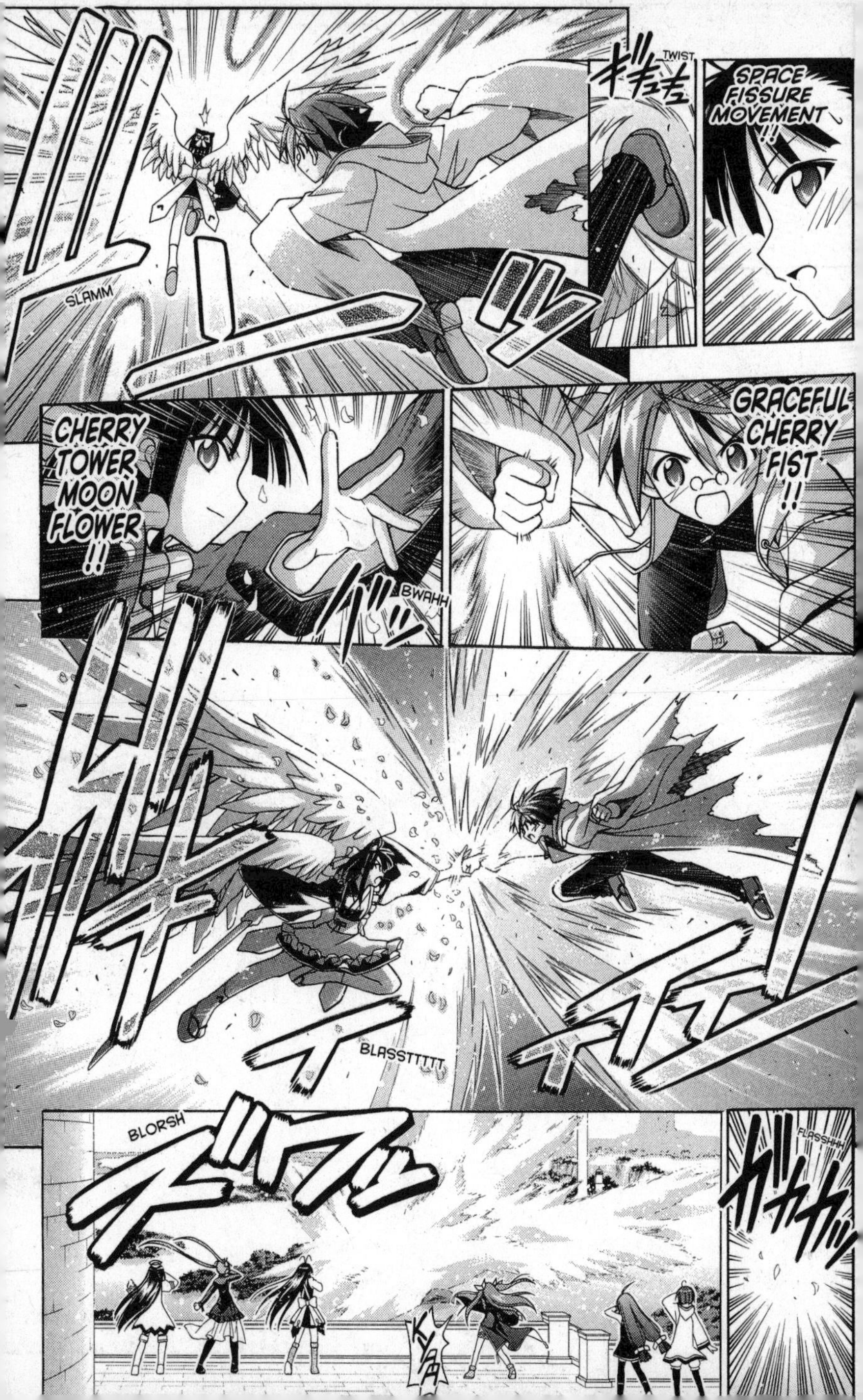
SPACE FISSURE MOVEMENT!!
TWIST
SLAMM
GRACEFUL CHERRY FIST!!
CHERRY TOWER MOON FLOWER!!
BWAHH
BLASSTTTTT
FLASSHHH
BLORSH

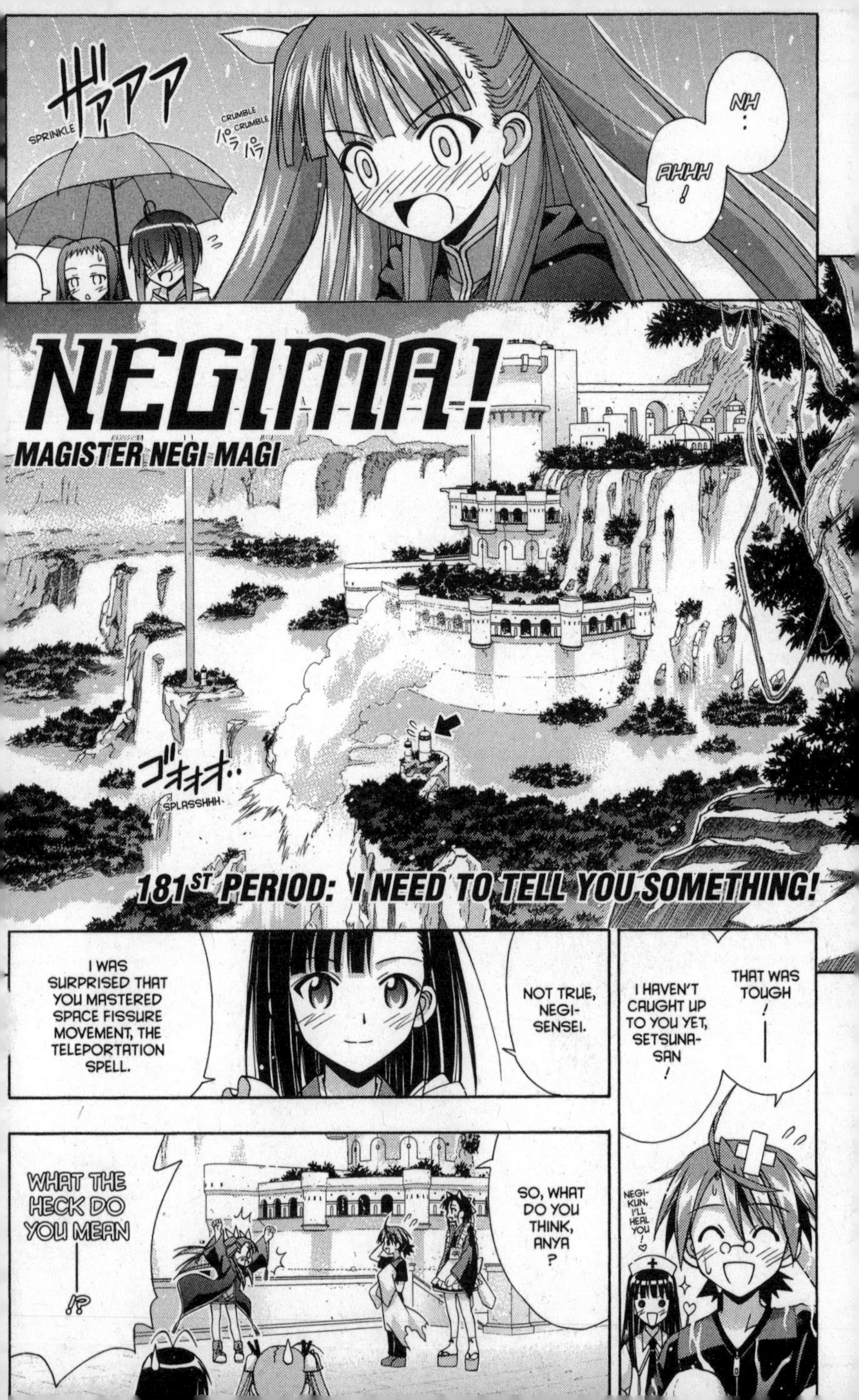

NH...
AHHH!
CRUMBLE CRUMBLE
パラパラ
ザァァァ
SPRINKLE
NEGIMA!
MAGISTER NEGI MAGI
ゴオオオ
SPLASSHHH
181ST PERIOD: I NEED TO TELL YOU SOMETHING!
THAT WAS TOUGH!
I HAVEN'T CAUGHT UP TO YOU YET, SETSUNA-SAN!
NEGI-KUN, I'LL HEAL YOU!
NOT TRUE, NEGI-SENSEI.
I WAS SURPRISED THAT YOU MASTERED SPACE FISSURE MOVEMENT, THE TELEPORTATION SPELL.
SO, WHAT DO YOU THINK, ANYA?
WHAT THE HECK DO YOU MEAN—!?

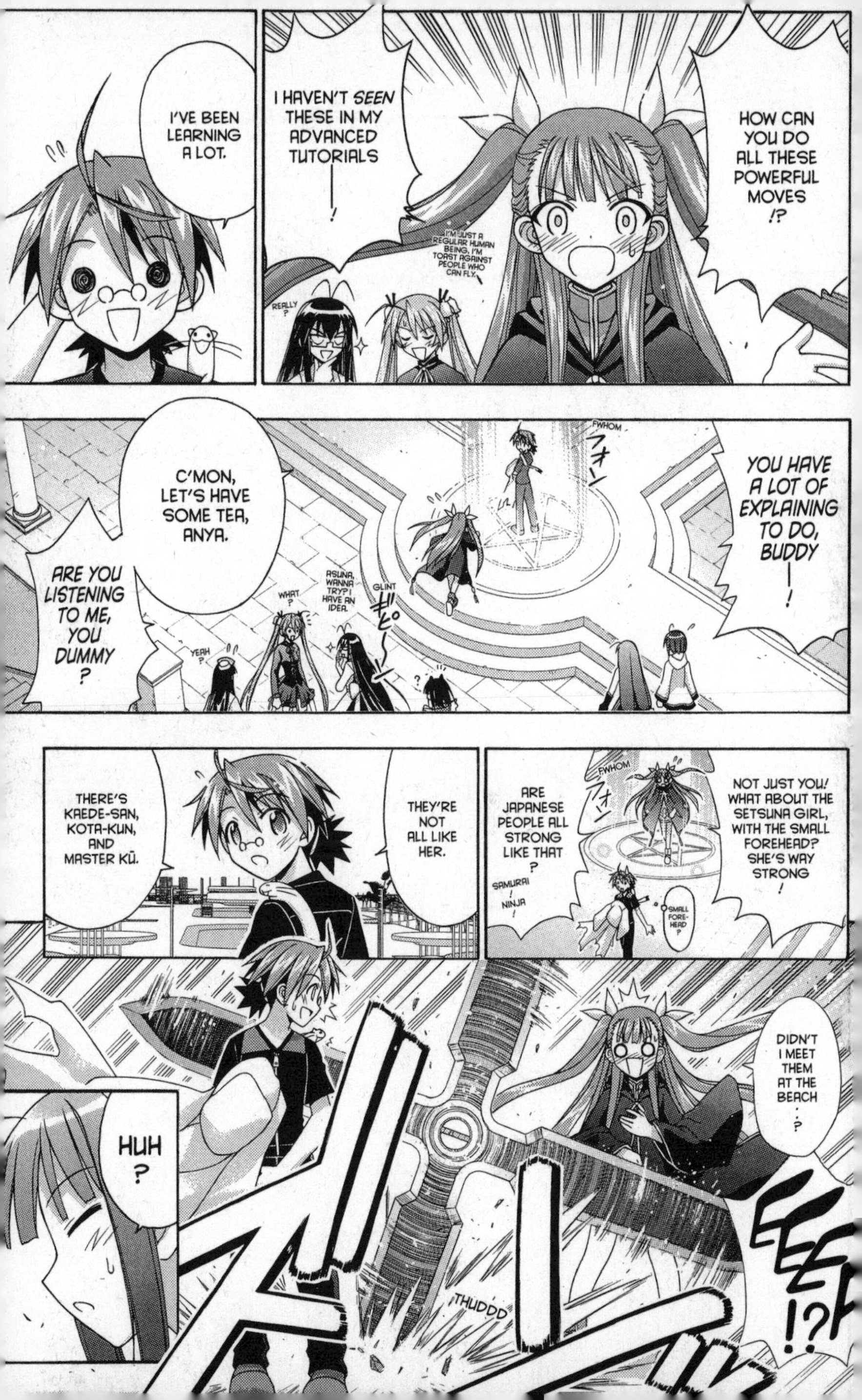
HOW CAN YOU DO ALL THESE POWERFUL MOVES !?
I HAVEN'T SEEN THESE IN MY ADVANCED TUTORIALS !
I'M JUST A REGULAR HUMAN BEING, I'M TOAST AGAINST PEOPLE WHO CAN FLY.
REALLY ?
I'VE BEEN LEARNING A LOT.
FWHOM
YOU HAVE A LOT OF EXPLAINING TO DO, BUDDY !
C'MON, LET'S HAVE SOME TEA, ANYA.
ARE YOU LISTENING TO ME, YOU DUMMY ?
ASUNA, WANNA TRY? I HAVE AN IDEA.
WHAT ?
GLINT
YEAH ?
NOT JUST YOU! WHAT ABOUT THE SETSUNA GIRL, WITH THE SMALL FOREHEAD? SHE'S WAY STRONG !
FWHOM
ARE JAPANESE PEOPLE ALL STRONG LIKE THAT ?
SAMURAI ! NINJA !
SMALL FOREHEAD ?
THEY'RE NOT ALL LIKE HER.
THERE'S KAEDE-SAN, KOTA-KUN, AND MASTER KŪ.
DIDN'T I MEET THEM AT THE BEACH ..?
EEE !?
THUDDD
HUH ?

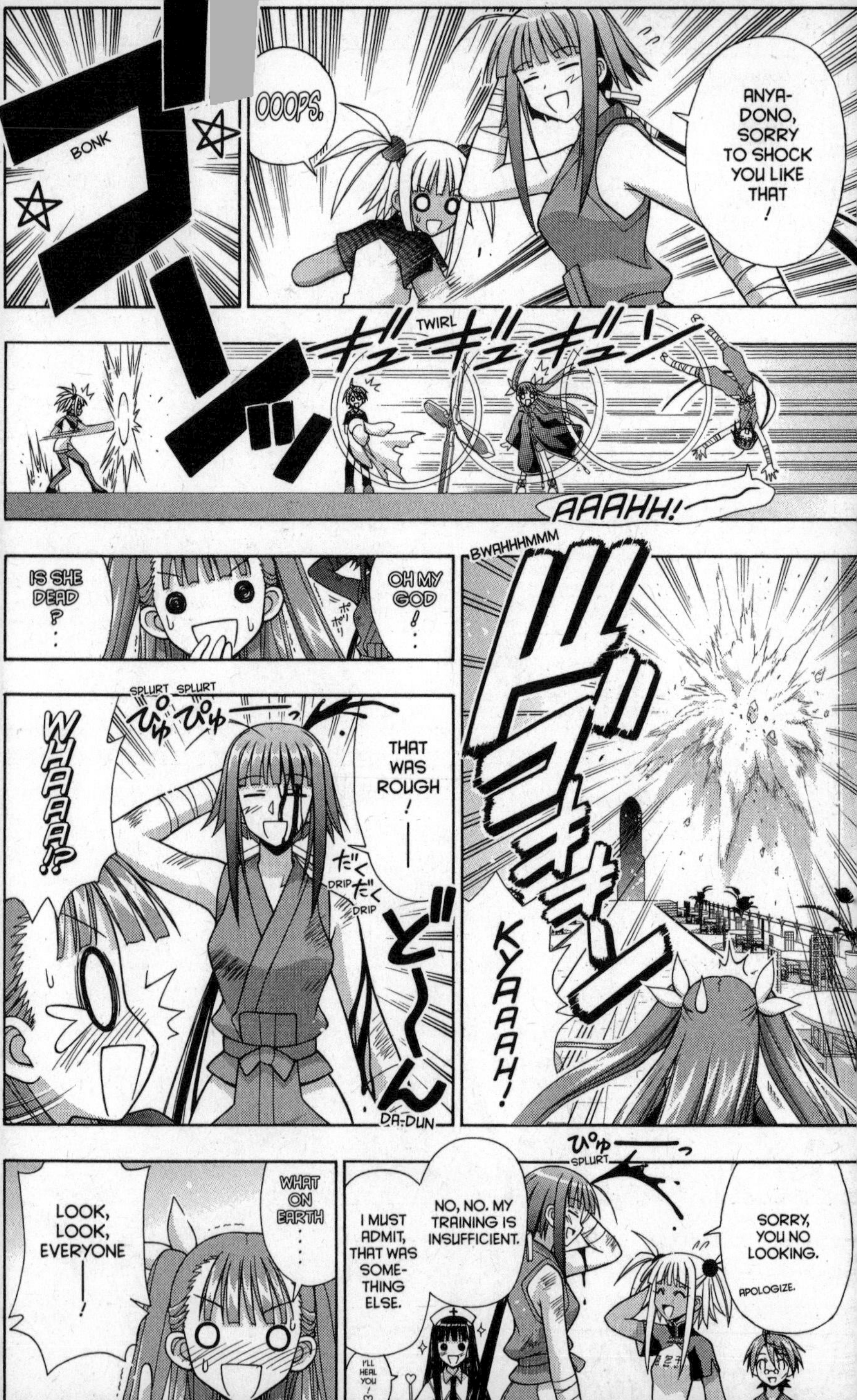
ANYA-DONO, SORRY TO SHOCK YOU LIKE THAT!
OOOPS.
BONK
TWIRL
AAAHH!
BWAHHHMMM
KYAAAAH!
OH MY GOD!..
IS SHE DEAD?..
SPLURT SPLURT
THAT WAS ROUGH!—
DRIP DRIP
DA-DUN
WHAAAAA!?
SPLURT
SORRY, YOU NO LOOKING.
APOLOGIZE.
NO, NO. MY TRAINING IS INSUFFICIENT.
I MUST ADMIT, THAT WAS SOMETHING ELSE.
I'LL HEAL YOU!
WHAT ON EARTH....
LOOK, LOOK, EVERYONE—!

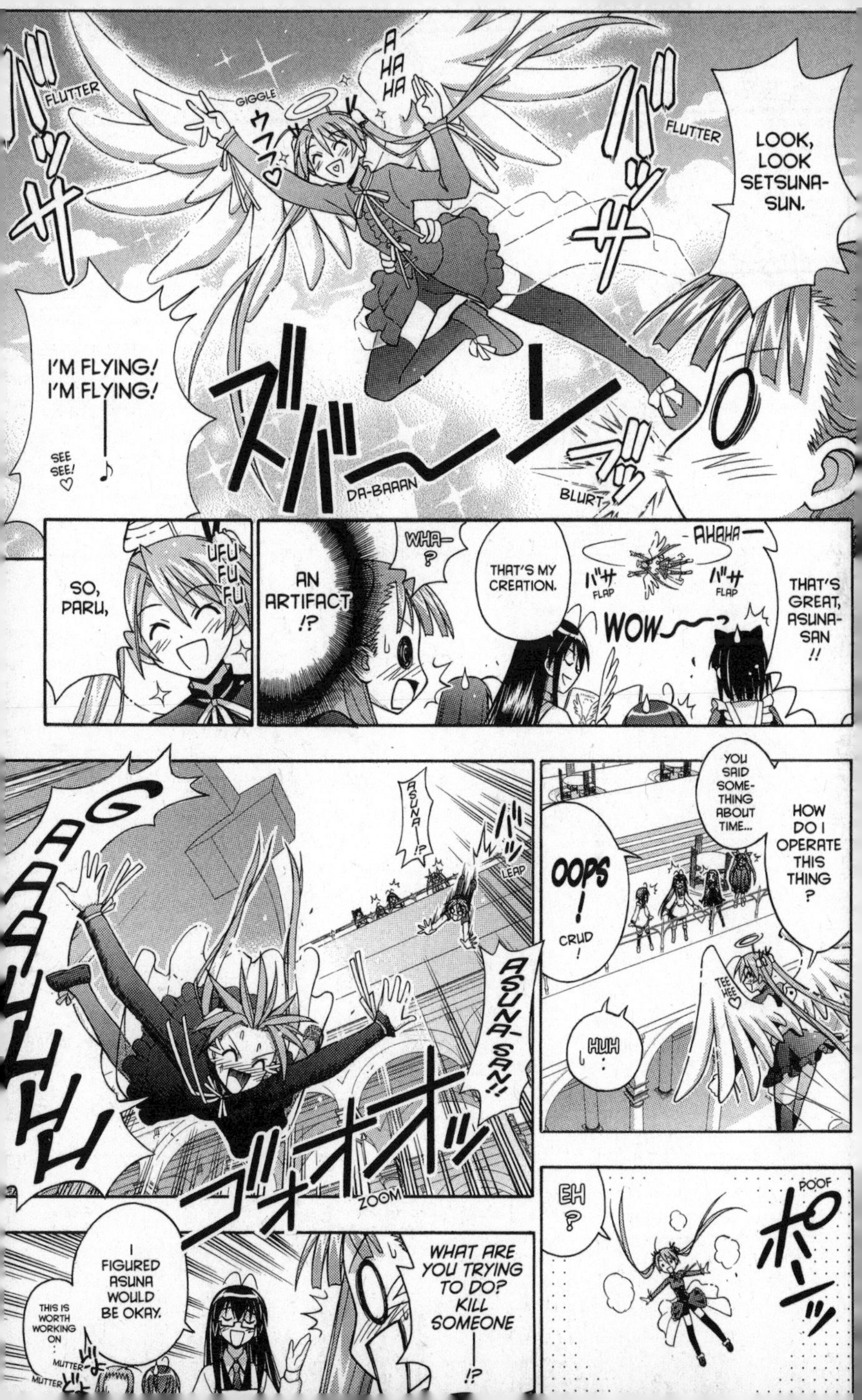

LOOK, LOOK SETSUNA-SUN.
FLUTTER
A HA HA
GIGGLE
FLUTTER
I'M FLYING! I'M FLYING!
SEE SEE!
DA-BAAAN
BLURT
THAT'S GREAT, ASUNA-SAN!!
AHAHA
FLAP
FLAP
WOW
THAT'S MY CREATION.
WHA-?
AN ARTIFACT!?
UFU FU FU
SO, PARU,
HOW DO I OPERATE THIS THING?
YOU SAID SOMETHING ABOUT TIME...
OOPS! CRUD!
TEE HEE
HUH...
POOF
EH?
ASUNA-SAN!!
LEAP
ASUNA—!?
GAAAAAAH
ZOOM
WHAT ARE YOU TRYING TO DO? KILL SOMEONE—!?
I FIGURED ASUNA WOULD BE OKAY.
THIS IS WORTH WORKING ON...
MUTTER
MUTTER

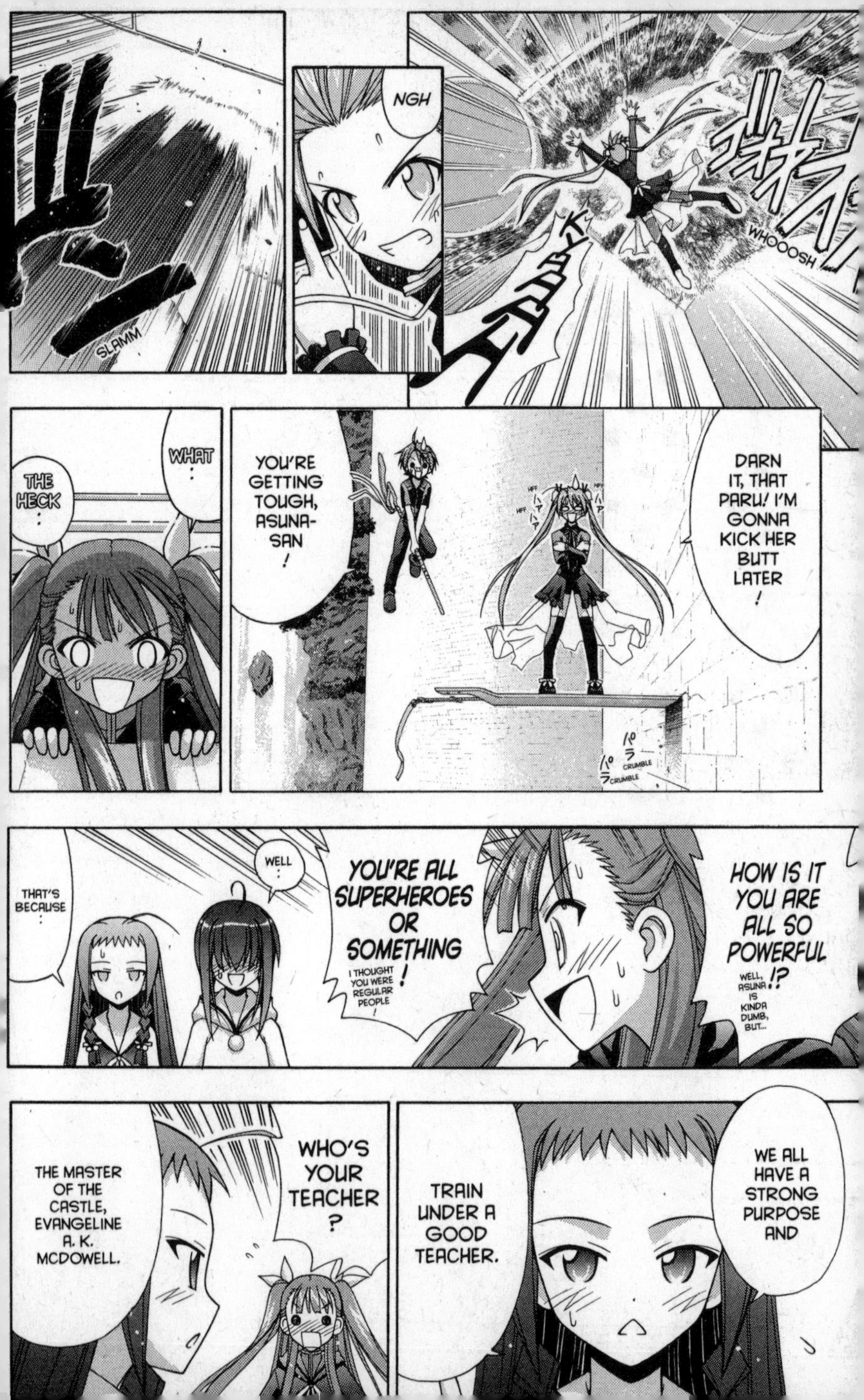
WHOOOSH
KYA
NGH
SLAMM
DARN IT, THAT PARU! I'M GONNA KICK HER BUTT LATER!
HFF HFF HFF
YOU'RE GETTING TOUGH, ASUNA-SAN!
CRUMBLE CRUMBLE
WHAT...
THE HECK...
HOW IS IT YOU ARE ALL SO POWERFUL!?
WELL, ASUNA IS KINDA DUMB, BUT...
YOU'RE ALL SUPERHEROES OR SOMETHING!
I THOUGHT YOU WERE REGULAR PEOPLE!
WELL...
THAT'S BECAUSE...
WE ALL HAVE A STRONG PURPOSE AND
TRAIN UNDER A GOOD TEACHER.
WHO'S YOUR TEACHER?
THE MASTER OF THE CASTLE, EVANGELINE A. K. MCDOWELL.

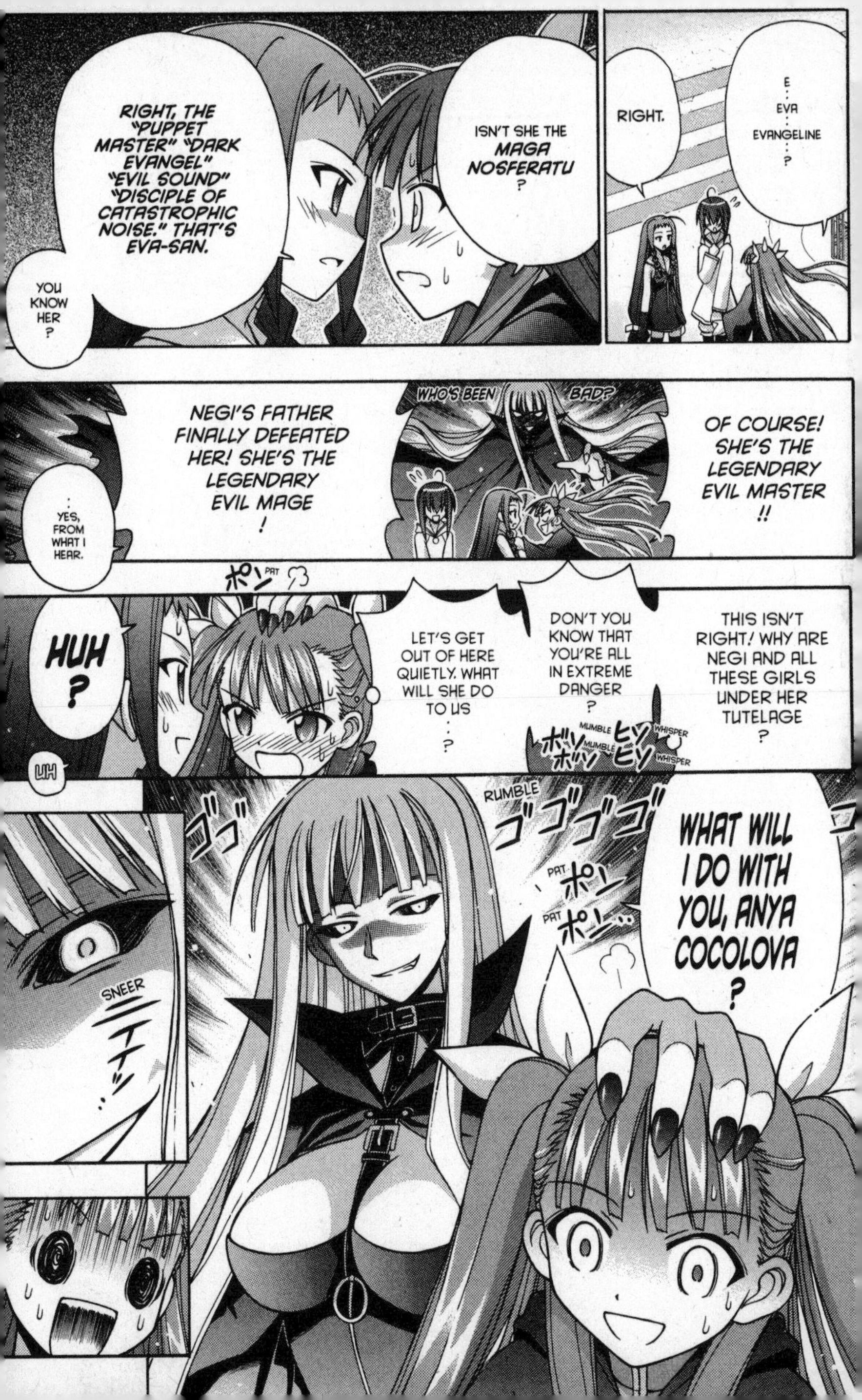
E... EVA... EVANGELINE...?
RIGHT.
ISN'T SHE THE MAGA NOSFERATU?
RIGHT, THE "PUPPET MASTER" "DARK EVANGEL" "EVIL SOUND" "DISCIPLE OF CATASTROPHIC NOISE." THAT'S EVA-SAN.
YOU KNOW HER?
OF COURSE! SHE'S THE LEGENDARY EVIL MASTER!!
WHO'S BEEN BAD?
NEGI'S FATHER FINALLY DEFEATED HER! SHE'S THE LEGENDARY EVIL MAGE!
...YES, FROM WHAT I HEAR.
THIS ISN'T RIGHT! WHY ARE NEGI AND ALL THESE GIRLS UNDER HER TUTELAGE?
DON'T YOU KNOW THAT YOU'RE ALL IN EXTREME DANGER?
LET'S GET OUT OF HERE QUIETLY. WHAT WILL SHE DO TO US...?
WHISPER
MUMBLE
PAT
HUH?
UH
WHAT WILL I DO WITH YOU, ANYA COCOLOVA?
RUMBLE
PAT
PAT
SNEER

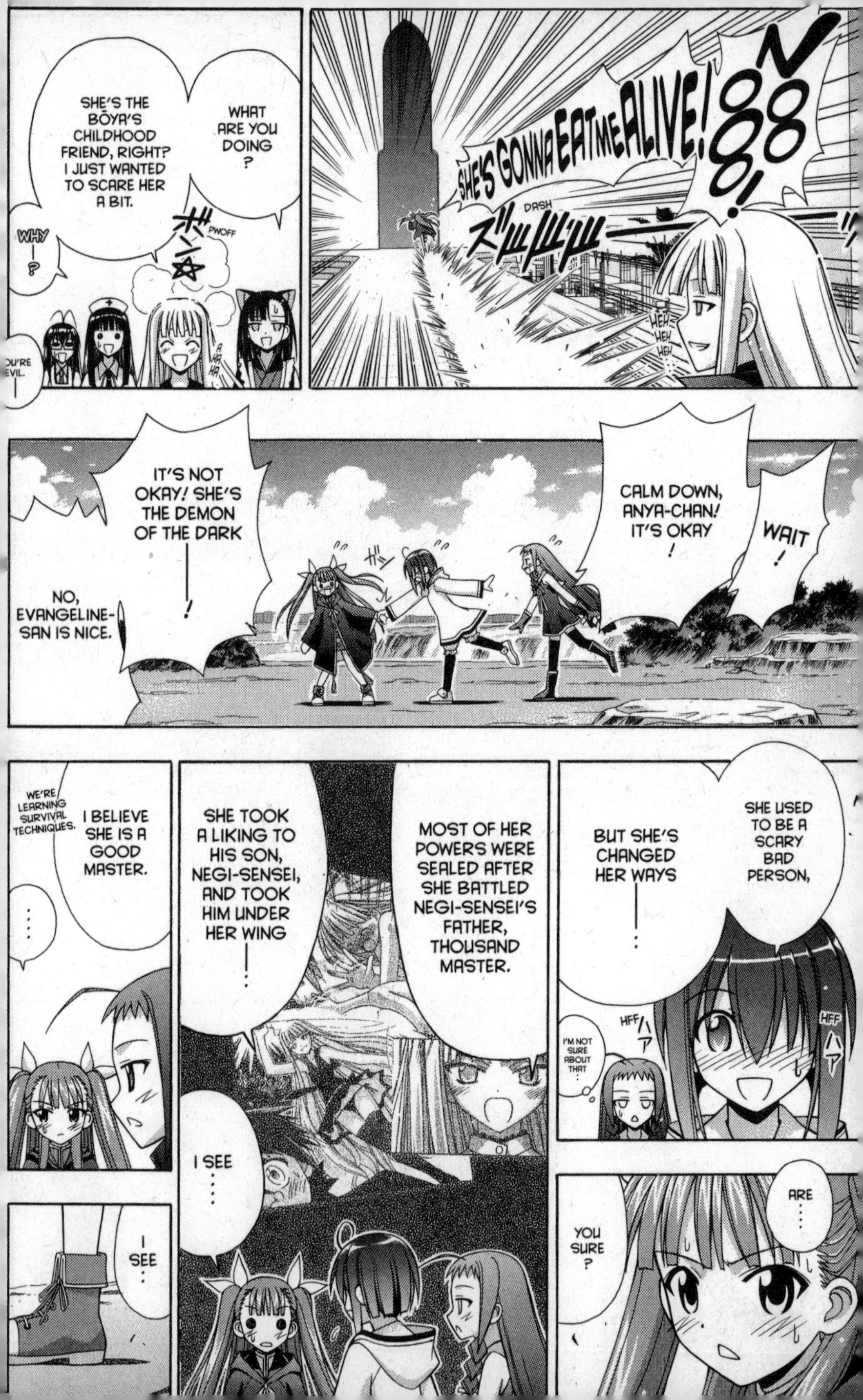
NOOOO!
SHE'S GONNA EAT ME ALIVE!
DASH
HEH HEH HEH
WHAT ARE YOU DOING?
SHE'S THE BŌYA'S CHILDHOOD FRIEND, RIGHT? I JUST WANTED TO SCARE HER A BIT.
PWOFF
WHY—?
A HA HA
OU'RE EVIL.—
WAIT!
CALM DOWN, ANYA-CHAN! IT'S OKAY!
IT'S NOT OKAY! SHE'S THE DEMON OF THE DARK—!
NO, EVANGELINE-SAN IS NICE.
SHE USED TO BE A SCARY BAD PERSON,
BUT SHE'S CHANGED HER WAYS—...
HFF
HFF
I'M NOT SURE ABOUT THAT...
MOST OF HER POWERS WERE SEALED AFTER SHE BATTLED NEGI-SENSEI'S FATHER, THOUSAND MASTER.
SHE TOOK A LIKING TO HIS SON, NEGI-SENSEI, AND TOOK HIM UNDER HER WING—...
I SEE....
I BELIEVE SHE IS A GOOD MASTER.
WE'RE LEARNING SURVIVAL TECHNIQUES.
....
ARE....
YOU SURE?
I SEE...

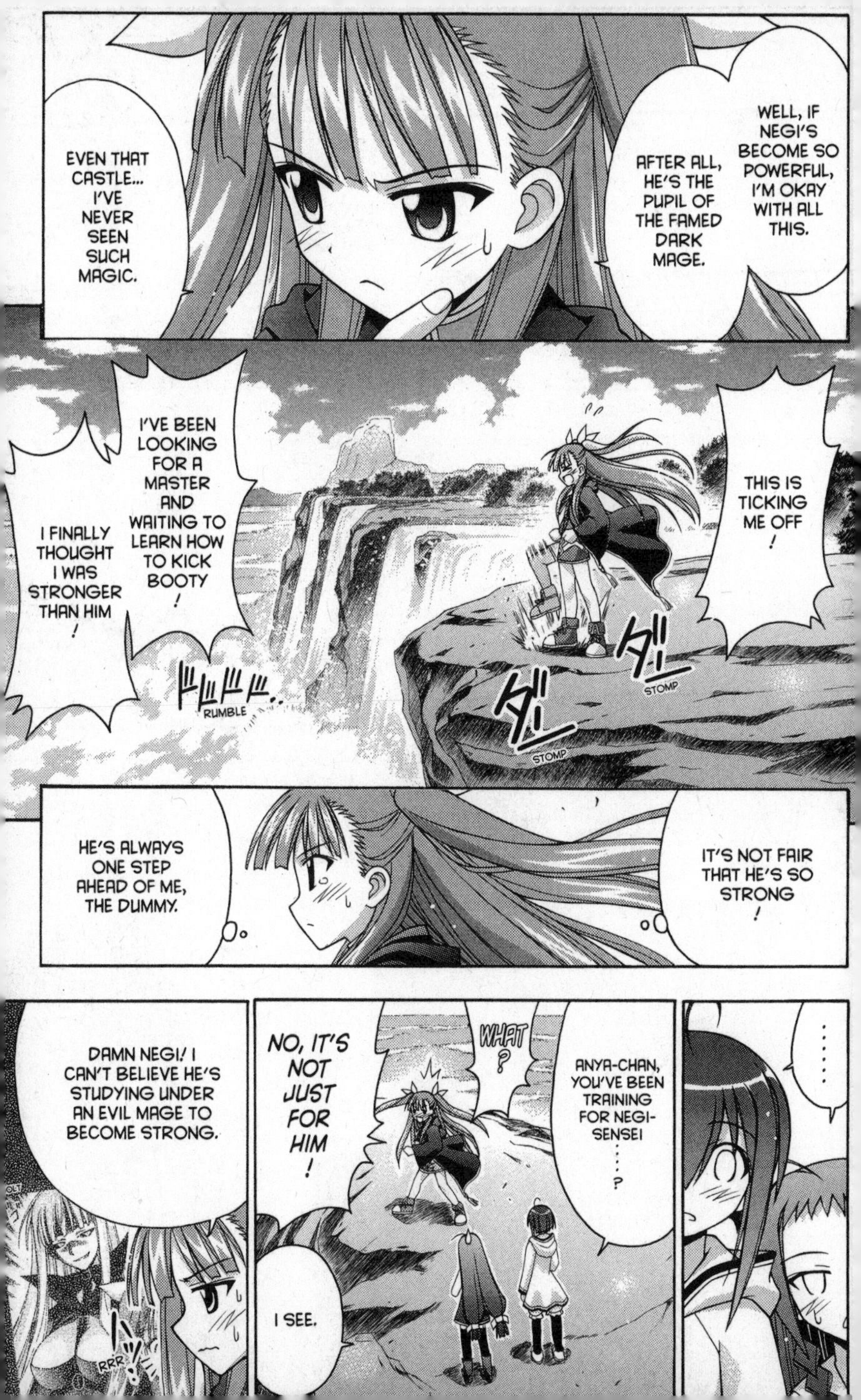
WELL, IF NEGI'S BECOME SO POWERFUL, I'M OKAY WITH ALL THIS.
AFTER ALL, HE'S THE PUPIL OF THE FAMED DARK MAGE.
EVEN THAT CASTLE... I'VE NEVER SEEN SUCH MAGIC.
THIS IS TICKING ME OFF!
STOMP
STOMP
I'VE BEEN LOOKING FOR A MASTER AND WAITING TO LEARN HOW TO KICK BOOTY!
I FINALLY THOUGHT I WAS STRONGER THAN HIM!
RUMBLE
IT'S NOT FAIR THAT HE'S SO STRONG!
HE'S ALWAYS ONE STEP AHEAD OF ME, THE DUMMY.
......
ANYA-CHAN, YOU'VE BEEN TRAINING FOR NEGI-SENSEI....?
WHAT?
NO, IT'S NOT JUST FOR HIM!
I SEE.
DAMN NEGI! I CAN'T BELIEVE HE'S STUDYING UNDER AN EVIL MAGE TO BECOME STRONG.
RRR

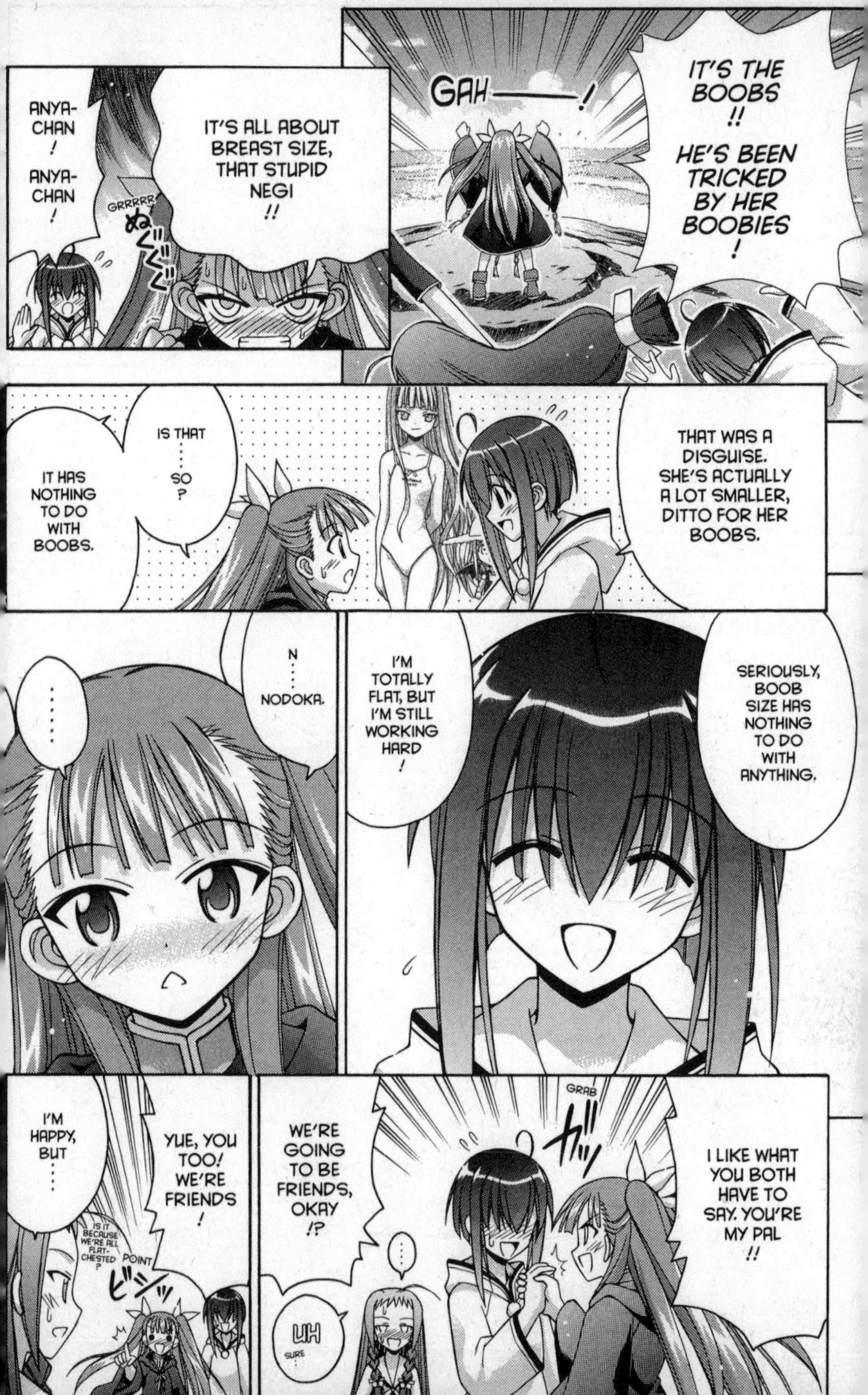
GAH———!
IT'S THE BOOBS!!
HE'S BEEN TRICKED BY HER BOOBIES!
IT'S ALL ABOUT BREAST SIZE, THAT STUPID NEGI!!
GRRRRR
ぬぐぐぐ
ANYA-CHAN!
ANYA-CHAN!
THAT WAS A DISGUISE. SHE'S ACTUALLY A LOT SMALLER, DITTO FOR HER BOOBS.
IS THAT... SO?
IT HAS NOTHING TO DO WITH BOOBS.
SERIOUSLY, BOOB SIZE HAS NOTHING TO DO WITH ANYTHING.
I'M TOTALLY FLAT, BUT I'M STILL WORKING HARD!
N... NODOKA.
......
I LIKE WHAT YOU BOTH HAVE TO SAY. YOU'RE MY PAL!!
GRAB
ガッ
WE'RE GOING TO BE FRIENDS, OKAY!?
......
UH
SURE
YUE, YOU TOO! WE'RE FRIENDS!
I'M HAPPY, BUT......
IS IT BECAUSE WE'RE ALL FLAT-CHESTED?
POINT
ビシッ

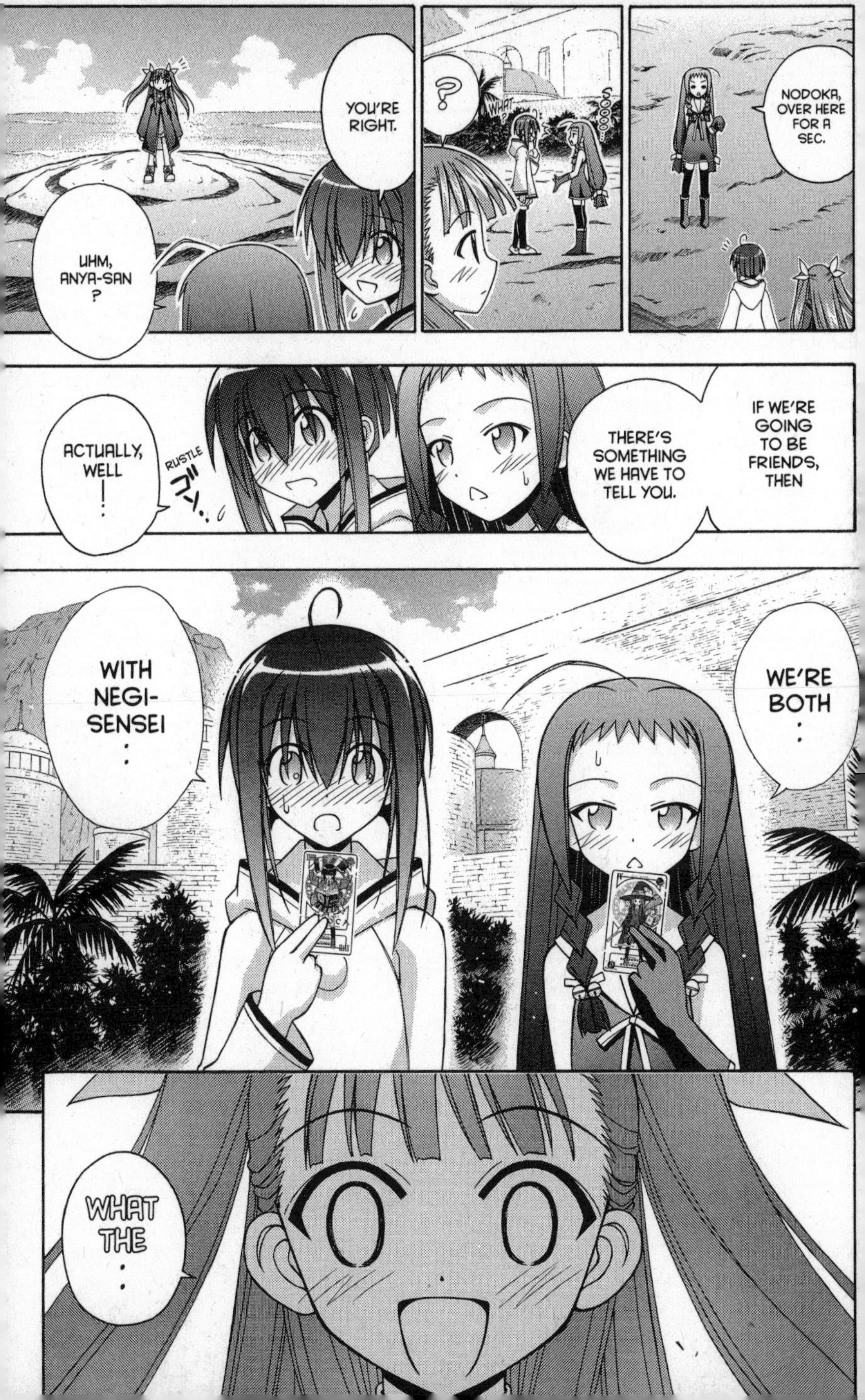

NODOKA, OVER HERE FOR A SEC.
?
WHAT
YOU'RE RIGHT.
UHM, ANYA-SAN ?
IF WE'RE GOING TO BE FRIENDS, THEN
THERE'S SOMETHING WE HAVE TO TELL YOU.
RUSTLE
ACTUALLY, WELL !
WE'RE BOTH ..
WITH NEGI-SENSEI ..
WHAT THE ..

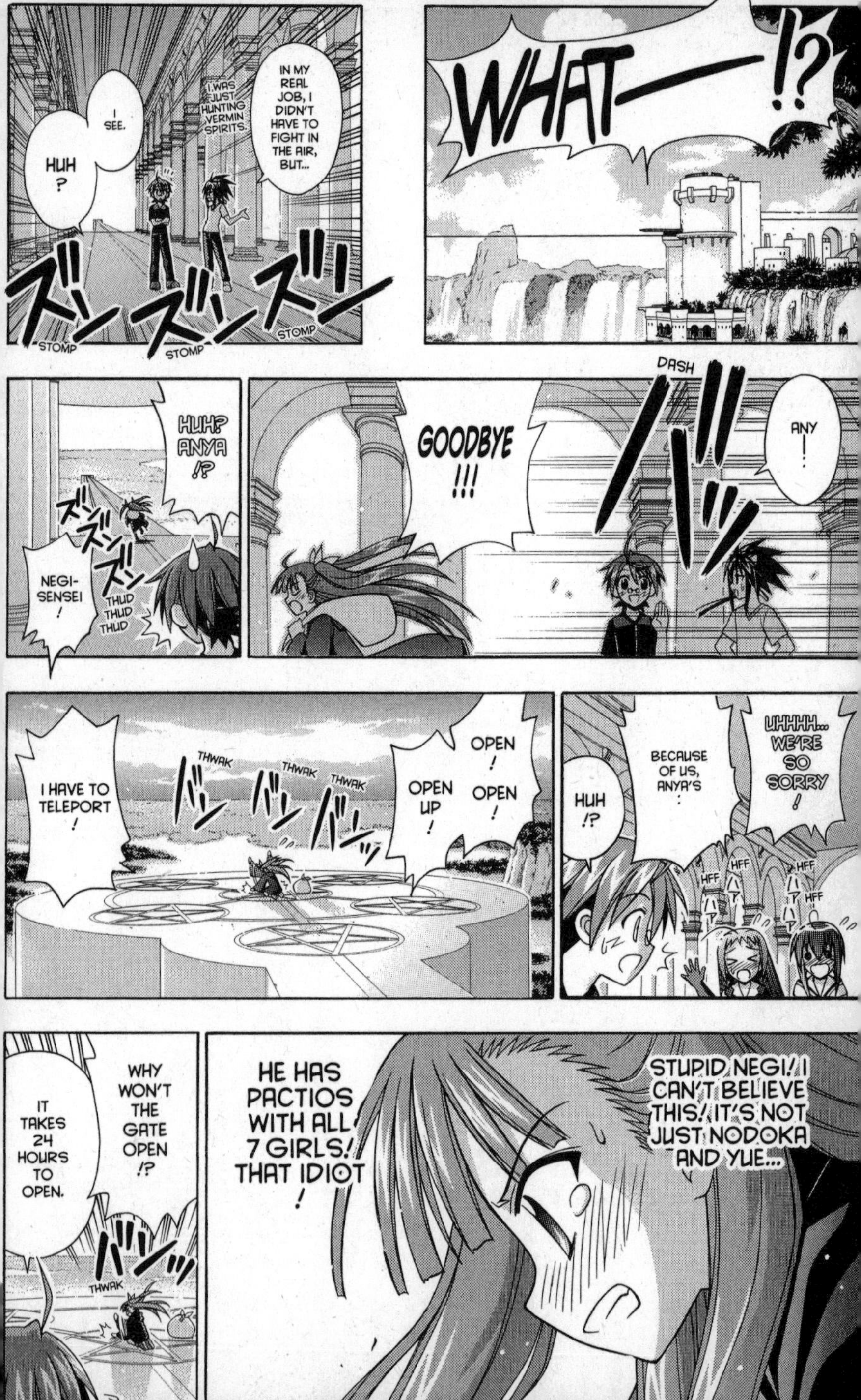
WHAT——!?
IN MY REAL JOB, I DIDN'T HAVE TO FIGHT IN THE AIR, BUT...
I WAS JUST HUNTING VERMIN SPIRITS.
I SEE.
HUH?
STOMP
STOMP
STOMP
DASH
ANY!
GOODBYE!!!
HUH? ANYA!?
NEGI-SENSEI!
THUD THUD THUD
UHHHH... WE'RE SO SORRY!
BECAUSE OF US, ANYA'S:
HUH!?
HFF
HFF
HFF
HFF
OPEN!
OPEN!
OPEN UP!
THWAK
THWAK
THWAK
I HAVE TO TELEPORT!
STUPID NEGI! I CAN'T BELIEVE THIS! IT'S NOT JUST NODOKA AND YUE...
HE HAS PACTIOS WITH ALL 7 GIRLS! THAT IDIOT!
WHY WON'T THE GATE OPEN!?
IT TAKES 24 HOURS TO OPEN.
THWAK

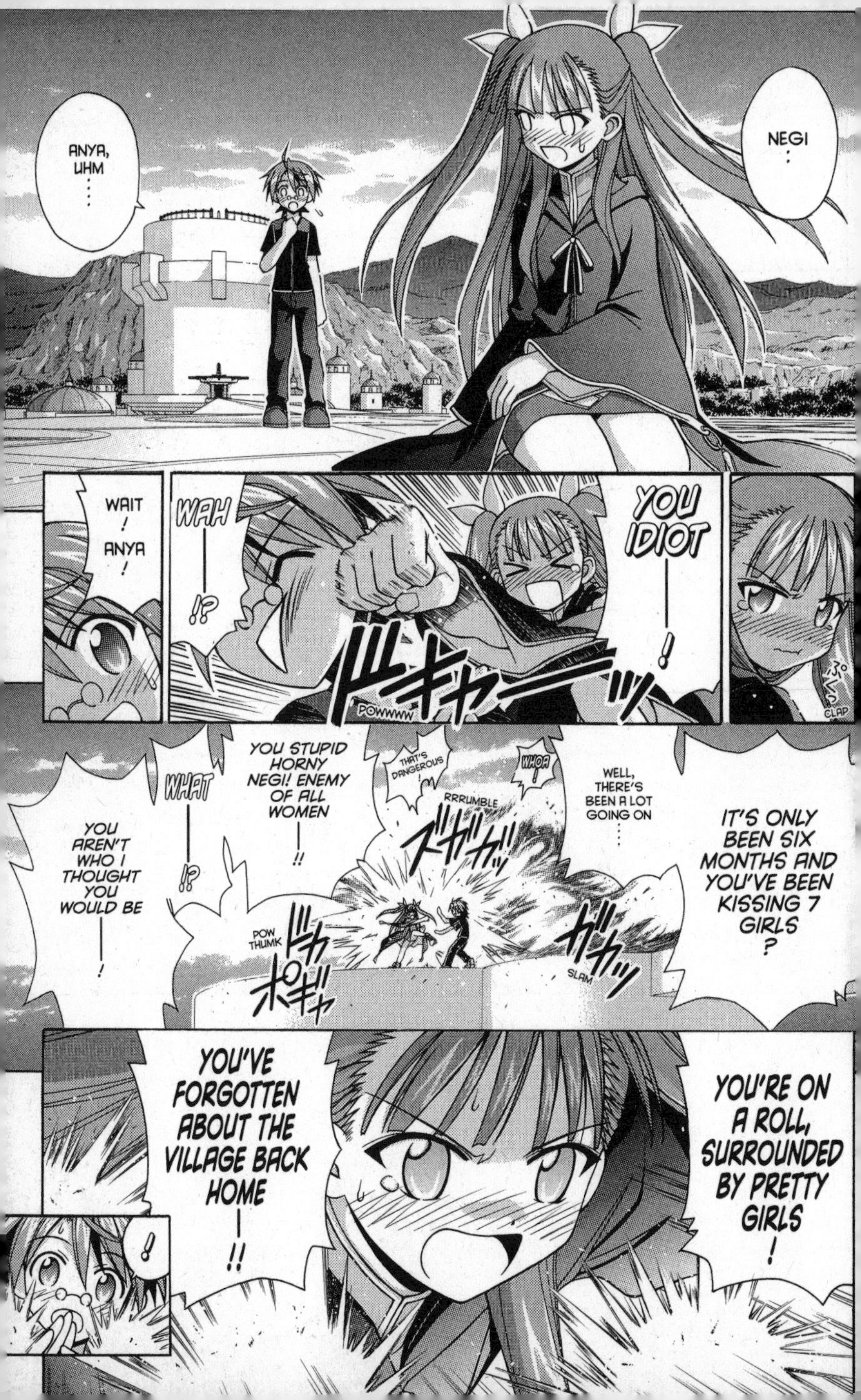
NEGI ...
ANYA, UHM ....
CLAP
YOU IDIOT —!
POWWWW
WAH —!?
WAIT! ANYA!
IT'S ONLY BEEN SIX MONTHS AND YOU'VE BEEN KISSING 7 GIRLS?
WELL, THERE'S BEEN A LOT GOING ON ...
WHOA!
THAT'S DANGEROUS!
RRRUMBLE
SLAM
YOU STUPID HORNY NEGI! ENEMY OF ALL WOMEN —!!
WHAT —!?
POW THUMK
YOU AREN'T WHO I THOUGHT YOU WOULD BE —!
YOU'RE ON A ROLL, SURROUNDED BY PRETTY GIRLS!
YOU'VE FORGOTTEN ABOUT THE VILLAGE BACK HOME —!!
!

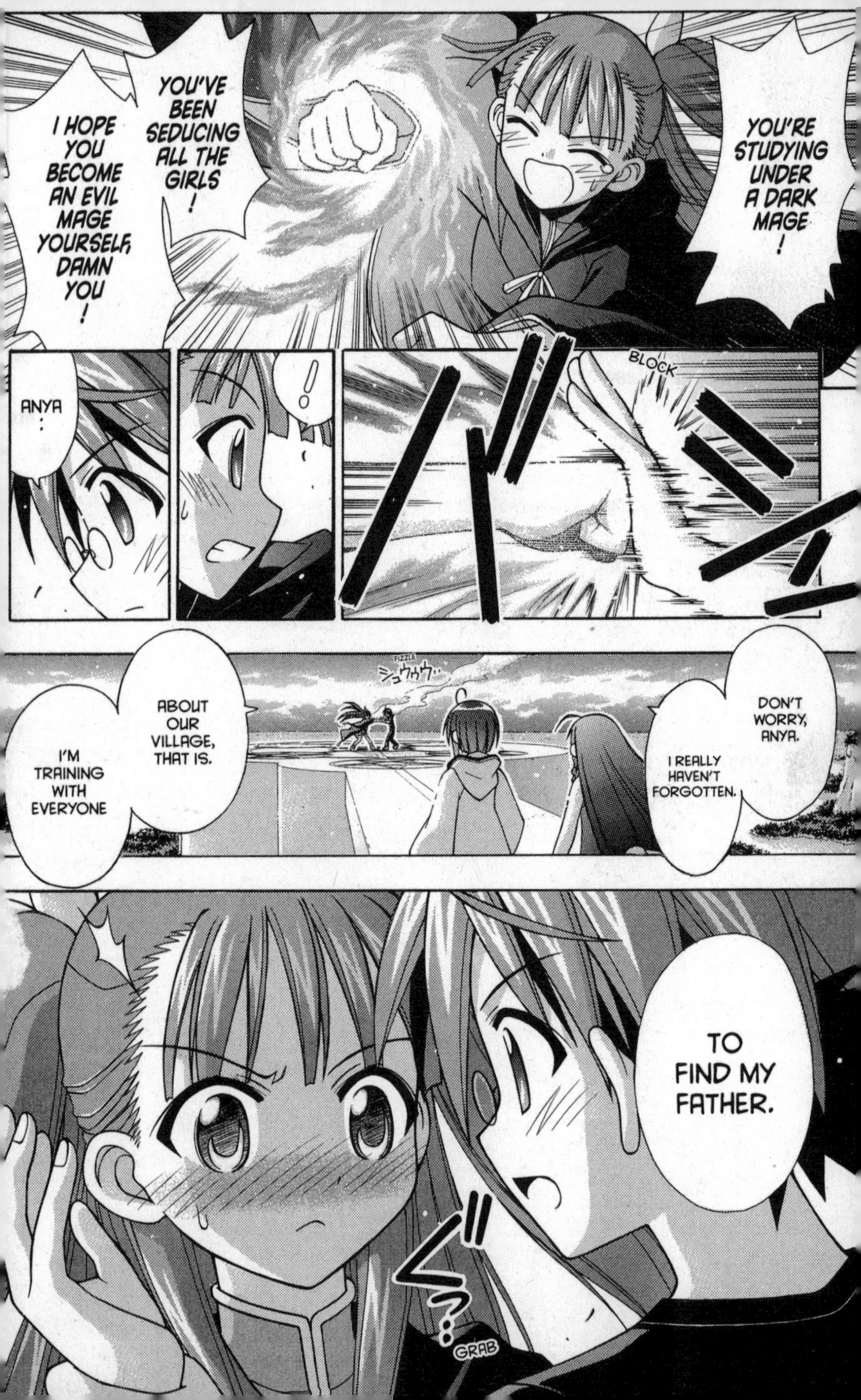
YOU'RE STUDYING UNDER A DARK MAGE!
YOU'VE BEEN SEDUCING ALL THE GIRLS!
I HOPE YOU BECOME AN EVIL MAGE YOURSELF, DAMN YOU!
BLOCK
!
ANYA...
DON'T WORRY, ANYA.
I REALLY HAVEN'T FORGOTTEN.
FIZZLE
ABOUT OUR VILLAGE, THAT IS.
I'M TRAINING WITH EVERYONE
TO FIND MY FATHER.
GRAB

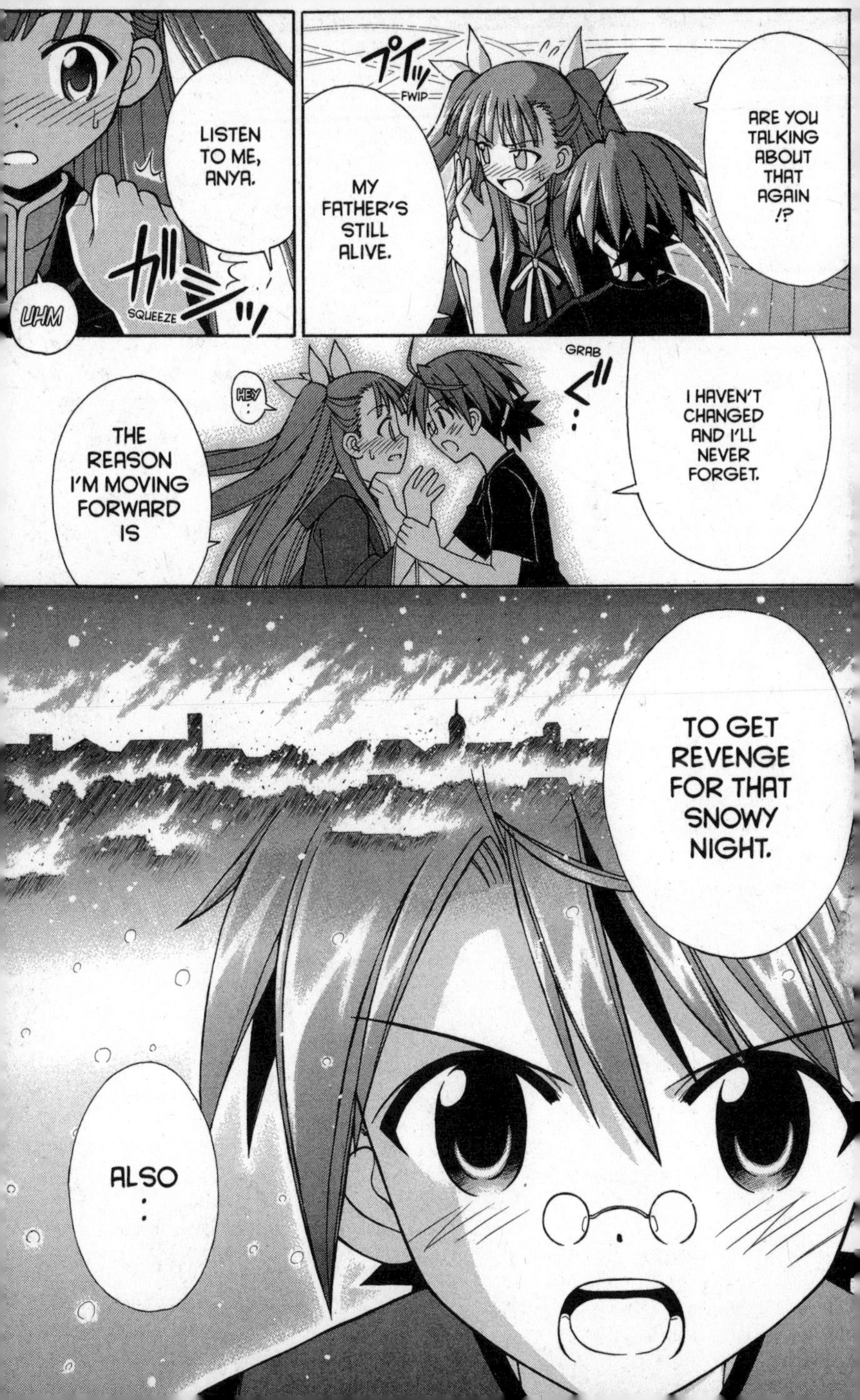
ARE YOU TALKING ABOUT THAT AGAIN !?
FWIP
MY FATHER'S STILL ALIVE.
LISTEN TO ME, ANYA.
UHM
SQUEEZE
GRAB
I HAVEN'T CHANGED AND I'LL NEVER FORGET.
HEY
THE REASON I'M MOVING FORWARD IS
TO GET REVENGE FOR THAT SNOWY NIGHT.
ALSO

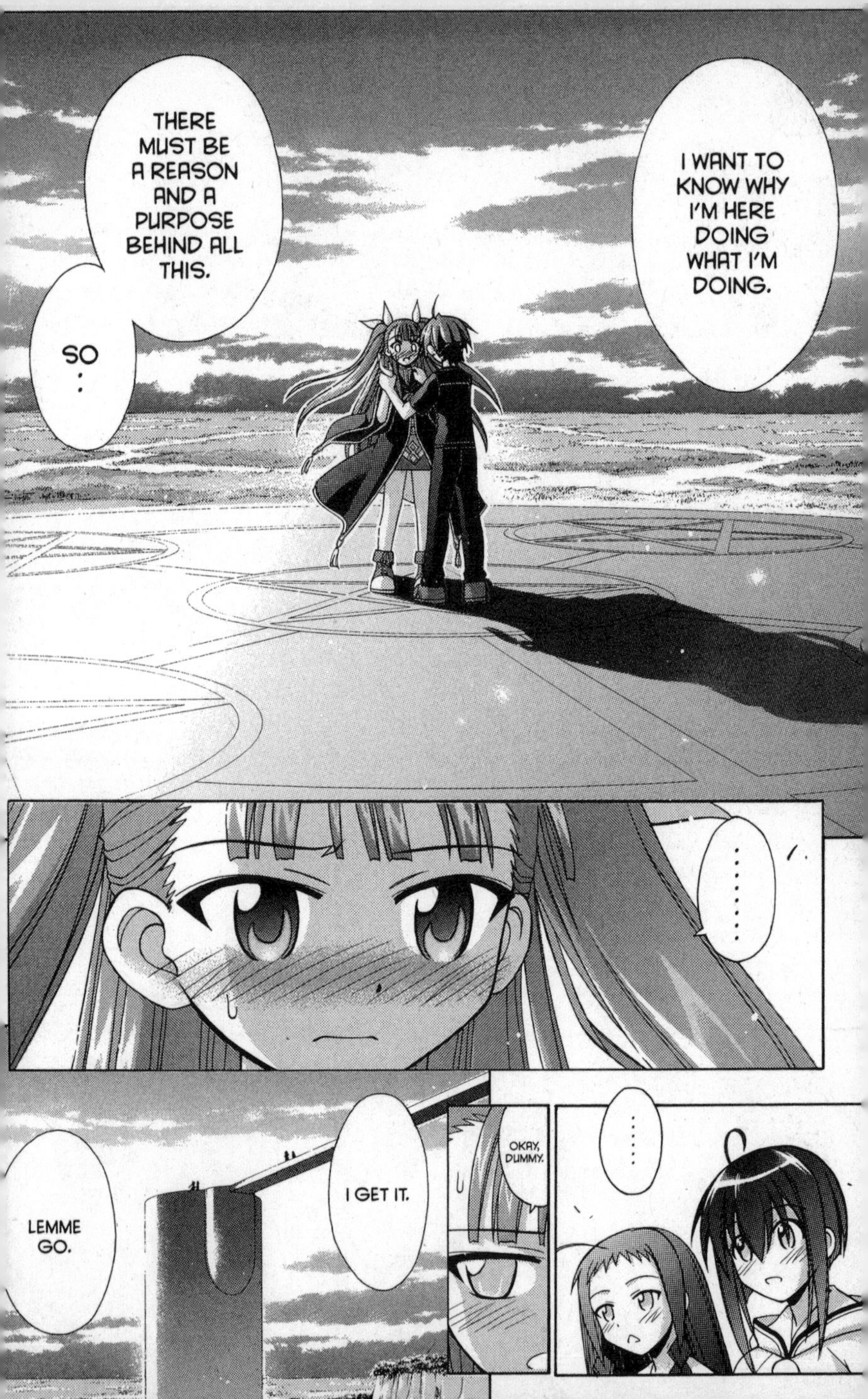
I WANT TO KNOW WHY I'M HERE DOING WHAT I'M DOING.
THERE MUST BE A REASON AND A PURPOSE BEHIND ALL THIS.
SO...
......
......
OKAY, DUMMY.
I GET IT.
LEMME GO.

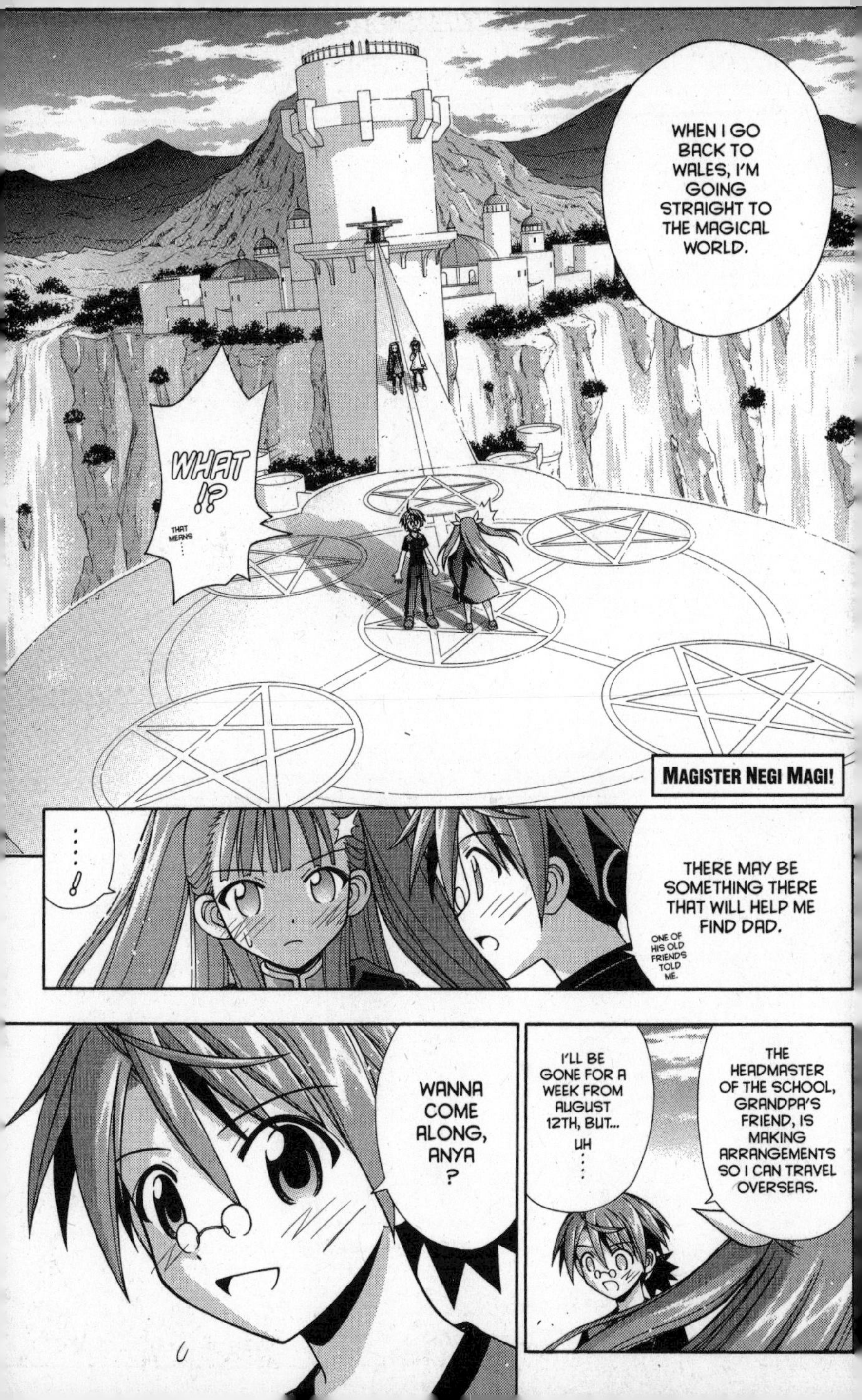
WHEN I GO BACK TO WALES, I'M GOING STRAIGHT TO THE MAGICAL WORLD.
WHAT!?
THAT MEANS....
MAGISTER NEGI MAGI!
THERE MAY BE SOMETHING THERE THAT WILL HELP ME FIND DAD.
ONE OF HIS OLD FRIENDS TOLD ME.
....!
THE HEADMASTER OF THE SCHOOL, GRANDPA'S FRIEND, IS MAKING ARRANGEMENTS SO I CAN TRAVEL OVERSEAS.
I'LL BE GONE FOR A WEEK FROM AUGUST 12TH, BUT... UH....
WANNA COME ALONG, ANYA?

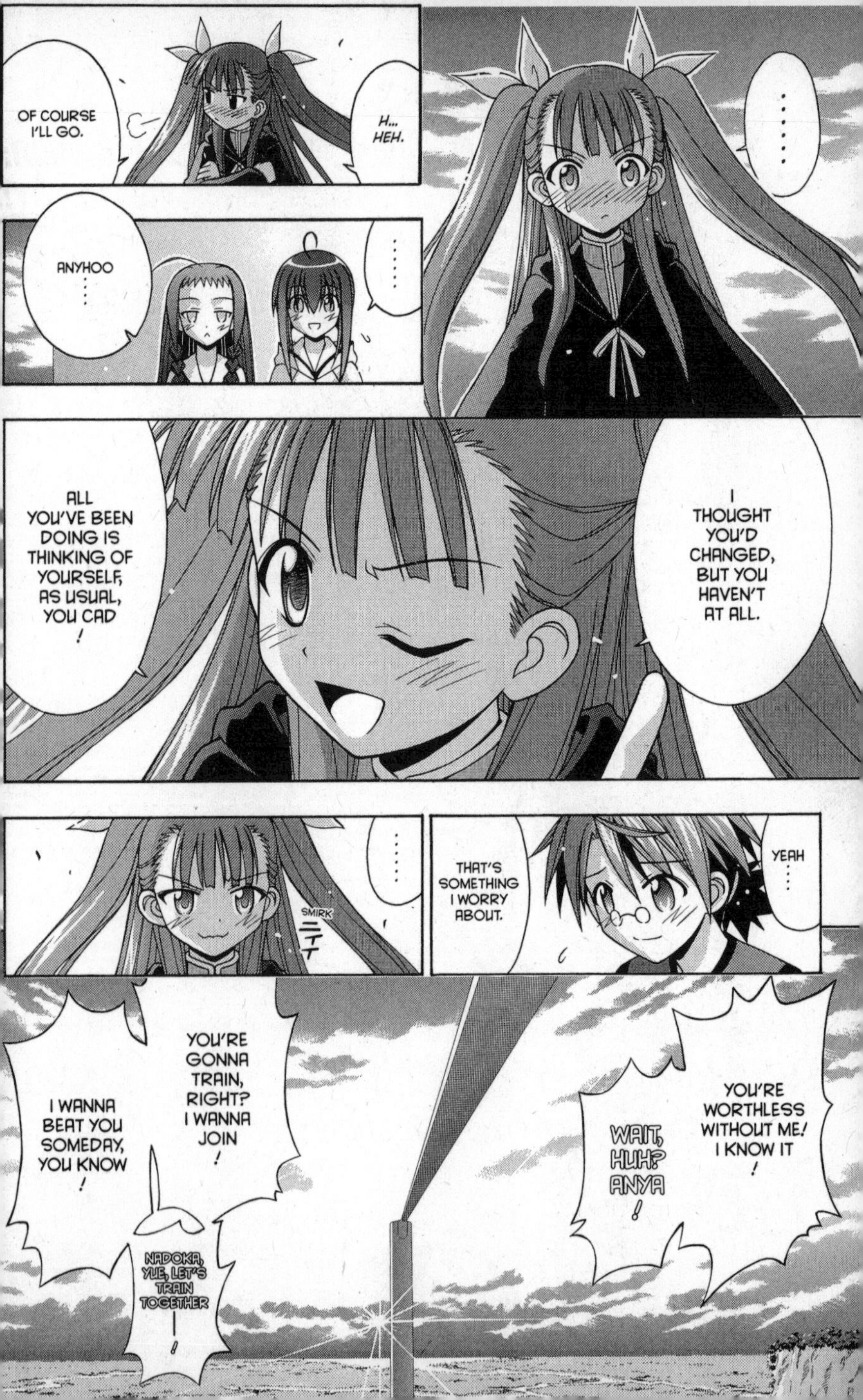
......
H... HEH.
OF COURSE I'LL GO.
......
ANYHOO ......
I THOUGHT YOU'D CHANGED, BUT YOU HAVEN'T AT ALL.
ALL YOU'VE BEEN DOING IS THINKING OF YOURSELF, AS USUAL, YOU CAD!
YEAH ......
THAT'S SOMETHING I WORRY ABOUT.
......
SMIRK
YOU'RE WORTHLESS WITHOUT ME! I KNOW IT!
WAIT, HUH? ANYA!
YOU'RE GONNA TRAIN, RIGHT? I WANNA JOIN!
I WANNA BEAT YOU SOMEDAY, YOU KNOW!
NADOKA, YUE, LET'S TRAIN TOGETHER—!

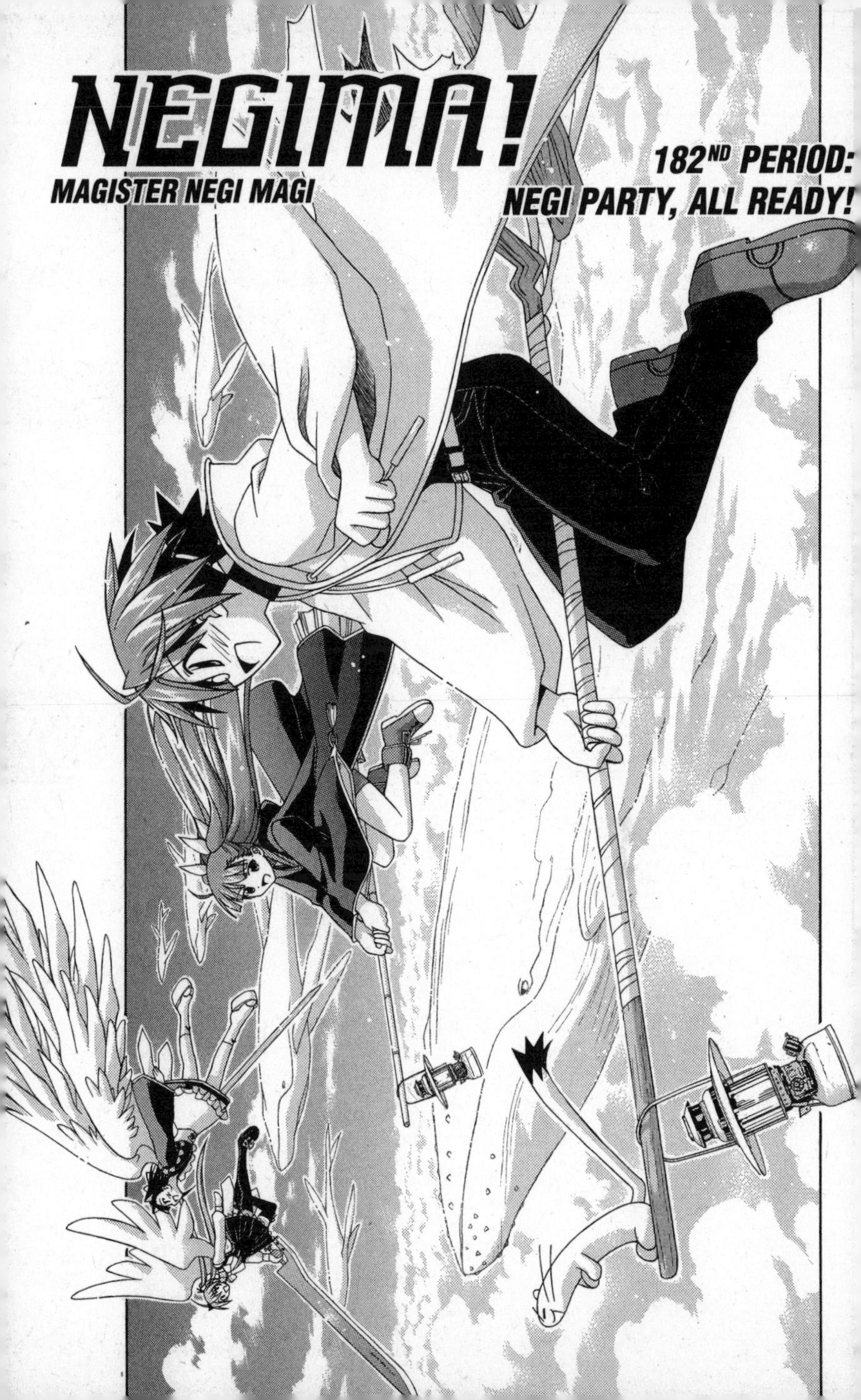
NEGIMA!
MAGISTER NEGI MAGI
182ND PERIOD:
NEGI PARTY, ALL READY!

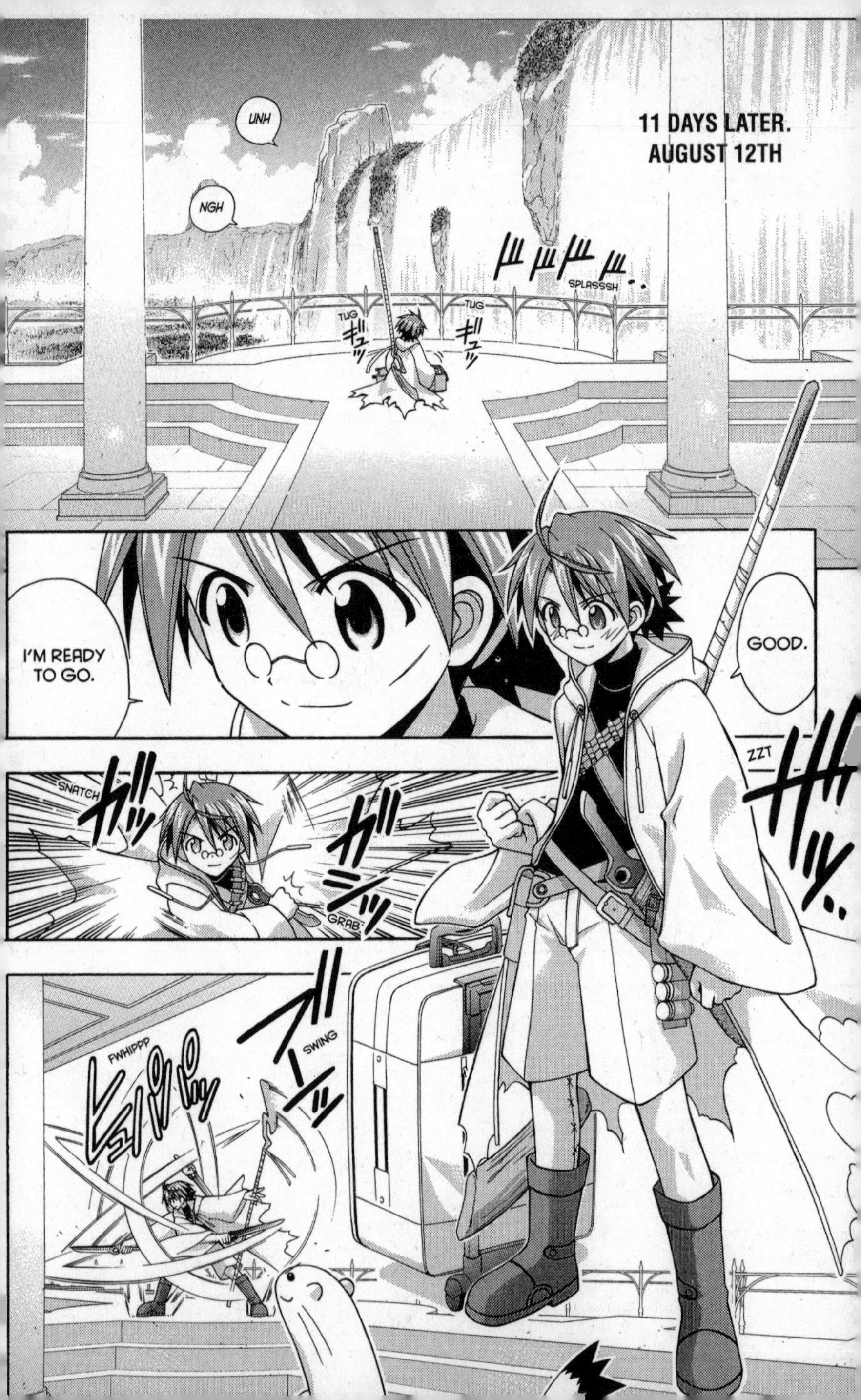
11 DAYS LATER. AUGUST 12TH
UNH
NGH
SPLASSSH
TUG
TUG
GOOD.
ZZT
I'M READY TO GO.
GRAB
SNATCH
SWING
FWHIPPP

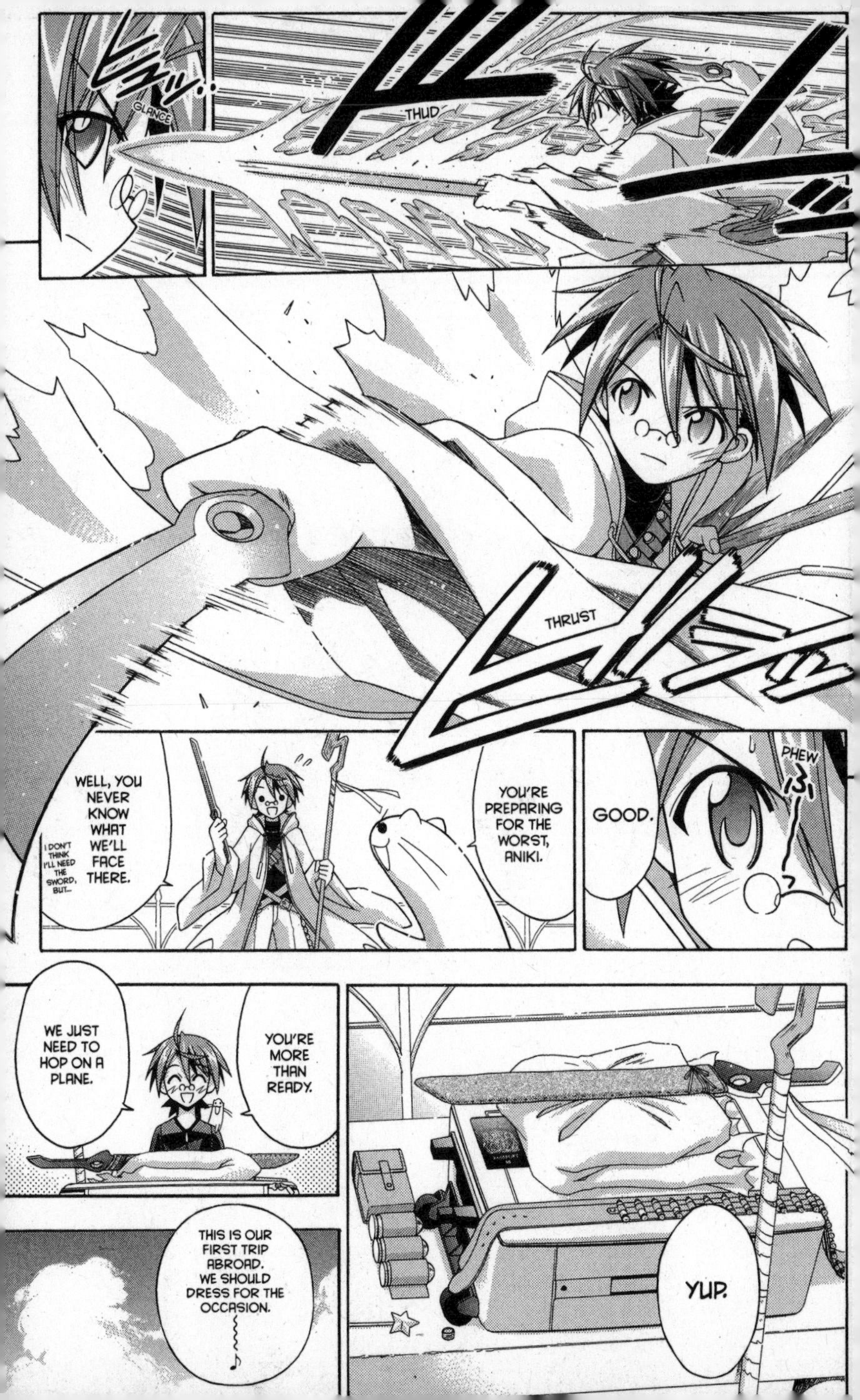
THUD
GLANCE
THRUST
PHEW
GOOD.
YOU'RE PREPARING FOR THE WORST, ANIKI.
WELL, YOU NEVER KNOW WHAT WE'LL FACE THERE.
I DON'T THINK I'LL NEED THE SWORD, BUT...
YUP.
YOU'RE MORE THAN READY.
WE JUST NEED TO HOP ON A PLANE.
THIS IS OUR FIRST TRIP ABROAD. WE SHOULD DRESS FOR THE OCCASION.

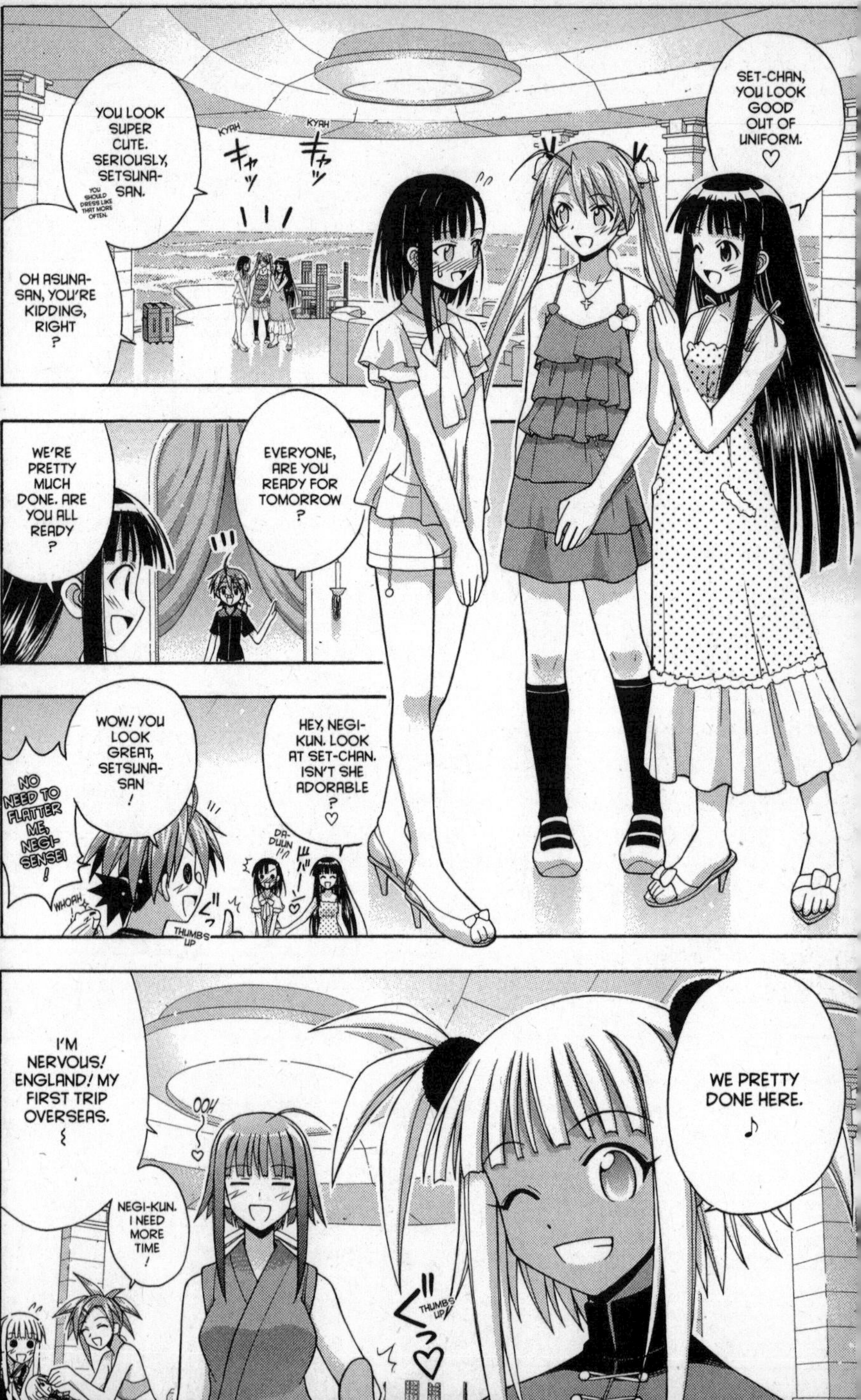
SET-CHAN, YOU LOOK GOOD OUT OF UNIFORM. ♡
KYAH
KYAH
YOU LOOK SUPER CUTE. SERIOUSLY, SETSUNA-SAN.
YOU SHOULD DRESS LIKE THAT MORE OFTEN.
OH ASUNA-SAN, YOU'RE KIDDING, RIGHT?
EVERYONE, ARE YOU READY FOR TOMORROW?
WE'RE PRETTY MUCH DONE. ARE YOU ALL READY?
HEY, NEGI-KUN. LOOK AT SET-CHAN. ISN'T SHE ADORABLE? ♡
DA-DUUN
WOW! YOU LOOK GREAT, SETSUNA-SAN!
THUMBS UP
WHOAH
NO NEED TO FLATTER ME, NEGI-SENSEI!
WE PRETTY DONE HERE. ♪
THUMBS UP
NEGI-KUN. I NEED MORE TIME!
OOH
I'M NERVOUS! ENGLAND! MY FIRST TRIP OVERSEAS.

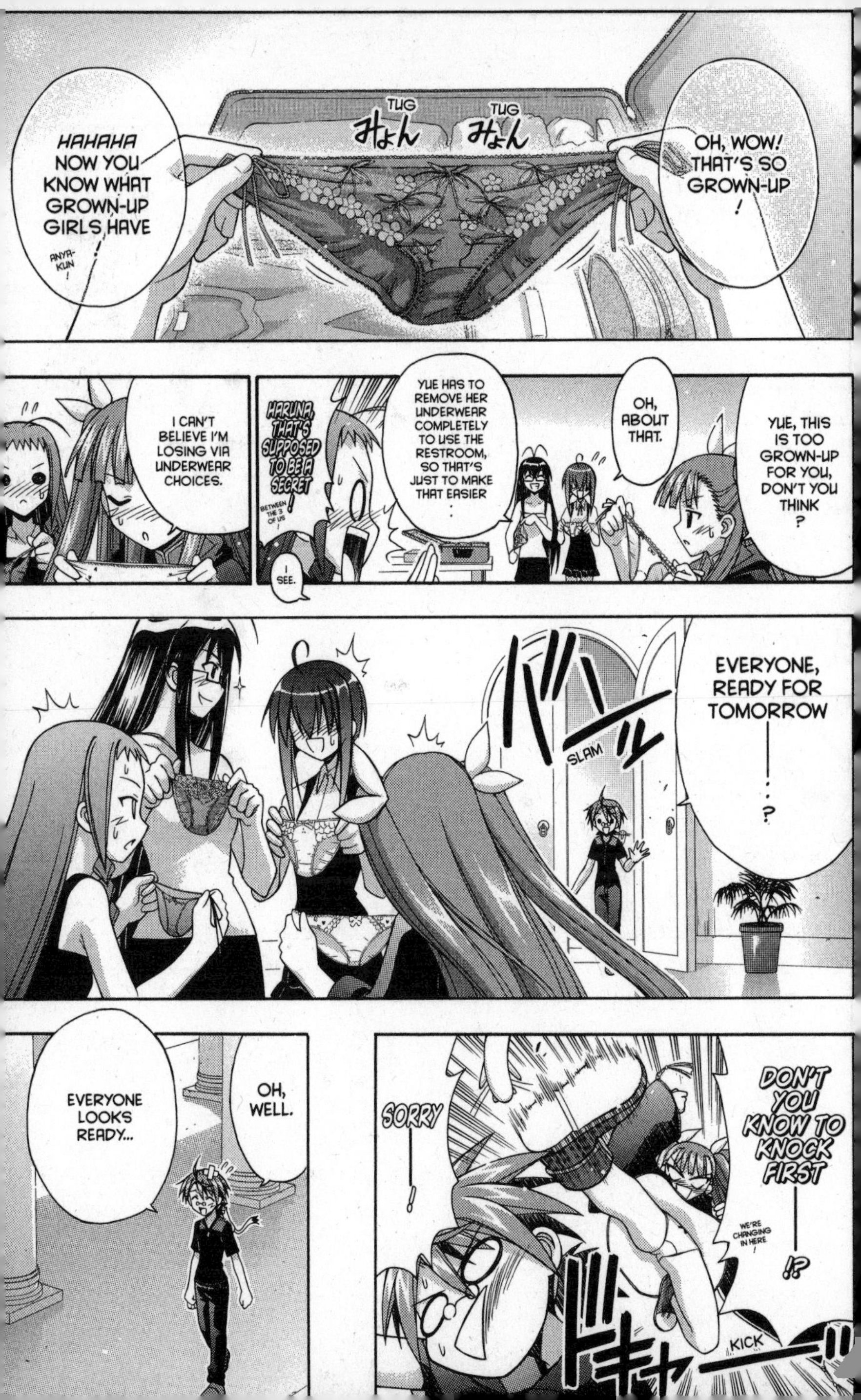
TUG
みょん
TUG
みょん
OH, WOW! THAT'S SO GROWN-UP!
HAHAHA NOW YOU KNOW WHAT GROWN-UP GIRLS HAVE!
ANYA-KUN!
YUE, THIS IS TOO GROWN-UP FOR YOU, DON'T YOU THINK?
OH, ABOUT THAT.
YUE HAS TO REMOVE HER UNDERWEAR COMPLETELY TO USE THE RESTROOM, SO THAT'S JUST TO MAKE THAT EASIER.
HARUNA, THAT'S SUPPOSED TO BE A SECRET!
BETWEEN THE 3 OF US!
I SEE.
I CAN'T BELIEVE I'M LOSING VIA UNDERWEAR CHOICES.
EVERYONE, READY FOR TOMORROW...?
SLAM
DON'T YOU KNOW TO KNOCK FIRST!?
WE'RE CHANGING IN HERE!
SORRY!
KICK
OH, WELL.
EVERYONE LOOKS READY...

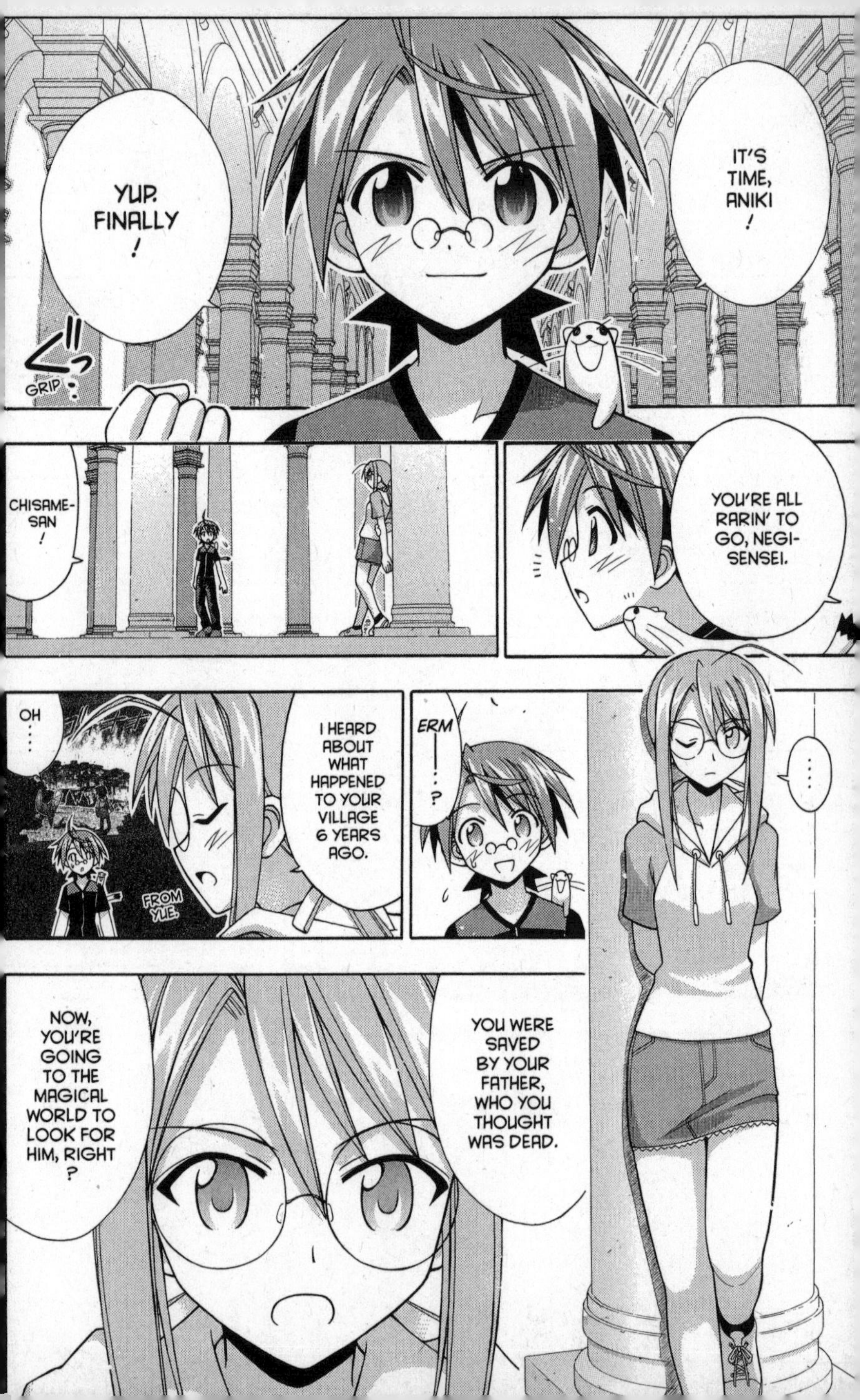
IT'S TIME, ANIKI!
YUP. FINALLY!
GRIP
YOU'RE ALL RARIN' TO GO, NEGI-SENSEI.
CHISAME-SAN!
......
ERM...?
I HEARD ABOUT WHAT HAPPENED TO YOUR VILLAGE 6 YEARS AGO.
OH......
FROM YUE.
YOU WERE SAVED BY YOUR FATHER, WHO YOU THOUGHT WAS DEAD.
NOW, YOU'RE GOING TO THE MAGICAL WORLD TO LOOK FOR HIM, RIGHT?

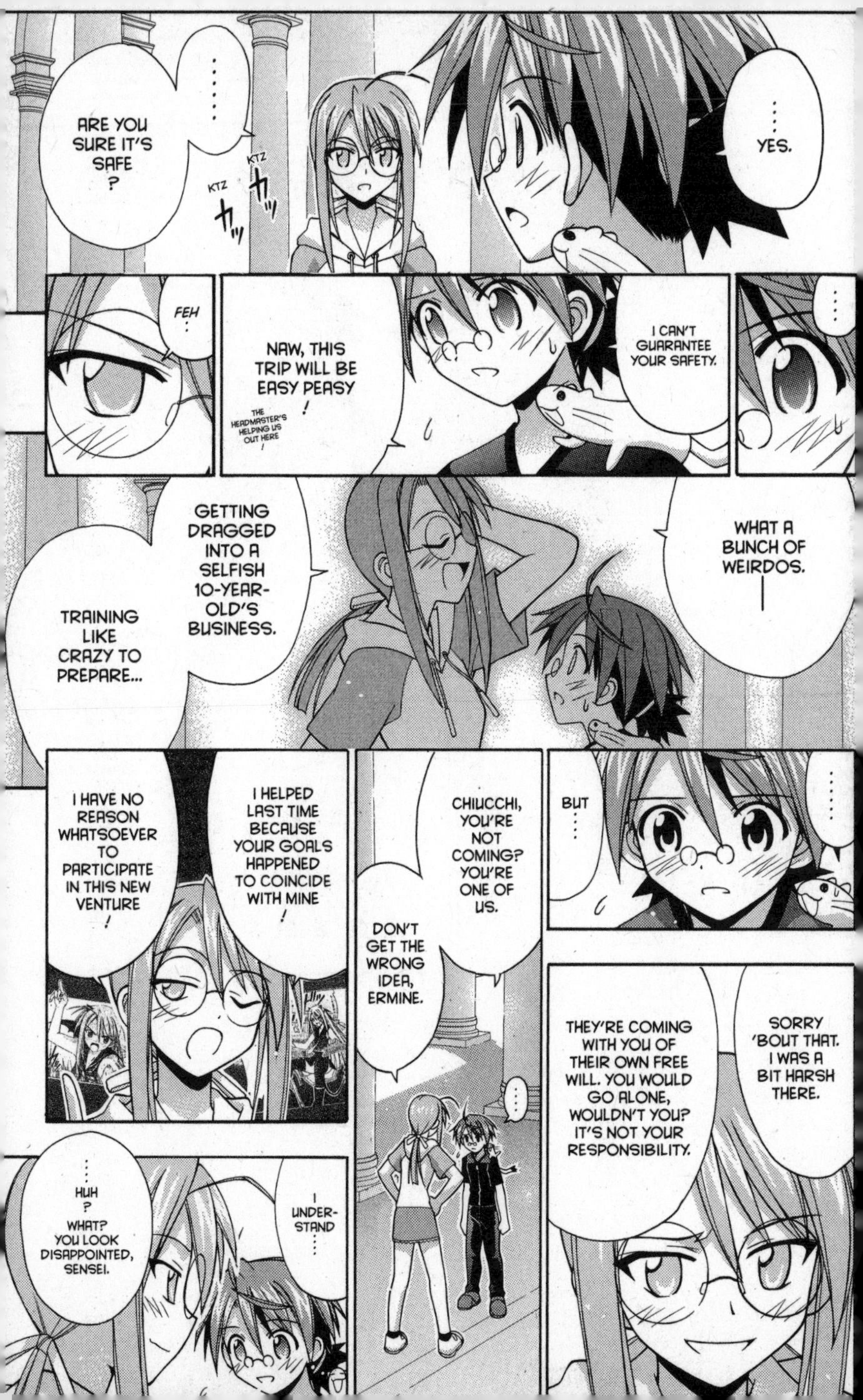
...YES.
......
ARE YOU SURE IT'S SAFE?
KTZ
KTZ
...
I CAN'T GUARANTEE YOUR SAFETY.
NAW, THIS TRIP WILL BE EASY PEASY!
THE HEADMASTER'S HELPING US OUT HERE!
FEH...
WHAT A BUNCH OF WEIRDOS—
GETTING DRAGGED INTO A SELFISH 10-YEAR-OLD'S BUSINESS.
TRAINING LIKE CRAZY TO PREPARE...
....
BUT....
SORRY 'BOUT THAT. I WAS A BIT HARSH THERE.
THEY'RE COMING WITH YOU OF THEIR OWN FREE WILL. YOU WOULD GO ALONE, WOULDN'T YOU? IT'S NOT YOUR RESPONSIBILITY.
CHIUCCHI, YOU'RE NOT COMING? YOU'RE ONE OF US.
DON'T GET THE WRONG IDEA, ERMINE.
...
I HELPED LAST TIME BECAUSE YOUR GOALS HAPPENED TO COINCIDE WITH MINE!
I HAVE NO REASON WHATSOEVER TO PARTICIPATE IN THIS NEW VENTURE!
I UNDERSTAND....
...HUH? WHAT? YOU LOOK DISAPPOINTED, SENSEI.

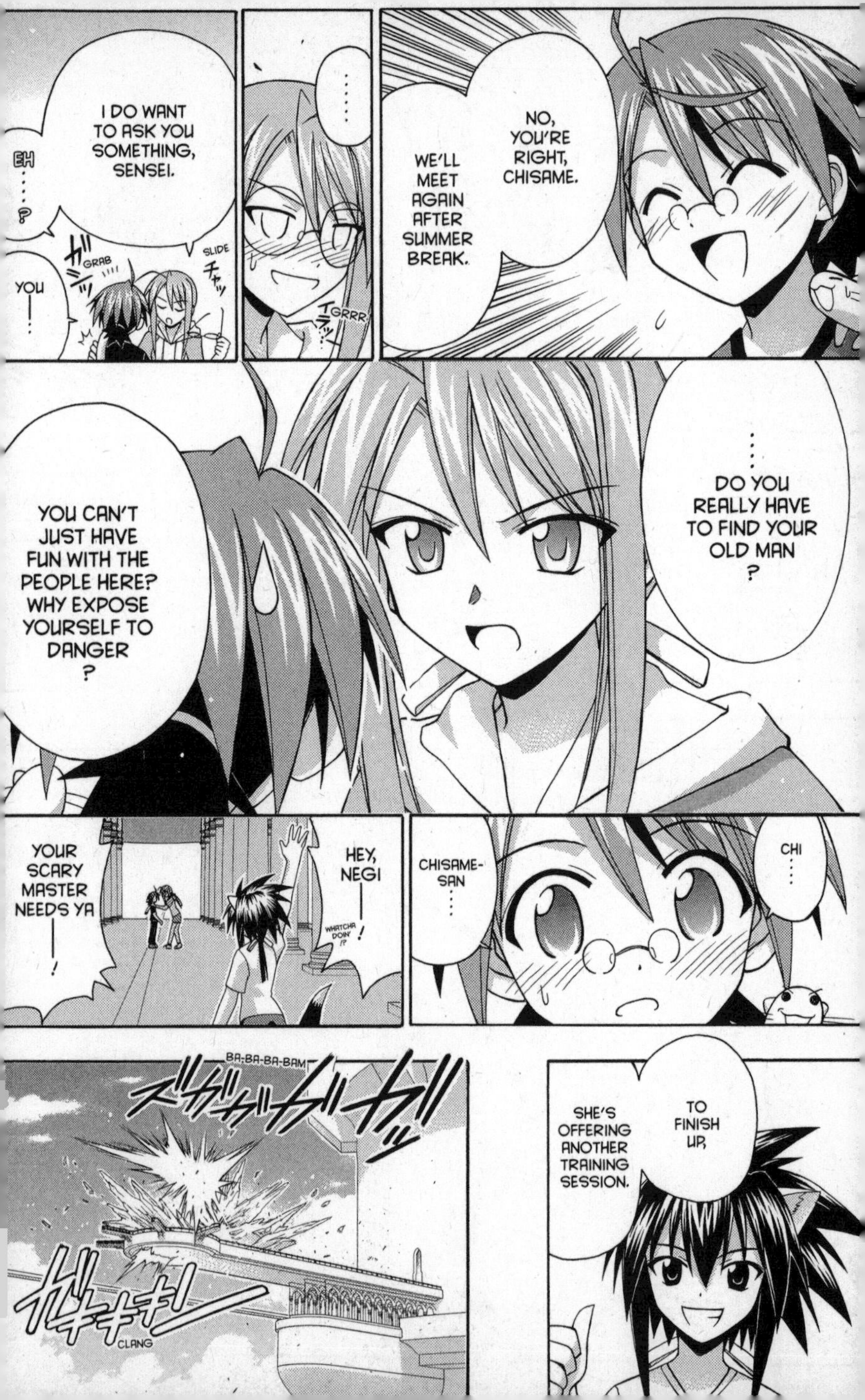
NO, YOU'RE RIGHT, CHISAME.
WE'LL MEET AGAIN AFTER SUMMER BREAK.
GRRR
......
I DO WANT TO ASK YOU SOMETHING, SENSEI.
EH....?
SLIDE
GRAB
YOU—...
...... DO YOU REALLY HAVE TO FIND YOUR OLD MAN?
YOU CAN'T JUST HAVE FUN WITH THE PEOPLE HERE? WHY EXPOSE YOURSELF TO DANGER?
CHI......
CHISAME-SAN......
HEY, NEGI—!
WHATCHA DOIN' !?
YOUR SCARY MASTER NEEDS YA—!
TO FINISH UP,
SHE'S OFFERING ANOTHER TRAINING SESSION.
BA-BA-BA-BAM
CLANG

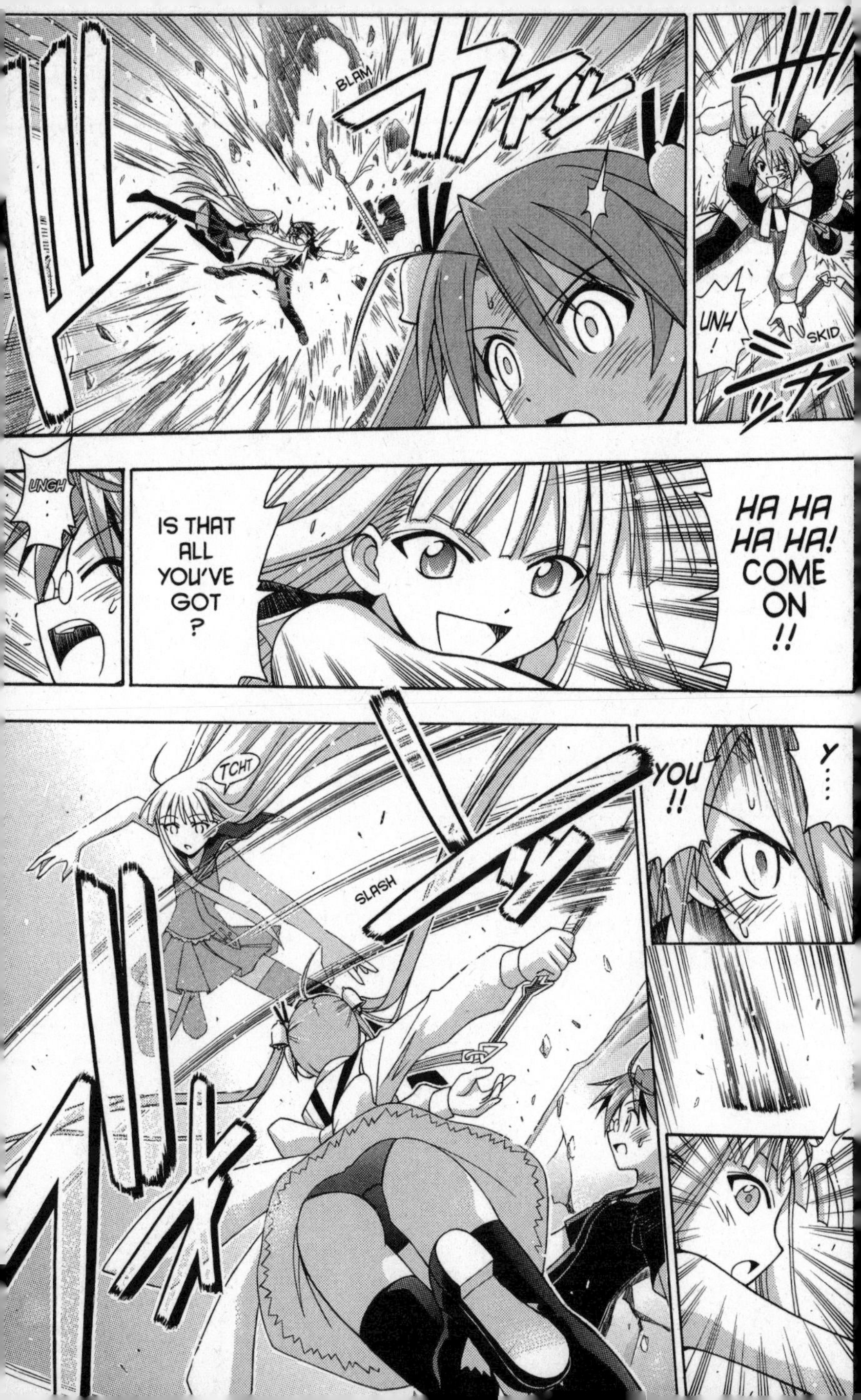
UNH !
SKID
BLAM
HA HA HA HA! COME ON !!
IS THAT ALL YOU'VE GOT ?
UNGH
Y....
YOU !!
TCHT
SLASH

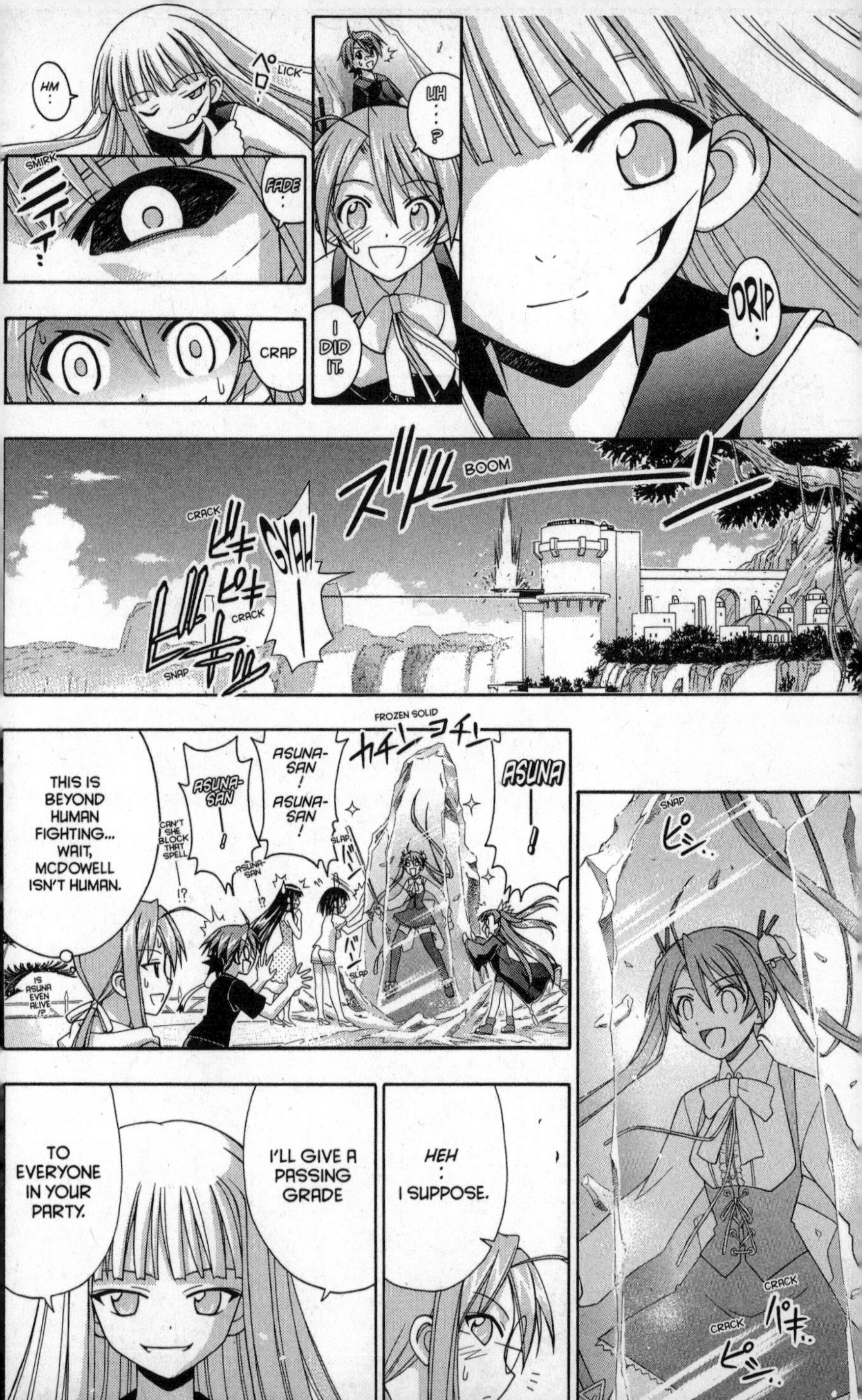
DRIP...
UH...?
I DID IT.
HM...
LICK
SMIRK
FADE...
CRAP
BOOM
GYAH!
CRACK
CRACK
SNAP
SNAP
CRACK
CRACK
ASUNA!
FROZEN SOLID
ASUNA-SAN! ASUNA-SAN!
ASUNA-SAN!
SLAP
SLAP
CAN'T SHE BLOCK THAT SPELL!?
ASUNA-SAN!?
THIS IS BEYOND HUMAN FIGHTING... WAIT, MCDOWELL ISN'T HUMAN.
IS ASUNA EVEN ALIVE!?
HEH I SUPPOSE.
I'LL GIVE A PASSING GRADE
TO EVERYONE IN YOUR PARTY.

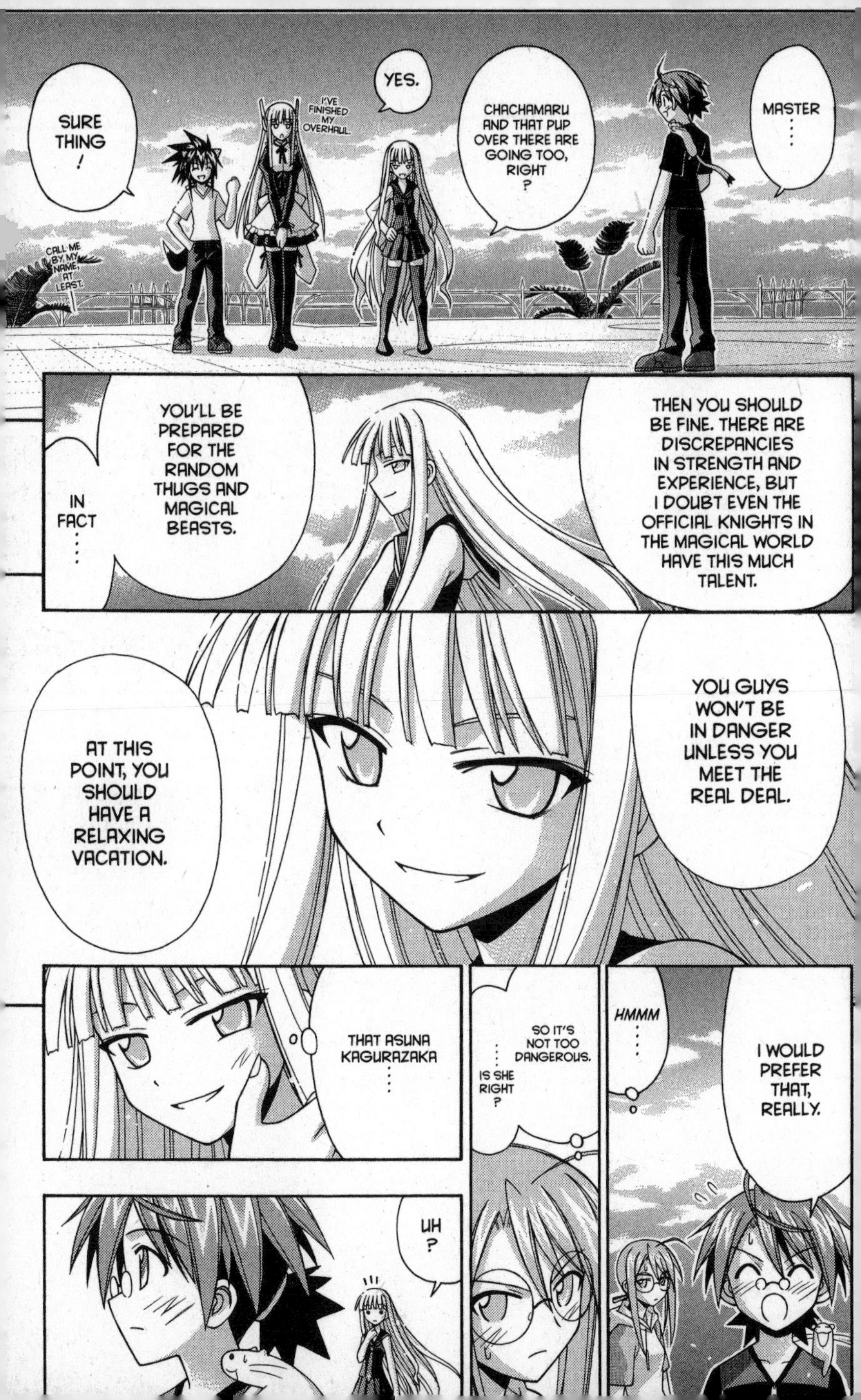
MASTER . . .
CHACHAMARU AND THAT PUP OVER THERE ARE GOING TOO, RIGHT?
YES.
I'VE FINISHED MY OVERHAUL.
SURE THING!
CALL ME BY MY NAME, AT LEAST.
THEN YOU SHOULD BE FINE. THERE ARE DISCREPANCIES IN STRENGTH AND EXPERIENCE, BUT I DOUBT EVEN THE OFFICIAL KNIGHTS IN THE MAGICAL WORLD HAVE THIS MUCH TALENT.
YOU'LL BE PREPARED FOR THE RANDOM THUGS AND MAGICAL BEASTS.
IN FACT . . .
YOU GUYS WON'T BE IN DANGER UNLESS YOU MEET THE REAL DEAL.
AT THIS POINT, YOU SHOULD HAVE A RELAXING VACATION.
I WOULD PREFER THAT, REALLY.
HMMM . . .
SO IT'S NOT TOO DANGEROUS.
. . . IS SHE RIGHT?
THAT ASUNA KAGURAZAKA . . .
UH?

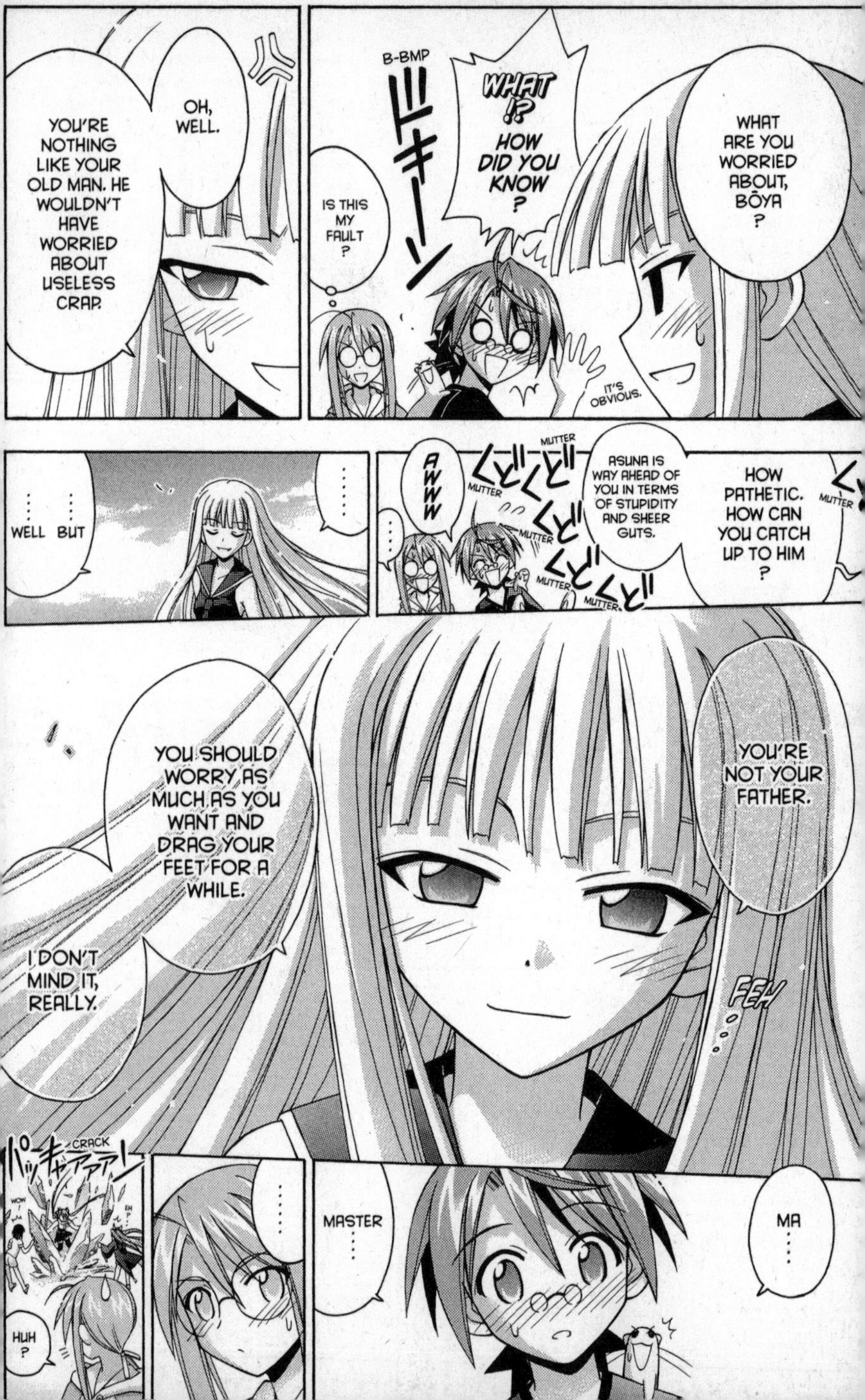
WHAT ARE YOU WORRIED ABOUT, BŌYA?
WHAT!? HOW DID YOU KNOW?
B-BMP
IS THIS MY FAULT?
IT'S OBVIOUS.
OH, WELL.
YOU'RE NOTHING LIKE YOUR OLD MAN. HE WOULDN'T HAVE WORRIED ABOUT USELESS CRAP.
HOW PATHETIC. HOW CAN YOU CATCH UP TO HIM?
MUTTER
ASUNA IS WAY AHEAD OF YOU IN TERMS OF STUPIDITY AND SHEER GUTS.
MUTTER
MUTTER
MUTTER
MUTTER
MUTTER
AWWW
...
......
...WELL ...BUT
YOU'RE NOT YOUR FATHER.
FEH
YOU SHOULD WORRY AS MUCH AS YOU WANT AND DRAG YOUR FEET FOR A WHILE.
I DON'T MIND IT, REALLY.
MA......
MASTER......
......
CRACK
EH?
WOW!
HUH?

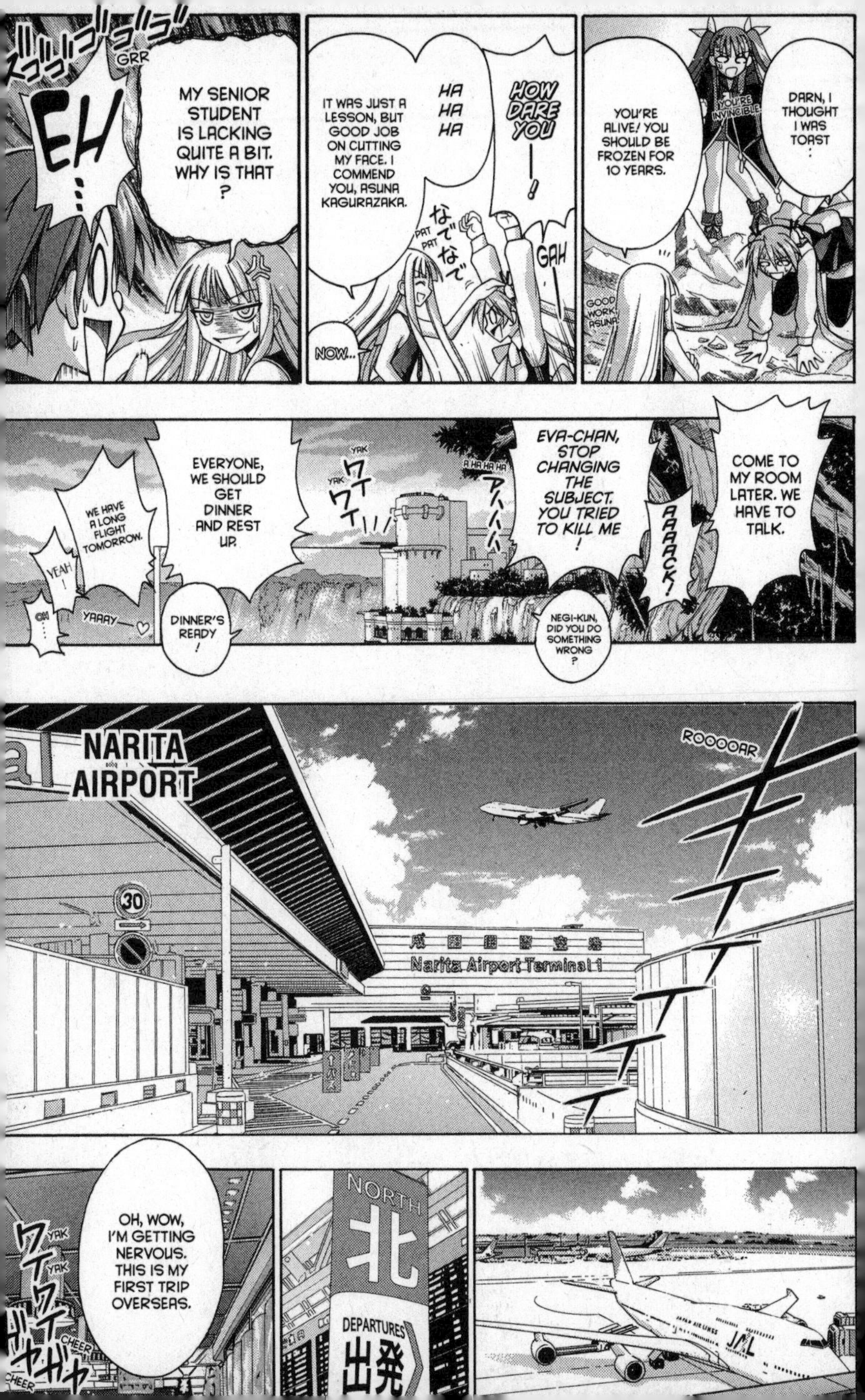
DARN, I THOUGHT I WAS TOAST :
YOU'RE INVINCIBLE
YOU'RE ALIVE! YOU SHOULD BE FROZEN FOR 10 YEARS.
GOOD WORK ASUNA
HOW DARE YOU —!
HA HA HA
IT WAS JUST A LESSON, BUT GOOD JOB ON CUTTING MY FACE. I COMMEND YOU, ASUNA KAGURAZAKA.
なでなで
PAT PAT
GAH
NOW...
GRR
MY SENIOR STUDENT IS LACKING QUITE A BIT. WHY IS THAT ?
EH...
COME TO MY ROOM LATER. WE HAVE TO TALK.
AAAACK!
EVA-CHAN, STOP CHANGING THE SUBJECT. YOU TRIED TO KILL ME !
A HA HA HA
アハハハ
NEGI-KUN, DID YOU DO SOMETHING WRONG ?
YAK YAK
ワイワイ
EVERYONE, WE SHOULD GET DINNER AND REST UP.
DINNER'S READY !
WE HAVE A LONG FLIGHT TOMORROW.
YEAH !
YAAAY♡
OH.....
ROOOOAR
キイイイイイ
NARITA AIRPORT
30
成田国際空港
Narita Airport Terminal 1
JAPAN AIRLINES
JAL
NORTH
北
DEPARTURES
出発
OH, WOW, I'M GETTING NERVOUS. THIS IS MY FIRST TRIP OVERSEAS.
YAK YAK
ワイワイ
CHEER CHEER
ガヤガヤ

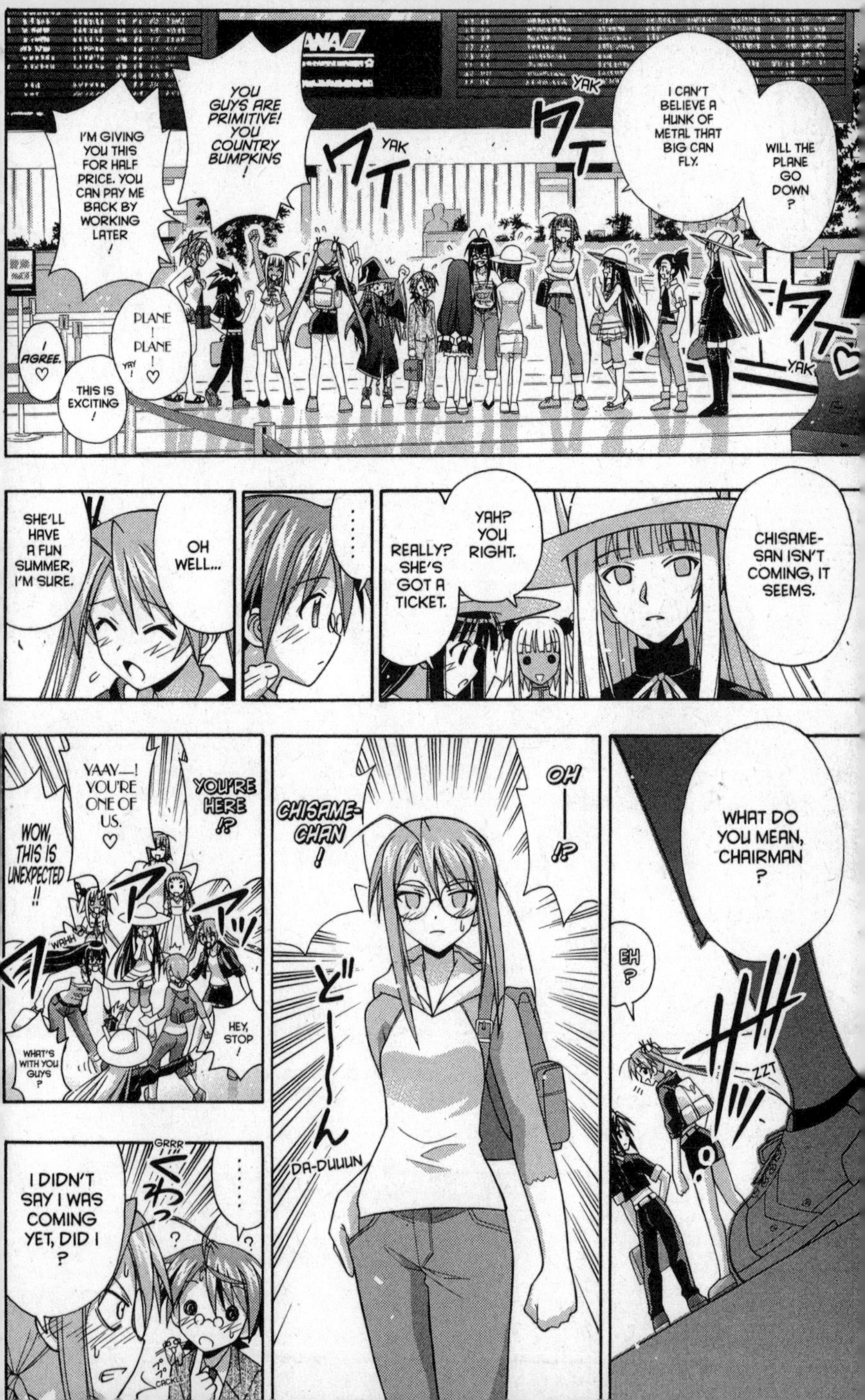
WILL THE PLANE GO DOWN?
YAK ♡
I CAN'T BELIEVE A HUNK OF METAL THAT BIG CAN FLY.
YAK
YAK
YOU GUYS ARE PRIMITIVE! YOU COUNTRY BUMPKINS!
I'M GIVING YOU THIS FOR HALF PRICE. YOU CAN PAY ME BACK BY WORKING LATER!
PLANE! PLANE! ♡
YAY!
I AGREE. ♡
THIS IS EXCITING!
CHISAME-SAN ISN'T COMING, IT SEEMS.
YAH? YOU RIGHT.
REALLY? SHE'S GOT A TICKET.
......
OH WELL...
SHE'LL HAVE A FUN SUMMER, I'M SURE.
WHAT DO YOU MEAN, CHAIRMAN?
EH?
ZZT
OH—!?
CHISAME-CHAN!
DA-DUUUN
YOU'RE HERE!?
YAAY—! YOU'RE ONE OF US. ♡
WOW, THIS IS UNEXPECTED!!
WAHH
HEY, STOP!
WHAT'S WITH YOU GUYS?
......
GRRR
I DIDN'T SAY I WAS COMING YET, DID I?
CRACKLE

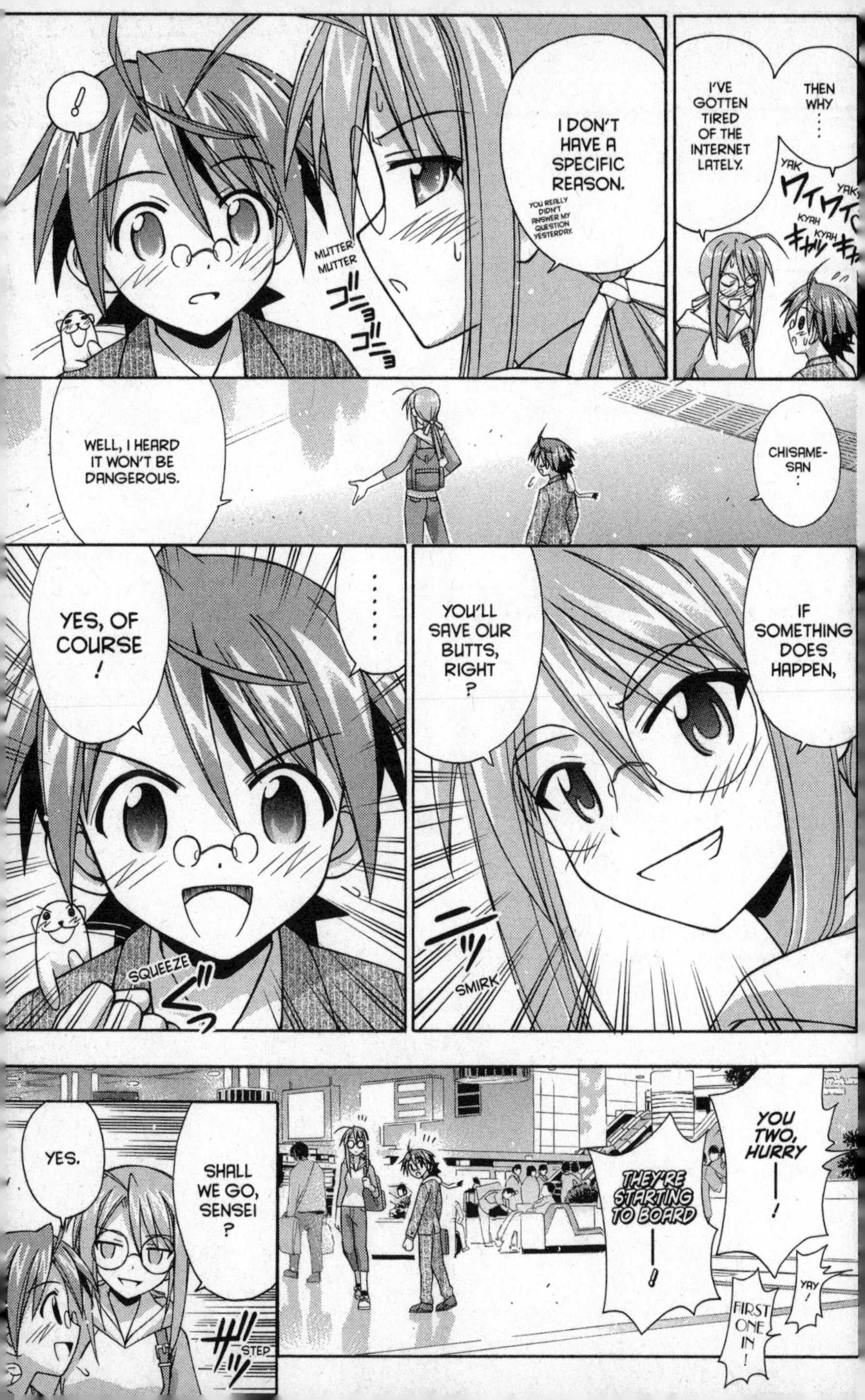
THEN WHY...
I'VE GOTTEN TIRED OF THE INTERNET LATELY.
YAK YAK
KYAH KYAH
I DON'T HAVE A SPECIFIC REASON.
YOU REALLY DIDN'T ANSWER MY QUESTION YESTERDAY.
MUTTER MUTTER
!
CHISAME-SAN...
WELL, I HEARD IT WON'T BE DANGEROUS.
IF SOMETHING DOES HAPPEN,
YOU'LL SAVE OUR BUTTS, RIGHT?
SMIRK
......
YES, OF COURSE!
SQUEEZE
YOU TWO, HURRY—!
THEY'RE STARTING TO BOARD—!
YAY!
FIRST ONE IN!
SHALL WE GO, SENSEI?
YES.
STEP

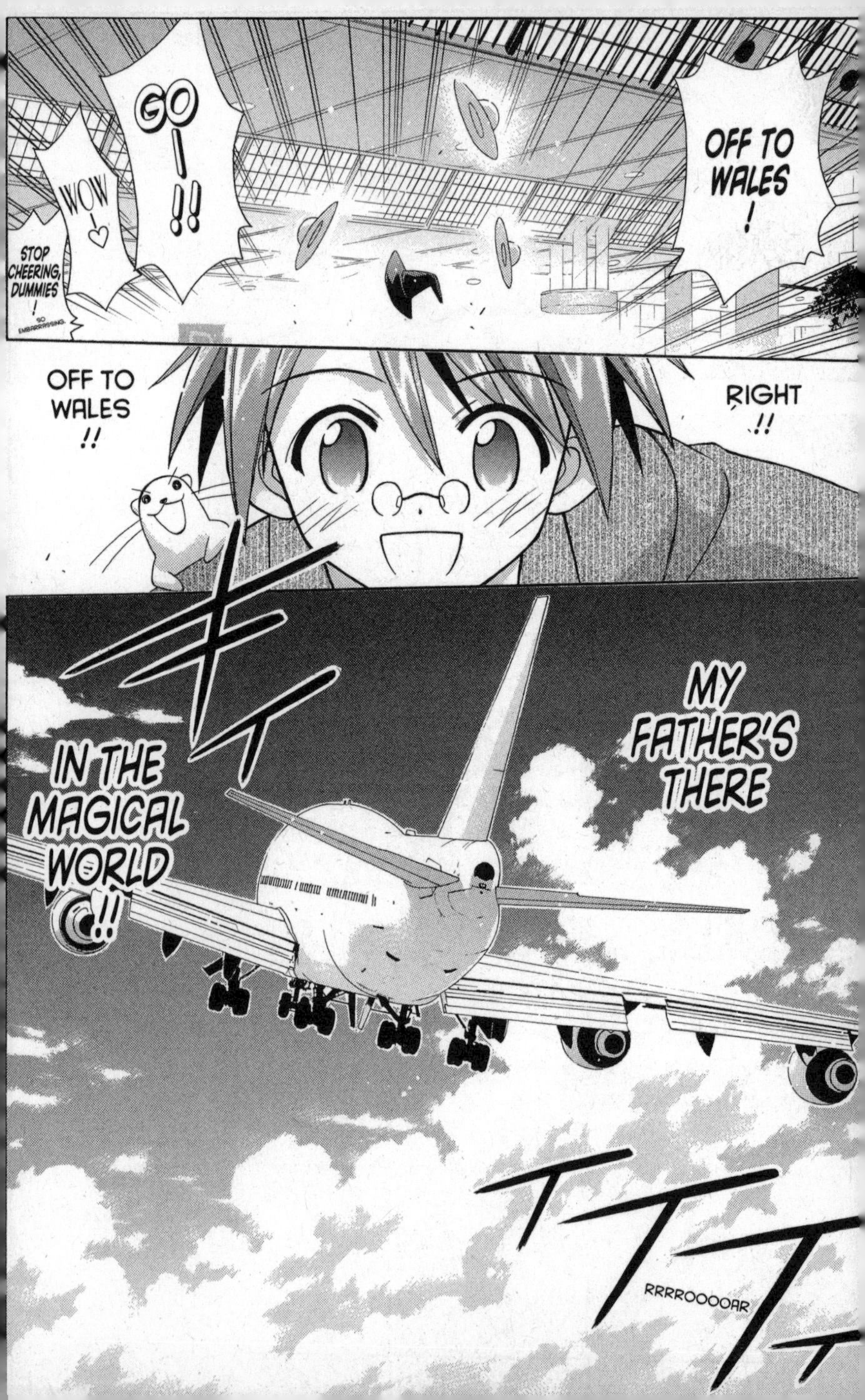
OFF TO WALES!
GO!!
WOW♡
STOP CHEERING, DUMMIES!
SO EMBARRRASSING.
RIGHT!!
OFF TO WALES!!
MY FATHER'S THERE
IN THE MAGICAL WORLD!!
RRRROOOOAR

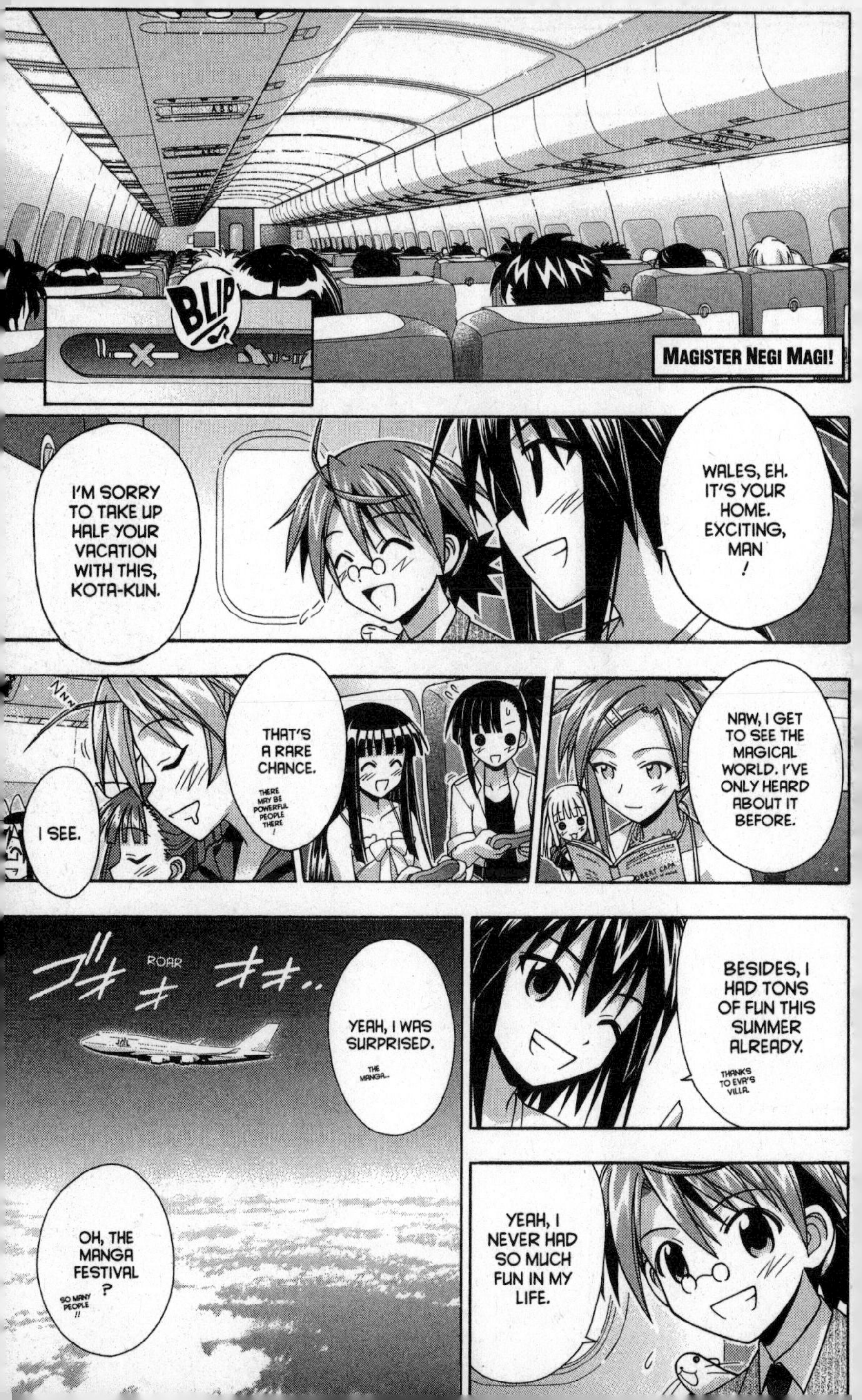
BLIP
MAGISTER NEGI MAGI!
WALES, EH. IT'S YOUR HOME. EXCITING, MAN!
I'M SORRY TO TAKE UP HALF YOUR VACATION WITH THIS, KOTA-KUN.
NAW, I GET TO SEE THE MAGICAL WORLD. I'VE ONLY HEARD ABOUT IT BEFORE.
THAT'S A RARE CHANCE.
THERE MAY BE POWERFUL PEOPLE THERE!
I SEE.
BESIDES, I HAD TONS OF FUN THIS SUMMER ALREADY.
THANKS TO EVA'S VILLA.
YEAH, I NEVER HAD SO MUCH FUN IN MY LIFE.
ゴオォォォ..
ROAR
YEAH, I WAS SURPRISED.
THE MANGA...
OH, THE MANGA FESTIVAL?
SO MANY PEOPLE!!

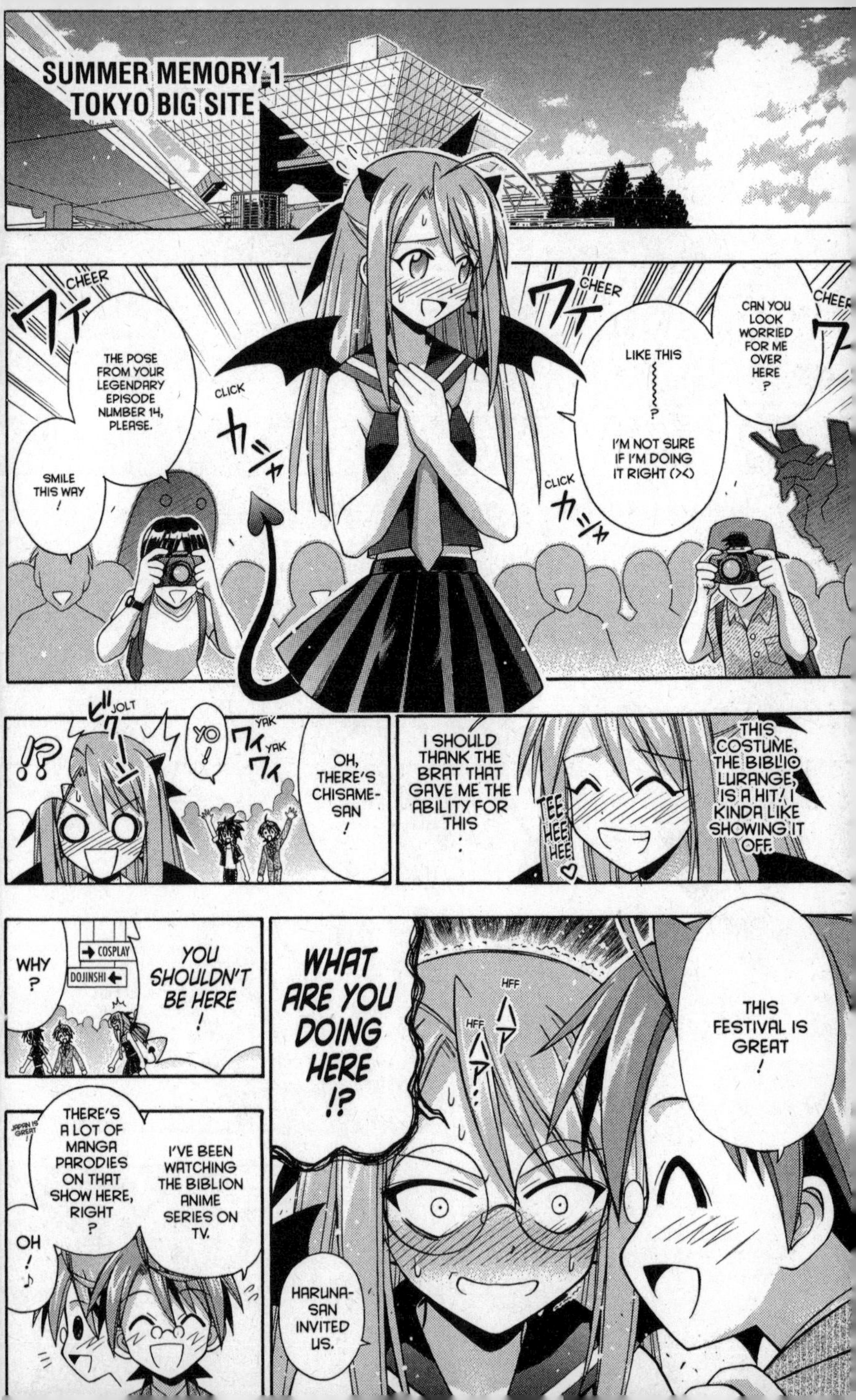
SUMMER MEMORY 1
TOKYO BIG SITE
CHEER
CAN YOU LOOK WORRIED FOR ME OVER HERE?
CHEER
LIKE THIS ~~~~?
I'M NOT SURE IF I'M DOING IT RIGHT (><)
CLICK
CLICK
THE POSE FROM YOUR LEGENDARY EPISODE NUMBER 14, PLEASE.
SMILE THIS WAY!
CHEER
THIS COSTUME, THE BIBLIO LURANGE, IS A HIT! I KINDA LIKE SHOWING IT OFF.
TEE HEE HEE
I SHOULD THANK THE BRAT THAT GAVE ME THE ABILITY FOR THIS...
OH, THERE'S CHISAME-SAN!
YAK YAK
YO!
JOLT
!?
THIS FESTIVAL IS GREAT!
HFF
HFF
WHAT ARE YOU DOING HERE!?
HARUNA-SAN INVITED US.
YOU SHOULDN'T BE HERE!
COSPLAY
DOJINSHI
WHY?
I'VE BEEN WATCHING THE BIBLION ANIME SERIES ON TV.
THERE'S A LOT OF MANGA PARODIES ON THAT SHOW HERE, RIGHT?
JAPAN IS GREAT!
OH!♪

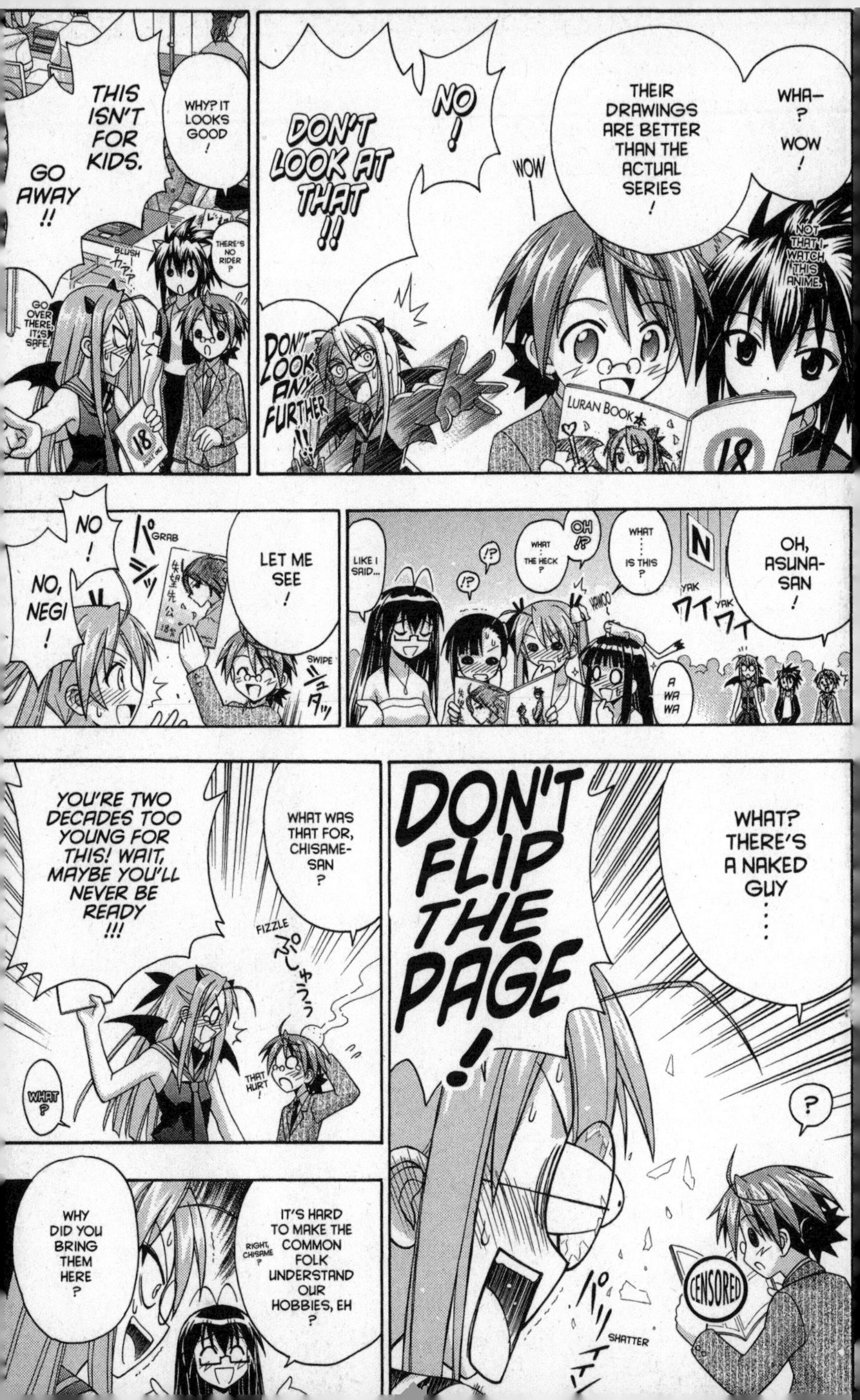

WHA— ? WOW !
THEIR DRAWINGS ARE BETTER THAN THE ACTUAL SERIES !
WOW !
NO !
DON'T LOOK AT THAT !!
NOT THAT I WATCH THIS ANIME.
DON'T LOOK ANY FURTHER !!
LURAN BOOK
18
WHY? IT LOOKS GOOD !
THIS ISN'T FOR KIDS.
GO AWAY !!
THERE'S NO RIDER ?
BLUSH
GO OVER THERE, IT'S SAFE.
18
OH, ASUNA-SAN !
YAK YAK
WHAT ... IS THIS ?
OH !?
WHAT ... THE HECK ?
!?
!?
LIKE I SAID...
KAMOO
A WA WA
LET ME SEE !
GRAB
NO !
NO, NEGI !
SWIPE
WHAT? THERE'S A NAKED GUY ....
DON'T FLIP THE PAGE !
?
CENSORED
SHATTER
WHAT WAS THAT FOR, CHISAME-SAN ?
YOU'RE TWO DECADES TOO YOUNG FOR THIS! WAIT, MAYBE YOU'LL NEVER BE READY !!!
FIZZLE
THAT HURT
WHAT ?
IT'S HARD TO MAKE THE COMMON FOLK UNDERSTAND OUR HOBBIES, EH ?
RIGHT, CHISAME ?
WHY DID YOU BRING THEM HERE ?

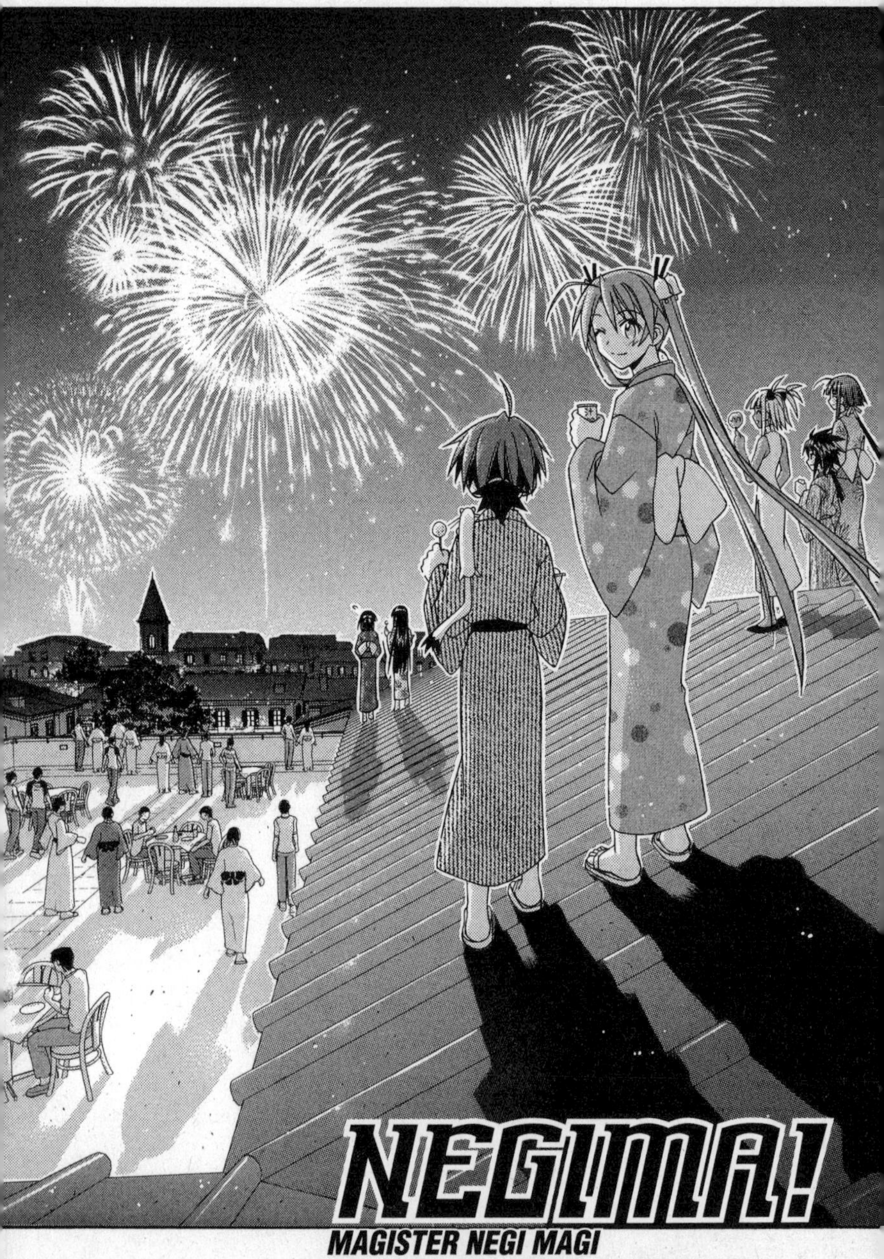
NEGIMA!

MAGISTER NEGI MAGI

183RD PERIOD: FULL OF MEMORIES♡

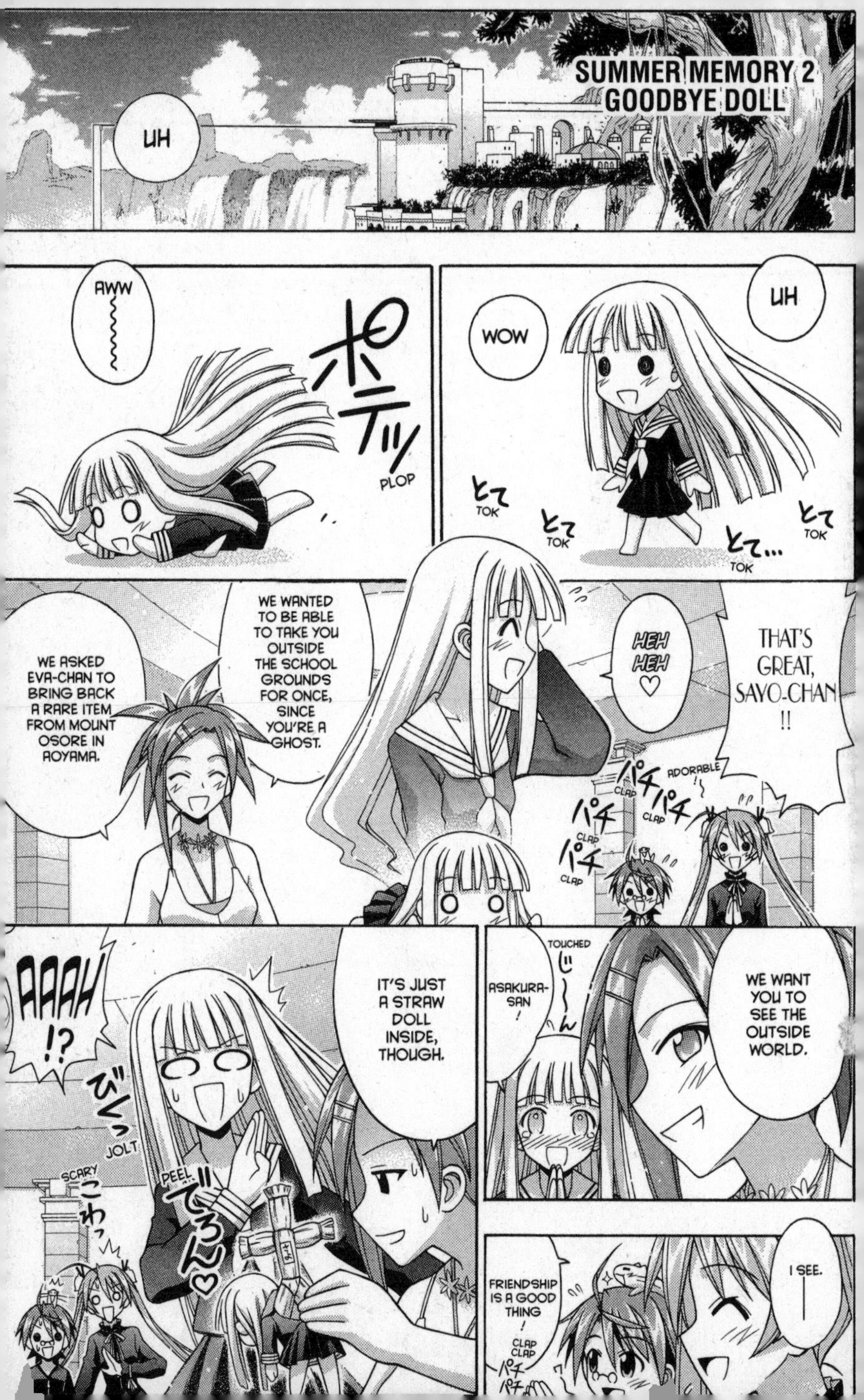
SUMMER MEMORY 2 GOODBYE DOLL
UH
UH
WOW
とて TOK
とて TOK
とて TOK
とて… TOK
AWW~
ポテッ PLOP
THAT'S GREAT, SAYO-CHAN!!
HEH HEH ♡
パチパチ CLAP CLAP
ADORABLE!
パチ CLAP
パチ CLAP
WE WANTED TO BE ABLE TO TAKE YOU OUTSIDE THE SCHOOL GROUNDS FOR ONCE, SINCE YOU'RE A GHOST.
WE ASKED EVA-CHAN TO BRING BACK A RARE ITEM FROM MOUNT OSORE IN AOYAMA.
WE WANT YOU TO SEE THE OUTSIDE WORLD.
TOUCHED じ~ん
ASAKURA-SAN!
I SEE.
FRIENDSHIP IS A GOOD THING!
CLAP CLAP パチパチ
IT'S JUST A STRAW DOLL INSIDE, THOUGH.
AAAH!?
びくっ JOLT
PEEL てろん♡
SCARY こわっ

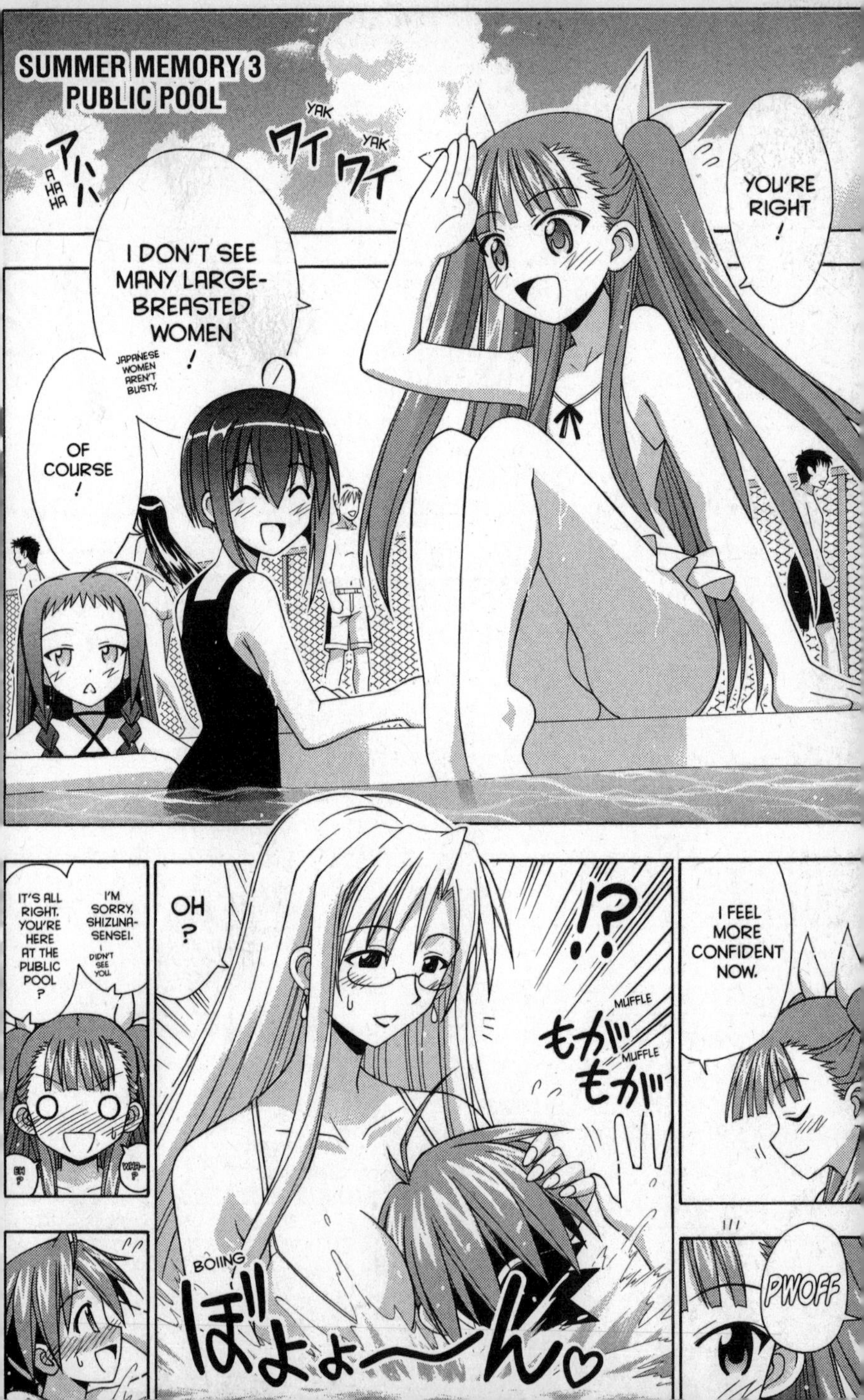
SUMMER MEMORY 3
PUBLIC POOL
YOU'RE RIGHT!
YAK YAK
ワイワイ
I DON'T SEE MANY LARGE-BREASTED WOMEN!
A HA HA
アハハ
JAPANESE WOMEN AREN'T BUSTY.
OF COURSE!
I FEEL MORE CONFIDENT NOW.
PWOFF
OH?
!?
MUFFLE MUFFLE
もがもが
BOIING
ぼよょ〜ん♡
I'M SORRY, SHIZUNA-SENSEI.
I DIDN'T SEE YOU.
IT'S ALL RIGHT. YOU'RE HERE AT THE PUBLIC POOL?
EH?
WHA-?

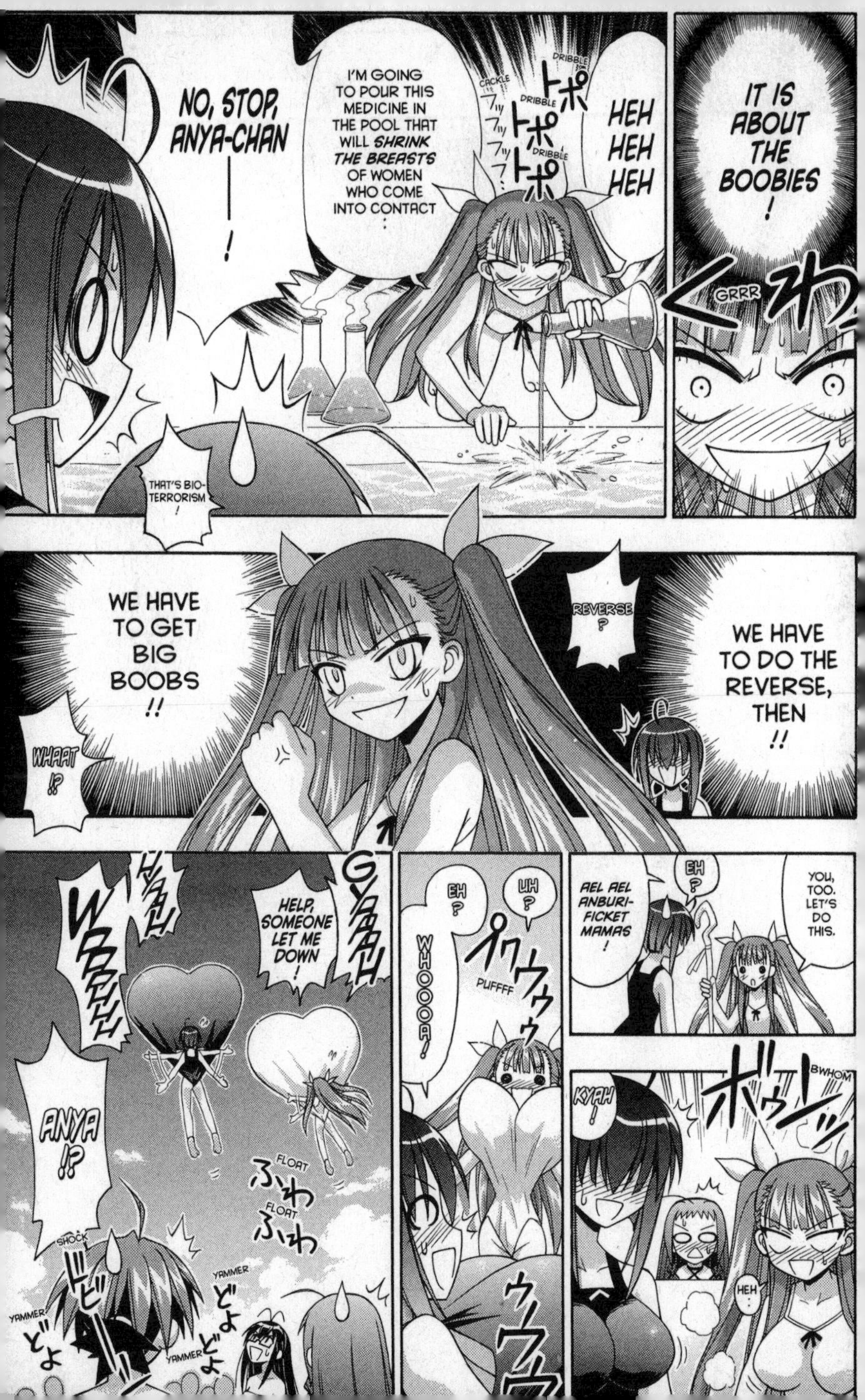
IT IS ABOUT THE BOOBIES!
GRRR
HEH HEH HEH
DRIBBLE
DRIBBLE
DRIBBLE
CACKLE
I'M GOING TO POUR THIS MEDICINE IN THE POOL THAT WILL SHRINK THE BREASTS OF WOMEN WHO COME INTO CONTACT...
NO, STOP, ANYA-CHAN—!
THAT'S BIO-TERRORISM!
REVERSE?
WE HAVE TO DO THE REVERSE, THEN!!
WE HAVE TO GET BIG BOOBS!!
WHAAT!?
YOU, TOO. LET'S DO THIS.
EH?
AEL AEL ANBURI-FICKET MAMAS!
BWHOM
KYAH!
HEH...
UH?
EH?
PUFFFF
WHOOOOA!
GYAAAH
HELP, SOMEONE LET ME DOWN!
ANYA!?
FLOAT
FLOAT
SHOCK
YAMMER
YAMMER
YAMMER

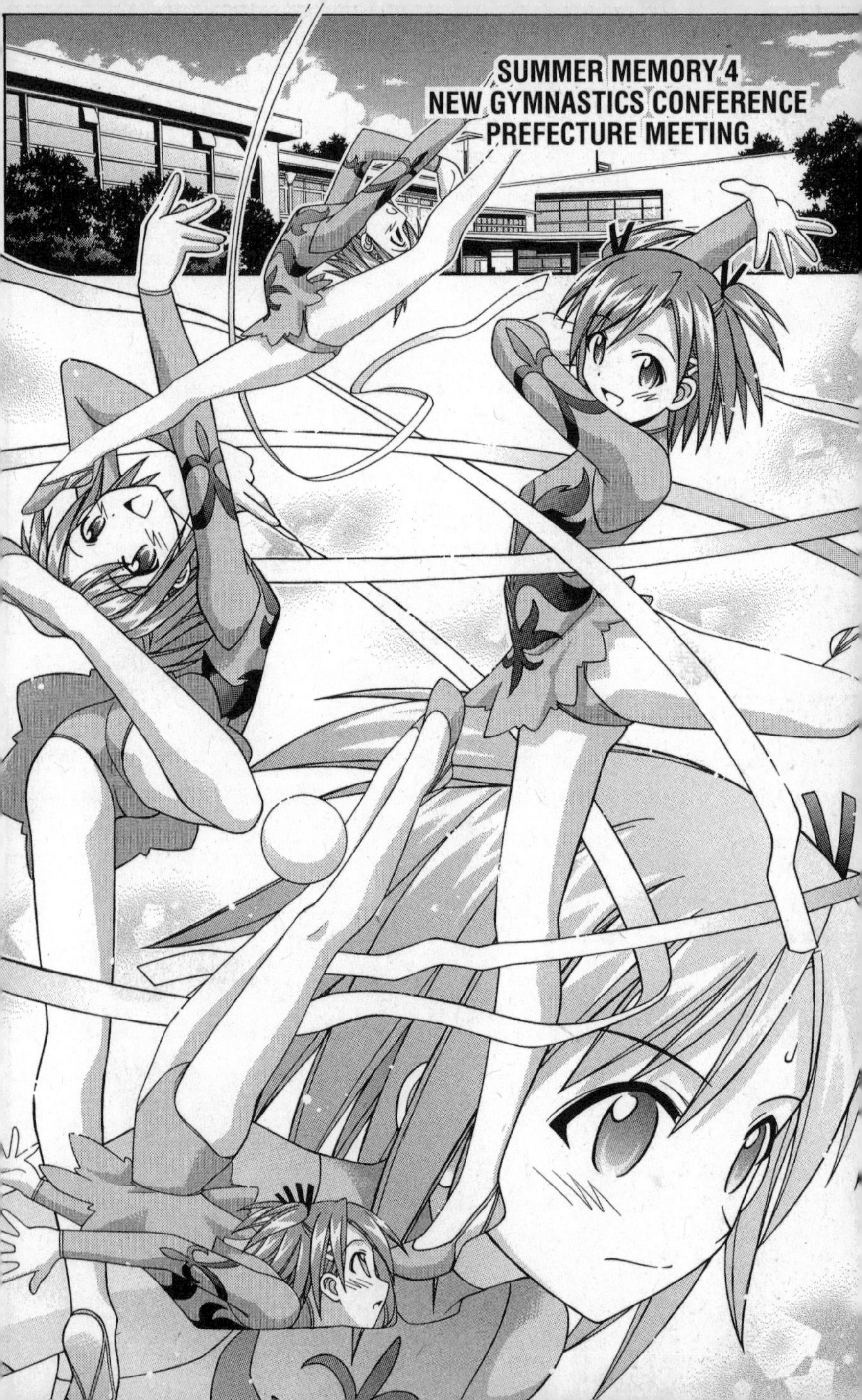
SUMMER MEMORY 4
NEW GYMNASTICS CONFERENCE
PREFECTURE MEETING

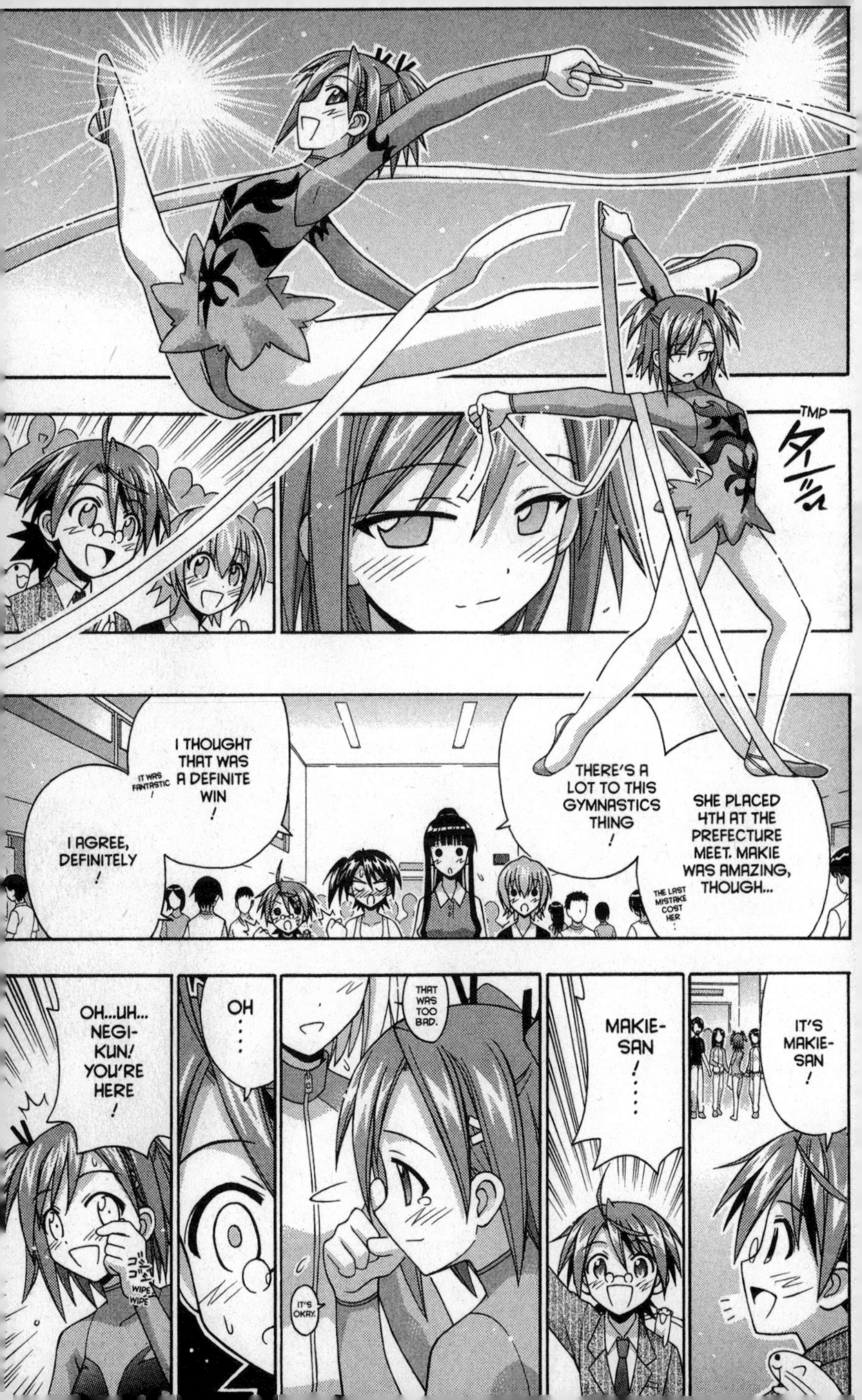
TMP
SHE PLACED 4TH AT THE PREFECTURE MEET. MAKIE WAS AMAZING, THOUGH...
THE LAST MISTAKE COST HER!
THERE'S A LOT TO THIS GYMNASTICS THING!
I THOUGHT THAT WAS A DEFINITE WIN!
IT WAS FANTASTIC!
I AGREE, DEFINITELY!
IT'S MAKIE-SAN!
MAKIE-SAN!.....
THAT WAS TOO BAD.
IT'S OKAY.
OH.....
OH...UH... NEGI-KUN! YOU'RE HERE!
WIPE WIPE

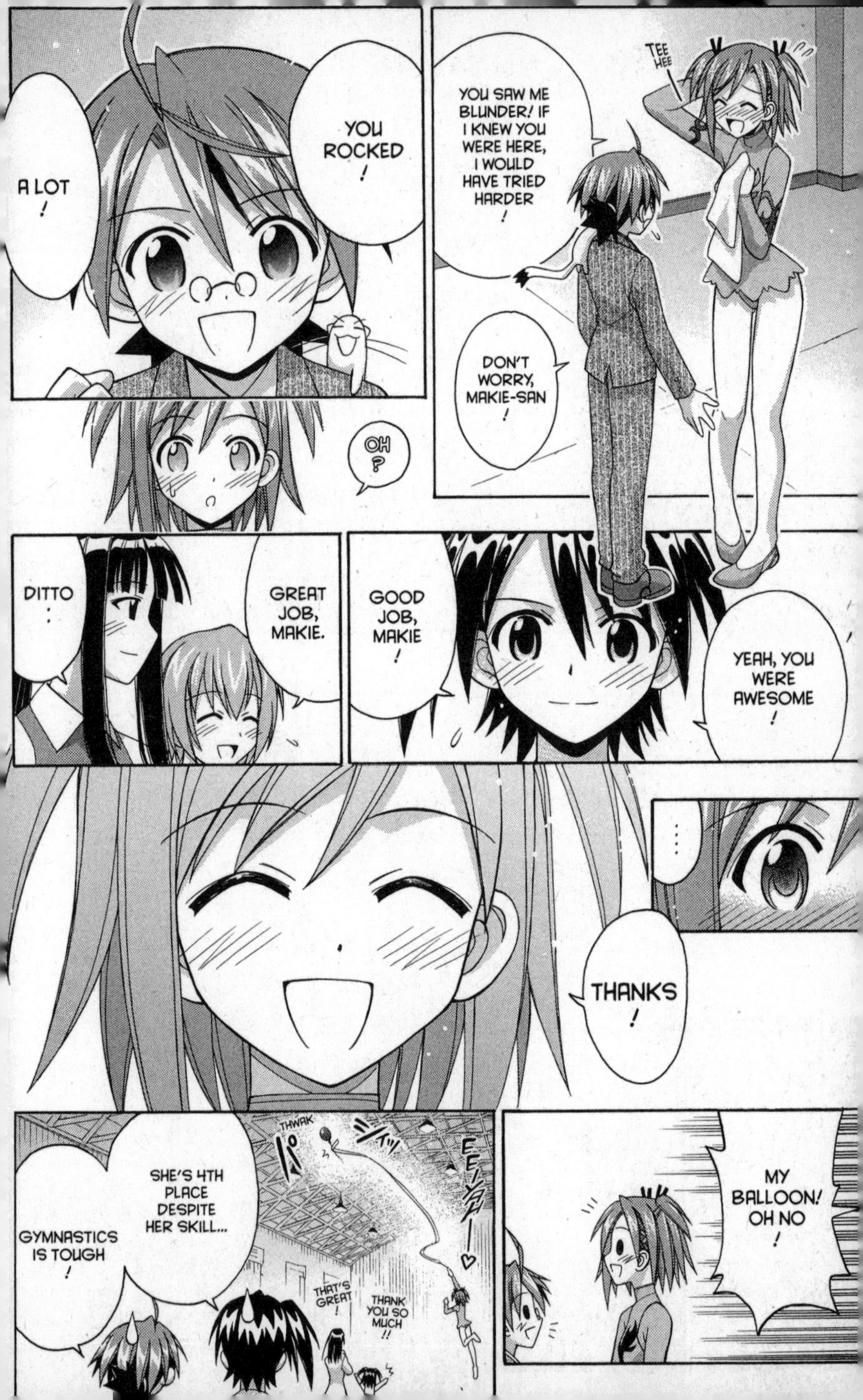
TEE HEE
YOU SAW ME BLUNDER! IF I KNEW YOU WERE HERE, I WOULD HAVE TRIED HARDER!
DON'T WORRY, MAKIE-SAN!
YOU ROCKED!
A LOT!
OH?
YEAH, YOU WERE AWESOME!
GOOD JOB, MAKIE!
GREAT JOB, MAKIE.
DITTO:
...
THANKS!
MY BALLOON! OH NO!
THWAK
SHE'S 4TH PLACE DESPITE HER SKILL...
GYMNASTICS IS TOUGH!
THAT'S GREAT!
THANK YOU SO MUCH!!

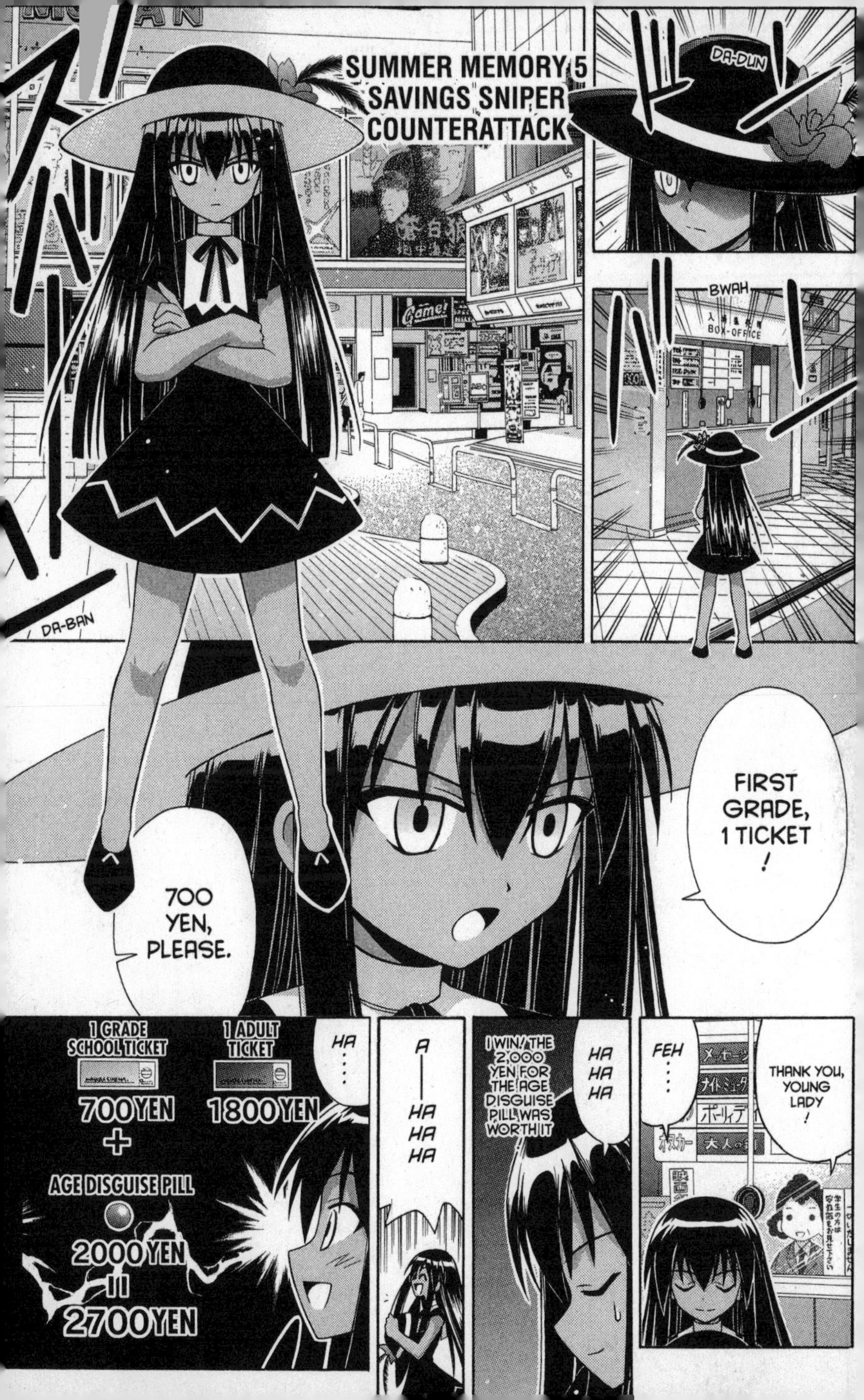
DA-DUN
BWAH
BOX-OFFICE
SUMMER MEMORY 5
SAVINGS SNIPER
COUNTERATTACK
Game!
DA-BAN
FIRST GRADE, 1 TICKET!
700 YEN, PLEASE.
THANK YOU, YOUNG LADY!
FEH...
HA HA HA
I WIN! THE 2,000 YEN FOR THE AGE DISGUISE PILL WAS WORTH IT
A—HA HA HA
HA...
1 GRADE SCHOOL TICKET
1 ADULT TICKET
700 YEN
1800 YEN
+
AGE DISGUISE PILL
2000 YEN
=
2700 YEN

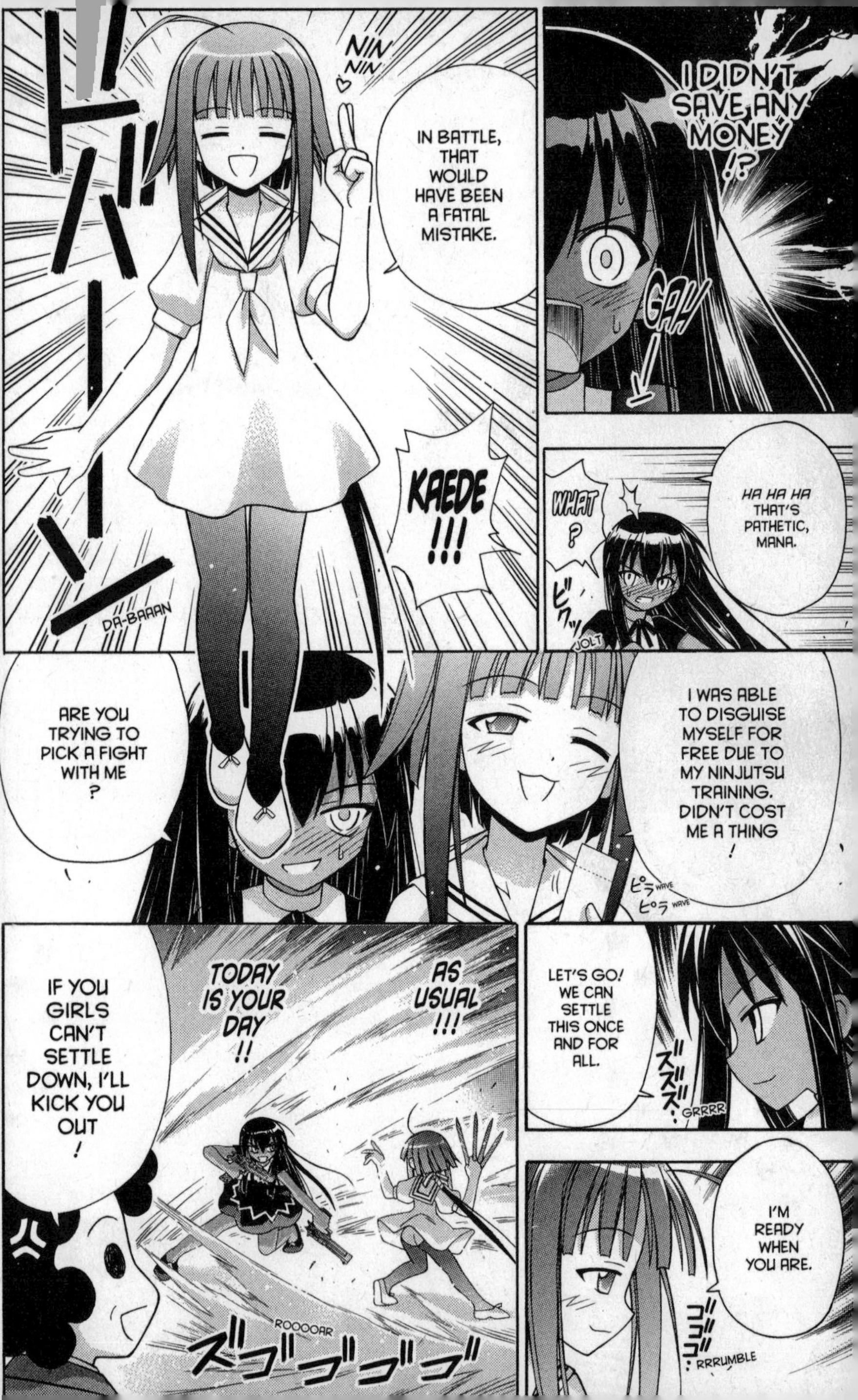
I DIDN'T SAVE ANY MONEY !?
GAH
HA HA HA THAT'S PATHETIC, MANA.
WHAT ?
JOLT
NIN NIN
IN BATTLE, THAT WOULD HAVE BEEN A FATAL MISTAKE.
KAEDE !!!
DA-BAAAN
I WAS ABLE TO DISGUISE MYSELF FOR FREE DUE TO MY NINJUTSU TRAINING. DIDN'T COST ME A THING !
WAVE WAVE
ARE YOU TRYING TO PICK A FIGHT WITH ME ?
LET'S GO! WE CAN SETTLE THIS ONCE AND FOR ALL.
GRRRR
I'M READY WHEN YOU ARE.
RRRUMBLE
AS USUAL !!!
TODAY IS YOUR DAY !!
IF YOU GIRLS CAN'T SETTLE DOWN, I'LL KICK YOU OUT !
ROOOOAR

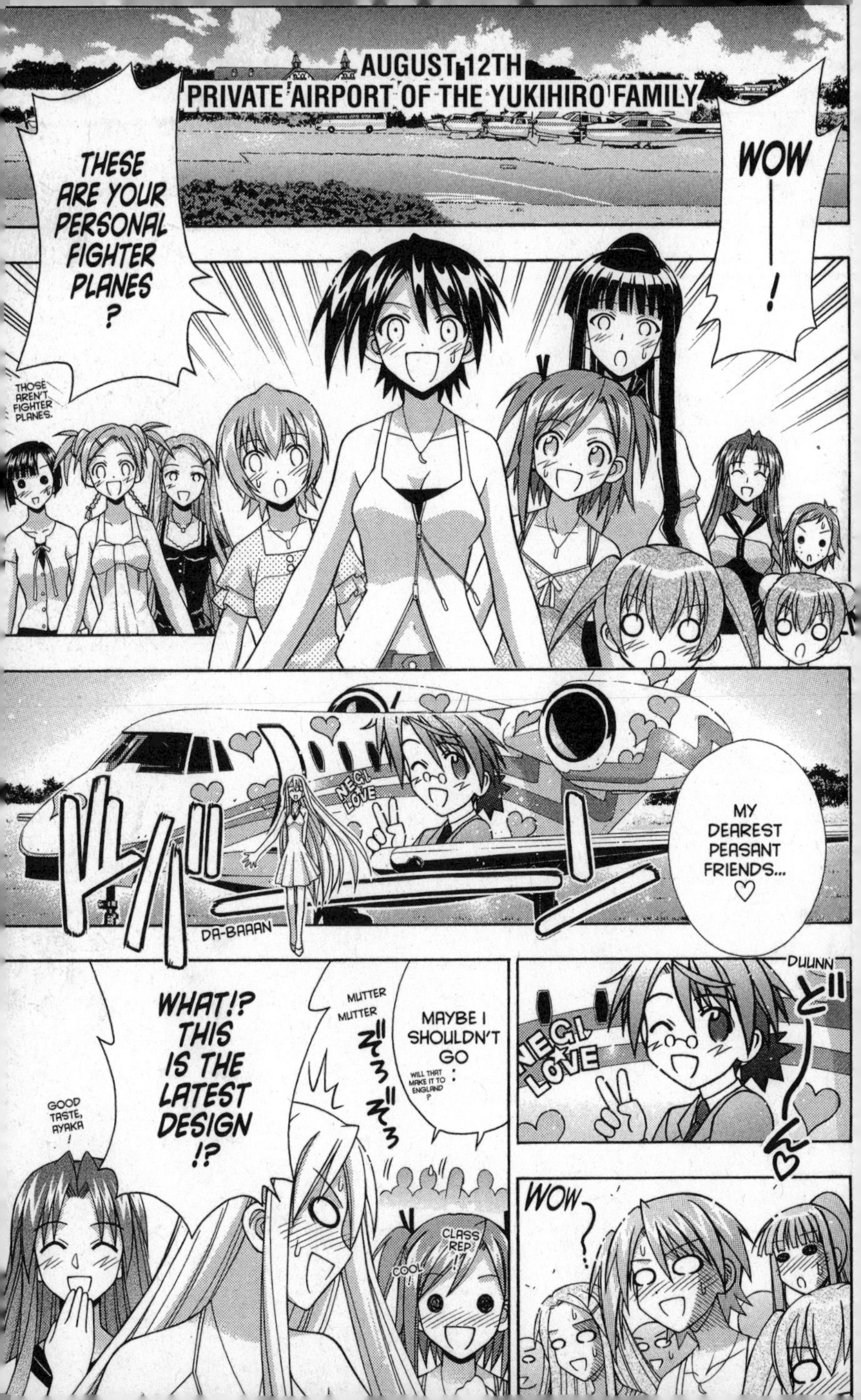
AUGUST 12TH
PRIVATE AIRPORT OF THE YUKIHIRO FAMILY
WOW—!
THESE ARE YOUR PERSONAL FIGHTER PLANES?
THOSE AREN'T FIGHTER PLANES.
MY DEAREST PEASANT FRIENDS... ♡
NEGI LOVE
DA-BAAAN
DUUNN
NEGI ☆ LOVE
WOW
MAYBE I SHOULDN'T GO
WILL THAT MAKE IT TO ENGLAND?
MUTTER MUTTER
WHAT!? THIS IS THE LATEST DESIGN!?
GOOD TASTE, AYAKA!
CLASS REP!?
COOL

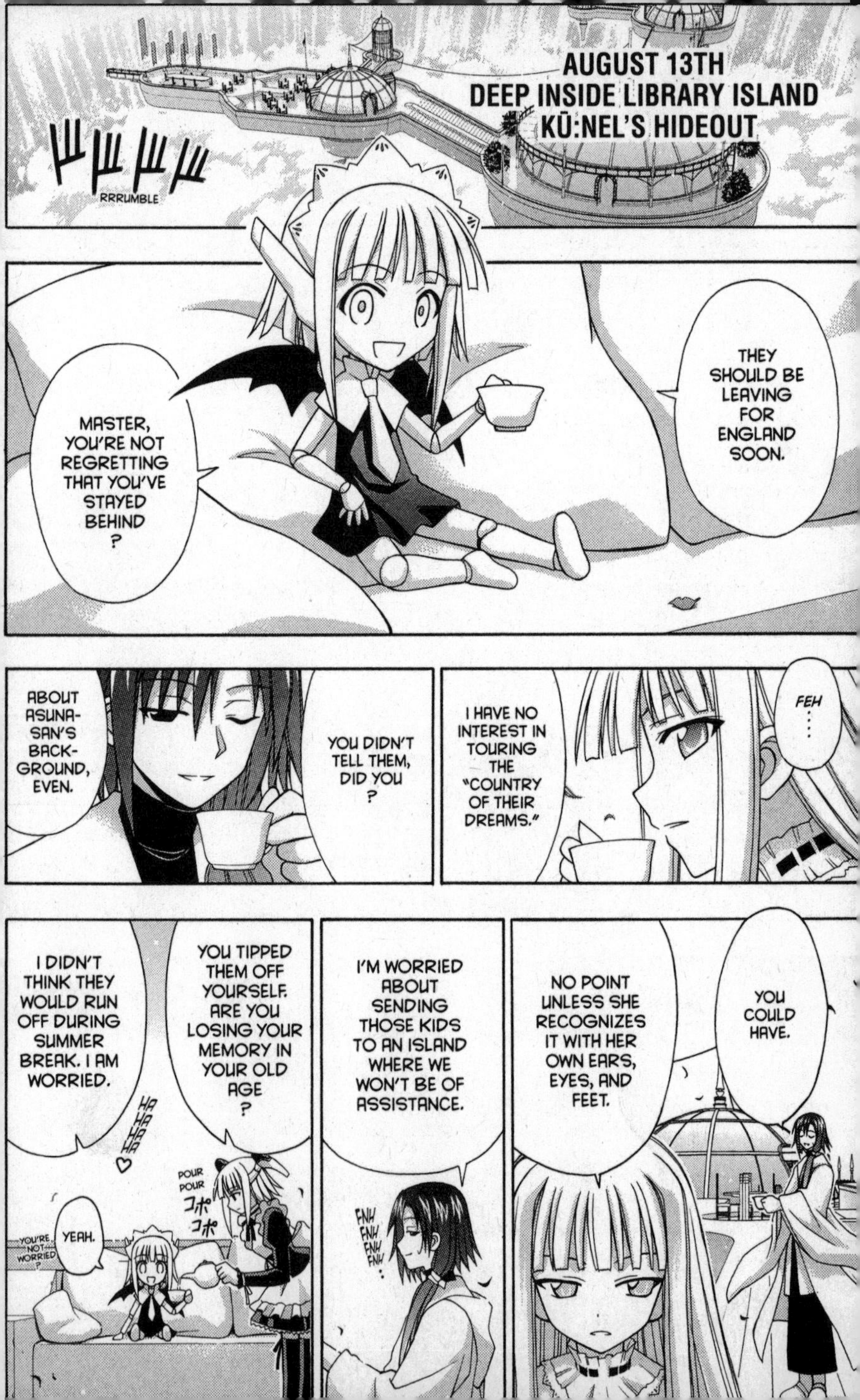
AUGUST 13TH
DEEP INSIDE LIBRARY ISLAND
KŪ:NEL'S HIDEOUT
RRRUMBLE
THEY SHOULD BE LEAVING FOR ENGLAND SOON.
MASTER, YOU'RE NOT REGRETTING THAT YOU'VE STAYED BEHIND?
FEH.....
I HAVE NO INTEREST IN TOURING THE "COUNTRY OF THEIR DREAMS."
YOU DIDN'T TELL THEM, DID YOU?
ABOUT ASUNA-SAN'S BACKGROUND, EVEN.
YOU COULD HAVE.
NO POINT UNLESS SHE RECOGNIZES IT WITH HER OWN EARS, EYES, AND FEET.
I'M WORRIED ABOUT SENDING THOSE KIDS TO AN ISLAND WHERE WE WON'T BE OF ASSISTANCE.
FNH FNH FNH FNH
YOU TIPPED THEM OFF YOURSELF. ARE YOU LOSING YOUR MEMORY IN YOUR OLD AGE?
I DIDN'T THINK THEY WOULD RUN OFF DURING SUMMER BREAK. I AM WORRIED.
HA HA HA HA ♡
POUR POUR
コポ コポ
YOU'RE NOT WORRIED?
YEAH.

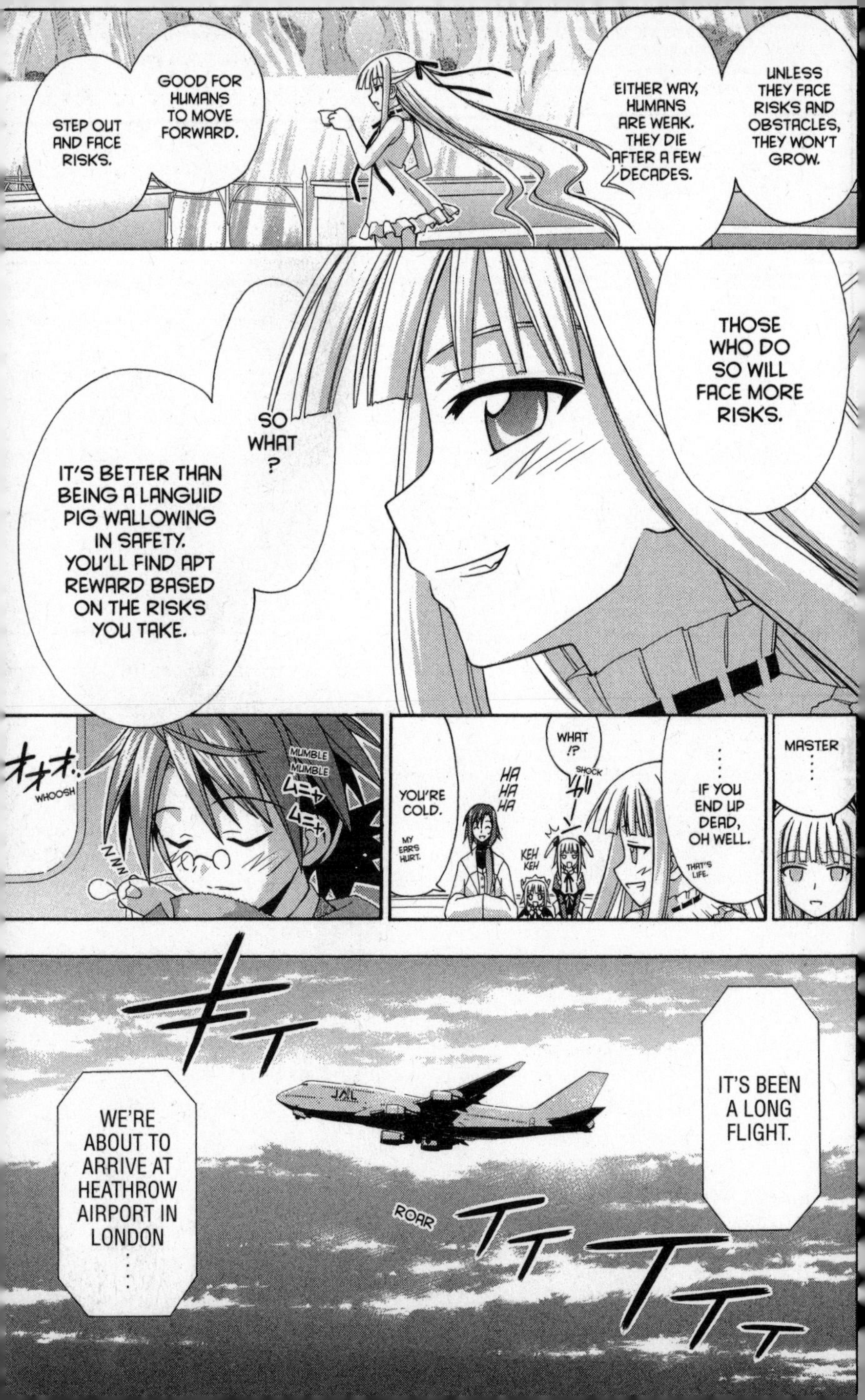
UNLESS THEY FACE RISKS AND OBSTACLES, THEY WON'T GROW.
EITHER WAY, HUMANS ARE WEAK. THEY DIE AFTER A FEW DECADES.
GOOD FOR HUMANS TO MOVE FORWARD.
STEP OUT AND FACE RISKS.
THOSE WHO DO SO WILL FACE MORE RISKS.
SO WHAT?
IT'S BETTER THAN BEING A LANGUID PIG WALLOWING IN SAFETY. YOU'LL FIND APT REWARD BASED ON THE RISKS YOU TAKE.
MASTER ...
... IF YOU END UP DEAD, OH WELL.
THAT'S LIFE.
WHAT!?
SHOCK
HA HA HA
KEH KEH
YOU'RE COLD.
MY EARS HURT.
MUMBLE MUMBLE
WHOOSH
IT'S BEEN A LONG FLIGHT.
WE'RE ABOUT TO ARRIVE AT HEATHROW AIRPORT IN LONDON ...
ROAR

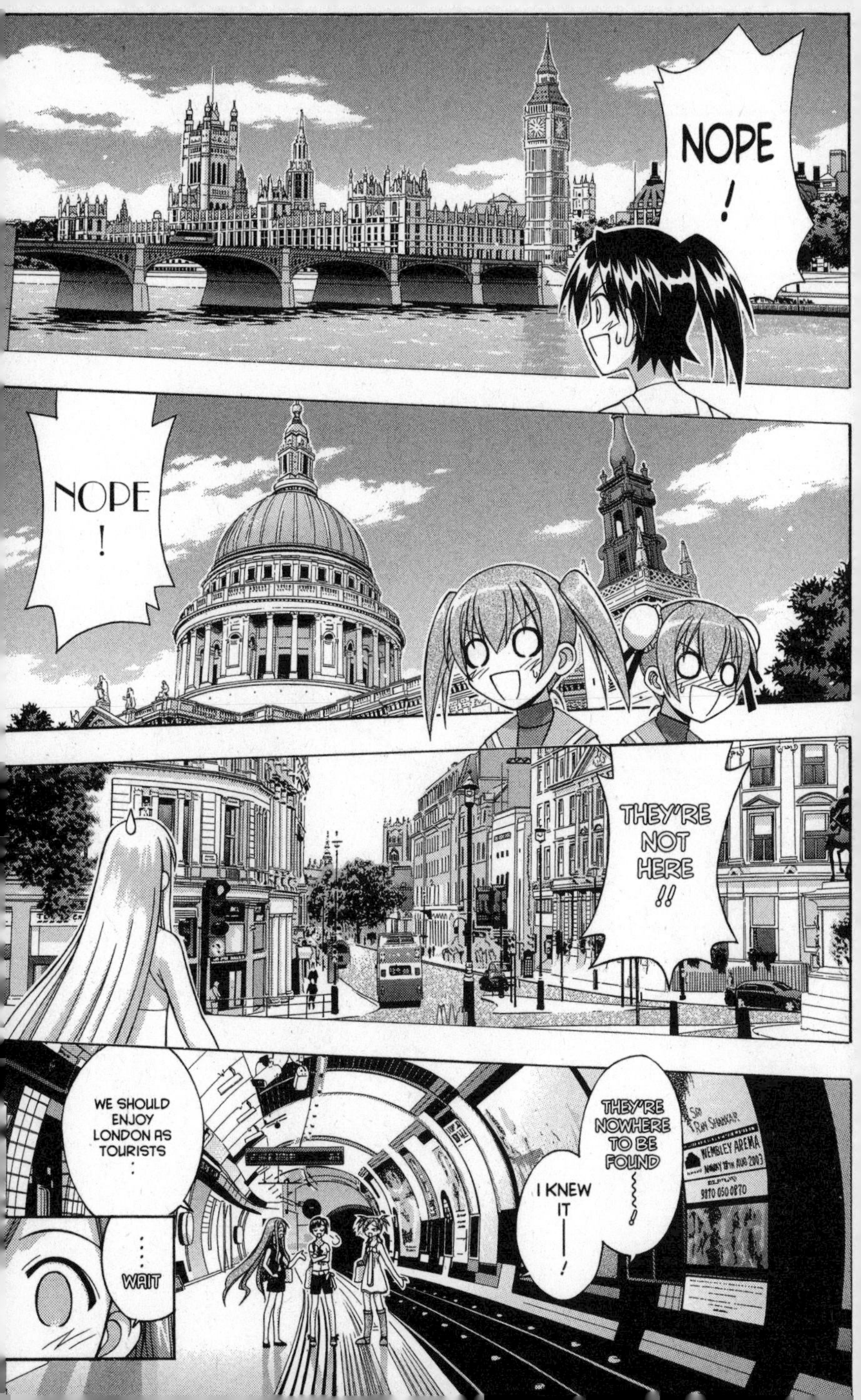
NOPE!
NOPE!
THEY'RE NOT HERE!!
THEY'RE NOWHERE TO BE FOUND~~~!
WEMBLEY ARENA
I KNEW IT—!
WE SHOULD ENJOY LONDON AS TOURISTS...
...WAIT

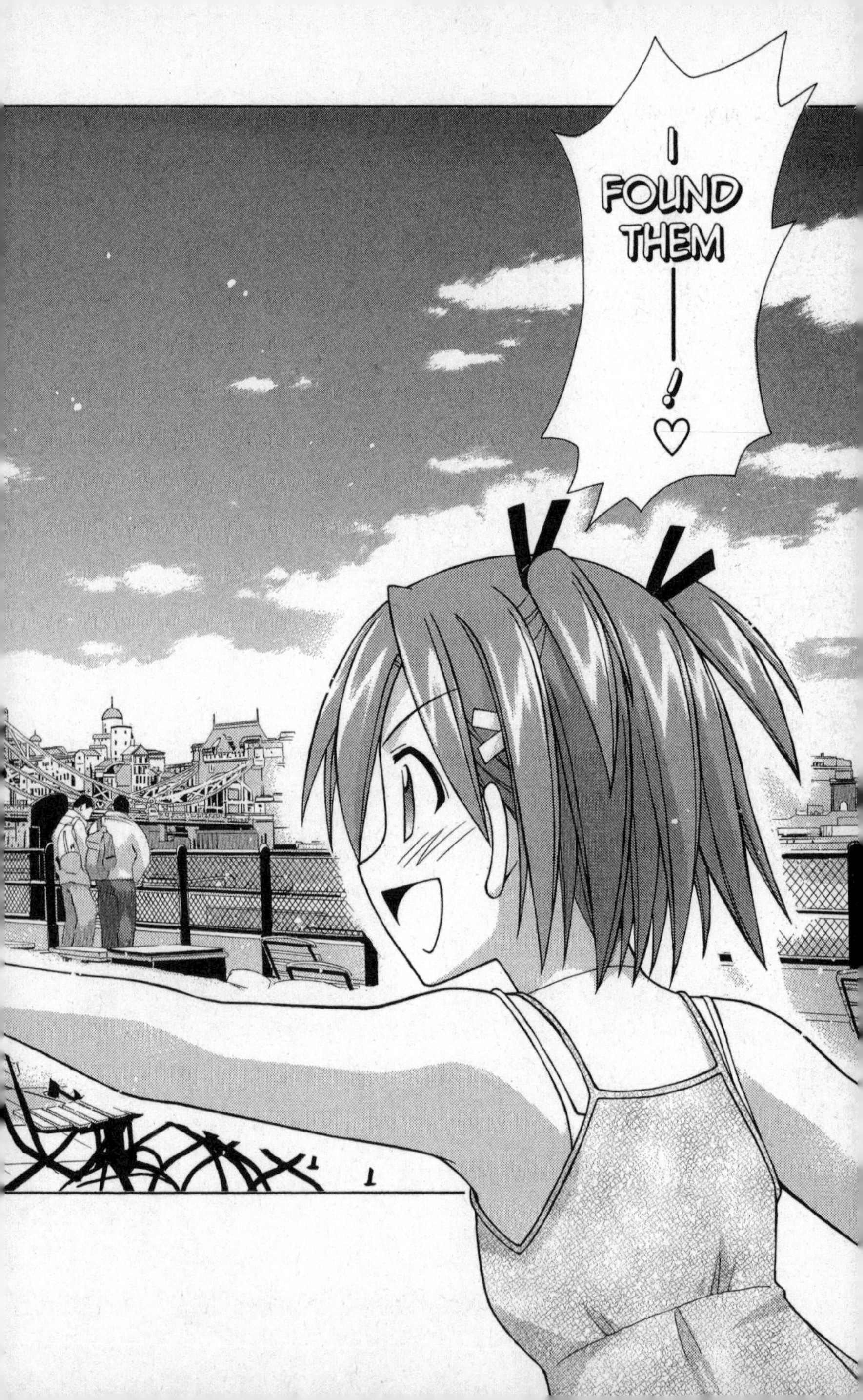
I FOUND THEM——!♡

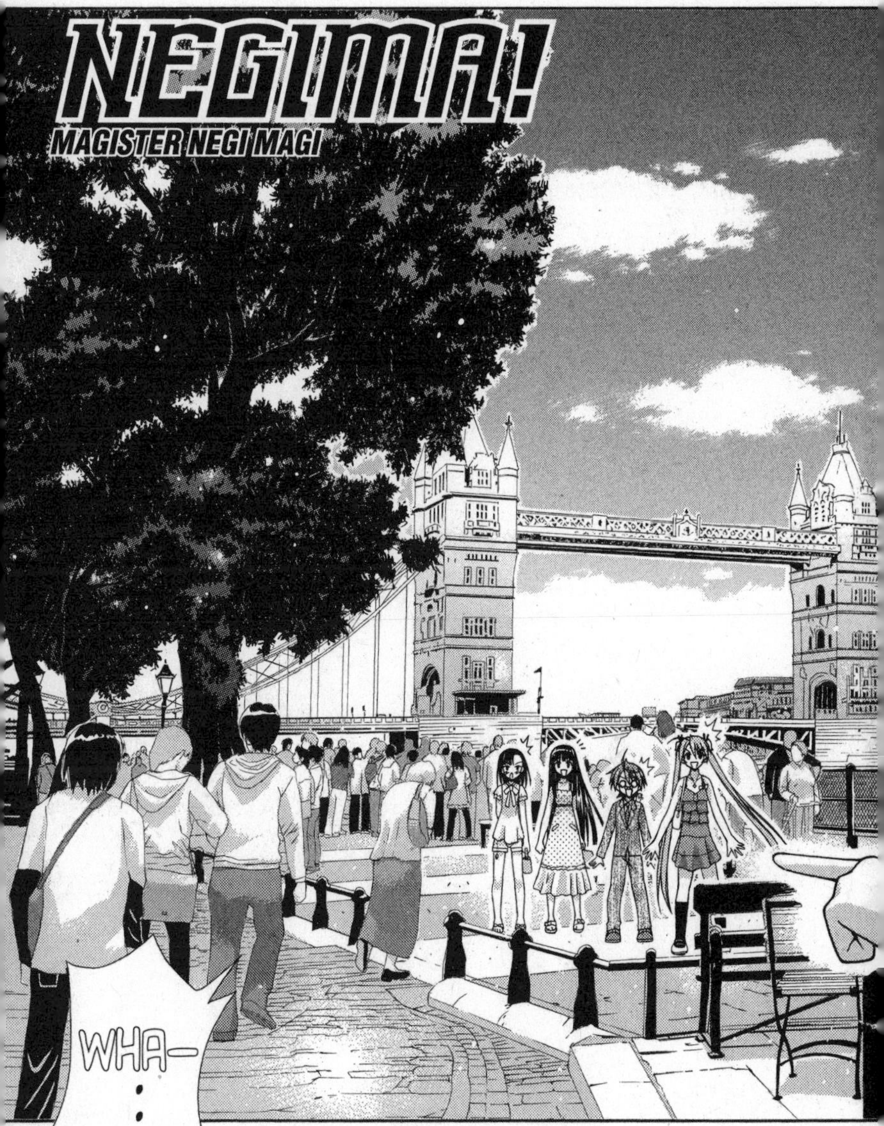
NEGIMA!
MAGISTER NEGI MAGI
WHA–

184TH PERIOD: NEGI PARTY DEPARTS TO LONDON!!

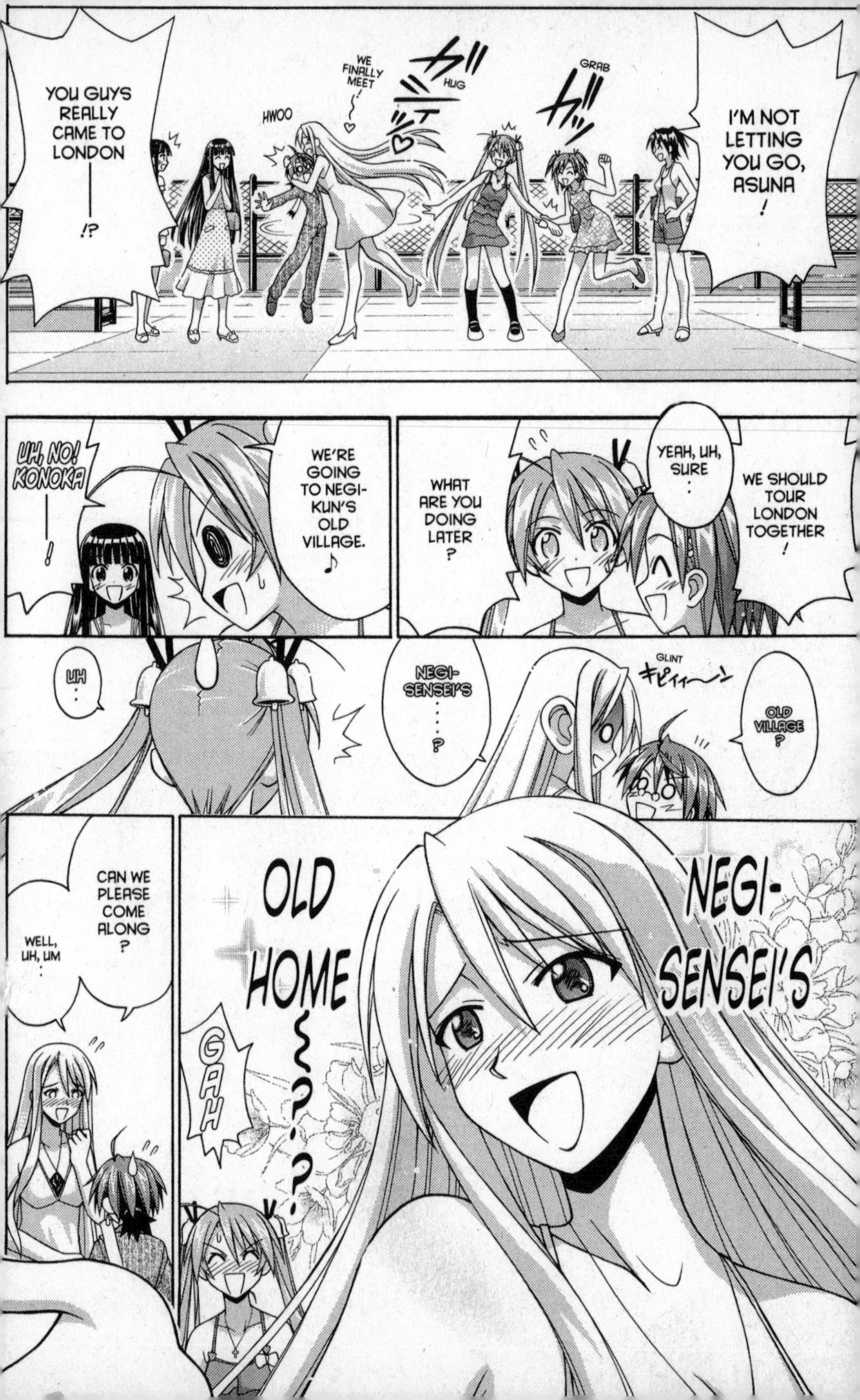
I'M NOT LETTING YOU GO, ASUNA!
GRAB
HUG
WE FINALLY MEET ♡
HWOO
YOU GUYS REALLY CAME TO LONDON—!?
WE SHOULD TOUR LONDON TOGETHER!
YEAH, UH, SURE...
WHAT ARE YOU DOING LATER?
WE'RE GOING TO NEGI-KUN'S OLD VILLAGE. ♪
UH, NO! KONOKA—!
GLINT
OLD VILLAGE?
NEGI-SENSEI'S....?
UH...
NEGI-SENSEI'S
OLD HOME~?!?
GAH
CAN WE PLEASE COME ALONG?
WELL, UH, UM...

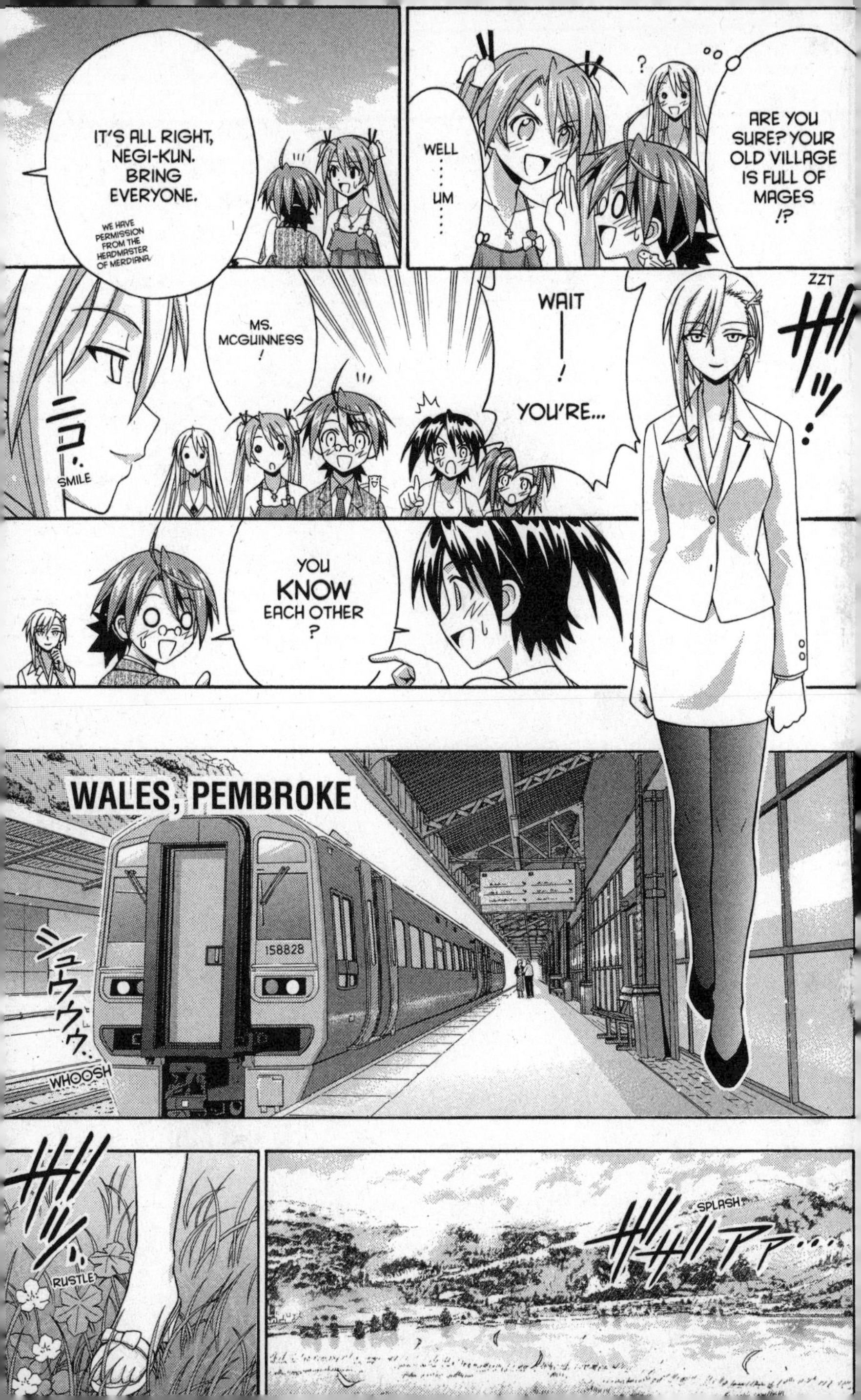
ARE YOU SURE? YOUR OLD VILLAGE IS FULL OF MAGES !?
WELL ...... UM ......
IT'S ALL RIGHT, NEGI-KUN. BRING EVERYONE.
WE HAVE PERMISSION FROM THE HEADMASTER OF MERDIANA.
ZZT
WAIT — ! YOU'RE...
MS. MCGUINNESS !
SMILE
YOU KNOW EACH OTHER ?
WALES, PEMBROKE
158828
WHOOSH
SPLASH
RUSTLE

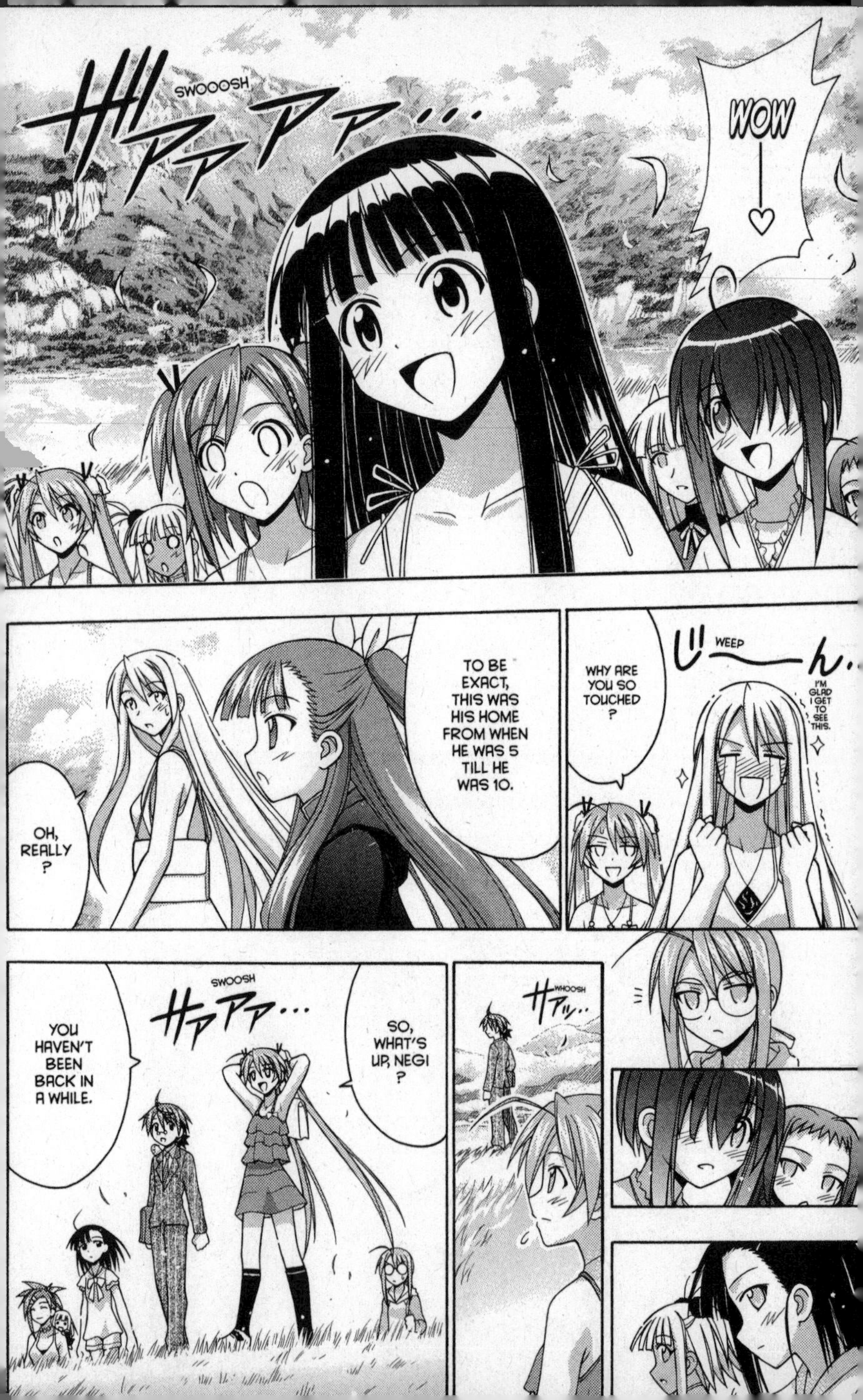
WOW
SWOOOSH
WEEP
WHY ARE YOU SO TOUCHED?
I'M GLAD I GET TO SEE THIS.
TO BE EXACT, THIS WAS HIS HOME FROM WHEN HE WAS 5 TILL HE WAS 10.
OH, REALLY?
WHOOSH
SO, WHAT'S UP, NEGI?
SWOOSH
YOU HAVEN'T BEEN BACK IN A WHILE.

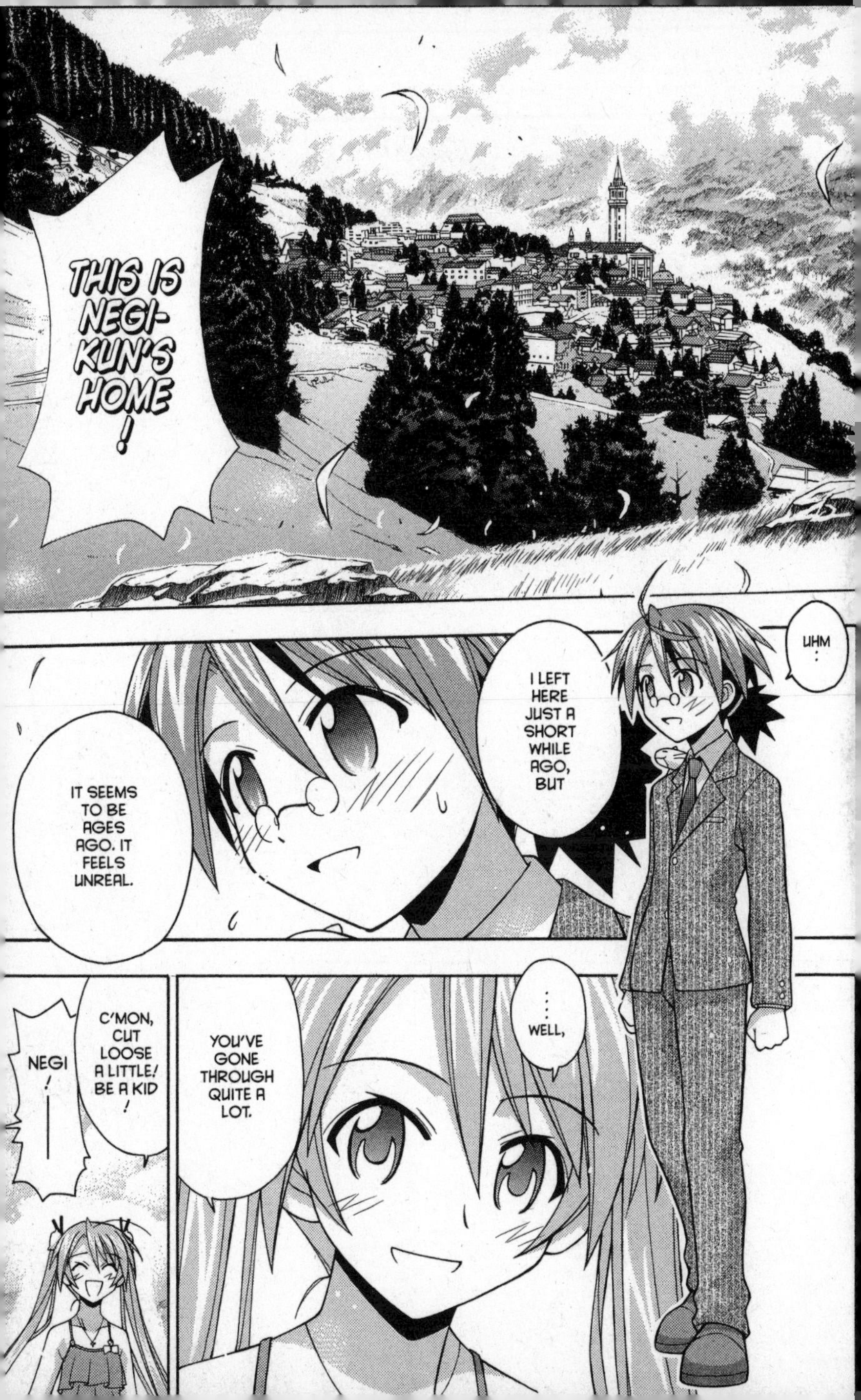
THIS IS NEGI-KUN'S HOME!
UHM...
I LEFT HERE JUST A SHORT WHILE AGO, BUT
IT SEEMS TO BE AGES AGO. IT FEELS UNREAL.
....WELL,
YOU'VE GONE THROUGH QUITE A LOT.
C'MON, CUT LOOSE A LITTLE! BE A KID!
NEGI!

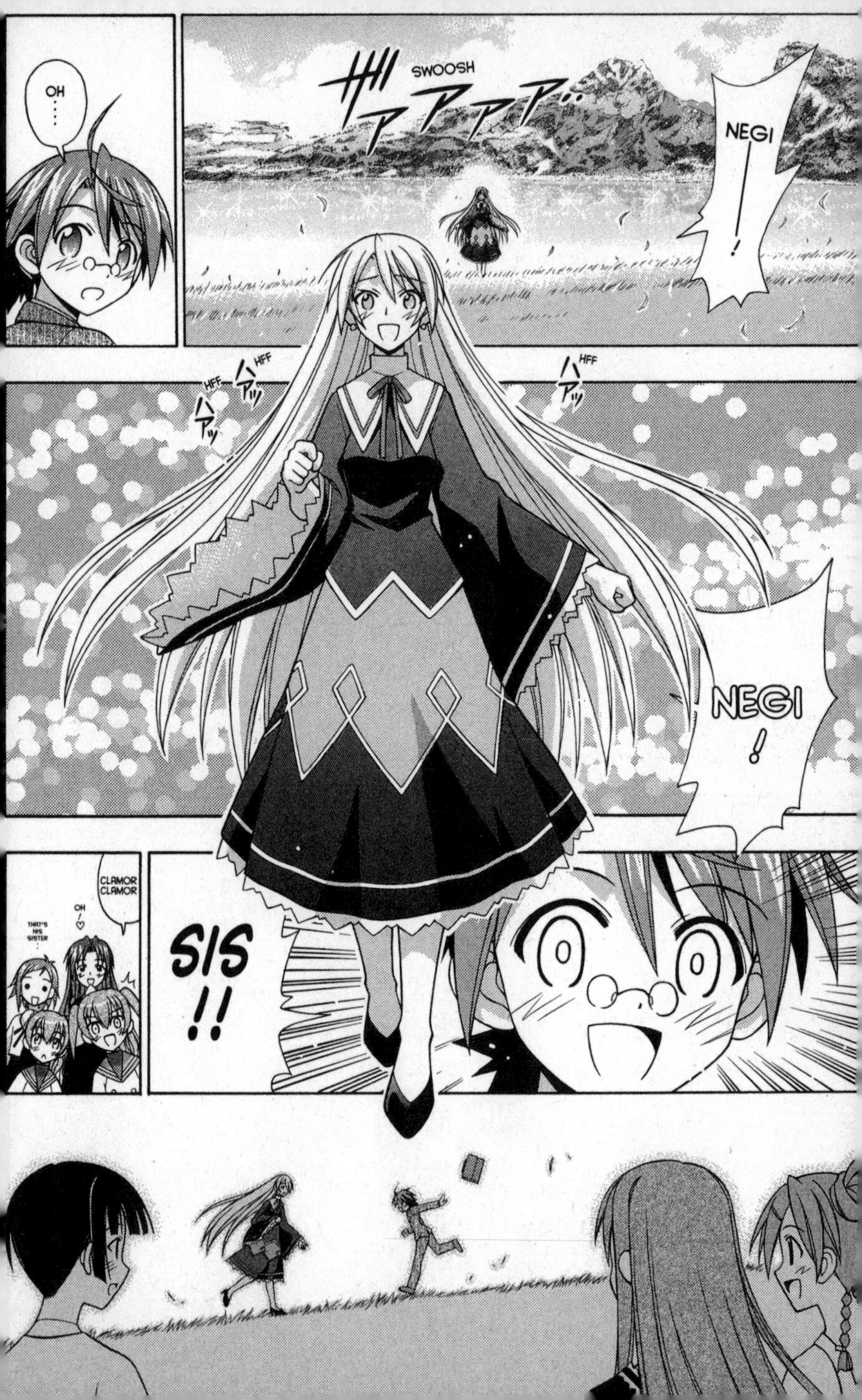
SWOOSH
NEGI—!
OH.....
HFF
HFF
HFF
NEGI!
SIS!!
CLAMOR CLAMOR
OH ♡
THAT'S HIS SISTER...

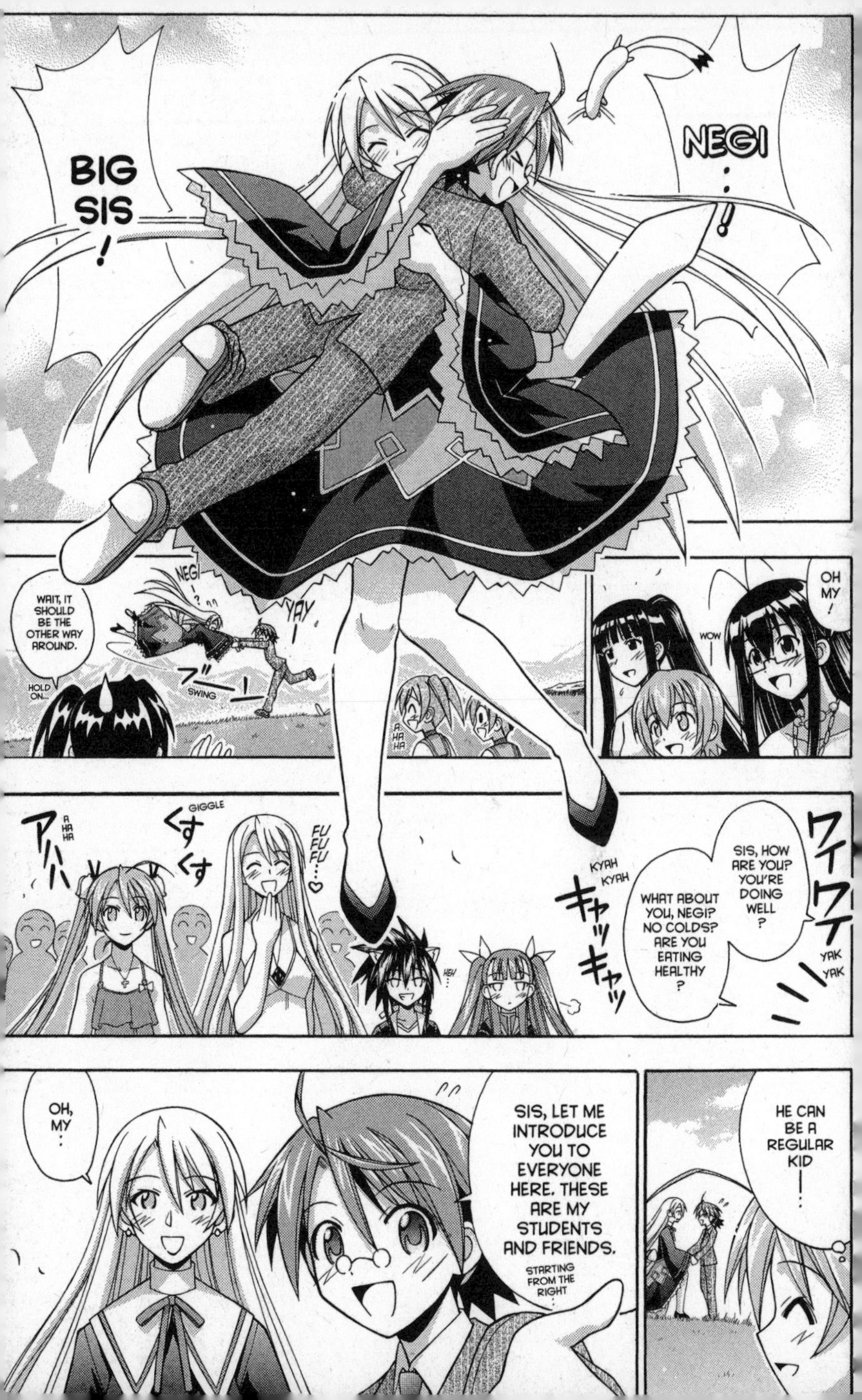
NEGI...!
BIG SIS!
OH MY!
WOW
NEGI!?
YAY!
WAIT, IT SHOULD BE THE OTHER WAY AROUND.
SWING
HOLD ON...
AHAHA
SIS, HOW ARE YOU? YOU'RE DOING WELL?
ワイワイ
YAK YAK
WHAT ABOUT YOU, NEGI? NO COLDS? ARE YOU EATING HEALTHY?
キャッキャッ
KYAH KYAH
HEY...
FUFUFU...♡
くすくす
GIGGLE
アハハ
AHAHA
HE CAN BE A REGULAR KID...!
SIS, LET ME INTRODUCE YOU TO EVERYONE HERE. THESE ARE MY STUDENTS AND FRIENDS.
STARTING FROM THE RIGHT...
OH, MY...

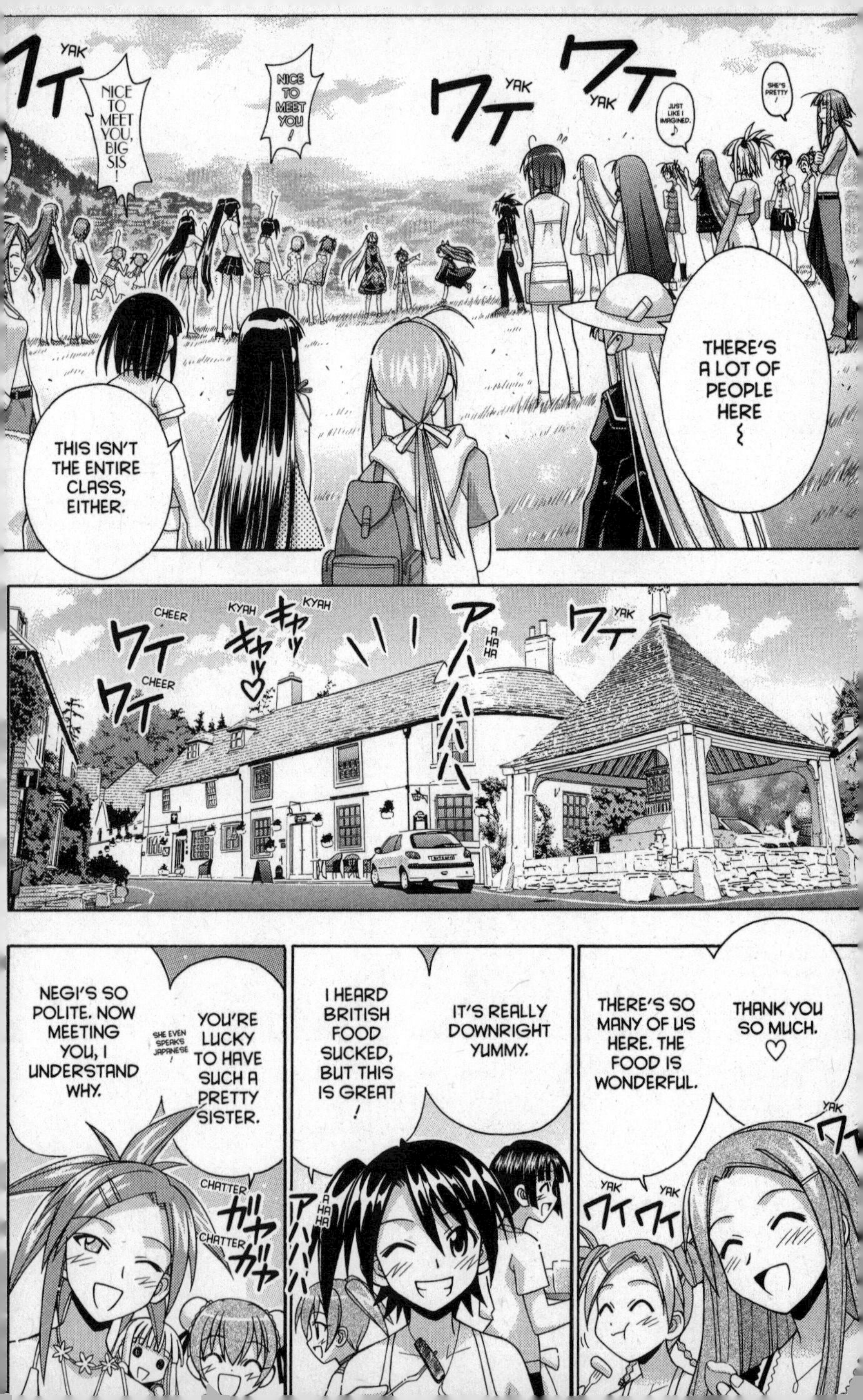
SHE'S PRETTY!
JUST LIKE I IMAGINED. ♪
YAK
YAK
NICE TO MEET YOU!
NICE TO MEET YOU, BIG SIS!
YAK
THERE'S A LOT OF PEOPLE HERE~
THIS ISN'T THE ENTIRE CLASS, EITHER.
YAK
A HA HA
KYAH
KYAH
CHEER
CHEER
THANK YOU SO MUCH. ♡
THERE'S SO MANY OF US HERE. THE FOOD IS WONDERFUL.
YAK
YAK
YAK
IT'S REALLY DOWNRIGHT YUMMY.
I HEARD BRITISH FOOD SUCKED, BUT THIS IS GREAT!
A HA HA
YOU'RE LUCKY TO HAVE SUCH A PRETTY SISTER.
SHE EVEN SPEAKS JAPANESE!
NEGI'S SO POLITE. NOW MEETING YOU, I UNDERSTAND WHY.
CHATTER
CHATTER

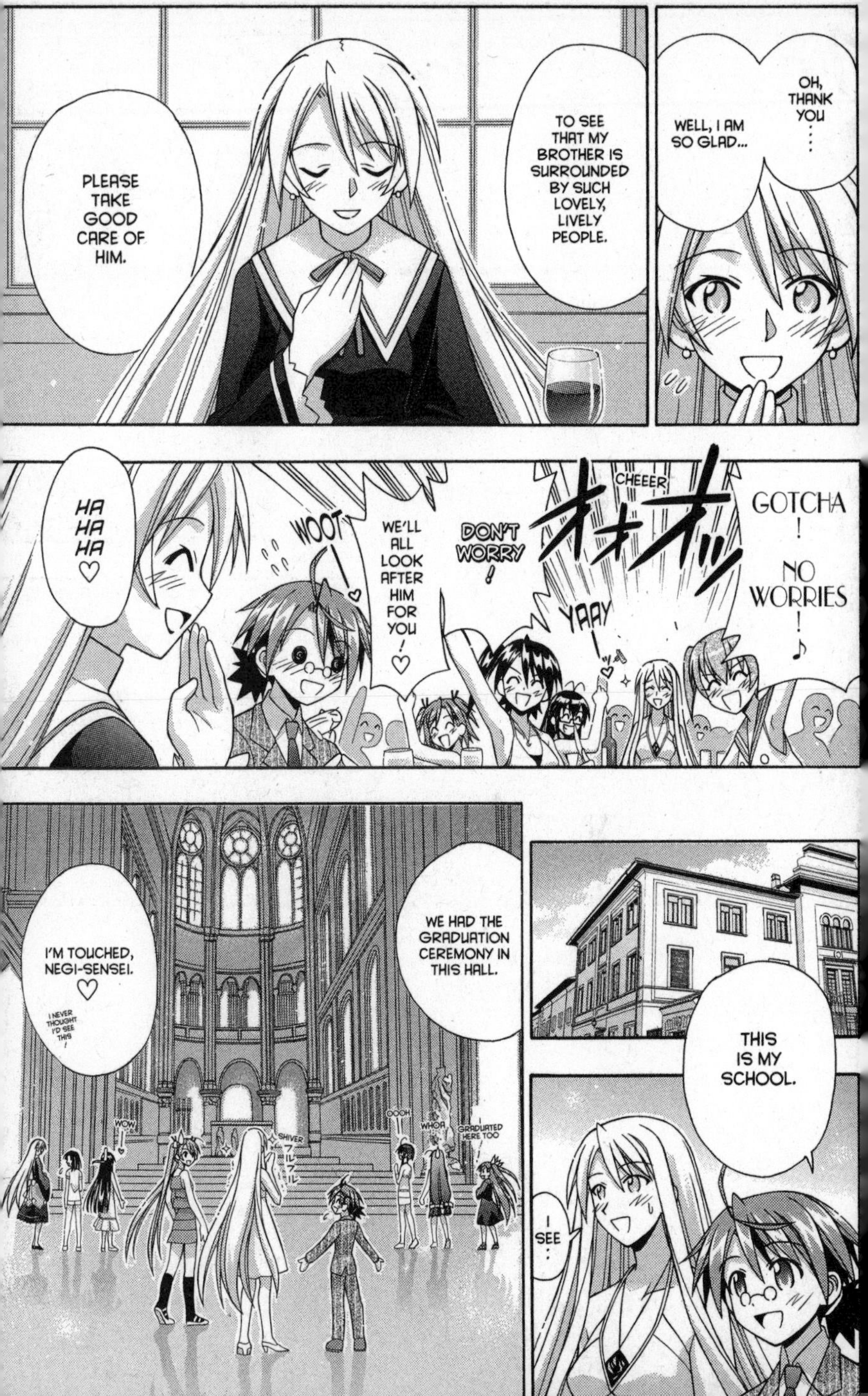
OH, THANK YOU....
WELL, I AM SO GLAD...
TO SEE THAT MY BROTHER IS SURROUNDED BY SUCH LOVELY, LIVELY PEOPLE.
PLEASE TAKE GOOD CARE OF HIM.
GOTCHA! NO WORRIES! ♪
CHEEER
YAAY!
DON'T WORRY!
WE'LL ALL LOOK AFTER HIM FOR YOU! ♡
WOOT!
HA HA HA ♡
THIS IS MY SCHOOL.
I SEE...
WE HAD THE GRADUATION CEREMONY IN THIS HALL.
I'M TOUCHED, NEGI-SENSEI. ♡
I NEVER THOUGHT I'D SEE THIS!
GRADUATED HERE TOO
WHOA
OOOH
SHIVER
WOW

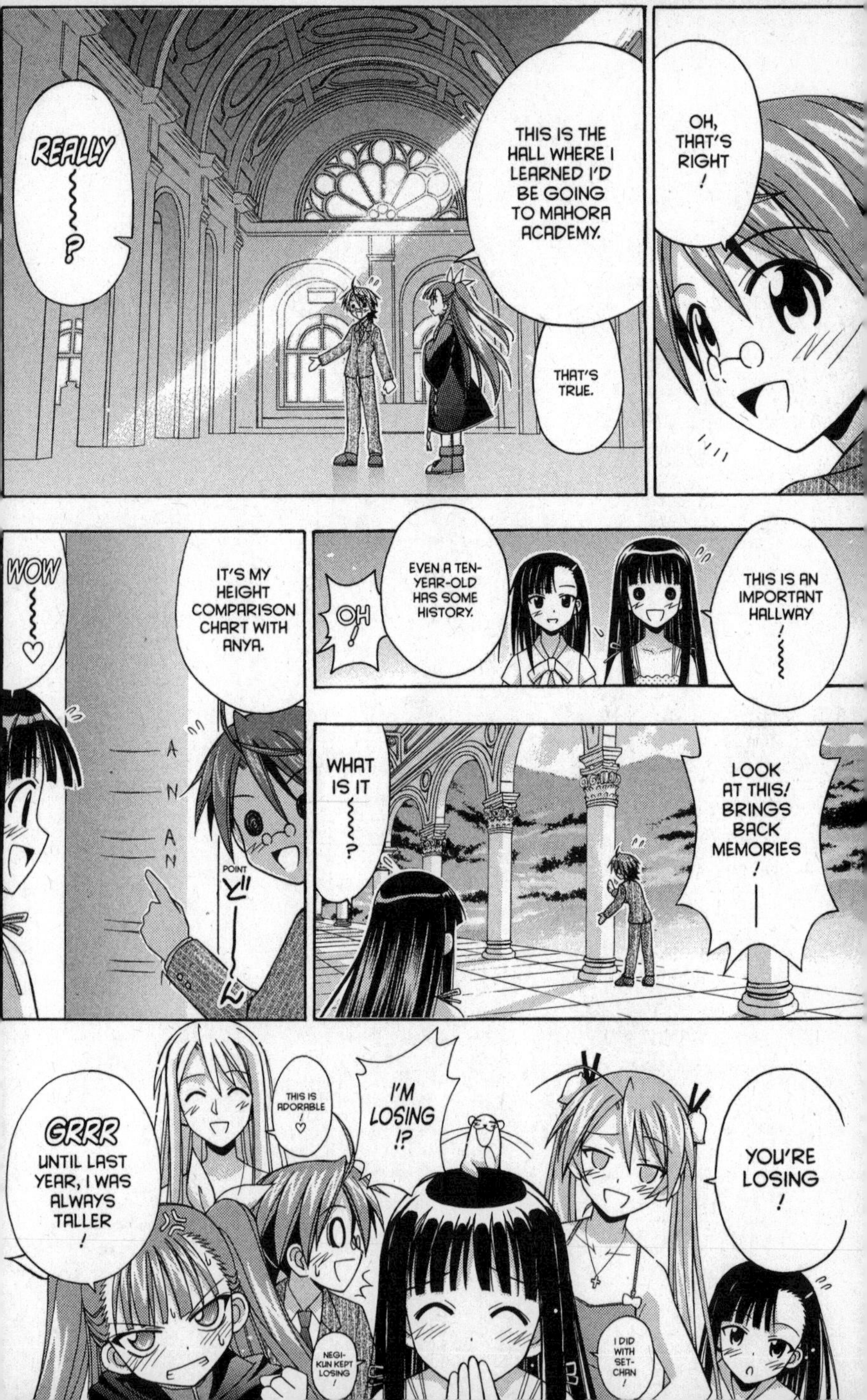
OH, THAT'S RIGHT!
THIS IS THE HALL WHERE I LEARNED I'D BE GOING TO MAHORA ACADEMY.
THAT'S TRUE.
REALLY~~~?
THIS IS AN IMPORTANT HALLWAY!~~~
EVEN A TEN-YEAR-OLD HAS SOME HISTORY.
OH!
LOOK AT THIS! BRINGS BACK MEMORIES!—
WHAT IS IT~~~?
IT'S MY HEIGHT COMPARISON CHART WITH ANYA.
A N A N
POINT
WOW~~~♡
YOU'RE LOSING!
I DID WITH SET-CHAN!
I'M LOSING!?
THIS IS ADORABLE!♡
NEGI-KUN KEPT LOSING!
GRRR UNTIL LAST YEAR, I WAS ALWAYS TALLER!

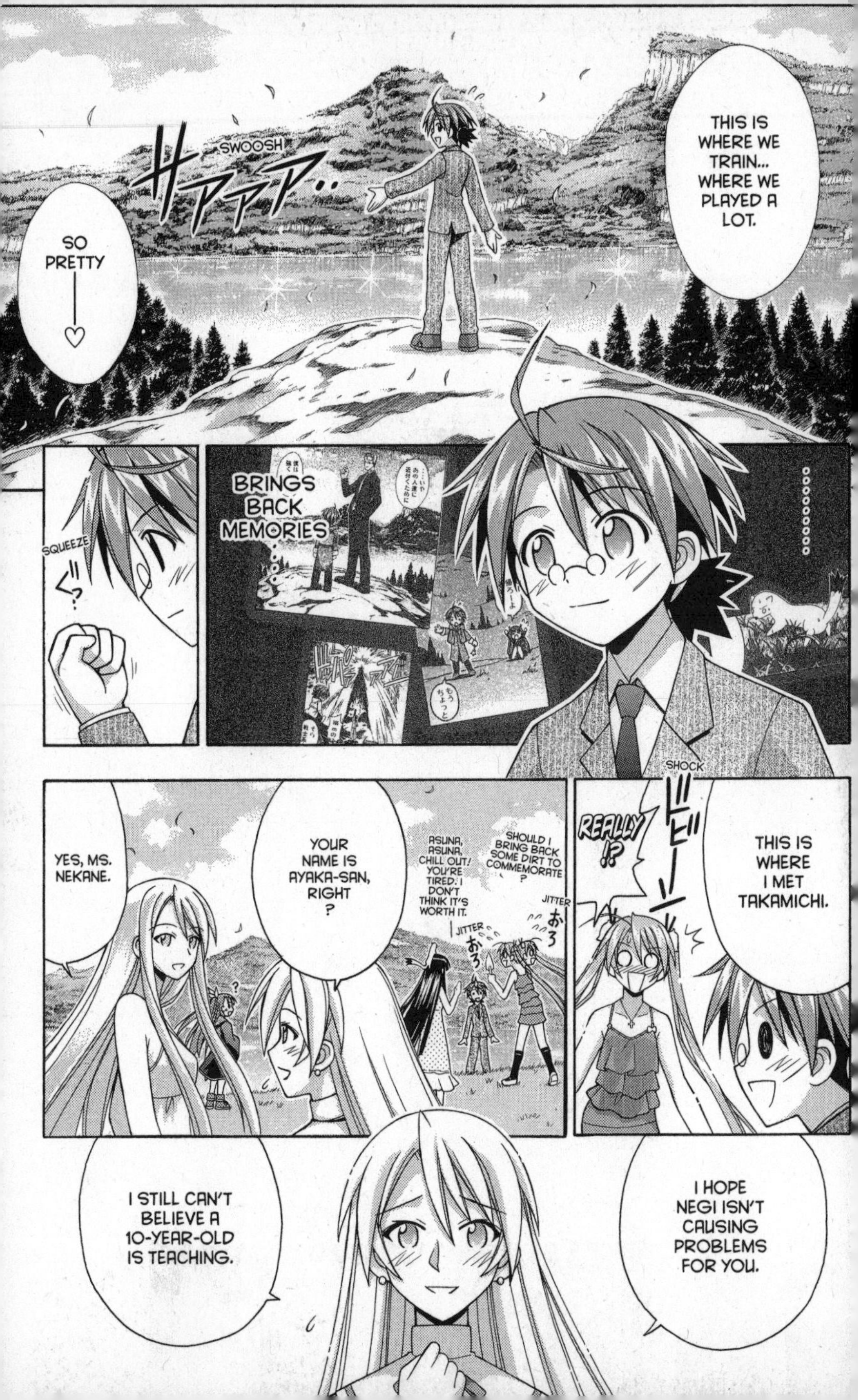

THIS IS WHERE WE TRAIN... WHERE WE PLAYED A LOT.
SWOOSH
SO PRETTY ♡
BRINGS BACK MEMORIES
SQUEEZE
THIS IS WHERE I MET TAKAMICHI.
SHOCK
REALLY!?
SHOULD I BRING BACK SOME DIRT TO COMMEMORATE?
JITTER
ASUNA, ASUNA, CHILL OUT! YOU'RE TIRED. I DON'T THINK IT'S WORTH IT.
JITTER
YOUR NAME IS AYAKA-SAN, RIGHT?
YES, MS. NEKANE.
I HOPE NEGI ISN'T CAUSING PROBLEMS FOR YOU.
I STILL CAN'T BELIEVE A 10-YEAR-OLD IS TEACHING.

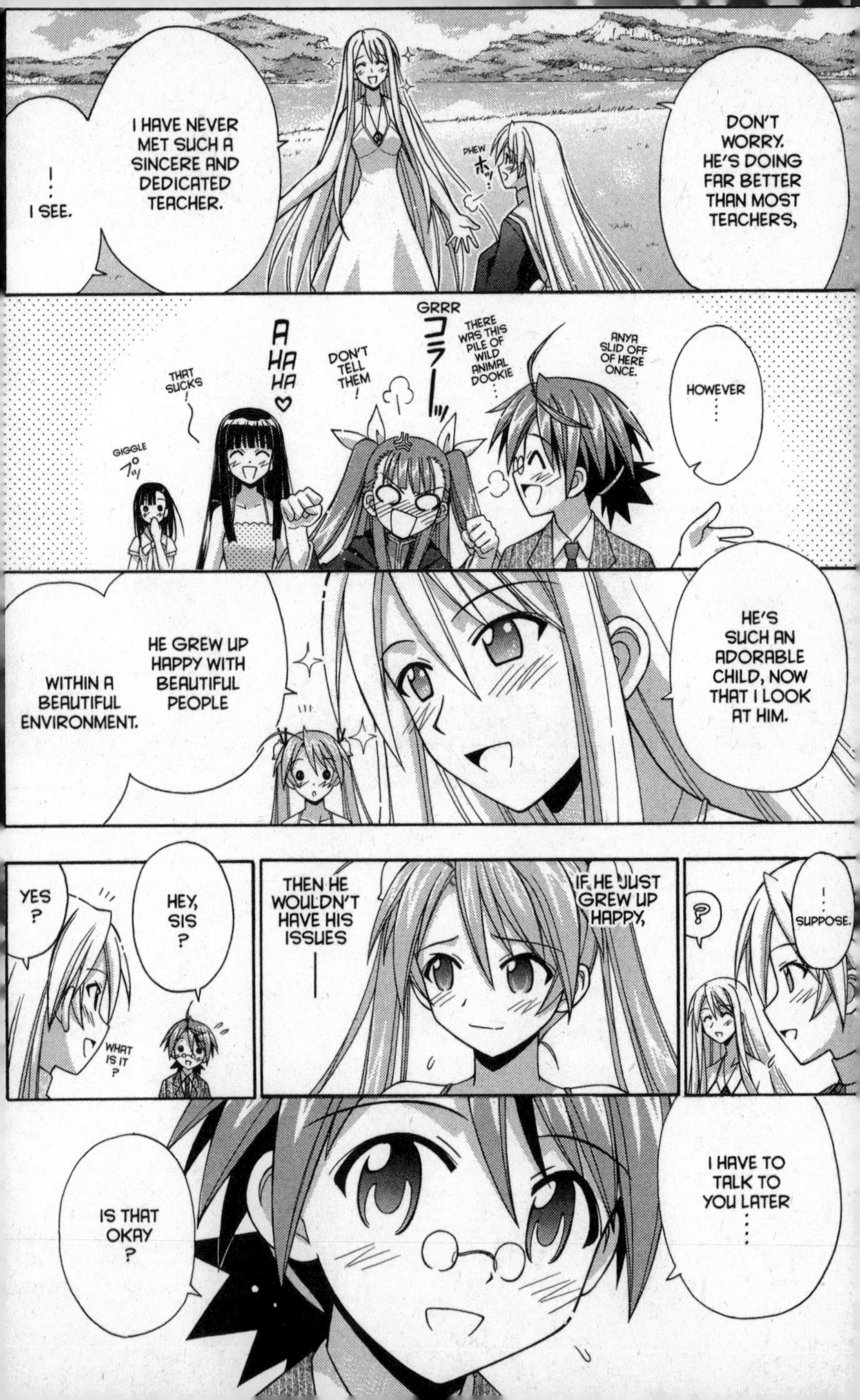
DON'T WORRY. HE'S DOING FAR BETTER THAN MOST TEACHERS,
PHEW
ホッ
I HAVE NEVER MET SUCH A SINCERE AND DEDICATED TEACHER.
...! I SEE.
HOWEVER...
ANYA SLID OFF OF HERE ONCE.
THERE WAS THIS PILE OF WILD ANIMAL DOOKIE...
GRRR
コラー
DON'T TELL THEM!
A HA HA ♥
THAT SUCKS!
GIGGLE
プッ
HE'S SUCH AN ADORABLE CHILD, NOW THAT I LOOK AT HIM.
HE GREW UP HAPPY WITH BEAUTIFUL PEOPLE
WITHIN A BEAUTIFUL ENVIRONMENT.
...I SUPPOSE.
?
IF HE JUST GREW UP HAPPY,
THEN HE WOULDN'T HAVE HIS ISSUES—
HEY, SIS?
YES?
WHAT IS IT?
I HAVE TO TALK TO YOU LATER...
IS THAT OKAY?

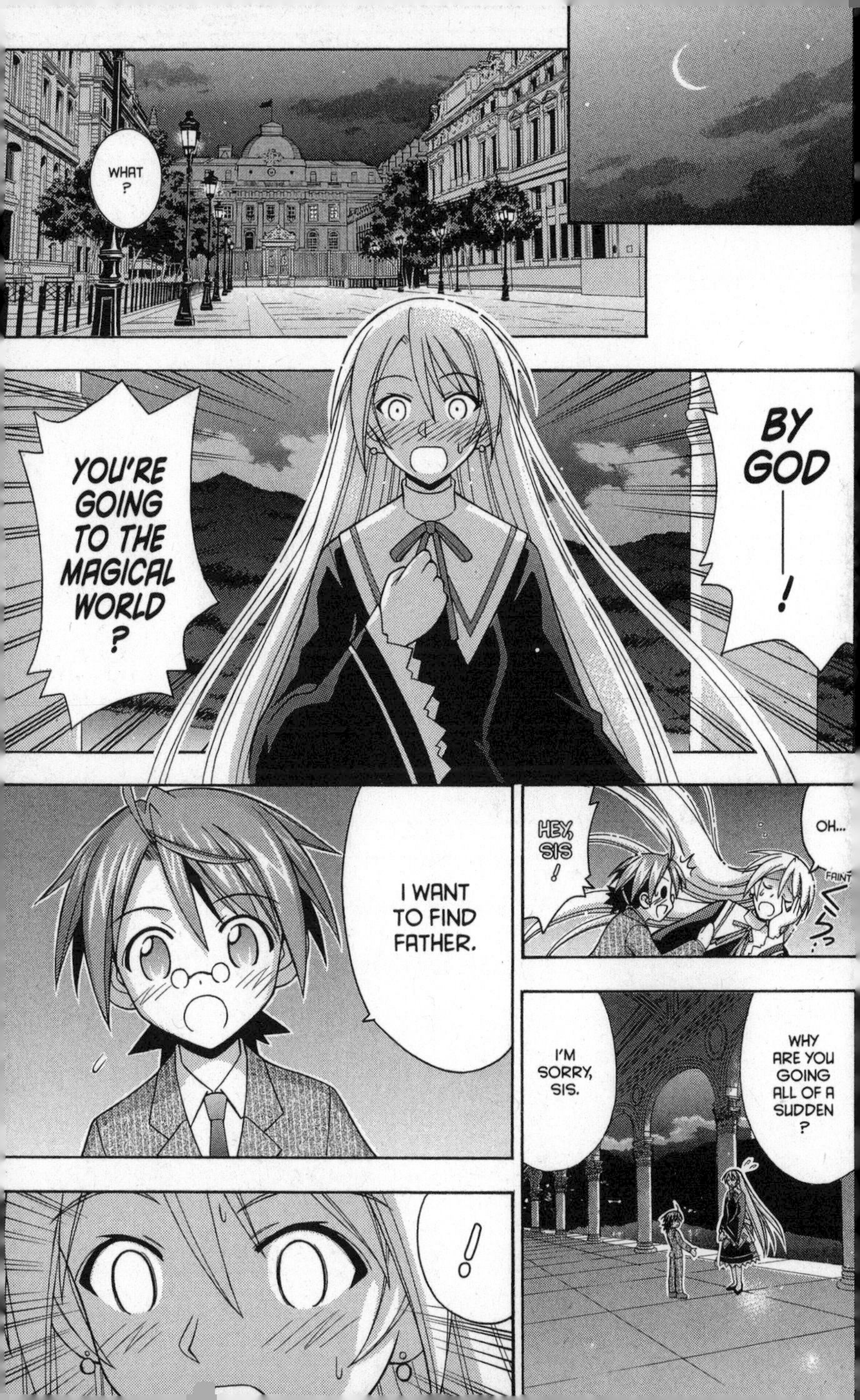
WHAT ?
BY GOD——!
YOU'RE GOING TO THE MAGICAL WORLD ?
OH...
FAINT
HEY, SIS !
WHY ARE YOU GOING ALL OF A SUDDEN ?
I'M SORRY, SIS.
I WANT TO FIND FATHER.
!

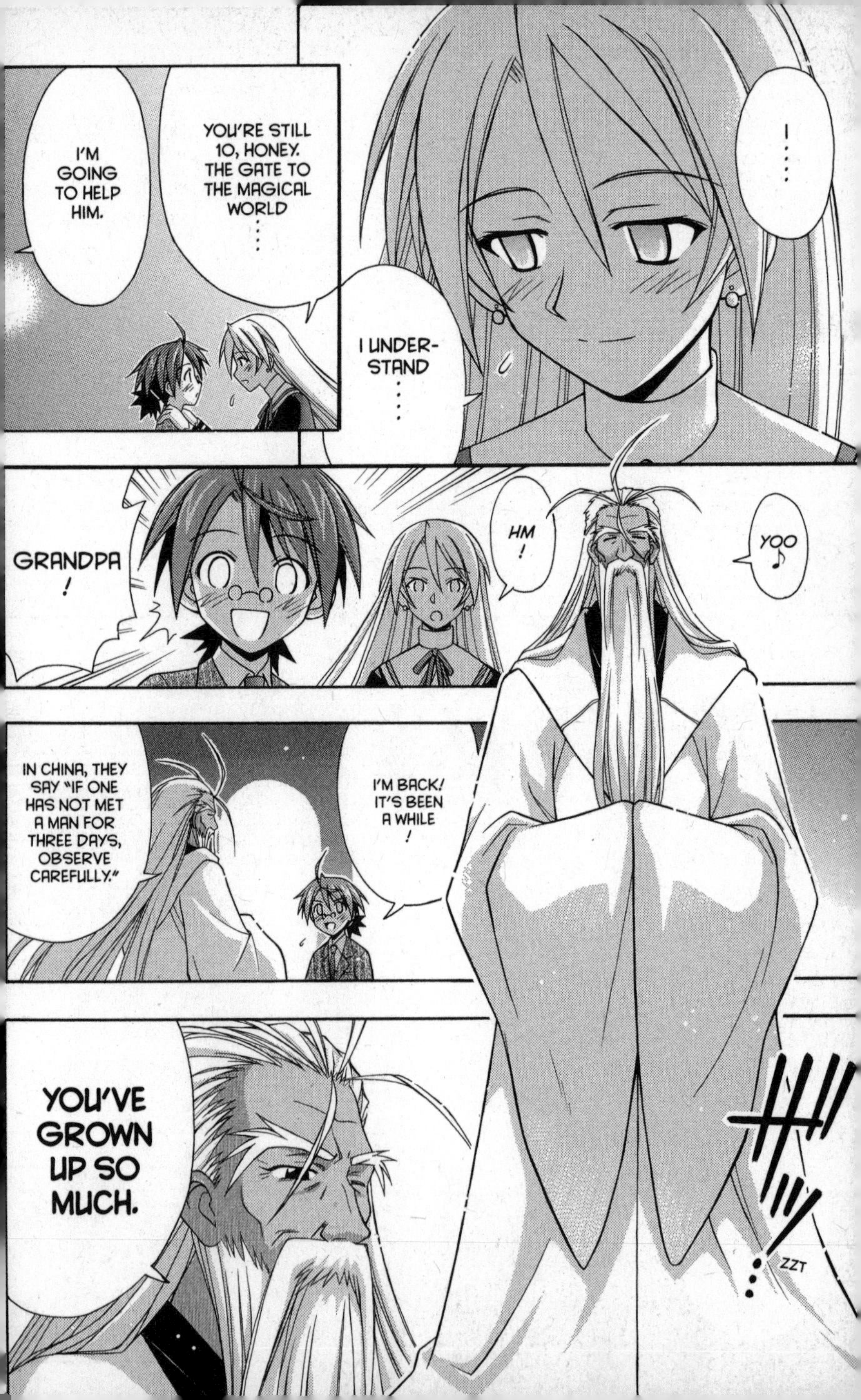

I......
I UNDER-STAND ......
YOU'RE STILL 10, HONEY. THE GATE TO THE MAGICAL WORLD ......
I'M GOING TO HELP HIM.
YOO ♪
ZZT
HM!
GRANDPA!
I'M BACK! IT'S BEEN A WHILE!
IN CHINA, THEY SAY "IF ONE HAS NOT MET A MAN FOR THREE DAYS, OBSERVE CAREFULLY."
YOU'VE GROWN UP SO MUCH.

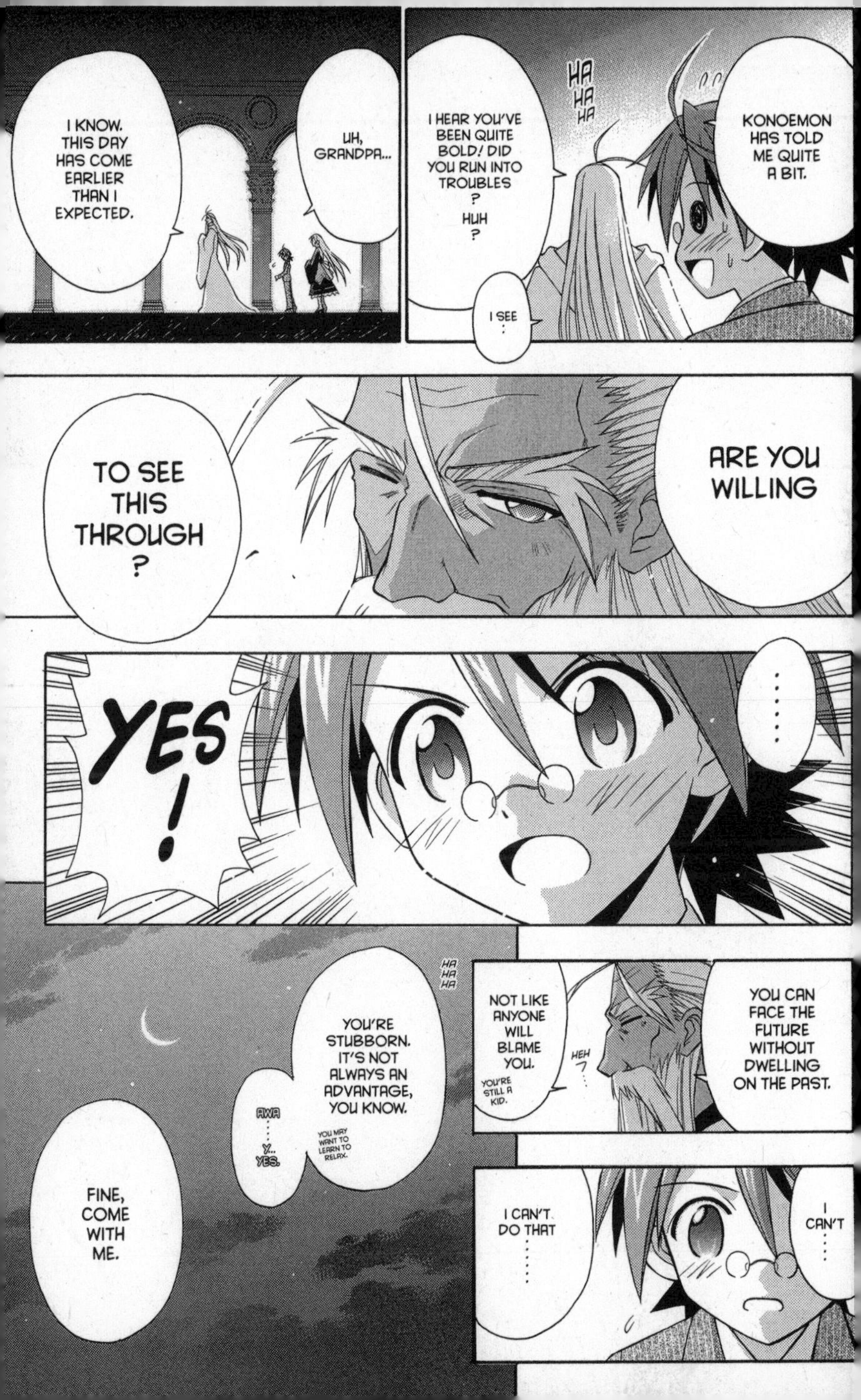
KONOEMON HAS TOLD ME QUITE A BIT.
HA HA HA
I HEAR YOU'VE BEEN QUITE BOLD! DID YOU RUN INTO TROUBLES? HUH?
I SEE...
UH, GRANDPA...
I KNOW. THIS DAY HAS COME EARLIER THAN I EXPECTED.
ARE YOU WILLING
TO SEE THIS THROUGH?
......
YES!
YOU CAN FACE THE FUTURE WITHOUT DWELLING ON THE PAST.
HEH...
NOT LIKE ANYONE WILL BLAME YOU.
YOU'RE STILL A KID.
I CAN'T...
I CAN'T DO THAT......
HA HA HA
YOU'RE STUBBORN. IT'S NOT ALWAYS AN ADVANTAGE, YOU KNOW.
YOU MAY WANT TO LEARN TO RELAX.
AWA... Y.. YES.
FINE, COME WITH ME.

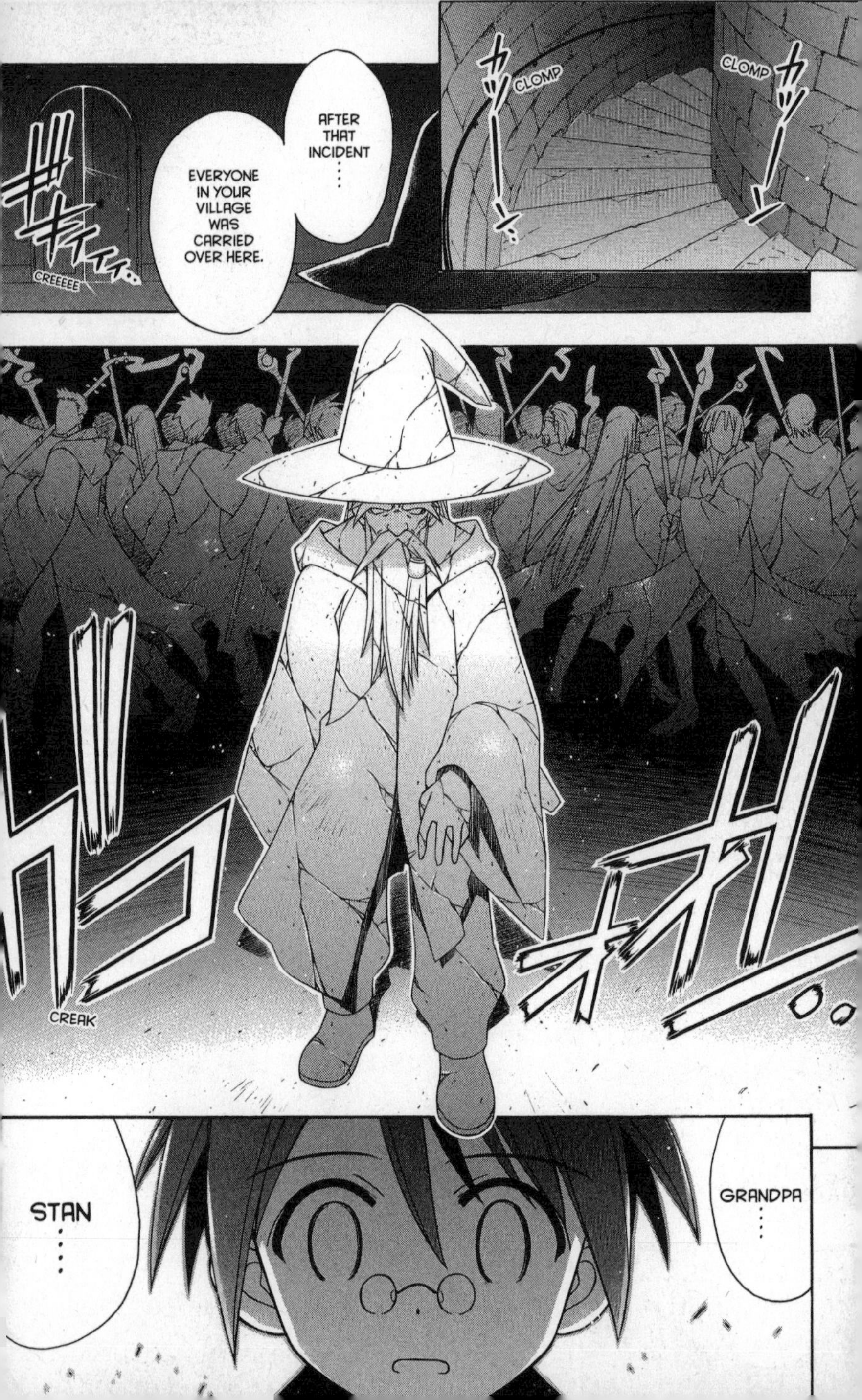
CLOMP
CLOMP
CREEEEE
AFTER THAT INCIDENT . . .
EVERYONE IN YOUR VILLAGE WAS CARRIED OVER HERE.
CREAK
GRANDPA . . .
STAN . . .

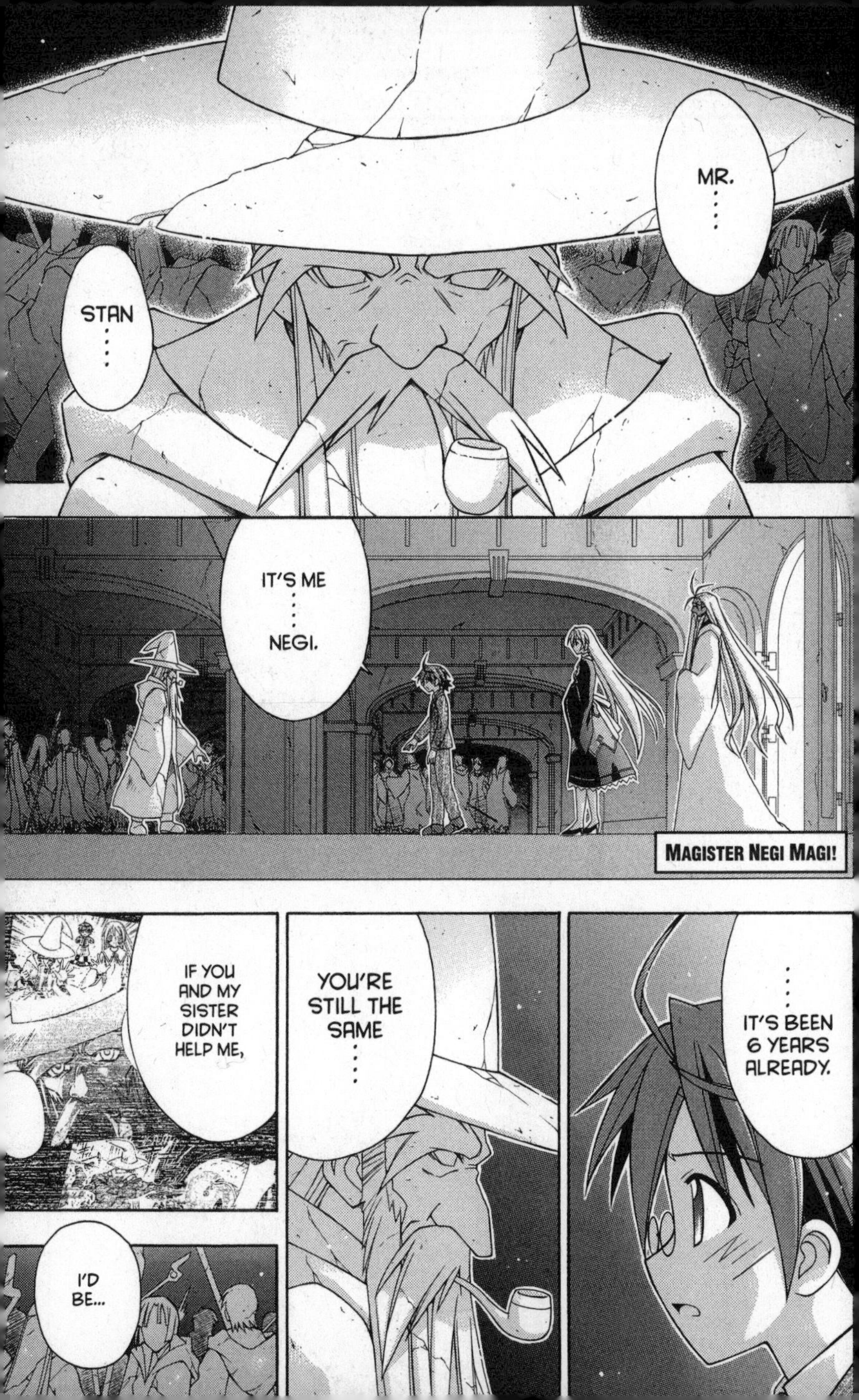
MR. ....
STAN ....
IT'S ME .... NEGI.
MAGISTER NEGI MAGI!
.... IT'S BEEN 6 YEARS ALREADY.
YOU'RE STILL THE SAME ....
IF YOU AND MY SISTER DIDN'T HELP ME,
I'D BE...

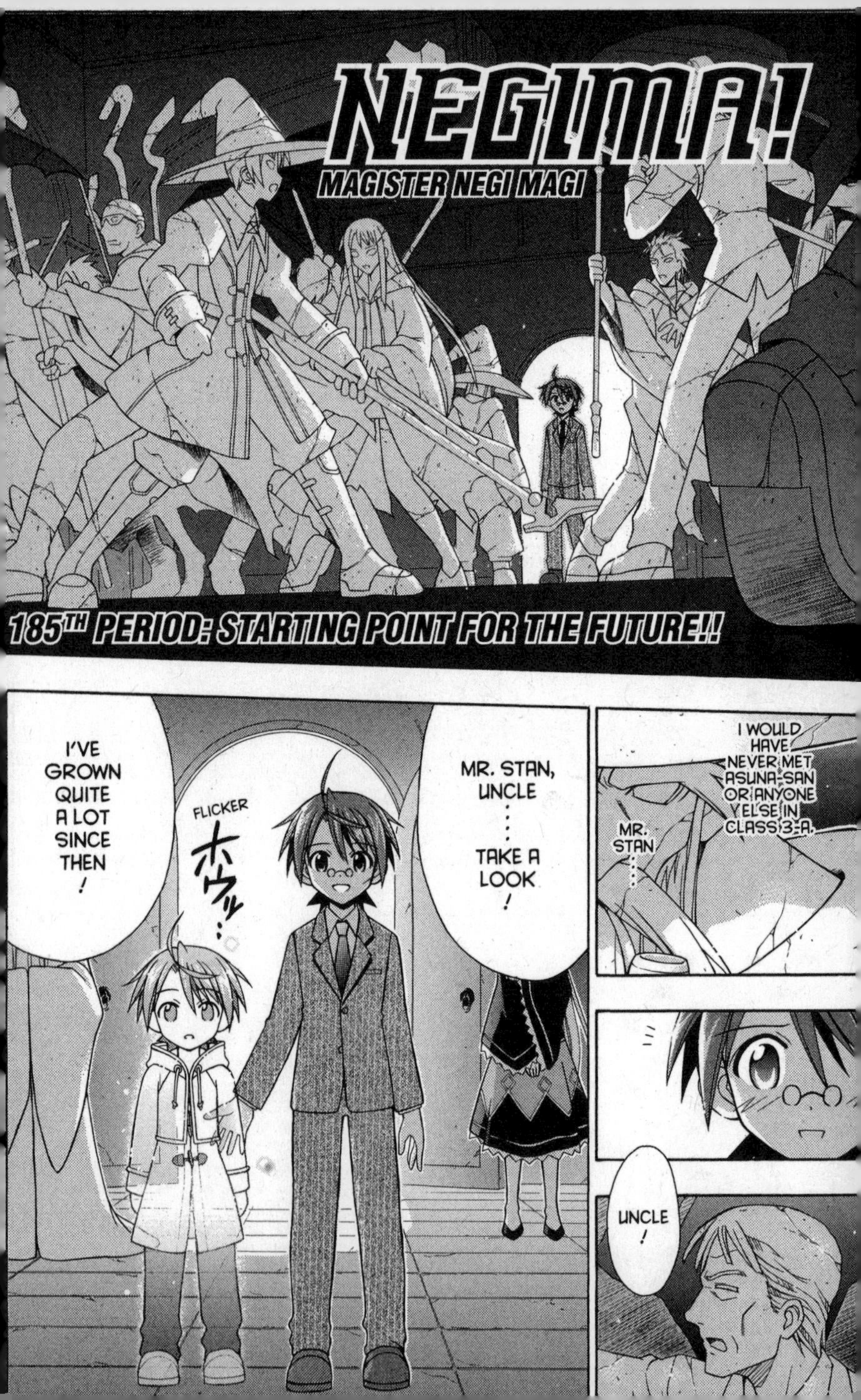
NEGIMA!
MAGISTER NEGI MAGI
185TH PERIOD: STARTING POINT FOR THE FUTURE!!
I WOULD HAVE NEVER MET ASUNA-SAN OR ANYONE ELSE IN CLASS 3-A.
MR. STAN ...
UNCLE !
MR. STAN, UNCLE ... TAKE A LOOK !
FLICKER
I'VE GROWN QUITE A LOT SINCE THEN !

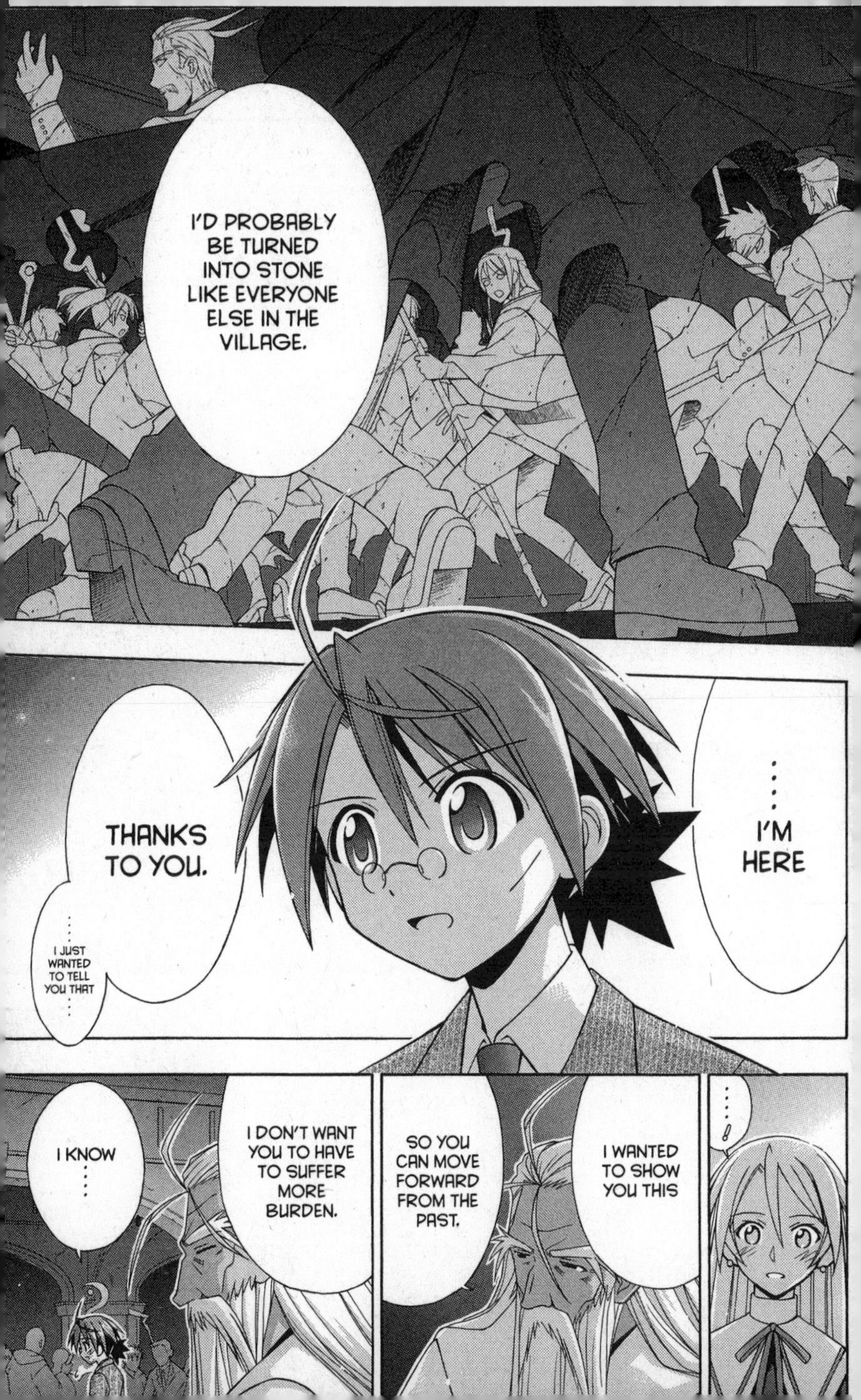
I'D PROBABLY BE TURNED INTO STONE LIKE EVERYONE ELSE IN THE VILLAGE.
....I'M HERE
THANKS TO YOU.
...I JUST WANTED TO TELL YOU THAT...
....!
I WANTED TO SHOW YOU THIS
SO YOU CAN MOVE FORWARD FROM THE PAST.
I DON'T WANT YOU TO HAVE TO SUFFER MORE BURDEN.
I KNOW...

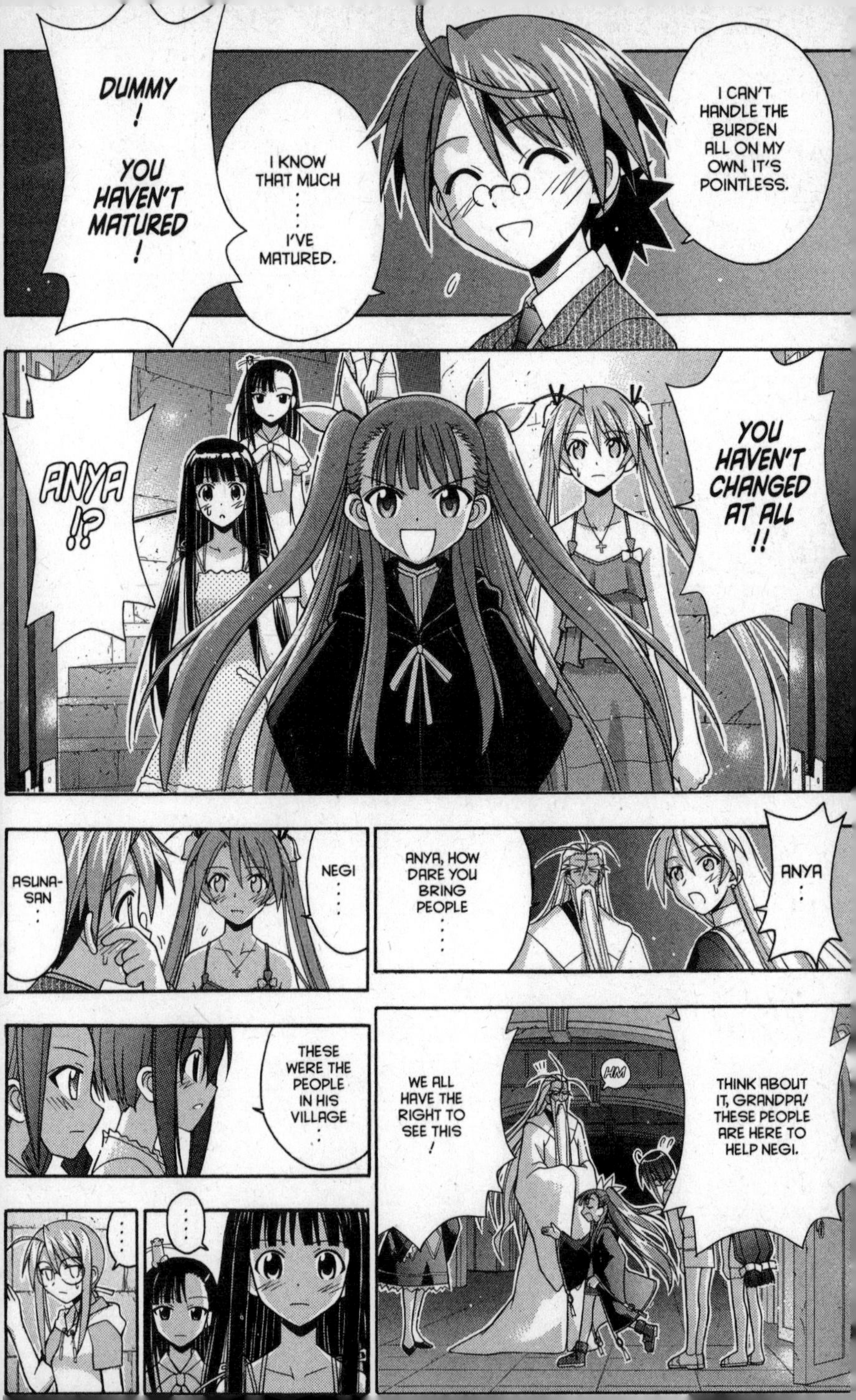
I CAN'T HANDLE THE BURDEN ALL ON MY OWN. IT'S POINTLESS.
I KNOW THAT MUCH... I'VE MATURED.
DUMMY! YOU HAVEN'T MATURED!
YOU HAVEN'T CHANGED AT ALL!!
ANYA!?
ANYA...
ANYA, HOW DARE YOU BRING PEOPLE...
NEGI...
ASUNA-SAN...
THINK ABOUT IT, GRANDPA! THESE PEOPLE ARE HERE TO HELP NEGI.
HM
WE ALL HAVE THE RIGHT TO SEE THIS!
THESE WERE THE PEOPLE IN HIS VILLAGE...
...
...

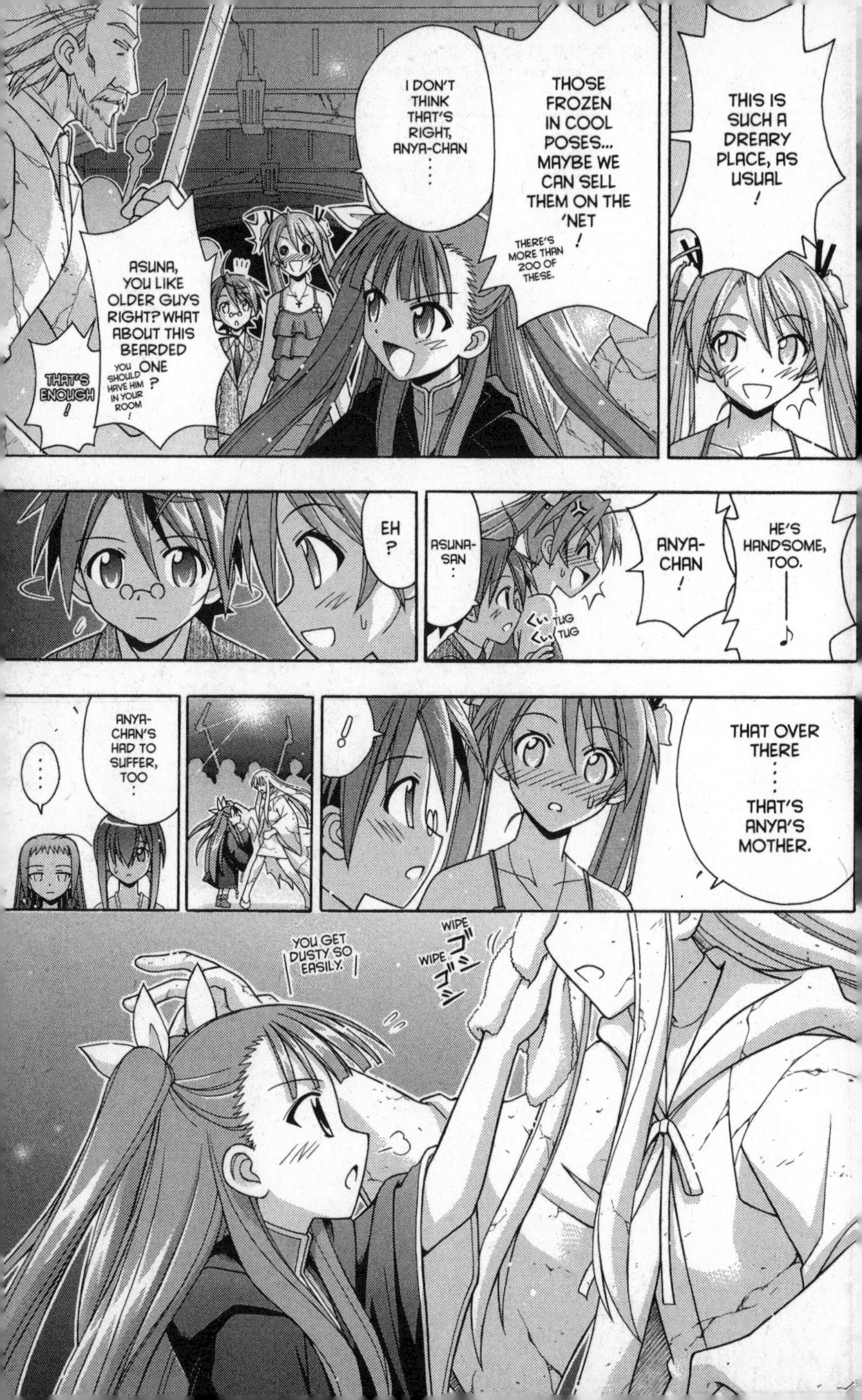
THIS IS SUCH A DREARY PLACE, AS USUAL!
THOSE FROZEN IN COOL POSES... MAYBE WE CAN SELL THEM ON THE 'NET!
THERE'S MORE THAN 200 OF THESE.
I DON'T THINK THAT'S RIGHT, ANYA-CHAN...
ASUNA, YOU LIKE OLDER GUYS RIGHT? WHAT ABOUT THIS BEARDED ONE?
YOU SHOULD HAVE HIM IN YOUR ROOM!
THAT'S ENOUGH!
HE'S HANDSOME, TOO. ♪
ANYA-CHAN!
ASUNA-SAN...
TUG TUG
EH?
THAT OVER THERE... THAT'S ANYA'S MOTHER.
!
ANYA-CHAN'S HAD TO SUFFER, TOO...
...
WIPE WIPE
YOU GET DUSTY SO EASILY.

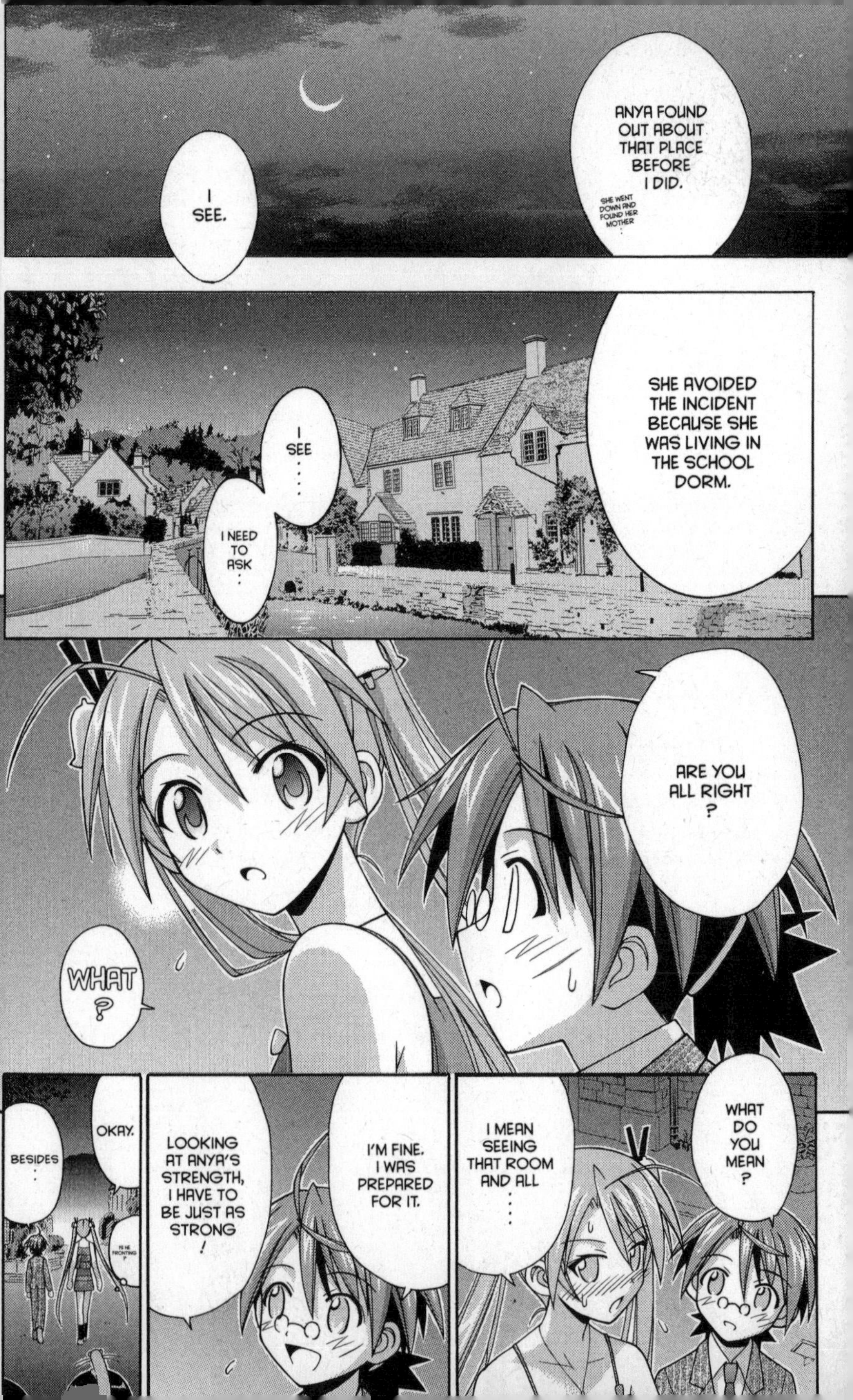
ANYA FOUND OUT ABOUT THAT PLACE BEFORE I DID.
SHE WENT DOWN AND FOUND HER MOTHER...
I SEE.
SHE AVOIDED THE INCIDENT BECAUSE SHE WAS LIVING IN THE SCHOOL DORM.
I SEE....
I NEED TO ASK...
ARE YOU ALL RIGHT?
WHAT?
WHAT DO YOU MEAN?
I MEAN SEEING THAT ROOM AND ALL....
I'M FINE. I WAS PREPARED FOR IT.
LOOKING AT ANYA'S STRENGTH, I HAVE TO BE JUST AS STRONG!
OKAY.
BESIDES...
IS HE FRONTING?

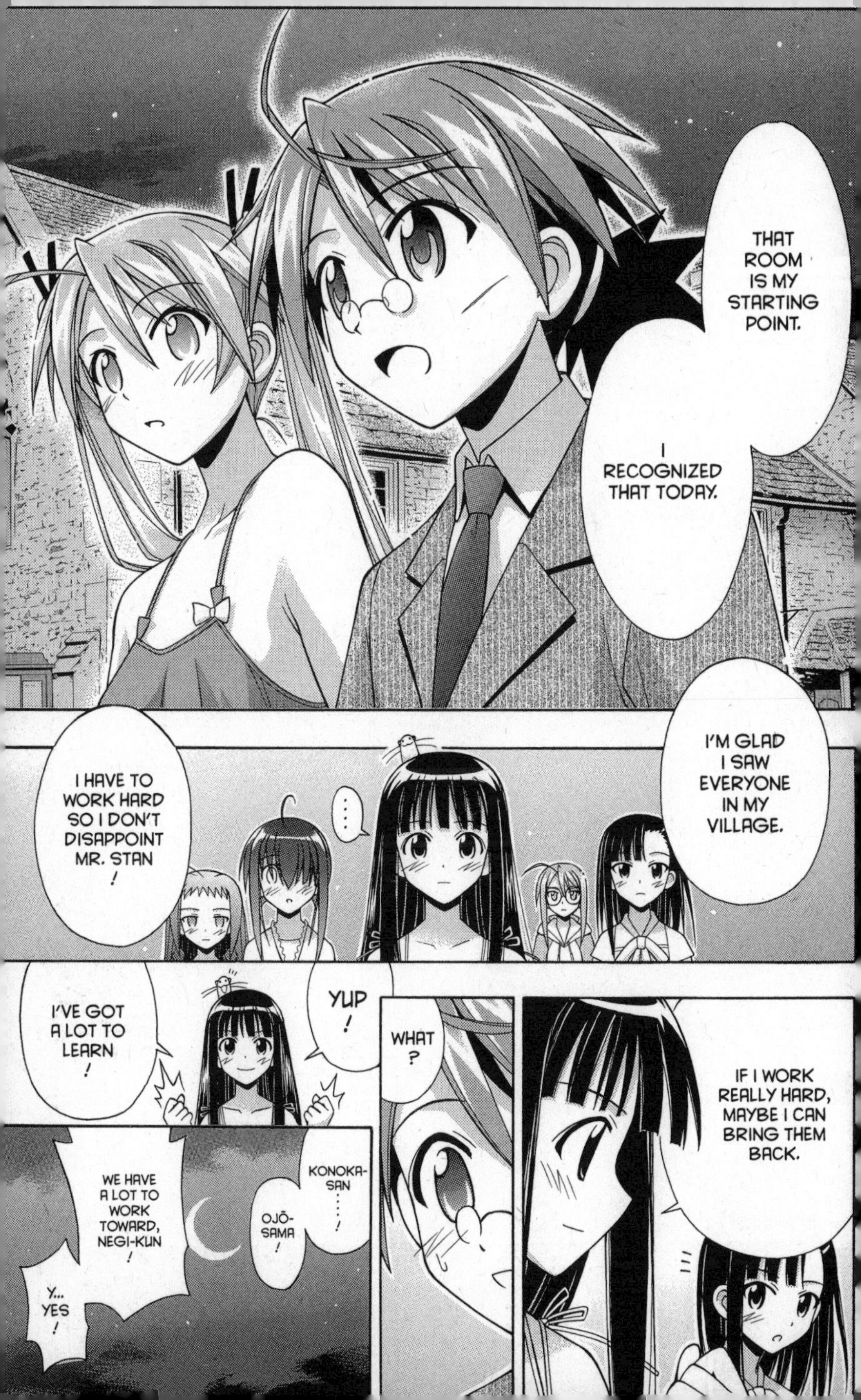
THAT ROOM IS MY STARTING POINT.
I RECOGNIZED THAT TODAY.
I'M GLAD I SAW EVERYONE IN MY VILLAGE.
....
I HAVE TO WORK HARD SO I DON'T DISAPPOINT MR. STAN!
IF I WORK REALLY HARD, MAYBE I CAN BRING THEM BACK.
WHAT?
YUP!
I'VE GOT A LOT TO LEARN!
KONOKA-SAN.....!
OJŌ-SAMA!
WE HAVE A LOT TO WORK TOWARD, NEGI-KUN!
Y... YES!

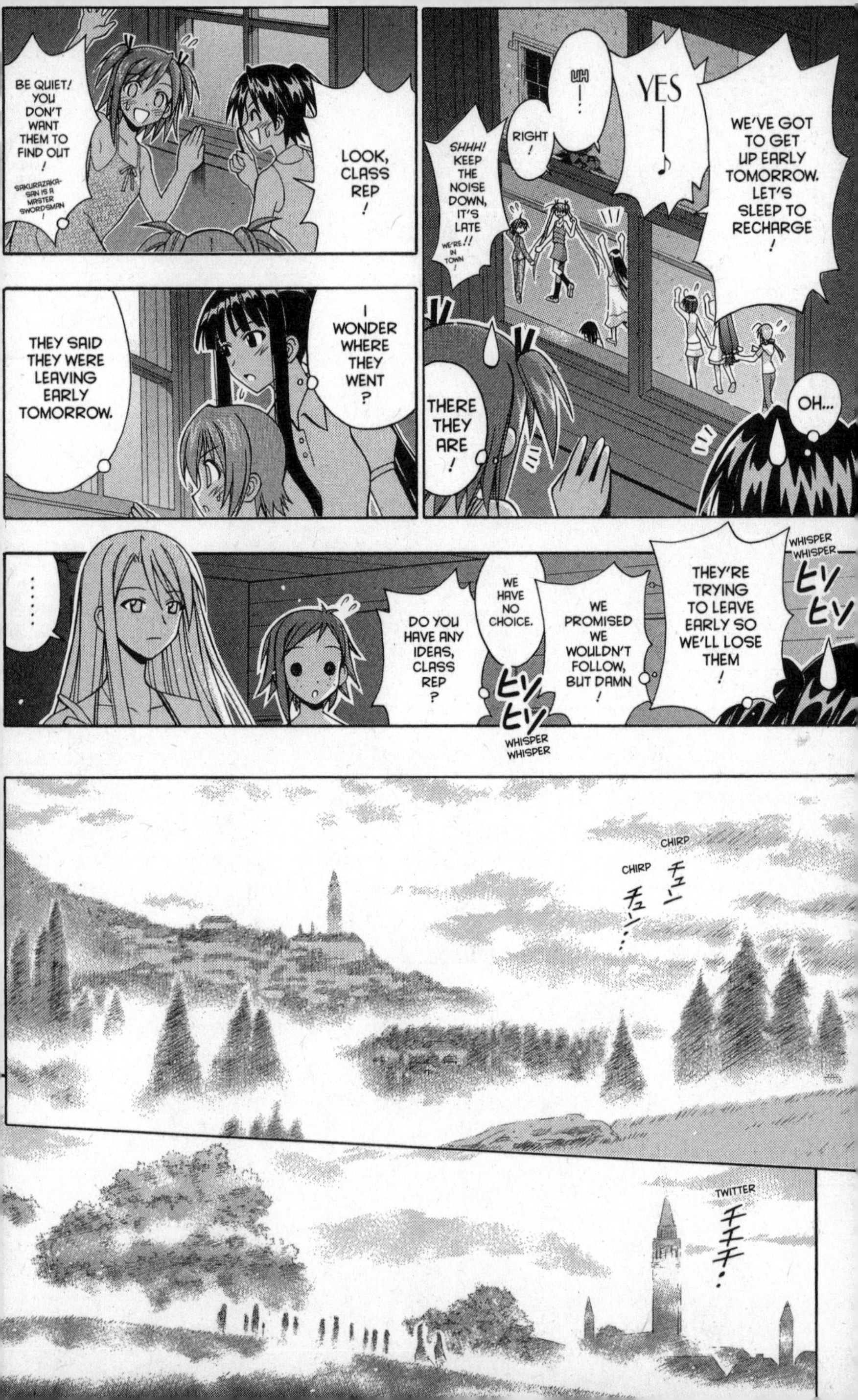
WE'VE GOT TO GET UP EARLY TOMORROW. LET'S SLEEP TO RECHARGE!
YES—♪
UH—!
RIGHT!
SHHH! KEEP THE NOISE DOWN, IT'S LATE!!
WE'RE IN TOWN!
LOOK, CLASS REP!
BE QUIET! YOU DON'T WANT THEM TO FIND OUT!
SAKURAZAKA-SAN IS A MASTER SWORDSMAN!
OH...
THERE THEY ARE!
I WONDER WHERE THEY WENT?
THEY SAID THEY WERE LEAVING EARLY TOMORROW.
WHISPER WHISPER
ヒソヒソ
THEY'RE TRYING TO LEAVE EARLY SO WE'LL LOSE THEM!
WE PROMISED WE WOULDN'T FOLLOW, BUT DAMN!
WE HAVE NO CHOICE.
DO YOU HAVE ANY IDEAS, CLASS REP?
ヒソヒソ
WHISPER WHISPER
......
CHIRP
チュン
CHIRP
チュン...
TWITTER
チチチ・

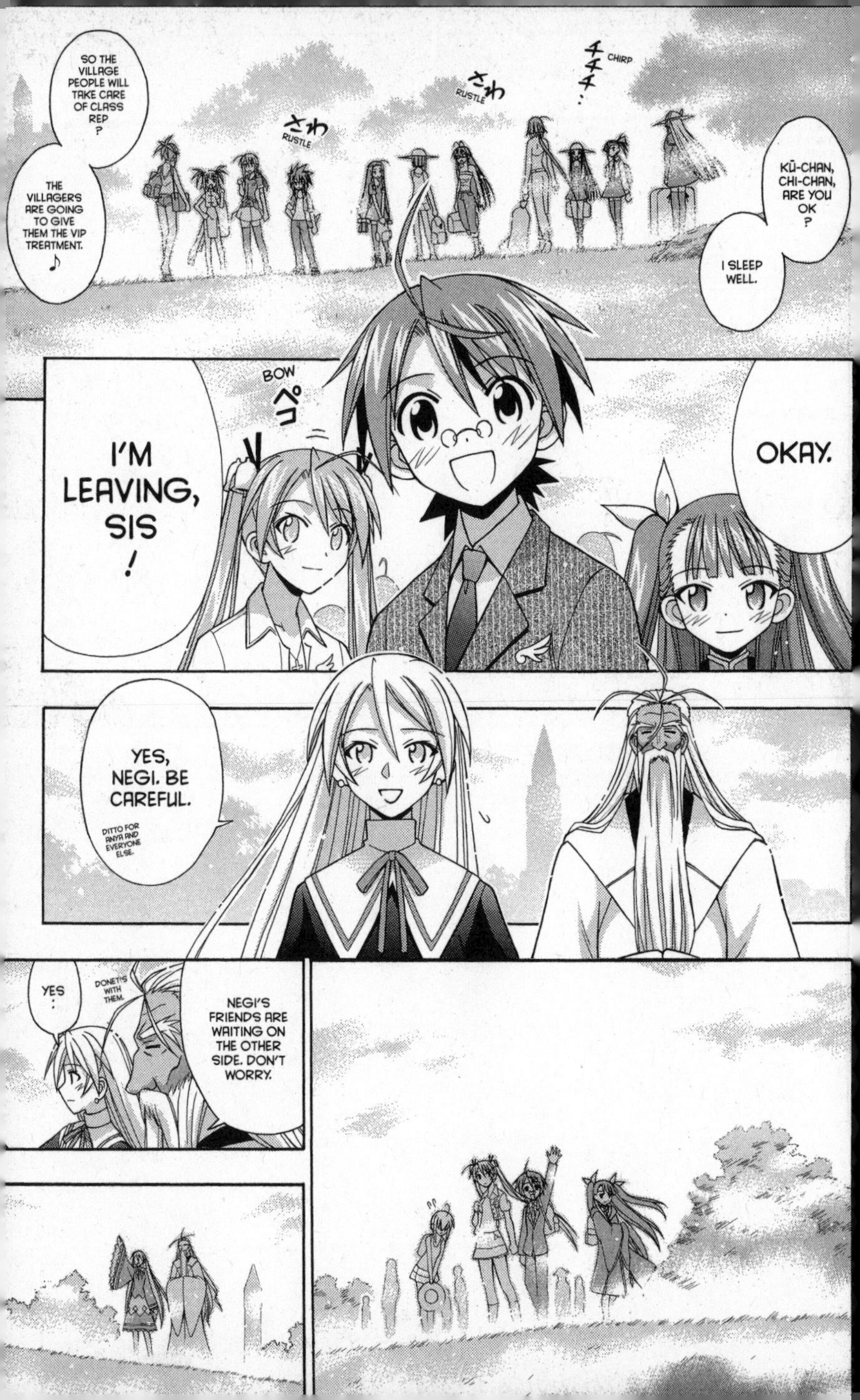
チチチ… CHIRP
さわ RUSTLE
KŪ-CHAN, CHI-CHAN, ARE YOU OK?
I SLEEP WELL.
さわ RUSTLE
SO THE VILLAGE PEOPLE WILL TAKE CARE OF CLASS REP?
THE VILLAGERS ARE GOING TO GIVE THEM THE VIP TREATMENT. ♪
OKAY.
BOW ペコ
I'M LEAVING, SIS!
YES, NEGI. BE CAREFUL.
DITTO FOR ANYA AND EVERYONE ELSE.
NEGI'S FRIENDS ARE WAITING ON THE OTHER SIDE. DON'T WORRY.
DONET'S WITH THEM.
YES…

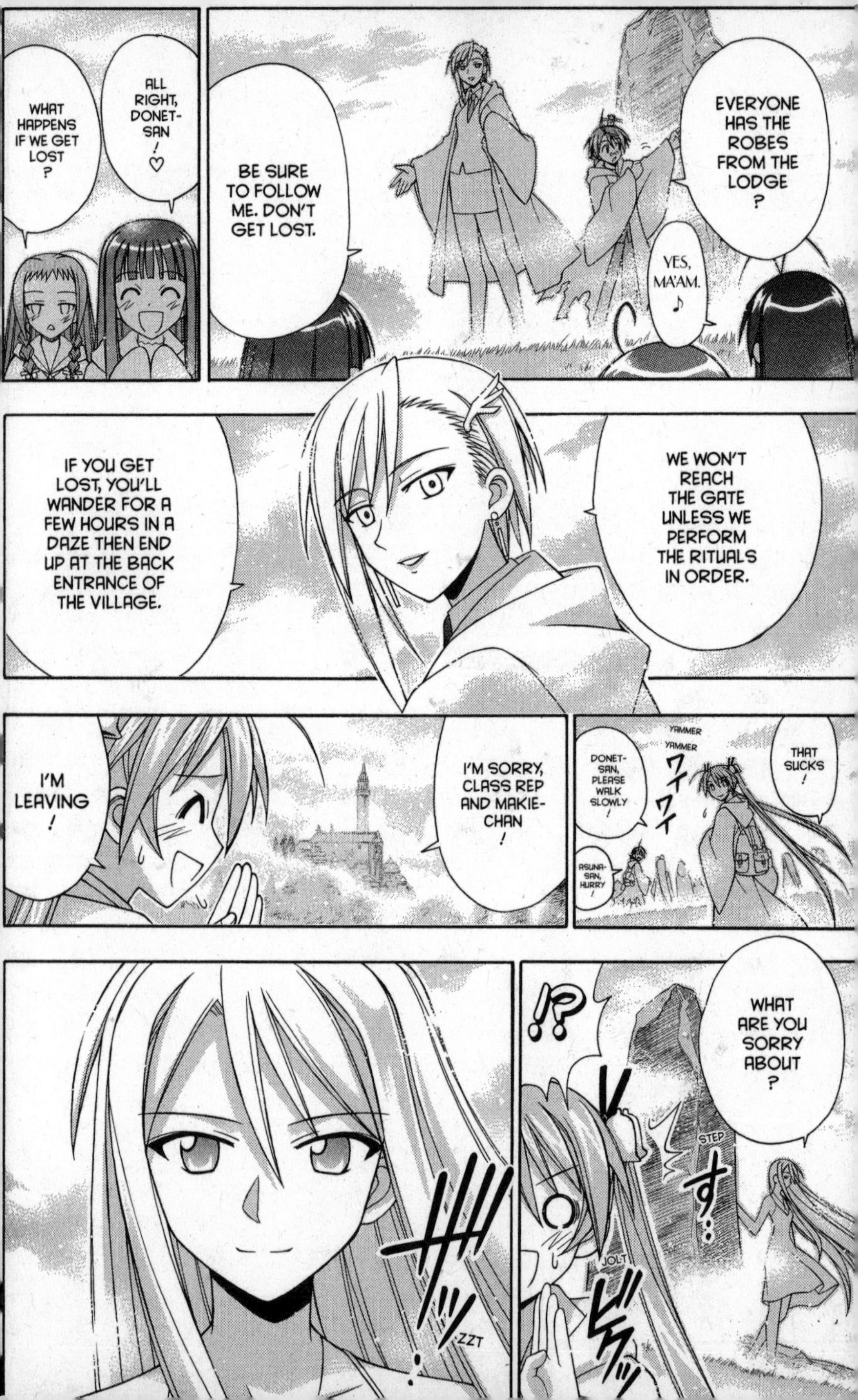
EVERYONE HAS THE ROBES FROM THE LODGE?
YES, MA'AM. ♪
BE SURE TO FOLLOW ME. DON'T GET LOST.
ALL RIGHT, DONET-SAN! ♡
WHAT HAPPENS IF WE GET LOST?
WE WON'T REACH THE GATE UNLESS WE PERFORM THE RITUALS IN ORDER.
IF YOU GET LOST, YOU'LL WANDER FOR A FEW HOURS IN A DAZE THEN END UP AT THE BACK ENTRANCE OF THE VILLAGE.
THAT SUCKS!
YAMMER YAMMER
ワイワイ
DONET-SAN, PLEASE WALK SLOWLY!
ASUNA-SAN, HURRY!
I'M SORRY, CLASS REP AND MAKIE-CHAN!
I'M LEAVING!
WHAT ARE YOU SORRY ABOUT?
!?
STEP
JOLT
ZZT

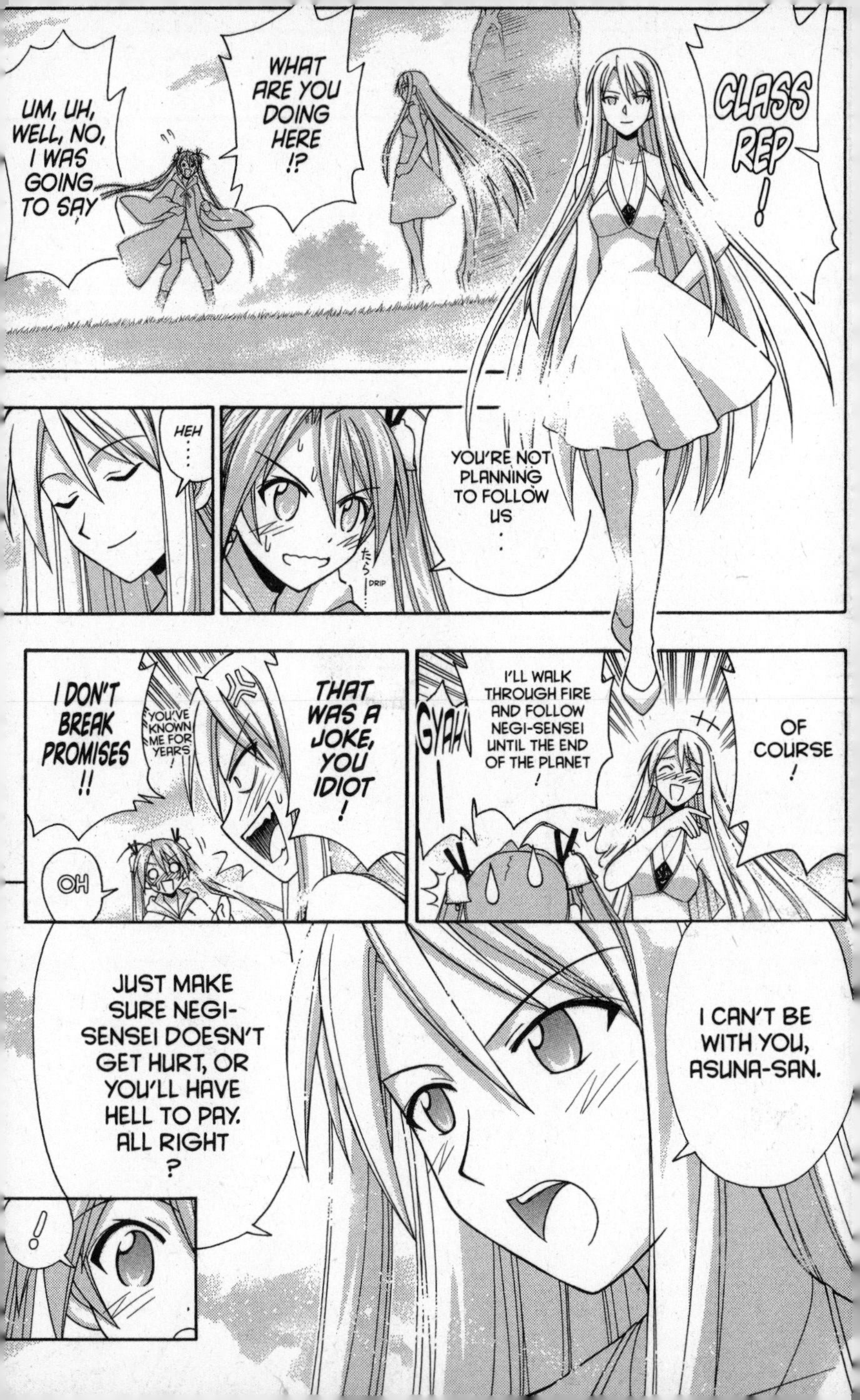
CLASS REP!
WHAT ARE YOU DOING HERE!?
UM, UH, WELL, NO, I WAS GOING TO SAY
YOU'RE NOT PLANNING TO FOLLOW US...
たら DRIP
HEH...
OF COURSE!
I'LL WALK THROUGH FIRE AND FOLLOW NEGI-SENSEI UNTIL THE END OF THE PLANET!
GYAH!
THAT WAS A JOKE, YOU IDIOT!
YOU'VE KNOWN ME FOR YEARS!
I DON'T BREAK PROMISES!!
OH
I CAN'T BE WITH YOU, ASUNA-SAN.
JUST MAKE SURE NEGI-SENSEI DOESN'T GET HURT, OR YOU'LL HAVE HELL TO PAY. ALL RIGHT?
!

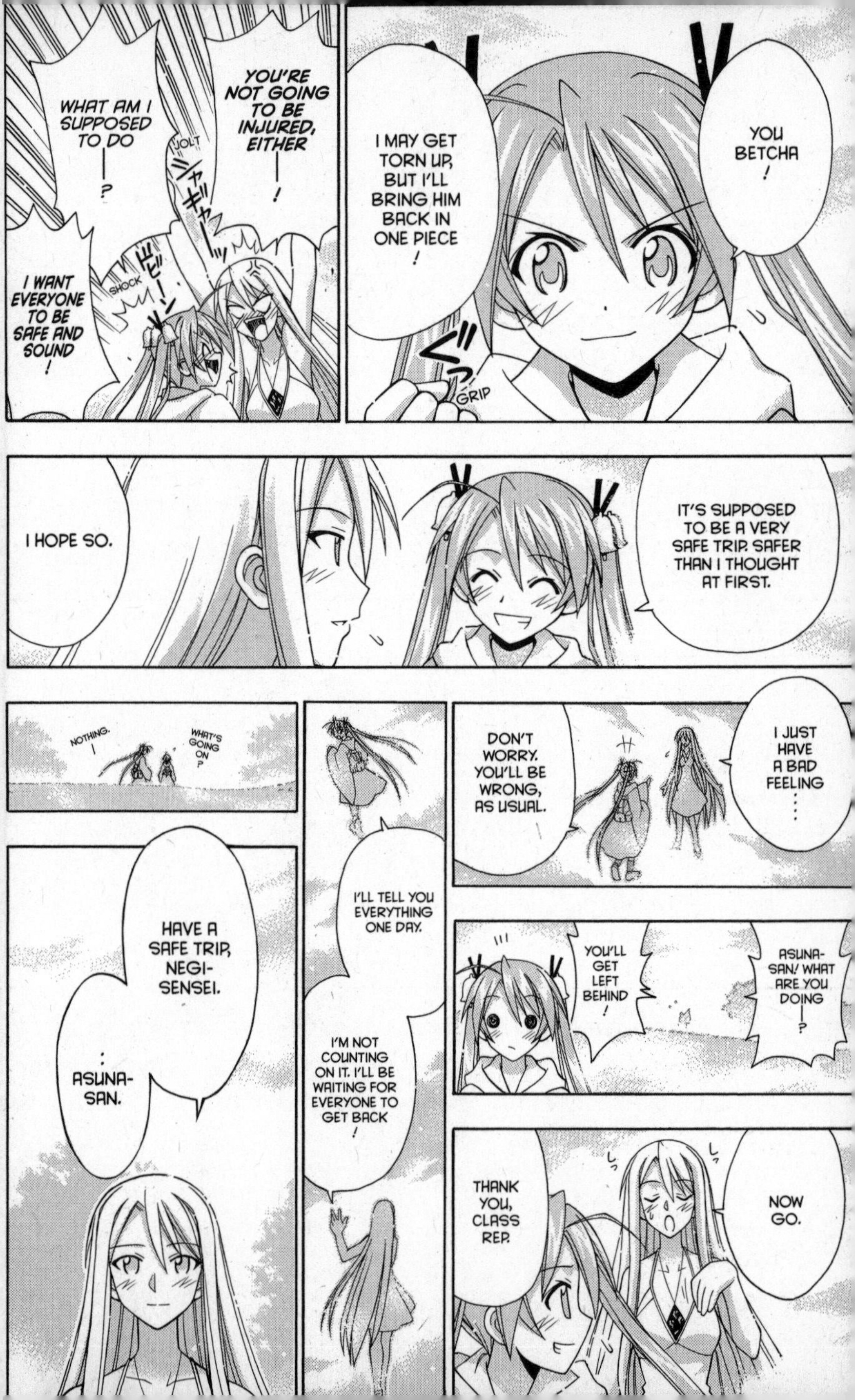
YOU BETCHA!
I MAY GET TORN UP, BUT I'LL BRING HIM BACK IN ONE PIECE!
GRIP
YOU'RE NOT GOING TO BE INJURED, EITHER—!
JOLT
WHAT AM I SUPPOSED TO DO—?
SHOCK
I WANT EVERYONE TO BE SAFE AND SOUND!
IT'S SUPPOSED TO BE A VERY SAFE TRIP. SAFER THAN I THOUGHT AT FIRST.
I HOPE SO.
I JUST HAVE A BAD FEELING....
DON'T WORRY. YOU'LL BE WRONG, AS USUAL.
ASUNA-SAN! WHAT ARE YOU DOING—?
YOU'LL GET LEFT BEHIND!
NOW GO.
THANK YOU, CLASS REP.
I'LL TELL YOU EVERYTHING ONE DAY.
I'M NOT COUNTING ON IT. I'LL BE WAITING FOR EVERYONE TO GET BACK!
WHAT'S GOING ON?
NOTHING.
HAVE A SAFE TRIP, NEGI-SENSEI.
: ASUNA-SAN.

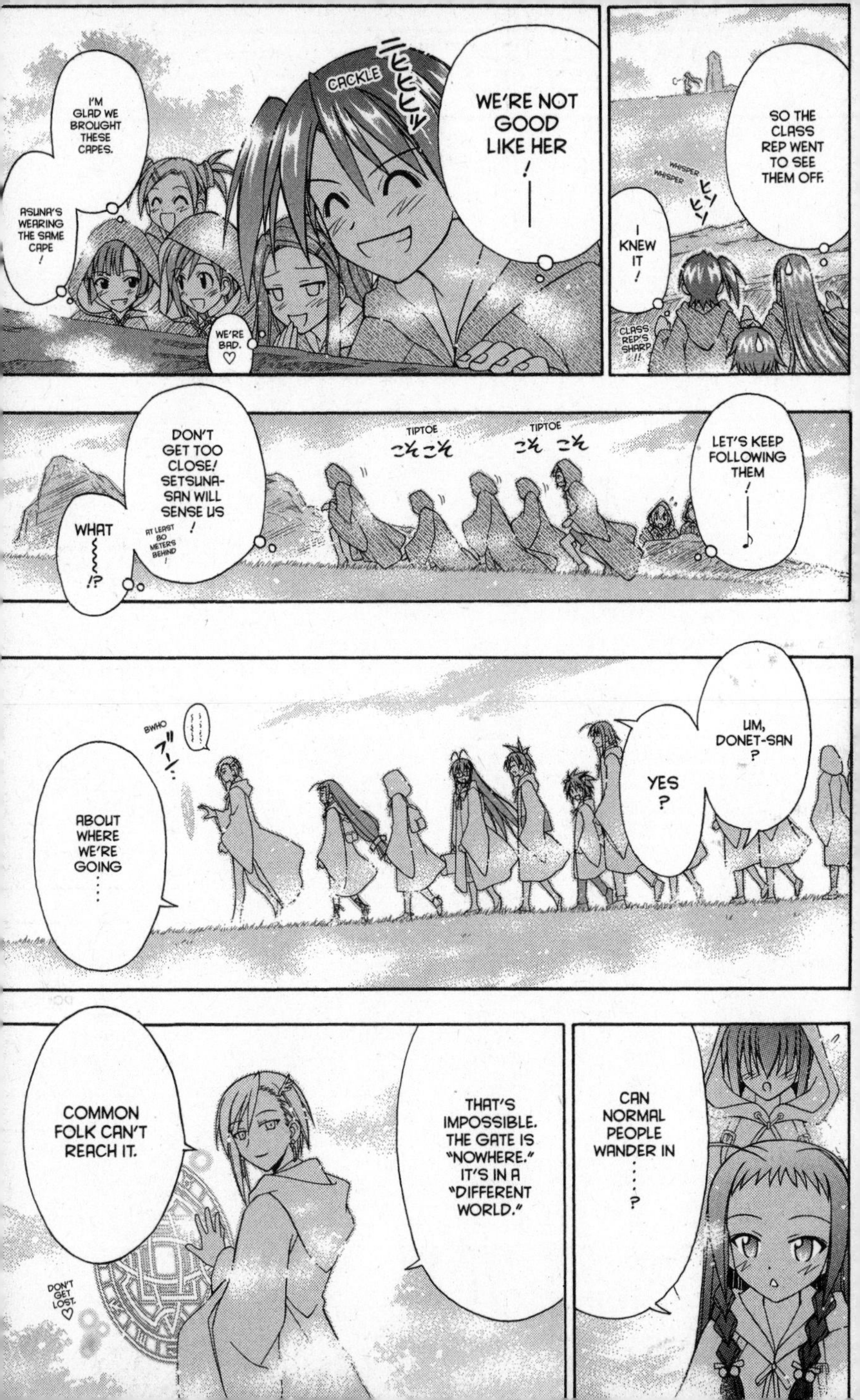
SO THE CLASS REP WENT TO SEE THEM OFF.
WHISPER WHISPER
ヒソヒソ
I KNEW IT!
CLASS REP'S SHARP!!
CACKLE
ニヒヒヒッ
WE'RE NOT GOOD LIKE HER!—
I'M GLAD WE BROUGHT THESE CAPES.
ASUNA'S WEARING THE SAME CAPE!
WE'RE BAD. ♡
LET'S KEEP FOLLOWING THEM!—♪
TIPTOE
こそ こそ
TIPTOE
こそこそ
DON'T GET TOO CLOSE! SETSUNA-SAN WILL SENSE US!
AT LEAST 80 METERS BEHIND!
WHAT~~~!?
UM, DONET-SAN?
YES?
ABOUT WHERE WE'RE GOING....
BWHO
CAN NORMAL PEOPLE WANDER IN....?
THAT'S IMPOSSIBLE. THE GATE IS "NOWHERE." IT'S IN A "DIFFERENT WORLD."
COMMON FOLK CAN'T REACH IT.
DON'T GET LOST. ♡

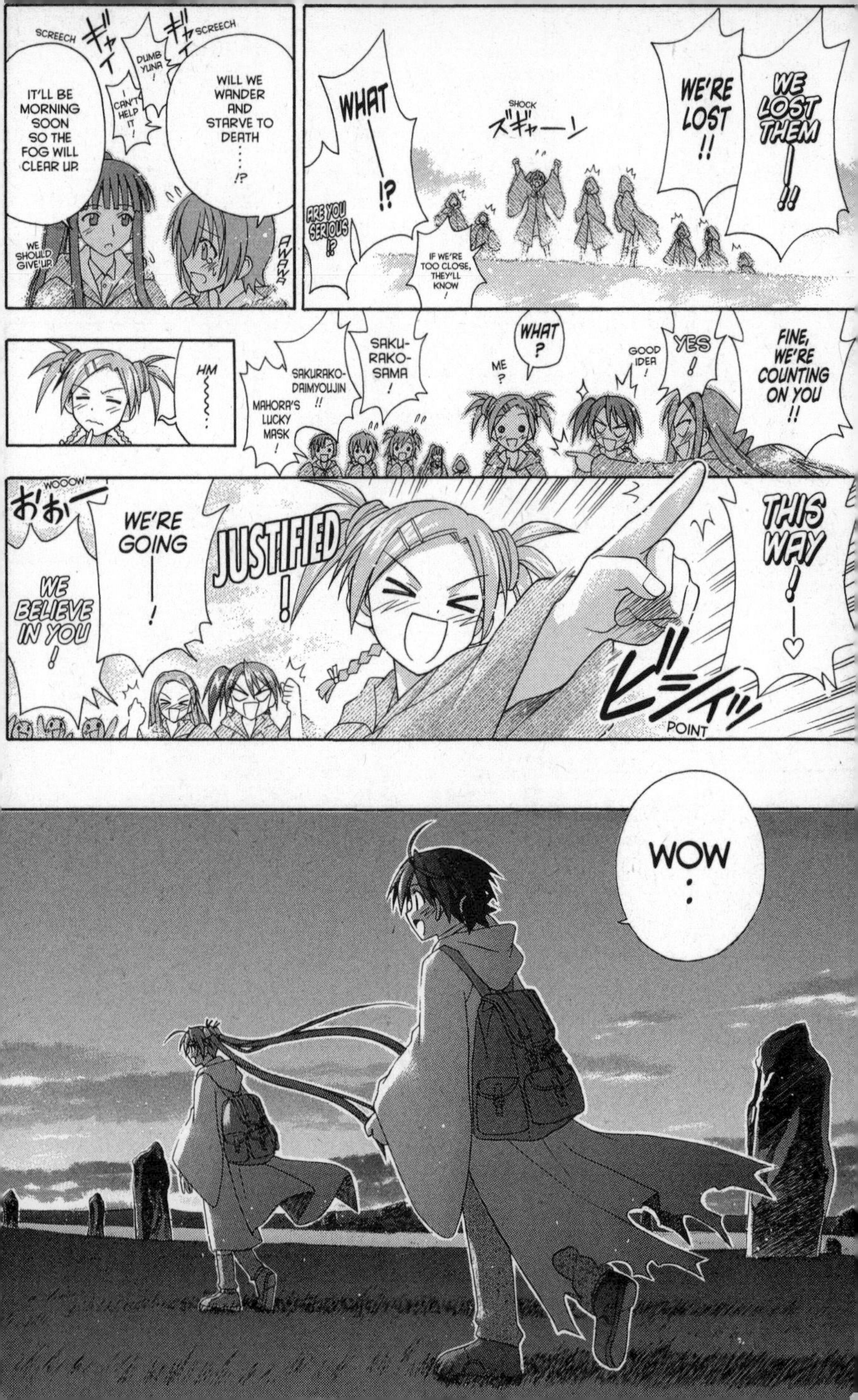
WE LOST THEM—!!
WE'RE LOST!!
SHOCK
ズギャーン
WHAT—!?
ARE YOU SERIOUS!?
IF WE'RE TOO CLOSE, THEY'LL KNOW!
SCREECH
ギャイ
SCREECH
ギャイ
WILL WE WANDER AND STARVE TO DEATH......!?
DUMB YUNA!
I CAN'T HELP IT!
IT'LL BE MORNING SOON SO THE FOG WILL CLEAR UP.
AWAWA
WE SHOULD GIVE UP.
FINE, WE'RE COUNTING ON YOU!!
YES!
GOOD IDEA!
WHAT?
ME?
SAKU-RAKO-SAMA!
SAKURAKO-DAIMYOUJIN!!
MAHORA'S LUCKY MASK!
HM~~...
THIS WAY!—♡
ビシイッ
POINT
JUSTIFIED!
WE'RE GOING—!
WOOOW
おぉー
WE BELIEVE IN YOU!
WOW...

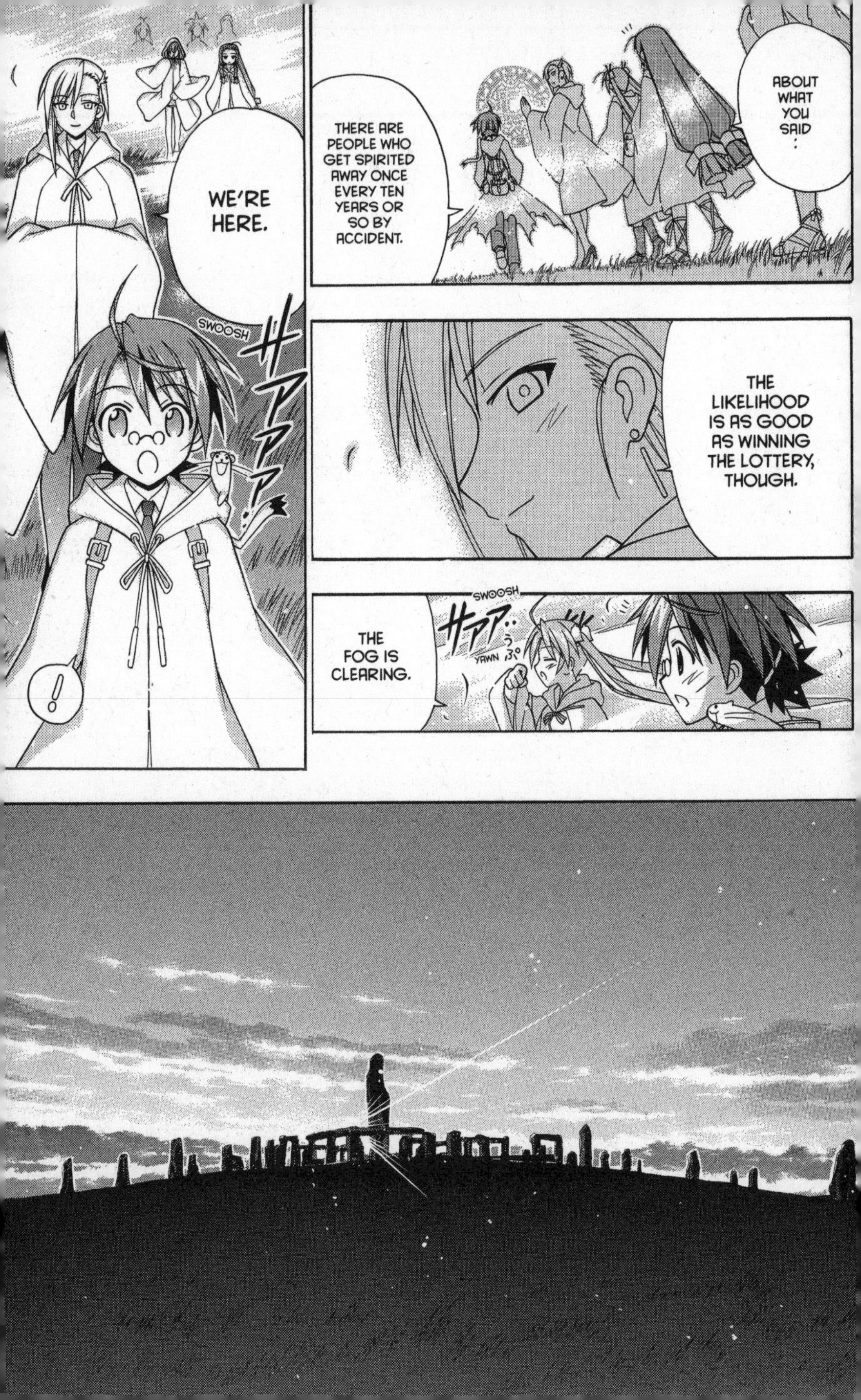
ABOUT WHAT YOU SAID...
THERE ARE PEOPLE WHO GET SPIRITED AWAY ONCE EVERY TEN YEARS OR SO BY ACCIDENT.
THE LIKELIHOOD IS AS GOOD AS WINNING THE LOTTERY, THOUGH.
THE FOG IS CLEARING.
SWOOSH
YAWN
WE'RE HERE.
SWOOSH
!

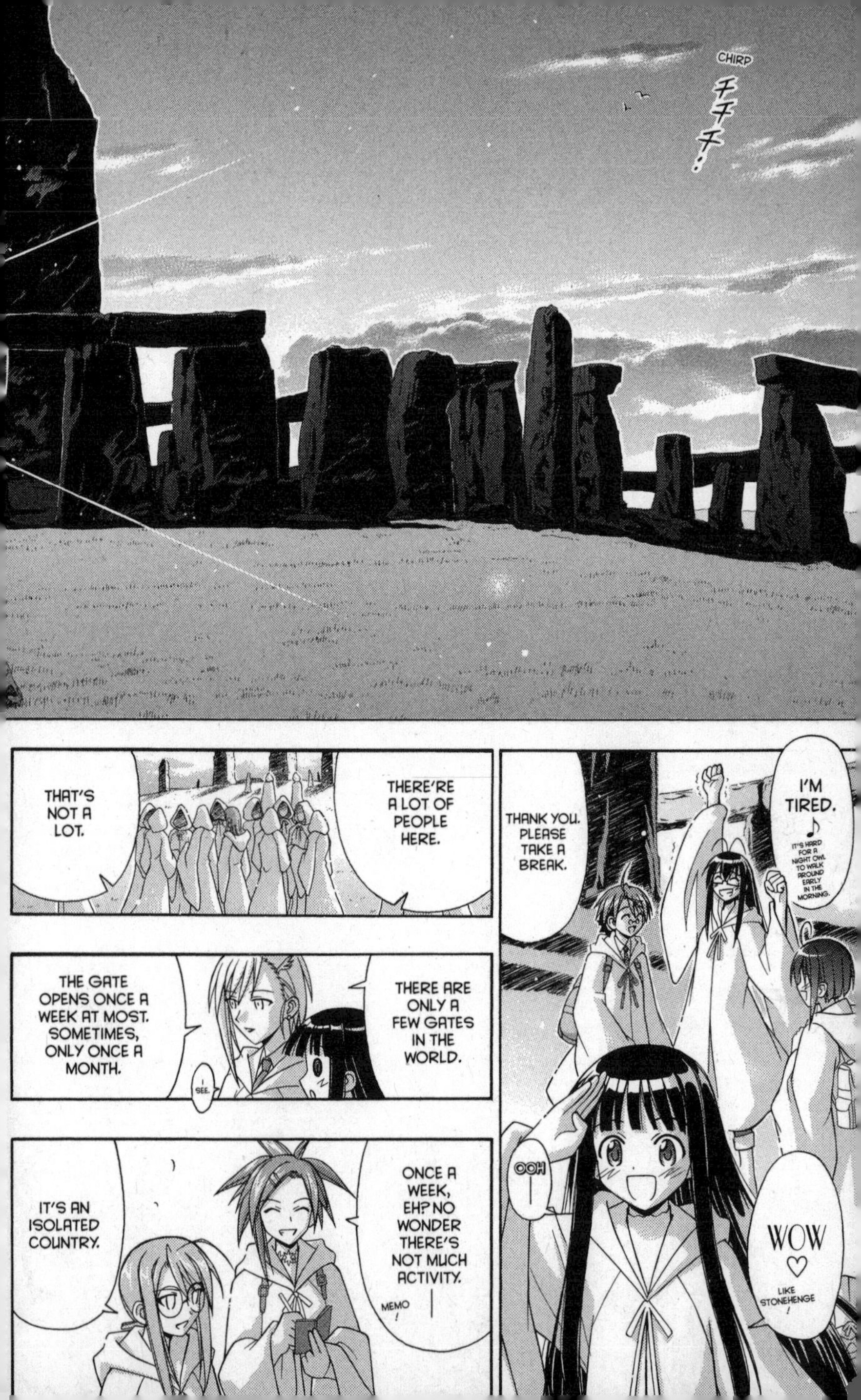
CHIRP
チチチ・
I'M TIRED. ♪
IT'S HARD FOR A NIGHT OWL TO WALK AROUND EARLY IN THE MORNING.
THANK YOU. PLEASE TAKE A BREAK.
OOH
WOW ♡
LIKE STONEHENGE!
THERE'RE A LOT OF PEOPLE HERE.
THAT'S NOT A LOT.
THERE ARE ONLY A FEW GATES IN THE WORLD.
THE GATE OPENS ONCE A WEEK AT MOST. SOMETIMES, ONLY ONCE A MONTH.
I SEE.
ONCE A WEEK, EH? NO WONDER THERE'S NOT MUCH ACTIVITY.
MEMO!
IT'S AN ISOLATED COUNTRY.

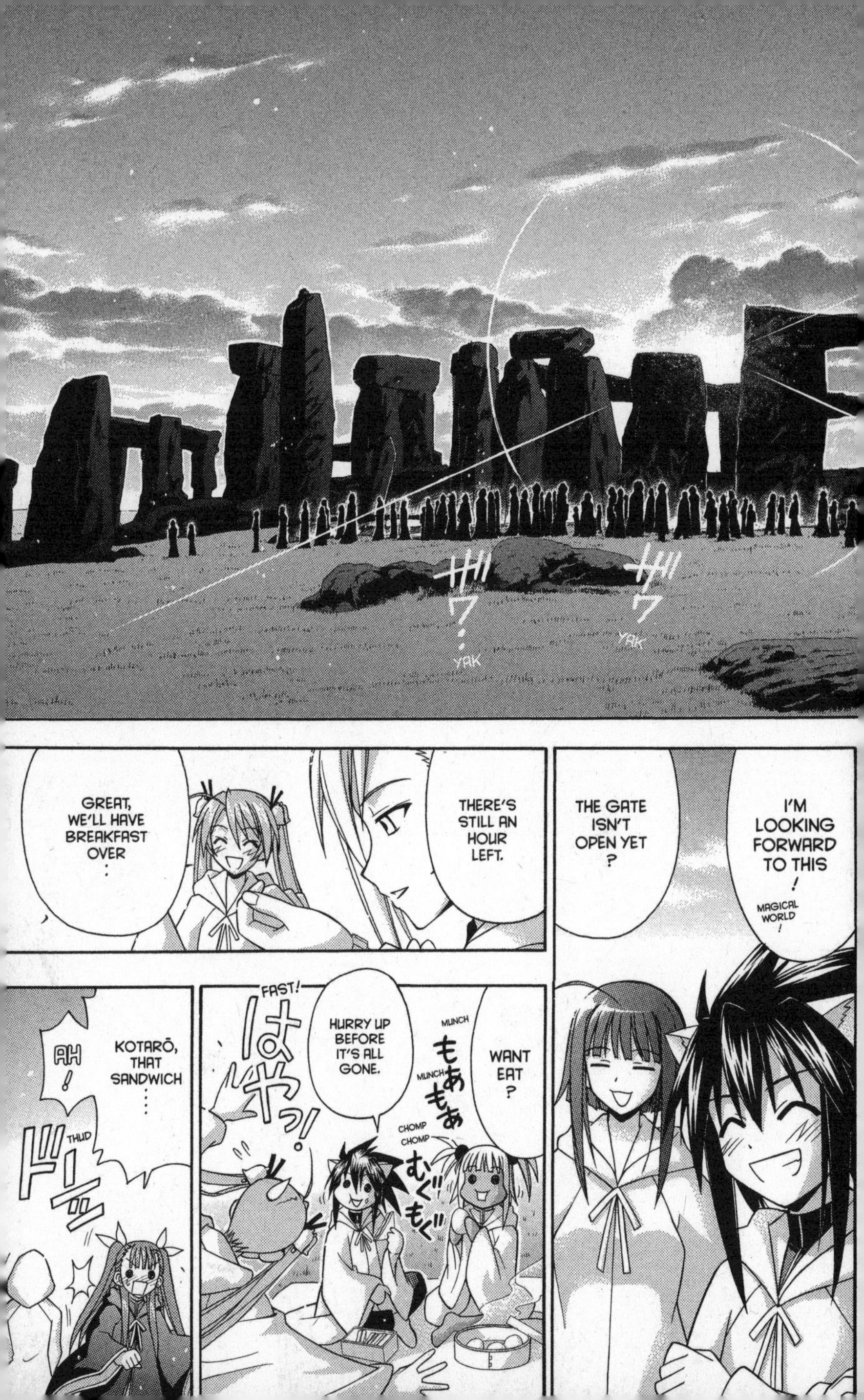
ザワ
YAK
ザワ!
YAK
I'M LOOKING FORWARD TO THIS!
MAGICAL WORLD!
THE GATE ISN'T OPEN YET?
THERE'S STILL AN HOUR LEFT.
GREAT, WE'LL HAVE BREAKFAST OVER...
WANT EAT?
もあもあ
MUNCH MUNCH
HURRY UP BEFORE IT'S ALL GONE.
はやっ!
FAST!
むぐ!! もぐ
CHOMP CHOMP
KOTARŌ, THAT SANDWICH...
AH!
ドーン
THUD

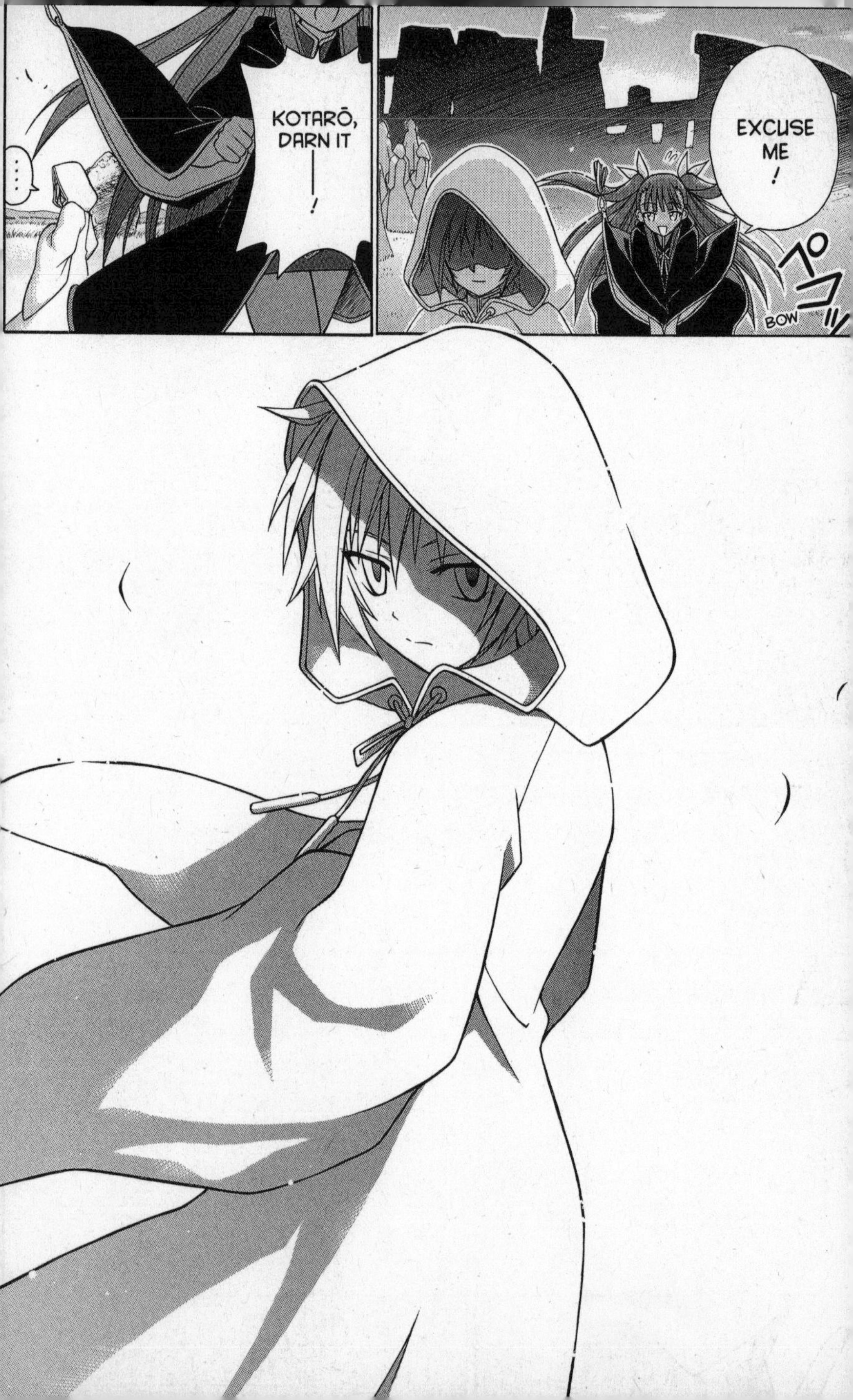
EXCUSE ME!
ペコッ
BOW
KOTARŌ, DARN IT—!
...

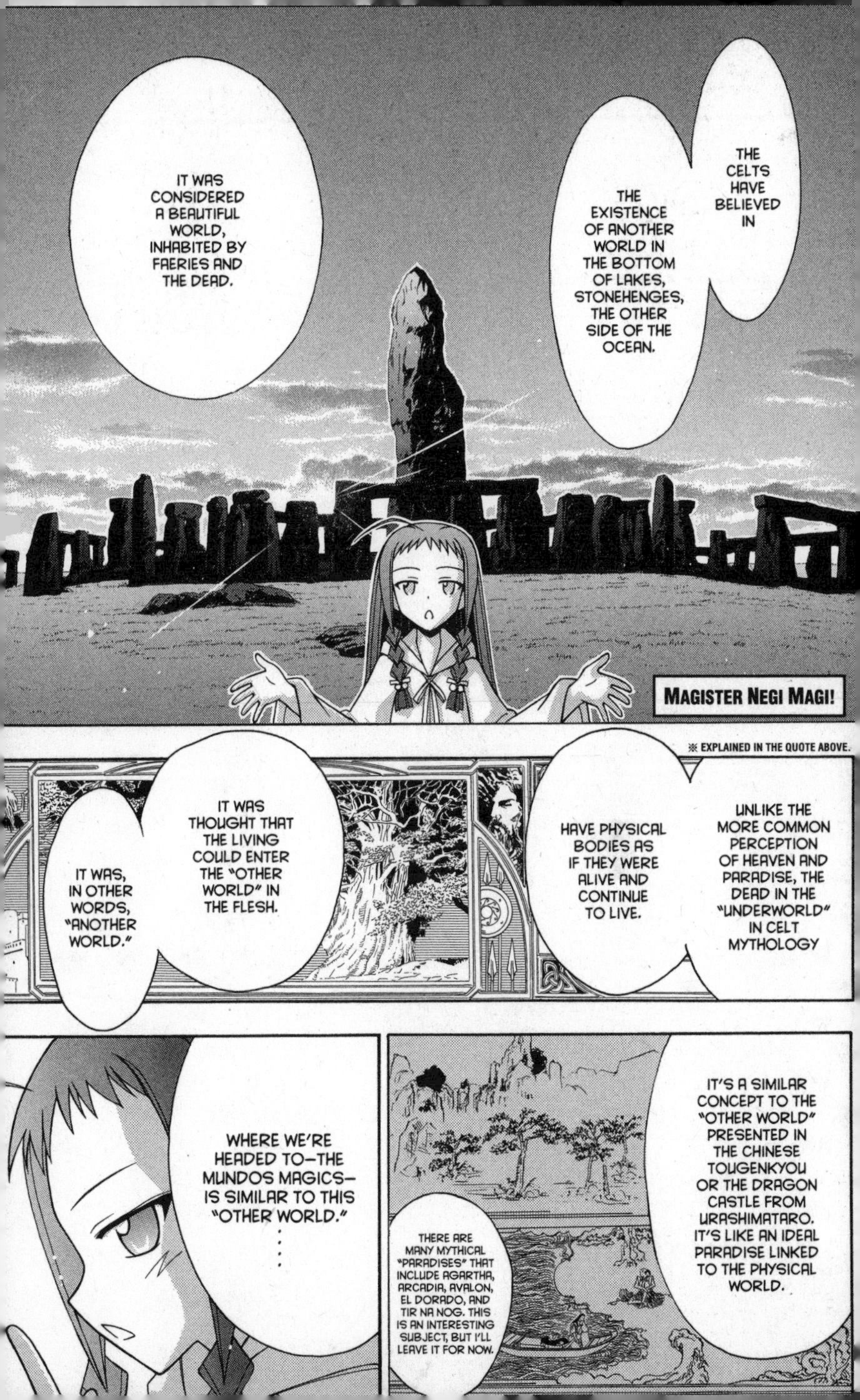
THE CELTS HAVE BELIEVED IN
THE EXISTENCE OF ANOTHER WORLD IN THE BOTTOM OF LAKES, STONEHENGES, THE OTHER SIDE OF THE OCEAN.
IT WAS CONSIDERED A BEAUTIFUL WORLD, INHABITED BY FAERIES AND THE DEAD.
MAGISTER NEGI MAGI!
※ EXPLAINED IN THE QUOTE ABOVE.
UNLIKE THE MORE COMMON PERCEPTION OF HEAVEN AND PARADISE, THE DEAD IN THE "UNDERWORLD" IN CELT MYTHOLOGY
HAVE PHYSICAL BODIES AS IF THEY WERE ALIVE AND CONTINUE TO LIVE.
IT WAS THOUGHT THAT THE LIVING COULD ENTER THE "OTHER WORLD" IN THE FLESH.
IT WAS, IN OTHER WORDS, "ANOTHER WORLD."
IT'S A SIMILAR CONCEPT TO THE "OTHER WORLD" PRESENTED IN THE CHINESE TOUGENKYOU OR THE DRAGON CASTLE FROM URASHIMATARO. IT'S LIKE AN IDEAL PARADISE LINKED TO THE PHYSICAL WORLD.
THERE ARE MANY MYTHICAL "PARADISES" THAT INCLUDE AGARTHA, ARCADIA, AVALON, EL DORADO, AND TIR NA NOG. THIS IS AN INTERESTING SUBJECT, BUT I'LL LEAVE IT FOR NOW.
WHERE WE'RE HEADED TO—THE MUNDOS MAGICS—IS SIMILAR TO THIS "OTHER WORLD."
...

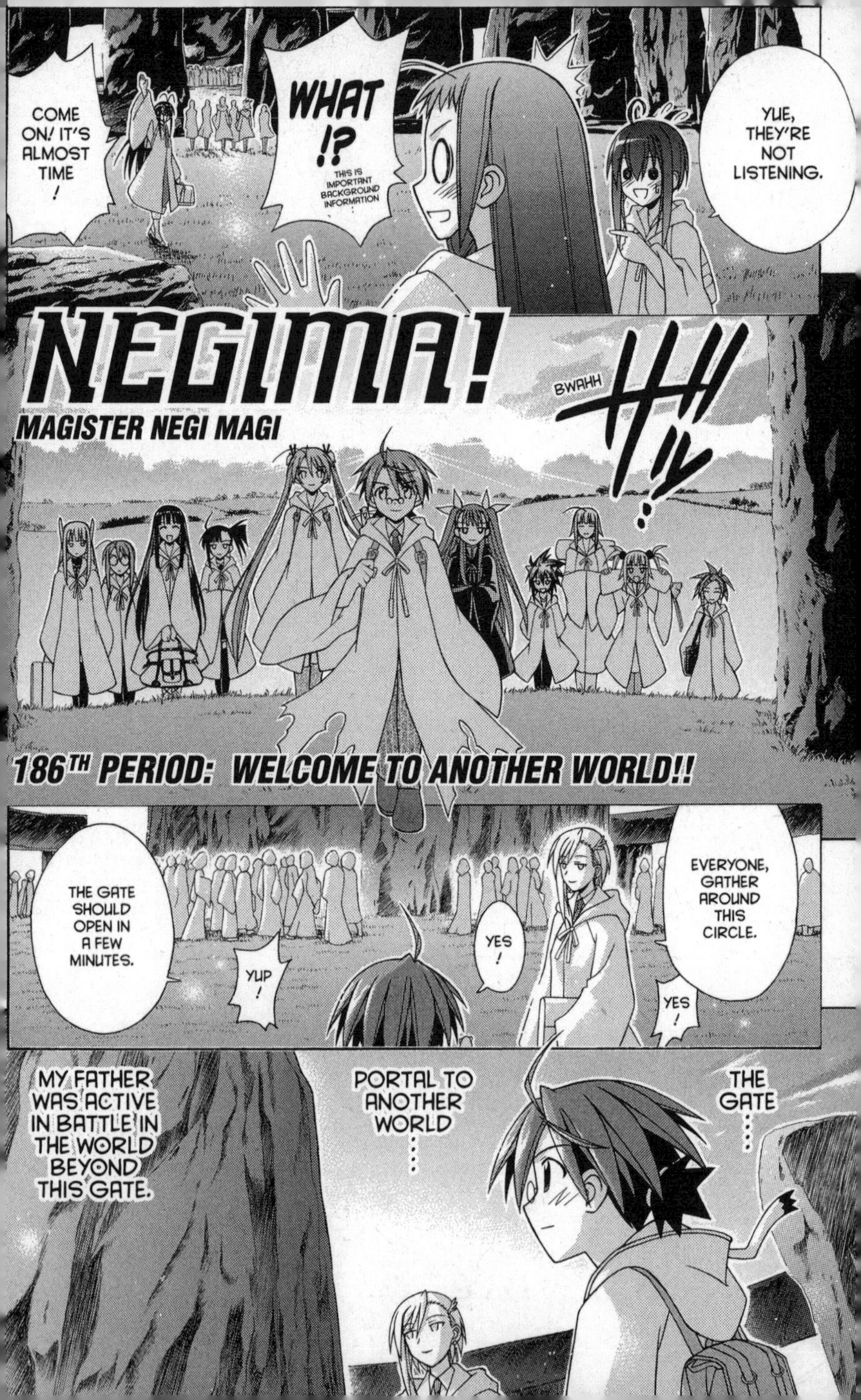
YUE, THEY'RE NOT LISTENING.
WHAT !?
THIS IS IMPORTANT BACKGROUND INFORMATION !
COME ON! IT'S ALMOST TIME !
BWAHH
NEGIMA!
MAGISTER NEGI MAGI
186TH PERIOD: WELCOME TO ANOTHER WORLD!!
EVERYONE, GATHER AROUND THIS CIRCLE.
YES !
YES !
YUP !
THE GATE SHOULD OPEN IN A FEW MINUTES.
THE GATE ...
PORTAL TO ANOTHER WORLD ...
MY FATHER WAS ACTIVE IN BATTLE IN THE WORLD BEYOND THIS GATE.

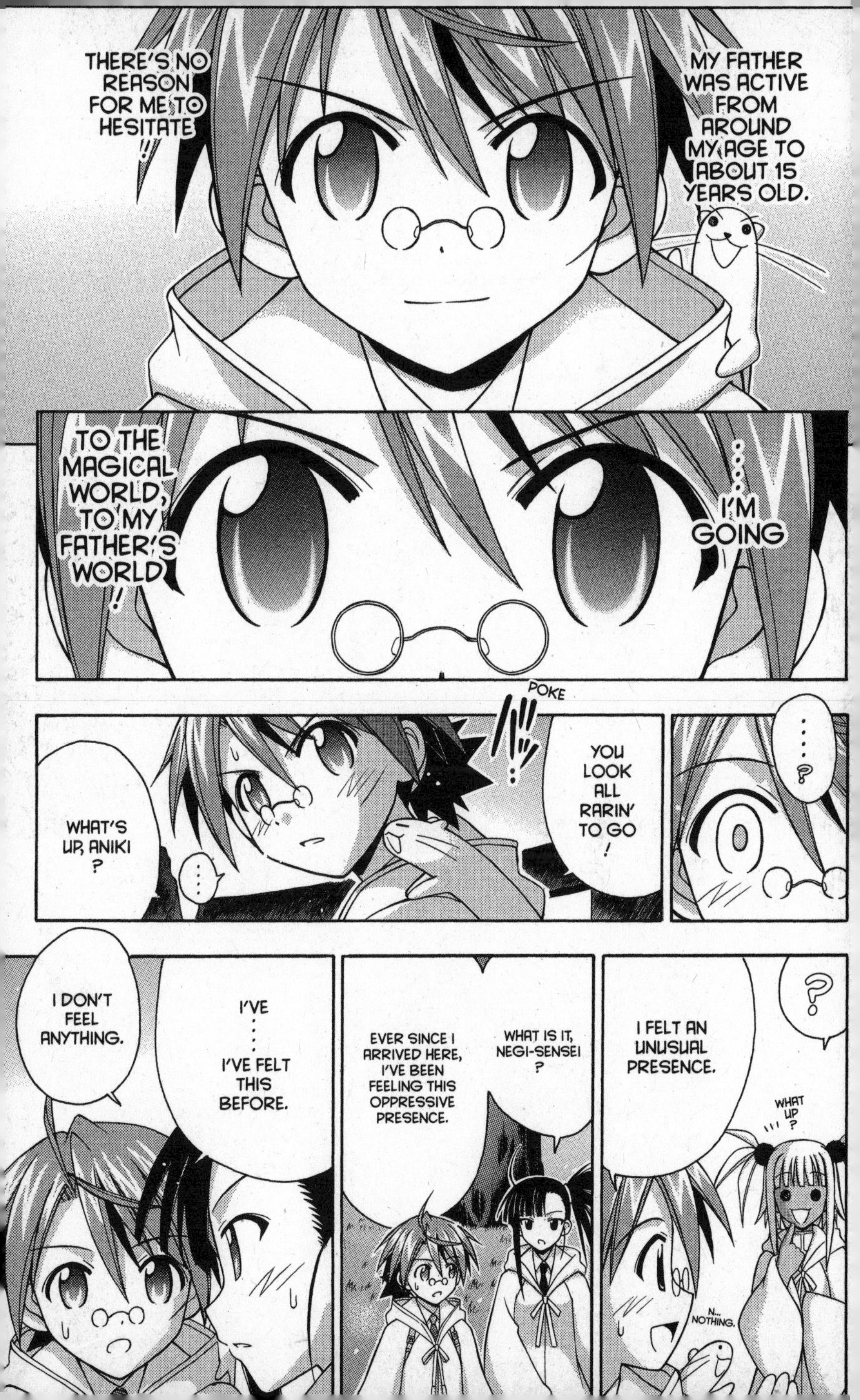
MY FATHER WAS ACTIVE FROM AROUND MY AGE TO ABOUT 15 YEARS OLD.
THERE'S NO REASON FOR ME TO HESITATE!
......I'M GOING
TO THE MAGICAL WORLD, TO MY FATHER'S WORLD!
....?
POKE
YOU LOOK ALL RARIN' TO GO!
WHAT'S UP, ANIKI?
...
?
I FELT AN UNUSUAL PRESENCE.
WHAT UP?
N... NOTHING.
WHAT IS IT, NEGI-SENSEI?
EVER SINCE I ARRIVED HERE, I'VE BEEN FEELING THIS OPPRESSIVE PRESENCE.
I'VE... I'VE FELT THIS BEFORE.
I DON'T FEEL ANYTHING.

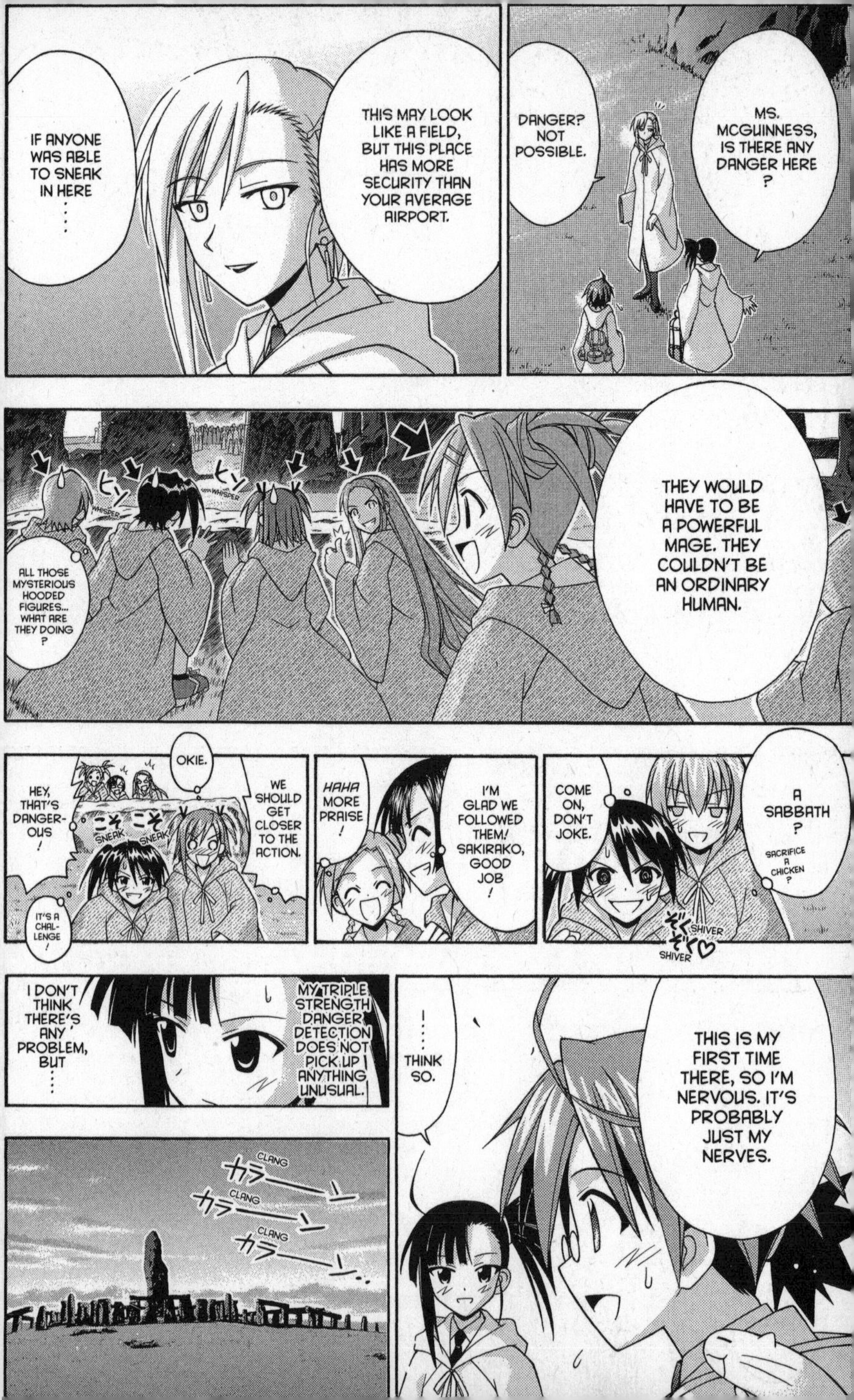
MS. MCGUINNESS, IS THERE ANY DANGER HERE?
DANGER? NOT POSSIBLE.
THIS MAY LOOK LIKE A FIELD, BUT THIS PLACE HAS MORE SECURITY THAN YOUR AVERAGE AIRPORT.
IF ANYONE WAS ABLE TO SNEAK IN HERE......
THEY WOULD HAVE TO BE A POWERFUL MAGE. THEY COULDN'T BE AN ORDINARY HUMAN.
ヒソ WHISPER
ヒソ WHISPER
ALL THOSE MYSTERIOUS HOODED FIGURES... WHAT ARE THEY DOING?
A SABBATH?
SACRIFICE A CHICKEN?
COME ON, DON'T JOKE.
ぞく SHIVER
ぞく SHIVER
I'M GLAD WE FOLLOWED THEM! SAKIRAKO, GOOD JOB!
HAHA MORE PRAISE!
WE SHOULD GET CLOSER TO THE ACTION.
OKIE.
HEY, THAT'S DANGEROUS!
こそ SNEAK
こそ SNEAK
IT'S A CHALLENGE!
THIS IS MY FIRST TIME THERE, SO I'M NERVOUS. IT'S PROBABLY JUST MY NERVES.
I...... THINK SO.
MY TRIPLE STRENGTH DANGER DETECTION DOES NOT PICK UP ANYTHING UNUSUAL.
I DON'T THINK THERE'S ANY PROBLEM, BUT......
CLANG カラーン
CLANG カラーン
CLANG カラーン

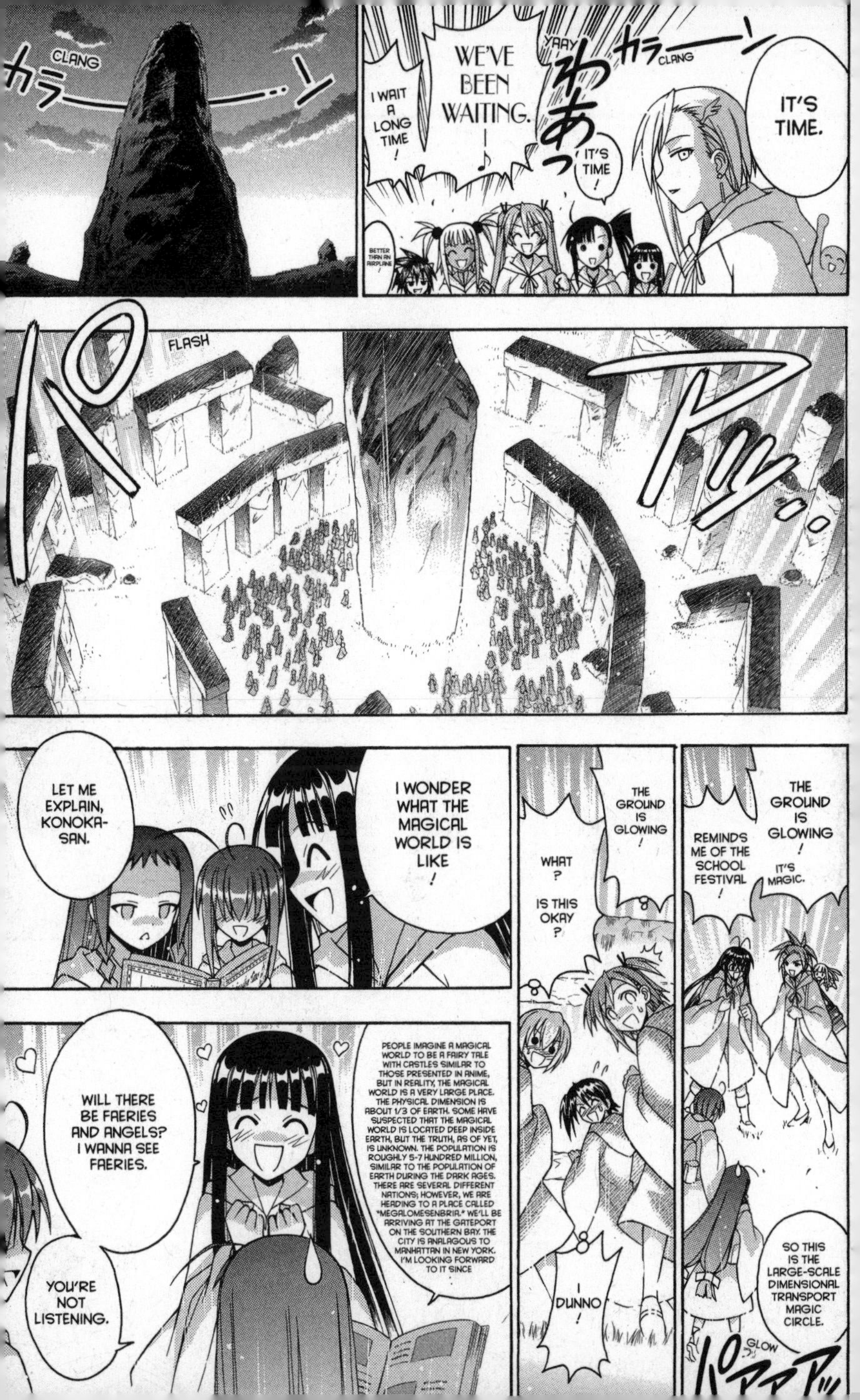
IT'S TIME.
カラーン CLANG
わあっ YAAY
IT'S TIME!
WE'VE BEEN WAITING!♪
I WAIT A LONG TIME!
BETTER THAN AN AIRPLANE!
CLANG
カラー…ン
パアッ
FLASH
THE GROUND IS GLOWING!
IT'S MAGIC.
REMINDS ME OF THE SCHOOL FESTIVAL!
SO THIS IS THE LARGE-SCALE DIMENSIONAL TRANSPORT MAGIC CIRCLE.
GLOW
パァァァッ
THE GROUND IS GLOWING!
WHAT? IS THIS OKAY?
I DUNNO!
I WONDER WHAT THE MAGICAL WORLD IS LIKE!
LET ME EXPLAIN, KONOKA-SAN.
PEOPLE IMAGINE A MAGICAL WORLD TO BE A FAIRY TALE WITH CASTLES SIMILAR TO THOSE PRESENTED IN ANIME, BUT IN REALITY, THE MAGICAL WORLD IS A VERY LARGE PLACE. THE PHYSICAL DIMENSION IS ABOUT 1/3 OF EARTH. SOME HAVE SUSPECTED THAT THE MAGICAL WORLD IS LOCATED DEEP INSIDE EARTH, BUT THE TRUTH, AS OF YET, IS UNKNOWN. THE POPULATION IS ROUGHLY 5-7 HUNDRED MILLION, SIMILAR TO THE POPULATION OF EARTH DURING THE DARK AGES. THERE ARE SEVERAL DIFFERENT NATIONS; HOWEVER, WE ARE HEADING TO A PLACE CALLED "MEGALOMESENBRIA." WE'LL BE ARRIVING AT THE GATEPORT ON THE SOUTHERN BAY. THE CITY IS ANALAGOUS TO MANHATTAN IN NEW YORK. I'M LOOKING FORWARD TO IT SINCE
WILL THERE BE FAERIES AND ANGELS? I WANNA SEE FAERIES.
YOU'RE NOT LISTENING.

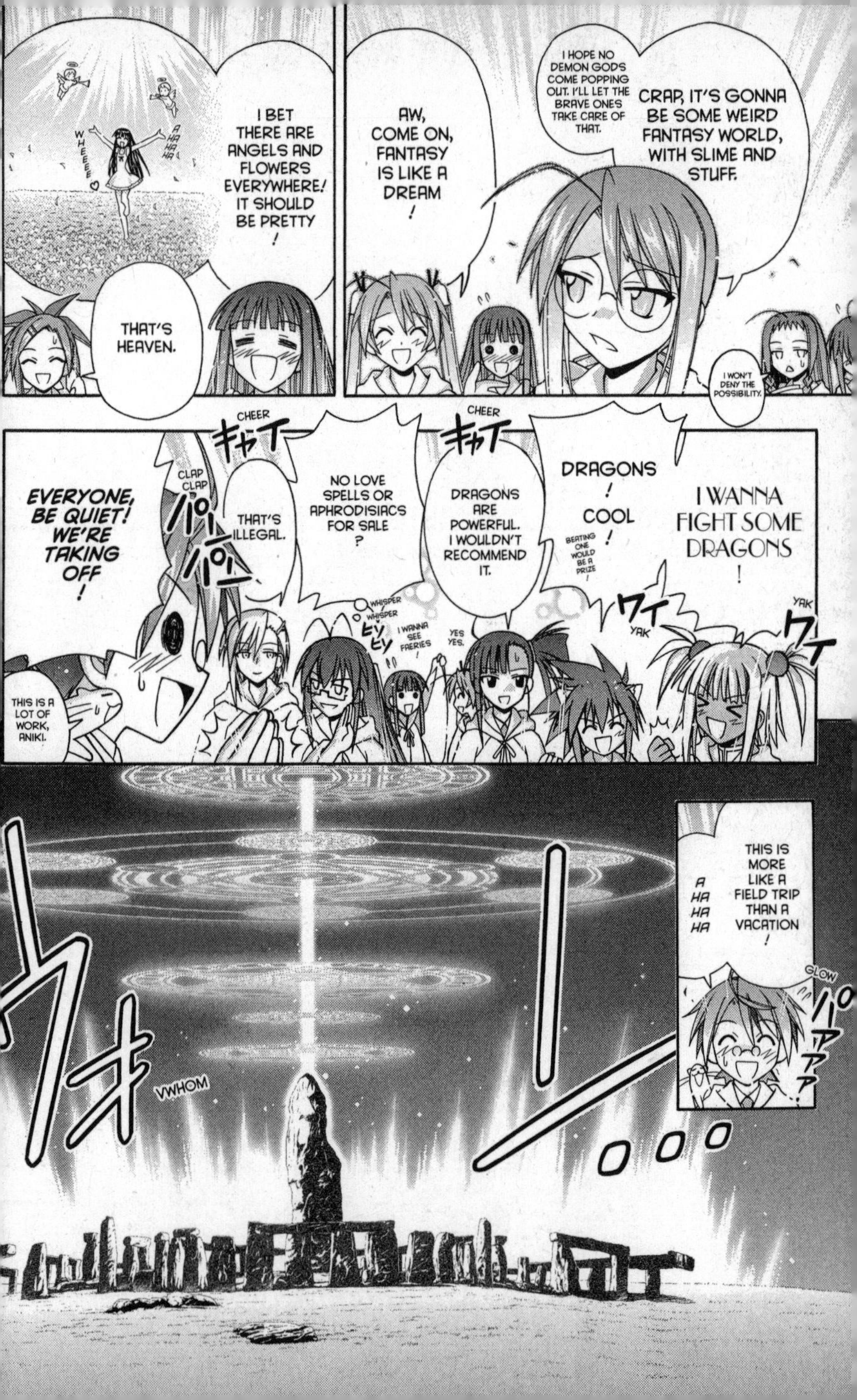
CRAP, IT'S GONNA BE SOME WEIRD FANTASY WORLD, WITH SLIME AND STUFF.
I HOPE NO DEMON GODS COME POPPING OUT. I'LL LET THE BRAVE ONES TAKE CARE OF THAT.
I WON'T DENY THE POSSIBILITY.
AW, COME ON, FANTASY IS LIKE A DREAM!
I BET THERE ARE ANGELS AND FLOWERS EVERYWHERE! IT SHOULD BE PRETTY!
A HA HA HA
WHEEEE ♡
THAT'S HEAVEN.
I WANNA FIGHT SOME DRAGONS!
YAK
YAK
DRAGONS! COOL!
BEATING ONE WOULD BE A PRIZE!
CHEER
DRAGONS ARE POWERFUL. I WOULDN'T RECOMMEND IT.
YES YES.
I WANNA SEE FAERIES!
WHISPER WHISPER
NO LOVE SPELLS OR APHRODISIACS FOR SALE?
CHEER
THAT'S ILLEGAL.
CLAP CLAP
EVERYONE, BE QUIET! WE'RE TAKING OFF!
THIS IS A LOT OF WORK, ANIKI.
THIS IS MORE LIKE A FIELD TRIP THAN A VACATION!
A HA HA HA
GLOW
VWHOM

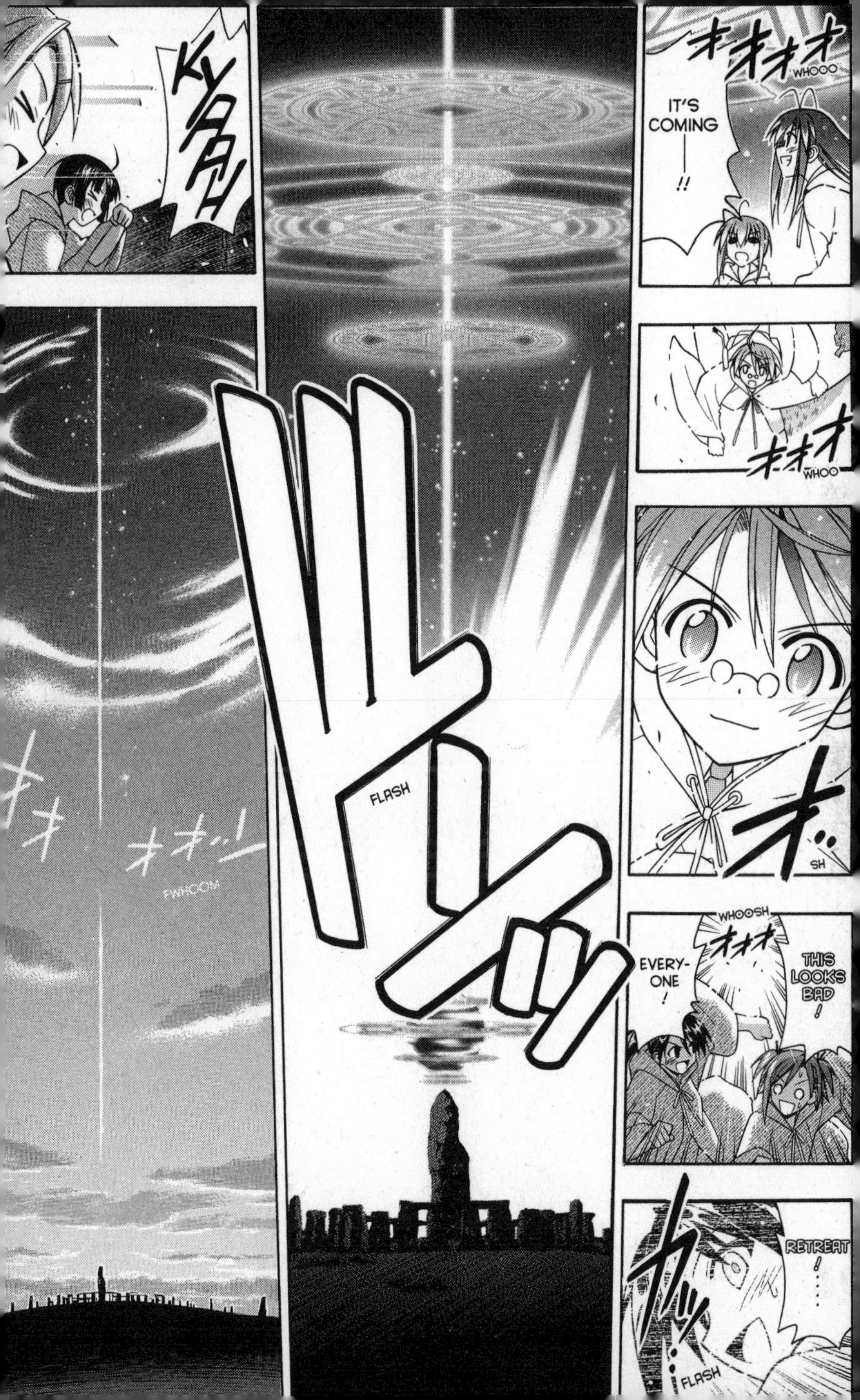
WHOOO
IT'S COMING —!!
WHOOO
SH
WHOOSH
THIS LOOKS BAD!
EVERY-ONE!
RETREAT!....
FLASH
FLASH
FWHOOM

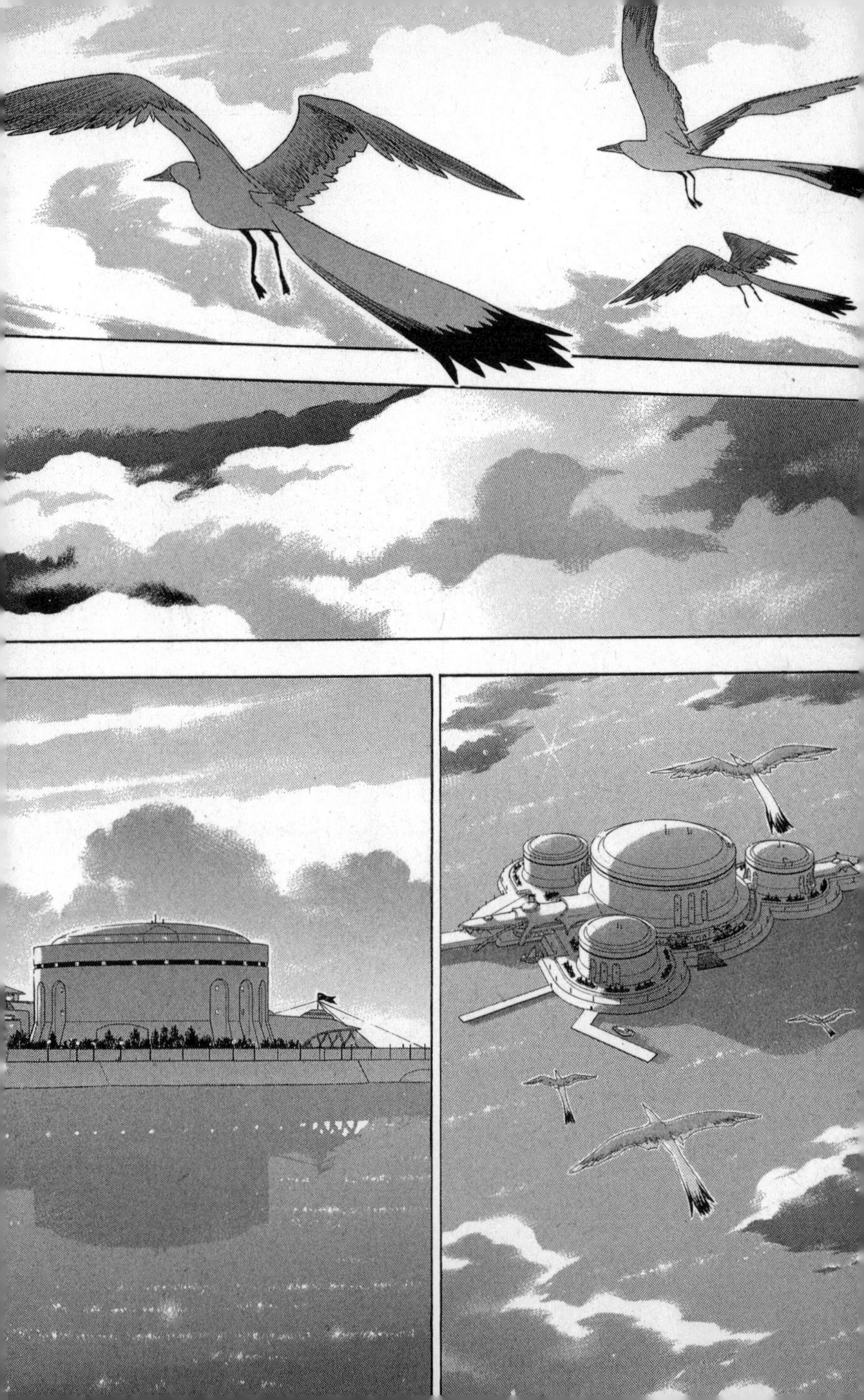

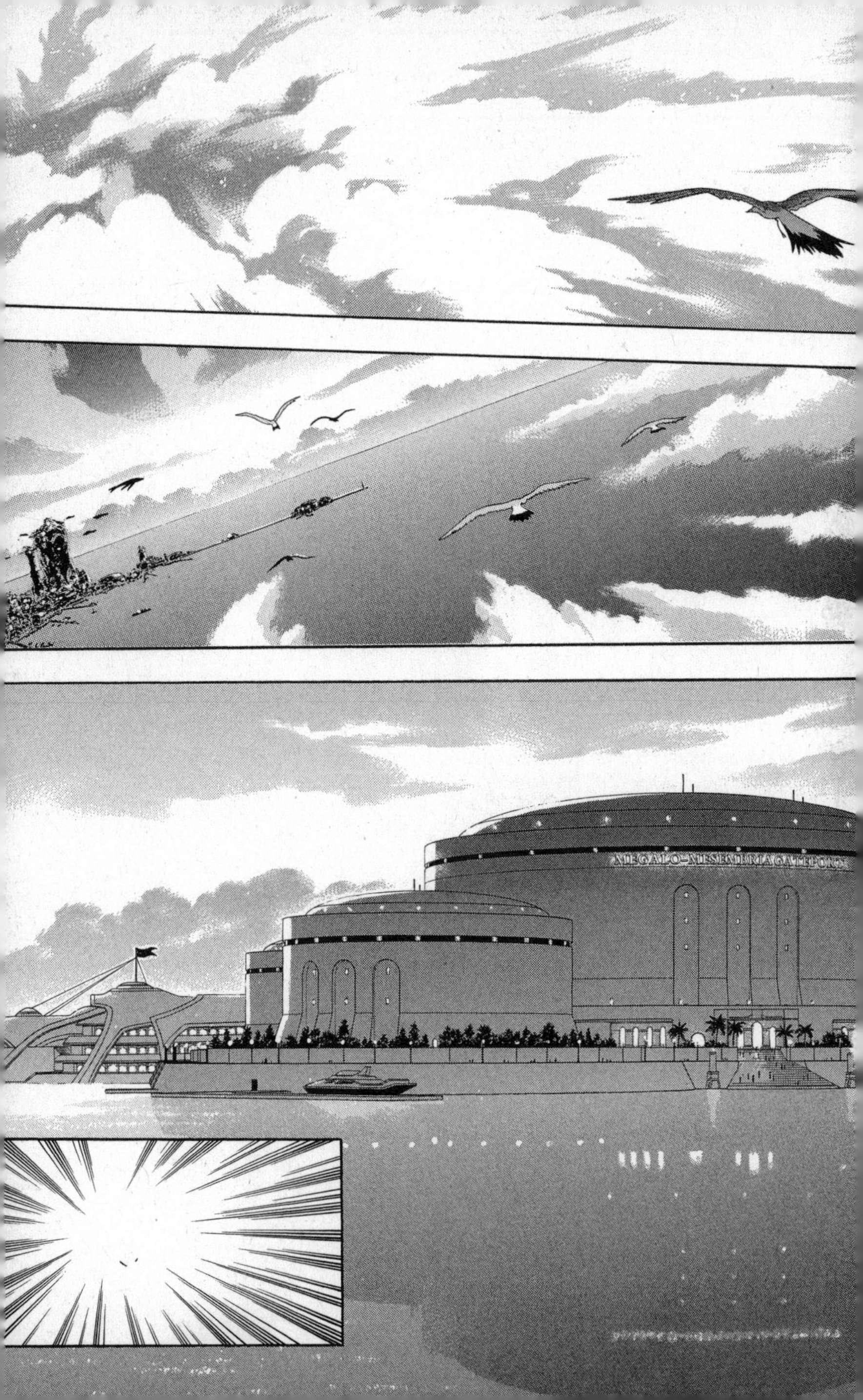
MEGALO-MESEMBRIA GATEPORT

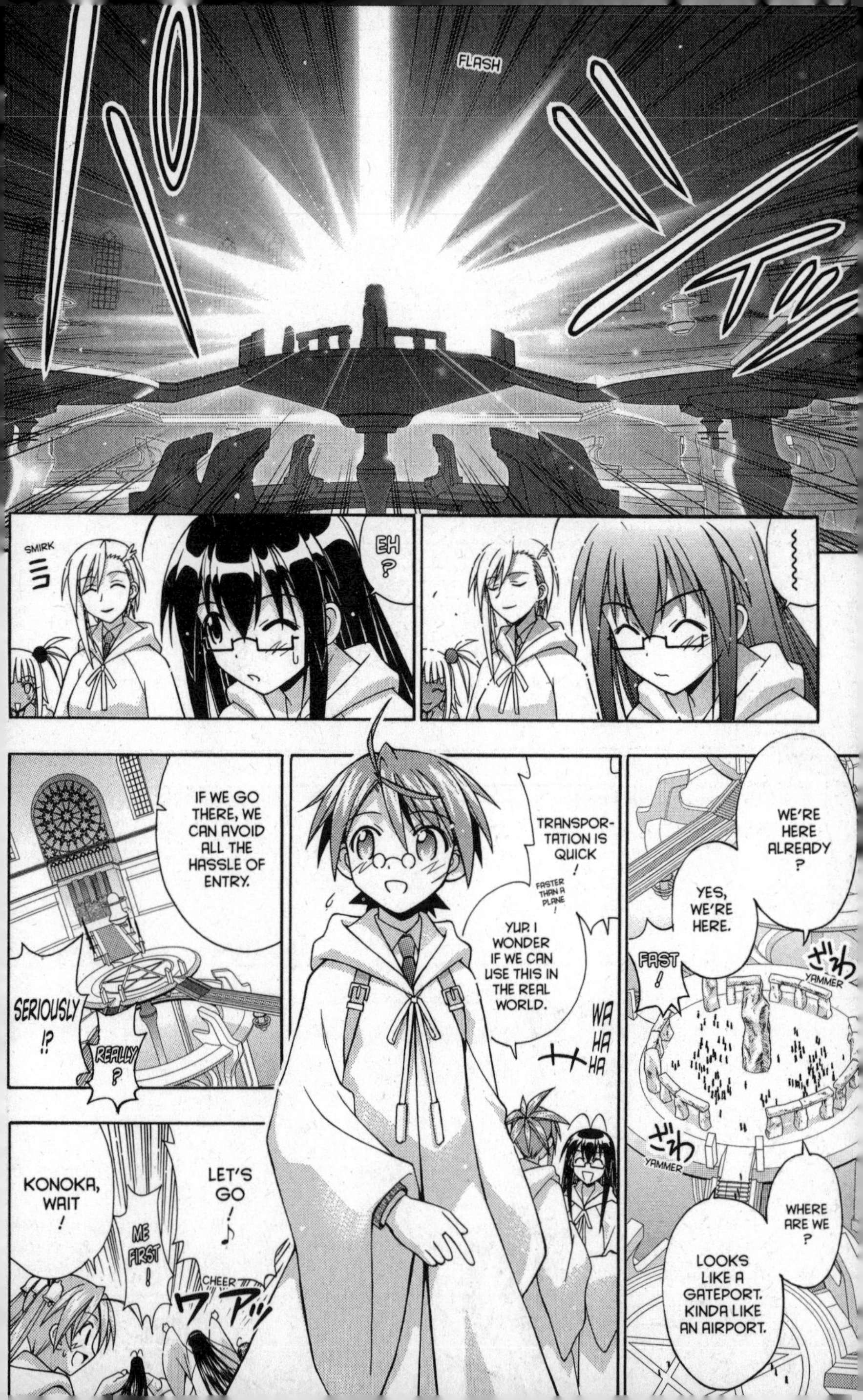
FLASH
......
SMIRK
EH ?
WE'RE HERE ALREADY ?
YES, WE'RE HERE.
FAST !
ざわ
YAMMER
ざわ
YAMMER
WHERE ARE WE ?
LOOKS LIKE A GATEPORT. KINDA LIKE AN AIRPORT.
TRANSPOR- TATION IS QUICK !
FASTER THAN A PLANE !
YUP. I WONDER IF WE CAN USE THIS IN THE REAL WORLD.
WA HA HA
IF WE GO THERE, WE CAN AVOID ALL THE HASSLE OF ENTRY.
SERIOUSLY !?
REALLY ?
LET'S GO ! ♪
KONOKA, WAIT !
ME FIRST !
CHEER

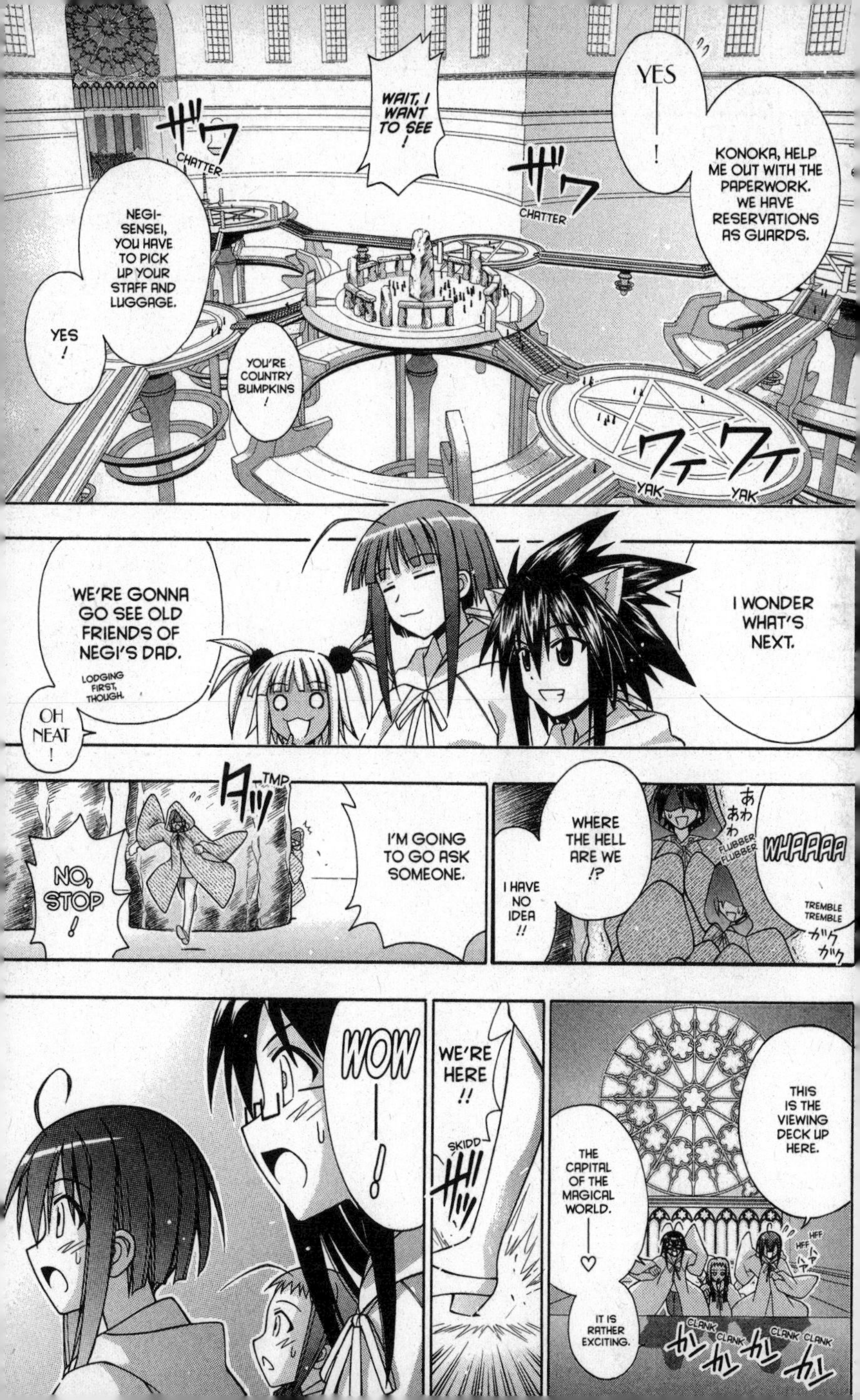

YES—!
KONOKA, HELP ME OUT WITH THE PAPERWORK. WE HAVE RESERVATIONS AS GUARDS.
ザワ
CHATTER
WAIT, I WANT TO SEE!
ザワ
CHATTER
NEGI-SENSEI, YOU HAVE TO PICK UP YOUR STAFF AND LUGGAGE.
YES!
YOU'RE COUNTRY BUMPKINS!
ワイワイ
YAK YAK
I WONDER WHAT'S NEXT.
WE'RE GONNA GO SEE OLD FRIENDS OF NEGI'S DAD.
LODGING FIRST, THOUGH.
OH NEAT!
WHAAAA
あわあわ
FLUBBER FLUBBER
WHERE THE HELL ARE WE!?
I HAVE NO IDEA!!
ガクガク
TREMBLE TREMBLE
I'M GOING TO GO ASK SOMEONE.
タッ
TMP
NO, STOP!
THIS IS THE VIEWING DECK UP HERE.
HFF HFF
THE CAPITAL OF THE MAGICAL WORLD.—♡
IT IS RATHER EXCITING.
CLANK CLANK CLANK CLANK
WE'RE HERE!!
SKIDD
WOW—!

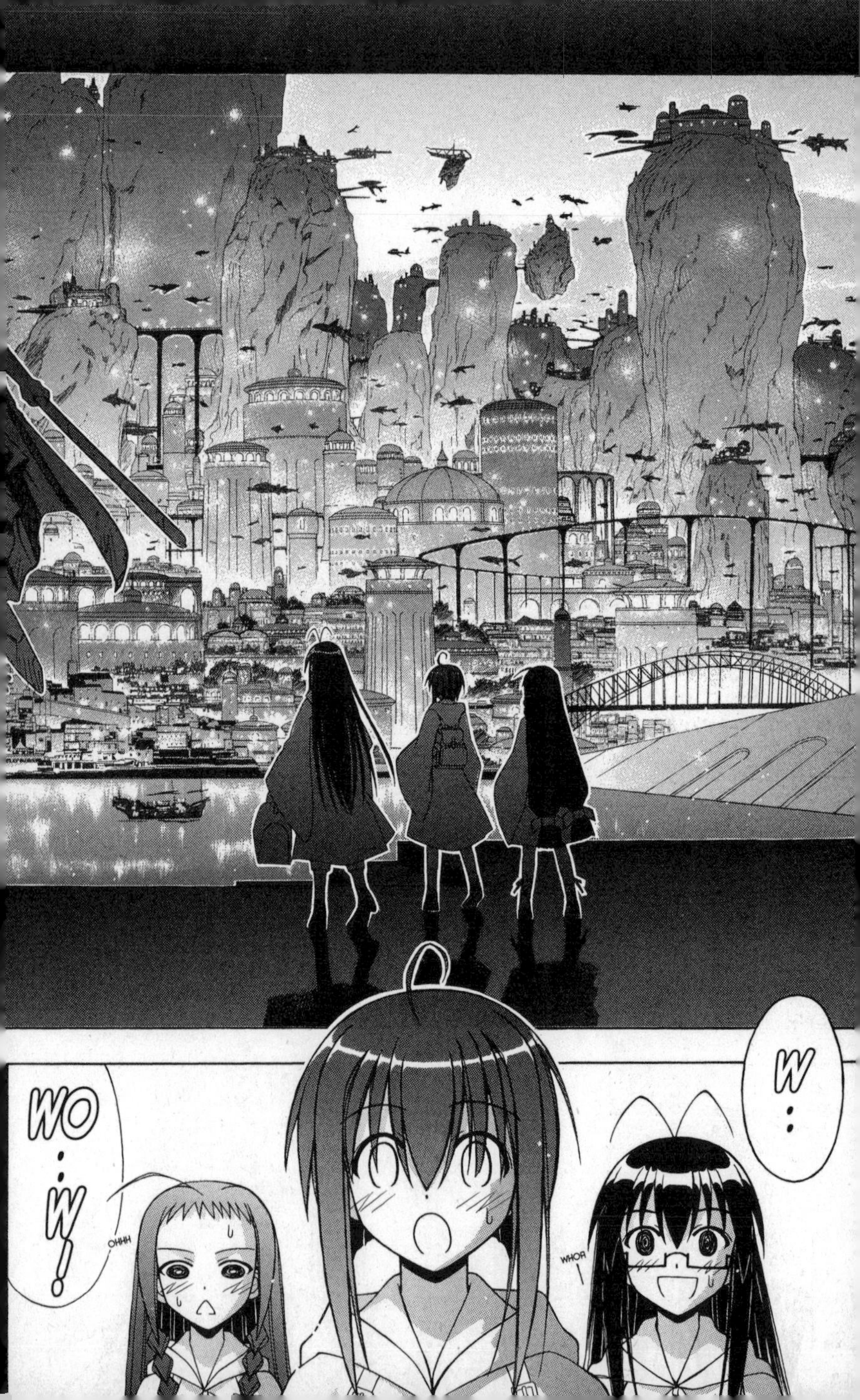
W...
WHOA
OHHH
WO...W!

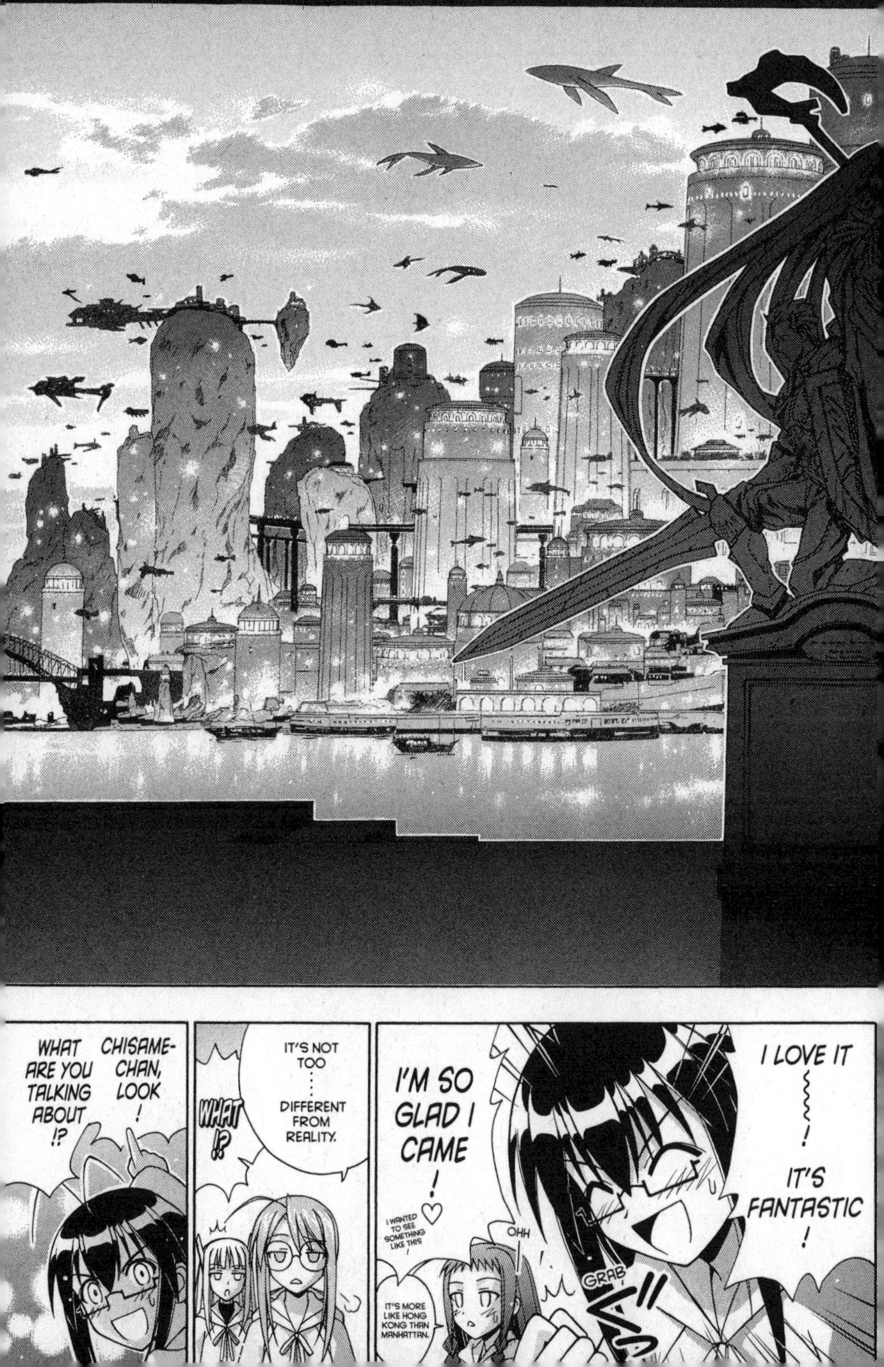
I LOVE IT ~! IT'S FANTASTIC!
I'M SO GLAD I CAME! ♡
GRAB
OHH!
I WANTED TO SEE SOMETHING LIKE THIS!
IT'S MORE LIKE HONG KONG THAN MANHATTAN.
IT'S NOT TOO... DIFFERENT FROM REALITY.
WHAT!?
CHISAME-CHAN, LOOK!
WHAT ARE YOU TALKING ABOUT!?

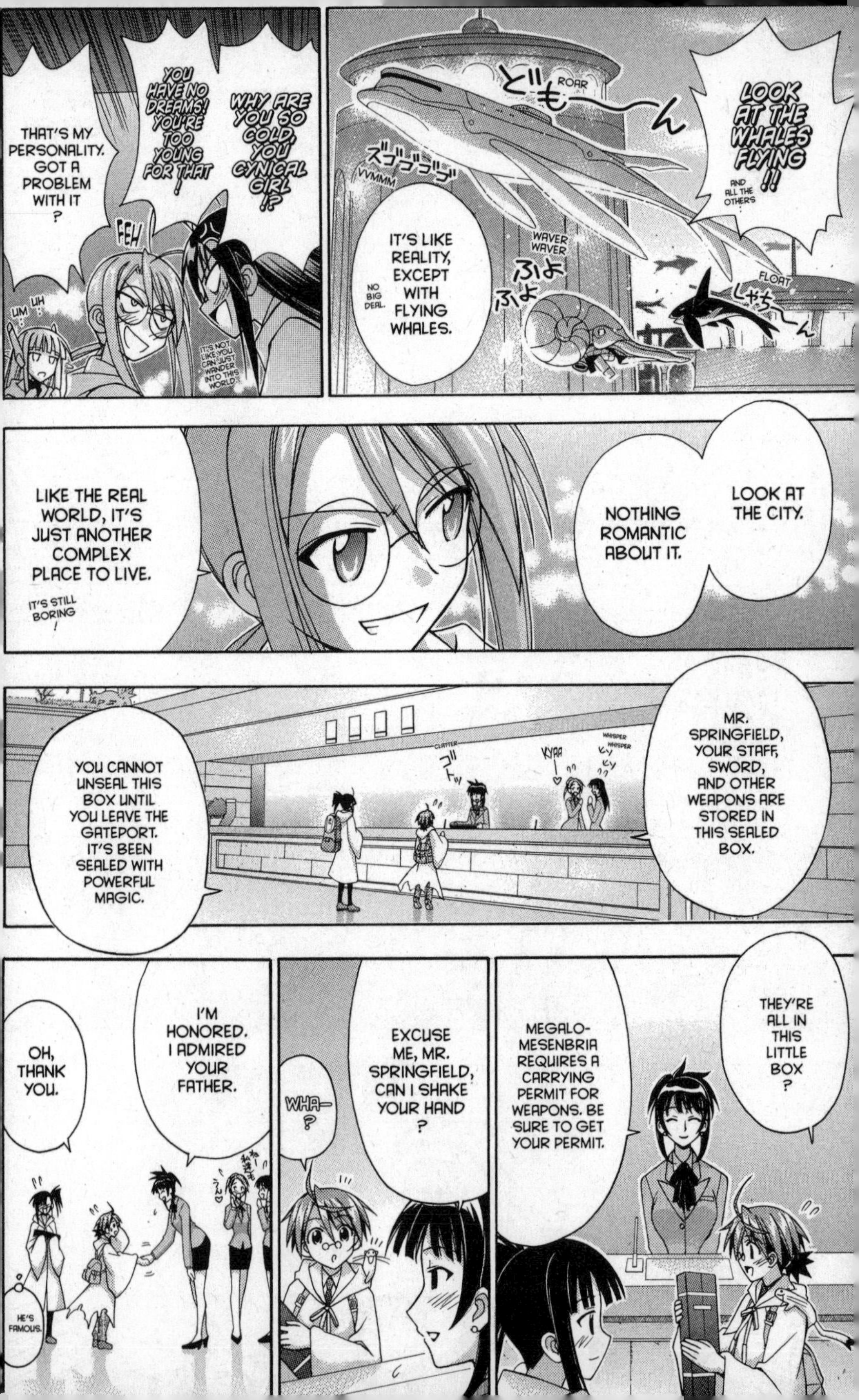
LOOK AT THE WHALES FLYING!!
AND ALL THE OTHERS
ROAR
VVMMM
IT'S LIKE REALITY, EXCEPT WITH FLYING WHALES.
NO BIG DEAL.
WAVER WAVER
FLOAT
WHY ARE YOU SO COLD, YOU CYNICAL GIRL!?
YOU HAVE NO DREAMS! YOU'RE TOO YOUNG FOR THAT!
THAT'S MY PERSONALITY. GOT A PROBLEM WITH IT?
FEH
IT'S NOT LIKE YOU CAN JUST WANDER INTO THIS WORLD.
UH
UM
LOOK AT THE CITY.
NOTHING ROMANTIC ABOUT IT.
LIKE THE REAL WORLD, IT'S JUST ANOTHER COMPLEX PLACE TO LIVE.
IT'S STILL BORING!
MR. SPRINGFIELD, YOUR STAFF, SWORD, AND OTHER WEAPONS ARE STORED IN THIS SEALED BOX.
WHISPER WHISPER
KYAA
CLATTER
YOU CANNOT UNSEAL THIS BOX UNTIL YOU LEAVE THE GATEPORT. IT'S BEEN SEALED WITH POWERFUL MAGIC.
THEY'RE ALL IN THIS LITTLE BOX?
MEGALO-MESENBRIA REQUIRES A CARRYING PERMIT FOR WEAPONS. BE SURE TO GET YOUR PERMIT.
EXCUSE ME, MR. SPRINGFIELD, CAN I SHAKE YOUR HAND?
WHA-?
I'M HONORED. I ADMIRED YOUR FATHER.
OH, THANK YOU.
HE'S FAMOUS.

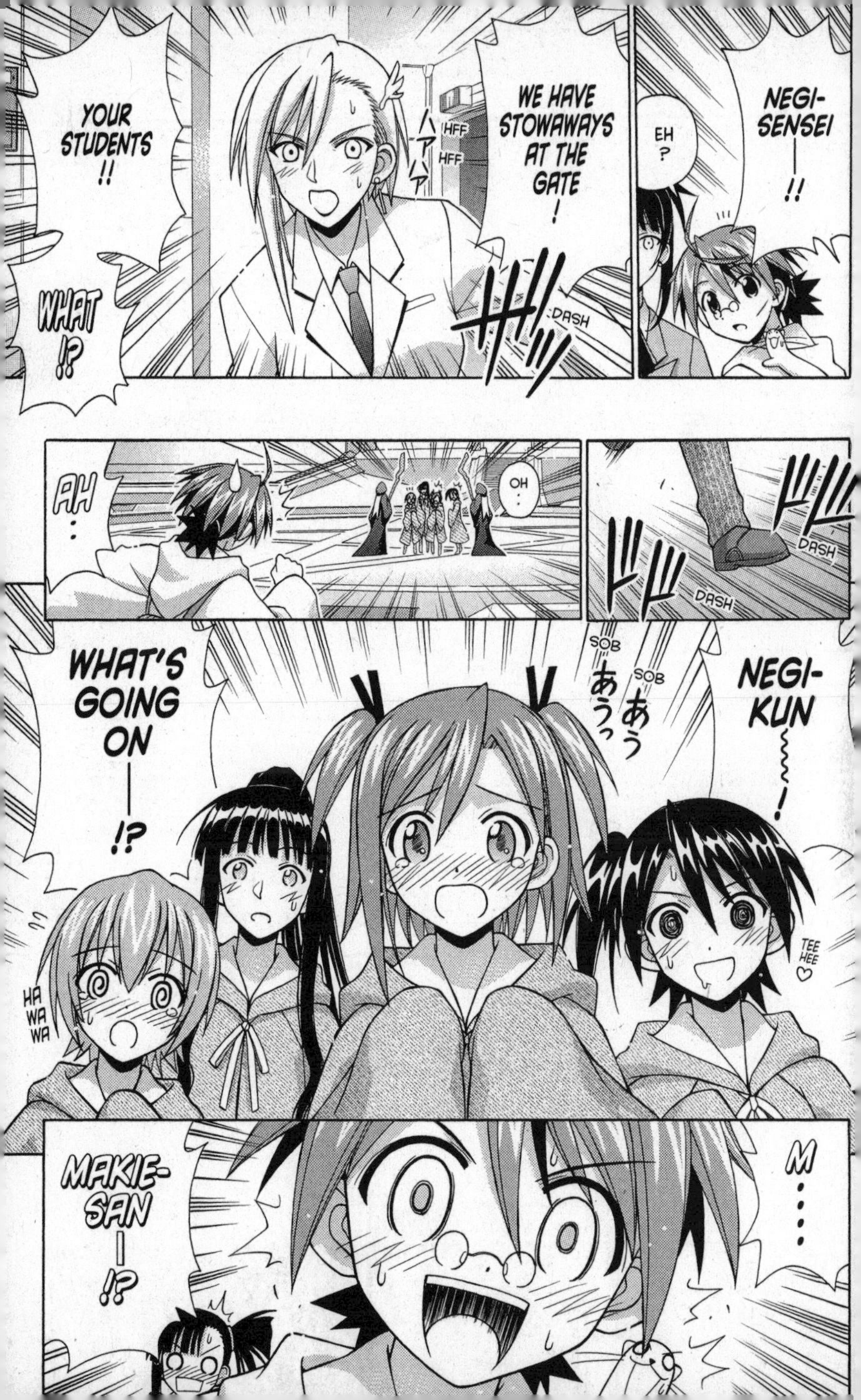
NEGI-SENSEI——!!
EH?
WE HAVE STOWAWAYS AT THE GATE!
ハァハァ
HFF HFF
DASH
YOUR STUDENTS!!
WHAT!?
DASH
DASH
OH..
AH..
NEGI-KUN~~~!
あうっ
SOB
あう
SOB
TEE HEE ♡
WHAT'S GOING ON——!?
HA WA WA
M....
MAKIE-SAN——!?

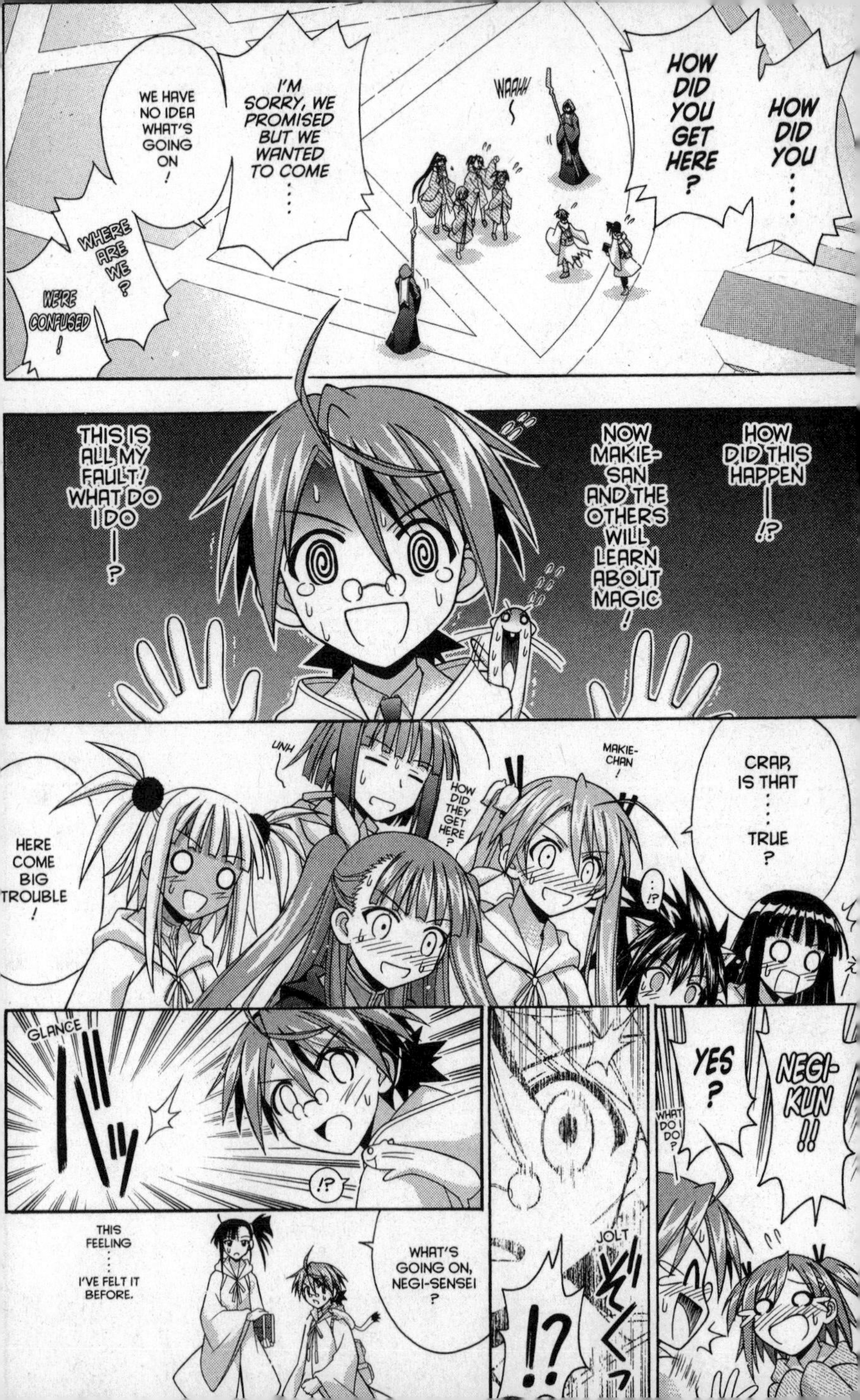
HOW DID YOU....
HOW DID YOU GET HERE?
WAAHH
I'M SORRY, WE PROMISED BUT WE WANTED TO COME....
WE HAVE NO IDEA WHAT'S GOING ON!
WHERE ARE WE?
WE'RE CONFUSED!
HOW DID THIS HAPPEN—!?
NOW MAKIE-SAN AND THE OTHERS WILL LEARN ABOUT MAGIC!
THIS IS ALL MY FAULT! WHAT DO I DO—?
CRAP, IS THAT.... TRUE?
...!?
MAKIE-CHAN!
HOW DID THEY GET HERE?
UNH
HERE COME BIG TROUBLE!
NEGI-KUN!!
YES?
WHAT DO I DO?
JOLT
!?
GLANCE
!?
WHAT'S GOING ON, NEGI-SENSEI?
THIS FEELING.... I'VE FELT IT BEFORE.

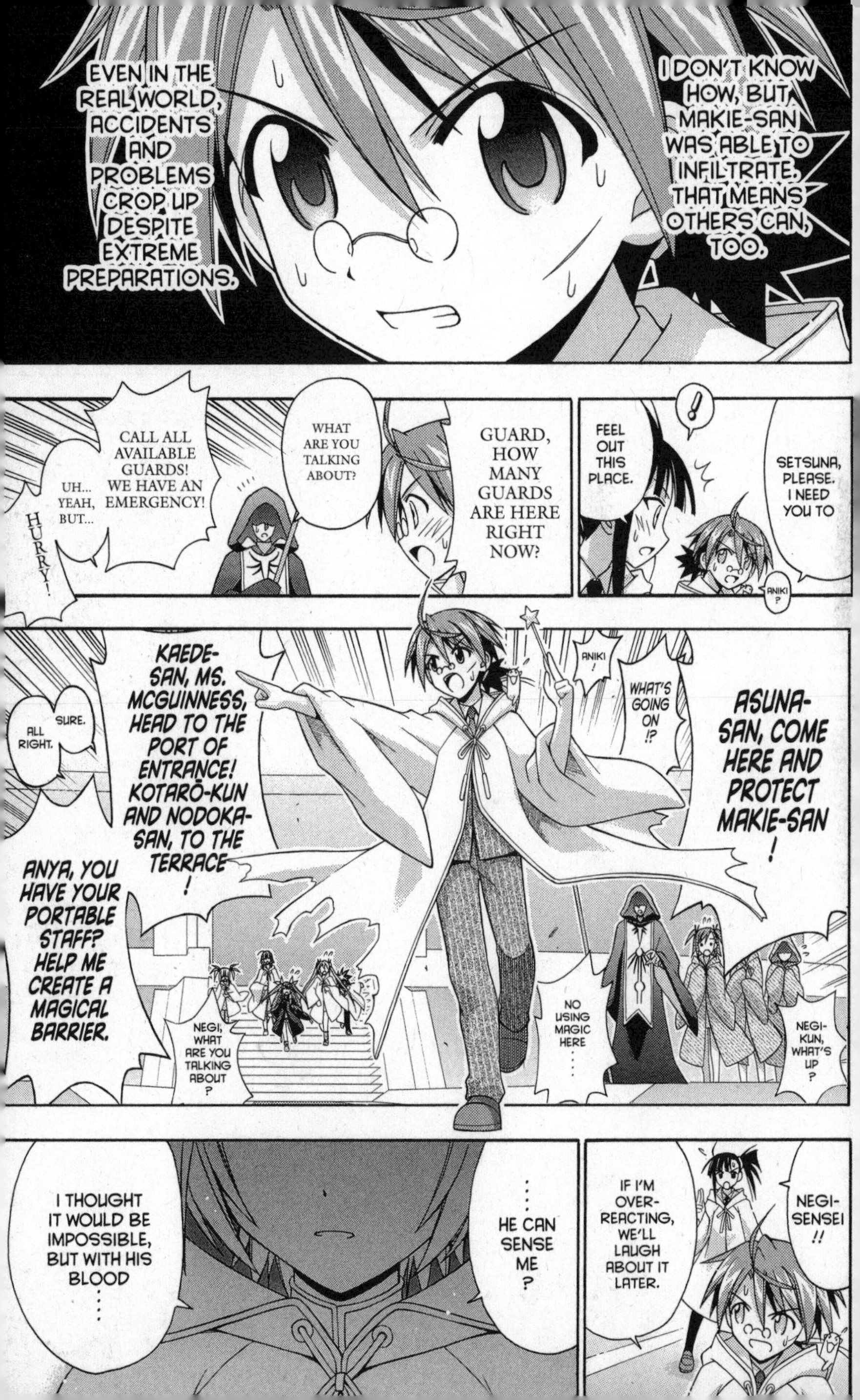
I DON'T KNOW HOW, BUT MAKIE-SAN WAS ABLE TO INFILTRATE. THAT MEANS OTHERS CAN, TOO.
EVEN IN THE REAL WORLD, ACCIDENTS AND PROBLEMS CROP UP DESPITE EXTREME PREPARATIONS.
!
SETSUNA, PLEASE. I NEED YOU TO
FEEL OUT THIS PLACE.
ANIKI?
GUARD, HOW MANY GUARDS ARE HERE RIGHT NOW?
WHAT ARE YOU TALKING ABOUT?
CALL ALL AVAILABLE GUARDS! WE HAVE AN EMERGENCY!
UH... YEAH, BUT...
HURRY!
ASUNA-SAN, COME HERE AND PROTECT MAKIE-SAN!
WHAT'S GOING ON!?
ANIKI!
KAEDE-SAN, MS. MCGUINNESS, HEAD TO THE PORT OF ENTRANCE! KOTARŌ-KUN AND NODOKA-SAN, TO THE TERRACE!
SURE.
ALL RIGHT.
ANYA, YOU HAVE YOUR PORTABLE STAFF? HELP ME CREATE A MAGICAL BARRIER.
NEGI-KUN, WHAT'S UP?
NO USING MAGIC HERE...
NEGI, WHAT ARE YOU TALKING ABOUT?
NEGI-SENSEI!!
IF I'M OVER-REACTING, WE'LL LAUGH ABOUT IT LATER.
... HE CAN SENSE ME?
I THOUGHT IT WOULD BE IMPOSSIBLE, BUT WITH HIS BLOOD...

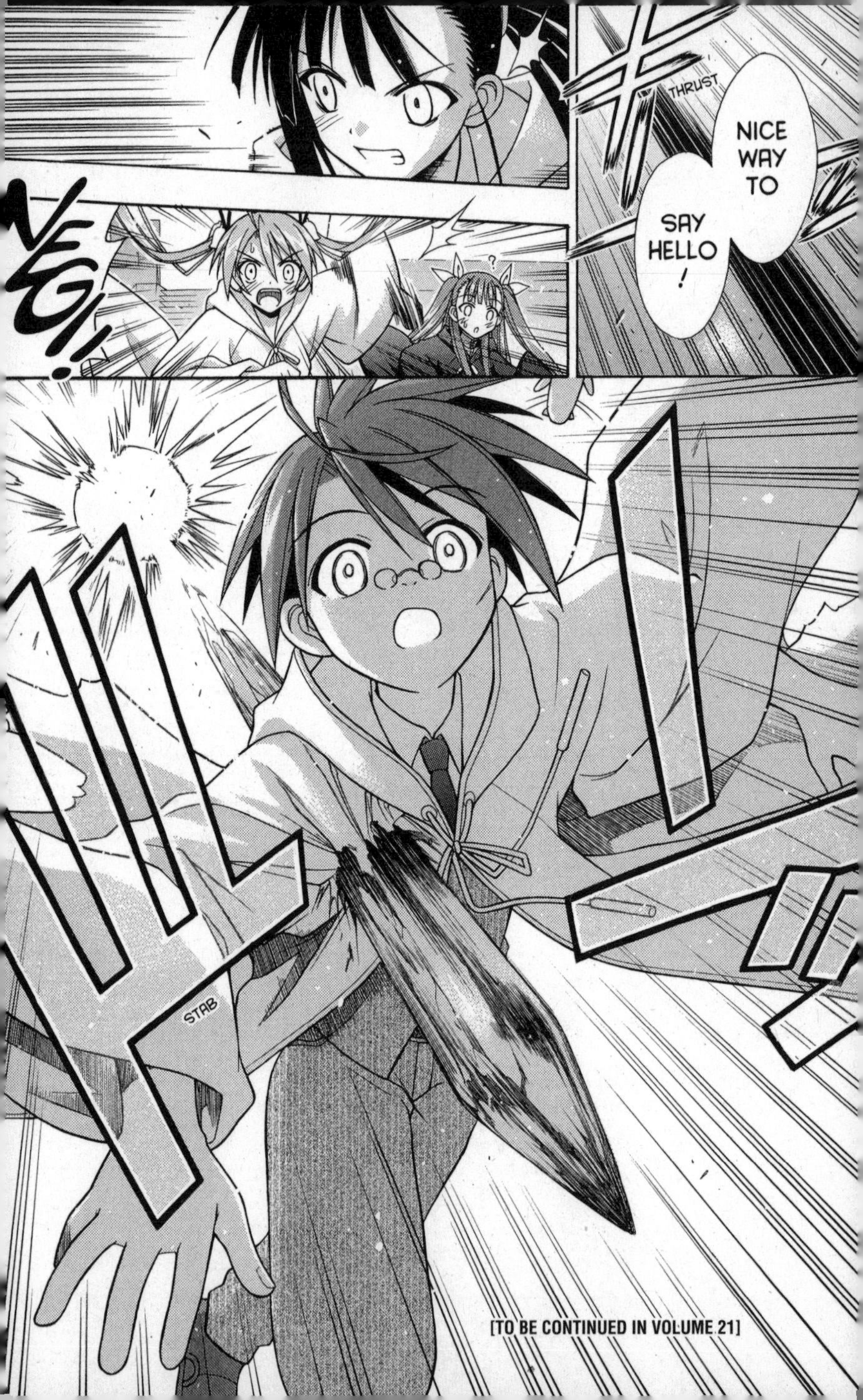
THRUST
NICE WAY TO
SAY HELLO!
NEGI!!
STAB
[TO BE CONTINUED IN VOLUME 21]

A Word from the Author

I'm pleased to present volume 21.

Negi and crew kick off their entry into the Magical World with a *major* incident. How will they find their way out of this mess? (^^;)

In these coming episodes, many mysteries surrounding Negi will be resolved, so stay sharp!

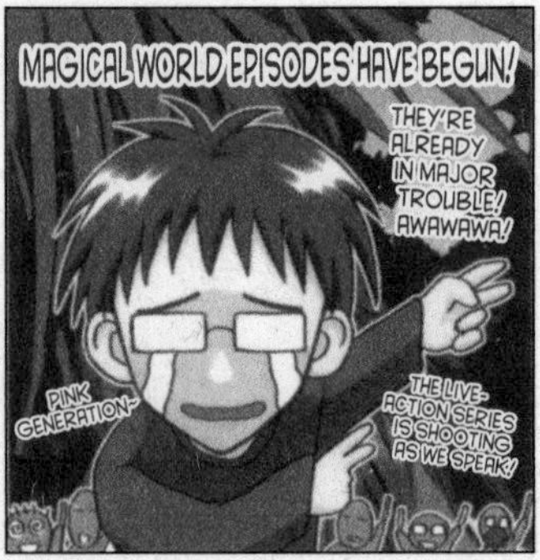
MAGICAL WORLD EPISODES HAVE BEGUN!
THEY'RE ALREADY IN MAJOR TROUBLE! AWAWAWA!
THE LIVE-ACTION SERIES IS SHOOTING AS WE SPEAK!
PINK GENERATION~

The shoots for the live-action drama version have been picking up steam! The drama series began in March of 2008! There will be cards available, similar to the manga series! I'm on fire!

Ken Akamatsu
www.ailove.net

21

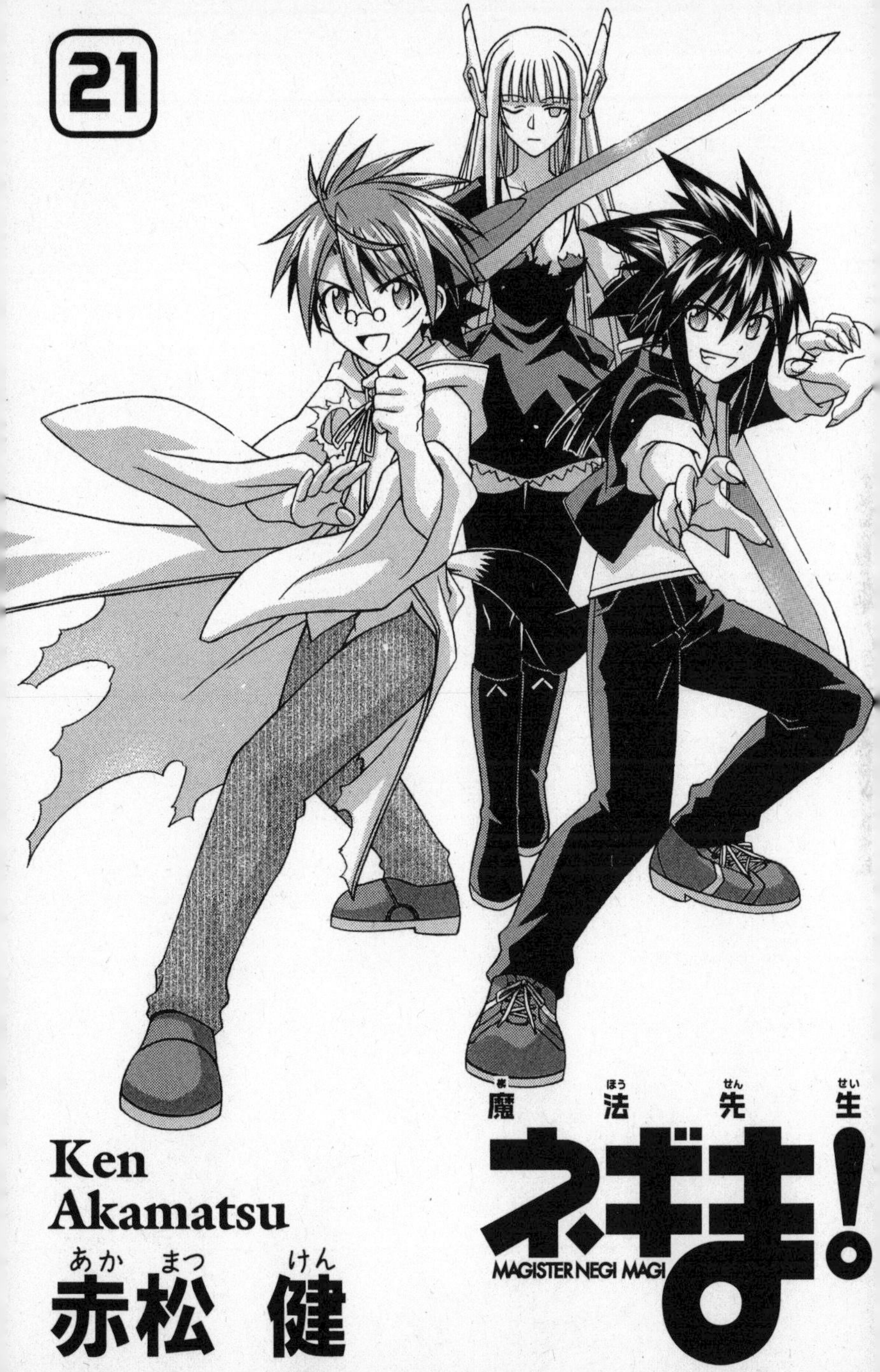

魔法先生ネギま!

MAGISTER NEGI MAGI

Ken Akamatsu

赤松 健

CONTENTS

187th Period – Fate Causes a Catastrophe........329

188th Period – Power Up, Negi Party!!..........347

189th Period – Destruction! Negi Party!!..........365

190th Period – Energy Recovered, 120% ♡..........383

191st Period – Promise from the Past........401

192nd Period – Hero's Duty........417

193rd Period – Wanted!!..........435

194th Period – Made in the Magical World........453

195th Period – 1,000,000 Dorakuma Repayment Plan.......471

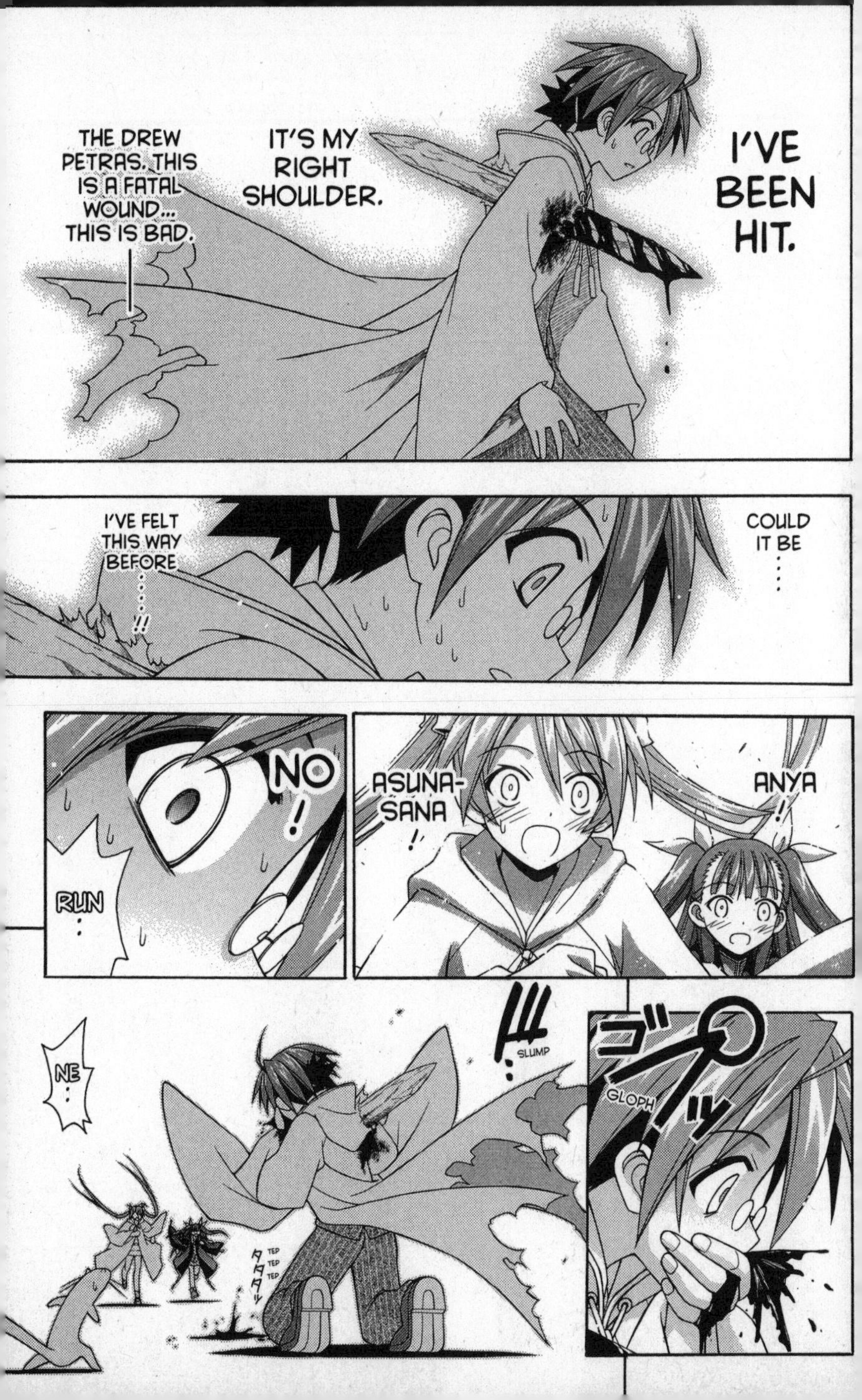
I'VE BEEN HIT.
IT'S MY RIGHT SHOULDER.
THE DREW PETRAS. THIS IS A FATAL WOUND... THIS IS BAD.
COULD IT BE ....
I'VE FELT THIS WAY BEFORE ....!!
ANYA!
ASUNA-SANA!
NO!
RUN..
GLOPH
SLUMP
TEP TEP TEP
NE..

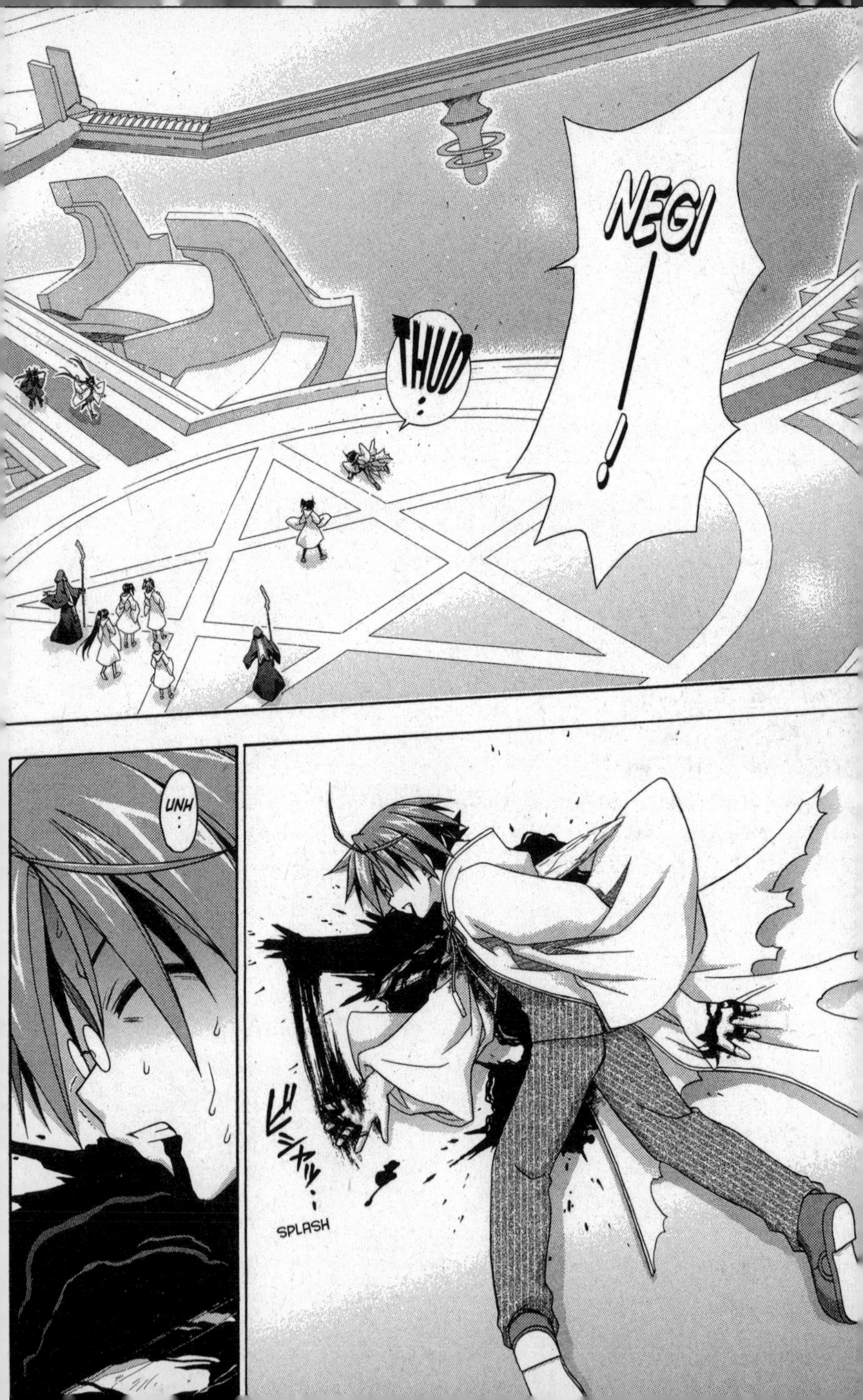
NEGI!!
THUD...
SPLASH
UNH...

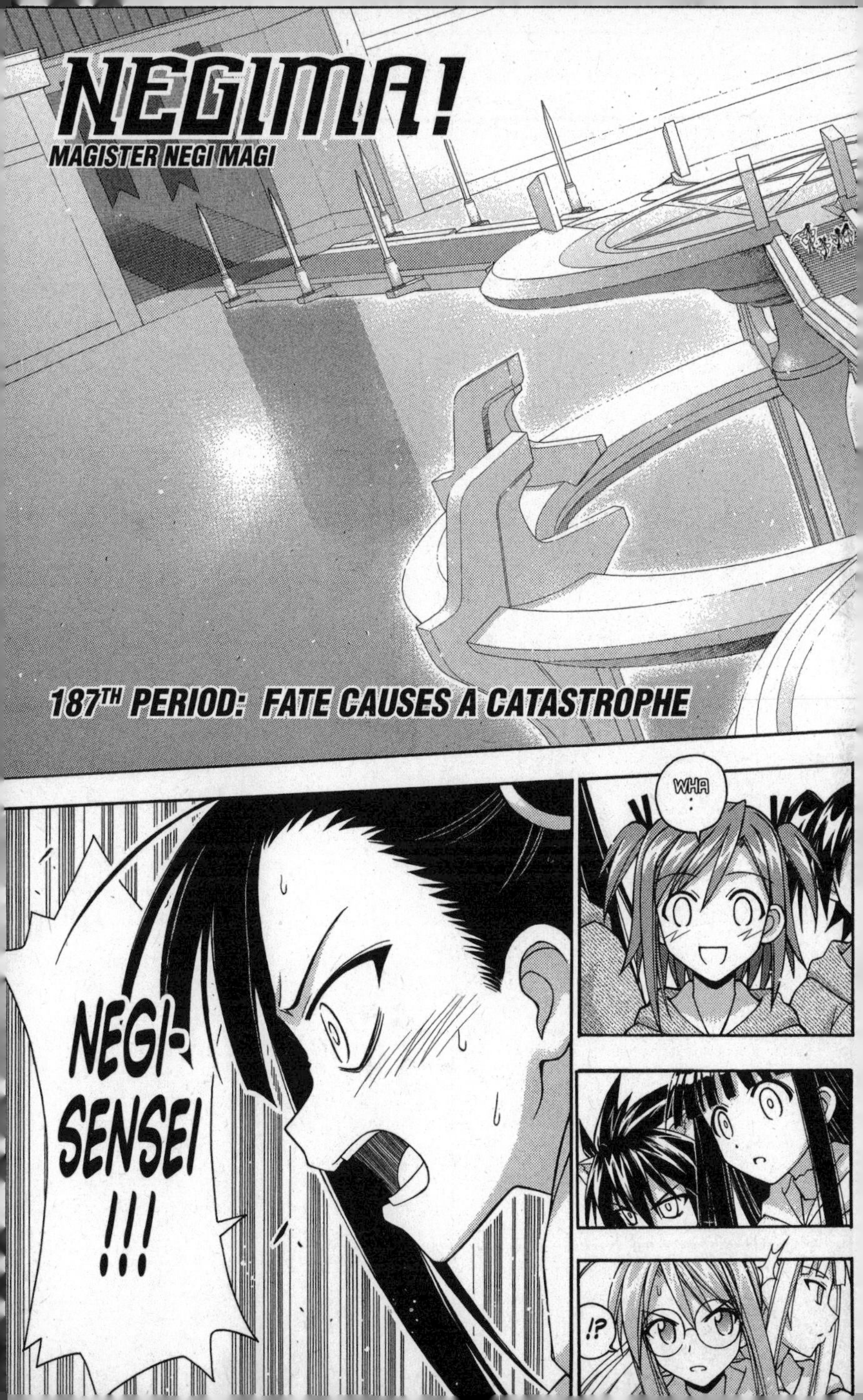
NEGIMA!
MAGISTER NEGI MAGI
187TH PERIOD: FATE CAUSES A CATASTROPHE
WHA
NEGI-SENSEI !!!
!?

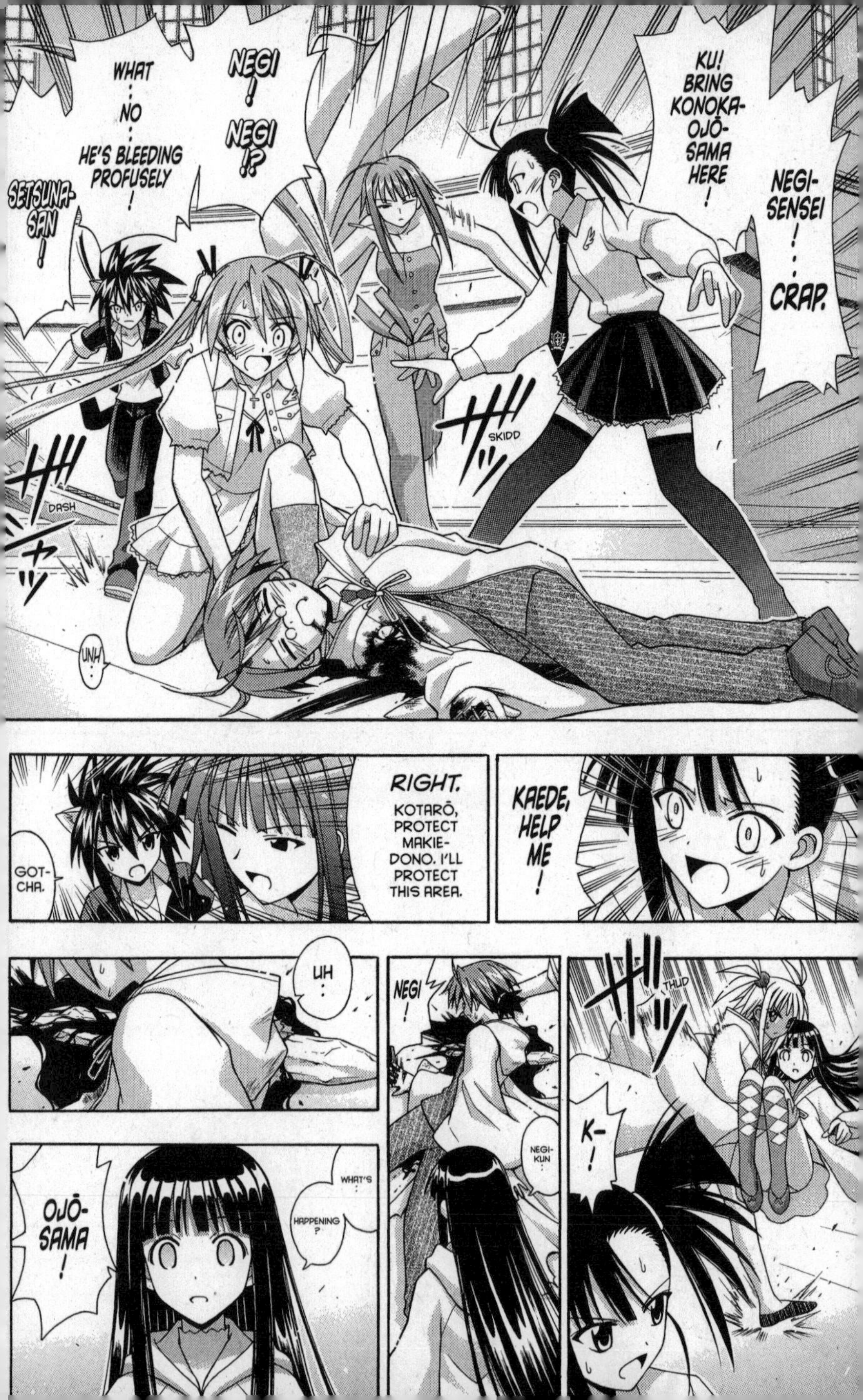
NEGI-SENSEI... CRAP.
KU! BRING KONOKA-OJŌ-SAMA HERE!
NEGI! NEGI!?
WHAT... NO... HE'S BLEEDING PROFUSELY!
SETSUNA-SAN!
SKIDD
DASH
UNH...
KAEDE, HELP ME!
RIGHT.
KOTARŌ, PROTECT MAKIE-DONO. I'LL PROTECT THIS AREA.
GOT-CHA.
THUD
K-!
NEGI!
NEGI-KUN...
UH...
WHAT'S... HAPPENING?
OJŌ-SAMA!

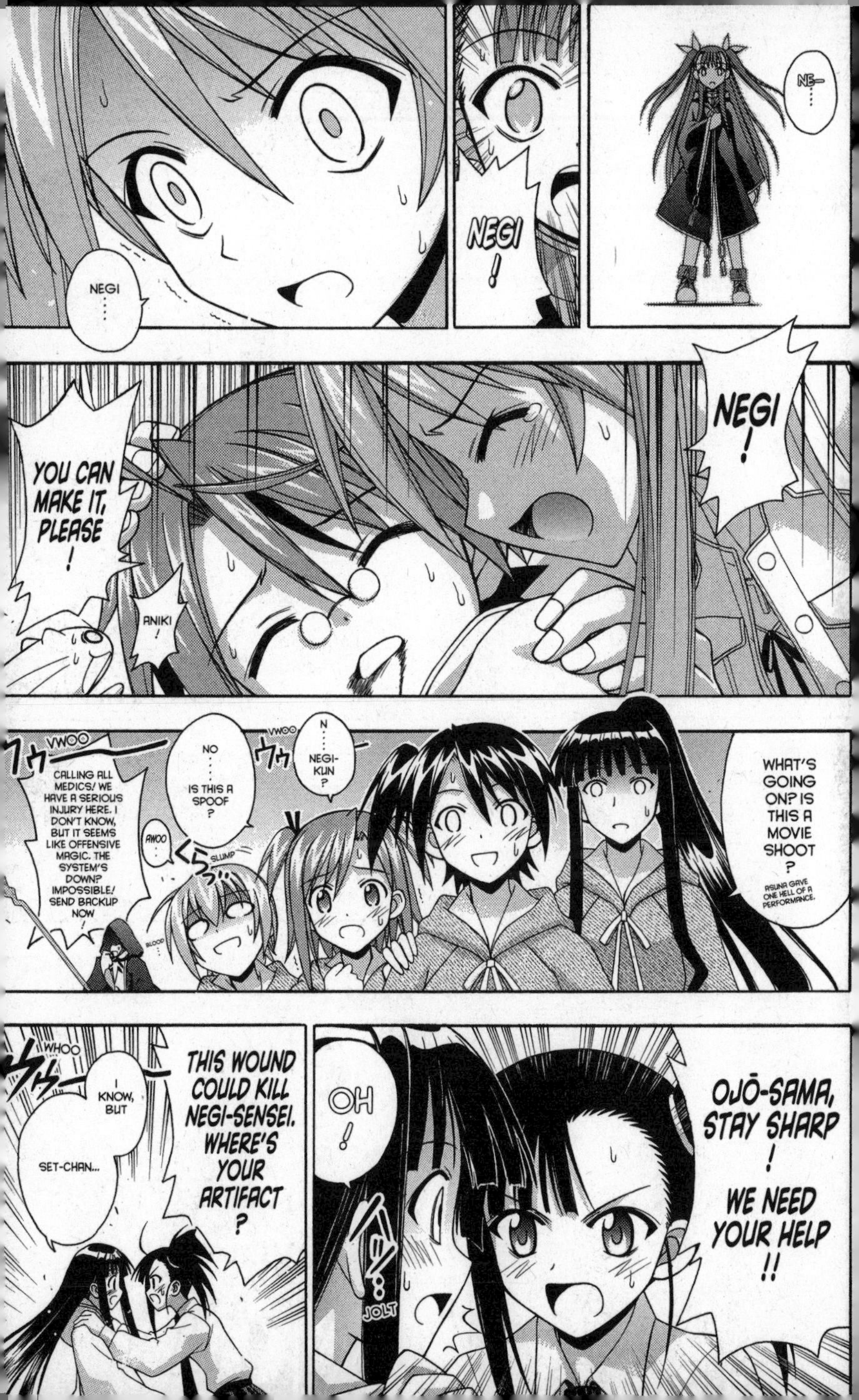
NE—......
NEGI!
NEGI......
NEGI!
YOU CAN MAKE IT, PLEASE!
ANIKI!
WHAT'S GOING ON? IS THIS A MOVIE SHOOT?
ASUNA GAVE ONE HELL OF A PERFORMANCE.
N...... NEGI-KUN?
VWOO
NO...... IS THIS A SPOOF?
SLUMP
AWOO......
BLOOD......
VWOO
CALLING ALL MEDICS! WE HAVE A SERIOUS INJURY HERE. I DON'T KNOW, BUT IT SEEMS LIKE OFFENSIVE MAGIC. THE SYSTEM'S DOWN? IMPOSSIBLE! SEND BACKUP NOW!
OJŌ-SAMA, STAY SHARP! WE NEED YOUR HELP!!
OH!
JOLT
THIS WOUND COULD KILL NEGI-SENSEI. WHERE'S YOUR ARTIFACT?
I KNOW, BUT
SET-CHAN...
WHOO

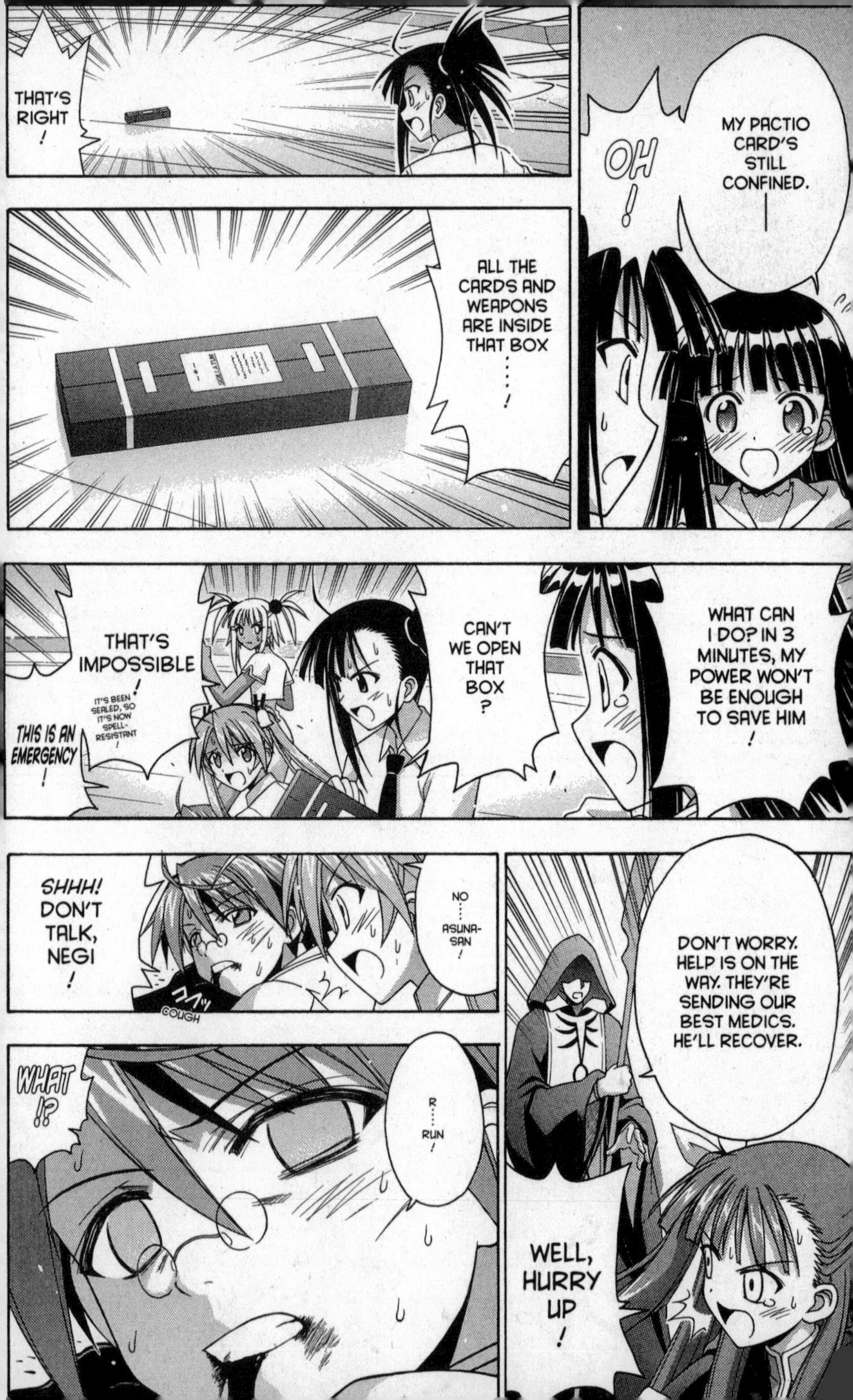
OH!
MY PACTIO CARD'S STILL CONFINED.
THAT'S RIGHT!
ALL THE CARDS AND WEAPONS ARE INSIDE THAT BOX...!
WHAT CAN I DO? IN 3 MINUTES, MY POWER WON'T BE ENOUGH TO SAVE HIM!
CAN'T WE OPEN THAT BOX?
THAT'S IMPOSSIBLE!
IT'S BEEN SEALED, SO IT'S NOW SPELL-RESISTANT!
THIS IS AN EMERGENCY!
DON'T WORRY. HELP IS ON THE WAY. THEY'RE SENDING OUR BEST MEDICS. HE'LL RECOVER.
WELL, HURRY UP!
NO... ASUNA-SAN!
SHHH! DON'T TALK, NEGI!
クハッ
COUGH
R... RUN!
WHAT!?

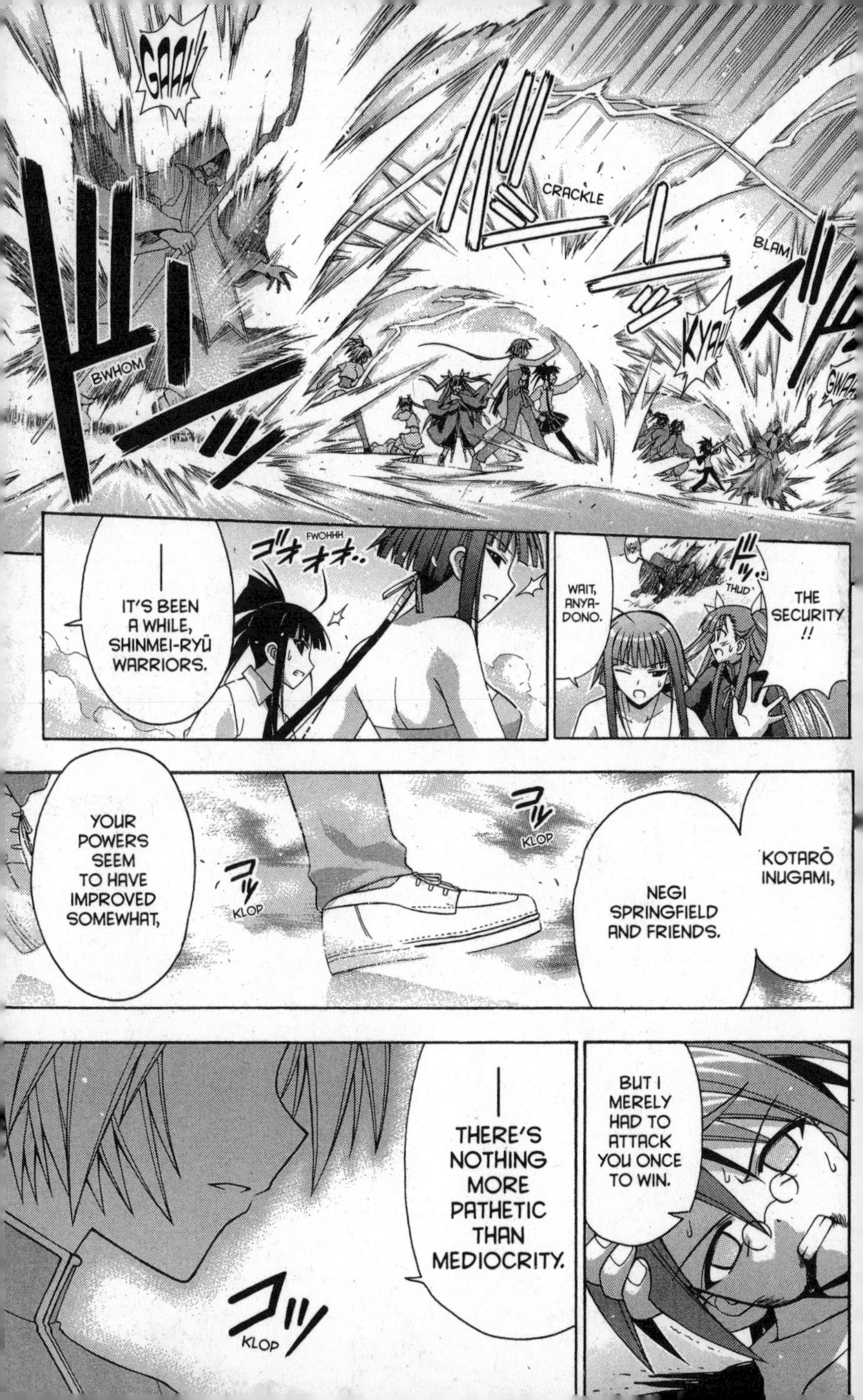
GWAH
KYAH
BLAM
CRACKLE
GAAH
BWHOM
THUD
THE SECURITY!!
WAIT, ANYA-DONO.
FWOHHH
IT'S BEEN A WHILE, SHINMEI-RYŪ WARRIORS.
KOTARŌ INUGAMI,
NEGI SPRINGFIELD AND FRIENDS.
KLOP
YOUR POWERS SEEM TO HAVE IMPROVED SOMEWHAT,
KLOP
BUT I MERELY HAD TO ATTACK YOU ONCE TO WIN.
THERE'S NOTHING MORE PATHETIC THAN MEDIOCRITY.
KLOP

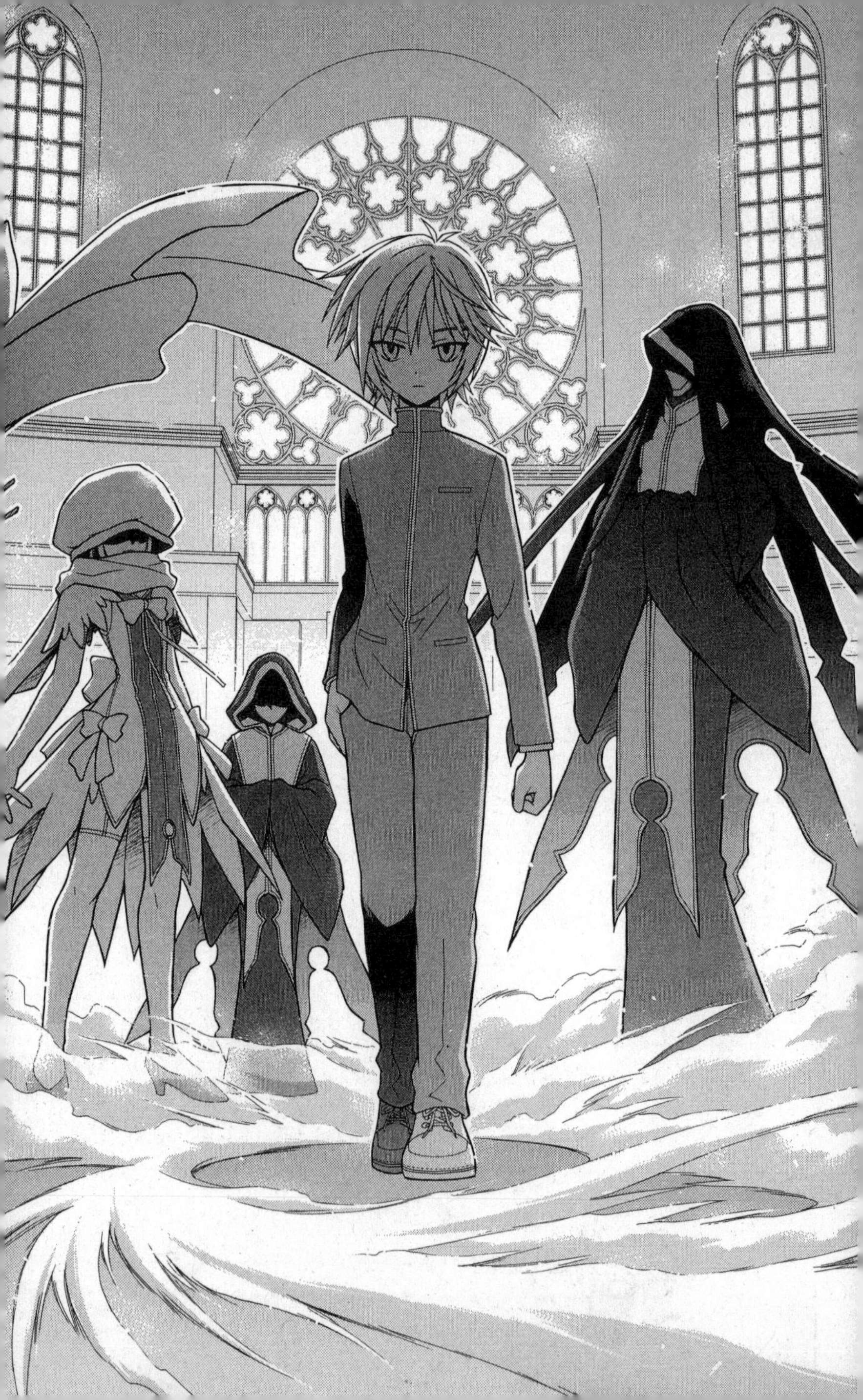

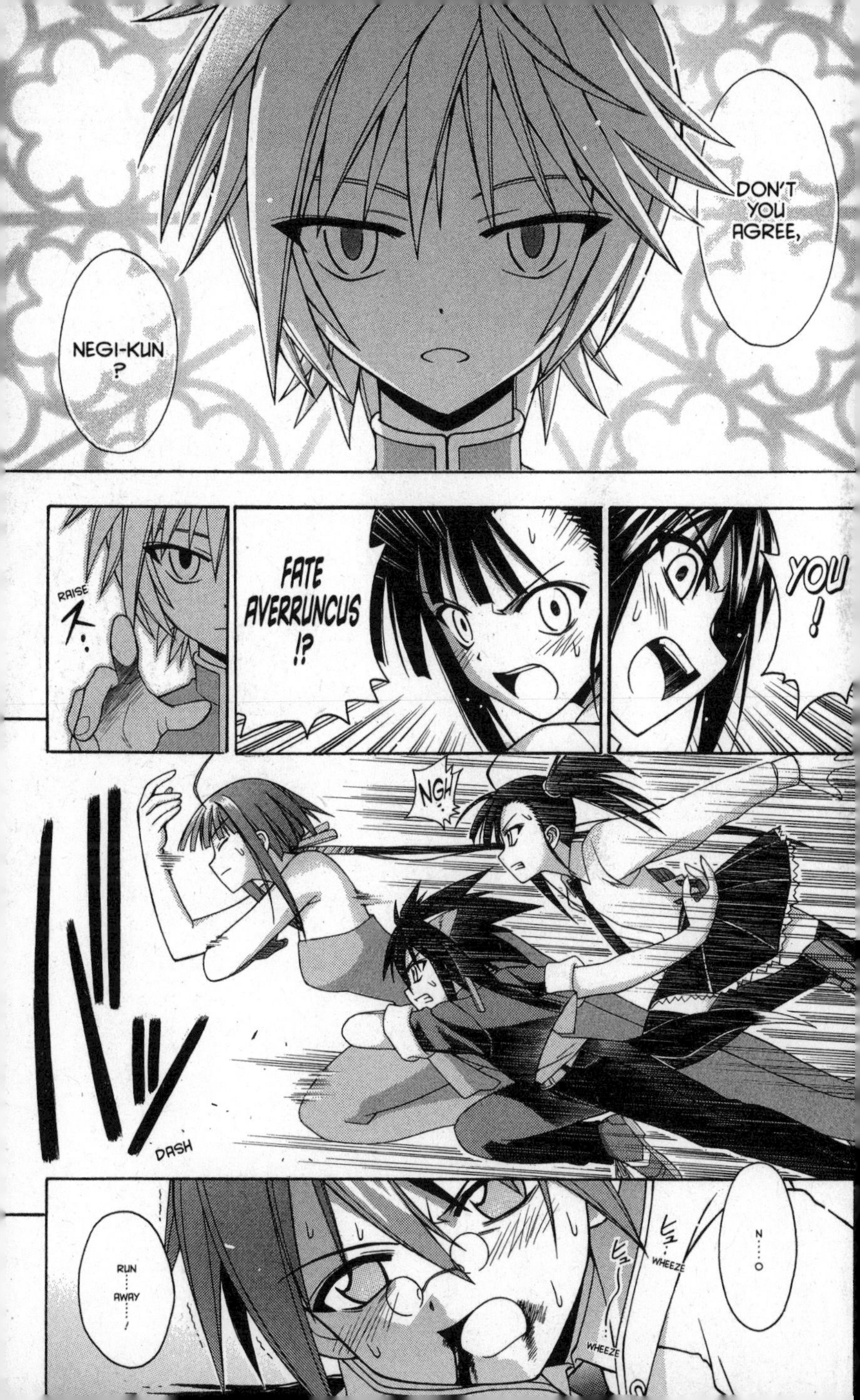
DON'T YOU AGREE,
NEGI-KUN ?
YOU !
FATE AVERRUNCUS !?
RAISE
NGH
DASH
N......O
WHEEZE
WHEEZE
RUN...... AWAY......!

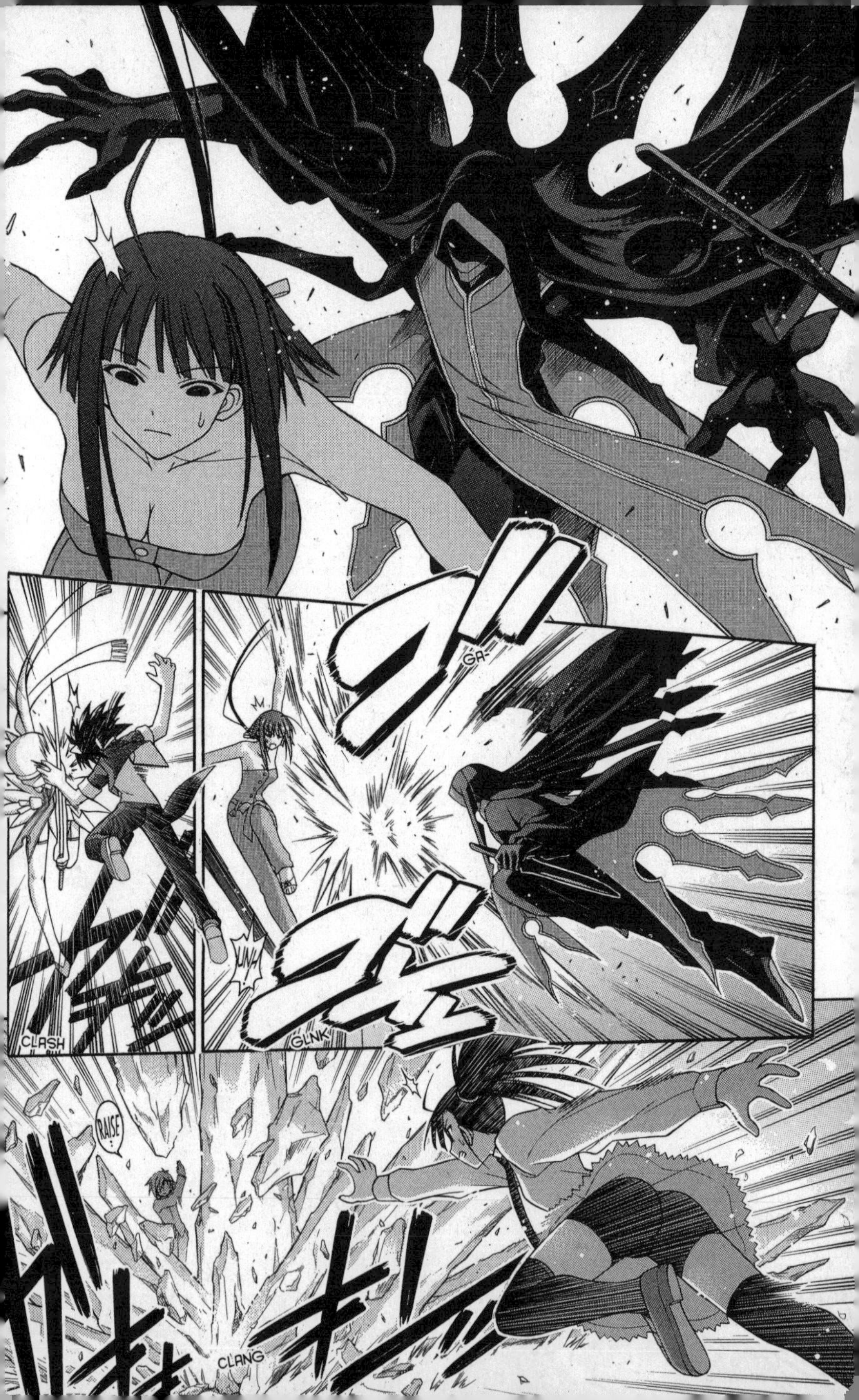
GA-
UNH!
GLNK
CLASH
RAISE
CLANG

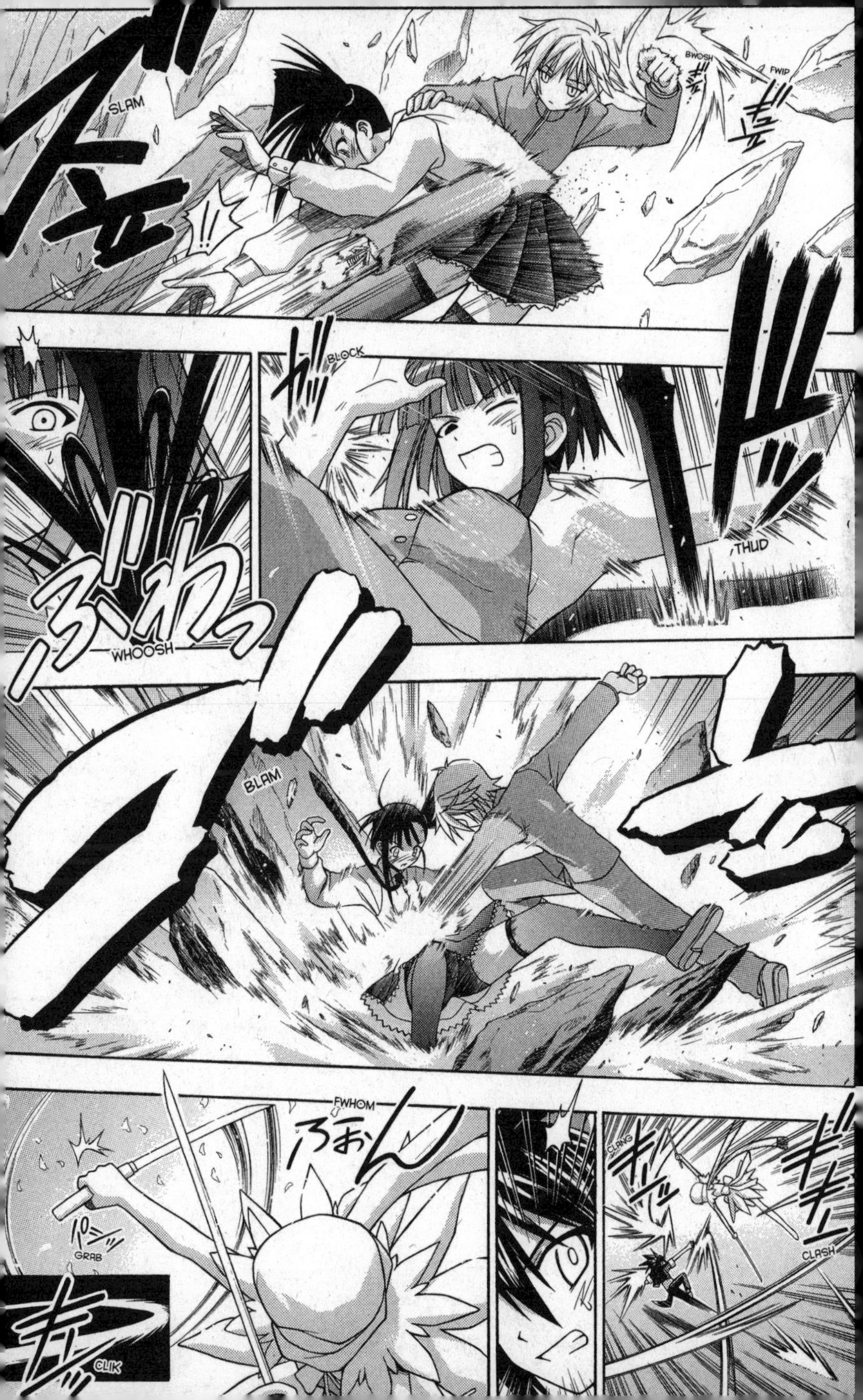
BWOSH
FWIP
SLAM
BLOCK
THUD
WHOOSH
BLAM
CLANG
CLASH
FWHOM
ろおん
GRAB
CLIK

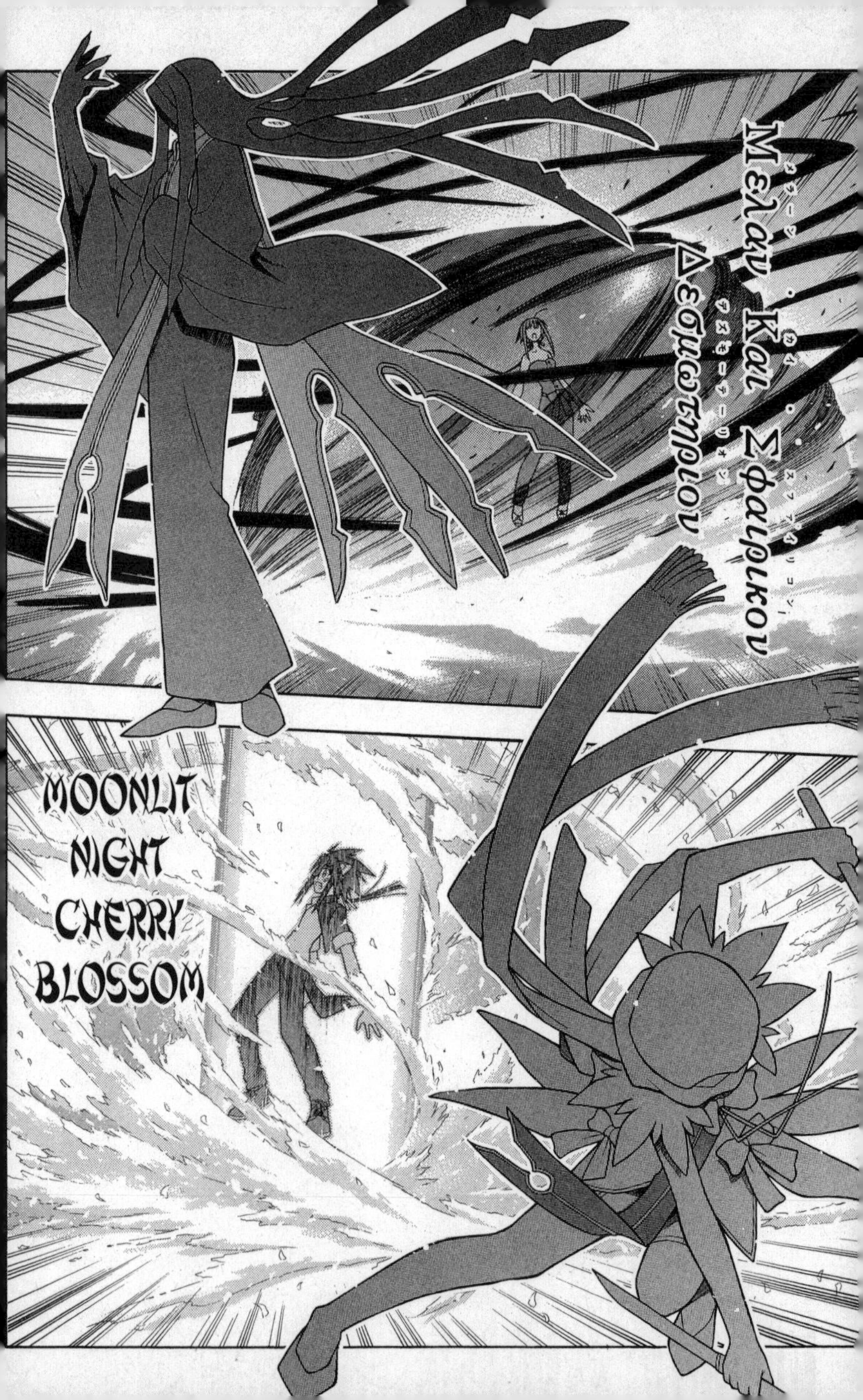
Μελαν · Και · Σφαιρικον
Δεσμωτηριον
MOONLIT NIGHT CHERRY BLOSSOM

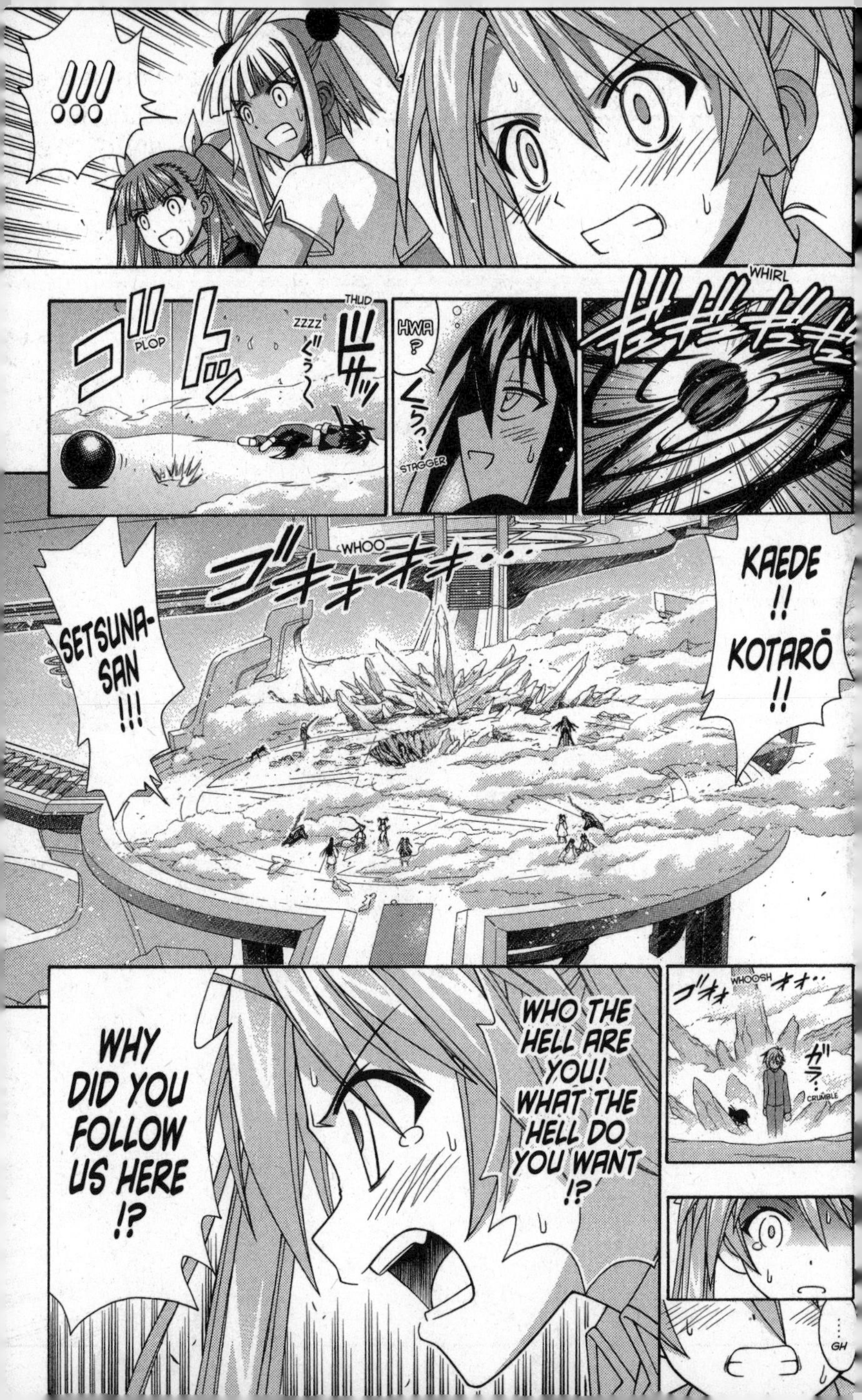

!!!!
WHIRL
HWA?
くらっ…
STAGGER
THUD
ジザッ
ZZZZ
ぐぅ～
ゴッ
PLOP
トッ
KAEDE!! KOTARŌ!!
ゴォォォォ…
WHOO
SETSUNA-SAN!!!
ゴォォ
WHOOSH
オォ…
ガラ…
CRUMBLE
WHO THE HELL ARE YOU! WHAT THE HELL DO YOU WANT!?
WHY DID YOU FOLLOW US HERE!?
……GH

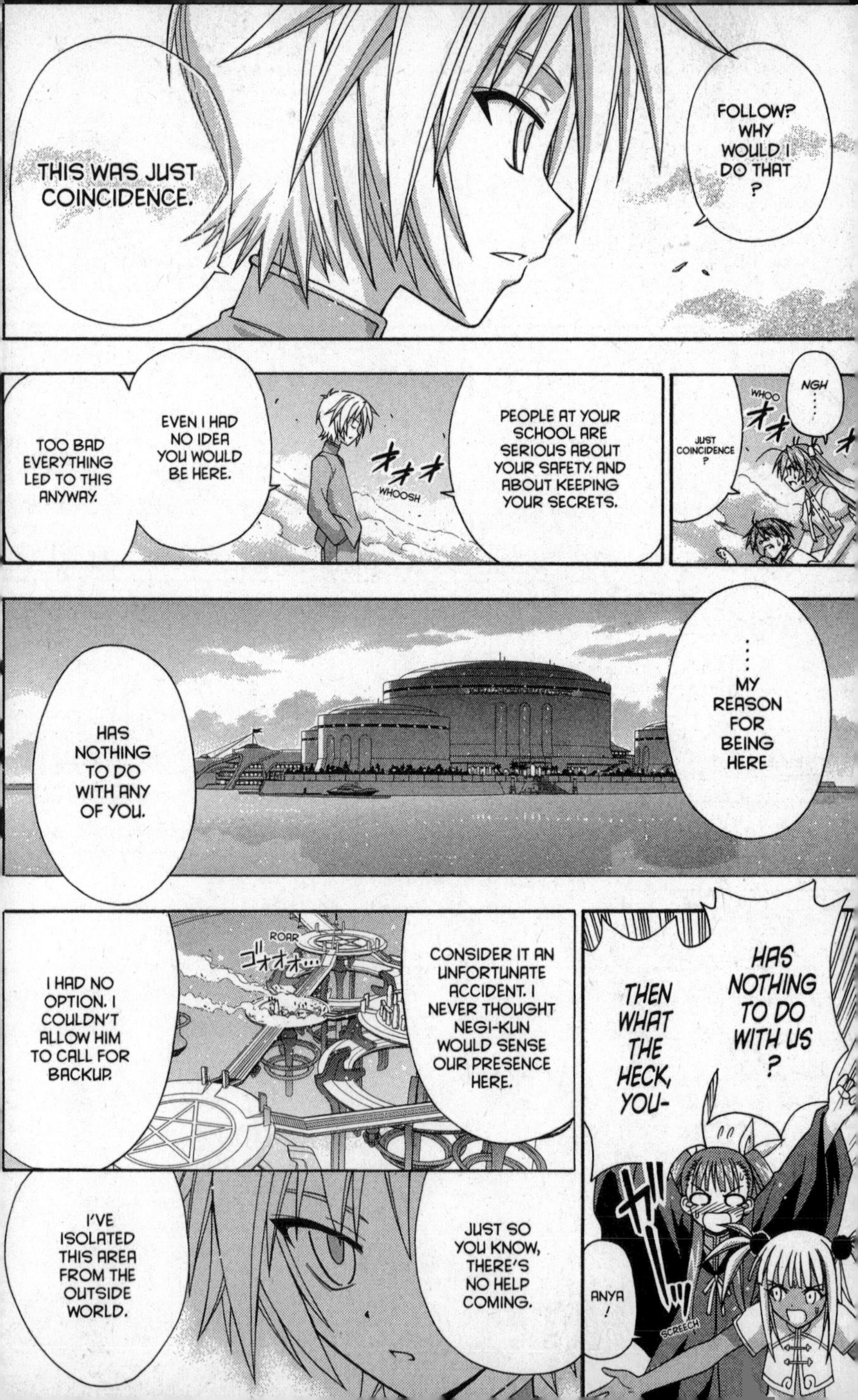
FOLLOW? WHY WOULD I DO THAT ?
THIS WAS JUST COINCIDENCE.
NGH ....
WHOO
JUST COINCIDENCE ?
PEOPLE AT YOUR SCHOOL ARE SERIOUS ABOUT YOUR SAFETY. AND ABOUT KEEPING YOUR SECRETS.
WHOOSH
EVEN I HAD NO IDEA YOU WOULD BE HERE.
TOO BAD EVERYTHING LED TO THIS ANYWAY.
... MY REASON FOR BEING HERE
HAS NOTHING TO DO WITH ANY OF YOU.
HAS NOTHING TO DO WITH US ?
THEN WHAT THE HECK, YOU-
ANYA !
SCREECH
CONSIDER IT AN UNFORTUNATE ACCIDENT. I NEVER THOUGHT NEGI-KUN WOULD SENSE OUR PRESENCE HERE.
ROAR
I HAD NO OPTION. I COULDN'T ALLOW HIM TO CALL FOR BACKUP.
JUST SO YOU KNOW, THERE'S NO HELP COMING.
I'VE ISOLATED THIS AREA FROM THE OUTSIDE WORLD.

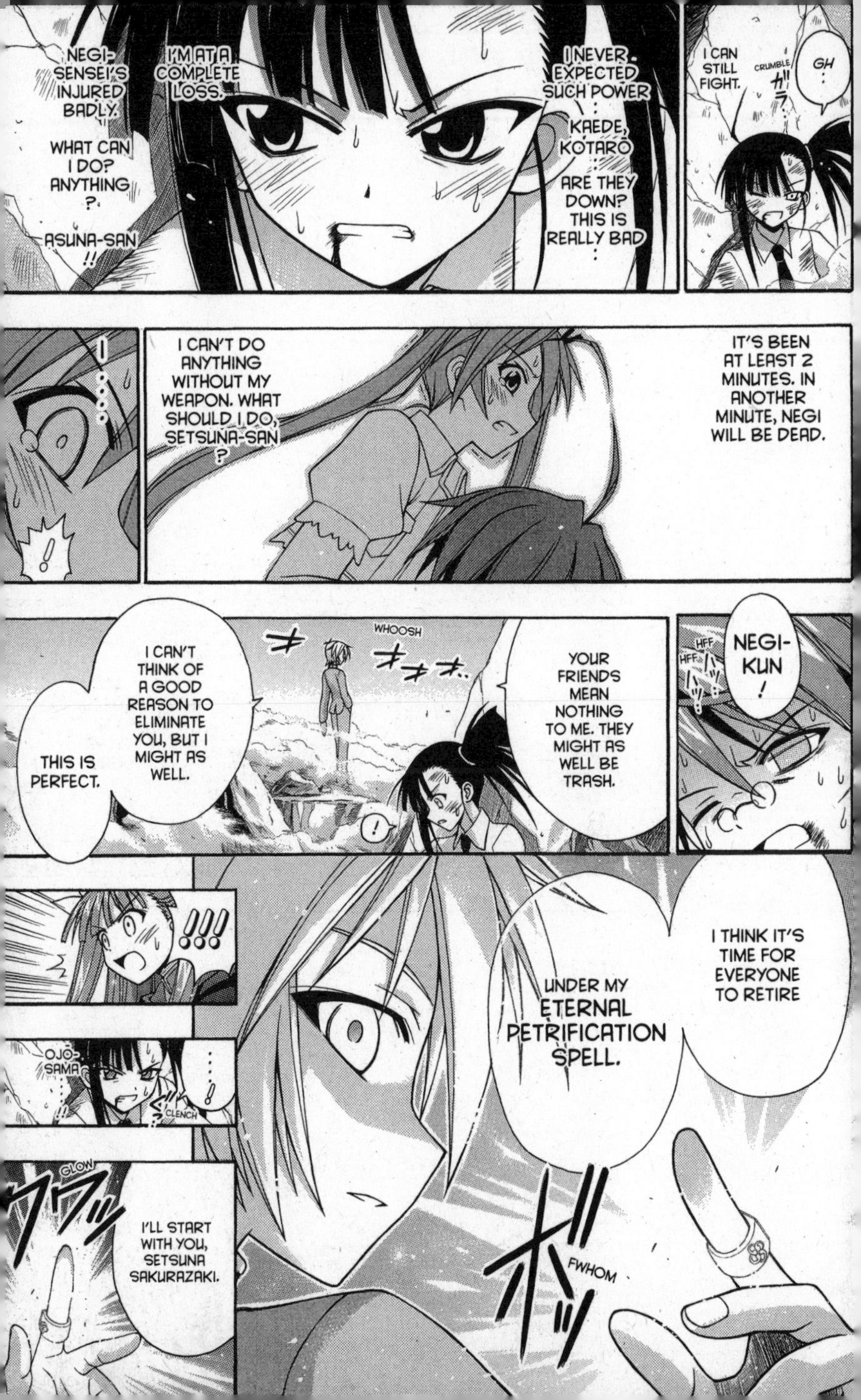

GH
CRUMBLE
I CAN STILL FIGHT.
I NEVER EXPECTED SUCH POWER...
KAEDE, KOTARO...
ARE THEY DOWN? THIS IS REALLY BAD...
I'M AT A COMPLETE LOSS.
NEGI-SENSEI'S INJURED BADLY.
WHAT CAN I DO? ANYTHING?
ASUNA-SAN!!
IT'S BEEN AT LEAST 2 MINUTES. IN ANOTHER MINUTE, NEGI WILL BE DEAD.
I CAN'T DO ANYTHING WITHOUT MY WEAPON. WHAT SHOULD I DO, SETSUNA-SAN?
!....
!
HFF HFF
NEGI-KUN!
WHOOSH
YOUR FRIENDS MEAN NOTHING TO ME. THEY MIGHT AS WELL BE TRASH.
!
I CAN'T THINK OF A GOOD REASON TO ELIMINATE YOU, BUT I MIGHT AS WELL.
THIS IS PERFECT.
I THINK IT'S TIME FOR EVERYONE TO RETIRE
UNDER MY ETERNAL PETRIFICATION SPELL.
FWHOM
GLOW
I'LL START WITH YOU, SETSUNA SAKURAZAKI.
!!!
...!
CLENCH
OJO-SAMA...!!

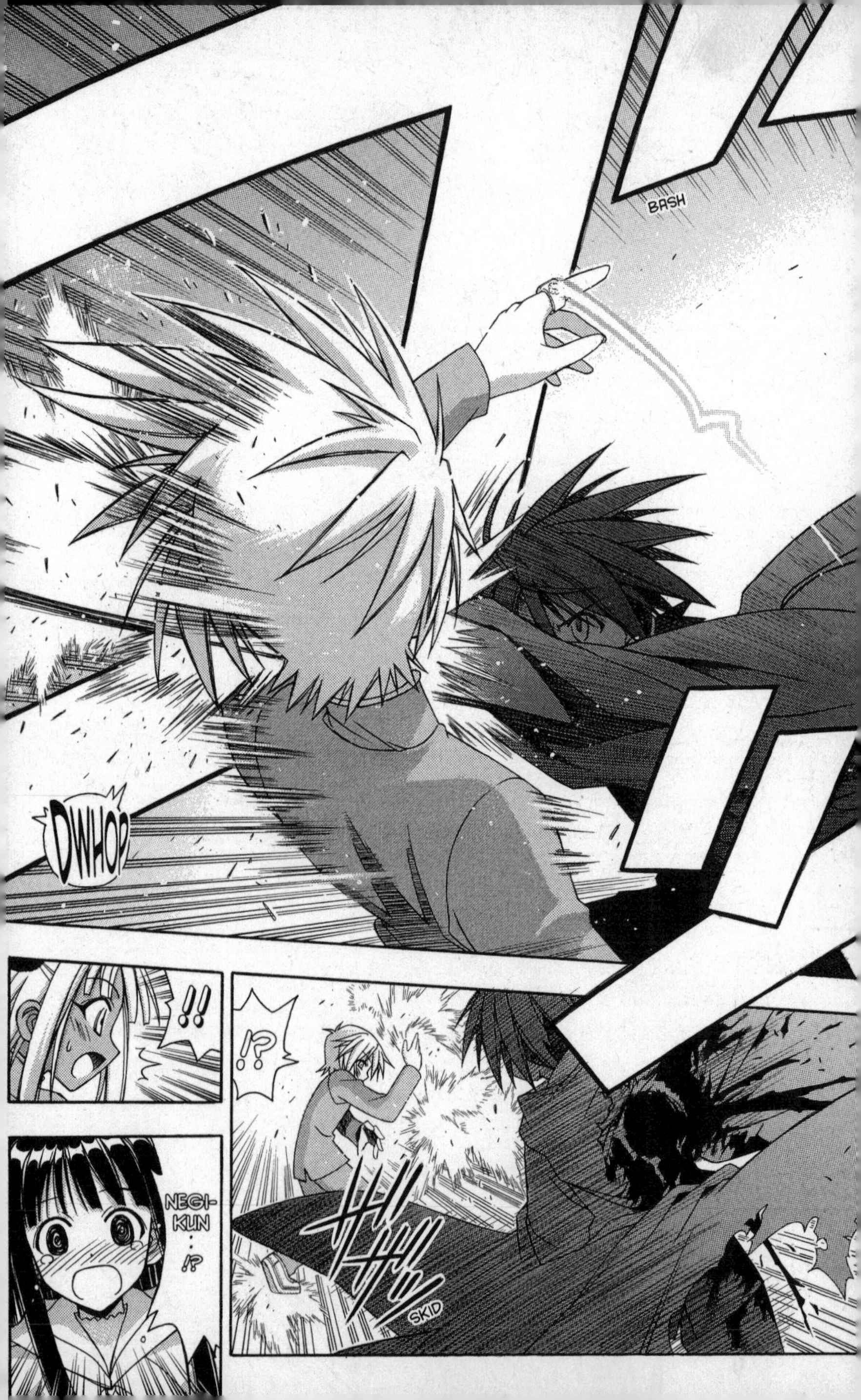
BASH
DWHOP
!!
!?
NEGI-KUN...!?
SKID

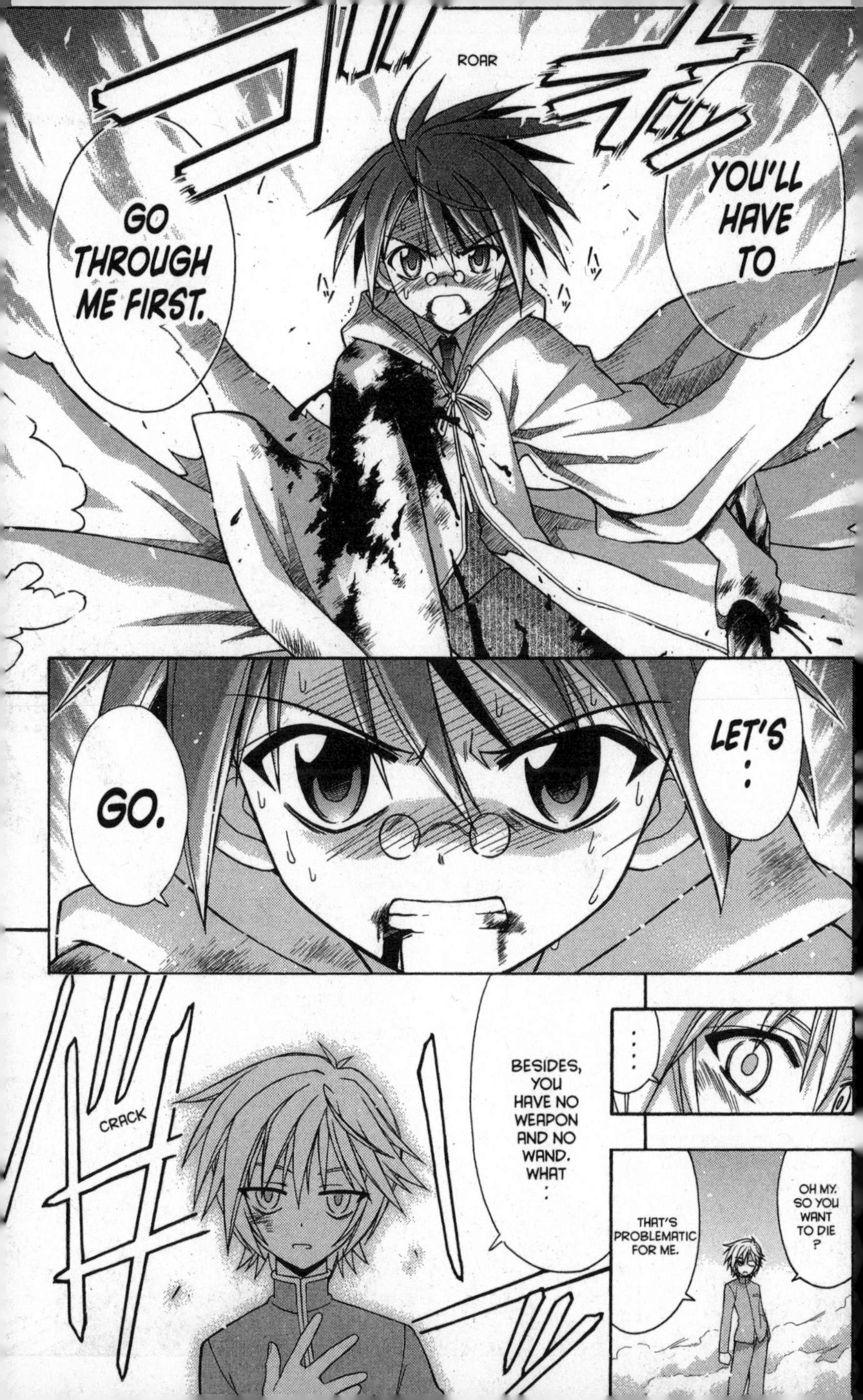
ROAR
YOU'LL HAVE TO
GO THROUGH ME FIRST.
LET'S
:
GO.
....
OH MY. SO YOU WANT TO DIE ?
THAT'S PROBLEMATIC FOR ME.
BESIDES, YOU HAVE NO WEAPON AND NO WAND. WHAT
:
CRACK

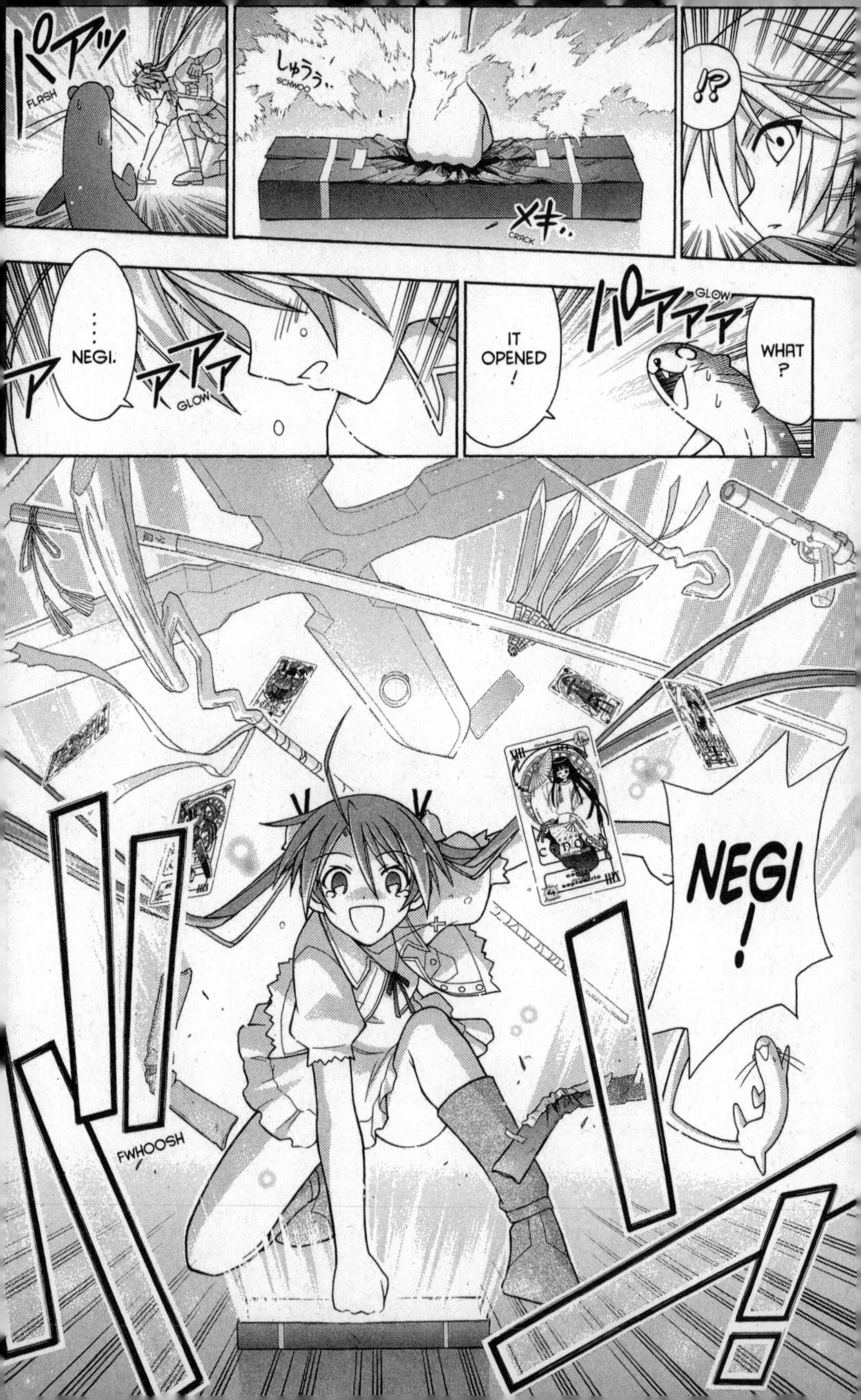
!?
しゅうう…
SCHWOO
メキ…
CRACK
パアッ
FLASH
WHAT?
パアアア
GLOW
IT OPENED!
…NEGI.
アアアア
GLOW
NEGI!
FWHOOSH

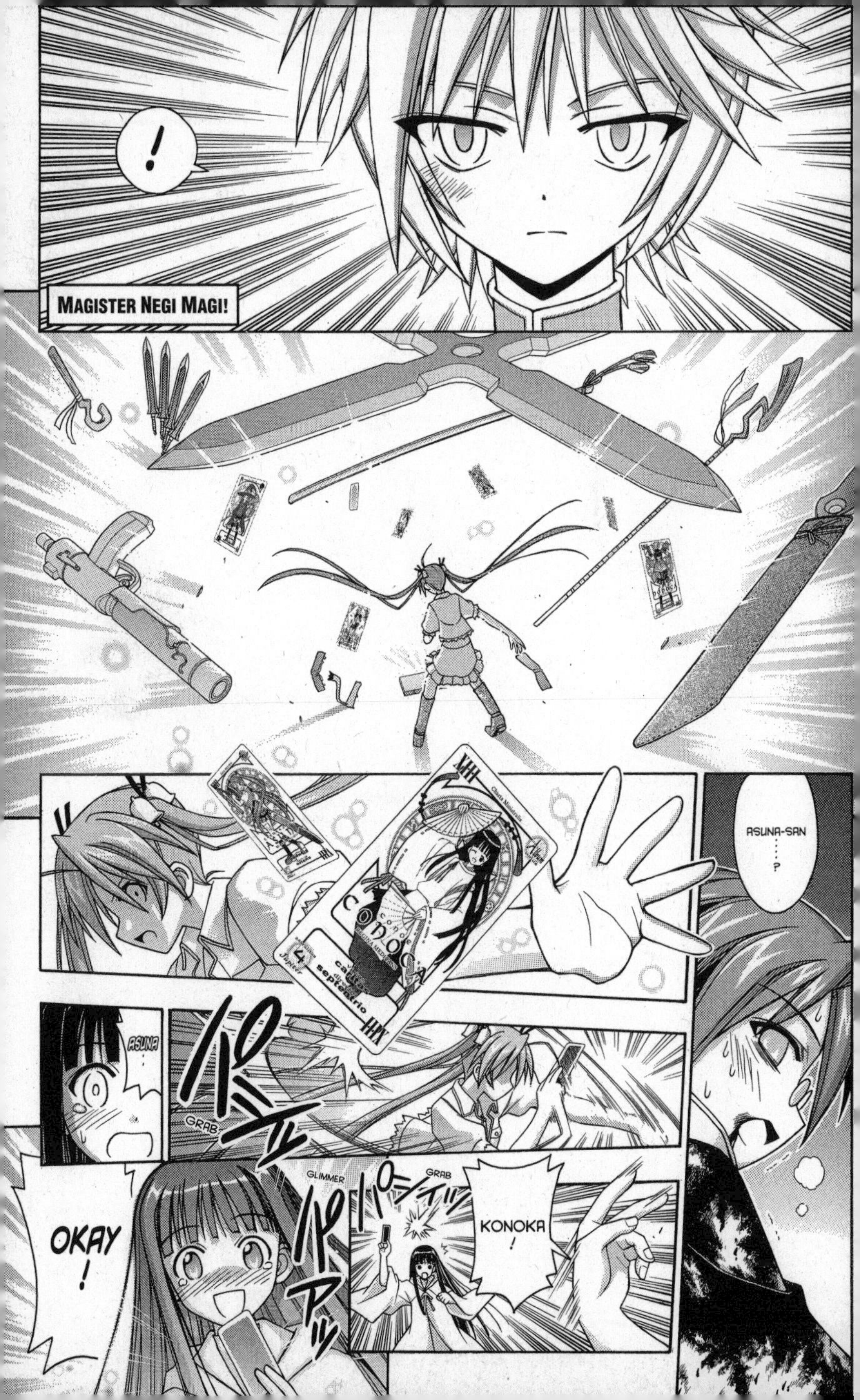
!
MAGISTER NEGI MAGI!
ASUNA-SAN ....?
GRAB
ASUNA!
GRAB
KONOKA!
GLIMMER
OKAY!

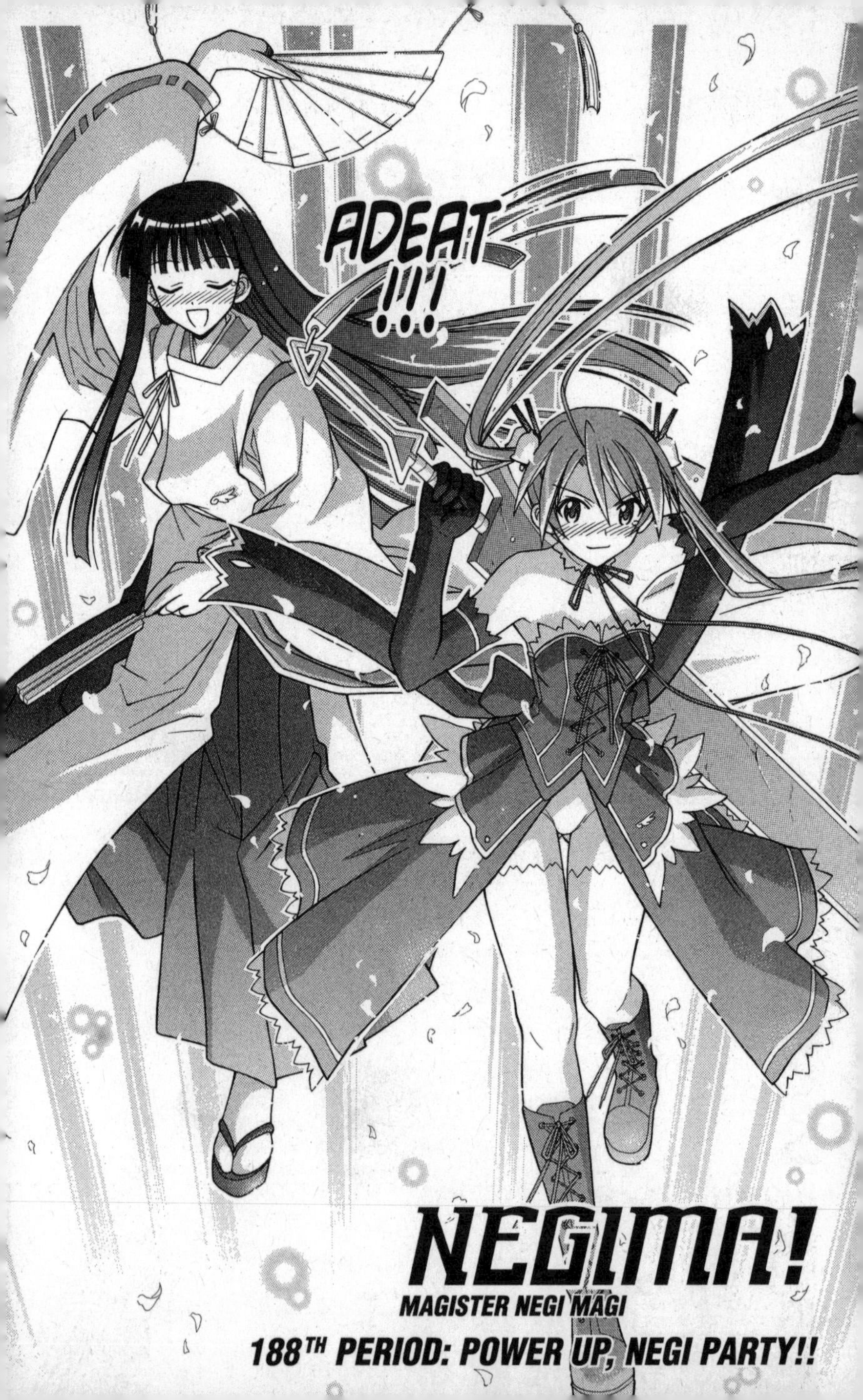
ADEAT !!!!

NEGIMA!

MAGISTER NEGI MAGI

188TH PERIOD: POWER UP, NEGI PARTY!!

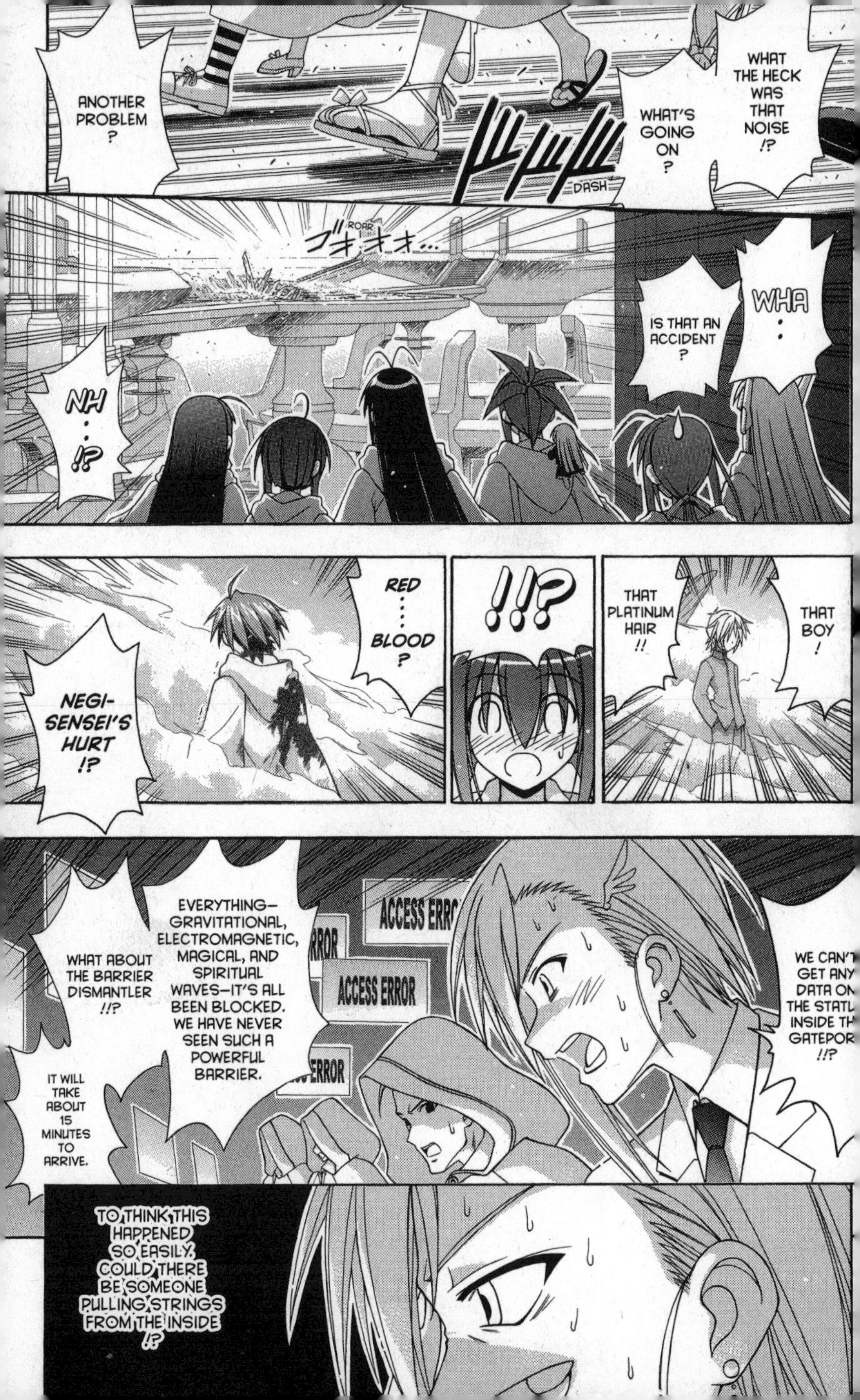
WHAT THE HECK WAS THAT NOISE !?
WHAT'S GOING ON ?
ドドドド
DASH
ANOTHER PROBLEM ?
WHA . .
IS THAT AN ACCIDENT ?
ゴオオオ...
ROAR
NH . . !?
THAT BOY !
THAT PLATINUM HAIR !!
!!?
RED . . . . BLOOD ?
NEGI-SENSEI'S HURT !?
WE CAN'T GET ANY DATA ON THE STATU INSIDE TH GATEPOR !!?
ACCESS ERROR
ACCESS ERROR
EVERYTHING— GRAVITATIONAL, ELECTROMAGNETIC, MAGICAL, AND SPIRITUAL WAVES—IT'S ALL BEEN BLOCKED. WE HAVE NEVER SEEN SUCH A POWERFUL BARRIER.
WHAT ABOUT THE BARRIER DISMANTLER !!?
IT WILL TAKE ABOUT 15 MINUTES TO ARRIVE.
TO THINK THIS HAPPENED SO EASILY. COULD THERE BE SOMEONE PULLING STRINGS FROM THE INSIDE !?

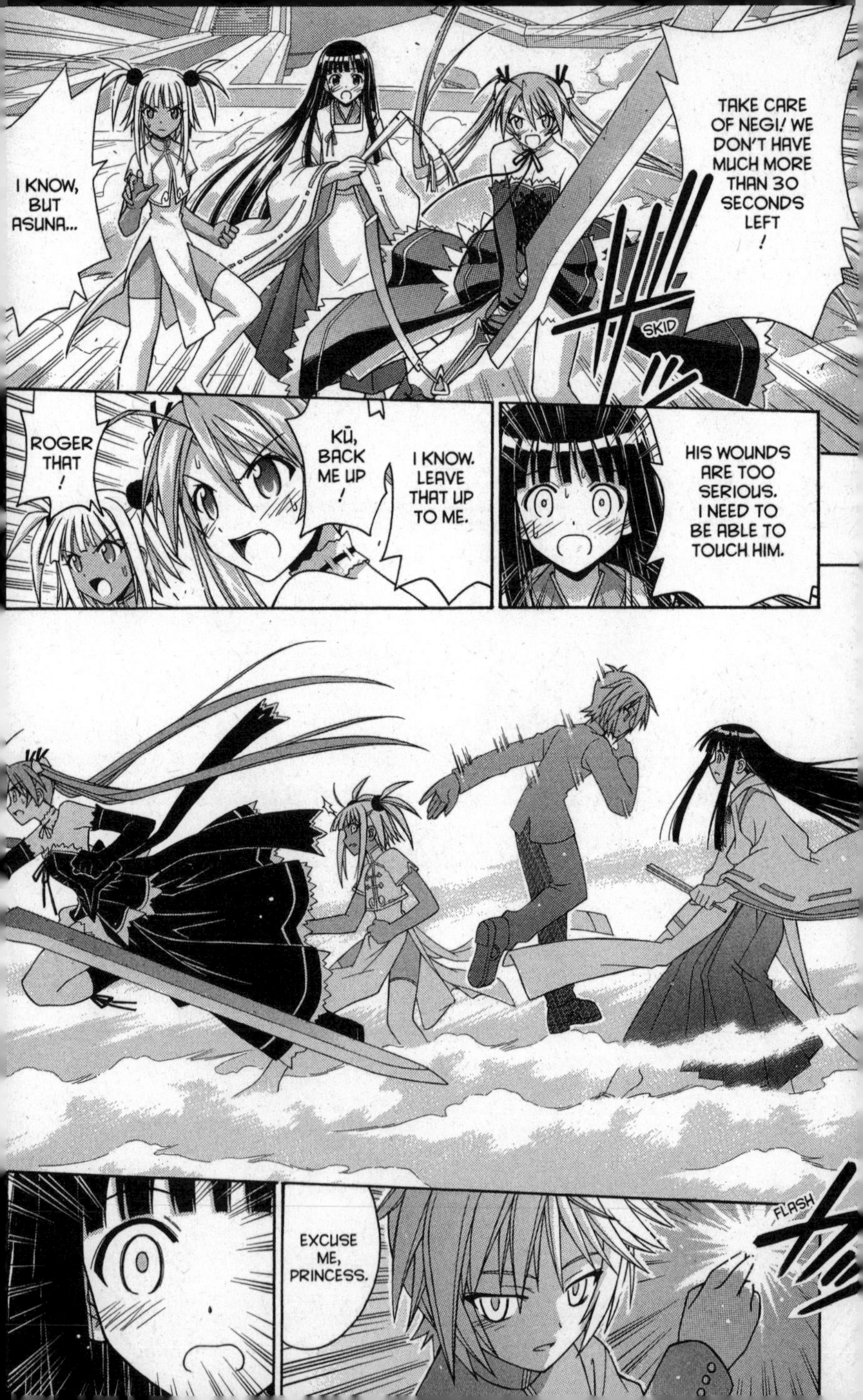
TAKE CARE OF NEGI! WE DON'T HAVE MUCH MORE THAN 30 SECONDS LEFT!
SKID
I KNOW, BUT ASUNA...
HIS WOUNDS ARE TOO SERIOUS. I NEED TO BE ABLE TO TOUCH HIM.
I KNOW. LEAVE THAT UP TO ME.
KŪ, BACK ME UP!
ROGER THAT!
FLASH
EXCUSE ME, PRINCESS.

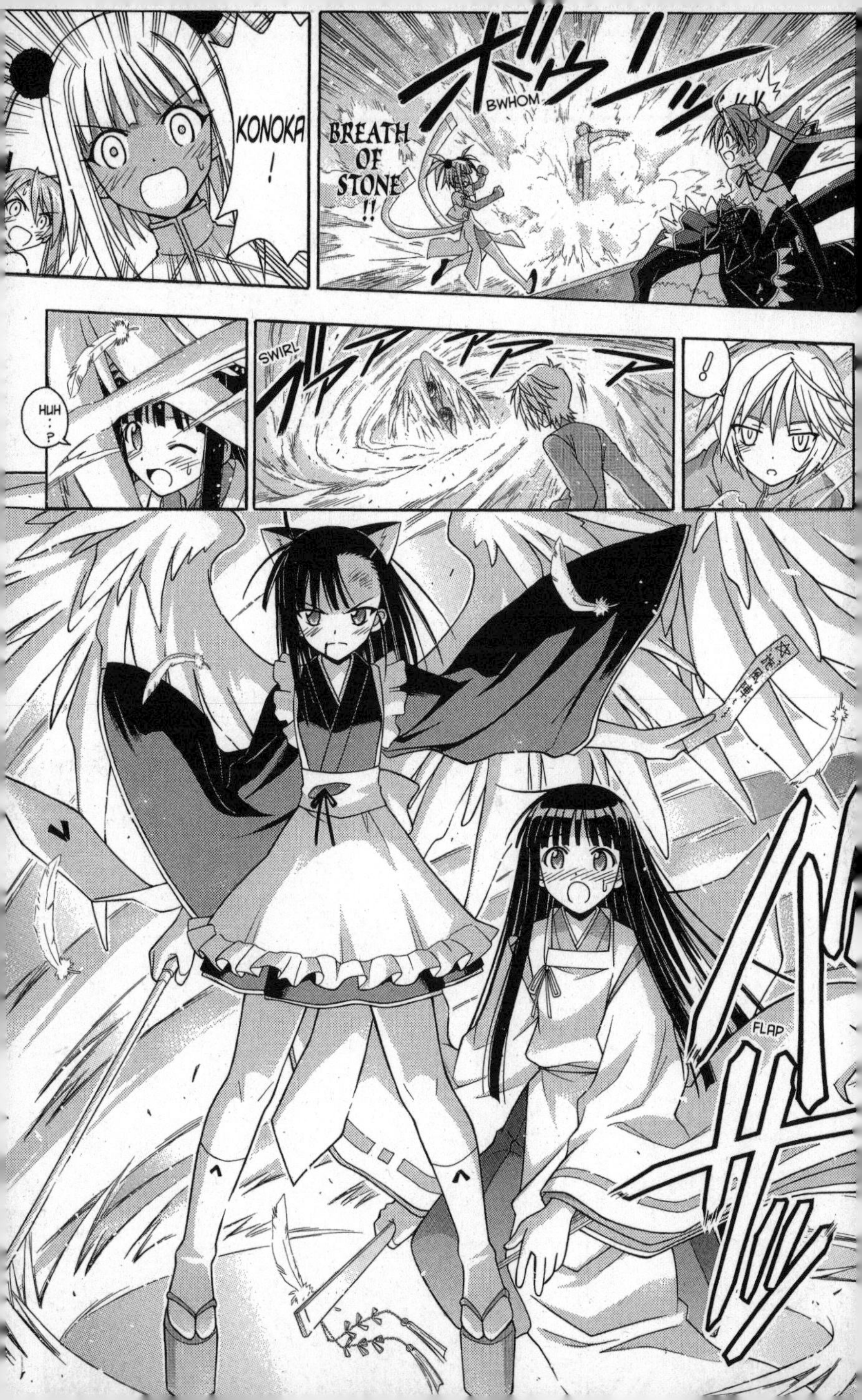
BWHOM
BREATH OF STONE!!
KONOKA!
!
SWIRL
HUH...?
FLAP

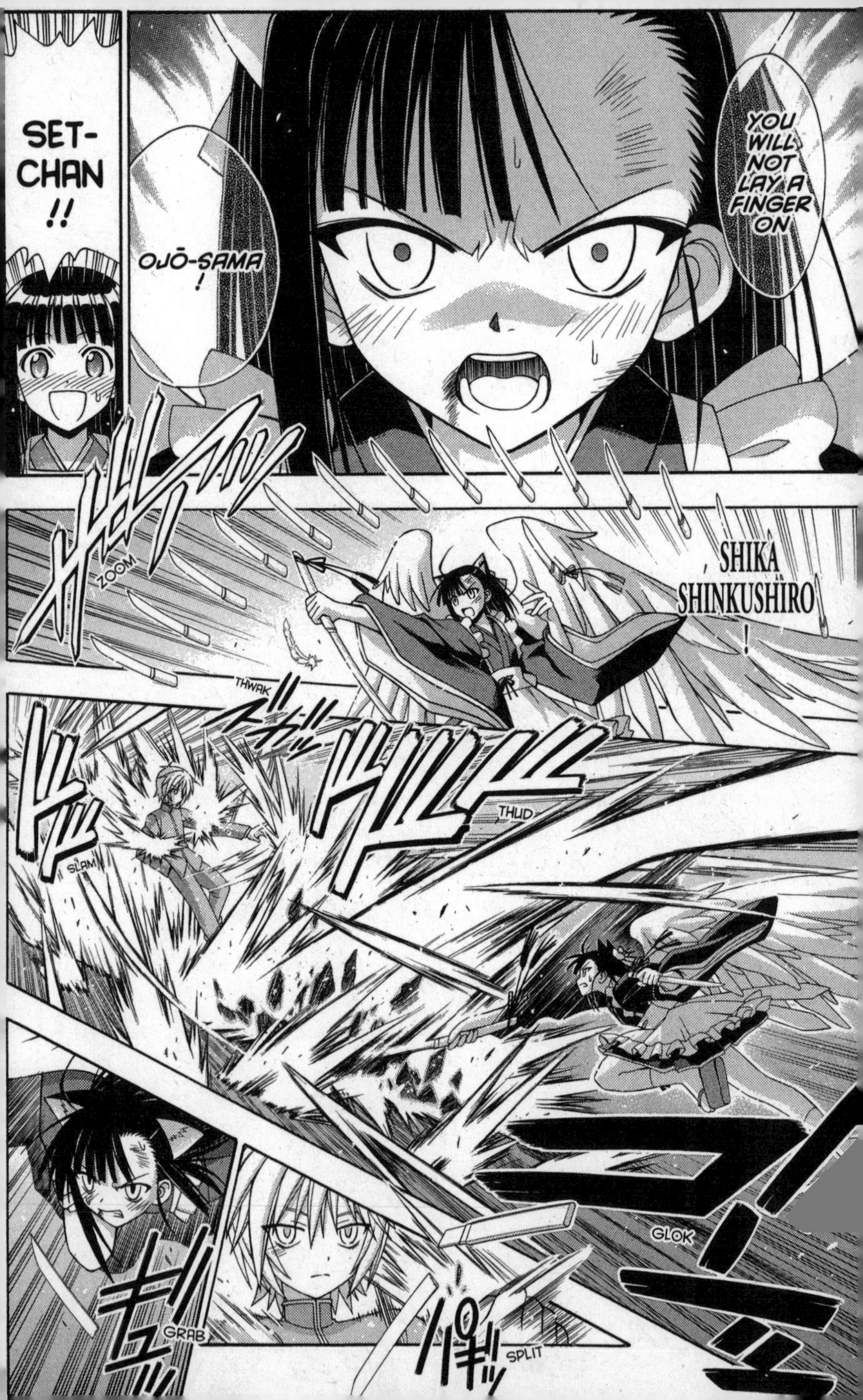

YOU WILL NOT LAY A FINGER ON
OJŌ-SAMA !
SET-CHAN !!
SHIKA SHINKUSHIRO !
ZOOM
THWAK
THUD
SLAM
GLOK
SPLIT
GRAB

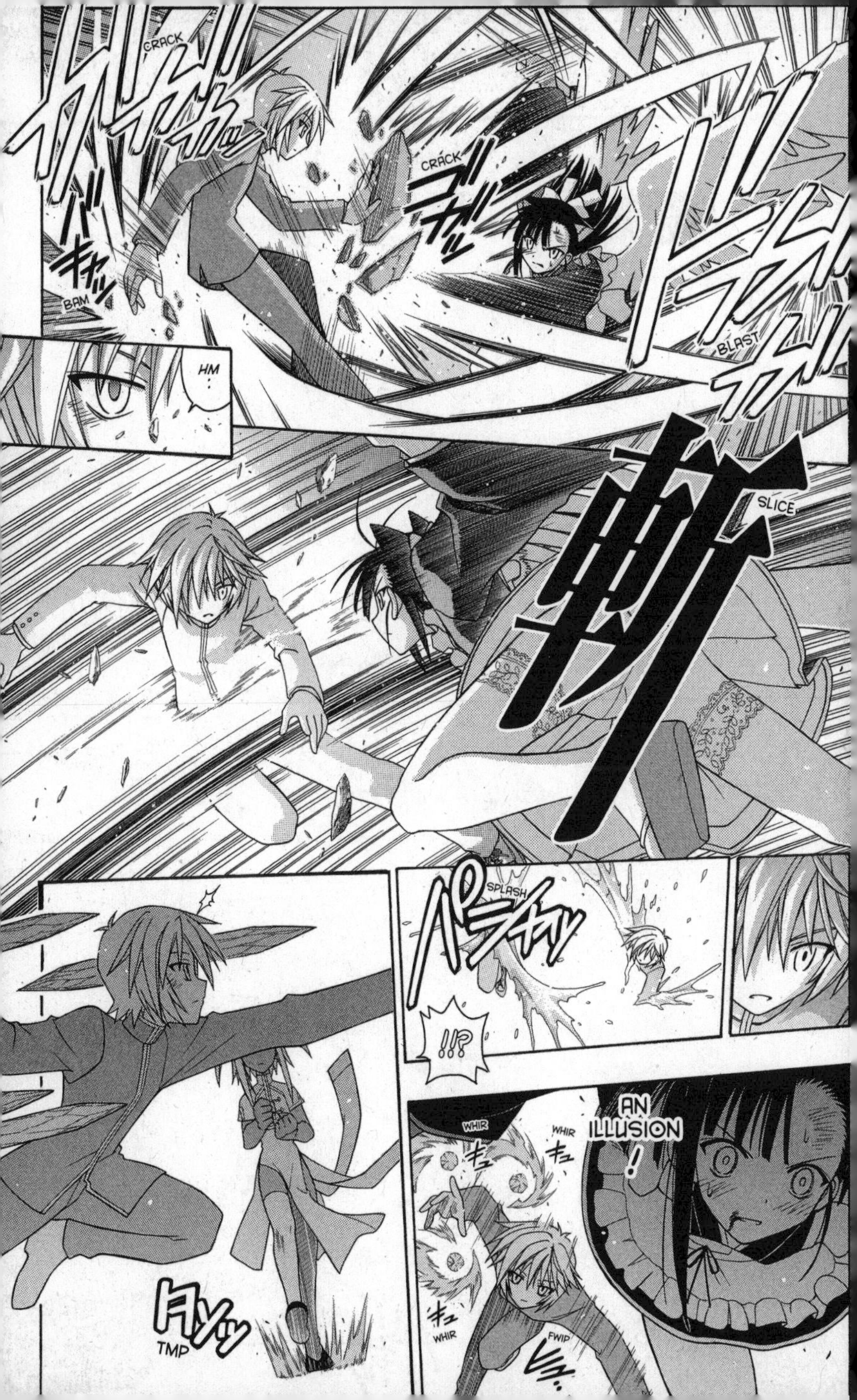
BLAST
CRACK
CRACK
BAM
HM
SLICE
SPLASH
!!?
AN ILLUSION!
WHIR
WHIR
WHIR
FWIP
TMP

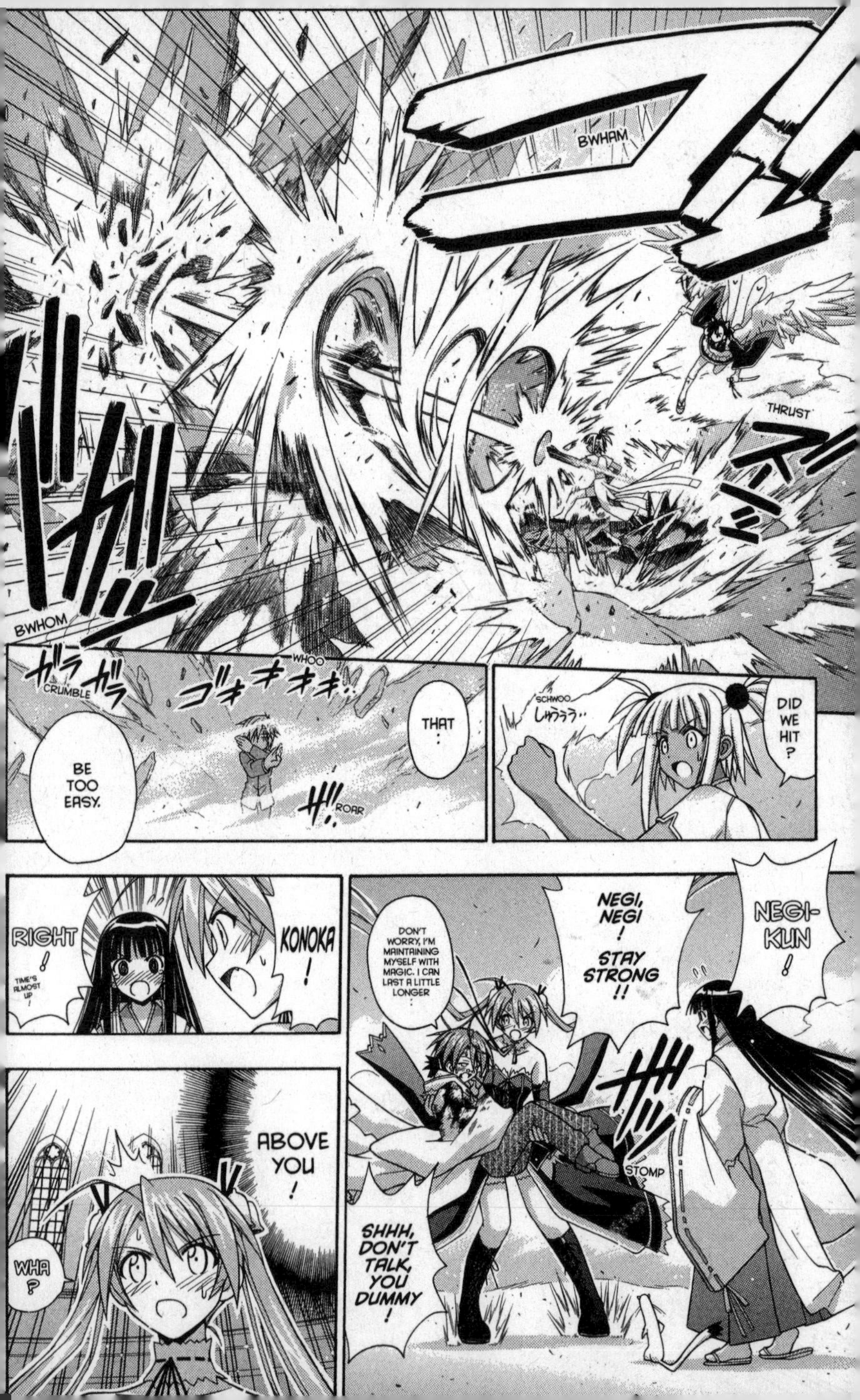
BWHAM
THRUST
BWHOM
SCHWOO
DID WE HIT?
WHOO
THAT...
CRUMBLE
BE TOO EASY.
ROAR
NEGI-KUN!
NEGI, NEGI! STAY STRONG!!
DON'T WORRY, I'M MAINTAINING MYSELF WITH MAGIC. I CAN LAST A LITTLE LONGER...
STOMP
SHHH, DON'T TALK, YOU DUMMY!
KONOKA!
RIGHT!
TIME'S ALMOST UP!
ABOVE YOU!
WHA?

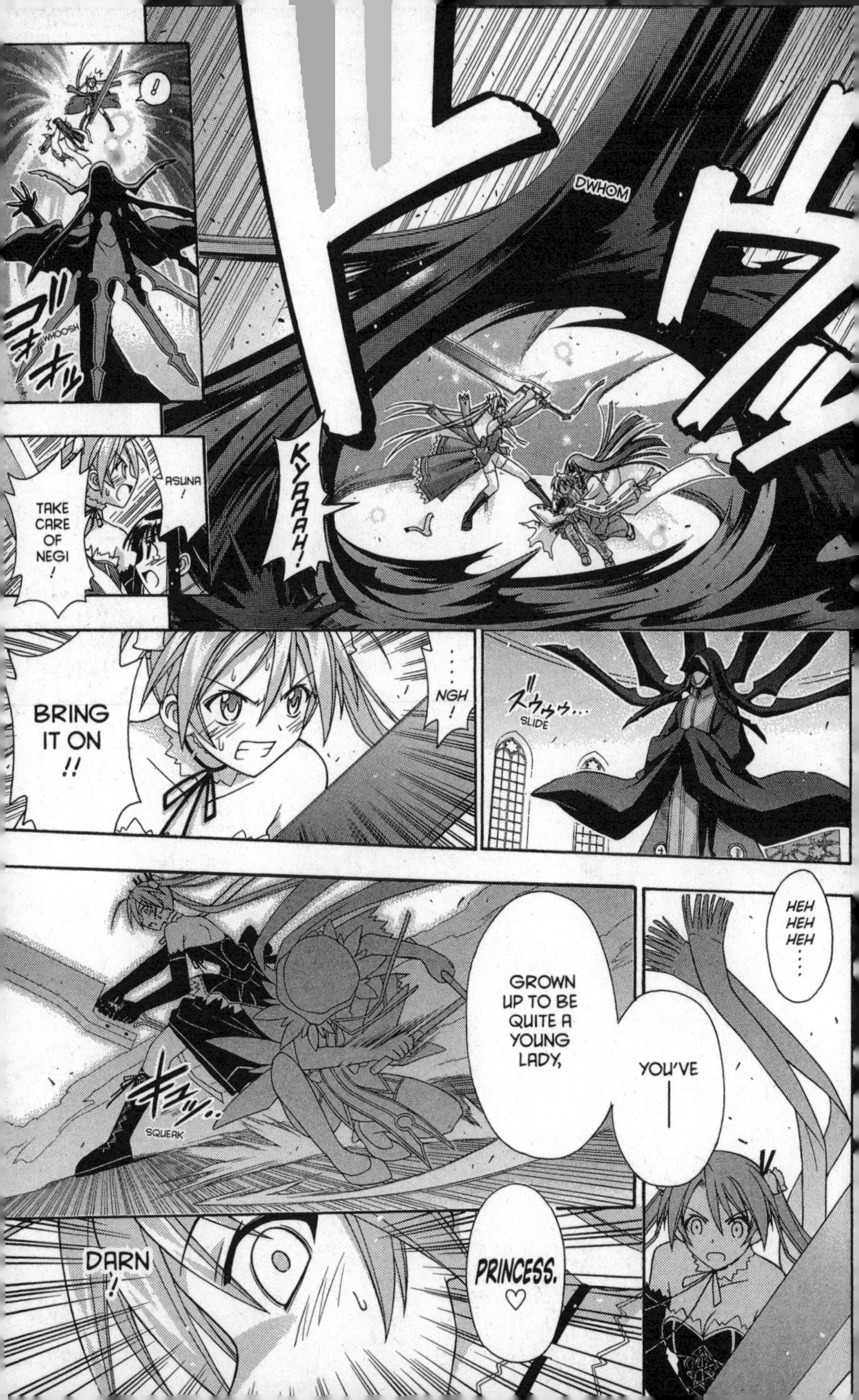
DWHOM
KYAAAH!
!
WHOOSH
ASUNA!
TAKE CARE OF NEGI!
SLIDE
...NGH!
BRING IT ON!!
HEH HEH HEH....
YOU'VE —
GROWN UP TO BE QUITE A YOUNG LADY,
PRINCESS. ♡
SQUEAK
DARN!

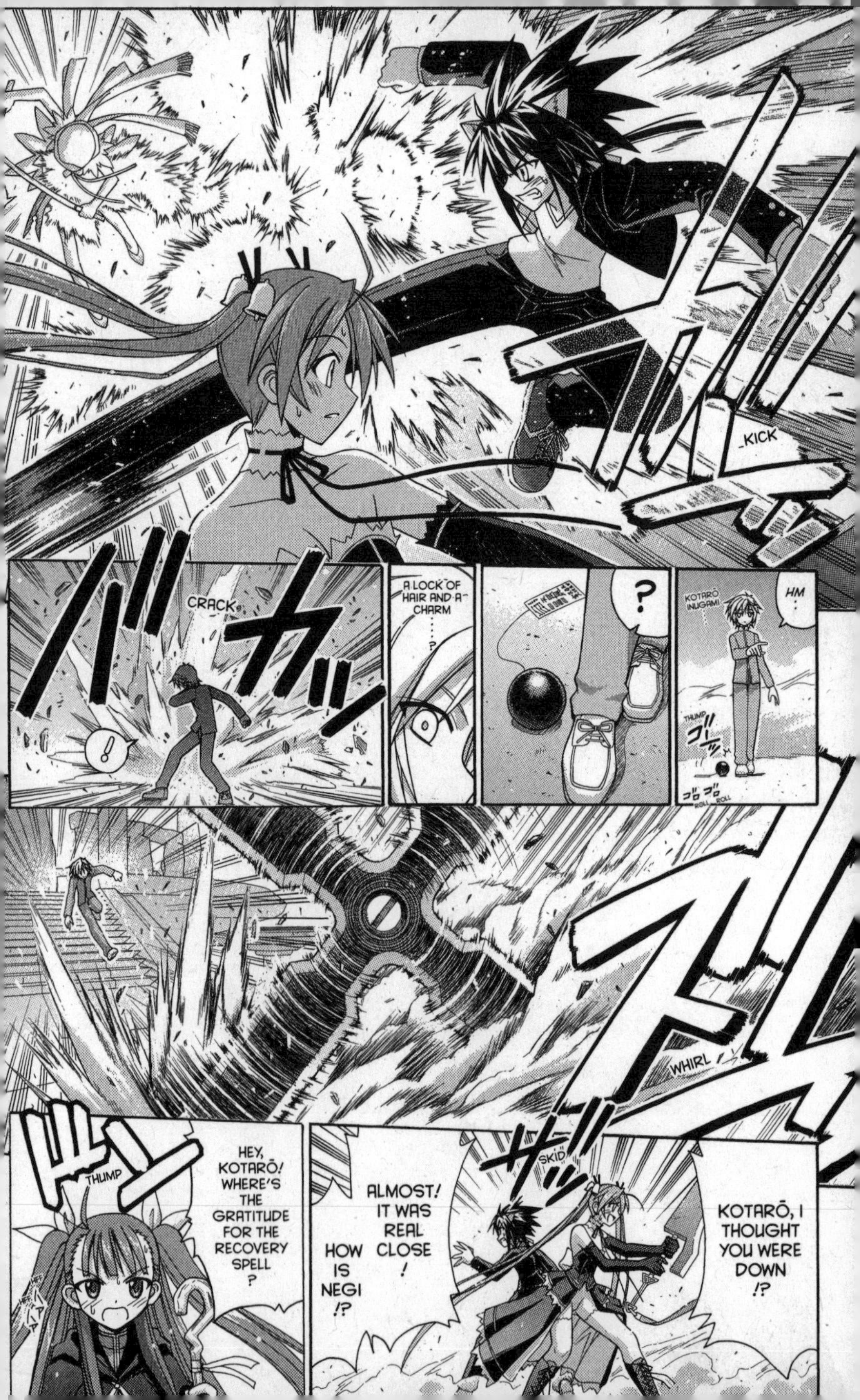
KICK
KOTARŌ INUGAMI ...
HM ...
THUMP
ROLL ROLL
?
A LOCK OF HAIR AND A CHARM ......?
CRACK
!
WHIRL
SKID
KOTARŌ, I THOUGHT YOU WERE DOWN !?
ALMOST! IT WAS REAL CLOSE !
HOW IS NEGI !?
THUMP
HEY, KOTARŌ! WHERE'S THE GRATITUDE FOR THE RECOVERY SPELL ?

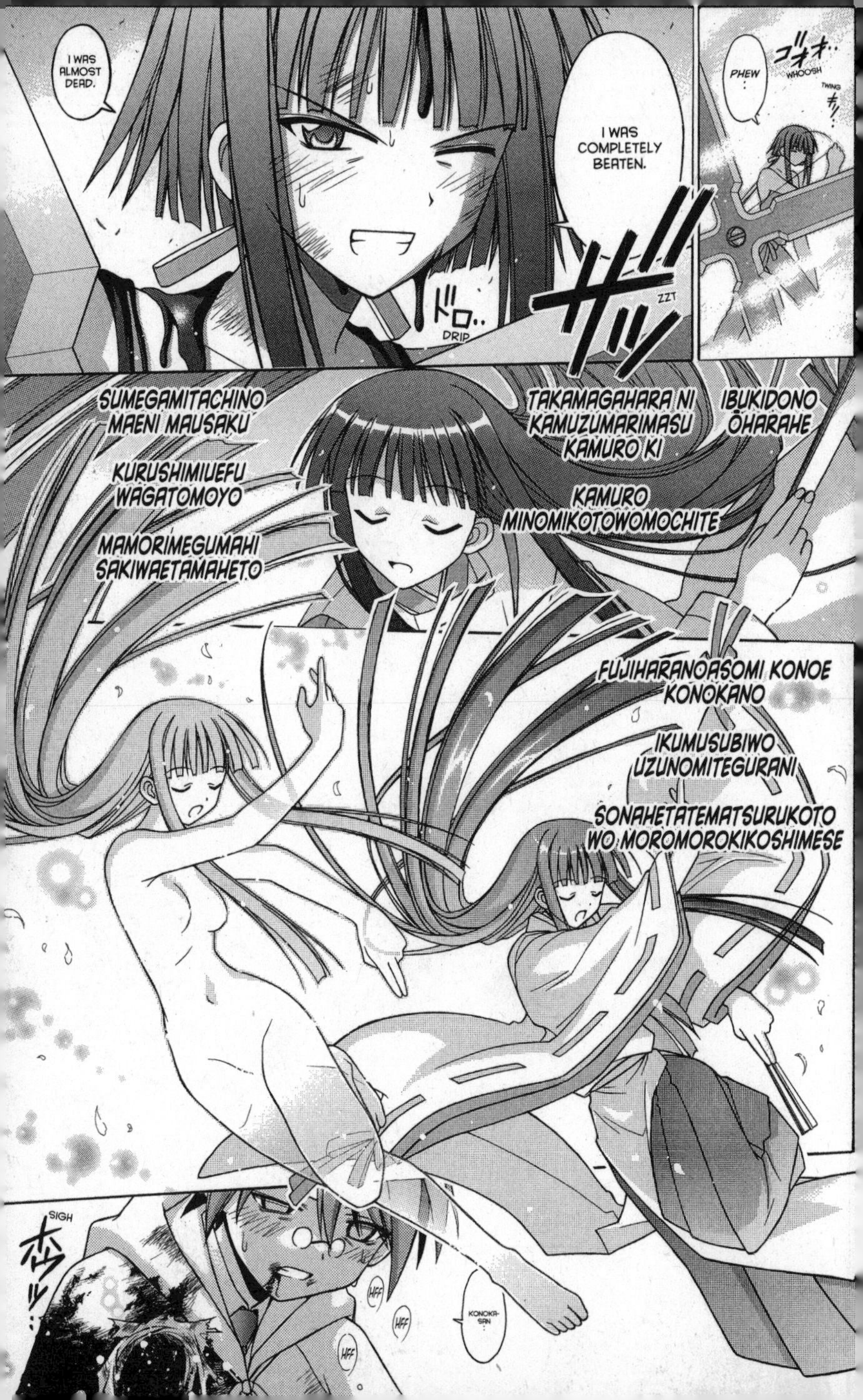
PHEW . . .
WHOOSH
TWING
ZZT
I WAS COMPLETELY BEATEN.
I WAS ALMOST DEAD.
DRIP
IBUKIDONO ŌHARAHE
TAKAMAGAHARA NI KAMUZUMARIMASU KAMURO KI
KAMURO MINOMIKOTOWOMOCHITE
SUMEGAMITACHINO MAENI MAUSAKU
KURUSHIMIUEFU WAGATOMOYO
MAMORIMEGUMAHI SAKIWAETAMAHETO
FUJIHARANOASOMI KONOE KONOKANO
IKUMUSUBIWO UZUNOMITEGURANI
SONAHETATEMATSURUKOTO WO MOROMOROKIKOSHIMESE
KONOKA-SAN . . .
HFF
HFF
HFF
SIGH

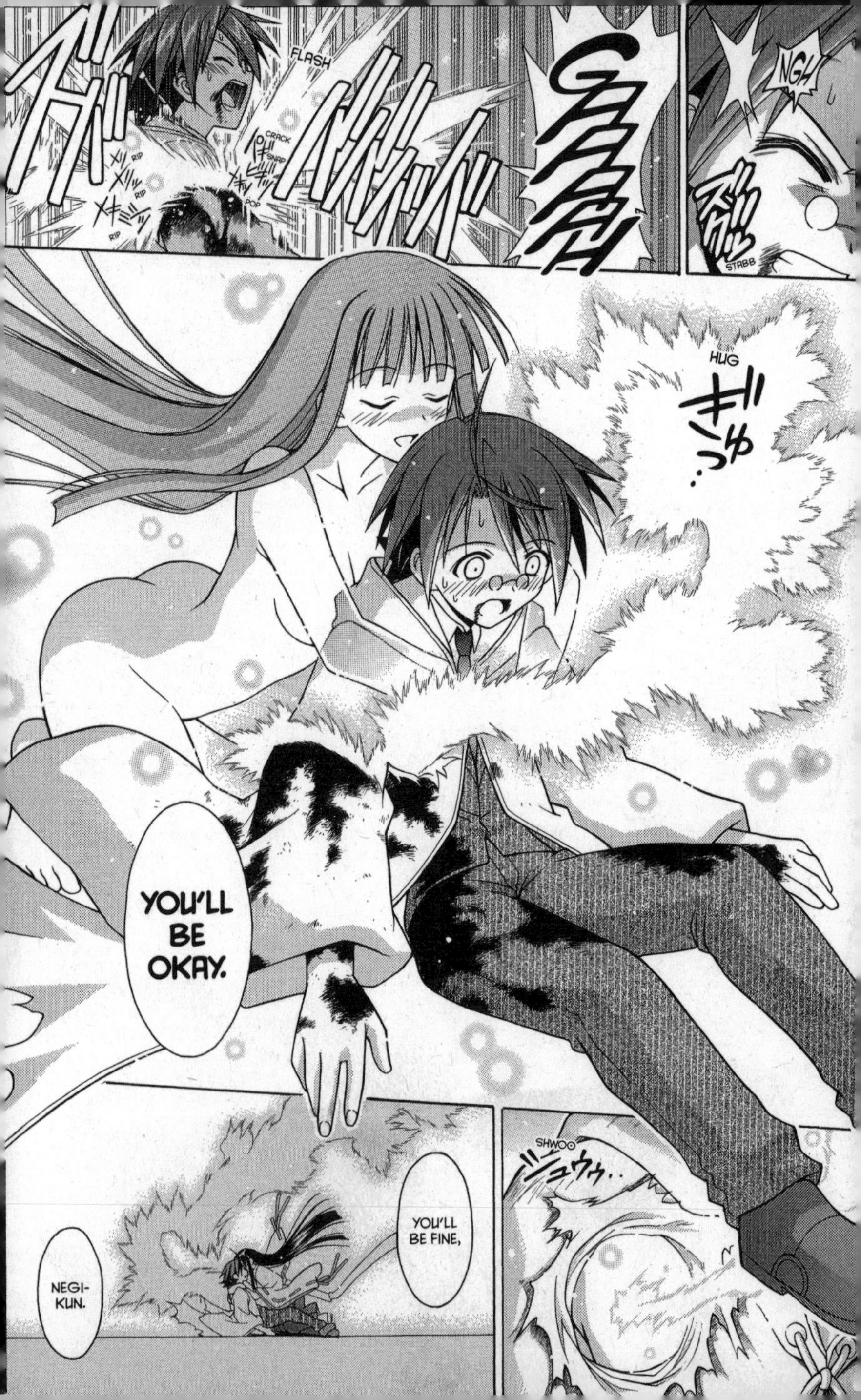
NGH
STABB
FLASH
CRACK
SNAP
POP
RIP
RIP
RIP
HUG
ぎゅっ…
YOU'LL BE OKAY.
SHWOO
YOU'LL BE FINE,
NEGI-KUN.

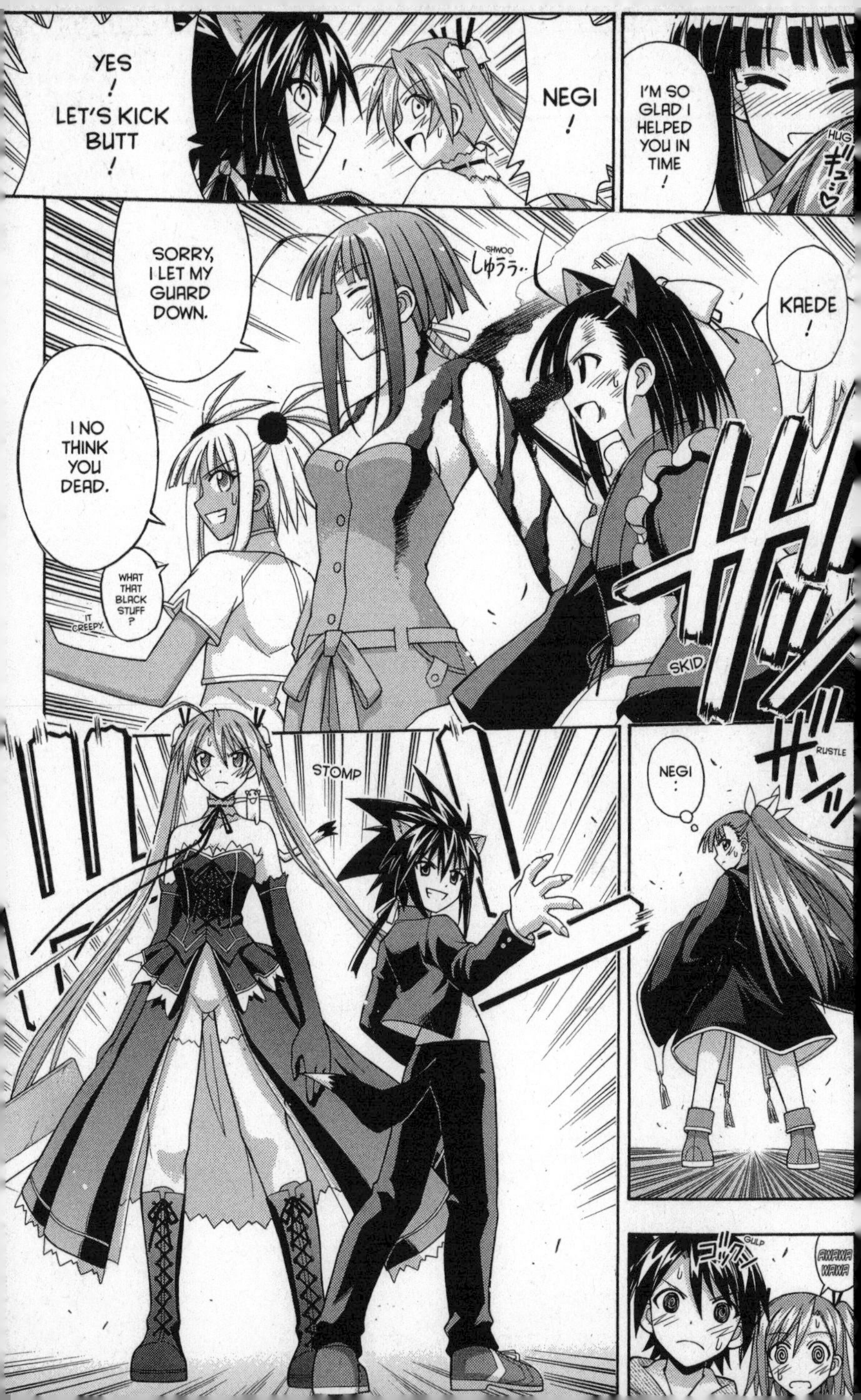
I'M SO GLAD I HELPED YOU IN TIME!
HUG
NEGI!
YES! LET'S KICK BUTT!
KAEDE!
SHWOO
SORRY, I LET MY GUARD DOWN.
I NO THINK YOU DEAD.
WHAT THAT BLACK STUFF?
IT CREEPY.
SKID
RUSTLE
NEGI...
GULP
AWAWA WAWA
STOMP

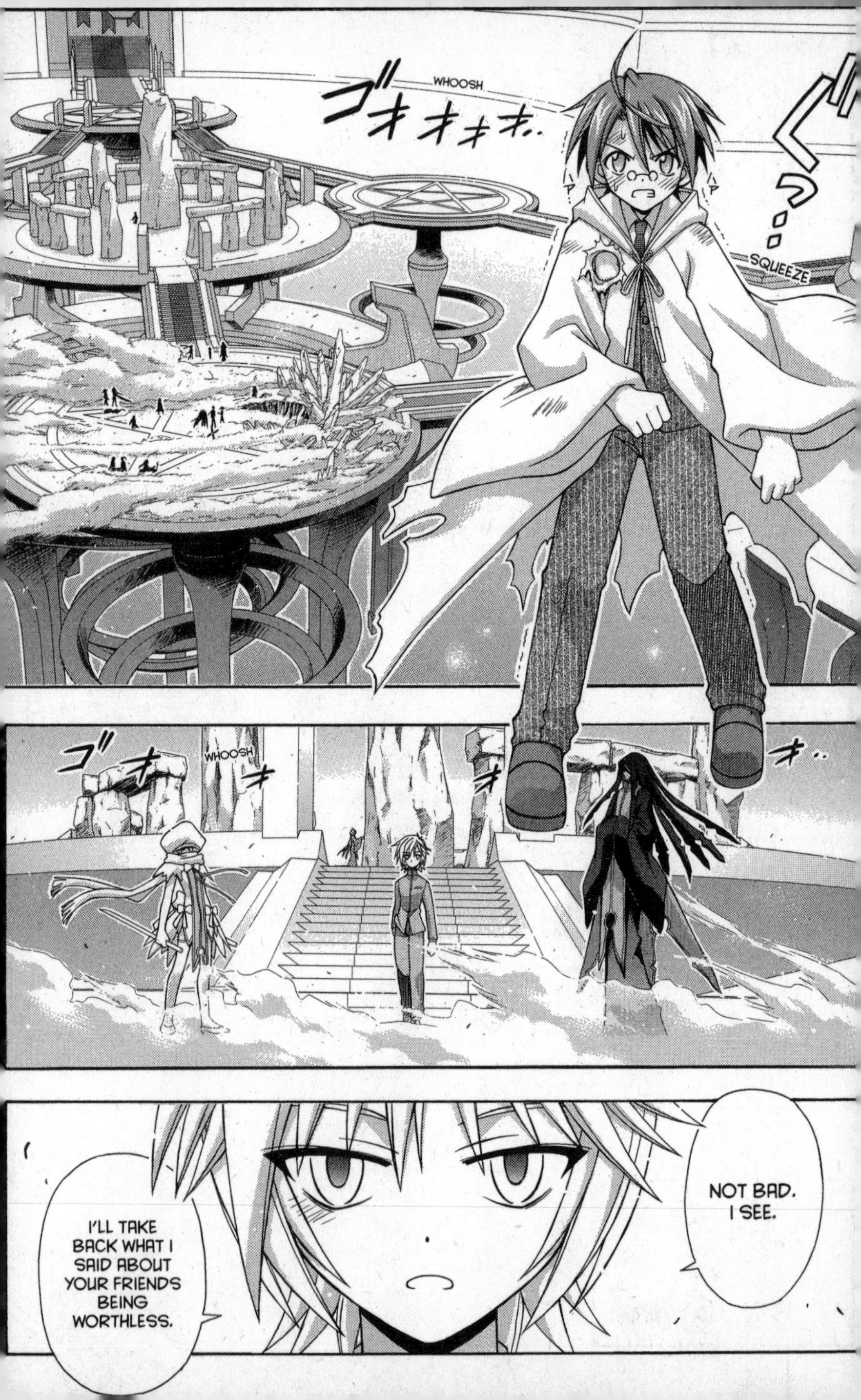

SQUEEZE
ゴオオォォォ..
WHOOSH
ォ..
ォ
ゴォ
WHOOSH
NOT BAD. I SEE.
I'LL TAKE BACK WHAT I SAID ABOUT YOUR FRIENDS BEING WORTHLESS.

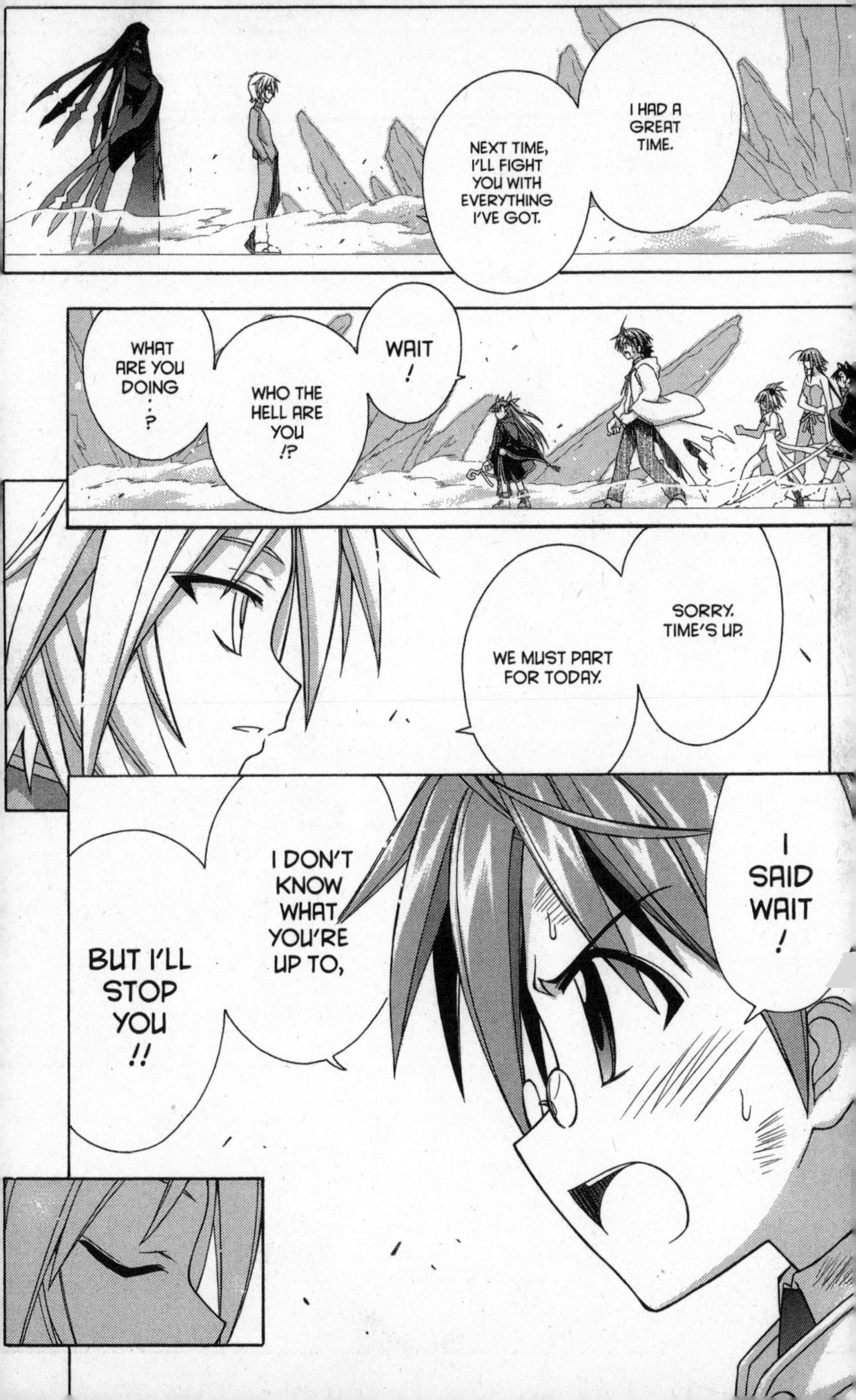
I HAD A GREAT TIME.
NEXT TIME, I'LL FIGHT YOU WITH EVERYTHING I'VE GOT.
WAIT!
WHO THE HELL ARE YOU!?
WHAT ARE YOU DOING...?
SORRY. TIME'S UP.
WE MUST PART FOR TODAY.
I SAID WAIT!
I DON'T KNOW WHAT YOU'RE UP TO,
BUT I'LL STOP YOU!!

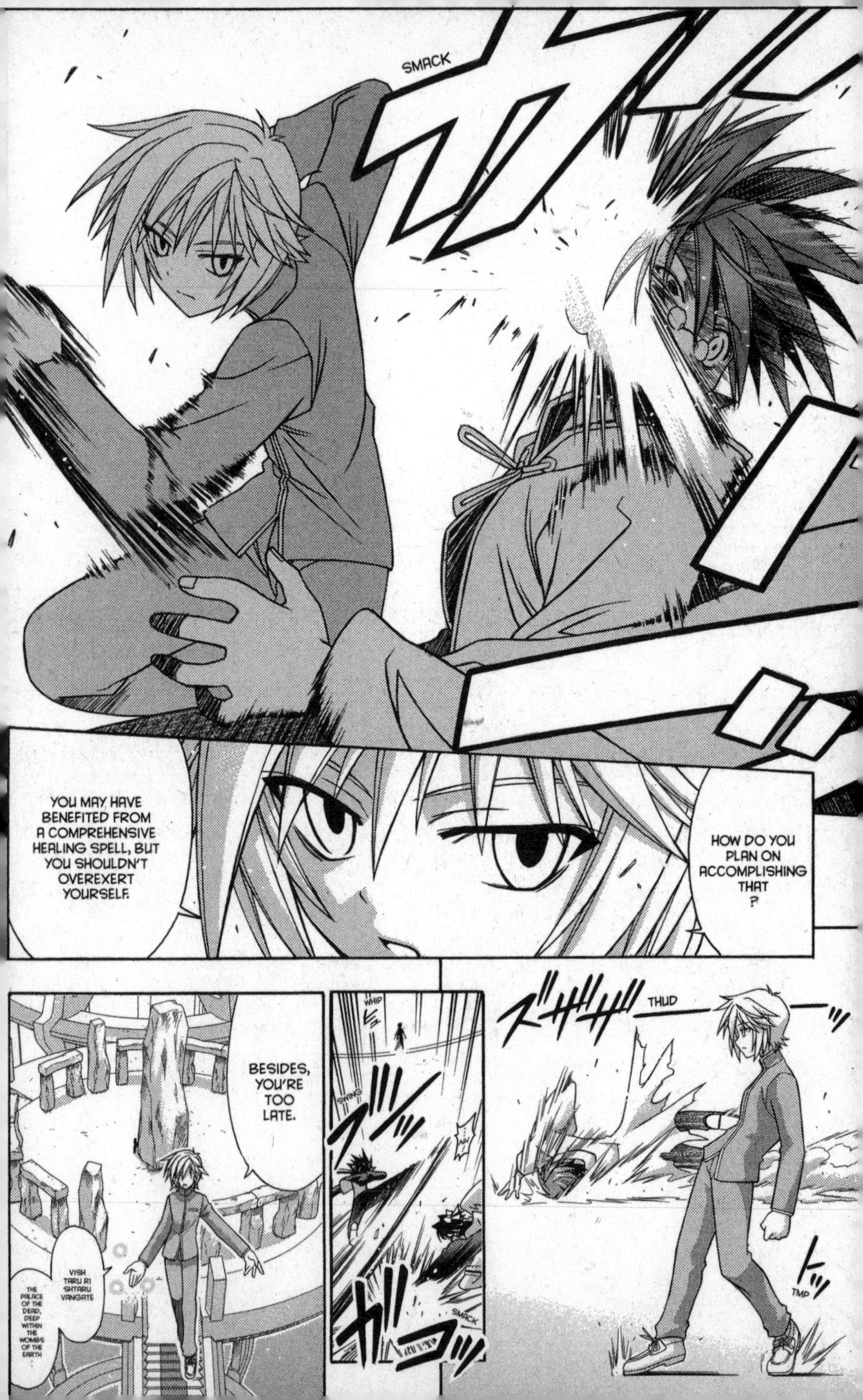
SMACK
HOW DO YOU PLAN ON ACCOMPLISHING THAT?
YOU MAY HAVE BENEFITED FROM A COMPREHENSIVE HEALING SPELL, BUT YOU SHOULDN'T OVEREXERT YOURSELF.
THUD
TMP
WHIP
SWING
SMACK
BESIDES, YOU'RE TOO LATE.
VISH TARU RI SHTARU VANGATE
THE PALACE OF THE DEAD, DEEP WITHIN THE WOMBS OF THE EARTH

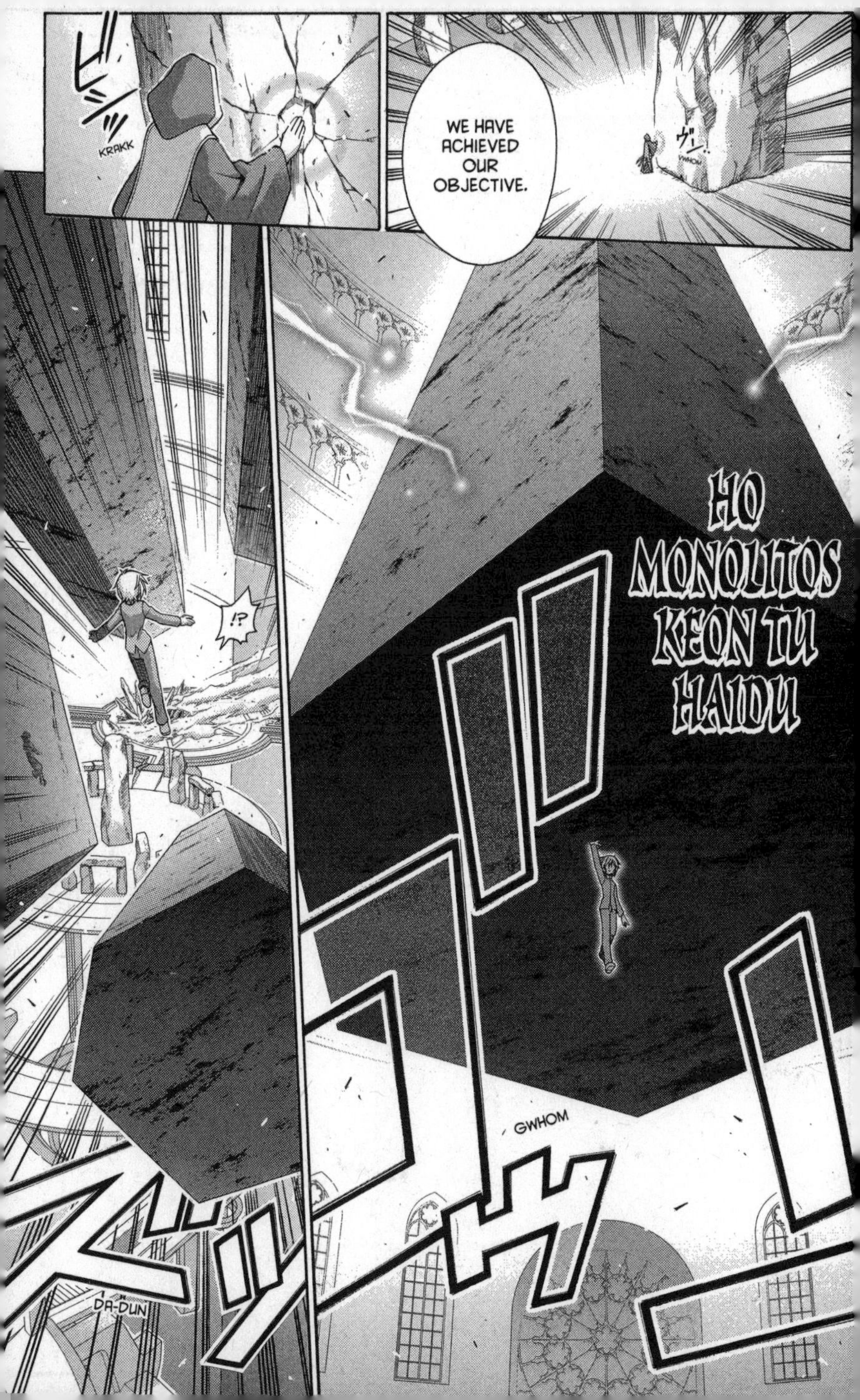
WE HAVE ACHIEVED OUR OBJECTIVE.
KRAKK
HO MONOLITOS KEON TU HAIDU
GWHOM
!?
DA-DUN

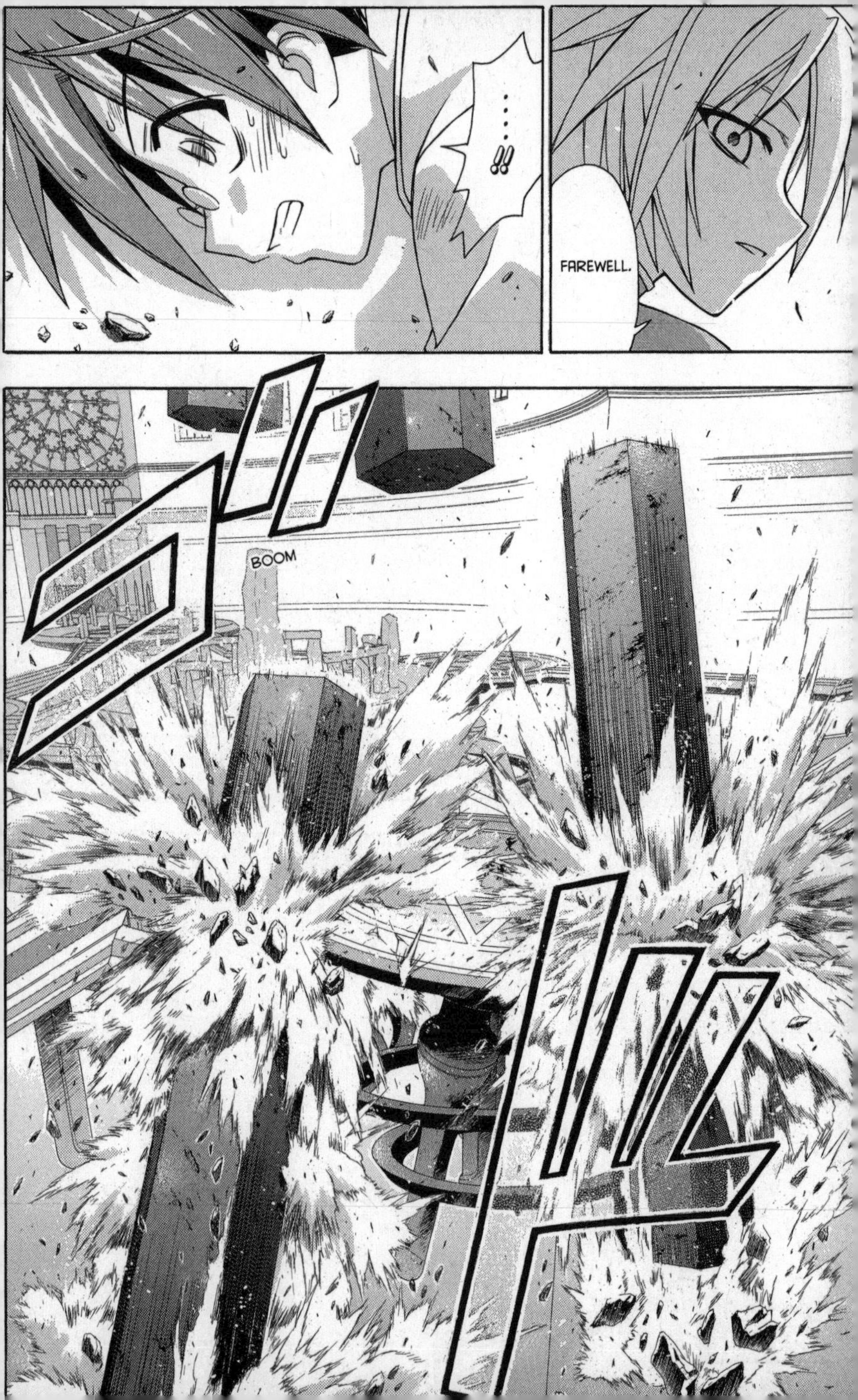
FAREWELL.
......!!
BOOM

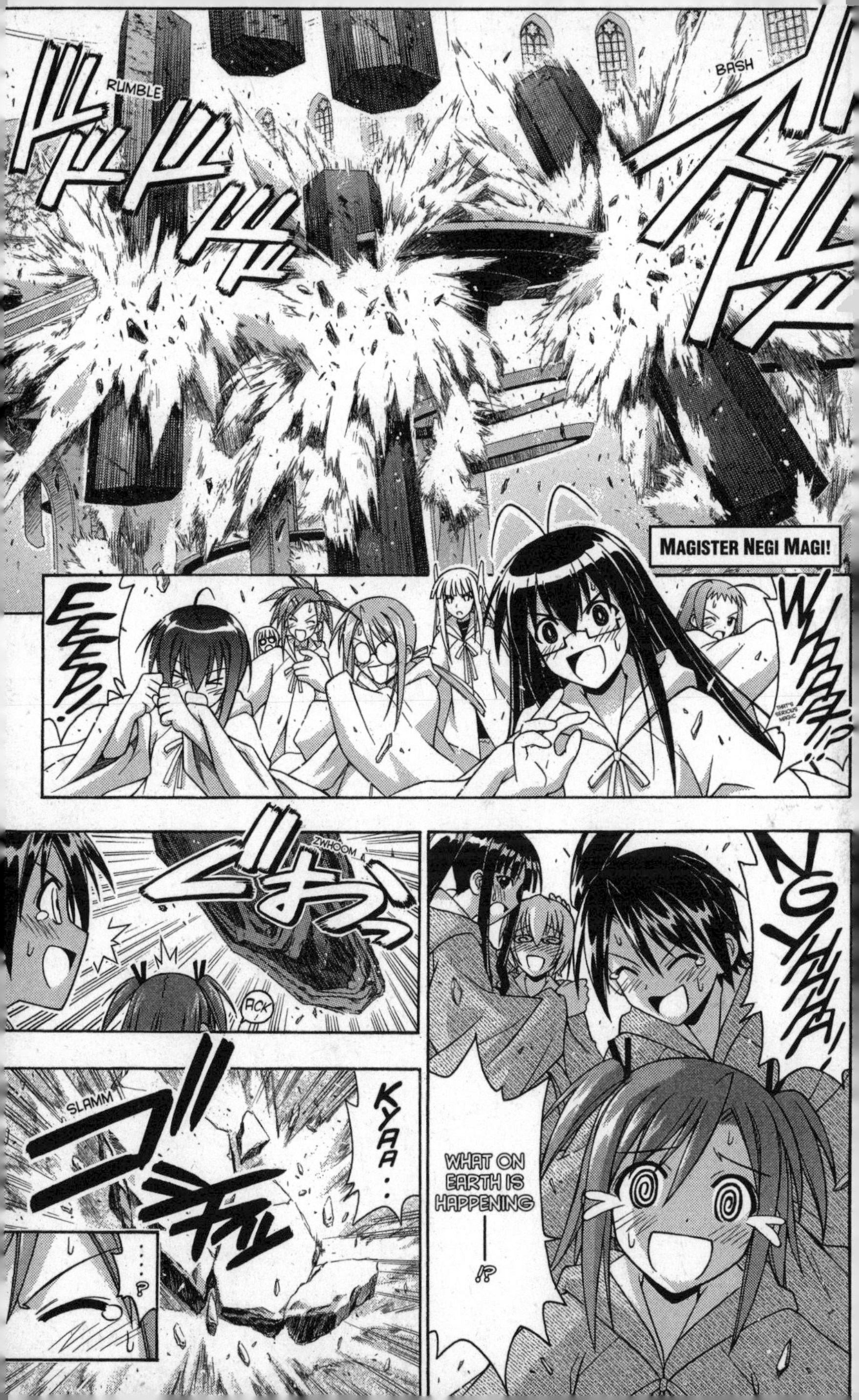
BASH
RUMBLE
Magister Negi Magi!
WHOOOA!?
THAT'S SERIOUS MAGIC!
EEEP!!
WHAT ON EARTH IS HAPPENING —!?
ZWHOOM
ACK
SLAMM
KYAA..
....?

NEGIMA!

MAGISTER NEGI MAGI

189TH PERIOD: DESTRUCTION! NEGI PARTY!!

I'M SORRY I GOT YOU INVOLVED IN THIS, MAKIE-SAN!

NEGI-KUN!!

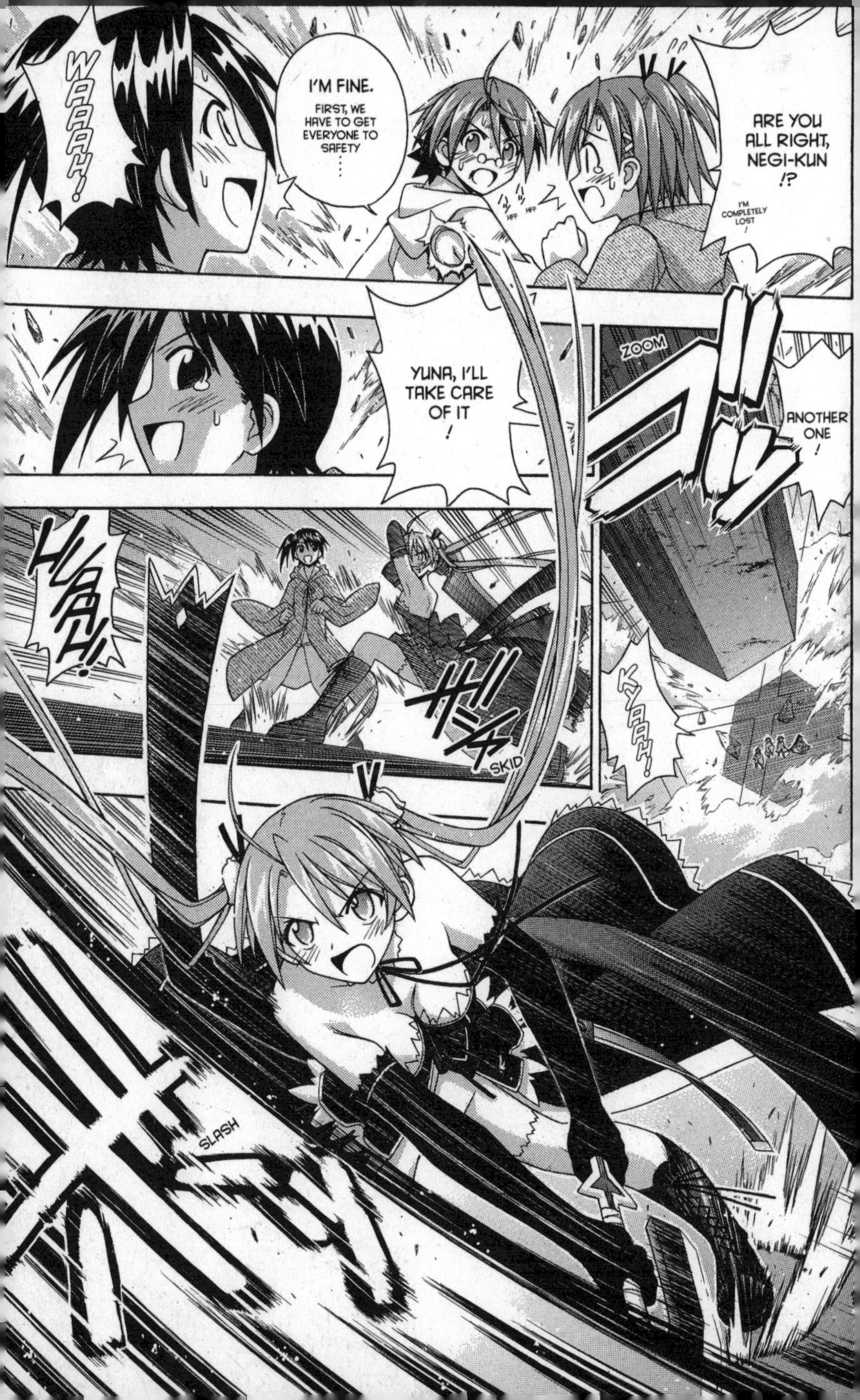
ARE YOU ALL RIGHT, NEGI-KUN!?
I'M COMPLETELY LOST!
HFF HFF
I'M FINE.
FIRST, WE HAVE TO GET EVERYONE TO SAFETY...
WAAAAH!
ZOOM
ANOTHER ONE!
YUNA, I'LL TAKE CARE OF IT!
KYAAAH!
SKID
HUAAAH!
SLASH

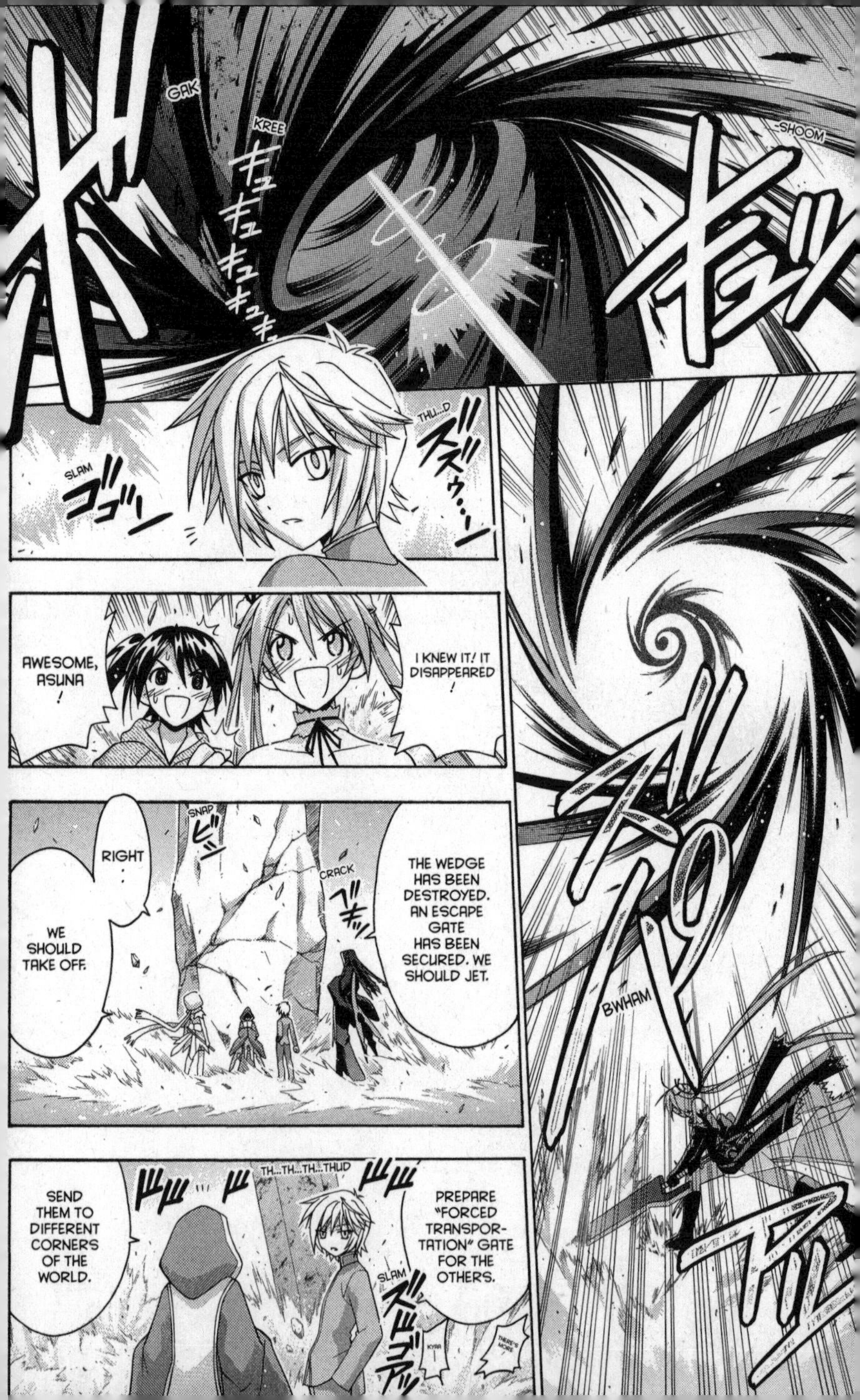
-SHOOM
GAK
KREE
BWHAM
THU...D
SLAM
I KNEW IT! IT DISAPPEARED!
AWESOME, ASUNA!
THE WEDGE HAS BEEN DESTROYED. AN ESCAPE GATE HAS BEEN SECURED. WE SHOULD JET.
CRACK
SNAP
RIGHT...
WE SHOULD TAKE OFF.
PREPARE "FORCED TRANSPORTATION" GATE FOR THE OTHERS.
TH...TH...TH...THUD
SEND THEM TO DIFFERENT CORNERS OF THE WORLD.
THERE'S MORE!
KYAA!
SLAM

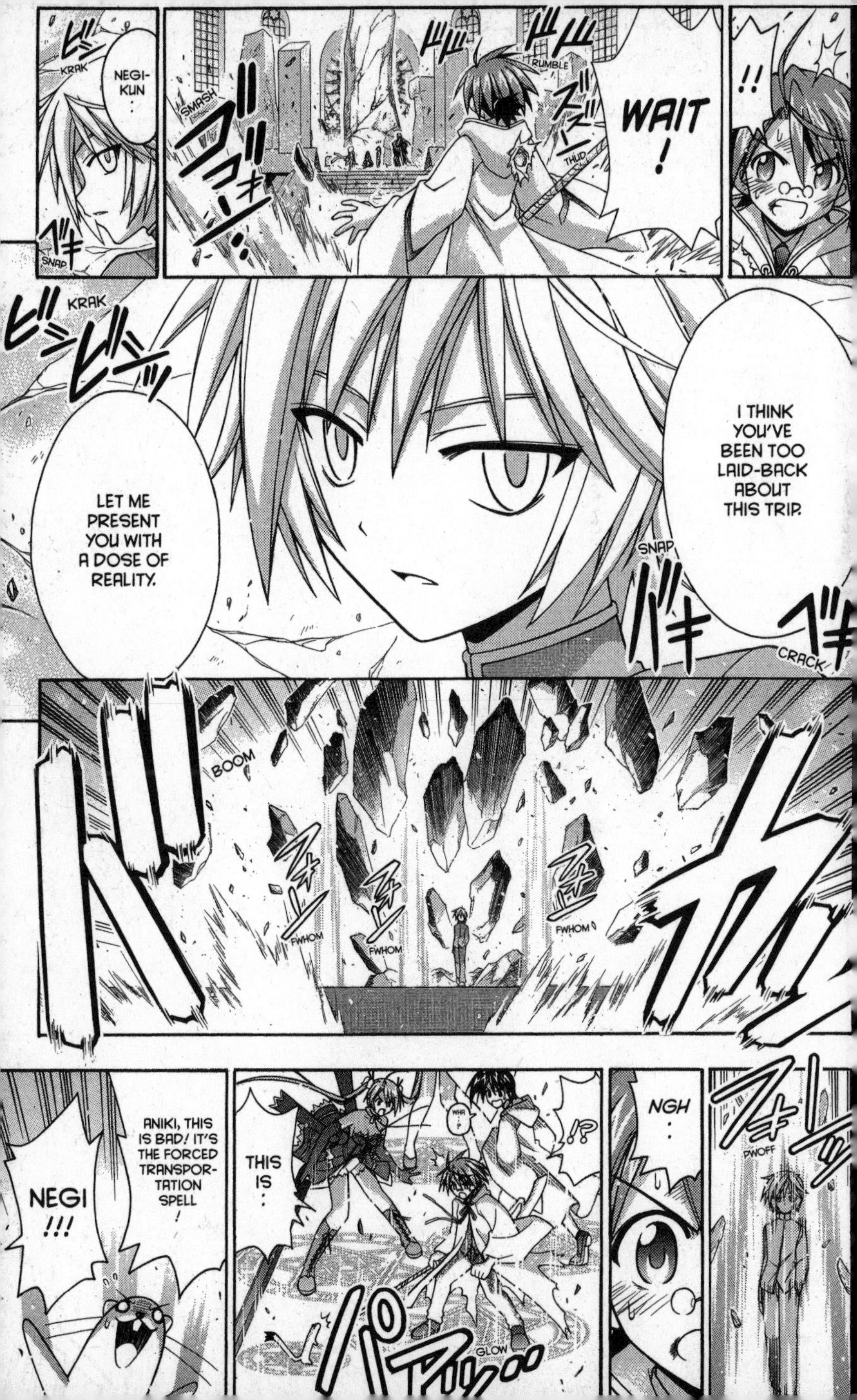
!!
RUMBLE
WAIT!
THUD
SMASH
KRAK
NEGI-KUN...
SNAP
I THINK YOU'VE BEEN TOO LAID-BACK ABOUT THIS TRIP.
SNAP
CRACK
KRAK
LET ME PRESENT YOU WITH A DOSE OF REALITY.
FWHOM
FWHOM
FWHOM
BOOM
PWOFF
NGH...
WHA...?
!?
THIS IS...
GLOW
ANIKI, THIS IS BAD! IT'S THE FORCED TRANSPORTATION SPELL!
NEGI!!!

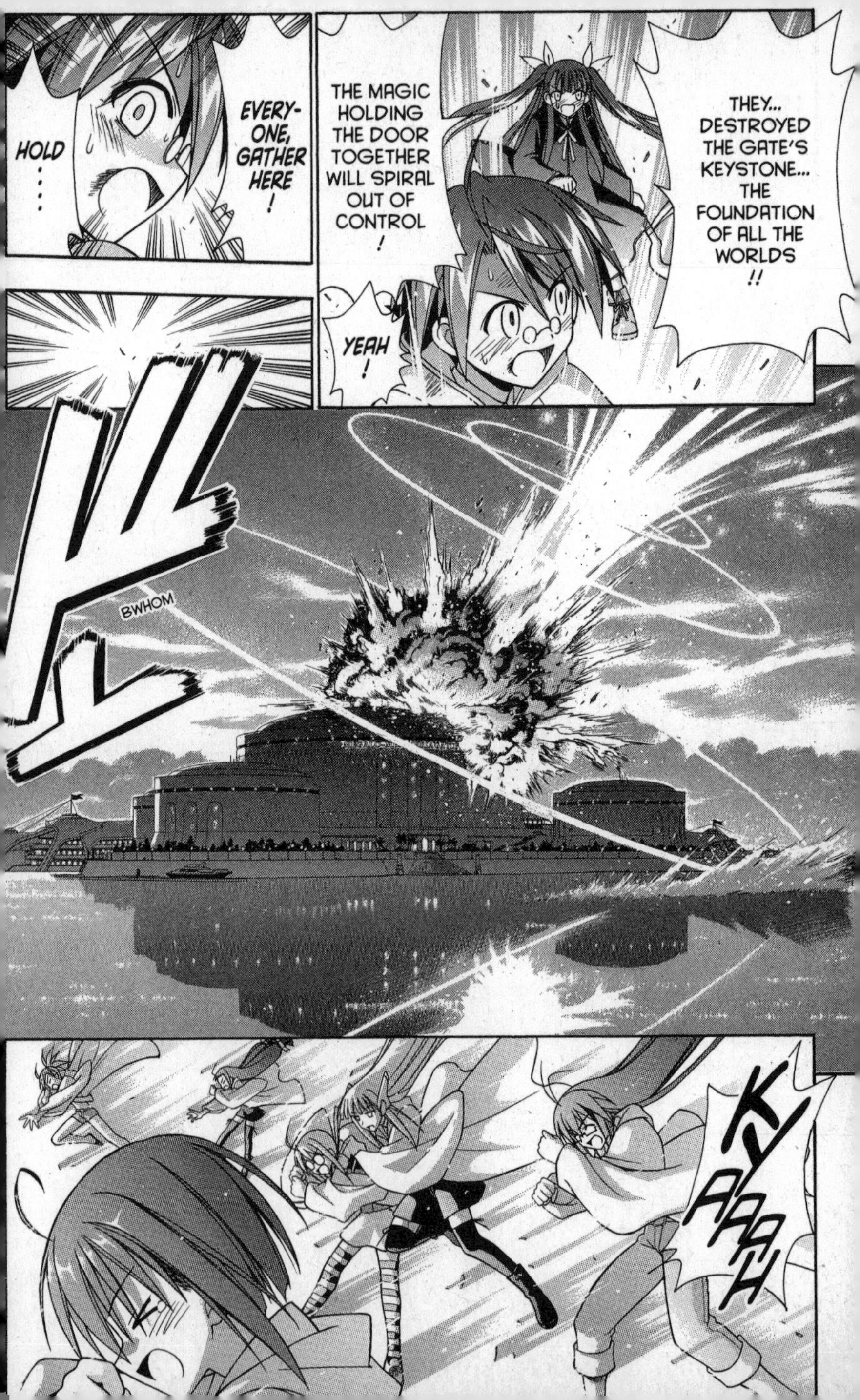
THEY... DESTROYED THE GATE'S KEYSTONE... THE FOUNDATION OF ALL THE WORLDS!!
THE MAGIC HOLDING THE DOOR TOGETHER WILL SPIRAL OUT OF CONTROL!
YEAH!
EVERY-ONE, GATHER HERE!
HOLD...
BWHOM
KYAAAAH

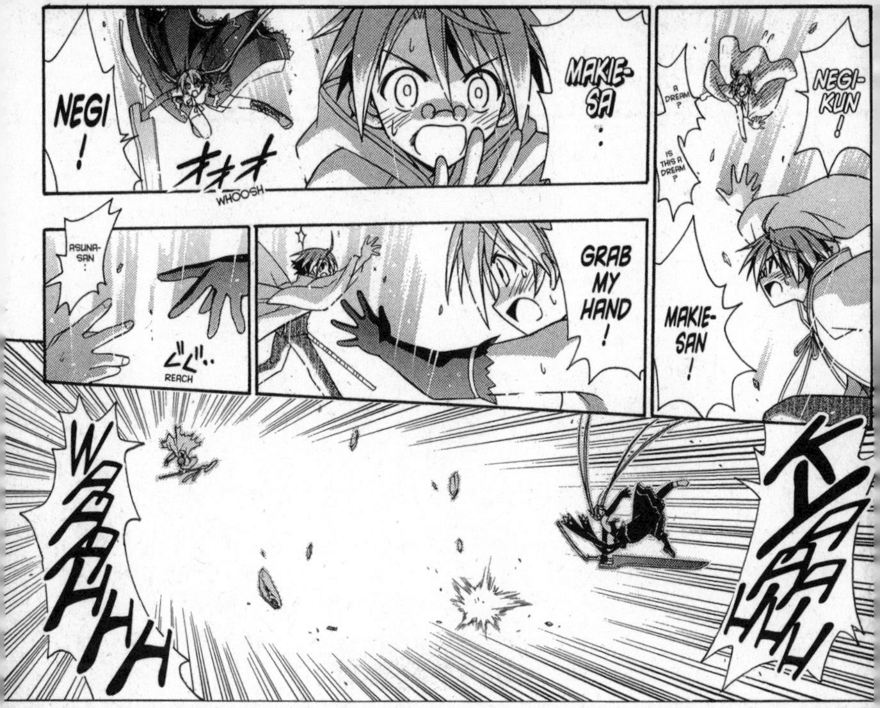
NEGI-KUN!
A DREAM?
IS THIS A DREAM?
MAKIE-SAN!
MAKIE-SA...
NEGI!
WHOOSH
GRAB MY HAND!
ASUNA-SAN...
REACH

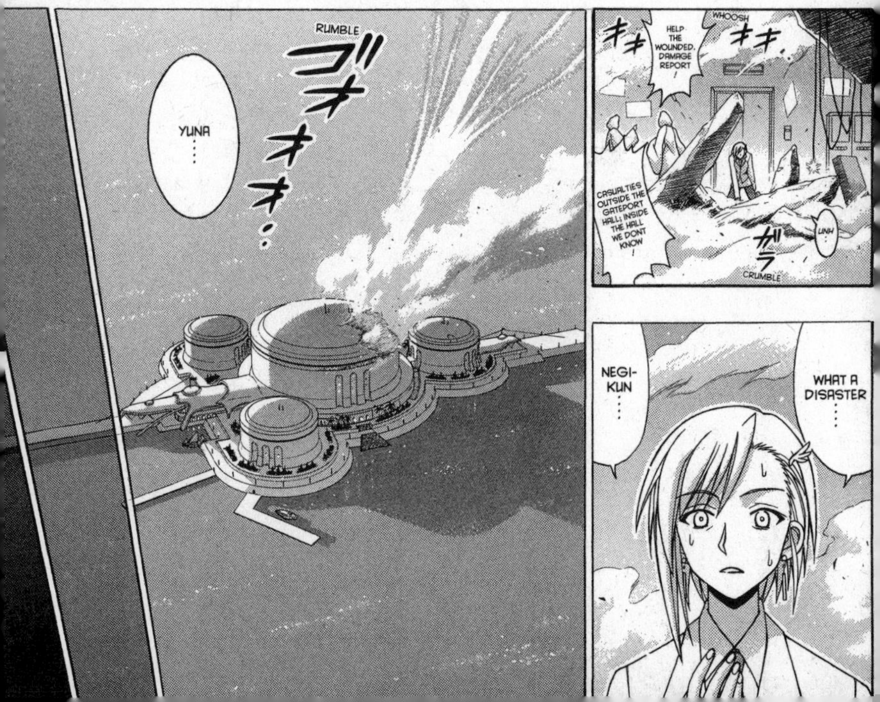
WHOOSH
HELP THE WOUNDED. DAMAGE REPORT!
CASUALTIES OUTSIDE THE GATEPORT HALL; INSIDE THE HALL WE DONT KNOW!
UNH
CRUMBLE
WHAT A DISASTER...
NEGI-KUN...
RUMBLE
YUNA...

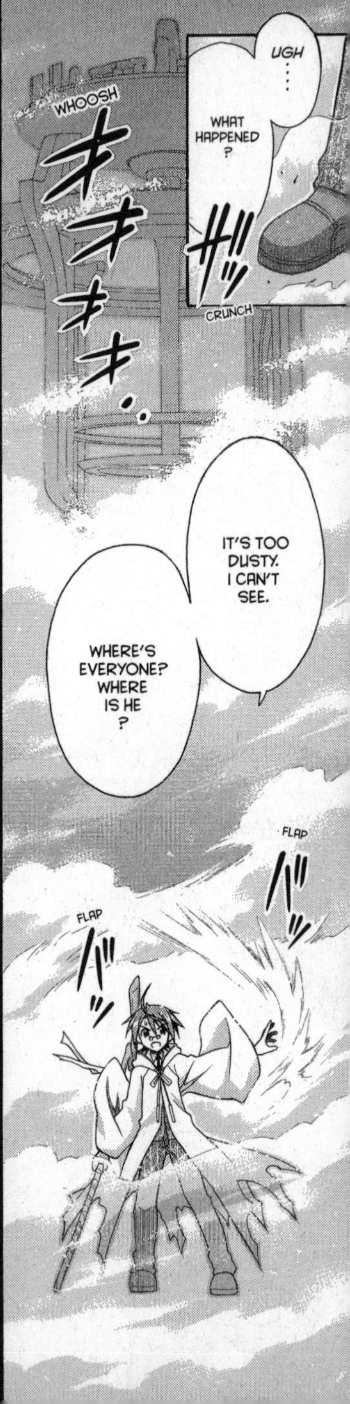
UGH...
WHAT HAPPENED?
CRUNCH
WHOOSH
IT'S TOO DUSTY. I CAN'T SEE.
WHERE'S EVERYONE? WHERE IS HE?
FLAP
FLAP

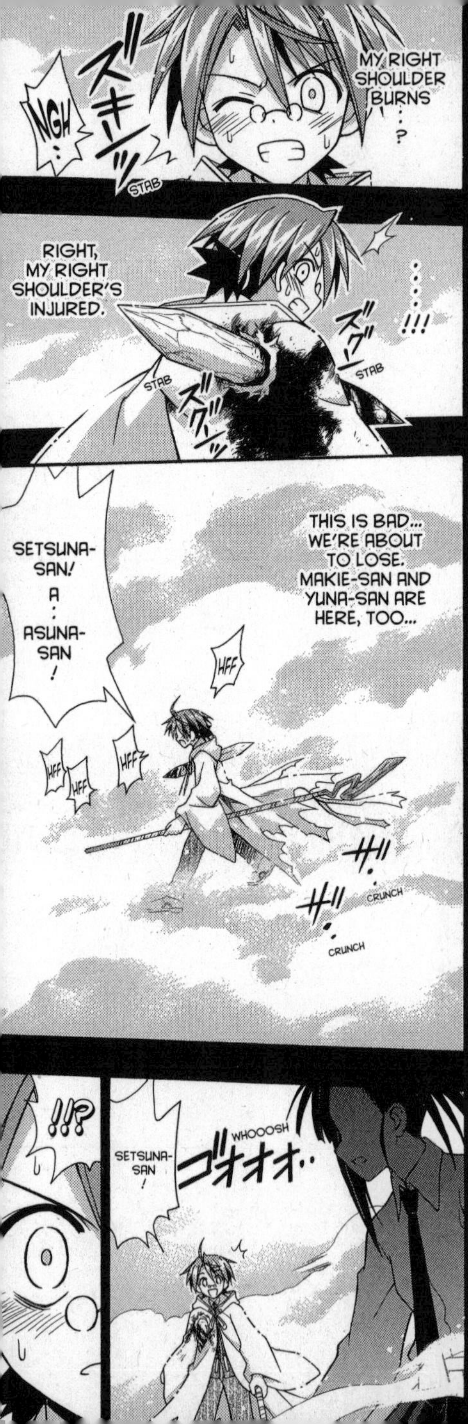
MY RIGHT SHOULDER BURNS...?
NGH...
STAB
RIGHT, MY RIGHT SHOULDER'S INJURED.
.....!!!
STAB
STAB
THIS IS BAD... WE'RE ABOUT TO LOSE. MAKIE-SAN AND YUNA-SAN ARE HERE, TOO...
SETSUNA-SAN! A... ASUNA-SAN!
HFF
HFF
HFF
HFF
CRUNCH
CRUNCH
SETSUNA-SAN!
WHOOOSH
!!?

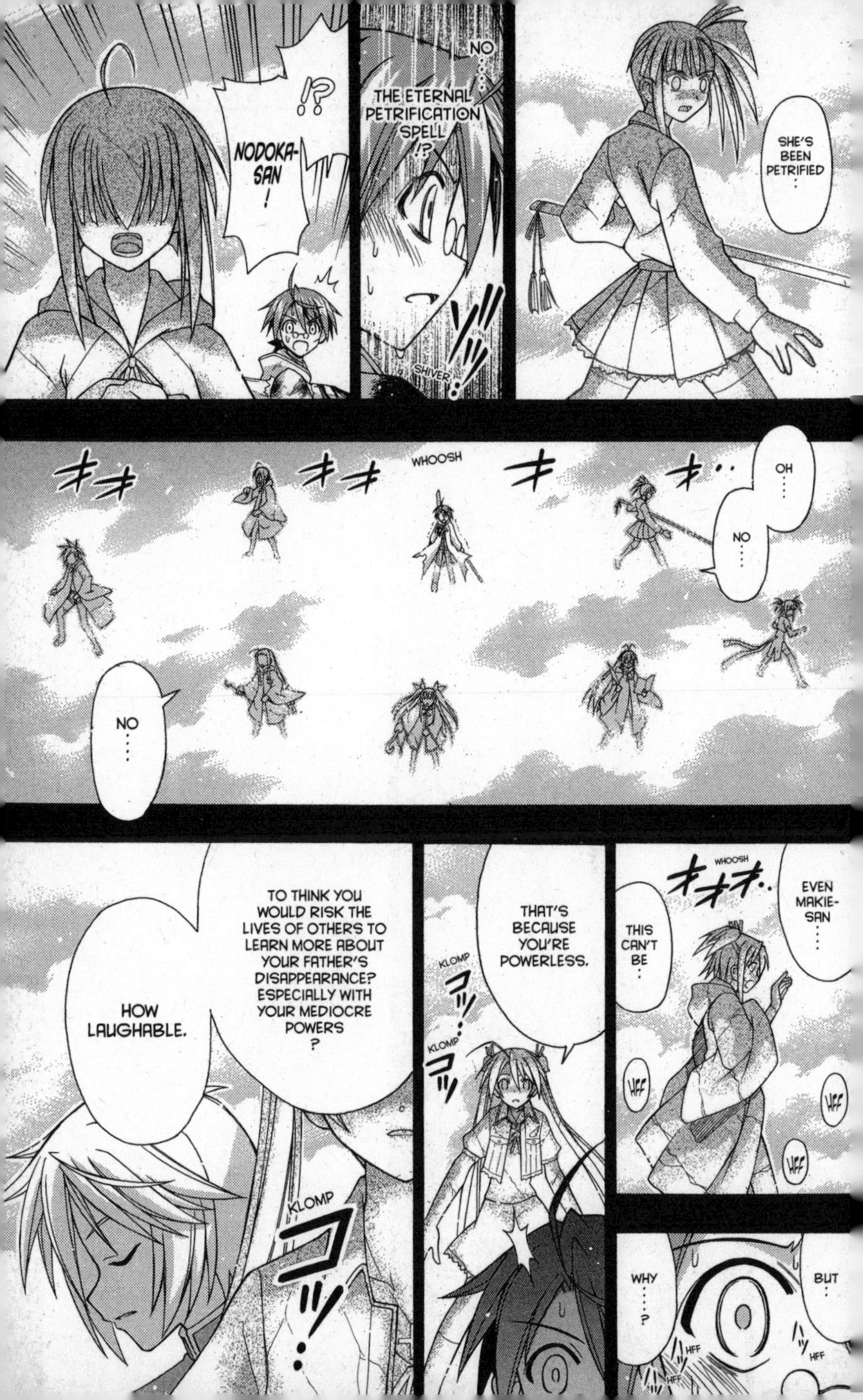

SHE'S BEEN PETRIFIED...
NO...
THE ETERNAL PETRIFICATION SPELL !?
SHIVER
!?
NODOKA-SAN!
OH... NO...
WHOOSH
NO...
EVEN MAKIE-SAN...
WHOOSH
THIS CAN'T BE...
HFF
HFF
HFF
BUT...
WHY...?
HFF
HFF
HFF
THAT'S BECAUSE YOU'RE POWERLESS.
KLOMP
KLOMP
TO THINK YOU WOULD RISK THE LIVES OF OTHERS TO LEARN MORE ABOUT YOUR FATHER'S DISAPPEARANCE? ESPECIALLY WITH YOUR MEDIOCRE POWERS?
HOW LAUGHABLE.
KLOMP

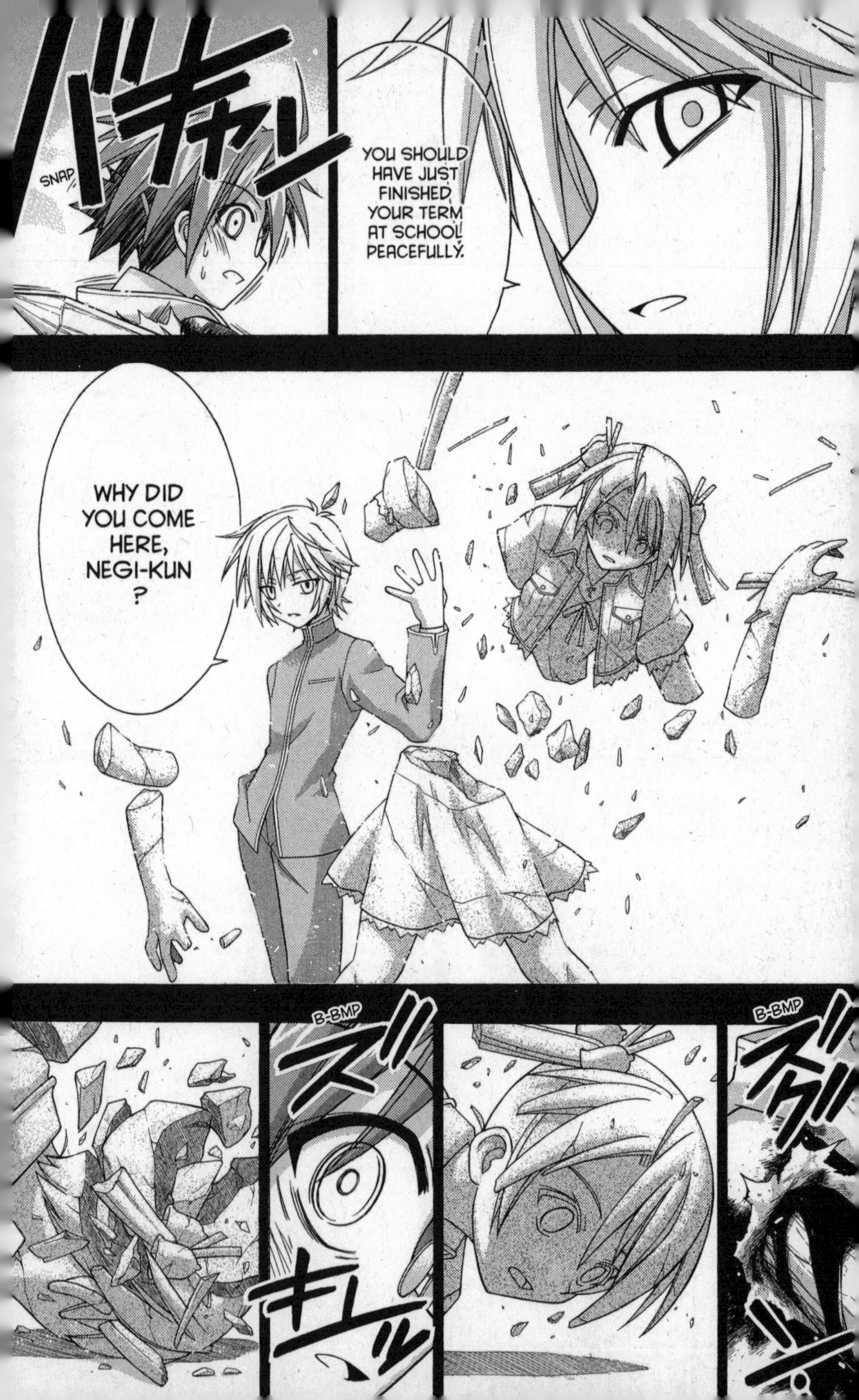
YOU SHOULD HAVE JUST FINISHED YOUR TERM AT SCHOOL PEACEFULLY.
SNAP
WHY DID YOU COME HERE, NEGI-KUN ?
B-BMP
B-BMP

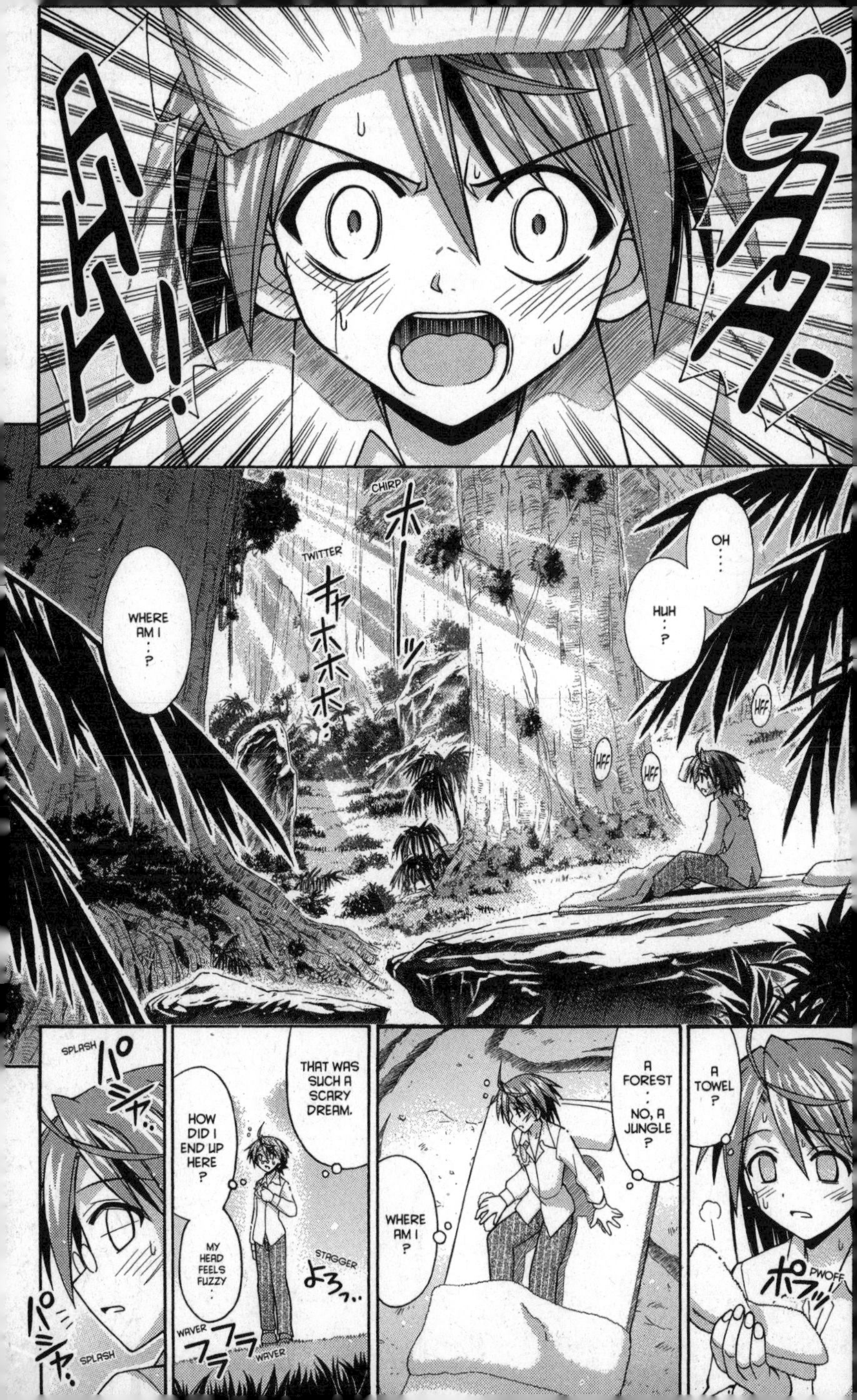
GAAA-
AAAH!
OH....
HUH...?
HFF
HFF
HFF
CHIRP
TWITTER
WHERE AM I...?
A TOWEL?
PWOFF
A FOREST... NO, A JUNGLE?
WHERE AM I?
THAT WAS SUCH A SCARY DREAM.
HOW DID I END UP HERE?
MY HEAD FEELS FUZZY...
STAGGER
WAVER
WAVER
SPLASH
SPLASH

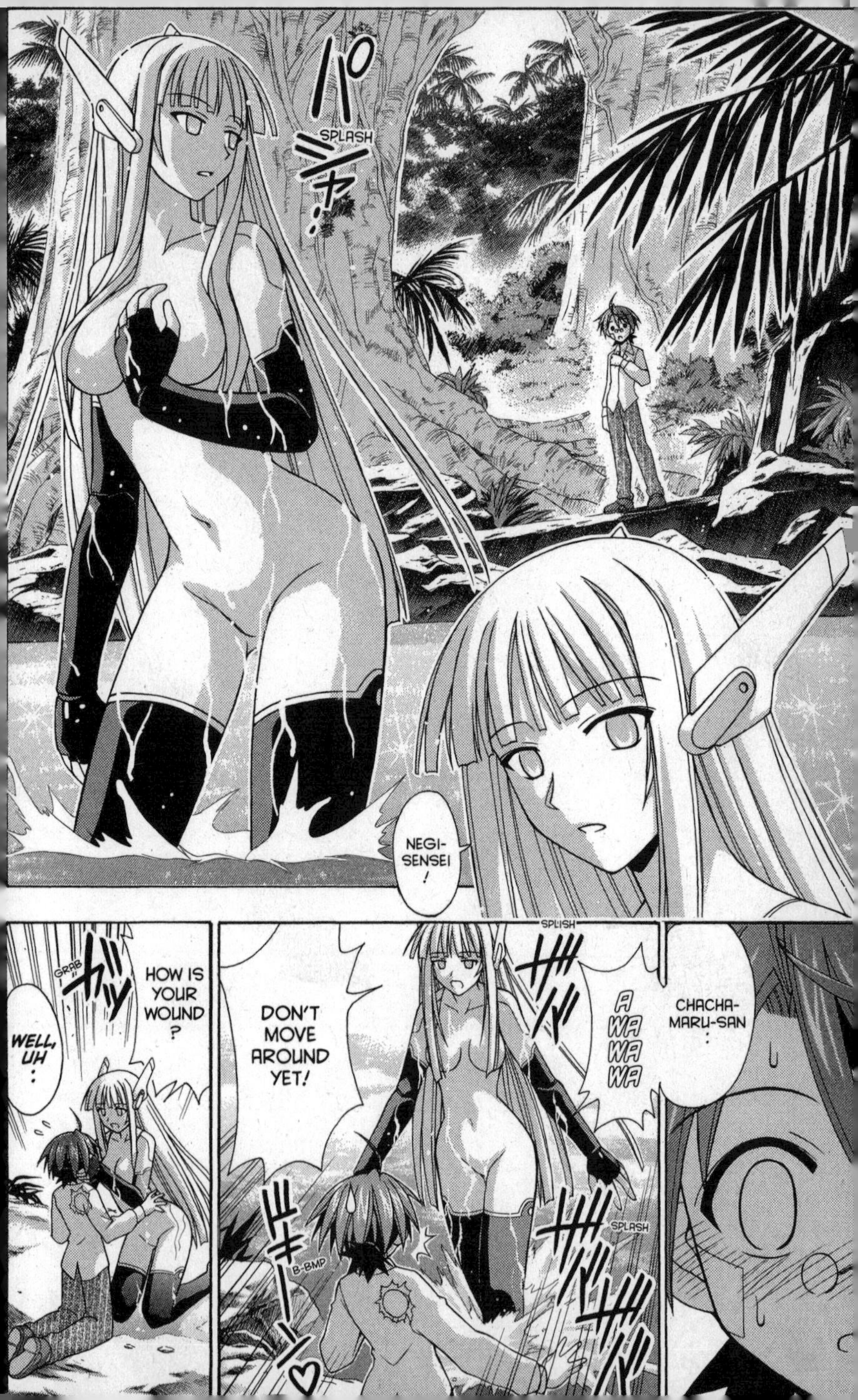
SPLASH
NEGI-SENSEI!
CHACHA-MARU-SAN...
SPLISH
A WA WA WA WA
DON'T MOVE AROUND YET!
SPLASH
B-BMP
GRAB
HOW IS YOUR WOUND?
WELL, UH...

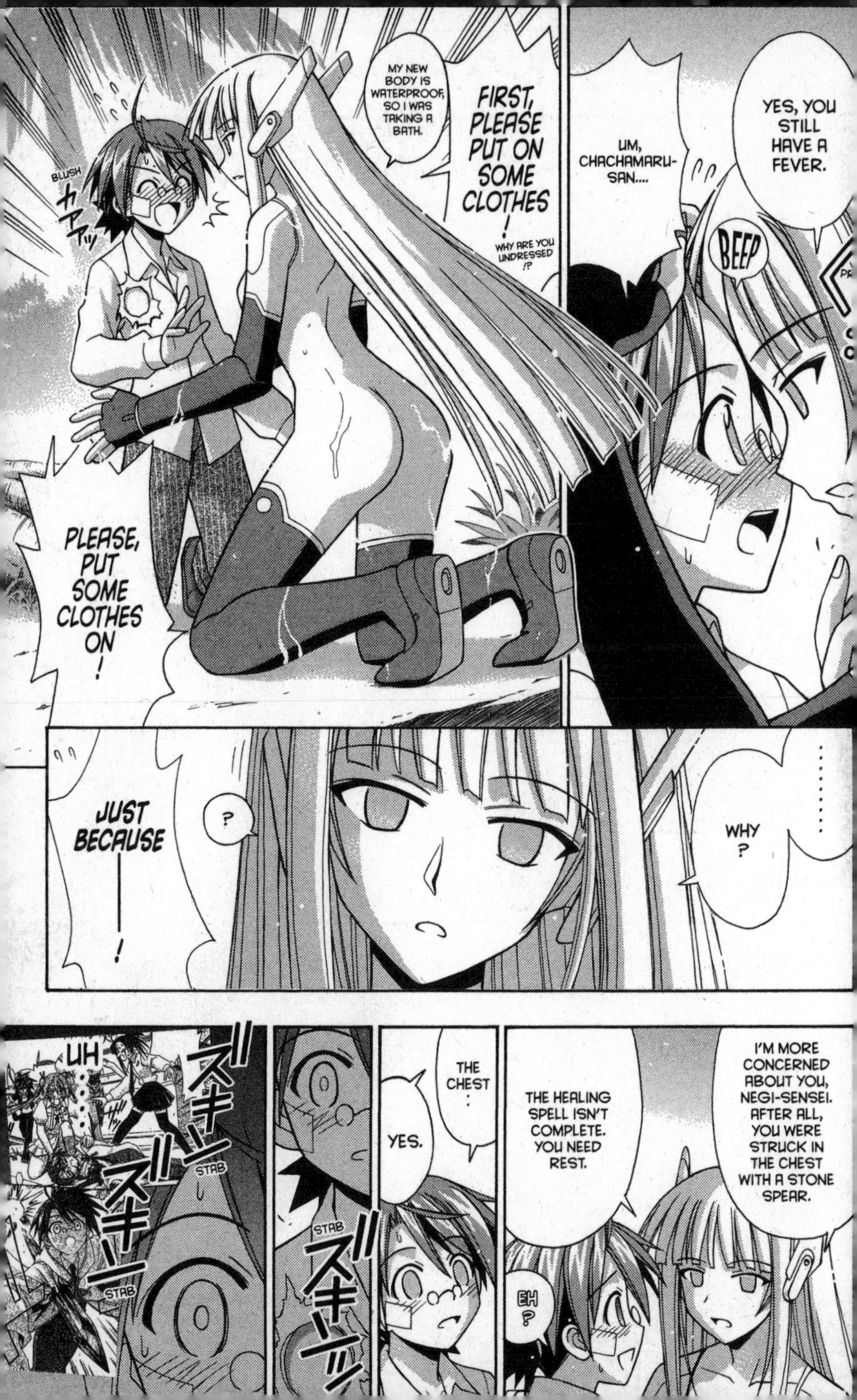
YES, YOU STILL HAVE A FEVER.
BEEP
UM, CHACHAMARU-SAN....
FIRST, PLEASE PUT ON SOME CLOTHES!
WHY ARE YOU UNDRESSED!?
MY NEW BODY IS WATERPROOF, SO I WAS TAKING A BATH.
BLUSH
PLEASE, PUT SOME CLOTHES ON!
......
WHY?
?
JUST BECAUSE——!
I'M MORE CONCERNED ABOUT YOU, NEGI-SENSEI. AFTER ALL, YOU WERE STRUCK IN THE CHEST WITH A STONE SPEAR.
THE HEALING SPELL ISN'T COMPLETE. YOU NEED REST.
EH?
THE CHEST...
YES.
STAB
UH...
STAB
STAB

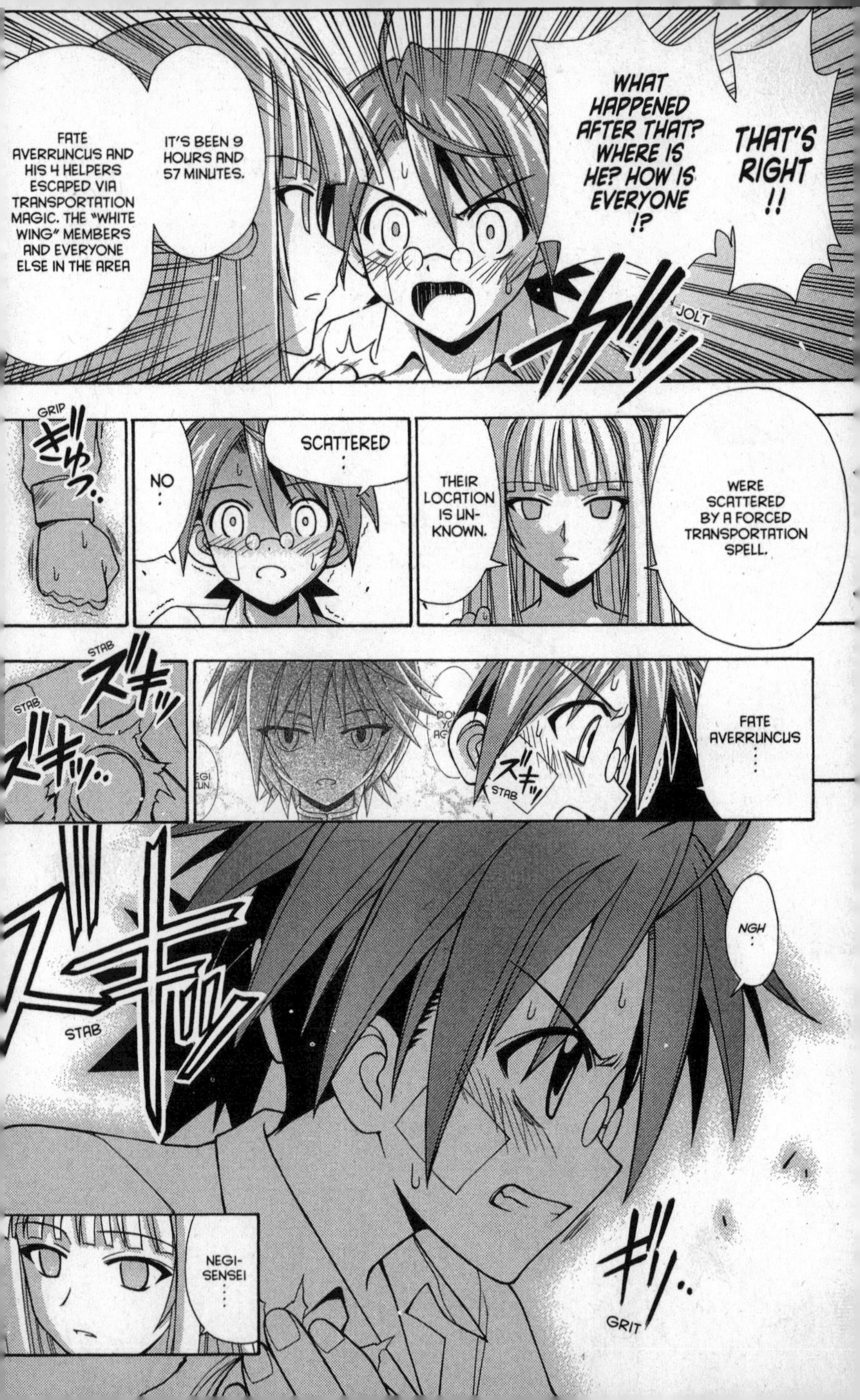

THAT'S RIGHT !!
WHAT HAPPENED AFTER THAT? WHERE IS HE? HOW IS EVERYONE !?
JOLT
IT'S BEEN 9 HOURS AND 57 MINUTES.
FATE AVERRUNCUS AND HIS 4 HELPERS ESCAPED VIA TRANSPORTATION MAGIC. THE "WHITE WING" MEMBERS AND EVERYONE ELSE IN THE AREA
WERE SCATTERED BY A FORCED TRANSPORTATION SPELL.
THEIR LOCATION IS UN-KNOWN.
SCATTERED ...
NO ...
GRIP
FATE AVERRUNCUS ....
STAB
STAB
STAB
NGH ...
STAB
GRIT
NEGI-SENSEI ....

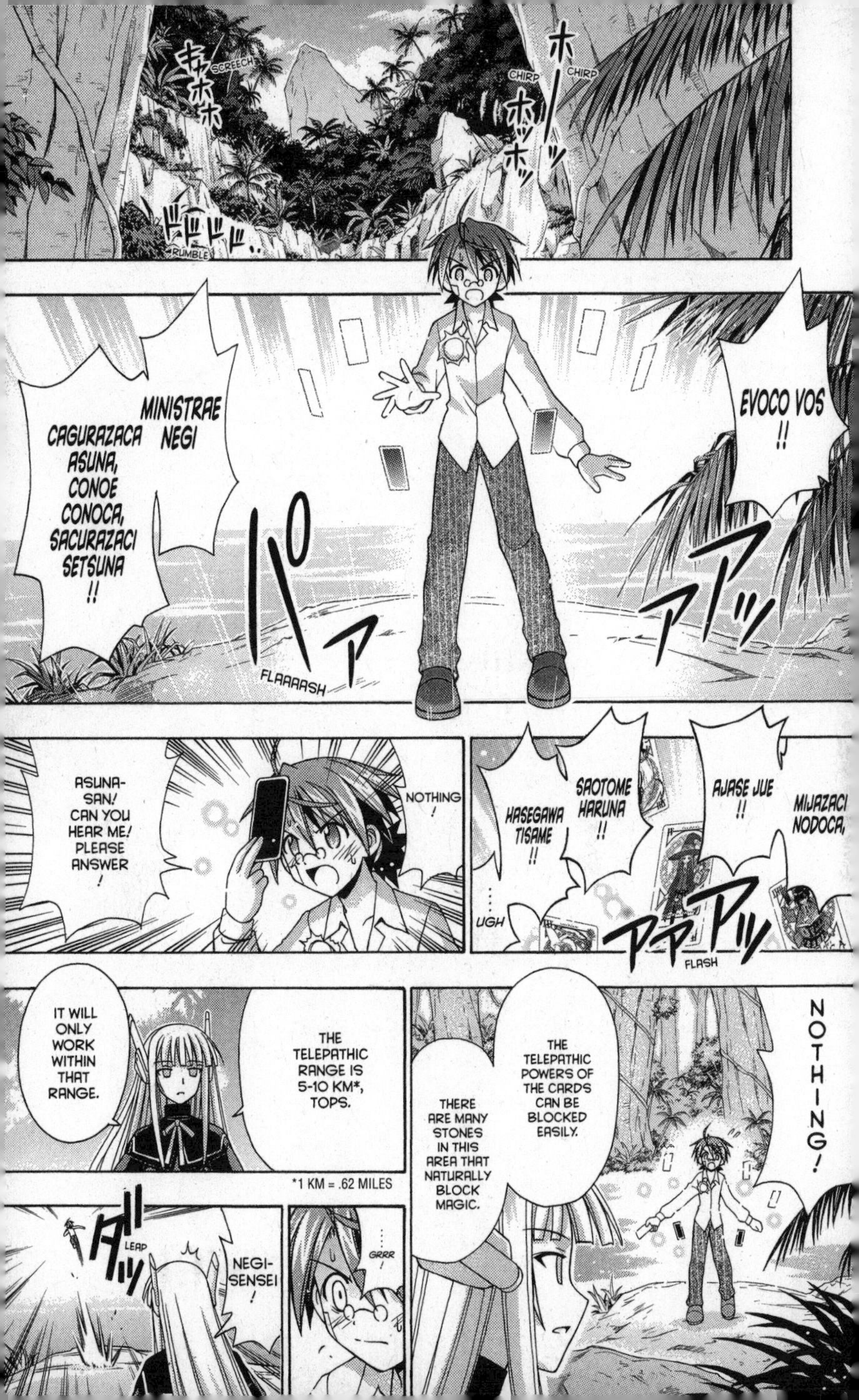

ホーッ ホッホッ
CHIRP
CHIRP
キャホホ
SCREECH
ドドドド..
RUMBLE
EVOCO VOS!!
MINISTRAE NEGI
CAGURAZACA ASUNA, CONOE CONOCA, SACURAZACI SETSUNA!!
パァ アァッ
FLAAAASH
MIJAZACI NODOCA,
AJASE JUE!!
SAOTOME HARUNA!!
HASEGAWA TISAME!!
...UGH
アァアッ
FLASH
NOTHING!
ASUNA-SAN! CAN YOU HEAR ME! PLEASE ANSWER!
NOTHING!
THE TELEPATHIC POWERS OF THE CARDS CAN BE BLOCKED EASILY.
THERE ARE MANY STONES IN THIS AREA THAT NATURALLY BLOCK MAGIC.
THE TELEPATHIC RANGE IS 5-10 KM*, TOPS.
IT WILL ONLY WORK WITHIN THAT RANGE.
*1 KM = .62 MILES
...GRRR!
NEGI-SENSEI!
ダッ
LEAP

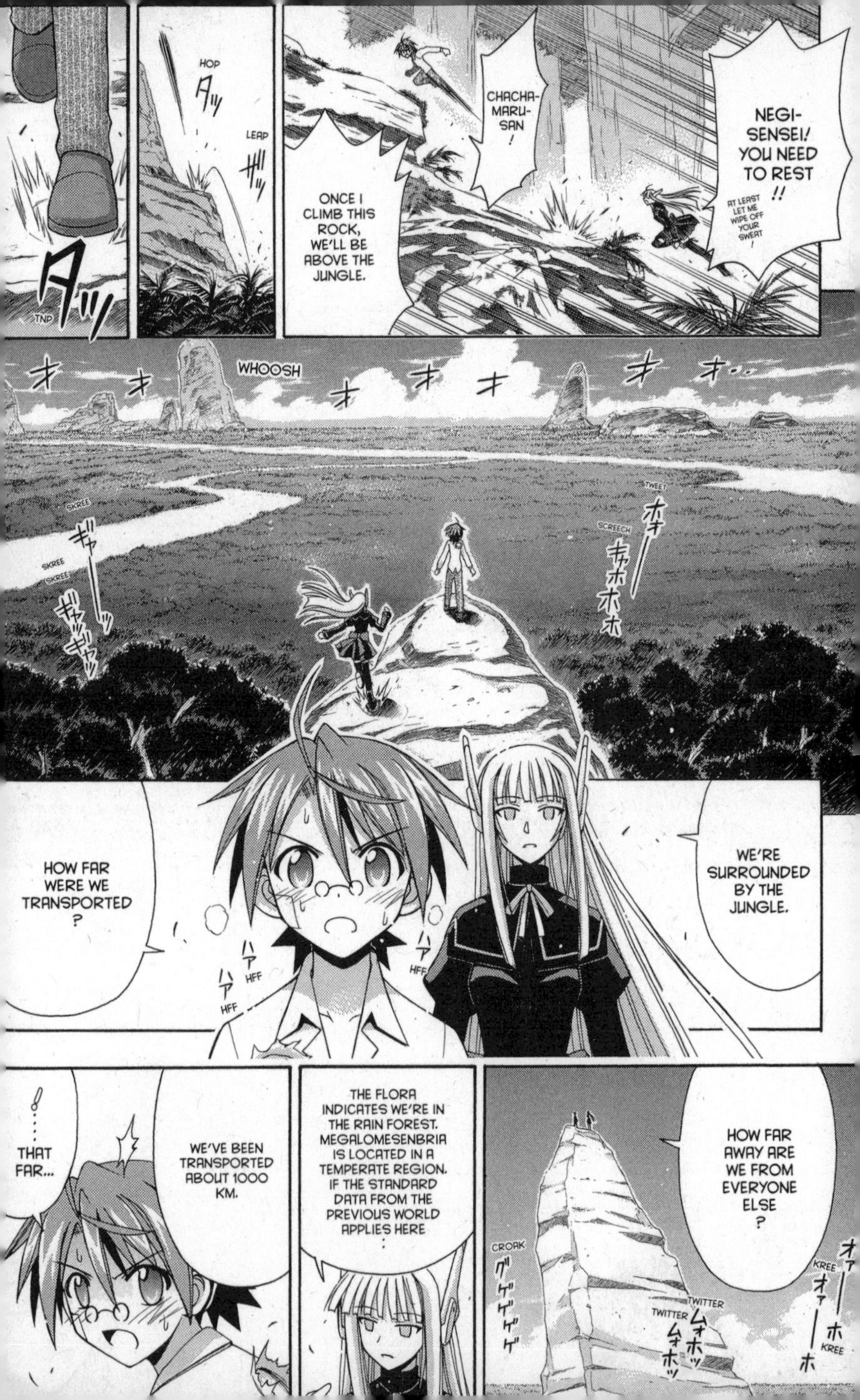
NEGI-SENSEI! YOU NEED TO REST!!
AT LEAST LET ME WIPE OFF YOUR SWEAT!
CHACHA-MARU-SAN!
ONCE I CLIMB THIS ROCK, WE'LL BE ABOVE THE JUNGLE.
LEAP
HOP
TNP
WHOOSH
TWEET
SCREECH
SKREE
SKREE
SKREE
WE'RE SURROUNDED BY THE JUNGLE.
HFF
HFF
HFF
HOW FAR WERE WE TRANSPORTED?
HOW FAR AWAY ARE WE FROM EVERYONE ELSE?
KREE
KREE
TWITTER
TWITTER
CROAK
THE FLORA INDICATES WE'RE IN THE RAIN FOREST. MEGALOMESENBRIA IS LOCATED IN A TEMPERATE REGION. IF THE STANDARD DATA FROM THE PREVIOUS WORLD APPLIES HERE:
WE'VE BEEN TRANSPORTED ABOUT 1000 KM.
!...... THAT FAR...

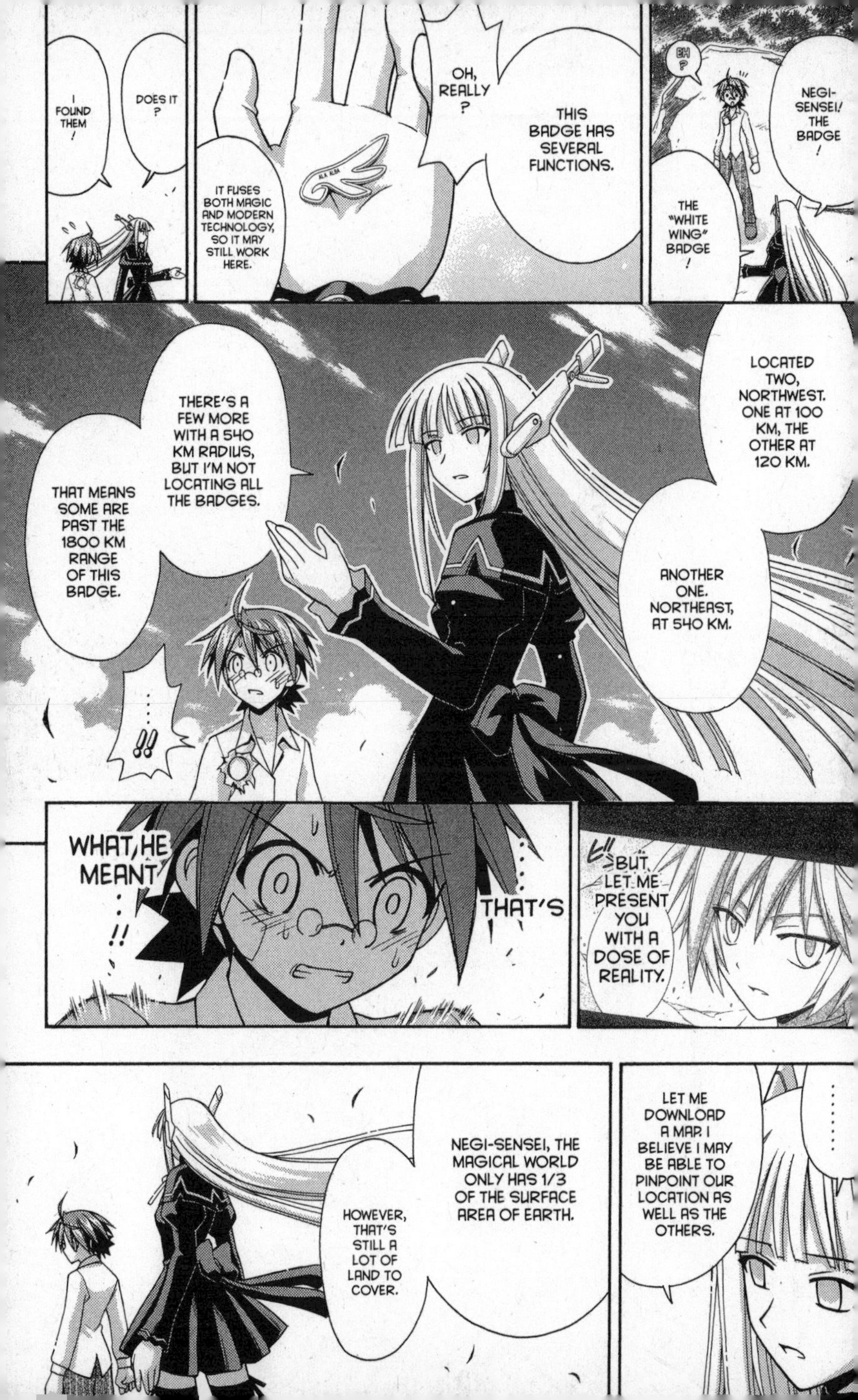
NEGI-SENSEI! THE BADGE!
EH?
THE "WHITE WING" BADGE!
THIS BADGE HAS SEVERAL FUNCTIONS.
OH, REALLY?
IT FUSES BOTH MAGIC AND MODERN TECHNOLOGY, SO IT MAY STILL WORK HERE.
ALA ALBA
DOES IT?
I FOUND THEM!
LOCATED TWO, NORTHWEST. ONE AT 100 KM, THE OTHER AT 120 KM.
ANOTHER ONE. NORTHEAST, AT 540 KM.
THERE'S A FEW MORE WITH A 540 KM RADIUS, BUT I'M NOT LOCATING ALL THE BADGES.
THAT MEANS SOME ARE PAST THE 1800 KM RANGE OF THIS BADGE.
......!!
BUT LET ME PRESENT YOU WITH A DOSE OF REALITY.
THAT'S...
WHAT, HE MEANT...!!
......
LET ME DOWNLOAD A MAP. I BELIEVE I MAY BE ABLE TO PINPOINT OUR LOCATION AS WELL AS THE OTHERS.
NEGI-SENSEI, THE MAGICAL WORLD ONLY HAS 1/3 OF THE SURFACE AREA OF EARTH.
HOWEVER, THAT'S STILL A LOT OF LAND TO COVER.

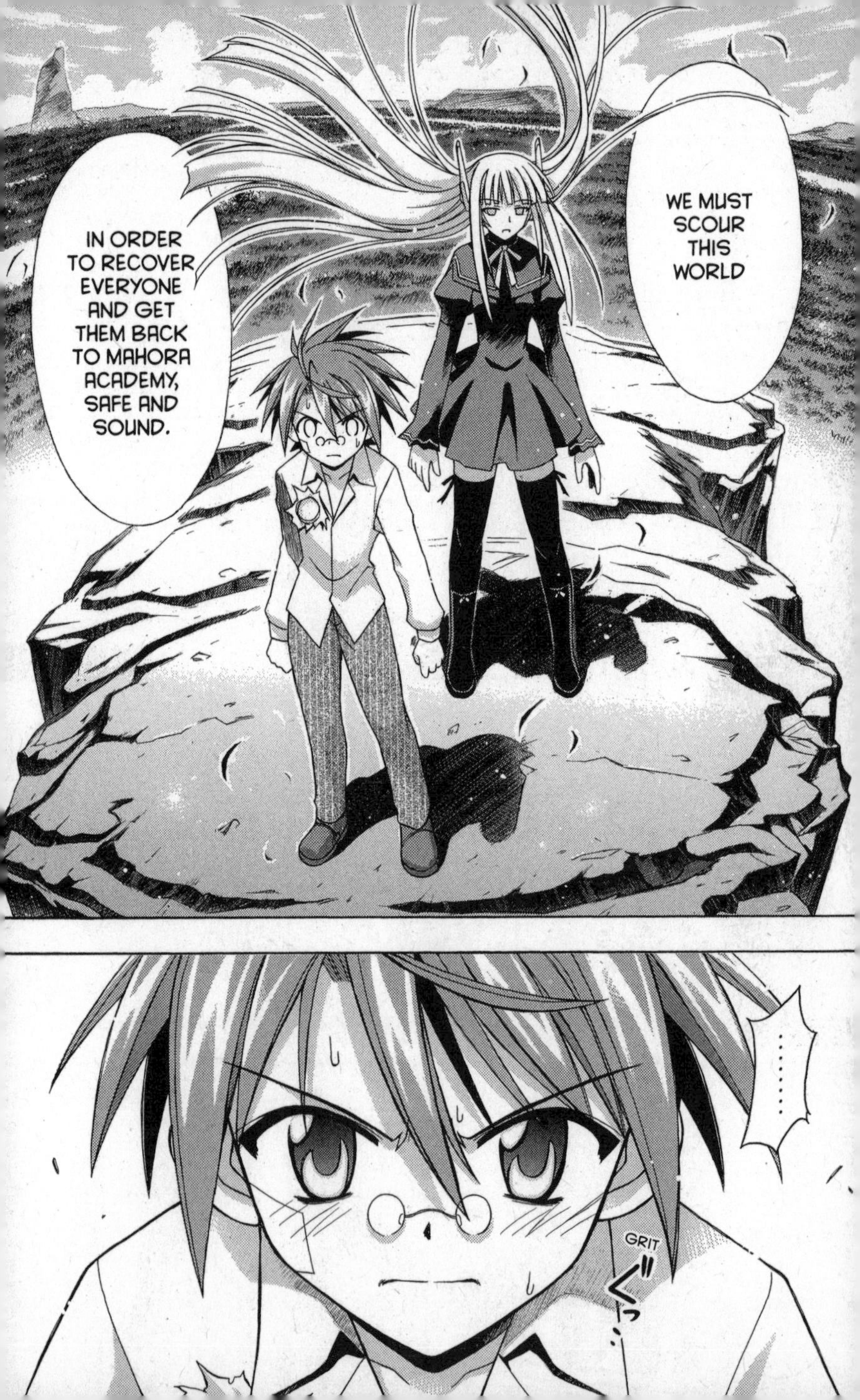
WE MUST SCOUR THIS WORLD
IN ORDER TO RECOVER EVERYONE AND GET THEM BACK TO MAHORA ACADEMY, SAFE AND SOUND.
.........!
GRIT

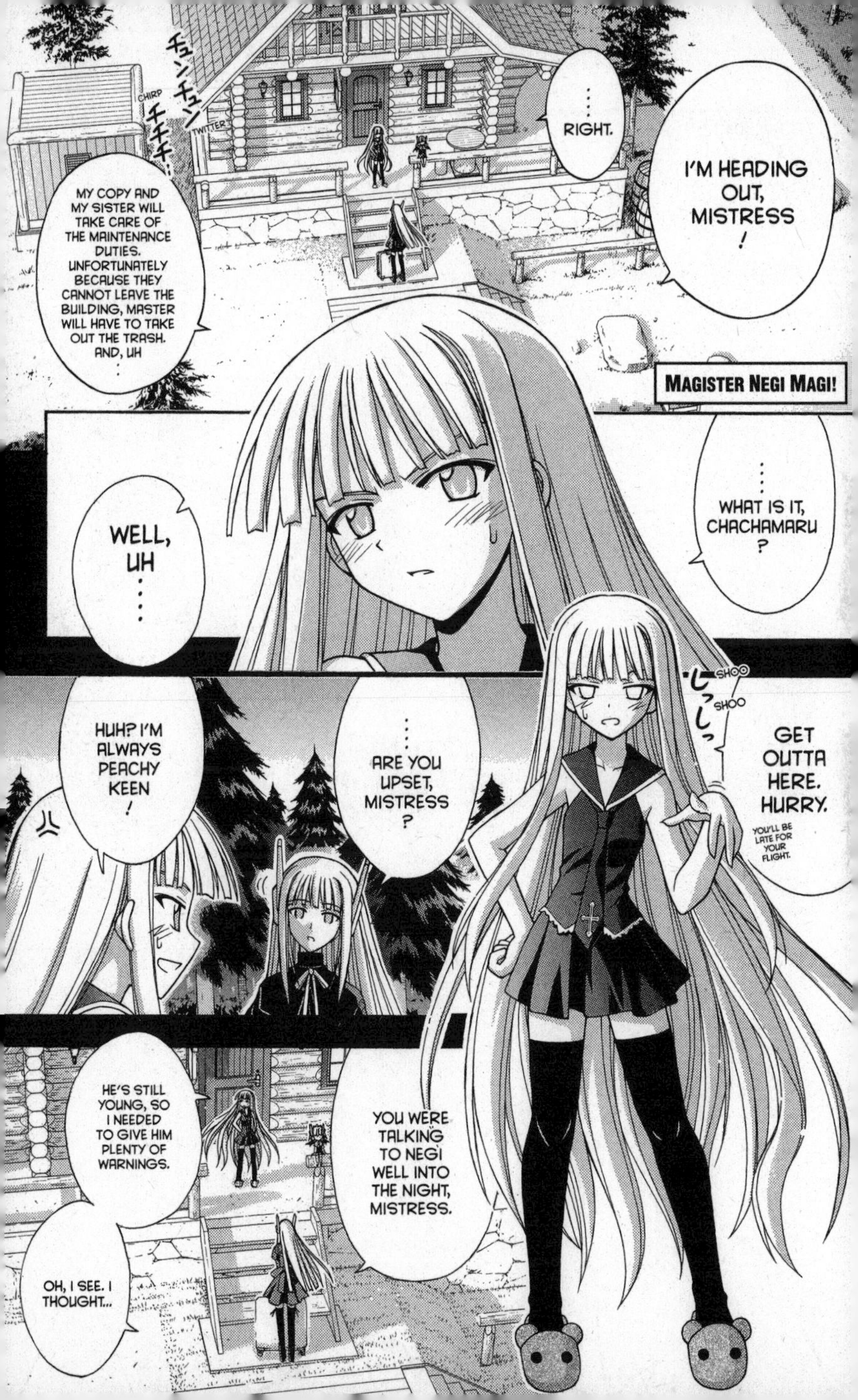I'M HEADING OUT, MISTRESS!
...RIGHT.
チュンチュン
CHIRP
チチチ
TWITTER
MY COPY AND MY SISTER WILL TAKE CARE OF THE MAINTENANCE DUTIES. UNFORTUNATELY BECAUSE THEY CANNOT LEAVE THE BUILDING, MASTER WILL HAVE TO TAKE OUT THE TRASH. AND, UH...
MAGISTER NEGI MAGI!
...WHAT IS IT, CHACHAMARU?
WELL, UH...
SHOO
SHOO
GET OUTTA HERE. HURRY.
YOU'LL BE LATE FOR YOUR FLIGHT.
...ARE YOU UPSET, MISTRESS?
HUH? I'M ALWAYS PEACHY KEEN!
YOU WERE TALKING TO NEGI WELL INTO THE NIGHT, MISTRESS.
HE'S STILL YOUNG, SO I NEEDED TO GIVE HIM PLENTY OF WARNINGS.
OH, I SEE. I THOUGHT...

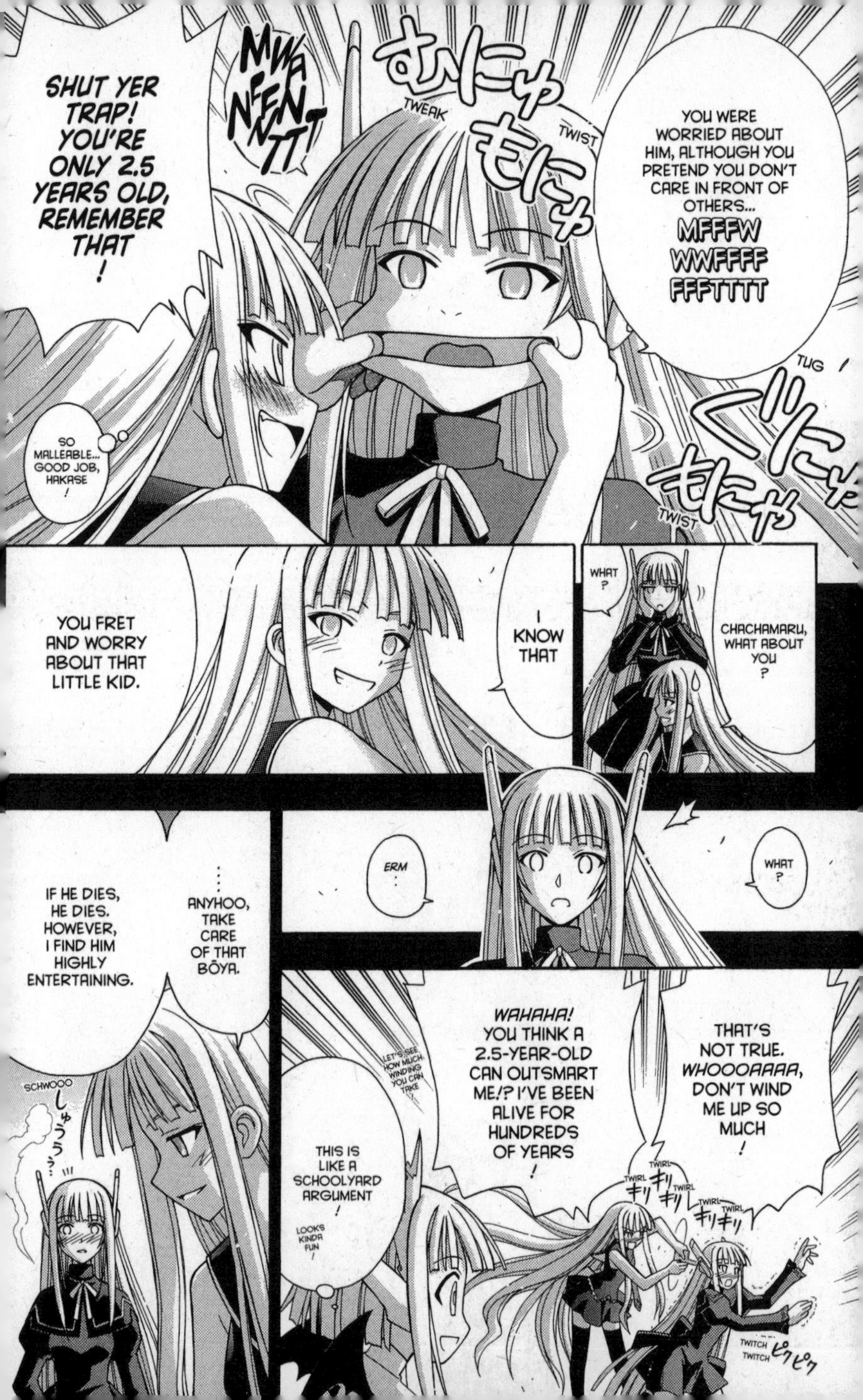
YOU WERE WORRIED ABOUT HIM, ALTHOUGH YOU PRETEND YOU DON'T CARE IN FRONT OF OTHERS... MFFFW WWFFFF FFFTTTT
むにゅ TWEAK
もにゅ TWIST
MWANFENNTTT
SHUT YER TRAP! YOU'RE ONLY 2.5 YEARS OLD, REMEMBER THAT!
TUG くりにゅ
もにゅ TWIST
SO MALLEABLE... GOOD JOB, HAKASE!
CHACHAMARU, WHAT ABOUT YOU?
WHAT?
I KNOW THAT
YOU FRET AND WORRY ABOUT THAT LITTLE KID.
WHAT?
ERM...
THAT'S NOT TRUE. WHOOOAAAA, DON'T WIND ME UP SO MUCH!
WAHAHA! YOU THINK A 2.5-YEAR-OLD CAN OUTSMART ME!? I'VE BEEN ALIVE FOR HUNDREDS OF YEARS!
LET'S SEE HOW MUCH WINDING YOU CAN TAKE
THIS IS LIKE A SCHOOLYARD ARGUMENT!
LOOKS KINDA FUN!
TWIRL キリ TWIRL キリ TWIRL キリ TWIRL キリ TWIRL キリ
TWITCH TWITCH ピクピク
...ANYHOO, TAKE CARE OF THAT BŌYA.
IF HE DIES, HE DIES. HOWEVER, I FIND HIM HIGHLY ENTERTAINING.
SCHWOOO しゅううう...

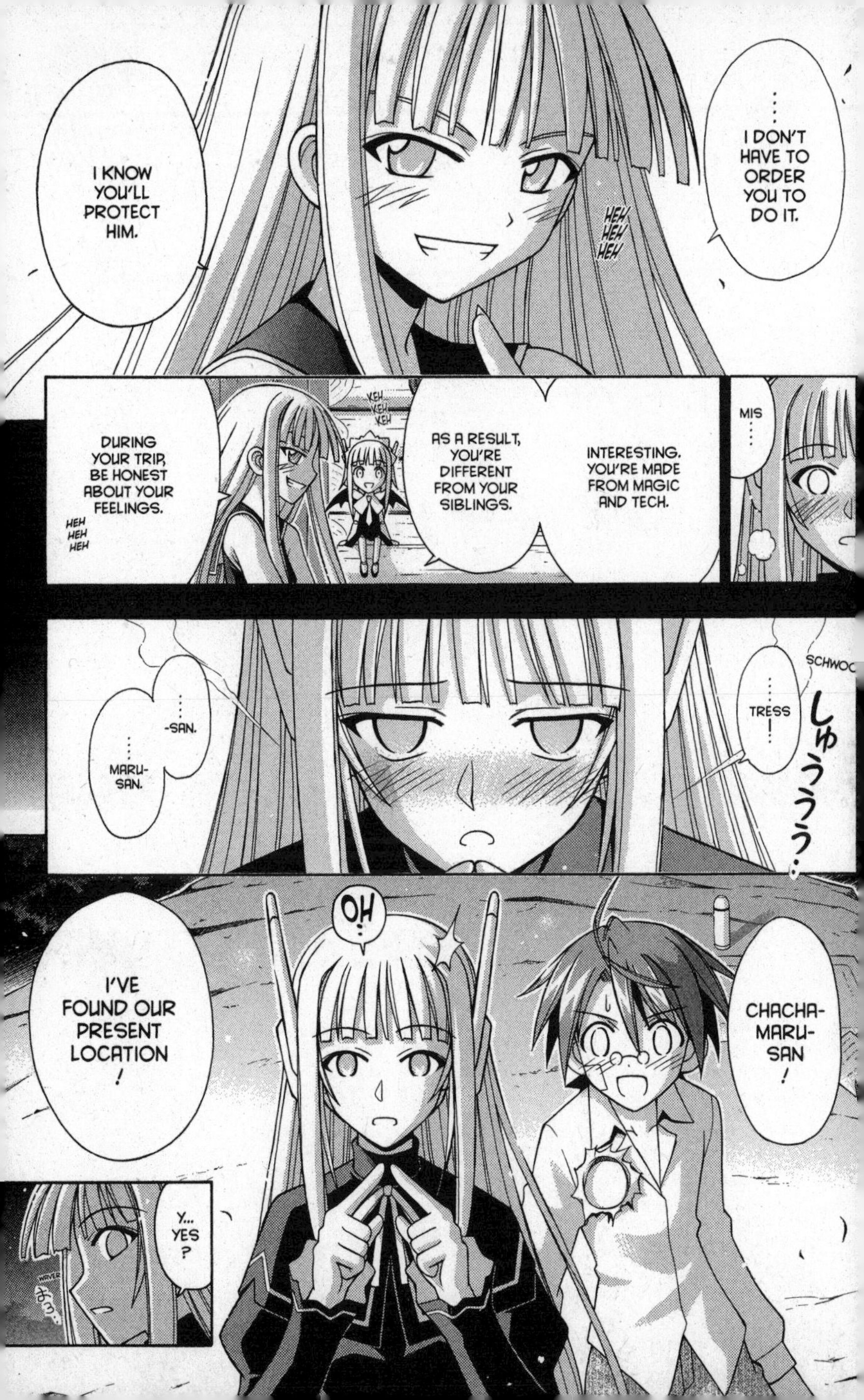
...... I DON'T HAVE TO ORDER YOU TO DO IT.
HEH HEH HEH
I KNOW YOU'LL PROTECT HIM.
MIS......
INTERESTING. YOU'RE MADE FROM MAGIC AND TECH.
AS A RESULT, YOU'RE DIFFERENT FROM YOUR SIBLINGS.
KEH KEH KEH
DURING YOUR TRIP, BE HONEST ABOUT YOUR FEELINGS.
HEH HEH HEH
SCHWOO
しゅううう・・
......TRESS!...
......-SAN.
......MARU-SAN.
OH!?
CHACHA-MARU-SAN!
I'VE FOUND OUR PRESENT LOCATION!
Y... YES?
WAVER

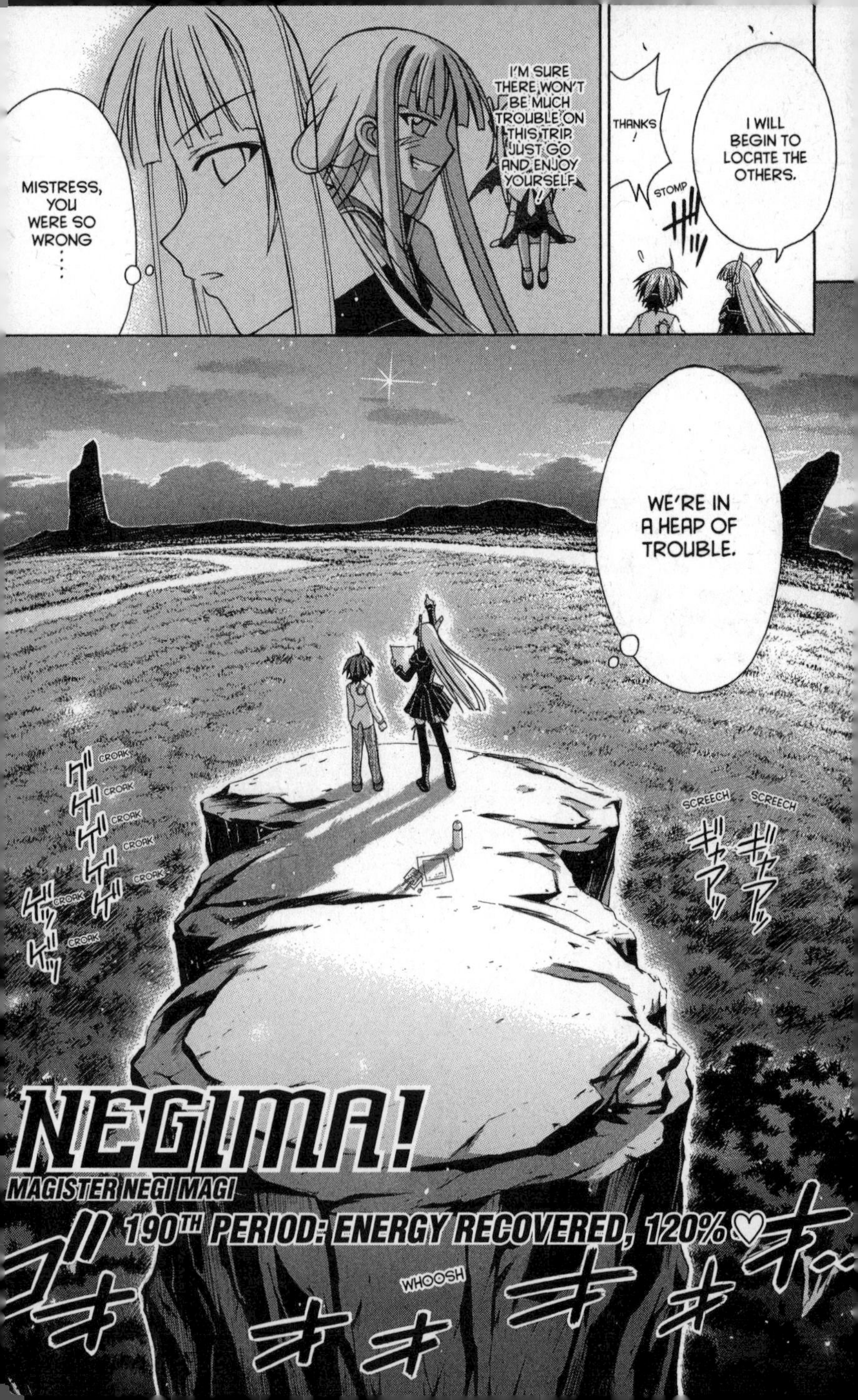
I WILL BEGIN TO LOCATE THE OTHERS.
THANKS!
STOMP
I'M SURE THERE WON'T BE MUCH TROUBLE ON THIS TRIP. JUST GO AND ENJOY YOURSELF!
MISTRESS, YOU WERE SO WRONG.......
WE'RE IN A HEAP OF TROUBLE.
SCREECH
SCREECH
CROAK
CROAK
CROAK
CROAK
CROAK
CROAK
CROAK
NEGIMA!
MAGISTER NEGI MAGI
190TH PERIOD: ENERGY RECOVERED, 120%♡
WHOOSH

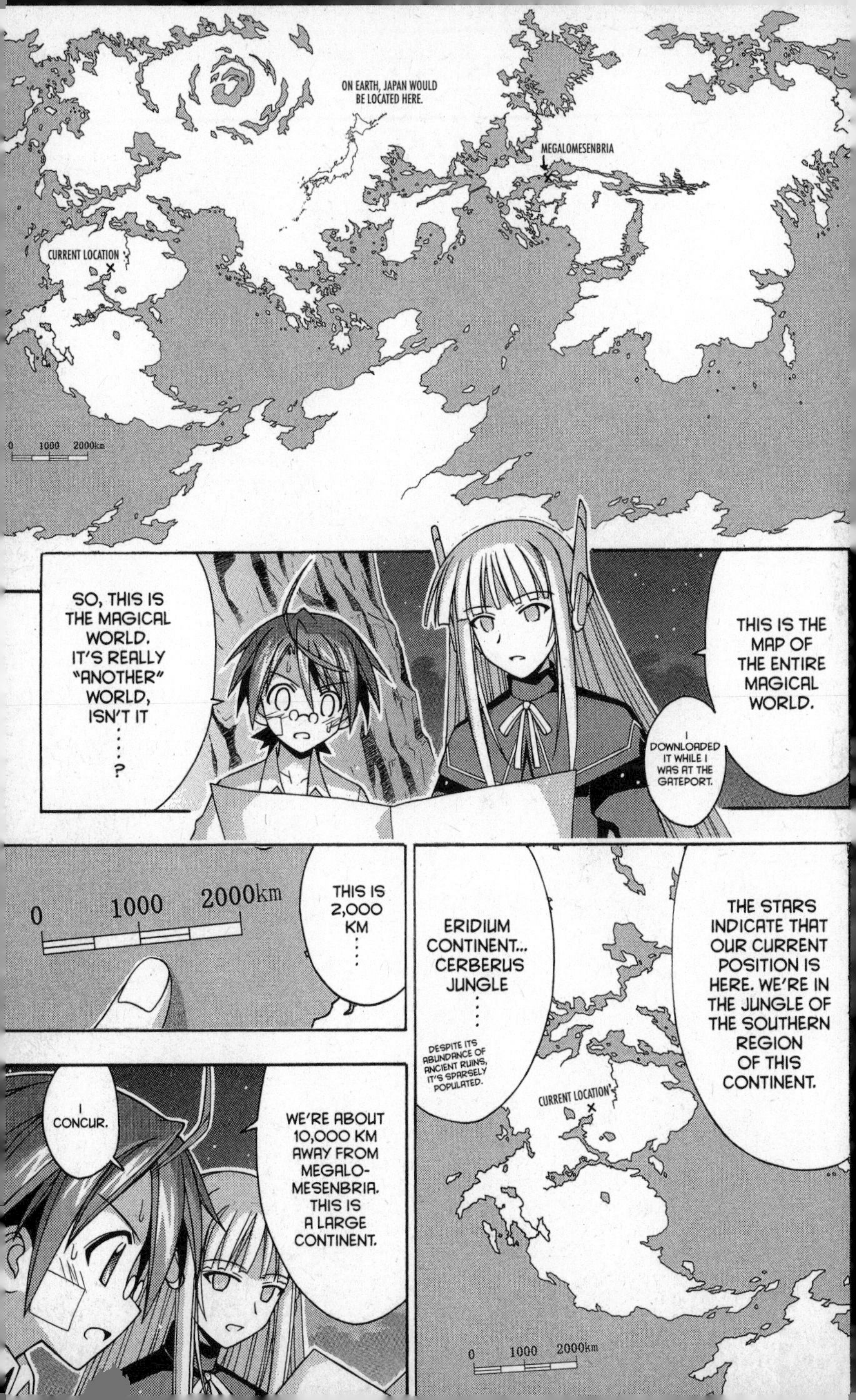
ON EARTH, JAPAN WOULD BE LOCATED HERE.
MEGALOMESENBRIA
CURRENT LOCATION
0 1000 2000km
THIS IS THE MAP OF THE ENTIRE MAGICAL WORLD.
I DOWNLOADED IT WHILE I WAS AT THE GATEPORT.
SO, THIS IS THE MAGICAL WORLD. IT'S REALLY "ANOTHER" WORLD, ISN'T IT .....?
THE STARS INDICATE THAT OUR CURRENT POSITION IS HERE. WE'RE IN THE JUNGLE OF THE SOUTHERN REGION OF THIS CONTINENT.
ERIDIUM CONTINENT... CERBERUS JUNGLE ....
DESPITE ITS ABUNDANCE OF ANCIENT RUINS, IT'S SPARSELY POPULATED.
CURRENT LOCATION
0 1000 2000km
THIS IS 2,000 KM ....
0 1000 2000km
WE'RE ABOUT 10,000 KM AWAY FROM MEGALO-MESENBRIA. THIS IS A LARGE CONTINENT.
I CONCUR.

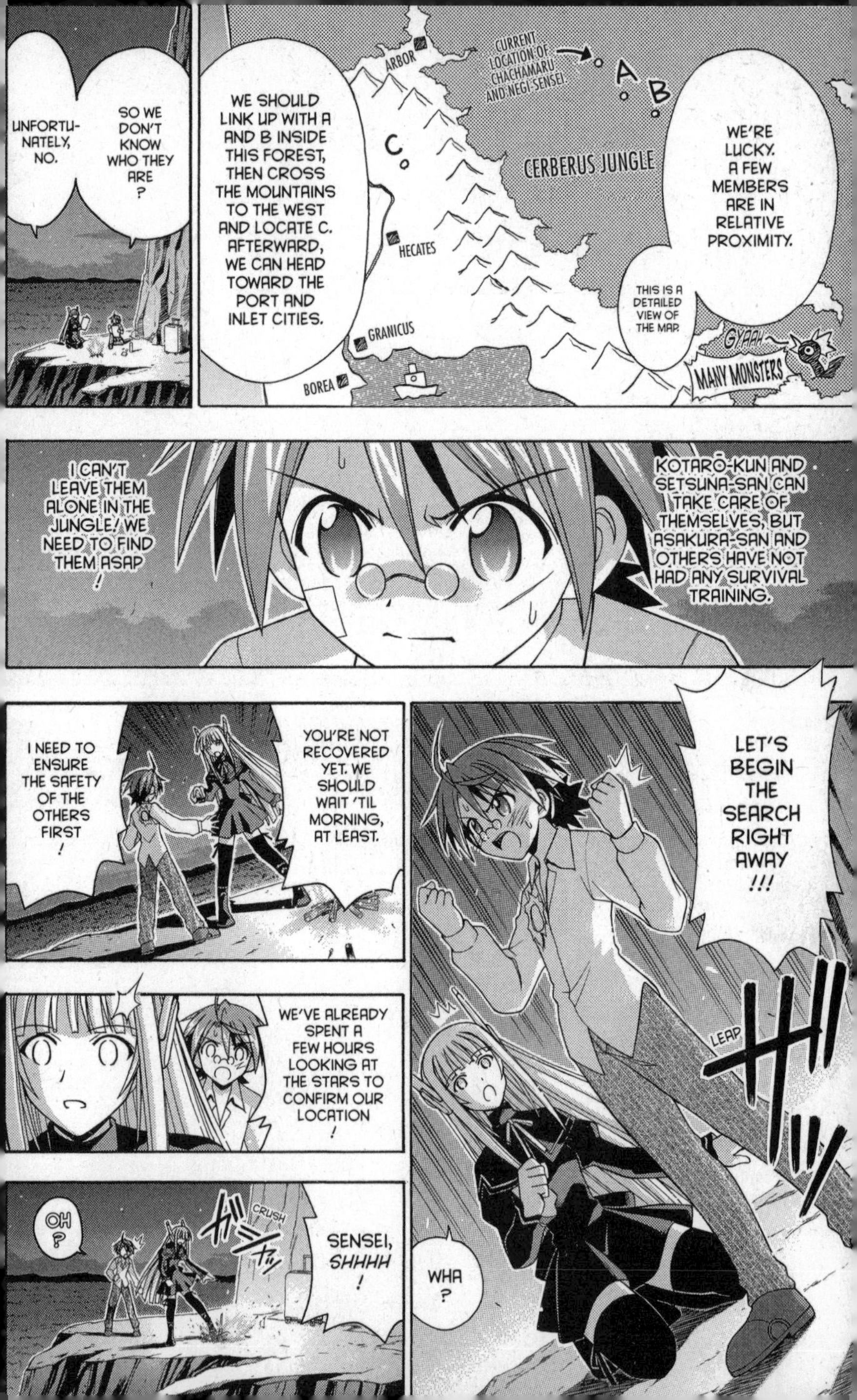
CURRENT LOCATION OF CHACHAMARU AND NEGI-SENSEI
A
B
WE'RE LUCKY. A FEW MEMBERS ARE IN RELATIVE PROXIMITY.
CERBERUS JUNGLE
ARBOR
C
THIS IS A DETAILED VIEW OF THE MAP.
GYAAH
MANY MONSTERS
WE SHOULD LINK UP WITH A AND B INSIDE THIS FOREST, THEN CROSS THE MOUNTAINS TO THE WEST AND LOCATE C. AFTERWARD, WE CAN HEAD TOWARD THE PORT AND INLET CITIES.
HECATES
GRANICUS
BOREA
SO WE DON'T KNOW WHO THEY ARE?
UNFORTU-NATELY, NO.
KOTARŌ-KUN AND SETSUNA-SAN CAN TAKE CARE OF THEMSELVES, BUT ASAKURA-SAN AND OTHERS HAVE NOT HAD ANY SURVIVAL TRAINING.
I CAN'T LEAVE THEM ALONE IN THE JUNGLE! WE NEED TO FIND THEM ASAP!
LET'S BEGIN THE SEARCH RIGHT AWAY!!!
LEAP
WHA?
YOU'RE NOT RECOVERED YET. WE SHOULD WAIT 'TIL MORNING, AT LEAST.
I NEED TO ENSURE THE SAFETY OF THE OTHERS FIRST!
WE'VE ALREADY SPENT A FEW HOURS LOOKING AT THE STARS TO CONFIRM OUR LOCATION!
SENSEI, SHHHH!
CRUSH
OH?

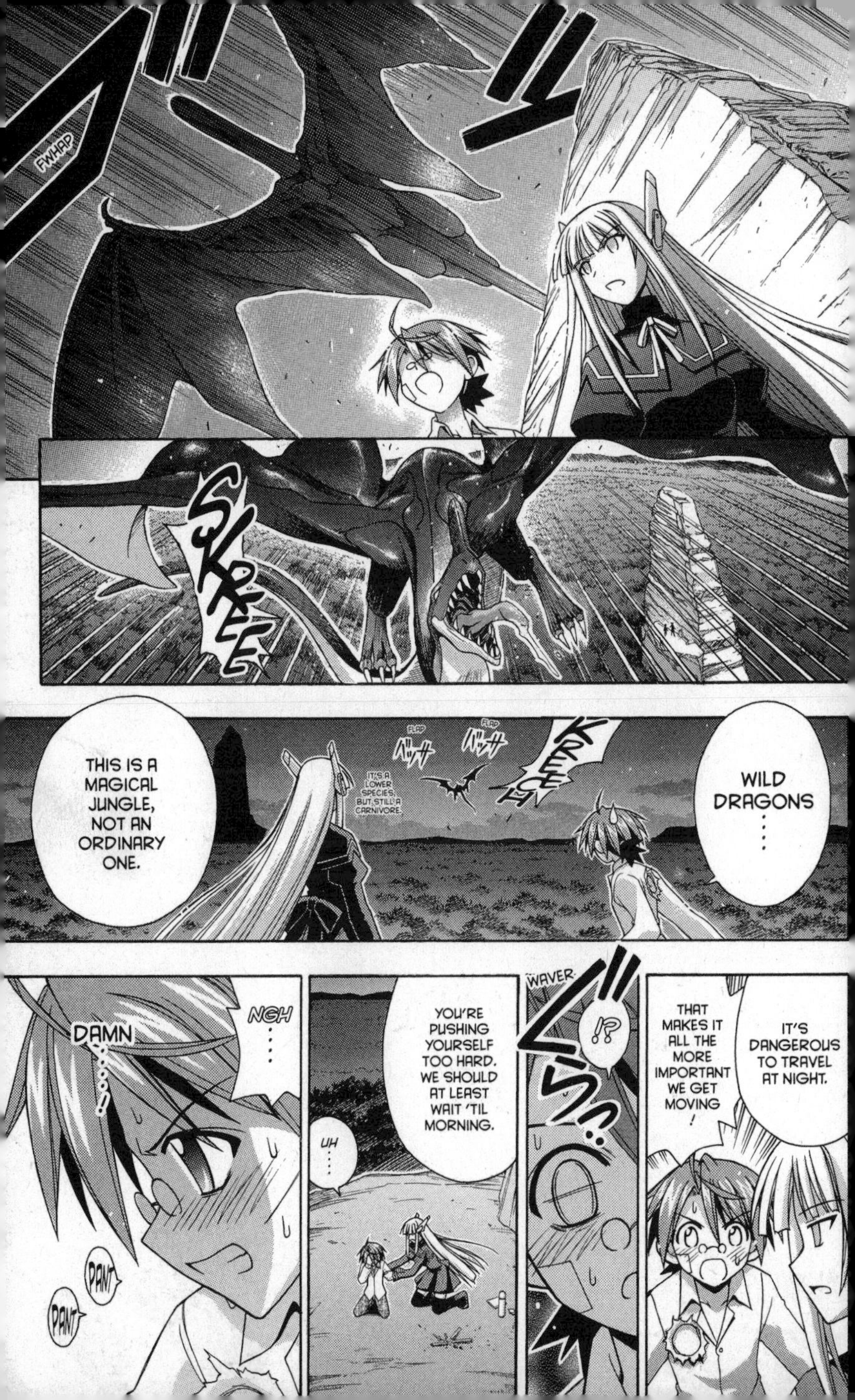
FWHAP
SKREE
WILD DRAGONS ....
KREECH
FLAP
バッサ
FLAP
バッサ
IT'S A LOWER SPECIES, BUT STILL A CARNIVORE.
THIS IS A MAGICAL JUNGLE, NOT AN ORDINARY ONE.
IT'S DANGEROUS TO TRAVEL AT NIGHT.
THAT MAKES IT ALL THE MORE IMPORTANT WE GET MOVING!
WAVER
!?
YOU'RE PUSHING YOURSELF TOO HARD. WE SHOULD AT LEAST WAIT 'TIL MORNING.
UH ....
NGH ....
DAMN ....!
PANT
PANT

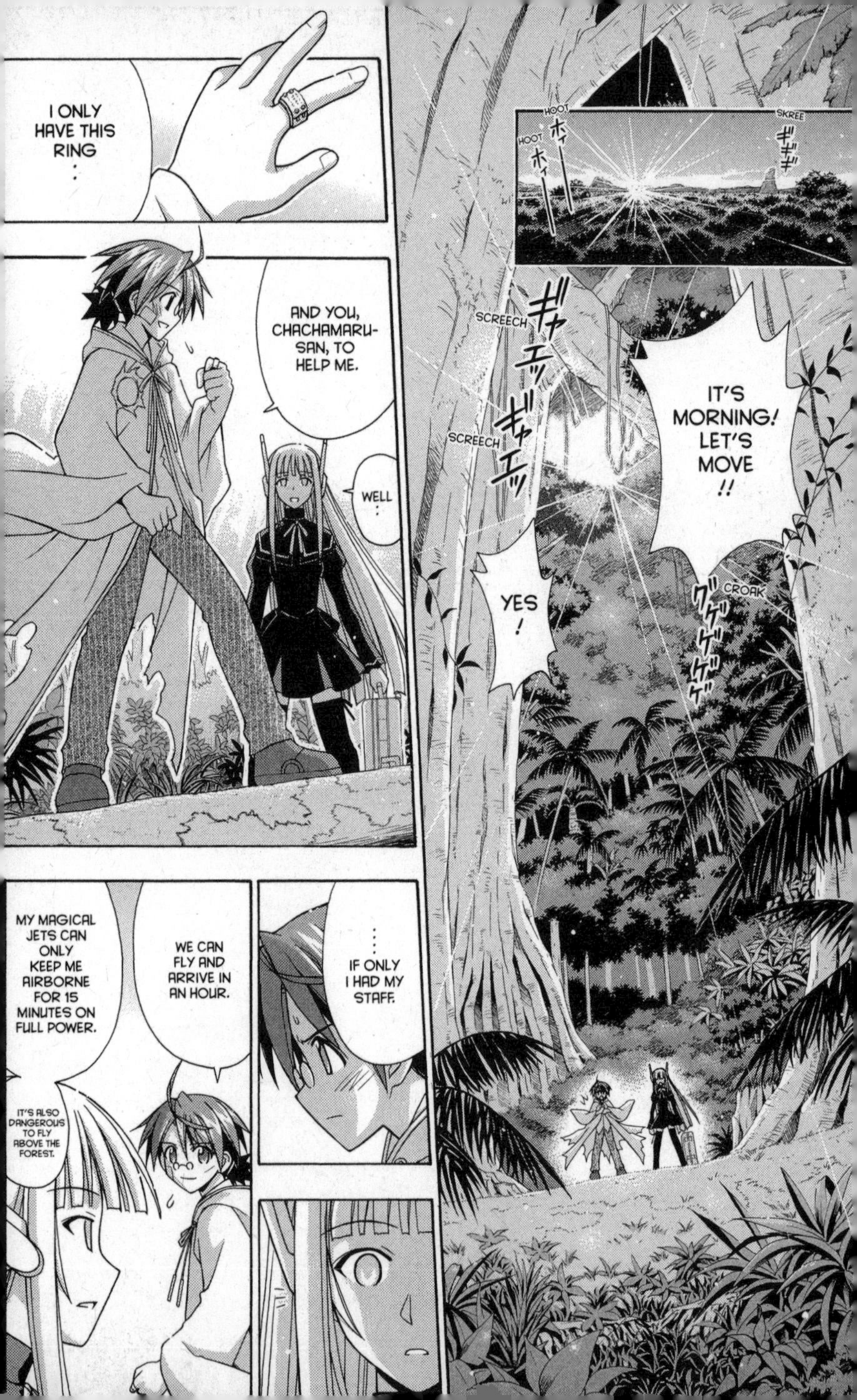

SKREE
ギギギ
HOOT
ホィー
HOOT
ホィー
IT'S MORNING! LET'S MOVE!!
SCREECH
ギャエッ
SCREECH
ギャエッ
YES!
CROAK
グゲゲゲゲ
I ONLY HAVE THIS RING...
AND YOU, CHACHAMARU-SAN, TO HELP ME.
WELL...
... IF ONLY I HAD MY STAFF.
WE CAN FLY AND ARRIVE IN AN HOUR.
MY MAGICAL JETS CAN ONLY KEEP ME AIRBORNE FOR 15 MINUTES ON FULL POWER.
IT'S ALSO DANGEROUS TO FLY ABOVE THE FOREST.

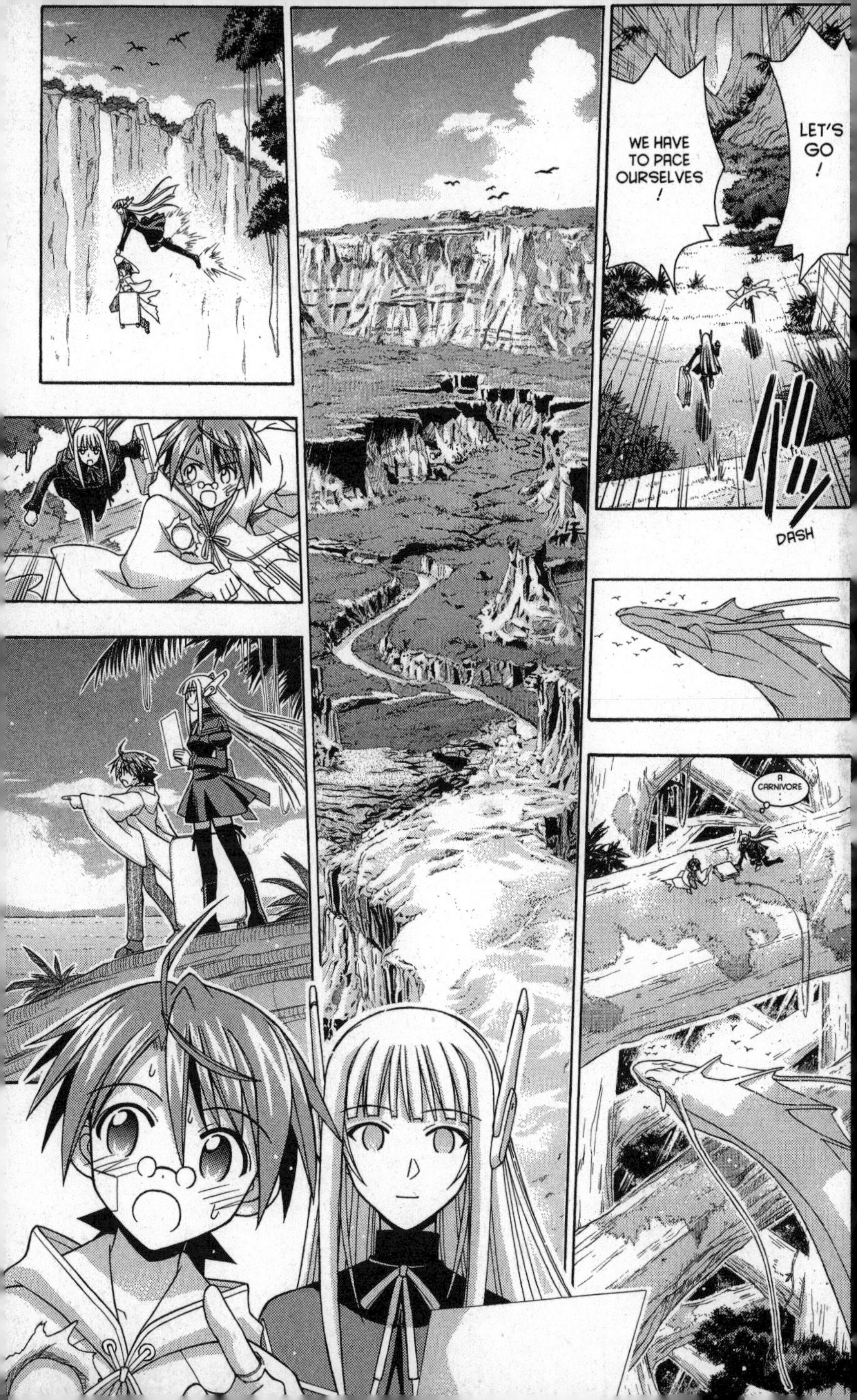
LET'S GO!
WE HAVE TO PACE OURSELVES!
DASH
A CARNIVORE...

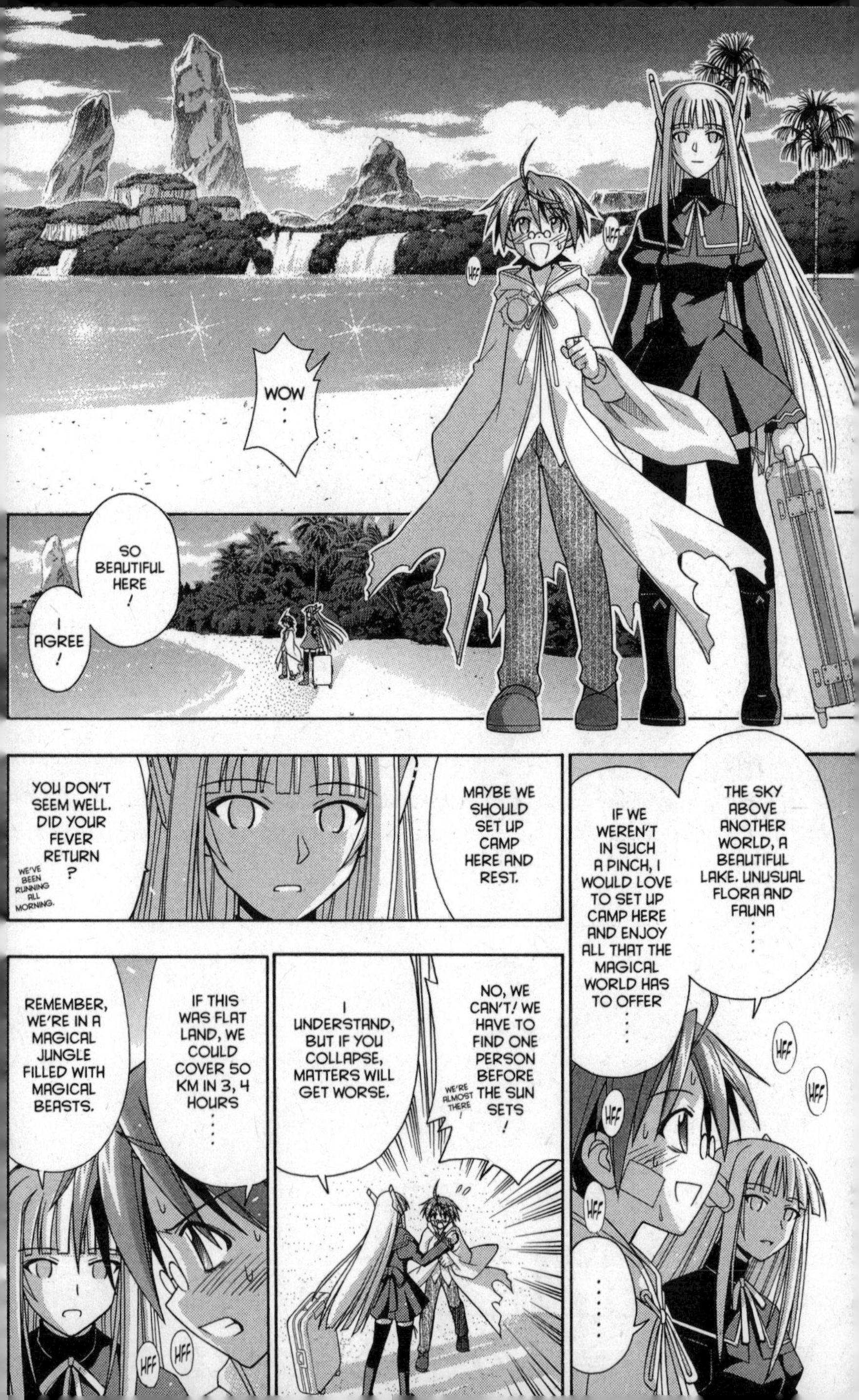
HFF
HFF
WOW
...
SO BEAUTIFUL HERE!
I AGREE!
THE SKY ABOVE ANOTHER WORLD, A BEAUTIFUL LAKE. UNUSUAL FLORA AND FAUNA...
IF WE WEREN'T IN SUCH A PINCH, I WOULD LOVE TO SET UP CAMP HERE AND ENJOY ALL THAT THE MAGICAL WORLD HAS TO OFFER...
HFF
HFF
HFF
HFF
......
MAYBE WE SHOULD SET UP CAMP HERE AND REST.
YOU DON'T SEEM WELL. DID YOUR FEVER RETURN?
WE'VE BEEN RUNNING ALL MORNING.
NO, WE CAN'T! WE HAVE TO FIND ONE PERSON BEFORE THE SUN SETS!
WE'RE ALMOST THERE!
I UNDERSTAND, BUT IF YOU COLLAPSE, MATTERS WILL GET WORSE.
IF THIS WAS FLAT LAND, WE COULD COVER 50 KM IN 3, 4 HOURS...
REMEMBER, WE'RE IN A MAGICAL JUNGLE FILLED WITH MAGICAL BEASTS.
HFF
HFF

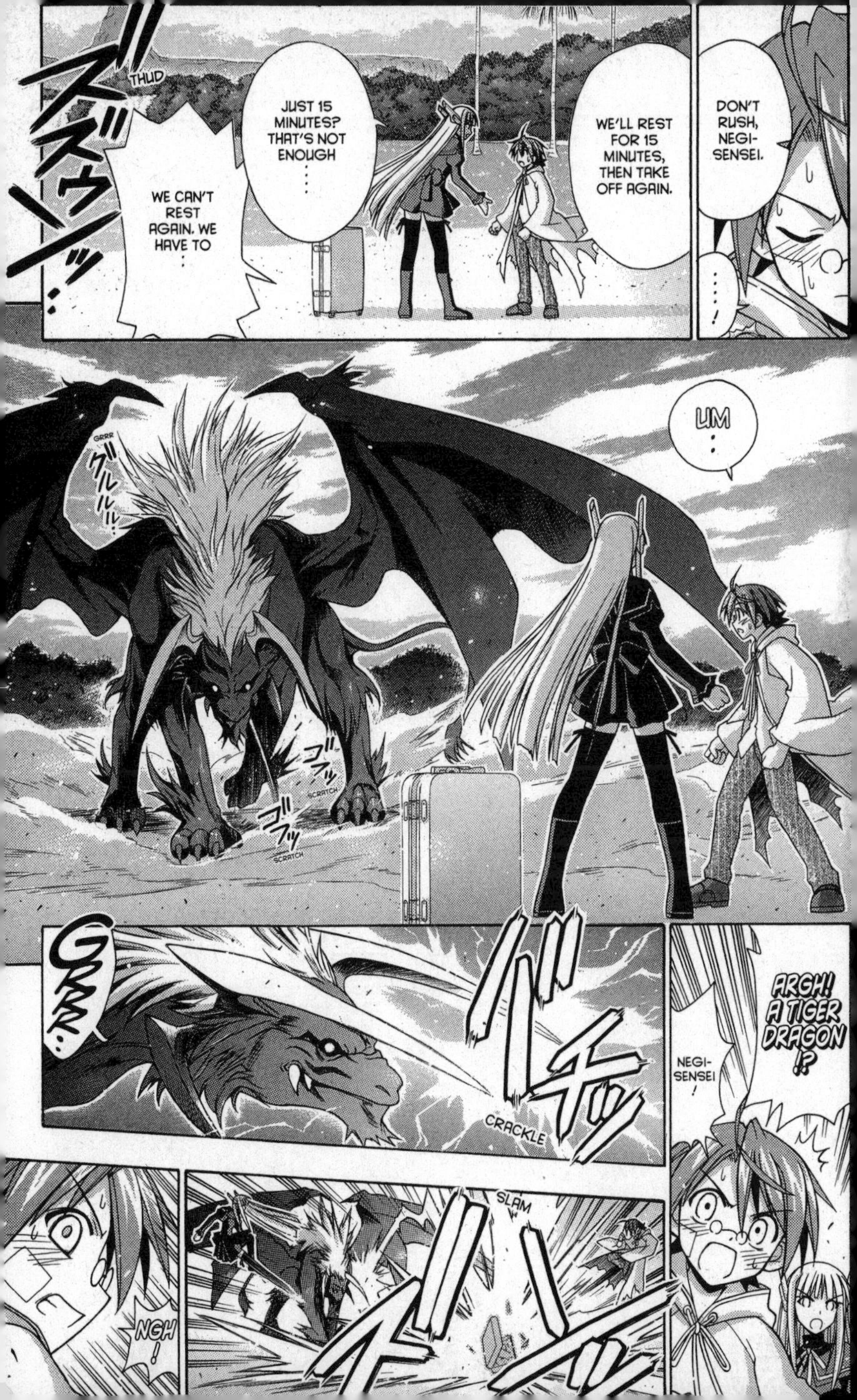
DON'T RUSH, NEGI-SENSEI.
...!
WE'LL REST FOR 15 MINUTES, THEN TAKE OFF AGAIN.
JUST 15 MINUTES? THAT'S NOT ENOUGH...
WE CAN'T REST AGAIN. WE HAVE TO...
THUD
UM...
GRRR
SCRATCH
SCRATCH
ARGH! A TIGER DRAGON!?
NEGI-SENSEI!
GRRR...
CRACKLE
SLAM
NGH!

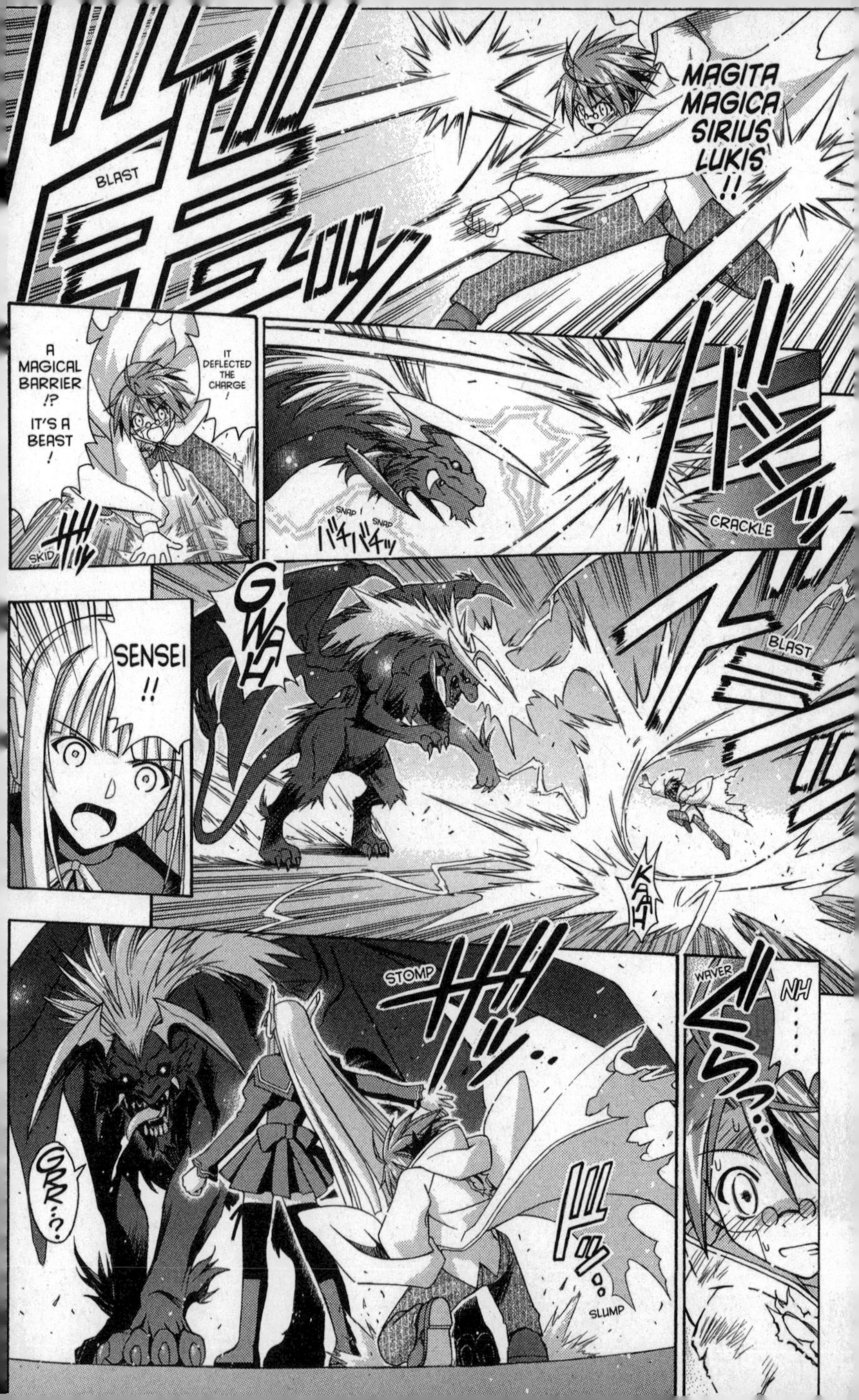

MAGITA MAGICA SIRIUS LUKIS !!
BLAST
CRACKLE
SNAP SNAP
バチバチッ
IT DEFLECTED THE CHARGE!
A MAGICAL BARRIER!?
IT'S A BEAST!
SKID
BLAST
GWAH
KRAH
SENSEI!!
WAVER
NH...
STOMP
SLUMP
GRR..?

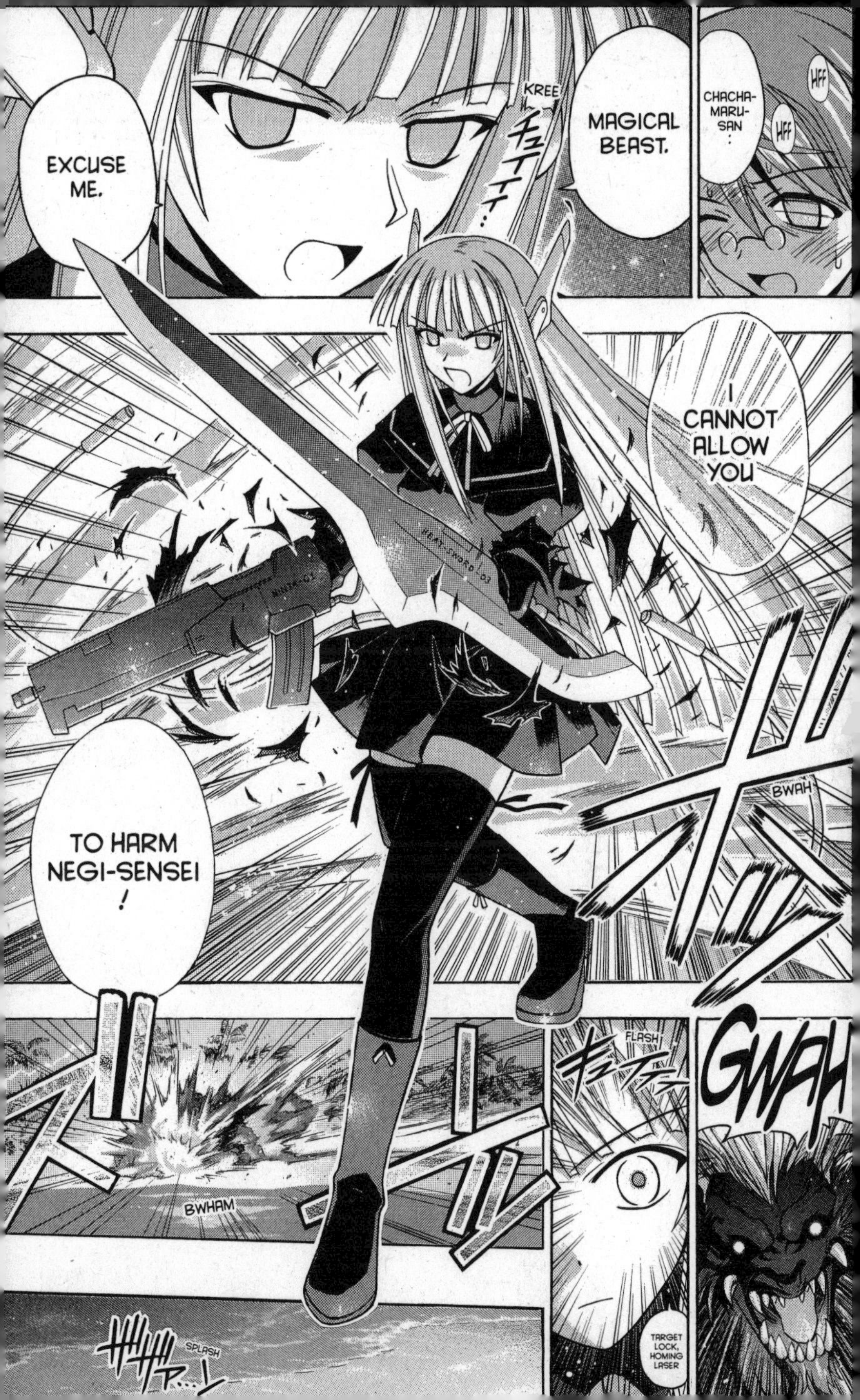
HFF
HFF
CHACHA-MARU-SAN...
MAGICAL BEAST.
KREE
EXCUSE ME.
I CANNOT ALLOW YOU
BWAH
TO HARM NEGI-SENSEI!
GWAH
TARGET LOCK, HOMING LASER
FLASH
BWHAM
SPLASH

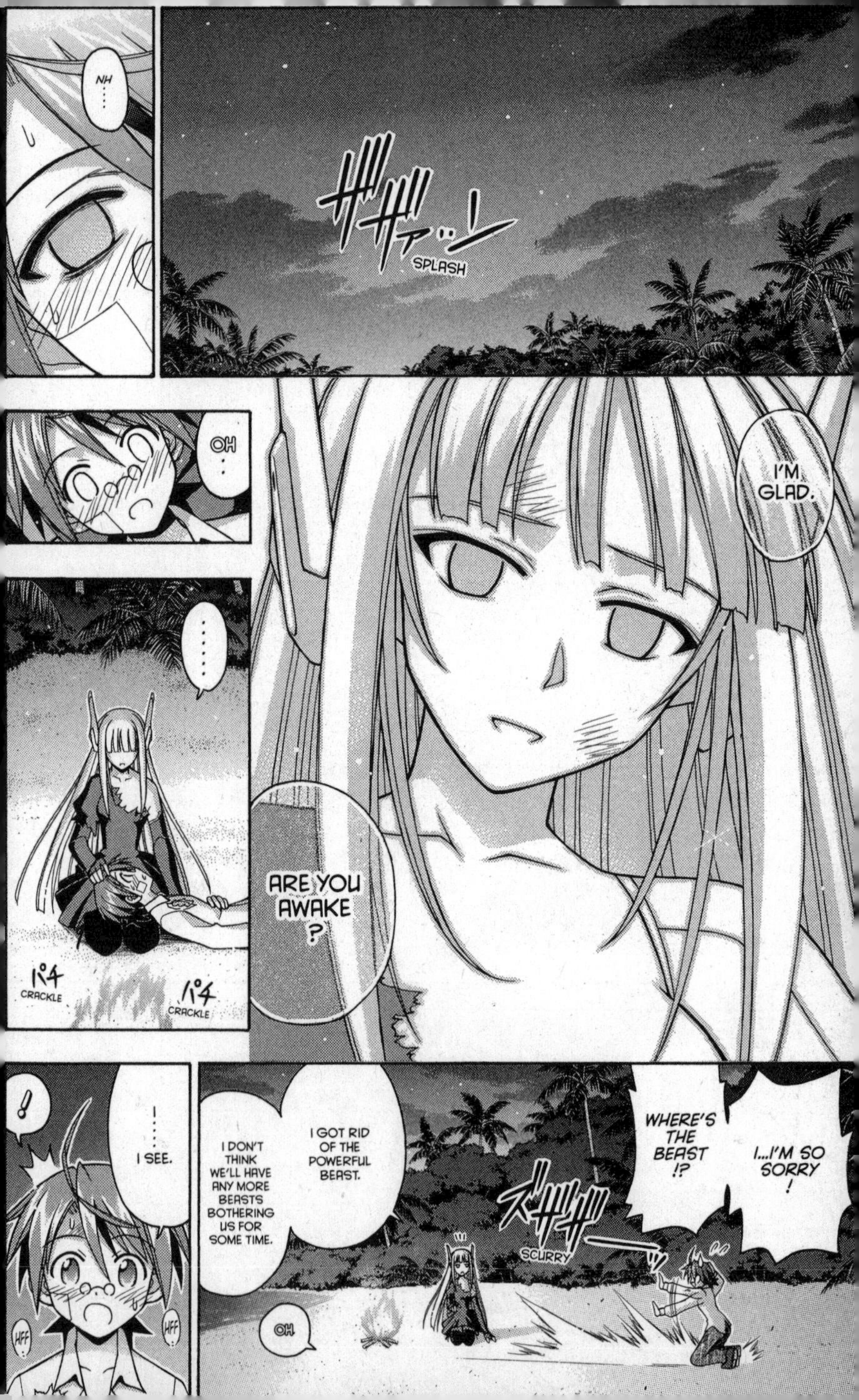
SPLASH
NH......
I'M GLAD.
ARE YOU AWAKE?
OH...
......
CRACKLE
CRACKLE
I...I'M SO SORRY!
WHERE'S THE BEAST!?
SCURRY
I GOT RID OF THE POWERFUL BEAST.
I DON'T THINK WE'LL HAVE ANY MORE BEASTS BOTHERING US FOR SOME TIME.
OH
!
I... I SEE.
HFF
HFF

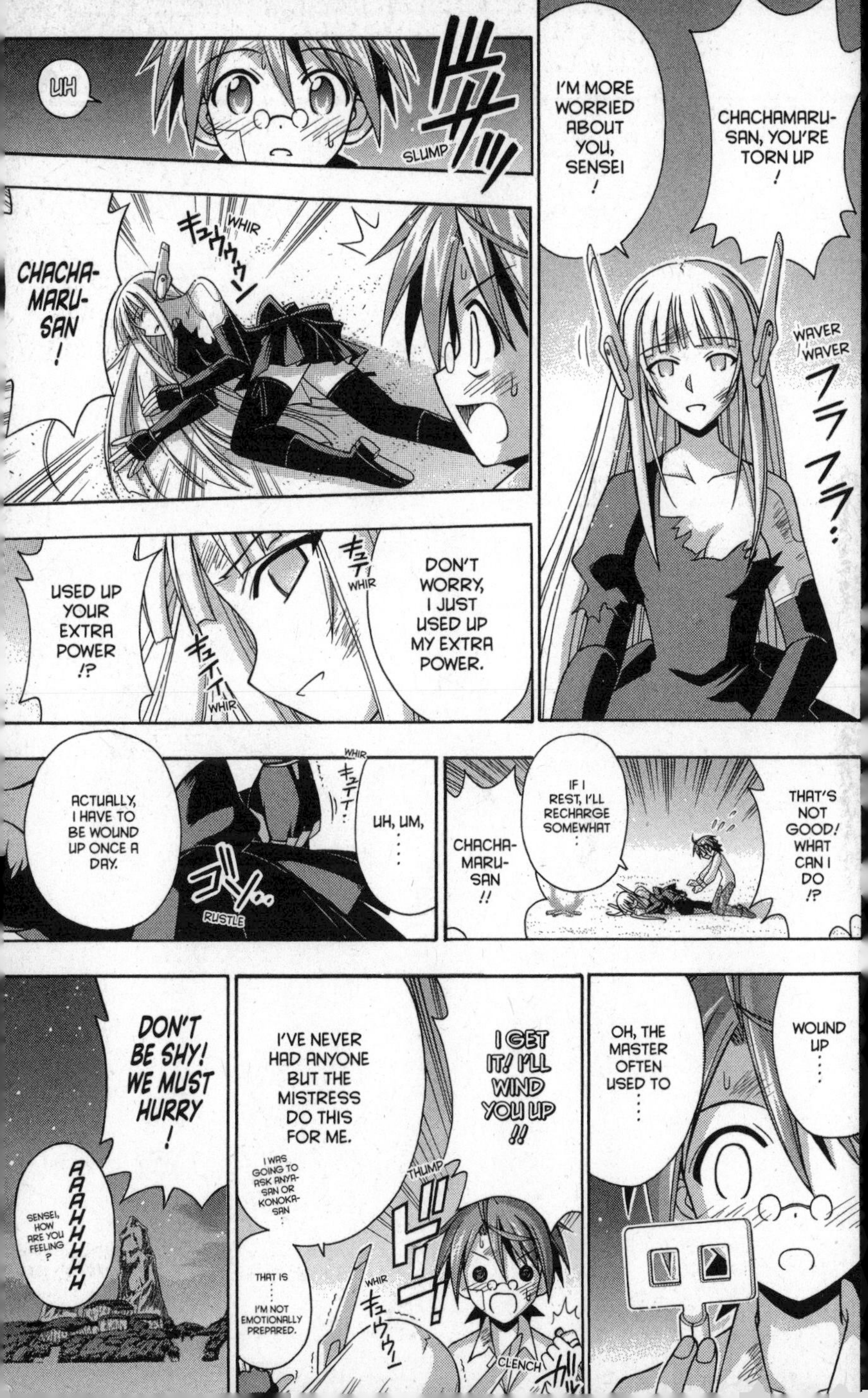
CHACHAMARU-SAN, YOU'RE TORN UP!
I'M MORE WORRIED ABOUT YOU, SENSEI!
WAVER WAVER
SLUMP
UH
WHIR
CHACHAMARU-SAN!
DON'T WORRY, I JUST USED UP MY EXTRA POWER.
WHIR
WHIR
USED UP YOUR EXTRA POWER!?
THAT'S NOT GOOD! WHAT CAN I DO!?
IF I REST, I'LL RECHARGE SOMEWHAT...
CHACHAMARU-SAN!!
WHIR
UH, UM, ...
ACTUALLY, I HAVE TO BE WOUND UP ONCE A DAY.
RUSTLE
WOUND UP....
OH, THE MASTER OFTEN USED TO....
I GET IT! I'LL WIND YOU UP!!
THUMP
I'VE NEVER HAD ANYONE BUT THE MISTRESS DO THIS FOR ME.
I WAS GOING TO ASK ANYA-SAN OR KONOKA-SAN...
THAT IS... I'M NOT EMOTIONALLY PREPARED.
WHIR
CLENCH
DON'T BE SHY! WE MUST HURRY!
AAAHHHHH
SENSEI, HOW ARE YOU FEELING?

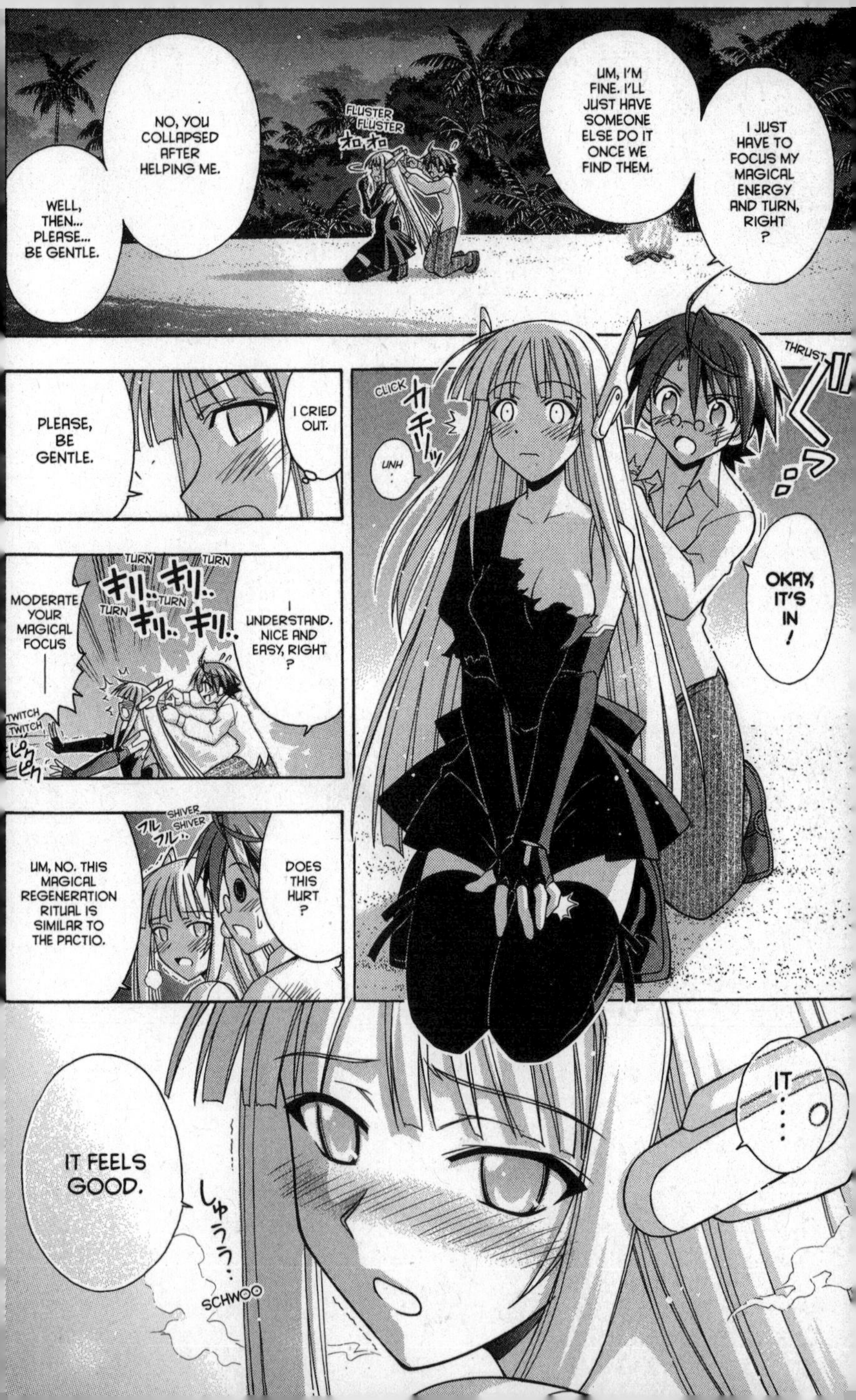
I JUST HAVE TO FOCUS MY MAGICAL ENERGY AND TURN, RIGHT?
UM, I'M FINE. I'LL JUST HAVE SOMEONE ELSE DO IT ONCE WE FIND THEM.
FLUSTER FLUSTER
NO, YOU COLLAPSED AFTER HELPING ME.
WELL, THEN... PLEASE... BE GENTLE.
THRUST
CLICK
UNH...
OKAY, IT'S IN!
I CRIED OUT.
PLEASE, BE GENTLE.
TURN TURN TURN TURN
I UNDERSTAND. NICE AND EASY, RIGHT?
MODERATE YOUR MAGICAL FOCUS—
TWITCH TWITCH
SHIVER SHIVER
DOES THIS HURT?
UM, NO. THIS MAGICAL REGENERATION RITUAL IS SIMILAR TO THE PACTIO.
IT...
IT FEELS GOOD.
SCHWOO

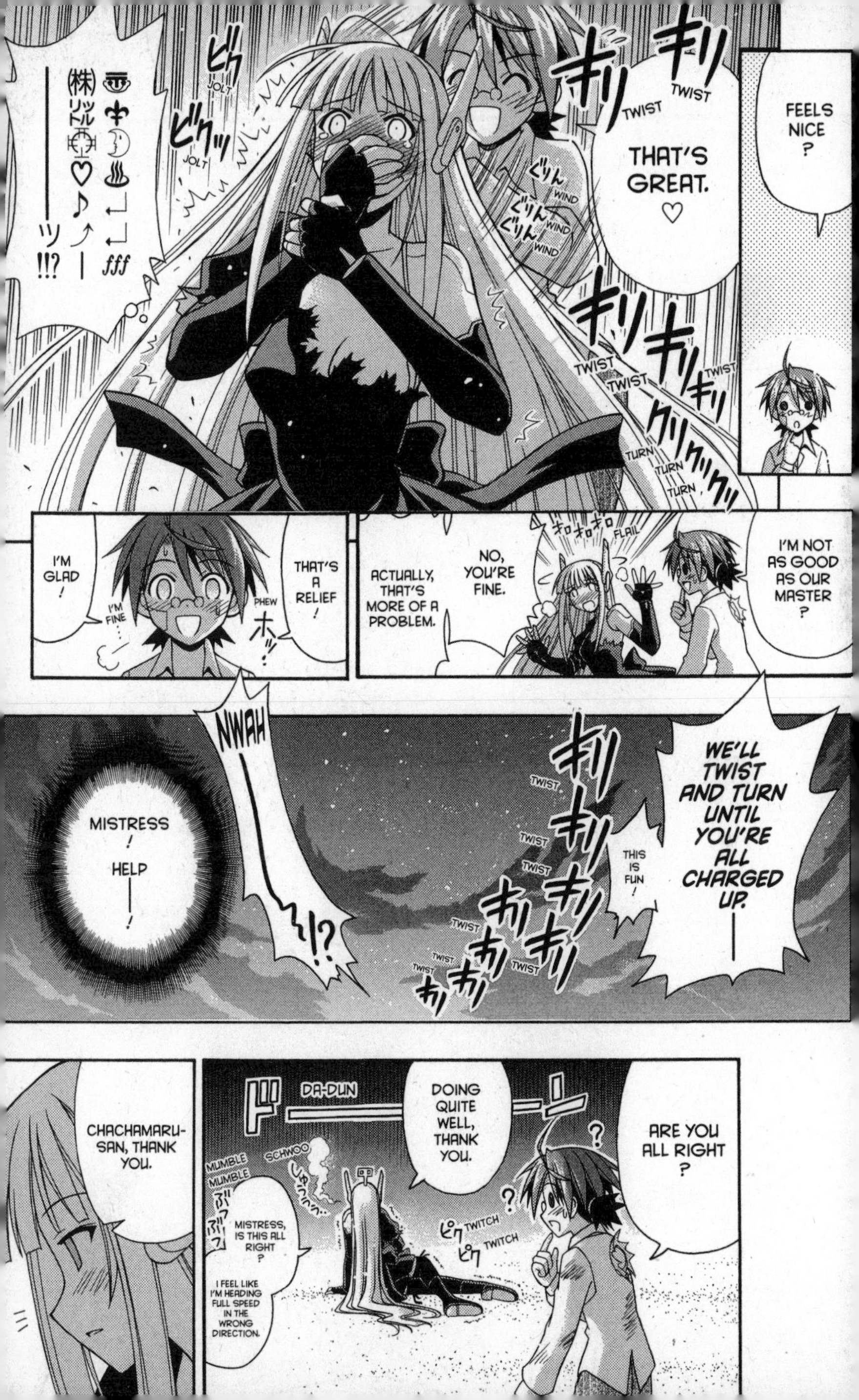
FEELS NICE?
TWIST
TWIST
THAT'S GREAT. ♡
WIND
WIND
WIND
JOLT
JOLT
(株)リットル
——ッ!!?
TWIST
TWIST
TWIST
TURN
TURN
TURN
I'M NOT AS GOOD AS OUR MASTER?
FLAIL
NO, YOU'RE FINE.
ACTUALLY, THAT'S MORE OF A PROBLEM.
THAT'S A RELIEF!
PHEW
I'M GLAD!
I'M FINE...
WE'LL TWIST AND TURN UNTIL YOU'RE ALL CHARGED UP.——
THIS IS FUN!
TWIST
TWIST
TWIST
TWIST
TWIST
TWIST
NWAH——~!?
MISTRESS! HELP——!
ARE YOU ALL RIGHT?
DOING QUITE WELL, THANK YOU.
DA-DUN
TWITCH
TWITCH
SCHWOO
MUMBLE
MUMBLE
MISTRESS, IS THIS ALL RIGHT?
I FEEL LIKE I'M HEADING FULL SPEED IN THE WRONG DIRECTION.
CHACHAMARU-SAN, THANK YOU.

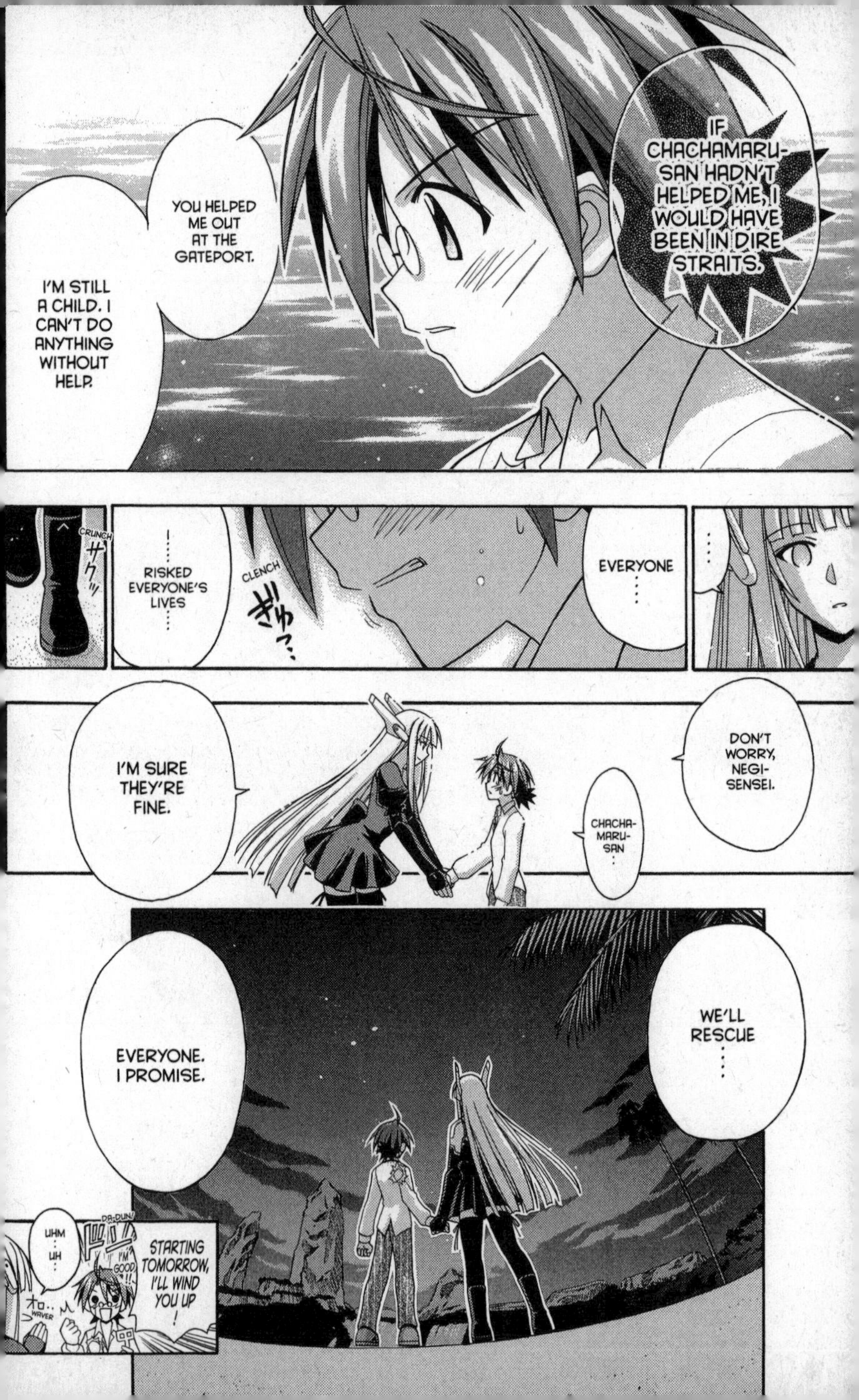
IF CHACHAMARU-SAN HADN'T HELPED ME, I WOULD HAVE BEEN IN DIRE STRAITS.
YOU HELPED ME OUT AT THE GATEPORT.
I'M STILL A CHILD. I CAN'T DO ANYTHING WITHOUT HELP.
......
EVERYONE ......
CLENCH
I ...... RISKED EVERYONE'S LIVES ......
CRUNCH
DON'T WORRY, NEGI-SENSEI.
CHACHAMARU-SAN ...
I'M SURE THEY'RE FINE.
WE'LL RESCUE ......
EVERYONE. I PROMISE.
STARTING TOMORROW, I'LL WIND YOU UP!
DA-DUN!
I'M GOOD!!
UHM ... UH ...
WAVER

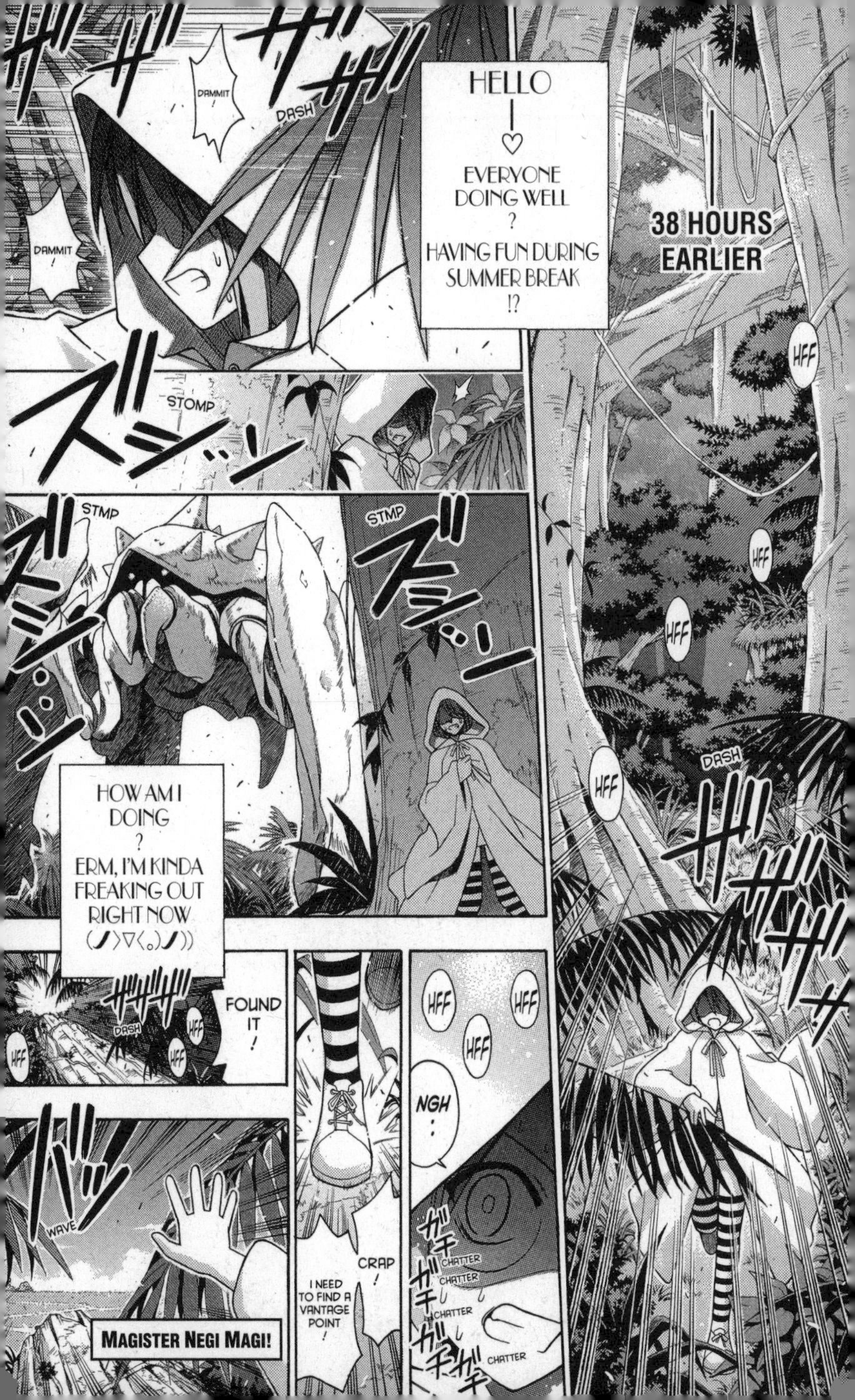

38 HOURS EARLIER
HFF
HFF
HFF
HFF
DASH
HELLO — ♡ EVERYONE DOING WELL ? HAVING FUN DURING SUMMER BREAK !?
DASH
DAMMIT !
DAMMIT !
STOMP
STMP
STMP
HOW AM I DOING ? ERM, I'M KINDA FREAKING OUT RIGHT NOW (ノ>▽<。)ノ))
HFF
HFF
HFF
NGH :
CHATTER
CHATTER
CHATTER
CHATTER
CRAP !
I NEED TO FIND A VANTAGE POINT
FOUND IT !
DASH
HFF
HFF
HFF
WAVE
Magister Negi Magi!

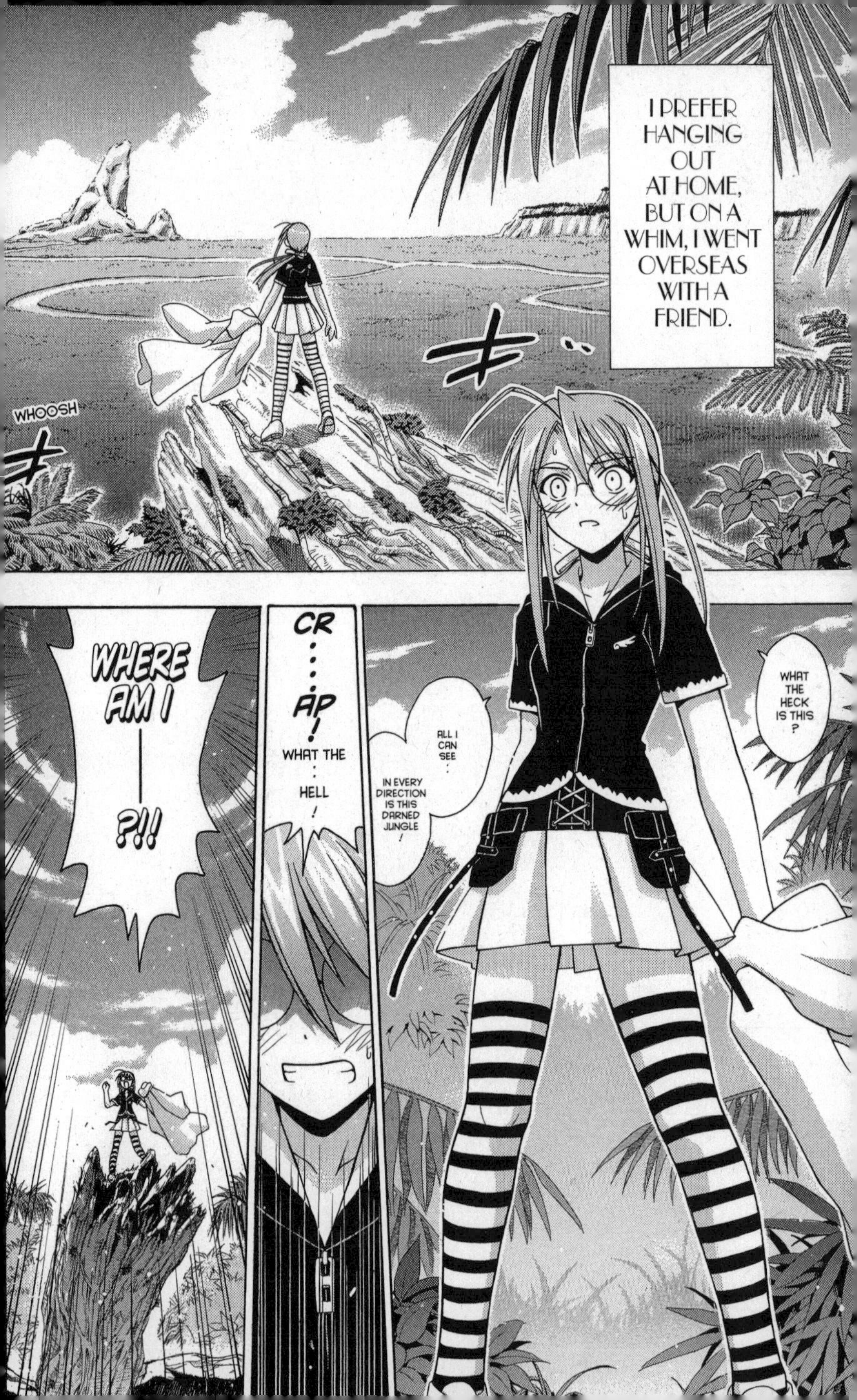
I PREFER HANGING OUT AT HOME, BUT ON A WHIM, I WENT OVERSEAS WITH A FRIEND.
WHOOSH
WHAT THE HECK IS THIS?
ALL I CAN SEE... IN EVERY DIRECTION IS THIS DARNED JUNGLE!
CR...AP! WHAT THE... HELL!
WHERE AM I——?!!

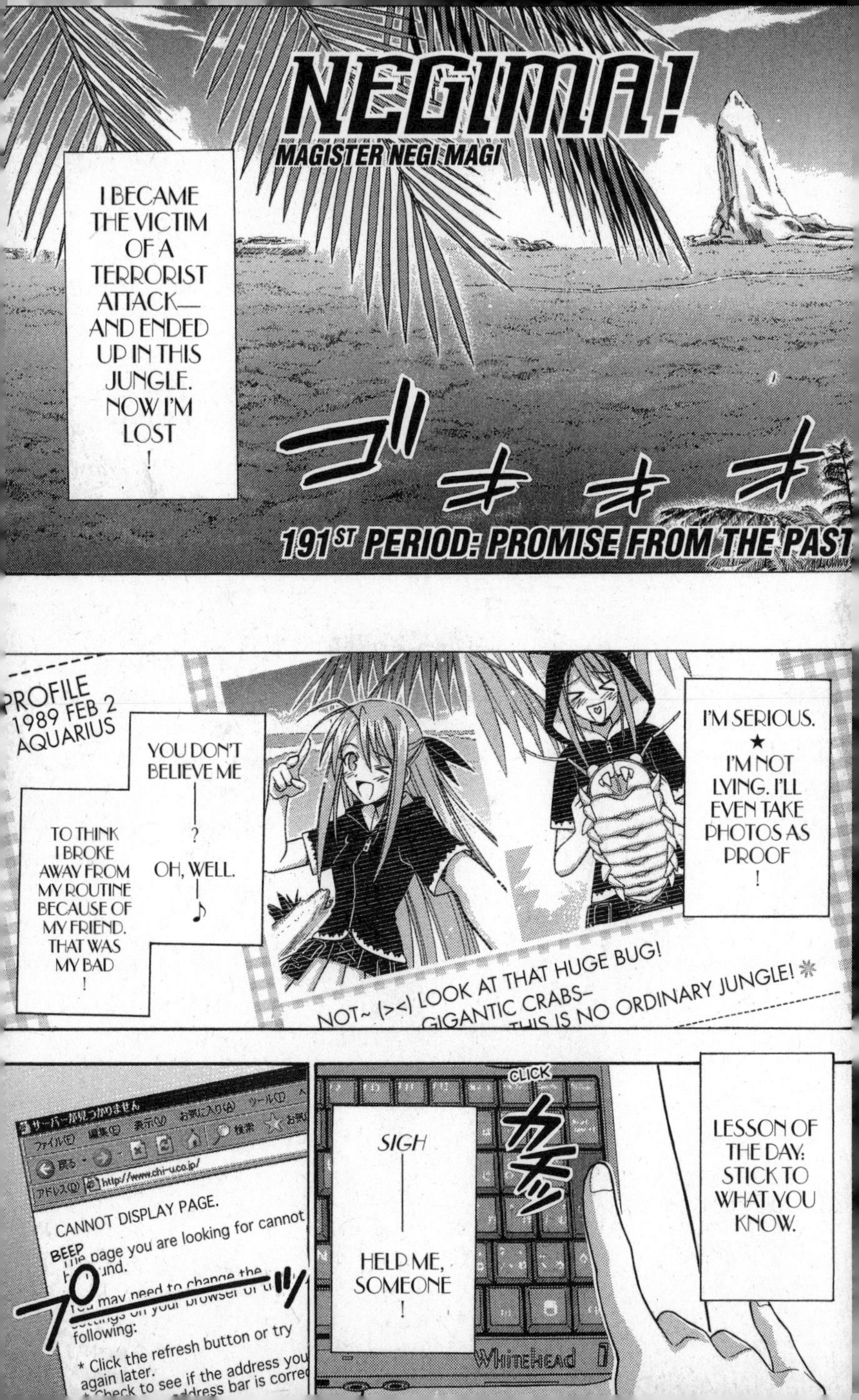
NEGIMA!
MAGISTER NEGI MAGI
I BECAME THE VICTIM OF A TERRORIST ATTACK— AND ENDED UP IN THIS JUNGLE. NOW I'M LOST !
191ST PERIOD: PROMISE FROM THE PAST
I'M SERIOUS. ★ I'M NOT LYING. I'LL EVEN TAKE PHOTOS AS PROOF !
YOU DON'T BELIEVE ME —? OH, WELL. —♪
TO THINK I BROKE AWAY FROM MY ROUTINE BECAUSE OF MY FRIEND. THAT WAS MY BAD !
PROFILE 1989 FEB 2 AQUARIUS
NOT~ (><) LOOK AT THAT HUGE BUG!
GIGANTIC CRABS–
THIS IS NO ORDINARY JUNGLE!
LESSON OF THE DAY: STICK TO WHAT YOU KNOW.
CLICK
SIGH — HELP ME, SOMEONE !
WHITEHEAD
サーバーが見つかりません
http://www.chi-u.co.jp/
CANNOT DISPLAY PAGE.
BEEP
The page you are looking for cannot be found.
You may need to change the settings on your browser or try the following:
* Click the refresh button or try again later.
* Check to see if the address you typed in the address bar is correct.

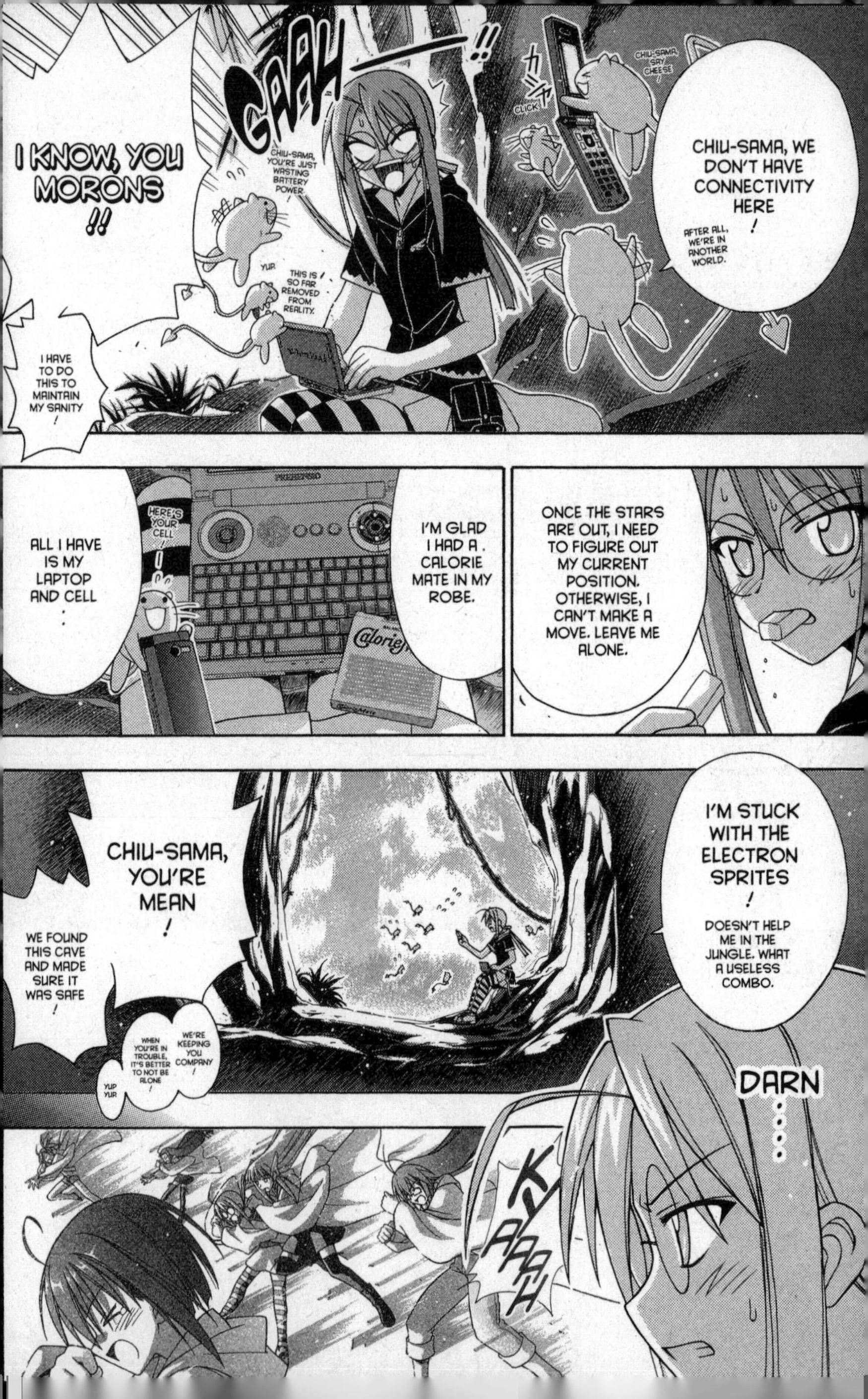

CHIU-SAMA, SAY CHEESE
CLICK
CHIU-SAMA, WE DON'T HAVE CONNECTIVITY HERE!
AFTER ALL, WE'RE IN ANOTHER WORLD.
GAAH—!!
CHIU-SAMA, YOU'RE JUST WASTING BATTERY POWER!
I KNOW, YOU MORONS!!
THIS IS SO FAR REMOVED FROM REALITY.
YUP
I HAVE TO DO THIS TO MAINTAIN MY SANITY!
ONCE THE STARS ARE OUT, I NEED TO FIGURE OUT MY CURRENT POSITION. OTHERWISE, I CAN'T MAKE A MOVE. LEAVE ME ALONE.
I'M GLAD I HAD A CALORIE MATE IN MY ROBE.
HERE'S YOUR CELL!
ALL I HAVE IS MY LAPTOP AND CELL...
I'M STUCK WITH THE ELECTRON SPRITES!
DOESN'T HELP ME IN THE JUNGLE. WHAT A USELESS COMBO.
CHIU-SAMA, YOU'RE MEAN!
WE FOUND THIS CAVE AND MADE SURE IT WAS SAFE!
WE'RE KEEPING YOU COMPANY!
WHEN YOU'RE IN TROUBLE, IT'S BETTER TO NOT BE ALONE!
YUP YUP
DARN....
KYAAAH

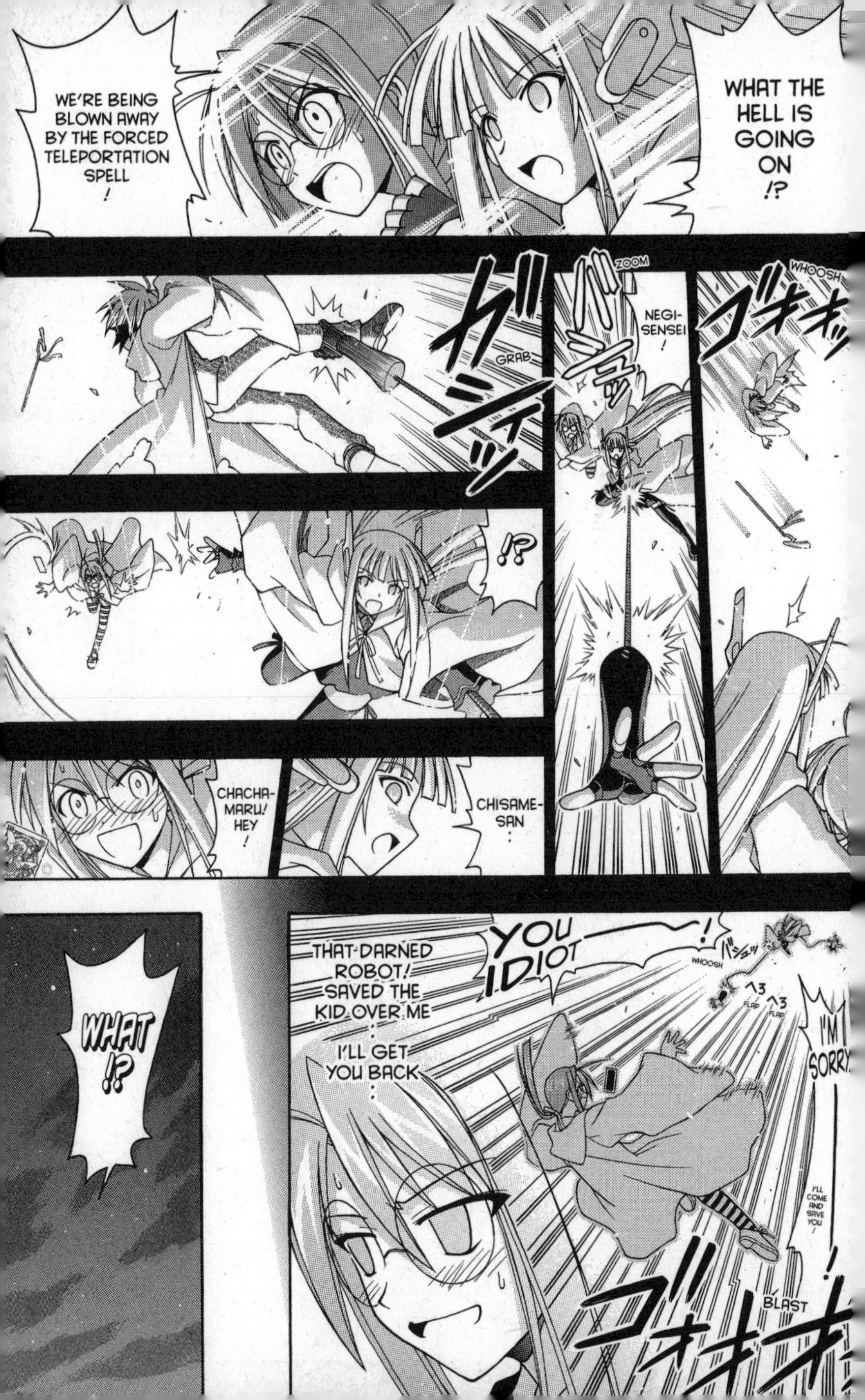
WHAT THE HELL IS GOING ON !?
WE'RE BEING BLOWN AWAY BY THE FORCED TELEPORTATION SPELL !
WHOOSH
ZOOM
NEGI-SENSEI !
GRAB
!?
CHISAME-SAN ...
CHACHAMARU! HEY !
WHOOSH
FLAP FLAP
I'M SORRY
YOU IDIOT—!
THAT DARNED ROBOT! SAVED THE KID OVER ME ...
I'LL GET YOU BACK ...
I'LL COME AND SAVE YOU !
BLAST
WHAT !?

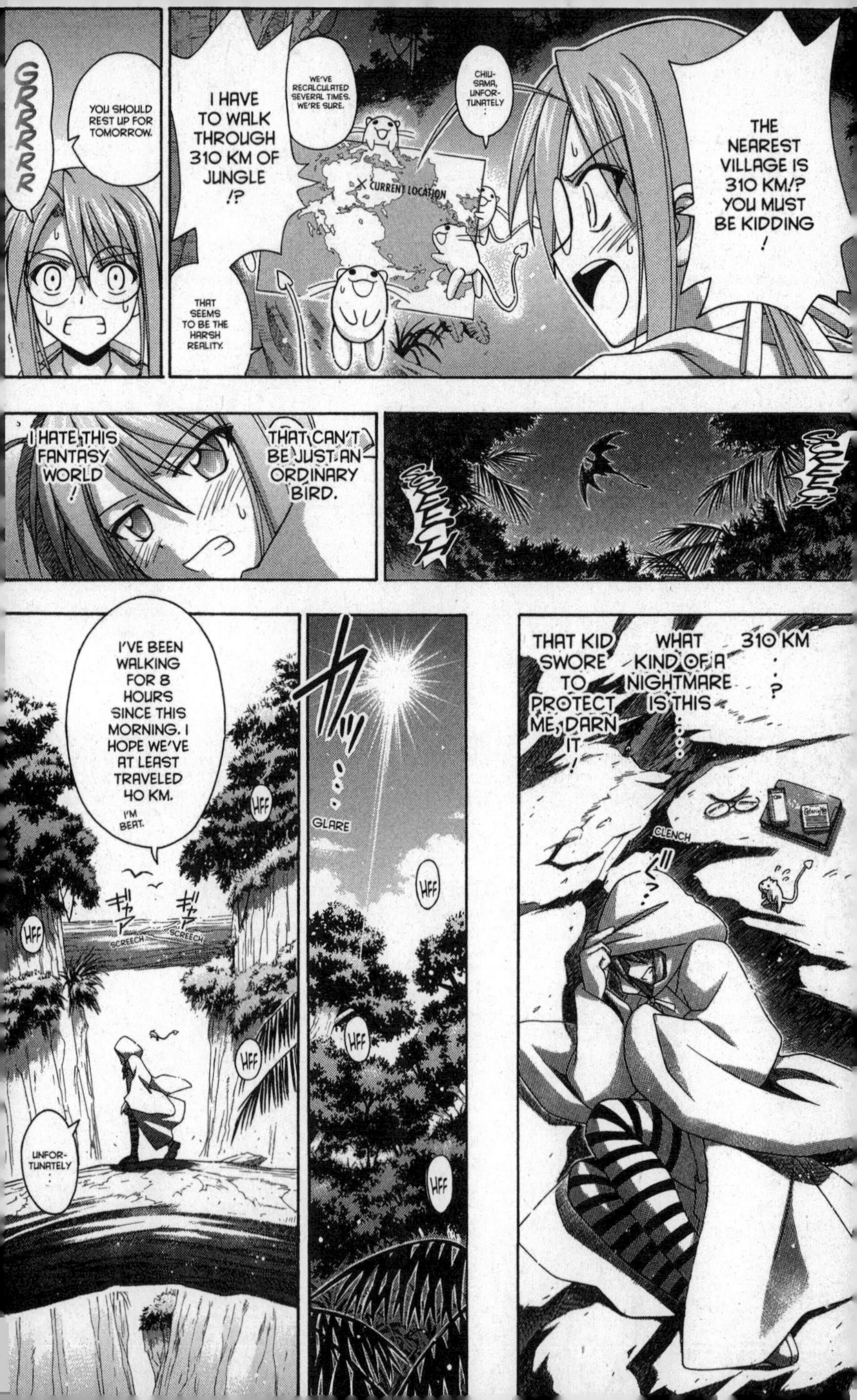

THE NEAREST VILLAGE IS 310 KM!? YOU MUST BE KIDDING!
CHIU-SAMA, UNFORTUNATELY:
WE'VE RECALCULATED SEVERAL TIMES. WE'RE SURE.
CURRENT LOCATION
I HAVE TO WALK THROUGH 310 KM OF JUNGLE!?
THAT SEEMS TO BE THE HARSH REALITY.
YOU SHOULD REST UP FOR TOMORROW.
GRRRRR
THAT CAN'T BE JUST AN ORDINARY BIRD.
I HATE THIS FANTASY WORLD!
310 KM...?
WHAT KIND OF A NIGHTMARE IS THIS.....
THAT KID SWORE TO PROTECT ME, DARN IT!
CLENCH
GLARE
HFF
HFF
HFF
I'VE BEEN WALKING FOR 8 HOURS SINCE THIS MORNING. I HOPE WE'VE AT LEAST TRAVELED 40 KM.
I'M BEAT.
HFF
HFF
SCREECH
SCREECH
HFF
UNFORTUNATELY...

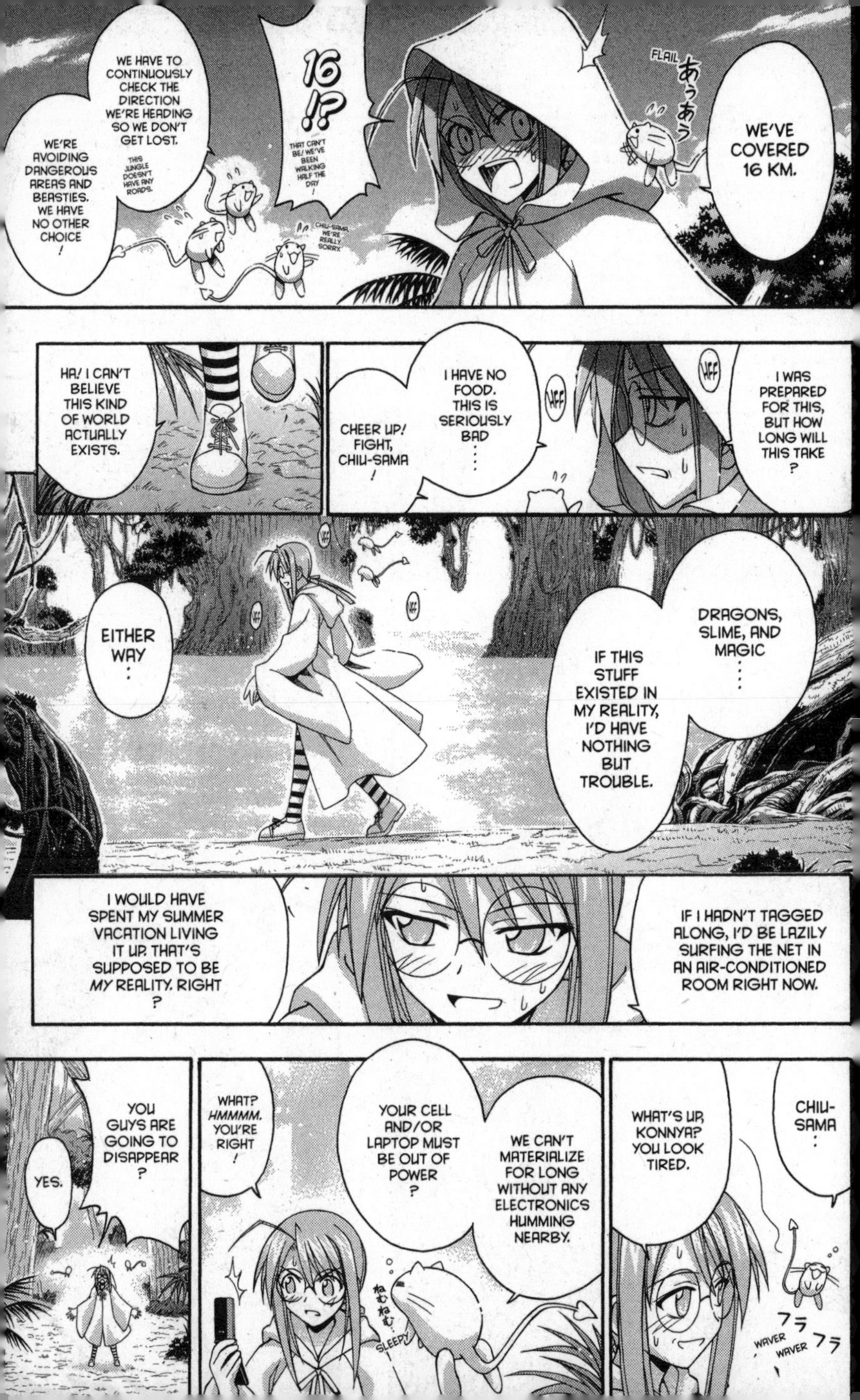
FLAIL あうあう
WE'VE COVERED 16 KM.
16!?
THAT CAN'T BE! WE'VE BEEN WALKING HALF THE DAY!
CHIU-SAMA, WE'RE REALLY SORRY.
WE HAVE TO CONTINUOUSLY CHECK THE DIRECTION WE'RE HEADING SO WE DON'T GET LOST.
THIS JUNGLE DOESN'T HAVE ANY ROADS.
WE'RE AVOIDING DANGEROUS AREAS AND BEASTIES. WE HAVE NO OTHER CHOICE!
I WAS PREPARED FOR THIS, BUT HOW LONG WILL THIS TAKE?
HFF
HFF
I HAVE NO FOOD. THIS IS SERIOUSLY BAD...
CHEER UP! FIGHT, CHIU-SAMA!
HA! I CAN'T BELIEVE THIS KIND OF WORLD ACTUALLY EXISTS.
DRAGONS, SLIME, AND MAGIC....
IF THIS STUFF EXISTED IN MY REALITY, I'D HAVE NOTHING BUT TROUBLE.
EITHER WAY...
IF I HADN'T TAGGED ALONG, I'D BE LAZILY SURFING THE NET IN AN AIR-CONDITIONED ROOM RIGHT NOW.
I WOULD HAVE SPENT MY SUMMER VACATION LIVING IT UP. THAT'S SUPPOSED TO BE *MY* REALITY. RIGHT?
CHIU-SAMA...
WHAT'S UP, KONNYA? YOU LOOK TIRED.
フラ WAVER フラ WAVER
WE CAN'T MATERIALIZE FOR LONG WITHOUT ANY ELECTRONICS HUMMING NEARBY.
YOUR CELL AND/OR LAPTOP MUST BE OUT OF POWER?
WHAT? *HMMMM.* YOU'RE RIGHT!
ねむねむ SLEEPY...
YOU GUYS ARE GOING TO DISAPPEAR?
YES.

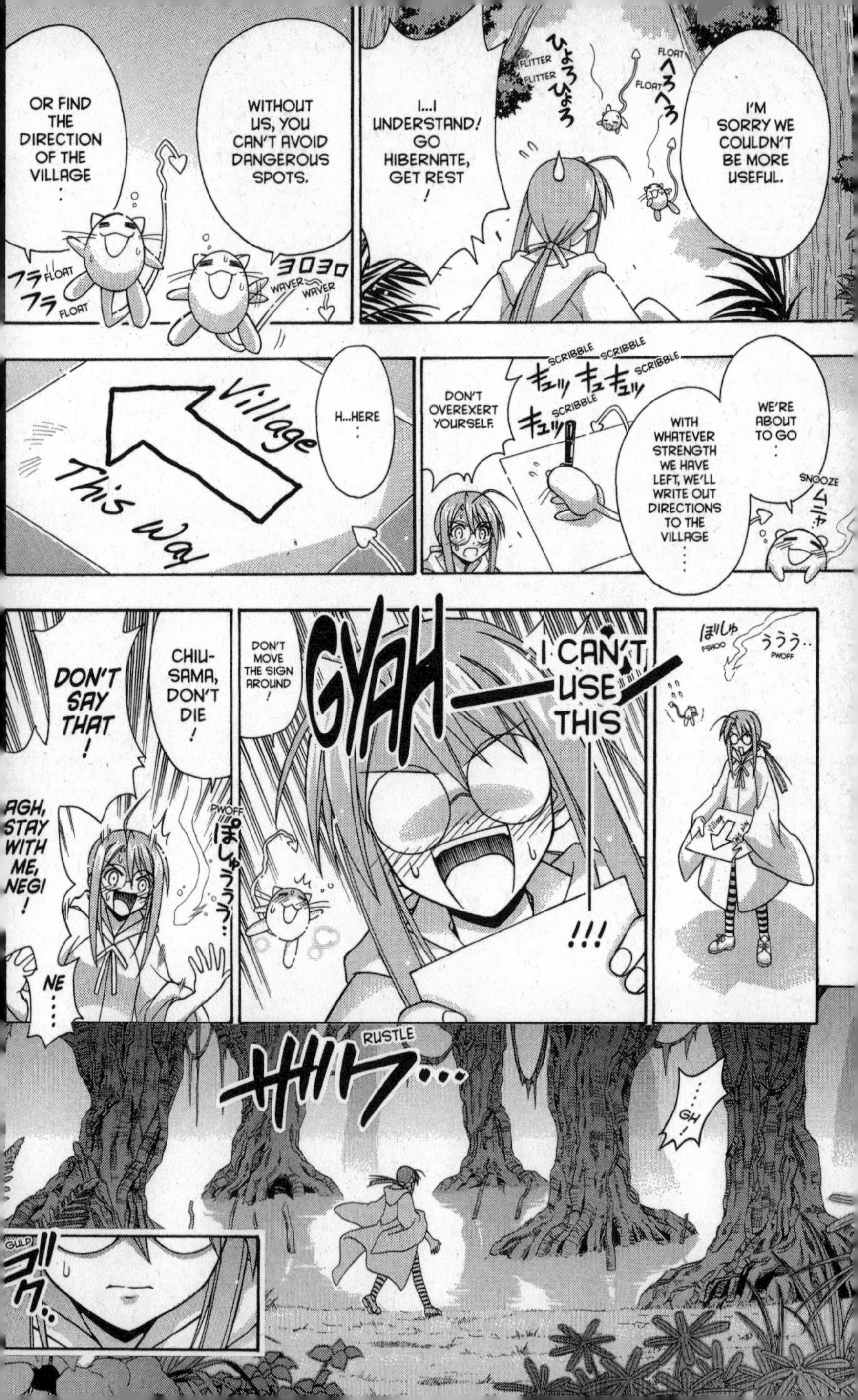
I'M SORRY WE COULDN'T BE MORE USEFUL.
へろへろ
FLOAT FLOAT
ひょろひょろ
FLITTER FLITTER
I...I UNDERSTAND! GO HIBERNATE, GET REST!
WITHOUT US, YOU CAN'T AVOID DANGEROUS SPOTS.
ヨロヨロ
WAVER WAVER
OR FIND THE DIRECTION OF THE VILLAGE...
フラフラ
FLOAT FLOAT
WE'RE ABOUT TO GO...
ムニャ
SNOOZE
WITH WHATEVER STRENGTH WE HAVE LEFT, WE'LL WRITE OUT DIRECTIONS TO THE VILLAGE...
キュッ キュ キュッ キュッ
SCRIBBLE SCRIBBLE SCRIBBLE SCRIBBLE
DON'T OVEREXERT YOURSELF.
H...HERE...
Village
This way
ぽしゅ
FSHOO
ううう..
PWOFF
I CAN'T USE THIS
GYAH—
DON'T MOVE THE SIGN AROUND!
!!!
CHIU-SAMA, DON'T DIE!
DON'T SAY THAT!
ぽしゅううう...
PWOFF
AGH, STAY WITH ME, NEGI!
NE...
ザザッ...
RUSTLE
...GH!
ゴクッ..
GULP

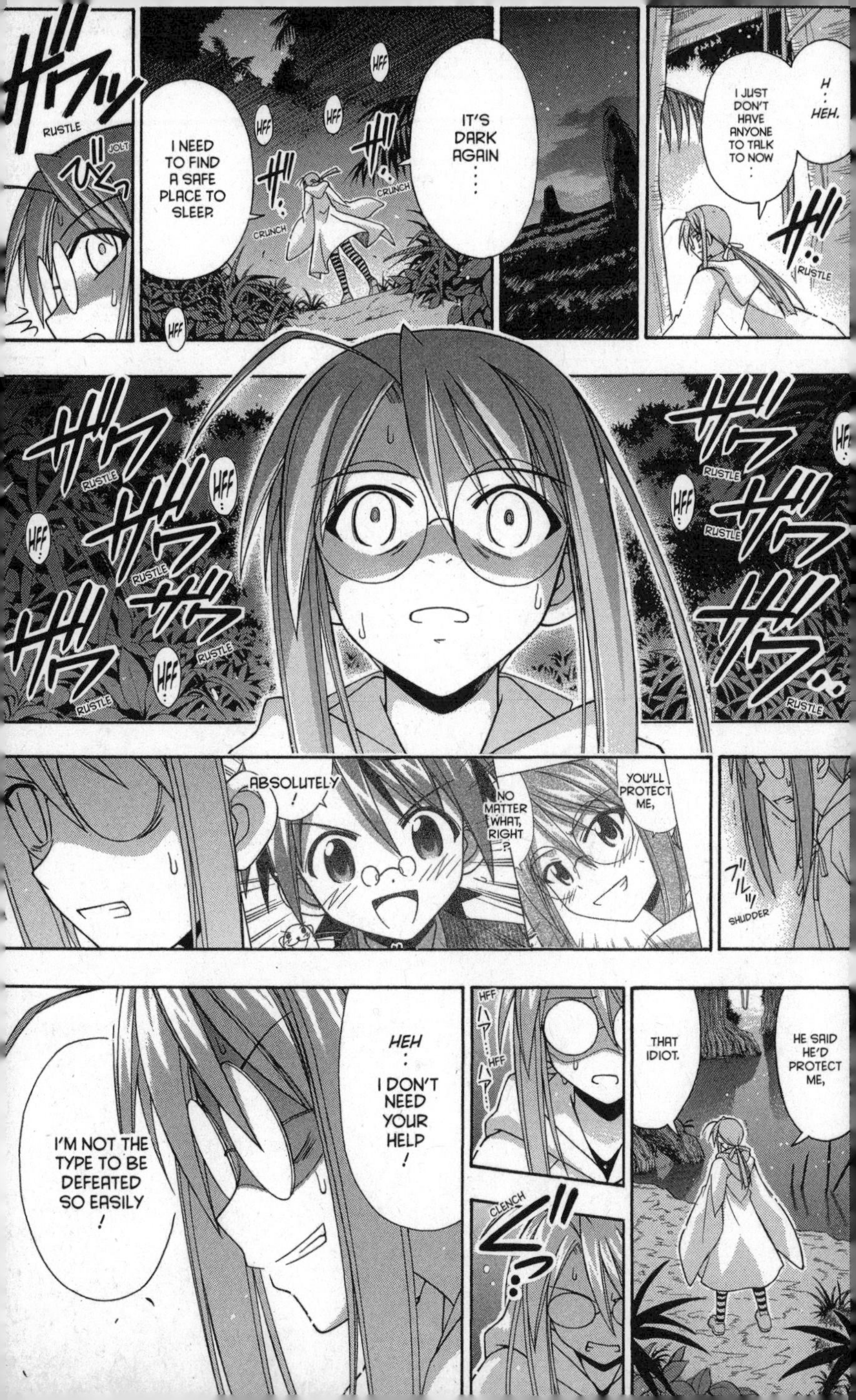

H... HEH.
I JUST DON'T HAVE ANYONE TO TALK TO NOW...
RUSTLE
IT'S DARK AGAIN...
HFF
HFF
CRUNCH
HFF
CRUNCH
I NEED TO FIND A SAFE PLACE TO SLEEP.
HFF
RUSTLE
JOLT
HFF
RUSTLE
HFF
RUSTLE
RUSTLE
HFF
RUSTLE
HFF
RUSTLE
HFF
RUSTLE
SHUDDER
YOU'LL PROTECT ME,
NO MATTER WHAT, RIGHT?
ABSOLUTELY!
HE SAID HE'D PROTECT ME,
THAT IDIOT.
HFF
HFF
CLENCH
HEH... I DON'T NEED YOUR HELP!
I'M NOT THE TYPE TO BE DEFEATED SO EASILY!

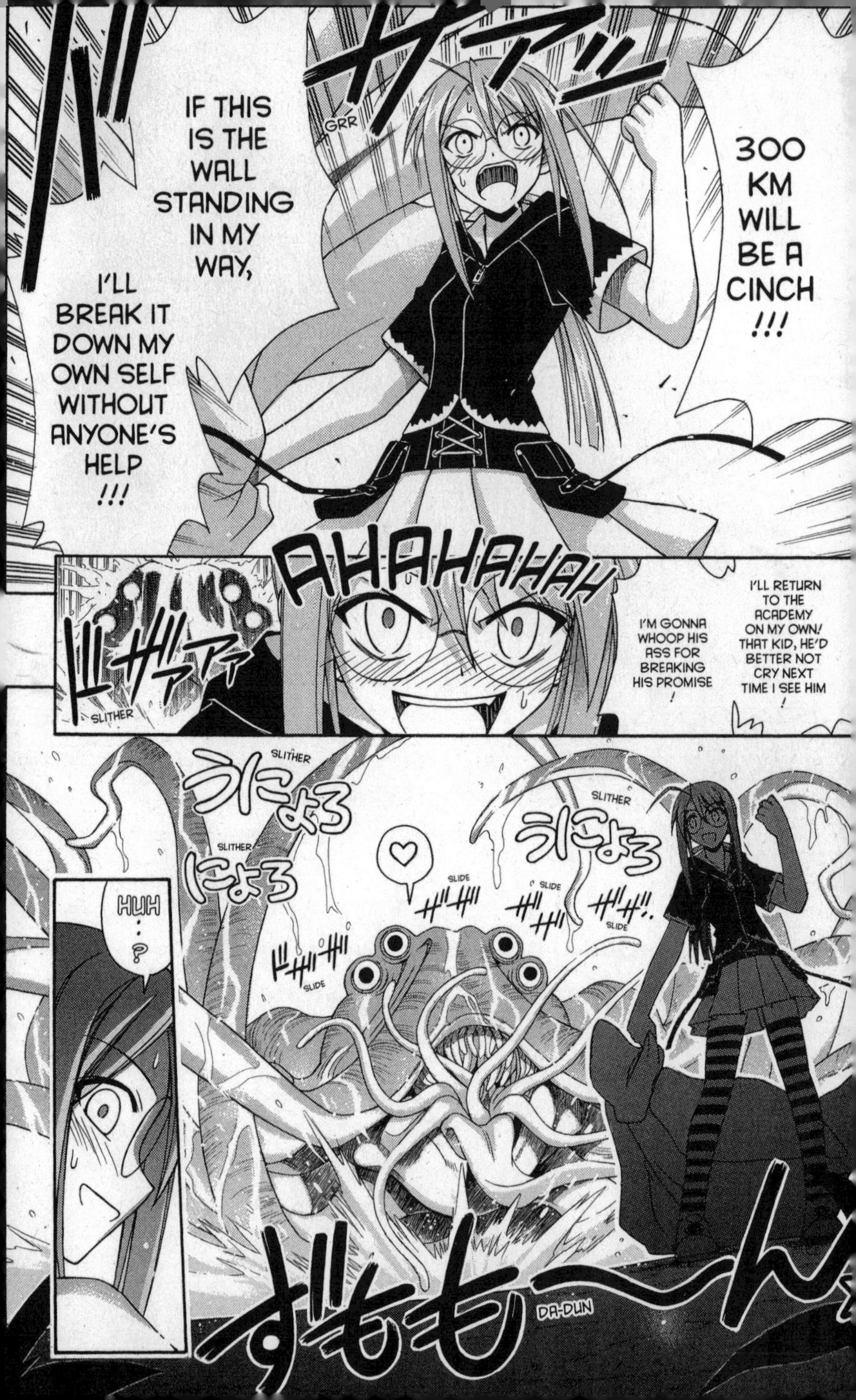

GRR
300 KM WILL BE A CINCH!!!
IF THIS IS THE WALL STANDING IN MY WAY,
I'LL BREAK IT DOWN MY OWN SELF WITHOUT ANYONE'S HELP!!!
AHAHAHAHAH
I'LL RETURN TO THE ACADEMY ON MY OWN! THAT KID, HE'D BETTER NOT CRY NEXT TIME I SEE HIM!
I'M GONNA WHOOP HIS ASS FOR BREAKING HIS PROMISE!
SLITHER
SLITHER
うにょろ
SLITHER
うにょろ
SLITHER
にょろ
SLIDE
SLIDE
SLIDE
SLIDE
DA-DUN
HUH...?

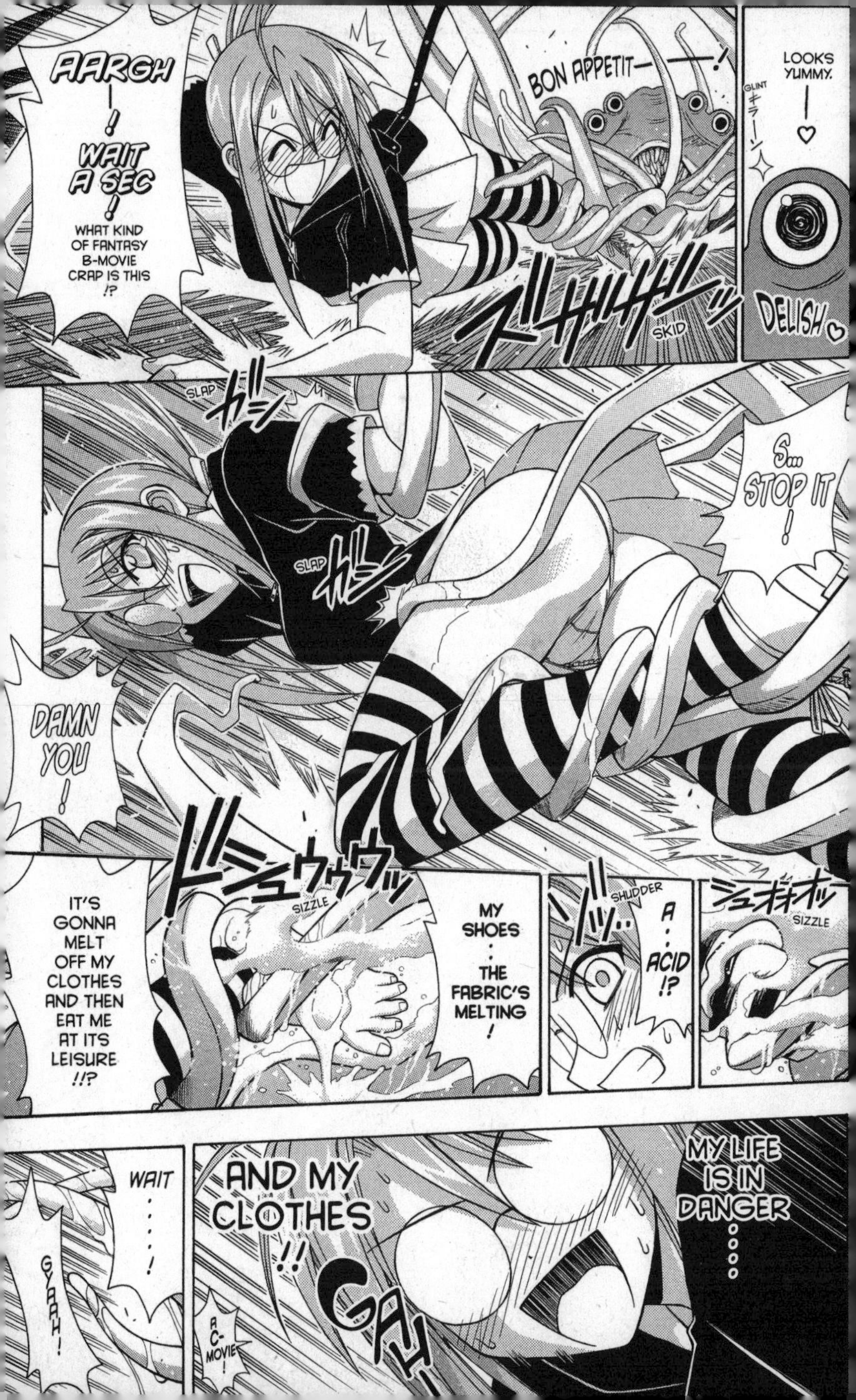
LOOKS YUMMY. ♥
GLINT
DELISH♥
BON APPETIT—!
AARGH! WAIT A SEC!
WHAT KIND OF FANTASY B-MOVIE CRAP IS THIS !?
SKID
SLAP
S... STOP IT!
SLAP
DAMN YOU!
SIZZLE
SHUDDER
A... ACID!?
MY SHOES... THE FABRIC'S MELTING!
SIZZLE
IT'S GONNA MELT OFF MY CLOTHES AND THEN EAT ME AT ITS LEISURE!!?
MY LIFE IS IN DANGER.....
AND MY CLOTHES!!
GAH
A C-MOVIE!
WAIT.....!
GYAAH!

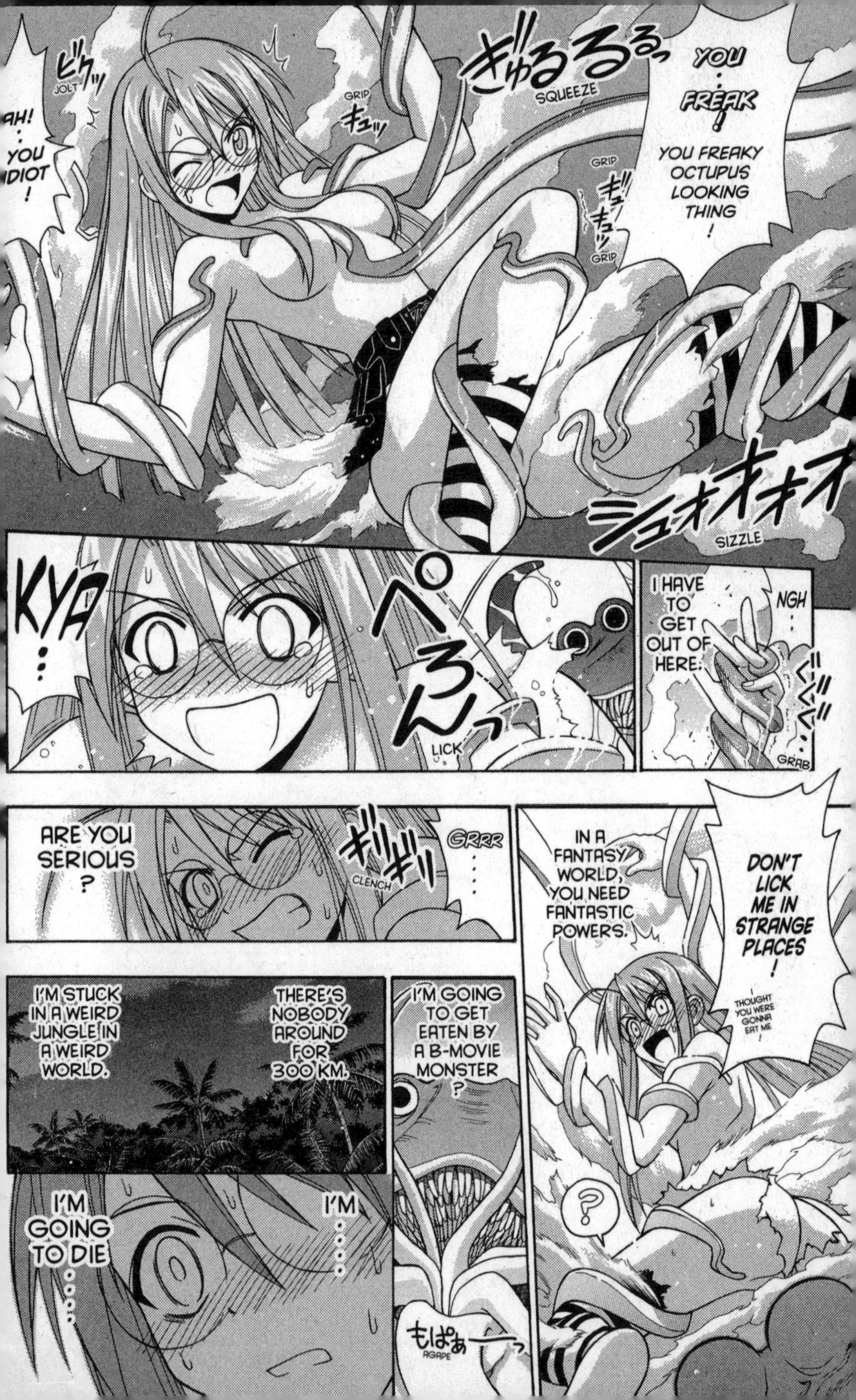

YOU... FREAK! YOU FREAKY OCTUPUS LOOKING THING!
きゅるるるっ
SQUEEZE
GRIP
ギュッ
GRIP
ギュ
ギュッ
GRIP
ビクッ
JOLT
AH!... YOU IDIOT!
シュオオオオ
SIZZLE
I HAVE TO GET OUT OF HERE.
NGH...
ぐぐぐ...
GRAB
ぺろんっ
LICK
KYA...
DON'T LICK ME IN STRANGE PLACES!
I THOUGHT YOU WERE GONNA EAT ME!
IN A FANTASY WORLD, YOU NEED FANTASTIC POWERS.
?
GRRR...
ギリギリ
CLENCH
ARE YOU SERIOUS?
THERE'S NOBODY AROUND FOR 300 KM.
I'M STUCK IN A WEIRD JUNGLE IN A WEIRD WORLD.
I'M GOING TO GET EATEN BY A B-MOVIE MONSTER?
もぱぁーっ
AGAPE
I'M....
I'M GOING TO DIE....

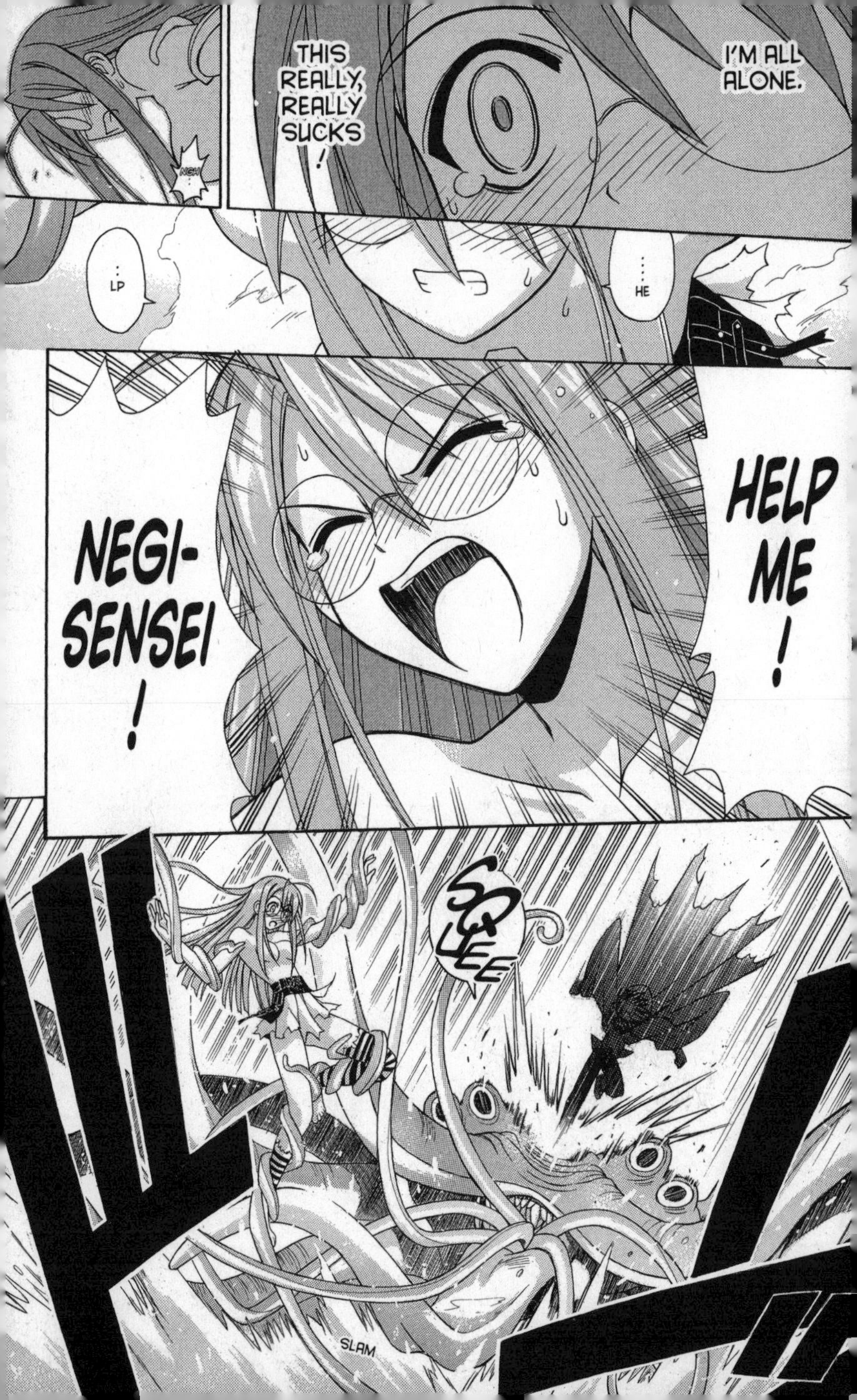
I'M ALL ALONE.
THIS REALLY, REALLY SUCKS!
NGH
...HE
...LP
HELP ME!
NEGI-SENSEI!
SQUEE
SLAM

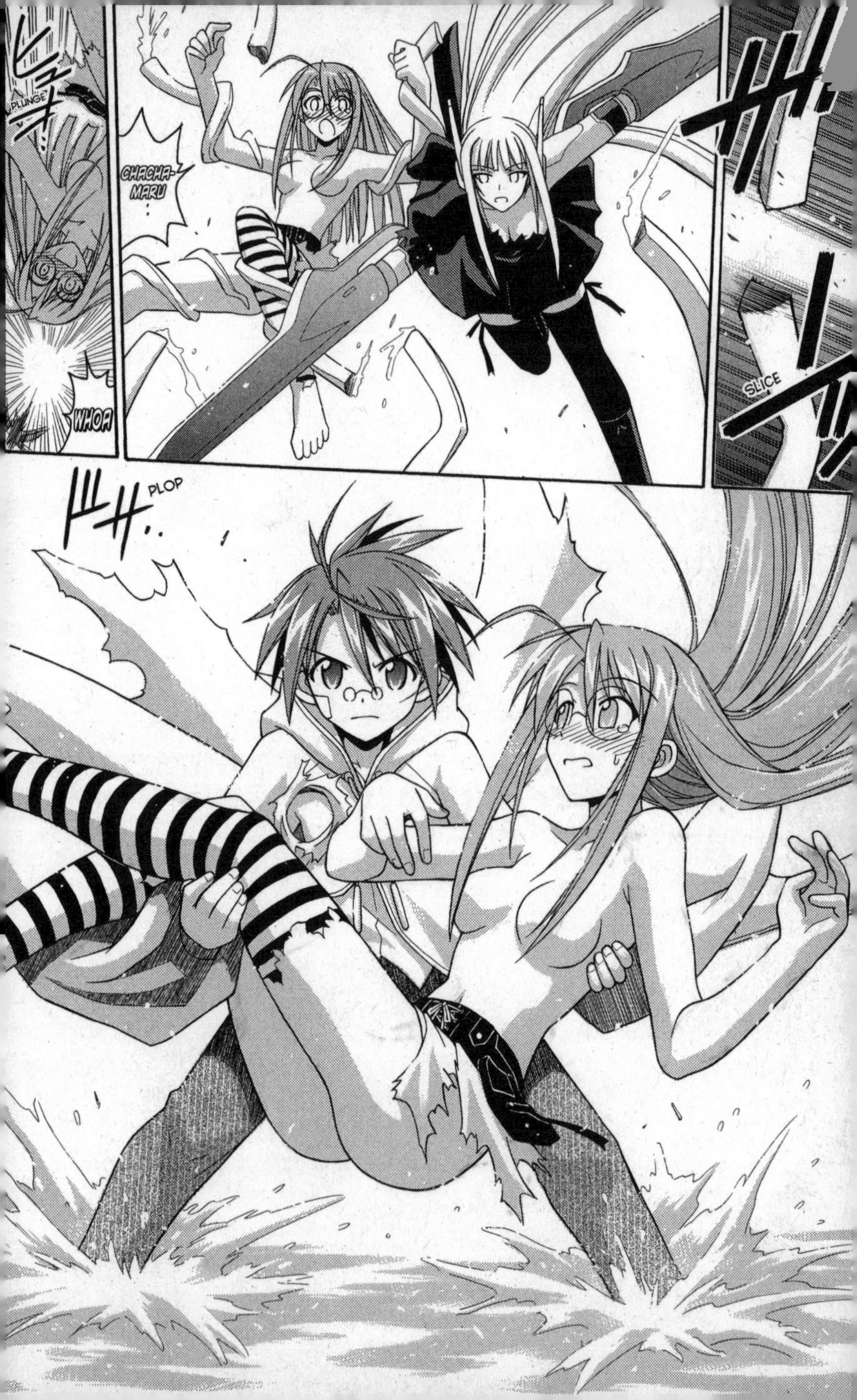
SLICE
CHACHA-MARU...!
PLUNGE
WHOA
PLOP

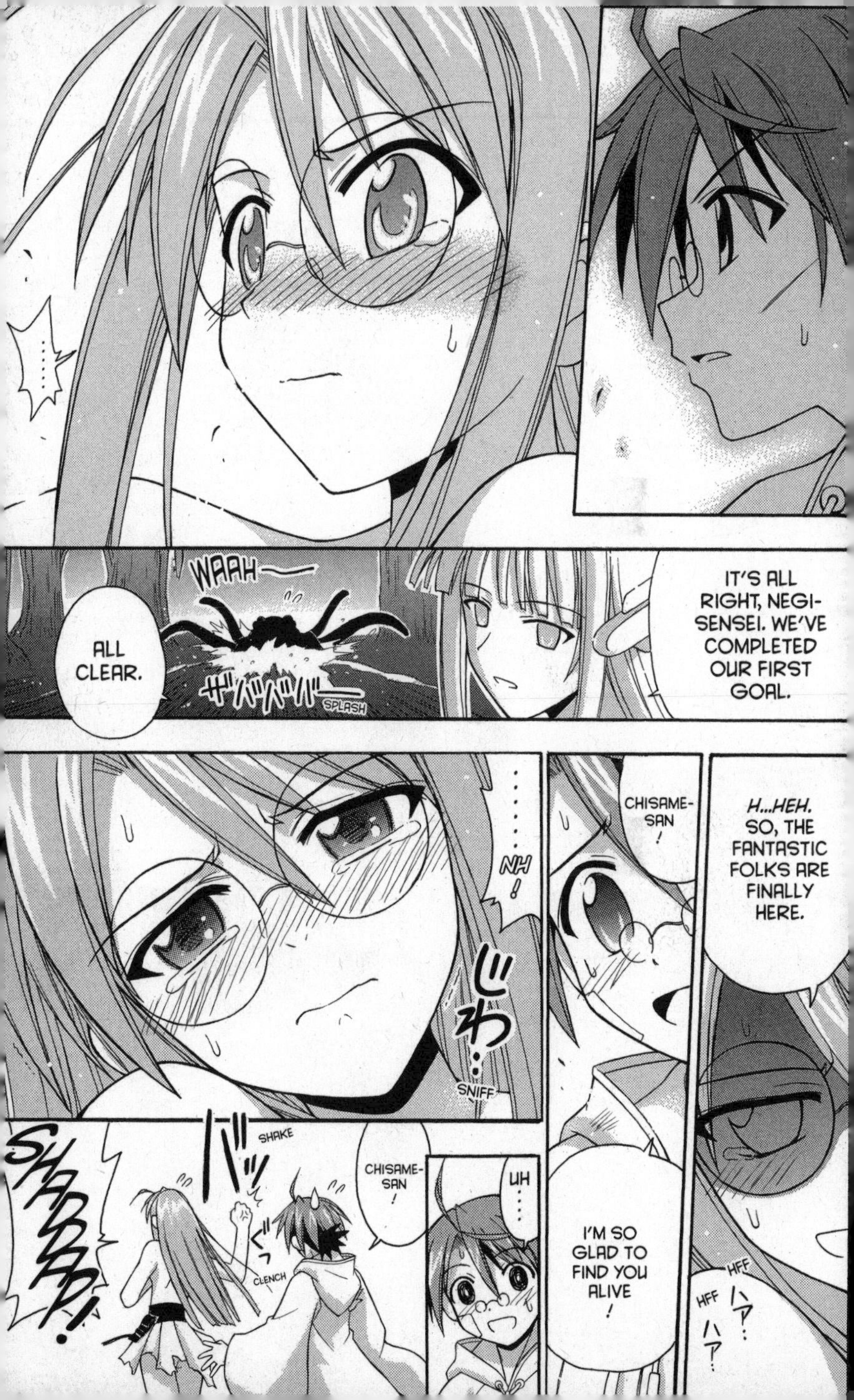
......!
IT'S ALL RIGHT, NEGI-SENSEI. WE'VE COMPLETED OUR FIRST GOAL.
WAAH—
ALL CLEAR.
ザバババー
SPLASH
H...HEH. SO, THE FANTASTIC FOLKS ARE FINALLY HERE.
HFF ハァ...
HFF ハァ...
CHISAME-SAN!
I'M SO GLAD TO FIND YOU ALIVE!
......NH!
じわ...
SNIFF
UH......
CHISAME-SAN!
SHAAAP!
バッ
SHAKE
ぐっ
CLENCH

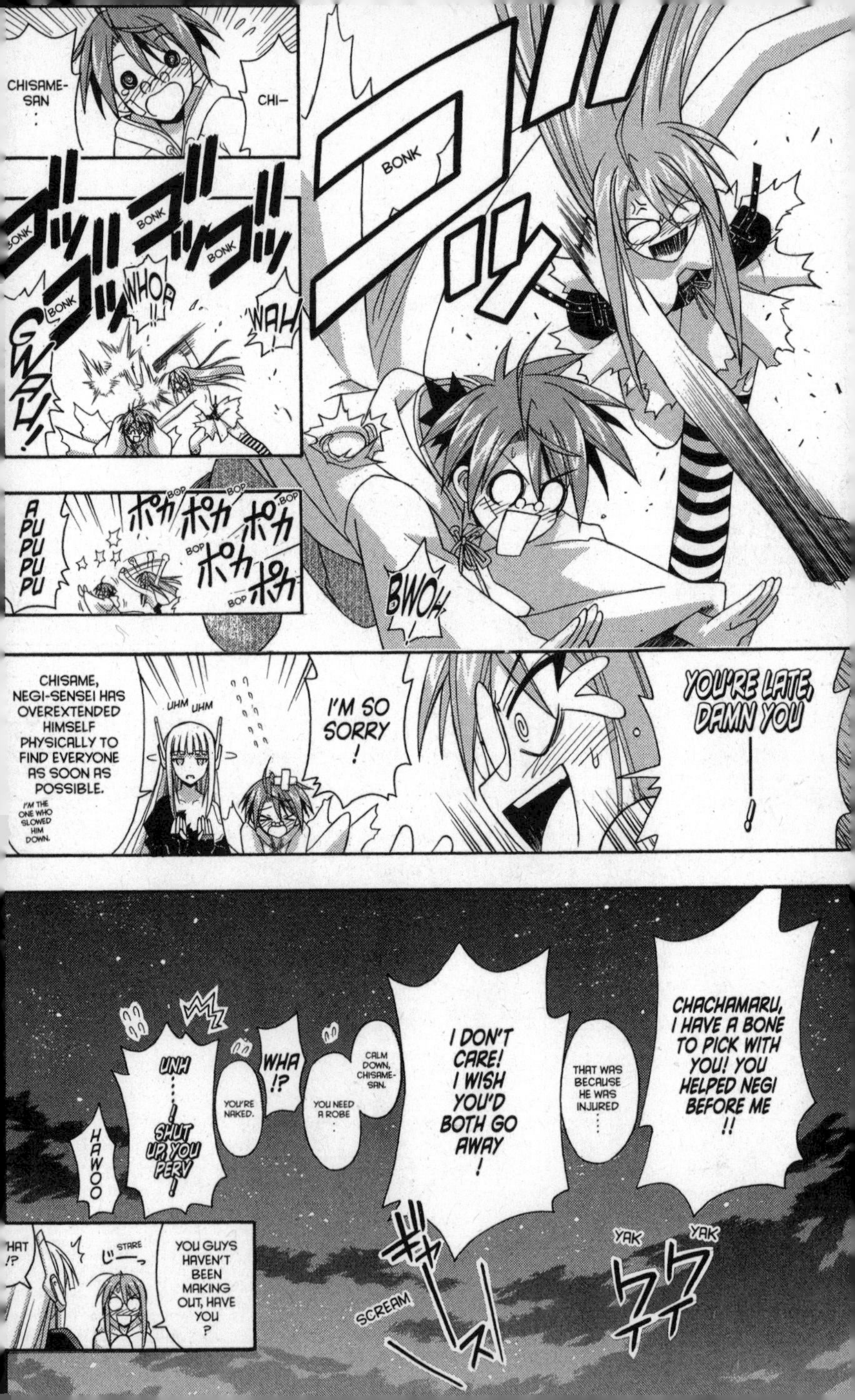
BONK
BWOH!
CHI–
CHISAME-SAN…
BONK
BONK
BONK
BONK
WAH!
WHOA!!
GWAH!
BOP BOP BOP BOP BOP
APUPUPUPUPU
YOU'RE LATE, DAMN YOU—!
I'M SO SORRY!
UHM UHM
CHISAME, NEGI-SENSEI HAS OVEREXTENDED HIMSELF PHYSICALLY TO FIND EVERYONE AS SOON AS POSSIBLE.
I'M THE ONE WHO SLOWED HIM DOWN.
CHACHAMARU, I HAVE A BONE TO PICK WITH YOU! YOU HELPED NEGI BEFORE ME!!
THAT WAS BECAUSE HE WAS INJURED…
I DON'T CARE! I WISH YOU'D BOTH GO AWAY!
CALM DOWN, CHISAME-SAN.
YOU NEED A ROBE…
WHA!?
YOU'RE NAKED.
UNH…! SHUT UP, YOU PERV!
HAWOO
YAK YAK
SCREAM
YOU GUYS HAVEN'T BEEN MAKING OUT, HAVE YOU?
STARE
HAT!?

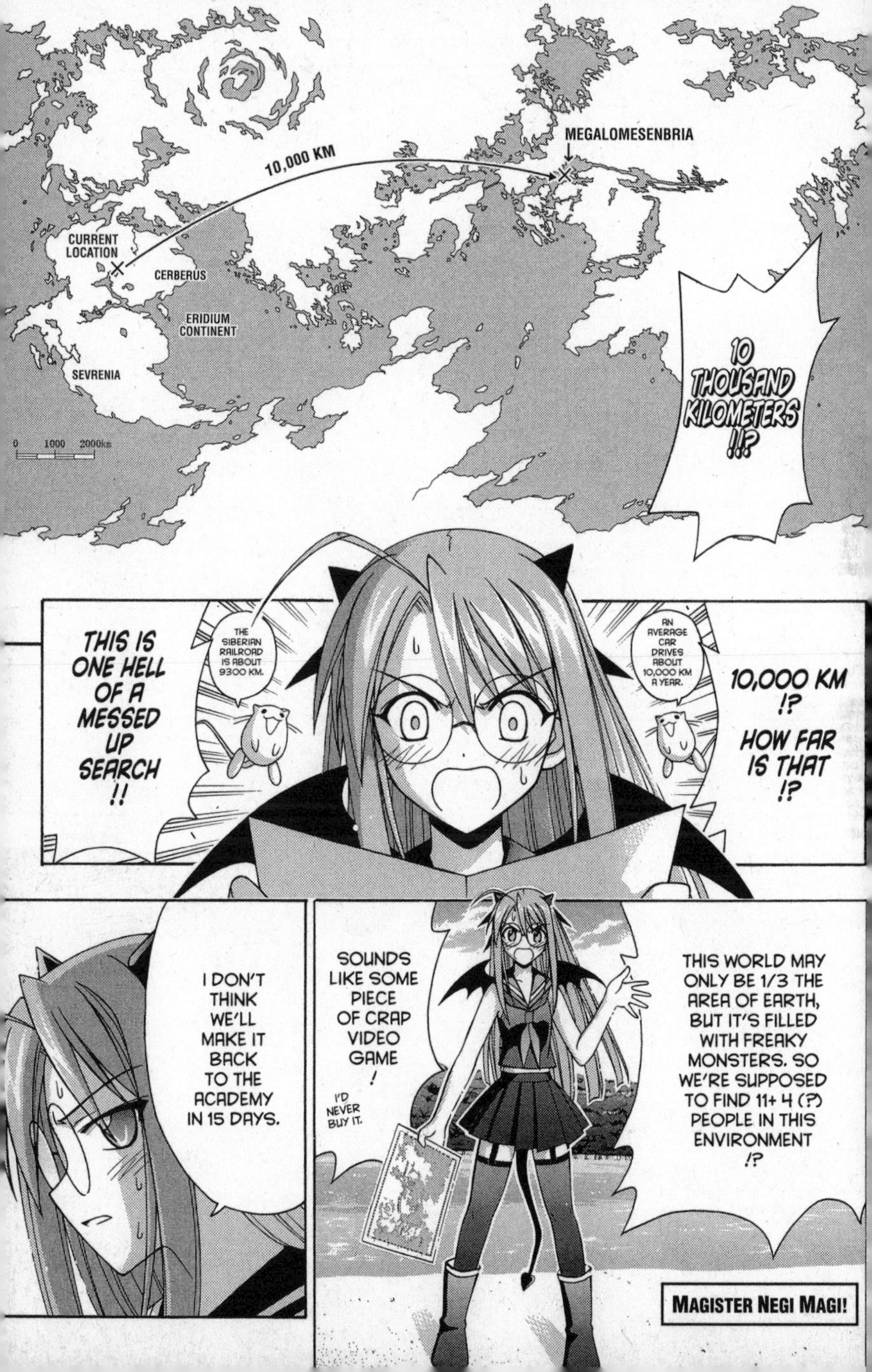
MEGALOMESENBRIA
10,000 KM
CURRENT LOCATION
CERBERUS
ERIDIUM CONTINENT
SEVRENIA
0 1000 2000km
10 THOUSAND KILOMETERS !!?
10,000 KM !? HOW FAR IS THAT !?
AN AVERAGE CAR DRIVES ABOUT 10,000 KM A YEAR.
THE SIBERIAN RAILROAD IS ABOUT 9300 KM.
THIS IS ONE HELL OF A MESSED UP SEARCH !!
THIS WORLD MAY ONLY BE 1/3 THE AREA OF EARTH, BUT IT'S FILLED WITH FREAKY MONSTERS. SO WE'RE SUPPOSED TO FIND 11+ 4 (?) PEOPLE IN THIS ENVIRONMENT !?
SOUNDS LIKE SOME PIECE OF CRAP VIDEO GAME !
I'D NEVER BUY IT.
MAGISTER NEGI MAGI!
I DON'T THINK WE'LL MAKE IT BACK TO THE ACADEMY IN 15 DAYS.

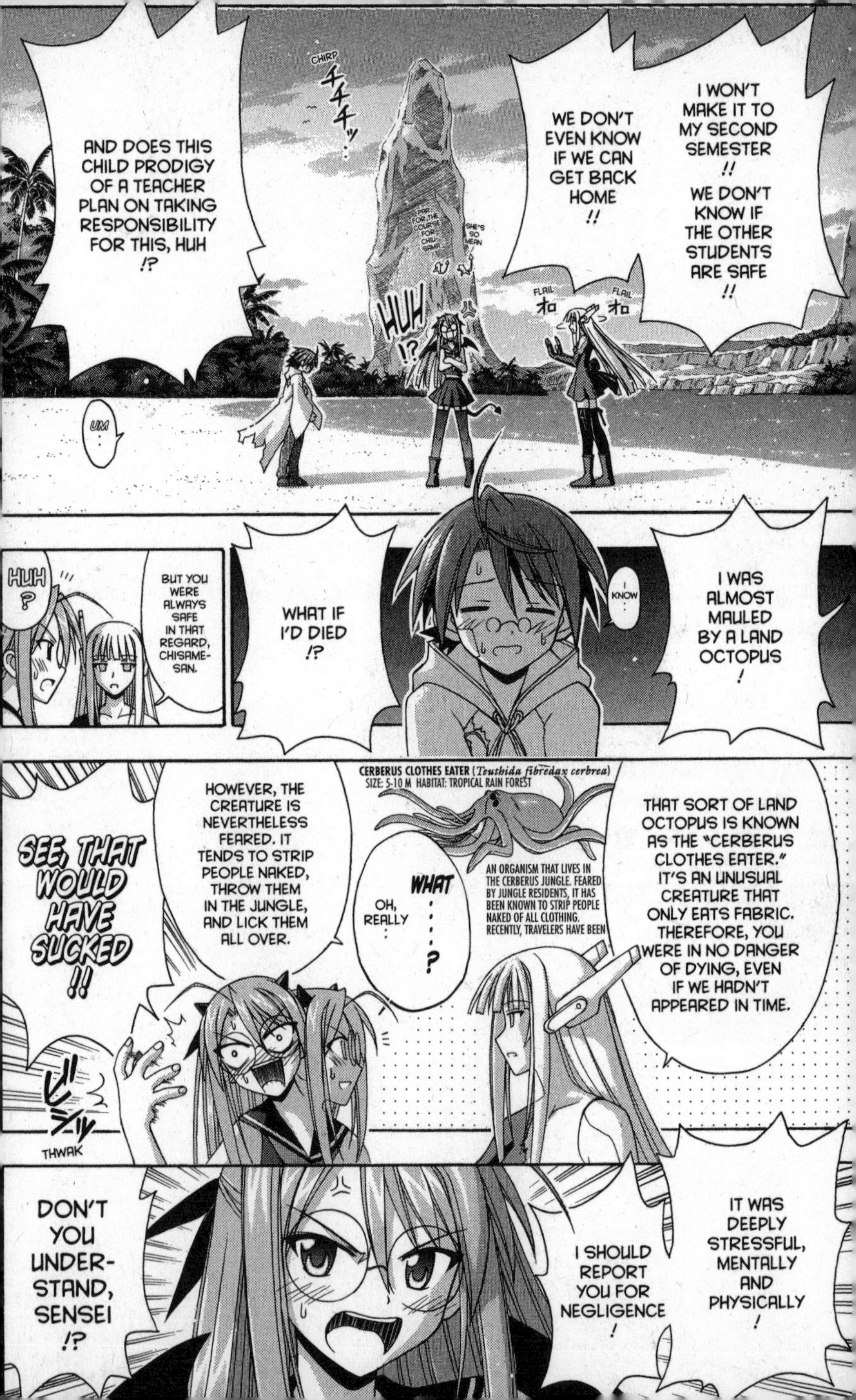
I WON'T MAKE IT TO MY SECOND SEMESTER!! WE DON'T KNOW IF THE OTHER STUDENTS ARE SAFE!!
WE DON'T EVEN KNOW IF WE CAN GET BACK HOME!!
FLAIL
FLAIL
SHE'S SO MEAN
PAR FOR THE COURSE FOR CHIU-SAMA
HUH!?
CHIRP
AND DOES THIS CHILD PRODIGY OF A TEACHER PLAN ON TAKING RESPONSIBILITY FOR THIS, HUH!?
UM...
I WAS ALMOST MAULED BY A LAND OCTOPUS!
I KNOW...
WHAT IF I'D DIED!?
BUT YOU WERE ALWAYS SAFE IN THAT REGARD, CHISAME-SAN.
HUH?
THAT SORT OF LAND OCTOPUS IS KNOWN AS THE "CERBERUS CLOTHES EATER." IT'S AN UNUSUAL CREATURE THAT ONLY EATS FABRIC. THEREFORE, YOU WERE IN NO DANGER OF DYING, EVEN IF WE HADN'T APPEARED IN TIME.
CERBERUS CLOTHES EATER (Teuthida fibredax cerbrea)
SIZE: 5-10 M HABITAT: TROPICAL RAIN FOREST
AN ORGANISM THAT LIVES IN THE CERBERUS JUNGLE. FEARED BY JUNGLE RESIDENTS, IT HAS BEEN KNOWN TO STRIP PEOPLE NAKED OF ALL CLOTHING. RECENTLY, TRAVELERS HAVE BEEN
WHAT...?
OH, REALLY...
HOWEVER, THE CREATURE IS NEVERTHELESS FEARED. IT TENDS TO STRIP PEOPLE NAKED, THROW THEM IN THE JUNGLE, AND LICK THEM ALL OVER.
SEE, THAT WOULD HAVE SUCKED!!
THWAK
IT WAS DEEPLY STRESSFUL, MENTALLY AND PHYSICALLY!
I SHOULD REPORT YOU FOR NEGLIGENCE!
DON'T YOU UNDERSTAND, SENSEI!?

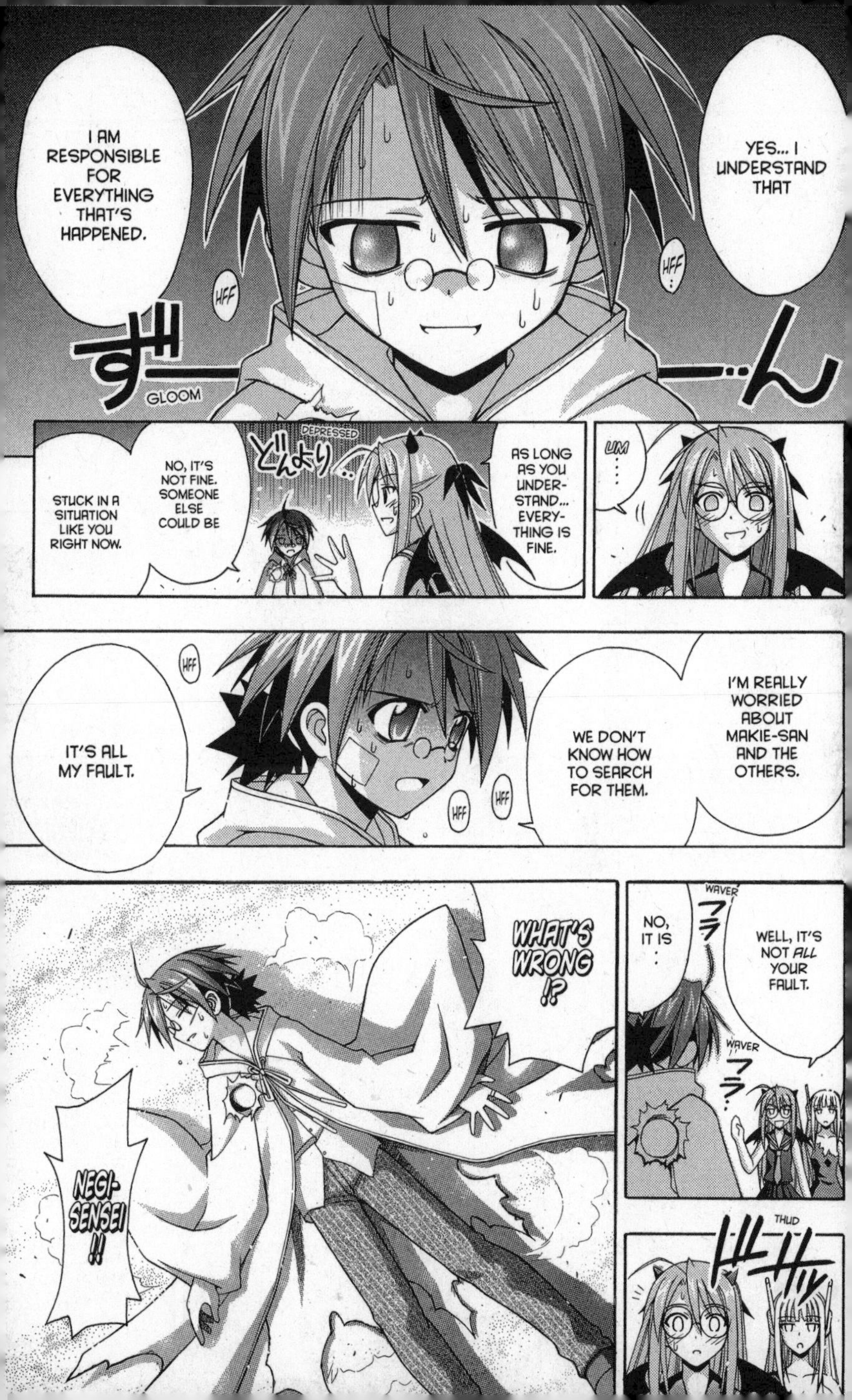

YES... I UNDERSTAND THAT
HFF...
I AM RESPONSIBLE FOR EVERYTHING THAT'S HAPPENED.
HFF
ずーー…ん
GLOOM
UM...
AS LONG AS YOU UNDERSTAND... EVERYTHING IS FINE.
どんより…
DEPRESSED
NO, IT'S NOT FINE. SOMEONE ELSE COULD BE
STUCK IN A SITUATION LIKE YOU RIGHT NOW.
I'M REALLY WORRIED ABOUT MAKIE-SAN AND THE OTHERS.
WE DON'T KNOW HOW TO SEARCH FOR THEM.
HFF
HFF
IT'S ALL MY FAULT.
HFF
WELL, IT'S NOT *ALL* YOUR FAULT.
フラ
WAVER
NO, IT IS...
フラ
WAVER
ドサッ
THUD
WHAT'S WRONG!?
NEGI-SENSEI!!

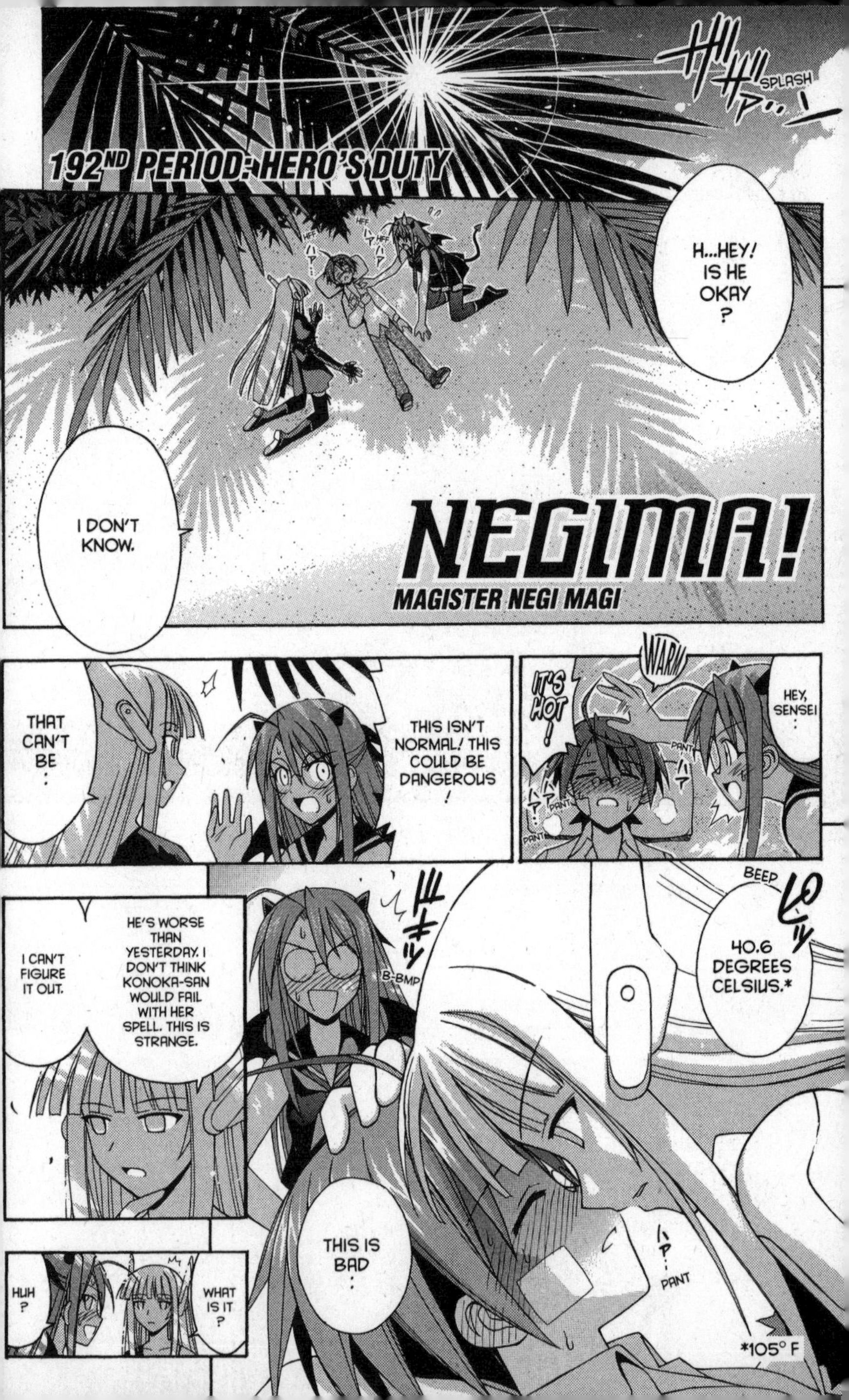
SPLASH
192ND PERIOD: HERO'S DUTY
HFF
HFF
H...HEY! IS HE OKAY?
I DON'T KNOW.
NEGIMA!
MAGISTER NEGI MAGI
HEY, SENSEI...
WARM
IT'S HOT!
PANT
PANT
PANT
THIS ISN'T NORMAL! THIS COULD BE DANGEROUS!
THAT CAN'T BE...
BEEP
40.6 DEGREES CELSIUS.*
B-BMP
HE'S WORSE THAN YESTERDAY. I DON'T THINK KONOKA-SAN WOULD FAIL WITH HER SPELL. THIS IS STRANGE.
I CAN'T FIGURE IT OUT.
PANT
THIS IS BAD...
WHAT IS IT?
HUH?
*105° F

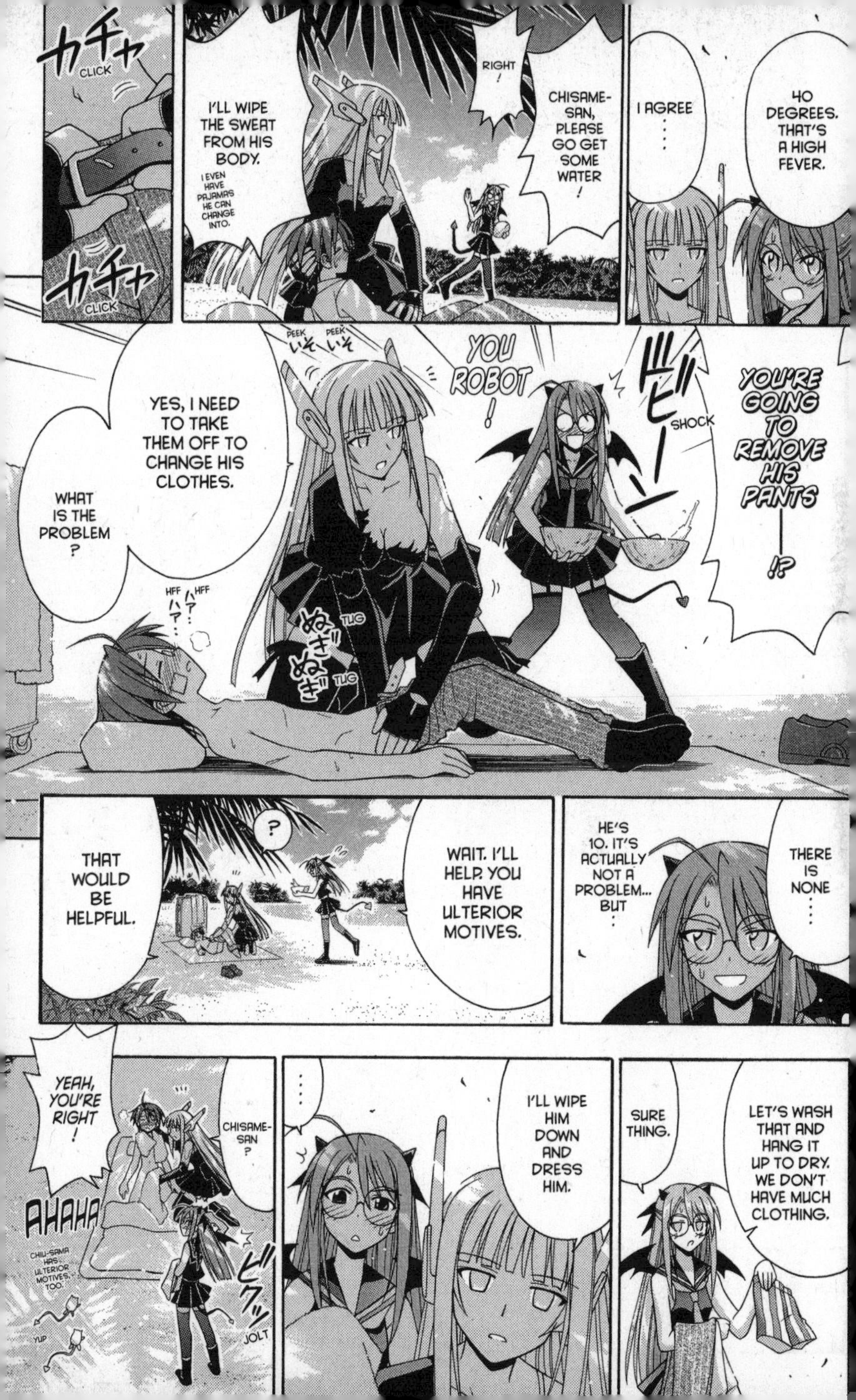
40 DEGREES. THAT'S A HIGH FEVER.
I AGREE...
RIGHT!
CHISAME-SAN, PLEASE GO GET SOME WATER!
I'LL WIPE THE SWEAT FROM HIS BODY.
I EVEN HAVE PAJAMAS HE CAN CHANGE INTO.
カチャ
CLICK
カチャ
CLICK
YOU'RE GOING TO REMOVE HIS PANTS――!?
ドビーン
SHOCK
YOU ROBOT!
いそ いそ
PEEK PEEK
YES, I NEED TO TAKE THEM OFF TO CHANGE HIS CLOTHES.
WHAT IS THE PROBLEM?
ハァ ハァ...
HFF HFF
ぬぎぬぎ
TUG TUG
THERE IS NONE...
HE'S 10. IT'S ACTUALLY NOT A PROBLEM... BUT...
WAIT. I'LL HELP. YOU HAVE ULTERIOR MOTIVES.
?
THAT WOULD BE HELPFUL.
LET'S WASH THAT AND HANG IT UP TO DRY. WE DON'T HAVE MUCH CLOTHING.
SURE THING.
I'LL WIPE HIM DOWN AND DRESS HIM.
...
CHISAME-SAN?
YEAH, YOU'RE RIGHT!
!!
AHAHA
ビクッ
JOLT
CHIU-SAMA HAS ULTERIOR MOTIVES, TOO.
YUP

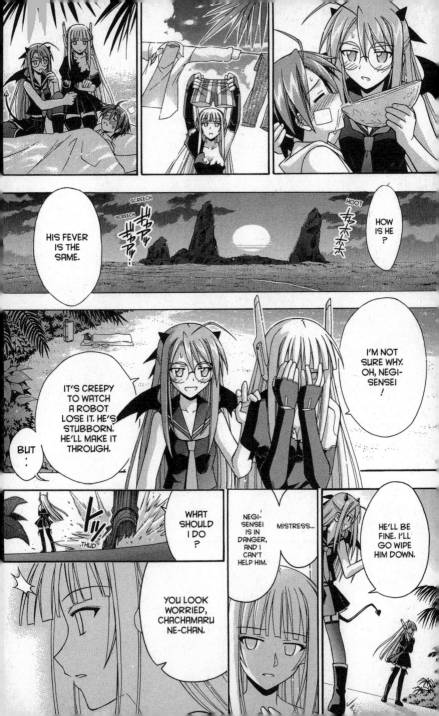

HOW IS HE?
HOOT
SCREECH
SCREECH
HIS FEVER IS THE SAME.
I'M NOT SURE WHY. OH, NEGI-SENSEI!
IT'S CREEPY TO WATCH A ROBOT LOSE IT. HE'S STUBBORN. HE'LL MAKE IT THROUGH.
BUT...
HE'LL BE FINE. I'LL GO WIPE HIM DOWN.
MISTRESS...
NEGI-SENSEI IS IN DANGER, AND I CAN'T HELP HIM.
WHAT SHOULD I DO?
THUD
YOU LOOK WORRIED, CHACHAMARU NE-CHAN.

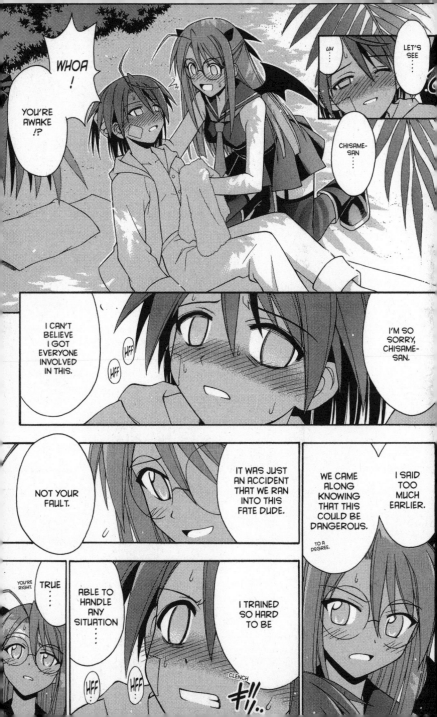

LET'S SEE...
UH...
CHISAME-SAN...
WHOA!
YOU'RE AWAKE!?
I'M SO SORRY, CHISAME-SAN.
I CAN'T BELIEVE I GOT EVERYONE INVOLVED IN THIS.
HFF
HFF
I SAID TOO MUCH EARLIER.
WE CAME ALONG KNOWING THAT THIS COULD BE DANGEROUS.
TO A DEGREE.
IT WAS JUST AN ACCIDENT THAT WE RAN INTO THIS FATE DUDE.
NOT YOUR FAULT.
I TRAINED SO HARD TO BE
ABLE TO HANDLE ANY SITUATION...
HFF
HFF
CLENCH
TRUE...
YOU'RE RIGHT.

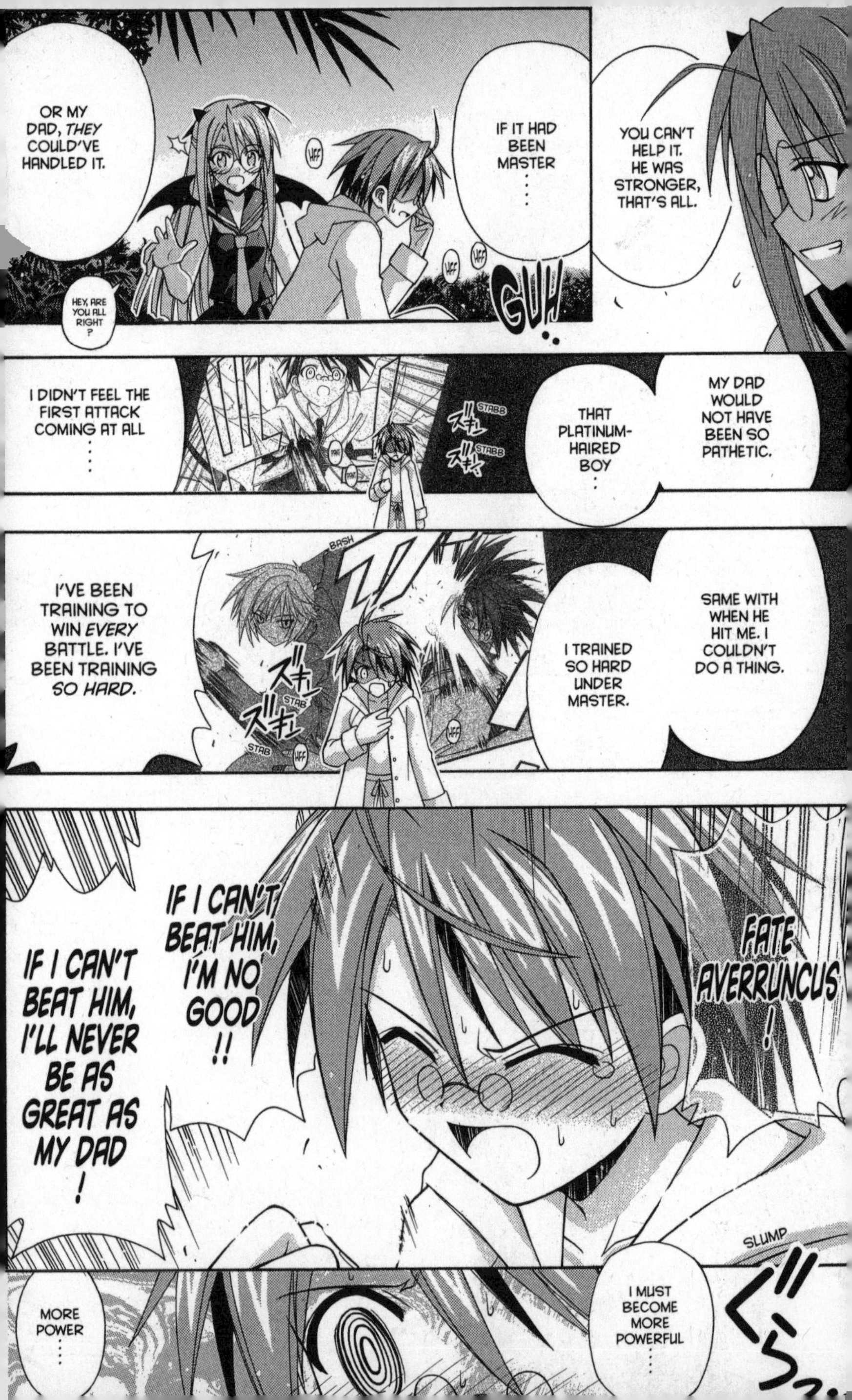
YOU CAN'T HELP IT. HE WAS STRONGER, THAT'S ALL.
IF IT HAD BEEN MASTER . . .
GUH..
HFF
HFF
HFF
OR MY DAD, *THEY* COULD'VE HANDLED IT.
HEY, ARE YOU ALL RIGHT?
MY DAD WOULD NOT HAVE BEEN SO PATHETIC.
THAT PLATINUM-HAIRED BOY . .
STABB
STABB
I DIDN'T FEEL THE FIRST ATTACK COMING AT ALL . . .
SAME WITH WHEN HE HIT ME. I COULDN'T DO A THING.
I TRAINED SO HARD UNDER MASTER.
BASH
HFF
STAB
STAB
HFF
I'VE BEEN TRAINING TO WIN *EVERY* BATTLE. I'VE BEEN TRAINING *SO HARD.*
FATE AVERRUNCUS!
IF I CAN'T BEAT HIM, I'M NO GOOD!!
IF I CAN'T BEAT HIM, I'LL NEVER BE AS GREAT AS MY DAD!
SLUMP
I MUST BECOME MORE POWERFUL . . .
MORE POWER . . .

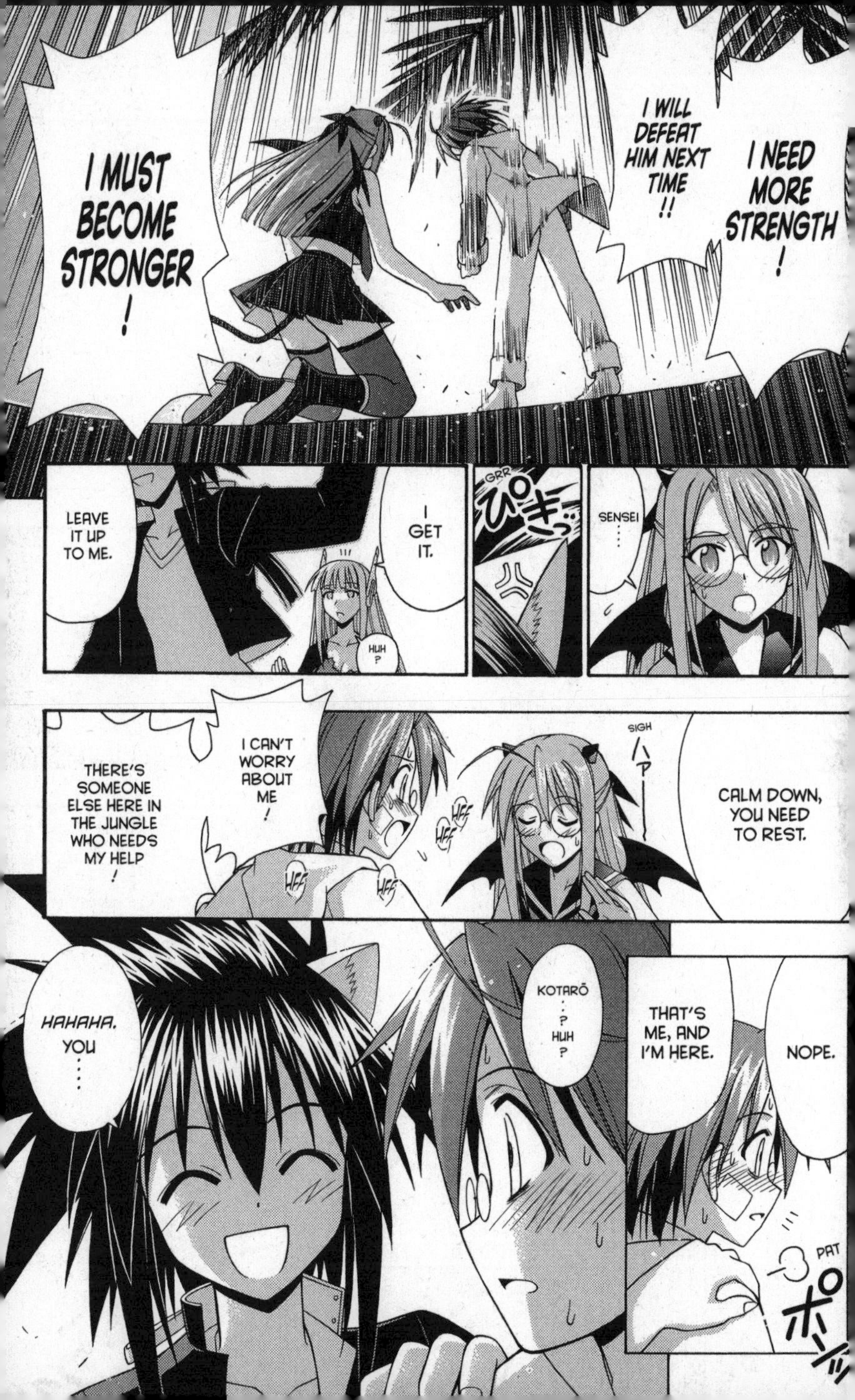
I NEED MORE STRENGTH!
I WILL DEFEAT HIM NEXT TIME!!
I MUST BECOME STRONGER!
SENSEI ......
GRR
ぴきっ
I GET IT.
LEAVE IT UP TO ME.
HUH?
CALM DOWN, YOU NEED TO REST.
SIGH
ハァ
HFF
HFF
I CAN'T WORRY ABOUT ME!
THERE'S SOMEONE ELSE HERE IN THE JUNGLE WHO NEEDS MY HELP!
HFF
HFF
NOPE.
THAT'S ME, AND I'M HERE.
PAT
ポンッ
KOTARŌ...? HUH?
HAHAHA. YOU....

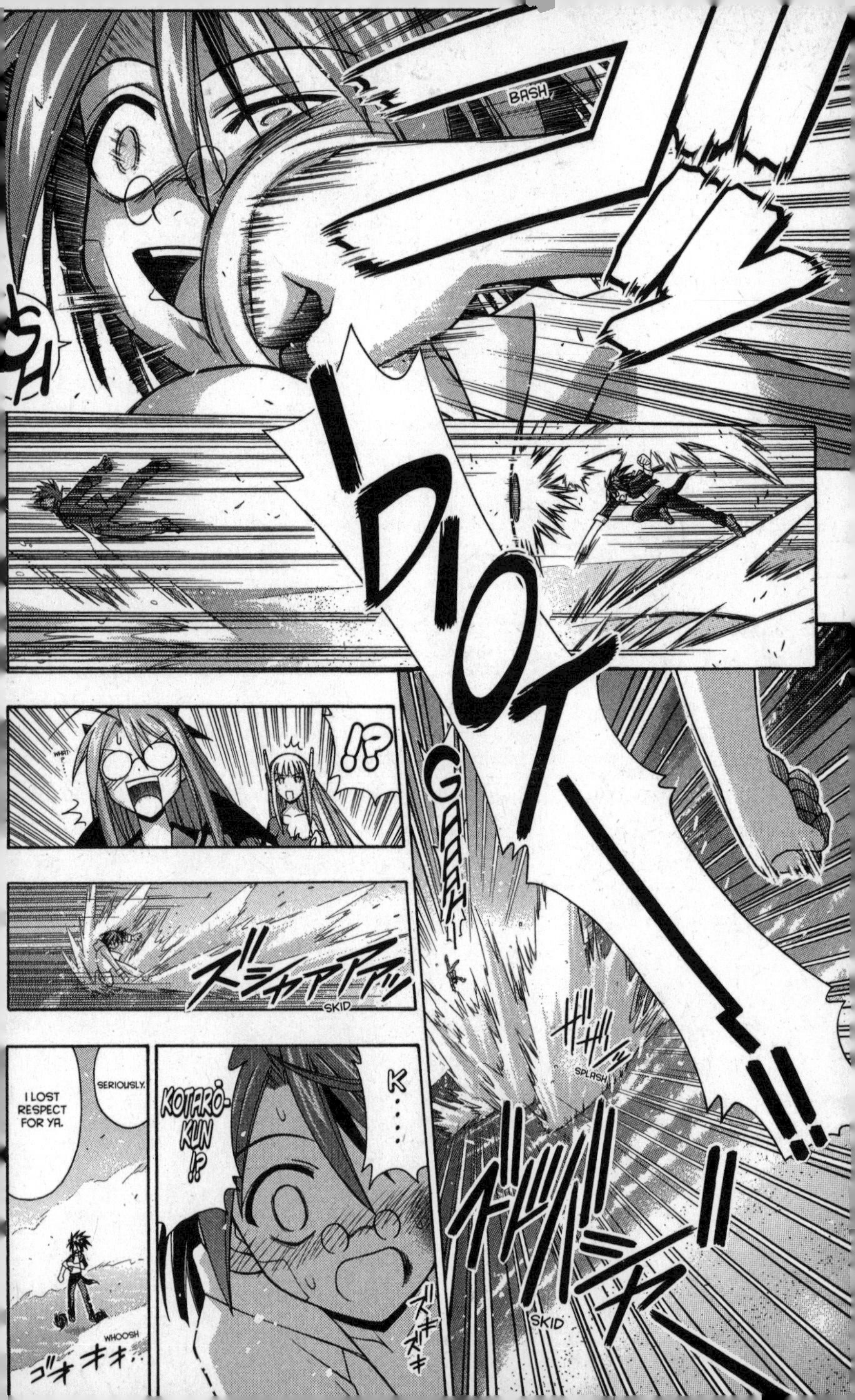
BASH
SH
IDIOT—!!
GAAAH!!
SPLASH
SKID
WHAT?...
!?
SKID
K....
KOTARÔ-KUN!?
SERIOUSLY.
I LOST RESPECT FOR YA.
WHOOSH

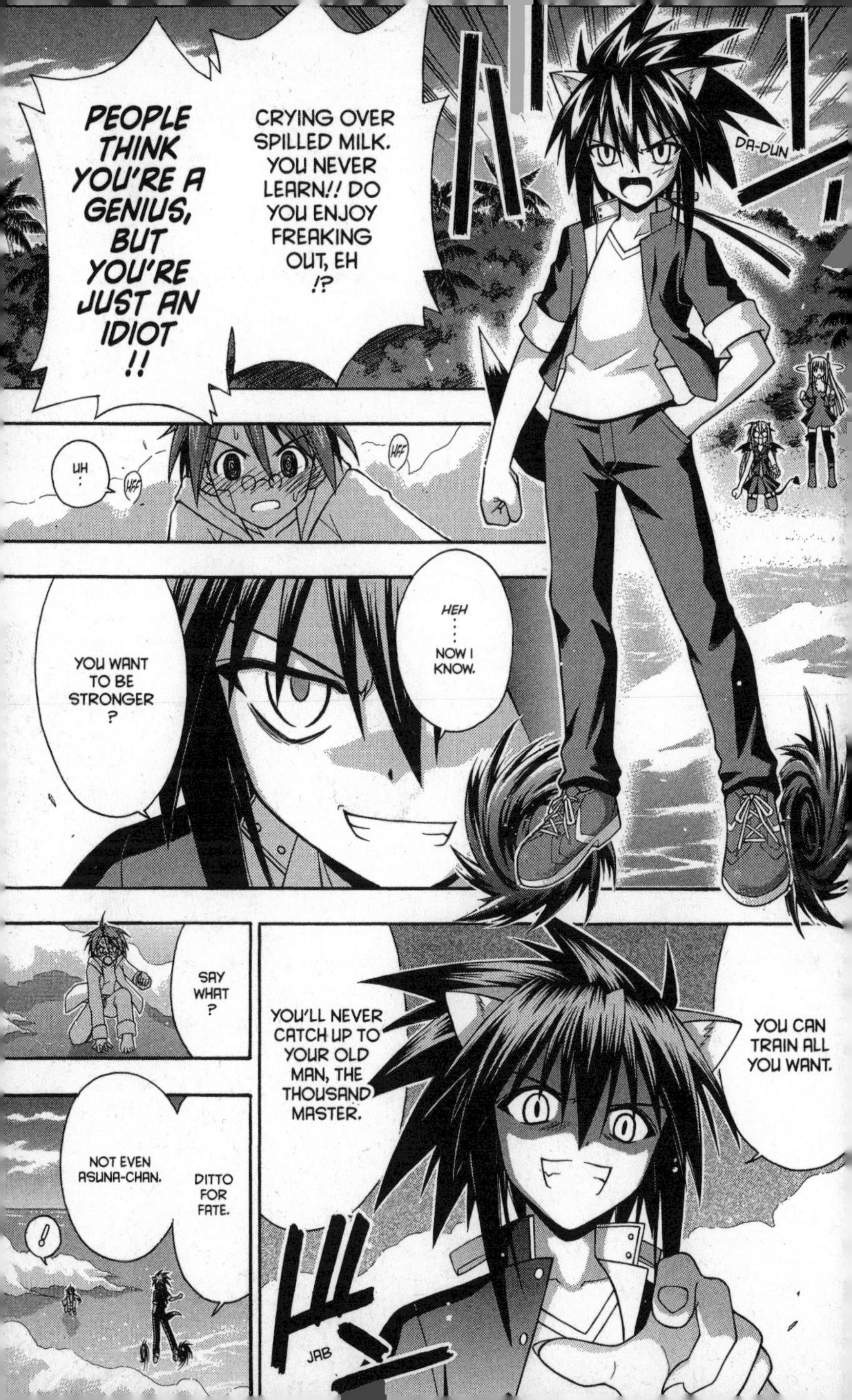
DA-DUN
CRYING OVER SPILLED MILK. YOU NEVER LEARN!! DO YOU ENJOY FREAKING OUT, EH !?
PEOPLE THINK YOU'RE A GENIUS, BUT YOU'RE JUST AN IDIOT !!
HFF
HFF
UH ...
HEH ... NOW I KNOW.
YOU WANT TO BE STRONGER ?
YOU CAN TRAIN ALL YOU WANT.
YOU'LL NEVER CATCH UP TO YOUR OLD MAN, THE THOUSAND MASTER.
JAB
SAY WHAT ?
NOT EVEN ASUNA-CHAN.
DITTO FOR FATE.
!

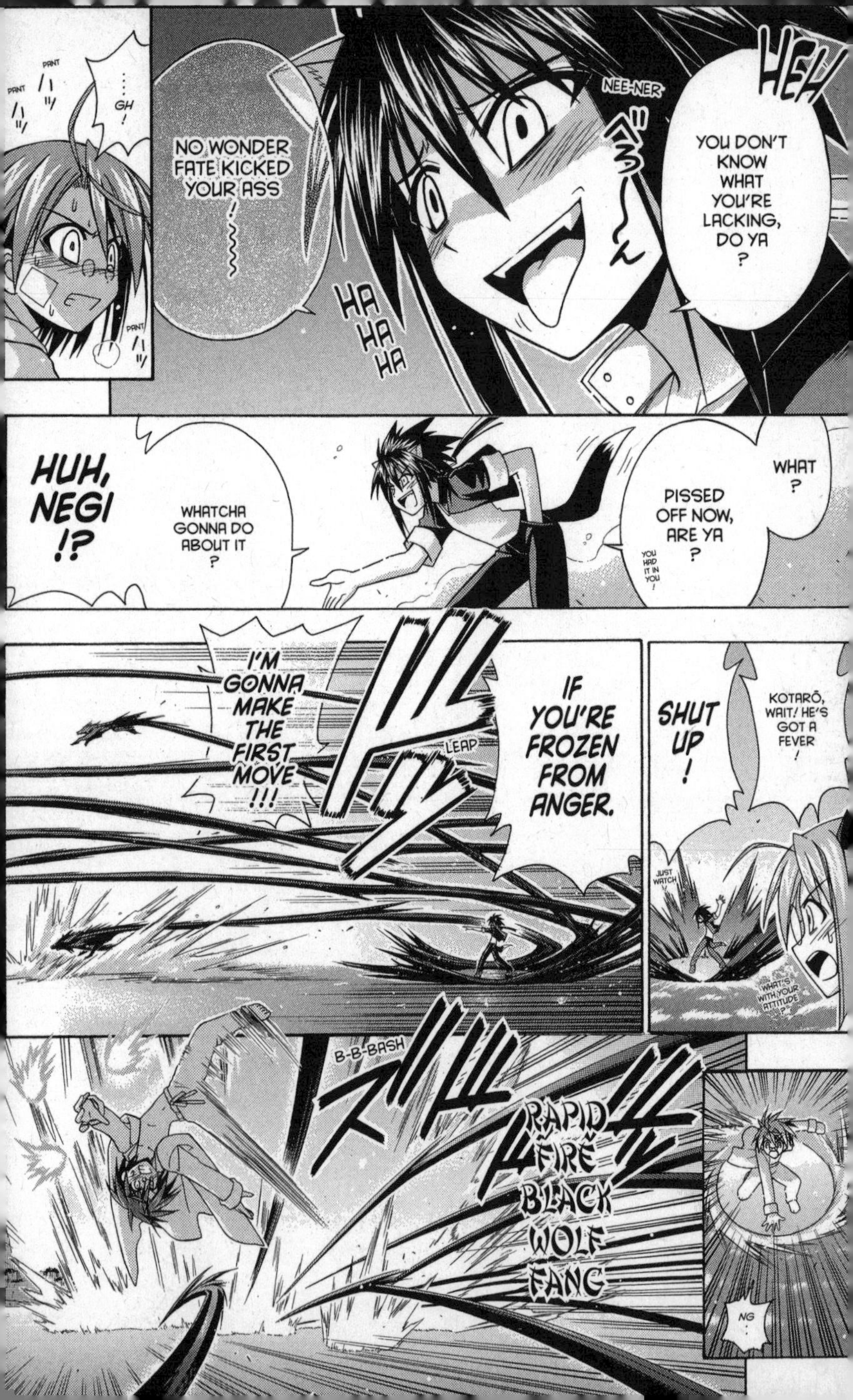
HEH
NEE-NER
YOU DON'T KNOW WHAT YOU'RE LACKING, DO YA?
HA HA HA
NO WONDER FATE KICKED YOUR ASS
...GH!
PANT PANT
PANT
WHAT?
PISSED OFF NOW, ARE YA?
YOU HAD IT IN YOU!
WHATCHA GONNA DO ABOUT IT?
HUH, NEGI!?
KOTARŌ, WAIT! HE'S GOT A FEVER!
SHUT UP!
JUST WATCH!
WHAT'S WITH YOUR ATTITUDE?
IF YOU'RE FROZEN FROM ANGER.
LEAP
I'M GONNA MAKE THE FIRST MOVE!!!
NG...
RAPID FIRE BLACK WOLF FANG
B-B-BASH

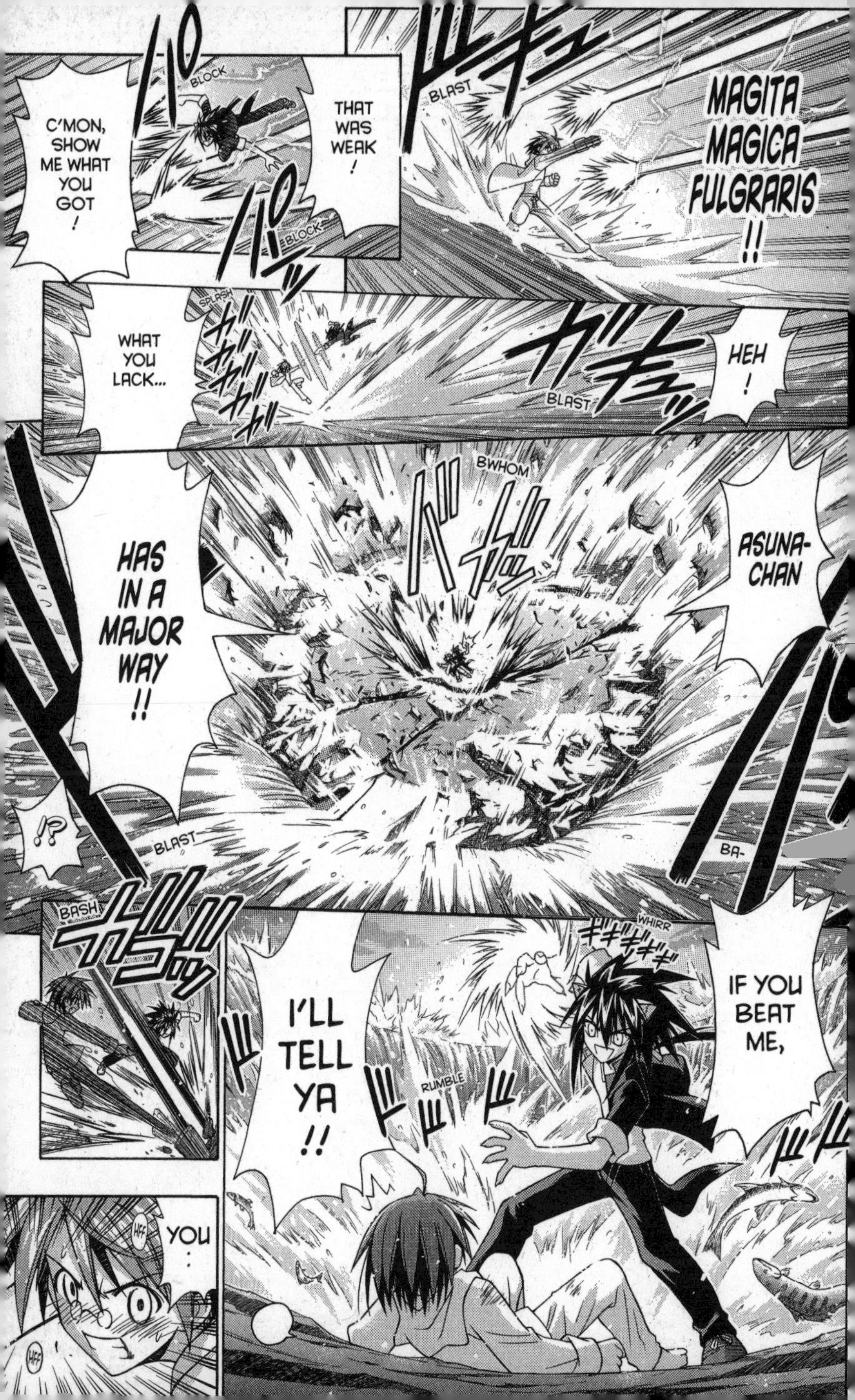
BLAST
MAGITA MAGICA FULGRARIS !!
BLOCK
THAT WAS WEAK !
C'MON, SHOW ME WHAT YOU GOT !
BLOCK
HEH !
BLAST
SPLASH
WHAT YOU LACK...
ASUNA-CHAN
BA-
BWHOM
HAS IN A MAJOR WAY !!
BLAST
!?
WHIRR
IF YOU BEAT ME,
RUMBLE
I'LL TELL YA !!
BASH
HFF
YOU :
HFF

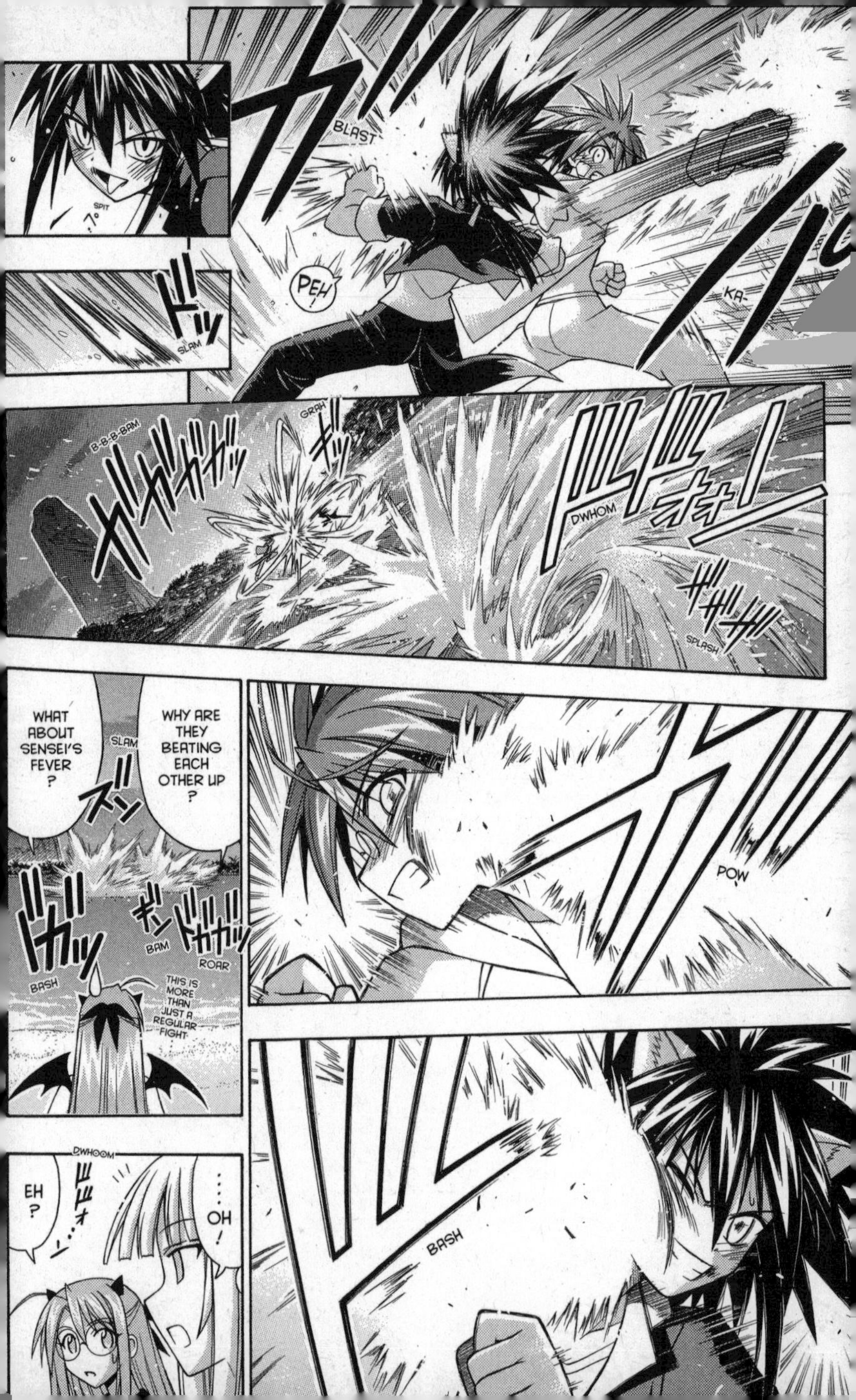

BLAST
KA-
PEH!
SPIT
SLAM
DWHOM
SPLASH
GRAH
B-B-B-BAM
POW
BASH
WHY ARE THEY BEATING EACH OTHER UP?
WHAT ABOUT SENSEI'S FEVER?
SLAM
ROAR
BAM
BASH
THIS IS MORE THAN JUST A REGULAR FIGHT...
DWHOOM
...OH!
EH?

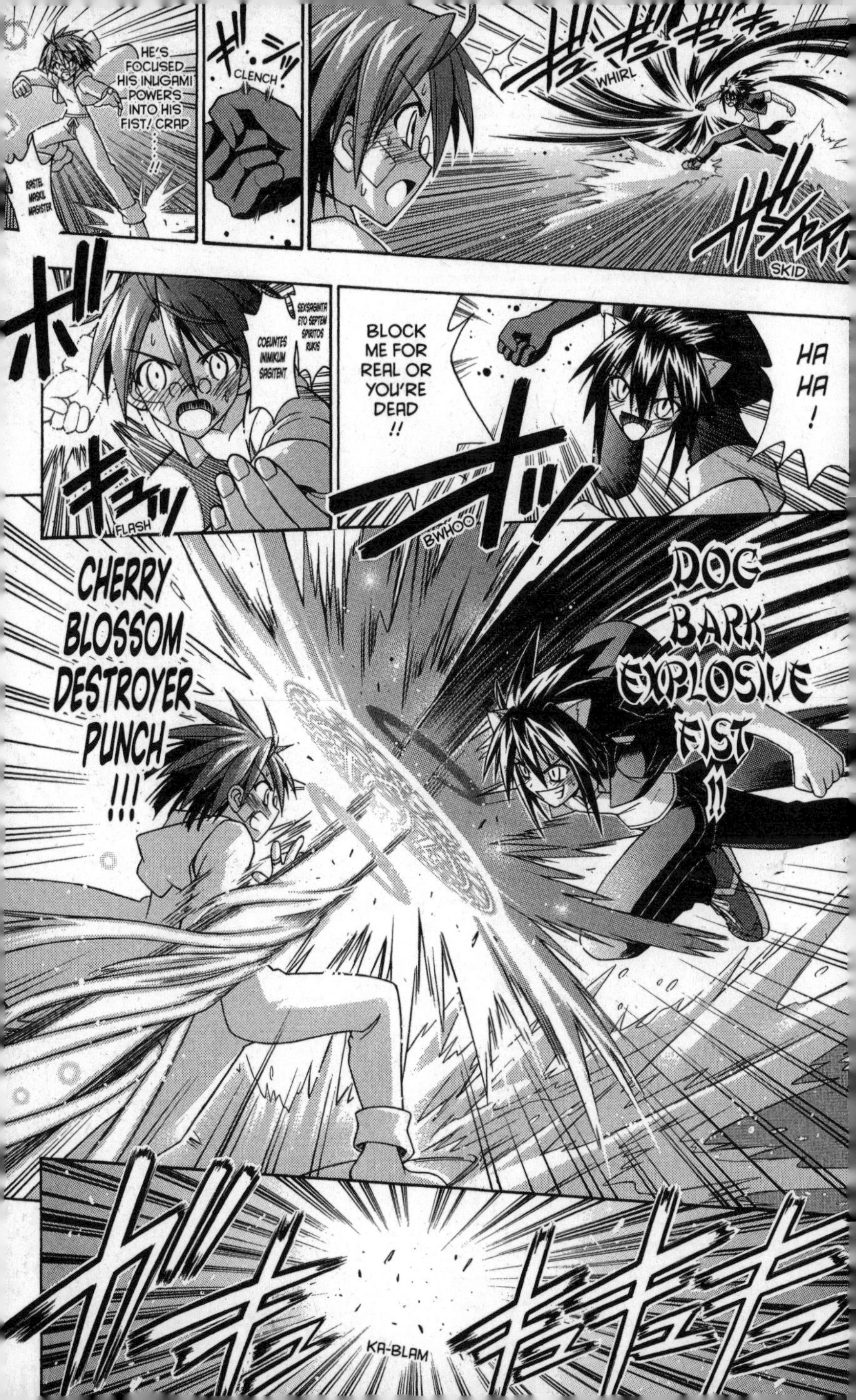
WHIRL
SKID
CLENCH
HE'S FOCUSED HIS INUGAMI POWERS INTO HIS FIST! CRAP......!!
RASTEL MASKIL MAGISTER
HA HA!
BLOCK ME FOR REAL OR YOU'RE DEAD!!
BWHOO
SEXSAGINTA ETO SEPTEM SPIRITOS RUKIS
COEUNTES INIMIKUM SAGITENT
FLASH
DOG BARK EXPLOSIVE FIST!!
CHERRY BLOSSOM DESTROYER PUNCH!!!
KA-BLAM

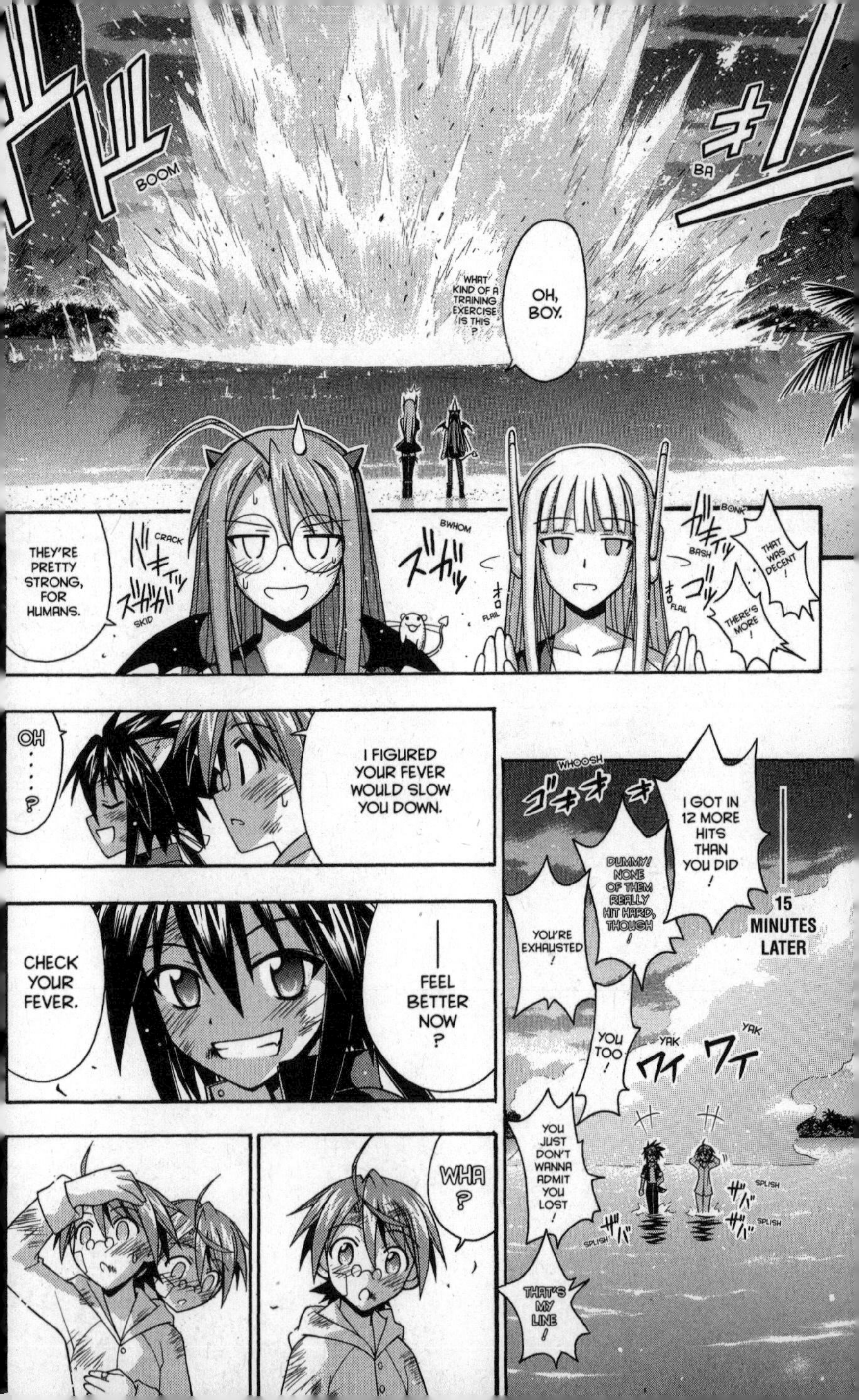
BA
BOOM
OH, BOY.
WHAT KIND OF A TRAINING EXERCISE IS THIS?
BONK
THAT WAS DECENT!
BASH
THERE'S MORE!
FLAIL
BWHOM
FLAIL
CRACK
SKID
THEY'RE PRETTY STRONG, FOR HUMANS.
15 MINUTES LATER
WHOOSH
I GOT IN 12 MORE HITS THAN YOU DID!
DUMMY! NONE OF THEM REALLY HIT HARD, THOUGH!
YOU'RE EXHAUSTED!
YAK
YAK
YOU TOO!
YOU JUST DON'T WANNA ADMIT YOU LOST!
SPLISH
SPLISH
SPLISH
THAT'S MY LINE!
I FIGURED YOUR FEVER WOULD SLOW YOU DOWN.
OH...?
FEEL BETTER NOW?
CHECK YOUR FEVER.
WHA?

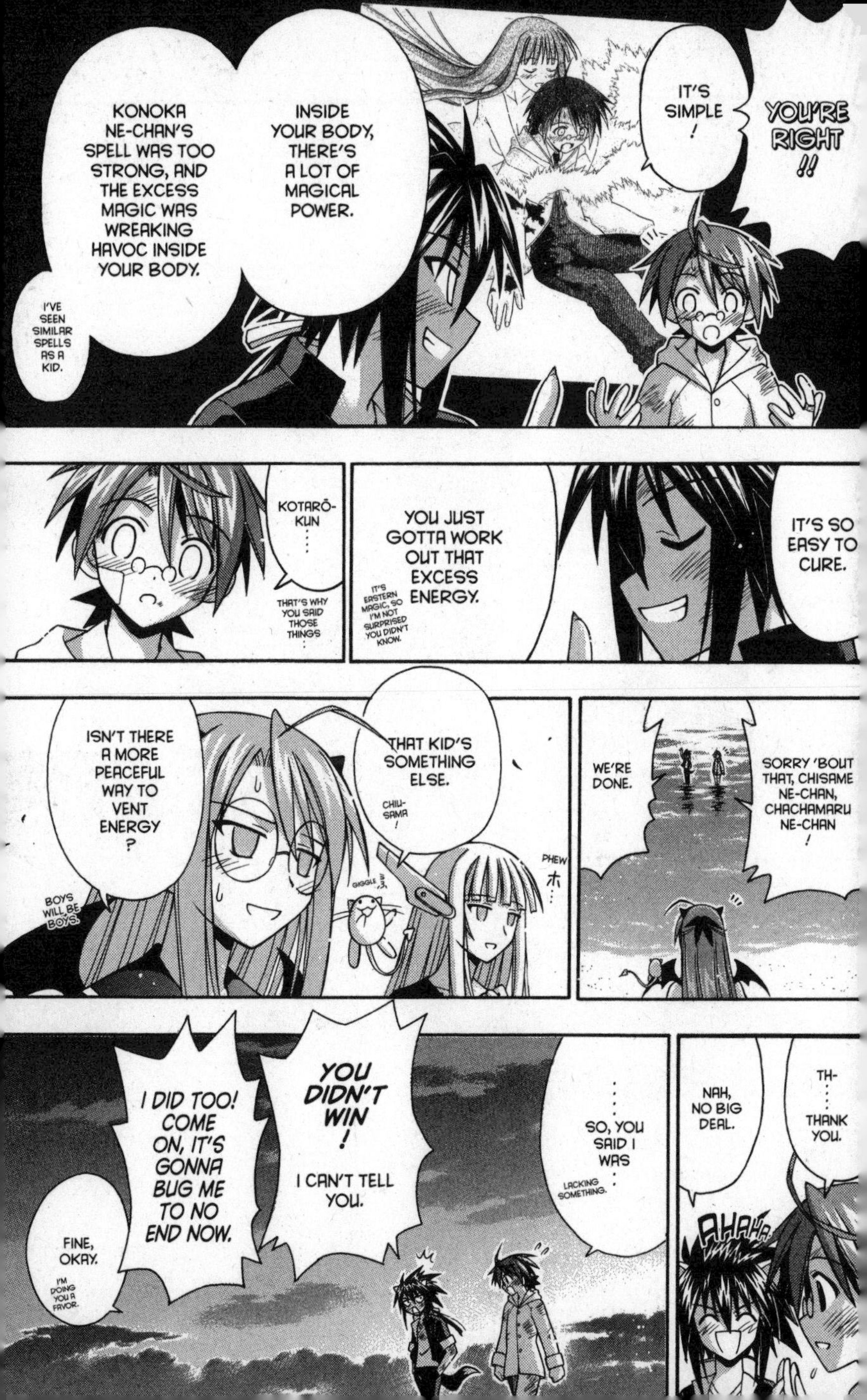
YOU'RE RIGHT!!
IT'S SIMPLE!
INSIDE YOUR BODY, THERE'S A LOT OF MAGICAL POWER.
KONOKA NE-CHAN'S SPELL WAS TOO STRONG, AND THE EXCESS MAGIC WAS WREAKING HAVOC INSIDE YOUR BODY.
I'VE SEEN SIMILAR SPELLS AS A KID.
IT'S SO EASY TO CURE.
YOU JUST GOTTA WORK OUT THAT EXCESS ENERGY.
IT'S EASTERN MAGIC, SO I'M NOT SURPRISED YOU DIDN'T KNOW.
KOTARŌ-KUN...
THAT'S WHY YOU SAID THOSE THINGS...
SORRY 'BOUT THAT, CHISAME NE-CHAN, CHACHAMARU NE-CHAN!
WE'RE DONE.
THAT KID'S SOMETHING ELSE.
CHIU-SAMA!
ISN'T THERE A MORE PEACEFUL WAY TO VENT ENERGY?
PHEW
GIGGLE
BOYS WILL BE BOYS.
TH-... THANK YOU.
NAH, NO BIG DEAL.
AHAHA
...SO, YOU SAID I WAS...
LACKING SOMETHING.
YOU DIDN'T WIN!
I CAN'T TELL YOU.
I DID TOO! COME ON, IT'S GONNA BUG ME TO NO END NOW.
FINE, OKAY.
I'M DOING YOU A FAVOR.

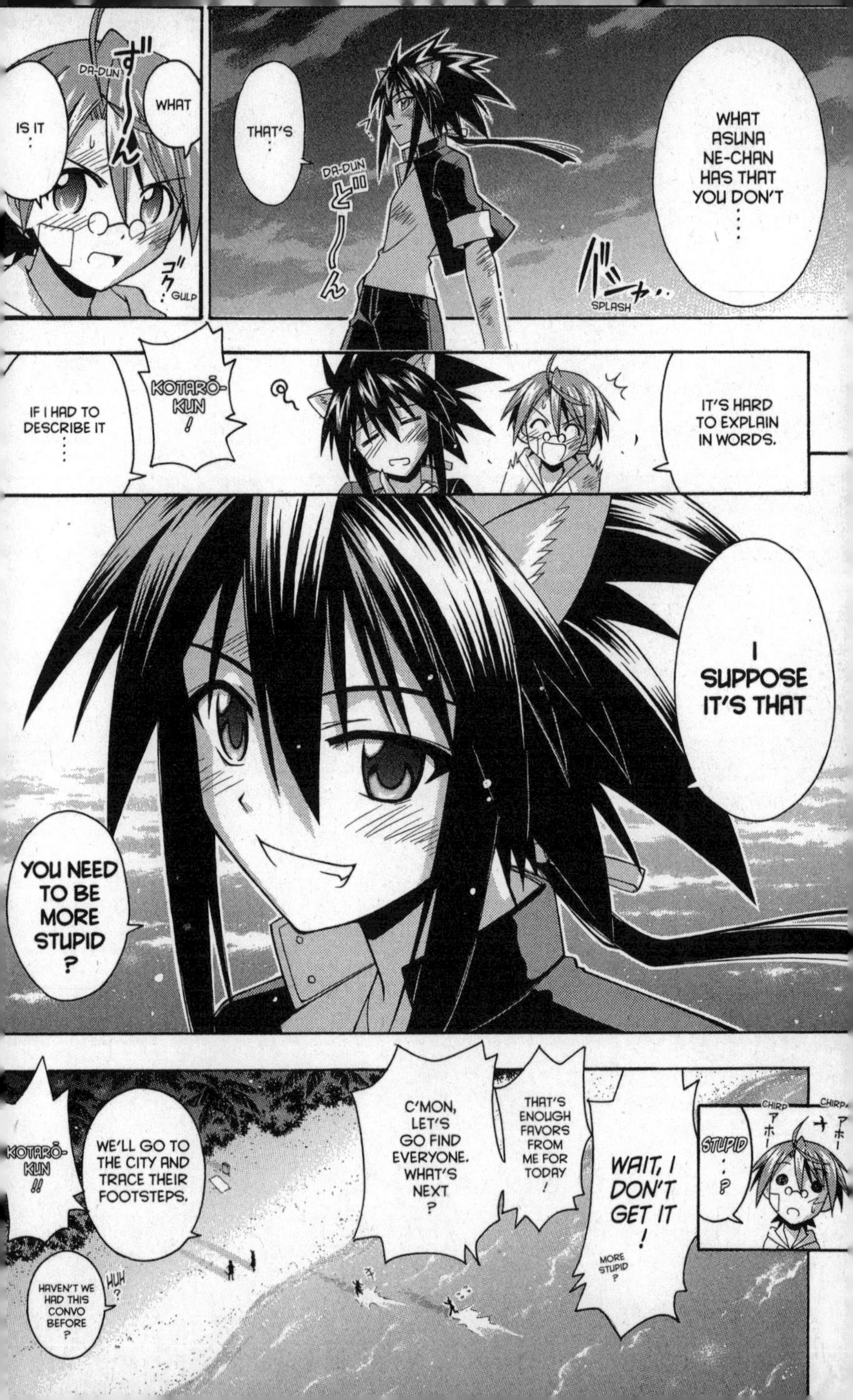

WHAT ASUNA NE-CHAN HAS THAT YOU DON'T ....
SPLASH
THAT'S ...
DA-DUN
WHAT
IS IT ...
DA-DUN
GULP
IT'S HARD TO EXPLAIN IN WORDS.
KOTARŌ-KUN!
IF I HAD TO DESCRIBE IT ...
I SUPPOSE IT'S THAT
YOU NEED TO BE MORE STUPID?
CHIRP
CHIRP
STUPID..?
WAIT, I DON'T GET IT!
MORE STUPID?
THAT'S ENOUGH FAVORS FROM ME FOR TODAY!
C'MON, LET'S GO FIND EVERYONE. WHAT'S NEXT?
KOTARŌ-KUN!!
WE'LL GO TO THE CITY AND TRACE THEIR FOOTSTEPS.
HUH?
HAVEN'T WE HAD THIS CONVO BEFORE?

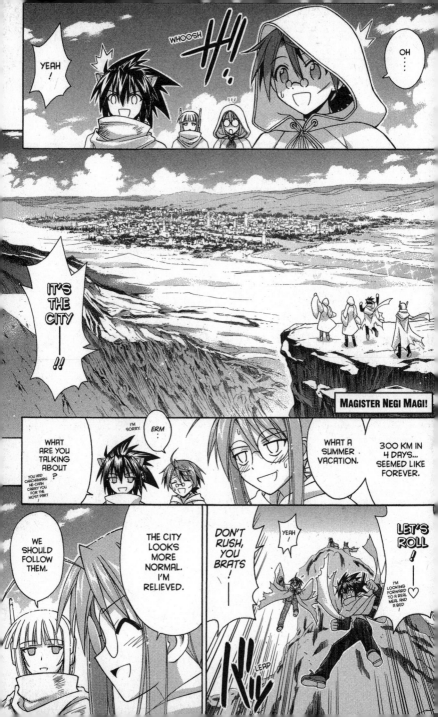

OH .....
WHOOSH
YEAH !
IT'S THE CITY ——— !!
MAGISTER NEGI MAGI!
300 KM IN 4 DAYS... SEEMED LIKE FOREVER.
WHAT A SUMMER VACATION.
ERM ..
I'M SORRY.
WHAT ARE YOU TALKING ABOUT ?
YOU HAD CHACHAMARU NE-CHAN CARRY YOU FOR THE MOST PART !
LET'S ROLL ! ——— ♡
I'M LOOKING FORWARD TO A REAL MEAL AND A BED
YEAH !
DON'T RUSH, YOU BRATS ! ———
LEAP
THE CITY LOOKS MORE NORMAL. I'M RELIEVED.
WE SHOULD FOLLOW THEM.

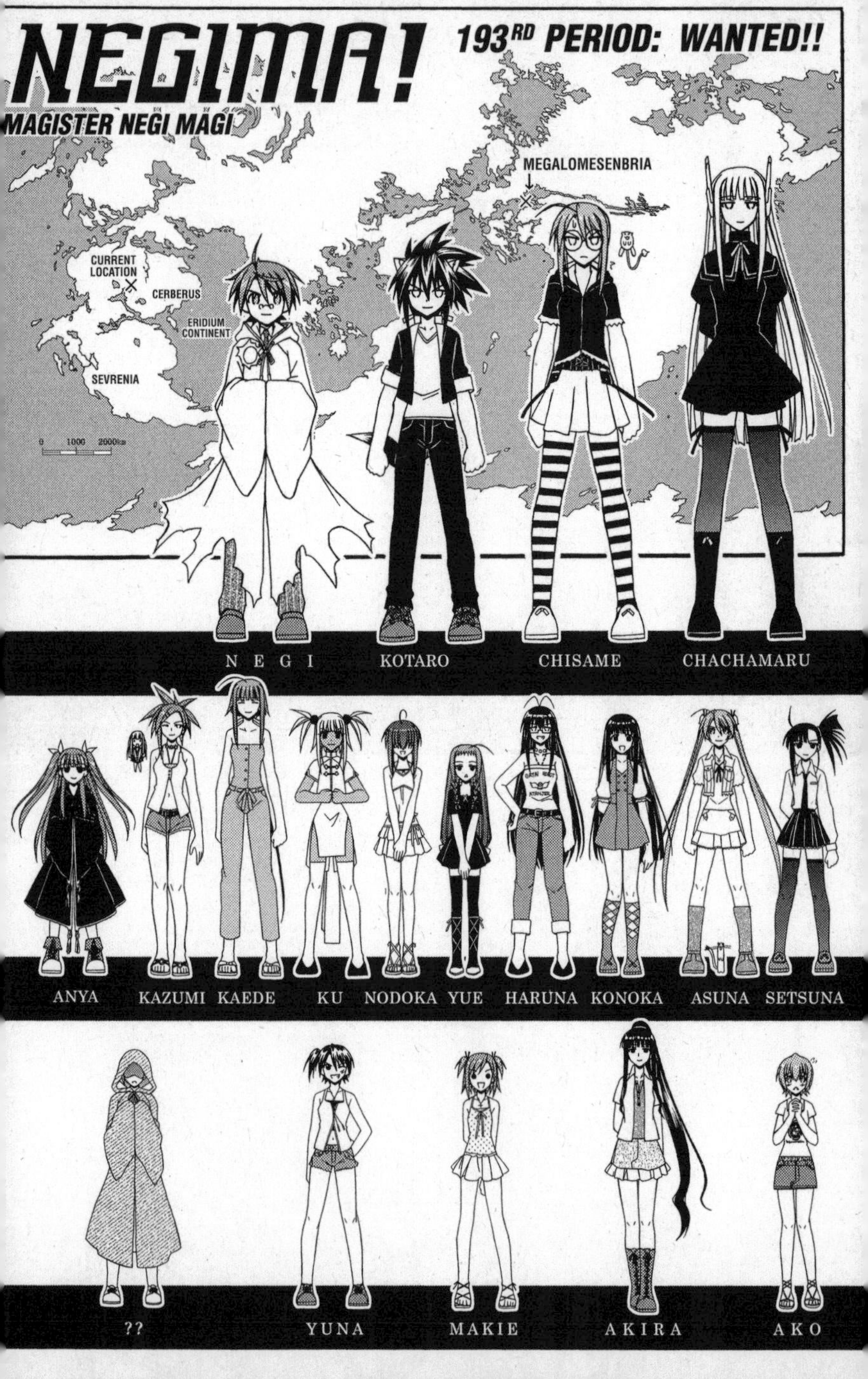

NEGIMA!
MAGISTER NEGI MAGI
193RD PERIOD: WANTED!!
MEGALOMESENBRIA
CURRENT LOCATION
CERBERUS
ERIDIUM CONTINENT
SEVRENIA
0 1000 2000km
NEGI
KOTARO
CHISAME
CHACHAMARU
ANYA
KAZUMI
KAEDE
KU
NODOKA
YUE
HARUNA
KONOKA
ASUNA
SETSUNA
??
YUNA
MAKIE
AKIRA
AKO

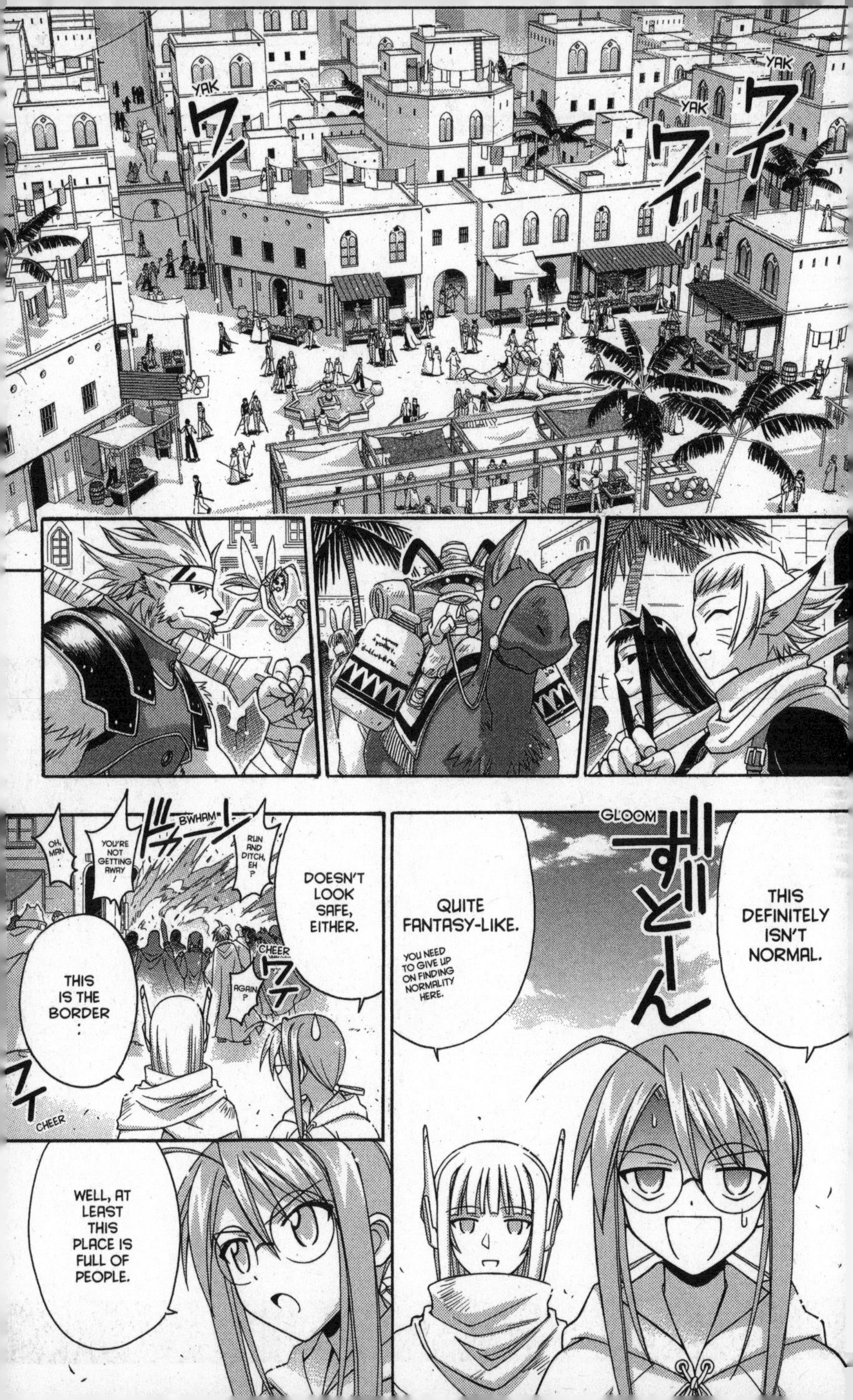

YAK
ワイ
YAK
ワイ
YAK
ワイ
GLOOM
THIS DEFINITELY ISN'T NORMAL.
QUITE FANTASY-LIKE.
YOU NEED TO GIVE UP ON FINDING NORMALITY HERE.
DOESN'T LOOK SAFE, EITHER.
RUN AND DITCH, EH?
BWHAM
YOU'RE NOT GETTING AWAY!
OH, MAN
CHEER
ワイ
AGAIN?
THIS IS THE BORDER:
ワイ
CHEER
WELL, AT LEAST THIS PLACE IS FULL OF PEOPLE.

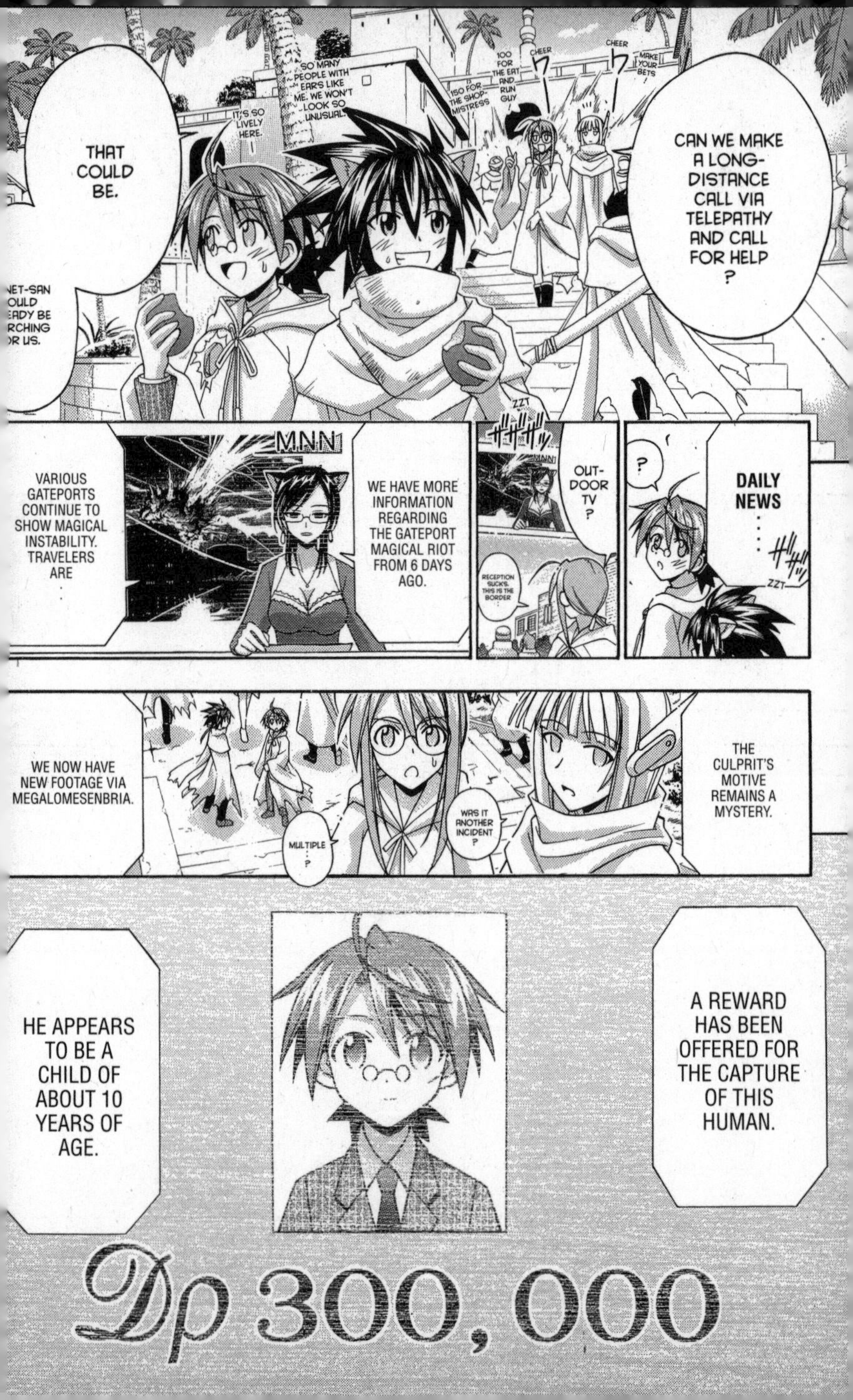
CAN WE MAKE A LONG-DISTANCE CALL VIA TELEPATHY AND CALL FOR HELP?
CHEER
MAKE YOUR BETS!
CHEER
100 FOR THE EAT AND RUN GUY
150 FOR THE SHOP-MISTRESS
SO MANY PEOPLE WITH EARS LIKE ME. WE WON'T LOOK SO UNUSUAL.
IT'S SO LIVELY HERE.
THAT COULD BE.
NET-SAN OULD EADY BE RCHING OR US.
DAILY NEWS...
?
ZZT
ZZT
OUT-DOOR TV?
MNN
RECEPTION SUCKS. THIS IS THE BORDER
MNN
WE HAVE MORE INFORMATION REGARDING THE GATEPORT MAGICAL RIOT FROM 6 DAYS AGO.
VARIOUS GATEPORTS CONTINUE TO SHOW MAGICAL INSTABILITY. TRAVELERS ARE...
THE CULPRIT'S MOTIVE REMAINS A MYSTERY.
WAS IT ANOTHER INCIDENT?
MULTIPLE...?
WE NOW HAVE NEW FOOTAGE VIA MEGALOMESENBRIA.
A REWARD HAS BEEN OFFERED FOR THE CAPTURE OF THIS HUMAN.
HE APPEARS TO BE A CHILD OF ABOUT 10 YEARS OF AGE.
Dp 300,000

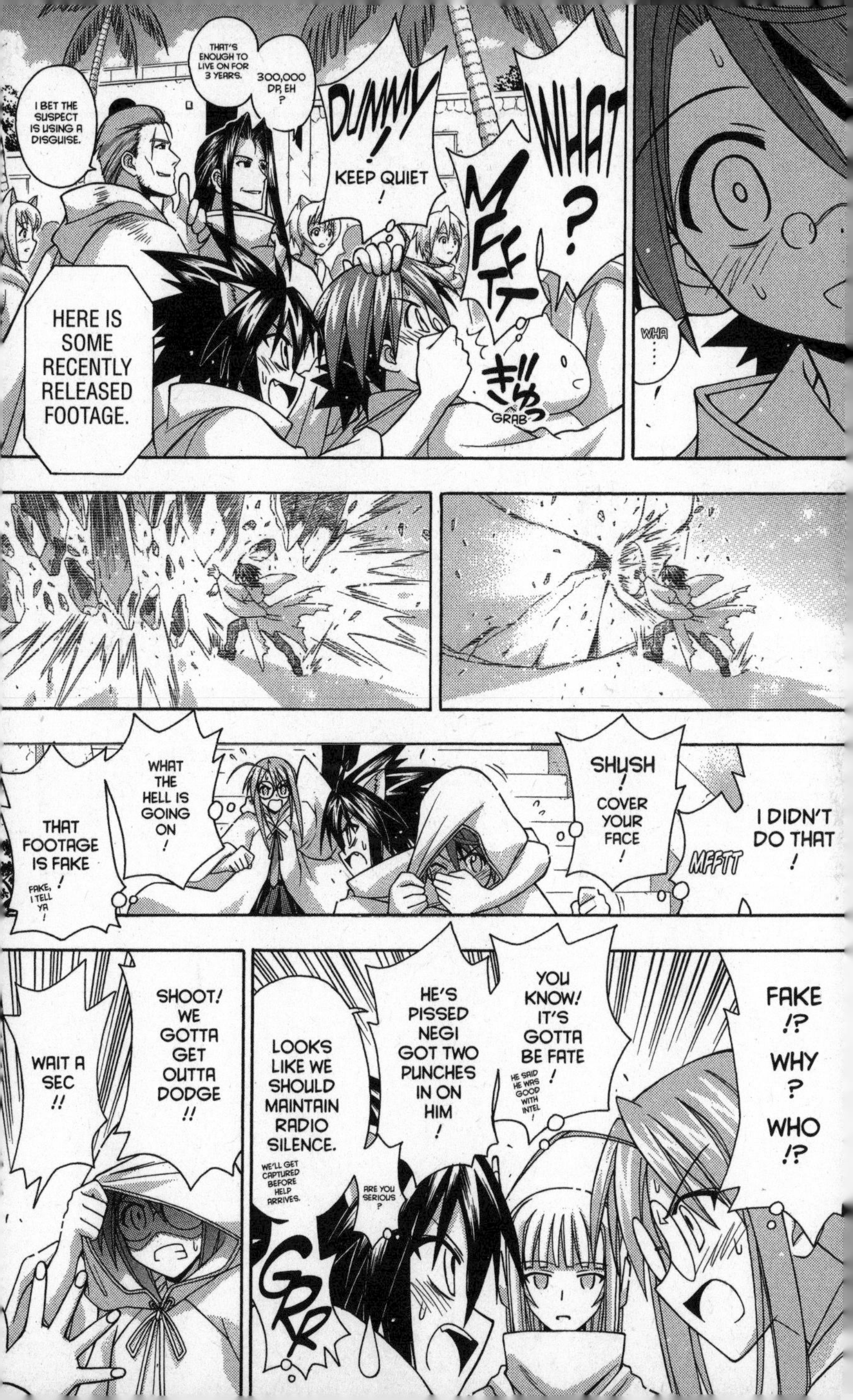
WHA...
WHAT?
MFFTT
DUMMY! KEEP QUIET!
300,000 DR, EH?
THAT'S ENOUGH TO LIVE ON FOR 3 YEARS.
I BET THE SUSPECT IS USING A DISGUISE.
HERE IS SOME RECENTLY RELEASED FOOTAGE.
ぎゅっ GRAB
I DIDN'T DO THAT!
MFFTT
SHUSH! COVER YOUR FACE!
WHAT THE HELL IS GOING ON!
THAT FOOTAGE IS FAKE!
FAKE, I TELL YA!
FAKE!? WHY? WHO!?
YOU KNOW! IT'S GOTTA BE FATE!
HE SAID HE WAS GOOD WITH INTEL!
HE'S PISSED NEGI GOT TWO PUNCHES IN ON HIM!
ARE YOU SERIOUS?
LOOKS LIKE WE SHOULD MAINTAIN RADIO SILENCE.
WE'LL GET CAPTURED BEFORE HELP ARRIVES.
GRR
SHOOT! WE GOTTA GET OUTTA DODGE!!
WAIT A SEC!!

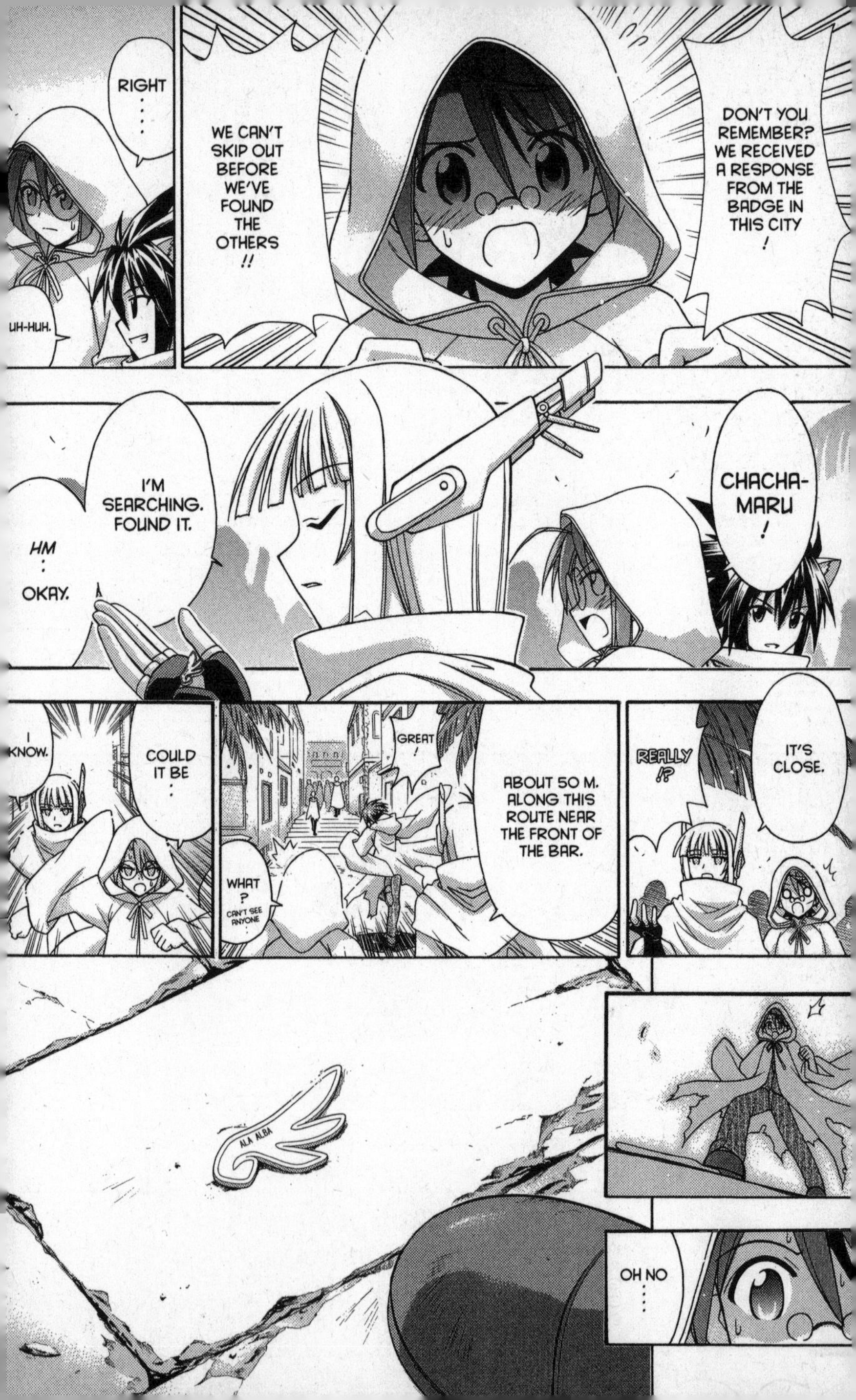
DON'T YOU REMEMBER? WE RECEIVED A RESPONSE FROM THE BADGE IN THIS CITY!
WE CAN'T SKIP OUT BEFORE WE'VE FOUND THE OTHERS!!
RIGHT....
UH-HUH.
CHACHA-MARU!
I'M SEARCHING. FOUND IT.
HM: OKAY.
IT'S CLOSE.
REALLY!?
ABOUT 50 M. ALONG THIS ROUTE NEAR THE FRONT OF THE BAR.
GREAT!
WHAT? CAN'T SEE ANYONE.
COULD IT BE...
I KNOW.
OH NO....
ALA ALBA

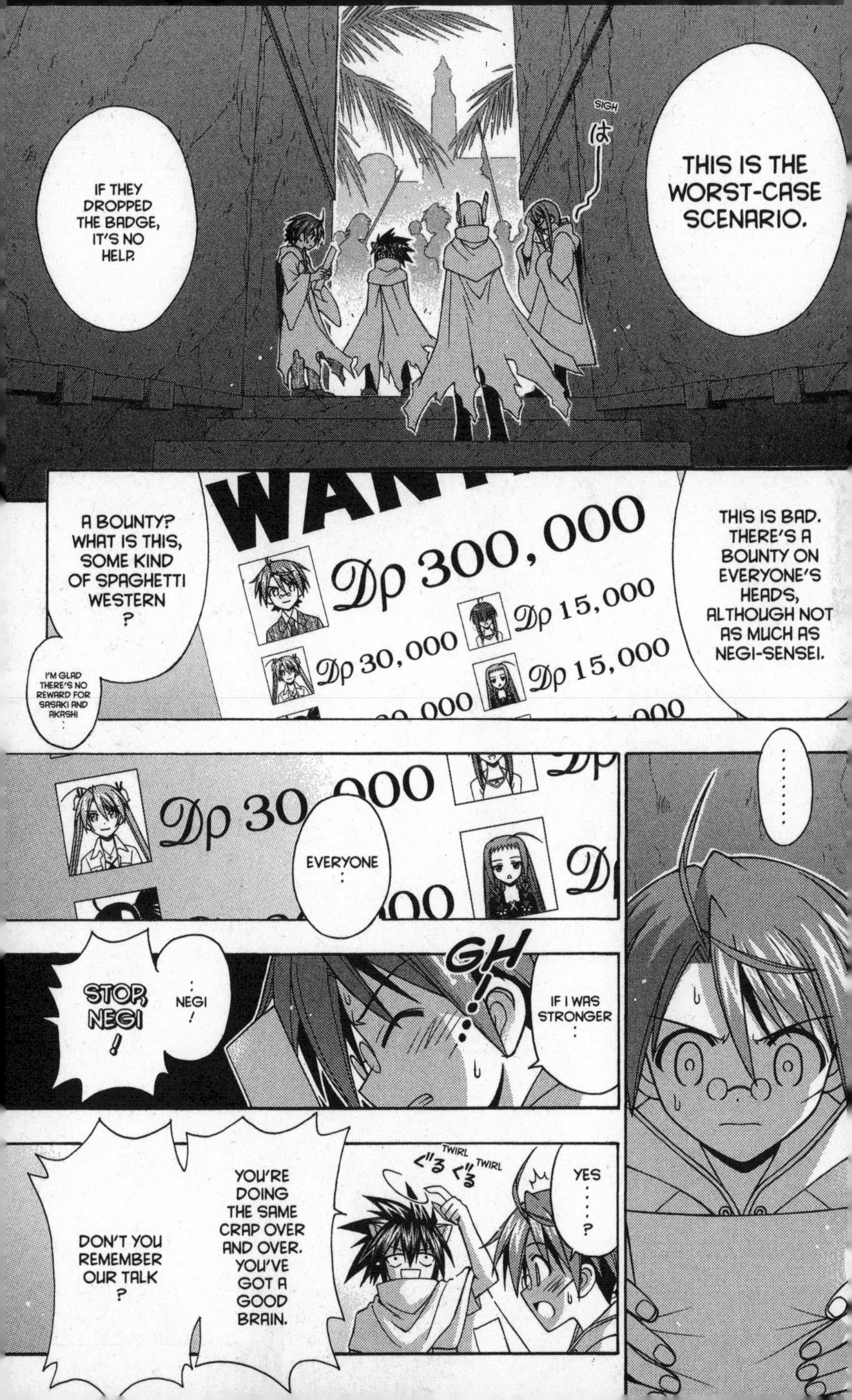
THIS IS THE WORST-CASE SCENARIO.
SIGH
は
IF THEY DROPPED THE BADGE, IT'S NO HELP.
THIS IS BAD. THERE'S A BOUNTY ON EVERYONE'S HEADS, ALTHOUGH NOT AS MUCH AS NEGI-SENSEI.
Dp 300,000
Dp 15,000
Dp 30,000
Dp 15,000
A BOUNTY? WHAT IS THIS, SOME KIND OF SPAGHETTI WESTERN?
I'M GLAD THERE'S NO REWARD FOR SASAKI AND AKASHI...
......
EVERYONE...
IF I WAS STRONGER...
GH!
...NEGI!
STOP, NEGI!
YES.....?
TWIRL
ぐる
TWIRL
ぐる
YOU'RE DOING THE SAME CRAP OVER AND OVER. YOU'VE GOT A GOOD BRAIN.
DON'T YOU REMEMBER OUR TALK?

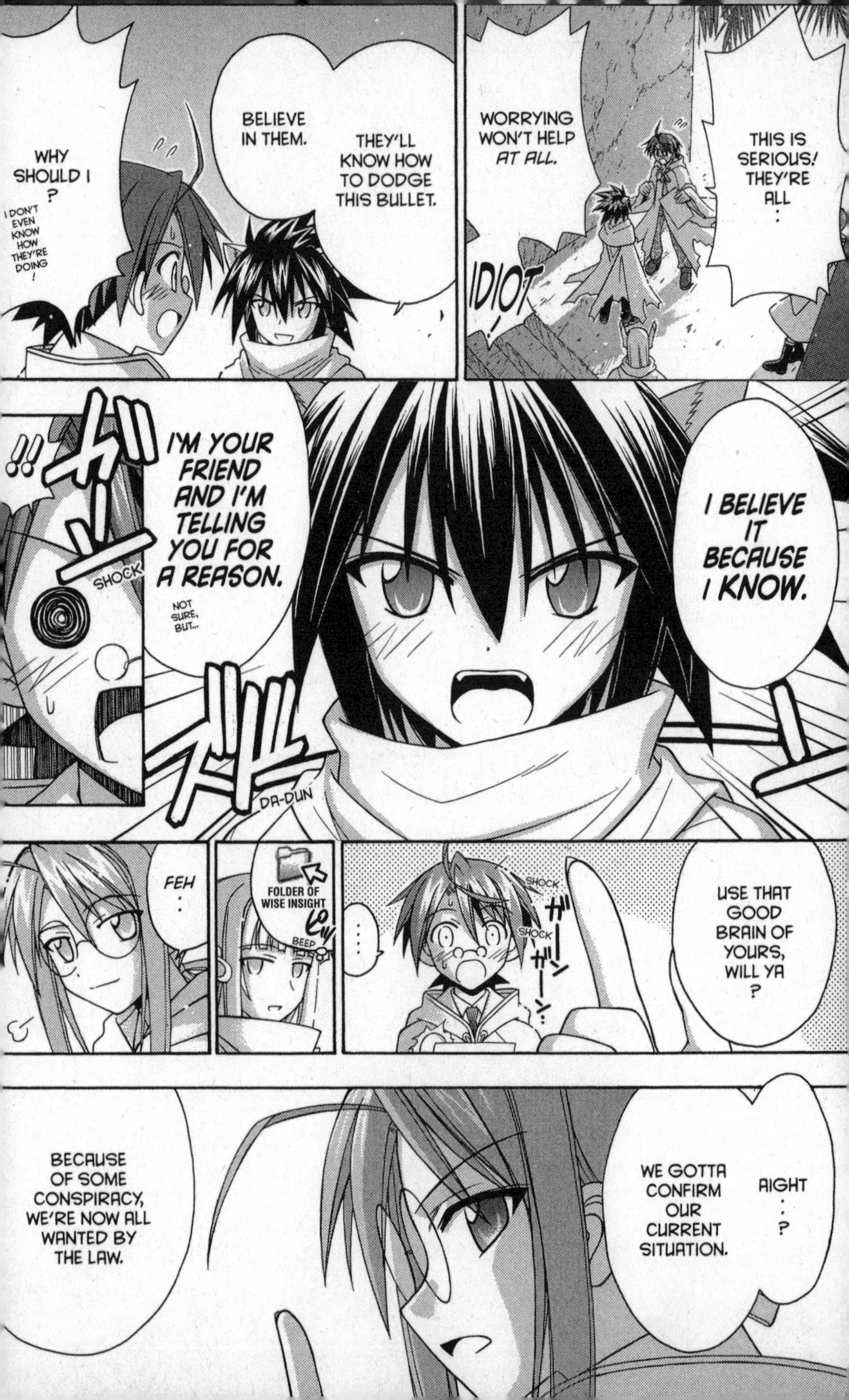
THIS IS SERIOUS! THEY'RE ALL...
IDIOT!
WORRYING WON'T HELP AT ALL.
BELIEVE IN THEM. THEY'LL KNOW HOW TO DODGE THIS BULLET.
WHY SHOULD I?
I DON'T EVEN KNOW HOW THEY'RE DOING!
I BELIEVE IT BECAUSE I KNOW.
DA-DUN
I'M YOUR FRIEND AND I'M TELLING YOU FOR A REASON.
NOT SURE, BUT...
!!
SHOCK
USE THAT GOOD BRAIN OF YOURS, WILL YA?
SHOCK
SHOCK
...
FOLDER OF WISE INSIGHT
BEEP
FEH...
AIGHT...?
WE GOTTA CONFIRM OUR CURRENT SITUATION.
BECAUSE OF SOME CONSPIRACY, WE'RE NOW ALL WANTED BY THE LAW.

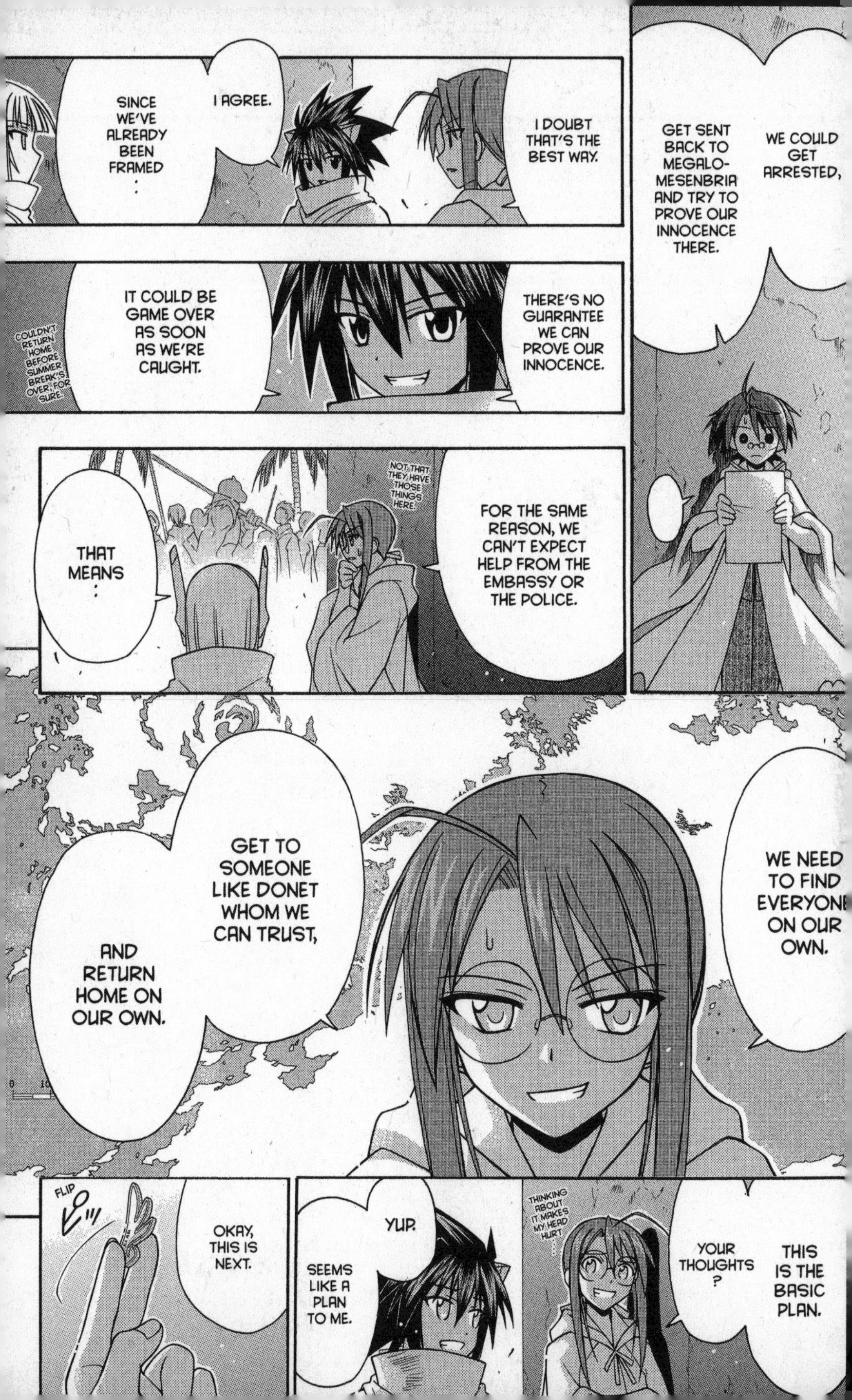
WE COULD GET ARRESTED,
GET SENT BACK TO MEGALO-MESENBRIA AND TRY TO PROVE OUR INNOCENCE THERE.
I DOUBT THAT'S THE BEST WAY.
I AGREE.
SINCE WE'VE ALREADY BEEN FRAMED
:
THERE'S NO GUARANTEE WE CAN PROVE OUR INNOCENCE.
IT COULD BE GAME OVER AS SOON AS WE'RE CAUGHT.
COULDN'T RETURN HOME BEFORE SUMMER BREAK'S OVER, FOR SURE.
FOR THE SAME REASON, WE CAN'T EXPECT HELP FROM THE EMBASSY OR THE POLICE.
NOT THAT THEY HAVE THOSE THINGS HERE.
THAT MEANS
:
WE NEED TO FIND EVERYONE ON OUR OWN.
GET TO SOMEONE LIKE DONET WHOM WE CAN TRUST,
AND RETURN HOME ON OUR OWN.
THIS IS THE BASIC PLAN.
YOUR THOUGHTS
?
THINKING ABOUT IT MAKES MY HEAD HURT
YUP.
SEEMS LIKE A PLAN TO ME.
OKAY, THIS IS NEXT.
FLIP

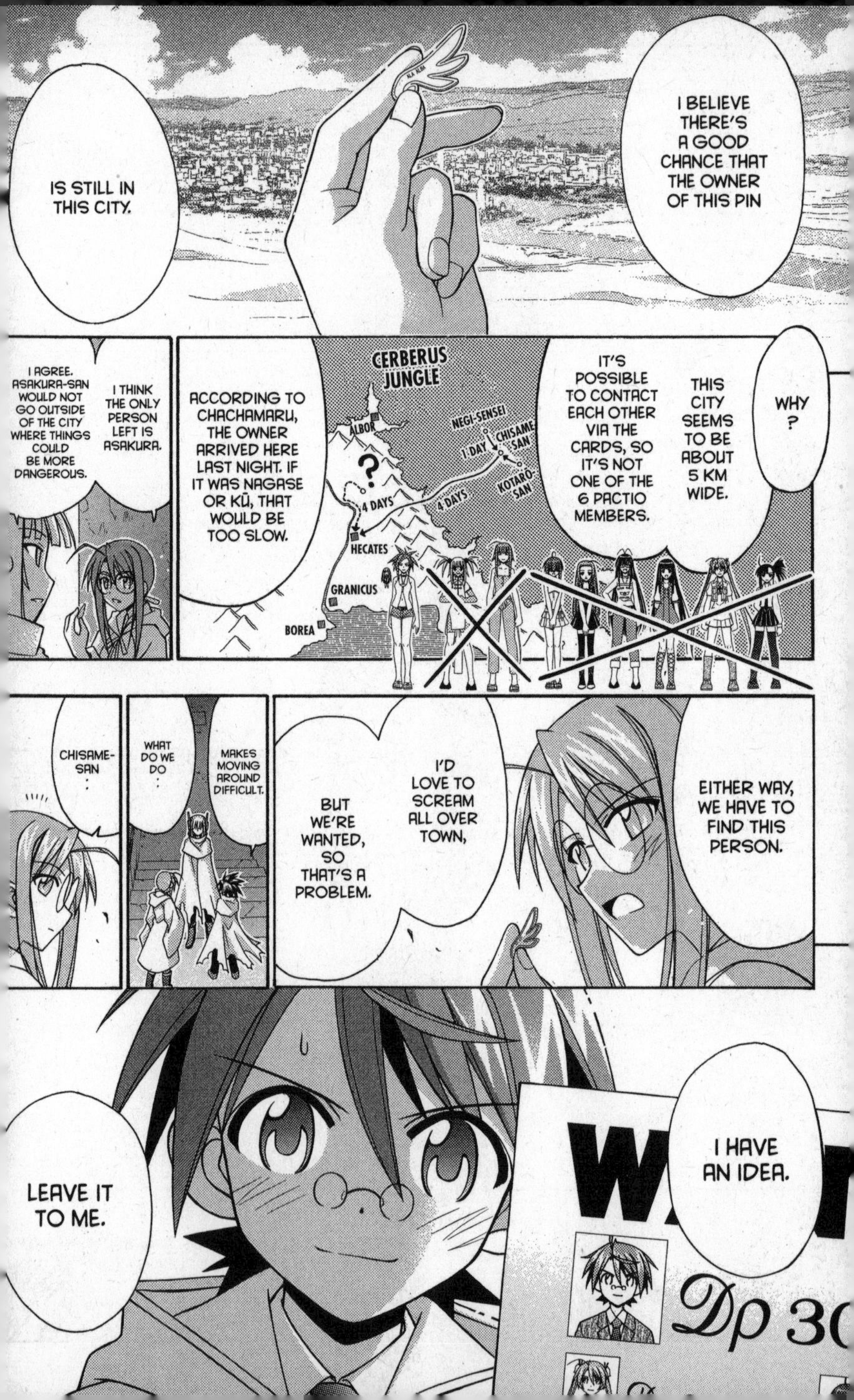
I BELIEVE THERE'S A GOOD CHANCE THAT THE OWNER OF THIS PIN
IS STILL IN THIS CITY.
WHY?
THIS CITY SEEMS TO BE ABOUT 5 KM WIDE.
IT'S POSSIBLE TO CONTACT EACH OTHER VIA THE CARDS, SO IT'S NOT ONE OF THE 6 PACTIO MEMBERS.
CERBERUS JUNGLE
ALBOR
NEGI-SENSEI
CHISAME-SAN
KOTARO-SAN
1 DAY
?
4 DAYS
4 DAYS
HECATES
GRANICUS
BOREA
ACCORDING TO CHACHAMARU, THE OWNER ARRIVED HERE LAST NIGHT. IF IT WAS NAGASE OR KŪ, THAT WOULD BE TOO SLOW.
I THINK THE ONLY PERSON LEFT IS ASAKURA.
I AGREE. ASAKURA-SAN WOULD NOT GO OUTSIDE OF THE CITY WHERE THINGS COULD BE MORE DANGEROUS.
EITHER WAY, WE HAVE TO FIND THIS PERSON.
I'D LOVE TO SCREAM ALL OVER TOWN,
BUT WE'RE WANTED, SO THAT'S A PROBLEM.
MAKES MOVING AROUND DIFFICULT.
WHAT DO WE DO...
CHISAME-SAN...
I HAVE AN IDEA.
LEAVE IT TO ME.

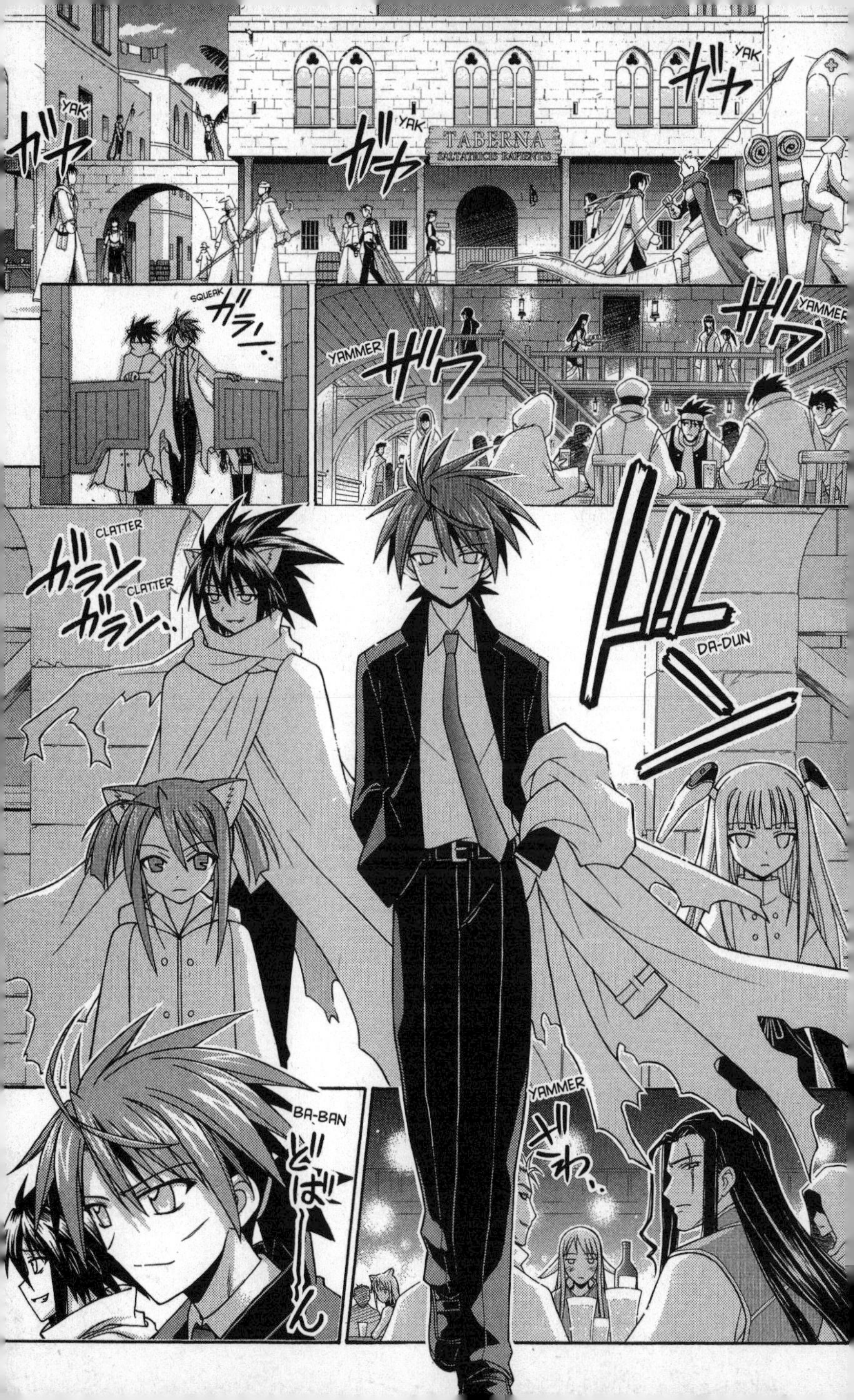
ガヤ
YAK
ガヤ
YAK
TABERNA
SALTATRICIS RAPIENTIS
ガヤ
YAK
ザワ
YAMMER
ザワ
YAMMER
ガラン…
SQUEAK
DA-DUN
ガラン
CLATTER
ガラン…
CLATTER
ざわ..
YAMMER
どばーん
BA-BAN

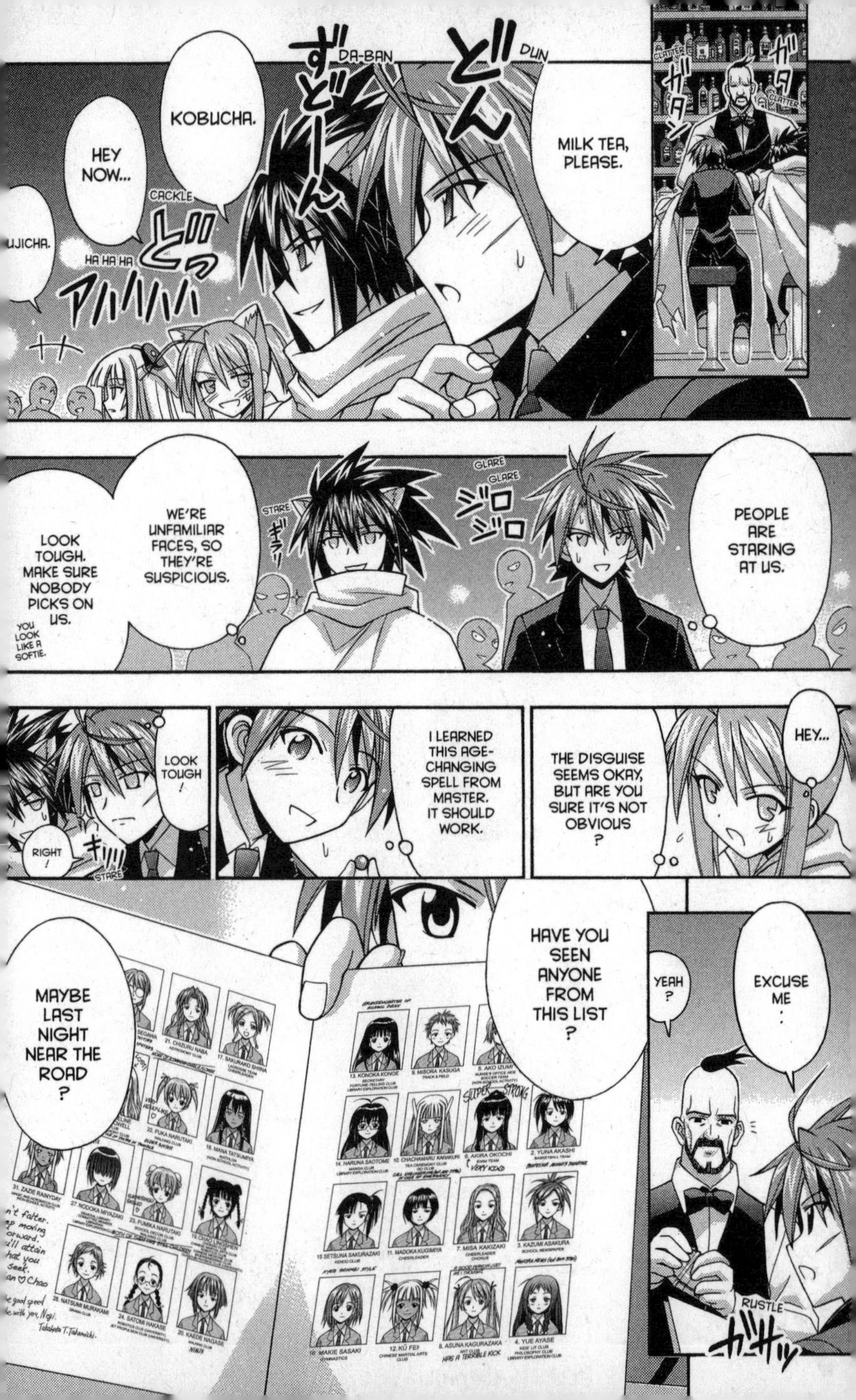
CLATTER
ガタ
ガタン
CLATTER
MILK TEA, PLEASE.
DUN
どん
DA-BAN
ずどーん
KOBUCHA.
HEY NOW...
CACKLE
どっ
HA HA HA
アハハハ
UJICHA.
PEOPLE ARE STARING AT US.
GLARE GLARE
ジロジロ
STARE
ギラ
WE'RE UNFAMILIAR FACES, SO THEY'RE SUSPICIOUS.
LOOK TOUGH. MAKE SURE NOBODY PICKS ON US.
YOU LOOK LIKE A SOFTIE.
HEY...
THE DISGUISE SEEMS OKAY, BUT ARE YOU SURE IT'S NOT OBVIOUS?
I LEARNED THIS AGE-CHANGING SPELL FROM MASTER. IT SHOULD WORK.
LOOK TOUGH!
RIGHT!
STARE
EXCUSE ME:
YEAH?
RUSTLE
ガサッ
HAVE YOU SEEN ANYONE FROM THIS LIST?
MAYBE LAST NIGHT NEAR THE ROAD?
13. KONOKA KONOE
9. MISORA KASUGA
5. AKO IZUMI
14. HARUNA SAOTOME
10. CHACHAMARU KARAKURI
6. AKIRA OKOCHI
2. YUNA AKASHI
15. SETSUNA SAKURAZAKI
11. MADOKA KUGIMIYA
7. MISA KAKIZAKI
3. KAZUMI ASAKURA
16. MAKIE SASAKI
12. KU FEI
8. ASUNA KAGURAZAKA
4. YUE AYASE
21. CHIZURU NABA
17. SAKURAKO SHIINA
22. FUKA NARUTAKI
18. MANA TATSUMIYA
31. ZAZIE RAINYDAY
27. NODOKA MIYAZAKI
23. FUMIKA NARUTAKI
19. CHAO LINGSHEN
28. NATSUMI MURAKAMI
24. SATOMI HAKASE
20. KAEDE NAGASE

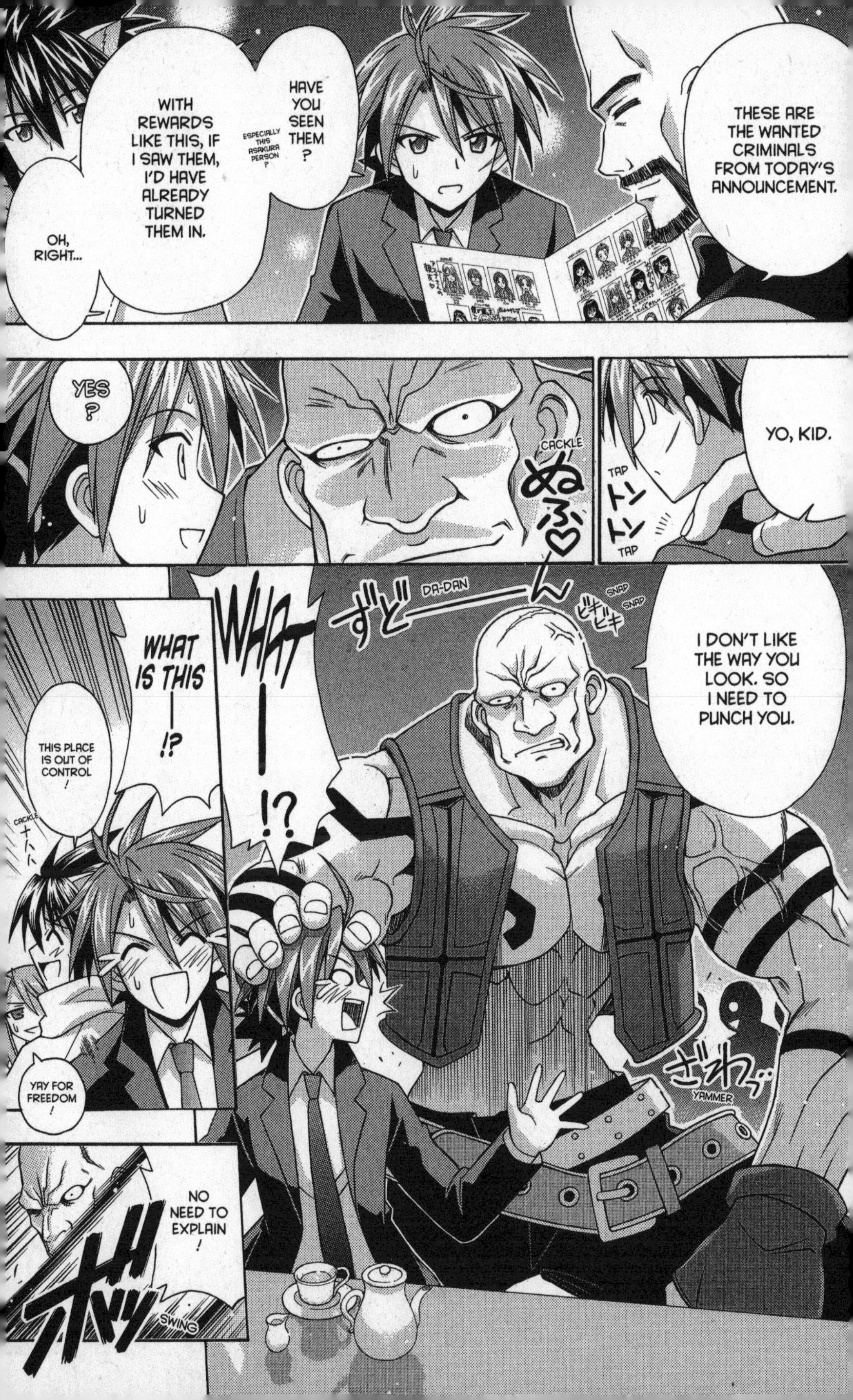

THESE ARE THE WANTED CRIMINALS FROM TODAY'S ANNOUNCEMENT.
HAVE YOU SEEN THEM?
ESPECIALLY THIS ASAKURA PERSON?
WITH REWARDS LIKE THIS, IF I SAW THEM, I'D HAVE ALREADY TURNED THEM IN.
OH, RIGHT...
YO, KID.
トントン
TAP TAP
ぬふ♡ん
CACKLE
YES?
I DON'T LIKE THE WAY YOU LOOK. SO I NEED TO PUNCH YOU.
ビキビキ
SNAP SNAP
ずど——ん
DA-DAN
WHAT—!?
WHAT IS THIS—!?
THIS PLACE IS OUT OF CONTROL!
ナハハ
CACKLE
ざわっ
YAMMER
YAY FOR FREEDOM!
NO NEED TO EXPLAIN!
SWING

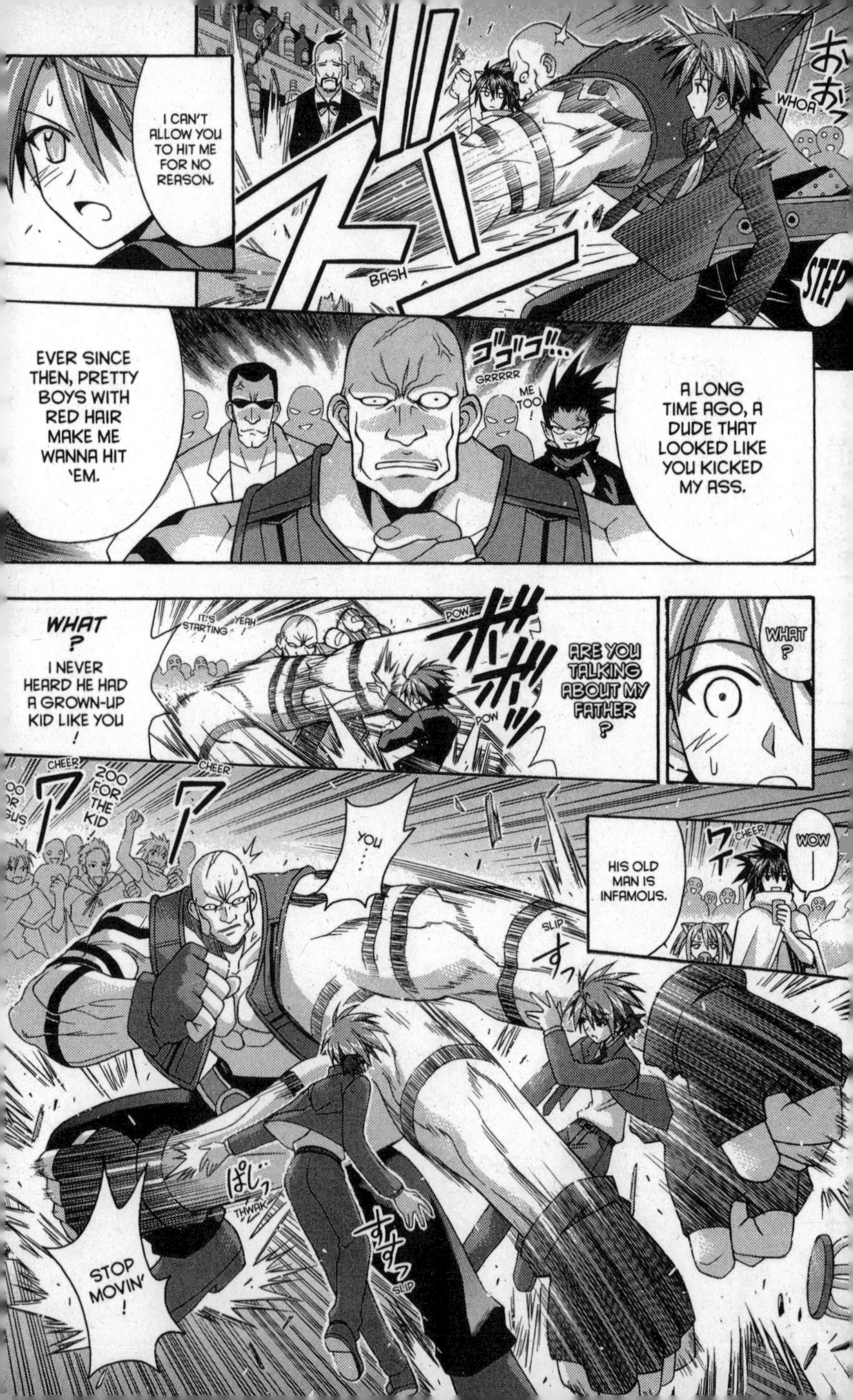
WHOA
BASH
STEP
I CAN'T ALLOW YOU TO HIT ME FOR NO REASON.
A LONG TIME AGO, A DUDE THAT LOOKED LIKE YOU KICKED MY ASS.
GRRRRR
ME TOO!
EVER SINCE THEN, PRETTY BOYS WITH RED HAIR MAKE ME WANNA HIT 'EM.
WHAT?
ARE YOU TALKING ABOUT MY FATHER?
POW
POW
IT'S STARTING!
YEAH
WHAT? I NEVER HEARD HE HAD A GROWN-UP KID LIKE YOU!
WOW—
CHEER
HIS OLD MAN IS INFAMOUS.
SLIP
YOU...
CHEER
200 FOR THE KID!
100 FOR GUS
CHEER
THWAK
SLIP
STOP MOVIN'!

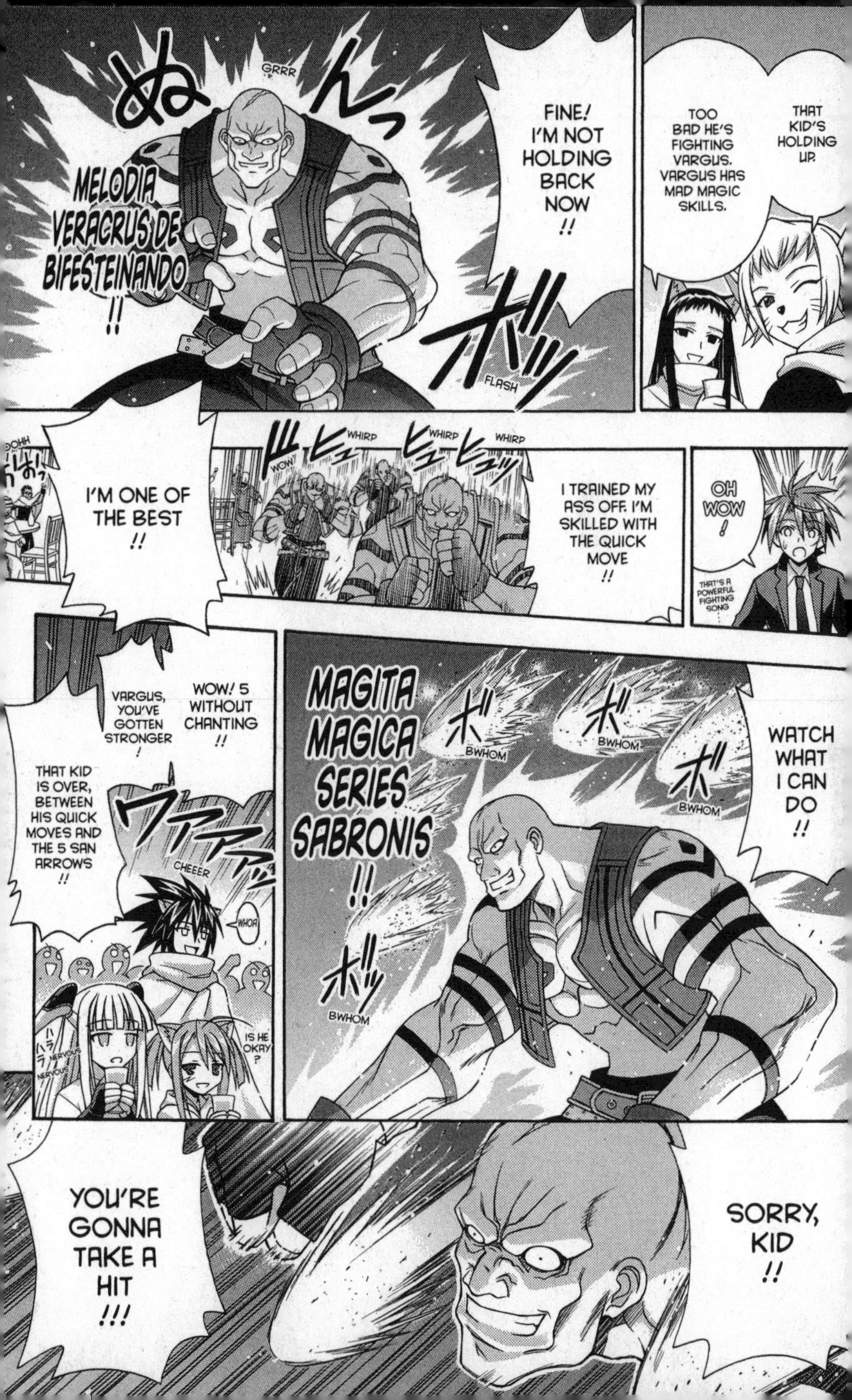
THAT KID'S HOLDING UP.
TOO BAD HE'S FIGHTING VARGUS. VARGUS HAS MAD MAGIC SKILLS.
FINE! I'M NOT HOLDING BACK NOW!!
んっ
ぬ
GRRR
MELODIA VERACRUS DE BIFESTEINANDO!!
ボッ
FLASH
OH WOW!
THAT'S A POWERFUL FIGHTING SONG...
I TRAINED MY ASS OFF. I'M SKILLED WITH THE QUICK MOVE!!
ヒュ WHIRP
ヒュ WHIRP
ヒュ WHIRP
ヒュ
WOW
I'M ONE OF THE BEST!!
WATCH WHAT I CAN DO!!
ボ BWHOM
ボ BWHOM
ボ BWHOM
MAGITA MAGICA SERIES SABRONIS!!
ボッ BWHOM
WOW! 5 WITHOUT CHANTING!!
VARGUS, YOU'VE GOTTEN STRONGER!
THAT KID IS OVER, BETWEEN HIS QUICK MOVES AND THE 5 SAN ARROWS!!
ワァァッ CHEEER
WHOA
IS HE OKAY?
ハラハラ NERVOUS NERVOUS
SORRY, KID!!
YOU'RE GONNA TAKE A HIT!!!

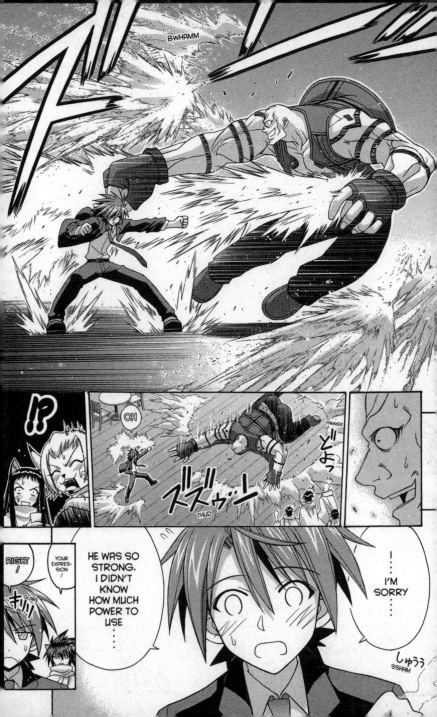

BWHAMM
!?
OH
どよっ
YAMMER
ズズゥ…ン
THUD
I'M SORRY……
しゅうう
SSHHM
HE WAS SO STRONG. I DIDN'T KNOW HOW MUCH POWER TO USE……
YOUR EXPRES-SION!
RIGHT!
キリリ
GLARE

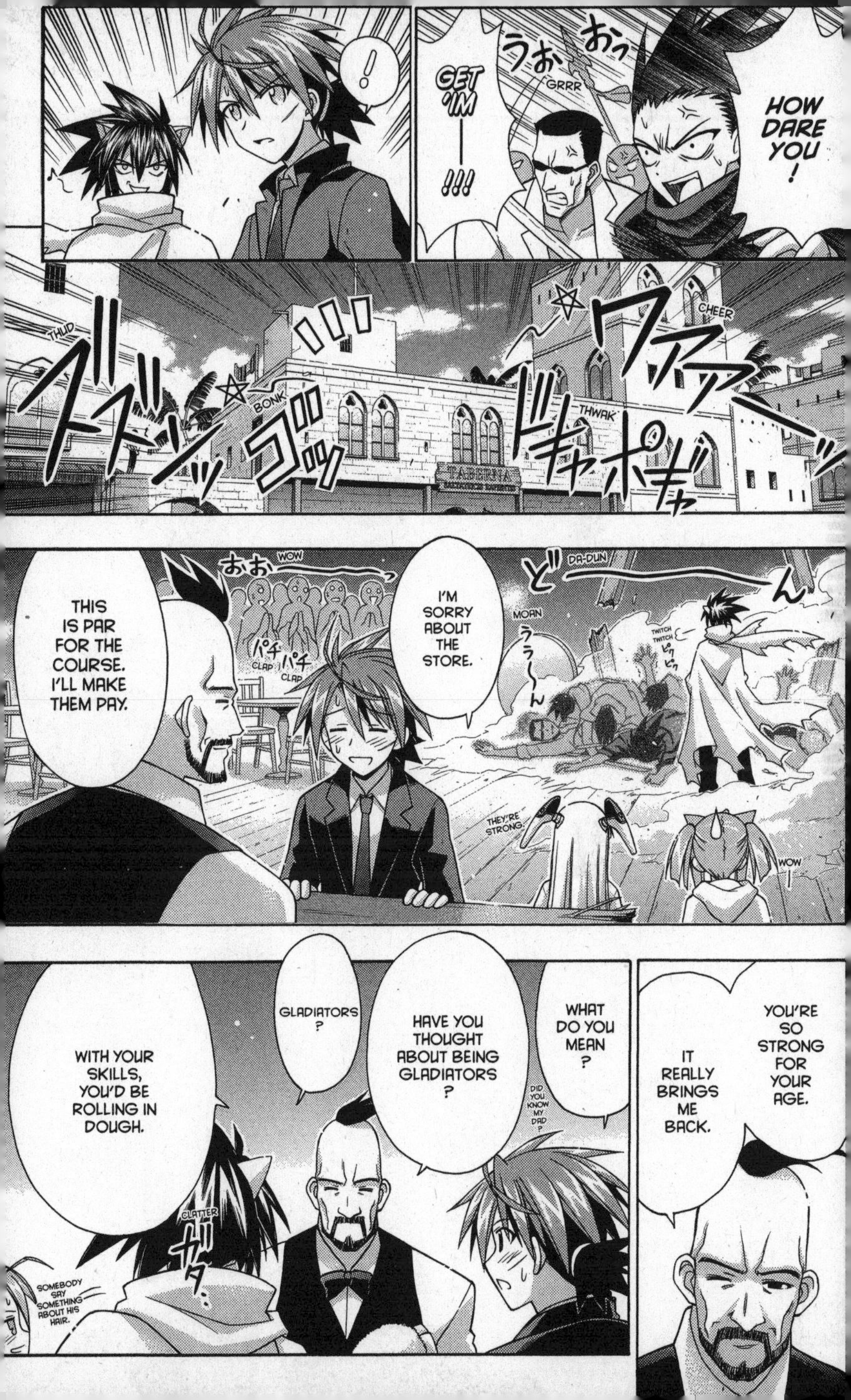
HOW DARE YOU!
うおおっ
GRRR
GET 'IM——!!!
!
ワアアーッ
CHEER
ドギャポギャ
THWAK
!!!
ゴッ
BONK
ズドッ
THUD
TABERNA
どーーん
DA-DUN
TWITCH TWITCH
ピクピク
MOAN
ウラ～ん
WOW!
THEY'RE STRONG
I'M SORRY ABOUT THE STORE.
おおー
WOW
パチパチ
CLAP CLAP
THIS IS PAR FOR THE COURSE. I'LL MAKE THEM PAY.
YOU'RE SO STRONG FOR YOUR AGE.
IT REALLY BRINGS ME BACK.
WHAT DO YOU MEAN?
DID YOU KNOW MY DAD?
HAVE YOU THOUGHT ABOUT BEING GLADIATORS?
GLADIATORS?
WITH YOUR SKILLS, YOU'D BE ROLLING IN DOUGH.
CLATTER
ガタ..
SOMEBODY SAY SOMETHING ABOUT HIS HAIR.

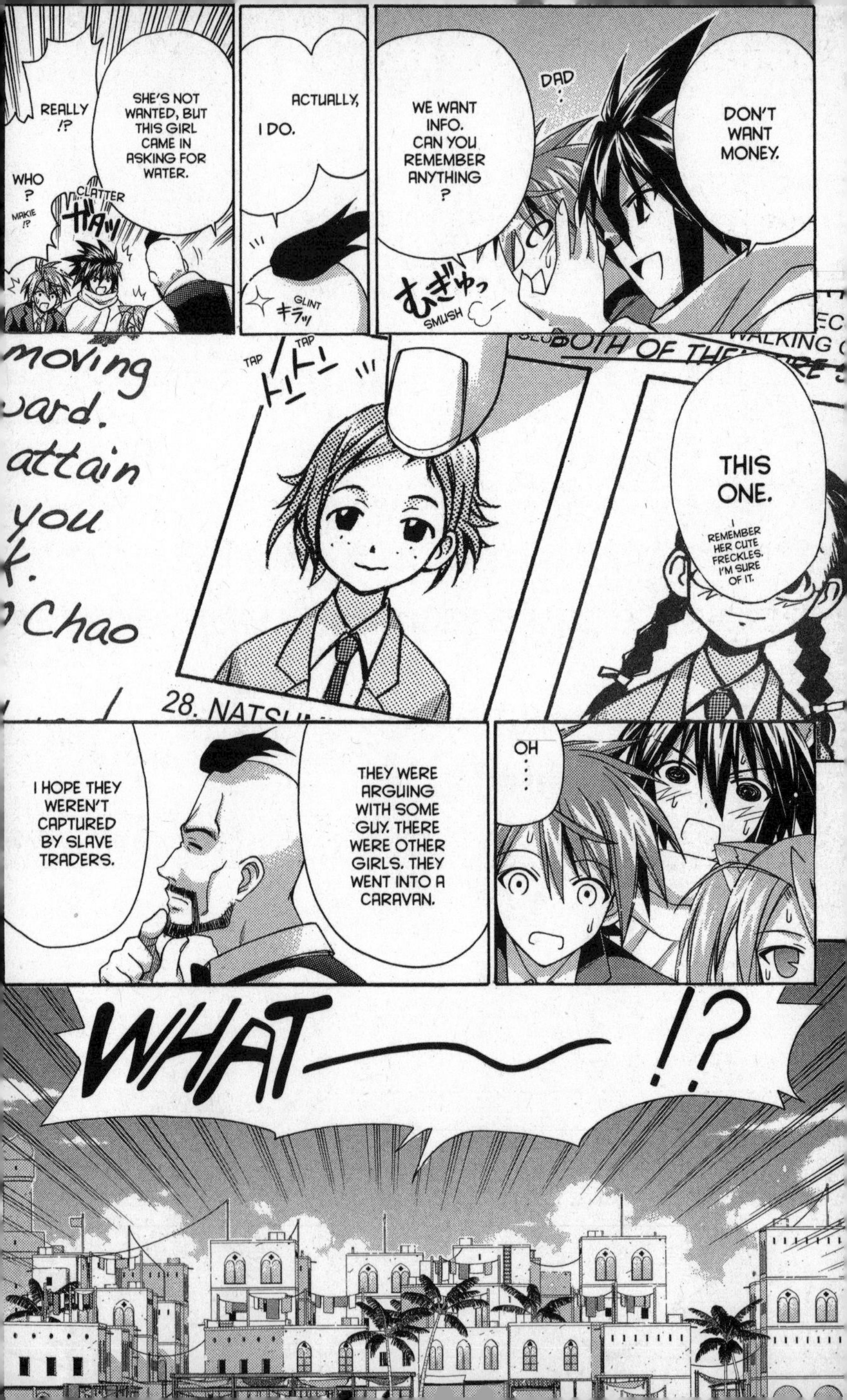
DON'T WANT MONEY.
DAD...
WE WANT INFO. CAN YOU REMEMBER ANYTHING?
むぎゅっ SMUSH
ACTUALLY, I DO.
キラッ GLINT
SHE'S NOT WANTED, BUT THIS GIRL CAME IN ASKING FOR WATER.
REALLY !?
ガタッ CLATTER
WHO ?
MAKIE !?
THIS ONE.
I REMEMBER HER CUTE FRECKLES. I'M SURE OF IT.
トントン TAP TAP
moving
attain
you
Chao
OH......
THEY WERE ARGUING WITH SOME GUY. THERE WERE OTHER GIRLS. THEY WENT INTO A CARAVAN.
I HOPE THEY WEREN'T CAPTURED BY SLAVE TRADERS.
WHAT——!?

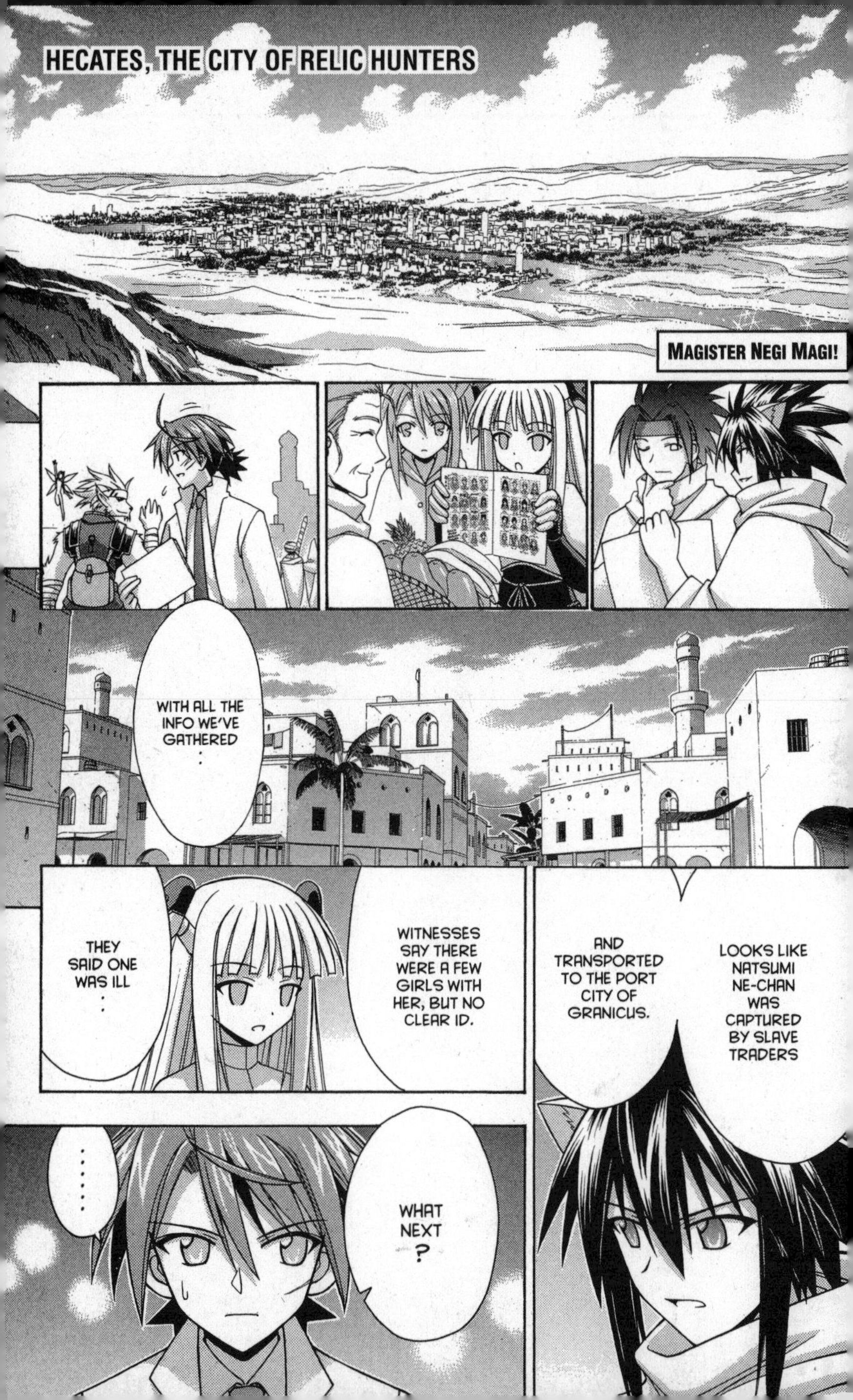
HECATES, THE CITY OF RELIC HUNTERS
MAGISTER NEGI MAGI!
WITH ALL THE INFO WE'VE GATHERED . . .
LOOKS LIKE NATSUMI NE-CHAN WAS CAPTURED BY SLAVE TRADERS
AND TRANSPORTED TO THE PORT CITY OF GRANICUS.
WITNESSES SAY THERE WERE A FEW GIRLS WITH HER, BUT NO CLEAR ID.
THEY SAID ONE WAS ILL . . .
WHAT NEXT ?
. . . . . .

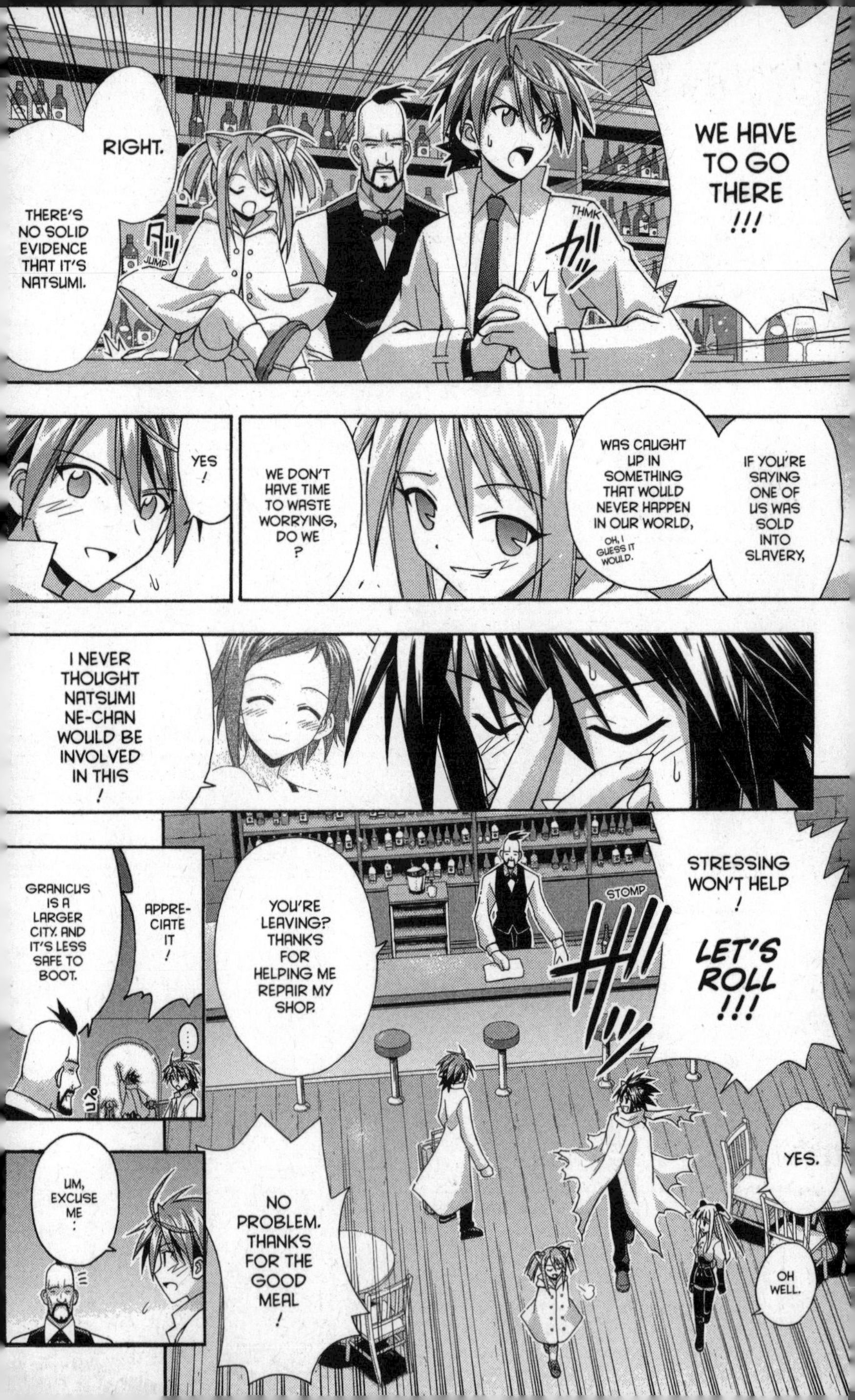
WE HAVE TO GO THERE!!!
THMK
RIGHT.
JUMP
THERE'S NO SOLID EVIDENCE THAT IT'S NATSUMI.
IF YOU'RE SAYING ONE OF US WAS SOLD INTO SLAVERY,
WAS CAUGHT UP IN SOMETHING THAT WOULD NEVER HAPPEN IN OUR WORLD,
OH, I GUESS IT WOULD.
WE DON'T HAVE TIME TO WASTE WORRYING, DO WE?
YES!
I NEVER THOUGHT NATSUMI NE-CHAN WOULD BE INVOLVED IN THIS!
STRESSING WON'T HELP!
LET'S ROLL!!!
STOMP
YES.
OH WELL.
YOU'RE LEAVING? THANKS FOR HELPING ME REPAIR MY SHOP.
APPRE-CIATE IT!
GRANICUS IS A LARGER CITY. AND IT'S LESS SAFE TO BOOT.
...
NO PROBLEM. THANKS FOR THE GOOD MEAL!
UM, EXCUSE ME...

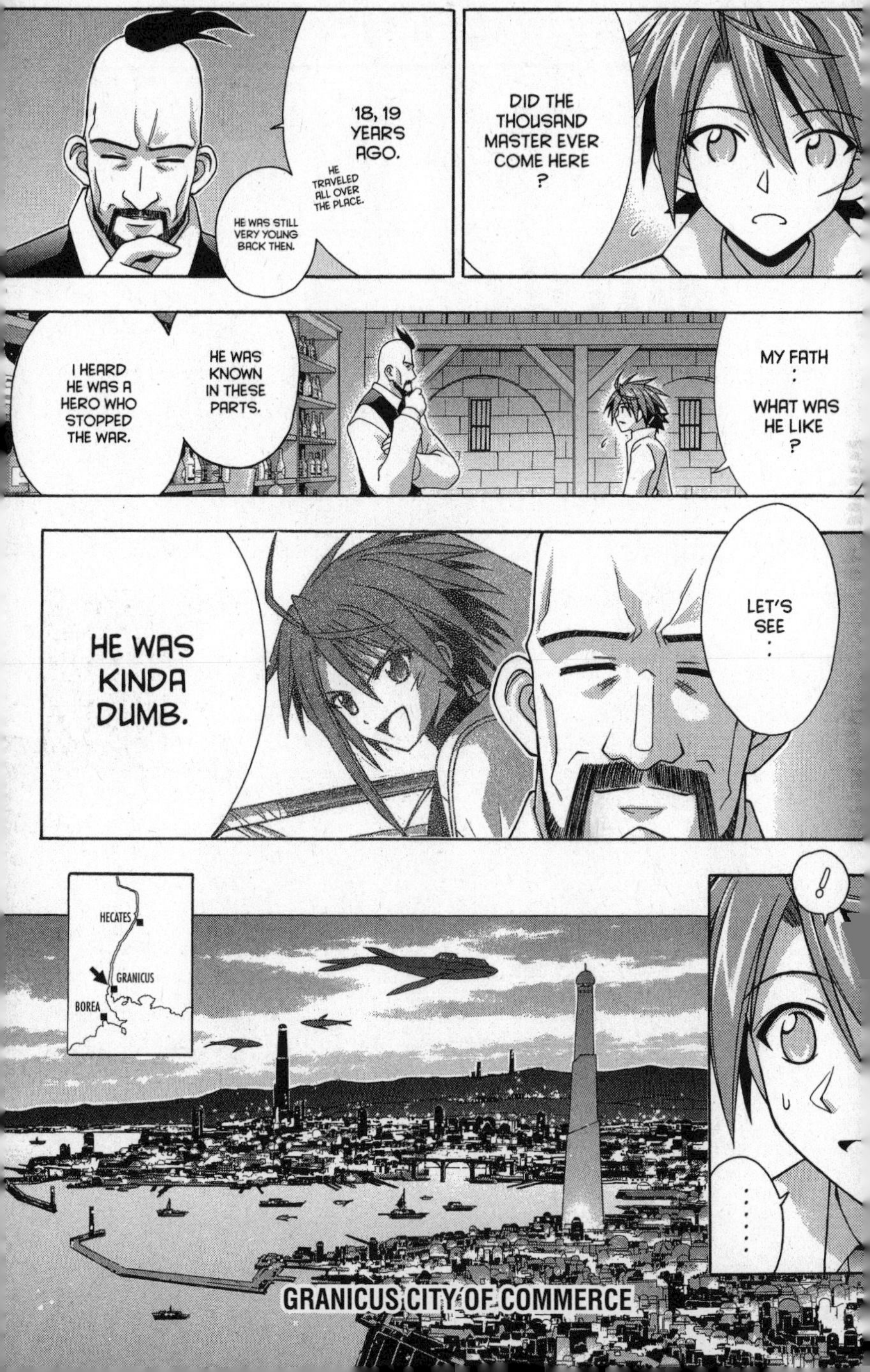
DID THE THOUSAND MASTER EVER COME HERE ?
18, 19 YEARS AGO.
HE TRAVELED ALL OVER THE PLACE.
HE WAS STILL VERY YOUNG BACK THEN.
MY FATH : WHAT WAS HE LIKE ?
HE WAS KNOWN IN THESE PARTS.
I HEARD HE WAS A HERO WHO STOPPED THE WAR.
LET'S SEE :
HE WAS KINDA DUMB.
!
......
HECATES
GRANICUS
BOREA
GRANICUS CITY OF COMMERCE

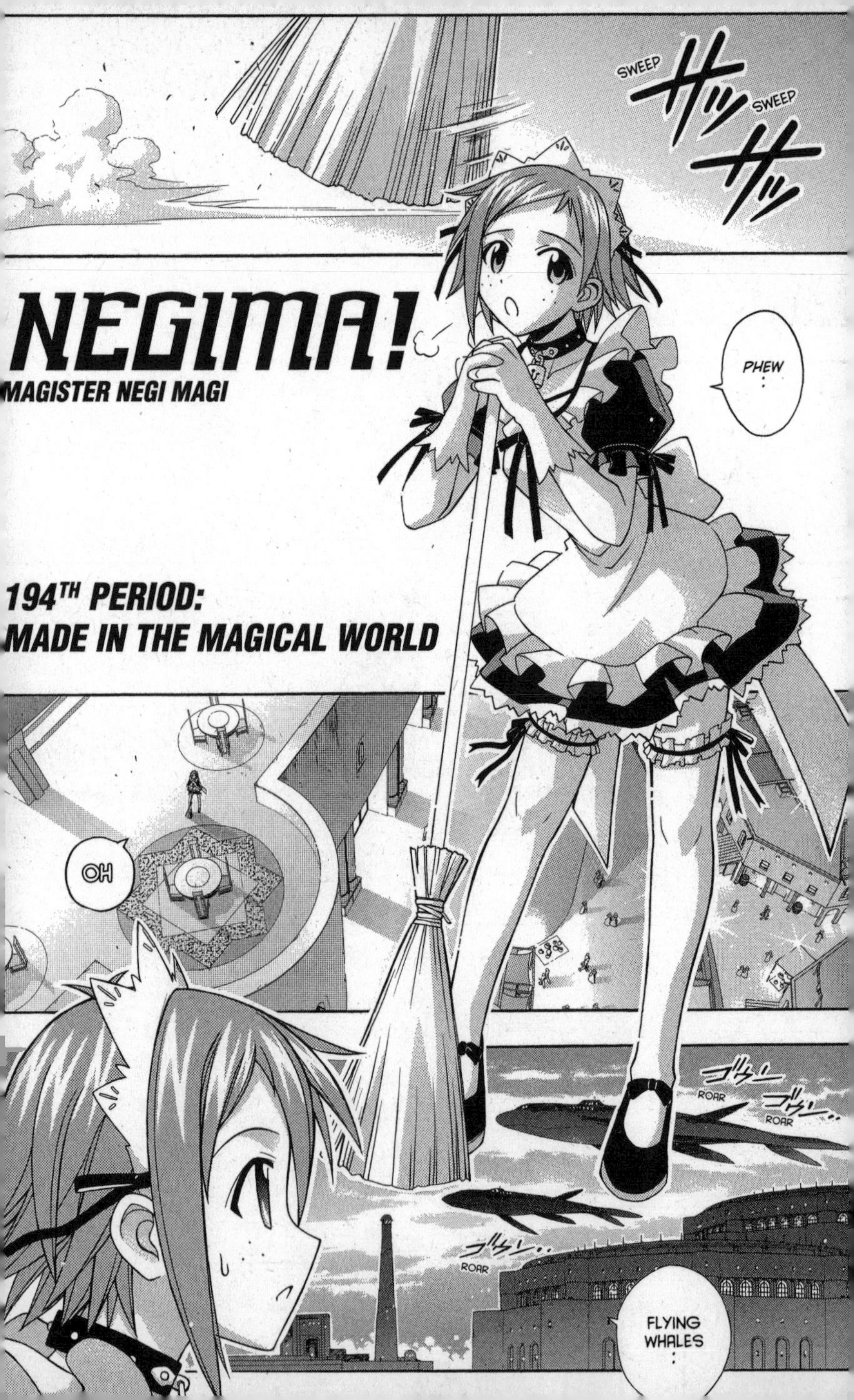
SWEEP
SWEEP
PHEW
NEGIMA!
MAGISTER NEGI MAGI
194TH PERIOD:
MADE IN THE MAGICAL WORLD
OH
ROAR
ROAR
ROAR
FLYING WHALES

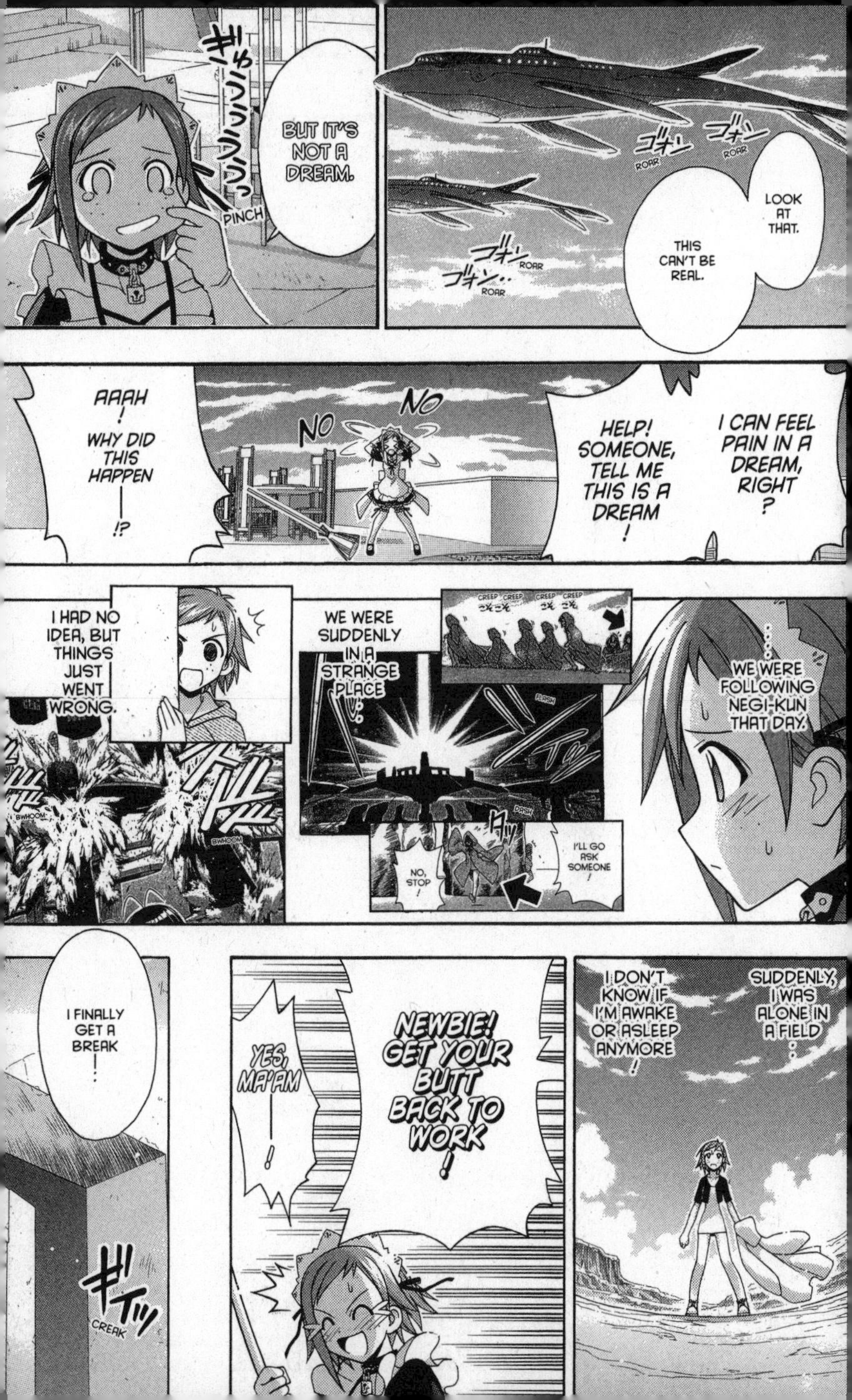
ROAR
ROAR
LOOK AT THAT.
THIS CAN'T BE REAL.
ROAR
ROAR
BUT IT'S NOT A DREAM.
PINCH
I CAN FEEL PAIN IN A DREAM, RIGHT?
HELP! SOMEONE, TELL ME THIS IS A DREAM!
NO
NO
AAAH! WHY DID THIS HAPPEN—!?
...WE WERE FOLLOWING NEGI-KUN THAT DAY.
CREEP CREEP CREEP CREEP
WE WERE SUDDENLY IN A STRANGE PLACE...
FLASH
DASH
I'LL GO ASK SOMEONE!
NO, STOP!
I HAD NO IDEA, BUT THINGS JUST WENT WRONG.
BWHOOM
BWHOOM
SUDDENLY, I WAS ALONE IN A FIELD...
I DON'T KNOW IF I'M AWAKE OR ASLEEP ANYMORE!
NEWBIE! GET YOUR BUTT BACK TO WORK!
YES, MA'AM—!
I FINALLY GET A BREAK!
CREAK

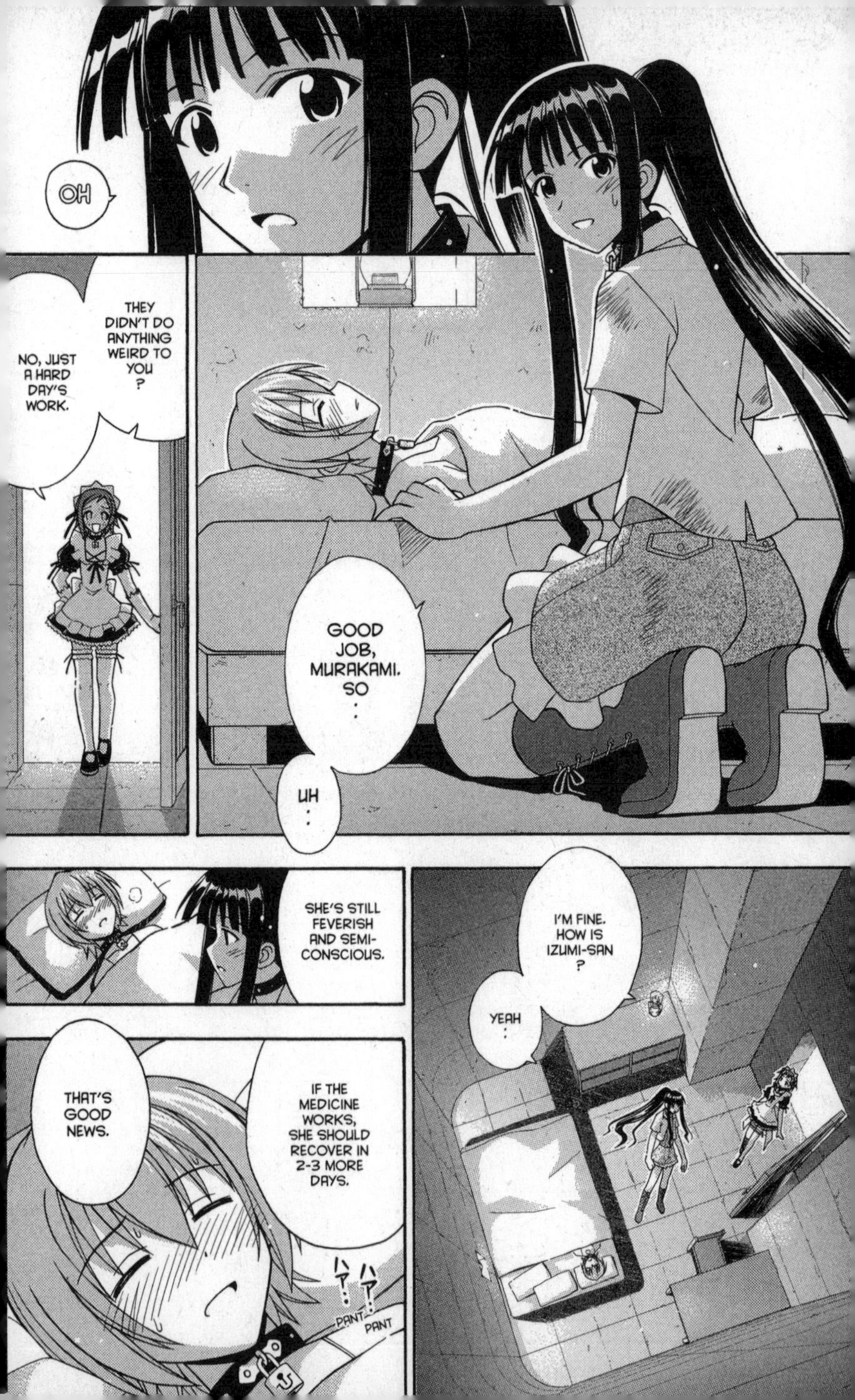
OH
GOOD JOB, MURAKAMI. SO . . .
UH . . .
THEY DIDN'T DO ANYTHING WEIRD TO YOU ?
NO, JUST A HARD DAY'S WORK.
I'M FINE. HOW IS IZUMI-SAN ?
YEAH . . .
SHE'S STILL FEVERISH AND SEMI-CONSCIOUS.
IF THE MEDICINE WORKS, SHE SHOULD RECOVER IN 2-3 MORE DAYS.
THAT'S GOOD NEWS.
ハァ . . . ハァ . . .
PANT PANT

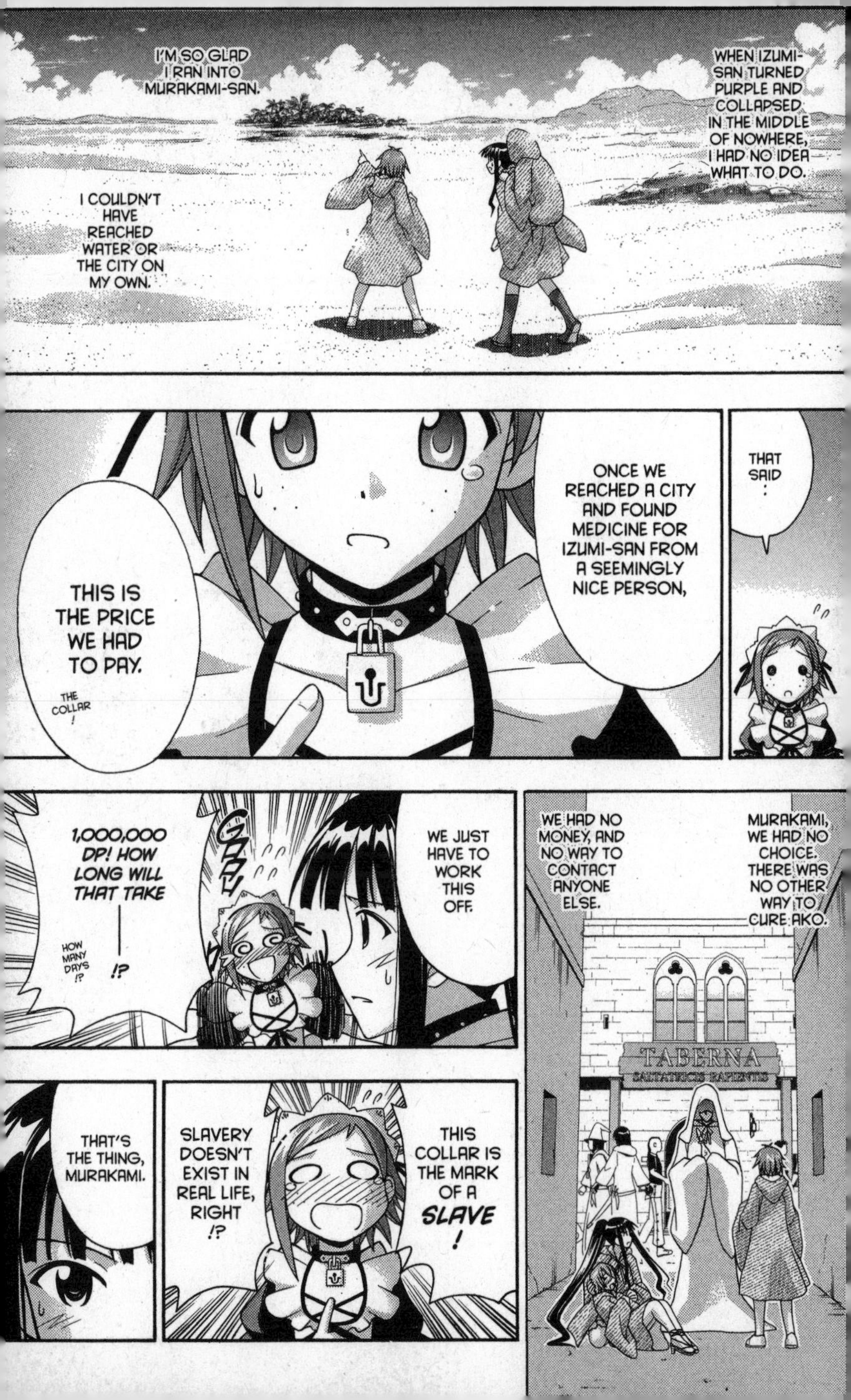
WHEN IZUMI-SAN TURNED PURPLE AND COLLAPSED IN THE MIDDLE OF NOWHERE, I HAD NO IDEA WHAT TO DO.
I'M SO GLAD I RAN INTO MURAKAMI-SAN.
I COULDN'T HAVE REACHED WATER OR THE CITY ON MY OWN.
THAT SAID :
ONCE WE REACHED A CITY AND FOUND MEDICINE FOR IZUMI-SAN FROM A SEEMINGLY NICE PERSON,
THIS IS THE PRICE WE HAD TO PAY.
THE COLLAR !
MURAKAMI, WE HAD NO CHOICE. THERE WAS NO OTHER WAY TO CURE AKO.
WE HAD NO MONEY, AND NO WAY TO CONTACT ANYONE ELSE.
TABERNA
SALTATRICIS RAPIENTIS
WE JUST HAVE TO WORK THIS OFF.
1,000,000 DP! HOW LONG WILL THAT TAKE —— !?
HOW MANY DAYS !?
THIS COLLAR IS THE MARK OF A SLAVE !
SLAVERY DOESN'T EXIST IN REAL LIFE, RIGHT !?
THAT'S THE THING, MURAKAMI.

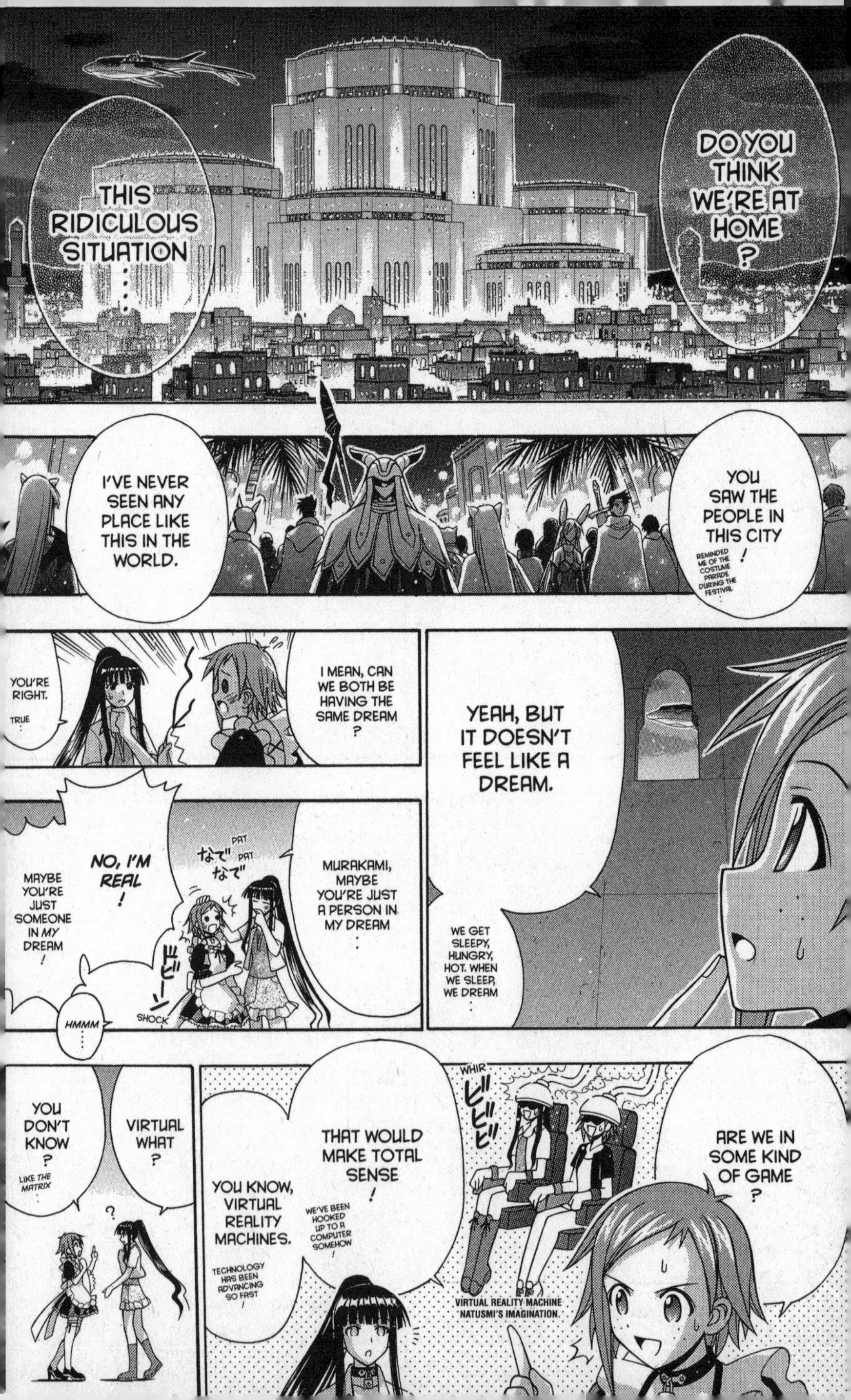
DO YOU THINK WE'RE AT HOME?
THIS RIDICULOUS SITUATION...
YOU SAW THE PEOPLE IN THIS CITY!
REMINDED ME OF THE COSTUME PARADE DURING THE FESTIVAL...
I'VE NEVER SEEN ANY PLACE LIKE THIS IN THE WORLD.
YEAH, BUT IT DOESN'T FEEL LIKE A DREAM.
WE GET SLEEPY, HUNGRY, HOT. WHEN WE SLEEP, WE DREAM...
I MEAN, CAN WE BOTH BE HAVING THE SAME DREAM?
YOU'RE RIGHT.
TRUE...
MURAKAMI, MAYBE YOU'RE JUST A PERSON IN MY DREAM...
なでなで PAT PAT
NO, I'M REAL!
ドビーン SHOCK
MAYBE YOU'RE JUST SOMEONE IN MY DREAM!
HMMM...
ARE WE IN SOME KIND OF GAME?
VIRTUAL REALITY MACHINE NATUSMI'S IMAGINATION.
ビビビ WHIR
THAT WOULD MAKE TOTAL SENSE!
WE'VE BEEN HOOKED UP TO A COMPUTER SOMEHOW!
YOU KNOW, VIRTUAL REALITY MACHINES.
TECHNOLOGY HAS BEEN ADVANCING SO FAST!
VIRTUAL WHAT?
YOU DON'T KNOW?
LIKE THE MATRIX...

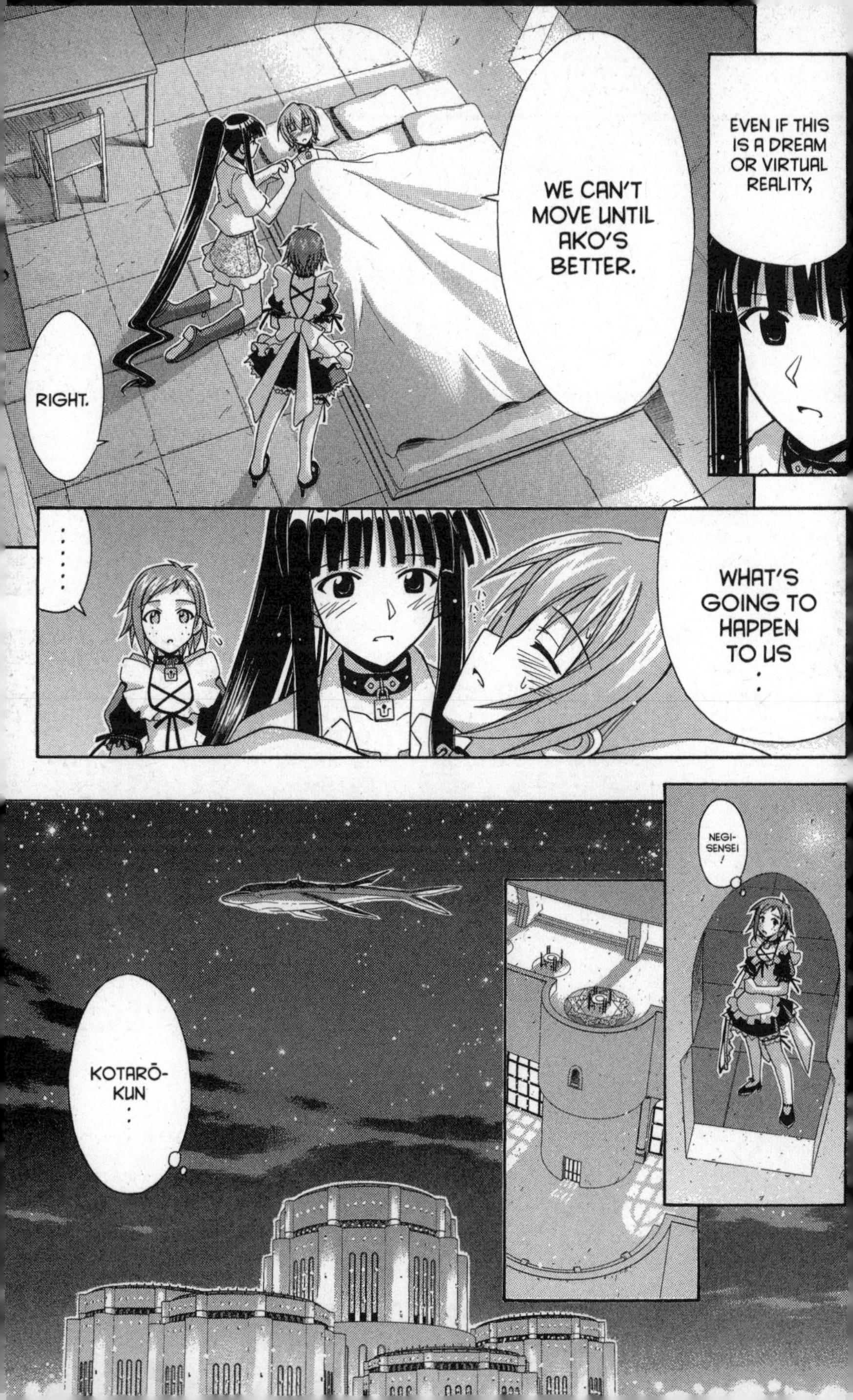
EVEN IF THIS IS A DREAM OR VIRTUAL REALITY,
WE CAN'T MOVE UNTIL AKO'S BETTER.
RIGHT.
WHAT'S GOING TO HAPPEN TO US..
......
NEGI-SENSEI!
KOTARŌ-KUN..

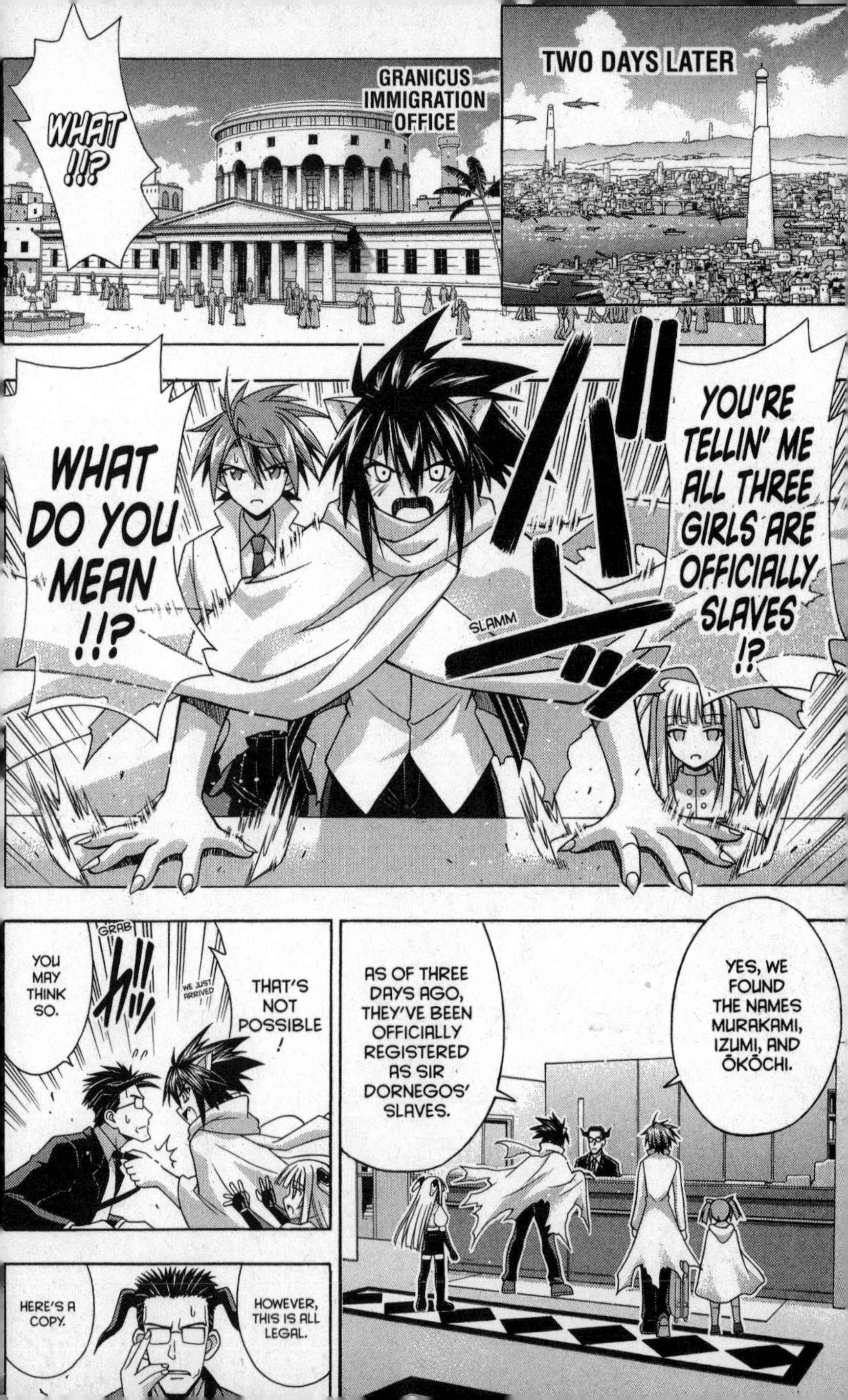

TWO DAYS LATER
GRANICUS IMMIGRATION OFFICE
WHAT !!?
YOU'RE TELLIN' ME ALL THREE GIRLS ARE OFFICIALLY SLAVES !?
SLAMM
WHAT DO YOU MEAN !!?
YES, WE FOUND THE NAMES MURAKAMI, IZUMI, AND ŌKŌCHI.
AS OF THREE DAYS AGO, THEY'VE BEEN OFFICIALLY REGISTERED AS SIR DORNEGOS' SLAVES.
THAT'S NOT POSSIBLE !
WE JUST ARRIVED !
GRAB
YOU MAY THINK SO.
HOWEVER, THIS IS ALL LEGAL.
HERE'S A COPY.

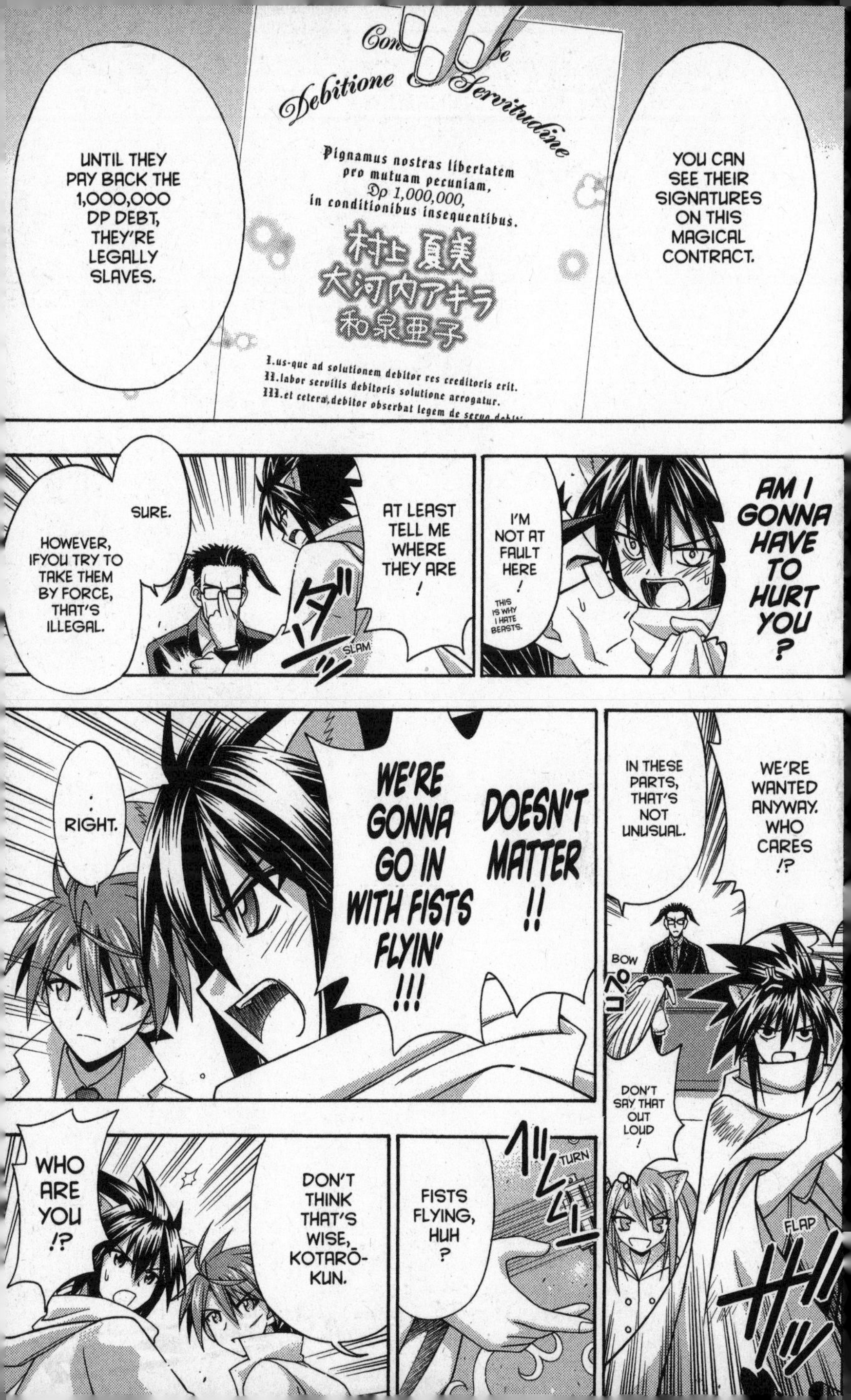
YOU CAN SEE THEIR SIGNATURES ON THIS MAGICAL CONTRACT.
Debitione
Servitudine
Pignamus nostras libertatem pro mutuam pecuniam, Dp 1,000,000, in conditionibus insequentibus.
村上夏美
大河内アキラ
和泉亜子
I.us-que ad solutionem debitor res creditoris erit.
II.labor servilis debitoris solutione arrogatur.
III.et cetera,debitor obserbat legem de servo
UNTIL THEY PAY BACK THE 1,000,000 DP DEBT, THEY'RE LEGALLY SLAVES.
AM I GONNA HAVE TO HURT YOU?
I'M NOT AT FAULT HERE!
THIS IS WHY I HATE BEASTS.
AT LEAST TELL ME WHERE THEY ARE!
SLAM
SURE.
HOWEVER, IFYOU TRY TO TAKE THEM BY FORCE, THAT'S ILLEGAL.
WE'RE WANTED ANYWAY. WHO CARES!?
IN THESE PARTS, THAT'S NOT UNUSUAL.
BOW
DON'T SAY THAT OUT LOUD!
FLAP
DOESN'T MATTER!!
WE'RE GONNA GO IN WITH FISTS FLYIN'!!!
: RIGHT.
FISTS FLYING, HUH?
TURN
DON'T THINK THAT'S WISE, KOTARŌ-KUN.
WHO ARE YOU!?

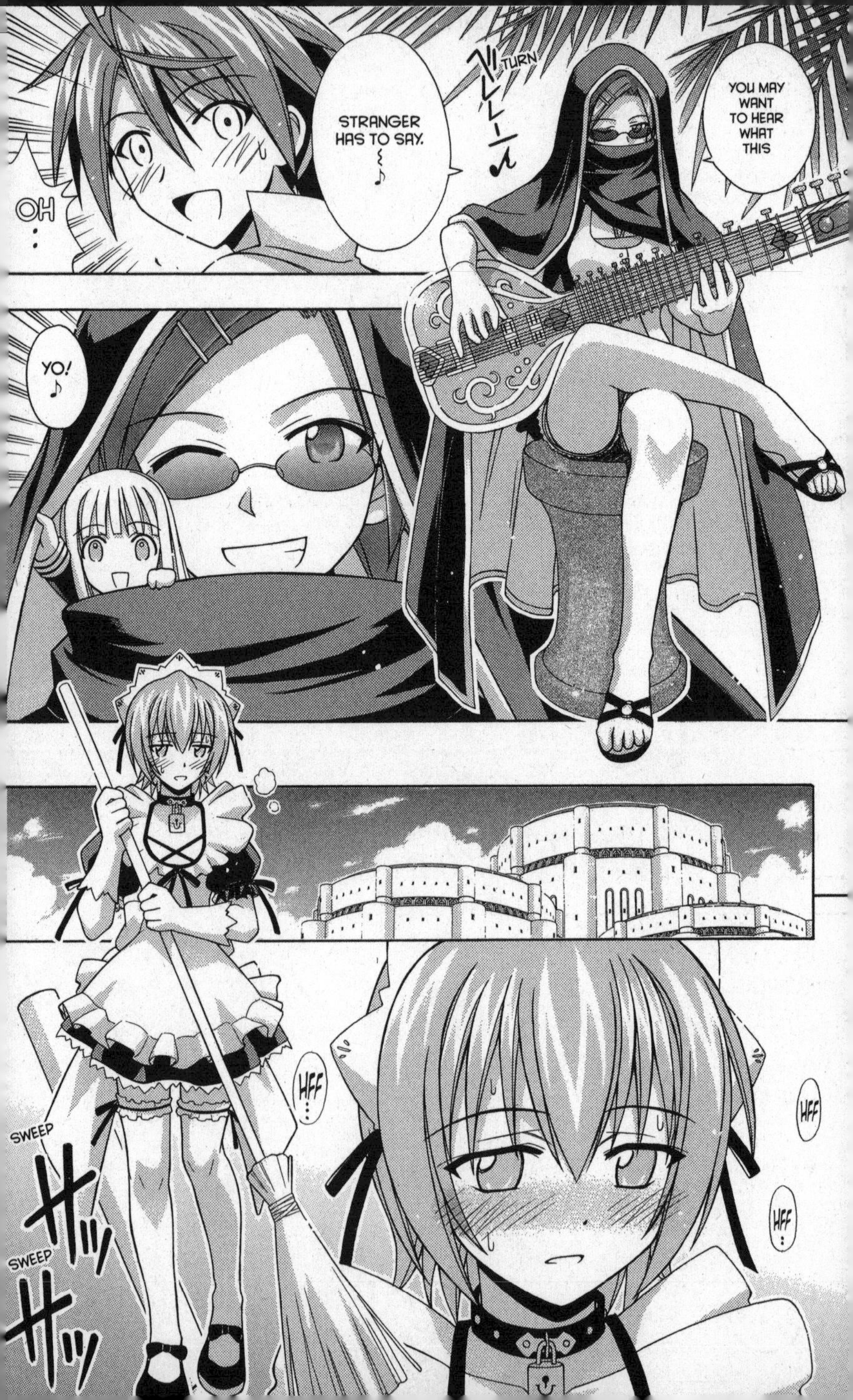
YOU MAY WANT TO HEAR WHAT THIS
TURN
STRANGER HAS TO SAY. ♪
OH...
YO! ♪
HFF
HFF...
HFF...
SWEEP
SWEEP

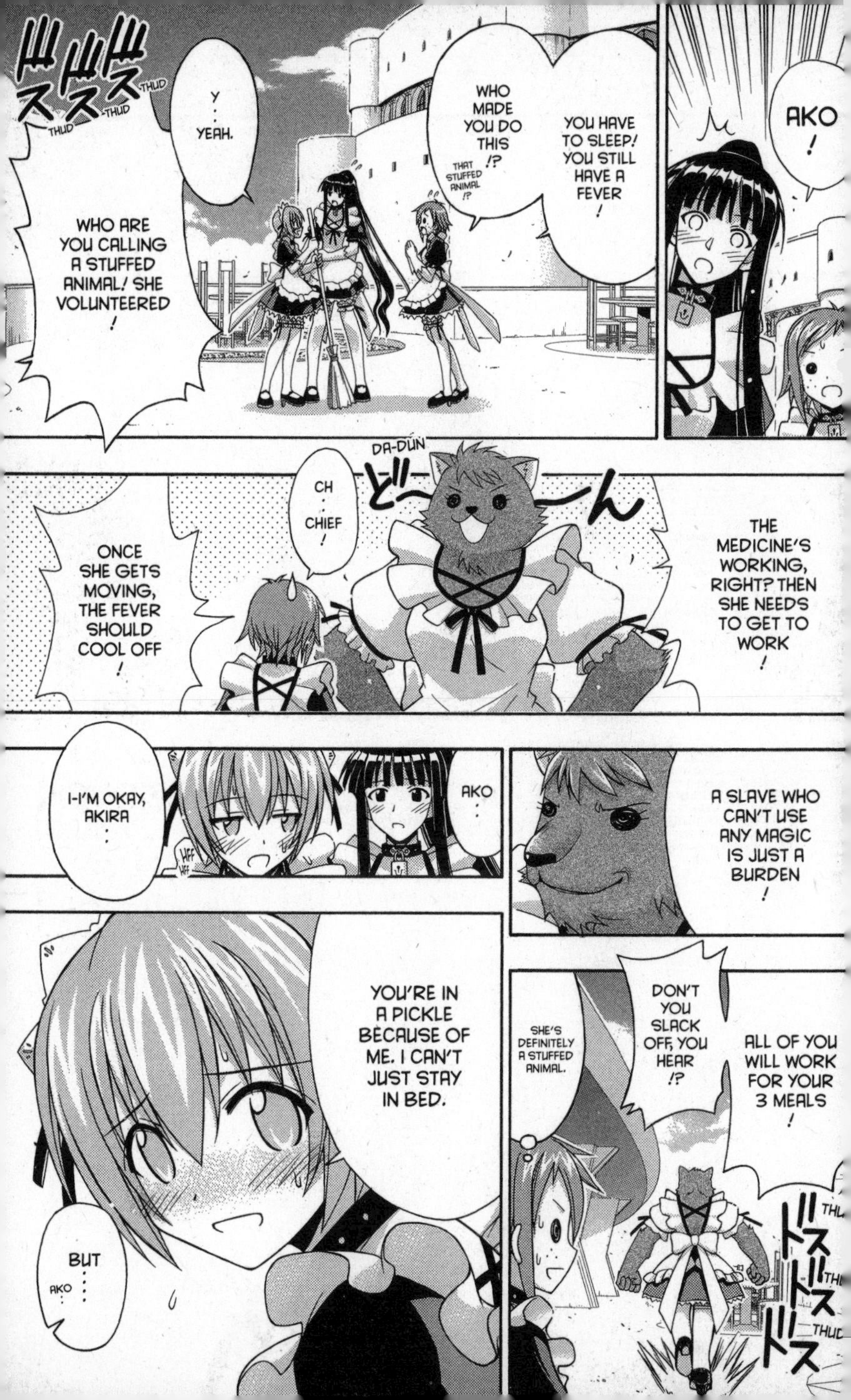
AKO!
THUD THUD THUD
YOU HAVE TO SLEEP! YOU STILL HAVE A FEVER!
WHO MADE YOU DO THIS!?
THAT STUFFED ANIMAL!?
Y... YEAH.
WHO ARE YOU CALLING A STUFFED ANIMAL! SHE VOLUNTEERED!
THE MEDICINE'S WORKING, RIGHT? THEN SHE NEEDS TO GET TO WORK!
DA-DUN
CH... CHIEF!
ONCE SHE GETS MOVING, THE FEVER SHOULD COOL OFF!
A SLAVE WHO CAN'T USE ANY MAGIC IS JUST A BURDEN!
AKO...
HFF HFF
I-I'M OKAY, AKIRA...
ALL OF YOU WILL WORK FOR YOUR 3 MEALS!
DON'T YOU SLACK OFF, YOU HEAR!?
SHE'S DEFINITELY A STUFFED ANIMAL.
THUD THUD THUD
YOU'RE IN A PICKLE BECAUSE OF ME. I CAN'T JUST STAY IN BED.
BUT...
AKO...

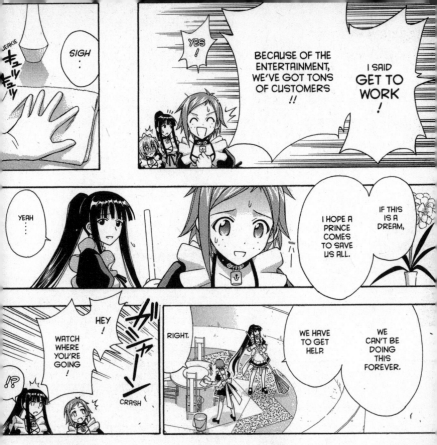

I SAID GET TO WORK!
BECAUSE OF THE ENTERTAINMENT, WE'VE GOT TONS OF CUSTOMERS!!
YES!
SIGH...
JEAKIE
キュッキュッ
IF THIS IS A DREAM,
I HOPE A PRINCE COMES TO SAVE US ALL.
SIGH
YEAH...
WE CAN'T BE DOING THIS FOREVER.
WE HAVE TO GET HELP.
RIGHT.
ガシャーン
CRASH
HEY! WATCH WHERE YOU'RE GOING!
!?
I'M SORRY!
THAT WON'T CUT IT! YOU'RE NEW? FREAKIN' SLOW!
OW!
CHILL OUT.
YOU SOILED MY CLOTHES!!
HAHA! LIKE YOU EVER WASH 'EM!
ドン
THUD
HM?

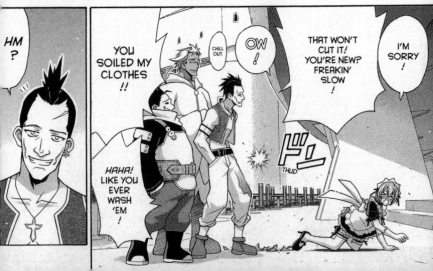

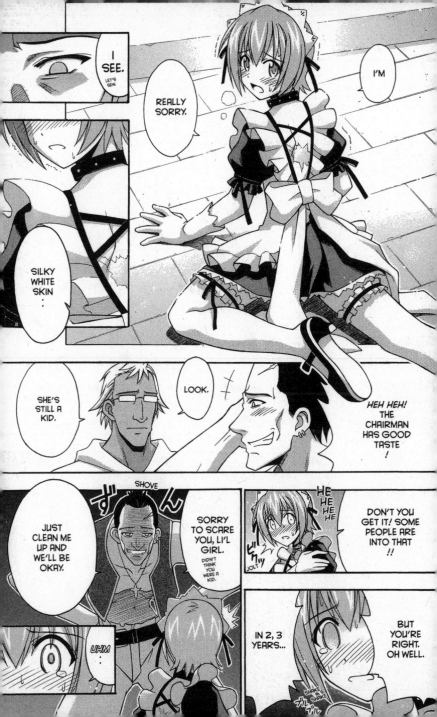

I'M
REALLY SORRY.
I SEE.
LET'S SEW.
SILKY WHITE SKIN :
HEH HEH! THE CHAIRMAN HAS GOOD TASTE !
LOOK.
SHE'S STILL A KID.
DON'T YOU GET IT! SOME PEOPLE ARE INTO THAT !!
HE HE HE HE
JOLT
SHOVE
SORRY TO SCARE YOU, LI'L GIRL.
DIDN'T THINK YOU WERE A KID.
JUST CLEAN ME UP AND WE'LL BE OKAY.
BUT YOU'RE RIGHT. OH WELL.
IN 2, 3 YEARS...
SHAKE SHAKE
UHM :

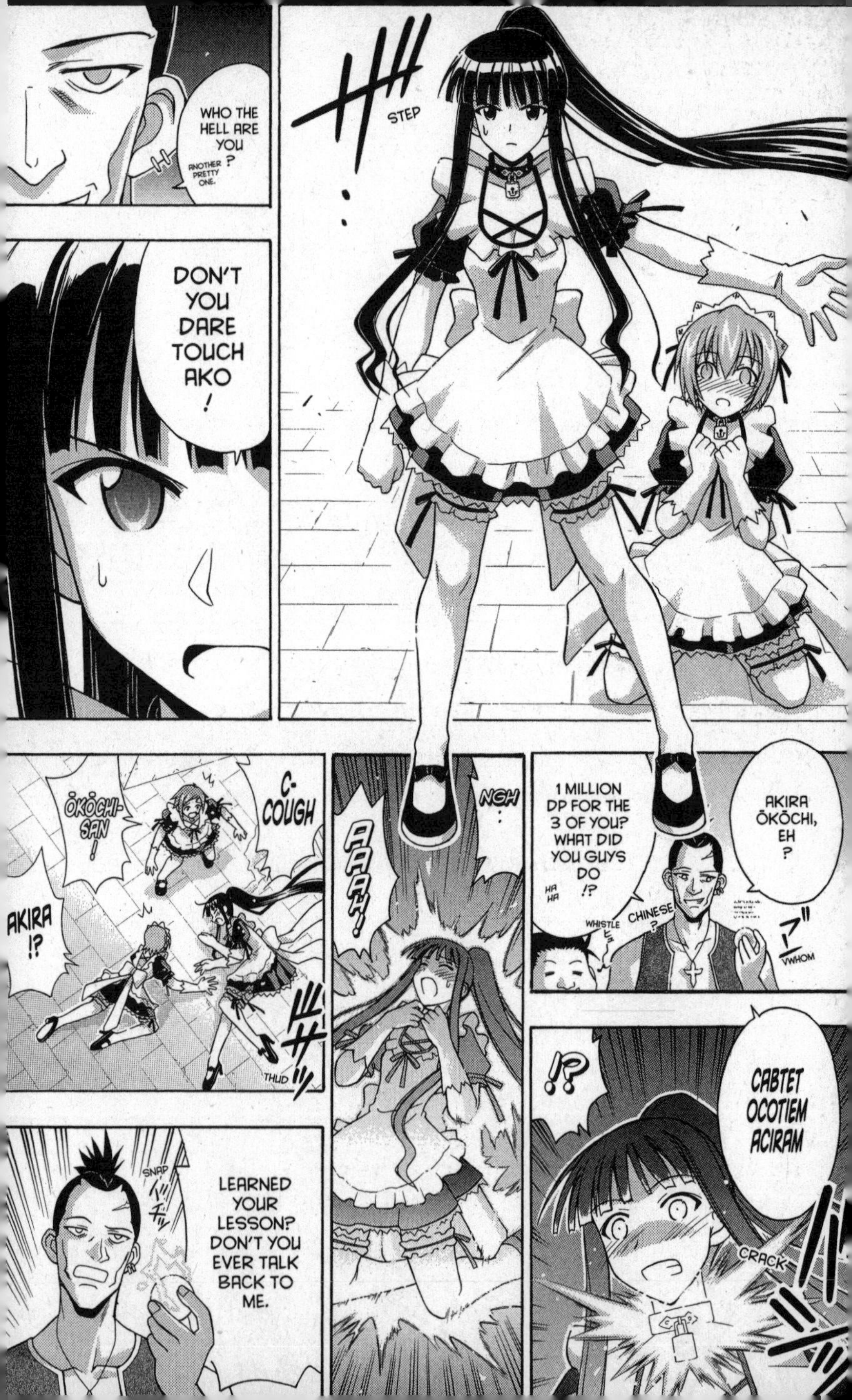
STEP
WHO THE HELL ARE YOU?
ANOTHER PRETTY ONE.
DON'T YOU DARE TOUCH AKO!
AKIRA ŌKŌCHI, EH?
VWHOM
CHINESE?
1 MILLION DP FOR THE 3 OF YOU? WHAT DID YOU GUYS DO!?
HA HA
WHISTLE
CABTET OCOTIEM ACIRAM
!?
CRACK
NGH...
AAAAH!
C-COUGH
ŌKŌCHI-SAN!
AKIRA!?
THUD
SNAP
LEARNED YOUR LESSON? DON'T YOU EVER TALK BACK TO ME.

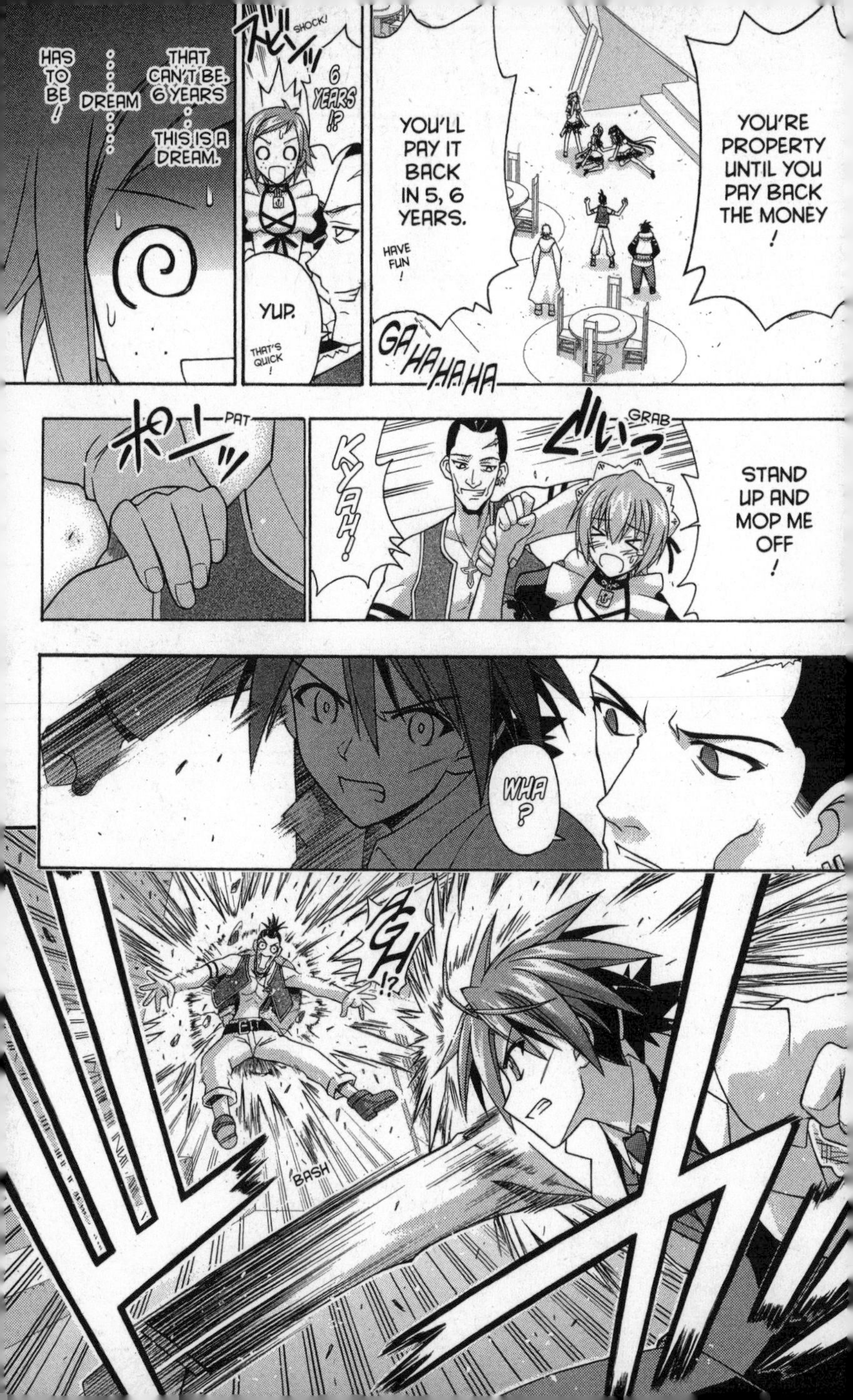

YOU'RE PROPERTY UNTIL YOU PAY BACK THE MONEY!
YOU'LL PAY IT BACK IN 5, 6 YEARS.
HAVE FUN!
GAHAHAHAHA
SHOCK!
6 YEARS!?
YUP.
THAT'S QUICK!
THAT CAN'T BE. 6 YEARS...
THIS IS A DREAM.
DREAM......
HAS TO BE!
STAND UP AND MOP ME OFF!
GRAB
KYAAH!
PAT
WHA?
AGH!?
BASH

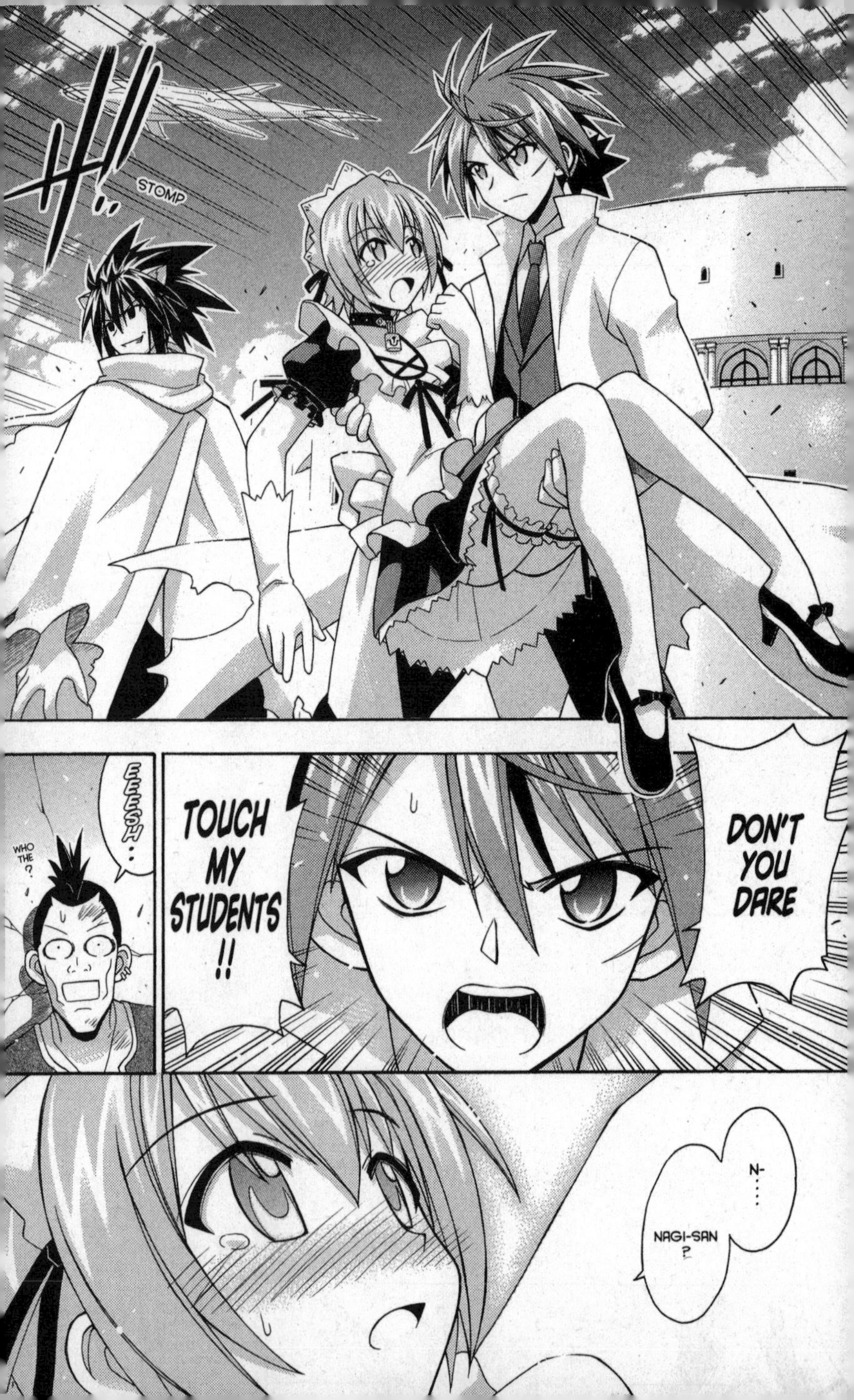
STOMP
DON'T YOU DARE
TOUCH MY STUDENTS !!
EEESH...
WHO THE ?
N-......
NAGI-SAN ?

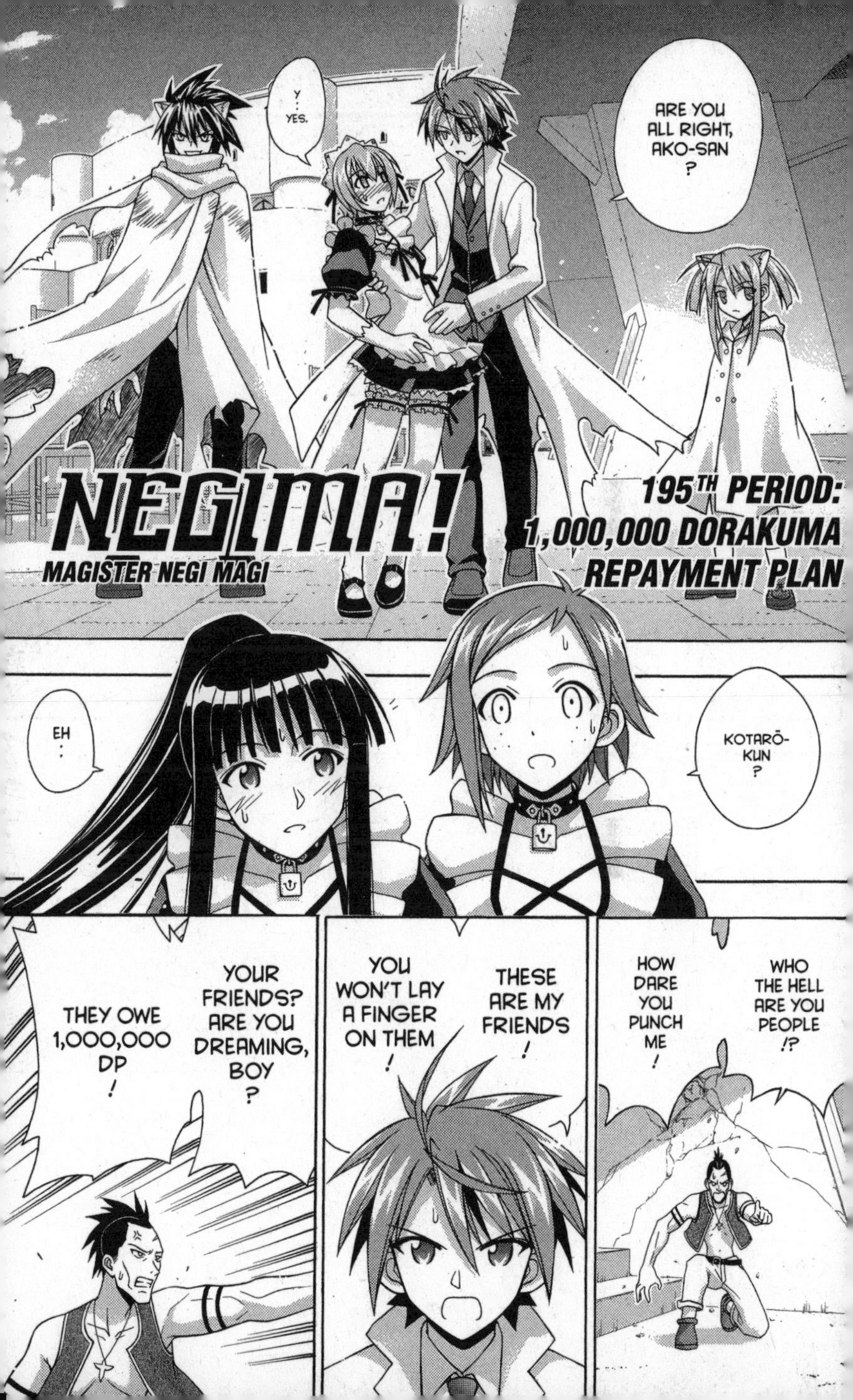
ARE YOU ALL RIGHT, AKO-SAN?
Y... YES.
195TH PERIOD: 1,000,000 DORAKUMA REPAYMENT PLAN
NEGIMA! MAGISTER NEGI MAGI
KOTARŌ-KUN?
EH...
WHO THE HELL ARE YOU PEOPLE!?
HOW DARE YOU PUNCH ME!
THESE ARE MY FRIENDS!
YOU WON'T LAY A FINGER ON THEM!
YOUR FRIENDS? ARE YOU DREAMING, BOY?
THEY OWE 1,000,000 DP!

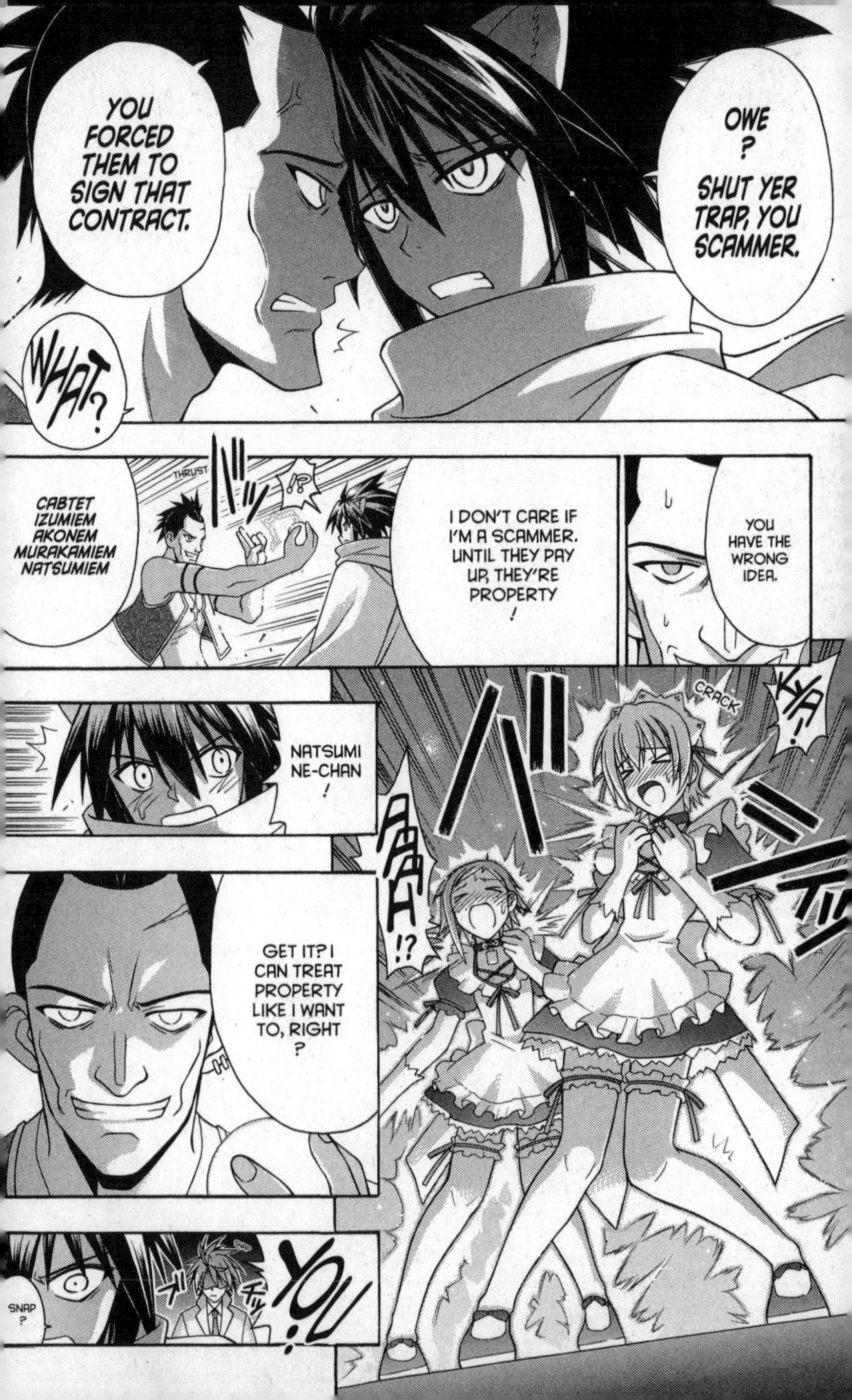
OWE? SHUT YER TRAP, YOU SCAMMER.
YOU FORCED THEM TO SIGN THAT CONTRACT.
WHAT?
YOU HAVE THE WRONG IDEA.
I DON'T CARE IF I'M A SCAMMER. UNTIL THEY PAY UP, THEY'RE PROPERTY!
!?
THRUST
CABTET IZUMIEM AKONEM MURAKAMIEM NATSUMIEM
KYA!
CRACK
AAAA!?
NATSUMI NE-CHAN!
GET IT? I CAN TREAT PROPERTY LIKE I WANT TO, RIGHT?
YOU!
SNAP?

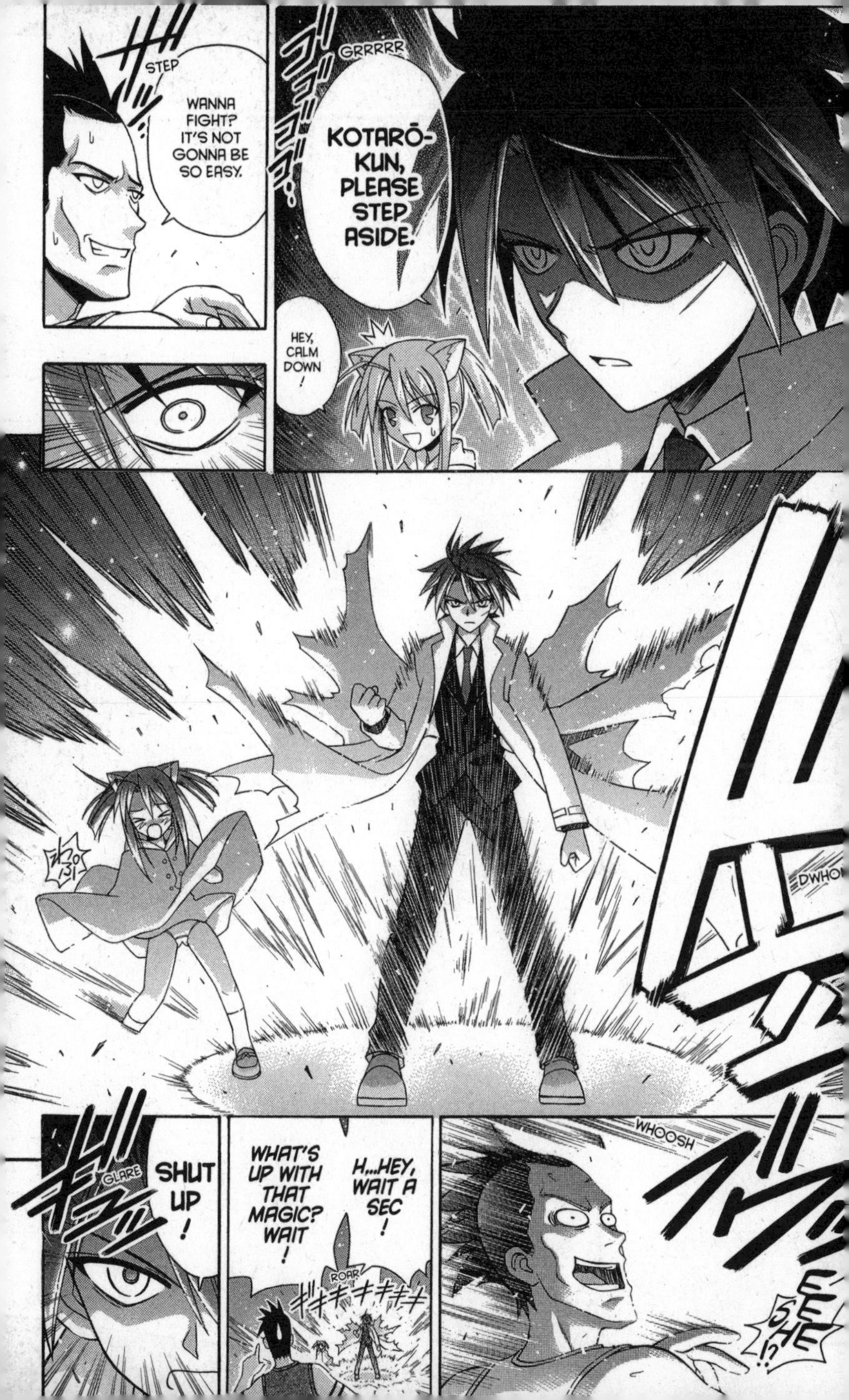
GRRRRR
KOTARŌ-KUN, PLEASE STEP ASIDE.
HEY, CALM DOWN!
STEP
WANNA FIGHT? IT'S NOT GONNA BE SO EASY.
WHOOSH
EEESHE!?
H...HEY, WAIT A SEC!
WHAT'S UP WITH THAT MAGIC? WAIT!
ROAR
GLARE
SHUT UP!

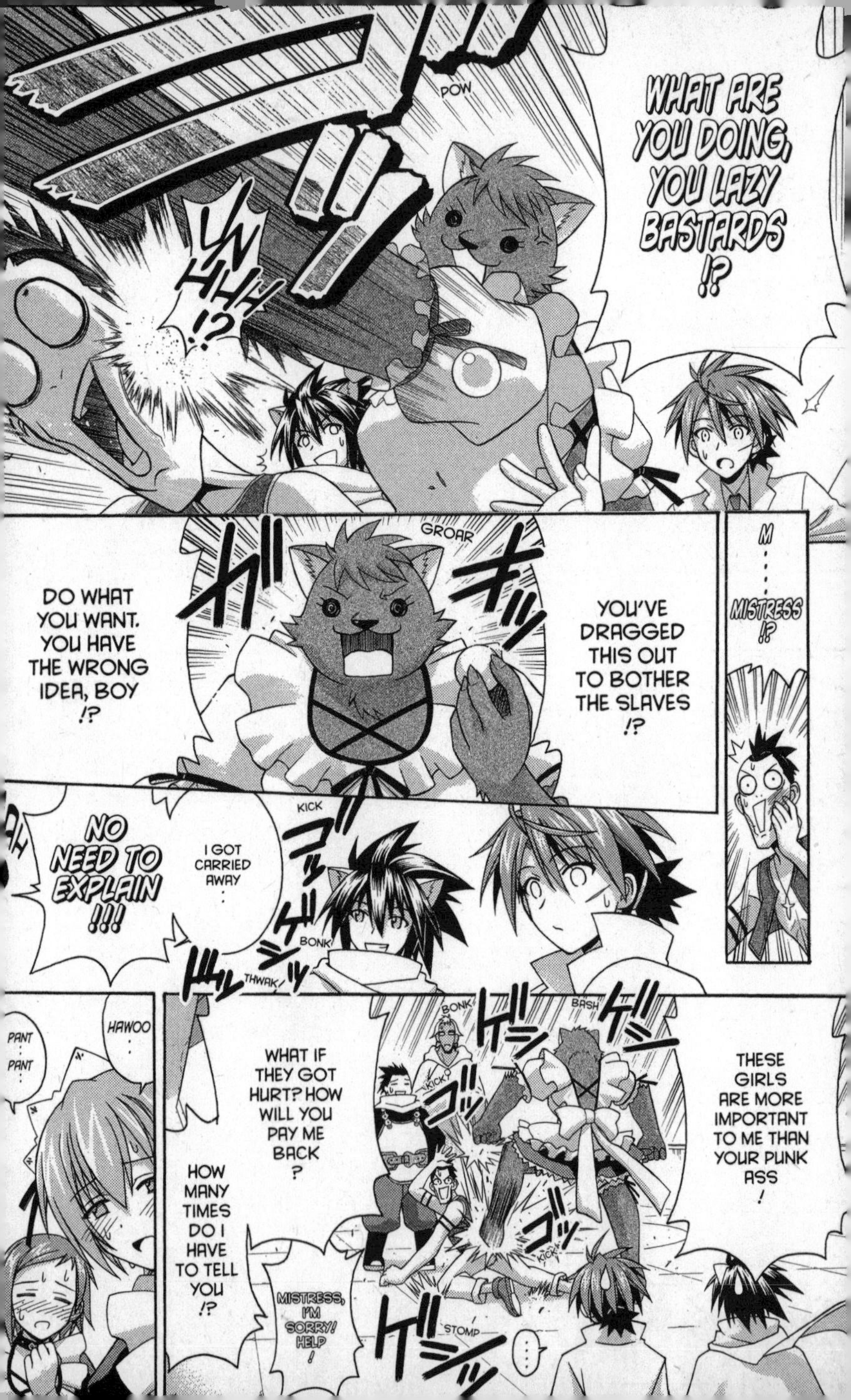
POW
WHAT ARE YOU DOING, YOU LAZY BASTARDS !?
UNHHH !?
M... MISTRESS !?
GROAR
YOU'VE DRAGGED THIS OUT TO BOTHER THE SLAVES !?
DO WHAT YOU WANT. YOU HAVE THE WRONG IDEA, BOY !?
KICK
I GOT CARRIED AWAY...
NO NEED TO EXPLAIN !!!
BONK
THWAK
BASH
BONK
THESE GIRLS ARE MORE IMPORTANT TO ME THAN YOUR PUNK ASS !
KICK
WHAT IF THEY GOT HURT? HOW WILL YOU PAY ME BACK ?
HOW MANY TIMES DO I HAVE TO TELL YOU !?
KICK
MISTRESS, I'M SORRY! HELP !
STOMP
...
HAWOO...
PANT... PANT...

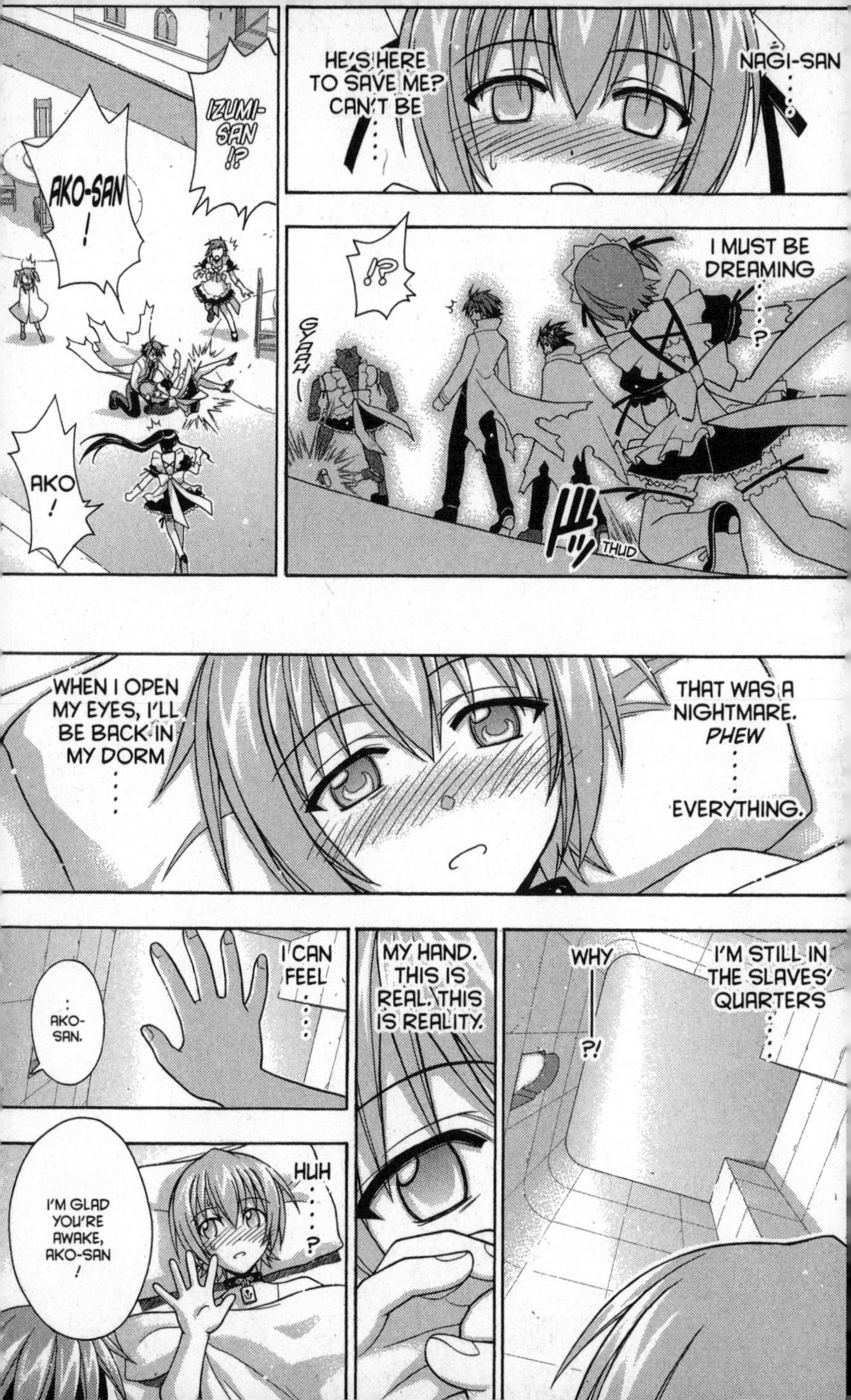

NAGI-SAN ...
HE'S HERE TO SAVE ME? CAN'T BE ...
I MUST BE DREAMING ...?
!?
GYAAH!
THUD
IZUMI-SAN !?
AKO-SAN !
AKO !
THAT WAS A NIGHTMARE. PHEW ... EVERYTHING.
WHEN I OPEN MY EYES, I'LL BE BACK IN MY DORM ...
I'M STILL IN THE SLAVES' QUARTERS ...
WHY ?!
MY HAND. THIS IS REAL. THIS IS REALITY.
I CAN FEEL ...
...AKO-SAN.
HUH ...?
I'M GLAD YOU'RE AWAKE, AKO-SAN !

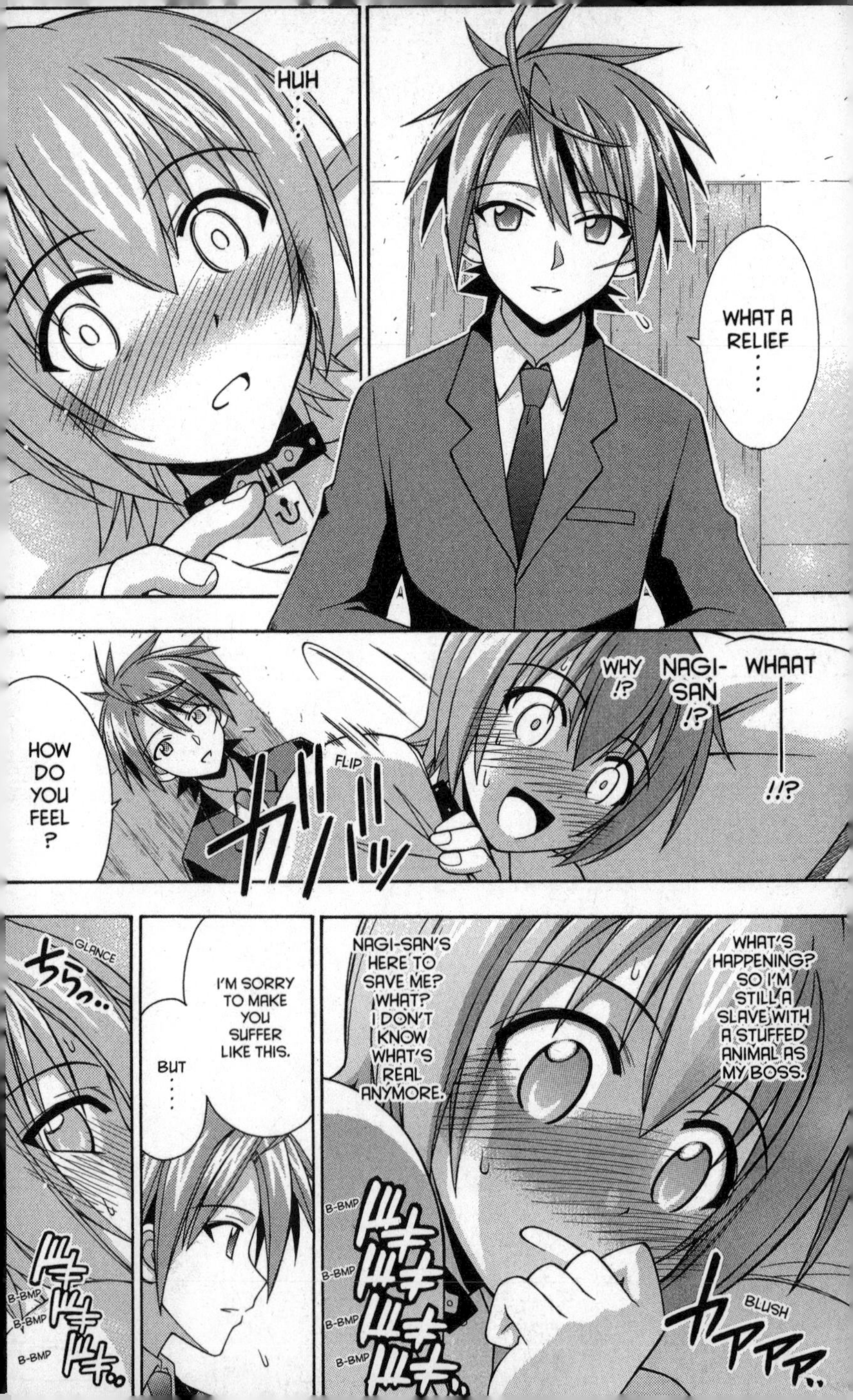

WHAT A RELIEF ....
HUH ...
WHAAT !!?
NAGI-SAN !?
WHY !?
FLIP
ガバッ
HOW DO YOU FEEL ?
WHAT'S HAPPENING? SO I'M STILL A SLAVE WITH A STUFFED ANIMAL AS MY BOSS.
NAGI-SAN'S HERE TO SAVE ME? WHAT? I DON'T KNOW WHAT'S REAL ANYMORE.
BLUSH
カァァァ..
B-BMP B-BMP B-BMP B-BMP
ドキドキドキドキ..
I'M SORRY TO MAKE YOU SUFFER LIKE THIS.
BUT ...
GLANCE
ちらっ..
B-BMP B-BMP B-BMP
ドキドキドキ..

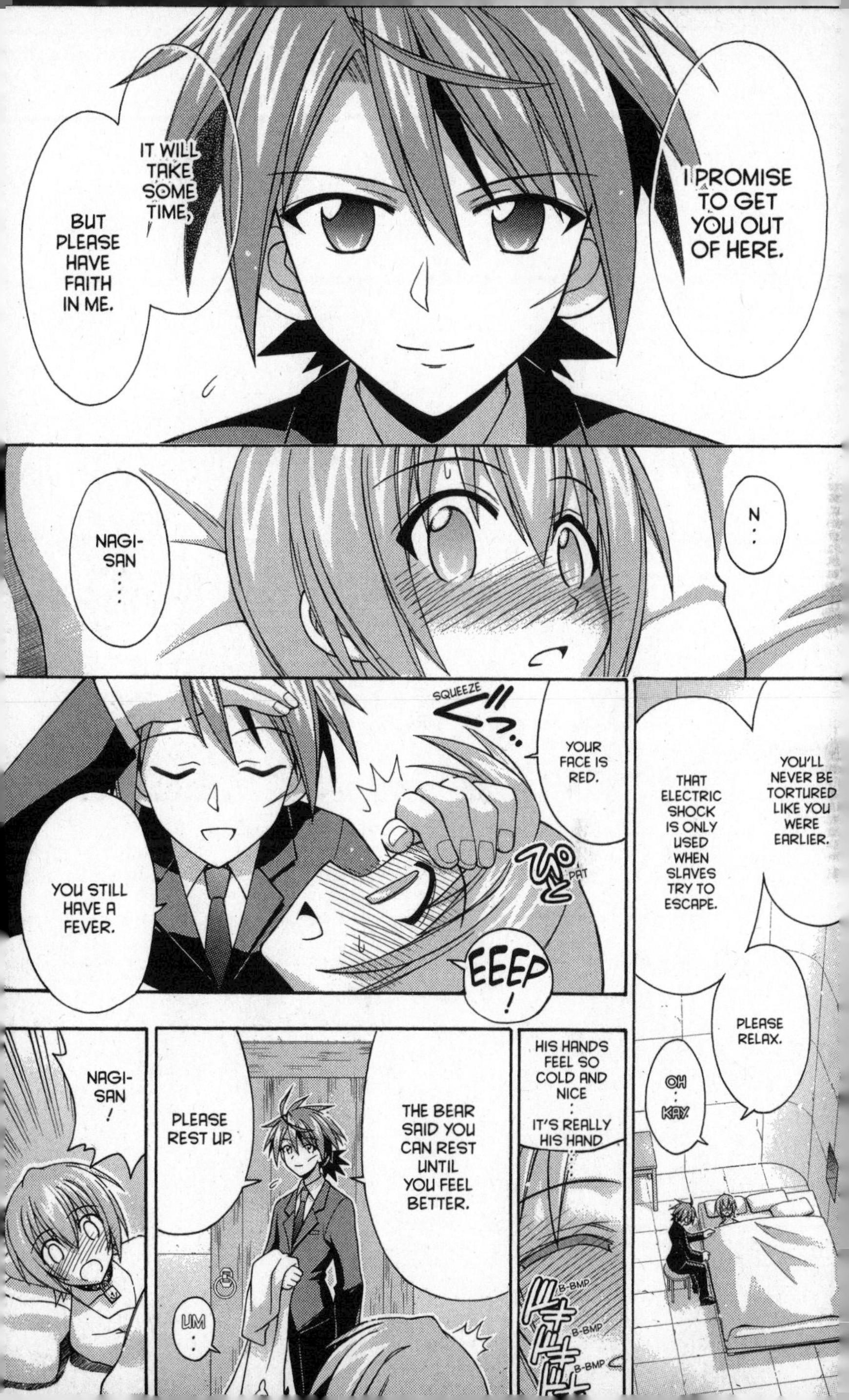
I PROMISE TO GET YOU OUT OF HERE.
IT WILL TAKE SOME TIME,
BUT PLEASE HAVE FAITH IN ME.
N...
NAGI-SAN....
YOU'LL NEVER BE TORTURED LIKE YOU WERE EARLIER.
THAT ELECTRIC SHOCK IS ONLY USED WHEN SLAVES TRY TO ESCAPE.
PLEASE RELAX.
OH...KAY.
SQUEEZE
YOUR FACE IS RED.
PAT
YOU STILL HAVE A FEVER.
EEEP!
HIS HANDS FEEL SO COLD AND NICE...
IT'S REALLY HIS HAND...
B-BMP
B-BMP
B-BMP
THE BEAR SAID YOU CAN REST UNTIL YOU FEEL BETTER.
PLEASE REST UP.
UM...
NAGI-SAN!

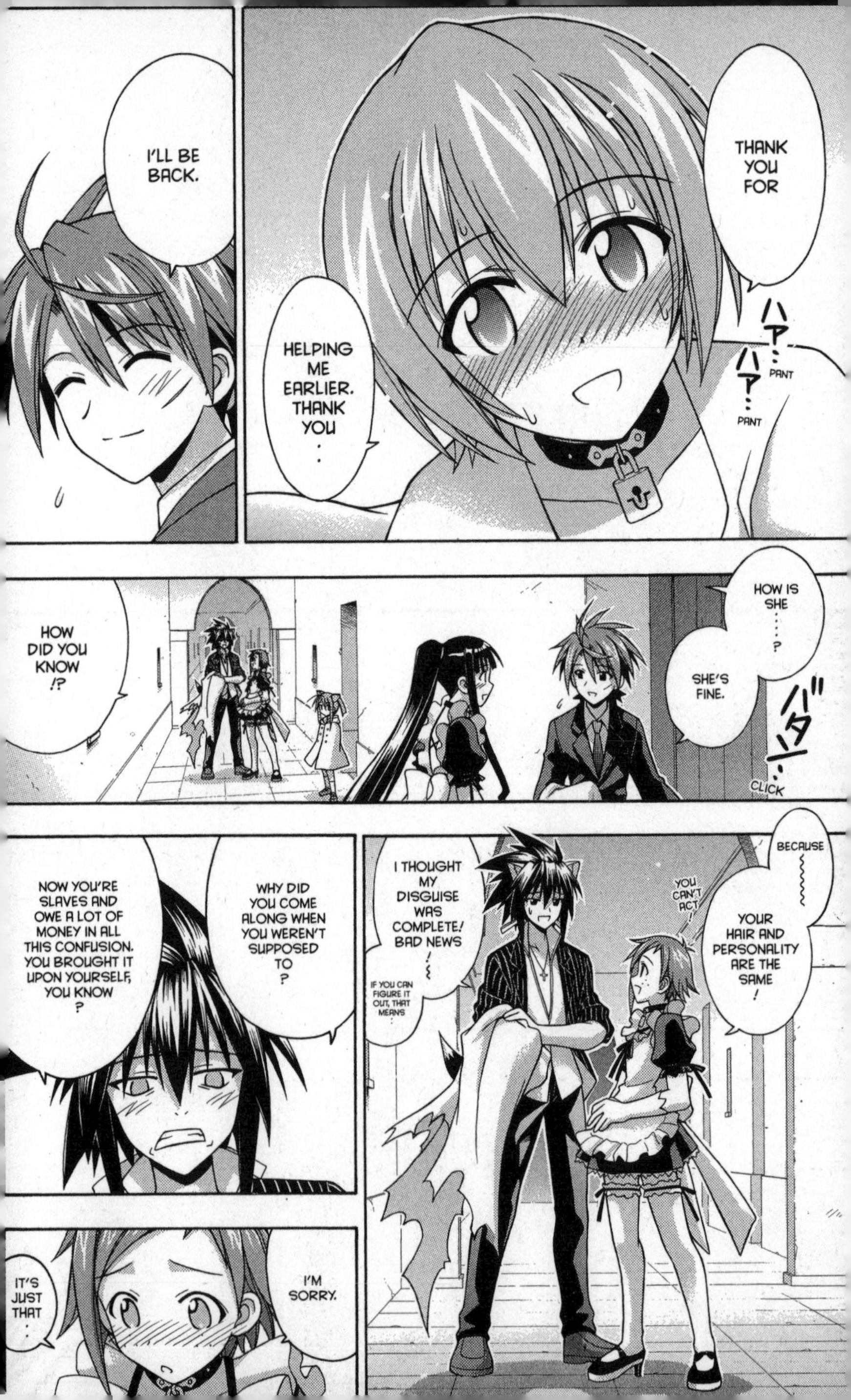
THANK YOU FOR
HELPING ME EARLIER. THANK YOU ...
ハァ... PANT
ハァ... PANT
I'LL BE BACK.
HOW IS SHE ...?
SHE'S FINE.
バタン... CLICK
HOW DID YOU KNOW!?
BECAUSE~
YOUR HAIR AND PERSONALITY ARE THE SAME!
YOU CAN'T ACT!
I THOUGHT MY DISGUISE WAS COMPLETE! BAD NEWS!~
IF YOU CAN FIGURE IT OUT, THAT MEANS...
WHY DID YOU COME ALONG WHEN YOU WEREN'T SUPPOSED TO?
NOW YOU'RE SLAVES AND OWE A LOT OF MONEY IN ALL THIS CONFUSION. YOU BROUGHT IT UPON YOURSELF, YOU KNOW?
I'M SORRY.
IT'S JUST THAT ...

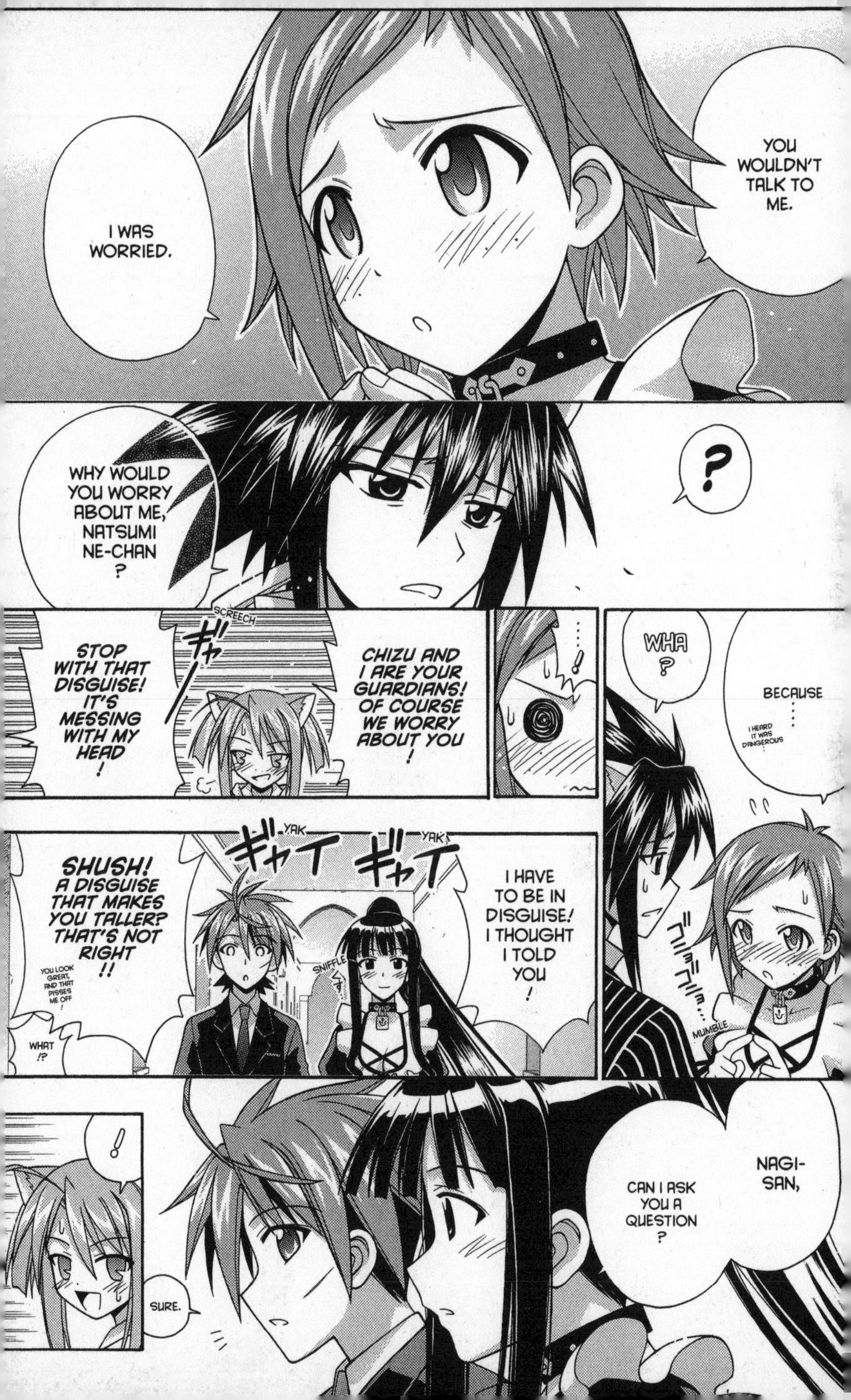
YOU WOULDN'T TALK TO ME.
I WAS WORRIED.
?
WHY WOULD YOU WORRY ABOUT ME, NATSUMI NE-CHAN?
WHA?
BECAUSE...
I HEARD IT WAS DANGEROUS...
MUMBLE
...!
CHIZU AND I ARE YOUR GUARDIANS! OF COURSE WE WORRY ABOUT YOU!
SCREECH
ギャー
STOP WITH THAT DISGUISE! IT'S MESSING WITH MY HEAD!
YAK YAK
ギャイ ギャイ
I HAVE TO BE IN DISGUISE! I THOUGHT I TOLD YOU!
SNIFFLE
SHUSH! A DISGUISE THAT MAKES YOU TALLER? THAT'S NOT RIGHT!!
YOU LOOK GREAT, AND THAT PISSES ME OFF!
WHAT!?
NAGI-SAN,
CAN I ASK YOU A QUESTION?
!
SURE.

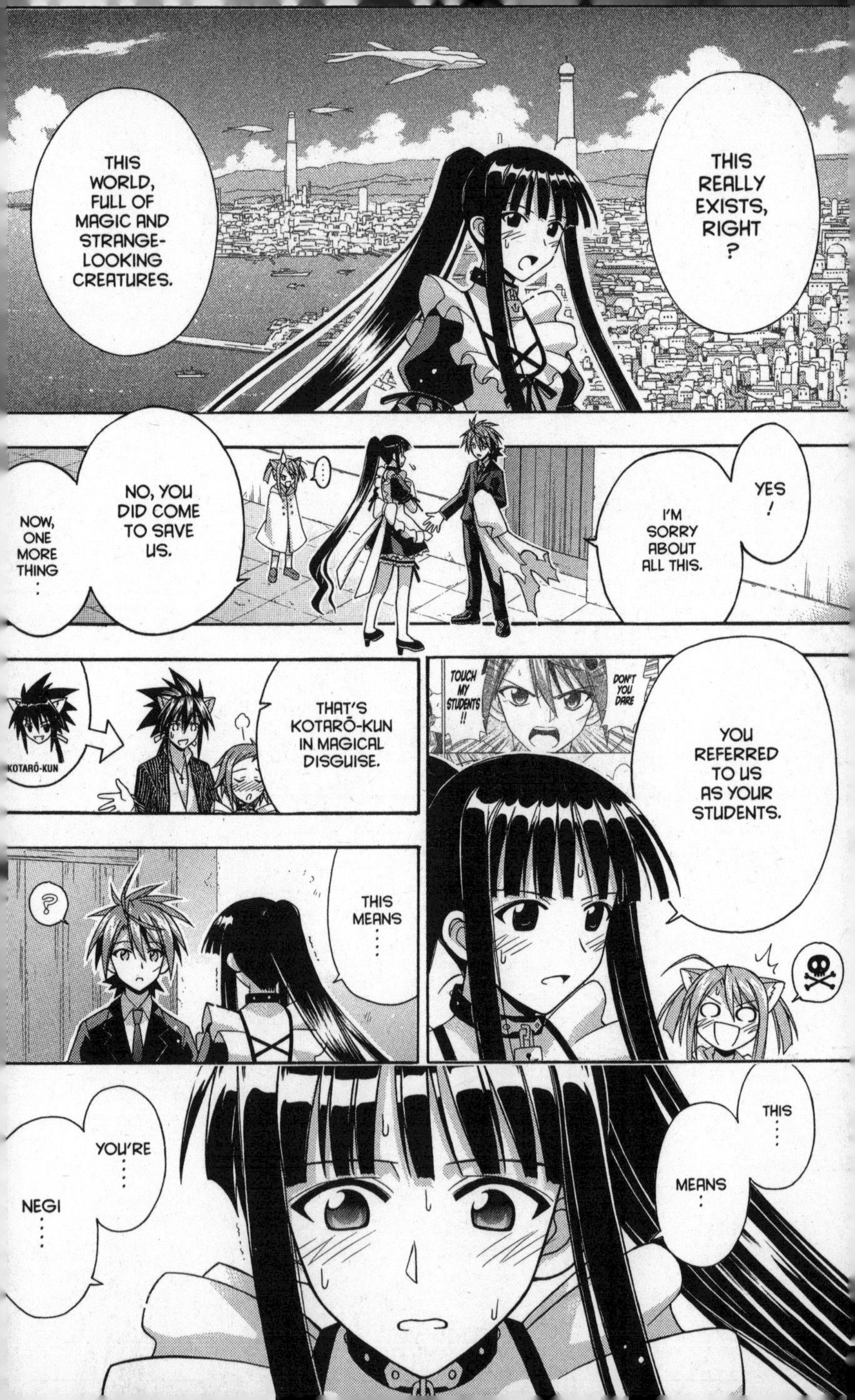
THIS REALLY EXISTS, RIGHT?
THIS WORLD, FULL OF MAGIC AND STRANGE-LOOKING CREATURES.
YES!
I'M SORRY ABOUT ALL THIS.
...
NO, YOU DID COME TO SAVE US.
NOW, ONE MORE THING...
DON'T YOU DARE
TOUCH MY STUDENTS!!
YOU REFERRED TO US AS YOUR STUDENTS.
THAT'S KOTARŌ-KUN IN MAGICAL DISGUISE.
KOTARŌ-KUN
THIS MEANS...
?
THIS... MEANS...
YOU'RE... NEGI...

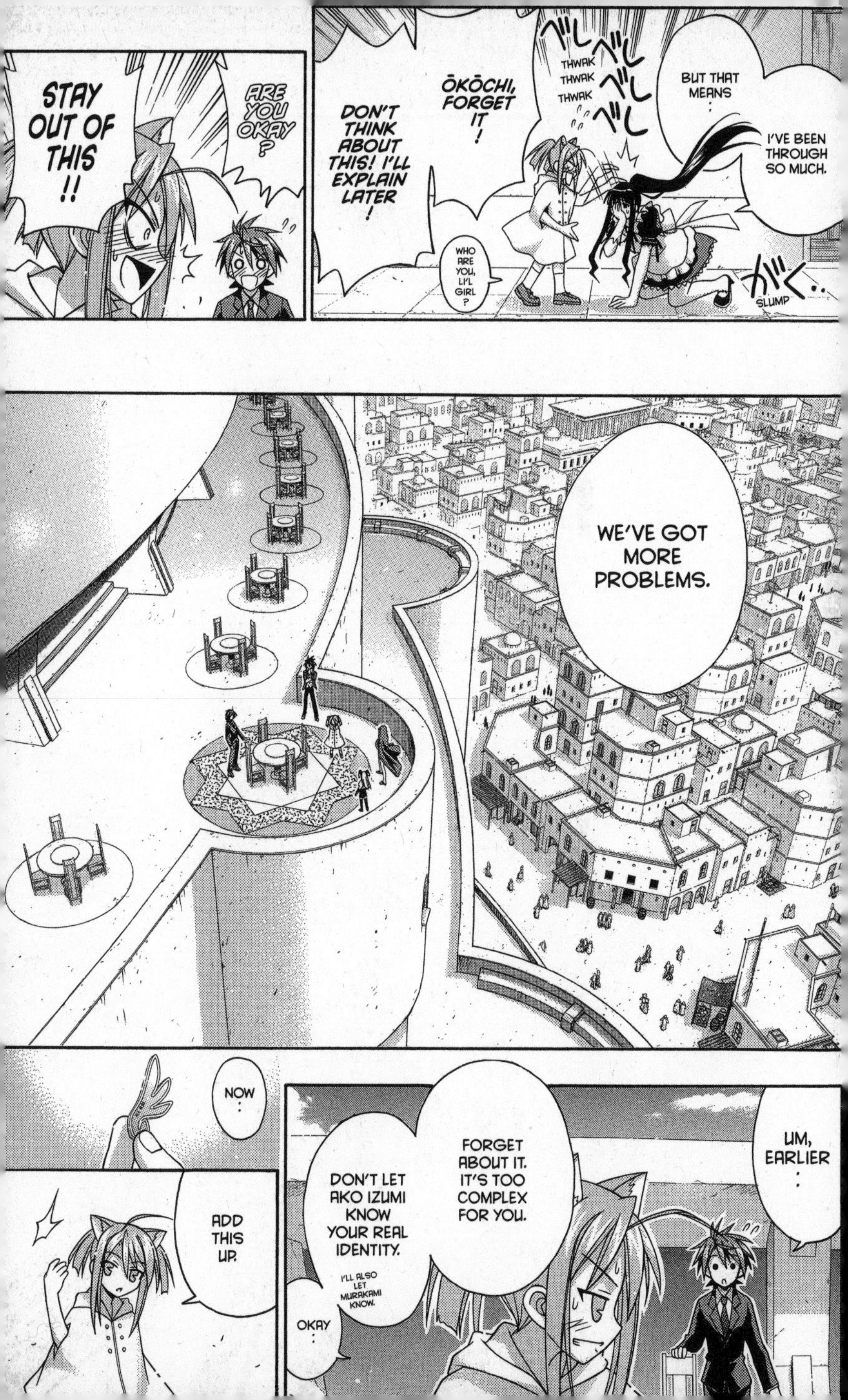
BUT THAT MEANS :
I'VE BEEN THROUGH SO MUCH.
べしべしべし
THWAK THWAK THWAK
ŌKŌCHI, FORGET IT!
DON'T THINK ABOUT THIS! I'LL EXPLAIN LATER!
がく…
SLUMP
WHO ARE YOU, LI'L GIRL?
ARE YOU OKAY?
STAY OUT OF THIS!!
WE'VE GOT MORE PROBLEMS.
UM, EARLIER :
FORGET ABOUT IT. IT'S TOO COMPLEX FOR YOU.
DON'T LET AKO IZUMI KNOW YOUR REAL IDENTITY.
I'LL ALSO LET MURAKAMI KNOW.
OKAY :
NOW :
ADD THIS UP.

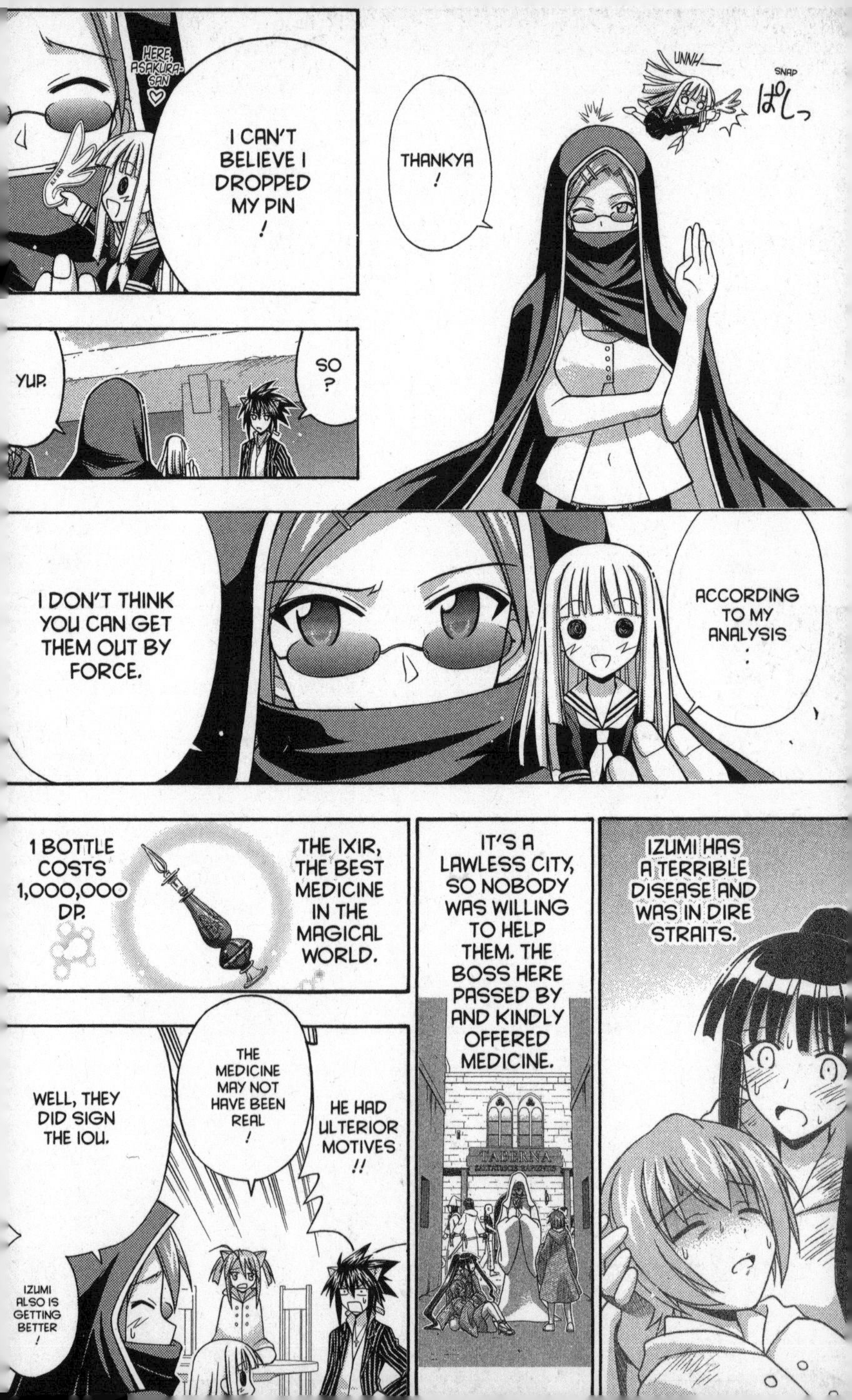
UNNH—
SNAP
ぱしっ
THANKYA!
HERE, ASAKURA-SAN ♡
I CAN'T BELIEVE I DROPPED MY PIN!
SO?
YUP.
ACCORDING TO MY ANALYSIS...
I DON'T THINK YOU CAN GET THEM OUT BY FORCE.
IZUMI HAS A TERRIBLE DISEASE AND WAS IN DIRE STRAITS.
IT'S A LAWLESS CITY, SO NOBODY WAS WILLING TO HELP THEM. THE BOSS HERE PASSED BY AND KINDLY OFFERED MEDICINE.
TABERNA
THE IXIR, THE BEST MEDICINE IN THE MAGICAL WORLD.
1 BOTTLE COSTS 1,000,000 DP.
HE HAD ULTERIOR MOTIVES!!
THE MEDICINE MAY NOT HAVE BEEN REAL!
WELL, THEY DID SIGN THE IOU.
IZUMI ALSO IS GETTING BETTER!

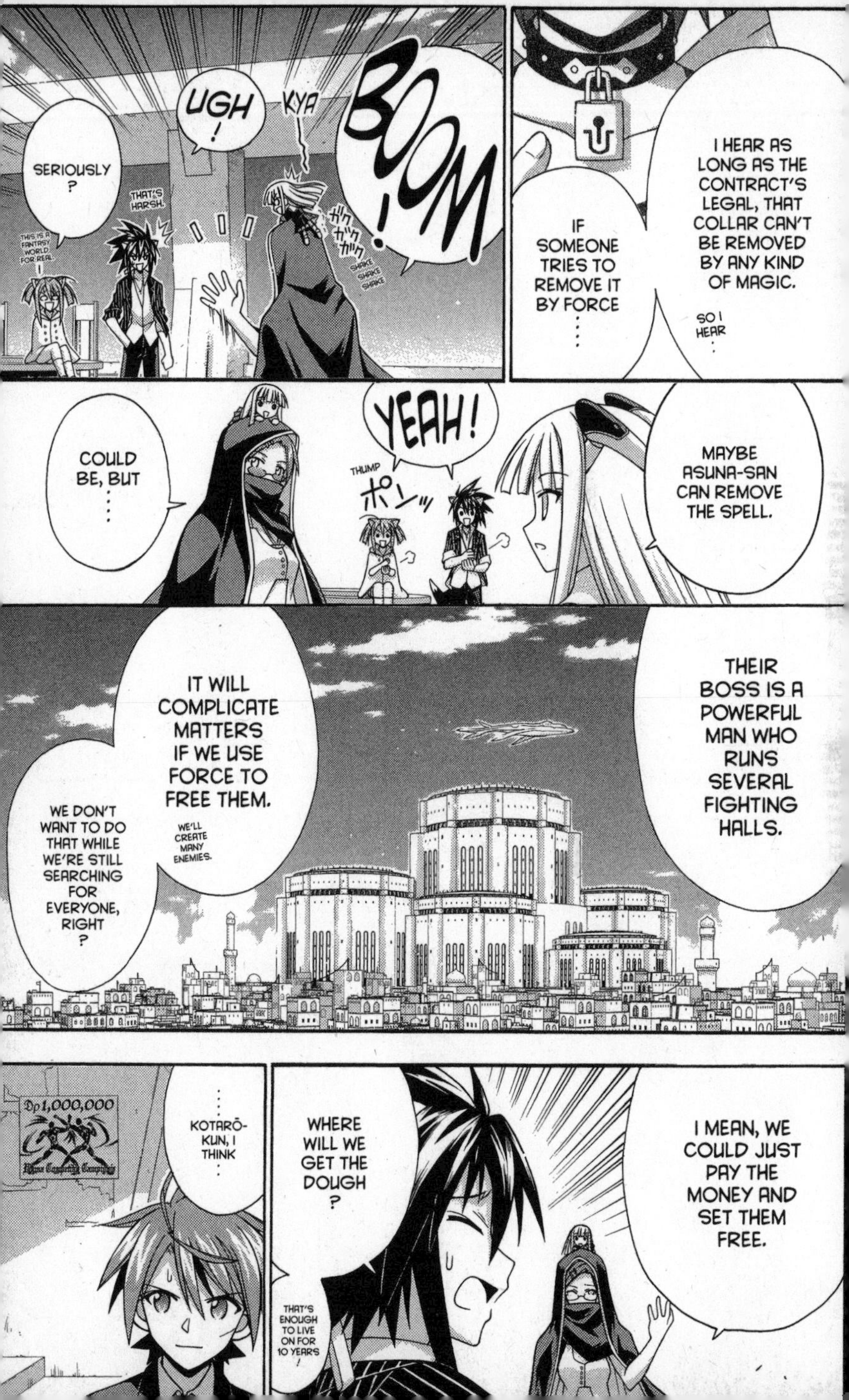
I HEAR AS LONG AS THE CONTRACT'S LEGAL, THAT COLLAR CAN'T BE REMOVED BY ANY KIND OF MAGIC.
SO I HEAR...
IF SOMEONE TRIES TO REMOVE IT BY FORCE...
BOOM!
KYA
ガク ガク ガク
SHAKE SHAKE SHAKE
UGH!
THAT'S HARSH.
SERIOUSLY?
THIS IS A FANTASY WORLD FOR REAL!
MAYBE ASUNA-SAN CAN REMOVE THE SPELL.
YEAH!
THUMP
ポンッ
COULD BE, BUT...
THEIR BOSS IS A POWERFUL MAN WHO RUNS SEVERAL FIGHTING HALLS.
IT WILL COMPLICATE MATTERS IF WE USE FORCE TO FREE THEM.
WE'LL CREATE MANY ENEMIES.
WE DON'T WANT TO DO THAT WHILE WE'RE STILL SEARCHING FOR EVERYONE, RIGHT?
I MEAN, WE COULD JUST PAY THE MONEY AND SET THEM FREE.
WHERE WILL WE GET THE DOUGH?
THAT'S ENOUGH TO LIVE ON FOR 10 YEARS!
...KOTARŌ-KUN, I THINK...
Dp1,000,000

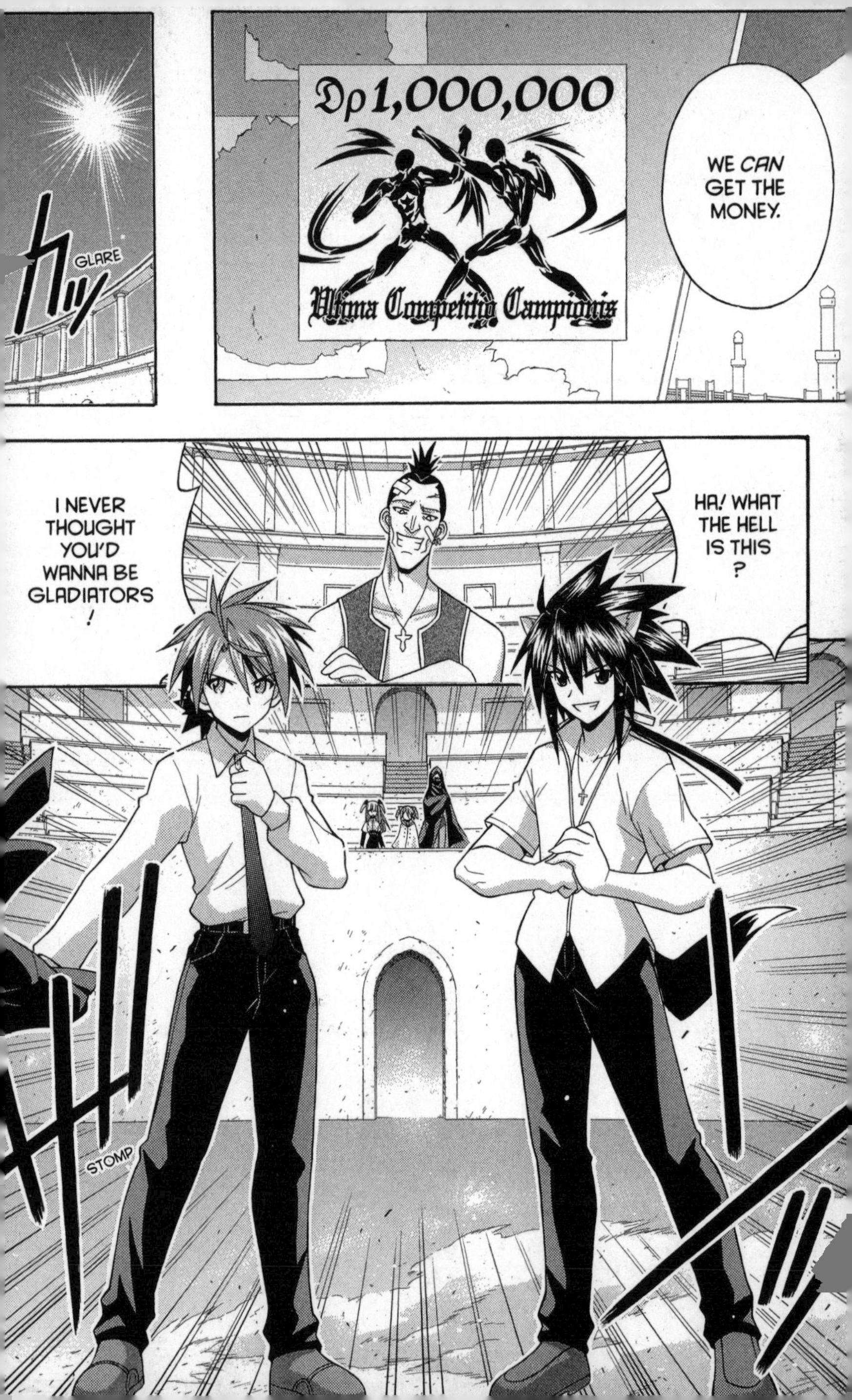
WE CAN GET THE MONEY.
Dp 1,000,000
Ultima Competitio Campionis
カッ
GLARE
HA! WHAT THE HELL IS THIS ?
I NEVER THOUGHT YOU'D WANNA BE GLADIATORS !
STOMP

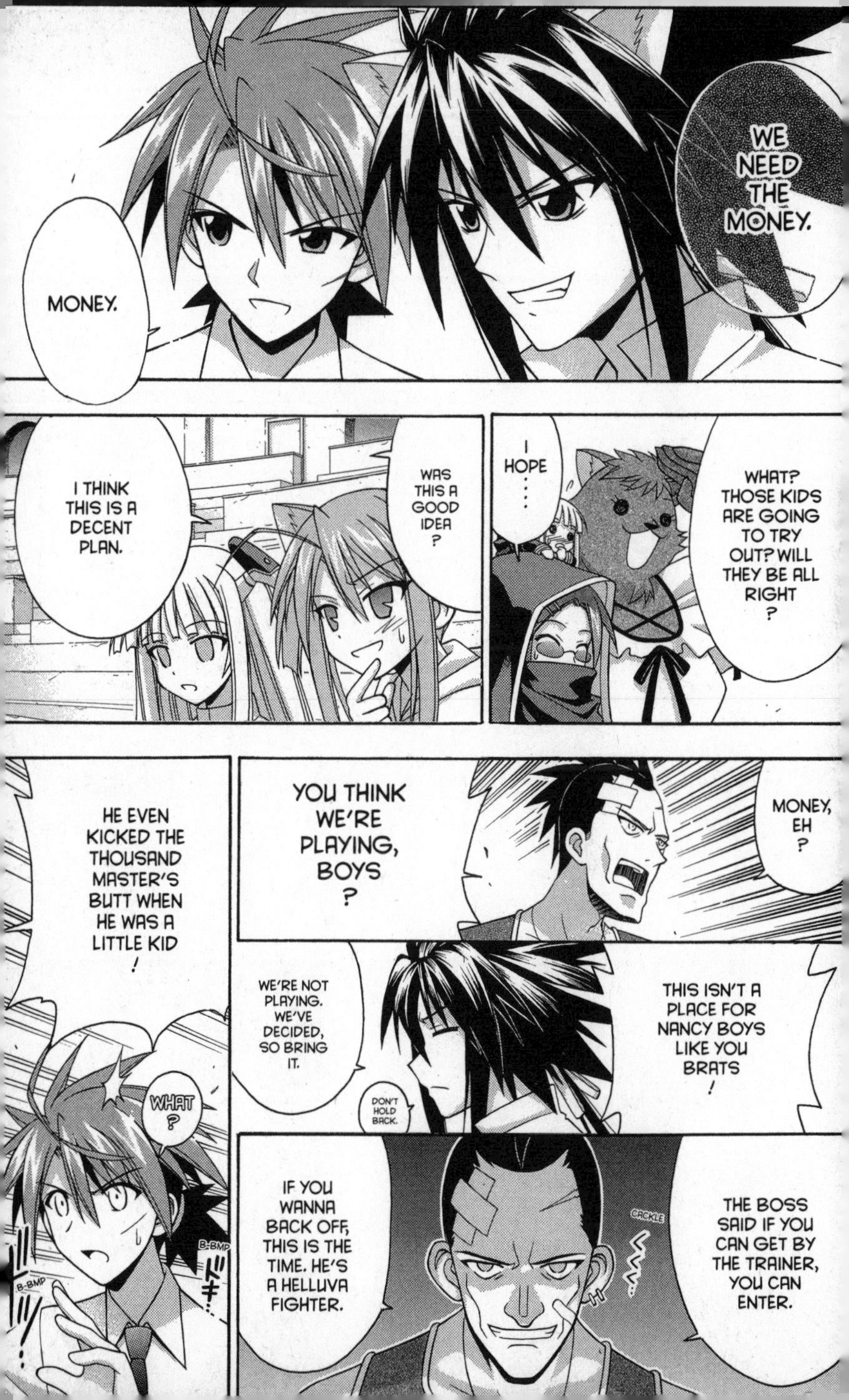
WE NEED THE MONEY.
MONEY.
WHAT? THOSE KIDS ARE GOING TO TRY OUT? WILL THEY BE ALL RIGHT?
I HOPE....
WAS THIS A GOOD IDEA?
I THINK THIS IS A DECENT PLAN.
MONEY, EH?
YOU THINK WE'RE PLAYING, BOYS?
THIS ISN'T A PLACE FOR NANCY BOYS LIKE YOU BRATS!
WE'RE NOT PLAYING. WE'VE DECIDED, SO BRING IT.
DON'T HOLD BACK.
THE BOSS SAID IF YOU CAN GET BY THE TRAINER, YOU CAN ENTER.
CACKLE
IF YOU WANNA BACK OFF, THIS IS THE TIME. HE'S A HELLUVA FIGHTER.
HE EVEN KICKED THE THOUSAND MASTER'S BUTT WHEN HE WAS A LITTLE KID!
WHAT?
B-BMP
B-BMP

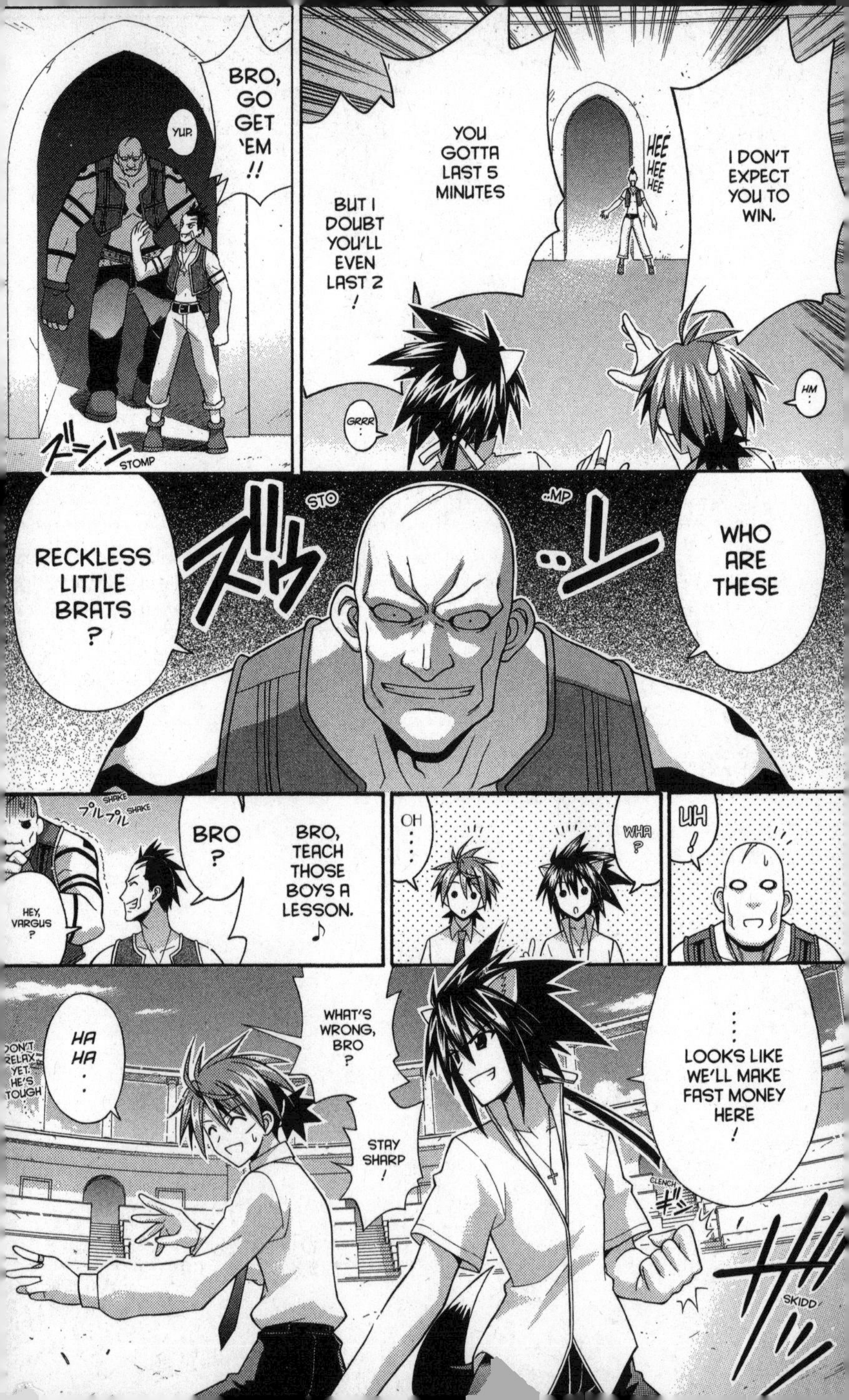
I DON'T EXPECT YOU TO WIN.
HEE HEE HEE
YOU GOTTA LAST 5 MINUTES
BUT I DOUBT YOU'LL EVEN LAST 2!
HM...
GRRR...
BRO, GO GET 'EM!!
YUP.
STOMP
WHO ARE THESE
..MP
STO
RECKLESS LITTLE BRATS?
UH!
WHA?
OH...
BRO, TEACH THOSE BOYS A LESSON. ♪
BRO?
SHAKE SHAKE
HEY, VARGUS?
...LOOKS LIKE WE'LL MAKE FAST MONEY HERE!
CLENCH
SKIDD
WHAT'S WRONG, BRO?
STAY SHARP!
HA HA..
DON'T RELAX YET. HE'S TOUGH

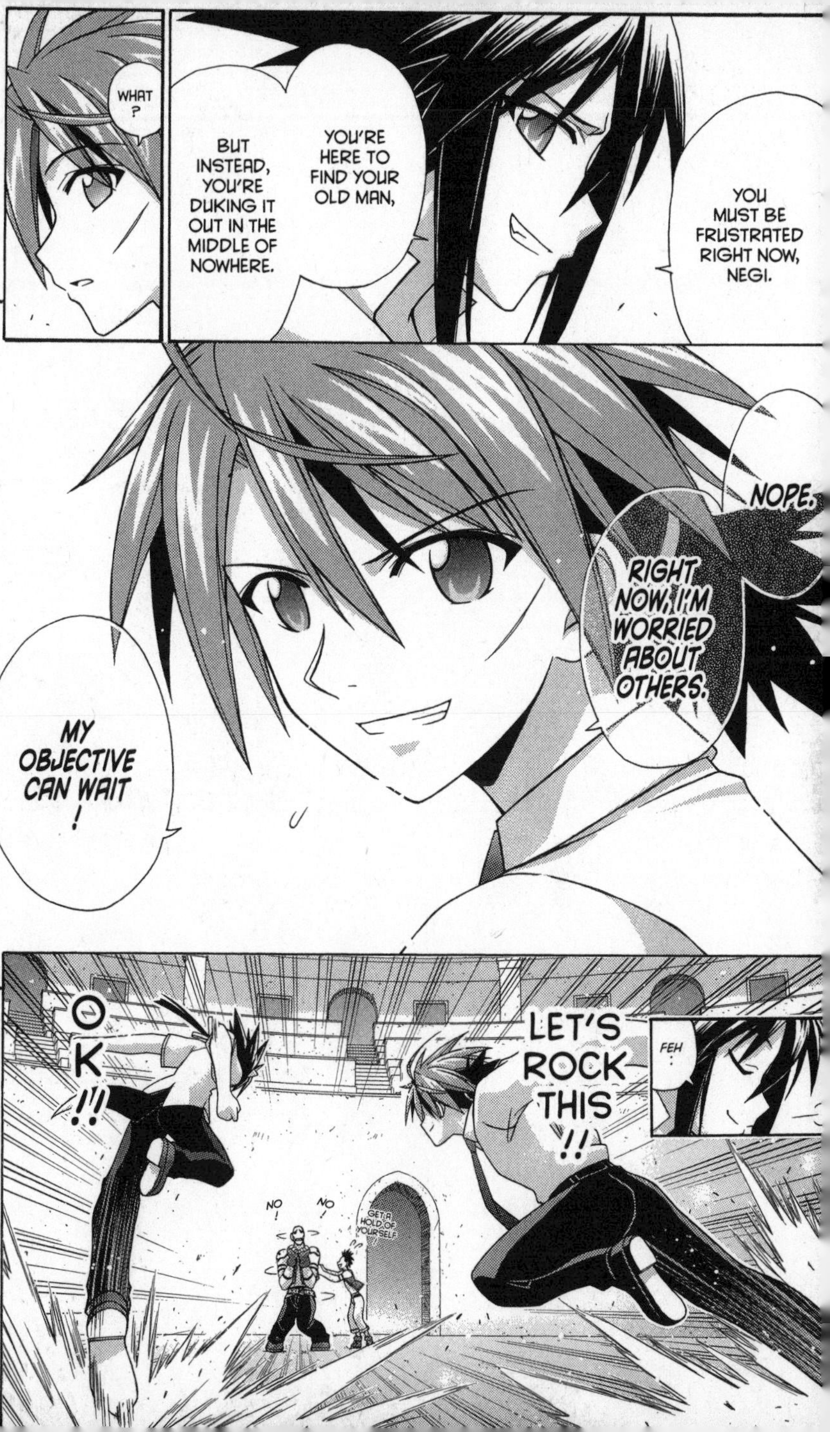
YOU MUST BE FRUSTRATED RIGHT NOW, NEGI.
YOU'RE HERE TO FIND YOUR OLD MAN,
BUT INSTEAD, YOU'RE DUKING IT OUT IN THE MIDDLE OF NOWHERE.
WHAT?
NOPE.
RIGHT NOW, I'M WORRIED ABOUT OTHERS.
MY OBJECTIVE CAN WAIT!
FEH...
LET'S ROCK THIS!!
OK!!
GET A HOLD OF YOURSELF
NO!
NO!

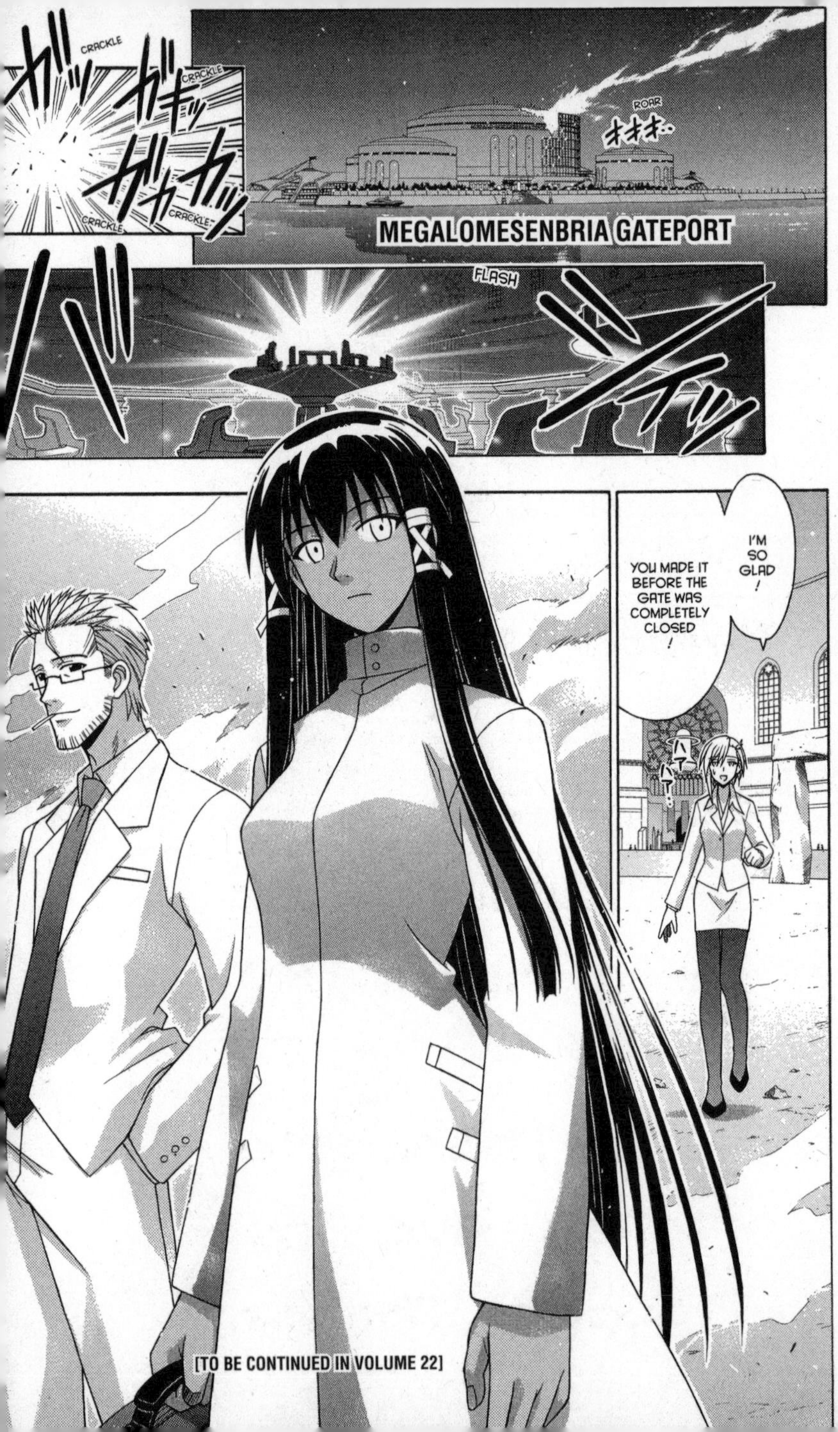
ROAR
MEGALOMESENBRIA GATEPORT
CRACKLE
CRACKLE
CRACKLE
CRACKLE
FLASH
I'M SO GLAD!
YOU MADE IT BEFORE THE GATE WAS COMPLETELY CLOSED!
[TO BE CONTINUED IN VOLUME 22]

-STAFF-

Ken Akamatsu

Takashi Takemoto

Kenichi Nakamura

Masaki Ohyama

Keiichi Yamashita

Tadashi Maki

Tohru Mitsuhashi

Thanks to

Ran Ayanaga

Sophie Thomas

NEGIMA!
FAN ART CORNER

I HAVE A HARD TIME ORGANIZING THIS SECTION IN EVERY VOLUME. (^^;) THERE ARE SO MANY PIECES OF ARTWORK I WANT TO INCLUDE, BUT I CAN'T! ☆ RECENT TRENDS: I'VE NOTICED LOTS OF PICTURES OF PEOPLE SAYING GOODBYE TO CHAO AND CUTE VERSIONS OF EVA. I REALLY ENJOY IT WHEN THE ARTWORK PEOPLE SEND IN ARE RELATED TO THE STORYLINE. ☆ PLEASE SEND YOUR CONTRIBUTIONS TO THE EDITORIAL OFFICES OF KODANSHA COMICS! ☆

TEXT BY ASSISTANT MAX

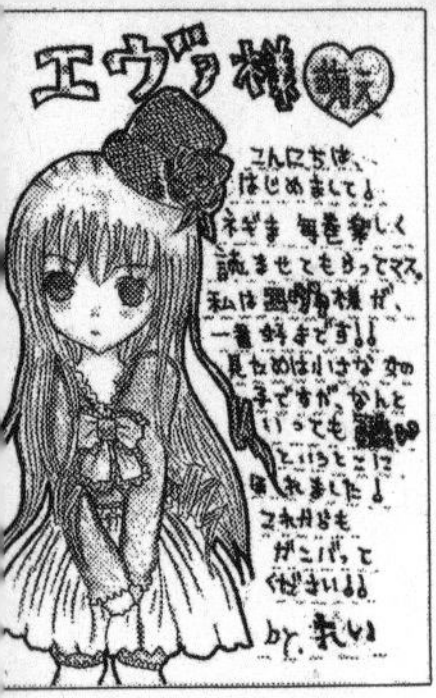

エヴァ様萌え
こんにちは，はじめまして。

▲ A VERY CUTE OUTFIT!

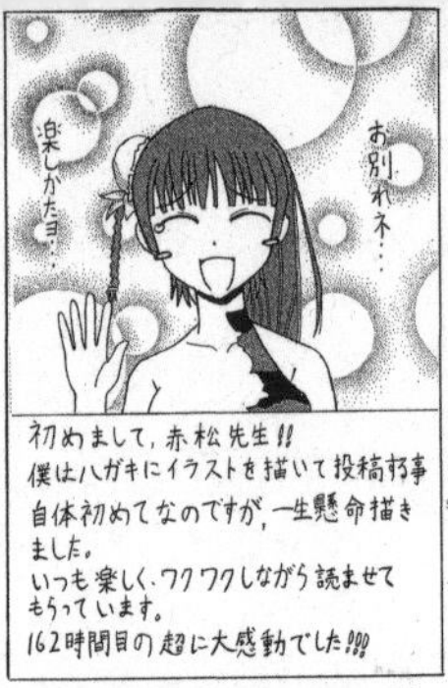

お別れネ…
楽しかたヨ…
初めまして，赤松先生!!
僕はハガキにイラストを描いて投稿する事
自体初めてなのですが，一生懸命描き
ました。
いつも楽しく，ワクワクしながら読ませて
もらっています。
162時間目の超に大感動でした!!!

▲ YOUR FEELINGS REALLY COME ACROSS ON THIS PICTURE.

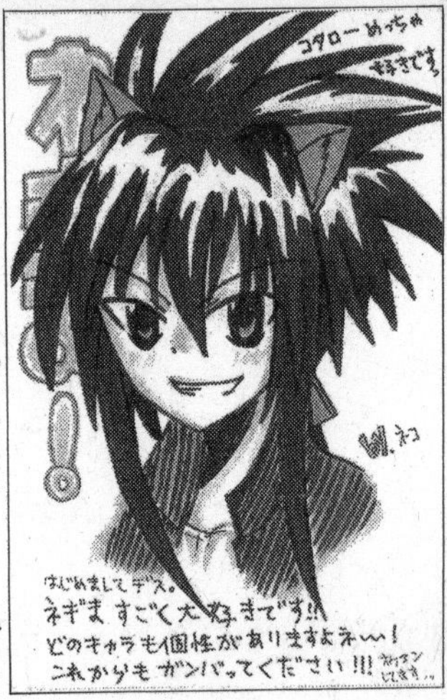

コタロー めっちゃ 好きです
はじめまして デス。
ネギま すごく大好きです!!
どのキャラも個性がありますよねぇ～!
これからも ガンバってください!!!

A VERY MANLY LOOKING KOTARŌ. ▶

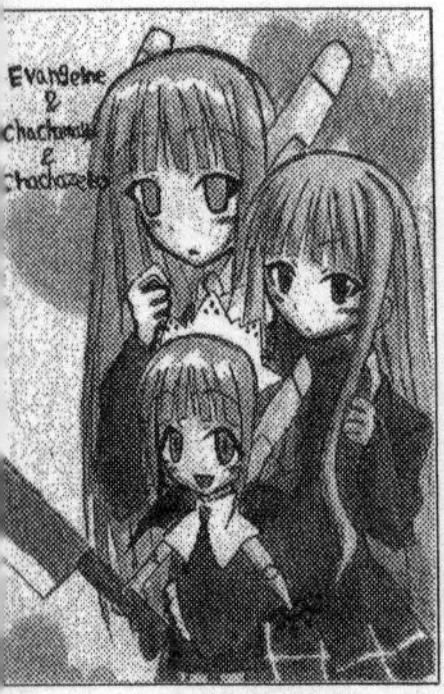

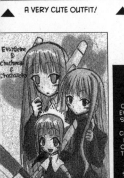

Evangeline & Chachamaru & Chachazero

▲ CHACHAZERO LOOKS REALLY CUTE! ★

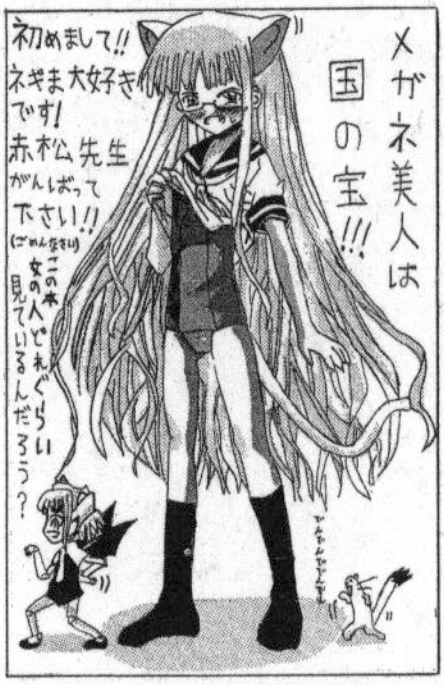

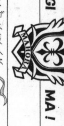

初めまして!!
ネギま大好きです!
赤松先生
がんばって
下さい!!
メガネ美人は
国の宝!!!

▶ I CAN FEEL YOUR PASSION IN THIS PICTURE!

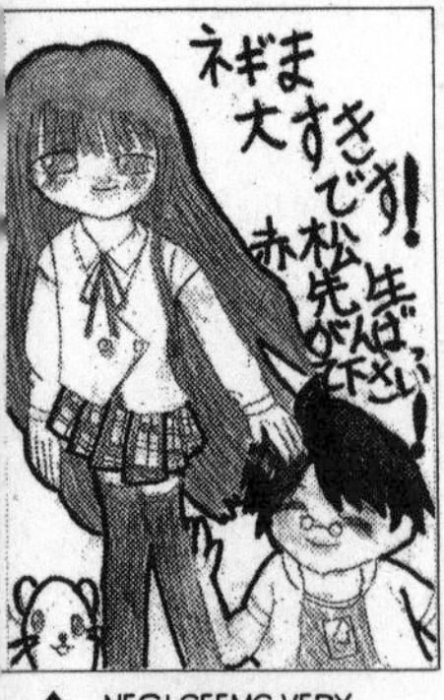

ネギま
大すき
です!
赤松
先生
がんばって下さい

▲ NEGI SEEMS VERY HAPPY.

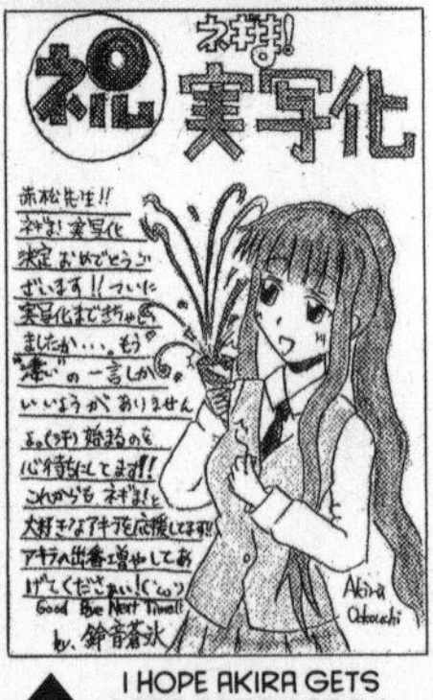

ネギま!
実写化
赤松先生!!
Good Bye Next Time!!

▲ I HOPE AKIRA GETS SOME ACTION SOON, TOO!

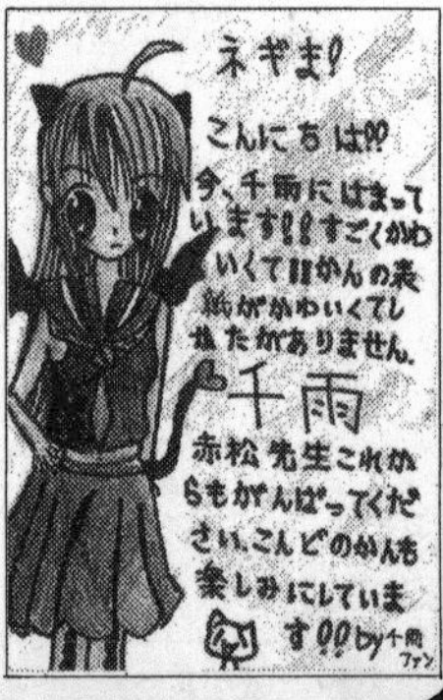

ネギま!
こんにちは!!
千雨

▶ A FAN OF CHIU, HUH?

NEGI MA!

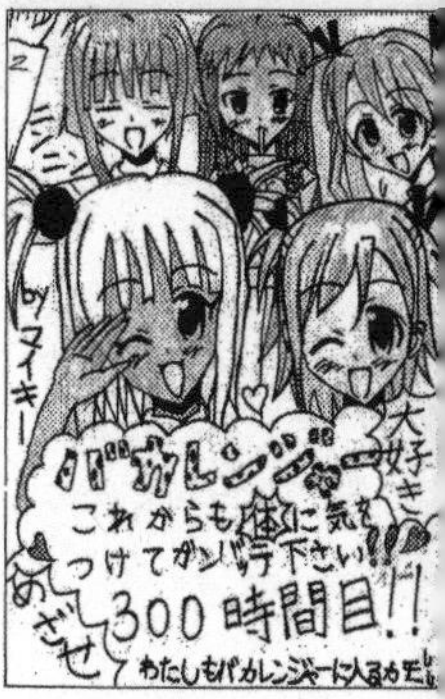
バカレンジャー大好き
これからも体に気をつけてガンバって下さい!!
めざせ300時間目!!
わたしもバカレンジャーに入るぞ!

▲ LOOKS LIKE THEY'RE HAVING FUN. ★

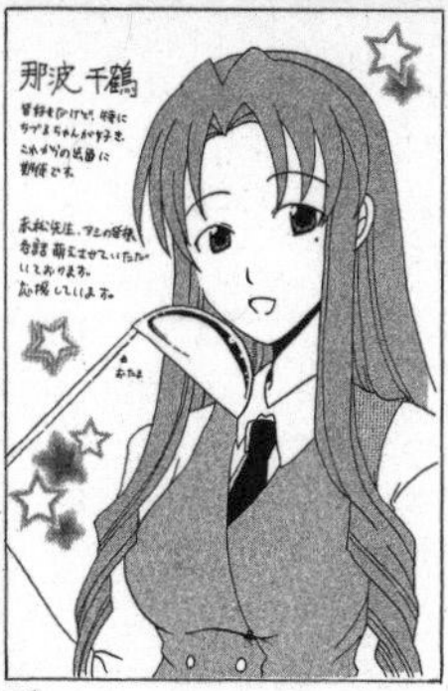
那波千鶴

◀ THIS IS VERY NEATLY DRAWN.

▼ THE ULTIMATE TEAM-UP. (^^)

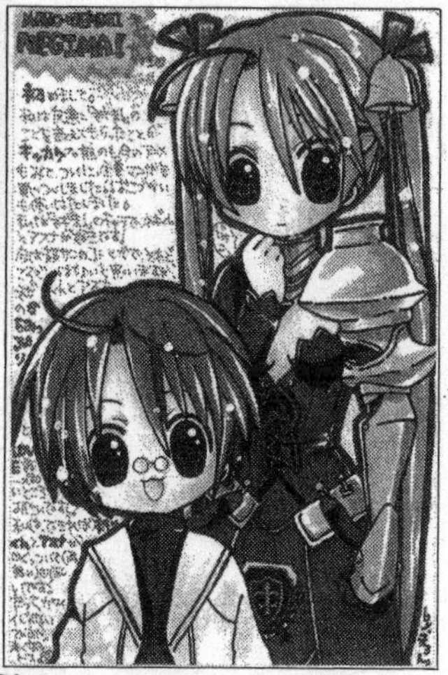
NEGIMA!

▶ THERE'S AN ELEGANT QUALITY TO THIS PICTURE.

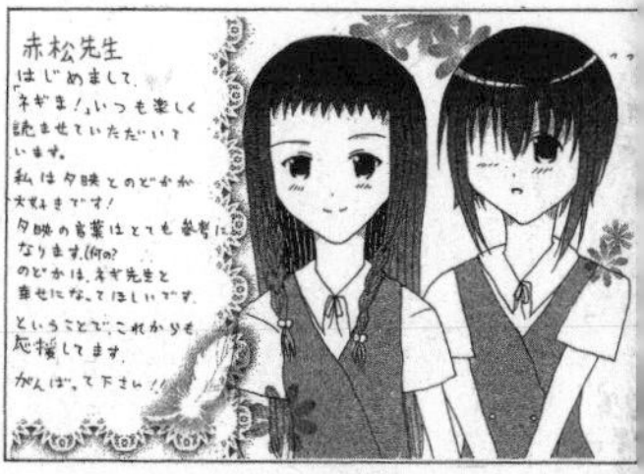
赤松先生
はじめまして。
「ネギま!」いつも楽しく読ませていただいています。
私は夕映とのどかが大好きです!
夕映の言葉はとても参考になります。(何の?)
のどかは、ネギ先生と幸せになってほしいです。
ということで、これからも応援してます。
がんばって下さい!!

▶ LET'S AVOID THE REALLY STRANGE BEVERAGES. (LAUGHS)

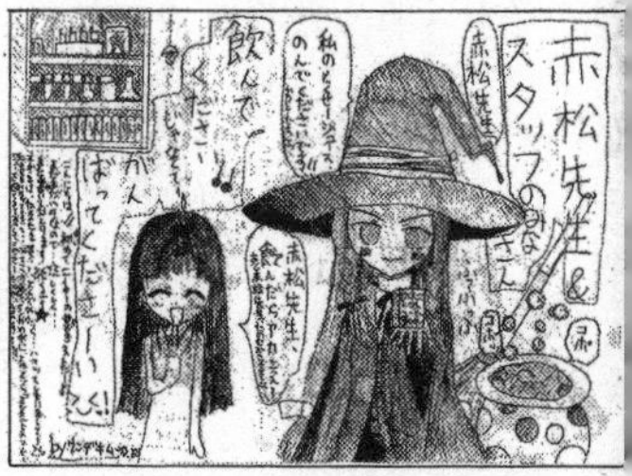
赤松先生&スタッフのみなさん
飲んでください
がんばってくださーい!

▶ HAPPY BIRTHDAY! ★

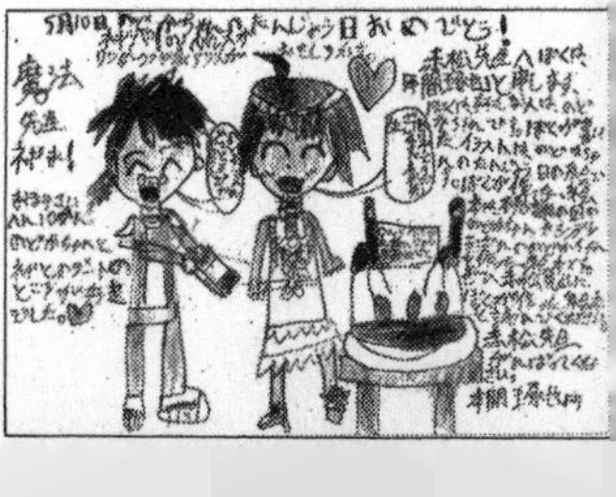
魔法先生ネギま!

▼ THEIR EXPRESSIONS ARE LOVELY.

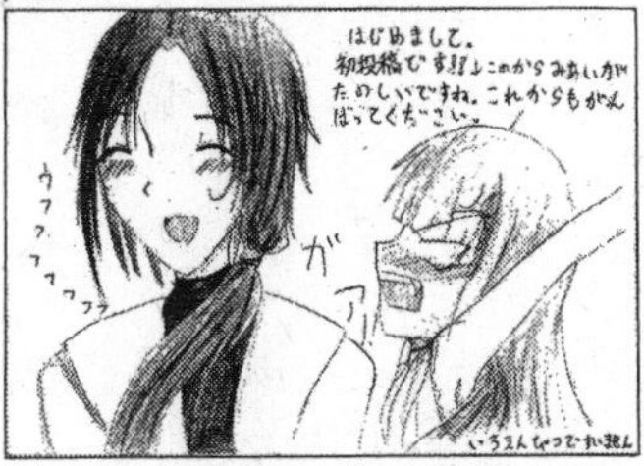
はじめまして。
ウフフフフフ
ガァ

▼ NOW THIS IS AN INTERESTING TRIO.

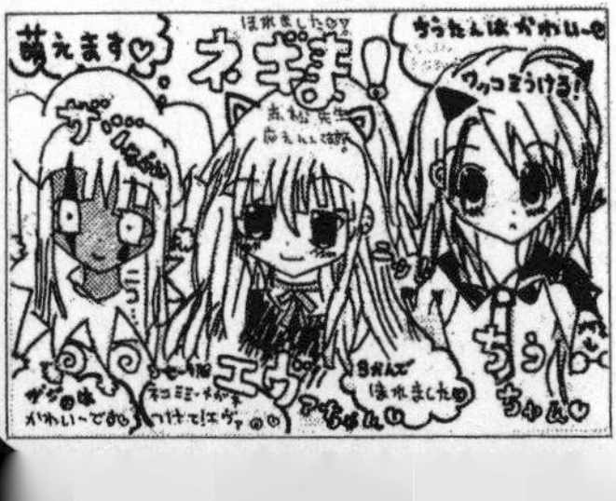
萌えます♡
ネギま!
エヴァちゃん
ちうちゃん

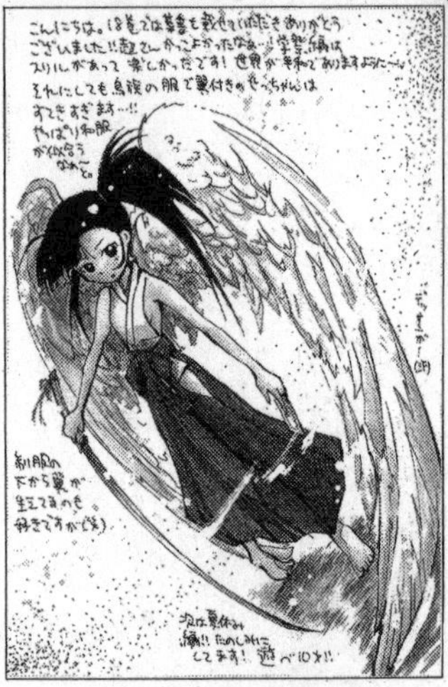

THE GENTLE USE OF COLOR IS WONDERFUL.

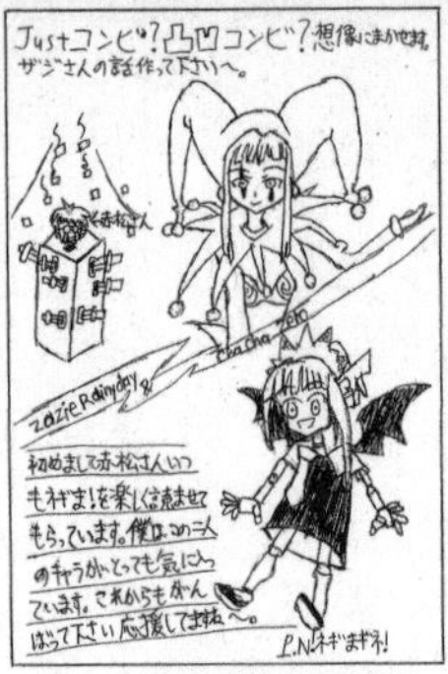

THEY MIGHT ACTUALLY MAKE A REALLY GOOD TEAM...

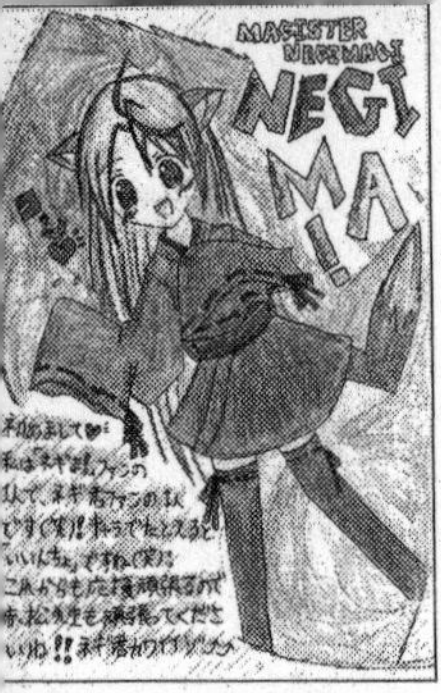
MAGISTER NEGI MAGI
NEGI MA!

THIS NEGI LOOKS VERY CUTE IN PINK!

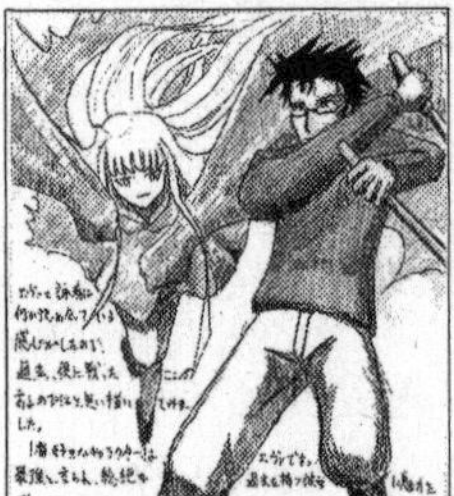

YOU CAN REALLY GET THE SENSE OF MOTION IN THIS PICTURE.

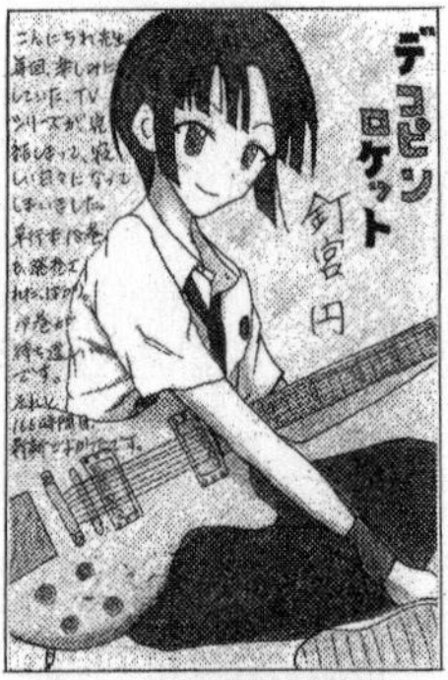
デコピンロケット
釘宮円

THE GUITAR REALLY SUITS HER IN THIS PICTURE. ★

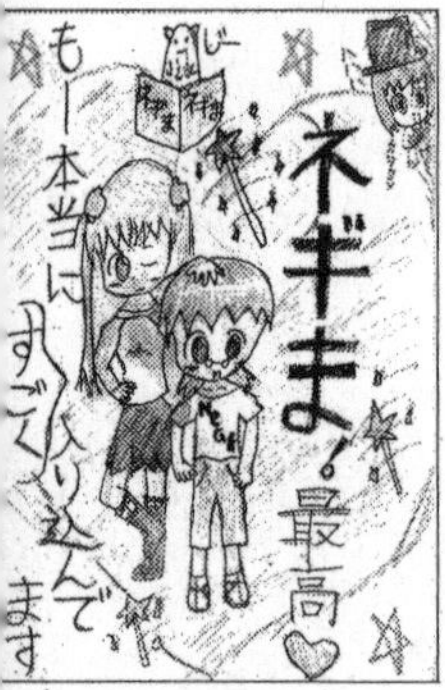
ネギま!最高
も一本当にすごく入り込んでます

PAT PAT. (^^)

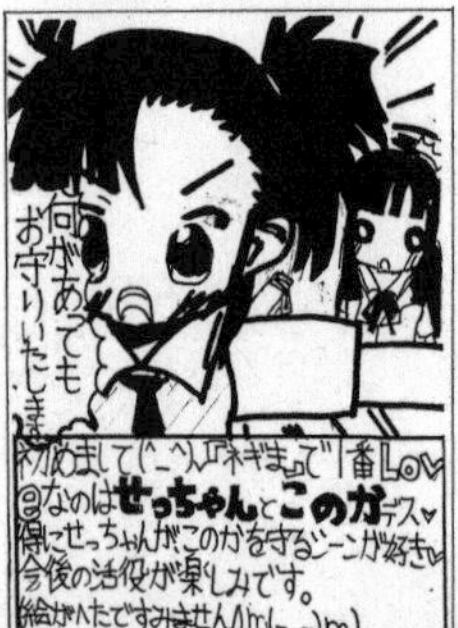
何があってもお守りいたします
by『ツンデレLove』でした。

A VERY HEROIC-LOOKING SETSUNA.

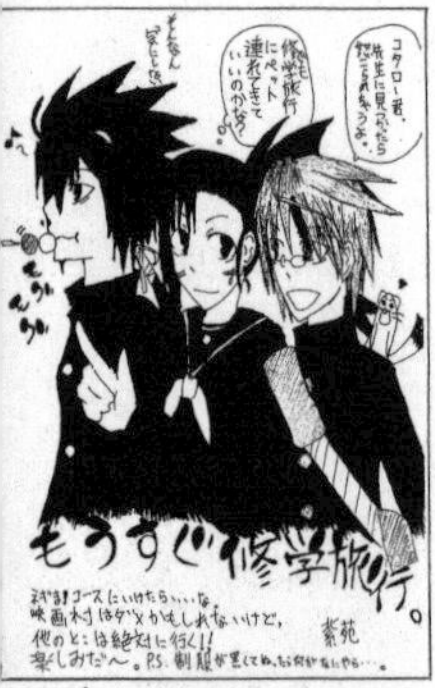
もうすぐ修学旅行。

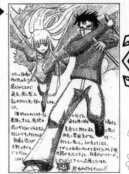

THEY REALLY LOOK THE PART OF BEING STUDENTS!

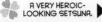

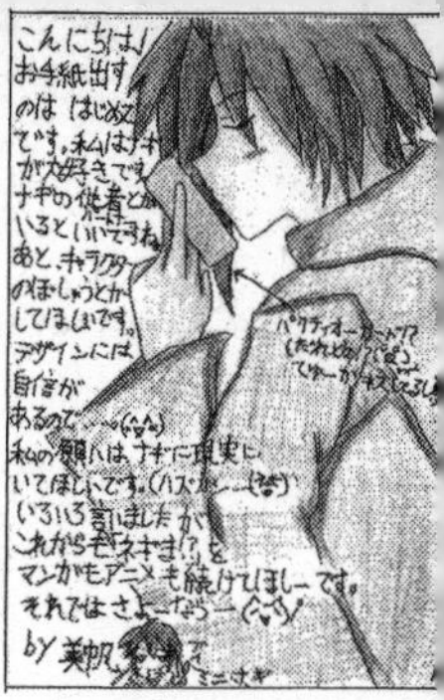

▲ NAGI'S EXPRESSION IS VERY NICE.

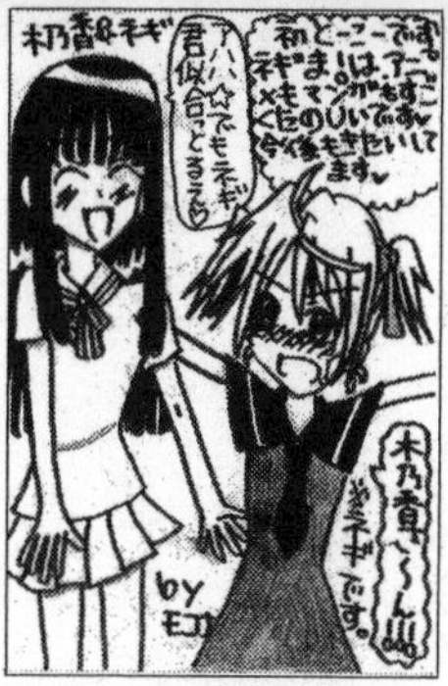

▲ WE DIDN'T REALIZE THIS WAS NEGI...

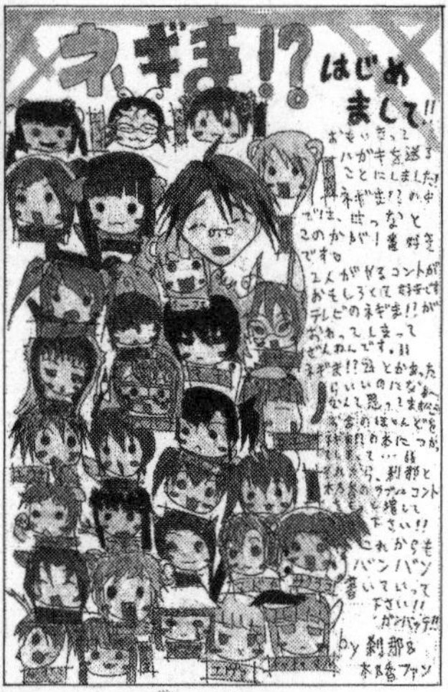

▲ EACH FACE IS SO CUTE. ★

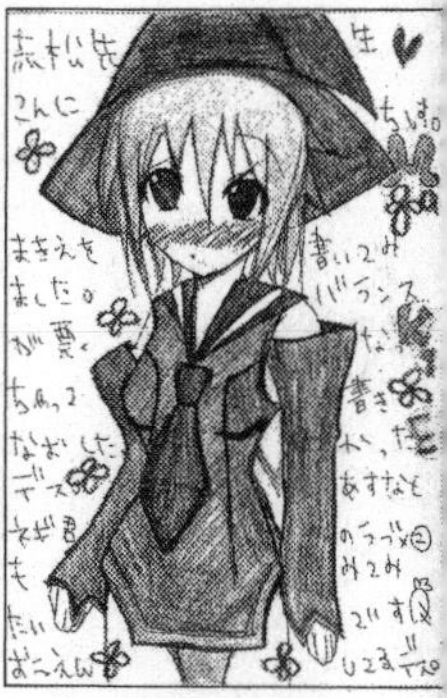

▲ MAKIE LOOKING VERY TIRED.

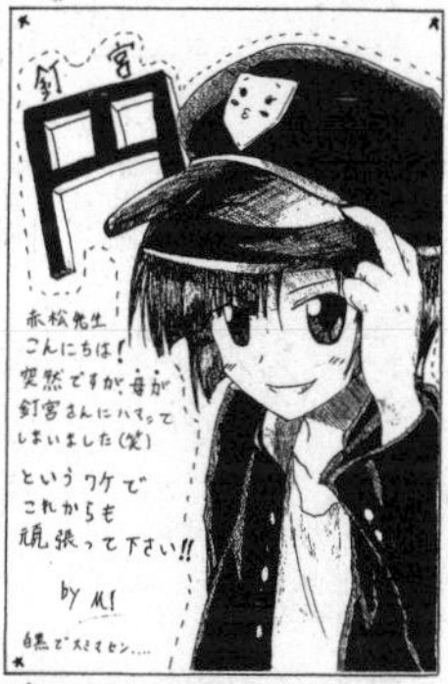

▲ A VERY COOL-LOOKING MADOKA!

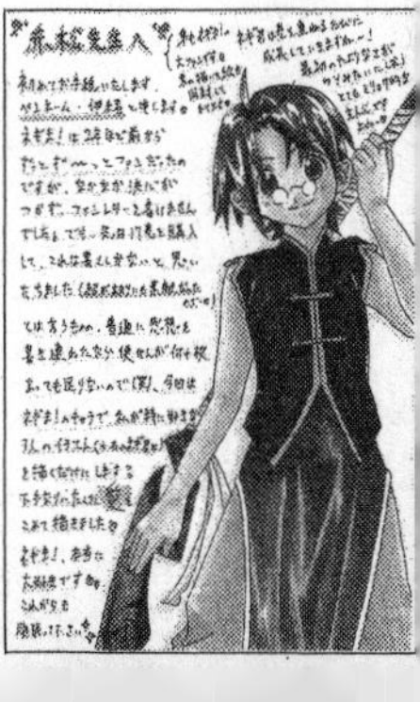

▶ A VERY MATURE-LOOKING NEGI.

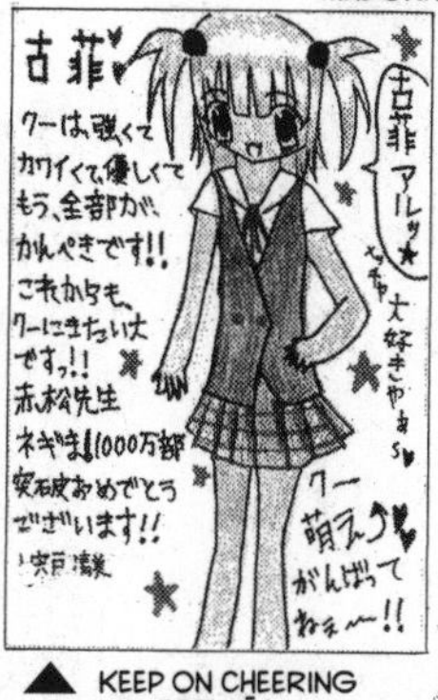

▲ KEEP ON CHEERING FOR KŪ! ★

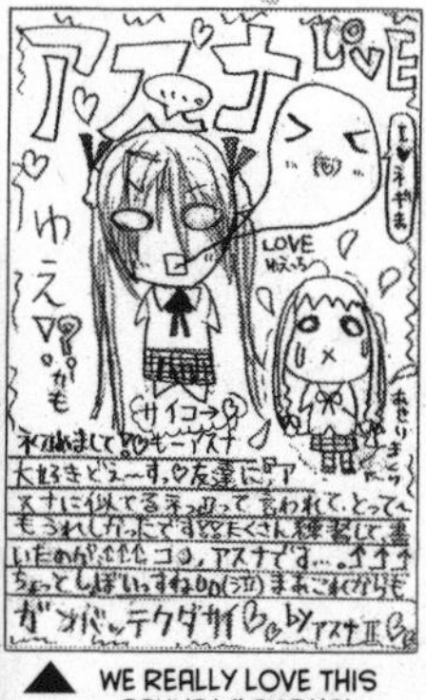

▲ WE REALLY LOVE THIS ASUNA! (LAUGHS)

3-D BACKGROUNDS EXPLANATION CORNER

IN THIS VOLUME, WE HAD A VARIETY OF VERY BIG STRUCTURES AND VERY SMALL ITEMS.

• LEBENS SCHULD CASTLE

SCENE NAME: EVA'S CASTLE

POLYGON COUNT: 576,479

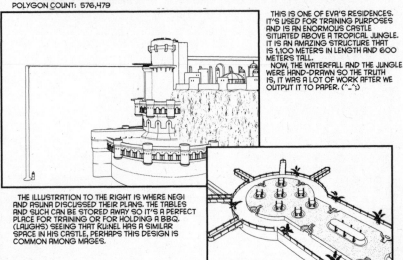

THIS IS ONE OF EVA'S RESIDENCES. IT'S USED FOR TRAINING PURPOSES AND IS AN ENORMOUS CASTLE SITUATED ABOVE A TROPICAL JUNGLE. IT IS AN AMAZING STRUCTURE THAT IS 1,100 METERS IN LENGTH AND 600 METERS TALL.

NOW, THE WATERFALL AND THE JUNGLE WERE HAND-DRAWN SO THE TRUTH IS, IT WAS A LOT OF WORK AFTER WE OUTPUT IT TO PAPER. (^_^;)

THE ILLUSTRATION TO THE RIGHT IS WHERE NEGI AND ASUNA DISCUSSED THEIR PLANS. THE TABLES AND SUCH CAN BE STORED AWAY SO IT'S A PERFECT PLACE FOR TRAINING OR FOR HOLDING A BBQ. (LAUGHS) SEEING THAT KU:NEL HAS A SIMILAR SPACE IN HIS CASTLE, PERHAPS THIS DESIGN IS COMMON AMONG MAGES.

• YŪNA'S HOUSE

SCENE NAME: YŪNA'S ROOM

POLYGON COUNT: 70,150

THIS IS THE APARTMENT THAT YŪNA'S FATHER, WHO IS A PROFESSOR AT MAHORA UNIVERSITY, RESIDES IN AND IS YŪNA'S HOME.

THE DESIGN INSIDE IS VERY COMMON LOOKING, BUT FOR THE STORY, THERE WERE SEVERAL ROOMS THAT WERE CREATED. YŪNA'S ROOM, THE STUDY, KITCHEN AND DINING ROOM, AND SO ON.

• KITCHEN & DINING ROOM

A KITCHEN THAT LOOKS LIKE IT CAN MAKE BETTER THINGS THAN JUST BOIL-A-BAG CURRIES. (LAUGHS)

AND AGAIN, A LOT OF THE MODELS USED IN THIS ROOM ARE FROM A ROOM THAT WASN'T USED PREVIOUSLY.

• YŪNA'S ROOM

IT'S A RATHER GIRLY ROOM WITH TEDDY BEARS AND ALL. THE TRUTH IS, MANY OF THE ITEMS IN THIS ROOM ARE RECYCLED FROM A ROOM THAT DIDN'T GET USED PREVIOUSLY. BUT THIS ISN'T A BAD-LOOKING ROOM, IS IT? (LAUGHS)

• GIRLS' DORMITORY LOBBY
SCENE NAME: LOBBY
POLYGON COUNT: 27,696

THIS IS THE SPACIOUS LOBBY LOCATED ON THE FIRST FLOOR OF THE GIRLS' DORMITORY. THIS IS WHERE THE RESIDENTS READ, EAT SNACK FOODS AND WHATNOT, DEPENDING ON THE STUDENT.

THERE'S A LARGE WINDOW IN THE ROOM AND IT MIGHT BE A NICE PLACE TO NAP NEAR AS EVANGELINE WAS DOING. (LAUGHS)

• SUMMER FESTIVAL
SCENE NAME: SUMMER FESTIVAL
POLYGON COUNT: 971,088

THIS IS THE ANNUAL SUMMER FESTIVAL HELD AT TATSUMIYA SHRINE. SHOPS LINE THE PATH FROM THE GATE ALL THE WAY TO THE TEMPLE AND ARE VISITED BY THE MANY PEOPLE LIVING IN MAHORA.

IN TRUTH, THERE WERE SEVEN DIFFERENT MODELS OF SHOPS AND THEY WERE ARRANGED RANDOMLY AND THEN DETAILS LIKE BANNERS AND SIGNS WERE DRAWN BY HAND AFTERWARD.

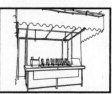

• SHOOTING GALLERY
IF YOU LOOK CAREFULLY, YOU MIGHT RECOGNIZE THE PRIZES... (LAUGHS)

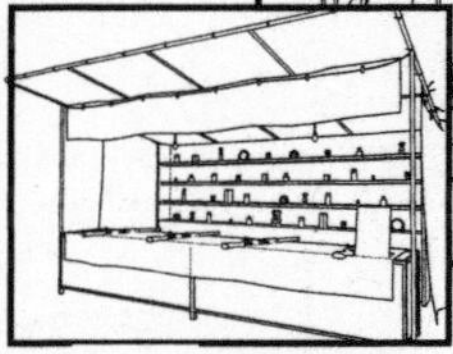

• CHOCO-BANANA STAND
WE EVEN PUT IN FINE DETAILS SUCH AS FOR THIS STAND.

POLY-MEN AND POLY-WOMEN WEARING *YUKATA*. THEN AGAIN, WITHOUT HAIR ON THEM, IT'S HARD TO TELL THEM APART. (^^;)

- BONUS -

• HAND BELL
IT'S A HASSLE TO DRAW THE FINE LINES EACH TIME SO WE MADE A 3-D VERSION. (LAUGHS)

• ALA RUBRA CLUB MEMBER PIN BADGE
SEE EXPLANATION TO THE LEFT. (LAUGHS)

PRELIMINARY DESIGN COLLECTION
~ CHARACTER ROUGH SKETCHES ~

NAME: YŪKO AKASHI
PERSONALITY: SORT OF RANDOM AND NOT FOCUSED
OCCUPATION: PRESCHOOL ASSISTANT (PART-TIME)

VERY INTENSE AT SCHOOL BUT TENDS TO BE A LITTLE UNFOCUSED ABOUT WHAT SHE DOES.

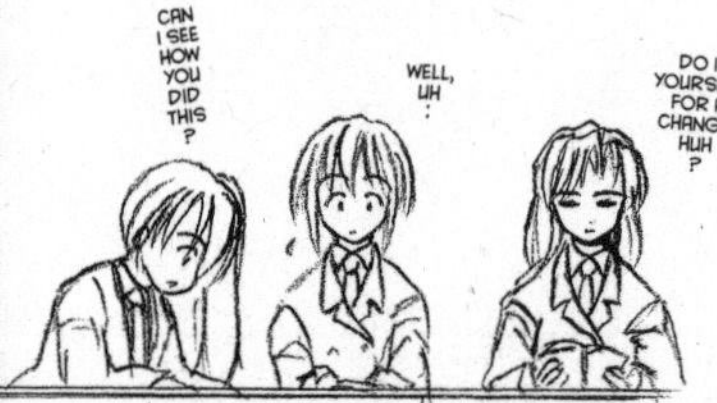
DO IT YOURSELF FOR A CHANGE, HUH?
WELL, UH...
CAN I SEE HOW YOU DID THIS?

[YŪKO AKASHI]

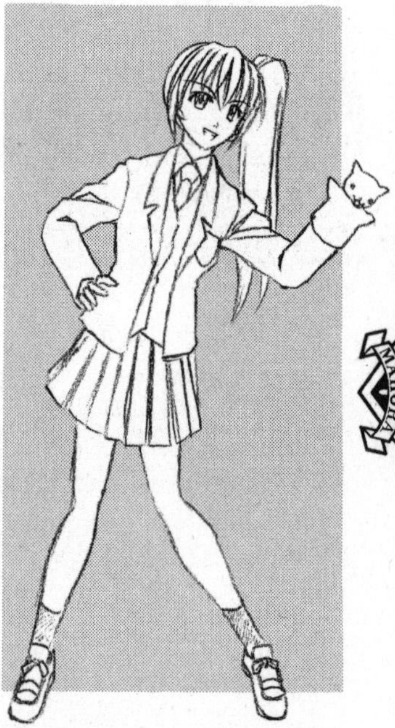

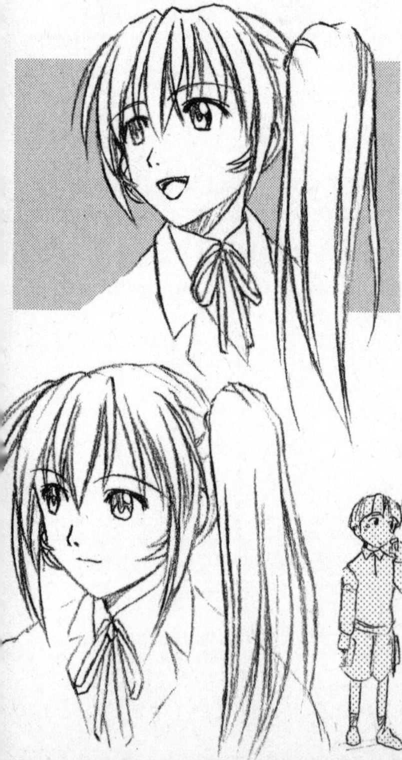

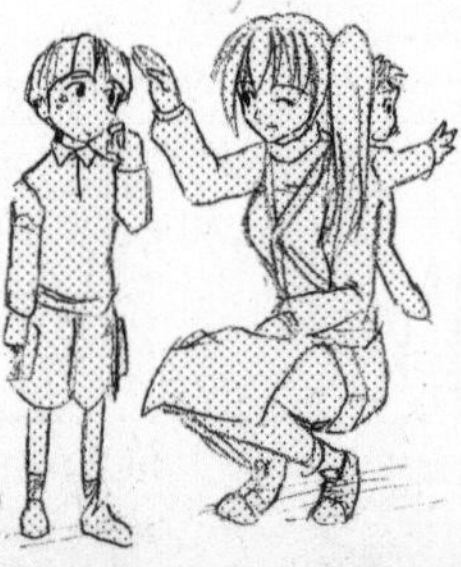

WHETHER SHE'S SERIOUS OR NOT, SHE'S WORKS PART-TIME AT A PRESCHOOL. SHE'S ACTUALLY REALLY GOOD WITH CHILDREN.

THE PRESCHOOL (BECAUSE OF TIME CONSTRAINTS SHE WORKS AT A PRESCHOOL INSTEAD OF A KINDERGARTEN) ACTUALLY COUNTS ON HER QUITE A BIT.

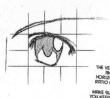

THE VERTICAL AND HORIZONTAL RATIO IS 2:3.
MAKE SURE YOU KEEP THE RATIO AND THE DETAILS EXACT.
NOSE FRONT VIEW
SLIGHTLY UPWARD POINTING.
SORT OF SHAPED LIKE THE KANJI CHARACTER FOR EIGHT.

THESE TWO BECOME YŪNA AND CHIZURU... BUT SOMETHING IS WRONG HERE! THE SECRET OF THAT IS ON THE NEXT PAGE. (LAUGHS) ACTUALLY THINGS LIKE THIS HAPPEN ALL THE TIME.

magister negi magi

HMM
MAKE SURE HIS NECKLINE IS ALWAYS SLIGHTLY SKEWED.
FATHER ... DO SOMETHING ABOUT YOUR COWLICKS.

TSUTSUMI NADAI
KATSUTOSHI NADAI (FATHER)

A DAUGHTER WHO HAS AN EXTREME FATHER COMPLEX, AND HER FATHER. THE FATHER IS A TEACHER AT THE SCHOOL WHERE THE MAIN CHARACTER TEACHES. POSSIBLY HAS A CONNECTION TO THE MAIN CHARACTER'S FATHER AS WELL?

IT'S A FATHER-DAUGHTER-ONLY FAMILY AND DESPITE THE CONSTANT COMPLAINING, SHE ENJOYS TAKING CARE OF HER FATHER. BECAUSE OF THAT, SHE'S VERY GOOD AT COOKING AND OTHER HOUSEHOLD CHORES. HER DREAM FOR HER FUTURE IS BECOMING HER FATHER'S WIFE (HEY NOW!). BUT HER FATHER'S SCHOOL HAS MANY FEMALE TEACHERS, AND THEY ARE A CONSTANT SOURCE OF JEALOUSY FOR HER.

FATHER, YOU FORGOT YOUR LUNCH...
OH! DID? THANKS.

INSIDE STORY: YŪNA AND CHIZURU WERE CREATED AFTER A PERSONALITY SWAP

character design

THE TWO CHARACTERS FEATURED IN THE PRELIMINARY DESIGN SECTION WERE BASICALLY BUILDING BLOCKS FOR THE FINAL CHARACTERS. THE ENERGETIC CHARACTER OF YŪKO AKASHI BECAME THE BASIS FOR YŪNA AKASHI, BUT SHE TAKES CARE OF CHILDREN FOR HER PART-TIME JOB! IN THE STORY, IT'S ACTUALLY CHIZURU NABA WHO IS THE VOLUNTEER NANNY. AND ON THE OTHER HAND, THE CONCEPT CHARACTER OF TSUTSUMI NADAI HAS YŪNA'S FATHER COMPLEX BUT ISN'T WELL PROPORTIONED OR ENERGETIC.

THE TRUTH IS, THE TWO CONCEPT CHARACTERS BECAME THEIR FINAL FORMS BY SWAPPING OUT THE "NANNY" AND "FATHER COMPLEX" TO END UP WITH:

THE ENERGETIC YET UNFOCUSED GIRL: YŪNA AKASHI

THE VOLUNTEER NANNY WHO WANTS TO TAKE CARE OF OTHERS: CHIZURU NABA.

LEXICON NEGIMARIUM

[*Negima!* 169th Period Lexicon Negimarium]

■ **(Let hundreds and thousands combine, run forth lightning. THOUSAND LIGHTNING BOLTS)**
 • An extremely destructive lightning-based attack spell that has a large area of effect. The spell is incanted in ancient Greek. From the highly destructive power of the spell, it is believed that it requires a great amount of magical power to cast.

[*Negima!* 177th Period Lexicon Negimarium]

■ *lux*
(light)
 • An entry-level spell that emits a small light. It is one of the first spells to be taught to a student mage. With experience and practice, the light can be maintained for a prolonged length of time, but for someone with Yue's experience level, only a momentary flash can be achieved. But in darkness, the sudden light can be used to blind an opponent.

■ *elementa aerialis, venti spirantes cito adeuntes ab inimicis meis me defendant LIMES AERIALES*
(Spirits of the air, breath of the winds, come forth and protect us from the enemy. BARRIER OF WIND)
 • This is the barrier magic used by Negi in *Negima!*, vol. 16, 145th Period. In this volume, the full incantation has appeared so it's listed here. For the description of the spell, see the lexicon in vol. 16

■ *Diaria Ejus Minora Quadrupla adeant tumcogitaiones vestigent de Makie Sasaki, Yūna Akashi, Akira Ōkōchi, Ako Izumi*
(Picture Diary of ID, four miniature simplified volumes, come forth. Follow the thoughts of Makie Sasaki, Yūna Akashi, Akira Ōkōchi, and Ako Izumi)
 • This spell allows Nodoka's artifact, Diarium Ejus (Picture Diary of ID), to separate to read the thoughts of multiple individuals. Adeant is the plural form of Adeat as she is calling forth multiple copies of her artifact. When reading the thoughts of multiple targets, the diary no longer contains pictures but is very effective when dealing with many opponents. Even still, it is difficult for the caster to follow the thoughts of multiple people.

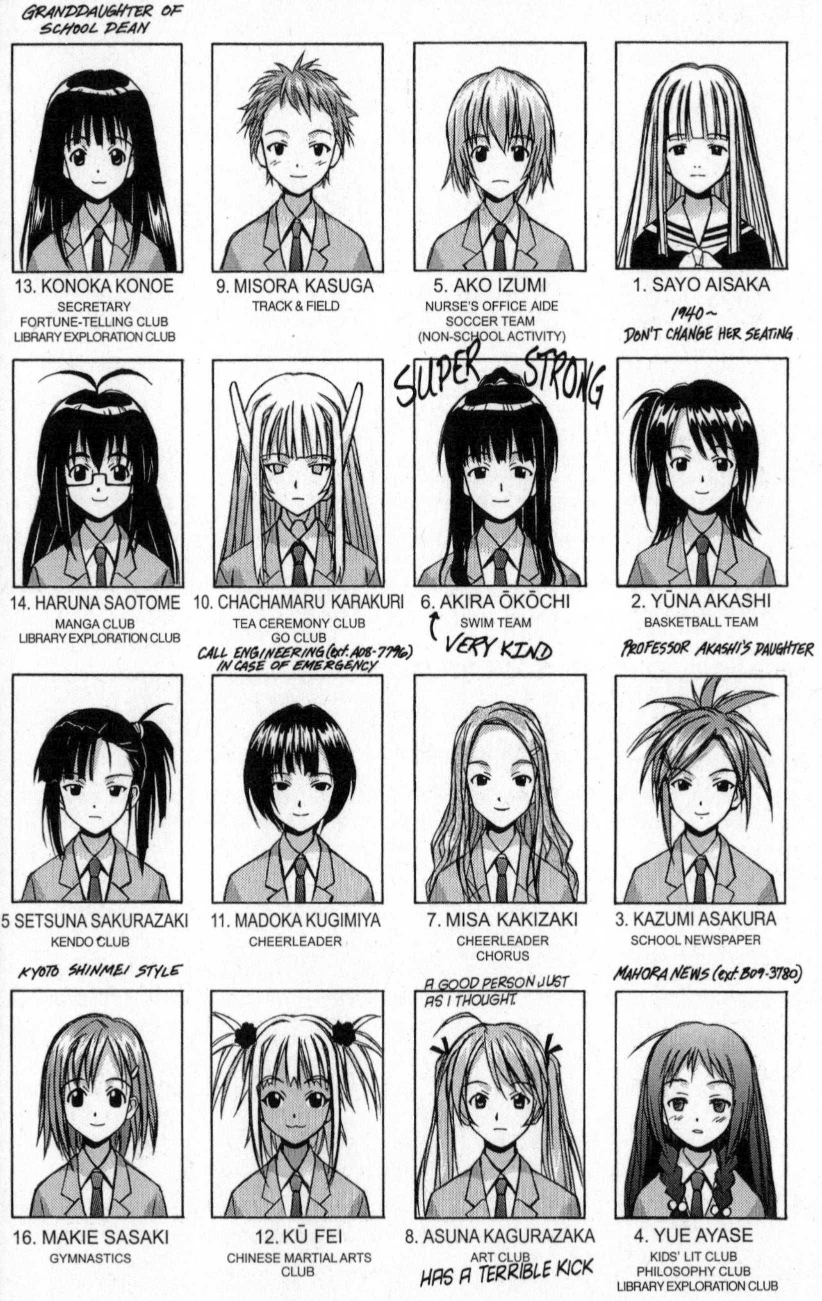
1. SAYO AISAKA
1940~
DON'T CHANGE HER SEATING
5. AKO IZUMI
NURSE'S OFFICE AIDE
SOCCER TEAM
(NON-SCHOOL ACTIVITY)
9. MISORA KASUGA
TRACK & FIELD
GRANDDAUGHTER OF SCHOOL DEAN
13. KONOKA KONOE
SECRETARY
FORTUNE-TELLING CLUB
LIBRARY EXPLORATION CLUB
2. YŪNA AKASHI
BASKETBALL TEAM
PROFESSOR AKASHI'S DAUGHTER
SUPER STRONG
6. AKIRA ŌKŌCHI
SWIM TEAM
VERY KIND
10. CHACHAMARU KARAKURI
TEA CEREMONY CLUB
GO CLUB
CALL ENGINEERING (ext. A08-7796) IN CASE OF EMERGENCY
14. HARUNA SAOTOME
MANGA CLUB
LIBRARY EXPLORATION CLUB
3. KAZUMI ASAKURA
SCHOOL NEWSPAPER
MAHORA NEWS (ext. 809-3780)
7. MISA KAKIZAKI
CHEERLEADER
CHORUS
11. MADOKA KUGIMIYA
CHEERLEADER
15 SETSUNA SAKURAZAKI
KENDO CLUB
KYOTO SHINMEI STYLE
4. YUE AYASE
KIDS' LIT CLUB
PHILOSOPHY CLUB
LIBRARY EXPLORATION CLUB
A GOOD PERSON JUST AS I THOUGHT.
8. ASUNA KAGURAZAKA
ART CLUB
HAS A TERRIBLE KICK
12. KŪ FEI
CHINESE MARTIAL ARTS CLUB
16. MAKIE SASAKI
GYMNASTICS

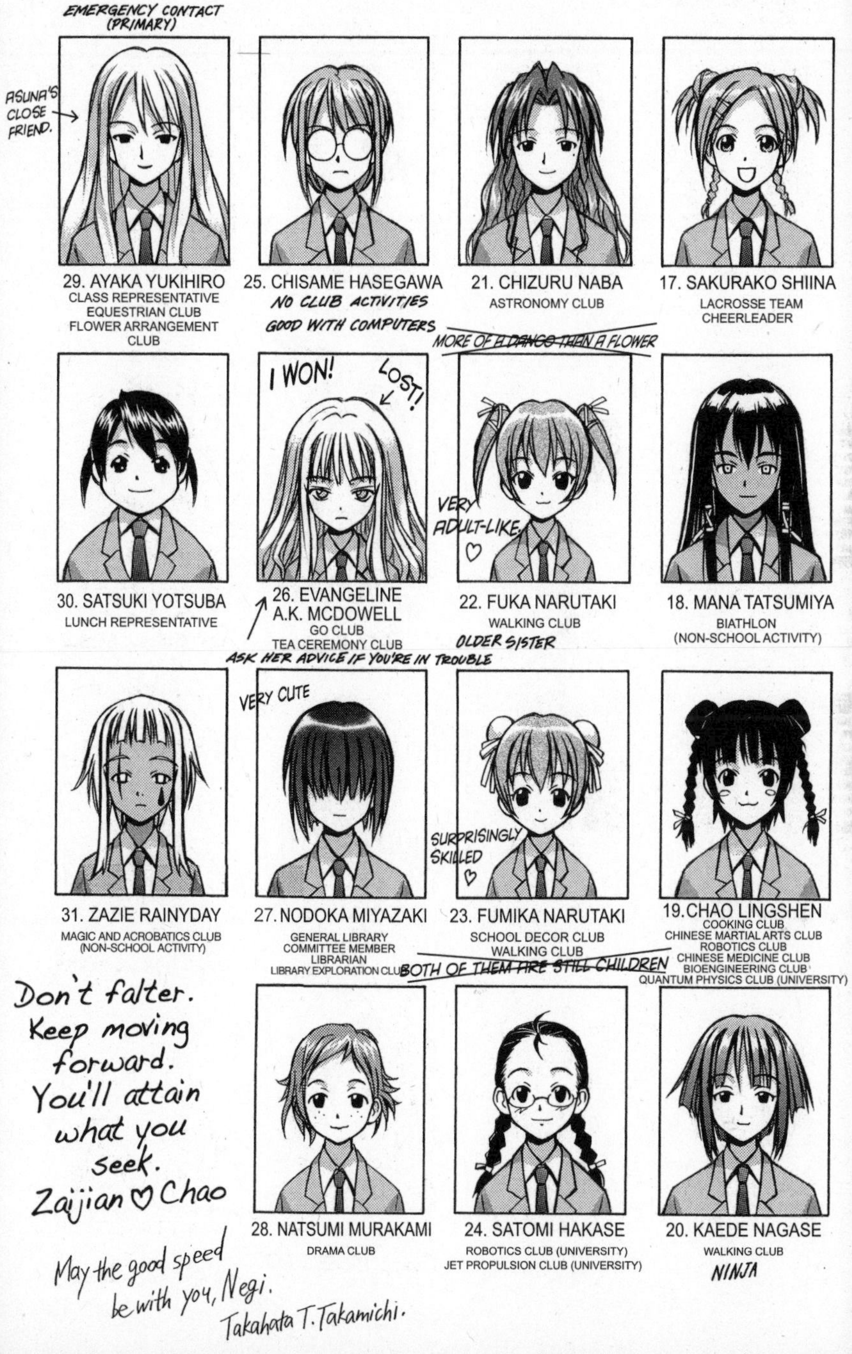
17. SAKURAKO SHIINA
LACROSSE TEAM
CHEERLEADER
21. CHIZURU NABA
ASTRONOMY CLUB
MORE OF A DANGO THAN A FLOWER
25. CHISAME HASEGAWA
NO CLUB ACTIVITIES
GOOD WITH COMPUTERS
EMERGENCY CONTACT (PRIMARY)
ASUNA'S CLOSE FRIEND.
29. AYAKA YUKIHIRO
CLASS REPRESENTATIVE
EQUESTRIAN CLUB
FLOWER ARRANGEMENT CLUB
18. MANA TATSUMIYA
BIATHLON
(NON-SCHOOL ACTIVITY)
VERY ADULT-LIKE.
22. FUKA NARUTAKI
WALKING CLUB
OLDER SISTER
I WON!
LOST!
26. EVANGELINE A.K. MCDOWELL
GO CLUB
TEA CEREMONY CLUB
ASK HER ADVICE IF YOU'RE IN TROUBLE
30. SATSUKI YOTSUBA
LUNCH REPRESENTATIVE
19.CHAO LINGSHEN
COOKING CLUB
CHINESE MARTIAL ARTS CLUB
ROBOTICS CLUB
CHINESE MEDICINE CLUB
BIOENGINEERING CLUB
QUANTUM PHYSICS CLUB (UNIVERSITY)
SURPRISINGLY SKILLED
23. FUMIKA NARUTAKI
SCHOOL DECOR CLUB
WALKING CLUB
BOTH OF THEM ARE STILL CHILDREN
VERY CUTE
27. NODOKA MIYAZAKI
GENERAL LIBRARY COMMITTEE MEMBER
LIBRARIAN
LIBRARY EXPLORATION CLUB
31. ZAZIE RAINYDAY
MAGIC AND ACROBATICS CLUB
(NON-SCHOOL ACTIVITY)
20. KAEDE NAGASE
WALKING CLUB
NINJA
24. SATOMI HAKASE
ROBOTICS CLUB (UNIVERSITY)
JET PROPULSION CLUB (UNIVERSITY)
28. NATSUMI MURAKAMI
DRAMA CLUB
Don't falter. Keep moving forward. You'll attain what you seek. Zaijian ♡ Chao
May the good speed be with you, Negi. Takahata T. Takamichi.

魔法先生ネギま! MAGISTER NEGI MAGI

赤松 健 SHONEN MAGAZINE COMICS KEN AKAMATSU

19

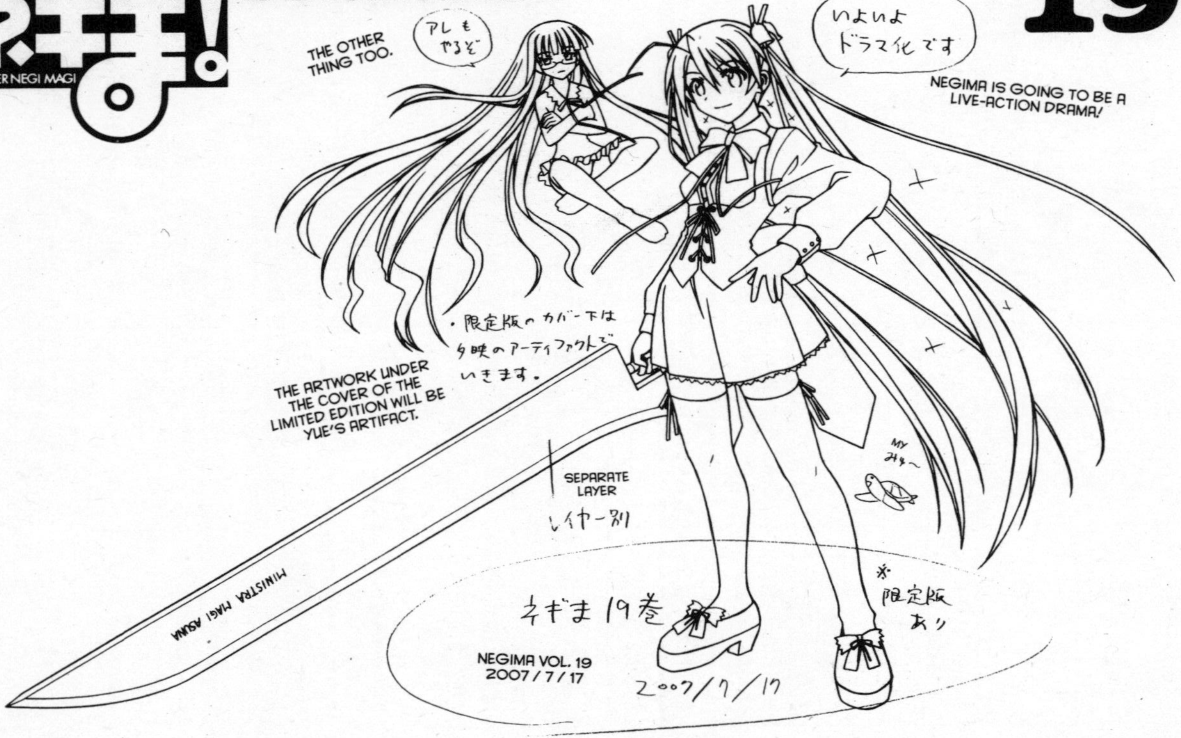

キャラ解説

CHARACTER PROFILE

㉘ 村上夏美

㉘ NATSUMI MURAKAMI

演劇部の夏美です。

THIS IS NATSUMI FROM THE DRAMA CLUB.

胸ペッタン、くせっ毛、そばかす、と 本人は色々

SHE SEEMS TO HAVE A BIT OF A COMPLEX ABOUT BEING FLAT-CHESTED, AND HAVING COWLICKS IN

気にしているようですが、周囲の人がすごすぎる

HER HAIR AS WELL AS FRECKLES, BUT MOST LIKELY IT'S BECAUSE THE OTHERS AROUND HER ARE A BIT

だけですよね。(笑)

OUT OF THE ORDINARY. (LAUGHS)

千鶴とか いいんちょとか

LIKE CHIZURU AND THE CLASS REP

どうやら、小太郎が気になってるみたい。

IT WOULD SEEM THAT SHE'S GOT A LITTLE THING FOR KOTARŌ

今後どうなるんでしょうね・・・!

I WONDER WHAT WILL BECOME OF THAT IN THE FUTURE?

何げにライバル多いし…

ESPECIALLY WITH ALL THE OTHER CONTENDERS...

くぎみやとか ちづるとか

SUCH AS KUGIMIYA AND CHIZURU

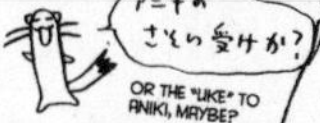

アニキの
さそい受けか?

OR THE "UKE" TO ANIKI, MAYBE?

髪型がむずかしくて、安定してません。

HER HAIRSTYLE IS DIFFICULT AND I REALLY

一巻よりかなり簡略化されています。

HAVEN'T MADE UP MY MIND ABOUT IT.

CVは、人気上昇中の 相沢舞ちゃん。

IT'S CHANGED PERIODICALLY SINCE VOLUME ONE.

こないだの打ち上げで「コタローくんと つきあわせてあげて下さい」

HER VOICE ACTOR IS MAI AIZAWA, WHO'S BEEN GETTING MORE POPULAR. DURING THE WRAP PARTY

と頼まれたけど、それムリっぽいかも。(笑)

SHE ASKED ME TO HAVE NATSUMI GO OUT WITH KOTARŌ, BUT THAT MIGHT BE A BIT DIFFICULT TO PULL OFF. (LAUGHS)

次の20巻で、またまた大発表があるかも?

I MIGHT HAVE ANOTHER BIG ANNOUNCEMENT TO MAKE IN VOL. 20...?

でも またあわないかも〜

THEN AGAIN, IT MIGHT NOT BE READY IN TIME...

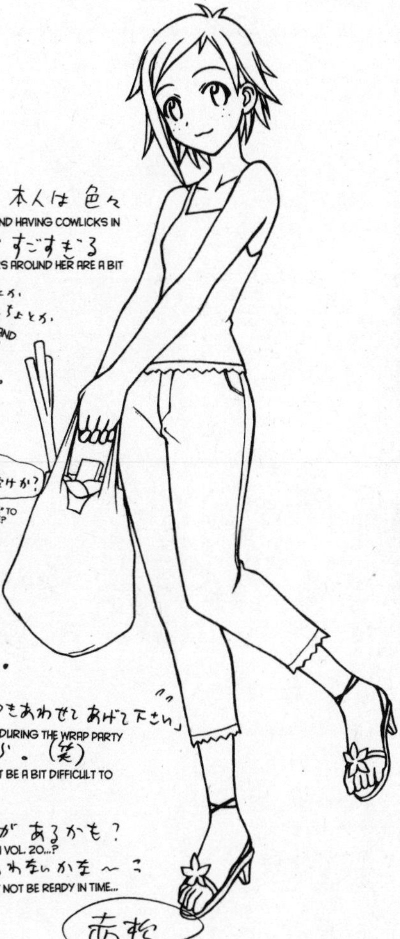

赤松

AKAMATSU

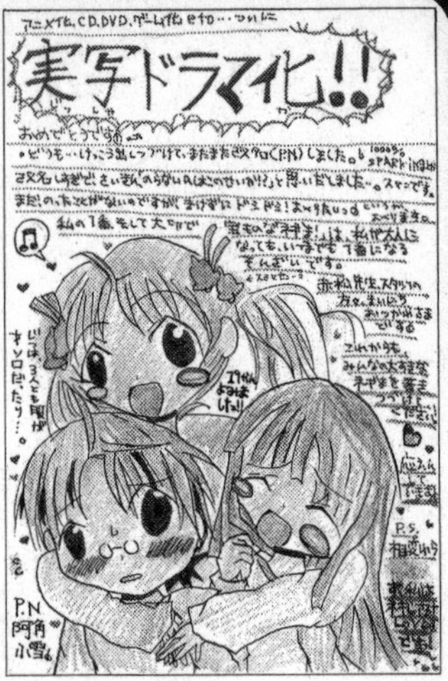
実写ドラマ化!!

▲ SO ADORABLE!

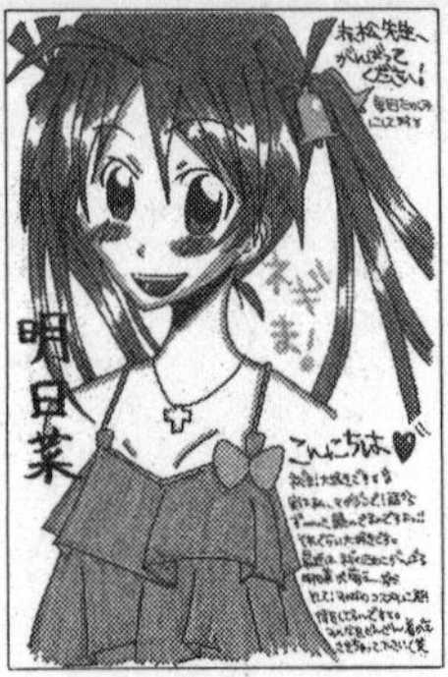
ネギま!
明日菜

▲ A HEALTHY-LOOKING ASUNA

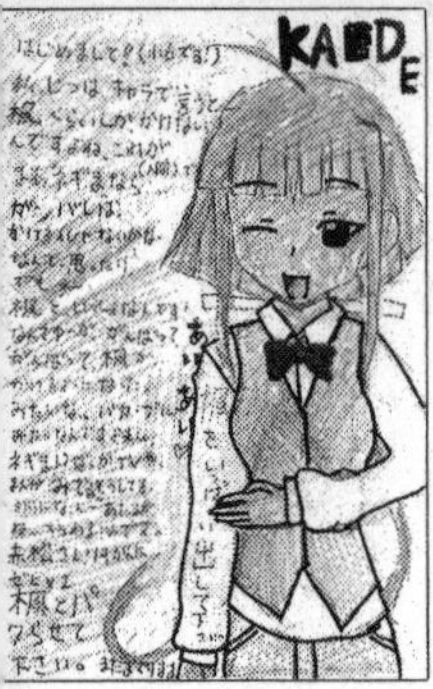
KAEDE

▲ THE WINK IS ADORABLE

NEGIMA!
FAN ART CORNER

EVERYONE, THANKS FOR YOUR LETTERS AND ILLUSTRATIONS AS ALWAYS. ☆ WE'VE BEEN GETTING MORE ASUNA ILLUSTRATIONS LATELY. I WONDER WHY? NOW, LET'S GET STARTED WITH TODAY'S ILLUSTRATIONS. PLEASE SEND YOUR CONTRIBUTIONS TO THE EDITORIAL OFFICES OF KODANSHA COMICS. ☆

TEXT BY ASSISTANT MAX

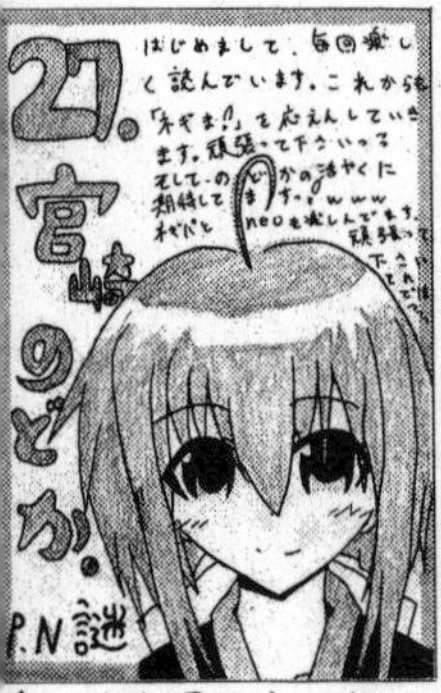
27.
宮崎のどか。
P.N 謎

▲ NODOKA LOOKS ALERT!

▼ SEXY NODOKA!

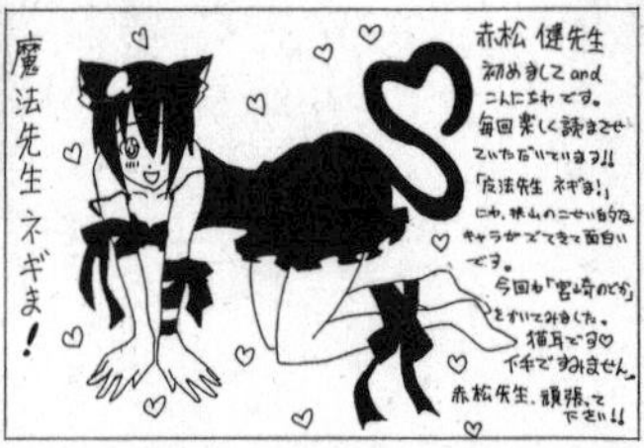
魔法先生ネギま!

▼ CUTE MANA!

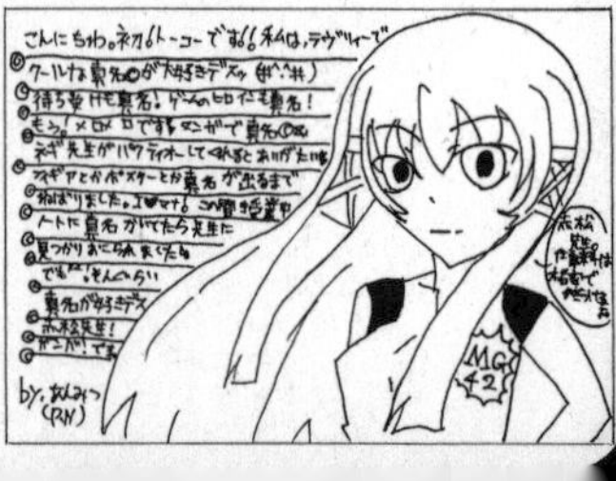
MG 42

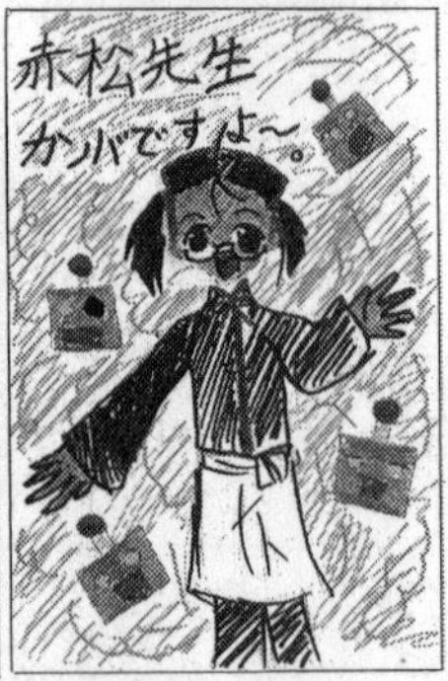
赤松先生
ガンバですよ~。

▲ A PLAYFUL CHAO

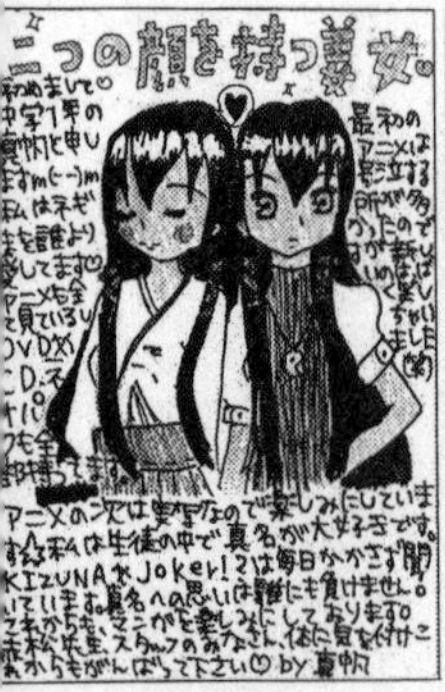
二つの顔を持つ美女。

▲ SUPER MANA LOVE

NEGI MAGI

MAGISTER

センせ
がんばって
…にゃ

Ako

▲ THE STEAMED PORK
BUNS LOOK WARM!

◀ ASUNA LOOKS LOVELY.

by 塩越 LOVE❤️
ナ
ギ
ス
タ

▲ LOOK'S HAPPY ☆☆

今日知り 赤松先生!
さっちゃんfan!
'SATUKI'

A 'SAT-CHAN FAN!'

赤松先生ガンばれ！！

▲ THE MOUTH IS CUTE!

暑中お見舞い
申し上げます

NO.25 長谷川千雨

▲ THE YUKATA IS SWEET!

タカミチ

COOL TAKAMICHI!

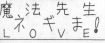

魔法先生
ネ。ギま！
L O V E

GOOFY ASUNA!

Asna

エヴァ
アスナ

▲ EVA AND ASUNA. WHAT
WILL BECOME OF THEM?

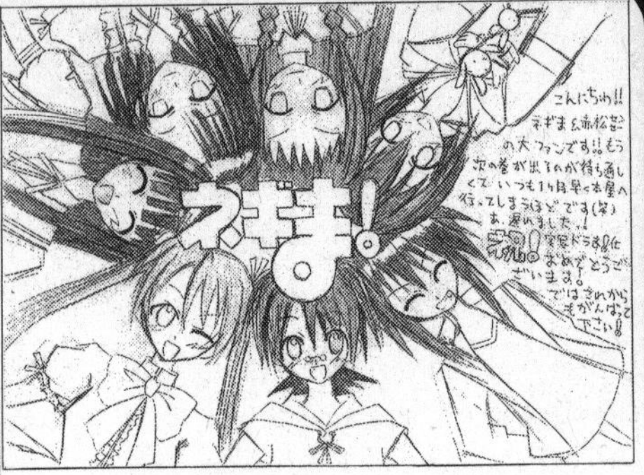
ネギま!
こんにちわ!! ネギま&赤松先生の大ファンです!! もう次の巻が出るのが待ち遠しくて いつも1ヶ月早く本屋へ行ってしまうほどです(笑)
あ、遅れました…実写ドラマ化 おめでとうございます! では これからもがんばって下さい!!

▲ WHAT A GOOD FEELING! ☆☆☆

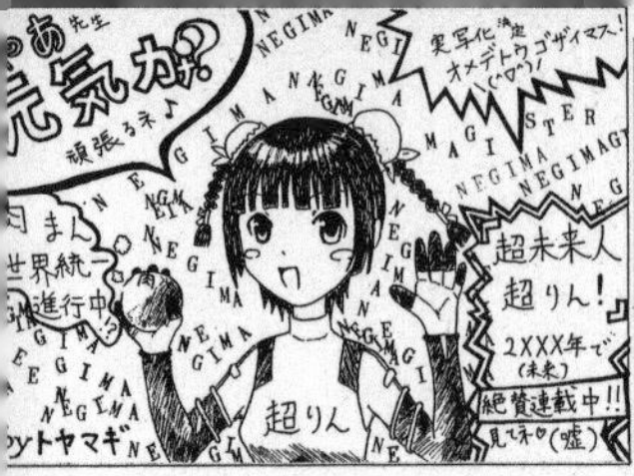
元気かな?
頑張るネ♪
実写化決定 オメデトウゴザイマス!
世界統一進行中
『超未来人 超りん!』
2XXX年で(未来)
絶賛連載中!!
見てネ。(嘘)
超りん
NEGIMA

▲ WHAT A SWEET CHAO. (LAUGH)

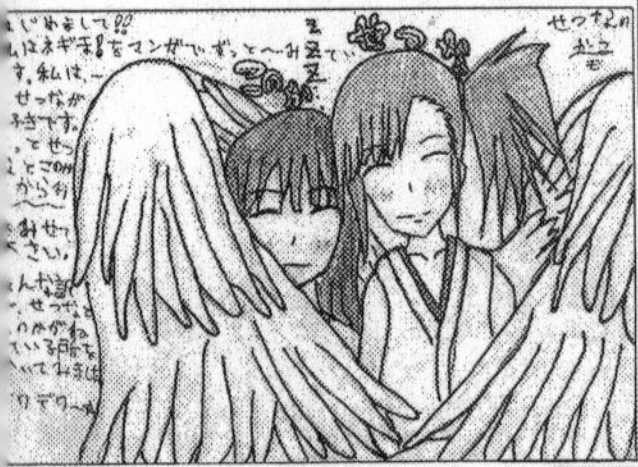

◀ THEY LOOK LIKE FRIENDS.

▼ I WAS WAITING FOR THIS. (LAUGH)

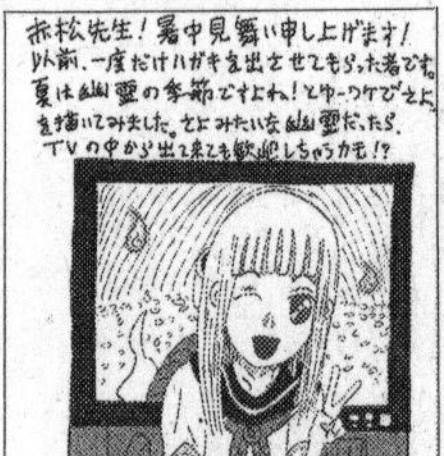
赤松先生!暑中見舞い申し上げます!
以前、一度だけハガキを出せてもらった者です。
夏は幽霊の季節ですよね!とゆーワケでさよを描いてみました。さよみたいな幽霊だったら、TVの中から出て来ても歓迎しちゃうかも!?
マンガに始まってナント実写にまで!表現の幅を広げて驀進する「ネギま!」を、これからも応援しています。それではお体に気をつけて!

▼ YES, IT'S HARD. (LAUGHS)

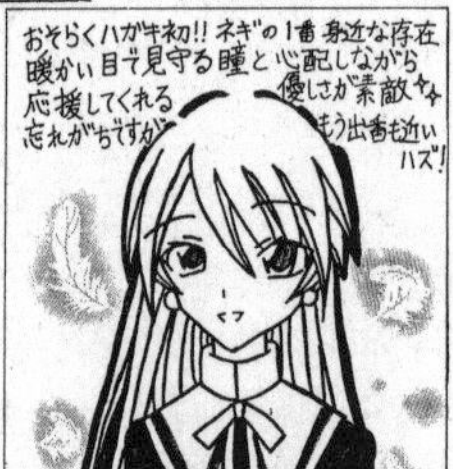
おそらくハガキ初!! ネギの1番身近な存在
暖かい目で見守る瞳と心配しながら応援してくれる優しさが素敵✧
忘れがちですが もう出番も近いハズ!
Nekane Springfield

◀ IT'S A LITTLE OFF. (LAUGH)

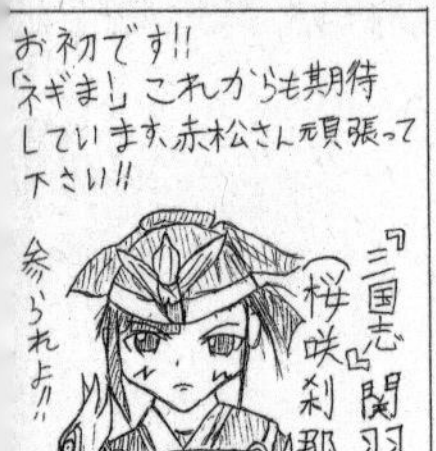
お初です!!
「ネギま!」これからも期待しています。赤松さん頑張って下さい!!
『三国志』関羽
桜咲刹那
参られよ!!
ネギま

▼ SHE LOOKS NERVOUS.

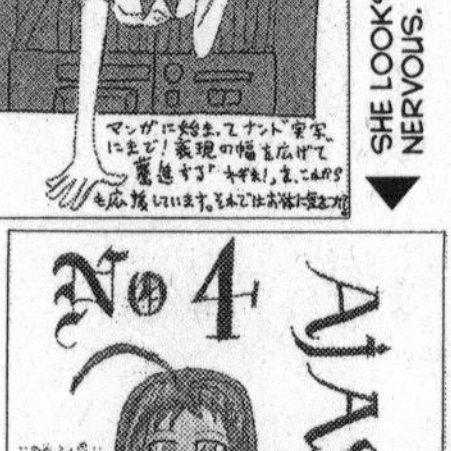
No 4
AYASE YUE

◀ YUNA IS LOOKING WELL!

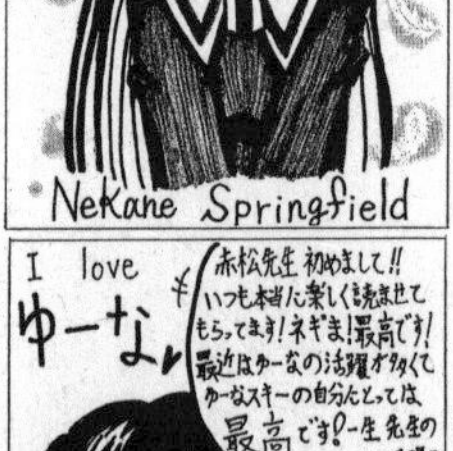
I love ゆーな
赤松先生 初めまして!! いつも本当に楽しく読ませてもらってます! ネギま!最高です! 最近はゆーなの活躍が多くてゆーなスキーの自分にとっては最高です! 一生先生の事応援してます! 頑張って下さい!!
MAHORA
by 朱旋律

◀ NICE AND RELAXED!

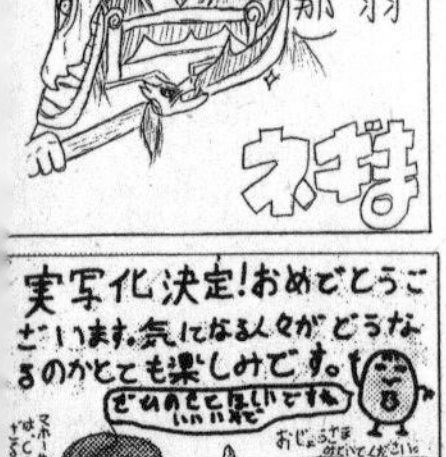
実写化決定!おめでとうございます。気になる人々がどうなるのかとても楽しみです。
わたしはどうなるのでしょうか?
そんなことしらん。

今回の
FEATURED CHARACTER EVANGELINE A. K. MCDOWELL RANKING

NEGI MAGI MAGISTER

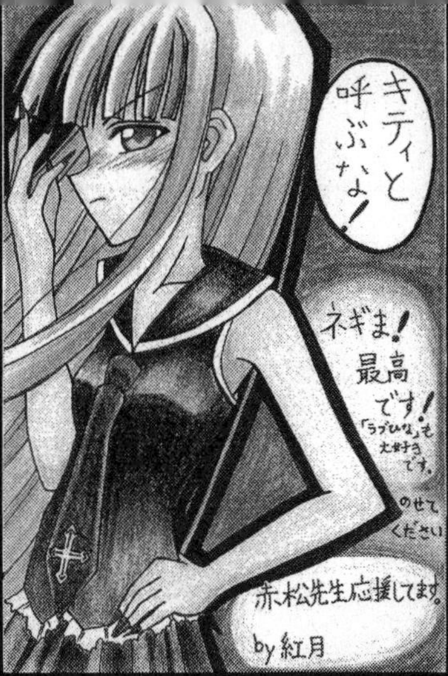

キティと呼ぶな！
ネギま！最高です！
「ラブひな」も大好きです。
のせてください
赤松先生応援してます。
by 紅月

第1位 ▶ EVA'S ATTITUDE SHOWS THROUGH HERE! (BY AKAMATSU)

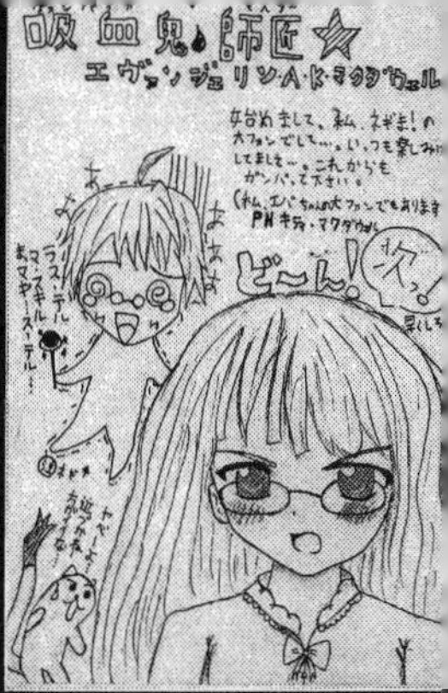

吸血鬼・師匠☆
エヴァンジェリン・A・K・マクダウェル
どーん！
次っ！

第2位 ▲ EVA IS POPULAR WITH GLASSES!

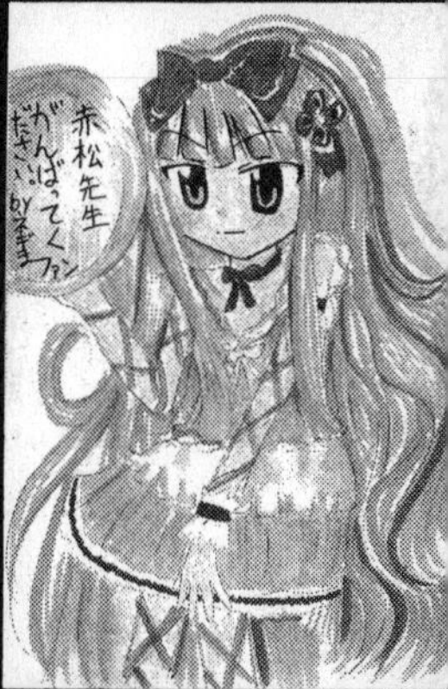

赤松先生がんばってください。by ネギまファン

第3位 ▶ EVA'S A GOTHIC LOLITA FAN. THE BIG RIBBON IS CUTE.

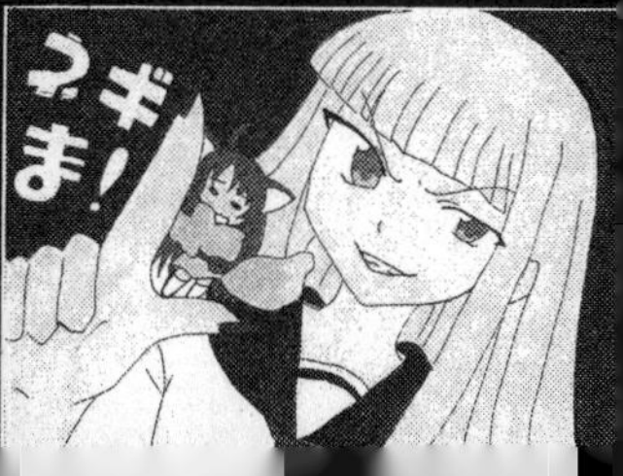

ネギま！

第4位 ▶ FOXY NEGI IS CUTE!

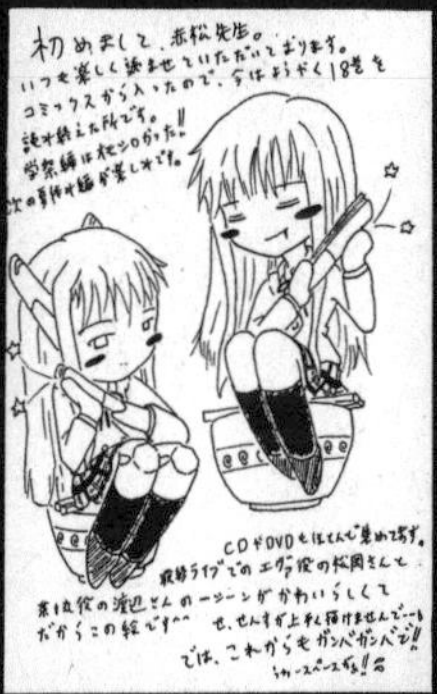

初めまして、赤松先生。

第5位 ▶ FOCUS ON THE VOICE ACTRESS—INTERESTING! THIS IS A PREFACE.

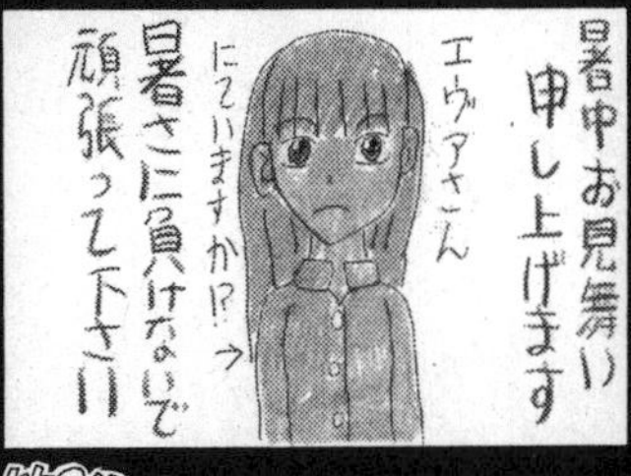

暑中お見舞い申し上げます
エヴァさん
にていますか!?
暑さに負けないで頑張って下さい!!

第6位 ▲ SHE LOOKS LIKE KONOKA...

THE VIEW FROM BA LONDON EYE. THE OFFICIAL NAME IS WEST-
MINSTER CASTLE, WHICH INCLUDES THE BRITISH PARLIAMENT
BUILDING. A FIRE IN 1834 DESTROYED THE BUILDING EXCEPT
OR THE WESTMINSTER HALL. IT WAS REBUILT IN 1860. THE TOWER
ON THE LEFT IS VICTORIA TOWER. THE TOWER ON THE RIGHT IS
IG BEN.

THE NEO-GOTHIC BUILDING ALONG
THE THAMES RIVER IN LONDON IS THE
BRITISH PARLIAMENT BUILDING. ALONG
WITH BIG BEN, IT IS ONE OF THE MOST
RECOGNIZABLE BUILDINGS IN LONDON. THE
HOUSE OF BRITISH PARLIAMENT, CREATED
IN 1295 BY EDWARD I, IS STILL ACTIVE. ON
THE FLOOR OF THE HOUSE, THERE ARE TWO
LINES THAT ARE SEPARATED BY A WIDTH
SLIGHTLY WIDER THAN THE SWORD. THESE
LINES ARE CALLED THE SWORDLINE. DURING
QUESTIONING, NO ONE IS ALLOWED TO
CROSS THIS LINE—TO AVOID BLOODSHED
DURING DEBATES. MODERN PARLIAMENTARY
GOVERNMENT WAS ESTABLISHED IN BRITAIN
AND SPREAD INTERNATIONALLY AFTER THE
PURITANICAL REVOLUTION.

THE LONDON SUBWAY SYSTEM IS KNOWN
COLLOQUIALLY AS THE TUBE. THE CENTRAL
MODE OF TRANSPORTATION IN LONDON,
IT IS EXPANSIVE AND TRAVELS IN VARIOUS
DIRECTIONS. UNLIKE IN TOKYO'S SYSTEM,
HERE IS NO CENTRAL LONDON STATION.
BRITAIN IS THE BIRTHPLACE OF THE RAILROAD,
AND INITIALLY, RAILROADS WERE NOT BUILT IN
N URBAN AREAS. AS A RESULT, MANY OF THE
STATIONS ARE BUILT OUTSIDE OF THE CITY. SO
LONDON-BOUND TRAINS CAN STOP AT VARIOUS
STATIONS, SUCH AS VICTORIA, WATERLOO,
PADDINGTON, AND KING'S CROSS. THE
SUBWAYS CONNECT THESE VARIOUS TERMINALS
TOGETHER TO HELP SMOOTH OUT TRAFFIC IN
LONDON.

VIEW OF THE TOWER BRIDGE FROM THE BACK OF THE LONDON
TOWER. IT IS ONE OF LONDON'S MOST POPULAR TOURIST
SPOTS, DUE TO ITS PROXIMITY TO THE TOWER OF LONDON. THE
BRIDGE CONNECTING THE TWO TOWERS IS LINED WITH GLASS.
THE CITY OF LONDON CAN EASILY BE VIEWED FROM THE BRIDGE.
THE ENGINE THAT OPERATES THE BASCULE BRIDGE IS VIEWABLE
BY THE PUBLIC.

ONE OF LONDON'S FAMOUS BRIDGES, THE
TOWER BRIDGE. IT IS NEAR THE LONDON
TOWER, WHICH USED TO BE THE RESIDENCE
FOR WILLIAM THE CONQUERER. IT WAS
CONSTRUCTED DURING THE LATTER HALF
OF THE 19TH CENTURY, BEGINNING IN 1886
AND COMPLETED IN 1898. COMMERCIAL
EXPANSION DURING THE 19TH CENTURY
NECESSITATED THE CONNECTION OF THE
NORTH AND SOUTH SIDES OF THE THAMES
RIVER. DUE TO THE LARGE SIZE OF THE
SHIPS TRAVELING THE RIVER, A BASCULE
BRIDGE WAS BUILT SO THE TRAFFIC ALONG
THE RIVER WOULD NOT BE BLOCKED.
HOWEVER, LARGE SHIPS NO LONGER
TRAVEL ALONG THE THAMES RIVER. AS
A RESULT, THE BASCULE BRIDGE IS NO
LONGER SEEN IN ACTION. HOWEVER, THE
BASCULE BRIDGE IS STILL COMPLETELY
FUNCTIONAL.

THERE ARE SEVERAL WAYS TO PRONOUNCE "CASTLE COMBE," BUT TAXI DRIVERS WILL KNOW WHERE YOU NEED TO GO. THE MARKET HALL IN THE MIDDLE OF MARKET CROSS WAS BUILT DURING THE 14TH CENTURY.

CASTLE COMBE IN COTSWOLD IS ONE OF THE MOST BEAUTIFUL VILLAGES IN ENGLAND. THE SCENERY IS BREATHTAKING, AND THE BUILDINGS IN THE CITY HAVE BEEN PRESERVED AS HISTORICAL LANDMARKS. TRAFFIC CAN BE HEAVY, HOWEVER, SINCE VISITORS FLOCK TO THIS VILLAGE ON WEEKENDS. THE VILLAGE WAS ONCE KNOWN FOR ITS WOOL INDUSTRY; A LARGE MARKET WAS HELD IN THE CENTER OF THE VILLAGE KNOWN AS MARKET CROSS. THE VILLAGE IS CURRENTLY RATHER SMALL—ONLY ABOUT 1/5 OF A MILE WIDE. THE ARISTOCRATIC MANOR NEAR THE VILLAGE HAS BEEN CONVERTED INTO A HOTEL. SURROUNDED BY IDYLLIC FARMS, THE SCENERY SHOWS US WHAT PRE-MODERN EUROPE MIGHT HAVE LOOKED LIKE.

FISHGUARD, LOCATED ON THE SOUTHEAST CORNER OF PEMBROKE, WALES. A FERRY THAT TRAVELS TO IRELAND DEPARTS FROM THE HARBOR NEAR FISHGUARD HARBOR TRAIN STATION.

WHILE THE TRAIN STATION IS AN IMPORTANT ONE IN TERMS OF TRAFFIC, NOT MANY TRAINS STOP AT THIS STATION. AS A RESULT, THE STATION IS VERY QUAINT. OCCASIONALLY, SEA BIRDS WILL OPEN THE AUTOMATIC DOORS TO THE STATION AND ENTER THE STATION LOBBY. PEMBROKE IS A NATIONAL PARK FROM THE HARBOR TO THE NEARBY HILLS. THE PARK IS ABOUT 620 SQUARE KILOMETERS IN SIZE. THE BEACH, SWAMP, AND FOREST WITHIN THE PARK ARE ALL VERY SCENIC.

THE PLATFORM FOR THE STATION AT FISHGUARD HARBOR. THE BUILDING ACROSS FROM THE EXIT IS THE LOBBY FOR THE FERRY. THERE ARE ONLY TWO PASSENGER TRAINS, ONE AT MIDNIGHT AND ONE AT NOON. AS A RESULT, THERE IS NO TICKET OFFICE. TICKETS ARE PURCHASED FROM TRAIN ATTENDANTS.

THE BEAUTIFUL DOLMENS IN THE NATIONAL PARK AT PEMBROKE ARE KNOWN AS PENTRE IFAN. THE STONE IS CALLED BLUESTONE, THE SAME STONE USED FOR THE FAMOUS STONEHENGE. PENTRE IFAN WAS A STONE ROOM THAT REPRESENTED REBIRTH AND THE WOMB.

THE STONES USED IN THE FAMOUS STONEHENGE ORIGINATE FROM PRESELI HILLS IN PEMBROKE. THE PRESELI HILLS ARE 125 MILES FROM STONEHENGE. PEMBROKE MUST HAVE BEEN AN IMPORTANT AREA, EVEN IN ANCIENT TIMES, FOR THE STONES TO BE CARRIED OVER SUCH A DISTANCE. BEAUTIFUL NATURAL DOLMENS REMAIN IN THE NATIONAL PARK IN PEMBROKE. WALES AND PEMBROKE ARE HOME TO THE MYSTERIOUS CULTURE THAT LEFT THE GIGANTIC STONE MONUMENTS.

DIRECTIONS TO FISHGUARD

2 HOURS AND 16 MINUTES FROM CARDIFF CENTRAL TO FISHGUARD CENTRAL ON THE ARRIVA TRAINS WALES.

3-D BACKGROUNDS EXPLANATION CORNER
THIS VOLUME HAS VARIOUS BACKGROUNDS, FROM JAPANESE-STYLE ROOMS TO THE MAGICAL WORLD.

● SCENE NAME: JAPANESE ROOM
POLYGON COUNT: 24,175

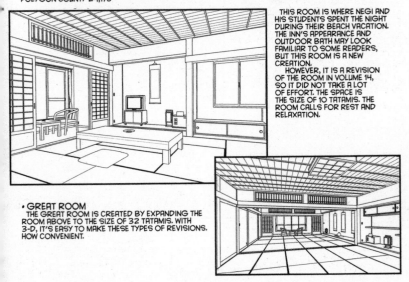

THIS ROOM IS WHERE NEGI AND HIS STUDENTS SPENT THE NIGHT DURING THEIR BEACH VACATION. THE INN'S APPEARANCE AND OUTDOOR BATH MAY LOOK FAMILIAR TO SOME READERS, BUT THIS ROOM IS A NEW CREATION.

HOWEVER, IT IS A REVISION OF THE ROOM IN VOLUME 14, SO IT DID NOT TAKE A LOT OF EFFORT. THE SPACE IS THE SIZE OF 10 TATAMIS. THE ROOM CALLS FOR REST AND RELAXATION.

• GREAT ROOM
THE GREAT ROOM IS CREATED BY EXPANDING THE ROOM ABOVE TO THE SIZE OF 32 TATAMIS. WITH 3-D, IT'S EASY TO MAKE THESE TYPES OF REVISIONS. HOW CONVENIENT.

● SCENE NAME: CATACOMB AT THE SCHOOL
POLYGON COUNT: 38,582

THIS IS THE BASEMENT WHERE THE STONE REMAINS OF THE VILLAGERS ARE STORED. THE EXISTENCE OF THIS ROOM IS ONLY KNOWN TO A FEW PEOPLE. GENERALLY, IT IS PROTECTED BY A MAGICAL BARRIER AGAINST INTRUDERS. ORIGINALLY, THE REQUEST WAS TO CREATE A CATACOMB-LIKE ROOM. HOWEVER, THE END RESULT IS MORE REMINISCENT OF A TEMPLE.

THE CREATION OF THIS ROOM WAS SIMPLE BECAUSE IT INVOLVED COPYING AND ROTATING ONE SECTION AND PUTTING THEM TOGETHER.

• CIRCULAR STAIRCASE
WE'LL KEEP THIS A SECRET. IN ONE FRAME, THE STAIRS WIND CLOCKWISE, AND IN ANOTHER FRAME, THE STAIRS WIND COUNTERCLOCKWISE. MAYBE THE MAGICAL BARRIER CREATES A TWIST IN THE PHYSICAL DIMENSION. (LAUGHS)

• SCENE NAME: GATEPORT EXTERIOR
POLYGON COUNT: 28,168

THIS IS THE GIGANTIC, CIRCULAR BUILDING INSIDE THE MAGICAL METROPOLIS OF MEGALOMESENBRIA. THIS GATEPORT CONNECTS IMPORTANT PLACES INSIDE THE MAGICAL WORLD. THIS GATEPORT ALSO CONNECTS THE MAGICAL WORLD TO THE HUMAN WORLD. MANY PEOPLE TRAVEL THROUGH THIS GATEPORT, AND THE GATEPORT IS ENORMOUS ENOUGH THAT IT CAN BE CONSIDERED A CITY BY ITSELF. THE CIRCULAR AREA AND THE BASE ARE IN 3-D, THE REST IS DRAWN BY HAND. THE BUILDING SHOWN HERE IS THE DRAWING BEFORE IT WAS REVISED, SO SOME DIFFERENCES CAN BE SEEN FROM THE FINAL VERSION.

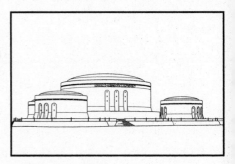

• SCENE NAME: IMMIGRATION GATE
POLYGON COUNT: 971,088

THIS IS THE INTERIOR OF THE GATEPORT. THE GATES ARE THE CIRCULAR LANDINGS SURROUNDING THE CENTRAL STONE. EACH LANDING CONNECTS TO A DIFFERENT LOCATION. THERE USED TO BE A WAY TO CHECK THE IDENTITY OF THE PEOPLE PASSING THROUGH THE PENTAGRAMS AS WELL AS THEIR DESTINATIONS, BUT FATE WAS ABLE TO CANCEL OUT THAT FUNCTION. THIS AREA IS LARGER THAN THE EXTERIOR BUILDING SURROUNDING IT. AS A RESULT, IT IS PRESUMED THAT SOME TYPE OF DIMENSIONAL ALTERING MAGIC WAS USED IN ITS CREATION. HOWEVER, THE DETAILS ARE NOT KNOWN AT THIS TIME.

• SCENE NAME: MAGIC TOWERS
POLYGON COUNT: 971,088

THIS IS THE VIEW OF THE CITY AS SEEN FROM THE GATEPORT. THERE ARE VARIOUS-SIZE BUILDINGS FILLING THE CITYSCAPE. CIRCULAR BUILDINGS ARE EASY TO CREATE IN 3-D. AFTER THE TOWERS WERE COMPLETED, THE ROCKY MOUNTAIN AND DETAILS WERE DRAWN BY HAND. THE PICTURE SHOWN IS THE SCENE BEFORE THE FINAL REVISION. AS A RESULT, THERE ARE FLOATING TOWERS. (^_^;)
THERE ARE 8 TYPES OF FLOATING TOWERS. THE TOWERS ARE TAKEN FROM THE TOWERS IN EVA'S GETAWAY.

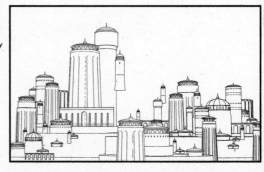

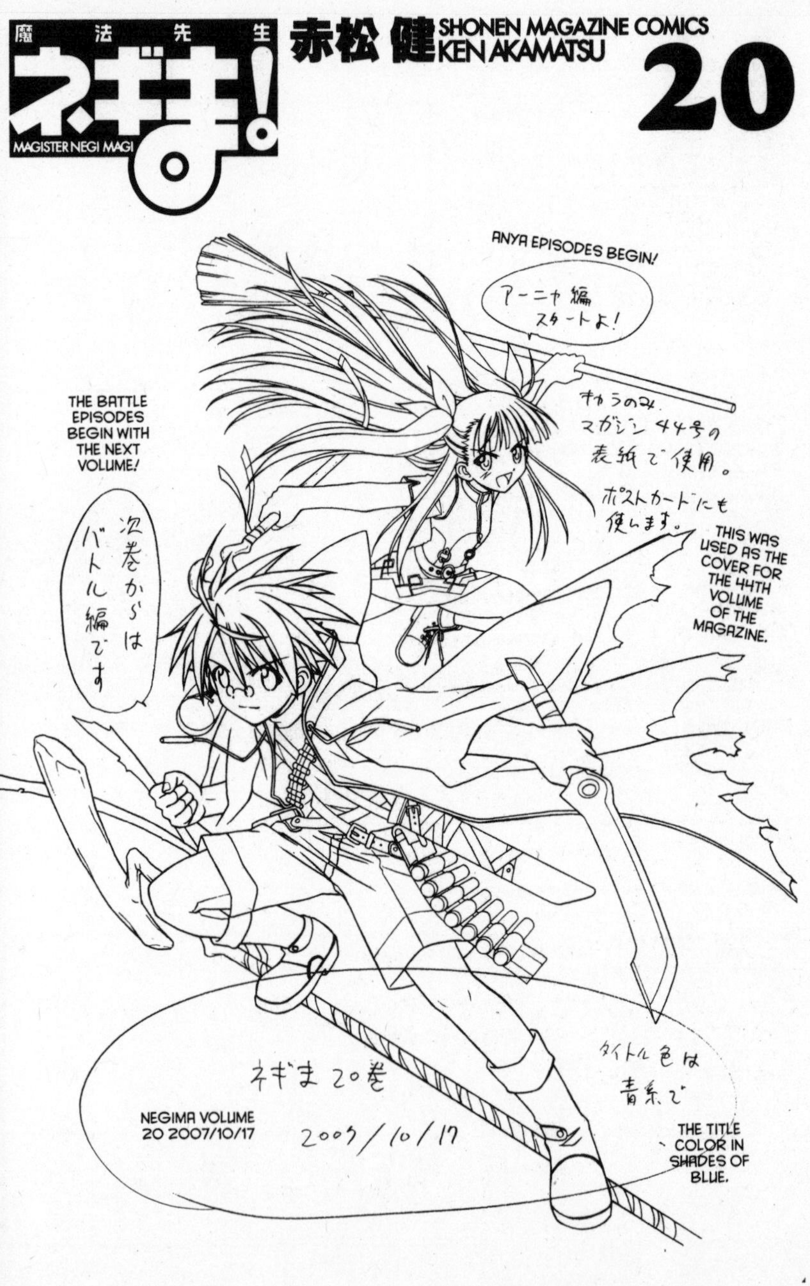

魔法先生
ネギま!
MAGISTER NEGI MAGI
赤松 健
SHONEN MAGAZINE COMICS
KEN AKAMATSU
20
ANYA EPISODES BEGIN!
アーニャ編 スタートよ!
キャラのみ。マガジン44号の表紙で使用。
ポストカードにも使います。
THIS WAS USED AS THE COVER FOR THE 44TH VOLUME OF THE MAGAZINE.
THE BATTLE EPISODES BEGIN WITH THE NEXT VOLUME!
次巻からはバトル編です
ネギま20巻
2007/10/17
NEGIMA VOLUME 20 2007/10/17
タイトル色は青系で
THE TITLE COLOR IN SHADES OF BLUE.

キャラ解説
CHARACTER PROFILE

⑰ 椎名 桜子
⑰ SAKURAKO SHIINA

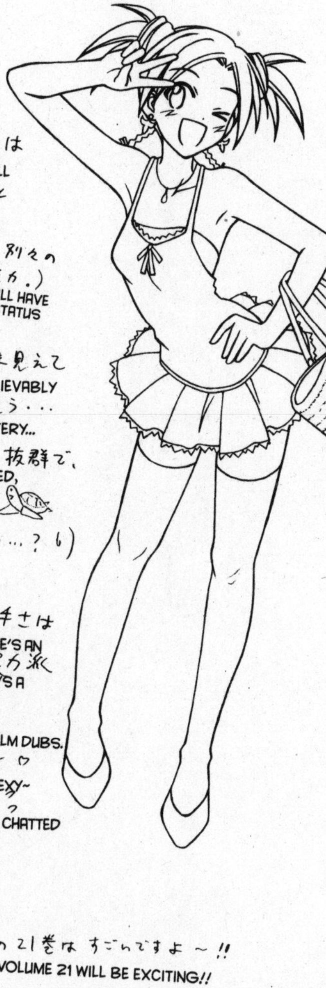

もしパクティオーしたら、桜子の能力は
IF SAKURAKO RECEIVES A PACTIO FROM NEGI, SHE'LL
「マスターのLUCK値（幸運度）アップ」と
RECEIVE AN INCREDIBLE NEW POWER: SHE'LL BE THE
すでに決まっています。（チア3名はそれぞれ別々のステータスUP能力。）
MASTER OF LUCK!
(THE 3 CHEERLEADERS WILL HAVE DIFFERENT, INCREASED STATUS ABILITIES.)

この巻でも、あふれる強運がかいま見えていますが。（笑）　宝クジ買ったらスゴそう…
IN THIS VOLUME, HER LUCK BECOMES ALMOST UNBELIEVABLY GOOD (LAUGHS). IF SHE DECIDES TO PLAY THE LOTTERY...
チアガールなだけあってプロポーション抜群で、いつも笑顔を絶やしません。
WATCH OUT! SHE'S A CHEERLEADER, AND AS EXPECTED, SHE'S ALWAYS CHEERFUL...AND HAS A GREAT BODY!
（口をとじてることってあるんでしょうか…？！）
(DOES SHE EVER CLOSE HER MOUTH?)

アニメCVは大前茜さん。絵の上手さはプロ級。吹き替えの出演も多い実力派なのです。（へ～）
THE VOICE ACTRESS FOR THE ANIME IS AKANE OOMAE. SHE'S AN EXCELLENT ARTIST—SHE COULD BE A PROFESSIONAL. SHE'S A TALENTED LADY WHO DOES A LOT OF VOICE-OVERS FOR FILM DUBS. (WOW)
ドラマ版は香山碧さん。セクシ～♡
AOI KAYAMA IS THE ACTRESS FOR THE DRAMA. SHE'S SEXY~
え…リネージュガールだったんですか？っ
I DIDN'T KNOW SHE WAS A LINEGE GIRL. I SHOULD HAVE CHATTED
ネットゲームの話すればよかったな。
ABOUT ONLINE GAMING WITH HER!

赤松
AKAMATSU

次の21巻はすごいですよ～!!
VOLUME 21 WILL BE EXCITING!!

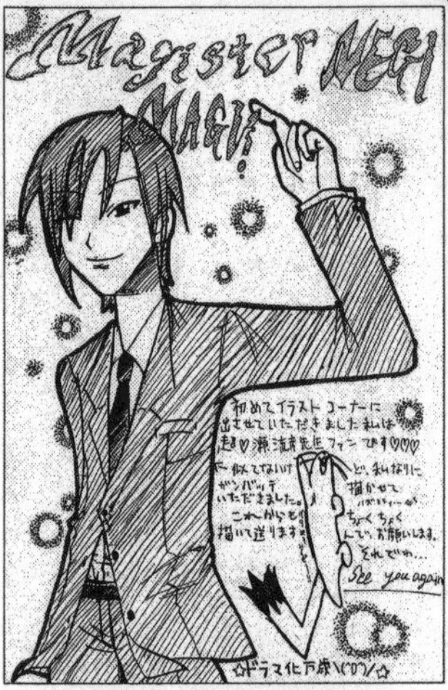

Magister NEGI MAGI!
See you again

HE'S SO COOL!

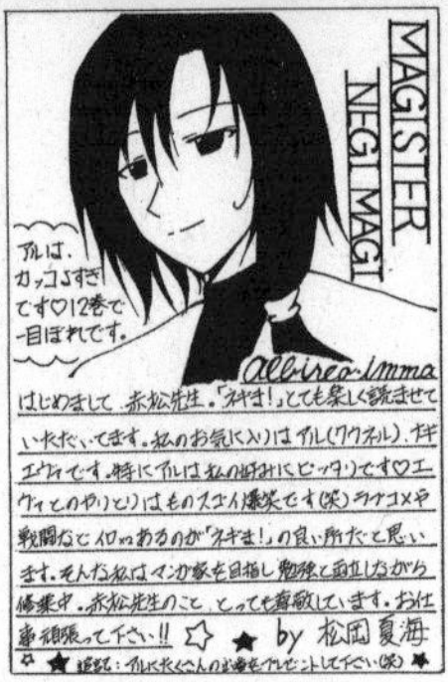

MAGISTER NEGI MAGI
アルは、カッコよすぎです♡12巻で一目ぼれです。
Albireo-Imma
by 松岡夏海

▲ SO HANDSOME!

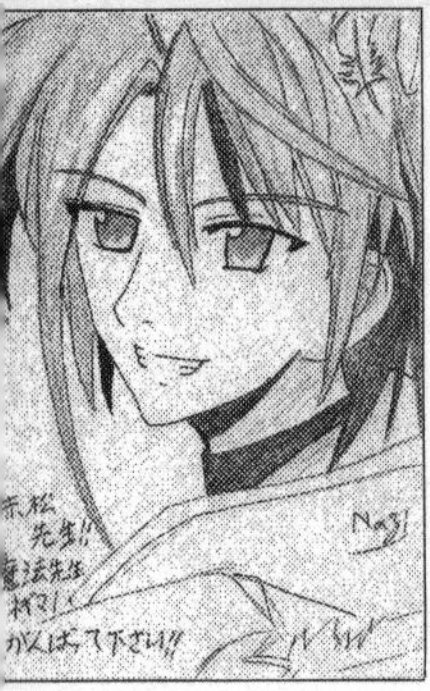

▲ PRETTY BOY!

THANKS FOR THE COLORFUL ARTWORK.

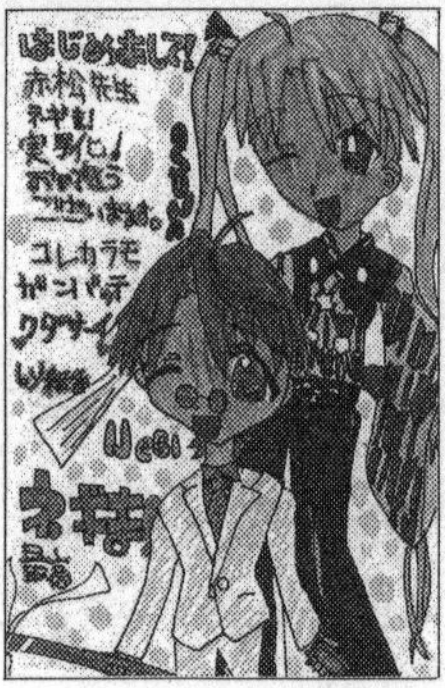

はじめまして!
Negi

NEGIMA!
FAN ART CORNER

FATE AND NAGI'S ARE BECOMING MORE AND MORE POPULAR FROM THE LOOKS OF IT (IN SECRET? (LAUGHS)) ASUNA IS AS POPULAR AS USUAL ★ HERE WE GO AGAIN FOR TODAY (^^)
★ BANA CREAM PUFF'S ILLUSTRATION FROM LAST TIME CAPTURED THE ESSENCE OF HAKASE (^^; I'M SORRY FOR THE MISTAKE.

TEXT BY ASSISTANT MAX

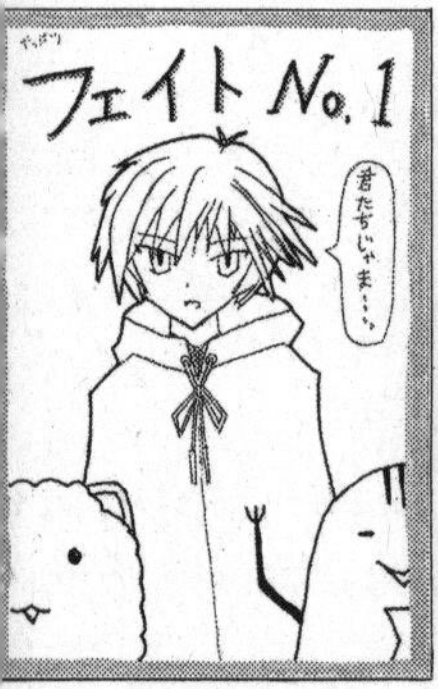

フェイト No. 1

▲ HE'S POPULAR.

NAGI'S ALSO IN THE LIVE-ACTION DRAMA!

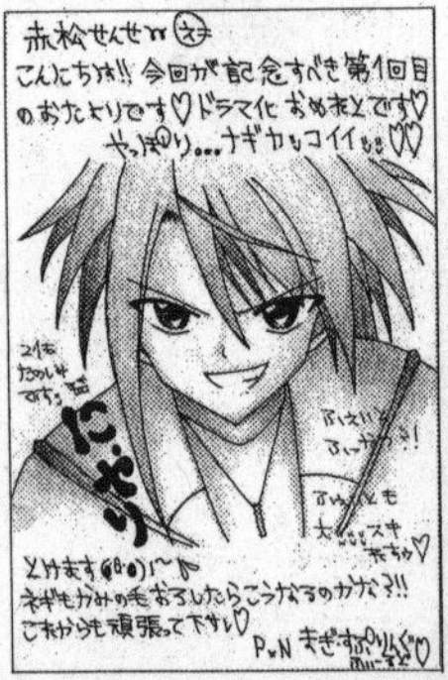

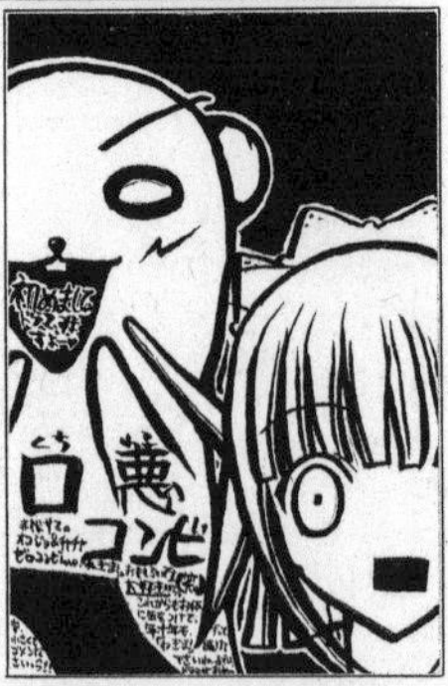

口悪コンビ

▲ GREAT COMBO

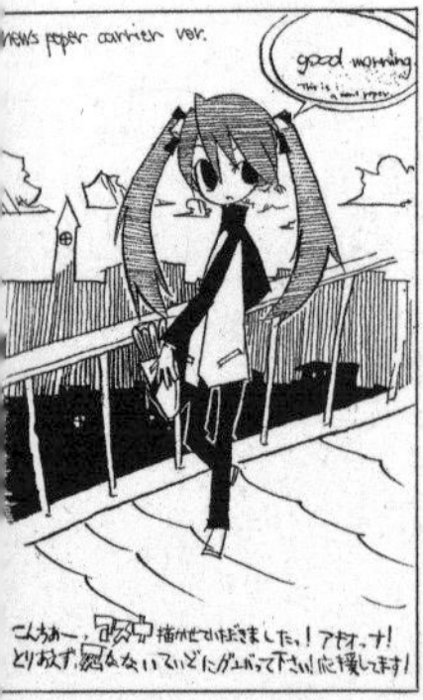

news paper carrier ver.
good morning

▲ HOW STYLISH

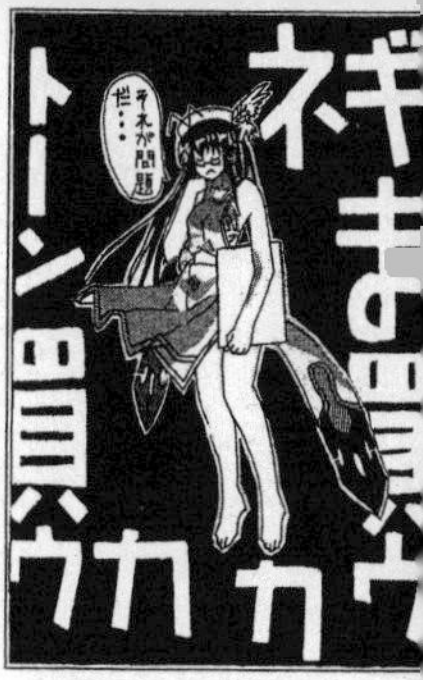

▲ LOOKS WORRIED

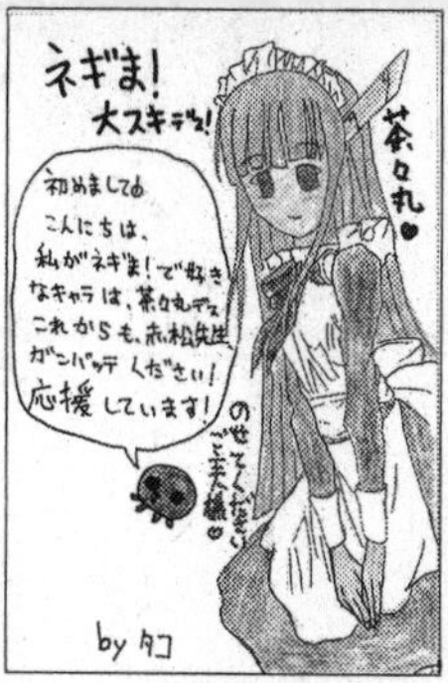
ネギま! 大スキデス!
茶々丸♥
初めまして。こんにちは、私がネギま!で好きなキャラは、茶々丸デス。これからも、赤松先生ガンバッテください! 応援しています!
by タコ

▲ I WANT HER TO POUR MY TEA!

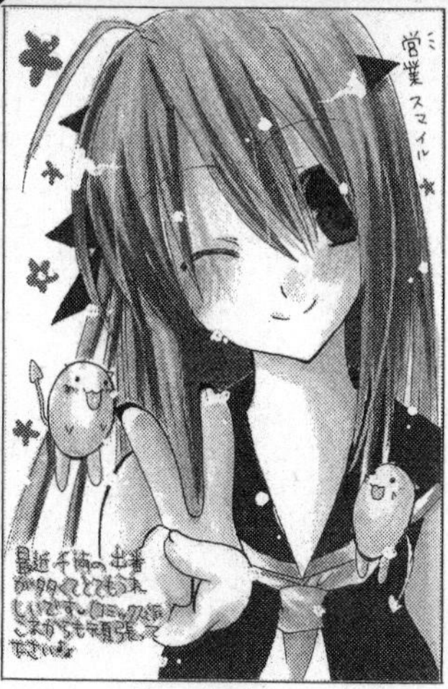
営業スマイル

▲ SUPERCUTE!

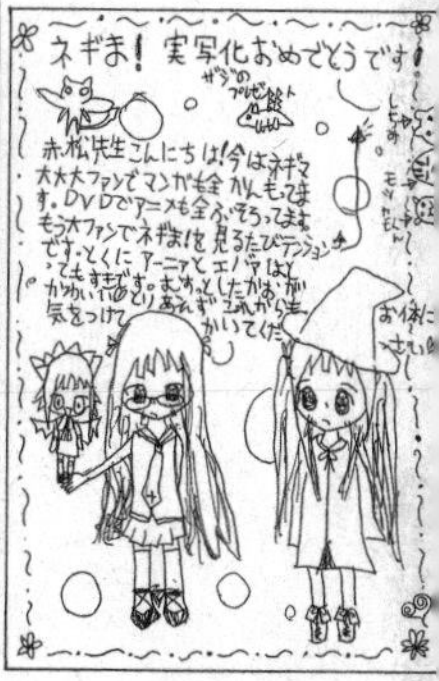
ネギま! 実写化おめでとうです!

▲ ADORABLE★

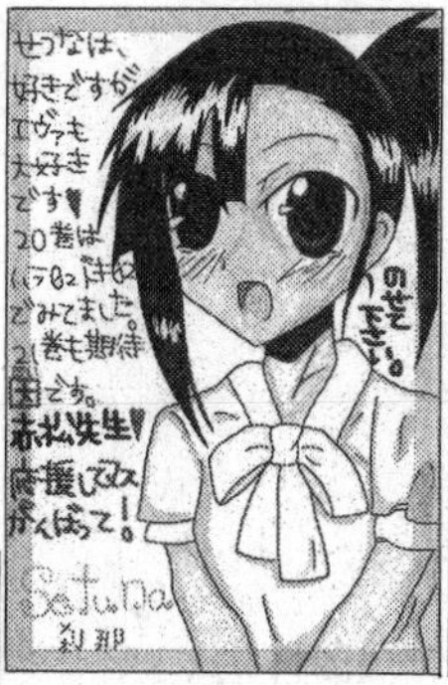
Setsuna
刹那

▲ SETSUNA-SAN LOOKS SO POLITE.

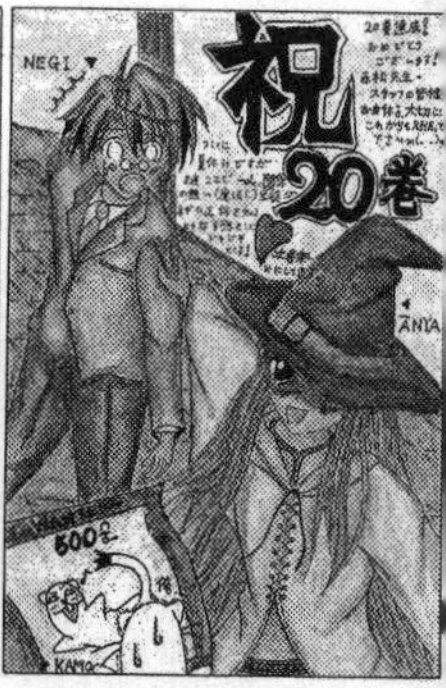
NEGI
祝20巻
ANYA
KAMO

▲ FRIENDS★ (^^)

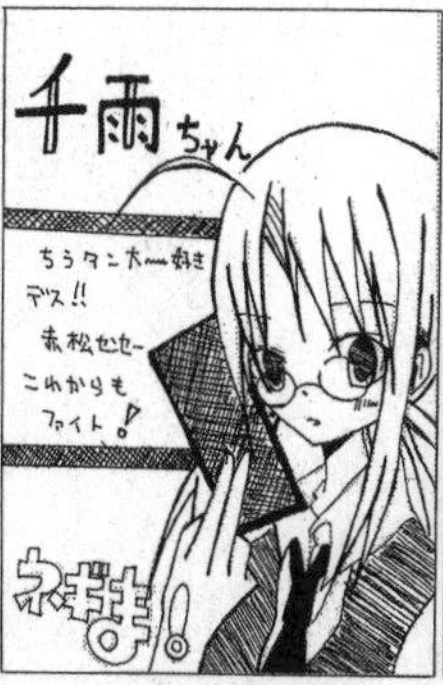
千雨ちゃん
ちうタン大ー好きデス!! 赤松センセー これからも ファイト!
ネギま!

▲ SHE'S A COOL BEAUTY (^^).

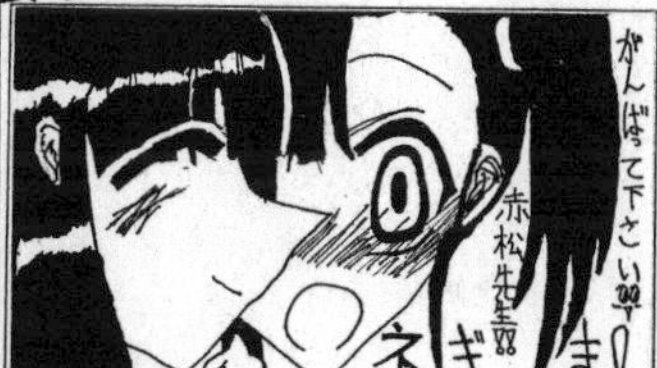
がんばって下さい!
赤松先生
ネギま!
チュッ
このか LOVE せつな

▲ LOVEY-DOVEY

▼ ZAZIE IS CUTE.★

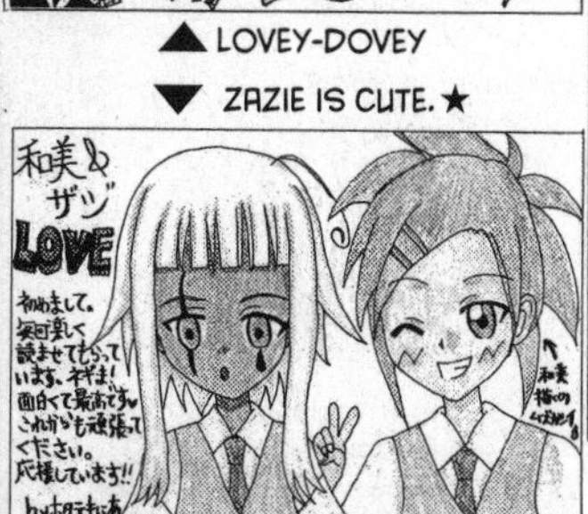
和美&ザジ LOVE

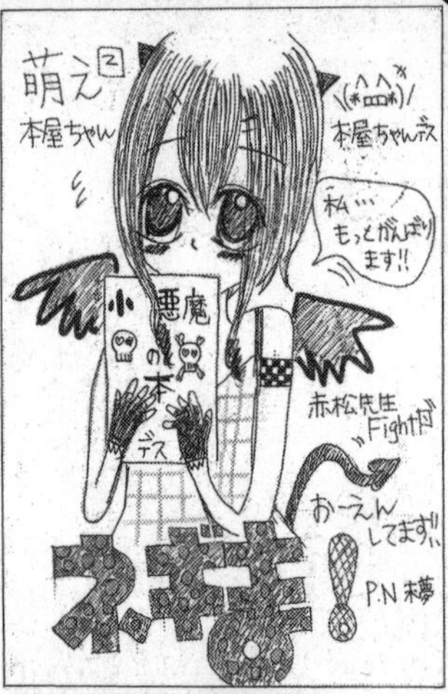
萌え²
本屋ちゃん
本屋ちゃんデス
私…もっとがんばります!!
小悪魔の本デス
赤松先生Fight!!
おーえんしてまず!!
ネギま!
P.N

GOOD BOOK (LAUGHS)

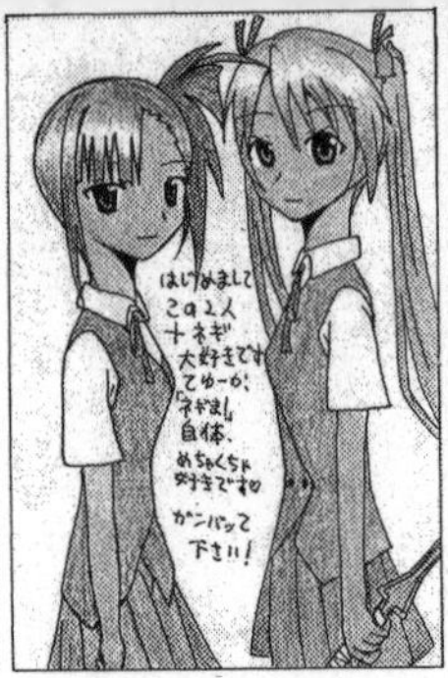

THEY'RE BOTH SO STRONG (^^).

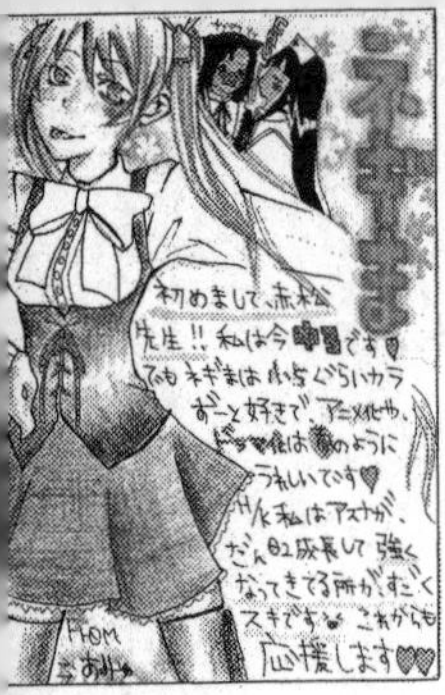

FLIRTY ASUNA (^^)

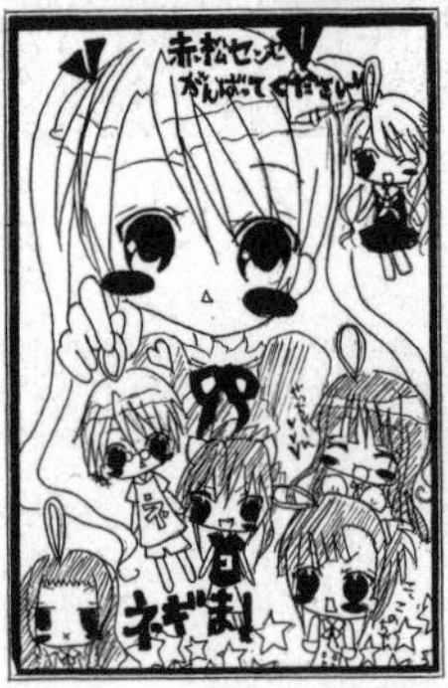
ネギま!

ASUNA'S CUTE.

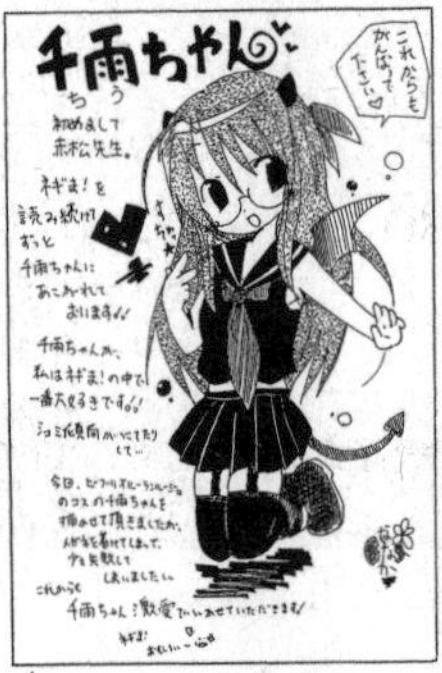
千雨ちゃん
初めまして
赤松先生。

LOVE THE TAIL

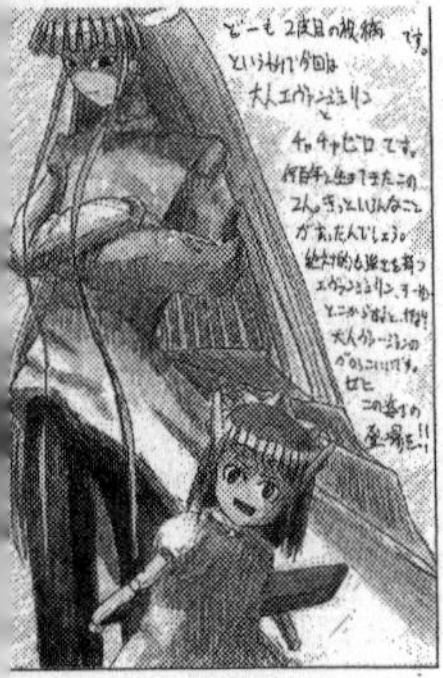

SERIOUS CHACHAZERO★

HOT AND COOL (^^)

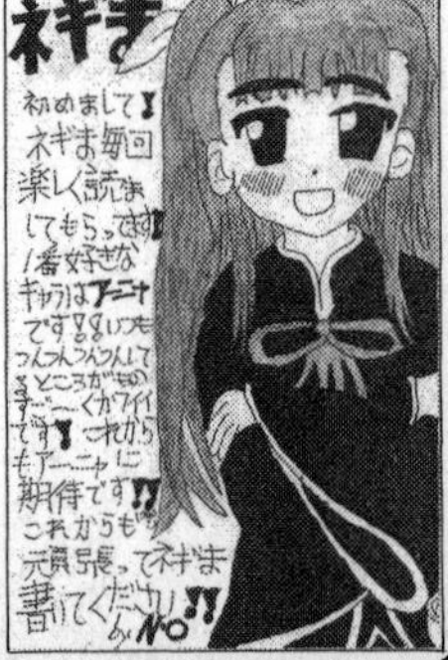
ネギま
初めまして!

SHE'LL BE ACTIVE.★

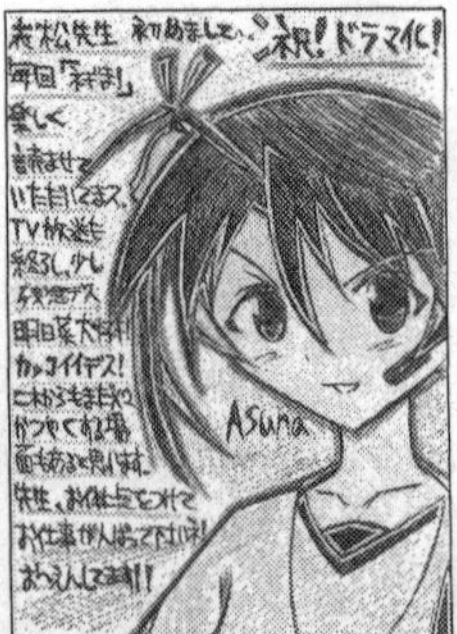
Asuna

NO NEED TO CRY (LAUGHS)

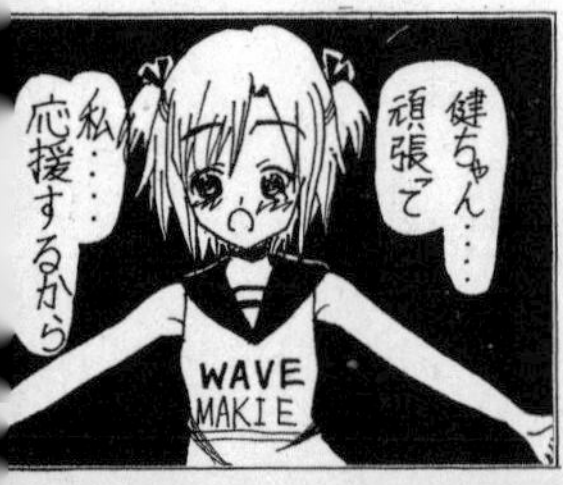
健ちゃん……
頑張って
私……
応援するから
WAVE
MAKIE

NEGI MAGI MAGISTER

今回の
FEATURED CHARACTER
KAEDE NAGASE
RANKING

FIRST PLACE

ネギまハマり中!!!
楓
楓の絵書くのはじめてです。
初めまして♪
私はヤバイほど楓好きデス!
20カンの子供の楓.スゴクカワユス〜でした!
20カン達成おめでとうございます
これからも.楓を.バンバン出して下さ〜い! お願いしますっ
あと.赤松さん.ガンバって下さい!
「ネギま!?」ドラマ見てます!!
応♥援してま〜す!!
楓とネギパクって〜
ぜひ.のせて下さい

WHAT AN ADORABLE KAEDE. A PACTIO WITH NEGI, EH... DON'T YOU THINK THAT WOULD MAKE HER TOO STRONG? (LAUGHS)

SECOND PLACE

KAEDE'S IMAGE IS ABOUT SUMMER IN THE MOUNTAINS. THE SD IS ADORABLE.

初夏
かえで
楓
でござるよ
楓に限るね
夏はやっぱり
by 睦月丸

by かかおでした〜。
楓姉さん!!
初めまして、赤松先生。
私は楓姉が大好きです♥ かっこよくてキレイで、ミステリアスな彼女がもう大好きです! (もちろん赤松先生も大好きですよ♥) 全巻買って秘密のスペースにかくしてます♥ これからもずっとおうえんしてます。なので、無理せずに、お体に気を付けてがんばって下さいね。
服は気にしないで下さい。
ドラマ化おめでとうございます♪ 見ます♪

THIRD PLACE

WHY DO YOU HIDE THEM IN A SECRET PLACE? (LAUGHS) IS IT TOO SEXY?

LEXICON NEGIMARIUM

[*Negima!* 187th Period Lexicon Negimarium]

■ **Μελαω Και Σφαιοιρικον Δεσμωτηριον**
- This is a spell that confines an object within a powerful boundary. It means "a black, round prison" in ancient Greek. The purpose of this magic is not for standard restraint, but rather to contain highly spiritual objects such as dragons and giants. Asphalt will be poured over the object, and it will be suffocated within the spheric borders. It looks like Kaede narrowly escaped. Unless the confined object has special magical survival abilities, it will suffocate to death.

[*Negima!* 188th Period Lexicon Negimarium]

■ **Ibukidono ōharahe**
Takamagahara ni kamuzumarimasu
kamuro ki kamuro minomikotowomochite
sumegamitachino maeni mausaku
kurushimiuefu wagatomoyo
mamorimegumahi sakiwaetamaheto
- Konoka Konoe's personal magical spell.

This spell activates the power of Kochinohiougi. This spell is incanted in the old Yamato dialect of Japanese. Magicians were given personalized spells that reflected their quality and character.

According to the Shinto ritual prayer in volume 8 of "Engishiki" called "Minazukinotsugomoriooharae" (what is called Nakatominoharae), "Ibukido" is a location where sin is dispersed to "Nenokuni" or "Sonokuni" by the "ibukidonushi," which is one aspect of the Haraedo Yohashi Ookami, a god. It's a place where all sins were erased. However, in ancient Japanese culture, sin is described more as corruption and catastrophe. In "Minazukinotsugomoriooharae," misfortune and vice are erased through the "Ibukido." Injuries and illness fall into this category and can also be erased through the "Ibukido."

During the Kamakura Era, in the sacred texts "Yamatohimenomiko" and "Nakatominoharahekunge," "Ibukidonushi" is the "Kamunahobinokami," a deity, in ancient Japanese mythology. An Edo era philosopher and scholar, Noringa Omoto, felt that in order for any healing to occur, one must think straightforwardly. This honesty can purge uncleanliness or misfortune and will the spirit from calamity to purification ("Kojikiden," volume 6). According to noringa, the "Ibukidonushi," aka "Kamunahobinokami," is a deity that "repairs" calamity. In the Yamato dialect, "to repair" also means "to heal." Therefore, the "Ibukidonushi" is also a healer.

Konoka's personalized spell is influenced by her teacher's magic (as a result, an inexperienced magician can still possess power similar to magic). However, Konoka's magical power exceeds that of Negi in this case, so her control over "Kochinohiougi" is rather unstable.

■ The Palace of the dead, deep within the wombs of the Earth...(appear below us) The Stone Pillar of Hades
(ω Ταρταρω κειμενον Βασιλειον νεκρων [Φαινσαοθω ημιν] Ο ΜΟΝΟΑΙΘΟΣ ΚΙΩΝ ΤΟΥ ΑΙΔΟΥ)
•This spell gives the ability to move enormous pillars of stone. A high-ranking mage can move and attack with this object via psychokinesis. Each pillar is enormous, hence the devastation is incredible. While these stones are moving through magic, magical barriers cannot prevent the damage due to the massive amount of energy produced by their impact.

[*Negima!* 193rd Period Lexicon Negimarium]

■ Melodia Bellax De Bi-Festinando
•A high-level magic used during close-contact fighting. It gives great agility to every movement of the mage's body.

■ Sagitta Magica Series Sabulonis
•An offensive magical spell that utilizes sand. The magical arrows created by sand are blasted shotgun style, spewing sand everywhere. It's nearly impossible to deflect the multiple sand projectiles. The sand granules are infused with magical power; hence, they have the ability to penetrate metal.

■ Iksir
(الإكسير, al-iksir)

• "Iksir" is an Arabic word referring to secret medicines used in alchemy. The word comes from the ancient Greek ξήριον (kseriou, medicinal powder for drying wounds) and originally meant nothing more than a powdered medicine. When given the Arabic article [الإكسير] al, "iksir" becomes "al-iksir," which then becomes the Latin "elixir."

A politician and historian active in North Africa, Ibn Khaldun (1332–1406), wrote the following in his book *The Muqaddimah: An Introduction to History*:

"Great alchemists consider iksir to be a substance composed of the four elements. When one applies special alchemic treatments, this substance gains specific traits and various natural powers. These powers cause anything the substance touches to assimilate with it, and change the thing, giving it the same traits and form as the substance. The powers transmit their various properties and powers to whatever they touch. It is exactly like the yeast in bread assimilating the dough, giving it its own traits, and making the bread loose and fluffy" (chapter 6, section 32[1]).

In regards to the effects of iksir, there are various alchemic theories, such as turning base metals into precious metals or granting ageless immortality, but it would seem that its essential function is to assimilate what it touches with its own traits. Then what are the traits of this iksir?

According to Ibn Khaldun, iksir is refined from a "noble stone" (ibid. ibidem). In layman's terms, this noble stone is the "wise man's stone (lapis sophorum)" or the "philosopher's stone (lapis philosophorum)," but these terms had not yet been coined in Ibn Khaldun's time. The reason the "stone" from which the iksir is derived is called the philosopher's stone is that the Spanish philosopher Maslama al-Majriti (approximately tenth century) and others considered alchemic knowledge to be absolutely essential to philosophy (ibid. section 29).

According to the written works of a pupil of Maslama al-Majriti, cited by Ibn Khaldun, as things created in the natural world go in order from mineral (earth) to vegetable to animal, their degree of purity goes up and they become higher quality (ibid. ibidem). This is because plants absorb their essence from the earth and animals

1. Section numbers in chapter 6 are from the Parisian edition (rev. by Quatremère, 1858).

prey upon those plants. And the philosopher's stone is inside the highest level of natural creations—namely, animal—and taking it apart would yield the four elements.

This work by Maslama al-Majriti's pupil gives a fascinating explanation about a treatment of a philosopher's stone:

"Take the noble stone. Place it in a cucurbit and an alembic. Divide it into the four elements: water, air, earth, and fire. Those are substance, spirit, soul, and dyeing. Once the water is separated from earth and the air from fire, keep them in their own individual containers. Take the dregs—that is, the sediment—from the bottoms of the containers. Purify in a hot flame until the blackness is removed and its coarseness and hardness disappear. Carefully bleach and evaporate the excess moisture hidden inside. Then it will become a white water, with no kind of darkness, dregs, or disharmony" (ibid. ibidem).

Here we can see the idea of "albedo," known by later generations as one of the four major stages of alchemy. This work does not clarify what the white liquid that is obtained after extracting the four elements from the philosopher's stone, but based on the fact that it is a substance gained from the philosopher's stone, assuming that it is iksir would not contradict Ibn Khaldun's report that iksir is refined from the philosopher's stone.

Nevertheless, even assuming that this white liquid is iksir, all we know is that it is a substance of extremely high purity, and it is still unclear what effects it has when used on other things. However, Ibn Khaldun says that iksir's power and the traits it transmits are not one, but many. It is possible that iksir does not have only one specific use but is used in many different ways. Therefore, it may not only change the qualities of minerals, but also function as a panacea to heal human flesh. This is because as long as alchemy is said to directly alter the elements, it would not only change the properties of minerals, but also of vegetables and animals.

Furthermore, Ibn Khaldun gives a stern warning that alchemy is harmful to monetary economies (ibid. section 32). Taking this into account, that is reason enough for the iksir to be extremely expensive. This is because if the iksir were to be sold at a low price, the value of precious metals such as gold and silver would plummet, throwing the economy into confusion. If the price of iksir was not set higher than the value of the precious metals that can be refined by it, the economy could fail.

2. There are strong suspicions that this work is apocryphal.

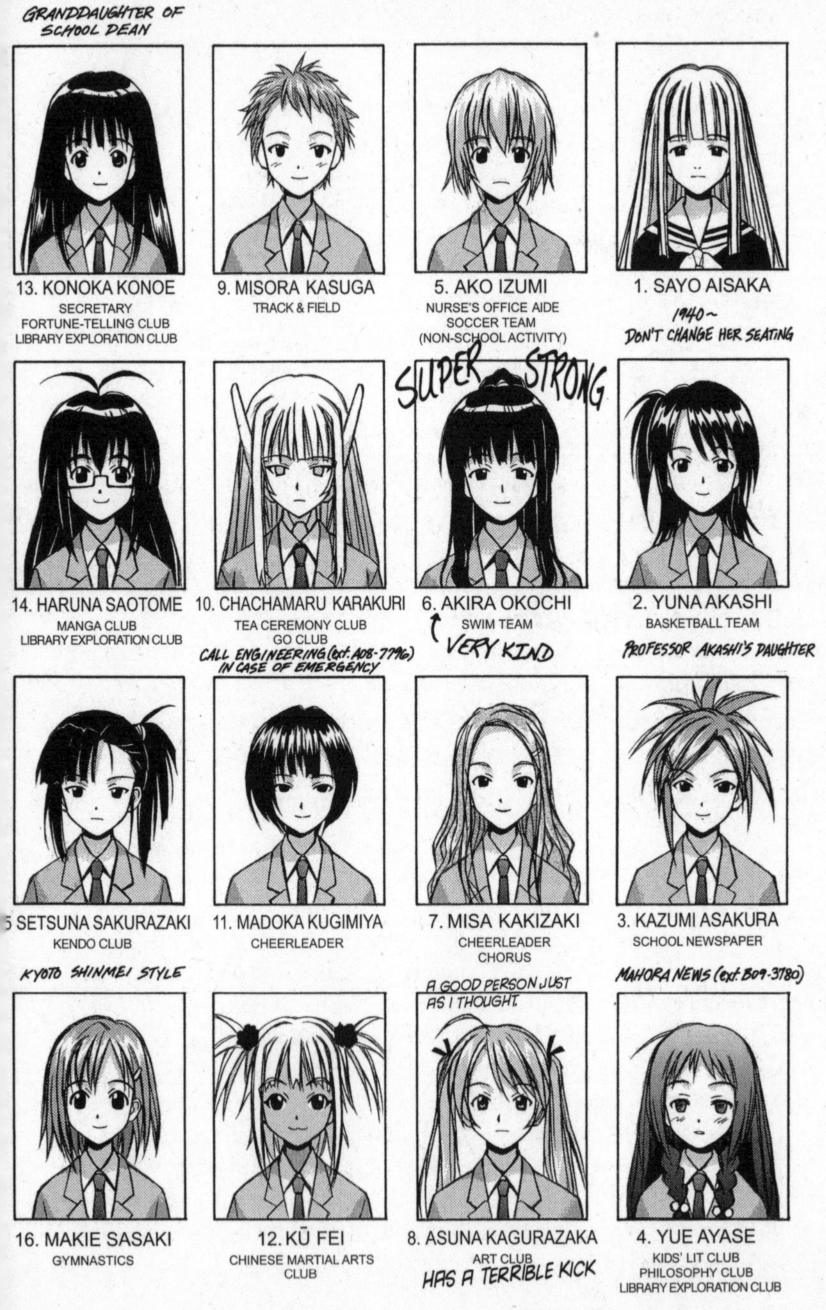
1. SAYO AISAKA
1940~
DON'T CHANGE HER SEATING
5. AKO IZUMI
NURSE'S OFFICE AIDE
SOCCER TEAM
(NON-SCHOOL ACTIVITY)
9. MISORA KASUGA
TRACK & FIELD
GRANDDAUGHTER OF SCHOOL DEAN
13. KONOKA KONOE
SECRETARY
FORTUNE-TELLING CLUB
LIBRARY EXPLORATION CLUB
2. YUNA AKASHI
BASKETBALL TEAM
PROFESSOR AKASHI'S DAUGHTER
SUPER STRONG
6. AKIRA OKOCHI
SWIM TEAM
VERY KIND
10. CHACHAMARU KARAKURI
TEA CEREMONY CLUB
GO CLUB
CALL ENGINEERING (ext. A08-7796) IN CASE OF EMERGENCY
14. HARUNA SAOTOME
MANGA CLUB
LIBRARY EXPLORATION CLUB
3. KAZUMI ASAKURA
SCHOOL NEWSPAPER
MAHORA NEWS (ext. B09-3780)
7. MISA KAKIZAKI
CHEERLEADER
CHORUS
11. MADOKA KUGIMIYA
CHEERLEADER
5 SETSUNA SAKURAZAKI
KENDO CLUB
KYOTO SHINMEI STYLE
4. YUE AYASE
KIDS' LIT CLUB
PHILOSOPHY CLUB
LIBRARY EXPLORATION CLUB
A GOOD PERSON JUST AS I THOUGHT.
8. ASUNA KAGURAZAKA
ART CLUB
HAS A TERRIBLE KICK
12. KŪ FEI
CHINESE MARTIAL ARTS CLUB
16. MAKIE SASAKI
GYMNASTICS

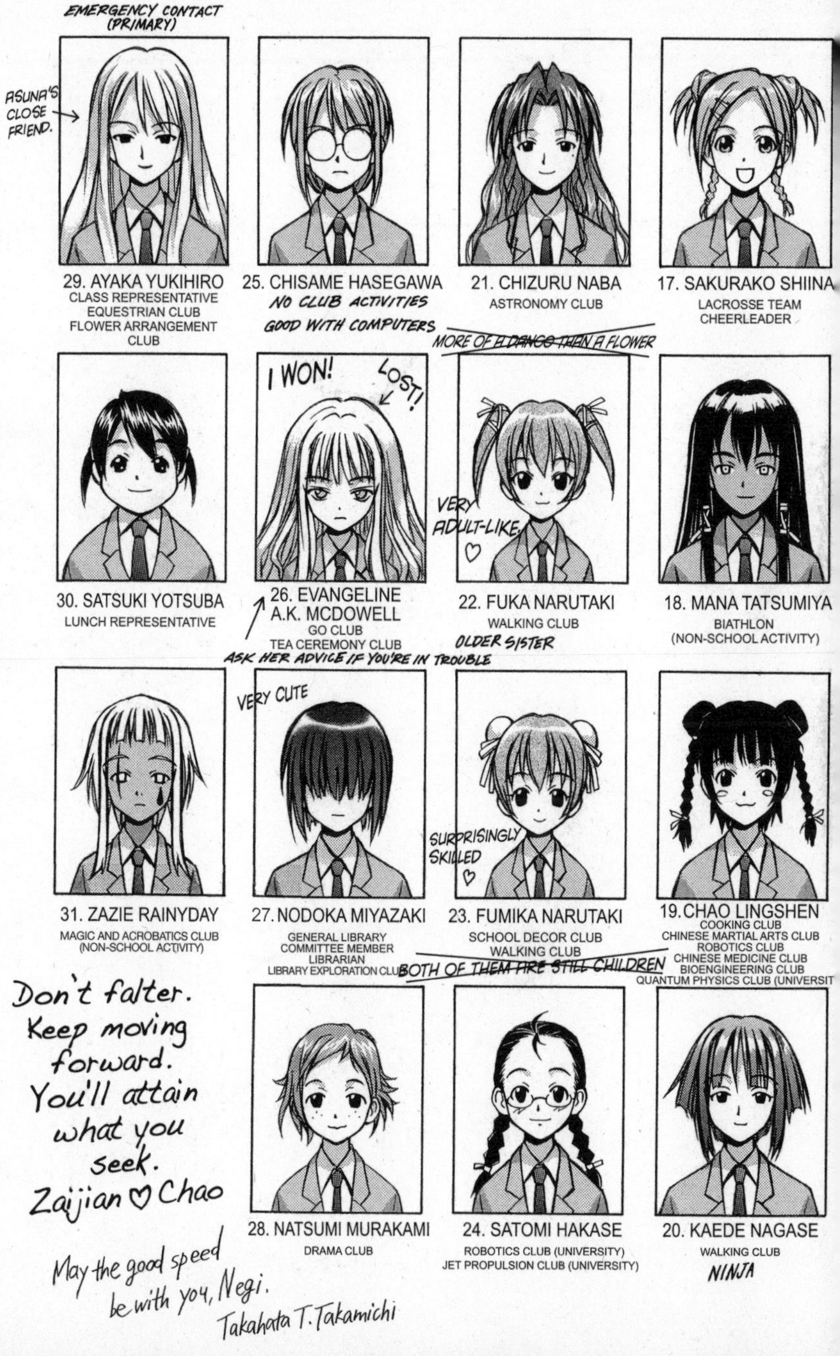

17. SAKURAKO SHIINA
LACROSSE TEAM
CHEERLEADER
21. CHIZURU NABA
ASTRONOMY CLUB
~~MORE OF A DANGO THAN A FLOWER~~
25. CHISAME HASEGAWA
NO CLUB ACTIVITIES
GOOD WITH COMPUTERS
EMERGENCY CONTACT (PRIMARY)
ASUNA'S CLOSE FRIEND.
29. AYAKA YUKIHIRO
CLASS REPRESENTATIVE
EQUESTRIAN CLUB
FLOWER ARRANGEMENT CLUB
18. MANA TATSUMIYA
BIATHLON
(NON-SCHOOL ACTIVITY)
VERY ADULT-LIKE. ♡
22. FUKA NARUTAKI
WALKING CLUB
OLDER SISTER
I WON!
LOST!
26. EVANGELINE A.K. MCDOWELL
GO CLUB
TEA CEREMONY CLUB
ASK HER ADVICE IF YOU'RE IN TROUBLE
30. SATSUKI YOTSUBA
LUNCH REPRESENTATIVE
19. CHAO LINGSHEN
COOKING CLUB
CHINESE MARTIAL ARTS CLUB
ROBOTICS CLUB
CHINESE MEDICINE CLUB
BIOENGINEERING CLUB
QUANTUM PHYSICS CLUB (UNIVERSIT
SURPRISINGLY SKILLED ♡
23. FUMIKA NARUTAKI
SCHOOL DECOR CLUB
WALKING CLUB
~~BOTH OF THEM ARE STILL CHILDREN~~
VERY CUTE
27. NODOKA MIYAZAKI
GENERAL LIBRARY COMMITTEE MEMBER
LIBRARIAN
LIBRARY EXPLORATION CLUB
31. ZAZIE RAINYDAY
MAGIC AND ACROBATICS CLUB
(NON-SCHOOL ACTIVITY)
20. KAEDE NAGASE
WALKING CLUB
NINJA
24. SATOMI HAKASE
ROBOTICS CLUB (UNIVERSITY)
JET PROPULSION CLUB (UNIVERSITY)
28. NATSUMI MURAKAMI
DRAMA CLUB
Don't falter. Keep moving forward. You'll attain what you seek. Zaijian ♡ Chao
May the good speed be with you, Negi.
Takahata T. Takamichi

魔法先生

ネギま!

MAGISTER NEGI MAGI

赤松 健 SHONEN MAGAZINE COMICS
KEN AKAMATSU

21

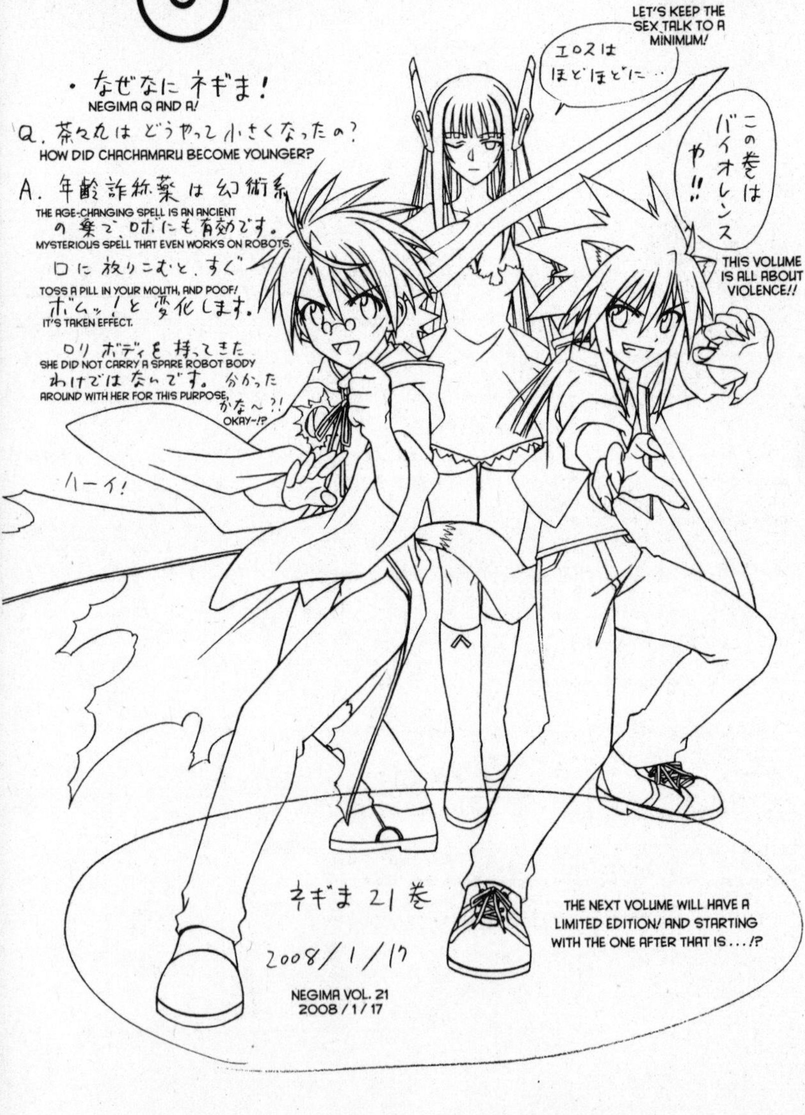

・なぜなにネギま!
NEGIMA Q AND A!
Q. 茶々丸は どうやって小さくなったの?
HOW DID CHACHAMARU BECOME YOUNGER?
A. 年齢詐称薬は幻術系の薬でロボにも有効です。
THE AGE-CHANGING SPELL IS AN ANCIENT MYSTERIOUS SPELL THAT EVEN WORKS ON ROBOTS.
口に放りこむと、すぐボムッ!と変化します。
TOSS A PILL IN YOUR MOUTH, AND POOF! IT'S TAKEN EFFECT.
ロリボディを持ってきたわけではないです。分かったかな~?!
SHE DID NOT CARRY A SPARE ROBOT BODY AROUND WITH HER FOR THIS PURPOSE. OKAY~!?
エロスはほどほどに…
LET'S KEEP THE SEX TALK TO A MINIMUM!
この巻はバイオレンスや!!
THIS VOLUME IS ALL ABOUT VIOLENCE!!
ハーイ!
ネギま 21巻
2008/1/17
NEGIMA VOL. 21
2008/1/17
THE NEXT VOLUME WILL HAVE A LIMITED EDITION! AND STARTING WITH THE ONE AFTER THAT IS . . .!?

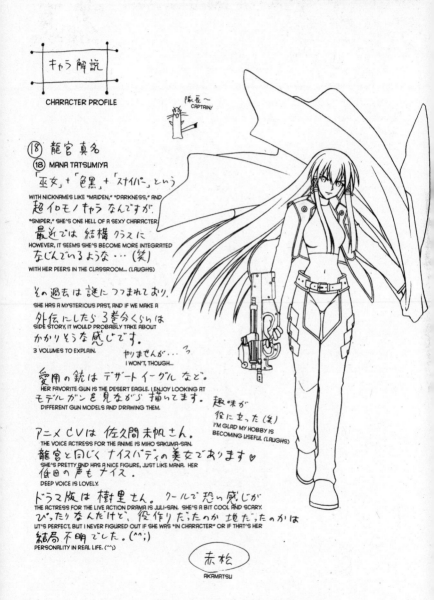

キャラ解説

CHARACTER PROFILE

隊長〜
CAPTAIN!

⑱ 龍宮真名

⑱ MANA TATSUMIYA

「巫女」＋「色黒」＋「スナイパー」という

WITH NICKNAMES LIKE "MAIDEN," "DARKNESS," AND

超イロモノキャラなんですが、

"SNIPER," SHE'S ONE HELL OF A SEXY CHARACTER.

最近では 結構 クラスに

HOWEVER, IT SEEMS SHE'S BECOME MORE INTEGRATED

なじんでいるような・・・(笑)

WITH HER PEERS IN THE CLASSROOM... (LAUGHS)

その過去は 謎につつまれており、

SHE HAS A MYSTERIOUS PAST, AND IF WE MAKE A

外伝にしたら 3巻分くらいは

SIDE STORY, IT WOULD PROBABLY TAKE ABOUT

かかりそうな感じです。

3 VOLUMES TO EXPLAIN.

やりませんが・・・

I WON'T, THOUGH...

愛用の銃は デザートイーグル など。

HER FAVORITE GUN IS THE DESERT EAGLE. I ENJOY LOOKING AT

モデルガンを 見ながら 描いてます。

DIFFERENT GUN MODELS AND DRAWING THEM.

趣味が

役に立った(笑)

I'M GLAD MY HOBBY IS
BECOMING USEFUL (LAUGHS)

アニメCVは 佐久間未帆さん。

THE VOICE ACTRESS FOR THE ANIME IS MIHO SAKUMA-SAN.

龍宮と同じく ナイスバディの美女であります♥

SHE'S PRETTY AND HAS A NICE FIGURE, JUST LIKE MANA. HER

低音の声も ナイス。

DEEP VOICE IS LOVELY.

ドラマ版は 樹里さん。クールで恐い感じが

THE ACTRESS FOR THE LIVE ACTION DRAMA IS JULI-SAN. SHE'S A BIT COOL AND SCARY.

ぴったりなんだけど、役作りだったのか 地だったのかは

IT'S PERFECT, BUT I NEVER FIGURED OUT IF SHE WAS "IN CHARACTER" OR IF THAT'S HER

結局 不明でした。(^^;)

PERSONALITY IN REAL LIFE. (^^;)

赤松

AKAMATSU

Translation Notes

Japanese is a tricky language for most Westerners, and translation is often more an art than a science. For your edification and reading pleasure, here are notes on some of the places where we could have gone in a different direction or where a Japanese cultural reference is used.

Volume 19

Yakitori eaters,
page 21

Negima is a common *yakitori* (BBQ) dish where meat is skewered alternately with sections of leeks or green onions.

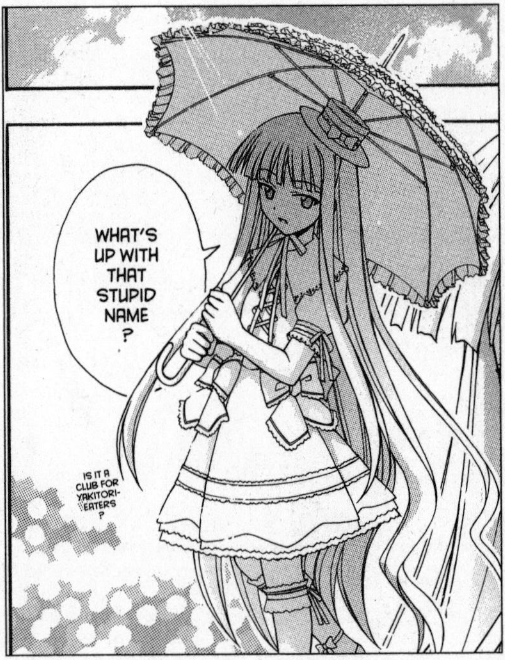
WHAT'S UP WITH THAT STUPID NAME ?
IS IT A CLUB FOR YAKITORI-EATERS ?

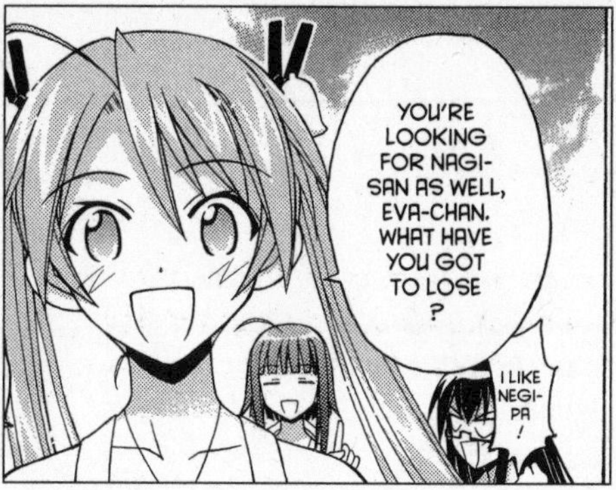
YOU'RE LOOKING FOR NAGI-SAN AS WELL, EVA-CHAN. WHAT HAVE YOU GOT TO LOSE ?
I LIKE NEGI-PA !

Negipa, page 22.

Negipa is a cute abbreviaton for Negima party. It's also the title of a series of official *Negima!* companion guides published in Japan.

Inferno aniki, page 60

The kanji in this spell reads literally "demon of the inferno," but the *furigana* notation indicates *aniki. Aniki* normally means "brother," but in this particular case, it means "a muscular man."

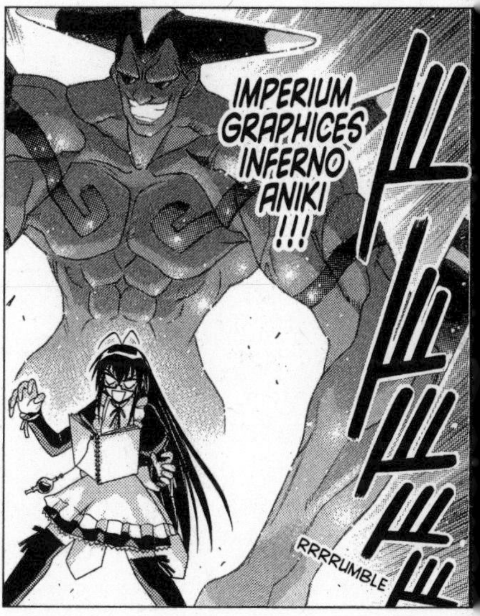
IMPERIUM GRAPHICES INFERNO ANIKI !!!
RRRRUMBLE

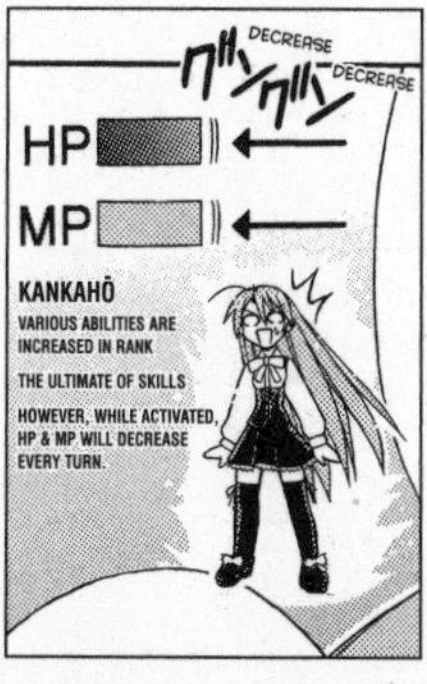
DECREASE
DECREASE
HP
MP
KANKAHŌ
VARIOUS ABILITIES ARE INCREASED IN RANK
THE ULTIMATE OF SKILLS
HOWEVER, WHILE ACTIVATED, HP & MP WILL DECREASE EVERY TURN.

HP and MP, page 68

Video-game fans will recognize this notation right away: it's "hit points" and "magic points," as used in an RPG.

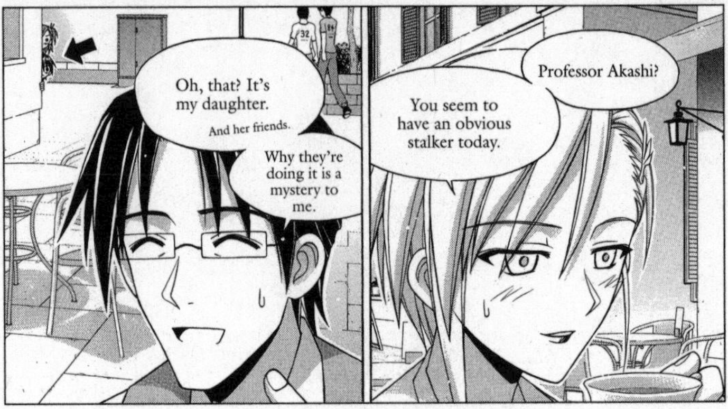
Professor Akashi?
You seem to have an obvious stalker today.
Oh, that? It's my daughter.
And her friends.
Why they're doing it is a mystery to me.

Donet and Akashi's conversation, page 102

Donet and Akashi's conversation was set in a special font in the Japanese edition to indicate that they were speaking in English, a convention which we've imitated here.

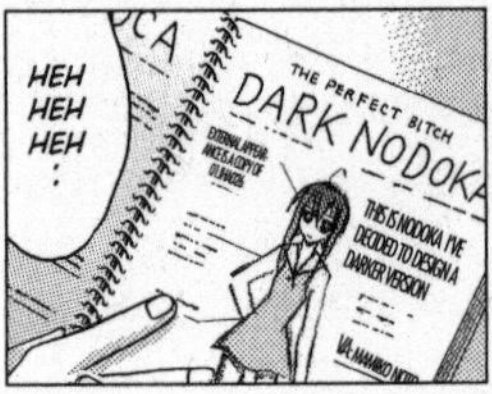
THE PERFECT BITCH
DARK NODOKA
THIS IS NODOKA I'VE DECIDED TO DESIGN A DARKER VERSION
HEH HEH HEH

VA: Mamiko Noto, page 116

VA stands for "voice actor." Mamiko Noto plays Nodoka in the *Negima!* anime; American *Negima!* fans know Leah Clark as the voice of Nodoka in the English-dubbed version.

Volume 20

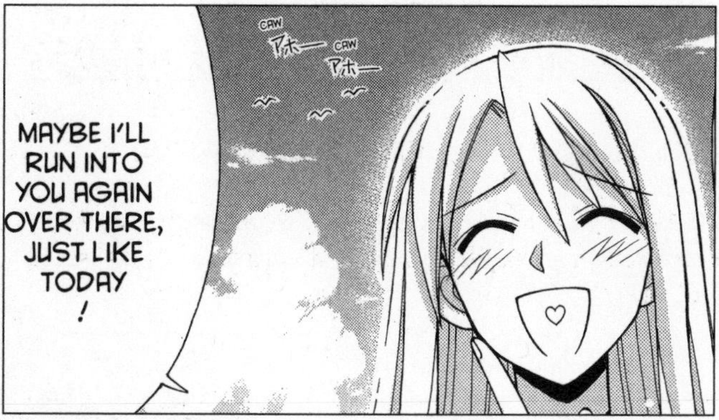
CAW
アホー
CAW
アホー
MAYBE I'LL RUN INTO YOU AGAIN OVER THERE, JUST LIKE TODAY!

Caw, page 175

The original Japanese says Ahō, which is a sound effect for a bird cawing as well as the word dummy in Japanese. In this case, it's a play on words.

Bourgeois, page 176

Bourgeois means "middle class." The word can also be used as a slight to describe something ordinary and commonplace.

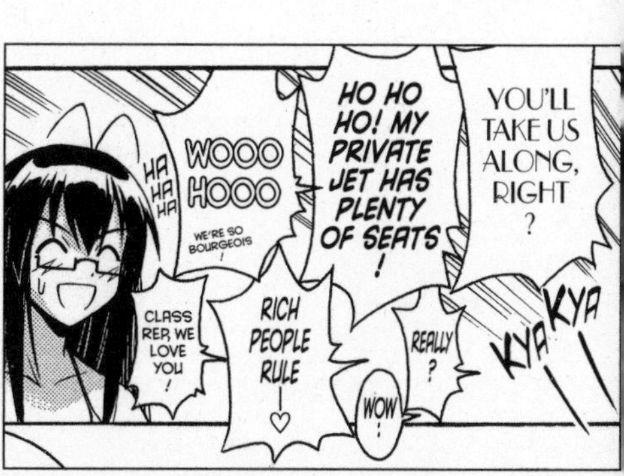
YOU'LL TAKE US ALONG, RIGHT?
HO HO HO! MY PRIVATE JET HAS PLENTY OF SEATS!
KYA KYA
REALLY?
WOW...
RICH PEOPLE RULE ♡
WOOO HOOO
WE'RE SO BOURGEOIS!
HA HA HA
CLASS REP, WE LOVE YOU!

Oden, page 179

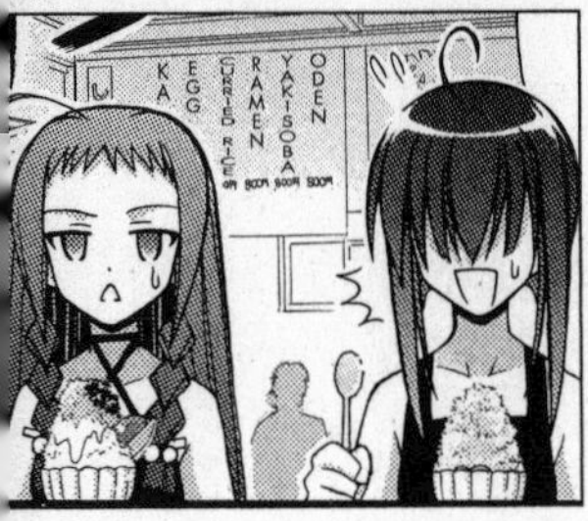
ODEN
YAKISOBA
RAMEN
CURRIED RICE
EGG
KA

Oden is a Japanese dish commonly available and consumed during the winter. Ingredients vary by home and region, but the basic ingredients consist of boiled eggs, various vegetables, and konjac jelly simmered in a light, fish and soy sauce-based broth.

Mount Osore, page 259

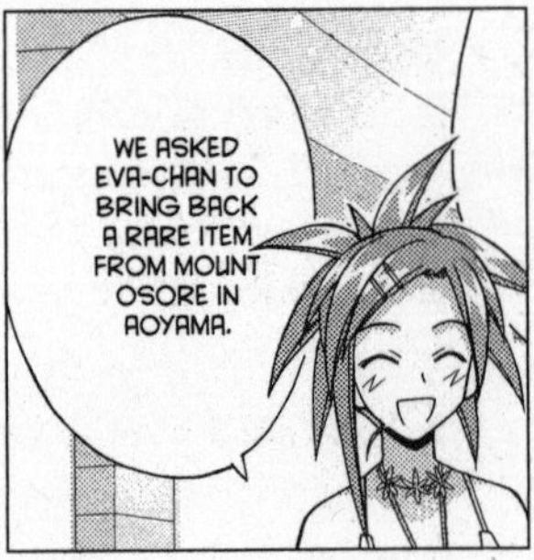
WE ASKED EVA-CHAN TO BRING BACK A RARE ITEM FROM MOUNT OSORE IN AOYAMA.

Mount Osore is located in Aomori Prefecture. Osore means "fear" in Japanese, and Mount Osore was considered the gateway to the underworld in Japanese mythology. The area is famous for the blind mediums who deliver messages from the dead called *itako*.

Daimyoujin, page 302

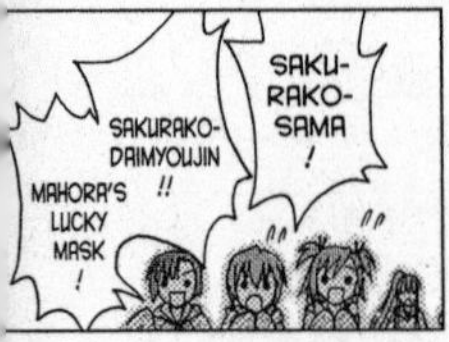
SAKU-RAKO-SAMA!
SAKURAKO-DAIMYOUJIN!!
MAHORA'S LUCKY MASK!

Daimyoujin, also spelled Daimyojin, is a title for Shinto demigods.

IT'S A SIMILAR CONCEPT TO THE "OTHER WORLD" PRESENTED IN THE CHINESE TOUGENKYOU OR THE DRAGON CASTLE FROM URASHIMATARO. IT'S LIKE AN IDEAL PARADISE LINKED TO THE PHYSICAL WORLD.
THERE ARE MANY MYTHICAL "PARADISES" THAT INCLUDE AGARTHA, ARCADIA, AVALON, EL DORADO, AND TIR NA NOG. THIS IS AN INTERESTING SUBJECT, BUT I'LL LEAVE IT FOR NOW.

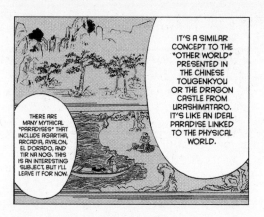

Urashimataro, page 307

Urashimataro is the name of a hero of a Japanese fairy tale. He's a young fisherman who, when he saves a turtle, discovers that it's actually a magical being who whisks him away to an underwater paradise. Urashimataro spends three heavenly days there, but when he returns home, he is distressed to find out that a hundred years have passed in the human world.

Agartha, Arcadia, Avalon, El Dorado, Tir Na Nog, page 307

These are names of legendary cities taken from several world folklore traditions. Agartha is located in the Earth's core. Arcadia is the name for a utopian ideal of a pastoral paradise. Avalon and Tir Na Nog come from the folklore from the British Isles. El Dorado is the legendary "City of Gold" that Spanish conquistadors searched for in South America.

Tatami count, page 332

Japanese room sizes are often described by the number of tatamis (straw mats) that fit into the room.

THIS ROOM IS WHERE NEGI AND HIS STUDENTS SPENT THE NIGHT DURING THEIR BEACH VACATION. THE INN'S APPEARANCE AND OUTDOOR BATH MAY LOOK FAMILIAR TO SOME READERS, BUT THIS ROOM IS A NEW CREATION.
HOWEVER, IT IS A REVISION OF THE ROOM IN VOLUME 14, SO IT DID NOT TAKE A LOT OF EFFORT. THE SPACE IS THE SIZE OF 10 TATAMIS. THE ROOM CALLS FOR REST AND RELAXATION.

Volume 21

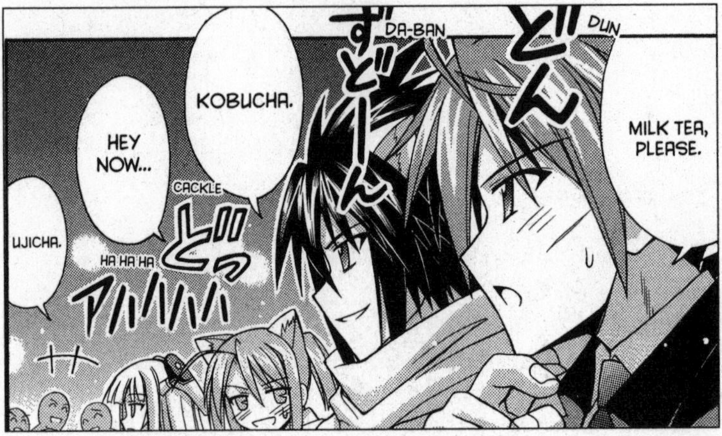
DUN
MILK TEA, PLEASE.
DA-BAN
KOBUCHA.
HEY NOW...
CACKLE
HA HA HA
UJICHA.

Kobucha and Ujicha, page 446

The Japanese kobucha is very different from what is known (and often mistakenly assumed to be the same) in the West as "kombucha." Kombucha is a sweetened tea made from bacteria and yeast fermentation. Kobucha is a slightly salty tea made from a type of kelp called konbu.

Ujicha is a type of green tea and one of the most popular green teas in Japan. The leaves are not covered by shade, so it has high quantities of caffeine and tannins. It is the most common type of tea produced in Japan.

Uji is a Southern city located in Kyoto Prefecture. Ever since Shigun Yoshimitsu encouraged tea cultivation in the city, Uji has been known as the Japanese epicenter for fine green tea.

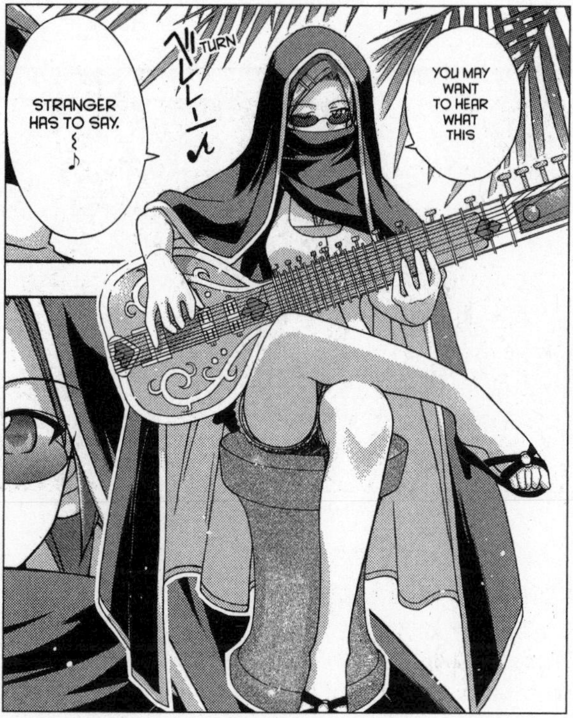
YOU MAY WANT TO HEAR WHAT THIS
TURN
STRANGER HAS TO SAY. ♪

Sitar, page 464

The instrument that Kazumi is playing on page 138 is very similar to a traditional Indian instrument called the sitar. The sitar has been present in India since the twelfth century. The instrument gained international attention through the work of Mr. Ravi Shankar, a prominent virtuoso. The sitar can be heard in popular music by artists such as the Beatles, Rolling Stones, and Metallica.

About the Creator

Negima! is only Ken Akamatsu's third manga, although he started working in the field in 1994 with *AI Ga Tomaranai* (released in the United States with the title *A.I. Love You*). Like all of Akamatsu's work to date, it was published in Kodansha's *Shonen Magazine*. *AI Ga Tomaranai* ran for five years before concluding in 1999. In 1998, however, Akamatsu began the work that would make him one of the most popular manga artists in Japan: *Love Hina*. *Love Hina* ran for four years, and before its conclusion in 2002, it would cause Akamatsu to be granted the prestigious Manga of the Year award from Kodansha, as well as going on to become one of the bestselling manga in the United States.

FROM HIRO MASHIMA,
CREATOR OF **RAVE MASTER**

Lucy has always dreamed of joining the Fairy Tail, a club for the most powerful sorcerers in the land. But once she becomes a member, the fun really starts!

Special extras in each volume! Read them all!

RATING T AGES 13+

VISIT WWW.KODANSHACOMICS.COM TO:
• View release date calendars for upcoming volumes
• Find out the latest about new Kodansha Comics series

Fairy Tail © Hiro Mashima / KODANSHA LTD. All rights reserved.

ANIMAL LAND

BY MAKOTO RAIKU

In a world of animals, where the strong eat the weak, Monoko the tanuki stumbles across a strange creature the likes of which has never been seen before—a human baby! While the newborn has no claws or teeth to protect itself, it does have the special ability to speak to and understand all different animals. Can the gift of speech between species change the balance of power in a land where the weak must always fear the strong?

ANIMAL LAND 1

MAKOTO RAIKU

Ages 13+

VISIT KODANSHACOMICS.COM TO:
- View release date calendars for upcoming volumes
- Find out the latest about upcoming Kodansha Comics series

© Makoto Raiku / KODANSHA LTD. All rights reserved.

MARDOCK

マルドゥック・スクランブル

SCRAMBLE

Created by
Tow Ubukata

×

Manga by
Yoshitoki Oima

"I'd rather be dead."

Rune Balot was a lost girl with nothing to live for. A man named Shell took her in and cared for her...until he tried to murder her. Standing at the precipice of death Rune is saved by Dr. Easter, a private investigator, who uses an experimental procedure known as "Mardock Scramble 09." The procedure grants Balot extraordinary abilities. Now, Rune must decide whether to use her new powers to help Dr. Easter bring Shell to justice, or if she even has the will to keep living a life that's been broken so badly.

Ages: 16+

VISIT KODANSHACOMICS.COM TO:
- View release date calendars for upcoming volumes
- Find out the latest about upcoming Kodansha Comics series

© Tow Ubukata / Yoshitoki Oima / KODANSHA LTD. All rights reserved.

TOMARE!

[STOP!]

You're going the wrong way!

Manga is a completely different type of reading experience.

To start at the *beginning*,
go to the *end*!

That's right! Authentic manga is read the traditional Japanese way—from right to left, exactly the *opposite* of how American books are read. It's easy to follow: Just go to the other end of the book, and read each page—and each panel—from right side to left side, starting at the top right. Now you're experiencing manga as it was meant to be.